Peace
and
World
Order
Studies

Fourth Edition

A Curriculum Guide

Barbara J. Wien, Editor

© World Policy Institute
777 United Nations Plaza
New York, NY 10017
(212) 490-0010

ISBN 0-911646-20-2

Table of Contents

I. Preface and Acknowledgments

II. Course Syllabi

A. Global Problems: A General Overview

B. Peacemaking and Nonviolence

III. Case Studies

IV. Resources

I
Preface and Acknowledgments

Editor's Note

Foreword

Introductory Essay

Editor's Note

Since the last edition of this book was published in 1981, political conflicts between groups and nation-states have become more pervasive and multi-faceted; struggles for liberation and domination have intensified; and assaults on the environment have mounted to some times irreversible proportions. It is my hope that this new volume can play at least a modest role in helping scholars and educators deepen their understanding and analyses of these social and political problems, with the eventual end of forging a peaceful and just world order.

The first three versions of *Peace and World Order Studies: A Curriculum Guide,* published in 1972, 1978 and 1981, have been used by over 6,000 college, university and secondary school educators in 42 countries to design and update new courses, familiarize themselves with new literature and resources, and plan and justify new academic programs in the study of global problems. To distinguish this Guide from the previous editions, I have added several new syllabi sections: Women and World Order; Hunger and the Politics of Food Distribution; World Political Economy; Religious Perspectives on Justice and Peace; Regional Studies; and Militarism and the Arms Race. All the former syllabus categories remain. An original list of Funding Sources and a Case Study section, describing the development and intellectual content of major curriculum programs in the U.S., also appear as new features of this book.

I am indebted to Adele Simmons and Peter Dale Scott for their insights, time, energy, warmth and wisdom. The encouragement and support of the staff of the World Policy Institute sustained me through the two years of conceptualization, compilation and production of the book and I thank them all very much. Jane Lawrence was invaluable in shaping the section on Funding Sources, and Kathy Sizemore researched the entire Filmography.

I do not believe it is humanly possible to thank Steve Maikowski enough for the hundreds of hours he put into proofreading, designing, laying out and editing the Guide. He sacrificed precious time with his family and many beautiful summer weekends in order for the production and printing of the Guide to proceed.

The 4th Edition would not have been possible without the assistance of my many student interns, all of whom I will name here—Shazie Prizade, Abdula Mohammed, Howard Kleinman, Leslie Taylor, Chin Choon Fong, Denneth Modeste, David Flythe, Anurada Seth, Laura Schisgall, Felisa Tibbits, Deborah Balk, Timothy Philipps, Lorna Simmons, Kristen Synder and Robert Jones—or without the incredible generosity of Earl D. Osborn who sponsored the promotion of the Curriculum Guide. I feel it is appropriate to thank in the same breath these young people and Mr. Osborn because during his 91 yearson this planet he has dedicated himself to the peaceful education of our youth.

Finally, I dedicate this book to overworked and underpaid teachers everywhere.

Foreword

As an outspoken advocate of the need to incorporate studies relating to peace and world order into the college curriculum, it is a pleasure for me to write an introduction to the fourth edition of *Peace and World Order Studies.*

The importance of including material relating to war and peace in the curriculum cannot be overstated. We live in a world in which our ability to live peacefully with other people and other nations is crucial. The alternative—conventional or nuclear war—is unthinkable. And yet, if we are to reduce conflicts among nations and perpetuate, however hostile, the peace between the superpowers, we must know much more about history, technology, decision-making, and the values and cultures of others; and we must be able to communicate with others in their own languages. The substance itself requires no justification.

At the same time, as an educator, I would like to suggest that few subjects help educators accomplish their most meaningful goals as much as this area of inquiry—the capacity to think critically, to analyze data and to reach independent conclusions; the need for different disciplines to work together; and the need to move beyond knowledge to understanding. Montaigne, in distinguishing between knowledge and understanding, wrote in his essay on pedagogy that both were necessary but concluded that "learning is less valuable than judgment. The latter can do without the former, and not the former without the latter."

A certain mystique has grown up around the fields essential to understanding the issues of peace and war, cultivated in part by the experts in those fields. Those of us who are nonexperts have encouraged the mystique by responding, "We leave it to you." The subject is too complicated.

In a democratic society, colleges have a responsibility to prepare nonspecialists to exercise informed judgment about such questions. That is a function of liberal education, and to fulfill this responsibility well may be the most important job of educators today. The subject may be complicated, but colleges have never rejected a subject simply because it could not be mastered perfectly by undergraduates. In short, undergraduates are ready and able to take on the study of peace and war.

To prepare to teach in this area, faculty members must read, talk to colleagues, learn along with their students, and look to the disciplines in which they were trained to provide a framework for addressing pertinent questions. This volume provides a good starting point.

Adele Simmons
President, Hampshire College
Amherst, MA

Please refer also to President Simmons' articles in *The Chronicle of Higher Education*, June 23, 1982, and *The New York Times*, September 12, 1982.

Introductory Essay

Peter Dale Scott†

Curriculum guides are not usually thought of as exciting reading. There is, however, an unmistakable sense of excitement, as well as urgency, about the book you are now holding. For this guide to peace studies is not only a reflection of the most important and far-reaching curricular development since the movements for women's studies, ethnic studies, and environmental studies, more than a decade ago; it is also a guide in a more dynamic sense, helping to lead this movement into new and more ambitious directions. Peace studies has evolved rapidly from the theoretical towards the practical, from the specialized towards the interdisciplinary, from futuristic world-order modelling towards a compelling engagement with the concrete issues of today's political processes.

In 1979, the editors of this guide sent out 7500 questionnaires to persons involved in peace studies programs, and they considered it a mark of this movement's growth that they received 400 responses. In 1983, they sent out 10,000 questionnaires, and received 12,000 responses. There is no doubt that the peace studies movement, like the peace movement, is larger and more serious than ever before. But that is, of course, no guarantee of its academic acceptability; on the contrary, what becomes challenging is likely, sooner or later, to be challenged.

When the first peace studies programs were launched after World War II*, by pioneers such as the distinguished economist Kenneth Boulding, their scope was both modest and noncontroversial. Courses were often devised as supplements to existing curricula in political science or international relations, while peace research became, in the hands of some academics, so theoretical it was virtually a form of mathematics. Rather like the 1950 intellectual's climate into which they were born, peace studies tended to avoid raising what might seem to be ideological or schismogenic issues, and instead sought peace through nonpolitical skills of conflict resolution, civility and consensus.

---

†Professor of English, University of California, Berkeley, and founder of the Program in Peace and Conflict Studies.

*If we consider the establishment of professional journals, university departments and international associations as the birthmarks of a new discipline, we may say that peace research was born in the late fifties, and was fully established by the late sixties. The first journals appeared in 1957 and 1959, international organization took place in 1963-64 (International Peace Research Association, IPRA), and by 1965 there were, according to UNESCO statistics, some 100 institutions in the world that devoted at least some effort to peace research—although only a small minority of them were occupied exclusively with peace research. The UNESCO statistics show that by 1978 there were 310 institutions of peace and conflict research in the world, employing approximately 5,000 researchers.   —*Department of Peace and Conflict Research Lund University, Sweden*

If, however, one looks at the successive curriculum guides which have been published, one can see a rapid expansion of peace studies from formal considerations of law and conflict resolution, into more substantial political questions. New areas of inquiry focus on human rights, ecology, and hunger, and even more recently on controversial issues such as the politics of energy exploitation, and the effects of socially reinforced sex roles. The result has been an evolution towards peace studies curricula that are more interdisciplinary, more holistic, more process-oriented, more relevant, and also, for many, more controversial.

The Need to Be Interdisciplinary

This evolution has not been gratuitous; it has resulted from a growing recognition that positive peace, as a stable system of process which consolidates all the conditions for human growth, will require more substantial adjustments to the status quo than those achievable by the fine-tuning of international law professors. Just as the search for peace in the real world requires a more capacious perspective integrating viewpoints previously discrete and in conflict, so a peace studies curriculum, to be serious, must integrate the results of many divergent disciplines into a less abstract, more holistic and far-reaching perspective.

This may sound pretentious, but consider the realities. A favorite topic for peace studies in the 1950's was disarmament, a topic to which I myself had some limited exposure when I was briefly a Canadian diplomat at the United Nations. Today, the topic of disarmament is so urgent as to have merited two Special Sessions of the United Nations; and the nuclear arms race has reached a point where many veteran diplomats are endorsing any stopgap measures to help restabilize a deteriorating global system. No one thinks, however, that stopgap measures to "freeze" or limit the production of arms will by themselves solve the arms race, or that significant disarmament can be achieved without a concomitant reduction of international tension in other areas.

Once it was thought that trade and development were an answer to international tension; but today they can be seen as part of a global struggle to dominate the world's peoples and raw materials. We are now far more conscious of our planet's finite resources and precarious environmental balance. Capital-intensive development, once looked to as a panacea, is now criticized for contributing to our ecological crisis. Yet that crisis itself is not simply a problem but also an opportunity for unprecedented global cooperation. As an example, we have just seen the important Third Conference on the Law of the Sea, dealing with such new problems as depleted fisheries and an international seabed. The resulting treaty is clearly a landmark in the search for transnational authority and cooperative development of the global commons.

There are, however, many thinkers who doubt that such ad hoc responses by governments are adequate to produce, by themselves, the changed political climate in which significant disarmament and justice would be possible. The existing system of large and small sovereign states, for which no rationale can be offered except the law of conquest the system memorializes, is seen by many to reflect a deeper system of social inequality in which structural violence is ingrained. For some, all existing ideological, social and technological systems, including both capitalism and Marxist-Leninism, are now exploitative, power- oriented contributions, and not solutions to the global problem.

The issues of social inequality and structural violence are of particular concern to the underprivileged majorities of the Third World, who have reason to view critically the "benefits" which Western technological civilization has so far bestowed upon them. Meanwhile, residents of more privileged nations, such as our own, increasingly recognize that a search for consensus and for conflict resolution, to be meaningful, cannot limit itself to our formal desires for an orderly and nonviolent international polity, but must somehow enlarge the dialogue of peace to engage Third World concerns. If not, peace studies would be no more than the privileged talking to themselves.

Thus, peace studies, while not necessarily committed to more radical proposals for amendment of global problems, still is committed to an enlarged intellectual viewpoint in which such radical critiques of the status quo can be contemplated and discussed. Indeed, the intellectual challenge and excitement of peace studies, justifying its inclusion among the academic offerings of colleges and universities, are not to be sought just in its "content" of solutions to problems of peace and conflict, but also in this very enlargement of global awareness and self-critical attitude. Undoubtedly this critical attitude must be projected, first and above all, on peace studies itself. If the frustration of our new discipline has been the inadequacy of the literature to be transmitted, the corresponding excitement today is the sense of participation in the creation of that literature.

The Need to Consider Values

Up to now I have been suggesting how a systematic approach to a traditional peace issue such as disarmament leads outward to more fundamental social, political, and ecological issues—issues of the large sort that require an interdisciplinary approach. But issues of war and peace are not all new, interdisciplinary, and problem-oriented; they are also raised by the world's oldest religions and literatures. As Richard Falk wrote in his introductory essay for the last *Curriculum Guide*:

> *Spiritual traditions and insights become relevant, especially as they shape cultural potentialities that draw on neglected aspects of national and civilizational heritage and posit a sound basis for [appropriate] forms of cultural renewal.*

The technological developments that led our culture to downplay the authority of religion in the last four centuries have now reached a crisis point, making the religious message of peace as an ultimate value an issue of the most practical relevance.

What religion and literature revive above all for us, in the face of all the detailed institutional arrangements of everyday life, are ultimate questions of value, personal choice and responsibility, and the use of freedom. Just as for technical and problem-solving reasons the modern sciences move towards a more interdisciplinary and integrative approach, so too, from a different starting point, the value-concerns of religion and literature are profoundly integrative, asking no less than what we should do with our lives. From one point of view our choices are new; from another viewpoint they engage values as old as the Bhagavad Gita, Homer, and Genesis.

The task of creating a more integrated global society will require not only collective but personal changes. As T.S. Eliot wrote a half century ago, you cannot build a peaceful order from individuals who are no more than aggregates of conflicting impulses, nor can the individual fully realize inner peace in a world that is tearing itself apart:

> *At the present time [he wrote] the problem of the unification of the world and the problem of the unification of the individual are in the end one and the same.*

Today, we might not put as much stress as Eliot on the word "unification," which suggests a model of order that is hierarchical rather than decentralized, authoritarian rather than (in the best sense) anarchic or self-sustaining. But the unifying perspective which religion and literature bring to our social and personal problems is perhaps indispensable.

Peace Studies and Existing Curricula

Peace, in other words, is not one more technical problem for institutional adjustment; if we are serious in studying it, we must go to fundamental questions about the arrangements of society and the priorities of personal life. But such an enlarged vision of peace studies will not fit as easily as a course on disarmament into the pluralist array of existing college and university curricula. Even far more modest interdisciplinary programs in limited areas such as ecology are finding it hard to survive in an era of budgetary retrenchment. The magnitude of the kind of integrated peace curriculum we have been considering here ensures that the task of easing it into existing academic programs will not be effortless.

We must face calmly but unevasively the fact that our colleges and universities are an important factor in, not just a symptom of, our dissociative, fragmented world in which human and spiritual priorities have so little sanction. For the most part we *train* students to look at parts of a problem rather than the whole, to survive within a system rather than to question it.

As the late Roy Preiswerk wrote in the last edition of this *Curriculum Guide*:

> *The dehumanization of the social sciences is partly the result of their fragmentation. Fragmentation prevents an understanding of what man is all about. To narrow the sphere of observation is considered a sign of seriousness in academic circles.... Fragmented social sciences can be useless, because they only provide information on minute issues, because other researchers often cannot build on the findings of their colleagues and because the degree of comparability across classes, nations, and cultures is low. It is simply absurd to invent a* homo oeconomicus, *a* homo psychologicus, *or a* homo sociologicus *and then refuse to relate these analytical abstractions to the totality of the real human beings.*

In voicing these important criticisms we must avoid any holier-than-thou Philistinism. It is unfortunately all too easy, in devising an alternative that is more integrative, to come up with a program that is full of moral uplift but devoid of intellectual seriousness and critical engagement. There are both good and bad reasons why our universities have moved towards greater and greater specialization: partial contributions that work are to be preferred over holistic overviews that offer the consolation of insight, but nothing more.

An integrative peace studies curriculum, to be serious, should emulate in a different way the intellectual modesty of the traditional disciplines. To avoid the illusion of teaching everything (and hence nothing), it should aim at the acquisition of a disciplined body of learning which, while allowing for individual variations of emphasis, is in the main manageable as well as coherently focused on peace.

Applications to Undergraduate Curricula

This will work out differently on the undergraduate and graduate levels. The undergraduate emphasis should be primarily on acquiring critical and integrative skills rather than objective content—skills which, as it happens, are often in greater demand in the outside world than mere familiarity with bodies of "fact" and information which are all too frequently dated. We should accept (as any honest discipline should accept) that in our undergraduate programs we can do little more than initiate the student to critical, evaluative, and research methods which hopefully will help him or her in a lifelong process of learning.

A necessary first step is the encouragement of the student to become more competent in analyzing, comparing, and verifying (or falsifying) competing claims of fact and viewpoint, not only from the media of various nations and factions, but also from more allegedly objective sources such as the peace studies instructors themselves. This will involve not just formal skills in analyzing arguments, and a developed tolerance for cognitive dissonance, but also research skills in exploiting library resources, telephone interviews, etc. The students should from the outset be helped to develop a sense of responsibility for their own education, to become active seekers after truth rather than passive receivers of it. To some extent this will involve demystification of academic disciplines currently treating political problems, where these disciplines have pursued the opposite academic strategy of presenting their introductory findings as "fact" or "science," while postponing the activity of research to the senior or graduate level.

Even an introductory course in peace studies, when it involves an investigation of competing explanations of human violence, can be a most fitting starting point for the exercise of such critical judgment and tolerance. After comparing the claims of sociobiology, political sociology, anthropology, social psychology, political economy, and political science, to say nothing of newer disciplines such as women's, ethnic, and environmental studies, the student should have gained a more discriminating perspective both on our own culture and on the various academic disciplines which are part of it.

From my own limited teaching experience I would conclude that this critical perspective is particularly helped by an objective consideration of small-scale alternatives to our present mass society, by studying both the admittedly problematic evidence from archaeology and early history, as Marija Gimbutas and Stanley Diamond have done, and also contemporary small-scale societies before and after they come into contact with the global technoculture. This helps the student to appraise both the alleged "facts" of the human condition, and just as importantly its values, with a more open mind.

However, a full introduction to the problems of peace and violence should be more than critical and analytical; it should go on to be constructive and imaginative in the consideration of alternatives. Here too a student can learn that theory and imagination, just as surely as the analysis of evidence, call for self-criticism and self-discipline. Here too there are competing alternatives to be evaluated, involving the methods, scale, and above all goals of desirable social change.

A high priority here is the issue of disarmament. Many students and professors in this country are still virtually unaware of the worldwide disarmament education campaign that has been launched under the auspices of the U.N. World Disarmament Campaign. By studying alternative disarmament proposals as part of this worldwide movement, the sense of participation in a global peace-oriented community can be strengthened. This is important in combatting the sense of powerlessness that so often results from thinking of peace in terms of our own nation's political processes.

I believe that whereas even a decade or two ago such wide-reaching discussions would have risked becoming so unmanageable as to be wholly profitless, real progress has been made in the *process* of conducting such a serious investigation of peace alternatives, a process which, I need hardly add, is also of the greatest importance for the consolidation of peace itself. Thus training in group process seems to be a desirable part of both the "content" and the "style" of peace studies.

Thus the skills acquired in peace studies can be practical as well as cognitive. More and more peace programs are offering options of practical field work in community conflict resolution, an opportunity to learn (and critically test) how nonviolent approaches to conflict can be applied in everyday life. Some will go further and focus directly on "process" within the program as well as outside it, developing the skills of awareness and affective sensitivity in human interaction and decision-making that have been refined recently by women's and nonviolent movements.

A consensus as to the content of undergraduate integrative peace studies curricula has been emerging at widely separated campuses over the past few years. It is encouraging to see how many different groups have, on their own, moved from specialized or futuristic courses towards more interdisciplinary, problem-oriented, practical syllabi. On the graduate level, the tasks are so numerous and pressing that as yet I detect far less consensus as to the chief priorities.

Graduate Research Possibilities

At one end of the spectrum, for example, are philosophical questions, already given academic refinement by thinkers such as Jurgen Habermas, about the relation of critical theory to human practice, such as Habermas' argument that a "human interest in emancipation" guides language and thought from their outset towards a universal and consensual society. Such questions have a more than theoretical importance: they can help integrate the language and ideas of peace studies more securely into the intellectual dialogue already established on the international university scene.

In addition, peace studies can give greater focus and integration to existing research into the sources of violence in both human and institutional behavior. It is, I suspect, no accident that so much of recent research and debate in this area has been interdisciplinary, from Stanley Milgram's celebrated experiments into how far the normal limits to human behavior can be broken down and dehumanized by obedience to social authority, to the recent spate of claims about genetically determined aggressive and/or territorial behavior.

From our point of view, one might argue that such research has not yet been interdisciplinary enough. For example, while there has been much response to Milgram's work in psychological literature, few academics have, like Daniel Ellsberg, applied Milgram's findings to the analysis of bureaucratic behavior in wartime, such as the U.S. Air Force's dropping of the equivalent of 7.5 million tons of TNT in Vietnam (or three and one-half times the total tonnage of World War II).

Research Into Experimental Peace Projects

Turning from violence to conciliation, we can also hope for more research into ways of encouraging human interaction between groups and interests previously separate or at odds. On the international level, one should think of experiments, not just in areas of acute conflict such as Northern Ireland or the Middle East, but for a general expansion of popular awareness of global community. Here the explosive developments in communications technology, so often seen as threatening dehumanization, can also prove an ally. Parochialism can become increasingly outmoded when we see not just all peoples, but the world itself, in the center of our television screen.

There is no ground for complacency about such developments. The century which has invented napalm, cluster bombs, and nerve gas, to say nothing of nuclear weapons, can hardly think of itself as having reached new heights of global humanitarianism. And yet it remains true that governments, which have invented strategic bombing and napalm for enemies abroad, have also moved towards wooden and rubber bullets at home. The most hateful products of the new weapons technology have been reserved for 'enemy' peoples defined as alien, in remote areas like East Timor or Afghanistan, with whom we have not yet identified.

Graduate peace research can continue, and integrate, the investigation of the extent to which improved domestic police recruitment and training can, for example, reduce conflict in areas where police and local populations have previously been at loggerheads. Such findings are useful not just in themselves but as a model for suggesting analogous improvements on the international level. If our society has gradually come to accept varieties of sensitivity training for our police officers, which would have seemed incongruous a generation ago, can we not guard against future My Lais, and eventually perhaps even Vietnams, by developing analogous programs for our military and even for our bureaucrats?

Even though we shall be far from sanguine in our expectations, the question seems serious enough to merit intellectual inquiry. The role of informal East-West meetings in furthering arms control suggests that other such meetings, for bureaucrats and intellectuals with other areas of international responsibility, would at least merit study. Another possible topic would be the consequences of recruiting officers precisely for their ruthless and aggressive potential, as the CIA is known to have done, and then putting such men in a position where they can increase their nation's involvement in conflict.

I myself dream of institutional support for historical research about such parapolitical escalation of local conflicts, in remote areas like Laos in 1959-61, or Chad in 1980-83, into international confrontations. Though I would not normally expect knowledge, in our present world, to have a limiting effect on warfare, there is perhaps hope with respect to such remote wars, because they were generated by a mixture of ignorance, on the one hand, and conscious deception of their own governments by self-aggrandizing intelligence agencies, on the other. These sources of conflict are more easily eliminated.

Up to now I have been sketching my purely hypothetical graduate program in peace studies, simply to argue to my more skeptical colleagues that abundant opportunities for such graduate research exist. In practice, graduate peace research will probably develop in a less utopian fashion. The fact is that in the world today there has been a veritable explosion of new peace programs, with a range of sponsors from established institutions to grassroots movements. Millions of dollars will be spent on generating such programs. Surely one can ask that some small portion of those millions be set aside, or matched, for an evaluation of these programs.

I have encountered many academics who clearly do not see the university as an appropriate place for such inquiry; and we must consider why not. The problem is not lack of intellectual challenge, nor am I frightened by charges that we in peace studies lack professional competence. No one at present has been trained to take on these intellectual tasks in a coherent way. But this great defect of peace studies is also its great opportunity.

Our Criteria for Being "Academic"

Peace studies has all the poverty of a new discipline, but also all the excitement. It knows that as yet it has only a few answers to the problem of peace and, indeed, is still in the process of refining what questions can be meaningfully posed. All scholars should consider the need for intellectual humility, but peace educators, especially so. Even on specific issues where we as individuals may be confident of our political priorities (for example, on the desirability of halting nuclear weapons development), it is important that our students be exposed to different viewpoints, so that they can learn to judge such issues for themselves and thereby enter competently into the social debate on such topics.

In other words, the relation of peace studies to divisive political issues must of necessity be two-sided. On the one hand, peace studies goes beyond the purely moralistic or "blueprint" approach to world order, and seeks understanding of the real sources of violent conflict in the world as it now exists. At the same time, as an academic program it must not lapse into the attitudes of a mere actor in the drama of world conflict. On the contrary, our commitment to nonviolent conciliation requires training in the understanding of alternative viewpoints, in the ability to translate blind opposition into a more reasonable dialectic. Our task as educators is to open minds, not to close them: we wish our students to acquire not only a viewpoint, but a self-critical perspective on that viewpoint. Thus, even while incorporating politics into our content, we must avoid being merely political in our process.

This sensitive balance has forced us to consider what it means to be, in the best sense, an *academic* program. Despite what some college deans and public relations officers may claim, to be academic does not have to mean that one must be without social relevance or practicality. Nor does it mean that one must pretend to study an issue as if one had no point of view about it, affecting a pseudo-neutrality which is misleadingly called "objectivity."

One will not find these associations with the academic or university approach before the capitalist era. Plato's school in the grove of Academe, from which we draw our name and even sometimes our inspiration, was explicitly directed to the study of the good life and how this could be realized in the social order. The revival of higher education (or *studium*) in the Carolingian era was even more consciously dedicated (along with the state, *imperium*, and church, *sacerdotium*) to the confirmation of a civilizing order in a barbarous world. The emergence of universities some three centuries later reflected a desire to adapt the learning of the church more directly to the needs of the emerging cities in which the universities were invariably based. One will search in vain for statements from that era that studies should be detached from life: theology, ethics, and law were not subjects about which schoolmen felt indifferent or "neutral."

The Controversy Over "Advocating Peace"

I offer these historical observations, with a little less charity than I can usually muster, to those academics who continue to object to the "political advocacy" of peace studies, even while condoning university management of some of the world's largest nuclear weapons laboratories. This double standard, or bad faith, has been defended by appeals to academic "tradition"—of the university's service to the state on the one hand (here the precedent of Nazi Germany can be solemnly cited), and of so-called academic neutrality on the other. Let us at least make it clear that both of these recent "traditions" turn their back on the historical inspirations for university studies.

Peace studies has no quarrel with the ideal of "objectivity," in the sense of striving to overcome the limitations of one's social perspective and to present opposing arguments as fairly as possible. Such objectivity is indeed part of our agenda. But we cannot avoid opposition to those ideologists who, by claiming that their own social perspective is "scientific," seek to impose their own ideology of pseudo-scientific neutrality as a requirement on the rest of the university.

A profound issue is at stake here. Even while avoiding the danger of mere political activism, peace studies must also steer clear of the opposite danger of total detachment from the issues of peace and war. It is true that we advocate peace, and deplore war as a social evil to be brought increasingly under control by the proper application of our intelligence and human feelings. There is no doubt that this advocacy is controversial in our society, where violence, in the name of "defense," "national security," and "the defense of civilization," has been so profoundly institutionalized into our way of life. (Among the opponents of peace studies have been those who argue that conventional war, after all, is "good" if it can forestall the nuclear alternative.)

I note here another interesting double standard in the position of my social scientist colleagues who are so militant about the "neutrality" of the university. No one seems to object to the advocacy of morality—only to the application of morality to serious political issues. Thus no controversy is stirred by moral philosophers who argue or teach conclusions opposing murder. Apparently, however, one should only study mass killing, not oppose it.

To argue that moral judgments hold sway in the political arena as well is rightly viewed as an adversarial challenge to both current political practice and the recent tradition of post-Machiavellian political science which blandly ratifies it. Above all, it is a challenge to programs which train students to be uncritical servants in the national security apparatus. In calm, constructive, and nonviolent language, we must make it clear that the University of California's nuclear weapons labs at Livermore and Los Alamos are only two visible symbols of the much deeper, even nationwide, involvement of universities in the lucrative business of war. If society's attitudes towards the legitimacy of the war business are to change, there is no doubt that the universities will have to change also.

The Controversy Over "Thinking Big"

But the academic resistance encountered by enlarged or integrative peace studies majors can have less to do with content than with the integrative approach itself. One recent critic of peace studies argued, "If the major talks about both food and Homer, then it isn't academic." He was not persuaded by assurances that we knew the risks of an interdisciplinary approach, and he would not give us the chance to show we could overcome them. Nor would he confess to any admission of deficiency in the academic status quo, a complacency which can hardly be characterized as self-critical or Socratic. Apparently, to him, being "academic" meant looking at isolable problems, and never at problems of our human and social condition as a whole.

Such a mentality, once again, is a source of the socio-intellectual predicament of our century: our institutions now train us *not* to look at the large questions which the Platonic Academy and universities originally addressed. This is, I think, a significant reinforcement to our acceptance of the status quo in which war and violence are part of our way of life.

Stanley Milgram (to say nothing of Eichmann) has alerted us to the dangers of excessive obedience, the extent to which obedience to authority can overcome our usual inhibitions against inflicting violence upon others. Educators have rightly asked whether such inhumanity from passive compliance cannot be blamed in part on our school system, whose goal too often "is to produce quiet, submissive students." But perhaps we should also see as complicit in this process of defective socialization the pseudo-scientific mentality of the university—that attitude which, having once taught us to question received ideas, more recently trains us not to.

The Need to Interface With Existing Programs

For these reasons I have to welcome the chief practical problem facing most peace studies programs: the problem of how to develop a significant peace curriculum within what are usually acute budgetary restraints. The resulting pressure to combine, as far as possible, the existing resources of the academy in a new perspective is probably a good experience, as well as a frustrating one. We do not wish to be utopian in the foolish sense, but to engage with the world as it now exists and, within our limited power, change it. For peace-minded faculty and students, this project can begin in no better place than with our colleagues.

As a former anti-war activist now struggling to win acceptance for peace studies at Berkeley, I confess that at times I feel a nostalgia for the easier, more simplistic politics of the sixties: it must have been more fun, back in those days, to sit in a dean's office when the dean himself was absent. But deans, provosts, and chancellors, along with the rest of our colleagues, are the kind of people we must learn to engage in the search for peace if someday we hope also to engage the governments and armies of this dark century. We must make the priorities of peace meaningful to those in power now. Otherwise we shall only begin to have an impact on the world after the next major war—a long perspective few of us are utopian enough to take.

It is too easy merely to write and read articles like the present one, or to share peaceful sentiments with those who already agree. It can be much more difficult to translate ideas about peace into new instructional programs; and those who encounter opposition may indeed wonder at times whether such a small step is worth so great an effort. But the translation of ideas into new institutional realities is precisely what the search for peace is all about. And the university, at least in past eras, has been the place not only to preserve ideals but also to give them life.

II
Syllabi

Global Problems: A General Overview

Approaches to World Order
Saul H. Mendlovitz, Columbia University

Global Issues: "Forward to Basics"
Walker Bush, University of California at Los Angeles

Problems of World Order
Clifton Wilson, University of Arizona

International Relations
Samuel S. Kim, Monmouth College

Toward A Just Society
Robert Elias et al., Tufts University

International Studies: A Global Perspective
Jerry W. Sanders, The City College of New York

Contemporary International Issues
Albert Eldridge and Gary Gereffi, Duke University

Global Issues: Energy, Food and the Arms Race
S.N. Leela and G.V. Stephenson, Millersville State College

International Relations
Marjorie Zamora, Moraine Valley Community College

Approaches to World Order

Saul H. Mendlovitz   *Fall 1984*
Ira D. Wallach Chair of World Order Studies
Department of Political Science/Columbia University/
New York, NY 10027

This course will attempt to provide an understanding of how the present system of international relations works, an appreciation of the major problems we will face over the next decade, and an opportunity to explore how we can intervene to bring about a more just world order.

The course is divided into three parts. The first part explores the evolution of the present international system and different theories and approaches to studying it. Further, it will develop the world order perspective by examining the writings of authors who are either witnesses to oppression or who speak on behalf of the oppressed. The second part will apply the world order perspective to each of the following world order problem areas: war, denial of human rights, poverty and underdevelopment, ecological balance, and the question of participation and governance. In the final section of the course we will explore the nature of change in the international system, its probable future consequences, and how human intervention can shape processes for a most just world order.

All readings for the course appear in Richard Falk, Samuel Kim and Saul H. Mendlovitz, eds., *Toward a Just World Order*, 1982.

Course Outline

Part I. A World Order Perspective

Week 1   Voices for the Oppressed
Introductory Remarks
Shariati, Ali, "Reflections of a Concerned Muslim: On the Plight of Oppressed People."
Biko, Steve, "Black Consciousness and the Quest for a True Humanity."
Charter 77, Czech Plea for Human Rights.
Manifesto of the Alliance for Human Rights in China.
Falk, Richard, "Invisible Oppression."
Lifton, Robert J., "Radiation and Nuclear-Age Victims."
"The Shimoda Decision."

Week 2   The Evolution of the State System
Carneiro, Robert L., "A Theory of the Origin of the State."
Diamond, Stanley, "Civilization and Progress."
Bull, Hedley, "The State's Positive Role in World Affairs."
Gilpin, Robert, "Three Models of the Future."

Week 3 Theories and Approaches
Galtung, Johan, "The Future of the International System."
Falk, Richard, "Contending Approaches to World Order."
Preiswerk, Roy, "Could We Study International Relations As If People Mattered?"
Mendlovitz, Saul H., The Transnational Program of the World Policy Institute
Wallerstein, Immanuel, "The Rise and Future of the World Capitalist System."

Part II. Analysis of World Order Values

Weeks 4 & 5   Peace
Boulding, Kenneth, "The War Trap."
Senghaas, Dieter, "Conflict Formations in Contemporary International Society."
Lewin, Leonard C., "War and Peace As Social Systems," and "The Functions of War."
Text of the "Joint Statement of Agreed Principles for Disarmament Negotiations" of the Soviet Union and the United States (The McCloy-Zorin Agreement).
Article 6 of the Non-Proliferation Treaty.
Johansen, Robert C., *Toward a Dependable Peace: A Proposal for an Appropriate Security System.*
Tolstoy, Leo, "The Beginning of the End."

Weeks 6 & 7   Economic Well-Being
Keyfitz, Nathan, "World Resources and the World Middle Class."
Cooper, Richard N., "A New International Economic Order for Mutual Gain."
Amin, Samir, "Toward a Structural Crisis of World Capitalism."
Kohler, Gernot, "Global Apartheid."
Salvador Allende's Address Delivered at the Inaugural Ceremony on 13 April, 1972, Third Session of UNCTAD.
Houari Boumedienne's Address at the Sixth Special Session of the General Assembly.
Fidel Castro's Speech before the Plenary of the 34th Session of the General Assembly.
Disarmament for a Just World: Declaration of Principles, Proposal for a Treaty, and Call for Action (the New Delhi Declaration).

Weeks 8 & 9   Justice
Introductory Remarks
Ajami, Fouad, "Human Rights and World Order Politics."
Universal Declaration of Human Rights.
The Lusaka Manifesto.
Universal Declaration on the Rights of People, Algiers, 4 July 1976.
Falk, Richard, "Comparative Protection of Human Rights in Capitalist and Socialist Third World Countries."

Weeks 10 & 11   Ecological Balance
Pirages, Dennis, "The Origins of Ecopolitics."
Lovins, Amory B., "Energy Strategy: The Road Not Taken?"
The Trilateral Commission, "Summary of the Report" and "Conclusions."
Christensen, Cheryl, "The Right to Food: How to Guarantee."

Cousins, Norman, "Who Owns the Ozone?"

Orr, David W. and Hill, Stuart, "Leviathan, the Open Society, and Crisis of Ecology."

Week 12 Participation and Governance

Crozier, Michael, Huntington, Samuel P. and Watanuki, Joji, "The Current Pessimism About Democracy" and "The Challenges Confronting Democratic Government."

Frakt, Phyllis, "Mao's Concept of Representation."

Ajami, Fouad, "Third World and World Order."

Alger, Chadwick F., "Role of People in the Future Global Order."

Falk, Richard, "Anarchism and World Order."

Part III. Toward a Just World Order

Week 13 Transition Strategies and Preferred Futures

Brzezinski, Zbigniew, "America in the Technetronic Age."

Bell, Daniel, "The Future World Disorder: The Structural Context of Crisis."

Montreal Statement of WOMP II (Fouad Ajami and Richard Falk).

Harman, Willis W., "The Coming Transformation."

Lakey, George, A Manifesto for Nonviolent Revolution.

Clark, Grenville and Sohn, Louis B., "Two Alternative Plans."

Ophuls, William, "Toward a Politics of the Steady State."

"To Set in Motion the Process of Change," The 1975 Dag Hammarskjold Report.

Kothari, Rajni, "Toward a Just World."

Global Issues: "Forward to Basics"

Walker Bush   *Fall 1983-Winter 1983*
Council on Educational Development/University of California/
Los Angeles, CA 90024

Globalizing the curriculum is viewed as a central mission of today's university community. Students, instructor, and guest seminar leaders will examine together some of the major issues which have transformed the globe into an interdependent planet, and explore opportunities available to students and campuses to prepare for international competence, citizen action and personal values for living in the 21st-century "global village."

This course is one contribution to the growing awareness that a central mission of today's postsecondary education is to bring a world view into all aspects of the university experience. "Whatever one's line of work," writes Harland Cleveland in his article "Forward to Basics" in *Change Magazine* for May/June 1981, "it will be more needful in the future to be interdisciplinary, interdepartmental, and international.... educators of the eighties and nineties are responsible for making sure that Americans enter the twenty-first century with a view as wide as the world. The implication is far-reaching: The widest and most neglected frontier of U.S. educational reform is no longer international studies. It is a global perspective on *all* studies."

This course is not meant to imply that UCLA neglects the world view in either curricular or extracurricular offerings; there is too much evidence to the contrary in the regional and area studies programs, the great variety of languages taught, the Education Abroad Program, the Office of International Students and Scholars, the inter-campus and worldwide outreach of faculty participation and publications. Rather, this course is focused on the specific educational objective of raising undergraduate awareness of the global perspectives available in *all* studies and majors, as noted above, and informing undergraduates that a decision to adopt this perspective will include them in a growing movement in higher education to study about and respond to global issues.

Burns H. Weston, professor of international law at the University of Iowa, describes this: "Significant inroads upon the global challenge, including the preparation of future citizens and leaders for executive coping, to say nothing of action, are scarcely going to materialize without substantial readjustments of this kind. It is not enough simply to marvel at what might be done were the $500 billion of annual world military expenditures allocated otherwise." His essay in *Peace and World Order Studies: A Curriculum Guide* (Third Edition, 1981) introduces a selection of 60—from over 400 submitted—course syllabi on global issues currently taught on campuses from the University of Santa Clara to Harvard.

Goals

We believe that a long-term goal of every campus will be to offer such an introductory course to lower-division undergraduates (also open to upper-division), in many cases as the second-half of a General Education requirement paired with the American History and Institutions requirement. In order to experiment with this concept, the Council on Educational Development has enabled this type of course to start at UCLA as an innovative, optional curricular offering directed toward lower-division students but open to all undergraduates.

An introductory undergraduate course examining "Global Issues" is unique and complementary to the rich variety of international studies, regional and area specializations which are offered in the graduate and undergraduate UCLA curriculum.

Does this course perform some functions which might be done by a College or departmental undergraduate adviser? This may be true, but the principle of complementarity still operates—together with the prospect that some students might first encounter the "global perspective" in a course format, while others meet it in discussions with advisers, classmates, or in readings. We have consciously designed this course as a complement to these other university experiences—with Harland Cleveland's goal-formulation in mind of undergraduates prepared to enter the twenty-first century "with a view as wide as the world." This may explain the kind of *students' term project* we have proposed: to have them each work through globalization of a topic in their major subject.

It is hoped that our rationale helps to explain the broad "survey" nature of this course. The course outline is divided in two roughly-equal parts: the first half of the course acquaints UCLA undergraduates with the main global issues confronting the world of the late 20th century and into the 21st century, grouped within *four* general areas (Weeks III, IV, V, VI). The prior sessions (Weeks I and II) are designed to stress the urgency of this subject matter and to demonstrate the inter-connectedness of issues at the global level as well as between local and global levels.

The second half of the course acquaints the students with some of the tools and locales available to the world's people in working on these issues: truly revolutionary and attitude-shaping revolutions in communications; the availability of existing international institutions and their malleability for improved operation and responsiveness; the special opportunities and obligations of working on global issues in a university setting; and the increasing (*not* decreasing) role individuals can play when they are aware of the issues; and the unprecedented tools available to them for addressing these issues (Weeks VII-X).

To those who may evaluate such a broad concept as a "shallow smorgasbord," I can only repeat that the introductory course nature and the inter-connectedness of the issues seem to us to mandate this breadth. Single-issue courses are already available through the regular University curriculum, University Extension, CED, etc.

Staffing & Resources

Weekly sessions of this course will employ a seminar format, with a gradual increase in the amount of time and quality of content expected from student discussions. A variety of presentation is evident including:

One (possibly two) simulation games to be modified to fit within a class session;

A built-in course evaluation through use of portions of the ETS "Survey of Global Understanding—College Students' Knowledge and Beliefs" at the first and last class sessions as pre-test and post-test. (Students themselves should also be interested in comparing their pre-test results with the nationwide survey data when this Test was given in 1981);

A student term project which requires each class member to design a class presentation or public program in their major subject (or major interest, if his or her major is undeclared) that will reflect a global perspective on their major subject or interest—thus gaining experience during the Quarter in the primary goal the course hopes to achieve at its conclusion;

Several guest lecturers to present the detailed knowledge (drawn in each case from extensive personal experience) in their subject fields:

Daniel Hirsch, CED lecturer in "Energy Alternatives and Public Policy" for *Week III* to discuss the global viewpoints on energy alternatives and the environment;

Amicus Most, professor (emer.) of international trade at NYU and Pace University for *Week V* to discuss international trade issues, questions of trade and development, the North-South debate, and UNCTAD;

Richard Byrne, professor and formerly ag. director, Annenberg School of Communications, USC to discuss in *Week VII* revolutions in communications and their implications for global issues, the ways in which the communications revolutions shape individuals and societies;

Norman Cousins, (UCLA faculty) professor in medical humanities and a leading world authority on the need for global problem-solving and the capacities of present international institutions to accomplish this.

Readings

Fortunately, there is a newly-published anthology containing most of the basic readings needed in this course Falk, Kim, and Mendlovitz, eds., *Toward a Just World Order* (Boulder, CO: Westview Press, 1982) which holds down the cost of textbook purchase and lends continuity in the presentation of readings.

Four other (shorter) works are on the Outline: Meadows, Myrdal, Schumacher, and Jacobson. The remaining readings—either pamphlets or chapters from other books—will be made available or xeroxed and included without additional cost.

Course Outline

1. Overview of the Course

Introduction to "global holism"—acting, thinking, feeling in a manner that spontaneously identifies *first* with the interests of the whole planet—as a way of approaching contemporary problem-solving at the personal, local, national, and international levels. Evaluating examples of each level.

Suggestion of the need for a global perspective in *all* studies and majors (as Harland Cleveland et al. have written); discussion of students' term projects: —to develop a global perspective in their respective declared majors (or, if undecided now, in a major field of interest they might have) through designing a class presentation, a public program, etc. that uses this perspective.

Evaluation of this course and the extent of its impact on the students—they are asked at this first meeting of the course to complete the General Background and Affective sections of the ETS nationwide 1981 "Survey of Global Understanding—College Students' Knowledge and Beliefs." Responses are of interest in comparing students in this course to the national results reported, as well as use of this tool or course evaluation at the last meeting to measure any opinion changes which might have occurred.

2. Global Issues

Examination of the international system as a set of inter-connected global problems of basic importance to the survival of mankind; problems incapable of solution if addressed singly or with old methodologies, capable of solution if addressed in concert and with "no-lose" holistic methodologies (e.g. Buckminster Fuller's concept of "four billion billionaires").

Film: "Survival of Spaceship Earth," a visualization of this class topic with presentations by the late Barbara Ward, Rene Dubos, Margaret Mead, Harrison Brown, Maurice Strong, and many others.

Presentation of Buckminster Fuller's "World Game" by the Friends of Buckminster Fuller, Inc. (Pacific Palisades, Calif.) as an approach to global problem-solving. (This presentation has been made throughout the U.S. at Univ. of Pennsylvania, U.I.U. in San Diego, So. Illinois University, etc. and for members of Congress at the beginning of 1983.)

READINGS: in Falk et al, "Alternative Images of the Future" and "Orientations to Transition" (Sec. 48), pp. 499-620. B. Fuller, *Critical Paths*, "Introduction" and "World Game" pp. 198-228.

3. Issues in Ecological Balance

Discussion of issues includes: concept of resource scarcity vs. inadequate distribution of plentiful resources; primacy of development through exploitation of available resources vs. the conservation equation and ecological balance; choices of "hard" energy vs. "soft" energy paths; and energy/resource cartels as a factor in the international system.

Guest: Daniel Hirsch, CED Lecturer on Energy Resource Alternatives

READINGS: in Falk et al, "Ecological Balance" (Sec. 7), pp. 435-499; Meadows, Donella & Dennis, *Limits to Growth*, 2nd ed. 1974.

4. Issues In Peace and Conflict Mediation

Discussion of issues includes: militarism as an instrument to ensure national security vs. alternative security proposals; comparison of world military expenditures vs. socio-development expenditures; negative peace (absence of war) vs. positive peace (improving economic well-being & ecological balance); professionalizing and internationalizing conflict intervention & mediation among nations.

Film: "Boom," a United Nations-produced brief summary of the global history and dimensions of the arms race.

(Simulation game on resources and their defense may be used in place of film, depending on class size and background information.)

READINGS: in Falk, et al, "Peace" (Sec. 4), pp. 219-288. Alva Myrdal, *The Game of Disarmament*, 1976. Ruth Sivard, *World Military and Social Expenditures*, 1983.

5. Issues in the Global Economy

Discussion of issues includes: the widening gap in economic well-being among (and within) nations; questions of internal reforms within developing nations; the "Physical Quality of Life Index" as a truer measure of national economic health; the population/food equation; the interdependent condition of all the world's economies today; transnational business as new actors in the global economy.

Guest: Amicus Most, professor (emer.) of international trade at NYU; career USAID officer and United Nations consultant.

READINGS: in Falk, et al, "Economic Well-Being" (Sec. 5), pp. 289-369. Keyfitz, Nathan, "World Resources and the World Middle Class," *Scientific American*, 235 (July 1976), pp. 28-35. Schumacher, E.F., *Small is Beautiful: Economics As If People Mattered*.

6. Issues of Human Rights

Discussion of issues includes: the human factors in demilitarization and in development; question of human rights as a factor in foreign policies of nation-states; efficacy of non-governmental international human rights efforts.

READINGS: in Falk, et al., "Social Justice" (Sec. 6), pp. 365-434. Fouad Ajami, "Human Rights and World Order Politics," *Alternatives*, 3, 3 (1978). Cyrus Vance, "Human Rights and Foreign Policy," *Dept. of State Bulletin*, Vol. 76 (May 23, 1977).

Midterm Examination

7. Roles of the Communications Revolution

Empowerment brought by the available (and nearly-available) communications technologies to work on global issues—environment and energy "worldwatches," potential for crisis-avoidance and human rights interventions, etc.; issues of ownership and control of news-gathering and disseminating agencies; problems of individual and societal influence and standard-setting—"communications imperialism."

Guest: Richard Byrne, professor and former director, Annenberg School of Communications, USC.

READINGS: Didsbury, Howard F. ed., *Communications and the Future: Prospects, Promises, and Problems*. Collected papers presented at the Fourth General Assembly of the World Future Society in Washington, D.C., July 1982.

8. Roles of International Institutions

Issues surrounding the United Nations (and the Specialized Agencies) record of accomplishment and areas lacking in sufficient mandate; potential for U.N. reform; regional and functional associations of nations; the contributions of non-governmental international associations.

Guest: Norman Cousins, UCLA Adjunct Professor in Medicine, Law and Human Values; president of the World Federalist Association; prolific author/editor on this theme (among others).

READINGS: in Falk, et al. "Approaches to World Order " (Sec. 3), pp. 141-215. Keys, Donald F. *Earth at Omega: Passage to Planetization.* Jacobson, Harold. *Networks of Interdependence: International Organizations and the Global Political System.* (also for Week 9).

9. Roles of Educational Institutions

Universities as non-governmental contributors to global problem-solving across national boundaries; discussion of higher education programs with stated goals of global awareness and education (e.g., Education Abroad Program, World Campus Afloat, etc.); the unique example of the United Nations University; examination of the University of California's *Institute on Global Conflict and Cooperation* as a case—initiative possible for higher education institutions to undertake.

READINGS: Tonkin, Humphrey and Jane Edwards. *The World in the Curriculum: Curricular Strategies for the 21st Century.* Ch. 2, 4, 6-11. Weston, Burns H. "Peace and World Order Education: An Optimal Design" in *Peace and World Order Studies,* pp. 55-72. Jacobson, Harold. *op. cit.,* chapter on educational institutions.

At this class session students should begin to draw from their term projects in the discussion.

10. Roles of Individuals

Discussion of individual responses to an understanding of "the basics" examined in the course: looking for global dimensions in a student's chosen major; choice of major (for undeclared students) involving global-awareness criteria; international opportunities available to students in business, the professions and other vocations; significance of individual choice and action in the world community.

At this final class session students should be able to contribute to the discussion by sharing from their term projects and what they learned in the process.

Students are asked in this session to again complete the Affective section of the ETS nationwide 1981 *Survey.* (see Week 1 desc.).

Problems of World Order

Clifton Wilson   *Spring 1983*
Political Science 459/University of Arizona/Tucson, AZ 85721

A. Nature of the World Order Approach
(See Richard Falk, et al., *Toward a Just World Order*, Vol. I. Boulder, CO: Westview Press, 1982)

1. Problem areas and

   a. militarism and war
   b. economic underdevelopment and poverty
   c. denial of human rights and underpresentation
   d. ecological decay

   World Order Values

   a. peace
   b. economic well-being
   c. social justice and participation
   d. ecological balance and stability

2. Obstacles to world order

   a. spreading of the arms race
   b. threat of nuclear destruction
   c. conflicts over resources
   d. economic difficulties
   e. revolutionary turbulence
   f. transnational terrorism
   g. expanding populations
   h. scarcity of land and water
   i. lack of constructive negotiations
   j. others?

3. Basic features of the World Order Approach

   a. unity of the human species—materially, ecologically and spiritually
   b. affirmation of values as essential goals of political action
   c. desirability and possibility of fundamental changes in the framework of international relations

B. Comparison of the World Order and International Relations Approaches
(From Norman V. Walbeck and Thomas G. Weiss, *A World Order Framework for Teaching International Politics*, NY: World Policy Institute, 1974, pp. 3-4)

World order is distinguished from international politics in a variety of ways. There are differences in focus, in the role of the investigator, and in definitions of actors, power, national interest, and other substantive areas. These are summarized in the chart below and discussed in detail in the pages which follow.

World order is a general field of inquiry for scholars and citizens seeking to explore possible ways to resolve complex and interrelated global problems. It focuses on

threats to survival and the general quality and dignity of human life. Value preferences are discussed openly; and past, present, and possible future activities are
explored for their potential ability to help resolve these problems. In short, the world
order framework is *systemic* in scope (dealing with global problems), normative in
its concerns, and *oriented* to shaping *the future*.

Differences in Overall Approach	Traditional International Politics	World Order
1) analysis is presumed	value-free	value-oriented
2) appropriate time-dimension is	past and present	past, present, and especially future
3) ultimate analytical goal is	description	prescription
Substantive Differences		
4) primary actors are	nation-states; government elites	continuum from individuals to supranational institutions
5) emphasis on	national interest	global interests
6) problems are seen as	discrete issues	interrelated issues
7) power is	basically military and economic manipulation	not only the ability to coerce
8) large scale violence is	an acceptable means to implement policy goals	ordinarily unacceptable
9) human survival is	assumed	problematical

C. World Order and the Present International Crisis

1. Global survival is an issue for the first time in history—the crisis is of planetary
   proportions.
   a. The crisis is the result of two revolutions: scientific-technological and
      egalitarian-ideological.
   b. Planetary destruction could result from either nuclear war or ecocide.
   c. The violent process of conflict has been rendered obsolete by nuclear war.
   d. The limits of planetary existence must be identified and we must live within
      these limits.

e. Survival requires that man live in harmony with nature as well as with man.

2. The present international system threatens human survival.

   "The global constellation of earthbound political communities stand to each other in what Raymond Aron calls an 'anarchical order of power.' It is a system lacking adequate areas of jurisdiction and structures of authority to set regional and global norms and to ensure compliance, to allocate resources among rich and poor, between as well as within particular communities, to regulate competition and resolve conflicts, and otherwise to safeguard the future of the human species and the habitat upon which we must all continue to depend for subsistence and survival." Sprout and Sprout, *Toward a Politics of the Planet Earth*, NY: Van Nostrand Reinhold, 1971, p. 8.

3. "The conditions of human existence could become safer and the quality of human life could be improved by inducing certain changes in the organization of world society." Richard Falk, *This Endangered Planet*, NY: Random House, 1971, p. 8.

   a. The sovereign state is unable to resolve the endangered-planet crisis.
   b. A dangerous time lag exists between technological advance and development of political institutions.
   c. The earth's population is more interrelated and interdependent, yet political fragmentation and parochial tribalism still characterize the system.

4. Under the world order concept, major threats to the planet are interrelated and require solutions which deal with all of these threats if man is to avoid catastrophe. The threats include:

   a. *The war system*. The constant threat of accidental, creeping or intentional nuclear destruction. Problem: Annihilation of the planet.
   b. *Poverty*. The inequitable distribution of wealth and economic power. Problem: Overpopulation, revolution, starvation, and large-scale human suffering.
   c. *Overpopulation*. The threat of overcrowding the earth by relentless breeding. Problem: Poverty and starvation.
   d. *Depletion of natural resources*. The threat that raw materials will be exhausted by ruthless exploitation. Problem: Social injustice (as well as poverty and starvation).
   e. *Pollution*. The fouling of the earth with waste products until the environment no longer will sustain life. This trend may be irreversible and the world already may have passed the point where a viable solution can be achieved. Problem: Ecocide.

5. Development of a world order system would permit humankind to resolve these threats and provide a positive program for the future.

   a. This system could be based upon plans ranging from "planned muddling through" to advocacy of a world government or world state.
   b. It is important that any world order system be politically feasible, and this requirement may require at least a minimum change in attitudes and institutions.
   c. Any process leading to a revised world order system can result only from the perception of the basic problems and the initiation of specific programs.

6. The world order system is used to describe past, present and future international systems and does not imply a utopian world government. The creation of international institutions (League of Nations, U.N., etc.) and the development of international "legislation" (nuclear test ban, space, sea and other great "law-making" treaties) have led to a stronger order system in recent history. It is assumed that national goals tend more toward survival than toward destruction and thus nations perceive at least the need for a minimum system of order. The thrust of this course is that the problems may be more dangerous than perceived and that more positive action may be required both to improve the quality of human life, and to lessen the threat of global nuclear destruction.

Texts

Richard Falk, Samuel S. Kim and Saul H. Mendlovitz (eds.), *Toward A Just World Order* (Vol. I, 1982). Cited as Reader.
Future Worlds (1979). Cited as Gribbon.
Jonathan Schell, *Fate of the Earth* (1982).
John Brunner, *Stand on Zanzibar (1968)*.

Reserve Readings

Wright, Quincy, *A Study of War* (Abridged ed.)
Stoessinger, John, *Why Nations Go to War* (2nd ed.)
Jacobson, Harold, *Networks of Interdependence*
Claude, Inis L., *Swords Into Plowshares* (4th ed.)
Brook, David, *Search for Peace*
Brown, Lester, *The Twenty-Ninth Day*
Ehrlich, Paul, et al., *Human Ecology*
Orr, David W. and Soroos, Marvin, *The Global Predicament*
Beitz, Charles R. and Herman, Theodore, *Peace and War*
Woito, Robert, *To End War*
Beres, Louis and Targ, Harry, *Reordering the Planet*
George, Susan, *How The Other Half Dies*
Paddock, William and Paul, *Time of Famine*

Section I. World Order and the International System

Week 1 Introduction

Week 2 (Jan. 18-20)   System Perspectives and Approaches to World Order

General Introduction—Reader, p. 1 (Numbers on left, 1 through 39, throughout the syllabus reflect sections of the Falk volume).
Introduction—Reader, p. 13
  1. "Reflections of a Concerned Muslim: On the Plight of Oppressed Peoples," Ali Shariati—Reader, p. 18
  2. "Black Consciousness and the Quest for a True Humanity," Steve Biko—Reader, p. 25
  3. "Charter 77: Czech Group's Plea for Human Rights"—Reader, p. 34
  4. "The Word to Black Women," Awa Thiam—Reader, p. 38
  5. "On Invisible Oppression and World Order," Richard Falk—Reader, p. 43
  6. "Pedagogy of the Oppressed," Paulo Freire—Reader, p. 47

Week 3 (Jan. 25-27)   The Sovereign State and the World System

Introduction—Reader, p. 55

Week 4 (Feb. 1 and 3)   Approaches to World Order

Section II. Problems and Issues of World Order

Week 5 (Feb. 8 and 10)   Economic Well-Being

Week 6 (Feb. 15 and 17)   Human Rights and Social Justice

Week 7 (Feb. 22 and 24)   Ecological Balance

Week 8 (March 1 and 3)   Overview on Economic, Social and Environmental Issues and Problems

John Brunner, *Stand on Zanzibar*

Week 9   Exam and Conferences

March 8—Midterm Exam

March 10—Individual Conferences on Semester Projects

Week 10 (March 15 and 17)   Spring Vacation

Week 11 (March 22 and 24)   Peace and the War System
Introduction—Reader, p. 219
15. "The War Trap," Kenneth Boulding—Reader, p. 225
16. "Conflict Formations in Contemporary International Society," Dieter Senghaas—Reader, p. 239
17. "The Beginning of the End," Leo Tolstoy—Reader, p. 265
18. "Toward a Dependable Peace: A Proposal for an Appropriate Security System," Robert Johansen—Reader, p. 271
19. "Disarmament for a Just World: Declaration of Principles, Proposal for a Treaty, and Call for Action"—Reader, p. 284
    Quincy Wright, Chap. 5, "Causation and War." (Reserve)

Week 12 (March 29 and 31)   Peace and the War System
Individual assignments:
From Stoessinger, *Why Nations Go To War*, (Reserve)
    1. World War I
    2. World War II
    3. Korea
    4. Vietnam
    5. India and Pakistan
    6. Middle East
Class assignments:
Stoessinger, Chap. 7, *Why Nations Go To War*
Schell, *The Fate of the Earth*

Section III. Toward a Future World

Week 13 (April 5 and 7)   Law, Organization and World Order
International Organization (April 5)

Jacobson, Ch. 1, "Nature of International Organization" and Ch. 16, "Formula for an Era of Interdependence" (Reserve)
Claude, Ch. 1 Introduction, and Ch. 19 "International Organization and World Order" (Reserve)
Levi, "What Underlying Conditions are Necessary for a More Effective United Nations?"—Brook, pp. 350-355 (Reserve)

International Law (April 7)

Corbett and Jessup, "Is International Law Really Law? A Challenging 'No' and a Defending 'Yes' ," Brook, pp. 270-281 (Reserve)
Oppenheim, Clark and Northrup, "Under What Conditions Can International Law Bring About Permanent Peace?—Three Different Approaches"—pp. 282-297 (Reserve)

Week 14 (April 2 and 14)   Alternative Futures (Boom or Gloom)
A. General

Gribbon. "Future Worlds," Part I, p. 23

Introduction (Alternate Images), Reader, p. 499
34. "The Global Futures Debate, 1965-1976," Sam Cole—Reader, p. 505
  Brown, *Twenty-Ninth Day*, Ch. 1 Introduction (Reserve)

B. Specific (Individual Assignments)

  1. Population and Food
    Gribbon, "Population and Food, The Malthusian Myth," Ch. 3, p. 77.
    Susan George, Ch. 2, "The Population Myth." (Reserve)
    Ehrlich, Ch. 1, "Population, Resources, Environment—Is Mankind Really in Trouble?" and Ch. 8 "Population Limitation." (Reserve)
    Brown, Ch. 4, "Population: Understanding the Threat." (Reserve)
    Paddock and Paddock, Ch. 9, "Triage." (Reserve)

  2. Energy and Environment
    Gribbon, Ch. 4, "Energy Alternatives."
    Brown, Ch. 5, "Energy: The Coming Transition." (Reserve)
    Ehrlich, Ch. 6, "Disruption of Ecological Systems" and Ch. 9, "Changing Human Behavior: Toward the Environment and Toward Our Fellow Man." (Reserve)

  3. Raw Materials
    Gribbon, Ch. 5, "The Raw Materials."
    Ehrlich, Ch. 3, "Carrying Capacity: Land, Energy and Mineral Resources" (Reserve)

  4. Lifeboat Ethics vs. One Worldism
    Garrett Hardin, "The Tragedy of the Commons," *Science*, p. 162 (Dec. 13, 1968) 1243-48.
    Marvin Soroos, "Lifeboat Ethics Versus One Worldism" in *International Food and Resource Policy*, Ch. 7 in Orr and Soroos (Reserve)

Week 15 (April 19 and 20)   Future Perspectives
A. Boom or Gloom or ???

  Gribbon, Part Three. "A Choice of Paths." (Intro and ch. 8 and 7)
  Brown, Ch. 12, "The Means of Accommodation." (Reserve)

B. What World Order?

  Beres and Targ, Ch. 6, "World Order Perspectives and Alternate World Futures." (Reserve)
35. "What New System of World Order?" Richard Falk—Reader, p. 537

C. Orientation for Transition

Introduction (Transition)—Reader, p. 559
36. "Towards a Just World," Rajni Kothari—Reader, p. 566
37. "Self-Reliance: An Overriding Strategy for Transition," Johan Galtung—Reader, p. 602
38. "Normative Initiatives and Demilitarization: A Third System Approach," Richard Falk—Reader, p. 623
39. "Manifesto for Nonviolent Revolution," George Lakey—Reader, p. 638

Week 16 (April 26 and 28)   Future Perspectives
Continue Week 15 and Individual Reports

Week 17 (May 3)
Review and Reflection

Resource List for Individual Projects

A. Approaches to Change
From Charles Beitz and Theodore Herman (eds.), *Peace and War* (Reserve)
Part I. Building a World Peace System: Approaches to Change

> Ch. 5 World Government
> Ch. 6 Reforming the State System
> Ch. 7 Domestic Change and World Peace
> Ch. 8 Civilian Defense and Nonviolence
> Ch. 9 Individual Action and Social Change

From Robert Woito, *To End War* (Reserve)
Part II. Building a World Peace System: Approaches to Change

> Ch. 4 Arms Control and Disarmament
> Ch. 5 International Organization and World Law
> Ch. 6 World Community and Human Rights
> Ch. 7 World Economic and Political Development

Part III. New Problems

> Ch. 12 The Changing World Economic Order
> Ch. 13 The Environment: A Limit to Growth

Part IV. Developing Capacities

> Ch. 15 Religious and Ethical Thoughts on War
> Ch. 16 Social Changes: Nonviolent Approaches

B. Future Alternatives: Boom or Gloom
1. Gloom

> Paul Ehrlich, *Population, Resources, Environment —Issues in Human Ecology* (1970) (Eco-catastrophe)
> Robert Heilbroner, *An Inquiry Into the Human Prospect* (1974) (Global predicament—population, weapons, environment)
> Donna Meadows et. al., *The Limits to Growth* (1972)
> E.F. Schumacher, *Small is Beautiful* (1973)
> Joseph Spengler, *Population Change, Modernization and Welfare* (1974) (Malthusian position)

2. Boom

> Herman Kahn et al., *The Next 200 Years* (1976)
> Arthur C. Clarke, *Profiles of the Future* (1964)
> V. Kosolapov, *Mankind and the Year 2000* (1976)
> John Maddox, *The Doomsday Syndrome* (1972)
> Herman Kahn, *The Coming Boom* (1982)
> Julian L. Simon, *The Ultimate Resource* (1981)
> Herman Kahn and Anthony Weiner, *The Year 2000* (1962)
> Y. Modrzhinskaya and C. Stephanyan, *The Future of Society* (1973)

C. Future Alternatives: Diverse News

Rene Dumont, *Utopia or Else* (1974) (plight of poor countries)

Mihajlo Mesarovic and Edward Pestel, *Mankind at the Turning Point* (1974) (strategy for survival model)

Wassily Leontief and others, *The Future of the World Economy* (1973) (UN world input-output model)

Amilcar Herrera, *Catastrophe or New Society* (1976) (Latin American model— redistribution and regional development)

Jan Tinbergen and others, *Reshaping the International Order* (RIO) (1976) (economic development)

Robert North, *The World That Could Be* (1976) (system change)

Richard Falk, *This Endangered Planet* (1971) (cultural perspective)

John McHale, *The Future of the Futures* (1971) (technology and ecology)

W. Warren Wager, *Building the City of Man* (1971) (universal cultural themes)

Carl Friedrich von Weizsacker, *The Politics of Peril* (1978) (transition to global solidarity)

Robert Cooley Angell, *The Quest for World Order* (1979) (organization and regionalism)

Hedley Bull, *The Anarchical Society* (1977) (the sovereign state and world order)

Paul Hawkins and others, *Seven Tomorrows* (1982) (future scenarios)

Gerald and Patricia Mische, *Towards a Human World Order* (1977) (religious and humanistic perspective)

Norman Adcock and others, *1982* (1978) (computer-based future scenarios)

D. The Nuclear Threat

1. Views from the 60s

Amitai Etzioni, *Winning Without War* (1964)

Charles O. Osgood, *An Alternative to War or Surrender* (1962)

Walter Mills and James Real, *The Abolition of War* (1963)

Robert Strauz-Hupe and others, *Protracted Conflict* (1958)

2. Views from the 80s

Ruth Adams and Susan Cullin (eds.), *The Final Epidemic* (1981)

Daniel Frei, *Risks of Nuclear War* (1983)

Robert J. Lifton and Richard Falk, *Indefensible Weapons* (1982)

Louis Rene Beres, *Apocalypse: Nuclear Catastrophe in World Politics* (1980) (Briefer studies)

E. P. Thompson and Dan Smith (eds.), *Protest and Survive* (1981)

Independent Commission on Disarmament and Security Issues, *Common Security* (1982)

Lewis A. Dunn, *Controlling the Bomb* (1982)

Nigel Calder, *Nuclear Nightmares* (1981)

Helen Caldicott, *Nuclear Madness* (1978)

James Avery Joyce, *The War Machine* (1980)

3. Action-Oriented

David Barash and Judith Lipton, *Stop Nuclear War* (1982)

Ground Zero, *Nuclear War: What's in it for You?* (1982)

Edward Kennedy and Mark O. Hatfield, *Freeze: How You Can Help Prevent Nuclear War* (1982)

International Relations

Samuel S. Kim   *Fall 1982*
Political Science 281/Monmouth College/West Long Branch, NJ 07764

This course is designed to study international relations from a world order perspective. The main objective of the course is to raise and explore some broad questions about the past, the present, and the future of the human condition on this planet with special attention to the historical roots and development of world politics, the present global issues and crises, and the future prospects for human survival. Part I is conceptual and methodological in focus, evaluating various ways and means of coming to terms with the "reality" of the human predicament in the world today. Part II probes the causes and dimensions of global crises and the responses of the present international system. Part III examines various proposals and images of preferred worlds, including contending global models, and transition politics.

Main Texts

Richard A. Falk, *A Study of Future Worlds* (New York: Free Press, 1975). (Paperback)
Charles W. Kegley, Jr. and Eugene R. Wittkopf, *World Politics: Trend and Transformation* (New York: St. Martin's Press, 1981). (Paperback)
Dennis Pirages, *The New Context for International Relations: Global Ecopolitics* (North Scituate, MA.: Duxbury Press, 1978). (Paperback)

Readings and Requirements

The reading selections in the following pages provide a guide for exploring various topical issues to be studied during the course. The items which are starred (*) constitute *the required readings* for the course. Each student should take into account his/her own background, area of interest, and future plans in determining the amount of additional reading beyond the required items. The requirements (and proportional grade value) for the course include a mid-term exam (20%), a term paper of about 15-20 typewritten pages on a topic germane to the course (30%), a final exam (30%), and contribution to class discussion (20%).

Schedule of Readings and Class Sessions

Part I. Conceptual Framework
1. The Transformation of World Politics
    *Falk, Chap. 2.
    *Kegley and Wittkopf, chap. 1, 5, 14.
    *Pirages, chap. 1.
    Joseph Camilleri, *Civilization in Crisis: Human Prospects in a Changing World* (New York: Cambridge University Press, 1976).
    Ole Holsti, Randolph Siverson, and Alexander George (eds.), *Change in the International System* (Boulder, CO: Westview Press, 1980).
    Evan Luard, *Types of International Society* (New York: Free Press, 1976).

Edward L. Morse, *Modernization and the Transformation of International Relations* (New York: Free Press, 1976).

Arthur Nussbaum, *A Concise History of the Law of Nations* (New York: The Macmillan Co., 1961).

Richard N. Rosecrance, *Action and Reaction in World Politics* (Boston: Little, Brown and Co., 1963).

2. Contending Theories of World Politics

Falk, pp. xvii-xxx, 1-5, chap. 1.

*Kegley & Wittkopf, chap. 2.

*Pirages, pp. 32-40.

James Dougherty and Robert Pfaltzgraff, *Contending Theories of International Relations* (2nd ed., New York: Harper & Row, 1981).

Klaus Knorr and James Rosenau (eds.), *Contending Approaches to International Politics* (Princeton, NJ: Princeton University Press, 1969).

Richard Mansbach, Yale Ferguson, and Donald Lamport, *The Web of World Politics* (Englewood Cliffs, NJ: Prentice-Hall, 1976).

3. Diverse Images of World Order

*Falk, chap. 7.

*Kegley & Wittkopf, chaps. 12-13.

*Pirages, chap. 2.

Hedley Bull, *The Anarchical Society: A Study of Order in World Politics* (New York: Columbia University Press, 1977).

Grenville Clark and Louis Sohn, *World Peace Through World Law* (3rd ed., Cambridge, MA: Harvard University Press, 1966).

Ian Clark, *Reform and Resistance in the International Order* (New York: Cambridge University Press, 1980).

Stanley Hoffman, *Primacy or World Order* (New York: McGraw-Hill, 1978).

Richard A. Falk and Samuel S. Kim, "An Approach to World Order Studies and the World System," in William Thompson (ed.), *Multiple Perspectives on the World System* (Beverly Hills, CA: Sage Publications, 1982).

Richard A. Falk, Samuel S. Kim, and Saul H. Mendlovitz (eds.), *Toward a Just World*, Vol. I in *Studies on a Just World Order* series (Boulder, CO: Westview Press, 1982).

A.J.R. Groom and Paul Taylor (eds.), *Functionalism: Theory and Practice in International Relations* (London: University of London Press, 1975).

Robert Johansen, *The National Interest and the Human Interest* (Princeton, NJ: Princeton University Press, 1980).

Robert Keohane and Joseph Nye, *Power and Interdependence* (Boston: Little, Brown and Co., 1977).

Samuel S. Kim, *China, the United Nations, and World Order* (Princeton, NJ: Princeton University Press, 1979).

Saul H. Mendlovitz (ed.), *On the Creation of a Just World Order* (New York: Free Press, 1975).

Immanuel Wallerstein, *The Capitalist World-Economy* (New York: Cambridge University Press, 1979).

Part II. The Causes of Global Crises and the Conditions of a Just World Order

4. Violence and War

*Falk, pp. 242-51.

*Kegley & Wittkopf, chaps. 3, 10-11.

Francis A. Beer, *Peace Against War: The Ecology of International Violence* (San Francisco: W.H. Freeman & Co., 1981).

Louis Rene Beres, *Apocalypse: Nuclear Catastrophe in World Politics* (Chicago: University of Chicago Press, 1980).

Richard A. Falk and Samuel S. Kim (eds.), *The War System: An Interdisciplinary Approach* (Boulder, CO: Westview Press, 1980).

J. David Singer and Melvin Small, *The Wages of War 1816-1965* (New York: John Wiley & Sons, 1972).

Ruth L. Sivard, *World Military and Social Expenditures 1981* (annual) (Leesburg, VA: World Priorities, 1981).

Quincy Wright, *A Study of War* (Chicago: University of Chicago Press, 1965).

5. Economic Poverty and Inequity

*Falk, chap. 6, pp. 251-62.

*Kegley & Wittkopf, chaps. 4, 6-7.

*Pirages, chap. 7.

Richard Barnet, *The Lean Years* (New York: Simon & Schuster, 1980).

George Modelski (ed.), *Transnational Corporations and World Order* (San Francisco: W.H. Freeman and Co., 1979).

North-South: A Programme for Survival [The Report of the Brandt Commission] (Cambridge, MA: M.I.T. Press, 1980).

Robert Rothstein, *Global Bargaining* (Princeton, NJ: Princeton University Press, 1979).

E.F. Schumacher, *Small is Beautiful: Economics as if People Mattered* (New York: Harper & Row, 1973).

Jan Tinbergen, et al., Reshaping the International Order (New York: E.P. Dutton, 1976).

World Development Report, 1981 (annual) (Washington, DC: The World Bank, 1981).

6. Human Rights Abuse

*Falk, pp. 262-68.

*Kegley & Wittkopf, chap. 8.

*Pirages, chap. 3.

Amnesty International Report 1980 (annual) (London: Amnesty International Publications, 1980).

Richard A. Falk, *On Human Rights* (New York: Holmes and Meier, 1981).

Louis Henkin, *The Rights of Man Today* (Boulder, CO: Westview Press, 1978).

Myres McDougal, et al., *Human Rights and World Public Order* (New Haven, CT: Yale University Press, 1980).

Barrington Moore, Jr., *Injustice: The Social Bases of Obedience and Revolt* (White Plains, NY: M. E. Sharpe, 1978).

John Rawls, *A Theory of Justice* (Cambridge, MA: Harvard University Press, 1972).

United Nations Action in the Field of Human Rights (New York: United Nations, 1980).

U.S. Department of State, *Country Reports on Human Rights Practices* (annual).

7. Ecological Degradation

*Falk, pp. 268-75.

*Kegley & Wittkopf, chap. 9.

*Pirages, chaps. 4-6.

Karl Deutsch (ed.), *Ecosocial Systems and Ecopolitics* (Paris: UNESCO, 1977).

Donella Meadows, et al., *The Limits to Growth* 2nd ed. (Washington, DC: Potomac Associates, 1974).

Michael M'Gonigle and Mark Zacher, *Pollution, Politics and International Law* (Berkeley, CA: University of California Press, 1979).

William Ophuls, *Ecology and the Politics of Scarcity* (San Francisco: W.H. Freeman and Co., 1977).

David Orr and Marvin Soroos (eds.), *The Global Predicament* (Chapel Hill, NC: The University of North Carolina Press, 1979).

Jan Schneider, *World Public Order of the Environment* (Toronto: University of Toronto Press, 1979).

Part III. Toward Alternative World Order Systems

8. The Promise and Prospects of a Just World Order

Falk, chap. 3; pp. 224-242.

*Kegley & Wittkopf, chap. 15.

Louis Rene Beres and Harry R. Targ (eds.), *Planning Alternative World Futures* (New York: Praeger Publishers, 1975).

Willis W. Harman, *An Incomplete Guide to the Future* (Stanford, CA: Stanford Alumni Association, 1976).

Robert Heilbroner, *An Inquiry into the Human Prospect* (New York: W.W. Norton, 1974).

Amilcar O. Herrera, et al., Catastrophe or New Society? A Latin American World Model (Ottawa, Canada: International Development Research Centre, 1976).

The Global 2000 Report to the President, 3 vols (Washington, DC: U.S. Government Printing Office, 1980-1981).

Robert Jungk and Johan Galtung (eds.), *Mankind 2000* (London: Allen and Unwin, 1969).

Herman Kahn, et al., *The Next 200 Years* (New York: William Morrow and Co., 1976).

Wassily Leontief, et al., *The Future of the World Economy* (New York: Oxford University Press, 1977).

H. Ornauer, et al., (eds.), *Images of the World in the Year 2000* (Atlantic Highlands, NJ: Humanities Press, 1976).

9. The Transition Politics

*Falk, chap. 5.

*Kegley & Wittkopf, chap. 14.

*Pirages, chap. 8.

S. N. Eisenstadt, *Revolution and the Transformation of Societies: A Comparative Study of Civilizations* (New York: Free Press, 1978).

Susanne Gowan, et al., *Moving Toward a New Society* (Philadelphia, PA: New Society Press, 1976).

George Lakey, *Strategy for a Living Revolution* (San Francisco: W.H. Freeman and Co., 1973).

Ervin Laszlo, *A Strategy for the Future* (New York: George Braziller, 1974).

Theda Skocpol, *States and Social Revolutions* (New York: Cambridge University Press, 1979).

Gene Sharp, *Social Power and Political Freedom* (Boston: Porter Sargent Publishers, 1980).

Toward A Just Society: Issues in Peace and Social Justice

Robert Elias (Coordinator)/Reverend Geoffrey/   *Spring 1983*
Hugo Bedau/Norman Daniels/Tad Akiba/Bobby Cooley/
Pearl Robinson/Gerald Gill/Francine Chew/Saul Slapikoff/
Maryanne Wolf/Susan Ostrander/Saul Schwartz/
Stephen Winter/Seymour Bellin
Political Science/Philosophy/Mathematics/International Relations/
History/Biology/Child Study/Sociology/Economics/Education/
Tufts University, Medford, MA 02155

It is not a happy thought, but it takes little insight to understand the serious-ness of the human predicament. Whatever progress we have made as a species, it is hard to deny that our failures and our human-made destructive-ness have been prominent. Problems such as racism, sexism, environmental decay, dwindling resources, starvation and poverty, world inequality and underdevelopment, the arms race, and nuclear proliferation all provide frightening indicators of the dangers we face. It is not true that we have always faced these problems, and that we are continually making progress. In fact, the threats are greater now than they ever were, despite our technological capabilities: in fact, such advances are often a part of the problem.

The Peace & Social Justice Program has been created by a group of faculty, students, staff, and administrators who believe that something must be done immediately to more successfully address and solve these problems. Through the educational system, we hope to generate new energy and enthusiasm toward grappling with world problems. We seek to make our existing courses more relevant to broad questions of peace and social justice, and to create new courses with these same goals in mind. And, we seek to build greater consciousness, responsibility, and social action among those who participate in the program.

This course is one of two, team-taught, interdisciplinary courses we have developed, the other ("The Quest for Peace") focusing entirely on peace studies. "Toward A Just Society" presents an introduction to peace, justice and human rights; to examine the threats (such as war, ecological decay, exploitation, poverty, sexism, racism) to these goals internationally; and to devise means (education, economic democracy, world-order systems, indi-vidual responsibility, social activism, etc.) to combat these threats. With these goals in mind, the course will be organized as follows:

General Readings

Richard Falk, *A Study of Future Worlds*
Gerald Mische & Patricia Mische, *Toward a Human World Order*
Saul Mendlovitz, ed., *On the Creation of a Just World Order*
Aldous Huxley, *Island*
Bernard Crick, *George Orwell: A Life*
Bertrand Russell, *Autobiography*

Week 1 Human Rights, Peace and Social Justice
by Professor Robert Elias, Department of Political Science
READ: Reza Baraheni, *God's Shadow*
   Richard Falk, "Theoretical Foundations of Human Rights"
   Christian Bay, "Universal Human Rights Priorities: Toward A Rational Order"
   Henry Shue, "Security and Subsistence" and "Correlative Duties"
   Noam Chomsky & Edward Herman, *The Washington Connection and Third World Fascism*, chap. 1.2.
   "Universal Declaration of the Rights of Peoples"
   "The International Bill of Rights"

Week 2 The Just Society
by Professor Hugo Bedau, Department of Philosophy
   Professor Norman Daniels, Department of Philosophy
READ: Arthur John and William Shaw, *Justice and Economic Distribution*

Week 3 Religion as Mediator for Social Justice
by Reverend Geoff Drutchas, University Chaplaincy
READ: Henry Scott Stokes, "Korea's Church Militants"
   Marlisse Simmons, "Latin America's New Gospel"
   Edwin Yoder, "The Bishops vs. the Bomb"
   Bill Kellerman, "The Heart of the Matter"

Week 4 The Threat of Nuclear War
by Jerome Grossman, Council for a Livable World
READ: Helen Caldicott, *Nuclear Madness*

Week 5 Consequences of Nuclear War: Hiroshima and Nagasaki
by Professor Tad Akiba, Department of Mathematics
READ: John Hersey, *Hiroshima*
   Masuji Ibuse, *Black Rain*
   Jonathan Schell, *The Fate of the Earth*

Week 6 World Order Systems
by Professor Bobby Cooley, International Relations Program
READ: Saul Mendlovitz, *On the Creation of a Just World Order*

Week 7 Third World Development and Food Policy
by Professor Pearl Robinson, Department of Political Science
READ: Pamela Moyer & Michael Haines, "How We Cause World Hunger"

Michael Lofchie, "Political and Economic Origins of African Hunger"

Frances Moore Lappé, *Aid As Obstacle*

Week 8   Race and Racism: America and South Africa
by Professor Gerald Gill, Department of History
   Professor Hugo Bedau, Department of Philosophy
READ: Study Commission on U.S. Policy Toward South Africa, *South Africa: Time Running Out*
   Gerry Gill and John Flemming, *The Case for Affirmative Action for Blacks in Higher Education*
   Barry Gross, *Reverse Discrimination*
   Robert O'Neil, *Discriminating Against Discrimination*
   Herbert Gans, *More Equality*

Week 9   Sexism and the Feminization of Poverty
by Professor Susan Ostrander, Department of Sociology
   Professor Saul Schwartz, Department of Economics
READ: Heather Ross, "Poverty: Women and Children Last"
   Robin Bartlett and Charles Poulton-Callahan, "Changing Family Structure & the Distribution of Income, 1951-76"
   Elizabeth Durbin, "The Vicious Cycle of Welfare"
   U.S. Department of Labor, "Twenty Facts on Women Workers"
   Ann Tickameyer, "Wealth and Power: A Comparison of Men and Women in the Property Elite"
   Donald Chambers, "Another Look at Poverty Lines in England and the United States"
   Lourdes Beneria, "Conceptualizing the Labor Force: The Underestimation of Women's Economic Activities"

Week 10   Environment as a Right: Ecological Threats
by Professor Saul Slapikoff, and Professor Francie Chew, Department of Biology
READ: Walter Westman, "How Much Are Nature's Services Worth"
   Anne & Paul Erlich, "The Snail Darter and Us"
   "Endangered Bird Species: Habitat Manipulation Methods"
   Norman Myers, "Playing God to Save Destiny"
   Council Report, "Health Evaluation of Energy-Generating Sources"
   Bernard Cohen & Ralph Nader, "Are Nuclear Side Effects Hazardous to Your Health?"
   Andre Gorz, "The Logic of Tools"

Week 11   Moral Development, Individual Responsibility, & Social Justice
by Professor Maryanne Wolf, Department of Child Study
   Professor John Powell, Department of Political Science
READ: Lawrence Kohlberg, "Moral Stages and Moralization"
   Lawrence Kohlberg and Carol Gilligan, "The Adolescent as Philosopher"

Week 12   Education and the Quest for Justice
by Professor Steven Winter, Department of Education

      READ: David Nasaw, *Schooled to Order*
              Colin Greer, *The Great School Legend*
              Henry Perkinson, *The Imperfect Panacea*
              Brian Wren, *Education for Justice*

Week 13   **Citizen Activism for Social Justice**
            by Professor Robert Elias, Department of Political Science
              Professor Seymour Bellin, Department of Sociology
            READ: Chadwick Alger, "Foreign Policies of U.S. Publics"
                   John Beam, "Solidarity Work and Community Organizing"
                   Harry Boyte, "The Formation of the New Peace Movement"
                   Samuel Day, "The New Resistance"
                   Richard Falk, "World Order Activism"
                   Susanne Gordon, "The Ultimate Single Issue"
                   Paul Wehr and Michael Washburn, "Working for Peace & Justice"
                   Christian Bay, *Strategies for Political Emancipation*
                   Susanne Gowan, et al., *Moving Toward A New Society*

Requirements

1) Regular attendance at presentations
2) General readings and reserve readings
3) Class participation
4) Two ten-page research papers—supervised by two different professors
5) Attendance at film series—"Protest and Progress"
6) *Active* interest and commitment
7) One short paper—social justice group investigation

International Studies: A Global Perspective

Jerry W. Sanders   *Fall 1983*
International Studies 201/The City College of New York/
New York, NY 10031

Global crisis is a phrase repeated often, but a phenomenon little understood. In this course we will examine contemporary crises in the present world order as they are manifested in the problems of war and militarism, economic stagnation and social inequality, and political repression of fundamental human rights.

Since these phenomena cross national borders, our point of departure will begin with the world as a social whole. Since the problems under study interrelate one with the other, our approach must also be interdisciplinary in nature. And finally, since the human suffering actual and potential in continuing present patterns of international relations is of such enormity, we will give equal concern to normative (what ought to be) as well as empirical (what is) inquiry.

Particular attention will be focused on the dynamics of U.S. foreign policy in the present context of global crisis, as well as to the differing perspectives for resolving these crises. Students will be encouraged to consider alternative policies that might better meet the needs of all peoples, as well as how they might be brought into being.

The course format is lecture, discussion, and special events, such as speakers and public forums.

The requirements for course credit are attendance at all class sessions and special events; participation in discussion; a term project which calls for critical evaluation and creative invention involving issues and concepts in the course; and mid-term and final essay exams over readings and lectures.

I. Introduction

September 27   Global Society, International (Dis)Order, and World Community
Reading:
Ruth Leger Sivard, *World Military and Social Expenditures, 1982*. Washington, D.C.: World Priorities Inc., 1982.
George F. Kennan, *A Proposal for International Disarmament.* Acceptance speech for the Albert Einstein Peace Prize. NY: World Policy Institute reprint, 1981.
Gernot Kohler, *Global Apartheid*. Working Paper #7, World Order Models Project, NY: World Policy Institute, 1978.
Roy Preiswerk, "Could We Study International Relations As If People Mattered?" in *Peace and World Order Studies: A Curriculum Guide*. NY: World Policy Institute, 1981, pp. 2-23.

September 30   U.S. Foreign Policy in Global Context
Reading:
Arthur Schlesinger, Jr. "Foreign Policy and the American Character," *Foreign Policy*, Fall 1983.
Norman Podhoretz, "Appeasement by Any Other Name," *Commentary*, July 1983.
Jerry W. Sanders, "Breaking Out of the Containment Syndrome," *World Policy*, Fall 1983, Vol. I, No. I.

II. Militarism

October 4   The Cold War and The Arms Race (Conservative view)
Reading:
The Committee on the Present Danger, *Common Sense and The Common Danger*, Washington D.C.: Committee on the Present Danger, 1976.
Countering The Soviet Threat: U.S. Defense Strategy for the 1980s. Washington, DC: CPD, 1980.
The 1980 Crisis and What We Should Do About It. Washington, DC: CPD, 1980.

October 11   The Cold War and The Arms Race (Liberal view)
Reading:
Leslie H. Gelb, "A Practical Way To Arms Control," *New York Times Magazine*, June 5, 1983.
Harry McPherson and Richard Holbrook, "A Foreign Policy For The Democrats," *New York Times Magazine*, April 10, 1983.

October 18   The Cold War and The Arms Race (Progressive view)
Reading:
Robert C. Johansen, *Toward A Dependable Peace*, World Policy Paper #8. NY: World Policy Institute, 1983.
Earl C. Ravenal, "The Case for A Withdrawal of Our Forces," *New York Times Magazine*, March 6, 1983.

III. Human Rights/Intervention

October 25   Current Policy Foundations
Reading:
Jeane Kirkpatrick, "Dictatorships and Double Standards," *Commentary*, November, 1979.
Jeane Kirkpatrick, "U.S. Security and Latin America," *Commentary*, January, 1981.

November 1   Critique of Current Directions
Reading:
Fouad Ajami, *Human Rights and World Order Politics*, Working Paper #4, World Order Models Project. NY: World Policy Institute, 1978.
Piero Gleijeses, *Tilting At Windmills: Reagan In Central America*, Occasional Papers in International Affairs, The Johns Hopkins Foreign Policy Institute, Washington, D.C., April 1982.

November 8   Midterm Exam

IV. World Economy

November 15   Decline of U.S. Hegemony
Reading:
"The Decline of U.S. Power," *Business Week*, March 12, 1979.
Immanuel Wallerstein, "Friends As Foes," *Foreign Policy*, Fall 1980, pp. 119-131.

November 22   North-South Inequality
Reading:
Daniel Chirot, *Social Change in the Twentieth Century*, "Comparative Sociology: Past Failures and New Ideas," pp. 1-15. "The Future and The Study of Social Change," pp. 248-256.
Willy Brandt, "A Plea for Change: Peace, Justice, Jobs," Introduction to *North-South: A Program for Survival* (The Report of the Independent Commission on International Development Issues, 1980), pp. 7-29.
Willy Brandt, *Common Crisis North-South: Cooperation For World Recovery* (The Brandt Commission, 1983), pp. 1-38.

November 29   Industrial Policy
Reading:
Sidney Blumenthal, "Drafting A Democratic Industrial Plan," *New York Times Magazine*, August 28, 1983.
Felix G. Rohatyn, "Alternatives to Reaganomics," *New York Times Magazine*, December 5, 1982.
Robert B. Reich, "The Next American Frontier," *The Atlantic Monthly*, April 1983.
Bob Kuttner, "An Interview with Bennett Harrison and Barry Bluestone," *Working Papers*, January-February 1983.

V. The Politics of Policy

December 6   Public Opinion
Reading:
Daniel Yankelovich and Larry Kaagan, "Assertive America," *Foreign Affairs*, Fall 1981.
John E. Rielly, "American Opinion: Continuity, Not Reaganism," *Foreign Policy*, Spring 1983.

December 13   Grassroots Movements
Reading:
Richard A. Viguerie, *The New Right: We're Ready to Lead*, "Our Primary Goal: Military Superiority," pp. 109-122; "1978: Our Critical Year," pp. 65-77; "The Four Keys To Our Success," pp. 78-98.
John Herbers, "Grass-Roots Groups Go National," *New York Times Magazine*, September 4, 1983.

December 20   The Intelligensia
Carl Gershman, "The Rise and Fall of the Foreign Policy Establishment," *Commentary*, July 1980.
Jerry W. Sanders, *Empire at Bay: Containment Strategies and American Politics at The Crossroads*, World Policy Paper #25. NY: World Policy Institute, 1983.

TERM PROJECT DUE

January 10   Final Exam

Socio-Biography Student Assignment

> Neither the life of an individual nor the history of a society can be
> understood without understanding both. The sociological imagi-
> nation enables us to grasp history and biography and the relations
> between the two within society. That is its task and its promise.
> —C. Wright Mills, *The Sociological Imagination* (1959)

Our lives take place in society, in history. Increasingly, since Mills wrote
the words above, we are aware that society is global in scope and that history
is also global in its sweep. Nonetheless, we often think of our biographies as
divorced from global events and lived outside history. When we think of the
forces shaping our lives most of our recollections involve other people—as
individuals or in groups—disconnected from social institutions, especially
those at the macro-level that transcend national boundaries such as the
economy and politics. Yet it is these large-scale institutions that so much
shape our values, communities, education, families, and life-chances. Your
task in this assignment is to trace your biography, demonstrating the intersection of history and social structure in your life, from a global perspective.

Some suggestions for organizing this paper:

I. Self-in-Society. In this section you locate yourself within the social structure.
Consider the stratification system and where you fit into it. Also, you should locate
the society into which you were born within the larger world system. (A helpful
source in this regard might be Daniel Chirot, *Social Change in The Twentieth
Century*, Harcourt Brace Jovanovich, 1977.)

Begin by considering your family's position in the social order by tracing its roots
back at least to your grandparent's generation. What type of social and geographical
mobility pattern emerges from your intergenerational analysis? What historical
forces (industrialization, urbanization, shifts in the international division of labor,
immigration, etc.) and big events (the Great Depression, wars, revolution, social
movements) help explain your family's history and present status?

II. Society-in-Self. The focus here is your socialization. What cultural values did
your family transmit to you? How were they reinforced, reinterpreted, or rejected in
your experiences in other institutional areas—school, religion, work, politics,
immigration to a new society? How did these values relate to the larger economic
and political realities and to your family's class position?

What expectations did (and does) your family have for you (regarding career, politics, marriage), and how have these been reinforced, reinterpreted, or rejected in
other subsequent institutional arenas and by historical events? (Refer to *The
Autobiography of Malcolm X* for this section and the next.)

III. Self vs. Society. The self is not simply made; it goes on making itself, amidst
subsequent experience. Consider biographical transitions that have brought you to
where you are today. Consider similarities and differences between your parents'
attitudes (on career, politics, religion, education, marriage) and your own. How do
larger historical processes help explain either the similarities or differences? What
sort of conflicts between your values and goals, your earlier socialization, and social
institutions do you see looming at present and in the future?

Contemporary International Issues

Albert Eldridge and Gary Gereffi   *Spring 1982*
History 109/Sociology 175/Political Science 160/Duke University/
Durham, NC 27706

This course is designed to introduce Duke undergraduates to some of the most important contemporary international issues. These are issues which daily fill our newspapers and television screens, which preoccupy private and public decision-makers, and which work to structure the patterns of our daily lives. That the international dimension of the basic problems which affect our lives has been growing is widely recognized. So also is the understanding that solutions to these problems will be forged on an international basis, as a result of attitudes and decisions made not only by individuals and social and political groups within single nation-states, but through conflict and compromise across national boundaries.

We live in an increasingly complex and integrated world divided into social groups, nations and blocs of nations by fundamental political, social and economic interests. These social groups, nations and blocs of nations have radically different understandings of the past and sharply divergent visions of the future. We use shorthand to summarize these differences. We speak of East-West tensions and North-South tensions. Along these two axes lie the five sets of contemporary international issues addressed in this course: (1) power and political interdependence; (2) dependency and underdevelopment in the Third World; (3) multinational corporations and international economic organization; (4) the new international military order; and (5) the political economy of development: industrialization and the erosion of democracy.

This course can only scratch the surface of conceptual and policy issues. It is designed to raise these issues in the minds of students, to encourage intellectual exchange among faculty across departmental and professional boundaries, and to stimulate students to pursue these issues in greater depth in the scores of specialized courses offered within the university which deal with international issues.

Reading Assignments

The following books should be purchased for the course. Other assigned reading can be found on 3-hour reserve in Perkins Library.

Crozier, Michel, Samuel Huntington, and J. Watanuki. *The Crisis of Democracy.* (New York: New York University Press, 1975).

Evans, Peter. *Dependent Development.* (Princeton, NJ: Princeton University Press, 1979).

Holsti, Ole, Randolph Siverson, and Alexander George. *Change in the International System.* (Boulder, CO: Westview Press, 1980).

Guest Lecturers

We are fortunate to be able to call upon the expertise of a number of guest lecturers in this course. Our guests will come not only from the faculty of Duke University, but also from other universities and institutions specializing in international issues. These guest lecturers will be available for small group discussions (at lunch and/or dinner) and scheduled small group appointments to discuss research topics.

Among the individuals who are likely to join us in the course are:

Professor John Odell, Center for International Affairs and Department of Government, Harvard University, on international trade.

Professor Peter Evans, Department of Sociology, Brown University, on Brazil.

Professor Douglas C. Bennet, Woodrow Wilson Center, Smithsonian Institution and Department of Political Science, Temple University.

Professor Richard Newfarmer, Overseas Development Council, Washington, D.C., on theories of state, the auto industry, Mexico, and political philosophy.

Professor Alfred Stepan, Councilium on International Studies and Department of Political Science, Yale University, on Latin America.

Professor Theodore Moran, School of Foreign Service, Georgetown University, Washington, D.C., on dependency theory.

Course Outline and Readings

There are five issue areas in the course: The Nature and Analysis of International Power; Dependency and Underdevelopment in the Third World; Multinational Corporations and Global Economic Organization; The New International Military Order; and The Political Economy of Development: Industrialization and the Erosion of Democracy. Each issue area is designated by a roman numeral. Within each of these issue areas are a number of interrelated topics. These topics are identified by the titles of the lectures presented on the specified dates. Assigned and suggested readings for each lecture topic are listed.

January 12   Course Introduction and Organization (Eldridge and Gereffi)

January 14   Conflict and International Relations: Perceptions and Decision-Making (Eldridge)

January 16   Conflict and International Relations: Structures and the Global Context (Gereffi)

I. The Nature and Analysis of International Power

January 19   The Conceptualization of International Power (Eldridge)
Required:
Steven J. Rosen and Walter S. Jones, "Power," *The Logic of International Relations* (Cambridge, MA: Winthrop Publishers, 1980) pp. 203-232.
David C. Baldwin, "Power Analysis and World Politics: New Trends vs. Old Tendencies," *World Politics* 31 (Jan. 1979), pp. 161-194.

Suggested:
David C. Baldwin, "Money and Power," *Journal of Politics*, XXXII (August, 1971), pp. 578-614.
Norman Alcock and Alan Newcombe, "The Perception of National Power," *Journal of Conflict Resolution*, 14 (Nov. 1970), pp. 335-343.

Bruce Russett (ed.), *Peace, War, and Numbers* (Beverly Hills, CA : Sage, 1972).

Ray S. Cline, *World Power Assessment: A Calculus of Strategic Drift* (Washington, D.C.: The Center for Strategic and International Studies, 1975).

January 21   The Structures of the International System (Eldridge)
Required:

Steven J. Rosen and Walter S. Jones,"The Balance of Power," *The Logic of International Relations* (Cambridge, MA: Winthrop, 1980), pp. 233-266.

Nils H. Wessell, "Soviet Views of Multipolarity and the Emerging Balance of Power," *Orbis*, Winter 1979, pp. 785-813.

Andrew J.R. Mack, "Why Big Nations Lose Small Wars: The Politics of Asymmetric Conflict," *World Politics* (January 1975), pp. 175-200.

Suggested:

Mary Kaldor, *The Disintegrating West* (New York: Hill and Wang, 1978).

Alex Inkeles, "The Emerging Social Structure of the World," *World Politics* 27 (July 1975), pp. 467-495.

John Burton, *Systems, States, Diplomacy and Rules* (New York: Cambridge University Press, 1968).

January 23   Discussion group

January 26   The Nature and Sources of Change in the International System (Professor Andrew Scott, Department of Political Science, University of North Carolina at Chapel Hill)
Required:

K.J. Holsti, "Changes in the International System," in Ole R. Holsti, et al., *Change in the International System* (Boulder, CO: Westview Press, 1980), pp. 23-54.

Arnfinn Jorgensen-Dahl, "Forces of Fragmentation in the International System: The Case of Ethno-nationalism," *Orbis* 19 (Summer 1975), pp. 652-674.

Randolph M. Siverson, "War and Change in the International System," in Holsti, et al., *Change*, pp. 211-232.

Suggested:

Robert O. Keohane and Joseph S. Nye, *Power and Interdependence: World Politics in Transition* (Boston: Little, Brown & Co., 1977).

J.J. Servan-Schreiber, *The American Challenge*, trans. Ronald Steel (New York: Avon Books, 1969).

George Modelski, "The Long Cycle of Global Politics and the Nation State," *Comparative Studies in Society and History*, 20(1978), pp. 214-235.

Robert O. Keohane, "The Theory of Hegemonic Stability and Changes in International Economic Regimes," in Holsti, et al., pp. 131-162.

January 28   The Internationalization of Domestic Concerns: The Core States (Eldridge)
Required:

Alexander L. George, "Domestic Constraints on Regime Change," in Holsti, et al., pp. 233-262.

Ole R. Holsti and James N. Rosenau, "Cold War Axioms in the Post-Vietnam Era," in Holsti, et al., pp. 263-298.

Robert W. Tucker, "Oil: The Issue of American Intervention," *Commentary* (January 1975), pp. 21-31.

Suggested:

Leon Lindberg, ed., *Politics and The Future of Industrial Society* (New York: David McKay Co., 1976).

James Caporaso, et al., *The New Nationalism*

Additional readings to be announced

January 30   Discussion group

II. Dependency and Underdevelopment in the Third World

February 2   The Capitalist World-System: Origins and Structure (Enrique Baloyra, Political Science Department, University of North Carolina at Chapel Hill)

Required:

Immanuel Wallerstein, "Three Paths of National Development in Sixteenth-Century Europe," in I. Wallerstein, *The Capitalist World Economy* (New York: Cambridge University Press, 1979), pp. 37-48.

Immanuel Wallerstein, "Dependence in an Interdependent World: The Limited Possibilities of Transformation Within the Capitalist World-Economy," in I. Wallerstein, *The Capitalist World Economy*, pp. 66-94.

Richard Rubinson, "Political Transformation in Germany and the United States," in Barbara Hockey Kaplan (ed.), *Social Change in the Capitalist World Economy* (Beverly Hills, CA: Sage Publications, 1978), pp. 39-73.

Suggested:

Immanuel Wallerstein, *The Modern World-System* (New York: Academic Press, 1974).

Immanuel Wallerstein, *The Modern World-System II* (New York: Academic Press, 1980).

Alexander Gerschenkron, "Economic Backwardness in Historical Perspective," in A. Gerschenkron, *Economic Backwardness in Historical Perspective* (Cambridge, MA: Harvard University Press, 1962), pp. 5-30.

February 4   The Dependent Development Debate (Gereffi)

Required:

Andre Gunder Frank, "The Development of Underdevelopment," in A.G. Frank, *Latin America: Underdevelopment or Revolution* (New York: Monthly Review Press, 1969), pp. 5-16.

Theotonio Dos Santos, "The Structure of Dependence," *American Economic Review*, Vol. 60, No. 9 (May, 1970), pp. 231-236.

Fernando Henrique Cardoso and Enzo Faletto, *Dependency and Development in Latin America* (Berkeley: University of California, 1979), pp. vii-xxv, 1-28, and 172-216.

Fernando Henrique Cardoso, "The Consumption of Dependency Theory in the United States," *Latin American Research Review*, Vol. 12, No. 3 (1977), pp. 7-24.

Suggested:

Samir Amin, *Unequal Development* (New York: Monthly Review Press, 1976).

Andre Gunder Frank, *Capitalism and Underdevelopment in Latin America* (New York: Monthly Review Press, 1967).

Osvaldo Sunkel, "Transnational Capitalism and National Disintegration in Latin America," *Social and Economic Studies*, Vol. 22, No. 1 (March, 1973), pp. 132-176.

Sanjaya Lall, "Is 'Dependence' a Useful Concept in Analysing Underdevelopment?" *World Development*, Vol. 3, Nos. 11 & 12 (Nov.-Dec., 1975), pp. 799-810.

February 6   Discussion group

February 9   The Case of Brazil (Peter Evans, Sociology Department, Brown Univ.)

Required:
Peter Evans, *Dependent Development: The Alliance of Multinational, State and Local Capital in Brazil* (Princeton, NJ: Princeton University Press, 1979).

Suggested:
Riordan Roett (ed.), *Brazil in the Seventies* (Washington, DC: American Enterprise Institute, 1976).
Pedro S. Malan and Regis Bonelli, "The Brazilian Economy in the Seventies: Old and New Developments," *World Development*, Vol. 5, Nos. 1/2 (Jan.-Feb., 1977), pp. 19-45.

February 11   The Case of Egypt (Nadia Farah, Political Science/Economic Departments, Duke University)
(Readings to be announced)

February 13   Discussion group

February 16   Developing Countries and International Trade: Dilemmas and Policy Responses (John Odell, Government Department, Harvard University)
Required:
Joan Spero, "The North-South System: Trade Strategy," in Joan Spero, *The Politics of International Economic Relations* (New York: St. Martin's Press, 1977), pp. 159-190.
Gottfried Haberler, "Dynamic Benefits of Trade," in Gerald Meier (ed.), *Leading Issues in Economic Development*, 3rd Edition (New York: Oxford University Press, 1976), pp.702-707.

Suggested:
Kathryn Morton and Peter Tulloch, *Trade and Developing Countries* (New York: John Wiley & Sons, 1977).
Benjamin J. Cohen, *The Question of Imperialism* (New York: Basic Books, 1973), Chapter 5.
Karl Sauvant and Hajo Hasenpflug (eds.), *The New International Economic Order* (Boulder, CO: Westview Press, 1977).
Thomas Biersteker, "Self-Reliance in Theory and Practice in Tanzanian Trade Relations," *International Organization*, Vol. 34, No. 2 (Spring, 1980), pp. 229-264.
Hollis Chenery et al., *Redistribution with Growth* (New York: Oxford University Press, 1974), pp. 280-290 (case studies of South Korea and Taiwan)
Robert Bond, "Regionalism in Latin America: Prospects for the Latin American Economic System," *International Organization*, Vol. 32, No. 3 (Spring, 1978), pp. 401-423.

III. Multinational Corporations and Global Economic Organization

February 18   Multinational Corporations: Distortion or Development? (Gereffi)
Required:
Stephen Hymer, "The Multinational Corporation and the Law of Uneven Develop-

ment," in J. Bhagwati (ed.), *Economics and World Order: From the 1970's to the 1990's* (New York: Macmillan, 1972), pp. 113-140.

Peter Evans, "National Autonomy and Economic Development: Critical Perspectives on Multinational Corporations in Poor Countries," in Robert O. Keohane and Joseph S. Nye, Jr. (eds.), *Transnational Relations and World Politics* (Cambridge, MA: Harvard University Press, 1971), pp. 325-342.

Raymond Vernon, "Multinational Enterprises in Developing Countries: Issues in Dependency and Interdependence," in David Apter and Louis Wolf Goodman, (eds.), *The Multinational Corporation and Social Change* (New York: Praeger, 1976), pp. 40-62.

Joan Spero, "The Western System: The Multinational Corporation and the Absence of Management" and "The North-South System: Managing the Multinational Corporation," in Joan Spero, *The Politics of International Economic Relations*, pp. 88-118 and 191-214.

Suggested:

Raymond Vernon, *Sovereignty at Bay: The Multinational Spread of U.S. Enterprises* (New York: Basic Books, 1971).

Raymond Vernon, *Storm over the Multinationals: The Real Issues* (Cambridge, MA: Harvard University Press, 1977).

Louis Turner, *Multinational Companies and the Third World* (New York: Hill and Wang, 1973).

United Nations, Centre on Transnational Corporations, *Multinational Corporations in World Development* (New York: United Nations, 1973).

United Nations, Centre on Transnational Corporations, *Transnational Corporations in World Development: A Re-Examination* (New York: United Nations, 1978).

February 20   Discussion group

February 23   The Automobile Industry (Douglas Bennett, Political Science, Woodrow Wilson International Center for Scholars, Washington, DC)

Required:

Louis T. Wells, Jr., "Automobiles," in Raymond Vernon (ed.), *Big Business and the State* (Cambridge, MA: Harvard University Press, 1978), pp. 229-254.

Joseph Kraft, "Annals of Industry: The Downsizing Decision," *New Yorker*, Vol. 56 (5 May 1980), pp. 134-154.

William Tucker, "The Wreck of the Auto Industry," *Harper's*, Vol. 26 (November, 1980), pp. 45-60.

Suggested:
On the U.S. Industry:

Robert F. Lanzillotti, "The Automobile Industry," in Walter Adams (ed.), *The Structure of American Industry* (New York: Macmillan).

On the Japanese Industry:

William Chandler Duncan, *U.S.-Japan Automobile Diplomacy: A Study in Economic Concentration* (Cambridge: Ballinger Publishing Co., 1973).

On the Auto Industry in Developing Countries:

Douglas Bennett and Kenneth Sharpe, "The World Automobile Industry and Its

Implications for Developing Countries in Latin America," (mimeo), June 1980.
Rhys Jenkins, *Dependent Industrialization in Latin America: The Automobile Industry in Argentina, Chile and Mexico* (New York: Praeger, 1977).

On the Consequences of Auto-Centered Industrialization in the U.S.:

Emma Rothschild, *Paradise Lost: The Decline of the Auto-Industrial Age* (New York: Random House, 1973).
Bradford C. Snell, *American Ground Transport: A Proposal for Restructuring the Automobile, Truck, Bus and Rail Industries* (Washington, DC: Government Printing Office, 1973).

February 25   Oil, Minerals, and Cartel Power (One, Two, or Many OPEC's?)
(Sheridan Johns, Political Science Department, Duke University)
Required:
Joan Spero, "Oil and Cartel Power," in Joan Spero, *The Politics of International Economic Relations*, pp. 215-242.
Edith Penrose, "No OPEC for Minerals," in S. Sideri and S. Johns, *Mining for Development in the Third World: MNCs, State Enterprises and the International Economy* (New York: Pergamon, 1980), pp. 256-265.
Carlos Fortin, "Changing Roles of MNCs in the Evolving World Mineral Economy," in Sideri and Johns, *Mining for Development in the Third World*, pp. 336-346.

Suggested:
C. Fred Bergsten, Thomas Horst, and Theodore H. Moran, "Access to Raw Materials," *American Multinationals and American Interests* (Washington, DC: The Brookings Institution, 1978), pp. 121-164.

February 27   Discussion group

March   2   MNCs, National Interests, and Basic Human Needs (Richard Newfarmer, Economist, Overseas Development Council, Washington, DC)
Required:
Michael Harrington, *The Vast Majority: A Journey to the World's Poor* (New York: Simon and Schuster, 1977), Chapters 1, 2, and 5.
Mark Green and Robert Massie (eds.), *The Big Business Reader* (New York: Pilgrim Press, 1980), pp. 399-430. ("How American Banks Keep the Chilean Junta Going," "U.S. Investments in South Africa: An Overview," and "Rabies, Bottles, and Breast Milk: The Nestle Syndrome.")
Richard Newfarmer, "Oligopolistic Tactics to Control Markets," *Journal of Development Studies* (April, 1979).

Suggested:
Richard Barnet and Ronald Muller, "Global Reach," *New Yorker*, December 2 and 9, 1974 (a two-part article).
Ronald Muller, "Poverty Is the Product," *Foreign Policy*, Vol. 13 (Winter, 1973-1974), pp. 71-102; Raymond Vernon, "Does Society Also Profit?" pp. 103-118; Richard Barnet, pp. 118- 123.

March   4   MNCs and Host Country Bargaining Strategies in the Third World (Theodore Moran, Director, Landegger Program in International Business Diplomacy, School of Foreign Service, Georgetown University)

Required:

Theodore Moran, "Multinational Corporations and Dependency: A Dialogue for Dependistas and Non-Dependistas," *International Organization*, Vol. 32, No. 1 (Winter, 1978), pp. 79-100.

Theodore Moran, "The International Political Economy of Cuban Nickel Development," in Cole Blasier and Carmelo Mesa-Lago (eds.), *Cuba in the World* (Pittsburgh, PA: University of Pittsburgh Press, 1979), pp. 257-273.

Paul Streeten, "Bargaining with Multinationals," *World Development*, Vol. 4, No. 3 (March, 1976), pp. 225-229.

Suggested:

On Extractive Industries:

Theodore Moran, *Multinational Corporations and the Politics of Dependence: Copper in Chile* (Princeton, NJ: Princeton University Press, 1974).

George Philip, "The Limitations of Bargaining Theory: A Case Study of the International Petroleum Company in Peru," *World Development*, Vol. 4, No. 3 (March, 1976), pp. 231-239.

On Manufacturing Industries:

Gary Gereffi, "Drug Firms and Dependency in Mexico: The Case of the Steroid Hormone Industry," *International Organization*, Vol. 32, No. 1 (Winter, 1978), pp. 237-286.

Douglas Bennett and Kenneth Sharpe, "Agenda Setting and Bargaining Power: The Mexican State Versus Transnational Corporations," *World Politics*, Vol. 32, No. 1 (October, 1979), pp. 57-89.

March 6   Discussion group

IV. The New International Military Order

March 16   Security in the Nuclear Age: The Nature of the Dilemma (Eldridge)
Required:

"The Balance of Terror," in Steven J. Rosen and Walter S. Jones, *The Logic of International Relations*, pp. 267-306.

Jan M. Lodal, "Deterrence and Nuclear Strategy," *Daedalus* 109 (Fall 1980), pp. 155-175.

Hedley Bull, "Arms Control and World Order," *International Security* 1 (Summer 1976), pp. 3-16.

Suggested:

Jerome Kahan, *Security in the Nuclear Age* (Washington, DC: Brookings Institution, 1975).

Michael Mandelbaum, *The Nuclear Question* (NY: Cambridge University Press, 1979).

March 18   The Use of Force in International Relations (Speaker to be announced)

Required (tentative):

Robert Art, "To What Ends Military Power?" *International Security* 4 (Spring 1980), pp. 3-35.

Ellen P. Stern, (ed.), *The Limits of Military Intervention* (Beverly Hills, CA: Sage, 1977), pp. 25-82.

David Holloway, "Military Power and Political Purpose in Soviet Policy," *Daedalus* 109 (Fall 1980), pp. 13-30.

Suggested:
Klaus Knorr. *The Power of Nations* (New York: Basic Books, 1975), pp. 3-26; 104-33.
Barry Blechman & Stephen Kaplan, "U.S. Military Forces as a Political Instrument Since World War II," *Political Science Quarterly* 94 (Summer 1979), pp. 193-209.
Raymond Garthoff, "Soviet Views on the Interrelation of Diplomacy and Strategy," *Political Science Quarterly* 94 (Fall 1979), pp. 391-405.

March 20   Discussion group

March 23   The Case for Arms Control (Professor Joseph Kruzel, Department of Political Science, Duke University)
Required:
Joseph Kruzel, "Arms Control and American Defense Policy: New Alternatives and Old Realities," *Daedalus* 110 (Winter 1980), pp. 137-157.
Dan Caldwell, "Strategic and Conventional Arms Control: An Historical Perspective," *Stanford Journal of International Studies* 14 (Spring, 1979), pp. 7-27.
Marshall D. Shulman, "Arms Control in an International Context," *Daedalus* 194 (1975), pp. 53-61.

Suggested:
Bernard Brodie, "On the Objectives of Arms Control," *International Security* 1 (Summer 1976), pp. 17-36.
John H. Barton and Lawrence D. Weiler, (eds.), *International Arms Control: Issues and Agreements* (Stanford, CA: Stanford University Press, 1976).
Andrew J. Pierre, (ed.), *Arms Transfers and American Foreign Policy* (New York: New York University Press, 1979).

March 25   The Dangers of Technology or What Lies Over the Horizon (Speaker to be announced)
Required:
Strategic Survey, 1977, "New Technology and Deterrence," pp. 114-118.
Harvey Brooks, "Notes on Some Issues on Technology and National Defense," *Daedalus* 110 (Winter 1980), pp. 129-136.
Harry Gelber, "Technical Innovation and Arms Control," *World Politics* 26 (July 1974), pp. 509-541.

Suggested:
Harvey Brooks, "The Military Innovation System and the Qualitative Arms Race," *Daedalus* 104 (1975), pp. 75-98.
Deborah Shapely, "Arms Control as a Regulator of Military Technology," *Daedalus* 109 (Winter 1980), pp. 145-57.

March 27   Discussion group

V. The Political-Economy of Development: Industrialization and the Erosion of Democracy

March 30   Economic Growth and Democracy: The Core States (Gereffi)
Required:
Seymour Martin Lipset, *Political Man* (Garden City, NY: Doubleday & Co., 1960),

Chapter 2, "Economic Development and Democracy," pp. 27-63.

Charles E. Lindblom, "The Close but Uneasy Relation Between Private Enterprise and Democracy," in *Politics and Markets* (New York: Basic Books, 1977), Part V, pp. 161-233.

Michael Walzer, "Must Democracy Be Capitalist?" *New York Review of Books*, July 20, 1978, pp. 40-42. (Review of Lindblom.)

Suggested:

Leon Lindberg, "Introduction: Politics and the Future of Industrial Society" in Leon Lindberg (ed.), *Politics and the Future of Industrial Society* (New York: David McKay Co., 1976).

Stanley Hoffmann, "Obstinate or Obsolete? The Fall of the Nation-State and the Case of Western Europe," *Daedalus* 95 (Summer 66), pp. 862-915.

Selected articles in either Pierre-Henri Laurent (ed.), "The European Community After Twenty Years," *The Annals of the American Academy of Political and Social Science* 440 (November 1978) or articles in "Looking for Europe," *Daedalus* 108 (Winter 1978).

Jack Lively, *Democracy* (New York: St. Martin's Press, 1975), pp. 60-88.

Ernest Gellner, "Democracy and Industrialization," *European Journal of Sociology*, Vol. 8, No. 1 (1967), pp. 47-70.

April 1   Return and Discussion of Section 2 of Research Paper

April 3   Discussion group

April 6   Democracy and Industry (Speaker and readings to be announced)

April 8   The Crisis of Democracy (Eldridge)

Required:

Michel Crozier, Samuel Huntington, and Joji Watanuke, *The Crisis of Democracy* (New York: New York University Press, 1975).

Suggested:

Peter Steinfels, *The Neo-Conservatives* (New York: Simon and Schuster, 1979).

April 10   Discussion group

April 13   Problems and Prospects of Redemocratization (Alfred Stepan, Political Science Department, Yale University)

Required:

Alfred Stepan, *Authoritarianism and Redemocratization* (book manuscript) Chapters 1 and 2.

Arend Liphart, "Consociational Democracy," *World Politics*, Vol. 21 (January, 1969), pp. 207-225.

Guillermo O'Donnell, "Tensions in the Bureaucratic-Authoritarian State and the Question of Democracy," in David Collier (ed.), *The New Authoritarianism in Latin America* (Princeton, NJ: Princeton University Press, 1979), pp. 285-318.

Suggested:

Fernando Henrique Cardoso, "Associated-Dependent Development: Theoretical and Practical Implications," in Alfred Stepan (ed.), *Authoritarian Brazil* (New Haven, CT: Yale University Press, 1973), pp. 142-176.

April 15   The Erosion of Democracy? (Gereffi)
Required:
Robert Lubar, "Making Democracy Less Inflation Prone," *Fortune*, September 22, 1980, pp. 78-86.
Everett Carl Ladd, "How to Tame the Special-Interest Groups," *Fortune*, October 20, 1980, pp. 66-80.
Samuel Bowles and Herbert Gintis, "The Invisible Fist: Have Capitalism and Democracy Reached a Parting of the Ways?" *American Economic Review*, Vol. 68, No. 2 (May, 1978), pp. 358-363.
Alan Wolfe, "Giving Up on Democracy: Capitalism Shows Its Face," *The Nation*, Vol. 22, No. 1 (November 29, 1975), pp. 557-563.
Walter Dean Burnham, "American Politics in the 1980s," *Dissent*, Vol. 27, No. 2 (Spring, 1980), pp. 149-160.

Suggested:
Robert A. Dahl, "On Removing Certain Impediments to Democracy in the United States," *Dissent*, Vol. 25, No. 3 (Summer, 1978), pp. 310-324.
Philip Green and Robert A. Dahl (an exchange) "What Is Political Equality?" *Dissent*, Vol. 26, No. 3 (Summer, 1979), pp. 351-368.
James R. Kurth, "The Political Consequences of the Product Cycle: Industrial History and Political Outcomes," *International Organization*, Vol. 33, No. 1 (Winter, 1979), pp. 1-34.

April 17   Discussion group

April 20   Course Overview I (Eldridge)

April 22   Course Overview II (Gereffi)

April 23   Discussion group

Global Issues: Energy, Food and the Arms Race

S.N. Leela and G.V. Stephenson   *Fall 1983*
Economics 206/Geography 201/Millersville State College/
Millersville, PA 17551

It is the objective of this course to acquaint the student with the various contemporary, interdependent global problems currently threatening our planet. Topics will cover the globalization of dangers such as war, famine, the energy crisis, the population explosion, and nuclear proliferation which call for policies that must go beyond mere national boundaries. Further topics pertaining to the challenges of economic development and North-South disparities, East-West tensions, the emancipation of women, and the establishment of a stable peace through the global acceptance of the equality of nations will also be discussed.

Progress towards this monumental task is slow. The dream of an international community remains too far off for the understanding of the vast majority of the world's peoples. Evidence of a lack of comprehension and communication in this respect is present also in the so-called "elite" class. Our educational processes have not caught up with these new dimensions of international order and therefore an ever-widening gap has developed in the ability of different cultures to resolve economic and political conflicts.

It is the objective of this interdisciplinary course to focus on international order issues through lectures, faculty dialogues, class discussions, encounter sessions, visual presentations, field trips, and other means of emphasizing the need for a global understanding of the human community rather than a weapons community.

Course Outline

1. World Economic Development: Its Origin, Development and Problems
A macro perspective of the present global order, its inequalities, diversities—geographic, political and economic. Analysis of theories both economic and geographic; interpretation of several peace and world order studies—*Global 2000 Report, North-South* (Brandt Commission) *Dialogue;* international world order projects; and Club of Rome studies.

2. World Population Problem and a Basic Human Needs Strategy
Economic and geographic dimensions of the world population problem. Examination of regional population perceptual differences and their effect on global conflict. Study of the dilemma of population increases and need for expanded development, employment and education. Relationships among population control programs, a basic needs strategy, and North-South economic interdependence.

3. The World Food Problem

Causes and consequences of world hunger. Analysis of food production, pricing, distribution and trade policies among the world's nations. Particular emphasis on environmental and accessibility factors in the distribution of the world's food supply. An assessment of the responsibility of the rich region in the elimination of world hunger. Relationships among export crop dependency, increasing lack of food self-sufficiency, and importance of a rural development strategy emphasizing ecological principles.

4. The World Energy Problem

Investigation of resource finiteness and global industrialization demands, emphasizing the issue of adequate energy supplies and an ecologically-sound approach to industrial development. Consideration of resource scarcities and non-Western industrial development models based on alternate energy sources. Attention to the "Less Is More" and "Small Is Beautiful" resource-use philosophies, especially their application to the role of industrialization in a basic human needs strategy.

5. Setting Global Priorities for a Safe and Sustainable World Order

Analysis of the economics and geography of the world military buildup versus the development of an ecological approach to peace. Critical evaluation of the various actors in the global system, especially the United Nations, the two rival superpowers, and transnational corporations. Discussion of the recommendations contained in several peace and world order studies, the Brandt Commission's *North-South Dialogue, Global 2000 Report*. Alternative models of international world order studies analyzed. The course will conclude in a dialogue among the participants concerning the development of a model for a preferred world order of stable and sustainable peace.

Required Reading Texts

1. Chichilnisky, Graciela. *Basic Needs and the North/South Debate*, World Order Models Project, Working Paper #21. NY: World Policy Institute, 1982.
2. Birdsall, Nancy. "Population Growth and Poverty in the Developing World," *Population Bulletin,* Vol. 35, No. 5, December, 1980.
3. Brown, Lester R. "World Food Resources and Population: The Narrowing Margin," *Population Bulletin*, Vol. 36, No. 3, September, 1981.
4. Christensen, Cheryl. *The Right to Food: How to Guarantee*, World Order Models Project, Working Paper #6. NY: World Policy Institute, 1978.
5. Mazrui, Ali A. *The Barrel of the Gun and the Barrel of Oil in the North-South Equation*, World Order Models Project, Working Paper #5. NY: World Policy Institute, 1978.
6. Sivard, Ruth Leger. *World Energy Survey*, Washington, DC: World Priorities Inc., June 1981.
7. Sivard, Ruth Leger. *World Military and Social Expenditures 1981*, Washington, DC: World Priorities, Inc., 1981.
8. Ridker, Ronald G.. "Resources, Environment and Population: The Nature of Future Limits," *Population Bulletin*, Vol. 34, No. 3, August 1979.
9. Mendlovitz, Saul H. *The Struggle for a Just World Order: An Agenda of Inquiry and Praxis for the 1980's*. World Order Models Project, Working Paper #20. NY: World Policy Institute, 1982.

Books on Reserve

Building a Sustainable Society—Brown, Lester; W.W. Norton, NY, 1981.
The Lean Years—Barnet, Richard J.; Simon & Schuster, NY, 1980.
The Twenty-Ninth Day—Brown, Lester; W.W. Norton, NY, 1978.
World Without Borders—Brown, Lester; Vintage Books, NY, 1972.
How The Other Half Dies—George, Susan; Allanheld, Osmun, NJ, 1977.
Food First—Lappé, Frances Moore and Collins, Joseph; Ballantine, NY, 1978.
Global Food Interdependence—Hopkins, Raymond and Puchala, Donald J.; Columbia University Press, NY, 1980.
The Poverty of Nations—Murdoch, William W.; Johns Hopkins University Press, Baltimore, 1980.
Rays of Hopes—Hayes, Dennis; W.W. Norton, NY, 1977.
North-South: A Program for Survival—Brandt, Willy; MIT Press, MA, 1980.
Small is Beautiful—Schumacher, E.F.; Harper & Row, NY, 1973.
Measuring the Condition of the World's Poor—Morris, David; Pergamon Press, NY, 1979.
Global 2000 Report of the President—Pergamon Press, NY, 1980.
Real Security—Barnet, Richard; Simon and Schuster, NY, 1981.
The Limits to Growth—Meadows, Donella H. et al.; Universe Books, NY, 1974.
Toward a Just World Order—Falk, Richard A., Kim, Samuel S. and Mendlovitz, Saul H., eds.; Westview Press, 1982.
"A Structural Theory of Imperialism"—Galtung, Johan; from Falk, Richard A. and Kim, Samuel S., eds. *The War System*, Boulder, CO: Westview Press, 1980.
Nuclear Weapons and World Politics—1980's Project of the Council on Foreign Relations, McGraw-Hill.
Farming for Profit in a Hungry World—Perelman, Michael; Montclair, NJ, Allenheld, Osmun, 1977.
Global Politics of Arms Race—Pierre, Andrew J.; Princeton University Press, 1982.
U.S. Foreign Policy and The Third World—*Agenda 1982*; Overseas Development Council, Washington, DC, 1982.

Articles on Reserve

"Economic Development," Dadzie, K.K.S.; *Scientific American*, September 1980.
"World Resources and the World Middle Class," Keyfitz, Nathan; *Scientific American*, July 1976.
"People," Mahler, Halfdan; *Scientific American*, September 1980.
"Supply-Side Ideas Challenge Old Population Theory," *Conservation Foundation*, February 1982.
"Resources, Population, Environment: An Oversupply of False Bad News," Simon, Julian L.; *Science*, June 1980.
"Food," Scrimshaw, Nevin S., Lance Taylor; *Scientific American*, September 1980.
"A General View of the World Food Situation," Panbro, Leonardo A.; *Food Situation and Potential in the Asian and Pacific Region*, Taipei, Taiwan, June 1980.
"The World Food Situation and Global Grain Prospects," Barr, Terry N.; *Science*, December 4, 1981.
"Water," Ambroggi, Robert A.; *Scientific American*, September 1980.
"Why Not Kill The Cow?" Economic Wing; Embassy of India, Washington, DC, September 23, 1975.
"Energy and the Oil Importing Developing Countries," Dunkerley, Jay and Welhaw Ramsey; *Science*, May 7, 1982.

International Relations

Marjorie Zamora   *Fall 1983*
Political Science 210/Moraine Valley Community College/
Palos Hills, IL 60465

This is a course to study comparative major political systems and ideologies. The emphasis is on current international problems and their possible solutions. There are no prerequisites since the course purpose is to help students broaden their understanding of world affairs.

General Course Objectives

1. To help the student develop tools for understanding the complexities of international power politics and distinguish "objective" and "ideological" components of world politics.
2. To promote in the student an appreciation for the differences among several major actors' perceptions of the international system: i.e., by looking at the world from each major nation's own viewpoint.
3. To aid the student in analyzing contrasting ideologies and foreign policies of capitalist, Communist, and Third World nations.
4. To enable the student to compare and contrast several approaches to balance of power, security, diplomacy, arms control, and war.
5. To develop in the student the ability to discuss the diffusion of international power, the shrinking and linking of the globe, and interdependence.

Texts

1. Required: Steven J. Rosen and Walter S. Jones: *The Logic of International Relations*, 4th ed., Cambridge, MA: Winthrop, 1982
2. Read in library: *The NACLA Report* on Central American, North American and Latin American current issues.

Schedule

Unit I: U.S. & Major Allies' Perspectives

Readings: Preface and Chs. 2, 3, & 6, Rosen and Jones, *Logic of International Relations*, 4th ed., 1982

A. Rationale

Each of us views our nation, state and politics from our own perspective: our political culture, our biases, our experiences. We frequently ask "Why can't others be more like us?" This first unit is structured to enable the student to see politics from different perspectives. In fact, one of the course goals is to help the student develop an international perspective similar to that of the inhabitants of other countries. The course goal is to stimulate your desire to continue learning about other countries long after this course.

In Unit I we will consider the causes of American and Western allies' perspectives toward each other and their concerns about foreign policies.

Ch. 2—US Perspectives

B. Objectives: At the end of this unit, you should be able to:

1. Discuss elements of the 1) perceptual analysis used by Rosen & Jones, 2) political system, 3) nation-state, 4) national power. (lecture and pp. X-XV)
2. Discuss: Who makes US foreign policy? (lecture)
3. Discuss the roots of the American worldview and our "aggressor" (p. 45) images of international relations. Ch. 2; Ch. 6 (lecture: "What's a Communist?")
4. Trace the history of US foreign policy from isolationism through commercial expansion to world leader. Ch. 2
5. Cite three causes of the Cold War from 1919 to 1945 and four causes from 1945 through the 1950's. (pp. 54-76)
6. Summarize the perceptual frames of these five major actors in international politics: (Ch. 6 and p. 209)
   a. United States
   b. US major allies
   c. Soviet Union
   d. China
   e. Third World countries
7. Distinguish the differences between subjective and objective "facts" and how these affect international actors' perceptions. (pp. 210-212)
8. Assess two valid but opposing views of a) American intervention in the Dominican Republic in 1965 and b) Soviet invasion of Czechoslovakia in 1968, Afghanistan in 1980 and their influence in Poland in 1980-84. (pp. 216-219)
9. Define:
   a. isolationism, p. 47
   b. appeasement, p.51, also "appeasers"
   c. Big Three Powers, p. 56
   d. Truman Doctrine, p. 58
   e. Containment policy, p. 58—George Kennan, keep Soviet expansion at their borders, "support people resisting attempted subjugation by armed minorities" (external or civil war)
   f. liberation policy,p. 60, J.F. Dulles
   g. Monroe Doctrine, p. 47
   h. hawk and dove, pp. 61-63
   i. hard vs. soft line, p. 62
   j. detente, p. 70—1970's; increased trade between US-USSR; Sino-US trade; Vietnam withdrawal
   k. monolithic vs. polycentric views of communism, pp. 71-75, Socialist Commonwealth

Ch. 3—Major Allies' Perspectives
1. Explain the reluctance of Japan to opening trade to the West. Then contrast Japan's pre-1854 policies with those during her expansionist period.
2. Discuss how American occupation policies helped Japan's postwar economic success. What were the American and international reasons for the "Nixon Shocks?"
3. Describe the Japanese worldview toward: remilitarization; nuclear proliferation; balance of trade; relations with US; USSR; and SE Asian nations.

4. Cite four major objections of Western Europe and Canada toward US commercial and military policies, and the US defense of these policies.
5. Define:
   a. most-favored-nation status 1858 with Japan
   b. rights of extraterritoriality, p. 82
   c. European Economic Community and EFTA; EEC (9 members), pp. 102-105
   d. NATO; p. 101 and pp. 108-111
   e. Customs unions, p. 105
   f. Eurocentric world politics, p. 100
   g. nationalists vs. continentalists, pp. 119-121
   h. portfolio vs. direct investments, pp. 122-124
   i. The Gray Report, p. 124
   j. NORAD, p. 126.

Unit II: Socialist & Third World Perspectives

Part I Rationale

Knowledge of the Soviet Union's history, culture, and mixed political and economic system is needed for understanding Soviet domestic and foreign policy. The Soviet perspective toward the West (capitalist countries) and its interpretation of communism, Marxism-Leninism differ from what we Americans have generally been taught. In this unit, we will explore these bases of Soviet perspectives and politics.

Reading: Ch. 1 of Rosen & Jones, *The Logic of International Relations*.

Objectives: At the end of this unit, you should be able to:

1. Trace the evolution of Russian nationalism and ideology through your historical knowledge of:
   a. Russian history (last 150 years). Lectures and Film: "Russian Revolution: World Turned Upside Down"
   —fears of the West (Ch. 1)
   —operation of Russian and Soviet govts. (Ch. 1)
   b. Marxism-Leninism: (Lecture & Ch. 1)
   —utopian vs. scientific socialism
   —communism vs. Communism
   —similarities and differences between Marxism and Leninism
2. State the major causes of territorial and ideological disputes between the USSR and China. (pp. 37-41)

Part II Rationale—Chinese and Third World Perspectives

The world perspectives of China and most developing (Third World) countries today derive from a "fusion of two great forces," nationalism and ideology. Both China and Third World countries share a history of struggles against oppressive colonial bureaucracies and the desire to modernize with or without benefits to the masses.

In this part of Unit II we will probe and evaluate the sources and effects of the forces of nationalism and ideology, especially the effects of these in international politics.

Readings: Rosen & Jones, Chs. 4, 5; magazine section; *NACLA* Report

Objectives

1. Trace the evolution of modern China through:
   a. Chinese contemporary history (last 150 years). (Videotape: "The Struggle for China" Pts. I and II) + (Ch. 4, R & J)
   b. Structure, operation and current policies of China's government
   c. Tribute system; Opium War; unequal treaties; extraterritoriality; Taiping Rebellion; Boxer Rebellion; KMT (Kuomintang); Dr. Sun Yat-sen; Chiang Kai Shek; Mao Tse Tung; Huo Kua Feng (Ch. 4 & lectures)
2. Describe contemporary Chinese foreign policy and Chinese relations with the USSR and with Japan. (pp. 154-158)
3. List six major improvements in Chinese society since the Revolution. (Readings, lectures)
4. Define Third World, list and elaborate nature of the "North-South" dialogue and several of the reasons for "underdevelopment" in the Third World. Ch. 5 (pp. 161-188)
5. Compare and contrast the conventional and radical or "revisionist" theories of development (pp. 188-198) (lecture).
6. Cite three major objections to foreign aid presented by radical theorists and assess the accuracy of their objections. (pp. 195-198)
7. Discuss Third World alternative solutions for development, including the Chinese model, regional integration, decentralization, people's revolutions, and the strengths and limitations of oil power and cartelization. (pp. 198-208)
8. (Optional) List several causes for rising prices in the US and abroad; the nature of conglomerate control of the source, supply, distribution, and price of goods; the effects of this control on Third World countries; and possible solutions to the "world food crisis." (lecture "Politics of World Food")
9. Define regional integration; "trickle-down theory" of development; bilateral and multilateral foreign aid; foreign investment viewpoints; OPEC petrodollars.
10. Compare and contrast differing views on the nature of terrorism.

Unit III: The Logic of Power and World Order

Reading: Rosen & Jones, Chs. 7, 8, 10, 11, 12, 13, 14, 17

Rationale
People often say, "War is inevitable," or "Man is by nature warlike." In this unit you will examine these popular beliefs and the multiple causes of international conflict. You will also study the nature of various forms of international control and their strengths and weaknesses. Finally, you will consider possible future forms of world order.

Objectives: At the end of this unit you should be able to:

Chs. 7 and 8: On Power
1. Define the nature of power in international politics, and list the ingredients of power potential. (lecture on Ch. 7)
2. Assess the significance of the "balance of power" theory as an analytical tool for equilibrium in world politics. List the varieties of balance of power theories. (lecture on Ch. 8)
3. Analyze the effects of these aspects of the film "The War Game":
   a. effects on individuals/on civilization of thermonuclear war

b. Soviet and US responses to E-W Berlin riots and potential for E-W exchange in 1980s

c. Civil Defense messages about preparedness

d. Continuing policies of overkill and MAD

4. Compare and contrast American and Soviet force and nuclear proposal levels, especially Reagan's START. (lecture and pp. 267-290)

5. Summarize the history and current status of chemical warfare and other conventional warfare arsenals. (pp. 340-343)

6. Discuss several human costs of nearly $500 billion year spent by nations of the world on military expenditures. (p. 291)

Ch. 10

1. Summarize these perceptions on balance of terror: (pp. 352-362)
   a. US
   b. Western allies
   c. Soviet
   d. Chinese
   e. Third World

2. Define START; RDF; MAD, MX, Salt I, II; megaton; overkill; mutual deterrence; brinkmanship; counterforce; MIRV; MARV; NPT; disarmament, arms control. (p. 345)

3. Define WAR. (lecture & pp. 343-34)

Ch. 11

1. Assess the implications of the following theories for causing and preventing war:
   a. power asymmetrics
   b. nationalism
   c. international Social Darwinism
   d. communications failure
   e. arms races
   f. internal cohesion
   g. aggression (instinctual); aggression (cultural)
   h. economics
   i. military-industrial complexes
   j. deprivation
   k. population limitation
   l. conflict resolution

2. Discuss: Is War a rational instrument for conflict resolution?

Ch. 12—International Trade and Exchange

1. Assess the significance of knowledge of international trade fundamentals for students of international relations. (pp. 399-405)

2. Ricardian theory of comparative advantage. (pp. 405-408)

3. Explain: Why must nations trade. (pp. 399-408)

4. Compare and contrast the operations and effects of global corporations (MNCs) on world politics, i.e., "foreign-oriented development." (lecture and pp. 415-416)

5. Summarize four types of trade restrictions and their effects. (pp. 408-415)

Ch. 13—International Monetary Exchange

1. Explore these ways for restraining the external behavior of states and for decreasing international anarchy: (pp. 441-494) (lecture)

a. autolimitation
b. positivist theory
c. neorealist theory
2. Assess these sources of international law for establishing international norms: (pp. 444-447) (lecture)
a. bilateral and multilateral treaties
b. custom
c. general principles
d. subsidiary sources
3. Analyze the effectiveness of several international sanctions: e.g., coercion; retorsions; reprisals; collective security; economic sanctions. (pp. 447-464)

Ch. 15—International Organization
1. Distinguish IGO's and NGO's. Cite examples of each. (pp. 475-482) (lecture)
2. Describe the founding, powers, structure, strengths and limitations of the United Nations. What are declarations, resolutions, and conventions? (lecture and pp. 480-503)
3. Compare the American, American allies', Soviet, Chinese, and Third World views and support of the United Nations. (pp. 503-517)

Ch. 17—Future World Order
1. Discuss the significance of these as supernational problems: (pp. 515-581)
a. ecology
b. population
c. food
d. autocratic governments
e. world economic anarchy
2. Evaluate these maximalist proposals for world order: (pp. 581-587)
a. world federalism (587)
b. separation of powers (588)
c. world government (590)
3. Summarize the minimalist proposal for world order based on world law and the elimination of armaments. (pp. 594-596)
4. Evaluate the strengths and weaknesses of the reformist proposal for world order. (pp. 596-604)
5. Your opinion: Should a student of international relations be concerned that the future of the world is narrowing to two alternatives, what the authors call "expansionist world government" or "systemic destruction?"

Peacemaking and Nonviolence

Politics of Nonviolence*
Ralph Summy, University of Queensland

Nonviolence and the New Society*
Sugata Dasgupta, University of Queensland

**Social-Psychological Approaches to
International Relations**
Herbert Kelman, Harvard University

Nonviolence—Meanings, Forms, and Uses
Theodore Herman and Nigel Young, University of Dubrovnik

Conflict and Violence in American Life
Paul Peachey, Catholic University

**The Ideology and Culture of Nonviolence
in Western Society**
Charles F. Howlett

Peace—Theories, Strategies, and Movements
Herbert Feith, Monash University

The Literature of Nonviolence
Ken Brown, Manchester College

Conflict Resolution: Theory and Technique
George Lopez, Earlham College

Imaging Security Alternatives to the Arms Race
Gerald and Patricia Mische, Viterbo College

Sociology of Nonviolence
Sevryn T. Bruyn, Boston College

*Companion Courses

Politics of Nonviolence*

Ralph Summy *Fall 1982*
External Studies XV201/University of Queensland/St. Lucia, Queensland, Australia, 4067

Every prospective student should be quite aware that this is a relatively new and hence experimental course. Although it has been offered four times at the University of Queensland, it is still very much in the developmental stage. There has been little in the way of precedence to build on. To my knowledge, neither it nor some close facsimile has ever been available to students at an Australian University. And though there are many courses overseas dealing with the topics of nonviolence—for instance, the School of Peace Studies at the University of Bradford which examines nonviolent movements in an historical context—it is doubtful if the particular format designed for this unit has been adopted elsewhere. Syracuse University in the United States has established an interdisciplinary major in nonviolent conflict and change that focuses—so it is stated in their prospectus—on "the identification of nonviolent action techniques, the study of them in their historical context, the evaluation of their psychological, ethical, and religious implications," and on "alternative means of waging conflict, and the nature and dynamics of conflict and change in relation to social, cultural, and political institutions."[1]

Since the Syracuse University initiative constitutes a series of interrelated courses extending over a number of years, it differs markedly from the limited scope and intensity of our effort where the emphasis is directed primarily at a single aspect of nonviolence, *viz.* the political process involved. Our study will also differ from the Syracuse major in that we shall be breaking new ground when we analyse nonviolent action in the context of the Australian political culture—e.g., in compiling the Australian case study that each student will be required to do.

The Challenge

The novelty and pioneering nature of this course provides a challenge that I hope we can all share and enjoy. Together, we shall be endeavouring to add a modest increment to the knowledge of nonviolence as a political technique. We shall be refining analytic categories, surveying case histories of nonviolent action, isolating and systematically relating "critical" variables, and compiling and interpreting the data of our own case studies. Despite the restrictive nature of the subject, ample opportunity exists for creativity in a field almost totally bereft of scholarly enquiry until the past few decades.

---

*Companion course to succeeding syllabus, "Nonviolence and the New Society."
[1]*International Peace Studies Newsletter.* University of Akron, Akron, Ohio, Spring 1975.

No doubt this previous lack of scholarly depth explains, in part, the reluctance of most Australian political science departments to incorporate the study of nonviolence into their curricula, though as Sir Mark Oliphant recently pointed out in an ABC lecture, the number one priority of our educational system should be the removal of violence from politics. Its existence threatens the survival of our civilization, indeed the human species itself.

Narrowing the subject matter

Let us be clear what the subject matter of this unit does not emphasise. As important and interesting as they may be, the various belief systems usually associated with nonviolence are not central to our enquiry. The Christian concept of redemption through suffering, the nonresistance creed of some religious sects, the "active reconciliation" practised by many Quakers, the selective nonviolence importuned by socialists, or the "satyagraha" and "ahimsa" of Gandhian philosophy are only examined in so far as they bear on the strategy and tactics of nonviolence—i.e. affect the resolve of the participants, the cohesion of the group, or the type of nonviolent action that may be engaged in. It is worth noting, as argued by Dave Dellinger, that "the major advances in nonviolence have not come from people who have approached nonviolence as an end in itself, but from persons who were passionately striving to free themselves from social injustice."[2] Their struggles have led to the need for more effective techniques so as to avoid the containment and co-optation of existing political systems, as well as the defeats inherent in the violent approach.

Social psychological factors are also excluded from our analysis unless they contribute substantially to an understanding of *why* some target groups relent while others hold fast, *why* some third parties can be activated on behalf of the actionists while others decline assistance or even prove hostile, and *why* some people are more effective in implementing the technique of nonviolence. For instance, we would want to consider the arguments of American sociologist George Lakey who claims that, if the goal is conversion or persuasion, "the task of the nonviolent campaigners, then, is to get the opponent to see them as human beings."[3] When this occurs, the chances for success apparently greatly increase.

For us, the key questions are invariably posed in terms of *how:* how does the technique of nonviolence operate in the political process; how can it effect social change or maintain the status quo; how can it affect power relations between political actors; how is it adapted to varying circumstances; how is it successful; how is it limited or inhibited? In short, how does the technique, as an instrument for resolving conflict, stand up to rigorous critical examination?

Why a Course in Nonviolence

Despite the fact that almost everyone has a moral aversion to violence, or simply views it as destructive and nonproductive, it is still widely advocated as an effective

[2] Dave Dellinger, "The Future of Nonviolence," cited in Bob Irwin & George Faison, *Why Nonviolence?: Nonviolence Theory & Strategy for the Anti-Nuclear Movement*, Movement for a New Society, Philadelphia, 1978, page 1.

[3] George Lakey, "Mechanisms of Nonviolent Action," in A. Paul Hare and Herbert H. Blumberg (eds), *Nonviolent Direct Action: American Cases, Social-Psychological Analyses*. Corpus Books, Washington, 1968, page 388.

means of controlling and exercising power whenever matters assumed to be of great import cannot be resolved through the normal institutional channels. If a conflict does not lend itself to compromise, people are inclined to think they have available a choice of only two responses: passive submission or the threat and willingness to use physical force. Yet there is also a third possibility: nonviolent resistance, the preservation or initiative of which has been comparatively little researched and studied.

Our undertaking is to contribute, albeit modestly, towards rectifying this academic deficiency. In the area of defence policy, Australians should be especially interested in seeking out alternatives other than submission and force. Since they obviously are not prepared to adopt a posture of surrender or submission with the prospect of future violent resistance, they have relied upon a strategy of "stabilising violence." Yet Australia's insufficient resources for the deployment of potential violence has proved a constant source of national anxiety throughout the 20th Century. The hordes of yellow and red men (what Dennis Altman has sardonically referred to as the "orange peril") have always been about to descend from the North. To compensate for its low resources in producing violence in an international system of anarchic states, Australia has turned to the formation of alliances with powerful, white, Anglo-Saxon nations—sometimes to the point of developing a sycophantic dependency. Furthermore, as Australians have ruefully discovered, allies are not always dependable. And alliances or "forward defence" positions can easily be interpreted by other nations as aggressive intentions. Therefore, there are good pragmatic reasons why the Australian government should be interested in investigating the feasibility of a defence policy that incorporates the technique of nonviolent resistance.

However, unless some of you wish to construct a plan of nonviolent civilian based defence as your major project—subjecting it to rigorous critical analysis—our course will mainly examine the nonviolent technique in the domestic context.

Defining Nonviolent Action

As a concept, nonviolent action can be defined as a type of behaviour seeking to control or exercise power without resorting to the threat or use of physical restraint, injury or destruction of persons in a context where violent action or such physical restraint etc. would generally be considered either legitimate or not unusual. Some students of nonviolence would also consider the destruction of property as violating the principle of nonviolence, whereas others would claim that the nonviolent commitment is basically to the dignity and preservation of the human being, not to a person's material possessions. The definition is subjective and interpretive inasmuch as you must determine what society accepts at the time as legitimate or not unusual. In a borderline case it may be necessary to justify your interpretation.

Our definitional problem is further complicated by the fact that virtually every nonviolent action contains an element of either conventional political behaviour or violent action, or of both. There are three broad categories of political action by which a ruler's power can be controlled:
1. by operating through the society's institutional and conventional arrangements that have developed to control the ruler's power—e.g., parliament, parties, lobbying, ombudsman, etc.

2. by resorting to the threat or use of superior violence against that which the ruler can muster at a particular time and place—e.g., rioting, terrorism, coup d'etat, civil war, international war, etc.
3. by engaging in nonviolent action that may take the form of
   a. protest and persuasion
   b. noncooperation
   c. intervention
   d. some combination of the above

The three broad categories of political action outlined above will tend to overlap in the concrete situation. Thus a nonviolent action may degenerate into violence, to a greater or lesser degree. A parliamentary action may be taken into the realm of nonviolence; or action may be conducted at both levels simultaneously. Action may even operate at all three levels. The question posed for the analyst: is the action primarily within the nonviolent sphere or one of the other two.

Another definitional problem besets the student of nonviolence. Our definition excludes the *threat* of physical restraint etc., yet theorists speak of coercion as one of the three nonviolent "ways success may be achieved" (the other two being conversion and accommodation). Nonviolent coercion, if successful, will force an opponent to capitulate against his/her will. As Sharp points out, this may occur when resistance becomes so widespread and massive as to render ineffective the opponent's powers of repression; when the social, economic or political system will not function unless the ruler accedes to the actionists' demands; and when the opponent's ability to command the agencies of repression is undermined. However, in any of these circumstances the key factor may be a subtle threat to use counter physical force by the actionists that determines the outcome. No matter how pure the intentions of the non-violent actionists, it may be the opponent's perception of a potential or possible use of violence that brings the struggle to a successful end. As well, the mechanism of nonviolent accommodation may entail an element of threatened violence. The opponent may be prepared to accommodate on the issue raised by the actionists, because he/she wishes to avert an unpleasantness or nuisance that is perceived, rightly or wrongly, to contain the seeds of violence. Nevertheless, though in cases of accommodation or coercion the threat of physical force may be the critical factor affecting the opponent's decision, it is suggested that for our purposes the criterion determining whether the political action falls within or outside the ambit of nonviolence should depend on the state of mind of the actionists and not the opponents. If a physical threat forms a part of the deliberate armoury of the actionists then (and only then) does the action fail to meet the specifications set out in our definition.

The problem of the "threat of violence" is compounded by still more difficulties. Some actionists have long term goals that involve the threat or use of violence, but their immediate goals, which they regard as stepping stones, are conducted within the framework of nonviolence. The actions of many Marxists follow this pattern.[4]

---

[4]For a different view, see E.G. Plimak et al., "Lenin on Peaceful & Nonpeaceful Forms of Revolutionary Transition to Socialism," *Excerpts from Paper Delivered at XI World Congress of International Political Science Association,* Moscow; 1979. The authors contend: "The idea of a peaceful path of revolution, the peaceful development of revolution, and a peaceful socialist revolution came into existence neither today nor yesterday. It was introduced by Marx and Engels. It was developed by V.I. Lenin. It is encountered in their works dozens of times." (page 1).

These revolutionists believe that ultimately, the capitalist exploiters will only relinquish power under the pressure of violent coercion. Since their revolutionary strategy is built around a violent uprising, and all their actions are theoretically directed toward this point, can the Marxists ever be said to engage in nonviolent action? I think the answer must be "yes," despite the fact their intentions may be to resort eventually to the threat or use of violence. In the first place, the strategy of revolution may change, as has happened recently in many communist parties, especially in Western Europe where the emphasis has shifted to nonviolently penetrating, initiating and controlling the various cultural and institutional components of the "superstructure," thereby eroding rather than forcefully destroying capitalism's economic base. For these Marxists the interdependence of the parts of a complex society opens the way to a revolutionary strategy that uses, in both the long and short terms, the weapons belonging to the armouries of nonviolent and conventional politics.

Moreover, if one is going to exclude from the politics of nonviolence Marxists because they ultimately subscribe to violence, the same argument must be applied to all nonpacifists. This would be true, then of the "just war" advocate who sanctions violence as long as it is proportional to what he/she or an authority determines is a moral goal, as well as of the individual (most of us) who foresees subconsciously the potential incompatibility of an ethic of noninjury with one of responsibility for the welfare of others, and thus would intercede violently if it became necessary in order to protect an abused child. One can cite many other groups of people who would have to be excluded along with the Marxists who prescribe ultimate violence; e.g., those who see the necessity of sometimes having to use physical force against the mentally deranged; those who judge a foe's goal to be annihilation, in which case nonviolence could merely provoke delight; and those whose experience and comprehension enable them to appreciate fully just what genuine evil is (an argument developed by Karl Jaspers in *The Future of Mankind*).

Required Texts

Sharp, Gene. *The Politics of Nonviolent Action*. Porter Sargent, Booton, MA, 1973.
Sharp, Gene. *Social Power and Political Freedom*. Extending Horizons Books, Boston, MA, 1980.

Finally, a purchase that students may find useful is the double issue of *Social Alternatives*, Vol. 1, Nos., 6&7, June 1980 ("World Peace: The Nonviolent Alternative").

Reference Materials
Whilst you will be relying chiefly on the basic Sharp texts, there are some other books and articles which you will find helpful. Those marked with an asterisk are especially recommended.

Books
Alexander, Horace. *Gandhi Through Western Eyes*, 1969.
Aron, Raymond. *History of the Dialectic of Nonviolence*, 1975.
Arrowsmith, Pat, (ed.) *To Asia in Peace*, 1972.
Ashe, Geoffrey. *Gandhi*, 1968.
Bedau, Hugo Adam, (ed.) *Civil Disobedience: Theory and Practice, 1969.*
Bhatyacharyya, B. *Satyagrahas in Bengal*, 1921-1939, 1977.

Blainey, Geoffrey. *The Causes of War*, 1977.
*Bondurant, Joan. *Conquest of Violence*, 1965.
*Bondurant, Joan, (ed.) *Conflict: Violence and Nonviolence*, 1971.
Boserup, A., et al. *War Without Weapons: Nonviolence in National Defence*, 1975.
Bosmajian, Haig. *Language of Oppression*, 1974.
Caron, Elsa, (ed.) *Fri Aiert*, 1974.
Carter, April. *Direct Action and Liberal Democracy*, 1973.
Carter, April. *Direct Action: Theory and Tactics*, [pamphlet] 1970.
Carter, April, et al. (eds.) *Nonviolent Action: Theory and Practice—A Selected Bibliography*, 1970.
Childress, James F. *Civil Disobedience and Political Obligation: A Study in Christian Social Ethics*, 1971.
Dellinger, Dave. *More Power Than We Know: The People's Movement Toward Democracy*, 1975.
Dellinger, Dave. *Revolutionary Nonviolence*, 1970.
Desai, Narayan. *Towards a Nonviolent Revolution*, 1972.
Dunn, Ted (ed.) *Foundations of Peace and Freedom*, 1975.
Erkison, Erik H. *Gandhi's Truth on the Origins of Militant Nonviolence*, 1969.
Gamson, Wm. A. *Strategy of Social Protest*, 1975.
Gandhi, M.K. *The Mind of Mahatma Gandhi*, 1967.
Gandhi, M.K. *For Pacifists*, 1971.
Gandhi, M.K. *Satyagraha*, 1951.
*Gandhi, M.K. *Nonviolent Resistance*, 1961.
Gandhi Peace Foundation. *Peace Research for Peace Action*, 1972.
*Gregg, Richard. *The Power of Non-Violence*, 1966.
*Hare, A. Paul and Blumberg, Herbert H. (eds) *Nonviolent Direct Action: American Cases; Social-Psychological Analyses*, 1968.
Hare, A. Paul and Bumberg, Herbert H. *Liberation Without Violence*, 1977.
Hyatt, John (ed.) *Pacificism: Its Ideas and History*, 1972.
Jezer, Marty. *The Power of the People: Active Nonviolence in the U.S.*, 1977.
Koch, Klaus-Friedrick. *War and Peace in Jalemo: The Management of Conflict in Highland New Guinea*, 1974.
Kripalani, J.B. *Gandhian Thought*, 1961.
Kumur, Satish (ed.) *School of Nonviolence*, 1969.
Lakey, George. *Readiness for Revolution*, 1971.
Lakey, George. *They Didn't Call It Violence But. . .*, *Three Cases of Civilian Insurrection in Latin America*, 1969.
*Lakey, George. *Strategy for a Living Revolution*, 1973.
Lanza, del Vasto. *Warriors of Peace: Writings on the Technique of Nonviolence*, 1974.
Leeds, Christopher. *The Teaching of Conflict Studies: An Introductory Guide*, [pamphlet] 1974.
Lynd, Staughton (ed.) *Nonviolence in America: A Documentary History*, 1966.
Muse, Benjamin. *The American Negro Revolution: From Nonviolence to Black Power*, 1968.
Narayan, Jayaprakash. *Towards Total Revolution*, 1978.
Nettleship, M.A., et al. (eds) *Pre-Congress Conference on War, Its Causes and Correlates*, 1973.

Olson, Theodore and Shivers, Lynne. *Training for Nonviolent Action*, 1970.

*Ostergaard, Geoffrey and Currell, M. *The Gentle Anarchists*, 1971.

Patwari, Prabhudas B. *Some Reflections on Gandhi's Relevance Today*, 1978.

Penter-Brick, Simone. *Gandhi Against Machiavellism*, 1966.

*Ramachandran, G. and Mahaderan,T. *Gandhi, His Relevance For Our Times*, 1971.

Rapoport, Anatol. *Conflict in Man-Made Environment*, 1974.

*Roberts, Adam (ed.) *The Strategy of Civilian Defense: Nonviolent Resistance to Aggression*, 1967.

Sadler, Chris. *On the Frontiers: Strategy for New Social Order*, 1977.

Satyapraksh. *Gandhiana 1962-1976*, 1977.

*Sharp, Gene. *Politics of Nonviolent Action*, 1973.

Sharp, Gene. *Exploring Nonviolent Alternatives*, 1970.

*Sharp, Gene. *Gandhi As a Political Strategist*, 1979.

*Sharp, Gene. *Social Power and Political Freedom*, 1980.

*Sibley, Mulford Q. (ed.) *The Quiet Battle: Writings on the Theory and Practice of Nonviolent Resistance*, 1968.

Sinha, Archana. *The Social and Political Philosophy of Sarvodaya*, 1978.

*Stiehm, Judith. *Nonviolent Power: Active and Passive Resistance in America*, 1972.

Tandon, Vishvanath. *The Social and Political Philosophy of Sarvodaya after Gandhi*, 1965.

Unnithan, T. *Gandhi and Social Change*, 1979.

Verma, V. *The Political Philosophy of Mahatma Gandhi and Sarvodaya*, 1965.

Woito, Robert (ed.) *World Disarmament Kit*, 1977.

Zinn, Howard. *Disobedience and Democracy*, 1968.

Zwieback, Burton. *Civility and Disobedience*, 1975.

Articles and Papers

*de Crespigny, Anthony. "The Nature and Methods of Nonviolent Coercion," *Political Studies*, Vol. 12, No. 2, June 1964, pages 256-265.

Galtung, Johan. "Violence, Peace and Peace Research," *Journal of Peace Research*, Vol. 6, 1969, pages 167-191.

Galtung, Johan. "A Structural Theory of Imperialism," *Journal of Peace Research*, Vol. 8, No. 2, 1971, pages 81-85.

Galtung, Johan. "On the Effects of International Economic Sanctions with Examples from the Case of Rhodesia," *World Politics*, Vol. 19, No. 3, April 1967, pages 378-416.

Hoffman, Frederick. "The Functions of Economic Sanctions: A Comparative Analysis," *Journal of Peace Research*, Vol. 4, No. 2, 1967, page 140-160.

*Jones, Lawrence. "A Nonviolent Civilian Defense Policy for New Zealand," *Social Alternatives*, Vol. 1, No. 1, Spring, 1977.

*Lakey, George. "The Sociological Mechanisms of   iolent Action," *Peace Research Reviews*, Vol. 2, No. 6, Dec. 1968.

Lipsky, Michael. "Protest as a Political Resource," *American Political Science Review*, Vol. 62, No. 4, 1968, pages 1114-1158.

*Marty, William R. "Nonviolence, Violence, and Reason," *Journal of Politics*, Vol. 33, No. 1, 1971.

*Overy, Bob. "How Effective Are Peace Movements?" *Peace Studies Papers*, No. 2, University of Bradford, 1980/81.

Plimak, E.G. and Karyakin, Yu. F. "Lenin on Peaceful and Nonpeaceful Forms of Revolutionary Transition to Socialism," *Excerpts from paper delivered at XIth World Congress of International Political Science Association*, Moscow, 1979.

*Randle, Michael. "Militarism and Repression," *Alternatives: A Journal of World Policy*, Vol. VII, No. 1, 1981, pages 61-144.

Yiping, Zhang. "Nonviolence Must be Basically Affirmed," *Shijie lishi* (World History), Vol. 16, No. 3, June 7, 1980, pages 78-80.

Young, Nigel. "Problems and Possibilities in the Study of Peace," *Peace Studies Papers*, No. 3, University of Bradford, 1980/81.

Although slightly outdated, an excellent selected bibliography entitled *Nonviolent Action* was prepared by April Carter, David Hoggett and Adam Roberts. Another useful bibliography, this one on the related subject of pacifism, is John Hyatt's *Pacifism, Its Ideas and History, A Selected Bibliography*. A more recently published bibliography on peace research can be found in Peter Van Den Dungen's *Foundations of Peace Research*, University of Bradford Peace Studies Paper No. 1, 1980/81.

Project Assignment
A large part of the course will be devoted to an original research project where you will be required to apply the analytic tools that you have learned from your reading to a case study of nonviolence. The nonviolent action that you choose to examine in detail can range from a minor local incident—such as the protest a few years ago by a handful of women in Ballon, Qld to preserve an avenue of wild plum trees, or the more recent hunger strikes of the Rumanian migrants—to a conflict of international proportions such as the "peace march" of thousands of Moroccans into the Spanish Sahara in November 1975, or the overthrow of the Thai military regime in 1973. The various forms of nonviolent action are described at great length in your basic text, and there is no dearth of events in Australia's history for you to choose from. In particular, Australia has been the scene of some interesting trade union strikes—e.g., the refusal of the Port Kembla waterside workers in 1938 to load pig-iron on the steamer *Delfram* bound for Japan, or the 1969 gaoling of Victorian Tramways Secretary Clairie O'Shea (by the then Mr. Justice Kerr, subsequently Governor-General of Australia), an event that led to a series of national stoppages and the *de facto* abolition of the penal powers in the Arbitration Act. In my view, the civil disobedience engaged by O'Shea and supported by many unions produced one of the most significant victories in the history of Australia's trade union movement.

The Vietnam anti-war movement utilized the technique of nonviolent direct action. Of course, well-intentioned actions may degenerate into violence on the part of some actionists, or they may provoke violence from the opponents. Simply because a nonviolent action fails to remain nonviolent is no reason for excluding it from the list of possible case studies. You would want to analyse the political process by which an action became violent. A student one year investigated the uprising at the Eureka Stockade, making comparisons with how similar type demands by miners at Bendigo were settled nonviolently.

When researching your topic here are a few points to remember:

- Your study involves interaction among groups, not just an analysis of what the nonviolent actionists are doing.
- Ask yourself if the actionists have clearly identified their target(s)—e.g., opponent(s), third parties, additional source of actionists, mass supporters.
- Is the objective clearly specified—to the leaders and to the supporters as well? Is the objective known to the other groups that interact with the actionists?
- Are the methods of nonviolence (see Sharp) and the mechanism employed (conversion, accommodation or coercion) intelligently and systematically related to the objective and target?
- Have the actionists been systematic in their approach to cutting off their opponent's sources of power (see Sharp for a list of these sources)?
- How do you evaluate the success or failure (again see Sharp)?

First Reading Assignment
As you read your basic text, consider the following questions (especially no. 4);
1. How would you define the terms power, authority and legitimacy?
2. What does Sharp describe as the "monolith theory" of power?
3. If one subscribes to the "monolith theory," what are the means available for controlling power?
4. What arguments does Sharp advance to support his contention that a ruler's power is dependent on the extent to which a society grants him/er that power—i.e., that all government is based on consent?
5. Why do people obey a ruler?
6. Do you agree that a power wielder who imposes sanctions relies essentially on the voluntary obedience of his/her subjects?

Nonviolence and the New Society*

Sugata Dasgupta   *Spring 1983*
External Studies XV202/University of Queensland/St. Lucia,
Queensland, Australia, 4067

Any study of nonviolence should be in three parts. First of all, it should analyse contemporary society in terms of violence and nonviolence, showing its movement outward or inward, towards violence or away from it. Secondly, it should provide a pointer to the direction of social growth that might lead to a less violent, if not to a "not", or a "non", violent society. Thirdly, the study should develop methods of social action for change that may bring into being a nonviolent society, or a social order where violence is reduced to the minimum.

A course on nonviolence has also to be normative in approach and positive in its treatment of the theme. It must implant faith in its recipients and not faithlessness or frustration. A course that deals with change and nonviolent social action is thus at its best only when it deals with the question of the formation of a new society, e.g., of the nonviolent society, or of the society of positive nonviolence. The course, whose outline is appended hereto, is such a course on the new society.

Introduction

One word now about the term "positive nonviolence." Nonviolence has always been associated with nonviolent action, action that means protest, action that negates something, say some system. Yet nonviolence does not mean protest. It is not wholly or ever partially a negative concept. It is, on the other hand, a positive concept. Nonviolence thus refers to a system under which violence cannot grow. If nonviolence therefore negates anything, it negates violence; and the way it does so is by building a new society where violence becomes impossible. It is the nonviolence of such constructive function that we call positive nonviolence. This course is about positive nonviolence.

The central theme of the course is the nonviolent society, non-violence being projected as a positive concept needed for the building of a nonviolent society. As the villain of a drama gets as much attention as its hero does, the course starts with a full appraisal of the role of violence, and of the structural stimuli that create such violence. It, in fact, does so even before it provides any substantial insight into the theory and practice of nonviolence. Since *development* creates violence, development, violence and nonviolence naturally provide the main emphasis of the course. For development, growth, and modernization also offer the central ethos of the contemporary society. If this ethos is evident in the developed societies of the north and the west, the east and the south, which are yet to be developed, follow closely the same pattern. They, indeed, find in development the goal of all their statecraft.

---

*Companion course to preceeding syllabus, "Politics of Nonviolence."

Yet it is "development" that creates maldevelopment. And it is maldevelopment that leads to tensions, peacelessness, violence and strife. (See the chart.)

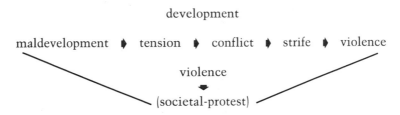

The type of society and the categories of institutions (societal, political, and economic) that support the end product of development, (e.g., violence) are thus responsible for the promotion of violence.

Violence, viewed in this context, has, however, a technical connotation. The course views violence from this specialized perspective and provides a macro review of the impact of development in order to examine how the institutions of development build the infrastructure of violence. In doing so it provides an analysis of some of the crucial institutions of the society (e.g., education, welfare, agriculture, industry, health services, technology, etc.) and on the basis of such analysis projects the following two paradigms:

1. Violence is a product of the type of institutions and policies we follow.
2. Nonviolence, the antonym of violence, can be reached only when we promote a different set of policies and institutions.

The course proceeds, thereafter, as follows:

1. It provides a typology of violence and an analysis of the culture that provides the roots of such violence.
2. It projects the type of institutional arrangements that perpetuate violence.
3. It analyses the role certain "myths" play.
4. It details the "methods" of change or the techniques of social action that may help to bring a nonviolent society into being.
5. It discusses the meaning, history, concept, philosophy and various ramifications of the phenomenon of nonviolence. Finally,
6. The course provides, in very rough outline, the schema of a nonviolent society and certain clear indicators that provide its identifying characteristics.

Those who join the course, however, need to be forewarned that the course offers no readymade blueprints for a definitive system. The "model" that it presents is likewise tentative, and not complete. It is far from being perfect. For if all ideas that the world cherishes as noble and worth striving for, (e.g., religion, democracy, socialism) still remain unrealized, nonviolence provides no exception to it. The goals of nonviolence have thus not only yet to be tested in practice but there is every reason to believe that they cannot claim to provide any readymade, straightjacket solutions for immediate transplantation everywhere. Theories of nonviolence only provide certain values with choices and options, which, within the framework of such leads, may help one to undertake nonviolence undeterred by the essence of nonviolence. Nonviolence thus preaches—if it must preach—the virtues of "swaraj" or of "autonomy" so that autonomous decisions by all concerned can help societies to choose their systems to suit their destiny, genius, culture, time and ecology.

One word more about the objectives of the course. Its main purpose is to develop a new perspective among its recipients, a perspective that will enable them to see the norms, techniques and ideologies in a new wholesome way. It is this perspective, more than the tailoring of any concrete model or technocratic knowhow, that provides the mainstay of the course.

The course leans heavily on the experience of some of the great philosophers and practitioners of our time, e.g., Tolstoy, Ruskin, Martin Luther King, E.F. Schumacher, and most of all Gandhi. The course likewise refers to concepts and theories that have direct relevance to the countries in which they functioned. Notwithstanding the difficulties that such an empirical treatment may entail, it will not be difficult, one hopes, to see in them the generic values of such specialized experiments. For the practitioners, referred to above, had always kept the whole of humankind in view. It is the latter, and not only the specific cultures in which they functioned, that are their beneficiaries, (vide Gandhi's dictum: "I hold that without Truth and Nonviolence there can be nothing but destruction of humanity; it is my bounden duty, therefore, up to my last breath, to try to protect India, and through India the entire world, from such a doom.")

Nonviolence and the New Society: Outline of the Theme

Violence and nonviolence. The meaning of nonviolence. Its evolution from an ethical phenomenon to an empirical reality—from an attitude of mind and philosophy of individual living to an applied political concept for social and economic change. The new meaning of nonviolence—the social scientists' approach to the theme.

Nonviolence as a lever of social action and as a methodology for social development—planning for the new society—an alternative model—the role of model building in nonviolence. Typology of violence and nonviolence; structural, societal violence, the violence of protest and of withdrawal from the society. Planning for a nonviolent society. Definitions, values, terminologies and concepts in nonviolence—e.g., means, ends, the individual, the collectivity, the society, the State, the civil authorities, the army, the organization, non-organization, power, democracy, freedom, majority, minority, races, secularism, God and truth—the new meaning of these terms and their role in the making of a nonviolent society.

Philosophy of social action for change—the new value system—competition, cooperation, conflict, harmony, aspiration, satisfaction, self abnegation and self fulfillment. Nonviolence and the culture of social action.

Nonviolence and the structure and function of the new society—enumeration of the criteria (value systems) of social action and of the indicators of a society of nonviolence—nonviolence and social organization, size structure, relationships, lines of command and control. Nonviolence and development, maldevelopment, peacelessness, development and the survival of the "least fit"—technology, economic patterns, health, education and their role in the determination of culture of development in a nonviolent society. The new political system and nonviolence. The explosion of violence in the "seventies" and "eighties," and the explosion of knowledge about the earth and its resources and the case for a new society. Its structure, function, process, relationship between material culture and non-material culture in non-violence. Evaluation and indicators of measurement of the new society.

Reading List
Whilst there are no prescribed texts in this course, the *essential* core of the reading includes the following:
*Bondurant, Joan. *Conquest of Violence: The Gandhian Philosophy of Conflict.*
*Dasgupta, Sugata. *Problems of Peace Research: A Third World View.*
Dasgupta, Sugata. *Gandhi for the Youth.*
*Desai, N. *Towards a Nonviolent Revolution.*
Freire, Paulo. *Pedagogy of the Oppressed.*
Galtung, Johan. *A Structural Theory of Revolution.*
*Gandhi, Mohandas K. *Hind Swarai.*
Gandhi, Mohandas K. *Village Health.*
*Illich, Ivan. *The De-Schooling Society.*
Narayan, J.P. *Socialism, Sarvodaya and Democracy.*
Ruskin, John. *Unto this Last.*
*Schumacher, E.F. *Small is Beautiful.*
Tolstoy, Leo. *The Kindom of God is Within You.*
1969 UNESCO Symposium. *Truth and Nonviolence.*
Van Gorcum, Koinkdrylee. *Development and Peace,* Vol. II.

The books marked with an asterisk have been ordered by the University Bookshop. The other books should be available through the Thatcher Library.

Assessment
Students are free to choose their own form of assessment—as long as it includes a minimum of two gradings. Thus you can opt to sit for the two-hour examination at the end of the year and submit an essay between 2,500-3,500 words at least one month before the exam; or you could decide to write two essays of approximately 4,000 words each.

Social-Psychological Approaches to International Relations

Herbert Kelman   *Spring 1982*
Psychology and Social Relations 2600/Harvard University/
Cambridge, MA 02138

The seminar will take up selected topics in the social psychology of international relations. One major focus will be on third-party intervention in conflict resolution, with special emphasis on the problem-solving workshop as an approach to conflict resolution.

A central feature of the seminar will be a problem-solving workshop on Arab-Jewish relations in Israel and the Israeli-Palestinian conflict. The workshop will include an Israeli-Jewish party and a Palestinian party; for the third party, the instructor will be joined by outside specialists in the workshop approach to conflict resolution and by the seminar members on a rotating basis. Seminar members will take part in planning the workshop, conducting pre-workshop sessions with the two parties, observing the entire workshop proceedings, serving on the third-party team for at least one workshop session, and evaluating the workshop.

Papers

Each seminar participant will prepare an individual paper (15-20 pages in length) on some aspect of the social psychology of international relations. Papers may deal with any topic within that field—either one of the topics covered during the seminar sessions or some other topic. There are a number of important topics in the social psychology of international relations that we will not be able to cover systematically in our seminar sessions and you are invited to take up one of these topics in your paper. They include, for example: bargaining and negotiation; decision-making in foreign policy; public opinion in the foreign policy process; cross-national contacts; strategies of conflict resolution; relations between domestic and international conflicts; transnational activities and international integration; and the development of a world society. Whatever your specific topic, the paper should focus on some conceptual and empirical problems.

Schedule and Reading List

February 3   Psychological Factors in War and Peace with Illustrations from the Middle East Conflict
Relevant references:
Kelman, H.C., and Bloom, A.H. "Assumptive Frameworks in International Politics." In J.N. Knutson (ed.), *Handbook of Political Psychology.* San Francisco: Jossey-Bass, 1973. Pp. 261-295.

Etzioni, A. "Social-Psychological Aspects of International Relations." In G. Lindzey and E. Aronson (eds.), *The Handbook of Social Psychology*, Vol. 5. Reading, Mass.: Addison-Wesley, 1969. Pp. 538-601.

Kelman, H.C. (ed.) *International Behavior: A Social-Psychological Analysis.* New York: Holt, 1965. Chapters 1 (pp. 3-35) and 16 (pp. 565-605).

February 10   International Conflict: Sources and Motives; Escalation and Perpetuation; Individual and Systemic Levels of Analysis

Pruitt, D.G., and Snyder, R.C. (eds.) *Theory and Research on the Causes of War.* Englewood Cliffs, NJ: Prentice-Hall, 1969. Introduction to Part Two (pp. 15-31).

Wright, Q. "The Escalation of International Conflicts." *Journal of Conflict Resolution,* 1965, 9, 434-449.

North, R.C. "Perception and Action in the 1914 Crisis." *Journal of International Affairs,* 1967, 21, 103-122.

Singer, J.D. "The Level-of-Analysis Problem in International Relations." In K. Knorr and S. Verba (eds.), *The International System.* Princeton, Princeton University Press, 1961, pp. 77-92.

Kelman, H.C. "The Role of the Individual in International Relations: Some Conceptual and Methodological Considerations." *Journal of International Affairs,* 1970, 24, 1-17.

Other relevant references:

Rapoport, A. *Conflict in Man-Made-Environment.* Baltimore: Penguin, 1974. Part Two (Sources and structure of conflict). Read especially Chapters 10 and 11 (pp. 109-134), 15 and 16 (pp. 166-183), and 20 (pp. 224-240).

Frank, J.D. *Sanity and Survival: Psychological Aspects of War and Peace.* New York: Vintage, 1967.

Galtung, J. "A Structural Theory of Aggression." *Journal of Peace Research,* 1965, 1, 95-119.

Holsti, O.R. *Crisis, Escalation, War.* Montreal, 1972.

Swingle, P.G. "Dangerous Games." In P. Swingle (ed.), *The Structure of Conflict.* New York: Academic Press, 1970. Pp. 235-276.

Holsti, O.R., Brody, R.A., and North, R.C. "The Management of International Crisis: Affect and Action in American-Soviet Relations." In D.G. Pruitt and R.C. Snyder (eds.), *Theory and Research on the Causes of War.* Englewood Cliffs, NJ: Prentice-Hall, 1969. Pp. 62-79.

McClelland, C.A. "The Beginning, Duration, and Abatement of International Crises: Comparisons in Two Conflict Areas." In C.F. Hermann (ed.), *International Crises: Insights from Behavioral Research.* New York: Free Press, 1972.

Azar, E.E. "Conflict Escalation and Conflict Reduction in an International Crisis: Suez, 1956." *Journal of Conflict Resolution,* 1972, 16, 183-201.

Wilkenfeld, J., Lussier, V.L., and Tahtinen, D. "Conflict Interactions in the Middle East." *Journal of Conflict Resolution,* 1972, 16, 135-154.

Pruitt, D.G., and Gahagan, J.P. "Campus Crisis: The Search for Power." In J. Tedeschi (ed.), *Perspectives on Social Power.* Chicago: Aldine, 1974. pp. 349-392.

Wolfers, A. "The Actors in International Politics." In W.T.R. Fox (ed.), *Theoretical Aspects of International Relations.* Notre Dame, Indiana: Univ. of Notre Dame Press, 1959. pp. 83-106.

Alger, C.F. "Comparison of Intranational and International Politics." *American Political Science Review,* 1963, 57, 406-419.

February 17   Perceptions and Images in International Conflict
Basic readings:
Jervis, R. "Hypotheses on Misperception." In J. Rosenau (ed.), *International Politics and Foreign Policy* (rev. ed.). New York: Free Press, 1969. Pp. 232-254.
Jones, E.E. "How do People Perceive the Causes of Behavior?" *American Scientist,* 1976, 64, 300-305.
White, R.K. "The Pro-Us Illusion and the Black-Top Image." In B.T. King and E. McGinnies (eds.), *Attitudes, Conflict, and Social Change.* New York: Academic Press, 1972. Pp. 211-221.
White, R.K. "Misperceptions in the Arab-Israeli Conflict." *Journal of Social Issues,* 1977, 33 (1), 190-221.
Silverson, R.M. "The Evaluation of Self, Allies, and Enemies in the 1956 Suez Crisis." *Journal of Conflict Resolution,* 1972, 16, 203-210.
Holsti, O.R. "Cognitive Dyanmics and the Image of the Enemy." *Journal of International Affairs,* 1967, 21, 16-39.
Heradstveit, D. *The Arab-Israeli Conflict; Psychological Obstacles to Peace.* Oslo: Universitetsforlaget, 1979 (Second edition: 1981), 48-76 and 107-120.
Fabian, L.L., and Schiff, A. (eds.) *Israelis Speak.* New York: Carnegie Endowment for International Peace, 1977. Pp. 1-11.
Other relevant references:
Jervis, R. *Perception and Misperception in International Politics.* Princeton, NJ: Princeton University Press, 1976. Chapter 4 (Cognitive consistency and the interaction between theory and data), esp. pp. 117-172.
White, R.K. "Images in the Context of International Conflict: Soviet Perceptions of the U.S. and U.S.S.R." In H.C. Kelman, *International Behavior: A Social-Psychological Analysis.* New York: Holt, 1965. Pp. 259-269. (Other chapters in Part I of this volume contain relevant discussions of national and international images.)
Bronfenbrenner, U. "The Mirror Image in Soviet-American Relations: A Social Psychologist's Report." *Journal of Social Issues,* 1961, 17 (3), 45-56.
Lumsden, M. "A Test of Cognitive Balance Theory in a Field Situation: A Factor-Analytic Study of Perceptions in the Cyprus Conflict." *Proceedings of the International Peace Research Association Third General Conference.* Assen, The Netherlands: Van Gorcum, 1970. Pp. 24-50.
Mandel, D. *Perception, Decision Making and Conflict.* Washington: University Press of America, 1979.

February 24   Nationalism and National Identity
Basic readings:
Kohn, H. "Nationalism." In D. Sills (ed.), *International Encyclopedia of the Social Sciences,* Vol. 11. New York: Macmillan, 1968. Pp. 63-69.
Deutsch, K.W. *Nationalism and Social Communication.* Cambridge, Mass.: MIT Press, 1966. Chapters 1 and 4 (pp. 15-28, 86-106).
Kelman, H.C. "Patterns of Personal Involvement in the National System: A Social-Psychological Analysis of Political Legitimacy." In J. Rosenau (ed.), *International Politics and Foreign Policy* (rev. ed.) New York: Free Press, 1969. Pp. 276-288.
Isaacs, H.R. "Nationality: 'End of the road'?" *Foreign Affairs,* 1975, 53, 432-449. (Adapted from *Idols of the Tribe: Group Identity and Political Change.* New York: Harper & Row, 1975.)

Fishman, J.A. *Language and Nationalism.* Rowley, Mass.: Newbury, 1973. Part I (pp. 1-38).

Kelman, H.C. "Israelis and Palestinians: Psychological Prerequisites for Mutual Acceptance." *International Security,* 1978, 3, 162-186.

Other relevant references:

Rustow, D.A. "Nation." In D. Sills (ed.), *International Encyclopedia of the Social Sciences,* Vol. 11. New York: Macmillan, 1968. Pp. 7-13.

Kuper, L., and Smith, M.G. (eds.), *Pluralism in Africa.* Berkeley, Calif.: University of California Press, 1969. Chapters 1 (pp. 7-26), 3 (67-81), and 10 (333-349).

Emerson, R. *From Empire to Nation.* Boston: Beacon, 1962. Part II (pp. 89-209).

Doob, L.W. *Patriotism and Nationalism: Their Psychological Foundations.* New Haven: Yale University Press, 1964. Chapters 1 and 13.

Smith, A.D. *Theories of Nationalism.* New York: Harper, 1972.

Katz, D. "Nationalism and Strategies of International Behavior: A Social-Psychological Analysis." In H. Kelman (ed.), *International Behavior: A Social-Psychological Analysis.* New York: Holt, 1965. Pp. 356-390.

Kelman, H.C. "Language as an Aid and Barrier to Involvement in the National System." In J. Rubin and B.H. Jernudd (eds.), *Can Language be Planned. Sociolinguistic Theory and Practice for Developing Nations.* Honolulu: University Press of Hawaii, 1971. Pp. 21-51.

Fishman, J.A. "Bilingualism with and without Diglossia; Diglossia with and without Bilingualism." *Journal of Social Issues,* 1967, 23 (2), 29-38.

March 3   Arab Nationalism and the Palestinian National Movement

This session of the Seminar will be led by Professor Bassam Tibi of the University Göttingen, who is currently a Visiting Scholar at the Center for International Affairs.

Basic readings:

Tibi, B. *Arab Nationalism: A Critical Inquiry.* New York: St. Martin's, 1981. Part IV (pp. 135-172) and Postcript (pp. 173-181). (Parts I-III of this book provide very useful theoretical and historical background information.)

Quandt, W.B., Jabber, F., and Lesch, A.M. *The Politics of Palestinian Nationalism.* Berkeley: University of California Press, 1973. Pp. 45-112.

Lesch, A.M. *Political Perceptions of the Palestinians on the West Bank and the Gaza Strip.* Washington: Middle East Institute, 1980. Pp. 51-78.

Other relevant references:

Khadduri, M. *Political Trends in the Arab World: The Role of Ideas and Ideals in Politics.* Baltimore: Johns Hopkins, 1970. Chapter 8 (pp. 176-211).

Haim, S. *Arab Nationalism: An Anthology.* Berkeley and Los Angeles: University of California Press, 1964. Introduction (pp. 3-72).

Cottam, R.W. "Arab Nationalism." In G.C. AlRoy (ed.), *Attitudes toward Jewish Statehood in the Arab World.* New York: American Academic Association for Peace in the Middle East, 1971. Pp. 165-180.

Sayigh, R. "Sources of Palestinian Nationalism: A Study of a Palestinian Camp in Lebanon." *Journal of Palestine Studies,* 1977, 6 (4), 17-40.

Barakat, H., and Dodd, P. "Palestinian Refugees: Two Surveys of Uprootedness." In P.Y. Hammond and S.S. Alexander (eds.), *Political Dynamics in the Middle East.* New York: American Elsevier, 1972. Pp. 325-349.

March 10   Jewish Nationalism and Current Trends in Zionist Ideology
The Seminar will be led by Professor Stephen P. Cohen of the Psychology Dept.,
City University of New York Graduate Center.
Basic readings:
Talmon, J.L. *Israel Among the Nations.* New York: Macmillan, 1970. Chapter 3 (pp. 130-191).
Hertzberg, A. *The Zionist Idea.* New York: Atheneum, 1973. Introduction (pp. 15-100).
Avni-Segre, D. "Israel: A Society in Transition." *World Politics,* 1969, 21, 344-365.
Other relevant references:
Baron, J.W. "The Modern Age." In L.W. Schwarz (ed.), *Great Ages and Ideas of the Jewish People.* New York: Modern Library, 1956. Pp. 315-484.
Tsur, J. *Zionism: The Saga of a National Liberation Movement.* New Brunswick, NJ: Transaction Books, 1977.
Memmi, A. *Jews and Arabs.* Chicago: J. Philip O'Hara, 1975. Pp. 19-29 and 69-98.
Herman, S.N. *Jewish Identity: A Social Psychological Perspective.* Beverly Hills, Calif.: Sage, 1977. Pp. 115-142 and 169-203.

March 17   The Arab-Jewish Encounter in Israel and the West Bank
Led by Professor Ian Lustick of the Department of Government, Dartmouth College.
Basic readings:
Lustick, I. *Arabs in the Jewish State: Israel's Control of a National Minority.* Austin: University of Texas Press, 1980. Pp. 1-81.
Lesch, A.M. *Political Perceptions of the Palestinians on the West Bank and the Gaza Strip.* Washington: Middle East Institute, 1980. Pp. 1-50.
Other relevant references:
Cohen, A. *Israel and the Arab World.* New York: Funk & Wagnalls, 1970.
Jiryis, S. *The Arabs in Israel.* New York: Monthly Review, 1976.
El-Asmar, F. *To Be an Arab in Israel.* London: Frances Pinter, 1975.
Nakhleh, K. *Palestinian Dilemma: Nationalist Consciousness and University Education in Israel.* Detroit: Association of Arab-American University Graduates, 1979.
Migdal, J.S. *Palestinian Society and Politics.* Princeton, NJ: Princeton University Press, 1980. Especially pp. 45-87 and 185-229.
Nakhleh, E.A. *The West Bank and Gaza: Toward the Making of a Palestinian State.* Washington: American Enterprise Institute, 1979.

March 24   Third-Party Intervention in Conflict Resolution: The Problem-Solving Workshop
The readings listed here provide the conceptual background for the workshop (scheduled for April 30-May 2), including the two pre-workshop sessions (April 14 and 21) and the planning session (April 28). You can spread out these readings over the next few weeks. However, read at least the first few items before March 24.
Basic readings:
Burton, J.W. *Conflict and Communication: The Use of Controlled Communication in International Relations.* London: Macmillan, 1969. Chapters 1-5 (pp. 1-87).

Kelman, H.C. "The Problem-Solving Workshop in Conflict Resolution." In R.L. Merritt (ed.), *Communication in International Politics*. Urbana: Univ. of Illinois Press, 1972. Pp. 168-204.

Cohen, S.P., Kelman, H.C., Miller, F.D., and Smith, B.L. "Evolving Intergroup Techniques for Conflict Resolution: An Israeli-Palestinian Pilot Workshop." *Journal of Social Issues*, 1977, 33 (1), 165-189.

Kelman, H.C. "An Interactional Approach to Conflict Resolution and Its Application to Israeli-Palestinian Relations. *International Interactions*, 1979, 6, 99-122.

Kelman, H.C. "Creating the Conditions for Israeli-Palestinian Negotiations." *Journal of Conflict Resolution*, 1982, 26.

deReuck, A. "Controlled Communication: Rationale and Dynamics." *The Human Context*, 1974, 6 (1), 64-80.

Mitchell, C.R. "Conflict Resolution and Controlled Communication." *Journal of Peace Research*, 1973, 10, 123-132. (This is a reply to an earlier article: Yalem, R.J. "Controlled Communication and Conflict Resolution." *Journal of Peace Research*, 1971, 8, 263-272.

Doob, L.W. (ed.) *Resolving Conflict in Africa: The Fermeda Workshop*. New Haven, Conn.: Yale University Press, 1970. Chapters 1-3 (pp. 1-56) and 6-8 (pp. 104-161). Skim the other chapters.

Levi, A.M., and Benjamin, A. "Focus and Flexibility in a Model of Conflict Resolution." *Journal of Conflict Resolution*, 1977, 21, 405-425.

Curle, A. *Making Peace*. London: Tavistock, 1971. Pp. 173-195 and 209-244.

Young, O.R. *The Intermediaries: Third Parties in International Crises*. Princeton: Princeton University Press, 1967. Pp. 49-68, 80-91.

Other relevant references:

Burton, J. *Deviance, Terrorism, and War: The Process of Solving Unsolved Social and Political Problems*. New York: St. Martin's, 1979.

Burton, J.W. "Resolution of Conflict." *International Studies Quarterly*, 1972, 16, 5-29.

Cot, J.P. Critical Remarks on John Burton's Paper, "Resolution of Conflict." *International Studies Quarterly*, 1972, 16, 31-39.

Doob, L.W. The Impact of the Fermeda Workshop on the Conflicts in the Horn of Africa. *International Journal of Group Tensions*, 1971, 1, 91-101.

Doob, L.W., and Foltz, W.J. "The Belfast Workshop: An Application of Group Techniques to a Destructive Conflict." *Journal of Conflict Resolution*, 1973, 17, 489-512.

Doob, L.W., and Foltz, W.J. "The Impact of a Workshop Upon Grassroots Leaders in Belfast." *Journal of Conflict Resolution*, 1974, 18, 237-256.

Boehringer, G.H., et al. "Stirling: The Destructive Application of Group Techniques to a Conflict." *Journal of Conflict Resolution*, 1974, 18, 257-275.

Alevy, D.I., Bunker, B.B., Doob, L.W., Foltz, W.J., French, N., Klein, E.B., and Miller, J.C. "Rationale, Research, and Role Relations in the Stirling Workshop." *Journal of Conflict Resolution*, 1974, 18, 276-284.

Doob, L.W. "A Cyprus Workshop: An Exercise in Intervention Methodology." *The Journal of Social Psychology*, 1974, 94, 161-178.

Doob, L.W. "A Cyprus Workshop: Intervention Methodology During a Continuing Crisis." *The Journal of Social Psychology*, 1976, 98, 143-144.

March 31, April 7   No Sessions

April 14   Pre-Workshop Session with Israeli-Jewish Participants in the Workshop
This will be a longer-than-usual session of the seminar, devoted to exploring Israeli-Jewish views of Arab-Jewish relations and the Israeli-Palestinian conflict, and to reviewing workshop goals, procedures, and ground rules with this group of participants. This session is an integral part of the workshop.

April 21   Pre-Workshop Session with Palestinian Participants in the Workshop
The length, purpose, and procedure will be those of the April 14 session.

April 28   Final Plans for the Workshop
Again, this will be a longer-than-usual session of the seminar, devoted to making final plans for the workshop itself. We will work out all the necessary details, review workshop procedures, and—as time permits—discuss theoretical issues.

April 30-May 2   Workshop on Arab-Jewish Relations and the Israeli-Palestinian Conflict
The workshop will begin toward the end of the afternoon, Friday, April 30, and end late Sunday afternoon, May 2. There will be a workshop session on Friday evening and a social gathering on Saturday evening. So please keep the entire weekend free.

May 5   Review and Evaluation of the Workshop
Review and complete readings on third-party approaches and on the Arab-Israeli conflict.

May 12   Overcoming Psychological Barriers to Change in a Conflict Relationship
Basic readings:
Deutsch, M. *The Resolution of Conflict: Constructive and Destructive Processes.* New Haven: Yale University Press, 1973. Chapter 13 (pp. 351-400).
Fisher, R. "Fractionating Conflict." In R. Fisher (ed.), *International Conflict and Behavioral Science.* New York: Basic Books, 1964.
Osgood, C.E. "Calculated De-escalation as a Strategy." In D.G. Pruitt and R.C.Snyder (eds.), *Theory and Research on the Causes of War.* Englewood Cliffs, NJ: Prentice-Hall, 1969. Pp. 213-216.
Sherif, M. "Superordinate Goals in the Reduction of Intergroup Conflict." *American Journal of Sociology,* 1958, 63, 349-356.
Baldwin, D.A. "The Power of Positive Sanctions." *World Politics,* 1971, 24, 19-38.
Lewis, A. "The Peace Ritual and Israeli Images of Social Order." *Journal of Conflict Resolution,* 1979, 23, 685-703.
Cohen, S.P., and Azar, E.E. "From War to Peace: The Transition Between Egypt and Israel." *Journal of Conflict Resolution,* 1981, 25, 87-114.
Other relevant references:
Pilisuk, M., and Skolnick, P. "Inducing Trust: A Test of the Osgood Proposal." In P. Brickman (ed.), *Social Conflict.* Lexington, Mass.: Heath, 1974. pp. 173-186.
Deutsch, M., and Krauss, R.M. "The Effect of Threat Upon Interpersonal Bargaining." In P. Brickman (ed.), *Social Conflict.* Pp. 161-172.
Kelley, H.H., and Stahelski, A.J. "Social Interaction Basis of Cooperators and Competitors Beliefs about Others." In P. Brickman (ed.), *Social Conflict,* pp. 242-260.

Note: Your papers are due at this session

Nonviolence—Meanings, Forms, and Uses

Theodore Herman and Nigel Young   *Summer 1983*

Inter-University Centre for Postgraduate Studies/Dubrovnik, Yugoslavia

The course directors set out from the realization that nonviolence is very little understood in its many forms and uses, and even less as a habit of alternative thinking about conflict at any level. In a world increasingly marked by violence, fear, and oppression, laws and arms control agreements have little prospect of being observed unless people and governments learn how to transform their differences into activities of mutual benefit. The more people learn how and where nonviolence has succeeded, the more they will become convinced of its worth. The course was designed to bring that knowledge into the open. It is the first time that this has been done by assembling organizers and examples from different parts of the world.

Content and Structure

The course was designed to offer a comprehensive view of nonviolence based on writings, experiences, and several training sessions. The detailed program shows the two-week session divided into four main parts of uneven length:

> I. Review of the Meanings of Nonviolence (1 day)
> II. Resolving Ongoing Conflict (4 days)
> III. Preventing Possible Conflict (1 day)
> IV. Social Change (4 days)

There were 14 sub-topics, with specific resource persons listed to speak on each in order to stimulate discussion either immediately thereafter or later on that day, and twelve discussion questions that often arise in any serious consideration of nonviolence. However, no attempt was made to answer them as given.

The course was not a formal academic event. Instead, it was intended primarily for those with little knowledge of the subject but with a sincere urge to find an alternative in outlook, in knowledge, and in methods to counter the sense of powerlessness that frustrates so many people today.

Participants

In addition to the two directors and 19 resource persons, there were 62 registered participants from 15 countries: United States (29); Canada, Denmark, W. Germany (5 each); Netherlands (4); Italy, Sweden (3 each); Belgium, England, France, Kenya, Pakistan, Philippines, Poland, Yugoslavia (1 each).

The occupations of those attending are as follows: students (16) postgraduate, 11; undergraduate, 5; college and university faculty (13); staff and peace organizations (12); school teachers and administrators (10); clergy (4); social workers (2); government official, lawyer, journalist (1 each).

Our 19 resource persons, two of whom were originally invited as interpreters in Italian and Serbo-Croatian, were from the following places: United States (6); England (4); Holland, Israel (2 each); Canada, India, Italy, W. Germany, UNESCO (1 each).

Each was chosen to present one or more specific topics in the program, to lead discussions upon it, and to join in the rest of the program as a regular participant. They were also chosen for their ability to present theory and practice based on their known experience in various parts of the world.

Topics presented at the course

The relation between education, creativity, and development—D. Dolci (Italy)
Gandhi and the ashram tradition—N. Desai (India)
NGO initiatives at the UN and outside—B. Hollister (USA)
Private negotiations with government leaders—K.A. Lee (UK)
The ombudsman in the government bureaucracy—R. Pelly (Canada)
Nonviolence training—H. Klinefelter (Holland) + 4 workshops
Gandhi on nonviolence training—N. Desai (India)
Civilian nonviolence action—G. Sharp (USA) + 4 workshops
Publicizing and communicating nonviolent action—P. Wehr (USA)
Principles of conflict resolution—P. Hare (Israel)
The Alternative Defense Commission—M. Randle (UK)
International Peace Brigades—P. Hare (Israel) and N. Desai (India)
Control of Mediterranean pollution as a step toward peace—T. Herman (USA)
Working for peace in the southern Philippines—N. Madale (Philippines)
Strengthening the impact of nonviolence networks—J. Forest (Holland)
Social regeneration in rural Sicily—D. Dolci (Italy)
Gandhi after Gandhi—N. Desai (India)
The civil rights struggle in the American South—B. LaFayette (USA)
Nonviolent action in Poland—P. Wehr (USA)
Imaging a world without weapons—M. Link (USA)
Role-playing and psychodrama against inner violence—J. Hare (Israel)
Nonviolence in Islamic teaching and action—S.S. Mehdi (Pakistan)
The Helsinki Process—J. Ernest (UK)
Feminism and nonviolence—L. Jones (UK) + 4 workshops
Deterrence by international hostage exchange—K. Smail (USA)
The potential for social structural change through training in nonviolence—N.L. Wood (USA)
The psychology of torture—J.P. Jensen (Denmark)
For women only—M. Bruemmer (US)
How to break down national identities—J. Forest (Holland)
Creative writing for training young children in nonviolence—J. Vitiello (USA) and H. Tempel (W. Germany)
Consensus process: tools for group communication—M. Bruemmer and P. Hare
Violence in the Third World—S.S. Mehdi (Pakistan) and J.B. Okubo (Kenya)
Development problems in Yugoslavia—C. Naef (USA) and V. Regjo (Yugoslavia)
Nonviolent action at Rocky Flats, Colorado—P. Wehr (USA)
Nonviolence and the development of the State—N. Young (UK)

Planning peace education—B. Hollister (USA), P. Hare (Israel), A. Lee (Canada), and
P. Wehr (USA)
A nonviolent political science and political action—G. Paige (USA)
How we learn nonviolence—N. Young (UK)
The religious basis of nonviolence—J. Forest (Holland)
Nonviolence and Euromissiles—H. and H.K. Tempel (W. Germany)

Course Program

Saturday, 25 June, Meeting of Resource Persons

Sunday, 26 June, Registration of Student-Participants
Antonia Young

Monday, 27 June (8:30—9:00)   Introduction to the Course
Theodore Herman, Nigel Young, Rosemary Pelly

I. Review of the Meanings of Nonviolence (9:00—12:00)

It does not enlighten us very much to define "nonviolence" as the opposite of
"violence." "Violence" can be used in several ways, nor do all people agree on the
meaning of such terms as "conflict," "force," "coercion," and "persuasion," or on
the difference between "inner" and "outer" violence, or between "structural" and
"overt" violence.

Since this course is about "nonviolence" it will be more useful to list some of the
commonest meanings and to explain them briefly. Four that concern individual
behavior come largely from the teachings of religion and philosophy, while four
touch on action by a group of people united more by a common need than by a
formal belief.

The designated resource persons will speak for about 10 minutes each in order to
clarify the meanings and offer examples. In the discussion that follows, other views
of "nonviolence" may be offered, thus starting us off on a lively two weeks of shared
learning.

A. Nonviolent action as a form of individual behavior
    1. Refusal to struggle openly against evil and injustice: Kenneth Lee, Paul Wehr
    2. Refusal to accept evil and injustice: Barrett Hollister
    3. Maintaining a loving relationship with others: Harcourt Klinefelter
    4. Reverence for a full life in a patriarchal world: June Hare

B. Nonviolent action by a *group* united for a common purpose
    1. To redress a grievance or defeat an adversary: Paul Hare, Michael Randle
    2. To grow with an adversary in a new relationship: Bernard LaFayette
    3. To work for conditions that remove the need for conflict: Petra Kelly, Narayan
    Desai
    4. To develop human potential in community living: Danilo Dolci, Justin
    Vitiello
    5. Discussion continued (3:30—6:00)

These several views of nonviolence will raise many questions for consideration and
deeper study. Here are some that often come up:
    1. Why pay attention to religious and philosophical teachings that seem to have
    no restraint on violence and oppression?

2. Do all religions, or all the formal religions, teach nonviolence?
3. What are some positive terms for "nonviolence"?
4. How can a responsible person accept inaction in the face of evil?
5. Does nonviolent resistance succeed only in certain cultures?
6. Is conflict always to be avoided, or can it produce some good?
7. Do oppression, injustice, and violence produce violent people?
8. Do good conditions produce nonviolent people?
9. How do certain people turn to nonviolence?
10. Can nonviolence be taught?
11. How do leaders in nonviolence arise? What is their role in building a lasting movement?
12. Who are some well-known leaders in nonviolence in your country or area, both past and present? Are such leaders admired as highly as are the military heroes? Are most such leaders men or women?

Tuesday, 28 June (8:30—12:00)

II. Resolving Ongoing Conflict

A. Through the political-administrative institutions
   1. Political campaigns and elections—Petra Kelly
   2. The ombudsman in the government bureaucracy—Rosemary Pelly

B. The uses of publicity and public witness
   1. Norway, Poland—Paul Wehr
   2. Gandhi's campaigns in South Africa and India—Narayan Desai
   3. Dr. King's efforts in the U.S.—Harcourt Klinefelter
   4. The relation between education, creativity, and development (3:30—6:00):
      Special session by Danilo Dolci, Justin Vitiello

Wednesday, 29 June (8:30—12:00)
C. Interposition between adversaries
   1. UN Emergency and Peacekeeping Forces—Paul Hare
   2. International Peace Brigades—Narayan Desai, Paul Hare

D. Third-party efforts at negotiation and mediation
   1. NGO initiatives at the UN and outside—Barrett Hollister
   2. Private efforts with government leaders—Kenneth Lee
   3. Private efforts in the Netherlands—Harcourt Klinefelter
   4. Training in individual and small group nonviolence (3:30—6:00): Harcourt Klinefelter, Narayan Desai

Thursday, 30 June (8:30—12:00)
E. Civilian nonviolent action
   1. Theory and practice—Gene Sharp
   2. Norway, Poland—Paul Wehr
   3. South Africa, Middle East—Paul Hare

Friday, 1 July (8:30—12:00)
F. Civilian nonviolent action (continued)
   1. Training—Gene Sharp
   2. The Alternative Defense Commission—Michael Randle

Monday, 4 July (8:30—12:00)

III. Preventing Possible Conflict

A. Deterrence by threat or reward
   1. Government power for law and order—Theodore Herman

B. Shared activities
   1. Intergovernmental via the UN—Paul Wehr
   2. Between countries—Nigel Young
   3. Control of Mediterranean pollution—Theodore Herman
   4. People-to-people projects—Barrett Hollister

C. Building new relationships 3:30—6:00
   1. Within countries—Petra Kelly, Nagasura Madale
   2. Between organizations—James Forest

D. UNESCO's Disarmament Education Program and nonviolence:
   Special session by Stephen Marks

Tuesday, 5 July (8:30—12:00)

IV. Social Change

A. Movements of social regeneration
   1. Gandhi's work in South Africa and India—Narayan Desai
   2. Work in rural Sicily—Danilo Dolci, Justin Vitiello
   3. The civil rights struggle in the American south (3:30—6:00)—Bernard La-
      Fayette; with film: "Amazing Grace—Martin Luther King From Montgomery
      to Memphis"

Wednesday, 6 July (8:30—12:00)

B. Religious influences
   1. Personal careers, past and present—Theodore Herman
   2. Conscientious objection to war—Kenneth Lee, Barrett Hollister

C. Secular education in nonviolence
   1. UNESCO's Disarmament Education Program and nonviolence—Nigel Young
   2. In universities and schools—Nigel Young, Theodore Herman
   3. Imaging a World Without Weapons (3:30—6:00)—Theodore Herman, Nigel
      Young

Thursday, 7 July (8:30—12:00)

D. Training in nonviolence
   1. Institute for Total Revolution—Narayan Desai
   2. Martin Luther King, Jr., Center for Non-Violent Social Change—Bernard
      LaFayette
   3. Self-training and community work—Theodore Herman

Friday, 8 July (8:30—12:00)

E. Intentional communities
   1. The tradition of the ashram—Narayan Desai
   2. Developing human potential in group living—James Forest, Danilo Dolci

Conflict and Violence in American Life

Paul Peachey   *Spring 1983*
Sociology 208/ Catholic University/ Washington, D.C. 20064

The oft repeated charge, "Violence is as American as cherry pie," sets the agenda for this course. Is this true? What kind of evidence is there to refute or to support this claim? What are the modes and sources of violence in American life, in American society? What light do the sciences shed on the problem? What are the countervailing forces? What are the solutions to the problems of violence? Each student will be asked to choose a problem area to investigate, to develop an appropriate bibliography (with Graduate Assistant help), and then to write a paper on a specific topic on the basis of the bibliography. Class sessions will be devoted to readings, lectures, and discussion. There will be a midterm test and a final.

Texts

Understanding Violence, Graeme Newman. New York: Harper & Row, 1979
Report of the National Advisory Commission on Civil Disorders. New York: New
   York Times, 1968 ("Kerner Report")

Course Agenda
Violence has been defined as "the exercise of physical force so as to inflict damage to persons or property." Violence used, *inter al.,* to "enforce" authority and to "challenge" authority. Newman, chap. 1.

January 12-16   Violence and Social Control
Newman, 1-37
Friedrich, "The Problem of Political Violence," 19-36
McFarlane, "The State of Violence," 55-98

January 19-23   Historical Violence I
Newman, 38-59
Hofstadter, ed., 3-43
Kerner Report, 1-31

January 26-30   Historical Violence II: Recent Cases
Rubenstein, 22-41
Kerner Report, 35-108, 203-250

February 2-6   Cultures and Subcultures of Violence
Newman, 89-115
Hackney in Graham/Gurr II: 387-404, "Southern Violence"
Raymond D. Gastil, "Homicide and a Regional Culture of Violence," *American
   Sociological Review* 36 (1971):412-427

February 9-11 Violence and the Roots of Culture: The Nature of American Society
Newman, 116-136
Connolly, "The Challenge to Pluralist Theory," 3-34
Pinkney, "Cultural Supports for Violence," 154-185
Ball-Rokeach in Short, "The Legitimation of Violence," 100-118

February 16-20 Recycling Violence: The Family and the Community
Newman, 137-153
Suzanne K. Steinmetz, Murray Strauss, "Social Myth and Social System in the Study of Intra-family Violence," in *Violence in the Family.* Ed. by Steinmetz & Strauss. New York: Harper & Row, 1974: 3-24
William Goode, "Force and Violence in the Family," *Journal of Marriage and the Family* 33 (1971): 624-636

March 2-4 Recycling Violence: The Community
Marvin B. Sussman, "Family, Kinship and Bureaucracy," in *Sourcebook in Marriage and the Family.* Ed. Sussman. Boston: Houghton, Mifflin, 1974: 232-251
James S. Coleman, "Community Conflict," *Politics of Metropolitan Areas.* Ed. by Philip Coulter. New York: Crowell, 1967:27-54

March 6-16 Violence: An Occupational Hazard
Newman, ch. 7
Allan Silver, "The Demand for Order in Civil Society," *The Police.* Ed. D. Bordua. New York: Wiley, 1967
Jesse Rubin, "Police Identity and the Police Role," in *The Police and the Community.* Baltimore: Johns Hopkins, 1972

March 18 Mobs, Riots and Gangs
Newman, ch. 8
Amitai Etzioni, "Collective Violence," *Contemporary Social Problems.* Ed. R.K. Merton, R. Nisbet. New York: Harcourt, Brace Jovanovich, 1976: 675-726

March 20 Violence of Strangers: Rape & Robbery
Newman, ch. 9
Harry Dienen, "Violence In the Ghetto," *Violence and Social Change.* Chicago: University of Chicago Press, 1968: 13-39
E. Hilberman, "Rape: The Ultimate Violation of Self," *American Journal of Psychiatry* 133 (1976): 436-7

March 23-25 Born to Kill?
Newman, ch. 10
Albert Bandura, "Theories of Aggression," *Aggression: A Social Learning Analysis.* Englewood Cliffs: Prentice Hall, 1973: 1-59
Samuel S. Kim, "The Lorenzian Theory of Aggression and Peace Research: A Critique," *Journal of Peace Research* 13 (1976):253-276

March 27-30 The Dynamics of Violence: Conclusions
Newman, 225-266
Hannah Arendt, David Riesman, et al., "Is America by Nature a Violent Society?" *New York Times Magazine,* April 28, 1968: 24; 111-119

April 1-24   Violence Reduction and Nonviolent Alternatives
Nonviolence: truth and strategy?; the concept of nonviolence; nonviolent direct action; Satyagraha—the salt march; Gandhi and Martin Luther King, Jr.; Birmingham.

Bibliography

Wilhelm Emil Mühlmann, "Pacifism and Nonviolent Movements," *Micropedia* 13:845-53

Joan V. Bondurant, *Conquest of Violence.* Berkeley & Los Angeles: University of California Press, 1965 (rev. ed.)

Eric H. Erikson, *Gandhi's Truth: On the Origins of Military Nonviolence.* New York: Norton, 1969

M.K. Gandhi, *Nonviolent Resistance.* New York. Schocken Books, 1961

A. Paul Hare, H.H. Blumberg, *Nonviolent Direct Action—American Cases: Social-Psychological Analysis.* Washington, D.C.: Corpus Books, 1968

Martin Luther King, Jr., "Letter from a Birmingham Jail," *The Christian Century,* June 12, 1963:767-772

Martin Luther King, *Why We Can't Wait.* New York: Signet Books, 1964

David Lewis, *King: A Critical Biography.* Champaign: University of Illinois Press, 1968

Staughton Lynd, *Nonviolence in America: A Documentary History.* Indianapolis: Bobbs-Merrill, 1966

E. Victor Wolfenstein, *The Revolutionary Personality.* Princeton: Princeton University Press, 1967

A. Nakhre, "Meanings of Nonviolence, A Study of Satyagraha Attitudes," *Journal of Peace Research* 13 (1976): 185-196

Giuliano Pontara, "The Rejection of Violence in Gandhian Ethics of Conflict Resolution," *Journal of Peace Research* 2 (1965): 197-215

Bo Wirmark, "Nonviolent Methods and the American Civil Rights Movement, 1955-1965," *Journal of Peace Research* 11(1974): 115-132

The Ideology and Culture of Nonviolence in Western Society

Charles F. Howlett   *Fall 1983*
West Islip, NY 11795

The occurrence of overt military hostilities between independent states alternates throughout history with periods free from such disruptions. Depending on the question posed, the war-peace dichotomy understood as the presence or absence of armed conflict between sovereign states or other large social entities proves inadequate for the description and explanation of the sequence of events in greater detail. When does war break out? When does peace begin or end? Are recurrent border conflicts still peace or already war? Can the balance of terror be called a condition of peace? Is war by proxy still peace even though the proxy gets massive arms support from its sponsor? Are struggles for national self-determination and liberation from colonial rule war? How does the idea of "just wars" fit in with the principle norm that war is to be avoided at all cost? In what way does the principle of conscientious objection threaten the legitimacy of the nation-state. How does war threaten the concept of individualism? Is a nation-state functioning on the basis of internal repression and external imperialism at peace as long as it does not get involved in armed hostilities beyond its borders?

One could easily propose more such questions, but the examples given demonstrate that the delineation between the two key concepts of war and peace is far from sufficient and that peace as non-war cannot serve as the single highest norm of peace research and education. Its relevance for a serious dilemma, the avoidance of nuclear war, is plain to see. But if we interpret peace as the absence of direct violence—a moral and social opprobrium placed on acts of violence—a more exacting definition of peace may be readily understood. Peace interpreted as absence of direct violence serves as a springboard for examining the ideological and cultural basis of war resistance in Western society. An examination of the issues of nonviolence may also tell us something about the nature and purposes of the nation-state, its political and moral obligations to humanity, and the troublesome dilemma of individual conscience versus service to the state.

Course Outline

Lesson 1   The Concept of Peace
Read: Select one of the following:
Norman Angell, *War and the Essential Realities.* London: Watts, 1913
Randolph Bourne, "War and the Intellectuals" in Carl Resek, ed. *War & the Intellectuals.* NY: Harper & Row, 1964

Allen Devere, *The Fight for Peace,* and E.P. Thompson "Letter to America," *New York Times,* April 1981

I. War: Strategies and Causes

Implicit in this section is a rejection of two frequently encountered views. The first posits a single cause of war, such as communism or capitalism. Proponents of such mono-casual explanations are, in a curious sense, optimists. They believe that war will end when the cause of war which they have singled out is destroyed. Consequently they often argue that war itself is the means that will end war. At the other end of the argument are the pessimists, those that survey history, discern the multiplicity of forces leading to war and conclude that this very multiplicity of causes demonstrates the inevitability of war. They find something in the nature of man, social organization or international relations that assures the continuation of war. If war *is* "in the nature of things" there is no way to eliminate it. But is it? Conflict certainly is, perhaps even violence. But there is a difference between personal or small group violence and the mass indiscriminate violence of war.

Lesson 2 The Causes and Nature of War
Quincy Wright, *A Study of War* (Parts 1 & 2). Chicago: Univ. of Chicago, 1964
Kenneth N. Waltz, *Man, The State and War.* NY: Columbia Univ. Press, 1965

Lesson 3 Multiple Causes
UN Report, *The Threat of Nuclear Weapons: Questions and Answers on the Effects of Their Possible Use.* NY: UN Publications, 1968.

Lesson 4 Deterrence
Philip Green, *The Deadly Logic.* NY: Schocken Books, 1967.
Film: "The Last Epidemic"

II. World Development and World Community

Those working for a world without war must understand alternative approaches to achieving world development and world community. How are the developing nations to meet the human needs of their people, now aware that "it doesn't have to be like this"? In a world ruled by nationalist and ideological passions, but made ever more interdependent by modern technological, communications and economic realities, how are we to achieve that recognition of interdependence that would make law possible? Can such a sense of world community make it possible for law to arise from consent instead of being imposed by violence?

Lesson 5 Human Rights
United Nations, *Universal Declaration of Human Rights.* NY: UN Publications, 1948
Luis Kutner, *World Habeas Corpus.* Los Angeles: Oceana, 1962

Lesson 6 Toward a World Community
Emile Benoit, *Interdependence on a Small Planet.* NY: Columbia Journal of World Business, 1966
William H. McNeil, *Past and Future.* Chicago: University of Chicago, 1954

III. International Organization and World Law

Pierre Dubois (1307), Dante Alighieri (1309), Erasmus (1517), Sully (1595), William Penn (1693), Hugo Grotius (1625), Abbe de Saint-Pierre (1716), Jean-Jacques Rousseau (1716) and Immanuel Kant (1795) each developed in their own way the idea of international law, binding arbitration between nation-states, supranational authority or world government. Studying the fate of their early plans for peace is a sobering experience. The history of the Hague Conference agreements, the League of Nations and our current experience with the International Court of Justice and the United Nations are not much more encouraging.

Given this history of international organizations many conclude that achieving world peace through world law is no more than an enduring illusion. Advocates of world law respond by pointing out that while the U.N. had failed to resolve conflicts between superpowers, it was not given the power to do so. In lesser conflicts, such as Iran (1946), Indonesia (1947), Suez (1956) and Cyprus (1968), the U.N. aided significantly in the nonviolent resolution of conflict.

Lesson 7 Law and Peace
Hugo Grotius, *Prolegomena to the Law of War and Peace*. Indianapolis: Bobbs-Merrill, 1957
Immanuel Kant, *On Perpetual Peace*. Indianapolis: Bobbs-Merrill, 1957
Nicholas M. Butler, *The International Mind*. NY: Scribner's Sons, 1913

IV. Moral, Religious, Philosophical and Ethical Thought on War

Moralistic slogans abound alike in the peace movement and in the statements of government leaders, but the question, "What is right?" is seldom seriously considered. Currently dominant ethical views, whether stated in theological or secular terms, argue that it cannot be answered. It cannot be answered, one hears, either because there is no way to justify ethical standards or because all ethical standards are situationally based and change as particular situations change. Some refuse to deal with this question because they feel that the danger of war comes precisely from those who *do* assert that they are right and therefore justified in violently imposing their views on others. Those seeking an end to war need to consider the other side of that argument, for without standards by which conflict can be arbitrated or resolved, there is left only the test of violence. Without standards other than history, i.e., who wins the battles, right becomes identified with might. Thus both the existence of standards for determining what is right and their absence can be considered causes of war.

Lesson 8 Christian Pacifism
Jo Ann O. Robinson, *Abraham Went Out*. Phila: Temple University Press, 1981
Kirby Page, *Must We Go to War?* NY: Larrar & Rinehart, 1937

Lesson 9 Judaism and War
Martin Buber, *I and Thou*. NY: Scribner's, 1958

Lesson 10 Moral, Philosophical, Ethical Issues
Albert Camus, *Neither Victims Nor Executioners*. NY: World Without War Council, 1968

Richard Wasserstrom, "Three Arguments Concerning the Morality of War," *Journal of Philosophy*, 1968

William James, "Moral Equivalent of War" in Ralph B. Perry, *Essays on Faith and Morals*. Cleveland: World Publishing, 1964

Jacob Bronowski, "The Abacus and the Rose" in Bronowski, *Science and Human Values*. NY: Harper & Row, 1965

Paul Edwards, *The Logic of Moral Discourse*

Film: "Non-Violence—Mahatma Gandhi and Martin Luther King"

V. Conscientious Objection

Wars are not only the sum total of numerous decisions by individuals; they are also the product of defective social institutions. Many pacifists tend to view problems of conscience and war only in a personal dimension, ignoring the social and political context of choice. The terrible reality confronting the conscientious objector is that even though he says no to war, even though he correctly asserts the importance of each individuals's moral choice, he must also recognize that, at least in the short run, war will continue despite his personal refusal to participate. C.O.'s who see this reality know that more is needed than simply a personal withdrawal. They seek ways to make their lives count in building the institutions of peace.

Understanding the C.O. position begins with one basic concept: a C.O. may regard the goals of a war as just (as some see our goals in World War II), but he will never countenance the means (warfare) as permissible in reaching these goals. The C.O. usually argues that means must be compatible with ends, or ends will never be achieved. He insists that organized mass violence will never bring peace or achieve justice.

Lesson 11 History

John Woolman, *The Journal of John Woolman*. NY: Cornith Books, 1961

Mulford Sibley & Philip Jacob, *Conscription of Conscience*. Ithaca: Cornell University Press, 1952

Lesson 12 Non-Cooperation and Resistance

A.J. Muste, *Of Holy Disobedience*. NY: Greenleaf, 1952

Film: "A Matter of Conscience"

VI. Social Change: The Nonviolent Approach

Advocates of nonviolence generally agree that nonviolence is preferable to violence because, when successful, its achievements are lasting. They do not deny that violence is sometimes successful in achieving political ends, although many doubt that violence has ever achieved progressive ends, particularly so when progress is defined as movement toward an "egalitarian society." As Mulford Sibley notes, "the utilization of violence tends to set up a kind of social logic which enhances class differentiation, promotes inequality, destroys the possibility of reconciliation, and in general undercuts revolutionary objectives."

Lesson 13 Theory and Practice

Richard Gregg, *The Power of Nonviolence*. NY: Schocken Books, 1966

Lesson 14 Civil Disobedience
Henry David Thoreau, *Civil Disobedience*
Leo Tolstoy, *Tolstoy on Civil Disobedience and Nonviolence.* NY: Signet Books,
    1968

VII. Political Process and the Peace Effort

A defense of democratic political processes and democratic norms begins with an
examination of the alternative political systems. On what values are they based?
What are their goals? How have they worked? A defense of democratic theory does
not require defense of past policies in a democratic society. Democracy does not
assure wise policy. It does assure that if a policy is unwise and if its consequences
affect many people, the policy can be changed without violence.

Advocates of a world without war need to understand democratic theory and
practice. They may disagree on capitalist or socialist forms of economic organization, for one could change the present American economic system enough to be
accurate in calling it either capitalist or socialist and not fundamentally affect the
chances for war or peace. But if democratic institutions are weakened, one effective
instrument for the nonviolent resolution of conflict is damaged. Increasing the
effectiveness of democratic institutions is one important part of work for a world
without war because democratic political processes recognize the inevitability of
conflict while institutionalizing some of the crucial insights of nonviolent conflict
resolution.

Lesson 15 Democracy and Its Critics
Raymond Aron, *Opium of the Intellectuals.* NY: W.W. Norton & Co., 1959
Randolph Bourne, *Untimely Papers.* NY: B.W. Huebsch, 1919

Lesson 16 The Peace Movement
Peter Brock, *Pacifism in Europe.* Princeton: Princeton University Press, 1972
Charles DeBenedetti, *The Peace Reform in America.* Bloomington: University of
    Indiana Press, 1980

Lesson 17 Organizing the Democratic Peace Movement: Problems and Prospects
George Orwell, *Homage to Catalonia.* Boston: Beacon Press, 1967

VIII. Literature—The Historical Novel

A world without war recognizes the need for literature which reaches across all
disciplines, mainly those in the Social Sciences and Humanities. Historical novels,
advocates of nonviolence maintain, present a humanistic picture of the realities of
war that supplement the scholarly documentation already undertaken. The use of
historical novels will prove effective in reaching a wider audience, academic and
nonacademic, as well as sensitizing the younger generation to the realities of death
in combat.

Lesson 18 Fear and Conscience
Erich Remarque, *All Quiet on the Western Front.*
Leo Tolsty, *War and Peace.* (abridged version)
Film: "All Quiet on the Western Front"

Lesson 19 Ideological and Cultural Impact of War on Humanity
Paul Fussell, *The Great War and Modern Memory*. NY: Oxford University Press, 1975

Select Bibliography

Adams, Robert P. *The Better Part of Valor: More, Erasmus, Colet and Vives on Humanism, War and Peace, 1496-1535.* Oshkosh, WA: University of Washington Press, 1962.

Addams, Jane. *Peace and Bread in Time of War.* New York: King's Crown Press, 1945.

Allen, Devere. *Pacifism in the Modern World.* Garden City, NY: Doubleday, Doran, 1929.

American Friends Service Committee. *Conscientious Objection to War: A Selected Bibliography.* Philadelphia: Central Committee for Conscientious Objectors, 1950.

Beales, A.F.C. *The History of Peace.* London: Dial Press, 1931.

Chatfield, Charles. Ed. *Peace Movements in America.* New York: Schocken Books, 1973.

Cook, Blanche W. *Bibliography on Peace Research in History.* Santa Barbara, CA: ABC-Clio, 1969.

Curti, Merle. *Peace or War: The American Struggle, 1636-1936.* New York: W.W. Norton, 1936.

Dowling, John. *War, Peace: Film Guide.* Chicago: War Resisters League, 1980.

Ekirch, Arthur A., Jr. *The Civilian and the Military.* New York: Oxford University Press, 1956.

Finn, James. Ed. *Protest, Pacifism and Politics.* New York: Random House, 1968.

Howlett, Charles F. and Glen Zeitzer. *The American Peace Movement: History and Historiography.* Washington: American Historical Association, 1984.

Horowitz, Irving. *The Idea of War and Peace in Contemporary Philosophy.* New York: Paine-Whitman, 1957.

Lynd, Staughton. Ed. *Nonviolence in America.* Indianapolis: Bobbs-Merrill, 1966.

Martin, David. *Pacifism: An Historical and Sociological Study.* New York: Schocken Books, 1966.

Mayer, Peter. Ed. *The Pacifist Conscience.* Chicago: Henry Regenery, 1967.

Millis, Walter. *Arms and Men.* New York: G.P. Putnam & Sons, 1956.

Newcomb, Hannah. *Bibliography on War and Peace.* Oakville, Ontario: Peace Research Abstracts, 1963.

Pickus, Robert and Robert Woito. *To End War.* New York: Harper & Row, 1970.

Sibley, Mulford Q. Ed. *The Quiet Battle.* New York: Doubleday, 1963.

Taylor, A.J.P. *The Troublemakers.* London: Hamish Hamilton, 1956.

Weinberg, Arthur and Lila Weinberg. Eds. *Instead of Violence.* Boston: Beacon Press, 1963.

Weston, Burns, et al. *Peace and World Order Studies: A Curriculum Guide.* 2nd ed. New York: World Policy Institute, 1978.

Peace: Theories, Strategies, and Movements

Herbert Feith   *Spring 1983*
Politics 378/Monash University/Melbourne, Australia 3168

"Peace: Theories, Strategies, Movements" is a new course. Its introduction in 1983 reflects the urgency and immediacy of peace issues. It also reflects my conviction that Australians interested in these issues can learn a lot from the traditions of peace studies, peace research and world order studies which have developed overseas.

The course is organized in two halves. In the first half of the year every seminar will begin with an interruptible lecture and end with general discussion. Students will be expected to have read one short piece to be ready to join in discussion.

The program for the second half of the year is more open, and the style will be more workshop-oriented. In this part of the course each seminar will start with one or (more often) two students introducing a topic, one selected from the long list in Section 5 of this guide. Students will be asked to consult with me extensively in advance on the way they propose to handle their seminar introductions. In the case of topics which lend themselves to antithesis-focussed discussion, two students will be asked to argue opposing positions. People will be expected to speak for between 10 and 20 minutes and encouraged to use films, videos, slide-sets, overhead projections, maps, charts and handouts distributed in the preceding week.

I will be asking seminar groups and individual students to make decisions on their second semester program by the beginning of second term. People will be free to write their major essays on the basis of the material they have presented at their seminars and they will be encouraged to write joint essays.

Objectives and Approach

Teachers are often asked to make their teaching objectives explicitly. Mine are four:
(i) to introduce students to some peace studies approaches;
(ii) to help students find their way through the burgeoning literature on war and peace issues which the New Cold War of the post-1979 period has spawned and give them a greater sense of competence in relation to technical terms which are so often mystifying,
(iii) to help people work out where they stand in relation to the intellectual and moral issues involved, specifically on the question of what peace strategies make sense and what individuals seeking to be peacemakers can do; and
(iv) to create an environment in which people work together cooperatively.

I should make it clear that technical aspects of weapons systems and arms control arrangements will get much less attention in this course than they deserve. So will much else, e.g., the question of how wars start, the sociology of military organizations, the economics of arms races and disarmament and the nexus between nuclear power and nuclear weapons. The area of peace studies is, of course, enormous, and our time is severely limited, as is my knowledge.

The approach I will be adopting will in some respects be interdisciplinary. Of the three peace theorists whose work we will consider in some detail, one, Johan Galtung, is a sociologist, another, Richard Falk, is an international lawyer, and the third, Edward Thompson, is an historian. But focus will be primarily on political aspects rather than on sociological, legal, historical or economic ones.

Outline of Seminars, First Half of the Year

March 7/10   Introduction to Peace Studies

March 14/17   Introduction to Global Politics since December 1979: What is the 'New Cold War'?

March 21/24   First of Four Historical Lectures: The Cold War and Detente

March 28/31   Deterrence and Counterforce

April 11/14   The Superpower Empires and their Challengers. Rivals and Peripheries

April 18/21   Peace Movements, Old and New

May 2/5   Edward Thompson as a Peace Theorist—The Exterminism Thesis

May 9/12   Edward Thompson as a Peace Theorist—Beyond the Cold War

June 6/9   Johan Galtung as a Peace Theorist—Structural Violence

June 13/16   Johan Galtung as a Peace Theorist—Peace Roles, Old and New

June 20/23   Richard Falk as a Peace Theorist—World Order Theory

June 27/30   Richard Falk as a Peace Theorist—Normative Initiatives and Demilitarization

Topics for Student-Initiated Seminars, Second Half of the Year

The Dynamics of the Current Arms Races

Can the power of America's military-industrial complex be broken or sidestepped?
Is there a military-industrial complex in the USSR?
Is there a Soviet threat?
Has the USSR been gaining an edge on the US in military capacity?
Can the US disengage from its empire?
What economic transformations would far-reaching disarmament require?
Is it possible to arrest the process whereby more and more states are acquiring nuclear weapons?

Accelerating arms sales to the Third World: Does the main impetus for these come from the arms selling states and companies or from the arms buying states?

Elements of the Counter-Dynamic
Western European peace movements 1980-83 (or a discussion of a particular country's movement)
The US peace movement
Independent peace groups in East Germany, Hungary and the USSR—Are they of real importance?
The peace politics of the Pacific

Arms Races and their Control
Are we close to a nuclear war?
How could a nuclear war start?
The issues of the Cruise and Pershing II missiles and the US-Soviet arms control negotiations
Could a nuclear war involving the superpowers remain limited?
Chemical and biological warfare

Global Reform, Global Transformation
Third World development vs. the arms race: Can Third World states be expected to take an active part in struggles for global demilitarization?
Is it feasible to work for the defanging of the KGB, CIA and similar organizations, particularly in relation to interventions outside their own states?
Is it possible to reform the United Nations or should one work for a global organization established on a new basis?
Should one work towards the establishment of a World Central Authority?

Peace Politics in Australia
The character and strength of the Australian peace movement
US bases in Australia and the politics of the ANZUS alliance
Arms production and arms exporting in Australia
Alternative defence and social defence proposals
What could Australia do in co-operation with other middle and small powers in support of global initiatives for peace?
What can Australia learn from the defence and foreign relations postures in Sweden, Switzerland, Austria, Yugoslavia, etc.
Civil defence issues and the survivalist argument

Consciousness Dimensions
Militarism, what is it?
Religious traditions and peace thinking
Feminism and peace thinking
New Age movements and peace thinking
The non-violence tradition
Peace movements as an increasingly important component of a larger alternative consciousness movement
Psychic numbing
Anti-nuclear dissidence within the military profession
Peace education as a new thrust in educational thought
Artists and writers and the transformation of consciousness

The Seminar Program in the First Two Weeks

Seminar 1 March 8/11   An Introduction to Peace Studies

Peace studies as an alternative to strategic studies. World order theory and theories of a trend to the eclipse of the nation state as one branch of peace studies.

Peter van den Dungen, *Foundations of Peace Research* (School for Peace Studies, University of Bradford, December 1980), 54 pp. An excellent introduction to the work of the great figures of peace thinking.

"Kenneth Boulding: A Discussion with Harry Redner," *Social Alternatives*, October 1982, pp. 15-20. One of the fathers of peace studies and research.

Kenneth Boulding, "The War Trap," in R. Falk, S. Kim and S.H. Mendlovitz (eds.), *Toward a Just World Order*, Boulder, CO: Westview Press, 1982, pp. 225-238.

Roy Preiswerk, "Could We Study International Relations as if People Mattered?" *ibid*, pp. 146-174; also in *Peace and World Order Studies: A Curriculum Guide*, (Third Edition, 1981), World Policy Institute, pp. 2-23.

Seminar 2 March 15/18   An Introduction to Global Politics since December 1979: What is the 'New Cold War'?

What is new about world polices since December 1979? How does this relate to what is new about the superpowers' weapons systems and strategic doctrines?

Newsweek, January 31, 1983, "An Arms Deal: Now or Never" and related articles, pp. 6-14 (handout from Politics Department Office).

New Internationalist, March 1981. This whole issue is on the superpowers strategic and political relations. Very readable and includes a layman's guide to nuclear stockpiles.

Alan Roberts, "Why we have a War to Stop," *Peace Dossier* 2 (Victorian Association for Peace Studies) 1982, 6 pp.

George F. Kennan, "A Proposal for International Disarmament" (address on receiving the Albert Einstein Peace Prize, Washington, May 19, 1981), 4pp.

Daniel Yankelovich and Larry Kaagan, "Assertive America," *Foreign Affairs*, December 1980, pp. 696-713.

Institute for Policy Studies, *Resurgent Militarism*, Washington, D.C. 1979.

John Kenneth Galbraith, "The Economics of the Arms Race—and After," *Development Dossier* No. 10 (Australian Council for Overseas Aid), September 1982, pp. 8-11. Also in *Bulletin of the Atomic Scientists*, June 1981.

Bibliographical Aids and Reference Material

The place to start is John Wiseman's *Peace and Disarmament Education: A Resource Kit and Annotated Bibliography* (Department of Politics, Monash University, December 1982). This 59-page guide was produced with the present course in view and copies will be distributed. Let me also draw your attention to:

Ruth Leger Sivard, *World Military and Social Expenditures*, published annually in the US. An excellent brief compendium of statistical and other factual material and valuable charts.

M. Kidron and R. Segal, *The State of the World Atlas*, London 1981, is an imaginative selection on military, political and cultural as well as economic and technological subjects.

The Literature of Nonviolence

Ken Brown   *Spring 1983*
SoSc333/ Manchester College Peace Studies Institute/
North Manchester, IN 46962

An introduction to the lives and thought of major practitioners of nonviolence, primarily Mahatma Gandhi and Martin L. King.

> "[Satyagraha] is a movement intended to replace methods of violence and a movement based entirely upon truth . . ."—Gandhi

> "The end is pre-existent in the means, and ultimately destructive means cannot bring about constructive ends."—King

Texts

Thoreau, *Essay on Civil Disobedience.*
Tolstoy, *The Law of Love and the Law of Violence.* NY: Rudolph Field, 1948.
Fischer, L., *Gandhi: His Life and Message for the World.* NY: Mentor, 1954.
Gandhi, *All Men are Brothers: Autobiographical Reflections.* NY: Continuum.
Bondurant, J., *Conquest of Violence: The Gandhian Philosophy of Conflict.* Revised ed. Berkeley: University of California, 1965.
Lewis, D., *King: A Critical Biography.* Baltimore: Penguin, 1970.
King, M., *Why We Can't Wait.* NY: Mentor, 1963.
Hope & Young, *Struggle for Humanity: Agents of Nonviolent Change in a Violent World.* Maryknoll, NY: Orbis, 1977.

Course Outline

January 31   Introduction to the Literature of Nonviolence

February 2   Thoreau
Essay on Civil Disobedience

February 7   Film: "Talking with Thoreau"

February 8   Film: Attenborough's "Gandhi"

February 9   Discussion of film

February 14   Gandhi: Early Life and Influences
Fischer, 1-93

February 16   Salt March and the Role of Fasting
Fischer, 93-137

February 21   Swaraj, Struggle Against Partition, Death
Fischer, 137-189

February 23   Film: "Gandhi's India"
All Men Are Brothers, 3-50

February 28   Gandhi and Religions
All Men Are Brothers, 51-97

March 2   Self-Discipline, Brahmacarya
All Men Are Brothers, 98-137

March 7   Aparigraha, Spinning
All Men Are Brothers, 138-178

March 9   Satyagraha: Progression, Distinction, Compulsion
Bondurant, 3-35

March 14   Five Satyagraha Campaigns
Bondurant, 36-104 (ind. report)

March 16   Gandhian Innovations, Film: "Gandhi"
Bondurant, 105-145

March 21   Gandhi and Politics
Bondurant, 146-188

March 23   Gandhi and Politics
Bondurant, 189-233; Exam

Spring Recess

April 6   Martin Luther King: Introduction
Lewis, 3-84

April 11   Film: "Satyagraha Home-Grown"
Lewis, 85-111

April 13   Atlanta, Albany, Birmingham; Film: "Strength of a Dream"
Lewis, 112-210 (ind. assign)
Lewis, 210-263

April 18   Selma, Chicago
Lewis, 264-296; 313-353 (ind. assign)

April 20   "The Fire Next Time"
Lewis, 297-312

April 25   "Killers of the Dream"
Lewis, 354-397

April 27   "Letter from a Birmingham Jail"
(library reserve)

May 2   Satyagraha and Duragraha
Why We Can't Wait

May 4   Comparison/Contrast of Gandhi, King

May 9, 11   Individual Papers on Practitioners of Social Change:
Muste, Day, del Vasto, Camara, Chavez, Kaunda, Esquivel, Douglass, Dolci, etc.

May 16   Final Examination

Film References
"Talking with Thoreau" (#32080)   Penn. State University
"Gandhi" (CS1124)   Indiana University
"Gandhi's India" (#CS2121)   Indiana University
"Martin Luther King: The Man & the March" (#CS1912)   Indiana University
"Martin Luther King, Jr.: From Montgomery to Memphis" (CS#2119)   Indiana University

Books by Mahatma Gandhi
Gandhi, Mahatma. *All Men are Brothers: Life and Thoughts of Mahatma Gandhi, As told in His Own Words.* Ahmedabad: Navajivan Publishing House, 1960.
An Autobiography: The Story of My Experiments with Truth. Boston: Beacon Press, 1957.
Collected Works. Delhi: Publications Division, Ministry of Information and Broadcasting, Gov't of India. 1958.
The Essential Gandhi. New York: Vintage, 1962.
For Pacifists. Ahmedabad: Navajivan Publishing House, 1949.
Gandhi on Non-violence. New York: New Directions Publishing Corp., 1965.
The Gandhi Reader: A Source Book of His Life and Writings. Bloomington: Indiana University Press, 1956.
Gandhi's Autobiography. Washington: Public Affairs Press, 1948.
Gandhi's Letter to a Disciple. New York: Harper, 1950.
100 Years. New Delhi: Gandhi Peace Foundation, 1968.
The Mind of Mahatma Gandhi. Ahmedabad: Navajivan Publishing House, 1967.
Non-violence in Peace and War. Ahmedabad: Navajivan Publishing House, 1942-49.
Non-violent Resistance. New York: Schocken Books, 1961.
Satyagraha in South Africa. Ahmedabad: Navajivan Publishing House, 1972.
Satyagraha. Ahmedabad: Navajivan Publishing House, 1952.
Swaraj in One Year. New York: AMS, 1972.
International Symposium on Truth and Nonviolence in Gandhi's Humanism. Paris, 1969.
What Does Gandhi Want. New York: Oxford University Press, 1942.
Young India, 1919-1922. N.Y.: Huebsch, 1923.

Secondary Works on Gandhi
Alexander, Horace Gundry. *Gandhi Remembered.* Wallingford, Pennsylvania: Pendle Hill Publications, 1969.
Andrews, Charles Freer. *Mahatma Gandhi at Work: His Own Story Continued.* New York: Macmillan, 1931.
Andrews, Charles Freer. *Mahatma Gandhi at Work: His Own Story, with an Introduction.* New York: Macmillan, 1930.
Ashe, Geoffrey. *Gandhi.* New York: Stein and Day, 1968.
Bhattacharyya, Sailendra Nath. *Mahatma Gandhi the Journalist.* Bombay: Asia Publishing House, 1965.

Bondurant, Joan Valerie. *Conquest of Violence: the Gandhian Philosophy of Conflict.* Princeton, N.J.: Princeton University Press, 1958.

Brown, Judith M. *Gandhi's Rise to Power.* Cambridge (Eng.): University Press, 1972.

Datta, Dhirendra Mohan. *The Philosophy of Mahatma Gandhi.* Madison: University of Wisconsin Press, 1953.

Devanesen, Chandra David Srinivasagam. *The Making of the Mahatma.* Cambridge: Harvard University Press, 1961.

Diwakar, Ranganath Ramachandra. *Is Not Gandhi the Answer?* Bharatiya Vidya Bhavan, 1966.

Eaton, Jeanette. *Gandhi, Fighter Without a Sword.* New York: Morrow, 1950.

Erikson, Erik Homburger. *Gandhi's Truth on the Origins of Militant Non-violence.* New York: Norton, 1969.

Fischer, Louis. *Gandhi and Stalin: Two Signs at the World's Crossroads.* New York: Harper and Row, 1947.

Fischer, Louis. *Gandhi: His Life and Message for the World.* New York: New American Library, 1954.

Fischer, Louis. *The Life of Mahatma Gandhi.* New York: Harper and Row, 1950.

Ghosh, Prafulla Chandra. *Mahatma Gandhi, As I Saw Him.* Delhi: S. Chand, 1968.

Green, Martin Brugess. *The Challenge of the Mahatmas.* New York: Basic Books, 1978.

Hall, Josef Washington. *Eminent Asians.* 1929.

Holmes, Patricia Hunt. (microfilm) Leo Tolstoi as a Theorist of Non-violent Social Revolution and his Relationship with Mohandas Gandhi, 1978.

Hosburgh, H. *Non-violence and Aggression: A Study of Gandhi's Moral Equivalent of War.* London: Oxford University Press, 1968.

Hoyland, John Somervell. *They Saw Gandhi.* New York: Fellowship Publications, 1947.

Hunt, James D. *Gandhi in London.* New Delhi: Promilla, 1978.

Hunter, Allan Armstrong. *Three Trumpets Sound: Kagawa, Gandhi, Schweitzer.* New York: Association Press, 1939.

Huthseeing, Krishna. *We Nehrus.* Bombay: Pearl Publications, 1968.

Jones, Eli Stanley. *Mahatma Gandhi: An Interpretation.* New York: Abingdon-Cokesbury Press, 1948.

Keer, Dhananjay. *Mahatma Gandhi: Political Saint and Unarmed Prophet.* Bombay: Popular Prakashan, 1973.

Kenworthy, Leonard Stout. *Twelve Citizens of the World: A Book of Biographies.* Garden City, New York: Doubleday, 1953.

Kripalani, Krishna. *Gandhi: A Life.* New Delhi: Orient Longmans, 1968.

Mahatma Gandhi: 100 Years. New Delhi: Gandhi Peace Foundation; Orient Longmans, 1968.

Malhotra, S. *Gandhi and the Punjab.* Chandigarh: Punjab University Publication Bureau, 1970.

Mallik, Basanta Kumar. *Gandhi: A Prophecy.* Oxford: Hall, 1948.

Maurer, Herrymon. *Great Soul: The Growth of Gandhi.* Garden City: Doubleday, 1948.

The Meanings of Gandhi. Honolulu: University Press of Hawaii, 1971.

Mohan Rao, U. *The Message of Mahatma Gandhi.* London: English Universities Press, 1968.

Muzumdar, Haridas Thakordas. *Gandhi Triumphant!* New York: Universal Publishing Co., 1939.

Naess, Arne. *Gandhi and the Nuclear Age.* Totowa, N.J.: Bedminster Press, 1965.

Nag, Kalidas. *Tolstoy and Gandhi.* Patna: Pustak Bhandar, 1950.

Nair, Pyarclal. *Mahatma Gandhi, The Last Phase.* Ahmedabad, India: Navajivan Publishing House, 1956.

Namboodripad, E. *The Mahatma and the Ism.* New Delhi: People's Publishing House, 1958.

Nanda, Bal Ram. *Mahatma Gandhi: A Biography.* Boston: Beacon Press, 1958.

Narasimhaiah, C. *The Writer's Gandhi.* Patiala: Punjab University, 1967.

Nehru, Jawaharlal. *Nehru on Gandhi.* New York: J. Day Company, 1948.

Oxnam, Garfield Bromley. *Personalities in Social Reform.* New York: Abingdon-Cokesbury Press, 1950.

Rajagopalachari, Chakravarti. *Gandhiji's Teachings and Philosophy.* Bombay: Bharatiya Vidya Bhaven, 1967.

Ramachandran, B. *Gandhi: His Relevance for our Times.* Bombay: Bharatiya Vidya Bhavan, 1967.

Reynolds, Reginald. *The True Story of Gandhi, Man of Peace.* Chicago: Children's Press, 1964.

Rolland, Romain. *Mahatma Gandhi: The Man Who Became One With the Universal Being.* New York: Century, 1924.

Rudolph, Lloyd I. *The Modernity of Tradition: Political Development in India.* Chicago: University of Chicago Press, 1967.

Russell, Bertrand. *Gandhi.* Brockway: Wallace, 1955.

Sheean, Vincent. *Lead, Kindly Light.* New York: Random House, 1949.

Sheean, Vincent. *Mahatma Gandhi: A Great Life in Brief.* Faridabad, India: Publications Division, 1968.

Shirer, William L. *Gandhi: A Memoir.* New York: Simon and Schuster, 1980.

Shridharani, Krishnalel Jethalal. *The Mahatma and the World.* New York: Duell, Sloan and Pearce, 1946.

Shridharani, Krishnalel Jethalal. *War Without Violence: A Study of Gandhi's Method and Its Accomplishments.* New York: Harcourt, Brace and Co., 1939.

Tendulkar, Dinanath Gopal. *Mahatma: Life of Mohandas Karamchand Gandhi.* Bombi, 1960.

Wadia, Ardeshir Ruttonji. *The Philosophy of Mahatma Gandhi, and Other Essays Philosophical and Sociological.* Mysore, India: University of Mysore, 1958.

Wolfenstein, E. Victor. *The Revolutionary Personality: Lenin, Trotsky, Gandhi.* Princeton, NJ: Princeton University Press, 1967.

Gauba, Khalid Latif. *The Assassination of Mahatma Gandhi.* Bombay: Jaico Publishing House, 1969.

International Symposium on Truth and Nonviolence in Gandhi's Humanism. *Truth and Nonviolence.* New Delhi: Gandhi Peace Foundation, 1970.

Sharp, Gene. *Gandhi as a Political Strategist: with Essays on Ethics and Politics.* Boston: P. Sargent Publishers, 1979.

Mahadevan, T.K. *Gandhi's Pivotal Year.* Chicago: World Without War Publications, 1983.

Books by Martin Luther King, Jr.

King, Martin Luther, Jr. *I Have a Dream*. (In Baird, Albert Craig, Comp Representative American Speeches.), 1964.

The Measure of a Man. Philadelphia: Pilgrim Press, 1968.

Strength to Love. New York: Harper and Row, 1963.

Stride Toward Freedom. New York: Harper and Row, 1958.

The Trumpet of Conscience. New York: Harper and Row, 1968.

Where Do We Go From Here: Chaos or Community. New York: Harper and Row, 1967.

Why We Can't Wait. New York: Harper and Row, 1964.

Secondary Works on King

Ansbro, John. *The Mind of Martin Luther King, Jr.* Maryknoll, N.Y.: Orbis Books, 1982.

Bennett, Lerone. *What Manner of Man*. Chicago: Johnson Publishing Co., 1968.

De Kay, James T. *Meet Martin Luther King, Jr.* New York: Random House, 1969.

King, Coretta Scott. *My Life with Martin Luther King, Jr.* New York: Holt, Rinehard and Winston, 1969.

Miller, William Robert. *Martin Luther King, Jr.* New York: Weybright and Talley, 1968.

Oates, Stephen B. *Let the Trumpet Sound: The Life of Martin Luther King, Jr.* New York: Harper and Row, 1982.

Peck, Ira. *The Life and Words of Martin Luther King, Jr.* New York: Scholastic Book Services, 1968.

Ramachandran G. *Nonviolence After Gandhi: A Study of Martin Luther King, Jr.* New Delhi: Gandhi Peace Foundation, 1968.

Reddick, Lawrence Dunbar. *Crusader Without Violence*. New York: Harper and Row, 1959.

Smith, Kenneth L. *Search for the Beloved Community*. Valley Forge, PA: Judson Press, 1974.

Taylor, Paula. *Coretta Scott King, A Woman of Peace*. Mankato, MN: Creative Education, 1974.

Walton, Hanes. *The Political Philosophy of Martin Luther King, Jr.* Westport, CT: Greenwood Publishing Corp., 1971.

Knight, Janet M. *3 Assassinations: The Deaths of John & Robert Kennedy and Martin Luther King*. New York: Facts on File, 1971.

Clayton, Edward Taylor. *Martin Luther King: The Peaceful Warrior*. Englewood Cliffs, NJ: Prentice-Hall, 1968.

Conflict Resolution: Theory and Technique

George Lopez   *Term III 1983*
Interdisciplinary 40/ Earlham College/Richmond, IN 47374

Probably no area of social theory is more pervasive than that which deals with the causes and consequences of conflict in its overt and its covert sense. Further, there is an emerging set of literature and practices in our society which examines the problems and practice of "dealing with" conflict. This course is an attempt to analyze how these two trends fit together and whether such a merger helps produce better analysts of conflict and better conflict resolvers. Specifically, the course attempts to answer a number of questions:

1. What, if any, are the differences among theories of social conflict? What does that mean for theories and techniques of conflict resolution?
2. What are the differences among the terms (and practice of) conflict management, conflict regulation and conflict resolution? Under what conditions is each possible and/or desirable? What approaches are available to conflict participants which differ from those available to neutral third parties.
3. What are the differences among *techniques* which have become prominent? Are there parallels, or at least parallel uses of techniques, across different arenas of conflict, that is, marriage difficulties; jail riots; labor-management disputes; community disputes; international negotiation?

Texts and resources

Louis Kriesberg. *Social Conflicts.* Prentice Hall, 1982.
Roger Fisher. *International Mediation: A Guide for Practitioners.* Harvard Negotiation Project, 1980
Maire Dugan (ed.) Conflict Resolution. Special Issue of *Peace and Change.* Summer, 1982.

For people interested in the "ministerial" approaches and aspects of conflict resolution, we will read Kraybill's *Repairing the Breach: Ministering in Community Conflict* which details both the overall approach and particular cases of conciliation and mediation in which the Mennonite Central Committee has been involved.

Course Requirements

There are a number of distinct course requirements. While I briefly state the rationale for each assignment below, I will further amplify their importance during the first class.

A. *Conflict Skills Workbook—20%—Collected every four or five classes*
This is a small notebook in which you are to make entries after each class or

experience (i.e., course reading; simulation; guest speaker; movie; etc.) It is not a diary! Rather, it is a handy guide to help you build, in a cumulative way, the various aspects of the course.
B. *Book Report*—15%
C. *Two exams*—mid-term and final; April 27 and June 1 or 2—50%
D. *Performance*—15%

Schedule and Assignments

Week I (March 23-April 1)   Conflict and How We Have Come to Study It
What is social conflict; across what levels of human interaction does it emerge; what controversies and problems surround the analysis of social conflict?
Readings:
Kriesberg—Preface (1, 2); 1-4
Kriesberg—5, 6, 8, 9 (begin)

Week II (April 4)   Processes of Handling Conflict
An examination of *your* predisposition to conflict/problem solving—distinctions among conflict management, redirection and resolution.
Reading:
Fisher, pp. 1-15
Kriesberg, 5, 6, 8, 9
Dugan—editor's introduction; all four essays in section entitled "Theoretical Perspectives"
Exercise: Complete Interaction Problem Solving Style Inventory

Week III (April 11)   People in Conflict (I)
Issues of trust, perception, on-going relationships, etc. some techniques like GRIT, US-Iran case study; some Middle East application.
Readings:
Fisher, pp. 17-60
Svenn Lindskold, "Trust Development, the GRIT Proposal, and the Effects of Conciliatory Acts on Conflict and Cooperation," *Psychological Bulletin*, Vol. 85
Herb Cohen, "Negotiating the Iranian Crisis" (4 papers on reserve)

Week IV (April 18)   People in Conflict (II)
Readings: Salem, Carpenter, Ray in Dugan
Exercise: Fisk Junior High School Dispute

Week V (April 25)   Negotiation
What does it mean to negotiate; what can a negotiator do to both advance or advocate their own cause and create conflict resolution; what are the various dimensions and interpretations of negotiation; what factors impact positively or negatively on the negotiation process?
Readings:
Fisher, part III
Bertram I. Spector, "Negotiation as a Psychological Process," *JCR*, Vol. xxi, No. 4
I. William Zartman, "Negotiation as a Decision-Making Process," *JCR*, Vol. xxi, No. 4

David A. Brookmire and Frank Sistrunk, "The Effects of Perceived Ability and Impartiality of Mediators and Time Pressure on Negotiation," *JCR*, Vol. xxiv, No. 2.

Week VI (May 2)   Mediation (I)
What do we know about intervention strategies; what factors assist and sustain this approach; what inventing tasks and communication tasks does the mediator perform?
Readings: Fisher, part II
Salem, "The Nazi-Skokie Dispute: A Mediators Perspective" (mimeo)
John Chace, "The Mediation Function of the Community Relations Service." Paper presented at the Society for Professionals in Dispute Resolution, Toronto, October, 1976 (on reserve)
D.G. Pruitt, and D.F. Johnson, "Mediation as an Aid to Face-Saving in Negotiation," *Journal of Personality and Social Psychology*, XXX 1970, 14, 239-246 (on reserve)
See: Skokie film

Week VII (May 9)   Mediation (II)
Readings:
Kriesberg, Chapter 7
Davis-Dugan, "Training the Mediator" in Dugan; review Lane in Dugan
G.A. Lopez, "Ceasefires" (mimeo)

Week VIII (May 16)   Controlled Communication and Resolution Workshops
Readings:
John W. Burton, "Resolution of Conflict," *International Studies Quarterly*, Vol. 16, (1972): 5-29
C.R. Mitchell, "Conflict Resolution and Controlled Communication: Some Further Comments," *Journal of Peace Research*, Vol. 10, (1973): 123-132
Herbert Kelman and Stephen Cohen, "Reduction of International Conflict: An Interactional Approach" (mimeo)
L. W. Doob and William Foltz, "The Belfast Workshop," *JCR*, Vol. 17, No. 3
Barbara J. Hill, "An Analysis of Conflict Resolution Techniques. From Problem-Solving Workshop to Theory," *JCR*, March, 1982

Week IX (May 23)   New Processes and Applications
An examination of emerging approaches including the futures invention workshop approach; the single text negotiation procedure, the negotiation investment strategy; non-violent direct action
Readings:
Coulson; Lewis; Wedge-Sandole in Dugan
Exercise: tracing application modes for the next 20 years—a role analysis

Imaging Security Alternatives to the Arms Race

Gerald and Patricia Mische   *Summer 1983*
Special Offering/ Viterbo College/La Crosse, WI 54601

The goal of this workshop is ultimately the empowerment of people to find a creative response to one of the gravest issues of our times—the unchecked and spreading arms race. This workshop thus has the following objectives:
1. To better understand the changing nature of security in an interdependent world.
2. To examine the current state of the arms race and its present and future impact on world security and peace.
3. To explore security alternatives that could make disarmament feasible.
4. To develop goals and strategies for realizing security alternatives.
5. To go beyond nuclear numbness and despair and discover ways to contribute to world peace and security.
6. To grow more deeply in the Spirit and open ourselves to God's creative action through us in forwarding life on the planet.

Outline

Day One   Introduction (a.m.)
How Do We Define Security in a Period of Global Transformation?
    Presentation & Group Discussion
State of the Arms Race: Are We More Secure?
The Breakdown of National Defense
Presentation
Psychological Effects of the Arms Race Dealing with Numbness and Despair
    (Afternoon)
    Presentation
    Series of Group Imaging Processes
Group Meditation/Reflection (Evening)
    Scripture and/or other readings

Day Two
The National Security Straitjacket: Social and Economic Effects of the Arms Race
    (a.m.)
    a. In the U.S.
    b. Worldwide
What About the Russians? The Soviet Security State (Afternoon)
Group Meditation/Reflection (Evening)

Day Three
War and Peace in the Bible (a.m.)
Christians and Disarmament—Past, Present, Tomorrow (a.m.)
Security Alternatives to the Arms Race—I (Afternoon)
  History of Disarmament Efforts
  Current Options for International Security and Disarmament
  World Order Movement
Great Alternative Dream Night (Evening)
  Discovering and Celebrating our own Images of Security Alternatives

Day Four
Inventing the Future: What Does a Secure World Look Like? (a.m.)
(group scenarios)
  If we can imagine what it is we seek to create we can begin to work toward it.
Future Histories: Strategies Toward World Security (Afternoon)
  Presentation followed by group process that places us in a future time when greater international security and disarmament has happened. From there we look backward to see how it happened and to get a handle on necessary steps in the present.
Group Meditation Reflection (Evening)

Day Five
Global Spirituality: The Inner Dimensions of World Security and Peace (a.m.)
Personal Empowerment: Let Peace Begin with Me (Afternoon)
  Individual and group processes designed to discover our own capacities for creative initiative as agents of creational history.

Closing Celebration

Texts
Gerald and Patricia Mische, *Toward A Human World Order*. New York/Ramsey, N.J.: Paulist Press, 1977.
Robert C. Johansen, *Toward a Dependable Peace: A Proposal for An Appropriate Security System*. New York: World Policy Institute, 1978.

Recommended:
Willy Brandt., et al. *North-South: A Programme For Survival*. Cambridge, MA.: MIT Press, 1980.
Helen Caldicott, *Nuclear Madness*. New York: Bantam, 1978.
James McGinnis, *Bread and Justice*. New York: Paulist Press, 1979.
Patricia Mische, "Global Spirituality" in *The Whole Earth Papers, No. 16*, E. Orange, N.J.: Global Education Associates. Patricia Mische, "Women, Power and Alternative Future," Parts I and II, *The Whole Earth Papers, No. 8 & 9*.
Earthscope: Transitions Toward World Order. A special issue for the Whole Earth Papers (No. 12), featuring articles by Thomas Berry, Robert Muller, Pat Mische and Robert Manley on global transformation.
Land and World Order. The Whole Earth Papers, No. 17, 1982.
Jonathan Schell, *The Fate of the Earth*. New York: Knopf, 1982.
J. Carter Swaim, *War, Peace and the Bible*. Maryknoll, New York: Orbis Books, 1982.
Mendlovitz, Saul H., ed. *On the Creation of a Just World Order*. New York: Free Press, 1975.

Sociology of Nonviolence

Sevryn T. Bruyn

Sociology 135/Boston College/Chestnut Hill, MA 02167

Fall 1982

Texts

Gene Sharp, *The Politics of Nonviolent Action*; Part One, "Power and Struggle" (Boston: Porter Sargent, 1973)

Sevryn Bruyn and Paula Rayman, *Nonviolent Action and Social Change* (NY: Irvington Press, 1979)

Marjoire Hope and James Young, *The Struggle for Humanity* (Orbis Books, 1977)

Suzanne Gowan, George Lakey, et al. *Moving Toward a New Society* (New Society Press, 1976)

Schedule of Readings

September 2
The Politics of Nonviolent Action, (Sharp), Ch. 1

September 7
"Technique of Struggle," (Sharp), Ch. 2

September 14
Nonviolent Action and Social Change (Bruyn-Rayman); "Social Theory," Ch. 1

September 21
"Social Mechanisms," (Bruyn-Rayman), Ch. 2

September 28
"Gandhi's Vision," (Bruyn-Rayman), Ch. 3

October 5
"In Jail," (Bruyn-Rayman), Ch. 4
"United Farm Workers," (Bruyn-Rayman), Ch. 5

October 12
"Georgia," (Bruyn-Rayman), Ch. 6
"Nuclear Power," (Bruyn-Rayman), Ch. 7

October 17
"Dolci in Italy," (Bruyn-Rayman), Ch. 8
Struggle for Humanity—Discussion

October 24
"Nkrumah in Africa," (Hope-Young), Ch. 9

November 2
"Norway and Czechoslovakia," (Hope-Young), Ch. 10

November 5
"Nonviolence as a Substitute for War," (Hope-Young), Ch. 11

November 11
"Veterans' Day," (Hope-Young)

November 16
"Feminist Perspectives," (Hope-Young), Ch. 12

November 23
"Theater," (Hope-Young), Ch. 13

November 25
Thanksgiving—classes resume Nov. 30th

November 30
Struggle for Humanity—Discussion 2nd half

December 7
Review

December 10-11
Study Days

December 12-18
Exam

Discussion Questions for *Nonviolent Action and Social Change*

Introduction
1. Discuss the key themes which link the book's chapters.
2. How does nonviolent change challenge three myths of our present society?

Chapter 1: Social Theory of Nonviolent Action
1. What are two functions of social theory?
2. What is distinctive about the "radical perspective?"
3. How is the professional definition of "conflict" challenged by the facts of nonviolent action?
4. What is nonviolence from the "principled" (or radical) perspective?
5. What are some requirements for acting on the causes of violence?
6. How is the definition of "power" challenged by nonviolent action?
7. What was the key issue to solve in the mind of Gandhi which was reflected in the theory of Emile Durkheim?
8. What are some radical implications of the concept of self-rule and social development?
9. What is structural violence?
10. Where does "structural dominance" exist in society?
11. What is "revolutionary reform"?
12. How does the "Salt March" contradict Smelser's theory of a social movement and advance our understanding of how basic change takes place?
13. How do "norms" function in society?
14. What are "elements of creative conflict"? (See also Notes; #22, 23)
15. How do Marxists criticize symbolic interaction theory?
16. How was "symbolic interaction" a key factor in creatively resolving conflict in the school yard?

17. What is an example of "de-bureaucratizing"? How does it follow the model of "organizational development"?
18. Select a proposition in organizational theory which you think especially needs further study. Why?
19. Explain the three principles of self-governance and how they apply to the analysis of political body.

Chapter 2: Sociological Mechanisms
1. What are three mechanisms of nonviolent action? (Give examples of each one.)
2. How are people persuaded?
3. Explain Gandhi's concept of Trusteeship.

Chapter 3: Gandhi's Vision
1. What are the three categories of Gandhism concepts? Give one example each.
2. What was the emphasis on Gandhi's ideal state and how would one attain this goal?

Chapter 4: Ten Days in Jail
1. How does Dellinger describe the jail? (e.g. differences between old fashioned jails and liberal correctional institutions, tough guard attitudes, the whole social system.)
2. Explain Dellinger's statement: "Being ready to go to jail is the only way of remaining free."

Chapter 5: United Farm Workers
1. What types of supporters did the United Farm Workers attract? (How did they see the strike?)
2. What were positive functions of the March to Sacramento in spite of the absent Governor?
3. Nonviolence is like a philosophy of life for the farm workers. What historical and cultural elements contribute to this philosophy to make nonviolent tactics more viable and compatible to workers in this case?
4. Why did Chavez fast?
5. Identify the following:
   a. Proposition 22
   b. El Teatro Campesino
   c. Dolores Huerta
   d. National Labor Relations Act of 1935
6. What were some of the factors working against the UFW? How did Chavez overcome them?

Chapter 6: Georgia, Civil Rights
1. What factors contributed to the "resolution" of conflict in Albany?
2. How do the authors apply Gene Sharp's theory to this case?
3. How did the following "actions" work:
   a. political jiu-jitzu
   b. fasting

Chapter 7: Nuclear Power
1. Describe the training program of the Clamshell Alliance (e.g. Affinity Groups.)

2. Describe the Alliance's main instruments of organization and decision-making. Do they demonstrate principles of self-governance?
3. What happened to Kasiwzaki?
4. What are the implications of nuclear power in the Third World?
5. Is nonviolent action a "principled" or "pragmatic" issue for Clamshell members?

Chapter 8: Danilo Dolci
1. Why was Dolci quick to win a following?
2. How did Dolci find Trapetto? How did he respond to it?
3. Describe the "reverse strike." (Note its relation to principles of nonviolent action.)
4. Describe Dolci's efforts to institute democratic control of Western Sicily's water supply and engage in community development.
5. How does Dolci view violence?
6. What is his hope for a "nonviolent revolution?"
7. What is your final evaluation of Dolci? (Drawn from the author's notes.)

Chapter 9: Nonviolence in Africa
1. What were the purposes of the World Peace Brigade? (What notables supported it?)
2. For what reasons is the proposal for land reclamation presented by the International Council of the W.P.B.?
3. Why did the W.P.B. begin to lose momentum as an international organization?
4. How can you evaluate what was gained?

Chapter 10: Norway and Czechoslovakia
1. What does "polarization" mean?
2. What is the basic objective of nonviolent national defense.
3. Discuss strategy and tactics of nonviolent action in Norway and Czechoslovakia. (In addition, note why one country succeeded, "schweikism," and the critical role of "symbolism.")
4. How does the author conclude this study? (What do you think about it?)

Chapter 11. Nonviolent Action as a Substitute for War
1. How does Merton's basic theorem relate to the function of defense and the military?
2. What are some forms of nonviolent action used internationally? How were the Gandhian struggles in India an example of international conflict?
3. What is required for a new effort to abolish war? What are some of the conditions that must be assumed to do this?
4. Since war is such a prominent institution of modern society, we must examine the functions of war in order to find alternative ways of fulfilling these functions. Identify the functions of war.
5. How is nonviolent action-struggle capable of severing the various sources of the opponent's power?
6. What is civilian defense? How is it a possible (functional) substitute for war?
7. According to Sharp, what are some of the unfavorable circumstances that have accompanied nonviolent techniques?

Chapter 12: Feminism
1. What potential do women have in relation to war?
2. Identify the following:
   a. ahimsa
   b. empowerment
3. What concept do most women share about themselves? Give an example.
4. Are there any non-biological differences between men and women on the deepest level?

Chapter 13: Theater for the Living Revolution
1. What are the goals and concepts of nonviolent action?
2. What is Swomley's definition of liberation?
3. What is Gandhi's view of violence in relation to being a coward?
4. What is the relationship between simplicity and nonviolence as stated by Schumacher?
5. Discuss briefly nonviolent action from two different perspectives.
6. What are Lakey's five stages necessary for the nonviolent revolution?
7. Should violent characters, or violence in general, be depicted in nonviolent theater?

Discussion Questions for *The Politics of Nonviolent Action*

I. The Nature and Control of Political Power
1. What is "social power"? Political power?
2. What are two (dualistic) views of power?
3. What are the sources of power? Explain their meaning.
4. How do these sources depend upon obedience?
5. How are "enforcement" and "obedience" interdependent?
6. Is there really any one-way relationship existing between rulers and subjects?
7. Why do people obey?
8. Explain the crucial role of "consent."
9. What are some concrete examples of bureaucratic obstruction?

II. Nonviolent Action: An Active Technique of Struggle
1. What is nonviolent action?
2. In what different ways does nonviolent action produce change?
3. What are some misconceptions about nonviolent action?
4. How may nonviolent action be compared to violent action (unfair) with different standards of assessment?
5. What are some early historical examples of nonviolent action?
6. What are some examples of the expansion of the nonviolent technique from the late eighteenth to the twentieth century?
7. What are some early 20th century cases?
8. What was Gandhi's contribution?
9. What are examples of struggles against the Nazis?
10. What is one example of Latin American nonviolent action?
11. What is one example of a nonviolent uprising against communist regimes?
12. What is one example in the United States?
13. Is nonviolent action always planned and organized? Does it require a high level of education?

Discussion Questions for *Struggle for Humanity*

1. The Philadelphia Life Center is in a racially mixed, low income area. How is this neighborhood organization different from conventional organizations? How is it also different from other nonviolent action movements?

2. Lanza del Vasto
   a. Why did Lanza decide to join Gandhi in India?
   b. What was Shantidas' (del Vasto's) view of nonviolence?
   c. From the term "L'Arche," how did Shantidas refer to the term "Ark"?
   d. What was the constant theme of Shantidas?
   e. Compare and contrast some of Shantidas' ideas with those of Marx.

3. Danilo Dolci: How did Danilo Dolci use *satyagraha* to bring about change?

4. Dom Helder Camara
   a. Why is Dom Helder Camara a significant figure in the study of non-violent action?
   b. What political, economic, and social conditions exist in Brazil?
   c. What is meant by *conscientizacion.*
   d. What are some of the methods Camara uses to raise consciousness and promote nonviolent change?
   e. What is Operation Hope?
   f. What is the philosophy of Dom Helder Camara on nonviolence?

5. Cesar Chavez
   a. Cesar Chavez has excluded the American dream of social and economic mobility from his life. What dream has he substituted and what Federal act is at the heart of his struggle?
   b. What are the provisions of the National Labor Relations Act as they pertain to unions?
   c. What is a *peregrinacion*? What event led to the call of a *peregrinacion*?
   d. What is the difference between a primary and a secondary boycott?
   e. What are the provisions of California's Agricultural Labor Relations Act of 1975?
   f. When the union is so small and agribusiness so big, how does Chavez maintain hope and how does this relate to nonviolence?
   g. What are some of the tangible gains achieved by Chavez since organizing the farmworkers?

6. Thich Nhat Hanh
   a. How can the successful revolution against president Diem in Vietnam be seen as truly a non-violent "people's revolution?"
   b. Though the self-immolation of the seven bonzes may be seen as violent, suicidal action, it inspired mutuality and responsibility among the Vietnamese people. How is this so?
   c. What is the cooperative division of labor between Buddhism and Communism?
   d. What was the danger of the U.S.'s one-sided view into the events of Vietnam during the 1960s?
   e. According to Nhat Hanh, how are "nationalism" and "Buddhism" combined?
   f. What was the "third force" in Vietnam during the 60's?

7. Kenneth Kaunda

a. What is meant by describing Kaunda's work in terms of "relative nonvio-lence?" (Note Kaunda's early life, later years, his government policies that are partly in the nonviolent tradition and others in opposition to it.)

Course Requirements

The following alternative ways of fulfilling the requirements for the course should be chosen by members in the course:

1. Research Paper, Oral Presentation, and Final Exam (No mid-term)
2. Action-Research Project, Oral Presentation, and Final Exam (No mid-term)
3. Book Report, Midterm, and Final Exam (No more than 5 pages on the Book Report)
4. Field Interviews, and Final Exam (Choice of mid-term)

Short Bibliography

Bauman, Margaret. *Kagaua*. N.Y.: Macmillan, 1936.

Bondurant, Joan. *Conquest of Violence*. Princeton, N.J.: Princeton University Press, 1958.

Bonhoeffer, Dietrich. *Letters and Papers from Prison*. N.Y.: Macmillan, 1967.

Dellinger, Dave. *Revolutionary Nonviolence*. N.Y.: Anchor Books, 1971; *More Power*, N.Y. Anchor Books, 1975.

Deming, Barbara. *Revolution and Equilibrium*. N.Y.: Grossman Publishers, 1971.

Estey, George and Hunter, Doris. *Nonviolence*. N.Y.: Ginn & Co., 1971.

Fischer, Louis. *Gandhi, His Life and Message for the World*. N.Y.: New American Library, 1954.

Gandhi, Mohandas, K. *An Autobiography, The Story of My Experiments With Truth*. Boston: Beacon Press, 1957.

Gandhi, Mohandas. *Non-Violent Resistance (Satyagraha)*. N.Y.: Schocken Books, 1951.

Gregg, Richard B. *The Power of Nonviolence*. Nyack, N.Y.: Fellowship Publica-tions, 1959.

Guinan, Edward, (ed.) *Peace and Nonviolence*. N.Y.: Paulist Press, 1973.

Hinton, William. *Fanshen*. N.Y.: Monthly Review Press, 1966.

King, Martin Luther, Jr. *Stride Toward Freedom: The Montgomery Story*. N.Y.: Harper and Row, 1958.

Lynd, Staughton. *Nonviolence in America: A Documentary History*. Indianapolis: Bobbs-Merrill, 1966.

Matthiessen, Peter. *Sal Si Puedes: Cesar Chavez and the New American Revolu-tion*. N.Y.: Dell Publishing Co., 1969.

Merton, Thomas. *Seeds of Destruction*. N.Y.: Farrar, Strauss and Giroux, 1961.

Muste, A.J. (ed. by Nat Hentoff). *The Essays of A.J. Muste*, Indianapolis: Bobbs-Merrill, 1967

Schumacher, E.F. *Small Is Beautiful*. N.Y.: Harper and Row, 1973.

Sharp, Gene. *The Politics of Nonviolent Action*. Boston: Porter Sargent, 1973.

Sibley, Mulford. *The Quiet Battle*. Boston: Beacon Press, 1963.

Swomley, John M., Jr. *Liberation Ethics*. N.Y.: Macmillan, 1972.

Thody, Philip. *Albert Camus: A Study of His Work*. N.Y.: Grove Press, 1957.

Tolstoy, Leo. *The Kingdom of God is Within You*. N.Y.: Farrar, Strauss, Cudahy, 1961.

Women
and
World Order

Women, Work, Wealth, and the Third World
Jill Gay, The Washington School

Sex Roles: Cross Cultural Perspectives
Janet Bauer, University of North Carolina, Chapel Hill

Anthropology of Women
Christine Ward Gailey, State University of New York,
Old Westbury

Women in Politics
Barbara J. Nelson, Princeton University

Women and Politics
Amrita Basu, Amherst College

Women, Work, Wealth, and the Third World

Jill Gay   *Spring 1983*
The Washington School/Institute for Policy Studies/
Washington, D.C. 20009

This course will identify central issues in development policies and effects on the lives of women in Latin America, Asia and Africa. It will explore alternative strategies that can be carried out equitably. The eight sessions will cover a range of concepts and issues such as health and family planning, domestic service and its implications for development, women and children at work and in the family, women and technology, women and revolution, and the program implications of women and energy.

Classes at the Washington School range from twenty to forty students. Students come from international organizations, public interest groups, community groups, church groups, universities, and congressional staff.

Each participant can expect the following questions to be addressed:

- What are the issues and concerns of your area (health, technology, domestic service, work, energy)? This will include a brief overview of the global situation and if you wish, a more in-depth look at a particular area or project. For example, in health, a major concern has been that women's health programs have focused on family planning.
- What needs to be done to improve conditions for women in the Third World?
- What national policies of Third World governments would result in a more equitable society?
- Would changes in United States policy positively affect Third World women?
- What U.S. development projects have successfully promoted equitable development? How?
- What positive impact could the people in this class have on the lives of Third World women?

Subtopics

The following subtopics will be explored initially through a few short, required readings; they will form the basis for the selection of areas to be researched. They should not be viewed as all inclusive and will hopefully be expanded through the progress of the course.

Population manipulation at home and abroad
What are the politics of population manipulation and population control programs? What is the history of population control organizations and programs, and why do governments push population control? What is the impact of population control on women and how much control do they have over public policy toward population manipulation?

The role of women in the church overseas—the missionary experience
What has been the participation of women in overseas church activities as well as at home? What images or ideas of women have been propagated by the church at home and abroad? What is the relation of the church and of missionary activities to the development of particular socio-economic policies and institutions in the Third World as well as at home?

Women and welfare—national and international
As most people on welfare or humanitarian relief programs are women and children, how do these institutions treat women? What are their attitudes toward women, in particular poor women, and how much do women participate in running these institutions? (Relate to population manipulation, as these are often linked.) What are the politics of humanitarian aid and the economics of welfare? How does the latter relate women on welfare to imperialism?

Cultural imperialism at home and abroad
What is the image of women projected at home and abroad through the media, life styles of the ruling class, socialization of children, etc.? Does the differential prevalence of different media in various countries make a difference in the type or degree of socialization of attitudes toward women?

Women and imperialist wars/women and liberation struggles
The role of women at home and abroad in the imperialist system—their particular oppression economically. The role of women at home and abroad in struggling for liberation from imperialism and from their own oppression.

Women's organizations
What are the spheres of power women have organizationally? How prevalent are women's organizations around the world and what are significant similarities or differences in their functioning or goals?

Additional subtopics
The differing economic roles of women in nations at different socioeconomic levels of development; socialist feminism and its relation to an anti-imperialist perspective.

Eight Sessions

1. Mervat Hatem, Political Science Department, Howard University, on Women in National and Global Development
2. Nancy Birdsall, Economist, World Bank, on Work
3. Kathleen Newland, Worldwatch Institute, author of *The Sisterhood of Man*, on The Family
4. Irene Tinker, Director, Equity Policy Center, co-editor of *Women and World Development*, on Energy

5. Elsa Chaney, author of *Supermadre,* on Migration
6. Caridad Inda, Director, Spanish Education Center, on Media
7. Barbara Ehrenreich, author of *For Her Own Good,* on Life on the Global Assembly Line
8. Jill Gay on Socialism, Cuba, Peoples Republic of China; Carol Collins on Insurgent movements in Africa

Reading List

Domitila Barros de Chungara with Mowma Vezzer, *Let Me Speak: Testimony of Domitila, a Woman of the Bolivian Mines,* Monthly Review Press, New York, 1978.

Ester Boserup, *Women's Role in Economic Development,* St. Martin's Press, New York, 1970.

Delia Davin, *Woman Work,* Clarendon Press, Oxford, 1976.

Susan George, *Feeding the Few: Corporate Control of Food,* The Institute for Policy Studies, Washington, D.C., 1978.

Susan George, *How the Other Half Dies: The Real Reasons for World Hunger,* Allanheld, Osmun, and Co., Montclair, 1976.

Nancy Hafkin and Edna Bay, eds., *Women in Africa: Studies in Social and Economic Change,* Stanford University Press, Stanford, CA, 1976.

Perdita Houston, *Third World Women Speak Out,* Praeger, New York, 1979.

Latin American Perspectives, *Women in Latin America,* Riverside, CA, 1979.

Beverly Lindsay, ed. *Comparative Perspectives of Third World Women: The Impact of Race, Class, and Sex,* Praeger, New York, 1980.

NACLA, Vol. XIV, No. 5, Sept.-Oct. 1980.

June Nash and Helen Safa, *Sex and Class in Latin America: Women's Perspectives on Politics, Economics, and the Family in the Third World,* J.F. Bergin Publishers, New York, 1980.

Kathleen Newland, *The Sisterhood of Man,* W.W. Norton and Co., New York, 1979.

Kathleen Newland, "Women, Men, and the Division of Labor," Worldwatch Paper 37, May 1980.

Margaret Randall, *Women in Cuba: Twenty Years Later,* Smyrna Press, New York, 1980.

Reina Rapp Reiter, ed., *Toward an Anthropology of Women,* Monthly Review Press, New York, 1975.

Nawal El Saadawi, *The Hidden Face of Eve,* Zed Press, London, 1980.

Adriana Santa Cruz, *Compropolitan: El orden transnacional y su modelo feminino, Un estudio de las revistas femeninas en latinoamericas,* Editorial Nueva Imagen, S.A., Mexico.

Signs: Journal of Women in Culture and Society, Vol. 3, No. 1, Autumn 1977.

Irene Tinker and Michèle Bo Bramser, eds., *Women and World Development,* Overseas Development Council, 1976.

Stephanie Urdang, *Fighting Two Colonialisms: Women in Guinea-Bissau,* Monthly Review Press, New York, 1979.

"Women and Work in the Middle East," *MERIP Reports,* No. 95, March-April, 1981.

Nadia Youssef, *Women and Work in Developing Societies,* Greenwood Press, Westport, Connecticut, 1974.

Sex Roles: Cross Cultural Perspectives

Janet Bauer   *Spring 1983*
Anthropology 140/University of North Carolina/Chapel Hill, NC   27514

This course examines social inequality through the study of gender roles. The material presents a comparative and evolutionary perspective on social roles as determined by sex in a range of human societies from preliterate hunter-gatherers through modern industrial nations. The elaboration of physiological differences into socially significant categories is examined through the ethnographic study of life cycle events, marriage, kinship and family, production and reproduction. The role of culture as symbolic and ideational systems which support sexual stratification is discussed. Likewise, attention is given to how structures of production and economic systems affect gender roles. Throughout the course the political aspects of gender, on both a personal and public level, will be explored toward understanding how gender systems (and other systems of inequality) are constructed, perpetuated and changed.

Class Format

Class sessions will be lecture/discussion. Study questions will usually be given out before each class period. In terms of earning discussion credit it would be helpful for you to read or skim over one or two of the recommended readings. These recommended readings also provide you with potential bibliographical selections for your research papers.

Because we will be discussing current sex role issues periodically, it would also be helpful for you to clip pertinent newspaper articles that you come across outside of class.

Required Readings

Full citations in accompanying bibliography.

Tavris and Offir, *The Longest War: Sex Differences in Perspective.*
Kingston, *Woman Warrior.*
E. Fernea, *Guests of the Sheik.*
Zaretsky, *Capitalism, The Family, and Personal Life.*
Anthropology 140. Collection of Readings in Comparative Gender Roles.

Course Outline

January 12   Introduction

Part I.   Sex Asymmetry in American Culture: Images and Issues

January 14   Overview: Noting the Differences in Sex Roles and Stereotypes
Required Reading: Tavris and Offir, Ch. 1,2
Recommended: Maccoby & Jacklin (1974)

January 17   Images in the Media and Popular Culture
Required Reading: Tavris and Offir, Ch. 3; Reinartz; Tong
Recommended: Komarovsky, Ch.1; Mason and Bumpass; Goffman (1979); Snow
Brown; Haskell; Farrell

January 19   Interpersonal Sexual Politics: Struggle and Violence
Required Reading: Komarovsky, Ch. 5; Hilberman//Wermuth (Note: // denotes
high recommendation)
Recommended: Dowling; Farrell; Goffman (1977); M. Mead (1942); Russell

January 21   Political Aspects of Gender in Family, Work and Reproduction
Required Reading: Cantarow, Rose, Judis *(In These Times)*; Lefkowitz; Mohr
Recommended: Sawhill; Kress; Ehrenreich and English; Snitow, Stansell and
Thompson; Godelier; Baruch

January 24   Class & Race Differences in Gender Relations
Required Reading: Lewis//Wittstock//Loo and Ong; Begin reading Kingston
Recommended: Puryear; The Combahee River Collective; Stack: Asian American
Women; Cotera (1977); Navarro; Cotera (1976); Gonzales; Nethamer; Moraga and
Azadna; Coles & Coles.

January 26   From the Outside Looking In: Third World Women in America
Required Reading: Maxine Hong Kingston (all)
Recommended: Kelly; Kingston (1977)

January 28   Theoretical Perspectives on Sexual Inequality
Required Reading: Rosaldo (1974)
Recommended: Quinn (1977); Schelegel; Smock; Berreman

Part II.   The Biological Basis for Differentiation: The Case for Universals

January 31   The Biology of Sex/Gender
Required Reading: Tavris and Offir, Ch. 4; Oakley, Ch. 1, Esp. pp. 19-27; Segal
Recommended: Money & Ehrhardt; Ehrhardt; Young; Hoffman; Vetterling-Braggin;
Shields; Brakke; Oakley, Ch. 6; Kessler and McKenna

February 2   Sociobiology and Bio-Social Perspectives
Required Reading: Wikan; Lambert//Rossi
Recommended: Harris; Divale & Harris; Leibowitz (1978); Dickerman Hardy;
MacCormack (1977); Parsons; Chagnon & Irons; Mead (1935)

Part III.   Cultural Explanations for Sex Roles

February 4   Nature, Culture, Honor: Symbolic Processes & Gender
Required Reading: Ortner (1974); Ahern//Wadley
Recommended: Webster; King; MacCormack & Strathern, eds.; Ortner & White-
head, eds., Newman; Gonzales; Beteille

February 7   Sexual Rites: Initiations and Mutilations
Required Reading: Pierce, pp. 4-7; Hayes; Jackson
Recommended: Herdt, G. (1982)

February 9   The Unconscious in Gender: Psychoanalytic Approaches
Required Reading: Chodorow (1974); Tavris & Offir, Ch.5
Recommended: Whiting and Child; Munro & Munro; Mitchell (1974 & 1971);
  Parker, Smith, and Ginat; Chodorow (1978); Slagter

February 11   Sex Role Socialization
Film on Sex Role Socialization and Sexuality
Required Reading: Begin Ch. 6, Tavris & Offir
Recommended: Kessler and McKenna

February 14   Cross-Cultural Studies of Early Learning of Gender Roles
Required Reading: Mead (1949), pp. 75-97; Pierce, pp. 9-25; Begin Fernea book
Recommended: Mead (1949), pp. 35-72 on anthropological questions; Maccoby
  (1966); Ember; Oakley

February 16   Social Learning Perspectives: Role Models, Non-verbal Communication and Language
Required Reading: Borker and Maltz//Bhatty; Webster
Recommended: Bandura (1977), parts; Roy; Vetterling-Braggin; Lakoff;
  Mary Henley

February 18   Sex Roles and Negotiation of Power: Family, Household and Mates
Required Reading: Youssef; Moses; Scrimshaw
Recommended: Topley; Bott; Campbell; Goldschmidt; Granzburg; Jacobson

February 21   Sex Roles and Society
Required Reading: Davis; Remy//MacIntyre
Recommended: Nelson, Maher; Lamphere; Granzburg; Frackenberg; Tiffany, ed.;
  Raphael, ed.

February 23   Gender in Middle Eastern Society
Required Reading: Fernea
Recommended: El-Saadawi

February 25   Theories of Sex Roles in Culture and Society
Required Reading: Rogers (1976)
Recommended: Rogers (1978); Schlegel (1972); Schlegal, ed. (1977); Lipshitz;
  Chetwynd; Smart & Smart; Rosaldo & Lamphere; Walum; Raphael; Friedl;
  Kessler; Murphy; Lapri; Burginon; Matthiasson

February 28   Midterm Exam

Part IV.   Evolutionary Perspectives, I. Sex Roles/Status in Different Types of Societies

March 2   Evolutionary Biology; Primate Sex Roles
Required Reading: McGrew
Recommended: Slocum; Zihlman

March 4   Simple Societies: Man The Hunter and Woman The Gatherer?
Slides/Cross Cultural Sex Roles
Required Reading: Tavis and Offir, Ch. 8; Griffin & Griffin//Leacock (1978)
Recommended: Lee (1981); Dahlberg, ed.; Leibowitz (1975); Sanday (1981); Giele
  (1972); Murphy & Murphy; Degler; Sacks (book)

March 14   Sedentarization and Sex Roles in Agricultural Societies
Required Reading: Draper; Michelson and Goldschmidt
Recommended: Pastner; Schneider; Lee (1972); Tiffany, ed.; Chinas; Whyte

Part V.   Economic Bases for M/F Differentiation: Production and Reproduction

March 16   The Effects of Economic Development on Gender Roles/Women
Panel Discussion
Required Reading: Bossen
Recommended: Elliot; Boserup; Tinker and Bo Bramsen; Pala

March 18   Structural and Marxist Critiques of Development
Required Reading: Giele & Smock; Sacks (1979)//Caulfield; Edholm, Olivia Harris, Kate Young
Recommended: Gayle Rubin; Kuhn and Wolpe, eds.; Reiter, ed.; Eisenstein, ed.

March 21   The Division of Labor: Work Roles and Status
Required Reading: Tavis and Offir, Ch. 7; Sanday (1974): Stoler
Recommended: Judith Brown; Murdock and Provost; Youssef (1974)

March 23   Capitalism and the Division of Labor: Class Differences
Required Reading: Carmen Diana Deere; Rubbo; Hull
Recommended: Chinchilla; Kandiyoti; Cain; K. Young (1978)

March 25   Film: "The Double Day"

March 28   The Political Economy of Housework (Public/Private Lives of Men and Women)
Required Reading: Gardiner; Reiter (article)
Recommended: Barron and Norris; Blexall and Reagan; Smith; Szalai

March 30   Reproduction and Women's Work
Required Reading: MacCormack (1982), pp. 1-19; Chaudhury
Recommended: Romaniuk; additional articles to be announced

April 1   Reproduction and Economic Development
Required Reading: Beneria and Sen
Recommended: Edholm, Olivia Harris and Kate Young

Part VI.   Evolutionary Perspectives, II. The Victorian Heritage: Family, Patriarchy and Capitalism

April 6   Women's Images in Western Society
Required Reading: Moller Okin, Ch. 5; Blum; Begin Zaretsky
Recommended: Rosenberg; Kern, Ch. 2; Vicinus

April 8   The Family and Patriarchy in Western Tradition
Required Reading: Zaretsky
Recommended: Moller Okin (1982); Tilly and Scott; Gough; Vogel; Rapp et al.; Poster

April 11   Capitalism, Patriarchy, and Socialist Feminism
Required Reading: H. Hartman
Recommended: Iris Young; Eisenstein, ed.; McDonough and Harris; Kuhn (1978)

Part VII.   The State as Patriarch: Public Policy and Changes in Sex Roles/ Status

April 13   The State as Patriarch: Philosophical Question on Inequality
Required Reading: Markovic; Mackinnon//Held
Recommended: Moller Okin, Ch. 11; Beteille; Berreman; Wolf

April 15   Planned Societies: Socialist States
Required Reading: Tavris and Offir, Ch. 9; Diamond//Molyneux
Recommended: Molyneux; Stacey; Cross

April 18   Planned Communities: Communes, Religious Sects
Required Reading: Spiro, Ch. 2; Kern, pp. 114-134//Abrams and McCulloch

April 20   Colonization, International Paternalism
Required Reading: Changing Role of Women in South East Asia; Minkon
Recommended: Fanon; family planning and development—to be announced

Part VIII.   Revolution, Protest; Change and Liberation

April 22   Women in Public Politics
Guest lecturer: M/F Relations in the Palestinian Political Movement
Required Reading: Fluehr-Lobban; Chai//first person accounts: Aminah el-Sa'id; Association of Salvadoran Women
Recommended: Fanon; Rein; Collier; Bauer; Caplan and Bujra, eds., Nashat, ed.

April 25   Panel on Women's Movements: ERA, Health Collectives (USA)

April 27   Consciousness, Change and Critiques of the Feminist Movement
Required Reading: Farrell, pp. 3-14; O'Brien, Slagter or Rosaldo
Recommended: Rowbatham; Barrett; Gould; Benston; Elstain; & 2 recent critiques: Balbus; McMillan

Bibliography

Abrams, P. and A. McCulloch. "Men, Women and Communes," in *Sexual Divisions and Society: Processes and Change*. Diana L. Barker and Sheila Allen, eds. London: Tavistock, 1976.

Ahern, Emily. "The Power and Pollution of Chinese Women," in *Women in Chinese Society*. Marjory Wolf and R. Witke, eds., pp. 193-214. Stanford: Stanford University Press, 1975.

Allman, James, ed. *Women's Status and Fertility in the Muslim World*. New York: Praeger, 1978.

Ardener, Shirley, ed. *Women and Space: Ground Rules and Social Maps*. New York: St. Martins Press, 1981.

Ardener, Shirley. *Defining Females: The Nature of Women in Society*. New York: John Wiley and Sons, 1978.

Asian American Women. Stanford: Stanford University Press, 1972.

Association of Salvadoran Women. "Participation of Latin American Women in Social and Political Organizations," *Monthly Review* 34 (2):11-23, 1982.

Babock, Barbara, Ann Freedman, Eleanor Norton and Susan Ross. *Sex Discrimination and the Law: Causes and Remedies.* Boston: Little, Brown and Co., 1975.

Balbus, Issac D. *Marxism and Domination: A Neo-Hegalian, Feminist, Psychoanalytic Theory of Sexual, Political and Technological Liberation.* Princeton: Princeton University Press.

Balzar, Marjorie. "Rituals of Gender Identity: Markers of Siberian Khanty, Ethnicity, Status, and Belief," *American Anthropologist* 83(4): 850-867, 1981.

Barash, David. *Sociobiology and Behavior.* New York: Elsevier, 1977.

Barrett, Michele. *Women's Oppression Today: Problems in Marxist Feminist Analysis.* London: NLB, 1980.

Barron, R.D. and G.M. Norris. "Sexual Divisions and the Dual Labour Market," *Dependence and Exploitation: Work and Marriage.* Diana Barker and Sheila Allen, eds., pp. 47-69. New York: Longman, 1976.

Baruch, Elaine Hoffman. "The Politics of Courtship," *Dissent* (Winter): 56-64, 1980.

Bauer, J. "Poor Women and Social Consciousness in Revolutionary Iran," in *Women and Revolution in Iran.* G. Nashat, ed., Boulder, CO: Westview Press, 1983.

Beneria, Lourdes and G. Sen. "Accumulation, Reproduction, and Women's Role in Economic Development," *Signs* 7(2):279-298, 1981.

Benston, Margaret. "The Political Economy of Women's Liberation," *Monthly Review* 2(1):13-27, 1969.

Berreman, Gerald. "Social Inequality: A Cross-Cultural Analysis," in *Social Inequality: Comparative and Developmental Approaches.* Berreman, G., ed., pp. 3-40. New York: Academic Press, 1981.

Beteille, Andre. "The Idea of Natural Inequality," in *Social Inequality: Comparative and Developmental Approaches.* G. Berreman, ed., pp. 59-80. New York: Academic Press, 1981.

Bhatty, Zarina. "Muslim Women in Uttar Pradesh: Social Mobility and Directions of Change," in *Women in Contemporary India: Traditional Images and Changing Roles.* de Souza, ed., pp. 25-36. New Delhi: Manoher Press, 1975.

Blaxall, Martha and Barbara Reagan, eds. *Women and the Workplace: The Implications of Occupational Segregation.* Chicago: University of Chicago, 1976.

Blum, Larry, Marcia Homiak, Judy Housman and Naomi Scleman. "Altruism and Women's Oppression," in *Women and Philosophy: Toward a Theory of Liberation.* Carol Gould and Marx Wartofsky, eds., pp. 222-247. Perigee Books, 1980.

Borker, Ruth and Daniel Maltz. *A Cultural Approach to Male-Female Miscommunication.* Gumperez, 1980.

Boserup, Ester. *Women's Role in Economic Development.* London: Allen and Unwin, 1970.

Bossen, Laurel. "Women in Modernizing Societies," *American Ethnologist* 2(4):587-601, 1970.

Bott, Elizabeth. "Urban Families: Conjugal Roles and Social Networks," *Human Relations* 8(4): 345-384, 1955.

Brake, Mike. "I May Be Queer But At Least I'm a Man: Male Hegemony and Ascribed vs. Achieved Gender," in *Sexual Divisions and Society: Processes and*

Change. Allen and Barker, eds., pp. 174-198. London: Tavistock, 1976.

Braybon, Gail. *Women Workers in the First World War.* New York: Barnes and Noble, 1981.

Brown, Lyvia Morgan. "Sexism in Western Art," in *Women: A Feminist Perspective.* Jo Freeman, ed., pp. 309-322. Palo Alto, CA: Mayfield Publishing Co., 1975.

Bullough, Vern. *Sexual Variance in Society and History.* New York: John Wiley and Sons, 1976.

Bourguinon, Erika, ed. *A World of Women: Anthropological Studies of Women in the Societies of the World.* New York: Praeger, 1980.

Bradly, David and Kent Tedin. "Ladies in Pink: Religion and Political Ideology in the Anti-ERA Movement," *Social Science Quarterly* 56:564-75, 1976.

Brown, Judith. "A Note on the Division of Labor by Sex," *American Anthropology* 72(5):1074-1078, 1970.

Burris, Val. "The Dialectic of Women's Oppression: Notes on the Relation Between Capitalism and Patriarchy," *Berkeley Journal of Sociology* 27:51-76, 1982.

Burton, Michael and Lorraine Kirk. "Sex Differences in Maasai Cognition of Personality and Social Identity," *American Anthropologist* 81(4):841-873, 1979.

Cain, Mead, S. Khanam, and S. Nahar. "Class, Patriarchy, and Women's Work in Bangladesh," *Population and Development Review* 5(3):405-437, 1979.

Campbell, J.K. *Honour, Family and Patronage.* New York: Oxford University Press, 1974.

Cantarow, Ellen. "Workers Not Wives," *In These Times*, p 11, Dec. 9-15, 1981.

Caplan, Patricia and Janet M. Bujra. *Women United; Women Divided.* Bloomington, IN: Indiana University Press, 1979.

Caulfield, Mina Davis. "Equality, Sex, and Mode of Production," in *Social Inequality: Comparative and Developmental Approaches.* Gerald Berreman, ed. New York: Academic Press, 1981.

Chai, Alice. "Korean Women in Hawaii, 1903-1945," in *Women in New Worlds.* Hilah Thomas and Rosemary Skinner Keller, eds., pp. 328-344, 1981.

Chaudhury, R.H. "Female Status and Fertility Behaviour in a Metropolitan Urban Area of Bangladesh," *Population Studies* 32(2):261-273, 1978.

Combahee River Collective. "The Combahee River Collective: A Black Feminist Statement," in *Capitalist Patriarchy and the Case for Socialist Feminism.* Zillah Eisenstein, ed. pp. 362-372. New York: Monthly Review Press, 1979.

Chagnon, Napoleon and William Irons. *Evolutionary Biology and Human Social Behavior: An Anthropological Perspective.* Belmont, CA: Wadsworth, Inc., 1979.

Chetwynd, Jane and O. Harnett, eds. *The Sex Role System: Psychological and Sociological Perspectives.* London: Routledge and Kegan Paul.

Chinas, Beverly. *The Isthmus Zapotecs: Women's Roles in Cultural Context.* New York: Holt, Rinehart and Winston, 1973.

Chinchilla, Norma. "Industrialization, Monopoly Capitalism and Women's Work in Guatemala," *Signs* 3(1):39-56, 1977.

Chodorow, Nancy, "Mothering, Male Dominance and Capitalism," in *Capitalist Patriarchy and the Case for Socialist Feminism.* Zillah Eisenstein, ed., pp. 83-106. New York: Monthly Review Press, 1979.

Chodorow, Nancy. *The Reproduction of Mothering: Psychoanalysis and the Sociology of Gender.* Berkeley: University of California Press, 1978.

Chodorow, Nancy. "Family Structure and Feminine Personality," in *Woman, Culture and Society*. Rosaldo and Lamphere, eds., pp. 43-66. Stanford: Stanford University Press, 1974.

Coles, R. and J. H. Coles. *Women of Crisis*. New York: Delacorte Press, 1978.

Collier, Jane. "Women In Politics," in *Woman, Culture and Society*. Rosaldo and Lamphere, eds. pp. 89-96. Stanford: Stanford University Press, 1974.

Cotera, Martha. *The China Feminist*. Austin, Texas: Informational Systems Development, 1977.

Cotera, Martha. *Profile of the Mexican-American Woman*. Austin, Texas: Informational Systems Development, 1976.

Cross, Elizabeth. "Women and Rural Production and Reproduction in the Soviet Union, China, Cuba, and Tanzania: Socialist Development Experiences," *Signs* 7(2):361-399, 1981.

Daly, Martin and Kargo Wilson. *Sex, Evolution and Behavior: Adaptations for Reproduction*. Duxbury Press, 1978.

D'Andrade, R. "Sex Differences and Cultural Institutions," in *The Development of Sex Differences*. Eleanor Maccoby, ed., pp. 174-204. Stanford: Stanford University Press, 1966.

Davis, Susan. "The Determinants of Social Position Among Rural Moroccan Women," in *Women In Contemporary Muslim Societies*. Jane A. Smith, ed., pp. 87-99. Lewisburg, PA: Bucknell University Press, 1980.

Deere, Carmen Diana. "Changing Social Relations of Production and Peruvian Peasant Women's Work," in Women and Class Struggle, *Latin American Perspectives* 4(1/2):48-69, 1977.

DeVos, G. "Conflict, Dominance and Exploitation," in *Human Systems of Social Segregation*. De Reuck et al, eds. Conflict in Society. Boston, 1966.

Diamond, Norma. "Collectivization, Kinship and the Status of Women in Rural China," in *Toward an Anthropology of Women*. R. Reiter, ed., pp. 372-395. New York: Monthly Review Press, 1975.

Dickeman, Mildred. "Female Infanticide and the Reproductive Strategies of Stratified Human Societies: A Preliminary Model," in *Evolutionary Biology and Human Social Behavior*. Chagnon and Irons, eds. Duxbury Press, 1978.

Divale and M. Harris. "Population, Warfare, and the Male Supremacist Complex," *American Anthropologist* 78:521-538, 1976.

Dowling, Colette. *The Cinderella Complex*. New York: Pocket Books, 1981.

Draper, Patricia. "!Kung Women: Contrasts in Sexual Egalitarianism in Foraging and Sedentary Contexts," in *Toward An Anthropology of Women*. R. Reiter, ed., pp. 77-109. New York: Monthly Review Press, 1975.

Edholm, Felicity, Olivia Harris, and Kate Young. "Conceptualizing Women," *Critique of Anthropology* 3:101-131, 1977.

Ehrenreich, Barbara and Deidre English. *Complaints and Disorders: The Sexual Politics of Sickness*.

Ehrhardt, Anke. "Prenatal Hormones and Human Behavior: Implications for the Status of Women," in *Being Female*. D. Raphael, ed., Hawthorne, NY: Mouton, 1975.

Eisenstein, Zillah, ed. *Capitalist Patriarchy and the Case for Socialist Feminism*. New York: Monthly Review Press, 1979.

Fernea, Elizabeth and Basima Bezigan, eds. *Middle Eastern Muslim Women Speak.* Austin: University of Texas Press, 1977.

Fluehr-Lobban, Carolyn. "The Political Mobilization of Women in the Arab World," in *Women in Contemporary Muslim Societies.* Jane Smith, ed., pp. 235-253. Lewisburg, PA: Bucknell University Press, 1980.

Frankenberg, Ronald. "In the Production of their Lives, Men(?) . . . , Sex and Gender in British Community Studies," in *Sexual Divisions: Processes and Change,* pp. 25-51. London: Tavistock, 1976. .

Friedl, Ernestine. *Men and Women.*

Gardiner, Jean. "Political Economy of Domestic Labour in Capitalist Society," in *Dependence and Exploitation in Work and Marriage.* Barker and Allen, eds. pp. 109-120. New York: Longman, 1976.

Giele, Janet. "Comparing Perspectives on Women," in *Women: Roles and Status in Eight Countries.* Giele and Smock, eds., pp. 1-32. New York: John Wiley and Sons, 1977.

Giele, Janet. "Centuries of Womanhood: An Evolutionary Perspective on the Feminine Role," *Women's Studies: An Interdisciplinary Journal* 1:97-110, 1972.

Giele, Janet and Audrey Smock, eds. *Women: Roles and Status in Eight Countries.* New York: John Wiley and Sons, 1977.

Godelier, Maurice. "Sex and Power," *New Left Review,* May-June, 1981.

Goffman, Erving. "The Arrangement Between the Sexes," *Theory and Society* 4(3):301-331, 1972.

Goffman, Erving. *Gender Advertisements.* Cambridge: Harvard University Press, 1979.

Gonzales, Sylvia. "La Chicana: Guadalupe or Malinche," in *Comparative Perspectives on Third World Women: The Impact of Race, Sex and Class.* Beverly Lindsay, ed., pp. 229-250. New York: Praeger, 1980.

Gough, Kathleen. "The Origin of the Family," in *Toward An Anthropology of Women.* R. Reiter, ed. New York: Monthly Review Press, 1975.

Gould, Carol and Marx Wartofsky, eds. *Women and Philosophy: Toward a Theory of Liberation.* New York: Putnam and Sons, 1976.

Granzkog, Jane. *The Power of Peasant Women: Implications of the Unforeseen,* Sacramento Anthropological Society. #15. pp. 27-49. Sacramento, CA., 1979.

Griffin, Agnes Estioko and P. Bion Griffin. "Woman the Hunter: The Agta," in *Woman, the Gatherer.* F. Dahlberg, ed. pp. 121. New Haven: Yale University Press, 1981.

Gurin, Joel. "Chemical Feelings," *Science* 80:28-33, 1979.

Haskell, Molly. *From Reverence to Rape: The Treatment of Women in the Movies.* New York: Holt, Rinehart and Winston.

Hayes, Rose O. "Female Genital Mutilation, Fertility Control, Women's Roles and the Patrilineage in Modern Sudan: A Functional Analysis," *American Ethnologist* 2(4):617-633, 1975.

Henley, Nancy. *Power, Sex, and Nonverbal Communication.*

Herdt, Gilbert, ed. *Rituals of Manhood: Male Initiation In Papua New Guinea.* Berkeley: University of California, 1982.

Hilberman, Elaine. "Overview: The "Wife-Beater's Wife" Reconsidered," *American Journal of Psychology* 137(11):1336-1346, 1980.

Hoffman, Joan. "Biorhythms in Human Reproduction: The Not-So-Steady State," *Signs* 7(4): 829-844, 1982.

Hopson, Janet. *The Silent Language of Sex*. New York: Wm. Morrow Publishing Co., 1979.

Hostetler, John and G. Huntington. *Children in Amish Society: Socialization and Community Education*. New York: Holt, Rinehart and Winston, 1971.

Hardy, Sarah B. *The Woman That Never Evolved*. Cambridge: Harvard University Press, 1981.

Huffman, S., A.K.M. Chowdhurty and W.H. Mosley. "Postpartum Amenorrhea: How is it Affected by Maternal Nutritional Status," *Science* 200:1155-1157, 1978.

Hull, Valerie. *A Woman's Place: Social Variations in Women's Work Patterns in a Japanese Village*. Population Studies Center, Gadjah Mada University, 1976.

Jacobson, Doranne. "The Chaste Wife: Cultural Norm and Individual Experience," in *American Studies in the Anthropology of India*. Sylvia Vatuk, ed. Manohar Press and American Institute of Indian Studies, 1978.

Joseph, Gloria. "Caribbean Women: The Impact of Race, Sex, and Class," in *Comparative Perspectives of Third World Women: The Impact of Race, Class, and Sex*. Beverly Lindsay, ed., pp. 160. New York: Praeger, 1980.

Judis, John. "One Too Many Nine-To-Fives," *In These Times*, Dec. 9-15, pp. 13 and 22, 1981.

Kandiyoti, Deniz. "Sex Roles and Social Change: A Comparative Appraisal of Turkey's Women," *Signs* 3:(1):57-73, 1977.

Kehoe, Alice and Dody Giletti. "Women's Preponderance in Possession Cults: The Calcium-Deficiency Hypothesis Explained," *American Anthropologist* 83(3):549-561, 1981.

Kelly, Gail. "The Schooling of Vietnamese Immigrants: Internal Colonialism and Its Impact on Women," in *Comparative Perspectives of Third World Women*. Beverly Lindsay, ed., pp. 276-296. New York: Praeger, 1980.

Kern, Louis. *An Ordered Love*. Chapel Hill: University of North Carolina Press, 1981.

Komarovsky, Mira. *Dilemmas of Masculinity: A Study of College Youth*. New York: W. W. Norton, 1976.

Kessler, S. and Wendy McKenna. *Gender: An Ethnomethodological Approach*. New York: John Wiley and Sons, 1978.

King, Ursula. "Women and Religion: The Status and Image of Women in Some Major Religious Traditions," in *Women in Contemporary India*. De Souza, ed., pp. 110-128.

Kingston, Maxine Hong. *The Woman Warrior: Memoirs of a Girlhood Among Ghosts*. New York: Vintage Books, 1977.

Kingston, Maxine Hong. *China Men*. New York: Ballantine Books, 1977.

Kuhn and Wolpe, eds. *Feminism and Materialism*. London: Routledge and Kegan Paul, 1978.

Kuhn, A. "Structures of Patriarchy and Capitalism in the Family," in *Feminism and Materialism*, Kuhn and Wolpe, eds., pp. 42-67. London: Routledge and Kegan Paul, 1978.

Lakoff, Robin. *Language and Woman's Place*.

Lambert, Helen. "Biology and Equality: A Perspective on Sex Differences," *Signs* 4(1):97-117, 1978.

Leacock, Eleanor. *Myths of Male Dominance*. New York: Monthly Review Press, 1981.

Leacock, Eleanor. "Women's Status in Egalitarian Society: Implications for Social Evolution," *Current Anthropology* 19(2):247-275, 1978.

Lee, Richard, B. "Politics, Sexual and Nonsexual, in an Egalitarian Society: The !Kung San," in *Social Inequality. Comparative and Developmental Approaches.* G. Berreman, ed., pp. 83-102. New York: Academic Press, 1981.

Lee, Richard B. "Population Growth and the Beginnings of Sedentary Life among the !Kung Bushman," in *Population Growth: Anthropological Implications.* B. Spooner, ed., pp. 329-342. Cambridge: MIT Press, 1972.

Lefkowitz, Rochelle. "NARAL's Shift to the Local Arena Provokes Palace Coup," *In These Times,* Oct. 28-Nov. 3, p. 6, 1981.

Leghorn and Parker. *Women's Worth.* London: Routledge and Kegan Paul, 1981.

Leibowitz, Lila. *Females, Males, Families: A Biosocial Approach.* Duxbury Press, 1978.

Leibowitz, Lila. "Perspectives on the Evolution of Sex Differences," in *Towards an Anthropology of Women.* R. Reiter, ed., pp. 20-35. New York: Monthly Review Press, 1975.

Lewis, D. K. "A Response to Inequality: Black Women, Racism and Sexism," *Signs* 3(2):339-361, 1977.

Lindsay, Beverly, ed. *Comparative Perspectives of Third World Women: The Impact of Race, Sex, and Class.* New York: Praeger, 1980.

Lipshitz, Susan, ed. *Tearing the Veil: Essays on Femininity.* London: Routledge and Kegan Paul.

Loo, Chalsa and Paul Ong. "Slaying Demons with a Sewing Needle: Feminist Issues for China Town's Women," *Berkeley Journal of Sociology* 27:77-88, 1982.

Lowe, Marian. "Sociobiology and Sex Differences," Signs 4(1):118-125, 1978.

Lupri, J., ed. *The Changing Role of Women in Family and Society: A Cross Cultural Comparison.* Leiden: Brill, 1979.

Maccoby, E.E., ed. *The Development of Sex Differences.* London: Tavistock, 1967.

Maccoby, E. and Carol Jacklin. *The Psychology of Sex Differences.* Stanford: Stanford University Press, 1974.

MacCormack, Carol P., ed. *Ethnography of Fertility and Birth.* New York: Academic Press, 1982.

MacCormack, Carol P. "Biological, Cultural and Social Adaptation in Human Fertility and Birth: A Synthesis," in *Ethnography of Fertility and Birth.* C. MacCormack, ed., pp. 1-23. New York: Academic Press, 1982.

MacCormack, Carol P. and Marilyn Stathern, eds. *Nature, Culture and Gender.* New York: Cambridge University Press, 1980.

MacIntyre, Sally. "Who Wants Babies? The Social Construction of Instincts," in *Sexual Divisions and Society: Process and Change.* D. Barker and Sheila Allen, eds. London: Tavistock, 1976.

MacKinnon, Katharine A. *Sexual Harassment of Working Women: A Case of Sex Discrimination.* New Haven: Yale University Press, 1979.

Maher, Vanessa. "Kin, Clients, and Accomplices: Relationships Among Women in Morocco," in *Sexual Divisions: Process and Change,* Barker and Allen, eds., pp. 52-75. London: Tavistock, 1976.

Markovic, Mikailo. "Women's Liberation and Human Emancipation," in *Women and Philosophy: Toward a Theory of Liberation.* Carol Gould and Marx Wartofsky, eds., pp. 145-167. Perigee Books, 1980.

Mason, Karen and Larry Bumpass. "US Women's Sex-role Ideology, 1970," *American Journal of Sociology* 80(5):1212-1219, 1975.

Mason, John P. "Sex and Symbol in the Treatment of Women: The Wedding Rite in a Libyan Oasis Community," *American Ethnologist* 2(4):649-661, 1975.

Matthiasson, Carolyn, ed. *Many Sisters: Women in Cross-Cultural Perspective.* New York: Free Press, 1974.

McDonough and Arrison. "Patriarchy and Relations of Production," in *Feminism and Materialism.* Kuhn and Wolpe, eds., pp. 11-41. London: Routledge and Kegan Paul, 1978.

McGilvray, D.B. "Sexual Power and Fertility in Sri Lanka: Batticaloa Tamils and Moors," in *Ethnography of Fertility and Birth.* MacCormack, ed., pp. 25-74. New York: Academic Press, 1982.

McGrew, W.C. "The Female Chimpanzee as a Human Evolutionary Prototype," in *Woman, The Gatherer.* F. Dahlberg, ed., pp. 35-73. New Haven: Yale University Press, 1981.

McMillan, Carol. *Women, Reason and Nature: Some Philosophical Problems with Feminism.* Princeton: Princeton University Press.

Mead, Margaret. *Male and Female: A Study of Sexes in a Changing World.* New York: Dell, 1949.

Mead, Margaret. *And Keep Your Powder Dry: An Anthropologist Looks at America.* New York: Wm. Morrow and Co, 1942.

Mead, Margaret. *Sex and Temperament in Three Primitive Societies.* New York: Wm. Morrow and Co, 1935.

Michaelson, Evalyn J. and Walter Goldschmidt. "Female Roles and Male Dominance Among Peasants," *American Anthropologist* 27(4):330-353, 1971.

Minkin, Stephen. "Nine Thai Women had Cancer, None of them Took Depo-Provera, Therefore, Depo-Provera is Safe," *Mother Jones,* 1981.

Mitchell, Juliet. *Psychoanalysis and Feminism: Freud, Reich, Laing and Women.* New York: Vintage Books, 1974.

Mitchell, Juliet. *Woman's Estate.* New York: Vintage Books, 1971.

Mohr, Richard. "Gay Rights," *Social Theory and Practice,"* 8(1):31-42, 1982.

Molyneux, Maxine. "Socialist Societies: Progress Toward Women's Emancipation," *Monthly Review* 3(34):56-100, 1982.

Money and Ehrhardt. *Man and Woman, Boy and Girl.* Baltimore, 1972.

Moraga, C. and G. Azaldna, eds. *This Bridge Called My Back: Writings by Radical Women of Color.* Watertown: Persephone Press, 1981.

Morgan, Kathryn P. "Androgyny: A Conceptual Critique," *Social Theory and Practice* 8(3):245-284, 1982.

Moses, Yolanda. "Female Status, the Family and Male Dominance in a West Indian Community," *Signs* 3(1):142-153, 1977.

Munro, Robert and Ruth Munro. "Psychological Interpretation of Male Initiation Rites: The Case of Male Pregnancy Symptoms," *Ethos* 1:490-8, 1973.

Murphy, R. *Social Structure and Sex Antagonism.*

Murphy, Yolanda and Robert Murphy. *Women of the Forest.* New York: Columbia University Press, 1974.

Nash, June. "The Aztecs and the Ideology of Male Dominance," *Signs* 4(2):349-62, 1978.

Nashat, Guity, ed. *Women and the Revolution in Iran.* Boulder, CO: Westview Press, 1983.

Navarro, Jovina. *Immigration of Filipino Women to America: Asian American Women.* Stanford: Stanford University Press.

Nelson, Cynthia. "Public and Private Politics: Women in the Middle Eastern World," *American Ethnologist* 1:551-563, 1974.

Nethamer, Carolyn. *Daughters of the Earth: The Lives and Legends of American Indian Women.* New York: MacMillan, 1977.

Newman, Philip. "Sexual Politics and Witchcraft in Two New Guinea Societies," in *Social Inequality: Comparative and Developmental Approaches.* G. Berreman, ed., pp. 103-121. New York: Academic Press, 1981.

Oakley, Ann. *Sex, Gender and Society.* New York: Harper & Row, 1972.

O'Brien, Mary. "Feminist Theory and Dialectical Logic," *Signs* 7(1):144-157, 1981.

Okin, Susan Moller. "Women and the Making of the Sentimental Family," *Philosophy and Public Affairs* 11(1):65-88, 1982.

Okin, Susan Moller. *Women in Western Political Thought.* Princeton: Princeton University Press, 1979.

Oppenheimer, Valerie. "Demographic Influence on Female Employment and the Status of Women," *American Journal of Sociology* 78(4):946-961.

Ortner, Sherry and H. Whitehead, eds. *Sexual Meanings: The Cultural Construction of Gender and Sexuality.* New York: Cambridge University Press, 1981.

Ortner, Sherry. "Is Female to Male As Nature is to Culture?" in *Woman, Culture and Society.* Rosaldo and Lamphere, eds., pp. 67-87. Stanford: Stanford University Press, 1974.

Pala, Achola O. "Definitions of Women and Development: An African Perspective," *Signs* 3:9-13, 1977.

Parker, S. and H. Parker. "The Myth of Male Superiority: Rise and Demise," *American Anthropologist* 81(2):289-309, 1977.

Parker, S., Janet Smith and Joseph Ginat. "Father Absence and Cross-Sex Identity: The Puberty Rites Controversy Revisited," *American Ethnologist* 2(4):687-706, 1975.

Parsons, Howard. "Gender, Sex Roles and Humanness: The Dialectics of Body, Culture and Human Fulfillment," in *Revolutionary World: An International Journal of Philosophy* 21/22:30-45, 1977.

Pierce, Joe. *Life in A Turkish Village.* New York: Holt, Rinehart and Winston, 1964.

Pitt-Rivers, Jr. "Honour and Social Status," in *Honour and Shame: The Values of Mediterranean Society.* J.G. Peristiany, ed., pp. 21-77. Chicago, IL: The University of Chicago Press, 1966.

Purvyear, Gwendolyn. "The Black Woman: Liberated or Oppressed?" in *Comparative Perspectives of Third World Women.* B. Lindsay, ed., pp. 251-275. New York: Praeger, 1980.

Quinn, Naomi. "Anthropolgical Studies in Women's Status," *Annual Review of Anthropology* 6:181-225, 1977.

Raphael, Dana, ed. *Being Female: Reproduction, Power and Change.* Hawthorne, NY: Mouton, 1975.

Rapp, Rayna, Ellen Ross, Renate Bridenthal. "Examining Family History," *Feminist Studies* 1:174-200, 1979.

Rassam, Amal. "Women and Domestic Power in Morocco," *International Journal of Middle East Studies* 12(2):171-179, 1980.

Rein, Natalie. *Daughters of Rachel: Women in Israel.* Penguin.

Reinartz, Kay. "The Paper Doll: Images of American Women in Popular Songs," in *Women: A Feminist Perspective*. Jo Freeman, ed., pp. 293-307. Palo Alto, CA: Mayfield, 1975.

Reiter, Rayna, ed. *Toward an Anthropology of Women*. New York: Monthly Review Press, 1975.

Reiter, Rayna. "Men and Women in the South of France," in *Toward an Anthropology of Women*. R. Reiter, ed., pp. 252-282. New York: Monthly Review Press, 1975.

Remy, Dorothy. "Underdevelopment and the Experience of Women: A Nigerian Case Study," in *Toward an Anthropology of Women*. R. Reiter, ed., pp. 358-371. New York: Monthly Review Press, 1975.

Ristorucci, Carmen. *Why We Oppose the ERA*.

Rogers, Barbara. *The Domestication of Women: Discrimination in Developing Societies*. London: Tavistock, 1981.

Rogers, Susan C. "Women's Place: A Critical Review of Anthropological Theory," *Comparative Studies in Society and History*, pp. 123-162, 1978.

Rogers, Susan C. "Female Forms of Power and the Myth of Male Dominance: A Model of Female/Male Interaction in Peasant Society," *American Ethnologist* 2(4):727-753, 1975.

Romaniuk, A. "Increase in Natural Fertility during the Early Stages of Modernization: Evidence from an African Case Study, Zaire," *Population Studies* 34(2):293-310, 1980.

Rosaldo, M. Z. "The Use and Abuse of Anthropology: Reflections on Feminism and Cross-Cultural Understanding," *Signs* 3(3):389-417, 1980.

Rosaldo, M. Z. "Women, Culture and Society: A Theoretical Overview," in *Woman, Culture and Society*. Rosaldo and Lamphere, eds., pp. 17-42. Stanford: Stanford University Press, 1974.

Rose, Diana. "Can Reagan Turn the Clock Back?," *In These Times*, Dec. 9-15, pp. 12-13, 1981.

Rosenberg, Carroll. "The Female World of Love and Ritual: Relations Between Women in 19th Century America," *Signs* 1:1-29, 1973.

Rosenfeld, Rachel. "Women's Intergenerational Occupational Mobility," *American Sociological Review*, 43:36-46, 1978.

Rossi, Alice. "A BioSocial Perspective on Parenting," *Daedalus* 106(2):1-25, 1977.

Roy, Manisha. "The Concepts of 'Femininity' and 'Liberation' in the Context of Changing Sex-Roles: Women in Modern India and America," in *Being Female*. D. Raphael, ed. Hawthorne, NY: Mouton, 1976.

Rowbotham, Sheila. *Women, Resistance and Revolution: A History of Women and Revolution in the Modern World*. New York: Pantheon, 1972.

Rubbin, Gayle. "The Traffic in Women: Notes on the 'Political Economy' of Sex," in *Toward an Anthropology of Women*. R. Reiter, ed., pp. 157-217. New York: Monthly Review Press, 1975.

Rubbo, Ann. "The Spread of Capitalism in Rural Columbia: Effects on Poor Women," in *Toward an Anthropology of Women*. R. Reiter, ed., pp. 333-357. New York: Monthly Review Press, 1975.

Russell, Diana. *The Politics of Rape*. 1975.

el-Saadawi, Nawal. *The Hidden Face of Eve: Women in the Arab World*. Boston: Beacon Press, 1982.

Sacks, Karen. *Sisters and Wives.*

Sacks, Karen. "Engels Revisited: Women, The Organization of Production, and Private Property," in *Issues in Cultural Anthropology.* McCurdy and Spradley, eds., pp. 189-201. Boston: Little, Brown and Co., 1979.

Safa, H., and J. Nash. *Sex and Class in Latin America.* New York: Praeger, 1976.

el-Sa'id, Aminah. "The Arab Woman and the Challenge of Society," in *Middle Eastern Muslim Women Speak.* Fernea and Bezirgen, eds., pp. 375-390. Austin: University of Texas Press, 1977.

Sanday, Peggy. *Female Power and Male Dominance: On the Degrees of Sex Inequality.* New York: Cambridge University Press, 1981.

Sanday, Peggy. "Female Status in the Public Domain," in *Issues in Cultural Anthropology.* McCurdy and Spradley, eds., pp. 175-201. Boston: Little, Brown and Co., 1979.

Sawhill, Isabel. "Discrimination and Poverty among Women who Head Families," in *Women and the Workplace.* Blaxall and Reagan, eds., pp. 201-211. Chicago: University of Chicago, 1976.

Schlegel, Alice, ed. *Sexual Stratification: A Cross-Cultural View.* New York: Columbia University Press, 1977.

Schlegel, Alice. *Male Dominance and Female Autonomy: Domestic Authority in Matrilineal Societies.* New Haven: HRAF, 1972.

Schneider, Jane. "Of Vigilance and Virgins: Honor, Shame, and Access to Resources in Mediterranean Societies," *Ethnology* 10:1-23, 1971.

Scrimshaw, Susan. "Stages in Women's Lives and Reproductive Decision-Making in Latin America," *Medical Anthropology* 2(3), 1978.

Segal, Sheldon, J. "The Physiology of Human Reproduction," in The Human Population, *Scientific American,* pp. 29-38, 1974.

Sharma, Ursula. "Women and their Affines: The Veil as a Symbol of Separation," *Man* 13(2):218-233, 1978.

Sharma, Ursula. *Women, Work, and Property in North-West India.* London: Tavistock, 1980.

Slagter, Janet Trapp. "The Concept of Alienation and Feminism," *Social Theory and Practice* 8(2):155-164, 1982.

Slocum, Sally. "Women the Gatherer: Male Bias in Anthropology," in *Toward an Anthropology of Women.* R. Reiter, ed., pp. 36-50. New York: Monthly Review Press, 1975.

Shields, Stephanie. "The Variability Hypothesis: The History of a Biology Model of Sex Differences in Intelligence," *Signs* 7(4):769-797, 1982.

Singer, Peter. "Ethics and Sociobiology," *Philosophy and Public Affairs* 11(1):40-64, 1982.

Smart, Carol and Barry Smart, eds. *Women, Sexuality, and Social Control.* London: Routledge and Kegan Paul.

Smith, Paul. "Domestic Labour and Marx's Theory of Value," in *Feminism and Materialism.* Kuhn and Wolpe, eds., pp. 198-219. London: Routledge and Kegan Paul, 1978.

Smock, Audry Chapman. "Conclusion: Determinants of Women's Roles and Status," in *Women: Roles and Status in Eight Developing Countries.* Giele and Smock, eds., pp. 385-421. New York: John Wiley and Sons, 1977.

Snitow, Ann, Christine Stansell, Sharon Thompson. *Powers of Desire: The Politics of Sexuality.* New York: Monthly Review Press, 1982.

Snow, Kimberly. "Women, in the American Novel," in *Women: A Feminist Perspective.* Jo Freeman, ed., pp. 279-308. Palo Alto, CA: Mayfield, 1975.

Srinivas, M. N. "The Changing Position of Indian Women," *Man* 12(2):221-238, 1977.

Southeast Asia Chronicle. "Changing Role of Southeast Asian Women: The Global Assembly Line and the Social Manipulation of Women on the Job." SRC Issue #66.

Spiro, Mel. *Gender and Culture: Kibbutz Women Revisited.* Durham, NC: Duke University, 1979.

Stacey, Judith. "When Patriarchy Kowtows: The Significance of the Chinese Family Revolution for Feminist Theory," in *Capitalist Patriarchy and the Case for Socialist Feminism.* Zillah Eisenstein, ed., pp. 299-348. New York: Monthly Review Press, 1979.

Stack, Carol. "Sex Roles and Survival Strategies in an Urban Black Community," in *Woman, Culture and Society.* Rosaldo and Lamphere, eds., pp. 113-128. Stanford: Stanford University Press, 1974.

Stimpson, C. "On the Women's Movement," *Dissent,* 1980.

Symons, Donald. *The Evolution of Human Sexuality.* New York: Oxford University Press, 1979.

Stoler, Ann. "Class Structure and Female Autonomy in Rural Java," *Signs* 3(1):75-89, 1977.

Szalai, Alexander. *The Situation of Women in the Light of Contemporary Time-Budget Research.* UNE/ConF/66/BP/6, 1975.

Talmon, Yonina. "Sex Role Differentiation in an Egalitarian Society," in *Life in Society.* T. E. Lasswell, J. H. Burma and S. H. Aronson, eds. Glenview, IL: Scott, Foresman, 1965.

Tanner, Nancy. "Matrifocality in Indonesia and Africa and Among Black Americans," in *Woman, Culture and Society.* Rosaldo and Lamphere, eds., pp. 129-157. Stanford: Stanford University Press, 1974.

Tavris, Carol and Carole Offir. *The Longest War: Sex Differences in Perspective.* 1977.

Tiffany, Sharon. "Introduction: Theoretical Issues in the Anthropological Study of Women," in *Women and Society: An Anthropological Reader.* Tiffany, ed., pp. 1-35. Montreal: Eden Press, 1979.

Tiffany, Sharon. "Models and the Social Anthropology of Women: A Preliminary Assessment," *Man* 13(2):34-51, 1978.

Tiffany, Sharon, ed. *Women and Society: An Anthropological Reader.* Montreal: Eden Press, 1979.

Tilly, Loruns and Joan Scott. *Women, Work and Family.* New York: Holt, Rinehart and Winston, 1978.

Tinker, Irene and Michele DoBranisen, eds. *Women and World Development.* Washington, D.C.: AAAS, 1976.

Tobach, Ethel. "Some Evolutionary Aspects of Human Gender," *American Journal of Orthopsychiatry* 41(5):710-715, 1971.

Tong, Rosemary. "Feminism, Pornography and Censorship," *Social Theory and Practice* 8(1):1-18, 1982.

Vetterling-Braggin, Mary. *Sexist Language: A Modern Philosophical Analysis.* Rowman and Littlefield, 1981.

Vetterling-Braggin, Mary. *"Femininity," "Masculinity" and "Androgeny": A Modern Philosophical Discussion.* Totowa, NJ: Rowman and Littlefield, 1982.

Vicinus, Martha. *Suffer and Be Still: Women in the Vietnam Age.* Bloomington: Indiana University Press, 1972.

Vogel, Lise. "The Contested Domain: A Note on the Family in the Transition to Capitalism," *Marxist Perspectives* 1(1):50-73, 1978.

Wadley, Susan. "Women and the Hindu Tradition," *Signs* 3(1):113-125, 1977.

Walum, Laurel R. *The Dynamics of Sex and Gender: A Sociological Perspective.* College Park, CO: Rand-MacNally, 1972.

Ware, Robert. "Marx, The Division of Labor and Human Nature," *Social Theory and Practice* 8(1):43-71, 1982.

Webster, Sheila. "Women, Sex and Marriage in Moroccan Proverbs," *International Journal of Middle East Studies* 14(2):173-184, 1982.

Wermuth, Laurie. "Domestic Violence Reforms: Policing the Private," *Berkeley Journal of Sociology,* 27:27-49, 1982.

White, Martin King. *The Status of Women in Pre-Industrial Societies.* Princeton: Princeton University Press, 1978.

Wikan, Unni. "Man Becomes Woman: Transsexualim in Oman as a Key to Gender," *Man* 12(2):304-319, 1977.

Winslow, Deborah. "Rituals of First Menstruation in Sri Lanka," *Man* 15(4):603-625, 1980.

Wittstock, Laura Waterman. "Native American Women: Twilight of a Long Maidenhood," in *Comparative Perspectives of Third World Women: The Impact of Race, Class, Sex.* B. Lindsay, ed., pp. 207-227. New York: Praeger, 1980.

Wolf, Margery. *Women and the Family in Rural Taiwan.* Stanford: Stanford University Press, 1972.

Whiting and Irving Child. *Child Training and Personality: A Cross-Cultural Study.* New Haven: Yale University Press, 1953.

Wolf, Eric R. "The Mills of Inequality: A Marxian Approach," in *Social Inequality: Comparative and Developmental Approaches.* G. Berreman, ed., pp. 41-57. New York: Academic Press, 1981.

Young, Iris. "Socialist Feminism and the Limits of Dual Systems Theory," *Socialist Review* 50/51: 169-188, 1980.

Young, Kate. "Modes of Appropriation and the Sexual Division of Labour: A Case Study from Oaxaca, Mexico," in *Feminism and Materialism.* Kuhn and Wolpe, eds., pp. 124-154. London: Routledge and Kegan Paul, 1978.

Youssef, Nadia. "Cultural Ideals, Feminine Behavior and Family Control: Comparative Studies," in *Society and History.* 15:326-347, 1973.

Youssef, Nadia. *Women and Work in Developing Societies.* Westport, CT: Greenwood Press, 1974.

Zaretsky, Eli. *Capitalism, the Family, and Personal Life.* New York: Harper and Row, 1976.

Zihlman, A. "Women as Shapers of the Human Adaptation," in *Woman the Gatherer.* Dahlberg, ed., pp. 75-120. New Haven: Yale University Press, 1981.

Zerelli, Linda. "Motionless Idols and Virtuous Mothers: Women, Art and Politics in France 1789-1848," *Berkeley Journal of Sociology* 27:89-126, 1982.

Anthropology of Women

Christine Ward Gailey   *Spring 1983*
Politics, Economics and Society 430/State University of
New York/Old Westbury/Long Island, NY 11568

This course examines the social and cultural status of women and of gender
relations in general, as these are associated with different levels of socio-
economic integration. Gender relations in the least stratified, kinship-
ordered societies are considered first. Then indigenous class and state
formation are analyzed as they change the content of gender relations and,
it is argued, involve the structural subordination of women. Processes such
as tribute extraction, commoditization, the removal of certain strata from
direct production, and the development of state ideologies are the major
aspects considered. The third part focuses on changes in women's status
with capitalist colonialization of both kinship-ordered societies and precapitalist states. Here processes such as commoditization, proletarianization,
differential migration of women and men to urban areas and/or internationally in search of employment, and rural immiseration and proletarianization provide the framework. The course is intended to complement
courses with a focus on women offered in other programs at the lower
division level. As an upper division course, it attracts an unusually diverse
group of students from other programs as well as from PES. The uniqueness
of the course is a result of the explicit integration of anthropological
perspective with political and economic concerns.

Required Readings

Books are limited, for reasons of students' financial situation. Texts are supplemented with articles and projects which involve library research.

Nisa: The Life and Words of a !Kung Woman, by Marjorie Shostak.
As an initial reading, the life-history format is involving for the students. The work
demonstrates, in a wide variety of contexts, the fundamentally egalitarian relations
of women and men in gatherer-hunter societies, so long as they are not forcibly
sendentarized. Shostak considers issues of individuation, autonomy, growing authority over one's own and others' actions as a life-long process.
    The book is supplemented with "!N'ai: Story of a !Kung Woman," a recent film
by John Marshall which discusses forced sedentarization of the !Kung by the
Namibian/South African government and the subsequent recruitment of the artifi-
cially improverished !Kung men for counterinsurgency warfare against SWAPO.
The shifts in gender relations with these ethnocidal policies are addressed directly.

Women of the Forest, by Robert and Yolanda Murphy. (An alternate is *To Hunt in
    the Morning,* by Janet Siskind.)
The Murphys' book discusses the inconsistency of gender ideologies (which present

women as subordinate) and structural features of an Amazonian horticultural/fishing/hunting people. The relative autonomy and solidarity of Mundurucu women is presented, as well as the absence of structural dependency or subordination. The Siskind work addresses the complementarity of women's and men's tasks and the absence of marked subordination, except as the Sharanahua become more integrated, in an inferior position, into the larger capitalist society. Either book provides an antidote to more widely read books, such as *The Fierce People* by Napoleon Chagnon, which tend to ignore the historical ethnocide in the Amazonian Basin and the effects that the colonization of the Amazon may have had on gender relations.

Women and Colonization, edited by Mona Etienne and Eleanor Leacock.
This collection of articles is the only one to consider the transformation of gender relations in a case-study format. Examples from gatherer-hunter, horticultural, precapitalist class societies are used to support the overall argument that 1) in previously kin-ordered societies, capitalist colonization rapidly creates a male-important gender hierarchy, or encapsulates the more egalitarian relations in a wider social formation characterized by gender hierarchy; and 2) in previously class stratified state societies, the character of the gender hierarchy shifts to provide less parallel authority for women, and to more approximate the type of gender relations which characterize the colonizing society.

Myths of Male Dominance, by Eleanor Leacock
A collection of essays which documents the historical nature of gender oppression and which critiques prevailing ahistorical explanations, such as structuralism and sociobiology. Clearly written and accessible, considering its theoretical thrust. Also useful in addressing the problems of feminist mythology in the form of matriarchy.

Course Requirements

Much will be covered in class. Four absences will be grounds for withdrawal.

Grades will be based on three assignments: two take-home essay exams and one research paper. These will be weighted equally. Class participation will help your grade, but I will not penalize those who are less vocal in their involvement.

Women in Politics

Barbara J. Nelson   *Fall 1983*
Politics 321/Department of Politics/Princeton University/
Princeton, NJ 08544

Politics 321 focuses on the women's movement as a social movement, investigating how the lives of individuals and the workings of the state have been affected by that movement. After defining a social movement, we recount the history of the American feminist movement, and compare it to other American social movements. With this background in mind, we cover the "nature vs. nurture" debate. This debate asks the fundamental question, "Is the social and political position of women more a function of biology or culture?" Next we cover the politics of family life, education, participation in the labor force and leisure activities. After that, we discuss three types of political participation: democratic participation (voting, campaign work, etc.), dependent participation (being a client of the state), and elite participation (political leadership). The course closes with a discussion of social policy in America as a reflection of the changes in the roles of women resulting from industrialization, urban growth, and the availability and reliability of contraception. This last section focuses on income tax policy, social security policy and welfare policy.

Course Requirements

The midterm will be announced at least one week in advance and will cover class lectures, precepts, readings, and guest lectures. The final will be comprehensive, covering the entire term's work. The analytic book review will be discussed at length in class, and an outline for its preparation will be distributed later in the term. Briefly, each student is required to read and review one additional book. Books are to be reviewed in terms of how they contribute to the understanding of the themes of the course.

To aid in book selection, four references have been put on reserve.

1. A typed list of books on a variety of topics relevant to women and politics entitled "Women and Politics Bibliography."
2. *Women and World Development: An Annotated Bibliography* (Mayra Buvinic, Overseas Development Council, 1976). This work is especially useful for those wanting to read about Third World women.
3. *The Women's Rights Movement in the United States: 1848-1940—A Bibliography and Sourcebook* (Albert Krichmar, Scarecrow Press, 1972).
4. *The Women's Movement in the 1970s: An International English Language Bibliography* (Albert Krichmar, Scarecrow Press, 1977).

Of course, students are free to choose books which are not on these lists.

Readings

The books for the course are:
1. Berg, Barbara. *The Remembered Gate: The Woman and the City, 1800-1860.* Oxford University Press, 1978.
2. Chafe, William H. *Women and Equality: Changing Patterns in American Culture.* Oxford University Press, 1977.
3. Chafe, William H. *The American Woman: Her Changing Social, Economic and Political Roles.* Oxford University Press, 1972. (Highly recommended).
4. Evans, Sara. *Personal Politics: The Roots of the Feminist Movement in the Civil Rights Movement and New Left.* Knopf, 1979.
5. Freeman, Jo. *The Politics of Women's Liberation.* David McKay Co., 1975.
6. Freeman, Jo. ed. *Women: A Feminist Perspective.* Mayfield, 1975.
7. LeGuin, Ursula K. *The Left Hand of Darkness.* Ace, 1974.

Course Outline and Reading

I. Week 1 September 15-19

A. Topics
1. Introduction to the course.
2. Defining social movements; the women's movements as social movements.
3. A social and political history of the women's movements in the U.S.

B. Readings
1. Chafe, *Women and Equality*, entire.
2. Morris, "The Public Definition of Social Movements: Women's Liberation," *Sociology and Social Research* (1973), pp. 526-543, on reserve.
3. Lavine, "The Idea of Revolution in the Women's Movement," *American Behavioral Scientist* (1977), pp. 535-566.

II. Week 2 September 22-26

A. Topics
1. Feminism as a social movement, cont'd.
2. History of feminism in America, cont'd.
3. Movie: "With Babies and Banners," Tuesday, September 23.

B. Readings
1. Hole and Levine, "The First Feminists," in Freeman, ed. *Women: A Feminist Perspective*, pp. 436-447.
2. Freeman, "The Women's Liberation Movement" in Freeman, ed. *Women: A Feminist Perspective*, pp. 448-460.
3. Freeman, *The Politics of Women's Liberation*, pp. vii-xvi, 1-11, 71-102 (optional: 1-169).
4. Berg, *The Remembered Gate*, pp. 3-7, 75-110, 145-175, 262-270 (optional: entire book).
5. Evans, *Personal Politics*, entire.
6. Painter, "The Black Woman in American Society," *Current History*, 1976, pp. 224-228, 234.
7. Sutherland, "Colonized Women: The Chicana," and Longauex Y. Vasquez, "The

Mexican-American Woman," in Morgan, ed. *Sisterhood is Powerful*, pp. 421-432.

8. Lorenzana, "La Chicana" in Snyder, ed. *The Study of Women*, pp. 336-341.

III. Week 3 September 20-October 3

A. Topics

1. Biological determinism as a way of excluding sex and race groups from full participation in political life.
2. What do we know about the cultural and biological antecedents of behavior?

B. Readings

1. LeGuin, *The Left Hand of Darkness*, entire.
2. Maccoby and Jacklin, "Myth, Reality and Shades of Gray: What We Know and Don't Know about Sex Differences," *Psychology Today*, Vol. 8, (December, 1974).
3. Chafitz, "Is Biology Destiny?" in *Masculine, Feminine or Human*, 1978, pp. 1-32.
4. Weisstein, "Kinde, Kuche, Kirche as a Scientific Law: Psychology Constructs the Female," in Morgan, ed., *Sisterhood is Powerful*, Vintage, 1970, pp. 223-245; on reserve.
5. Lydon, "The Politics of Orgasm," in Morgan, ed., *Sisterhood is Powerful*, Vintage, 1970, pp. 219-228; on reserve.

IV. Week 4 October 6-10, Book Choices Due This Week

A. Topics

1. Nature vs. Nurture, cont'd.
2. Women in the Family. The political significance of patterns of power in the household, the care of children, and the economic basis of the family.

B. Readings

1. Gillespie, "Who Has the Power? The Marital Struggle," in Freeman, ed., *Women: A Feminist Perspective*, pp. 64-87.
2. Bem and Bem, "Case Study of a Nonconscious Ideology: Training the Woman to Know her Place," in Bem and Bem, *Beliefs, Attitudes, and Human Affairs*, Brooks Cole, 1970, pp. 89-100; on reserve.
3. Shear, "Stoolies, Ciphers and Alibis: Women in the White House Transcripts," *ETC*, March 1976, pp. 88-92.
4. Hershey, "Racial Differences in Sex Role Identities and Sex Stereotyping . . ." *Social Sciences Quarterly*, March 1978, pp. 583-596.
5. Murray, "The Liberation of Black Women" in Freeman, ed. *Women: A Feminist Perspective*, pp. 351-363.
6. Ross and Sawhill, "Families Headed by Women: Their Growth and Changing Composition" in *Time of Transition*, 1975, pp. 9-30.

V. Week 5 October 13-16

A. Topics

1. Women in the Family: Sources of Political Socialization.

B. Readings
1. Kraus, "Political Implications of Gender Roles," *American Political Science Review*, Dec. 1974, pp. 1706-1723.
2. Orum, et al, "Sex, Socialization and Politics," *American Sociological Review*, 1974, pp. 197-209.
3. Greenstein, "Sex-Related Political Differences in Childhood," *Journal of Politics*, Vol. 23 (May, 1961), pp. 353-371; on reserve.
4. Jennings and Langton, "Mothers vs. Fathers: The Formation of Political Orientations Among Young Americans," *Midwest Journal of Politics*, Vol. 31, (May, 1969), pp. 329-357; on reserve.
5. Flora and Lynn, "Women and Political Socialization: Considerations of the Impact of Motherhood," in Jacquette, ed., *Women in Politics* (Wiley, 1973), pp. 37-53.

VI. Week 6 October 20-24

A. Tuesday, October 21. Midterm in class.
B. Thursday, October 23. Guest speaker—to be announced.
C. No Precepts!

VII. Week 7 October 27-31

Midterm Break—No Classes

VIII. Week 8 November 3-7

A. Topics
1. Women in School.
2. Women at Work.
3. Women at Leisure.

B. Readings
1. Chafitz, "Educational Institutions," in *Masculine, Feminine or Human*, 1978, pp. 142-148.
2. Roby, "Structural and Internalized Barriers to Women in Higher Education" in Freeman, ed. *Women: A Feminist Perspective*, pp. 171-193.
3. Homer, "A Bright Woman is Caught in a Double Bind," *Psychology Today*, November 1969.
4. Olsen and Willemsen, "Fear of Success—Fact or Artifact," *Journal of Psychology*, 1978, pp. 65-70.
5. Barrett, "Women in the Job Market: Occupations, Earnings, and Career Opportunities" in Smith, ed. *The Subtle Revolution*, 1979, pp. 31-62.
6. Vickery, "Women's Economic Contribution to the Family," in Smith, ed. *The Subtle Revolution*, 1979, pp. 159-200.
7. Singer, "Undervalued Jobs—What's a Woman (and Government) to Do?" *National Journal*, 5/24/80, pp. 858-862.

IX. Week 9 November 10-14

A. Topics
1. Democratic Political Participation: Voting, campaign work, party activism.

B. Readings
1. Welch, "Women as Political Animals: A Test of Some Explanations for Male/Female Participation Differences," *American Journal of Political Science,* November 1977, pp. 711-30.
2. Margolis, "Invisible Hands: Sex Roles and the Division of Labor in Two Local Political Parties," *Social Problems,* February 1979, pp. 314-324.
3. Porter and Matasar, "The Role and Status of Women in the Daley Organization," in Jacquette, ed. *Women in Politics,* pp. 85-108; on reserve.
4. Lynn, "Women in American Politics: An Overview," in Freeman, ed. *Women: A Feminist Perspective,* pp. 364-385.
5. Andersen, "Working Women and Political Participation," *American Journal of Political Science,* Vol. 19 (August 1975), pp. 439-453; on reserve.

X. Week 10 November 17-21

A. Topics
1. Dependent political participation: Women as clients of the State.

B. Readings
1. Nelson, "Helpseeking From Public Authorities: Who Arrives at the Agency Door? " *Policy Sciences,* 1980, pp. 418-441.
2. Ban and Nelson, "Decision by Line Bureaucrats: Do Sex and Race Affect the Results of Applications for Public Social Benefits or Services?" paper delivered at the 1977 APSA meeting.
3. Placek and Hendershot, "Public Welfare and Family Planning: An Empirical Study of the Brood Sow Myth," *Social Problems,* Vol. 21 (June 1974), pp. 658-673.
4. Iglitzen, "A Case Study in Patriarchal Politics: Women on Welfare," in Githens and Prestage, eds. *A Portrait of Marginality,* David McKay Co., 1977, pp. 96-112.
5. Rein and Rainwater, "Patterns of Welfare Use," *Social Services Review,* 1978, pp. 511-534.

XI. Week 11 November 21-28

A. Topics
1. Women and elite participation.
2. Women as elected leaders.
3. Women as appointed leaders.

B. Readings
1. Neuse, "Professionalism and Authority: Women in Public Service," *Public Administration Review,* 1978, pp. 436-441.
2. Lee, "Why Few Women Hold Public Office: Democracy and Sex Roles," *Political Science Quarterly,* 1976, pp. 297-314.
3. Merritt, "Winners and Losers: Sex Differences in Municipal Elections," *American Journal of Political Science,* 1977, pp. 731-743.
4. "Why Aren't There More Women in Congress?" *Congressional Quarterly,* August 12, 1978, pp. 2108-2110.
5. Ferree, "A Woman for President? Changing Responses: 1958-1972," *Public Opinion Quarterly,* 1974, pp. 390-399.

6. Perkins and Fowlkes, "Opinion Representation vs. Social Representation: Why Women Can't Run as Women and Win," *American Political Science Review,* 1980, pp. 92-103.
7. Darcy and Schramm, "When Women Run Against Men," *Public Opinion Quarterly,* 1977, pp. 1-12.

XII. Week 12 December 1-5

A. Topics
1. Women as leaders, cont'd.
2. Women and Social Policy.

B. Readings
1. See Week 11.
2. Hansen, et al., "Women's Political Participation and Policy Preferences," *Social Sciences Quarterly,* 1976, pp. 576-90.

C. Guest Lecturer, Thursday, December 4
Lecturer: Dr. Carolyn Ban, (Federal) Office of Personnel Management, "Women in the Federal Executive Service."

XIII. Week 13 December 8-12

A. Topics
1. Women and Social Policy.
2. Conclusion and Summary: From Social Movement to Social Policy.

B. Readings
1. Gordon, "Institutional Responses: The Federal Income Tax System," in Smith, ed. *The Subtle Revolution,* 1979, pp. 201-222.
2. Gordon, "Institutional Responses: The Social Security System," in Smith, ed. *The Subtle Revolution,* 1979, pp. 223-256.
3. Handout: Summary of the Denver/Seattle Income Maintenance Experiments.

XIV. Week 14 December 15-16

A. No Classes
B. Book Reviews are due

Women and Politics

Amrita Basu   *Spring 1982*
Political Science 40/Amherst College/Amherst, MA   01002

Course Materials

Zillah Eisenstein, ed., *Capitalist Patriarchy and The Case for Socialist Feminism*
Juliet Mitchell, *Woman's Estate*
Perdita Huston, *Third World Women Speak Out*
Leghorn and Roodkowsky, *Who Really Starves: Women and World Hunger*
Lydia Sargent, *Women and Revolution*

In addition, multilith readings can be purchased from the Political Science department office, Clark 103. Readings marked: (P) are recommended purchase, (R) are
available on reserve and (M) are compiled in the multilith.

Course Outline

Part I.   The Origins of Sexual Inequality

1. Introduction
2. Sexual Inequality and Private Property
Engels, *The Origin of the Family, Private Property and the State*, pp. 110-146. (R)
Gough, "The Origin of the Family" in Reiter, ed., *Toward An Anthropology of
   Women*, pp. 51-76. (R)

3. Biological Sex and Cultural Gender
Tiger and Fox, "Mother and Child Bonding," and Bettleheim, "Fathers Shouldn't
   Try to Be Mothers," in *Feminist Frameworks*, pp. 226-235. (M)
Rubin, "The Traffic in Women" in Reiter, ed., *Toward An Anthropology of Women*,
   pp. 157-210. (R)
Chodorow, "Mothering, Male Dominance and Capitalism," in Eisenstein, ed.,
   Capitalist Patriarchy and The Case For Socialist Feminism, pp. 83-106. (P,R)

4. Engels Revisted: Capitalism versus Patriarchy
Firestone, *The Dialectic of Sex*, pp. 130-135. (M)
Millett, "The Sexual Revolution," pp. 108-127. (M)
Reed, "In Defense of Engels on the Matriarchy," in Jenness, ed., *Feminism and
   Socialism*, p. 108-112.
Mitchell, *Woman's Estate*, pp. 76-84, 99-122, 152-158. (P,R)

5. Production and Reproduction
Benston, "The Political Economy of Women's Liberation" (M)
Zaretsky, "Socialist Politics and The Family" (M)
Larguia, "The Economic Basis of the Status of Women," in Rohrlich-Leavitt, eds.,
   Women Cross Culturally, pp. 281-295. (M)
Fee, "Domestic Labour: An Analysis of Housework and Its Relation to the Produc-
   tion Process" (M)

Lopate, "Women and Pay for Housework," in *Feminist Frameworks,* pp. 211-217. (M)

6. Women and The Family in the Third World
Huston, *Third World Women Speak Out,* pp. 33-43, 55-61. (P,R)
Boserup, *Woman's Role in Economic Development,* pp. 37-52. (R)
Das, "Marriage Among Hindus," in Jain, ed., *Indian Women, pp. 71-86. (M)*
El Saadawi, "Marriage and Divorce," *The Hidden Faces of Eve,* pp. 194-209. (M)

Part II.   The Impact of Capitalist Development in the West

7. The Black Female Slave
Davis, "The Black Woman's Role In The Community of Slaves," pp. 2-14. (M)
Hooks, *Ain't I a Woman,* chapter 1. (R)
Hine and Wittenstein, "Female Slave Resistance: The Economics of Sex," Steady, ed., *The Black Woman Cross Culturally,* pp. 289-299. (R)

8. Capitalist Industrialization and The Sexual Division of Labor: Historical Perspectives I
Rowbotham, *Hidden from History,* chapters, 1, 5, 6, 11, 12, 19. *(R)*

9. Capitalist Industrialization and The Sexual Division of Labor: Historical Perspectives II
Hartmann, "Capitalism, Patriarchy and Job Segregation By Sex," and Davies, "Woman's Place Is At the Typewriter," in Eisenstein, ed., *Capitalist Patriarchy,* pp. 206-247. (P,R)
Milkman, "Organizing the Sexual Division of Labor: Historical Perspectives on Women's Work and The American Labor Movement." (M)

10. Sexual and Social Relations of Production
Gates, "Occupational Segregation and The Law," in Blaxall and Reagan, *Women and The Workplace,* pp. 61-74. (M)
Deckard and Sherman, "Monopoly Power and Sex Discrimination" (M)
Stevenson, "Women's Wages and Job Segregation," *Politics and Society,* pp. 83-96. (M)
Ervin, "The Equal Rights Amendment" and Ginsberg, "Equal Opportunity" in English, ed., *Sex Equality,* pp. 183-195. (M)
Baxandall et al., ed., *America's Working Women,* pp. 376-381. (M)

Part III.   Creating The Periphery: Colonialism and Its Legacy

11. The Colonization of Women
Rothenberg, "The Mothers of The Nation;" Buenaventura-Posso and Brown, "Forced Transition From Egalitarianism to Male Dominance;" Etienne, "Women and Men, Cloth and Colonization," and Gailey, "Putting Down Sisters and Wives," in Etienne and Leacock, ed., *Women And Colonization,* pp. 63-87, 109-133, 214-238, 294-322. (R)

12. Double Dependency
Von Allen, "African Women, 'Modernization' and National Liberation," in Iglitzin and Ross, eds., *Women in The World,* pp. 25-44. (M)
Tinker, "The Adverse Impact of Development on Women," in Tinker and Bramsen

eds., *Proceedings of the Seminar on Women and Development*, pp. 22-34. (M)

Nash, "A Critique of Social Science Roles in Latin America," Nash, ed., *Sex and Class in Latin America*, pp. 1-21. (R)

Rogers, *The Domestication of Women*, Ch. 5, pp. 79-107. (R)

13. The Production of Hunger

Boserup, *Woman's Role in Economic Development*, pp. 15-35, 53-64, 66-81. (R)

Leghorn and Roodkowsky, *Who Really Starves: Women and World Hunger*, pp. 8-10, 15-26. (P, R)

14. The Commercialization of Subsistence

Deere, "Rural Women's Subsistence Production In The Capitalist Periphery," *Review of Radical Political Economics*, pp. 9-17. (M)

Rogers, *The Domestication of Women*, pp. 152-176. (R)

Stoler, "Class Structure and Female Autonomy in Rural Java," in *Women and National Development: The Complexities of Change*, pp. 74-89. (R)

15. The Global Assembly Line

Arizpe, "Women In The Informal Labor Sector;" Chinchilla, "Industrialization, Monopoly Capitalism and Women's Work in Guatemala;" and de Miranda, "Women's Labor Force Participation In a Developing Society: The Case of Brazil," in *Women and National Development: The Complexities of Change*, pp. 25-56, 261-277. (R)

Kelly, "The 'Maguila' Women," in *Latin American Women: One Myth—Many Realities*, pp. 14-17. (M)

Grossman, "The Changing Role of Southeast Asian Women," in *Southeast Asia Chronicle Report*, pp. 24-26. (M)

Part IV.   Sexual Politics

16. Reproduction Politics I

Gordon, "The Struggle for Reproductive Freedom," in Eisenstein, ed., *Capitalist Patriarchy*, pp. 107-132. (P,R)

Oliker, "Abortion and the Left: The Limits of Pro-Family Politics," *Socialist Review*, pp. 71-95. (M)

17. Reproduction Politics II

Rogers, *The Domestication of Women*, pp. 107-115. (R)

Leghorn & Roodkowsky, *Who Really Starves*, pp. 29-33. (R,P)

Huston, *Third World Women Speak Out*, pp. 72-83. (P,R)

Birdsall, "Women and Population Studies," in *Signs*, pp. 669-712. (M)

18. Sexual Exploitation I

Brownmiller, *Against Our Will*, pp. 375-404. (R)

Barnett, "The Political Economy of Rape and Prostitution," *Review of Radical Political Economics*, pp. 59-66. (M)

Robert Victor in Terkel, ed., *Working*, pp. 91-103.

Southeast Asia Chronicle Report, pp. 15-25, 18-23. (M)

19. Sexual Exploitation II

Brownmiller, *Against Our Will*, pp. 140-170, 210-255. (R)

Hooks, *Ain't I A Woman*, pp. 51-63. (R)

20. The Commodification of Women

Joseph and Lewis, *Common Differences: Conflicts in Black and White Feminist Perspectives*, pp. 151-176. (R)

Multilith articles on The Nestles Infant Formula

Part V. The Struggle for Political Representation

21. The Suffrage Movement in the West I

O'Neill, *Everyone Was Brave*, pp. 49-76. (R)

Kraditor, Up From the Pedestal, pp. 183-203, 253-265.

Terborg-Penn, "Discrimination Against Afro-American Women in the Women's Movement," Steady, ed., *The Black Woman Cross Culturally*, pp. 301-315. (R)

22. The Suffrage Movement II

O'Neill, *Everyone Was Brave*, pp. 264-294. (R)

Elshtain, "Moral Man and Immoral Woman: Consideration of The Public-Private Split and Its Political Ramifications" (M)

Du Bois, "The Nineteenth Century Woman Suffrage Movement and the Analysis of Women's Oppression" in Eisenstein, ed., *Capitalist Patriarchy*, pp. 137-150. (P,R)

23. The Apostles of Non-Violence: Women In the Indian Nationalist Movement

Forbes, "Indian Women's Movement: A Struggle for Women's Rights or National Independence? " and Pearson, "Nationalism, Universalization and the Extended Female Space in Bombay City," in Minault, ed., *The Extended Family: Women and Political Participation in India and Pakistan*, pp. 49-82, 174-91. (R)

Everett, *Women and Social Change In India*, pp. 190-199. (M)

24. The Contradictory Legacy of the Indian Nationalist Movement

Katzenstein, "Towards Equality? Cause and Consequence of the Political Prominence of Women in India," in Minault, ed., *The Extended Family*, pp. 286-303. (R)

Omvedt, "Women and Rural Revolt in India," *Journal of Peasant Studies* (M)

25. The Suffrage Movement and Its Aftermath in Latin America

Chaney, *Supermadre*, pp. 67-106, 131-166. (R)

26. Legal and Political Rights

27. Visibility and Invisibility: Female Political Participation

Bourque and Grossholtz, "Politics, An Unnatural Profession: Political Science Looks at Female Participation." (M)

Jacquette, "Female Political Participation in Latin America," in Nash and Safa, eds., *Sex and Class in Latin America*, pp. 221-244.

28. Female Elites and Leaders

29. International Women's Year and Its Critics

"World Plan of Action of the World Conference of the International Women's Year," in Tinker, ed., *Proceedings of the Seminar on Women and Development*, pp. 191-223. (M)

Barry, "International Feminism: Sexual Politics and The World Conference of Women in Copenhagen," in *Feminist Studies*, pp. 37-50. (M)

Tinker, "A Feminist View of Copenhagen," and "Comments on Tinker's 'A Feminist View of Copenhagen' ," *Signs*. (M)

Part VI.   The Struggle for Liberation: The Politics of Class, Race and Gender

30. The Resurgence of Feminism in The West
Mitchell, *Woman's Estate*, pp. 11-66, 173-182. (P,R)

31. Alternative Feminist Strategies: Radical and Socialist Feminist Perspectives
Hartmann, "The Unhappy Marriage of Marxism and Feminism," Riddiough, "Socialism, Feminism and Gay/Lesbian Liberation," and Vogel, "Marxism and Feminism," in Sargent, ed., *Women and Revolution*, pp. 1-41, 72-89, 196-217. (P,R)

32. Alternative Feminist Strategies: Liberal, Anarchist and Black Feminist Perspectives
Joseph, "The Incompatable Menage A Trois;" Ehrlich, "The Unhappy Marriage of Marxism and Feminism;" and Eisenstein, "Reform and/or Revolution," in Sargent, ed., *Women and Revolution*, pp. 91-107, 109-133, 339-362. (P,R)

33. Anti-Feminist Perspectives
Readings to be assigned.

Part VII.   The Struggle for Liberation: Fighting Two Colonialisms

34. African Women in Struggle
Steady, "The Black Woman Cross Culturally;" Lapchik, "The Role of Women in the Struggle against Apartheid;" and Urdang, "The Role of Women in the Revolution in Guineau-Bissau," in Steady, ed., *The Black Woman Cross Culturally*, pp. 28-36, 119-139, 231-261. (R)

35. Women in Revolution: China
Belden, "Gold Flower's Story" (M)
Stacey, "When Patriarchy Kowtows," in Eisenstein, ed., *Capitalist Patriarchy*, pp. 299-312. (R)

36. Women in Revolution: Cuba
Rowbotham, *Women, Resistance and Revolution*, chapter 8. (R)
Randall, *Cuban Women*. (M)

37. After the Revolution
Delia Davin, "The Women's Movement In the People's Republic of China." (M)
Bengelsdorf and Hageman, "Emerging From Underdevelopment;" Randall, "Introducing The Family Code;" Stacey, "When Patriarchy Kowtows," in Eisenstein, ed., *Capitalist Patriarchy*, pp. 271-298, 312-348. (P,R)

38. Women in Anti-Revolutionary Movements
Mattelart, "Chile: The Feminine Version of the Coup d'Etat." in Nash and Safa, eds., *Sex and Class in Latin America*, pp. 279-301. (R)

39. Towards A Unified Women's Movement?

World Order Education: Teacher Training

Education and the World Community
Arthur J. Newman, University of Florida

International Development Education
Frank A. Stone, The University of Connecticut

Issues in Contemporary Education:
Educating for Peace and Justice
David Shiman and David Conrad, University of Vermont

Global Perspectives in Citizenship Education
Dorothy I. Seaberg, Northern Illinois University

Teaching About Nuclear War
Robert W. Shuford, National College of Education

Comparative and International
Perspectives in Education
Donna Cole, Wittenberg University

Developing a Global Perspective:
Instructional Materials and Strategies
Jan Tucker, Florida International University

Education for Peace, Disarmament
and the Control of Nuclear Weapons
Betty Reardon, Willard Jacobson and Douglas Sloan,
Columbia University Teachers College

Building Toward Peace—A Curriculum
for Public School Teachers
Gwen Minkler, Western Washington University

Education and the World Community

Arthur J. Newman   *Fall 1982*
Education 4780/University of Florida/Gainesville, FL 32611

It is increasingly apparent that the problems with which the peoples of the world are today saddled are predominantly global in scope and can be solved only by concerted international effort. Whatever our most awesome problems—be they armed conflict, environmental pollution, a depletion of natural resources, over-population, disease, economic ills; the underdevelopment which afflicts most of the world's peoples—their nature, scope, and possibility of solution are clearly worldwide. It would appear that our planet's continued viability demands the presence of people possessed of a cosmopolitan disposition, i.e., people who are aware of, sensitive to, and committed to humankind as a whole.

The implications for education are profound and far-reaching. Assuming that educational provisions—on whatever level—can facilitate the student's cultivation of the needed world-minded disposition, we must have on hand sensitive, imaginative teachers who are equal to the task.

This course is designed primarily to help the practicing educator or the aspiring teacher master the tools of inquiry and develop the mindset which are prerequisites for guiding the student in the direction of cosmopolitanism. While written with the educator in mind, the course's value is not restricted to those in the teaching profession. If diligently pursued, this learning experience will prove to be liberalizing and sensitizing for layman and professional alike.

The course is thoroughly multidisciplinary in intent and scope. It draws upon concepts and insights from, among other areas, those of philosophy, religion, the arts, anthropology, political science, and psychology, as well as those richly varied areas of inquiry such as social foundations of education, which are traditionally found in colleges of education. The only prerequisite is an open, probing mind.

Reading Assignments

For each subtopic, appropriate reading materials are assigned. You will find these varied materials to be intellectually exciting and clearly presented. While the length and depth of these assignments vary somewhat from week to week, an effort has been made to make them as uniform as possible in these respects.

Course Materials

I. To be purchased

1. *Schooling for a Global Age*, J. Becker, ed. (N.Y.: McGraw Hill, 1979) (book).

2. *The World: Context for Teaching in the Elementary School*, E. King, (Dubuque, Iowa: William C. Brown, 1971) (book).

3. *The Interdependence of Nations*, Lester Brown, (N.Y.: Foreign Policy Assoc., 1972) (booklet).

4. *An Attainable Global Perspective*, R. Hanvey, (N.Y.: Global Perspectives in Education, 1979) (pamphlet).

5. *On Recognizing the Human Species*, Harold Courlander, (N.Y.: B'nai B'rith, 1960) (booklet).

6. *Internationalizing the Curriculum and the Campus*, M.Harari, (Washington: American Assoc. of State Colleges and Universities, 1981) (booklet).

II. Provided by the instructor
1. UNICEF material.
2. "Global Perspectives in the Social Studies," Becker and Anderson.
3. "Global Perspectives in Education: Questions People Ask."
4. "Implicit Culture: Some Educational Implications," A. Newman.
5. "Ideology: A Necessary Tool for Understanding International Political Dynamics," A. Newman.
6. *West Virginia State Board of Education vs. Barnette.*
7. Poetry Anthology on Universal Humankind.
8. Patriotic Quotations.
9. "The Historical Meaning of Sovereignty," E. Reves.
10. "Promoting Intercultural Understanding Through Art," A. Newman.
11. Article by Felix Robb.

III. On library reserve
1. "Should the Nation-State Give Way to some Form of World Organization?" W. Nesbitt and C. Bloomstein.
2. "Toward a Definition of Nationalism," B. Shafer.
3. "Children and War," N. Law.
4. "The New Economic and Political Order of the 1980's," J. Naisbitt.
5. Article by Mehlinger.
6. Chapter 8 of Kenworthy book.

Week One   Homo Sapiens: A Single Species
Study
1. *On Recognizing the Human Species*, Harold Courlander.
2. At least one of the following: (1) pp. 326-327 of Ralph Linton's *The Study of Man*; (2) pp. 239-257 of Carl Roger's *Freedom to Learn*; (3) pp. 25-30,"The Child as a Moral Philosopher," *Psychology Today*, 2, August, 1968 by Lawrence Koglberg; (4) Any other article which deals with the theme of human universality.

Discussion
Throughout recorded history, people from many walks of life have suggested that we homo sapiens—while diverse culturally—are in many crucially significant ways identical. Among the more eloquent recognitions of the universality of the human condition is the United States Declaration of Independence which states " . . .that all men are created equal, that they are endowed. . . ." In addition to and supportive of this concept of moral equality is a treasure trove of evidence derived from the physical, biological, and social sciences which points to the essential sameness of

all human creatures. For example, we know unequivocally that all people, whenever and wherever, are blood type A, B, AB, or O (plus RH or minus RH). The consensus among anthropologists, sociologists, psychologists and others is that all have biological and psychological needs which, while satisfied in myriad ways, are significantly universal.

We also know only too well that our species has, for myriad reasons and in many ways, denied the sanctity of this human condition. For too many, concepts like "the brotherhood of man" operate as empty abstractions or convenient clichés.

We need not belabor the point that among the cultural imperatives for insuring the continued survival of our species is a full recognition, in word and in deed, of the inherent dignity of all. And, the quality of our continued survival is crucial. Along with peace must come social justice and economic prosperity.

While the world's schools (and less formal educational provisions) cannot "go it alone," we can reasonably assume that they can play a significant role in initiating and accelerating the process of humanizing our globe.

Discussion Questions
1. After having read thoroughly the pamphlet by Courlander, briefly sum up his position. Do you support this conviction? Why or why not?
2. Briefly discuss the other reading you have chosen. Focus upon the type of evidence drawn upon by the author (biological, linguistic, or whatever). Is this reading convincing to you as support for the proposition that humankind is one?

Week Two   The Earth as a Single System

Study
1. *The Interdependence of Nations*, Lester Brown.

Discussion
Increasingly our single species daily participates on and in earth, a single system. No clearer example can be found of this interdependence than the energy crisis of the 1970's and 1980's. In innumerable ways, what we and our brothers and sisters abroad do (or fail to do) affects one another in profound and far-reaching ways. An infant's milk can contain traces of strontium 90 due to a nuclear explosion on a remote Pacific atoll. More positively, the Soviets can (and do daily) instantaneously transmit crucially important weather information to the U.S. Weather Bureau.

This lesson, like the former, is a prelude to a consideration of how educational provisions might best contribute to the emergence of a peaceful, just, global village. We are caught up in the midst of a global society. How can we transform this interdependent society into a dignified condition of community?

Discussion Questions
1. Drawing upon your readings and own observations, discuss six examples of increasing interdependence among the world's people.
2. Drawing upon your insights and imagination, discuss what you believe are the educational implications of this increasing condition of interdependence.

Week Three   The Rationale for Global Education

Study
1. *Global Perspectives in Social Studies*, (handout) by Becker and Anderson.

2. *An Attainable Global Perspective*, Robert Hanvey.
3. *Global Perspectives in Education: Questions People Ask.*

Discussion
It is obvious that humankind, the single species who participates in earth, the single system, has failed to create the conditions necessary for the establishment of an ongoing world community (by world community, we mean a social and political condition wherein the culturally diverse peoples of the world can enjoy peace, economic prosperity, and social justice, while maintaining their distinct cultural identities).

Our main concern at this stage of the course is to suggest that education is *among* the social institutions which can facilitate the attainment of world community. As the Preamble to the Constitution of UNESCO so eloquently puts it: "Since wars begin in the minds of men, it is in the minds of men that the defenses of peace must be constructed." We wish to make clear one point: It is unquestionably wrong to assume naively that the world's schools are able to wave a magic wand and usher in the new millennium. On the other hand, it is just as inexcusable to suggest the converse, i.e., that the schools are impotent as regards engendering an awareness of, identification with, and commitment to universal humankind.

Discussion Questions
1. Why is it necessary to engender a global perspective among today's students?
2. Is the public school an appropriate place to stimulate this process?

Week Four, Five and Six   Some of the Forces Which Might Impede the Emergence of a World Community

Lesson I: The Case of Implicit Culture

Study
1. The Newman article on Implicit Culture.

Discussion
In order to interpret meaningfully ourselves and our relationship to our environment, we are oriented by a worldview (or global outlook). This orienting set of beliefs helps us come to grips with fundamental questions such as: What is morally good? What type of government is most desirable? What is the most reliable source of knowledge? The rich cultural pluralism manifested by the earth's peoples is testimony to the extremely variegated nature of these worldviews. Quite often these differing philosophies of life complement and supplement one another. Frequently they conflict (and even contradict) one another. Obviously, in the absence of sensitivity to ways of life which differ from our own, we are bound to flounder, whether as visiting tourists or foreign policymakers. This lack of penetrating insight is among the conditions which give rise to international stress and strife.

An important part of the global educator's job is that of acquainting students with varying and differing world views. The objective is not necessarily to encourage the student to accept and approve all the belief and attitudinal systems subscribed to by others, but to stimulate him/her to recognize and appreciate that her/his culture's philosophy of life is but one among many. We might say that the objective here is to stimulate a comprehensive, flexible disposition toward others' points of view.

Discussion Questions
1. Relating to Newman's article, discuss:
   a. Some of your (implicit) philosophic assumptions.
   b. Some of the major philosophic premises subscribed to by members of your local community and/or geographic region.
   c. Do these premises which you have identified in parts (a) and (b) conduce to the establishment of a condition of global community? Why or why not?

Lesson II: Political Ideology: A Component of Varying Global Outlooks

Study
1. The Newman article on Political Ideology.

Discussion
Every one of the earth's nations proudly proclaims an official political ideology. As the essay on ideology indicates, this network of beliefs provides each nation's peoples with a sense of political direction and destiny. While less abstract than the underlying global outlook we explored in the previous lesson, the political ideology must be reasonably congruent with a people's basic philosophic premises if it is to be sustained. Whether we are discussing the varying interpretations of American democracy as they have obtained at any particular time or the officially favored version of Soviet Marxism, a prerequisite for the development of a cosmopolitan attitude is a reasonable working knowledge of and sensitivity to different nations' political ideologies. The student can neither understand intellectually nor appreciate empathically culturally different people without a grasp of their political ideology.

Discussion Questions
1. Interpret and describe some of the distinguishing characteristics of the contemporary American political ideology (ies).
2. Critically react to what you have written by focusing upon the serviceability of this ideology in the interest of global education (i.e., does it tend to lend support to a global educational thrust).

Lesson III: Nationalism As An Ideological Component

Study
1. Nesbitt—Bloomstein Article (on reserve).
2. Shafer Article (on reserve).

Discussion
As we noted in the last lesson, one of the key functions of a political ideology is justifying (legitimizing) a given nation's cultural ethos and mode of political operation. To put it another way, one might say that a given people's nationalistic sentiments and behaviors are legitimized by appeal to its political ideology. The concept of nationalism is an elusive one and admits of varying interpretations. We shall be somewhat arbitrary and define nationalism as does Boyd Shafer, in his *Nationalism: Myth and Reality:* "That sentiment unifying a group of people who have a real or imagined common historical experience and a common aspiration to live together as a separate group in the future."

Quite clearly, nationalism as thus defined is neither morally good nor bad in the abstract. One must look carefully at each particular case of nationalism to judge whether it tends to enhance or impede the development of a cosmopolitan disposition. Those interested in promoting cosmopolitanism must be acutely aware of and sensitive to the operation of nationalistic sentiments.

Discussion Question

1. Do you feel one can be at one and the same time a loyal nationalistic citizen and a committed citizen of the world? Why and/or why not?

Nationalism: The Concept of Political Sovereignty

Study

1. The essay by Emory Reves.

Discussion

A key concept in our inquiry is that of nationalistic sovereignty. While the idea of sovereignty is exceedingly complex (for example, one can distinguish between political and legal sovereignty), for our purposes it is convenient to regard the term as synonymous with autonomy (or, if you like, independence). That is, a nation can be described as sovereign if it is free politically and legally to forge its own domestic and foreign policies. Of course, no nation is (or could be) absolutely sovereign. For reasons we have already pondered, this is truer today than in the past. But, while no nation can be absolutely sovereign, it is a glaring fact that the concept of sovereignty is constantly being invoked to protect this or that alleged national interest. This is true, whether one is talking about prohibiting fishing vessels within the 200-mile limit of one's coast, or of exercising the veto in the UN Security Council.

For our purposes, we want to give careful consideration to the contention of some that global education programs will tend to unduly and unfairly undermine or debunk national sovereignty. Is this probably or necessarily the case? Might not an appreciable reduction of national sovereignty enhance the prospects of attaining world peace? These are among the over-arching questions which all concerned with global education must ponder carefully.

Discussion Questions

1. React to Reve's contention that:
   "But to transfer certain aspects of our sovereign rights from national legislative, judiciary and executive bodies to equally democratically elected and democratically controlled universal legislative, judiciary and executive bodies in order to create, apply and execute law for the regulations of human relationships in the international field—in a field where such law has never existed—is not 'surrender' but *acquisition*. It is an exchange of a phantom asset, a product of unfulfilled and unfulfillable promises, for a real and tangible asset."

Lesson IV: Patriotism

Study

1. Excerpts from *West Virginia vs. Barnette.*
2. Audiotape (National Public Radio).
3. Compilation of Quotations.

Discussion

Nationalistic patriotism is a term to which people attach many different meanings. As the enclosed quotations point up, it has been thoroughly praised and roundly damned. For purposes of this course, the term is best regarded as the emotion people invest in their particular nation-state. This positive attachment to nation has historically been among the most important attitudes the schools have been called upon to engender. It is clear that all citizens, whether within or without the educational progression, should come to grips with the concept toward the end of examining critically their own interpretations.

Patriotism usually implies loyalty to country. It is clear, however, that one can be loyal to many things other than country: e.g., family; religion; profession; mankind. We all have our own hierarchy of such loyalties. Some put country at the top of the hierarchy; some unequivocally do not. For example, the conscientious objector frequently insists that loyalty to religious and/or philosophic principle supersedes obligation to country. It is instructive to observe, along with Morton Grodzins *(The Loyal and the Disloyal)*, that to say that another is disloyal is to insist on one thing: his loyalties are antagonistic to your own.

The educator's posture regarding the process of development of a wholesome disposition of loyalty is of critical importance to those concerned with globalizing student horizons. We must forever guard against educators who insist that this or that object of loyalty (whether country or some form of world federal government or whatever) ought to be regarded alike by each and every student.

Discussion Questions

1. Reflecting upon the *West Virginia vs. Barnette* case, critically assess the majority opinion (from a moral, not a legal perspective).
2. Do you think colleges of education ought to filter out aspiring teachers who are narrowly ethnocentric (extremely patriotic)? Why and/or why not?

Lesson V: Political Socialization: Some General Considerations

Study

1. Pages 139 to 143 in the Edith King Book.
2. Torney Article in Becker Book.
3. "Children and War," Norma Law (on reserve).

Discussion

Obviously, if we are to come to grips with attitudes such as those represented by nationalistic patriotism, we have to understand the process by which these dispositions are acquired. This lesson is designed to provide us with an elemental working knowledge of this process.

Every one of us is born into the world innocent of any and all attitudes and beliefs. This vacuum is of exceedingly short duration, however. At an early, tender age the cultural inductee begins to take on many of the beliefs, customs and attitudes to which he or she is exposed. Whether done deliberately or inadvertently, this process of socialization is inevitable and unavoidable. One dimension of the attitudinal and belief system which the young imbibe is political in nature. Social scientists describe this taking on of peculiarly political convictions as political socialization. While there is no universally accepted definition of the process, the following one, suggested by Robert Cleary in *Political Education in the American Democracy,* will stand us in good stead. Political socialization is the "development of politically relevant knowledge, attitudes, and values . . ."[1]

Discussion Questions
1. Identify and briefly discuss at least three social institutions which have a politically socializing impact on young people.
2. In a two-page essay respond to the following question: What do Kohlberg's stages (pages 141 to 142 in Edith King) imply for those who are committed to a global educational curriculum?

Week Seven   General Curriculum Considerations

Study
1. Chapter 1, 2, 4 of Becker Book.

Discussion
Having done the spade work which points up the need for a globally-oriented educational curriculum, we are now in a position to consider some of the broad contours such a program of instruction might assume. Among the crucially important points to ponder in this context is whether global education should be represented by a discrete "course" or whether this (global) perspective should infuse the entire curriculum. Another important consideration is whether global education content should be of a required or an elective nature. And, we would want to reflect upon an appropriate agency (whether student, teacher, parent, board of education, state legislature or a combination of some or all) for assuming the responsibility of providing globally-oriented learning experiences.

Discussion Question
1. If you were on a committee charged with the responsibility of formulating the broad contours of such a curriculum (on the elementary or secondary level—your choice), discuss some of the substantive considerations you would ponder.

Week Eight   A Futuristic Perspective

Study
1. Review and discuss film, "Future Shock."
2. Read and discuss "The New Economic and Political Order of the 1980's" by J. Naisbitt.

Discussion
Toward the end of *An Attainable Global Perspective,* Robert Hanvey observes that those who are globally disposed adopt a futuristic perspective. They are committed to making reasonable, responsible projections as guides for contemporary policy and practice. Quite clearly this futuristic point of view avoids any notion of imposing a blueprint for the future. What most futurists do insist upon is that our present social policies be illuminated by the beacon which suggests a "relevant utopia." This means every policy decision ought to be anchored to and inspired by reasonable well-grounded empirical projections.

---

[1]Cleary, Robert E., *Political Education in the American Democracy* (Scranton, PA: Intest, 1971).

Those of us concerned with education will presumably find the development of a futuristic orientation a desireable learning objective. (Indeed, intelligent behavior means, in part, anticipating future consequences!) In this course we can only hint at a few of the curriculum approaches the futuristic teacher might wish to adopt. One fertile source of firing the imagination is science fiction enterprise. On the later elementary levels and up, the students can be encouraged to extrapolate probable future conditions from respectable data which address the present. They should be guided to reflect upon these probable futures and ponder whether or not such scenarios represent desireable ways of life.

Discussion Questions
1. What do you think might be some possible obstacles to the stimulation of a futuristic perspective?
2. Discuss curriculum measures you might adopt were you charged with the responsibility of helping students develop a futuristic perspective.

Weeks Nine and Ten   Elementary Education

Study
1. Read King's book.
2. Read Chapter 5 of Becker's book.
3. Read UNICEF material.

Discussion
It is axiomatic that the attitudinal and belief systems which are internalized at young, tender ages are the mortar out of which most adult life styles are forged. We need not belabor the critical impact of home influences. In this lesson we shall ponder—more as an article of faith than a firmly demonstrated empirical observation—the potential effect of school learning experiences on the evolution of global dispositions. What might we do, what can we do, what dare we do in the elementary school toward the end of enhancing cosmopolitanism?

As we explore this area we should be ever mindful of the thin line between obvious brainwashing, subtle propagandizing, and responsible democratic education efforts. How can we promote, in an effective and responsible way, cosmopolitanism while avoiding a violation of the child's dignity?

Discussion Questions
1. Discuss and critically react to some of the early education learning approaches suggested by Professor King. Would you feel comfortable in the capacity of a facilitator of these processes? Why or why not?
2. What curriculum measures might suggest themselves for the early childhood level?
3. Critically assess the UNICEF material from the perspective of meaningfulness, practicality, and usability.

Week Eleven   Secondary Education

Study
1. The article by Mehlinger in *Social Education.*
2. Chapter 6 of Becker's book.

Discussion

Having attended to some of the considerations involved in "globalizing" the elementary educational curriculum, we are now prepared to "graduate" to the secondary level. While scholars disagree regarding the impact of secondary school experiences on adolescent attitudes, we shall proceed as if such experience can play an appreciable role in facilitating the development of a world-minded disposition. As many researchers have observed, our secondary schools have not exactly distinguished themselves in the area of global education. As your readings reflect, this is due to a welter of interrelated factors,not the least of which is the resistance of community pressure groups (you might wish to review the Torney chapter in Becker). Our major concern in these lessons is coming to grips with two interrelated questions: (1) What are among the more effective and humanistic curriculum measures which the globally-minded high school teacher might adopt toward the end of stimulating world mindedness? (2) How might such proposals be formulated so as to gain acceptance and approval by local school districts?

Another very crucial consideration which you might ponder is the feasibility of stimulating a global disposition among those thousands of adolescents who are **poverty stricken** and all too frequently alienated from the American social fabric.It is not surprising that many poor ghetto youth are quite suspicious and untrusting of the political authority (local, state and national) which affects their lives. Can we reasonably expect these youth (whether American or whatever) to expand their loyalties to the world community when their basic biological and psychological needs remain unsatisfied?

In the secondary school context we might also wish to give some thought to the feasibility of infusing predominantly-vocational high school courses with a global perspective. Can learning experiences which are essentially geared to teaching trade skills be related meaningfully to the global context?

Yet another important consideration on the secondary school level is that of meaningfully relating globally-oriented learning experiences to the perceptual field of those thousands of adolescent activists who plead for educational "relevancy." How might the secondary school educator effectively demonstrate the "relevancy" of constructs and modes of inquiry integral to the global perspective? These are but a few of the exciting questions with which those concerned with globalizing secondary school education must cope.

Discussion Questions

1. Drawing upon your readings and personal experience, do you think global education on a secondary level should be: (a) embraced by a discrete, one-shot course required of all students? (b) a series of such courses extending throughout the high school experience required of all students? (c) An all-pervasive dimension of the entire secondary school curriculum?

2. How might an imaginative secondary school teacher design a science course to stimulate global awareness?

3. a. Focusing on the Mehlinger article, critically react to the suggestions for changing American history and civics courses. Are such modifications in the best interests of our country?

   b. Suggest some preliminary ideas of your own (other than those proposed by Dr. Mehlinger) which might augment the global orientation of such high school courses.

Week Twelve   Global Education on the University Level

Study
1. Read the Harari booklet.

Discussion
Our inquiry has been focused almost exclusively on the global dimension of elementary and secondary school learning experiences. A consideration of some of the problems which beset global education on the university level will lend an exciting dimension to our studies. Our focus in this lesson will be on higher education in general. Among the major questions you might wish to ponder in this lesson are:
1. How might our universities best, i.e., most effectively, efficiently, and responsibly, use their resoures in the interest of promoting global outlooks?
2. What are some approaches a university—in conjunction with the federal government and outside non-governmental funding agencies—might adopt toward the end of better serving the underdeveloped peoples of the world?
3. Can our universities do a better job of accommodating and drawing upon the insights of our foreign student population?

Week Thirteen   The Global Dimension of Teacher Education

Study
1. Chapter 8 of Kenworthy's book (on reserve).
2. Chapter 10 of King's book.
3. The mimeographed article by Robb.

Discussion
As Professor King so trenchantly points out: "if we accept the premise that the early years of life are crucial in forming attitudes, beliefs, and values, then we must also accept the proposition that teachers of young children are the most important elements in shaping the future of mankind." (page 203) While our colleges of education obviously aren't independent causal variables that can work some kind of globalizing magic, it's just as clear that they can aid immeasurably in facilitating the aspiring teacher's development of a cosmopolitan disposition. The readings for this lesson highlight some of the weaknesses and strengths of our teacher preparation programs. As all three authors conclude, a vast amount of work remains to be done if we are to get on with the job of preparing our teachers to cope adequately with our increasingly fragile "spaceship earth."

Discussion Questions
1. Drawing upon your readings and personal experience, discuss how we might better adapt our pre-service and in-service teacher preparation programs to the goal of stimulating world-mindedness among our nation's youth.
2. Suggest and discuss at least three curriculum measures not found in your readings which teacher preparation institutions might adopt toward the end of globalizing the outlook of prospective teachers.

Week Fourteen   Aesthetic Approaches to Global Education

Study
1. The Newman article.

2. All of the Edith King book (review).

3. Poetry Anthology (handout).

Discussion
As we have observed throughout this course, global education is concerned primarily and predominantly with student attitudinal change. Attitudes, we know, are a highly intricate fabric woven of strands which are at one and the same time cognitive (or intellectual) and affective (or emotional). If we are to stimulate effectively an attitudinal change, our learning experiences must embrace both domains. We must, as it were, involve the student's head, heart, and gut. One predominantly affective learning approach is aesthetic. In its simplest terms, by aesthetic we mean "that which is present to our consciousness immediately and sensuously."[2] To perceive an object—be it a painting, nature, one's fellow man—aesthetically is to permit it to flow into and "flood" one's consciousness. In the process, we and the object(s) become an intimate bond.

An aesthetic approach to global education is admittedly rather unconventional (in some circles, perhaps iconoclastic). It is, however, a richly compelling orientation which the imaginative educator can adopt as a complement to predominantly-cognitive approaches. A predominately intellectual approach to global education, while crucially necessary, is not sufficient when it comes to facilitating the student's development of a humane, empathic disposition.

Discussion Question
1. Having read Professor King's book, choose a chapter from among Chapters 4 and 7 which most clearly reflects your interests and background and respond to the following:
   a. What are the strengths and weaknesses of this approach?
   b. How might the high school teacher adopt this approach?
   c. Drawing on your pool of knowledge and insights, enlarge upon this approach, i.e., suggest related pedagogical orientations, materials not mentioned.

Week Fifteen   Review

Study
1. Review and tie together all course materials.

Discussion Questions
Having completed successfully all lessons, it is now appropriate to step back a few paces and engage in a comprehensive overview of our learning experience. Please respond to the following questions:
1. As presented in this course, what do you feel are among the strengths and weaknesses of global education? (Methodologically, contentwise, administratively, politically).
2. Carefully reflecting on your own value commitments, do you feel prepared (whether as active teacher or concerned lay person) to stimulate a global disposition among the young? Why and/or why not?
3. Which of the sub-topics have proven the most exciting and helpful? Why? Which areas seemed to be boring or wasteful?

---

[2]Tsugawa, Albert, "The Nature of the Aesthetic and Human Values," *The Bulletin of the National Association of Secondary School Principals,* 53, Nov., 1969, p. 52.

International Development Education

Frank A. Stone   *Spring 1983*
ESIM 408/I.N. Thut World Education Center/University of Connecticut/
Storrs, CT 06268

This seminar is intended for both American and international students enrolled in fields such as Educational Administration, Curriculum Development, Higher Education Administration, or Educational Studies where there is concern to relate educational policies and programs to social aims and objectives. It is a study of educational approaches to community and society planning, types of impact assessments, as well as the moral issues related to development programs. The focus is on less-developed areas of the United States, as well as Third World societies.

Outline

1. Interdisciplinary Methods of Studying the Processes of International Development Education
2. Investigating How Education Functions as an Instrument of Development
3. Planning Education Development Projects and Programs
4. Implementing and Assessing Education for Development
5. Basic Issues in International Development Education
6. Exploring Specialized Sectors such as Village Revitalization, Appropriate Technologies, Mass Media and Literacies, Urban Renewal, and Women's Role in Development

Description
A study of educational processes for international development in light of alternative strategies for improving society and contemporary development theories. The aim of this advanced graduate level seminar will be three-fold:
(1) To increase the knowledge of in-service educators from the United States and overseas regarding the perspectives concerning development that are advocated by theorists in the 1980's.
(2) To enhance the practical understanding of what is involved in effective international development education.
(3) To prepare professional educators with the competencies and skills that they will need in order to plan, implement and evaluate projects in educational development.

Textbooks
Ahmed, Manzoor and Philip H. Coombs, (eds.) *Education for Rural Development: Case Studies for Planners.* New York: Praeger Publishers, 1975.
Bauer, P.T. *Dissent on Development*, Revised Edition. Cambridge, MA: Harvard University Press, 1976.
Harbison, Frederick H. *Human Resources as the Wealth of Nations.* New York: Oxford University Press, 1973.

P.D. Dunn, *Appropriate Technology: Technology with a Human Face.* New York: Schocken Books, 1978.

John Simmons, (ed.) *The Education Dilemma: Policy Issues for Developing Countries in the 1980's.* New York: Pergamon Press, 1980.

Requirements

1. Regular attendance and participation by sharing your experience, knowledge and cultural understanding. It is not expected that you will be absent from more than two evenings for any reason, and you are requested to make prior arrangements with the instructor if you anticipate not being able to attend.
2. Knowledge of the contents of the three core textbooks, which may be tested by quizzes or examinations.
3. Familiarity with the material presented in the seminar by films, slides or special informants.
4. Acquaintance with the information and interpretation given by the instructor in lectures or by other members of the seminar to their presentations.
5. Reading of a minimum of six additional articles, books or monographs aside from the textbooks, to be evidenced by "reading reaction cards."
6. Prepare one Case Study of an International Development Education Project. It is to have three components that will be due at stated times during the semester.
   6.1 A General Situation Profile. Please make this four to six pages in length.
   6.2 An Educational Needs and Resources Assessment. Keep this short.
   6.3 A Project Plan and Implementation Design, including a Means of Evaluating Its Effectiveness. This may be a tentative exploration if you hope to initiate the project, or it can be an analysis of a project that has been undertaken. Again, please try to be brief. Eight to ten pages, at most, should do it.
7. Each seminar member will be expected to orally present their case studies during the last meetings of our group. Therefore, please plan ahead to have the information ready at the time when it will be needed.

All materials that you prepare will be handed in at the last seminar meeting.

Seminar Program

1. Interdisciplinary Methods of Studying International Development Education Processes

1.1   Economic Efficiency Cost/Benefit Analysis
1.2   Educational Policy Studies
      1.21   Evaluations of National Development Plans
      1.22   Project Case Studies
1.3   Educational Anthropology
1.4   Action Research in Education

2. Comprehending Concepts of How Education Functions as a Tool for Development

2.1   Terms that are used in Current Theories of Education and Development
2.2   Development Processes in the History of Education
2.3   Some Alternative Development Rationales Today
2.4   Educational Development in Traditional Societies

3. Studying Educational Development as it has been Implemented by Colonial and Imperial Powers

3.1	Belgium	3.7	The Netherlands
3.2	France	3.8	Ottoman
3.3	Germany	3.9	Portugal
3.4	Great Britain	3.10	Spain
3.5	Italy	3.11	U.S.A.
3.6	Japan	3.12	U.S.S.R.

4. Loci for Planning Development Education Projects
4.1   National (Comprehensive Development Plans)
4.2   Regional
4.3   Community or Neighborhood
4.4   Institutional (Model Sub-systems)
4.5   Personal (Human Resources)

5. Organizations that Participate in Educational Development Efforts
5.1   Voluntary Groups that Operate Projects
5.2   Development Research Centers
5.3   National Authorities
5.4   Personnel Training and Preparation
5.5   Bilateral and Multinational Agencies

6. Planning, Carrying Out and Assessing Educational Development Projects
6.1   Preparing a Situation Profile
6.2   Compiling Needs Assessments
6.3   Identifying Available Resources
6.4   Establishing Aims and Priorities
   6.41   Mission Statements
   6.42   Measurable Objectives
6.5   Using Redeployment, Reform and Innovation Strategies
6.6   Implementing the Project
6.7   Evaluating Its Outcomes

7. A Survey of Some Common Educational Development Sectors
7.1   Urban Planning and Renewal
7.2   Rural Village Revitalization
7.3   Population and Family Life Education
7.4   Integrating Women into Development
7.5   Finding and Applying Appropriate Technologies
7.6   Literacies and Languages as Development Vehicles
7.7   Mass Media in Educational Development
7.8   Improving Vocational/Technical Education
7.9   The Role of Higher Education in Development
7.10   Curriculum Reform
   7.11   Math and Science Education
   7.12   Social Studies Education
7.11   Special Education in Developing Countries

8. Basic Issues in International Development Education
8.1   Educational Wastage

8.11   Lack of Retention
8.12   Inefficient Management
8.13   Poor Interfacing with Employment Demands

8.2   Absorption of Human Resources
8.3   Competition among Educational Sectors
8.4   Inequities in Disseminating Educational Opportunities
8.5   Non-Formal Approaches versus Formal Schools
8.6   Shortages of Qualified Educators
8.7   Effectiveness of Schools and the Educational Investment
8.8   Clashes among Educational, Political and Social Ideologies

9. Specific Case Studies of Educational Development Projects (Student Reports)

**10. Proposals for International Development Education Activities
(Student Reports)**

A Glossary of Terms Frequently Used by International Development Educators
Compiled by Frank A. Stone, 1982

1. *absorptive capacity*—the amount of resources that a community, institution or society can effectively utilize within a given period of time.
2. *adult education*—opportunities for general rather than specific vocational/technical education provided citizens after the school leaving age. Other terms that are used for similar processes are: continuing education, further education, lifelong education, education permanente, recurrent education and tertiary education.
3. *aid*—programs of assistance and support by an institution to individuals; a local, regional or national government to school systems or educational organizations; or transfers through binational or multinational agreements from donors to recipients through allotments, appropriations, grants or technical know-how to further educational goals.
4. *appropriate technology*—methods, techniques or machines that function effectively within a particular social context without causing difficulties or distortions.
5. *aspirations*—an individual's ambitions which in educational usage are usually perceived as academic, occupational, or social, and are concerned with performance, prestige or status goals.
6. *assistance*—taking part in or collaborating with a program or project by contributing financial, personnel, material or technical support.
7. *basic education*—the fundamental knowledge, skills and understanding that are regarded as being necessary in order to get along, be productive, and function as a citizen in a particular society.
8. *bilingualism*—the ability to use two languages fluently, either as co-mother tongues when they have been learned at about the same time, or when one of the tongues has been acquired as a second language after the first one.
9. *brain drain*—the departure of highly educated professional people for localities or countries that offer them greater incentives in the form of bigger challenges, better working conditions or higher remuneration. "Brain drain" can be internal within a nation as well as among nations.

10. *career education*—comprehensive learning programs that focus on occupational options that are systematically investigated through actual or simulated work experiences so that the learners have a basis for making decisions regarding their careers from childhood through the adult years.

11. *community*—"a wide grouping of people, located within fairly recognizable boundaries and related to each other by social, economic, and civil activities which produce cohesiveness sufficient to develop a history and recognizable identity." *School and Community*. Paris: CERI, OECD, Volume II, 1980, p. 12.

12. *community development education*—activities and processes of an educational nature that are undertaken by local people, embodying the principles of self-help, in order to improve the conditions in their neighborhood.

13. *compensatory education*—instructional programs whose ultimate objective is equalizing the performance of all the population attending school by improving the experience of those who have previously been deprived or disadvantaged.

14. *"completed" students*—learners who have finished the prescribed course of study at any level in an educational system and received a certificate, credential or degree attesting to this fact. For every "completed" student there will be nonfinishers who attended school, but were not graduated for various reasons. Educational attainments and the proportions of "finished" and "unfinished" products, borrowed from production management approaches, are sometimes also used to assess the efficiency of school systems.

15. *conscientization*—education aimed at raising the learners' awareness of their situation and the conditions within which they are living in a socio-economic system. The goal is then to empower these marginal citizens so that they can improve their lot.

16. *convivial society*—a social system that fulfills human needs for companionship, both in the variety of contacts and the constancy of relationships that it provides.

17. *critical size*—the point at which numbers involved are sufficient to make a process cost effective, after which the problems of that aggregation are created by its proportions rather than as a result of bureaucratic, human or institutional shortcomings.

18. *curriculum*—all of the contents and instructional process that are involved in a learning program, both intentional and unintentional or "hidden" curriculum.

19. *custodial function*—the care provided to children or youths in schools or non-formal programs freeing their parents or other family members for productive employment or leisure while keeping the young people out of the labor market.

20. *deschooling*—a movement whose advocates contend that conventional schools are archaic and ought to be replaced with self-mediated learning resources such as media centers and personal mentors.

21. *development*—efforts to move from a condition that is regarded as less than satisfactory toward one that is closer to optimum through planned change or growth.

22. *development education*—learning that has been designed to improve the cultural, economic, political or social condition of a community, region or nation.

23. *development studies*—investigations of the cultural, economic, political, social and technological problems and issues that are encountered in societies in which people are trying to improve the conditions of life for most citizens.

24. *devolution*—a form of bureaucratic decentralization in which some basic policy making and implementation authority is re-located outside of the central agencies in the national capital or downtown headquarters to regional centers or outlying areas. It is the opposite of consolidation.

25. *education permanente*—extra-school, life-long learning opportunities as they have been developed in Cuba.

26. *educational production function*—"EPF is used to determine the maximum product which can be derived from a given combination of inputs within the existing state of technical knowledge." John Simmons, (ed.) *The Education Dilemma.* Oxford: Pergamon Press, 1980, p. 78.

27. *educational reconstruction*—restructuring institutions and programs of learning to make them more relevant to desirable social change and justice.

28. *elite*—any leadership that wields power or authority based on its prestige, economic advantage, superior knowledge or social position. There are various kinds of elites that have different functions: managerial elites, military elites, political elites, and intellectual elites. Some may be relatively open to access by upward mobility that is based on merit, others are closed systems.

29. *enterprise zones*—specially designated areas in a city or country in which commercial and industrial entrepreneures are given abatements of regulations and/or tax incentives to attract them to locate there and employ local residents in their operations.

30. *external productivity*—the relationship between the cumulative benefits derived from an educational system over a given period of time, and the corresponding inputs that were used earlier to produce them.

31. *factor costs*—the expenditures of human resources, materials and money to provide a sub-section or sub-sectors of a system, such as floorspace, places for students, personnel, or fields of instruction.

32. *fotonovela*—pictures and captions arranged to narrate a story that can communicate development concepts to a broad population.

33. *functional literary*—the ability to read and write at about what is considered to be the average proficiency for fourth or fifth grade students in that society. It is a relative concept of the cognitive and communicative skills that will meet all of the individual's normal daily needs.

34. *green revolution*—increased agricultural production due to using better fertilizers, improved seed and stock, and the application of other techniques such as drainage and irrigation.

35. *Harambee School Movement*—a program of village revitalization in Kenya that was based on indigenous African values.

36. *headstart*—pre-school learning opportunities for disadvantaged children funded by the United States Department of Education.

37. *human capital theory*—a rationale of investment in upgrading the knowledge, skills and understanding of human beings in order to allow them to contribute to economic development and a more equitable income distribution.

38. *imperfect development*—any development that fails to bring about the anticipated and desired results.

39. *informal education*—learning within one's family or peer group; or through relatively unplanned interpersonal and intergroup processes within the community.

40. *internal efficiency*—the relationship between the outputs of a system and the corresponding inputs that were necessary to produce them.

41. *language maintenance*—keeping up fluency in a minority tongue within the given social context, especially when it is not used for formal instruction or as the vehicle of political communication as an "official" tongue.

42. *LDC* or *LDS*—less developed country or less developed society. This is the designation used by the United Nations for nations or societies in which the GNP is less than $500 per capita and a modern industrial infrastructure doesn't exist.

43. *legitimization*—achieving credibility for a development policy, program or project by exercising either persuasive authority or coercive power.

44. *manpower planning*—forecasting or projecting the human resource needs of a community or society in order to meet them by preparing people with the knowledge, skills and talents that will be required.

45. *meritocracy*—a system in which it is claimed that authority and power are achieved purely on the basis of demonstrated superior ability.

46. *metropole economies*—the "center" industrial or post-industrial powers of modern societies located largely in the northern hemisphere as contrasted with "satellite" or "peripheral" economies of eastern Europe and the southern hemisphere. According to the proponents of this model, there is often an auto-centric surplus drain from the periphery toward the center, within LDC's, as well as among developing and developed nations.

47. *misschooled*—peope who are unable to find employment in the field for which they were prepared in an educational institution.

48. *model cities*—an urban renewal program in the United States funded by the federal government in the 1960's and 1970's.

49. *modern*—"the form of civilization that is characteristic of our current historical epoch. Economic modernity is typified by the intense application of scientific technology, inanimate sources of energy, high labor specializations, the interdependence of impersonal markets, large scale financing, the concentration of decision making, and rising levels of material well being. A process of change in which ways of perceiving, expressing and valuing are altered toward a stress on individual functioning, an emphasis on empirical and rational evidence, and a disposition to act in certain ways." Alex Inkeles and David H. Smith, *Becoming Modern* (Cambridge, MA: Harvard University Press, 1974), pp. 15-16.

50. *non-formal education*—out-of-school planned learning and training that is relatively less institutionalized than schooling and open to all.

51. *obsolesence*—falling into disuse, being regarded as archaic, or becoming no longer the most efficient type or kind.

52. *'open' system*—educational programs that are available to all qualified applicants with little or no screening by means of standardized testing or other selection procedures. The other end of this spectrum is a highly selective system where intensive screening is applied to make it relatively 'closed.' Open education can also refer to the arrangement of space, movement within the learning place that is less prescribed, greater flexibility of the curriculum or more varied methods of instruction.

53. *over-developed*—societies with high affluence and huge rates of mass consumption that are post-industrial in their means of production and experiencing

problems of pollution, imbalance, economic stagflation and social turbulence.

54. *paucity of savings*—insufficient capital for use in development investment due either to a lack of cash surplus or to a preference for other types of investment such as in precious metals and real estate.

55. *personal costs of education*—the investment that individuals have made in their learning through the effort expended, time deployed, possible income lost, inability to help with their family's work load, and the funds that were directly or indirectly spent to educate them by themselves or their families. The other aspect of the costs of education is social.

56. *philosophy*—all of one's personal educational beliefs and commitments; or the stated mission of an educational institution or system—its aims and objectives.

57. *policy*—a general statement of the action, type of conduct, or management approach—based on principles or a rationale—that will be pursued under stated circumstances.

58. *policy formation*—decision making processes that include assessing alternative options, negotiating differences, making choices, articulating the chosen position, implementing and evaluating it.

59. *policy studies*—research and investigation into institutional and organizational decision making in order to better understand its processes and outcomes.

60. *population education*—the transmission of knowledge about demographic changes and characteristics along with better understandings of the causes of population fluctuations and their consequences for individuals and societies.

61. *progress*—aspects that are regarded as improvements in the socio-economic and technological dynamics of a social system because they contribute to greater opportunity and mobility for human beings.

62. *recurrent education*—a system that provides for re-entry into formal educational programs for those who left school early at any point in their careers.

63. *revolution*—a turnover in the power structure of a society in which an old elite or technology is displaced by a new one with a greater or lesser amount of violence and upheaval.

64. *underdevelopment*—lack of an industrial and consumption infrastructure in comparison with industrialized, high consumption societies. The indicators of underdevelopment are usually relatively low per capita income, high illiteracy, poor nutrition, limited mobility, and high mortality.

65. *undeveloped*—societies that are largely untouched by the values and ways of doing things brought about by the enlightenment and the industrial revolution.

66. *underemployment*—persons who are working on a casual or part-time basis below the optimum for their levels of energy, learning and skills.

67. *unemployment*—people who previously had a recognized job in the production or service sectors of the economy, but have temporarily or permanently been laid off.

68. *Village Institute*—a movement for rural revitalization and modernization that was pioneered in Turkey during the 1930's by Ismail Hakki Tonguch and other indigenous educators.

69. *wastage*—the degree of inefficiency in an educational institution or system due to drop-outs, lack of retention of the learning, or excessive costs in relation to the desired outcomes.

Issues in Contemporary Education: Educating for Peace and Justice

David Shiman and David Conrad   *Spring 1983*

Education and Social Science 200/University of Vermont/
Burlington, VT 05405

Global struggles for peace and justice touch our lives in many ways. Questions related to conflict, violence, and the threat of nuclear war confront us at the international negotiating table, within the classrooms, and in the community. Similarly, issues of discrimination, stereotyping, and human rights violations exist at both global and local levels.

This course will strive to help elementary, secondary, and adult educators increase their understanding of these issues and translate their concerns into action. Curriculum materials wil be developed and shared. Ways of teaching about peace and justice issues will be stressed.

Introduction to the Course

This course will examine relationships between two central issues of our time. We hope that the way this course is organized will help teachers and community educators explore connections between peace and justice issues in new and constructive ways.

The manner in which we pose our questions about the world profoundly influences the sorts of answers or solutions which we are capable of generating. Any curriculum or change strategy concerned with peace and justice is an expression of one's experience, knowledge, beliefs and global vision. Through this course we hope to develop new ways of thinking about issues of peace and justice and new strategies for action. In our explorations, we will keep in mind a quote by Simone de Beauvoir: "All oppression creates a state of war" and another by A.J. Muste: "There is no way to Peace, Peace is the way."

Course Outline

January 18   Introduction
Overview of Course
Creating a Peace & Justice Web
Visit to the Center

January 25   Peace and Justice: A Framework for Understanding Education as Dialogue
Wren, 1-29
Shiman/Conrad article

February 1   Peace and Justice: Exploring Alternative Frameworks
Wren, 30-78
Sloan, 1-14, 102-114

February 8   Linking Understanding and Action
What Can Be Done?
Curriculum in its Broadest Sense
Examining Existing Curriculum
Wren, 79-126
Assignment #1 Due

February 15   Peace and Justice: One Perspective
Film: "Controlling Interest"
Kohler article
Sloan, 65-78, 137-151
Assignment #3 Due

February 22   Peace and Justice: Another Perspective
Film: "War Called Peace"
Selected articles

March 1   Focus on the Arms Race
Film: "War Without Winners"
Sloan, 15-49, 79-101

March 8   Focus on Peace and Disarmament
Curriculum and Practice in Vermont Schools

March 15   Militarism and Racism in School and Society
Boyer, *Education* for *Annihilation*, "Definitions of Racism"
William's article
Assignment #3 Due

March 22   Developing Curriculum around Military and Social Issues
Sivard, *World Military* . . .
Assignment #2 Due

April 5   Perspectives on Justice: Classroom Activities

April 12   Human Rights and Human Needs
Branson and Torney-Purta, *International Human Rights* . . .

April 19   Institutional Violence as a Threat to Peace
Assignment #3 Due

April 26   Future Visions/Future Actions
Sloan, 199-209, 240-276

May 3   Presentations

Books to Purchase
Brian Wren,*Education for Justice* (New York: Orbis Books, 1977).
Douglas Sloan (ed.), *Education for Peace and Disarmament: Toward A Living World* (N.Y.: Teachers College Press, 1983).
Margaret Branson and Judith Torney-Purta, *International Human Rights, Society and the Schools* (Washington: National Council for the Social Studies, 1982).
Ruth Leger Sivard, *World Military and Social Expenditures, 1983* (Washington, D.C.: World Priorities, 1983).

William H. Boyer, *Education for Annihilation* (Honolulu: Hogarth Press, 1972.)
Plus a book on the Arms Race to be selected by you.

Articles

"Definitions of Racism," New York: Foundation for Change Inc., March 1974.

Gernot Kohler, *Global Apartheid* (New York: World Policy Institute, 1978).

David Shiman and David Conrad, "Awareness, Understanding, and Action: A Global Conscience in the Classroom," *New Era*, Vol. 58, No. 6, December 1977.

Greg Williams, "Racism and Militarism—Exploring the Links," *Interracial Books for Children Bulletin*, Vol. 13, Nos. 6-7, 1982.

Assignments

1. Evaluation of Curriculum

   Select a curriculum resource from the Center for World Education which relates to a peace or justice theme. Write a 2-3 page critical review of the resource. Discuss its goals, age-level appropriateness, activities, political or philosophical orientation, and strengths and weaknesses. *Due: February 8*

2. Development of Curriculum

   Drawing on the information presented in Sivard's *World Military and Social Expenditures 1983*, create a curriculum activity. Indicate its goal(s), age-level appropriateness, political or philosophical orientation, and ways in which it might be integrated into existing curriculum content areas. Length 1-3 pages. *Due: March 22*

3. Critical Reactions to Readings

   During the course of the semester, select *three* articles or chapters from the readings assigned (from three different weeks) and write 2-3 page reactions. Reflect on the readings in terms of your own work and political/philosophical orientation. *Due: February 15, March 15, April 19*

4. Curriculum Project

   This project should embody a program or plan for action. For many of you, this will involve action within the classroom and will probably take the form of instructional activities for children. For others, your "curriculum" might involve an educational plan for work with some group of people outside the context of the school, e.g., church, legislature, TV or radio, study group, social group. Collaborative projects are strongly encouraged. *Due: May 3*

Whichever direction you move, your curriculum project should contain the following characteristics:

Rationale—Statement explaining the need for this project and reasons for selecting your target population.

Statement of Goals—Identification of those understandings, skills, feelings, attitudes, and values that you hope will be acquired, expanded, or exhibited by the target population.

Activities—These might be original activities developed by you or ones derived from other sources. Several should be described in some detail while others might merely be mentioned.

Resources—An annotated list of resources, including books, curriculum guides, games, films or filmstrips.

Evaluation—Some discussion of how you are going to determine whether or not you have been successful in achieving your goals.

Global Perspectives in Citizenship Education

Dorothy I. Seaberg *Fall, 1982*

Curriculum and Instruction in Early Childhood Education 535/
Northern Illinois University/DeKalb, IL 60115

We will explore in this course the implications of emerging global trends and problems for social education in the elementary and middle school, and the creation of interdisciplinary activities and units to develop the global perspective.

Texts
Brown, Lester R. *Building a Sustainable Society.* New York: W.W. Norton, 1981.
Hanvey, Robert G. *An Attainable Global Perspective.* New York: Center for Global Perspectives, 1976.

Objectives
The student will:
1. identify emerging global problems and trends and recognize the needs they will create for future society.
2. develop an understanding of the earth and its inhabitants as parts of an interrelated network.
3. develop an awareness that there are alternatives facing individuals/nations and that choices will shape our future world; recognize that other peoples and cultures may have different perceptions and may prefer different choices.
4. increase his/her capacity to analyze controversy surrounding an issue, problem or policy, to engage in reflective moral reasoning and to make judgments or decisions on the basis of critical analysis. Explore ways to develop these capacities in children.
5. develop an appreciation for social participation in creating a desirable future.
6. assess the place of global understanding in the curriculum; examine and critique curriculum innovations with the global perspective and create materials for classroom use.

Course Requirements
1. Active participation in class.
2. Careful reading of the text and *assigned* handout material.
3. Locate, read and critique a minimum of five journal articles or chapters in books. These articles should be read in conjunction with session topics and your critiques turned in on 5 x 8 cards on the evening the topic is discussed in class. You are expected to assume responsibility for informal sharing. Specifically, read one article on each of the following topics:
   Energy
   Food/population
   Environmental issues

Read two articles selected from the following topics:
Scarce resources (exclusive of energy)
Multinational corporations
World economic problems
Problems of developing countries/or a selected developing country
Articles contributing to cultural awareness or about some other culture
International human rights
Military build-up and problems of peacekeeping
General article contributing to an understanding of the global system
Views of futurists about a stablilized global system
Note: These should be by-line articles.
4. Individual project. (Note: In some cases, two or three students may wish to work together on a project.)

Suggestions
A. Community research project. Select a product imported from a foreign country which is sold in the local community. Make a survey to gather the following kinds of data:
   1. Quantity of products sold in the community during the last 12 months or fiscal year.
   2. Financial impact on the community as a result of the product's being sold in the community (number of persons employed as a direct result of the product's sales, approximate amount of dollar sales during the last 12 months or fiscal year, who usually buys the product, impact on the community if the product were not available for purchase in the community, etc.).
   Develop a written report about the survey and also give a short verbal report to the class about the results of the survey, or you might wish to make a more general survey of as many links to the world as you can find in your community. Develop a plan showing how you could use these links to the world in a unit of study.
B. Create a teaching unit or learning center related to the global perspective.

Ideas
   1. Use a concept such as interdependence, systems, change, conflict, appreciating differences as your organizer.
   2. Use a theme such as "global connections."
   3. Create a study of a particular culture giving emphasis to concepts developed in class regarding cross-cultural awareness.
C. Develop a set of activities to infuse your existing curriculum with the global perspective.
D. Read a book(s) that relates to global problems/futures. Review and critique.
E. Develop an annotated resource guide of books, A-V materials, field trips, etc. that could be used to develop the global perspective in your curriculum.
F. Read the article, "A Practical Guide to Critical TV Viewing Skills." (Secure from instructor.) Design a TV project for viewing, logging and reporting your findings. The project might take one of the following forms:
   —View random programs and analyze how certain concepts (or misconceptions) are developed or conveyed, e.g.: stereotypes—Afro-American, Asian-American, Chicano, other ethnic groups, and sex-roles. Other themes might be ethnocen-

trism (closely related to stereotyping), interdependence, conflict. Or you might analyze propaganda techniques, decision-making processes as depicted on TV, or values exemplified and how these are shown.

—View selected programs and design a TV viewing project that you could use with the age group you teach.

G. Develop a slide show on "Global Connections," or some other aspects pertaining to global education.

H. Tape record several (at least three or four) interviews with people having global connections or who come from different cultural backgrounds. Plan your interview questions in advance. Transcribe the highlights of each interview. Share your project in class.

I. Other (you decide).

Agenda

Theme I: The Global Perspective

August 31   Orientation
What is the global perspective?
Activity: Attitudes we value

September 7   Global 2000 Report
Futuring activities
Activity: Global issues
Reading: Brown, Part I: Chap. 16

September 14   The Global System
Filmstrip: "Interdependence and Systems"
Links-to-the-World Concept
Film: "Ecology: Barry Commoner's Viewpoint"
Reading: Hanvey, An Attainable Global Perspective (synopsis); Seaberg, Social Systems: Paradigm for a New Social Studies

Theme II: State of the Planet Awareness

September 21   Discussion: Energy
Energy Environment Simulator
Film: "Energy Sources of the Future"
Reading: Brown, Chap. 8 and 9

September 28   Discussion: Food/Population
Films: "Tragedy or Triumph;" "Diet for a Small Planet"
Filmstrip: "The Giant and the Dwarf"
Reading: Brown, Chap. 7

October 5   Global Futures Simulation Game
Reading: Brown, Chap. 10

October 12   Discussion: Environmental Concerns
Value Clarification Activities: Planetary Awareness
Film: "To Live on Earth;" "Recycling Waste"
Reading: Brown, Chap. 11

Theme III: Cross-Cultural Awareness

October 23   Problems of a Developing Country: What Have They Done To My Village?
Radolfo S. Sanchez, Consul General, Philippines
Discussion: What should be studied about developing countries?

November 2   International Understanding
Guest Speaker: Professor Marjorie Dixon Zamora, Moraine Valley Junior College
Reading: Brown, Chap. 12

November 9   Cross-Cultural Awareness: Perceptions of other Cultures
Perception exercises
Slides: Images of China
Film: "Colonialism: A Case Study of Namibia"

November 16   Perspective Consciousness
Guest Speaker: Johann J. Grobler, Consul (information, South Africa)

November 23   Approaches in Studying Cultures
India: A Case Study
Film: "India: Customs in the Village;" "Image India: Radha's Day"
Slides: India
Reading: Harvey, Cross-Cultural Awareness

November 30   Glimpses of Cultures: Potpourri
Slides: China
Selected films and slides or resource persons
Projects welcome

Theme IV: Human Rights/Peace Education

December 7   Human Rights/ Peace Education
Discussion: "Futures" articles
UNICEF: Rights of the Child Exercise: Peace Begins at Home
Reading: Brown, Chap. 13
Assigned futures articles
Projects due

December 14   Synthesis: Infusing the Curriculum with the Global Perspective
Group sharing
Film: "Soviet Union: Faces of Today"

Teaching About Nuclear War

Robert W. Shuford   *Fall 1983*
Center for International Cooperation/National College of Education/
Evanston, IL 60201

The course will prepare teachers at K-12 levels to deal with the issue of nuclear war in the classroom in a constructive, positive way. Topics include a survey of the history of nuclear arms competition between the U.S. and the U.S.S.R., the technology of the arms race and relevant terminology, the psychological impact on children of living with the prospect of nuclear war, and classroom approaches to teaching about nuclear war and alternatives of peaceful conflict resolution.

Topic Outline

1. **History of the Nuclear Arms Race**
   Current Strategic Doctrine
2. **Nuclear Proliferation**
   Arms Control and Disarmament Efforts
3. **Ethical and Philosophical Issues**
4. **Review and Test**
5. * **Teaching about Nuclear War: The Elementary Level**
   a. The K-3 Classroom
   Developmental Factors
   Starting Points
   Activities: Books, Songs, Creative Writing, Story Telling and Art
   b. Grades 4-6
   Developmental Factors
   Starting Points
   Activities: Brainstorming, Monsters, Stories, Negotiations, Cooperative
   Games, and others
   Follow-up Activities for Information, Expression and Action

6. * **Teaching about Nuclear War: Grades 7-12**
   Developmental Factors in Junior High School
   Developmental Factors in High School
   Starting Points for Junior High and High School
   Teaching About Dialogue
   Using Community Resources and Speakers
   Using Printed Materials
   Content Area Subjects
   Taking Action
   Projects for Further Research

---

*Based on "Day of Dialogue Planning Manual," Educators for Social Responsibility, Brookline, MA, October 1982

7. Teaching about Nuclear War: Student Curriculum Projects (Students will develop curriculum materials appropriate for their needs)

8. Review and Conclude

Competencies
1. Develop familiarity with issues associated with modern defense technologies, with special emphasis on strategic nuclear weapons systems.
2. Gain the ability to present major issues associated with attempts to control nuclear arms, and the positions held by key individuals and organizations.
3. Be able to outline the major issues associated with the proliferation of nuclear weapons, contrasting positions held by significant contributors to the debate.
4. Gain familiarity with the issues associated with child development and the psychological impact which knowing about nuclear weapons has upon children's development.
5. Gain familiarity with available curriculum materials designed to help teachers face the nuclear issue in the classroom.

Required Reading
Richard J. Barnet, *The Giants: Russia and America* (NY: Simon and Schuster, 1977)
Robert C. Aldridge, *The Counterforce Syndrome* (Washington, DC: Institute for Policy Studies, 1978)

Bibliography
(See list of periodicals, books and pamphlets available through the Center for International Cooperation)

Choices: A Curriculum on Conflict and Nuclear War (National Education Association, Massachusetts Teachers Association, Union of Concerned Scientists, 1983) A two-to-three week curriculum for junior high designed to illustrate the dynamics of conflict resolution and peaceful means of settling disputes. Activities encourage students to analyze conflict on the personal, national, and international levels. Games, readings and projects are suggested to help students value the role of mediation, negotiation, and problem-solving in non-violent ways.

Decision-Making in a Nuclear Age (Facing History and Ourselves Resource Center, Brookline, MA, 1982) Examines topics including the history of the nuclear arms race; the nuclear bombing of Japan; the technology and physical effects of a nuclear explosion; the psychological effects of living in the presence of nuclear arms; the conflicting approaches to insuring against actual use of nuclear weapons in the future; negotiations and conflict resolution; roots of the Cold War; and the moral and ethical decisions confronting scientists, politicians, military leaders and citizens.

"Toward a Human World Order" (East Orange, NJ: Global Education Associates, 1982) Presents issues of international justice and security in a four-part filmstrip series, concluding with a consideration of the moral and religious implications of these issues.

Comparative and International Perspectives in Education

Donna Cole   *Spring 1982*
Education 390/Wittenberg University/Springfield, OH 45501

> As the interdependence of nations grows in all areas of our existence—political, economic, social, and ecological—the astronaut's image of our fragile globe floating in space jolts us into awareness that the threats to human survival are global and that we need to be educated about the world as a single unit, not as a collection of separate entities. In an editorial in the *New York Times*, James Reston called for new directions in American education. He asked whether a six-year-old child who entered the first grade in 1973—who will be 33 at the end of the Twentieth Century—will be ready to meet the problems of a new world in a new century. He admonished that whether or not the children of today will be prepared "depends largely on whether they are educated for the world that is coming or for the world that is going . . . In the field of education the 21st century is now . . . For what the six-year-olds learn between now and then, what view they have of life in that century, what knowledge, skills and attitudes they acquire in the next two decades will obviously determine their capacity for leadership, and certainly influence their personal happiness."
>
> —*James P. Grant*

This course is designed to allow students to examine various societies through historical, religious, political, economic, societal, geographic and educational perspectives. Emphasis will be placed on the relationship of societal factors (which influence change in developed and developing countries) to the educational institution.

Rationale

An undisputable fact of life in the early 1980's is that we are living in an increasingly interdependent world. Evidence of that fact surrounds us. Virtually all aspects of human activity, be they political, environmental, economic, or cultural are influenced by our growing and unavoidable interdependence with other nations and other ways of life. A decision in the Middle East to increase the price of crude oil affects the amount we pay for fuel at the gasoline pump; the Soviet invasion of Afghanistan results in a firming up of the defense posture of the United States and the cancellation of American participation in the Olympic Games; economic decisons made in the international financial community trigger suspicion of the American dollar, resulting in increased unemployment and inflation in the United States; the airing on American television of the drama, "The Death of a Princess," results in bruised feelings among Saudi Arabians who threaten retaliation; a hit musical opens on Broadway, and within weeks its songs are being played and sung around the world.

Interdependence in the world community is not a new development, of course. What is new is the extent to which the phenomenon has increased in recent years and the pace at which it continues to grow. To a greater degree than ever before the day-to-day lives of average citizens as well as the lives of nations are being influenced by our growing international, cross-cultural linkages. Our global ties appear to be here to stay, and in fact, to continue to expand at an ever increasing rate in the future.

Definitions of international education abound, but in essence it can be thought of as those educational efforts designed to cultivate in young people an international perspective and to develop in them the knowledge, skills, and attitudes needed to live effectively in a world possessing limited natural resources and characterized by ethnic diversity, cultural pluralism, and increasing interdependence. Although international education recognizes the importance of commonalities among mankind, it also is concerned with the differences among peoples and nations. A person with an international perspective recognizes that we are all members of a single species, enriched by diversity. As Lee Anderson puts it, we are ". . . both 'culture borrowers' and 'culture depositors' who draw from and contribute to a 'global bank of human culture' that has been and continues to be fed by contributions from all peoples in all geographical regions, and in all periods of history." (Anderson, 1979)

A basic assumption underlying global education is that no society has a corner on truth and wisdom and that no nation's view of the world is universally shared.

Rather it is recognized that other cultures possess unique value systems, different modes of thought and action, and different world views. It is the recognition and acceptance of these realities—an acceptance of the fact that there are many ways of being human—that is the hallmark of international education. Students who develop an understanding of an appreciation for these differences are well on their way to achieving an international perspective.

Text
Other Schools and Ours: Comparative Studies for Today, Edmund S. King, Holt, Rinehart and Winston, 1979.

Course Requirements
1. Participation. Involvement is expected and will be evaluated.
2. 7 short papers.
3. One quiz—April 16th.
4. One test—June 4th.

Course Outline

Week One   An International Perspective
March 30 pretest
     31 introduction
April 1 interdependence
    2 a World Village

Week Two   Developed and Developing Countries
April 6 definitions to develop
    7 developing countries
    8 culture
    9 poverty

Week Three   Education: A Means to an End or an End in Itself?
April 13 why educate
    14 purposes
    15 methods
    16 quiz

Week Four   How an Historian Approaches an International Issue
April 20 Dr. Huffman, guest
    21 studying history
    22 group analysis
    23 group analysis

Week Five   A Look at the Influence of Religion on Society
April 27 Dr. Swanger
    28 religion defined
    29 group analysis
    30 group analysis

Week Six   Politics and National Development
May 4 Dr. Mao
    5 political impact
    6 group analysis
    7 group analysis

Week Seven   Economic Evaluation
May 11 Dr. Weeks
    12 Dr. Cheema
    13 economic review
    14 discussion
    15 Dr. Barman

Week Eight   Sociology: Studying a Society
May 18 Dr. McEvoy
    19 societal attributes
    20 group analysis
    21 group analysis

Week Nine   Geographic Implications
May 25 Dr. Brown
    26 geography
    27 group analysis
    28 group analysis

Week Ten   Relating Cross-discipline Information to Education
June 1, 2, 3, 4 test

Developing a Global Perspective: Instructional Materials and Strategies

Jan Tucker   *May and June 1983*
Social Studies Education 4380/Florida International University/
Miami, FL 33199

Teacher education in the United States is a low priority on the public's agenda. The record of colleges and universities in the U.S. in providing leadership in teaching, research, and scholarship to cope with the "world problematique" is discouraging. The curriculum of higher education is fragmented and only rarely includes interdisciplinary approaches to global issues.

The following facts underscore the problem in higher education:

- Less than one percent of U.S. college-aged students are enrolled in any courses which specifically feature international issues or areas
- Only about one percent of college and university faculty members go abroad each year
- Of the 10 million students enrolled in higher education in the U.S., only one to two percent participate in study programs abroad
- Fewer than five percent of the teachers being trained today have any exposure whatsoever to international, comparative, area, and other intercultural courses in their work for certification (Hayden, 1979).

This course is part of the Global Awareness Program (GAP) in the School of Education at Florida International University. We take the approach that the long-term validity of higher education in the U.S. as a shaper of global futures hinges on whether educational institutions can become more globally-minded.

The course is based on three major premises: first, teacher education is an honorable and functional endeavor in the U.S.; second, the nature of global education as a grassroots movement requires a rethinking of teacher education; and third, higher education must assume a leadership role in teacher education with a global outlook.

Our perspective in global education can fortunately draw upon the idealism and pithy views of Harold Taylor (1969), whose observations on the importance of teachers and teacher education ring true even more clearly today. This course will share the spirit of some of the following excerpts:

- Education is only as good or bad as the teachers who plan it and carry it out.
- What teachers or anyone else can learn about world affairs depends on how sensitive they are to political, social and cultural life around them in their own society and in the world at large.
- Whatever they teach, teachers should be educated in a way calculated to raise awareness of what is happening to mankind in the world contemporary circumstances.

● What we need to do first if the American teacher is to be brought into the mainstream of contemporary culture and world affairs is to create a radically new conception of what a college for teachers should be.

One need not agree with every detail of these views to appreciate the gap between the reality of teacher education in the U.S. and what may be required to institutionalize even a modicum of a global perspective in these programs. But the effort is crucial.

—excerpted from "Developing a Global Dimension in Teacher Education" by Jan Tucker, *Theory into Practice*, 21:2 (Summer 1982), 213-217

Books

Botkin, James W., Mahdi Elmandjra, and Mircea Malitza. *No Limits to Learning: Bridging the Human Gap*. Pergamon Press, 1979.

Brown, Lester. *Building A Sustainable Society*. W.W. Norton and Company, Inc., 1981.

Naisbitt, John. *Megatrends: Ten New Directions Transforming Our Lives*. Warner Books. 1982.

In addition, there will be handouts. Students will make extensive use of the collections of print and non-print resources on global education in the FIU library.

Requirements

● One exam covering two books and lectures/discussions.
● One book review or three journal article reviews.
● Materials development.

Course Outline

I. Theory and Goals of Global Education
A. Historical and Social Forces Giving Rise to the Need for Global Education
B. Learning Theory and Global Education

II. The Content of Global Education
A. Perception and Perspective
B. Conceptual Understanding: Culture, Conflict, Change, Communication, and Interdependence
C. Global Issues: Population, Food, Energy, Human Rights, and others

III. Teaching Global Perspectives
A. Concept Development
B. Thinking and Valuing Skills
C. Using the Contemporary Media
D. Extant Materials and Resources

IV. Development of Materials and Lessons
A. Applications to Various Subject Areas
B. Demonstration and Sharing of Materials
C. Further Research and Development

SSE 4380 is acceptable as "infield" credit for social studies, early childhood education, and elementary education teachers. It is categorized as "basic skills education " for all other teachers.

Education for Peace, Disarmament and the Control of Nuclear Weapons

Betty Reardon, Willard Jacobson and Douglas Sloan *Fall 1982*
TF 4061X/Teachers College/Columbia University/New York, NY 10025

Course Schedule

September 13   Introduction
Overview and description of organization, objectives, and requirements for the
course.

September 20   The Nature of Nuclear War
Readings: Schell, Ch. 1
Geyer, Ch. 1
Thee, Part 1, Ch. 1 (on reserve)
U.N. Fact Sheet on Nuclear Weapons
World Military and Social Expenditures—Supplement on Nuclear War
(latter two readings will be provided on request)

September 27   Deterrence, Defense, and the Arms Race
Readings: Geyer, Ch. 2, 3, 4
Thee, Part III, pp.97-216

October 4   Weapons Development
Readings: Riverside Disarmament Reader (on reserve)
Kaplan, "Enhanced Radiation Weapons"
Paine, "Pershing II: The Army's Strategic Weapons"

October 11   United States Security Policy
Readings: Riverside Disarmament Reader
Drell and Von Hippel, "Limited War"
President Carter, "National Security Policy"
Eagleburger, "Preserving Western Independence and Security"

October 18   Nuclear Literary
Presentation by Edwin A. Deagle, Jr., Director, International Relations, Rockefeller
Foundation
Readings to be announced before Oct. 1

October 25   Economic Consequences of the Arms Race
Readings: *World Military and Social Expenditures*
Melman, Ch. 1
Clyde Sanger, *Safe and Sound* (on reserve)

November 1   Economic Consequences of the Arms Race
Presentation by Seymour Melman
Reading: Melman, complete book

November 8   Arms Control
Readings: Geyer, Ch. 5
Haig, "Arms Control for the '80's: An American Policy" (will be provided)
Thee, Part II and Parv IV

November 15   Disarmament
Readings: Geyer, Ch. 6
Final Document, S.S.D.I.
Johanson, *Towards a Dependable Peace* (on reserve)

November 22   Legal and Ethical Issues
Presentation by Elliot Meyrowitz, Lawyers Committee on Nuclear Policy
Readings: Briefs Prepared by Lawyers Committee
"War Criminals, War Victims"

November 29   Psychological Consequences
Readings: Schell, Ch. II
Escalone, "Effects on Children"
Macy, "Dealing with Despair"
Robert Lifton, any relevant works

December 6   Disarmament Education
Presentation by Swadesh Rana, U.N. Disarmament Centre
Readings: Rana, Ch. 2, pp. 105-150 (on reserve)
Thee, Part III (on reserve)
Final Document of World Congress on Disarmament Education (will be provided)
Reardon, Session 5 (on reserve)

December 13   Disarmament Education
Reading: *Teachers College Record*, Fall 1982 (on reserve)

December 20   Summary and Review
Deadline For Handing in Papers!

Building Toward Peace—A Curriculum for Public School Teachers

Gwen Minkler   *Fall 1983*
Education 164/Western Washington University/Bellingham WA   98225

Course Goals

1. To build a concept of world citizenship.
2. To demonstrate the use of a variety of peace-oriented educational materials and show how they can be used in the classroom and fit into the curriculum.
3. To explore methods of conflict resolution.
4. To inspire a beginning in "building toward peace."

Requirements

1. Keep a journal during the seven weeks of class including your reflections and evaluation of the weekly presentation. Also, write of your daily awareness and experiences in peace building. Due dates: November 4th, November 18th
2. Write a 2-3 page typewritten paper describing conflict resolution in your class-room and/or family, how satisfactory the method is, and possible changes you could make. Due November 17th.
3. Use "peace-oriented" material which will initiate discussion in your classroom. Give an oral report in class.
4. Participate in culminating activity: "In Celebration of Our World."

October 7   Introduction and Overview of Course

1. Definitions of "peace"
2. Peacemaking in daily life
3. "Creating the Future" cassette/slides
4. Present Curriculum Materials: "A Repertoire of Peacemaking Skills" by Susan Carpenter,available from the Consortium on Peace Research, Education, and Development (COPRED), University of Illinois at Urbana-Champaign.
   "A Manual on Nonviolence and Children" by Stephanie Judson, Fellowship of Reconciliation, Nyack, New York.

October 14

Art/Dr. Tom Schlotterback, WWU
To acquaint people with art as a major factor of beauty and peace.
Music/Dr. Robert Scandrett, WWU
To introduce musical materials which were written with the goal of fostering brotherhood and presenting ideals of peace.
Curriculum Materials:

1. "Building Blocks for Peace" by Margaret Comstock (K)
2. "Decision Making in a Nuclear Age" by Elizabeth Lewis and Roberta Snow (High School) available from Educators for Social Responsibility, Boston, Massachu-setts.

October 21
Drama/Karen Crawford, Children's Theater
To present the concept of drama that imagination helps an individual transform his
environment. It helps him refurnish his home and surroundings and he gradually
develops a power to touch and transform things that make up his environment.
Curriculum Materials:
1. "Peace Is In Our Hands" by Grace C. Abrams and Fran C. Schmidt (K-6)
2. "Learning Peace" by Grace C. Abrams and Fran C. Schmmidt (7-12) both
available from Grace Contrino Abrams Peace Foundation, Miami Beach, Florida
Resources
Bellingham Public Library/Bruce Radtke

October 28
Peace Persons
1. Literature and History
2. Noble Peace Prize

Exploring and Understanding the Roots of Conflict
1. "Educating for Peace and Justice" by James and Kathleen McGinnis, Institute for
Peace and Justice, St. Louis, Missouri.
2. "The Friendly Classroom for a Small Planet" by Prutzman, Burger, Bodenhamer
and Stern Publ.
3. "Conflict and Aggression" by Abrams and Schmidt, 50 copy masters, J. Weston
Walch, Publ.

November 4
Conflict Resolution
Mediation/Elisabeth Starnes, Mediator, Creative Conflict Resolution
Experiences from Your Classrooms

November 11
A View from a Political Scientist/Dr. Maurice Foisy, WWU
1. Cultural Bias
2. Ideology of Materialistic Individualism and It's Limits
3. Theories of Society
4. Political Responses

November 18
Concepts of Patriotism/World Citizenship
1. Discussion
2. Culminating Activity: "In Celebration of Our World"

Hunger
and the
Politics of
Food Distribution

Political Economy of World Food Problems
Sheridan Johns, Duke University

The Politics of Food
Joyce Livak, University of Vermont

Constructive Alternatives to Destructive Weaponry
William Eisinger/Dennis Gordon/Richard Pefley,
University of Santa Clara

Starvation: A Sociological Analysis
Richard Wells, University of South Alabama

World Food Politics
William Alexander, California Polytechnic State University

Global Issues
Glenn Mitchell/Ollie Ahrens/Virginia McKinley/Bill Mosher
Warren Wilson College

World Nutrition
Sondra King, Northern Illinois University

The World Food Crisis
Frank Holmquist and Ray Coppinger, Hampshire College

Hunger for Justice
Donald Clifford, Saint Joseph's University

Political Economy of World Food Problems

Sheridan Johns   *Fall 1982*
Political Science 173S/Duke University/Durham, NC 27706

How do governmental policies, technological change, international trading patterns, and private interests (both corporate and individual) affect the way in which food is produced, processed, and distributed in the world's richest agricultural power, the United States, and in the world's poorer, often food-short states, the underdeveloped countries of the Third World? It is this question, considered in the light of global food interdependence, which will be the focus of this seminar.

In the opening section of the course the question will be posed with respect to the agricultural system of the United States, with particular attention to the transformation of the last decades. Primary concern will be to gain appreciation of the changing structure of the agricultural system and the involvements and interests of the major public and private actors involved through examination of contending analytical perspectives.

The second section of the course will consider United States "food power" in the context of the world food system. Essential features of the global food and hunger situation will be delineated with special reference to countries in Africa, Asia, and Latin America. The role of the United States government and private interests in addressing global food problems will then be assessed from diverse critical perspectives.

In the third and concluding section of the seminar each student will have the opportunity to examine the food and agricultural policies of a particular Third World country with attention to both its national and international dimensions. The countries to be studied will be chosen from a select list of African, Asian, and Latin American countries. Several students will be assigned to study each country. The country "team" will share responsibility for a report to be presented to the seminar upon the country; each student will then have responsibility for his own individual research paper to be submitted at the end of the semester.

The Format of the Course

The seminar will meet weekly for approximately 150 minutes. During the first two sections of the course weekly discussion will focus upon common readings to be done by all students, with individual students being assigned more specialized readings from time to time. In the last section of the course (in November and December) seminar meetings will consist of student presentations and discussion.

Requirements of the Course

The success of any seminar is dependent, *inter alia*, upon the informed participation of all its members. Accordingly, all will be expected to complete assigned weekly readings in order to engage in the weekly discussions central to the seminar.

Each student will submit a 10-15 page analytical essay at the end of the second section of the seminar addressed to topics handled in the assigned readings for sections one and two. In preparation for the paper each student will complete the assigned reading; no additional reading will be expected.

During the third section of the course each student will join with others conducting research upon the same Third World country to prepare and make an oral presentation upon the salient features of that country's food and agricultural policies.

At the end of the seminar each student will submit a 20-25 page research paper assessing his/her country's policy. The paper will certainly draw upon the "team" country report, but will be an individual analysis elaborating and expanding upon the country report and based upon additional research and reflection.

Reading Assignments

(Books Suggested for Purchase Noted by Asterisks)

September 16   The American Agricultural System
Jules Billard, "The Revolution in American Agriculture," *National Geographic*, February, 1970, pp. 147-185 (Reserve)
Earl Heady, "The Agriculture of the US," *Scientific American*, September, 1976, pp. 106-127 (Reserve)
*Lyle Schertz et al., *Another Revolution in US Farming!*, Washington, DC: U.S. Dept. of Agriculture, 1979, Part I and one chapter from both Part II and Part III
*Sterling Wortman and Ralph Cummings, *To Feed This World*, Baltimore, MD: Johns Hopkins Univ. Press, 1978, Ch. 3

September 23   A Critical Perspective on the American System
*Wendell Berry, *The Unsettling of America*. San Francisco, CA: Sierra Club Books, 1977

September 30   World Food Problems
*Raymond Hopkins and Donald Puchala, *Global Food Interdependence*, New York, NY: Columbia Univ. Press, 1980, Ch. 1
International Food Policy Research Institute, *Food Needs of Developing Countries: Projection of Production and Consumption to 1990*, pp. 17-23 (Reserve)
*Sterling Wortman and Ralph Cummings, *To Feed This World*, Chs. 1-2, 4-7

October 7   The American Role in the World Food System
Raymond Hopkins and Donald Puchala, *Global Food Interdependence*, Chs. 2-3, 5-7
One of the following pair of articles:
1. Food Power
   a. "US Food Power: Ultimate Weapon in World Politics?" *Business Week*, December 15, 1975, pp. 54-60 (Reserve)
   b. Robert Paarlberg, "Food, Oil, and Coercive Resource Diplomacy," *International Security*, Fall, 1978, pp. 3-19 (Reserve)

2. The Private Sector and Government Involvement

a. Victor Ferkiss, "Intervening in the Market," in Peter Brown and Henry Shue (eds), *Food Policy*, NY: Columbia Univ. Press, 1977, pp. 164-182 (Reserve)

b. Charles Shuman, "Food Aid and the Free Market," in Peter Brown and Henry Shue (eds), *Food Policy*, pp. 145-163 (Reserve)

3. Corporations Overseas

a. Presidential Commission on World Hunger, *Overcoming World Hunger*, Washington, DC: U.S. Government Printing Office, 1980, Ch. 2 (Reserve)

b. U.N. Commission on Transnational Corporations, *Transnational Corporations in Food and Beverage Processing*, pp. 8-22 (Reserve)

October 14   Critical Perspectives on the American Role
*Frances Lappé et al., *Aid as Obstacle*
Daniel Shaughnessy, "The Political Uses of Foreign Aid: Are Criteria Necessary?" in Peter Brown and Henry Shue (eds), *Food Policy*, pp. 94-102 (Reserve)
Peter Timmer, "Food Aid and Malnutrition," in *International Food Policy Issues, A Proceedings*, Foreign Agricultural Economic Report No. 143, pp. 29-35 (Reserve)

October 21   Case Studies in Foreign Aid and Agricultural Development
Walter Falcon, "Food Self-Sufficiency: Lessons From Asia," in *International Food Policy Issues, A Proceedings*, Foreign Agricultural Economic Report No. 143, pp. 13-20 (Reserve)
Nathan Koffsky, "Food Needs of Developing Countries" and "Comments" by John Lewis and John Mellor, in *International Food Policy Issues, A Proceedings*, Foreign Agricultural Economic Report No. 143, pp. 21-28 (Reserve)
Francis Lappé and Joseph Collins, *Food First*, Boston, MA: Houghton-Mifflin, 1977, Chs. 46-49 (Reserve)
Ume Lele and Mohan Agarwal, "Food Grain Imports: Whether? When? Where?" *Ceres*, November-December, 1979, pp. 20-25 (Reserve)
J.P. O'Hagan, "National Self-Sufficiency in Food," *Food Policy*, November, 1976, (Reserve)
*Sterling Wortman and Ralph Cummings, *To Feed This World*, Chs. 8-10

November 4   Presentation by Daniel Shaughnessy
*Raymond Hopkins and Donald Puchala, *Global Food Interdependence*, Ch. 4

November 11-December 9   Individual Country Studies
*Sterling Wortman and Ralph Cummings, *To Feed This World*, Chs. 11-15

The Politics of Food

Joyce Livak   *Fall 1983*
Human Nutrition & Food 237/University of Vermont/
Burlington, VT 05405

The major objective of this course is to investigate the policies which are affecting our current food system, i.e. the production, processing and marketing of food. We have been hearing about the high cost of food, processing of food and the possible effect on nutritional quality and the controversial aspects of additives. Joan Gussow has written that it is important for nutrition educators to be concerned now with access to food. This course will deal with policies involved with our food supply. We will become informed so that we may become more effective in making sure that food of a good quality is available to everyone and in a price range that everyone can afford.

The topics with which this course will deal will begin with I) The Family Farm, The Small Farm. What has happened and is happening to the small farms? What are the factors which have eroded the small farm in the past? II) What role has the USDA and The Landgrant Colleges played in the demise of the small farm? III) The Growth of Agribusiness and its effect on food and nutrition has become inextricably intertwined with the corporations so we will take a look at IV) Corporations. This will lead us deeply into V) Third World and Its Politics as we find most corporations are multinational. By this point most students are discouraged and frustrated about the seriousness and magnitude of the problem which appears to be not the corporation, not the USDA, but an entrenched political and economic system. Most students at this time are ready to look at what the individual can do and what are some possible alternatives.

We then will return to an in-depth study of the general role of corporations followed by some case studies of specific foods. How does what we eat affect life in Third World countries? What can our VI) Regulatory Agencies Do? Again the focus will be on the USDA, FDA, FTC, etc.

Throughout, we are especially interested in those factors which are affecting *prices* of food such as monopolies, advertising, corporate takeovers, differentiation and super process foods and supermarket chain takeovers. What does the production and processing do to the nutritional quality? HN&F 237 takes a detailed look at food technology but the broad picture will emerge in this class. The politics of VII) Additives and VIII) Nutrition Education will be discussed in-depth. The "What can I do?" aspect will be strengthened by speakers, films, and readings as we explore alternatives.

Requirements (Bases for evaluation)

An action project: Objectives, abstract, scope, learning outcomes.

Participation on information panels on a rotating basis. Participation in class discussions and/or discussion debate panels.

Worksheet for each topic to be checked off on a weekly basis. Class attendance to be documented in diary form. A three- to five-page position paper to be written to a specific person.

Class Format

Tuesdays: Information panels

Everyone will have access to the readings but panels function is to summarize and clarify using guideline sheets.

Fill out worksheets on Tuesdays and Thursdays to hand in on the following Tuesday. (Some exceptions depending on flow.)

Thursday: Films, speakers, discussion/debate panels or individual presentations

Class Schedule

Introduction to the Course (Sept. 1)

Slideshow: "Hamburger USA"

Topic I—The Farm—Small and Disappearing, Large and Corporate; The Farm—In Transition (Sept. 6 and 8)

Readings:

"Food for People, Not for Profit," pp. 35-44 in *The Case for the Family Farmer* by Jim Hightower

"Eat Your Heart Out" in *Farmers: Death of American Gothic*, pp. 128-157, by Jim Hightower

Agribusiness Manual—Big Business Down On the Farm—Part V, pv 1-pv 30

Radical Agriculture, Richard Merrill, ed.—Chapter 4, pp. 43-63

New Directions In Farm, Land and Food Policies—A Time for State and Local Action, p. 9, 10, 15

Agribusiness in the Americas by Burbach and Flynn—Chapter I

Three Farms by Mark Kramer

Slideshow: "Who Butters Our Bread?"

Panels

1. Historical perspectives: What has happened to agriculture and the small farms since 1942? As farmers leave the land what happens to rural and small town life? What have been some causes of declining small farms?
2. Define agribusiness. Define vertical integration. What is the effect of agribusiness and vertical integration on the nutrition and cost of food?
3. This panel will tell you about chicken vertical integration from the article "Super Chickens and Super Profits"—pp. 23-27, in *Food Monitor*, May/June 1982.
4. Discuss ramifications and effect of conglomerate firms on input prices for farmers. (Seeds, fuel, fertilizer, etc.)
5. Describe the kinds (size, etc.) of farms in the U.S. Have large corporations taken over ownership of farms?

Topic II—USDA and the Land Grant College Complex (Sept. 13, 15 and 20)

Readings:
Radical Agriculture, p. 88 or
Hard Tomatoes, Hard Times or
Eat Your Heart Out also
New Directions in Farm, Land and Food Policies

Information Panels

1. Land Grant Complex System
   Brief history and description of original purposee
   Definition of land grant complex (3 components)

2. Research at land grant colleges
   What kind of research—links to land grant colleges?
   Who has it helped?
   How do agribusiness and petrochemical companies influence research?
   Readings from above: Article "Agribusiness on Campus" by Al Meyerhoff

3. Who are the victims of the current work on mechanization?
   Describe types of research and results, especially on nutrition, quality and cost of
      food.
   Describe briefly tomatoes and lettuce. I will give you an article on lettuce.
   Readings: "Agribusiness in the Lettuce Fields," *New Directions*, p. 67-69

4. What kinds of research are being done that affect consumers? To whom is this
   information most useful? How well has the extension service lived up to its
   mandate for service to rural people?
      Describe funding of land grant complex (role of state, county and federal). What
   role does Congress have for its accountability? What suggestions do you have for
   increasing accountability of this process?
   Readings:
   New Directions, p. 57
   Also in *Radical Agriculture*, etc.
   Film: "Green Grows the Profits"

Topic III—The Corporation—General Overview (Sept. 22 and 27)

1. Short History
   The Big Business Reader by Green and Massie, pp. 1-8
   "Corporations: The Domestic Experience," in *The Corporate Action Guide*, pp.
      9-16

2. The Global Corporation
   How it differs from the corporation of the past
   How it is able to transform the world political economy through control of
      resources?
   How it has weakened the power of the nation-state, pp. 5-12 in *Crisis of the
      Corporation* by Richard Barnet

3. "Four Myths to Legitimize the Role of the Corporation in Society," pp. 13-23 in
      The Crisis of the Corporation
   "Effect of the Corporation on Cost of Food"—pp. 9-18 in the *Big Business Reader*
   "The Food Monsters" by Daniel Zwerdling from *The Progressive*, p. 16, March
      1980

Effect of the supermarket oligopoly on food prices—*The Food Monsters* and also a chapter in *Eat Your Heart Out* by Jim Hightower

What is the effect on quality of food?

Article: "Let Them Eat Junk," by William Serrin, *Saturday Review* 2/2/80, p. 17

4. What can be done? Alternatives?

Crisis of the Corporation, pp. 24-26

Corporate Action Guide, pp. 63-74

Corporate Action Guide, pp. 83-88

Film: "Multinationals, Controlling Interests"

Topic IV—Role of Corporation in Foods Available in Third World Countries (Sept. 29)

Readings:

Food First by Frances M. Lappé, pp. 277-336 and 183-194

Agribusiness in the Americas by Burbach et al., pp. 108-126 *

Hungry for Profits by Robert Ledogar, pp. 108-126

1. Multinationals and Third World Development

Multinationals play a crucial role in the food production and distribution system. Their role as global food producers, processors and distributors is increasing. What are the major effects of these corporations, in general, in Third World Countries?

Readings:

"Multinationals and Third World Development," by Richard Barnet, *Multinational Monitor* 2/80, pp. 13-14

"The Profits of Hunger," by Richard Barnet, *The Nation*, Feb. 9, 1980, p. 129

2. The Global Farm for the Global Supermarket

Basic Concept

Describe how Del Monte and other corporations have created a Global Farm to serve a global supermarket (Mexico, Central America, Dominican Republic, Columbia, etc.)

3. Discuss the marketing strategies of multinationals in developing countries and their effect on:

—local agricultural development

—on employment

—on diet and the nutritional quality of food

—on income distribution

4. Farm Exports: "Force Feeding the World," by Jack Doyle, *The Progressive*, March 1982, p. 35

What are some of the long-term consequences of promoting foreign dependence on U.S. farmers and resources?

What % of various U.S. food crops is grown on 100 billion acres of U.S. farm land?

What are Agriculture Secretary Block's beliefs about farm exports?

How did the 1981 farm bill improve the lot of farm exporters?

Discuss market development in Japan, China, West Germany, Europe, Britain.

What impact might the food export business have on railroads, refrigerators, water, etc.?

What might be some of the social costs on the American public?

Describe the kind of farms that we might see with the growth of farm exports.
Slideshow: "Guess Who's Coming to Breakfast?"

Topic IV: A—Role of World Bank (Oct. 4)

Aid As Obstacle by Frances Moore Lappé, Joseph Collins and David Kinley
Development Debacle—The World Bank in the Philippines by Walden Bello, David
  Kinley and Elaine Elinson
The Trojan Horse by Steve Wirssman and Members of Pacific Studies Center and the
  North American Congress in Latin America
Against the Grain by Tony Jackson (Oxfam: England)

Topic IV: B—Pesticides in Third World Seed Patenting (Oct. 6)

Pesticides in Third World
Readings:
"A Critical Look at Castle and Cook: Blemishes on the Top Banana," by Ian Lind
  Multinational Monitor, July 1981, p. 10. "Administration to Act on Heptachlor,"
  CNI, Vol. xii, No. 36, p. 4, Sept. 16, 1982
Circle of Poison by David Weir and Mark Schapiro

Seeds
Readings:
Seeds of the Earth by Pat Mooney
"Patenting of Seeds Threatens Plant Extinction, Famine," by Gary Fowler in *Food
  Monitor*, May/June 1981, p. 5
"Seeds: The final round?" In *Circle of Poison* (Weir and Schapiro) pp. 43-46

Topic V—U.S. Foreign Policy in Third World Countries (Oct. 11)

Brief overview of three countries:
Nicaragua
Bangladesh
Chile or El Salvador

Speaker: Dr. Willard Miller

Questions:
1. A brief history
2. Who owns the land?
3. What are the main crops?
4. Who gets the benefits?
5. How is the nutrition?
6. What corporations are involved? Their effects?
7. How is the United States involved?

Resources:
Bangladesh
Hartmann, Betsy and James Boyce. *Needless Hunger: Voices from a Bangladesh
  Village*, San Francisco, CA: Institute for Food and Development Policy, 1979

Nicaragua
"Nicaragua, The Revolution was The Easy Part,"—*Food First Action Alert*

"Nicaragua Revolution," *NACLA*, May/June 1980
"The Somoza Apparatus," *NACLA*, Nov./Dec. 1978
"Aid No Obstacle," *Food Monitor*, Mar./Apr. 1982, p.9
What Difference Could A Revolution Make?, Collins and Lappé
Now We Can Speak: A Journey Through the New Nicaragua, Frances Moore Lappé and Joseph Collins
El Salvador
Food First Action Alert, March 1981
Chile
Agrarian Reform and Counter-Reform in Chile by Joseph Collins
Guatemala
Food First News, "Farming and Fighting," Issue No. 14, Spring 1983
Bitter Fruit, Stephen Schlesinger, Doubleday, 1982

Topic VI—Politics of Infant Feedings (Oct. 13 and 18)

Readings:
Food First by Frances Moore Lappé, pp. 336-348
Folder on Infant Formula or Infant Formula Action Packets
"Formula for Malnutrition," in *Hungry For Profits* by Robert Ledogar, pp. 127-145
The Promotion of Bottle Feedings by Multinational Corporations: How Advertising and the Health Professions Have Contributed, by Ted Greiner, Cornell International Monograph Series #2 (1975)

Panels:
1. Evidence that links marketing of bottle formulas to increased infant death.
2. Advantage of breast milk over formulas in Third World.
3. Marketing techniques used by the multinational corporations.
4. How does company advertising undermine the mother's confidence? (See pictures in Ted Greiner's monograph)
5. Pretend you are Nestle's officials and defend what you are doing. I will give you material from the company.
6. What are the products in the Nestle boycott? How effective has this been?
7. What is the WHO code? What would it do? Describe U.S. position on the international code to restrict marketing of infant formula. What was Lefever's role in the Nestle controversy? "Infant Formula: A Threat to Third World Babies," by Nanci Hartwick, *Graduate Woman*, Nov./Dec. 1981.
8. Summarize how formula firms control their markets. You will be given a recent article on this: "How Formula Firms Control Their Market," by James E. Post, *CNI*, Vol. XI, No. 28, p. 4.

   Summarize about the baby formula here in the United States: "Here's Looking At You, Kid," by Mary Ellen Schoonmaker, *The Progressive*, Dec. 1981, p. 42.

Film: "Bottle Babies"

Topic VII—What Can We Do? (Oct. 20)

1. Chapter 50, pp. 491-504 in *Food First* by Frances Moore Lappé
2. Chapter 12 (What Can I Do), p. 252 etc. in *How The Other Half Dies* by Susan George. Please summarize

3. Read Part I, pp. 3-8 in *What Can We Do: Food and Hunger: How You Can Make a Difference* by Valentine and Lappé

4. *Taking Charge*, a paperback by the American Friends Service Committee, has some excellent suggestions on personal action

5. Changing a Corporation
   Crisis of The Corporation —Richard Barnet, pp. 24-26
   Corporate Action Guide by Corporate Action Project, pp. 63-74
   Corporate Action Guide by Corporate Action Project, pp. 83-88

6. Chapter X, "Food Self-Reliance," in *Food First* by Frances Moore Lappé, pp. 457-504

7. Book I, Part I, II, III and IV in *Diet For A Small Planet* by Frances Moore Lappé (1982)

8. *Moving Toward a New Society* by Susanne Gowan, George Lakey, William Moyer & Richard Taylor

9. Building Social Change Communities by the Training/Action Affinity Group of Movement for a New Society, Chapter 1, 6, and 7

10. *New Age Politics—Healing Self and Society* by Mark Satin

11. *The Aquarian Conspiracy* by Marilyn Ferguson

Film (videotape): "Edge of Survival"

Topic VIII—Politics of Regulatory Agencies—Emphasis on FDA and USDA. Topic—Additives. Also FTC (Oct. 25 and 27-Nov. 1 and 3)

Readings:

Eater's Digest, by Michael Jacobsen. Introduction pp. 3-38. Appendix I and II pp. 226-228

Food for Nought: The Decline of Nutrition, by Ross Hume Hall, Chapter 4

Eating May be Hazardous to Your Health, by J. Verret, Chapter 3, p. 66

The Brain Bank by Philip Boffey, Chapter 8; also introduction by Ralph Nader XVII-XXIII

The Mirage of Safety, by Beatrice Trum Hunter, Chapter 12

The Great Nutrition Robbery, by Beatrice T. Hunter, for colors, flavors etc

"Company Town at FDA," in *Food for People, Not Profit*, pp. 372-386

Speaker: Ray Maggio, FDA

Panels:

1. Why are additives used? What are unintentional additives? What is the regulatory responsibility of each of the following agencies as regarding food—FDA, USDA, EPA, FTC? What is meant by "company town" at FDA?

2. What is the Delaney Clause? Why does food industry want to get rid of it? What foods are exempt from the Delaney Clause? Define Gras additives.

3. Does everything cause cancer? Fact sheet and an analysis of the bill S1442. I suggest that people who have been working on this do this panel. Discuss risk-benefit issue.

4. What are some policies and politics involved in color additives; DES, pesticides (you may want to bring in some things from *Circle of Poison* here).

5. What are some policies and politics involved in antibiotics in cattle, feed, nitrates, lead, mechanically-deboned meat?

6. Review the history of the FDA as to policies of the last four Commissioners and the present one. (I will give you material.)

Slideshow: "Food Technology"

Topic IX: Politics of National Nutritional Policy (Nov. 15 and 17)

Readings:

Mottern, Nicholas. *Inside the Governmental Community.* East-West Foundation, 1978

Hegsted, D. Mark, "Priorities in Nutrition in the U.S.," *JADA*, Vol. 71, pp. 9-13, July 1977

Hegsted, D. Mark, "U.S. Dietary Goals," *Family Economics Review* (Winter and Spring 1978)

Leveille, Gilbert A. "Establishing and Implementing Dietary Goals," *Food and Nut-rition News* 49 (Dec. 1977)

Hausman, Patricia. "The Dairy Lobby: Battling for America's Hearts and Minds," *Nutrition Action*, pp. 13-17, March 1981

Groves, Bob. "Looking Towards a Healthy Future in Fjord Country," *Nutrition Action*

"Block Upholds Dietary Guidelines," Consumer Nutrition Institute Newsletter, October 1, 1981, p. 6

"USDA Abolishes Nutrition Center in Reorganization," *CNI*, June 25, 1981

"Academy Gets Egg on Its Face," *Nutrition Action*, p. 10

Leveille, Gilbert A. *The American Diet—Congressional Hearings*, pp. 108-115

Mottern, Nick. "Dietary Goals Food Monitor," *Food Monitor*, March/April 1978, pp. 8-10

"The AMA and Nutrition," *Nutrition Action*, September 1980

Panels:

1. What was the Senate Select Committee? How permanent was it? What, in brief, were the original dietary goals. See page III of *The American Diet* by Gilbert Leveille. The original "Dietary Goals for the U.S."
2. Describe Norway's nutrition policy. What is its focus? Discuss differences and similarities between the two countries as to factors affecting food policy.
3. Contrast the two viewpoints about the dietary goals of Hegsted and Leveille. Read both articles by Hegsted and discuss briefly.
4. Discuss the effect of the dairy lobby on food policy in the U.S. See "The Dairy Lobby" by Hausman.
5. Describe the USDA-HHS Dietary Guidelines for Americans. Why are these still controversial? Who is supporting them at present? What things are left out of these guidelines? What was the role of the Human Nutrition Center in formulating these guidelines?
6. What appears to be the politics of Food and Nutrition Board of the National Academy of Science. (Not composition of the Board.)
7. Describe the role of the AMA in nutrition policy as regards to sugar, fat and additives.

Topic X: Politics of Nutrition Education (Nov. 22 and 29-Dec. 1 and 6)

Speaker: Suzanne Terry, Movement Toward a New Society—How to Effect Social Change.

Panel 1. Nutritionists
Readings:
"IFT Honors Theodore B. Labuza for Teaching," in Michigan State Newsletter
Harvard's Sugar Pushing Nutritionist by John L. Hess
Professors on the Take by Benjamin Rosenthal, Michael Jacobson and Mary Bohm
Junk Foods Talk by F.M. Clydesdale

1. What evidence is there that the nutrition and food science communities have fallen under the food industries' influence?
2. Discuss briefly each of the following as to who they are and their possible relationship with industry.
3. Define the Food and Nutrition Board. Is there evidence of conflict of interests?

Panel 2. Textbooks
Analyze some college textbooks in food and nutrition. Subjects to check out are additives, basic flour, white flour, sugar vs. honey, quality of food supply, infant feeding, etc.

Read: "School Daze" by Greg Moyer, *Nutrition Action*, p. 7, Sept. 1982

Panel 3. Nutrition Education in Public Schools
Readings:
"The Dairy Lobby: Battling for America's Hearts and Minds"
The Nutrition Education Gospel According to NDC
Editorial: Corporation in the Classroom by Sr. Valerie Heinonen R.U.
School Children Learn to Sell Pepsi
Walt Disney Filmstrips
"The Third Grade Has Been Brought To You," by Natalie Rothstein

1. Discuss the dairy council's curriculum for nutrition as to good and bad points.
2. What are some flaws with the use of the Basic Four Food Groups?
3. Discuss use of food industry materials in the public schools.

Panel 4. Consumer Groups
Readings:
"New Consumer Groups Confuse Public Debate," *CNI*, Vol. VIII, No. 44, Nov. 9, 1978
CSPI: "Ready for the Reagan Era," *CNI*, Vol. X, No. 49, Dec. 11, 1980
"What, Me Worry," by Peter Harnik, *Nutritional Action*, Feb. 1982
"Voodoo Science vs. Sour Grapes," p. 4, *CNI*, Vol. XII, #9, March 4, 1982

1. Discuss the membership, projects and goals of CSPI.
2. Discuss the American Council on Science and Health.
3. Discuss briefly the Calorie Control Council.

Panel 5. Society of Nutrition Education
Readings:
SNE Considers "Access to Food" from *CNI*, Vol. XI, No. 35, Sept. 3, 1981, p. 4, and 5
"Society for Nutrition Education: Ten Years Old and Troubled," from *Nutrition Action*, pp. 6-10, July 1979

Contrast some of the changes from 1979 to 1981 in this professional society.

Constructive Alternatives to Destructive Weaponry

William Eisinger/Dennis Gordon/Richard Pefley   *Fall 1983*
Biology/Political Science/Engineering/University of Santa Clara/
Santa Clara, CA 95053

This course re-evaluates the traditional reliance on weapons of destruction and addresses the possibility of using our leadership in food production, high technology and alternative sources of energy to influence international relations.

To assess the need for weapons, it is important to understand the nature of power in the international system. The relative decline in the utility of military instruments of power has increased the importance of economic interdependence as an aspect of national influence. Creative use of economic and technological resources to further the developmental goals of other nations can provide an alternative to a large U.S. weapons industry, and replace our present role abroad with a more positive influence and image.

Our present technology has evolved to meet the needs of our wealthy society and seemingly limitless natural resources. Not surprisingly, most attempts to directly transplant this technology into developing countries has not been successful. An important challenge for the future will be matching technology to the resources, culture and needs of each individual developing country.

The agricultural system in the United States is the most productive in the world. The infusion of technology during the past 50 years has greatly increased the productivity, but American agriculture has become very energy-intensive. The emerging biotechnology industry promises a true revolution in agriculture. High yields of high quality foods could be produced at low cost and with minimal damage to the environment. If this kind of biotechnology could be applied to Third World countries, many might be able to meet the food needs of their people. America's technological and economic resources could thus be used as a constructive alternative to weaponry in international diplomacy.

Texts

Maarten J. Chrispeels and David Sadava, *Plants, Food, and People*. San Francisco: W.H. Freeman, 1977.

James A. Stegenga and W. Andrew Axline, *The Global Community*, 2nd ed. New York: Harper & Row, 1982.

Project Mechanics

The purpose of a class project is to achieve, through interdisciplinary effort, a balanced report on an issue relating to constructive alternatives to atomic war.

Credit for the project will consist of two parts: a weekly progress statement and a final report. The progress statements are due on Fridays and the authorship is to be rotated among the group members. Each statement is worth 3% of the project grade. The report is worth the balance.

Possible Project Topics

Professor Eisinger

1. Select a country which has a problem feeding its people. Propose a "package" to improve the nutrition of the people based on what new crop could be grown — consider:
    a. Agricultural aspects like climate, soil type, rain fall, etc.
    b. Nutritional needs of people like, "Are there just certain amino acids lacking or vitamines, etc.?"
    c. Cultural aspects like religious restrictions on diet, traditional methods of food preparation which might have to be changed, etc.
    d. Mechanical problems like the kinds of equipment and skills that the new crop might require, etc.
    e. Economic aspects like "How would this new crop affect the production and sales of current crops? Might excess production of the new crop disrupt the agricultural economies of neighboring countries, etc.?"
    f. Political problems like "If you operate through the existing government, might that result in a political imbalance which could result in rivalry — the group with the food would have the power over the peasants?"
    g. Any other aspect you might like to consider.
2. I do not expect one group to cover all aspects in detail. As a group select those aspects of greatest interest and deal with them in depth. However, I do want a complete "package" which at least considers each of the above problems.
3. Examine the Green Revolution — what is it, how was it brought about, what good did it do, what harm did it do, how might it be improved in the future?
4. What are the real facts on the interrelationship between diet and human behavior? I would like to see social science majors give this evidence a critical evaluation. If the reports in the literature are correct, the long term political and social consequences could be monumental.
5. What really happened in Third World countries where infant formulas were introduced as a substitute for breast feeding? Investigate all aspects and points of view.

Professor Gordon

1. Many important technological developments have been the result of military related research. What sorts of political, economic, and technological changes would be required to maintain U.S. competitiveness in technological innovation if the need for weapons research was diminished by meaningful arms control agreements?
2. It is commonly assumed that the economy of the Santa Clara valley would suffer significantly should a peace race replace the present arms race. Through a survey of one or more local firms, determine the attitudes of labor and management towards arms control. To what extent are local firms prepared for a transition to non-weapons related products and projects?
3. Many Third World nations spend a high proportion of their G.N.P. on imported arms. Are such expenditures beneficial for their economic development? What are the internal and external pressures which encourage arms purchases in the Third

World? Is it politically realistic to expect Third World leaders to break dependency on imported weapons and technology?

4. Many argue that the United States should use its "commodity power" as a weapon in the international arena. What is the agricultural and economic basis of commodity power? Are there political and/or technological barriers to its use as a policy instrument in lieu of destructive weapons?

Professor Pefley

1. Examine the natural gas pipeline from Siberia to Western Europe in the context of constructive alternatives to war. How do the Russians view it, the Europeans, the Americans and the rest of the world?
2. Determine the amount of energy required to produce a megaton hydrogen bomb and how much energy must be used to repair the damage it will cause if burst strategically over a city. Then compare that energy if it were used for constructive alternatives.
3. Consider the question: Could the United States restore its liquid energy independence and, if so, what would be the risks and benefits in a war related sense?
4. Can nationalistic policies result in food being used as fuel to the economic benefit of the country? If there are such examples, examine a selected example as to its potential for reducing or increase risk of war.

Course Outline

I. An Analysis of Power—Dr. Gordon, Political Science
A. Power in the International System
  1. Definitions of Power
    a. Natural Sources of Power
    b. Social and Psychological Components of Power
    c. Synthetic Components of Power
  Readings: Stegenga & Axline, Chapter 1, "The State in Global Politics."

B. Power and the Nuclear Arms Race
  Readings: Stegenga & Axline, Chapter 3, "International Tensions."

II. Applications of Technology to Agriculture—Dr. Eisinger, Biology
A. Introduction
  Reading: Chrispeels and Sadava, Chapter 1, "The Problem."

B. Human Nutrition
  Reading: Chrispeels and Sadava, Chapters 2, "Human Nutrition" and Chapter 3, "Plants as a Source of Food."

C. Agricultural Practices
  Readings: Chrispeels and Sadava, Chapter 7, "Modern Agricultural Practices."

D. Pest Control
  Readings: Chrispeels and Sadava, Chapter 8, "Strategies for Pest Control."

E. Plant Breeding
  Readings: Chapters 9, "Plant Breeding and the Green Revolution" and Chapter 10, "The Impact of the Green Revolution."

F. Recombinant DNA

G. Future Foods
   Readings: Chrispeels and Sadava, Chapter 11, "Alternative Sources of Food" and Chapter 12, "Conclusion: The Prospects."

III. An Analysis of Energy—Dr. Pefley, Engineering
A. Energy, its basic principles and world energy resources

B. Energy use for destructive purposes—historic and present
   Reading: Jonathan Schell, *The Fate of the Earth*, Chapter 1, "A Republic of Insects and Grass."

C. Energy use for constructive purposes—historic and present

D. Alternative energy resources

E. Planning potential for future use of alternate energy resources for constructive alternatives to weapons

IV. The Political Economy of Alternatives to Weaponry—Dr. Gordon
A. Political Economy of the Arms Race
   1. Military Spending
      Reading: Stegenga and Axline, Chapter 2, "The International System."

   2. Arms Sales
      Reading: Joseph S. Nye, "Nuclear Weapons Proliferation: Too Late to Stop It?" and "Arming the World," *Time* (Oct. 26, 1981).

   3. Conversion to Peaceful Industry

B. Political Economy of Development
   1. Global Economic Issues
      Reading: Allan F. Matthews, "World North-South Issues at the Cancun Conference," and "Third World Development: A U.S. Perspective," *The Interdependent* (July 1981).

   2. Alternate Models of Development: The Basic Needs Approach
      Reading: Dennis R. Gordon, "The Andean Auto Program and Peruvian Development," *Journal of Developing Areas*, (Jan. 1982).

Alternate Readings for Gordon
James Fallows, *National Defense*. New York: Vintage Books, 1981.
Richard Barnet, *Real Security: Restoring American Power in a Dangerous Decade*. New York: Touchstone Books, 1981.
Andrew J. Pierre, *The Global Politics of Arms Sales*. Princeton: Princeton University Press, 1982.
George McRobie, *Small is Possible*. New York: Harper and Row, 1981.
Barbara Ward, *Progress for a Small Planet*. New York: W.W. Norton, 1982.
Mahbub ul Haq, *The Poverty Curtain: Choices for the Third World*. New York: Columbia University Press, 1976.

Selected References for Energy Discussions
Palmer Putnam, *Energy in the Future*. New York: D. Van Nostrand Co., 1953.
Lon C. Ruedisili and Morris W. Firebaugh, *Perspectives on Energy*. New York: Oxford University Press, 1975.
Morris West, *The Clowns of God*. New York, Bantam Books, 1982.

Starvation: A Sociological Analysis

Richard Wells   *Spring 1983*
Sociology 292/University of South Alabama/Mobile, AL 36688

We will examine the extent of hunger, malnutrition and starvation in the United States and abroad. The past, present, and future world food supply will be considered in terms of the social factors that determine food production and distribution. Both the sociological causes and consequences of hunger will be identified. Political, economic, religious, historical, geographic, and other dimensions of hunger will be reviewed. In sum, our major objective for this course is to develop a general sociological perspective of world hunger.

Outline of Lecture

I. How easily and for how long can we digest the following facts?
A. Before we finish our discussion almost 1,000 people will have died of starvation or hunger-related illness.
B. For at least half a billion people in the "mis"-developed countries, hunger and malnutrition are daily facts.
C. Other facts provided throughout the course.

II. Statement of specific problem:
There are gross inequities in the per capita consumption of food. Consequently, the rates of hunger, malnutrition and starvation vary tremendously from country to country.

III. Hunger, Malnutrition and Starvation: What type of problems?
A. Personal problems?
Personal problems are characteristics of individuals which are consequences of the individual's personality structures. Solutions to this type of problem are within one's personal orbit.
B. Social problems?
Social problems are related to conditions of an institution, community, society or world system which have negative effects on large numbers of people. Solutions to these types of problems are primarily beyond one's personal orbit. Collective action is needed to resolve a social problem.
C. Hunger, malnutrition and starvation are best considered as social problems.
D. What type of social problem—micro or macro—are hunger, malnutrition and starvation?
   1. Micro social problems are those problems arising from the actions of large numbers of individuals which are considered troublesome and troubled behavior. That is to say, millions of people are believed to be somewhat voluntarily engaging in behavior that adversely affects other people and/or is at times self-destructive. Criminal behavior, suicide, and drug abuse are examples of micro social problems.

2. Macro social problems are those problems rooted in social organizations such as communities, societies and world systems. That is, certain economic, social and technological arrangements that have come to prevail say in a given society such as the United States are problematic because these fundamental organizational features harm millions of people. Concentration of power, gross economic inequities, and militarism are examples of macro social problems.

E. Hunger, malnutrition and starvation as macro social problems for whom?
1. "Mis"-developed countries?
2. Dominant countries?
3. The world system?

IV. World Systems and National Autonomy: How "together" is today's world?

A. World systems?
A world system consists of a set of interconnected societies. The state of being of each of these societies depends to some extent on its relative position in the world system, which has strong, middling and weak members.

B. World system characteristics:
A world system is characterized by three interdependent classes or groups of societies united by common economic interests as well as similar cultural values, beliefs, etc. The classes that make up a world system are as follows:
1. Core societies (upper class) or economically diversified, rich, powerful societies that are relatively independent of outside control. The United States, United Kingdom, Canada, Australia and France are some of the members of this class.
2. Semi-peripheral societies (middle class) or societies in the mist of industrializing and diversifying their economies. This class of societies is relatively weaker than the core or upper class societies, but they are not as subject to outside control as are the lowest class of societies. Saudi Arabia, Brazil, Turkey, Egypt and India are some of the members of this class.
3. Peripheral societies (lower class)—economically overspecialized, relatively poor and weak societies—are subject to manipulation or direct control. Guatemala, Biafra, Cambodia and South Korea are some of the members of this class.

C. Interdependence is the basic characteristic of a world system.

D. Put simply, a world system is designed so as to ensure the continual existence of winners and losers.

V. World Systems and Macro Social Problems

A. Hunger, malnutrition and starvation are macro social problems basically attributable to the structure of the world system. From this perspective:
1. Hunger, malnutrition and starvation of the distant past were macro social problems basically traceable to the organizational features of relatively autonomous tribes and countries.
2. As modern macro social problems, hunger, malnutrition and starvation are traceable to the organizational features of individual societies as well as the prevailing world systems.

B. Individual guilt and macro social problems: Social problems, especially macro level social problems, will not yield to simplistic individual, psychological and/or genetic level theories nor "solutions." Such approaches often eradicate individuals' guilt, while hunger, malnutrition and starvation not only persist but continue to rise.

C. What is needed to resolve macro social problems? Major reform or revolution of the existing capitalist world system and its major competitor—a (potential) communist world system—are needed.

VI. The Consideration of Existing Policy Suggestions:

Overcoming World Hunger: The Challenge Ahead
(Excerpts from the Report of the Presidential Commission
on World Hunger: Abridged Version,
Washington, DC: Government Printing Office, 1980)

Alleviating Hunger in the Short Run

The short-term goal of alleviating the hunger of those who are poor is sometimes criticized as attacking the symptom rather than the disease. Yet it would be arrogant and unfair to talk only of preventing hunger in the future and to ignore the pain of those who suffer now. Taking immediate action to alleviate hunger even before poverty is eradicated involves four areas:

Ensuring that poor people are not hungry

Food suplements and income supplements (on the model of the U.S. food stamp program, which enables participants to stretch their food dollars) can help the poor to obtain both more food and more nutritious food.

Assuring that infants and children are adequately nourished

Malnutrition takes its greatest toll among infants and young children. For those who do not die from it, the adverse effects of malnutrition are lifelong. Nutrition programs directed at pregnant and nursing women and pre-school children can help to ensure that malnutrition will not impair the lives of yet another generation.

Eliminating diseases resulting from specific nutritional deficiencies

Nutritional deficiencies currently devastate millions through such diseases as blindness, goitre, and anemia. These can be prevented in the near term—long before poverty is eliminated—through some very specific health and nutrition programs. Such programs can be implemented relatively quickly and inexpensively.

Providing disaster relief

Effective international relief efforts undertaken in response to wars, famine, earthquakes, and other natural and man-made disasters can and do prevent mass starvation. To be effective, however, such efforts require food reserves, fast transport, efficient administration, and the cooperation by and with local authorities.

Building A World Without Hunger

In the long run, hunger will be eliminated only when the poor countries have the opportunity to develop and when all countries work together to ensure that global food supplies are large enough to meet global needs. Building a world without hunger requires action toward four goals.

Equitable economic growth

Even if the poorest countries achieve the highest economic growth rates possible between now and the year 2000, at least 470 million people will still be living in the conditions of stark poverty. Yet this figure could be reduced by at least 120 million (about the population of Japan) if these countries start increasing the share of income going to their poorest people. This would require policies in these countries specifically designed to meet the "basic human needs" of the poorest people by redirecting income from the rich to the poor.

Redistributing existing wealth

Redistributing existing wealth is as important as redistributing income resulting from new growth. Redistribution, however, requires changes in existing economic and political systems. (Examples of such changes are land reform and the creation of new jobs through expanded public services.) Because these actions are so politically difficult, such changes require extraordinary commitment from local leaders. Political, financial and technical support from the more developed countries can assist local governments to make the required changes.

Producing enough food

By the year 2000, the world will have at least six billion people, and nearly 8 out of every 10 of them will live in the developing world. The world has the physical capacity to grow enough food to feed all these people. Yet more food must be grown in the developing countries themselves. Since the poorest countries cannot afford to import all the food they need to feed their populations—and because the need for increased production is greatest in these countries—it is vital that they achieve significant increases in food production. This will require both reform in domestic agricultural policies and supportive international structures.

Why Should The United States Care About World Hunger?

...failure to assure adequate world food supplies will have far more serious global implications for the future than even the current energy crisis.

Most (but not all) of the world's hungry people live outside the borders of the United States. They do not vote in our elections or participate in our economy. Many of us may never have direct contact with poor and hungry people overseas. While it is clear that we, in the United States, have a moral obligation and special capability to work actively and vigorously toward eliminating world hunger wherever it exists, it is also in our own national interest to do so. In view of the combined humanitarian, political and economic interests at stake, the major recommendation of the Presidential Commission on World Hunger is that the United States make the elimination of hunger the primary focus of its relationships with the developing countries, beginning with the decade of the 1980s. Living up to this commitment, however, will not be easy. It will require action in all of the areas related to the world hunger problem.

Moral Obligation and Responsibility

The right to food is the most basic right of all. If we are truly committed to the cause of human rights, we must exercise initiative and leadership and work to eliminate world hunger. The United States has long been committed in rhetoric—if not always in its actions—to eliminating hunger both in this country and in other places. Following through on past promises will be the strongest possible proof of our renewed dedication to human rights.

Moreover, as the most powerful actor in the world's increasingly interdependent food system, the United States is in a particularly good position to take the lead.

More than half the grain that crosses international borders has been harvested in the United States. U.S. grain reserves are the largest in the world, and the United States has high levels of agricultural productivity, advanced technologies, and extraordinary market power—all of which confer responsibility to act in ways that will have beneficial, rather than detrimental, effects on the world's hungry.

U.S. Economic Self-Interest and National Security

A vigorous attack on the world hunger problem will have a positive effect on both the national security and the continued economic vitality of the United States.

Hunger is only one of a number of global issues which aggravate relationships between the developed and the developing countries. Like widespread hunger, the growing scarcity of energy and other non-renewable resources, environmental hazards, the pollution of the seas, and international terrorism are all global problems that threaten national security as much as military confrontation. The developed and developing countries have been hostile to and suspicious of one another during various global conferences held in recent years. The developing countries have looked at developed-country proposals for regulation in these areas as simply new attempts to keep the poor countries from improving their economic situations. The United States and the other developed countries, on the other hand, have been afraid that if they "give in" to demands by the developing countries for a greater voice in international decisions they will lose too much.

Unless we begin to find ways of resolving these tensions, we face the likelihood of increasing chaos and belligerence from large segments of the world. Because hunger offers the most powerful point for attacking the many problems related to poverty and underdevelopment—and because the United States is in an excellent position to provide leadership in solving the hunger problem—U.S. action could contribute greatly to solving the current deadlock between the two economically diverse groups of countries. The developing countries are likely to respond positively to the issues of importance to the United States, if we respond quickly and cooperatively on this issue of critical importance to them.

The U.S. economy will also benefit from a concerted attack on worldwide hunger. It is more and more evident that for the international economic system to be healthy and growing, all countries must be able to buy and sell products. In order to buy American products, other countries must be able to earn needed foreign exchange by selling their own products. The more rapidly the agricultural and industrial sectors of the now-poor countries develop, the sooner they will be able to participate fully in international markets.

Some people fear that if the economies of other countries grow, American farmers and industry workers will lose their jobs because consumers in the United States and elsewhere will buy imports rather than equivalent American products. There will be some short-term costs. But over the long term, if other countries can produce particular goods more cheaply than the United States, Americans will benefit. It will dampen inflation by making low-cost goods available and will ensure that other countries are able to purchase those products in which the United States is more competitive.

American farmers will continue to benefit even when other countries greatly increase their own agricultural productive capacity. The United States depends on world markets to maintain its strong farm economy. American farmers export two-thirds of their wheat, half their rice and soybeans, and a quarter of their corn and other coarse grains. In fact, even though farm products represent only 3 percent of the country's GNP, they represent nearly 25 percent of U.S. exports. Many of these products are purchased by the developing countries. Studies show that these countries will continue to import increasing amounts of food (because of population growth as well as changing food consumption patterns), even as they increase their own agricultural output.

Neither the United States nor the rest of the world can afford another food crisis like that of 1972-74. But if food production is not improved in the world as a whole, and in the poor countries in particular, another food shortage could have serious consequences for all countries and could be more devastating than the current energy crisis. In the developed countries, it could cause prices to skyrocket. In the poor countries, it could push millions more to the brink of starvation.

The Need for Action
Eliminating at least the very worst aspects of hunger by the year 2000 is possible—if the United States and others make it a major policy objective. We have the technical know-how and the resources to do so. What we lack is the political will to act upon this commitment with sufficient vigor.

Eliminating hunger will not be an easy task, however. Nor will it be accomplished just by growing more food on American farms to ship overseas. In the short run, more foreign aid and more food are needed to keep the poor from starvation and to make sure that children born today do not suffer life-long harm from early malnutrition. But these are palliatives to keep the problem from getting worse. They are not genuine, long-lasting solutions.

Over the longer term, hunger can be eliminated only by eliminating its causes— poverty and insecure food supplies. This requires that the poor countries increase agricultural productivity and develop in ways that allow them to distribute the gains from development equitably throughout the population. Achieving such equitable and self-reliant development is to a large extent the task of the poor countries themselves. But they cannot do it alone. The actions of the rich countries—and of the United States in particular—have important effects on whether and how well these countries develop.

How much we export to and import from the developing countries; what kinds of things we export and import; what kinds of investments our large corporations make and how much return they get from those investments; and how much grain we, the "breadbasket of the world," are willing to store for hard times—all of these can have either a positive or a negative effect on the world's hungry. What the U.S. Government and private industry do (or don't do) will greatly affect the lives of millions of people in the poor countries.

What You Can Do As A Concerned Citizen
Inform yourself about world hunger because hunger affects the quality of life and security of the United States, your community and your family. Become knowledgeable about the issues of hunger at home and abroad.

Join a community group that is doing something about hunger at home or abroad such as a neighborhood organization, a civic group, a church group, or an advocacy group for a specific program such as School Lunch. Who's Involved in Hunger is available for purchase from World Hunger Education Service, 2000 P St., NW, Washington, DC 20036.

Form a group for study or action if none exists in your community. Consult *Who's Involved in Hunger* for groups who can provide information on how to set up a study or action organization.

Find out what resources our library has on world hunger and ideas about how to end it. Find out what resources your school libraries have for different ages. Recommend additional resources.

Ask your school officials to include programs on world hunger in their own professional meetings and in assemblies for students. Ask that world hunger issues be included in the school curriculum.

Course Books

Loretta Schwartz-Nobel, *Starving in the Shadow of Plenty*, New York: G.P. Putnam's Sons, 1981. (Required)

Richard J. Barnet, *The Lean Years: Politics in the Age of Scarcity*, New York: Simon and Schuster, 1980. (Required)

Dan Morgan, *Merchants of Grain*, New York: Penguin Books, 1979. (Optional)

Frances Moore Lappé, *Diet For a Small Planet*, New York: Ballantine Books, 1975. (Optional)

Jack A. Nelson, *Hunger for Justice: The Politics of Food and Faith*, Maryknoll, New York: Orbis Books, 1980. (Required)

Pitirim A. Sorokin, *Hunger as a Factor in Human Affairs*, Gainsville, Florida: Univ. Press of Florida, 1975. (Required)

Tentative Reading Schedule and Seminar Topics

January 12 — I. Educational Philosophy and Course Expectations
A. Course syllabus
B. Begin reading Schwartz-Nobel

January 14 — II. A Challenge for Sociologists
A. "The Role of Sociology in Ending World Hunger" by Earl Babbie, pp. 4-8 in *The Humanist Sociologist*, vol. 6, no. 4.
B. "What Americans Think About Hunger" by James B. Chapin, pp. 18-19 in *Food Monitor*, May/June 1980.

January 19-21 — III. Types of Hunger
A. Five types of hunger: a handout
B. *Starving in the Shadow of Plenty*, pp. 11-104.
C. "Famine: Problems in Definition" by William A. Dando, pp. 57-67 in *The Geography of Famine*.
D. "Nutrition and Staple Foods" by Dando, pp. 35-53 in *The Geography of Famine*.

January 26-February 9 — IV. Extent of Hunger and World Food Production: Past, Present and Future
A. "The Nature and Extent of World Hunger," pp. 15-18 in *Overcoming World Hunger: Report of the Presidential Commission on World Hunger* (1980).
B. "Domestic Hunger and Malnutrition: Overcoming Hunger at Home" pp. 153-169 in *Overcoming World Hunger* (1980).
C. "What? Hunger In My Town?" by Jeri Barr, pp. 5-7 in *Food Monitor*, Jan./Feb. 1979.
D. *Hunger U.S.A.* report of CBIHM, pp. 7-10.

E. "The Difficulty of Documenting Hunger and Malnutrition in the United States" in *Hunger U.S.A.*, pp. 39-48.

F. "The Threat of Increasing Hunger" by Schwartz-Nobel, pp. 105-195 in *Starving in the Shadow of Plenty*.

G. *The Geometry of Famine* by William A. Dando, Chapter 1, 2, and 5.
   a. "Parameters for Food Production" (Chapter 1)
   b. "Crops and Man" (Chapter 2)
   c. "Famine Regions and Types" (Chapter 5)

H. "The Struggle Over Hunger: Social and Ecological Dimensions" by Humphrey and Buttel, pp. 195-219 in *Environment, Energy, and Society* (1982)

February 11-March 4 — V. The Economics of Hunger

A. "The Bottle Baby Scandal: Milking the Third World for All Its Worth" by Barbara Barson, pp. 238-246 in *The Feeding Web*.

B. "Engines of Development" by Barnet and Muller, pp. 234-237 in *The Feeding Web*.

C. "Imperialism and Hunger" by Alexander Liagor, pp. 135-166 in *People First: An Introduction to Social Problems* (1982).

D. "The Economics of Hunger" and "Hunger Today" by Jack A. Nelson, pp. 10-55 in *Hunger for Justice* (1980).

E. *Merchants of Grain* by Dan Morgan. Introduction, pp. 13-24; "Glenas, Inc., of Panama," pp. 25-52.

F. "When More Food Means More Hunger" by Lappé and Collins, pp. 90-93 in *The Futurist*, (April, 1977).

G. *Starving in the Shadow of Plenty*, pp. 181-236.

March 16-25 — VI. The Politics of Hunger

A. "The Politics of Hunger" by Ron Freund, pp. 38-39 in *Progressive* (Dec., 1979).

B. "Hunger, Politics and Security" by Thomas W. Wilson, pp. 1-12 in *Technical Papers: Presidential Commission on World Hunger* (1980).

C. "The Food Weapon" by Dan Morgan, pp. 334-365 in *Merchants of Grain* (1975).

D. "The Diplomatic Crop" by Dan Morgan, pp. 366-404 in *Merchants of Grain* (1975).

E. "Food: Sowers, Reapers, Ranchers and Eaters" by Richard Barnet, pp. 151-190 in *The Lean Years: Politics in the Age of Scarcity*.

F. *Hunger for Justice*, pp. 56-131.

March 30-April 6 — VII. Hunger, Religion and Morality

A. *Hunger for Justice*, pp. 1-9 and 132-208.

B. "Introduction" by William Aiken and Hugh LaFollette, pp. 1-10 in *World Hunger and Moral Obligation*.

C. "Lifeboat Ethics: The Case Against Helping the Poor" by Garrett Hardin, pp. 11-21 in *World Hunger and Moral Obligation*.

D. "The Right to Be Saved From Starvation" by William Aiken, pp. 85-102 in *World Hunger and Moral Obligation*.

E. "Give if it Helps But Not if it Hurts" by Joseph Fletcher, pp. 103-114 in *World Hunger and Moral Obligation*.

April 8-22 — VIII. General Explanations for Hunger

A. "Rich Man, Poor Man: Who's the Thief?" by Susan George, pp. 3-27 in *How the Other Half Dies: The Real Reasons for World Hunger* (1977).

B. "The Causes of Hunger" pp. 19-28 in *Overcoming World Hunger* report of the

Presidential Commission on World Hunger (1980).

C. "Conflicting Interpretations of the Contemporary World Food Problems" by William A. Dando, pp. 95-110 in *The Geography of Famine* (1980).

D. "Population Growth and World Hunger" by Lawrence R. Kegan, pp. 35-67 in *Technical Papers: Presidential Commission on World Hunger* (1980).

E. "World Hunger: Its Causes, Its Alleviation" by Martin McLaughlin, pp. 13-24 in *Technical Papers: Presidential Commission on World Hunger* (1980).

F. "On the Causes and Solution to the Problem of World Hunger and Starvation" by Shirley Ceresto, pp. 33-52 in the *Insurgent Sociologist* (1977:7,3).

G. "Material Determinants of the World Food Crisis" by Alain de Janvry, pp. 3-26 in the *Berkeley Journal of Sociology* (1976- 77, 21).

H. "Silent Violence: Famine and Inequality" by Pierre Spitz, pp. 867-892 in *International Social Science Journal* (1978/30/4).

April 27—IX. Hunger Solutions

A. "World Hunger: Putting Development Ethics to the Test" by Denis Goulet, pp. 3-9 in *Sociological Inquiry* (1975/45/4).

B. "Population and Hunger: Whose Problems Are the World's Hungry?" by Marjorie Kensell, a paper printed at the Illinois Sociological Association Meetings (1981).

C. "Food First" by Lappé and Collins, pp. 101-108 as reprinted in *The Feeding Web* (1978).

E. "Major Findings and Conclusions" pp. 1-5 in *The Global 2000 Report to the President of the U.S.* (1980).

May 2,—X. Final Exam Due

The final exam will be a 1,000-1,200 word book review and critique of Pitirim A. Sorokin's *Hunger as a Factor in Human Affairs*, pp. 3-319.

World Food Politics

William Alexander   *Fall 1983*
Political Science 371/California Polytechnic State University/
San Luis Obispo, CA 93407

We have recently discovered that there are no natural or physical reasons why all men, women, and children in the world cannot have enough food to eat. At the same time, we find that the adequate feeding of people constitutes a goal of nearly universal acceptability. Whether a half billion humans may have sufficient food in any year is, however, a political choice made by another 4 billion humans who do have sufficient food.

The course in *World Food Politics* explains and demonstrates the political processes which Americans can use to support the legitimate desires of the half billion hungry to feed themselves. Such political support may begin by refraining from those actions which prevent the hungry poor from feeding themselves, it will continue to the restraint of those who limit the opportunity of the hungry to feed themselves, and may lead to positive assistance in those cases where forebearance and restraint have failed.

World food politics will be studied in three interacting parts. First, knowledge of the cultural, political and resource situation within the several LDCs as it applies to the food available to the poor. Second, how the concern and good will of Americans may be effectively applied to these conditions, and how to find the most effective actions. Third, knowledge about the existing political structures within the U.S. with particular attention to the many interest and pressure groups active in the field of world hunger—how they function and how the American citizen can use them in effective political actions benefiting the hungry poor in the LDCs.

The student who completes this course of study will be able to explain and demonstrate the political processes Americans may use to support and maintain conditions which will allow the hungry poor of the world to feed themselves.

Text and References

William W. Murdoch, *The Poverty of Nations: The Political Economy of Hunger and Population* (Johns Hopkins University Press, 1980)

Dudley Kirk and Ellen Eliason, Editors, *Food and People* (Boyd and Fraser, 1982)

Jack A. Nelson, *Hunger for Justice: The Politics of Food and Faith* (Orbis, 1980)

Elaine M. Murphy, *World Population: Toward the Next Century* (Population Reference Bureau, 1981)

Bruce F. Johnson and William C. Clark, *Redesigning Rural Development: A Strategic Perspective* (Johns Hopkins University Press, 1982)

Roland Bunch, *Two Ears of Corn: A Guide to People-Centered Agricultural Improvement* (World Neighbors, 1982)

Cheryl Christensen, *The Right to Food: How to Guarantee* (World Policy Institute, 1978)

Jeffery M. Berry, *Lobbying for the People* (Princeton University Press, 1977)

Linda Worthington, *Who's Involved in Hunger: An Organization Guide* (World Hunger Education Service, 1982)

Frances Moore Lappé, Joseph Collins and David Kenley, *Aid as Obstacle: Twenty Questions about our Foreign Aid and the Hungry* (Institute for Food and Development Policy, 1980)

A.I.D. Policy Papers on *Food and Agricultural Development, Nutrition, and Private and Voluntary Organizations* (Bureau for Program and Policy Coordination, U.S. Agency for International Development, 1982)

An enormous variety of other materials are used in the preparation of individually designed term papers.

Minimum Student Materials Required
Assigned texts, notebooks and blue books.

Minimun Facilities Required
Classroom with blackboard, maps, and audio-visual equipment.

Expanded Description of Content and Method of Instruction
A. There are three topics essential for the understanding of World Food Politics which cannot be pursued in detail within a 3-unit course.
 1. The cultural and philosophical roots of the belief that food is a preeminent human right.
 2. The science and technology of effective methods for production, distribution, and utilization of food by the world's hungry poor.
 3. The current distribution of food and food producing resources among the various nations of the world and the current systems of control of food and food producing resources within the various LDCs.
 Our teaching of World Food Politics will assume that our students have some appreciation of these topics: only a brief review can be included.

B. In recent years there has developed a huge body of scientific knowledge on the subject of population stabilization. Familiarity with this knowledge cannot be assumed and a study of this field must be included with an emphasis on those factors which appear to cause fertility decline, i.e., equity factors, changing women's roles, family planning, and anti-fertility incentives. The connections between the availability of adequate food and fertility decline will be especially noted.

C. Based on the above knowledge, a self-reliant, food-first policy will be studied. This policy in its barest form may be stated as: Every human being on earth should have sufficient control over some of the earth's resources so that he (or she) can produce (or provide) adequate nutrition for self and personal dependents.

D. Central to an effective food-first policy is support of the self-reliant activities of the poor in the LDCs. These activities show where external support can be applied with greatest effect to increase food productivity, facilitate food distribution, improve food utilization, and decrease food demand distribution, improve food utilization, and decrease food demand through population stabilization. Study of these self-reliant activities will be included, i.e., organizational work, educational programs, government support functions, and the support activities of private voluntary organizations.

E. The essential political process to be taught in World Food Politics is the process which connects each responsible citizen in America to those conditions which may make it possible for the hungry poor to feed themselves on a permanent basis. This will be taught in terms of the political network of national and international institutions, both public and private, which directly and indirectly influence the conditions under which the hungry poor may become food self-reliant. These institutions will include education and research groups, political advocacy groups, the U.S. and other MDC governments, international governmental institutions, international commercial institutions, governments of LDCs, and private voluntary organizations.

F. The methods of instruction are adapted to the subject matter, the materials available, and to the students. The subject of world food politics is expanding very rapidly with a new book or major article published each week. New material from authoritative sources will be introduced as soon as available. In addition there are some very good instructional films available. These films fill in visual images needed to support comprehension of the written material. They are particularly useful as an aid to the understanding of food production and consumption within the cultures of the hungry poor of the LDCs. The student will be given lectures, assignments, and quizzes which cause him to locate himself within the larger political processes which define the conditions under which the hungry poor are permitted to produce their own food. The method of instruction assumes that as a responsible citizen, each student wants to alleviate the misery of the hungry poor and shows him how to implement that object.

Global Issues

Glenn Mitchell (Coordinator)/Ollie Ahrens
Virginia McKinley/Bill Mosher   *Term III, Fall 1982*
Social Studies 110/Warren Wilson College/Swannanoa, NC 28778

This is a synoptics core course designed to integrate our understanding and analysis of contemporary world issues in the context of change. We will look at history, the modern world system and strategies for change, to understand the broad origins of today's problems, how they relate to each other, and what can be done to meet them as informed citizens.

Course Objectives

We will first examine the underlying issues of energy and population throughout history. Then we will examine the current problems of oil and natural resources, food production and the transnational control of the world economy. Food, poverty and world hunger will be taken as a case study. Given these problems we will then examine approaches toward solutions, through appropriate development at the local level, and peace through a new world order.

Methods

We will develop our understanding of these issues primarily through reading, discussion, and analysis of information on different aspects of the problems. This will involve writing and examination on course material and lectures, guest speakers, and films. The writing will include two, two-page typed critical papers over class readings, and a five-page typed research paper on any topic related to the course. At midterm you will hand in a typed thesis paragraph for the paper and a tentative bibliography. The research paper will be presented in class. The examination will include three quizzes over class reading, lectures and films, and three essay and short answer examinations over each third of the course.

Texts

R. Barnet, *The Lean Years*
C. Cipolla, *The Economic History of World Population*
F. Lappé and J. Collins, *Food First*
G. Mische and P. Mische, *Toward a Human World Order*
E. Schumacher, *Small is Beautiful*

Course Schedule

Week 1   1/17-21
A. Introduction: What are Global Issues?

B. Energy, Technology and Population: Agricultural and Industrial Societies
(What is the historical relation of population and energy in the two world technological revolutions? What is the present result of the demographic transition from agricultural to industrial societies?)

Reading: Cipolla: Preface and Chapters 1, 2, 4, 5, 6.
Films: "Powers of Ten," "Growth Dilemma," "Industrial Revolution in England" and "Population and the American Future."
Assignments: Friday quiz on readings and lecture, and handout on paper writing.

Week 2   1/24-28
C. The Organization of the Modern World System: Its Origins and the Present Control of Resources and the Environment
(What are the scarce resources of the world and what are the social economics and political issues of their control? What are the problems with limits to growth argument of the neo-Malthusians and what are the alternatives for a politics of survival?)

1. Energy and Minerals.
Reading: Barnet: Chapters 1, 2, 3, 4, 5.
Films: "Sharing Global Resources," "Energy for the 80's," "This River Must Live."
Assignments: Friday: Two page typed paper over Cipolla/Barnet on issue of energy, technology, population and control.

Week 3   1/31-2/4
2. Scarce Resources and The Global Factory—transnational division of labor, and the politics of survival and/or limits to growth
Reading: Barnet: 6, 7, 8, 9, 10, 11, notes and bibliography.
Films: "Song of the Canary," "South: Roots of the Urban Crisis."
Assignments: Friday: First examination, short answer and essay.

Week 4   2/7-11
D. Case Study of Food: Third World Poverty and World Hunger
(What are the myths of hunger and population as problems? What are the problems and how can they be met?)

1. The Development of Underdevelopment
Reading: Lappé and Collins: Chapters 1, 4, 8 (rec. 35).
Films: "Grain of Conscience," "A Day Without Sunshine."
Assignments: Monday: handout on research paper. Friday: quiz.

Week 5   2/14-18
2. Aid and/or Self Reliance
Reading: Lappé and Collins, Chapters 9, 10, Appendix A and B.
Films: "Rich and Poor," "Hope For Life," "Something for Everyone," "Nuclear Energy."
Assignments: Monday: Typed thesis paragraph and bibliography for research paper. Friday: Second examination.

Week 6   2/21-25
E. Approaches towards Solutions I: Local level development, appropriate technology and Buddhist economics
(What are the relations between modern world problems and the organization of technology in the Third World? In what way are appropriate or intermediate technology and Buddhist economics solutions? Are self sufficiency and decentralizing the system the same thing?)

Reading: Schumacher: Intro and Chapters I, 4 (rec. 1, 2, 3), II, 4, III 2 (rec. 1, 3, 4), IV 4, 5 (rec. 2), epilogue.

Films: "Manika Villages in Transition," "Man and Nature," "Juggernaut," "Tools of change: A.T."

Assignments: Friday: Two page typed paper on Schumacher.

Week 7   2/28-3/4
F. Approaches Towards Solutions II: Global Level Interdependence and Peace
(What is the "crisis of growth" and the issue of national security? What are alternative strategies for a new world order, and what is the role of religion and values?)

1. War and the International Order
Reading: Mische and Mische: Intro and chapters, 1, 3, 4, 7.

Films: "Essay on War," "Interviews with My Lai Vets."

Assignments: All week: presentation of research papers. Friday: quiz.

Week 8   3/7-11
2. Networks and Coalitions: Reorganizing Interdependence
Readings: Monday: Five page typed research paper due.

Friday: Final examination.

World Nutrition

Sondra King

Fall 1983

Department of Home Economics/Northern Illinois University/
DeKalb, IL 60115

Topics to be Covered

I. Malnutrition
A. Physiological impact—Film: "Hunger in America"
B. Mental and physical consequences—Slide set: Dr. Myron Winnick on Malnutrition & Development
C. Protein deficiency
D. Vitamin and mineral deficiencies—Slide set: Deficiency Diseases

II. Assessment
A. Community
B. Individual and family

III. What causes malnutrition?
A. Geographic and climatic factors—speakers from Dept. of Geography—Film: "Drought in Africa"
B. Economics and politics—speaker from Economics Dept.
C. Religious influences
D. Socio-cultural influences—Film: "What's to Eat"

IV. The impact of multinational business
A. The bottle feeding problem—Film: "Into the Mouths of Babes"
B. The price of the development miracle—speaker from Dept. of Management—Film: "Multinational Corporation"

V. Population Dynamics
A. Fertility
B. Morality

VI. Feeding a hungry world
A. Agricultural considerations—speaker from DeKalb Agriculture Research
B. Staple foods of the world
C. Unorthodox means of meeting food needs—Films: "Diet for a Small Planet;" "Food Revolution"

VII. Interventions
A. Education
B. International agencies—speaker & film from Peace Corps
C. Private agencies—speaker: returned missionary
D. Policy making—speaker: Bread for the World

Final Examination

Tests:

Throughout the semester, 2-3 exams will be announced to cover material on the various units. The Final Exam will be comprehensive.

Nutrition Niche:

In this project, each student will select a country and develop a paper concerning the unique problems and various factors which lead to the particular nutritional status of that country. It is expected that the student will explore all aspects of a country that relates to the nutritional well-being or lack thereof in their specific country.

Book Report:

A book of your choosing should be read with an awareness of how food or its absence affects the daily lives of the persons in the story. You may choose a novel set in another country or culture, or read a specific book on hunger or food problems. Dr. King has a number of books which you can check out for this purpose.

Outside readings:

As appropriate, outside readings will be assigned. Some are on reserve in the library. Abstracts will be required for some assignments, others will be made to increase your general awareness. Both kinds of assignments may be covered on tests.

The World Food Crisis

Frank Holmquist and Ray Coppinger   *Fall 1983*
School of Social Science 151/Hampshire College/Amherst, MA 91002

The course is intended to provide an interdisciplinary and historical look at food production and distribution at home (New England), the U.S. as a whole, and the Third World. Class time will be spent with a combination of lectures and discussion and will include guest speakers and three films. Evaluations for students will require three brief essays, one each in the natural and social sciences, with the third in either category. We will discuss possible paper themes in class.

Texts
Joe Belden et al., *Farm, Land, and Food Policies*
Wendell Berry, *The Unsettling of America*
Betsy Hartman and James Boyce, *Needless Hunger*
Michael Perelman, *Farming for Profit in a Hungry World*
Frances Moore Lappé and Joseph Collins, *Food First*
I. G. Simmons, *Biogeography: Natural and Cultural*

1. An Extended Introduction
—The Modern New England Farm
—Is There a World Food Crisis? Facts, Figures and Trends

Other General Books on the World Food Crisis
Sterling Wortman and Ralph Cummings, *To Food This World*, 1978
René Dumont and Nicolas Cohen, *The Growth of Hunger: A New Politics of Hunger*, 1980
Raymond Hopkins and Donald Puchala (eds.), *The Global Political Economy of Food*, 1978
Raymond Hopkins and Ross Talbot (eds.), *Food Politics and Agricultural Development*, 1979
Lester Brown, *The Twenty-Ninth Day: Accommodating Human Needs and Number to the Earth's Resources*, 1978.
Susan George, *Feeding the Few: Corporate Control of Food*, 1979
Susan George, *How the Other Half Dies: The Real Reasons for World Hunger*, 1976
The State of Food and Agriculture, FAO, 1977
World Development Report (World Bank Annual Report)
National Research Council, *World Food and Nutrition Study*, 1977 (esp. pp. 1-32)
Wassily Leontief et al., *The Future of the World Economy*, 1977 (esp. Chapter 9)
"Food and Agriculture" (Special issue) *Scientific American*, September, 1976
Global Food Assessment, 1980, USDA: Economics, Statistics and Cooperative Service, Foreign Agricultural Economic Report #159, 1980.

2. Agriculture in Antiquity
Required:
I. G. Simmons, *Biogeography: Natural and Cultural*

Other:
Mark Nathan Cohen, *The Food Crisis in Prehistory: Overpopulation and the Origins of Agriculture*, 1977

3. Evolution of U.S. Agriculture
—Export thrust and relation to foreign policy
—Populism and tensions of capitalist growth
—Rise and role of agribusiness
—Evolution of technology
—Energy dependence
—Ecological decline
—Biogeography

Required:
Wendell, Berry, *The Unsettling of America* (whole book)
Michael Perelman, *Farming for Profit in a Hungry World* (Parts I, II and III)
I. G. Simmons, *Biogeography: Natural and Cultural* (to be assigned)

Other:
Willard Cochrane, *The Development of American Agriculture: A Historical Analysis*, 1979
Willard Cochrane and Mary Ryan, *American Farm Policy: 1948-1973*, 1976
Mark Kramer, *Three Farms*, 1979
Dan Morgan, *Merchants of Grain*, 1979
Peter Barnes (eds.), *The People's Land: A Reader on Land Reform in the U.S.*, 1975
Grant McConnell, *The Decline of Agrarian Democracy*, 1953
Lawrence Goodwyn, *The Populist Moment: A Short History of the Agrarian Revolt in America*, 1978. Contains excellent bibliographical essay on populism
S. R. Eyre, *Vegetation and Soils: A World Picture*, 1968
John Shover, *First Majority—Last Minority: The Transforming of Rural Life in America*, 1976
John Shover, *Cornbelt Rebellion: The Farmer's Holiday Association*, 1965
Douglas North, *Growth and Welfare in the American Past*
William Appleman Williams, *The Contours of American History*, 1973
James Green, *Grass-Roots Socialism: Radical Movements in the Southwest: 1895-1943*, 1978.
Garin Burbank, *When Farmers Voted Red: The Gospel of Socialism in the Oklahoma Countryside, 1910-1924*, 1976
Michael Schwartz, *Radical Protest and Social Structure: The Southern Farmers Alliance and Cotton Tenancy, 1880-1890*, 1976
Leo McGee and Robert Boone, *The Black Rural Landowner—Endangered Species*, 1979
Developments in American Farming, Contains: M. R. Cooper et al., "Progress of Farm Mechanization," and Sherman Johnson, "Changes in American Farming," 1976
Wendell Berry, *The Unsettling of America: Culture and Agriculture*, 1977
Charles Schultz, *The Distribution of Farm Subsidies: Who Gets the Benefits?*, 1971
"The New Rural America" (special issue), *The Annals*, vol. 429, Jan., 1977
Ross Hume Hall, *Food for Nought: The Decline of Nutrition*, 1974
Jim Hightower, *Hard Tomatoes, Hard Times*, 1973
Jim Hightower, *Eat Your Heart Out*, 1979

Lawrence Goodwyn, "The Cooperative Commonwealth and Other Abstractions: In Search of a Democratic Promise," *Marxist Perspectives*, Summer, 1980

John Tarrant, *Food Policies*, 1980

Don Parlberg, *Farm and Food Policy: Issues of the 1980s*, 1980

Robert Parlberg, "Lessons of the Grain Embargo," *Foreign Affairs*, Fall, 1980

Richard Gilmore, "Grain in the Bank," *Foreign Policy* No. 38, Spr., 1980.

Vivek Bammi, "Nutrition, The Historian, and Public Policy: A Case Study of U.S. Nutrition Policy in the 20th Century," *J. of Social History* 14:4, Summer, 1981.

John Young and Jan Newton, *Capitalism & Human Obsolescence*, 1980

D. Zwerdlin, "Curbing the Chemical Fire," *The Progressive*, Dec., 1978

Peter Meyer, "Land Rush: A Survey of America Land," *Harper's*, Jan., 1979

Robert Coppedge and Carlton Davis (eds.), *Rural Poverty and The Policy Crisis*, 1977

Frederick Buttel (ed.), *The Rural Sociology of the Advanced Societies: Critical Perspectives*, 1979

R. D. Rodefeld et al., (ed.), *Change in Rural America*, 1978

R. A. Brink et al., "Soil Deterioration and the Growing World Demand for Food," *Science* 197, August, 1977

Frederick Buttel, "Agricultural Structure and Energy Intensity: A Comparative Analysis of the Developed Capitalist Societies," *Comparative Rural and Regional Societies* 1, 1980

Frederick Buttel, "Farm Size, Structure, and Energy Intensity: An Ecological Analysis of U.S. Agriculture," *Rural Sociology* 44, 1979

Walter Goldschmidt, *As You Sow: Three Studies in the Social Consequences of Agribusiness*, 1978

Neal Jensen, "Limits to Growth in World Food Production," *Science* 201, 1978

Howard Newby, "The Rural Sociology of Advanced Capitalist Societies," in his (ed.), *International Perspectives on Rural Sociology*, 1978

Kevin Goss, et al. (ed.), *The Political Economy of Class Structure in U.S. Agriculture*, Penn State U. Experimental Sta., 1979

Clifton Luttrell, "The 'Middleman': A Major Source of Controversy in the Food Industry," *Federal Reserve Bank of St. Louis*, May, 1980

Richard S. Street, *Into a Good Land: The Emergence of California Agriculture, 1850-1920*

Dick Meister and Anne Loftis, *A Long-Time Coming: The Struggle to Unionize America's Farm Workers*, 1977

Ron Taylor, *Sweatshops in the Sun*

Eugene Nelson, *Huelga: The First Hundred Days of the Delano Grape Strike*

John G. Dunne, *Delano*

Carey McWilliams, *Factories in the Fields*

Paul Gates, *The Farmers Age: Agriculture 1815-1897*, 1945

Wayne Rasmusson, "The Impact of Technological Change on American Agriculture, 1862-1962," *Journal of Economic History*, Dec., 1962

Richard Merrill (ed.), *Radical Agriculture*, 1976

Ted Bradshaw and Edward Blakely, *Rural Communities in Advanced Industrial Societies*, 1979

John Warnock, *Profit Hungry: The Food Industry in Canada*, 1978

4. Evolution of New England Agriculture: A Regional Case Study

—Rise and decline of sheep farming
—Changing land tenure, technology and land use paterns
—The future of the small farm: should and can it be revived?

Required:
Joe Belden, et al., *Farm, Land and Food Policies* (whole book)

Other:
Robert Mutch, *Class and Region in American Political Development: 1750-1850*, 1976
Robert Mutch, "Yeoman and Merchant in Pre-Industrial America," *Societas*, 1979
Stephen Davis, *From Plowshares to Soindles: Dedham, Massachusetts, 1790-1840*, 1973
Harold Wilson, "The Rise and Decline of the Sheep Industry in Northern New England," *Agricultural History* 9:1, Jan. 1935
Steve Turner, "The Colonization of New England Farms," *New Roots*, Mar.-April, 1980
John Finck, et al., "Where Have All The Farmers Gone?" *Western Massachusetts*, May-June 1976
Christopher Clark, "The Household Economy, Market Exchange and the Rise of Capitalism in the Connecticut Valley, 1800-1860," *Journal of Social History*, 1980
Clarence Danhoff, *Change in Agriculture: The Northern U.S., 1820-1870*, 1969
James Henretta, "Families and Farms: Mentality in Pre-Industrial America," *William and Mary Quarterly*, Jan., 1978
Kenneth Lockridge, *A New England Town: The 1st 100 Years*, 1970
Michael Merrill, "Cash in Good to Eat: Self Sufficiency and Exchange in the Rural Economy of the U.S.," *Radical History Review*, Winter, 1977
Tamara Hareven et al., *Amoskeog*, 1979
Anthony Wallace, *Rockdale: The Grow of an American Village in the Early Industrial Revolution*, 1978
Howard Russell, *The Long Deep Furrow*
Richard Dourghty, (on leadership and power in 6 towns in early 19th century Mass.)
Jon Butler, "A Bicentennial Harvest: Four Studies of the Early American Community," *Journal of Urban History*, Aug., 1978
Paul Glen Munyon, *A Reasessment of New England Agriculture in the Last Thirty Years of the 19th Century*, 1978

5. Third World Agriculture
—Case Studies: Turkey, Portugal, St. Kitts, and the Sahel
—The Green Revolution
—The population issue
—The position of women in Third World agriculture
—Land reform: past and present
—Ecological decay
—Crisis of arid and semi-arid regions
—International relationships: trade and aid
—An example of socialist agriculture

Required:
Frances Lappé and Joseph Collins, *Food First* (whole book)
Michael Perelman, *Farming for Profit in a Hungry World* (remainder of book)
Betsy Hartman and James Boyce, *Needless Hunger* (whole book)

Other:

Ross Talbot (ed.), *The World Food Problem and U.S. Food Politics and Problems, 1977: A Reading Book*, 1978

Raymond Hopkins and Donald Puchala, *Global Food Interdependence: Challenge to American Foreign Policy*, 1980

Radha Sinha, *Food and Poverty: The Political Economy of Confrontation*, 1976

Marylin Chou and David Harmon (eds.), *Critical Food Issues of the Eighties*, 1979

Robert Ledogar, *Hungry for Profit: U.S. Food and Drug Multinationals in Latin America*, 1975

"Food Policy and World Hunger," (special issue), *National Forum*, 69:2, 1979

Errol Black, "Seeds of Destruction?" *Monthly Review* 31:11, April, 1980

"Agribusiness Targets Latin America" (special issue) 12:1, Jan.-Feb., 1978

John Tosh, "The Cash Crop Revolution in Tropical Africa: An Agricultural Reappraisal," *African Affairs*, Jan., 1980

Kenneth Anthony, *Agricultural Change in Tropical Africa*, 1979

Michael Lipton, *Why Poor People Stay Poor*

Michael Lipton, "Inter-Farm, Inter-regional farm, Non-farm Income Distribution: The Impact of the New Cereal Varieties," *World Development* 6:3, 1978

Michael Lipton, "The New Technology, the System and the Poor: The Case of New Cereal Varieties," in *Development of Societies: The Next Twenty-Five Years*, 1979

Michael Lipton, "Technological Cures for Social Pathologies?" *The Journal of Development Studies*, July, 1979

Proceedings of The World Food Conference of 1976, 1977

Jerry Stockdale, "Technology and Change in United States Agriculture: Model of Warning?" *Sociological Ruralis* 12:1/2 (1977)

Leslie Stein, "The Green Revolution and Asian Development Strategy," *Studies in Comparative International Development* 12:2 (Summer 1977)

Andrew Pearse, "Technology and Peasant Production: Reflections on a Global Study," *Development and Change* 8:2 (1977)

Keith Griffin, *The Political Economy of Agrarian Change: An Essay on the Green Revolution*, 1974

Keith Griffin, *Land Concentration and Rural Poverty*, 1976

Keith Griffin and Azizur Rahman Khan (eds.), *Poverty and Landlessness in Rural Asia*, 1976

Keith Griffin, "Poverty in the Third World: Ugly Facts and Fancy Models," *World Development* 6:3 (1978)

Alan Berg, *The Nutrition Factor: Its Role in National Development*, 1973

A. Pacey, et al., *Seasonal Dimensions to Rural Poverty*, 1980

Ernest Feder, *Strawberry Imperialism*, 1978

Frederick Clairmonte and John Cavanaugh, "The Anatomy of Multi-Commodity Trading Conglomerates: A Case Study" (cotton), *Journal of Contemporary Asia* 8:3 (1978)

Umberto Colombo, D. Gale Johnson, Tashio Shishido, *Reducing Malnutrition in Developing Countries: Increasing Rice Production in South and Southeast Asia*, The Trilateral Commission, The Triangle Papers, 1978

Review of Radical Political Economy (issues on women) 8:1 (1976)

David Feldman and Peter Lawrence, *Africa Report*, Global II Project on the Social and Economic Implications of Large-Scale Introduction of New Varieties of Food Grains, 1975 U.N. Study

Alain de Janvry, "Material Determinants of the World Food Crisis," *Berkeley Journal of Sociology* (1976)

Alain de Janvry, "The Political Economy of Rural Development in Latin America: An Interpretation," *American Journal of Agricultural Economies* 57:3 (Aug. 1975)

Alain de Janvry, and Carlos Garramon, "The Dynamics of Rural Poverty in Latin America," *Journal of Peasant Studies* 4:3 (April 1977)

Harry Cleaver, "The Contradictions of the Green Revolution," *Monthly Review* 24:2 (1972)

Harry Cleaver, "Food, Famine and the International Crisis," *Zerowork: Political Materials*, 2, Fall, 1977

Donald Cruise O'Brien, "Ruling Class and Peasantry in Senegal, 1960-1976: The Politics of a Monocrop Economy," in Rita Cruise O'Brien (ed.), *The Political Economy of Underdevelopment: Dependence in Senegal*, 1979

Roger Burbach and Patricia Flynn, *Agribusiness in the Americas*, 1980

Dari Sharma, "The Green Revolution in India: Prelude to a Red One?" in Kathleen Gough and Sharma (eds.), *Imperialism and Revolution in South Asia*, 1973

E. H. Jacoby, "Transnational Corporations and Third World Agriculture," *Development and Change* 6:2 (July 1975)

E. H. Jacoby, "Structural Changes in Third World Agriculture as a Result of Neo-Capitalist Developments," *Developing Economies* 12:1 (June 1974)

Bruce Johnson and Peter Kilby, *Agriculture and Structural Transformation: Economic Strategies in Late-Developing Countries*, London: Oxford U., 1975

Ernest Feder, "How Agribusiness Operates in Underdeveloped Agricultures: Harvard Business School Myths and Reality," *Development and Change* 7 (1976)

Erik Eckholm and Frank Record, "The Two Faces of Malnutrition," *Worldwatch Paper-9*, Dec., 1976

Rick Doner, "The Development of Agribusiness in Thailand," *Bulletin of Concerned Asian Scholars* 6:1 (Jan.-March 1974)

Shelton H. Davis, *Victims of the Miracle: Development and the Indians of Brazil*, N.Y.: Cambridge University Press, 1977

Francis Aylward and Mogens Jul, *Protein and Nutrition Policy in Low-Income Countries*, N.Y.: Halsted Press, 1975

Francis Aylward, "New World Bank Programs for the Liquidation of the Third World Peasantry," *Journal of Peasant Studies* 3:3 (1976)

T. J. Byres, "Of Neo-Populist Pipe-Dreams: Daedalus in the Third World and the Myth of Urban Bias," *Journal of Peasant Studies*, 1978

T. J. Byres, "The Green Revolutions Second Phase," *Journal of Peasant Studies*, 1980

David Lehman (ed.), *Agrarian Reform and Agrarian Reformism*. Faber, 1974

David Lehman, "The Death of Land Reform: A Polemic," *World Development* 6:3 (1978)

June P. Morgan, "The Green Revolution in Asia: False Promise of Abundance," *Bulletin of Concerned Asian Scholars* 10:1 (1978)

Kenneth Backman and Leonardo Panlino, "Rapid Growth in Food Production in 16 Developing Countries, 1961-76," *Development Digest* 17:2, April, 1980

T. Towning and I. Restrepo, "New Technology and Dry Land Agriculture," *Culture and Agriculture* 7, Winter, 1980

Patrick Marnham, *Nomads of the Sahel*

Lakshman Yapa, "Ecopolitical Economy of the Green Revolution," *Professional Geographer* 31:4, 1979

Georganne Chapin and Robert Wasserstrom, "A Bitter Harvest: Pesticide Pushers are Sowing the Seeds of Disease in the Third World," *The Progressive*, March, 1980

Phil O'Keefe and Ben Wisner, *Landuse and Development*, 1977

Thomas Robert Malthus, *Populations: The First Essay*. Written in 1798 seeing food supply always lagging behind production

Bonnie Mass, *Population Target: The Political Economy of Population Control In Latin America*, 1976

National Academy of Sciences, *Population and Food: Crucial Issues*, U.S. Department of Commerce, Sept., 1975

R. L. Meeks (ed.), *Marx and Engels on the Population Bomb*. Berkeley: Ramparts Press, 1971

Albert Szymanski, "Economic Development and Population," *Studies in Comparative International Development* 9:2 (Summer 1974)

Paul Ehrlich, *The Population Bomb*. N.Y.: Ballantine Books, 1968

Scientific American (special issue on population) September, 1974

Mahmood Mamdani, *The Myth of Population Control: Family, Class and Caste in an Indian Village*, 1972

Lester Brown, "World Population Trends: Signs of Hope, Signs of Stress," *World Watch Paper* 9, World Watch Institute, Oct. 1976

Current History 68:406 (June 1975). Special issue on population. Articles by Heisel on Africa, Sanchez-Albormoz on Latin America, and Thomas Dow on the World

"Population and Imperialism." (A special issue). *Latin American Perspectives* IV:4 (Fall 1977)

Alan Chase, *The Legacy of Malthus: The Social Costs of the New Scientific Racism*. N.Y.: Alfred Knopf, 1977

Carter Marshall, "Health, Nutrition and Results of World Population Growth," *International Journal of Health Services*, 4:4 (1974)

T. Lynn Smith, *The Race Between Population and Food Supply in Latin America*. Albuquerque: University of New Mexico Press, 1976

Ralph Thomlinson, *Population Dynamics: Causes and Consequences of World Demographic Change*. N.Y.: Random House, 1976

Samuel Lieberman, "Rural Development and Fertility Transition in South Asia: The Case for a Broad-based Strategy," *Social Research* 47:2, Summer, 1980

William Petersen, *Malthus*, 1979

"Symposium" (on Malthus), *Contemporary Sociology* 9, July, 1980

Robert Cassen, "Population and Development: A Survey," *World Development*, 1977

Mitchell Kellman and Dan Landau, "Economic Development and Population: Further Empirical Tests of the Malthusian Hypothesis," *Studies in Comparative International Development* 13:3, Fall, 1978

John Hunter and George Ntiyi, "Speculations on the Future of Shifting Agriculture in Africa," *Journal of Developing Areas*, 12:2, Jan., 1978

R.J.S. Baker, "FAO and the World Food Situation," *Political Quarterly* 50:2, April-June, 1979

Christopher Stevens, "Food Aid: Good, Bad, or Indifferent?" *Journal of Modern African Studies*, 16:4, Dec., 1978

M. R. Redclift, "The Influence of the Agency for International Development on Ecuador's Agrarian Development Policy," *Journal of Latin American Studies*, May, 1979

Yash Tandon, "The Food Question in East Africa: A Partial Case Study of Tanzania," *Africa Quarterly* 17:4, 1978

Aruna Nayyar Mitchie, "Agricultural Policy and Political Viability in Rural India," *Comparative Political Studies* 12:3, Oct., 1979

Cheryl Payer, "The World Bank and the Small Farmers," *Journal of Peace Research* 16:3, 1979

"Capitalist and Socialist Agriculture in Asia," (special issue) *World Development* 7:4-5, April-May, 1979

Richard Franke and Barbara Chasin, *The Political Economy of Ecological Destruction*, 1979

James Scott, *The Moral Economy of the Peasant*

Samuel Popkin, *The Rational Peasant*

Luis A. Serron, *Scarcity, Exploitation and Poverty: Malthus and Marx in Mexico*, 1980

Vilho Harle (ed.), *The Political Economy of Food*, 1978

Barbara Huddleston and Jon Mehin (eds.), *Political Investments in Food Production: National and International Case Studies*, 1979

Richard M. Fraenkel et al., (eds.), *The Role of U.S. Agriculture in Foreign Policy*, 1979

Lars Bondestam and Staffen Bergstrom (eds.), *Poverty and Population Control*, 1980

Andrew Pearse, *Seeds of Plenty, Seeds of Want: Social and Economic Implications of the Green Revolution*, 1980

David Weir and Mark Shapiro, *Circle of Poison: Pesticides and People in a Hungry World*, 1981.

Frances Moore Lappé et al., *Aid as Obstacle: Twenty Questions about Our Foreign Aid and the Hungry*, 1980

Prannoy Roy, "Transition in Agriculture: Empirical Indicators and Results (Evidence from Punjab, India)," *Journal of Peasant Studies* 8:2, Jan., 1981

Bonnie Nardi, "Modes of Explanation in Anthropological Population Theory: Biological Determinism vs. Self-Regulation in Studies of Population Growth in Third World Countries," *American Anthropologist* 83:1, March, 1981

Hunger for Justice

Donald Clifford   *Spring 1983*
Faith-Justice Institute/Saint Joseph's University/Philadelphia, PA 19131

This seminar aims at probing the ethical dimensions of hunger and justice from a variety of disciplines. This course reflects the heart of the Jesuit vision "to serve faith and promote justice" by giving students a clearer understanding of some ethical problems in this complex world and by exploring moral strategies for change.

January 12   Introduction
Fr. Donald Clifford S.J. (Director)
Human Needs for Physical and Emotional Nourishment
Dr. Carole Regan (Psychology)

January 19   Living in an Age of Violence
Dr. Daniel Curran (Sociology)

January 26   Seeing the World Justly: The Esthetic Dimension
Prof. Robert McGovern; Artist & Lecturer Philadelphia College of Art

February 2   Justice and Sacred Scripture
Dr. Thomas Ryan (Theology)

February 9   Technology and Justice in Nepal
Dr. Shakya (Minister of Education, Nepal)

February 16   World Hunger: Moral Response
Fr. Joe Godfrey S.J. (Philosophy)

February 23   World Hunger: Political Response
Dr. James Dougherty (Politics)

March 9   Spiritual Values in our Nurturing Earth
Dr. Paul Dietrich (Theology)

March 16   Competitiveness in the North American's Life
Dr. Dan Dombrowski (Philosophy)

March 23   The Latin American's Experience: Response to Liberation
Mr. Charles Schreiner and Fr. Ventura (El Salvador)

March 30   Urban Justice through Community Organizing
Fr. Joseph Katalec S.J.; Director, Philadelphia Council of Neighborhood Organizations

April 6   Strategies for Change: The Political Process
Mr. Jack Holenstein, Bread for the World

April 13   Seder Meal; Responsible Living in an Age of Scarcity
Dr. Dom Roberti (Chemistry)

April 27   Prospects for the Future: Excuse Me America

All lecturers are invited to attend any of the lectures this Spring. The schedule will follow this format:

2:00-3:00—Discussion on previous weeks' lecture
3:00-3:30—Break, informal discussion
3:30-4:30—Guest Lecturer
4:30-5:00—Questions

Assignments:

Reflection Papers: (approximately 500 words) will be due for each discussion session, and should be based on the previous week's discussion, assigned readings, and include a report of a related experience.

Related Experience: a personally selected experience, involving a minimum of 2 hrs. a week. They can include reading, personal interaction with others, an encounter with oppressed social conditions....

Attendance: As the class only meets once a week, students must attend all classes. Any absence must be for a sufficient reason, and must be explained in the weekly reflection paper and substituted with an appropriate activity.

Readings:
Marstin, Ronald. *Beyond our Tribal Gods*
Nelson, Jack. *Hunger for Justice*

Ecological Balance

Teaching World Environmental Strategies: One University's Experience
Hermann H. Field, Tufts University

Planned Urban Growth and Conservation of Natural Resources
Donald Miller, University of Washington at Seattle

Global Environmental Politics
Marvin S. Soroos, North Carolina State University at Raleigh

Environmental Ethics
L. Shannon Jung, Concordia College

Social Ecology
Joseph Miller, St. Mary's College

International Politics and the Physical Environment
David Rosen, Ramapo College of New Jersey

Environmental Policy Analysis
Richard Andrews, University of North Carolina at Chapel Hill

Teaching World Environmental Strategies: One University's Experience

Hermann H. Field *Spring 1981*
School of Urban and Environmental Policy/Tufts University/
Medford, MA 02155

On January 28, 1981, nearly 100 university students and environmental professionals gathered at Tufts University for the first session of a 14-week experimental course—"Global Environmental Strategies in the New England Context." The course was offered by the Tufts Department of Urban and Environmental Policy, under the auspices of the International Union for the Conservation of Nature and Natural Resources (IUCN). Its sponsors saw it as a first step in bringing an important document, the *World Conservation Strategy*, into an educational setting.

This section describes the Tufts experience and suggests guidelines for others who may want to prepare similar courses. Because this was a pilot project, it received more attention and resources than usual for a university course. While this allowed the inclusion of lecturers for whom most schools would not have the funds, a similar course could be quite adequately designed with far fewer resources. Therefore, where appropriate, alternatives to the resource-intensive approaches are suggested.

Finally, it is important to remember the university is only one forum in which global environmental strategies can be taught. Community organizations, public interest groups, government departments and agencies, and elementary and secondary schools could also host workshops, seminars, and discussions on such strategies.

We hope this course will lead to the sharing of different approaches to teaching the concepts of the *World Conservation Strategy* in other cultural and ecological settings.

Why This Course?

The *World Conservation Strategy (WCS)* was published in 1980 as a response to the need for a clear statement of environmental priorities within a framework of sustainable development.

This document, a joint project of the IUCN, the United Nations Environment Programme (UNEP), the Food and Agriculture Organization (FAO), UNESCO, and the World Wildlife Fund (WWF), was initiated when 450 governmental and nongovernmental agencies in more than 100 countries were asked to define their environmental concerns. Drafts of the document were sent to more than 700 experts on ecology, endangered species, protected areas, environmental education, environmental law, and environmental planning. The result of the two-year review period was a consensus document, the *WCS*.

The *WCS* was distributed to policymakers at top levels in government, banking, and development sectors who were considered the direct route to supportive legislation, resource management, and international agreement. However, there became a growing awareness among the *WCS*'s promoters that to be effective the ideas contained in the *WCS* must penetrate not only at the international and national levels, but also at the regional and local levels where environmental perception tends to be removed from any overall strategic framework for resource conservation. Without this grassroots support and understanding of global interdependence, any strategies imposed from above were likely to fail.

Assignments

The *WCS* would be the text for the course, supplemented by the summary of the *Global 2000 Report to the President of the U.S.*, prepared by the Council on Environmental Quality and the State Department (1980). Additional readings recommended by the lecturers and the staff would cover the specific topic under discussion in a particular session. A term paper relating a global aspect of the *WCS* to a specific local context would be required of all university students taking the course for credit.

January 28   Session 1   Introduction
Historical background of the world conservation movement. The World Conservation Strategy is premised on the unity of international, national, and local efforts, and it emphasizes the critical linkage between conservation and development as components of a sustainable future. Through the integration of conservation and development, its goal is to ensure that modifications to the planet do indeed secure the survival of all people. The Strategy has three main objectives: to maintain essential ecological processes and life support systems, to preserve genetic diversity, and to promote the sustainable utilization of species and ecosystems. *Harold J. Coolidge, Honorary President IUCN and Prof. Raymond F. Dasmann, U.C. Santa Cruz, international ecologist, author*

The Objectives of Conservation and Requirements for Their Achievement

February 4   Session 2   Maintenance of Essential Ecological Processes and Life Support Systems
At present rates nearly one-third of the world's available land and one-half of the tropical forests will be destroyed by the end of the century. The productivity of aquatic ecosystems continues to decline. Highest priority must be given to the most significant and urgent environmental problems if we are to prevent further irreversible damage to our basic life support systems. Our health and well-being are dependent on theirs. *Dr. Gerard A. Bertrand, President, Mass. Audubon Society; former chief for Intern. Affairs, U.S. Fish and Wildlife Service*

February 11   Session 3   Preservation of Genetic Diversity
More than 26,000 species are threatened with extinction. The loss of genetic diversity among both cultivars and wild species is the most irreversible problem that we face. We need to expand our commitment to the preservation of the entire range of living resources: crop plants, forage, timber trees, livestock, animals for

aquaculture, microbes, wild species and prime ecosystems. It is the base also for much of our scientific and medical advance and technical innovation dependent on these resources. *Dr. F. Wayne King, Director, Florida State Museum; Deputy Chairman, IUCN Species Survival Commission*

February 18   Session 4   Sustainable Utilization of Species and Ecosystems
Between 1970 and 1976 the world catch of fish declined from 4.3 to 3.5 metric tons; in Gambia it now takes 360 woman days a year for a family to find its firewood. Both developed and developing countries are taxing ecosystems beyond their capacity to regenerate. We must develop resource policies that allow nature to sustain itself and to provide for us. *Prof. Gerardo Budowski, Head, Natural Renewable Resources Program, CATIE, Costa Rica*

Priorities for National Action

February 25   Session 5   A Framework for National and Subnational Conservation Strategies
Few, if any, countries take adequate account of ecological considerations when they are making policy or planning development. Often conservation is viewed as a narrow interest that stands in opposition to change or resource use. National agencies that coordinate conservation and development must oversee each stage of the planning and implementation processes. Sound living resource management requires effective legislation and governmental organization. *Prof. Kenton R. Miller, School of Natural Resources, Univ. of Michigan; Chairman, IUCN Parks Commission*

March 4   Session 6   Environmental Planning and Rational Use Allocation
An environmental assessment takes only a small fraction of a project's costs, between .05% and 2% of the total outlay, and it is an essential tool for national resource allocation. Ecosystem Evaluations (EEs) and resource planning will have to take their place among engineering, economic, and socio-political assessments so that informed choices can be made before resources are irrevocably committed. *Prof. Peter Jacobs, University of Montreal; Chairman, IUCN Environmental Planning Commission*

March 11   Session 7   Building Support for Conservation
Ultimately, the behavior of entire societies must be transformed to assure the achievement of conservation objectives. This begins with building environmental awareness into all levels of the educational process. This must be accompanied by development of a solid research base, and better training and education for professional conservationists, technicians, and resource users. Its ultimate success, however, is dependent on an enlightened citizenry through its own knowledge, participation and concern. *Prof. William Stapp, Chairperson, Behavior and Environment Program, Univ. of Michigan; former Director of Environmental Education UNESCO*

March 18   Session 8   Conservation-based Rural Development
500 million people are malnourished. Many more sustain themselves on a deteriorating resource base. There is an urgent need for rural development that combines

short term measures to ensure human survival with long term measures to safeguard the resource base. The traditional ecological relationship between a people and their environment will have to be the foundation for these measures. *Dr. Naseeb Dajani, Executive Officer, IUCN, formerly Coordinator of Integrated Rural Projects, UNESCO; and Dr. David Western, N.Y. Zoological Society, Research Zoologist in East Africa*

Priorities for International Action

April 1   Session 9   Law and Assistance
Although there are more than 40 multinational conventions concerning the management of living resources, few of them have conservation as their primary goal. We will have to establish new law, institutions, and procedures built upon the international agreements which we do have because so many environmental problems reach beyond individual national boundaries. *Dr. Wolfgang Burhenne, Director, Environmental Law Center, Bonn; Chairman, IUCN Commission on Environmental Policy, Law and Administration*

April 8   Session 10   The Global Commons
Much of the ocean remains open for unchecked exploitation by anyone with the technology to do so; the chemical composition of the atmosphere is changing alarmingly, yet there are few effective international controls; Antarctica is a land threatened because it has no government. The international community is only now beginning to move toward the sustainable use of these common resources at a time when there is a pressing need for effective action. *Prof. Ann Hollick, Director, Policy Assessment Staff, Oceans International Environment; Scientific Affairs, Department of State*

April 15   Session 11   Protection of Drylands, Genetic Resource Areas, and Tropical Forests
An area twice the size of Canada is threatened with desertification; 40% of the world's biomes are inadequately represented in national parks or equivalent reserves; and, at present rates, the last tropical forests will be destroyed in 85 years. Protection of the resources contained in these areas will depend on expanded international encouragement and support, but the industries that profit from the use of these resources should share the cost of our common responsibility. *Dr. Thomas Lovejoy, Vice President-Science WWF-US*

Reflections
The primary purpose of the seminars was to make the linkage between the global perspective of a particular session's topic and the local perspective of the same topic. The one overriding criticism, most strongly voiced by the professionals in the class, was the repeated failure to make strong linkages.

The problems were fourfold: (1) the visiting lecturers often raised specific international issues in their lectures that captured the interest of the participants and dominated the greater part of the seminar discusssions; (2) the lecturers and local experts only had the presession dinner to plan together how the linkage could be accomplished; (3) the role of moderator was more passive than active; (4) the participants' questions often did not reveal much concentrated thought on the possible linkages.

Planned Urban Growth and Conservation of Natural Resources

Donald Miller   *Spring 1982*

Urban Planning 598/College of Architecture and Urban Planning/
University of Washington/Seattle, WA 98195

In this student initiated seminar, we will investigate the interactions between urban and rural areas, focusing on the goals and strategies of accommodating urban growth while conserving agricultural, forestry and natural areas that contribute to the economy and to environmental quality. The Puget Sound Basin will be used as the context and source of cases for this inquiry. Most class sessions will include invited speakers representing a variety of views, followed by a discussion of the presentation and supplementary readings. A term paper or two shorter papers, providing a critical synthesis on a topic(s) of interest, will be required.

Objectives for this seminar include:

1. Defining and assessing the major issues of rural land conversion for urban uses.
2. Identifying rural uses that are being threatened.
3. Focusing on cases in the Puget Sound Basin.
4. Developing alternative strategies and tactics for accommodating growth while conserving natural qualities of rural areas.
5. Methods of evaluating development strategies to appropriately account for cost/revenue implications, and for resource and environmental quality objectives.
6. Equity implications of development strategies.
7. Identifying effective political approaches to gaining approval of resource conserving policies and programs.

Course Outline

April 1

A. What values are served by conserving rural land uses and natural resources (e.g., land use ethics, aesthetics, variety, economics)? Brief overview of historical background of interest in rural conservation. How can we translate long-term goals into useful and effective short-term justifications for conservation actions? What should be the professional's role in determining these values?
Invited Speaker: Estella Leopold

B. What rural and natural land uses, and areas of the Puget Sound region are being threatened by development; why, and what are the conditions of these resources? How to determine what will be threatened? What are ways of mitigating conflicts between urban and these rural land uses?

April 8
 1. Forest Lands (publically and privately held and managed)
 Invited Speakers: John Chambers, Gordon Bradley
April 15
 2. Agricultural Lands: which, why, and where; and Water Resources Management: water quality issues; coastal areas; etc.
 Invited Speakers: Pat van Almkirk, Brian Mar
C. What are alternative strategies and state and local intervention tactics for accommodating growth while conserving natural qualities of rural areas?
April 22
 1. Growth Management: regulation, service provision, and tax incentives. What are developers' views of these? What has worked in various cases and why? What models do we have that apply to the Puget Sound region?
 Speaker: Mary Bundy
April 29
 2. Public Ownership: partial or fee simple, purchase options, leases, dedication, etc. What are owners' views of these? What are the fiscal implications?
 Invited Speaker: Elliot Marks
May 6
 3. Regulation: other existing and promising forms—e.g., registration, designation, environmental review, performance standards, planned unit development, etc. How effective are these? What are developers' views of these?
 Invited Speaker: Keith Dearborn
D. How can alternative development strategies and land use schemes be best evaluated? How can these evaluations be used to shape decisions?
May 13
 1. Environmental Quality Analysis Techniques: capacity studies, landscape resource analysis, potential surface analysis, etc. How effective is the EIS process in assisting conservation of rural land uses? Speaker: David Streatfield
May 20
 2. Revenue/Cost, Benefit/Cost, and Multi-Criteria Methods of Evaluation. How can environmental qualities be addressed by these? Are there reliable short-cut methods that do not require elaborate modeling? What are effective tactics for presenting these to decision makers?
 Invited Speakers: Richard Zerbe, Don Miller
May 27
E. What are the equity implications of development schemes—e.g., availability of land for residential development and role in cost of housing, access to open spaces and recreational resources? Who benefits and who pays? Methods of treating distribution of benefits and subsidy payments.
 Speakers: David Hodge, Don Miller
June 3
F. What are effective political and legal approaches to gaining approval of resource conserving policies and programs? What are the arguments to which public officials and the electorate are responsive? Speaker: Alan Merson

Reading List

In the following bibliography, starred (*) items are required reading on which seminar discussion will be based. The additional items are a beginning resource dealing with the seminar topics for the quarter. Each participant will be expected to develop a fuller, selective bibliography on the topic of her or his choice, and to assume the role of leading the discussion of that topic.

1. Values, Ethics and Purposes
*Phillip M. Hoose, *Building an Ark: Tools for the Preservation of Natural Diversity Through Land Protection* (Covelo, CA: Island Press, 1981), pp. 1-5.
*T. O'Riordan, *Environmentalism* (New York: Methuen, 1981, 2nd Ed.), pp. 1-36, 200-227, 300-315.
Charles A. Lewis, "Comment: Healing in the Urban Environment," *Journal of the American Planning Association (JAPA)* 45:3 (July 1979), pp. 330-338.

2. Forest Lands
*Robert G. Healy and James L. Short, *The Market for Rural Land: Trends, Issues, and Policies* (Washington, D.C.: Conservation Foundation, 1981), pp. 1-23, 27-67, 77-90, 138-156.
Robert G. Healy and James L. Short, "Rural Land: Market Trends and Planning Implications," *Journal of the American Planning Association (JAPA)* 45:3 (July 1979), pp. 305-317.
Marion Clawson, *Suburban Land Conversion in the United States* (Baltimore: The John Hopkins Press, 1971).
Department of Natural Resources, Washington State, *Lands in Transition* (Olympia: DNR, December 1981).
E. M. Sterling, "Forestry in Austria: Small Cuts and Grand Vistas," *Sierra Club Bulletin* (November/December 1981), pp. 40-42.
Richard Plochmann, "Forestry in the Federal Republic of Germany," *Journal of Forestry* (July 1981), pp. 451-454.
Robert M. Press, "Rural America is Disappearing—in 5- or 10-acre Pieces," *Christian Science Monitor* (November 24, 1981).
Robert Kilborn, Jr., "Giant Forest Companies Help Small Landowners Harvest Their Trees," *Christian Science Monitor* (November 24, 1981).
William E. Bruner, et al., *Alternative Forest Policies for the Pacific Northwest* (Pullman: Washington State University, 1981).
Forest Practices Board, State of Washington, *Proposed Forest Practices, Rules and Regulation Changes* (Olympia: Department of Natural Resources, 1980).
William Koss and Billy Dean Scott, *A Profile of Western Washington's Nonindustrial Forest Landowners* (Olympia: Department of Natural Resources, State of Washington, March 1978).

3. Agricultural Lands and Water Resources Management
*Healy and Short, op. cit., 93-119, 129-138, 168-201, 207-230.
*Brian W. Mar, "Dead is Dead—An Alternative Strategy for Urban Water Management," *Urban Ecology*, 5(1980/1981), pp. 103-112.
Raymond J. Burby and Steven French, "Coping with Floods: The Land Use Management Paradox," *JAPA* 47:3 (July 1981), pp. 289-300.
Bruce Lindeman, "Anatomy of Land Speculation," *Journal of the American Institute of Planners, (JAIP)* 42:2 (April 1976), pp. 142-152.

Symposium: Agriculture and Urbanization, Special Issue of the *JAIP*, 41:6 (November 1975), including:
  Philip Roup, "Urban Threats to Rural Lands: Backgrounds and Beginnings," pp. 371-378;
  Gregory Gustafson and L. T. Wallace, "Differential Assessment as Land Use Policy: The California Case," pp. 379-389;
  William Bryant and Howard Conklin, "New Farmland Preservation Programs in New York," pp. 390-396.
Michael F. Brewer (Ed.), *Agricultural Land Availability*, "Papers on the Supply and Demand for Agricultural Lands in the United States," (Washington, D.C.: United States Senate, Committee on Agriculture, Nutrition, and Forestry, July 1981).
Charles Benbrook and Allen Hidlebaugh, *The Economic and Environmental Consequences of Agricultural Land Conversion*, National Agricultural Lands Study Technical Paper XIV (Washington, D.C.: NALS, 1982).
William H. Gray, *Methods of Agricultural Land Preservation*, Cooperative Extension Service, Report N.E.M. 3906 (Pullman: Washington State University, 1975).
George Peterson and Harvey Yampolsky, *Urban Development and the Protection of Metropolitan Farmland* (Washington, D.C.: The Urban Institute, 1975).
Puget Sound Governmental Conference, *Regional Agriculture Land Use Study* (Seattle, Washington: the Conference, 1974).
Robert E. Coughlin, et al., *The Protection of Farmland: A Reference Guidebook for State and Local Governments*, Report of the National Agricultural Lands Study (Washington, D.C.: USGPO, 1981), pp. 31-55.
National Agricultural Lands Study, *Final Report 1981* (Washington, D.C.: USGPO, 1981).
National Agricultural Lands Study, *Agricultural Land Retention and Availability: a Bibliographic Source Book* (Washington, D.C.: USGPO, 1981).
American Planning Association, *Saving Farms and Farmlands*, Planning Advisory Service Report (Chicago: APA, 1978).
National Association of Counties Research Foundation, *Disappearing Farmlands: A Citizen's Guide to Agricultural Land Preservation*, Second Edition (The Association, August 1980).

4. Growth Management Strategies

*Frank Schnidman, Jane A. Silverman and Rufus C. Young, Jr. (Eds.), *Management and Control of Growth*, Volume IV, *Techniques in Application* (Washington, D.C.: Urban Land Institute, 1978).
*O'Riordan, op. cit., pp. 127-140, 157-163.
Public Technology, Inc., *Land Management: A Technical Report on Selected Analytical Techniques for State and Local Governments* (Washington, D.C.: Public Technology for National Science Foundation, 1977).
Paul Enales, "Environmentally Sensitive Area Planning in Ontario, Canada," *JAPA* 47:3 (July 1981), pp. 313-323.
H. James Brown, Robyn Phillips and Neal Roberts, "Land Markets at the Urban Fringe," *JAPA* 47:2 (April 1981), pp. 131-144.
Donald C. Hagman, *Public Planning and Control of Urban and Land Development, Cases and Materials*, Second Edition, Chapter VIII, "Uses and Effects of Plans," (St. Paul: West Publishing Co., 1980).
Sullivan and Kressel, "Twenty Years After: Renewed Significance of the Comprehensive Plan," 9 *Urban Law Annual* 33, 1975.

Robert E. Coughlin, et al., op. cit., pp. 16-21, 56-75, 188-203.

Richard W. Dunford, "Circuit-Breaker Rebates for Farmland Tax Relief," Paper presented at the Statewide Conference on Land Use, held at the University of Washington, Seattle, November 6-7, 1981.

B. Chavooshin, et al., "Growth Management Program: A New Planning Approach," in Randall W. Scott, et al. (eds.), *Management and Control of Growth*, Volume III (Washington D.C.: The Urban Land Institute, 1975), pp. 114-126.

Michael Gleeson, et al., *Urban Growth Management Systems: An Evaluation of Policy-Related Research* (Chicago: American Society of Planning Officials, August 1975).

Tom Walsh, "Urban Growth Management: Techniques and Legal Issues," Staff Report to the Seattle City Council (Seattle: City Council, November 1975).

Frederic O. Sargent, *Rural Environmental Planning* (Published by author, 1976).

5. Public Ownership Strategies

*O'Riordan, op. cit., pp. 140-141.

*Healy and Short, op. cit., pp. 283-301.

*Hoose, op. cit., pp. 25-32, 81-145.

Adolf W. Ratyka, "Land Banking in Stockholm: An Evaluation of Municipal Residential Leasehold as a Public Finance and Housing Subsidy Instrument," *JAPA* 47:3 (July 1982), pp. 279-288.

Robert E. Coughlin and Thomas Plant, "Less-than fee Acquisition for the Preservation of Open Space: Does It Work?" *JAIP* 44:4 (October 1978), pp. 452-462.

James Lemonides and April Young, "Provision of Public Open Space in Urban Areas: Determinants, Obstacles, and Incentives," *JAIP* 44:3 (July 1978), pp. 286-296.

Robert E. Coughlin, et al., *The Protection of Farmland*, op. cit., pp. 76-92, 148-187.

6. Regulation Strategies

*Hoose, op. cit., pp. 35-79, 171-179.

*O'Riordan, op. cit., pp. 144-157.

*Healy and Short, op. cit., pp. 251-283.

David Callies, "The Quiet Revolution Revisited," *JAPA* 46:2 (April 1980), pp. 135-144.

Richard Liroff, "NEPA—Where Have We Been and Where are We Going?" *JAPA* 46:2 (April 1980), pp. 154-161.

Kenneth Pearlman, "State Environmental Policy Acts: Local Decision Making and Land Use Planning," *JAIP* 43:1 (January 1977), pp. 42-53.

Daniel R. Mandelker, "Critical Area Controls: A New Dimension in American Land Development Regulation," *JAIP* 41:1 (January 1975), pp. 21-31.

William Toner, "Zoning Alone Won't Save our Farmland," *Planning* 45 (January 1979), pp. 13-14.

Robert E. Coughlin, et al., *The Protection of Farmland*, op. cit., pp. 21-24, 104-47.

Charles Thurow, William Toner and Duncan Erley, *Performance Controls for Sensitive Lands: A Practical Guide for Local Administrators*, Planning Advisory Service Reports Nos. 307-308 (Chicago: American Planning Association, 1979).

Judith Getzels and Charles Thurow (eds.), *Rural and Small Town Planning* (Chicago: APA, Planners Press, 1980).

Lane H. Kendig, et al., *Performance Zoning* (Chicago: APA, Planners Press, 1980).

Charles M. Harr, *Land Use Planning: A Casebook on the Use, Misuse, and Re-Use of Urban Land,* Third Edition (Boston: Little, Brown and Co., 1977).

Clifford L. Weaver and Richard F. Babcock, *City Zoning: The Once and Future Frontier* (Chicago: APA, Planners Press, 1980).

7. Environmental Quality Analysis Techniques

*Hoose, op. cit., pp. 7-12, 15-22, 181-195.

*O'Riordan, op. cit., pp. 163-167, 193-199.

Steven Gordon and Gaybrielle Gordon, "The Accuracy of Soil Survey Information for Urban Land Use Planning," *JAPA* 47:3 (July 1981), pp. 301-312.

Robert Fleming, David Varnes, and Robert Schuster, "Landslide Hazards and Their Reduction," *JAPA* 45:4 (October 1979), pp. 428-439.

Lewis D. Hopkins, "Methods for Generating Land Suitability Maps: A Comparative Evaluation," *JAIP* 43:4 (October 1977), pp. 386-400.

Paul Mansel, et al., "Regional Land Use Classification Derived from Computer-processed Satellite Data," *JAIP* 42:2 (April 1976), pp. 153-164.

Frederick Steiner, *Ecological Planning for Farmlands Preservation* (Chicago: APA, Planners Press, 1981).

American Planning Association, *The Carrying Capacity as a Planning Tool* (Chicago: APA, Planners Press, 1978).

Julius G. Fabos, Christopher Greene, and Spencer Joyner, Jr., *The Metland Landscape Planning Process: Composite Landscape Assessment, Alternative Plan Formulation and Plan Evaluation;* Part 3 of the Metropolitan Landscape Planning Model (Amherst, MA: Massachusetts Agricultural Experiment Station, September 1978).

Edward J. Kaiser, et al., *Promoting Environmental Quality Through Urban Planning and Controls* (Chapel Hill, NC: University of North Carolina, Center for Urban and Regional Studies, 1973).

Michael Romanos and Linda Keesler, "Planning with the Environmental Technical Information System," *Planning and Public Policy* 8:1 (February 1982).

8. Evaluation Techniques: Revenue/Cost, Benefit/Cost, Multi-Criteria

*O'Riordan, op. cit., pp. 141-144, 168-193.

*Donald Miller, "Project Location Analysis Using the Goals Achievement Method of Evaluation," *JAPA* 46:2 (April 1980), pp. 195-208.

Duane Windsor, "A Critique of The Costs of Sprawl," *JAPA* 45:3 (July 1979), pp. 279-292.

Dean Runyan, "Tools for Community-Managed Impact Assessment," *JAIP* 43:2 (April 1977), pp. 125-134.

John W. Krutilla and Anthony C. Fisher, *The Economics of Natural Environments: Studies in the Valuation of Commodity and Amenity Resources* (Washington, D.C.: Resources for the Future, 1975).

W. R. Derrick Sewell, "Broadening the Approach to Evaluation in Resources Management Decision-Making," *Journal of Environmental Management* 1(1973), pp. 33-60.

9. Equity Implications and How to Assess Them

*O'Riordan, op. cit., pp. 85-126, 37-84.

*Healy and Short, op. cit., pp. 230-245.

Ronald A. Foresta, "Comment: Elite Values, Popular Values, and Open Space Policy," *JAPA* 46:4 (October 1980), pp. 449-456.

Franklin James, Jr., with Oliver Windsor, "Fiscal Zoning, Fiscal Reform, and Exclusionary Land Use Controls," *JAIP* 42:2 (April 1976), pp. 130-141.

Daniel R. Mandelker, *Environment and Equity: A Regulatory Challenge* (New York: McGraw-Hill Book Co., 1981).

James Noel Smith (ed.), *Environmental Quality and Social Justice in Urban America* (Washington, D.C.: Conservation Foundation, 1974).

Bernard J. Frieden, *The Environmental Protection Hustle* (Cambridge: MIT Press, 1980).

10. Political and Legal Approaches to Gaining Approval

*Hoose, op. cit., pp. 147-169.

*O'Riordan, op. cit., pp. 228-299.

Alan Hahn and Cynthia Dybella, "State Environmental Planning and Local Influence: A Comparison of Three Regional Resource Management Agencies," *JAPA* 47:3 (July 1981), pp. 324-335.

W. Patrick Beaton, "Regional Tax Base Sharing: A Conceptual Analysis," *JAPA* 46:3 (July 1980), pp. 315-322.

Andrew Reschovsky and Eugene Knaff, "Tax Base Sharing: An Assessment of the Minnesota Experience," *JAIP* 43:4 (October 1977), pp. 361-370.

Bruce Weber and Kathleen Peroff, "Local Government Response to State-mandated Land Use Laws," *JAIP* 43:4 (October 1977), pp. 352-360.

Robert E. Coughlin, et al.,*The Protection of Farmland*, op. cit., pp. 93-97, 254-277.

Judith Getzels and Charles Thurow (eds.), *Rural and Small Town Planning*, (Chicago: APA, Planners Press, 1980).

Robert G. Healy, *Land Use and the States* (Baltimore: John Hopkins University Press, 1976).

Global Environmental Politics

Marvin S. Soroos   *Spring 1983*
Political Science 336/North Carolina State University/Raleigh, NC   27650

"One rules Nature only by obeying it."—Sir Francis Bacon

The course explores the political aspects of the ecological problems that confront humanity. Emphasis is placed upon the international politics of population, food, energy and non-fuel resources, and pollution. Conflict over the use of resources of the ocean and other non-national areas, such as Antarctica and outer space, will be examined with special attention to efforts to establish a new international law of the seas. In addition, comparisons will be made between the domestic energy and environmental policies of a number of countries of varying levels of economic development.

Books to Purchase

Lester R. Brown, *Building a Sustainable Society*, Norton, 1981.
Raymond F. Hopkins, Robert L. Paarlberg, and Mitchel B . Wallerstein, *Food in the Global Arena*, Holt, Rinehart and Winston, 1982.
Parker G. Marden, Dennis G. Hodgson, and Terry McCoy, *Population in the Global Arena*, Holt, Rinehart and Winston, 1982.

Papers

Each student will write two papers (1) an essay on "The Tragedy of the Commons" and (2) an analysis of an international or foreign environmental problem.

Course Outline and Schedule

Readings marked with an asterisk (*) are optional.

January 13   Course Introduction
Brown, chapter 1

I. The Fundamentals of Global Environmental Politics

Before examining specific problems it is important to know something about the overall terrain of global environmental politics. Toward this end, consideration will be given to what is known as the global "problematique," the interrelated group of environmental concerns which are further complicated by economic and political realities, such as the phenomenon of the "tragedy of the commons."

January 18   The Global Problematique and its Skeptics
The Global 2000 Report, pp. 1-5 (skim rest of booklet) (on reserve)
Simon, "Global Confusion 1980: A Hard Look at the Global 2000 Report," *The Public Interest*, Winter 1981 (photocopy on reserve)

Gillman, "Julian Simon's Cracked Crystal Ball," *The Public Interest*, Fall 1981
*Falk, *This Endangered Planet*, 1971.
*Meadows et al., *The Limits to Growth*, 1972.
*Mesarovic and Pestel, *Mankind at the Turning Point*, 1974.
*Heilbroner, *An Inquiry into the Human Prospect*, 2nd edition, 1980.
*Beckerman, *Two Cheers for the Affluent Society*, 1974.
*Simon, *The Ultimate Resource*, 1981.

January 20   Actors and Arenas in Global Environmental Politics
Marden et al., chapter 2
Hopkins et al., chapter 2
Handleman, *Introductory Case Studies for International Relations*, chapter 4
Brown, chapter 12

January 25   The Environment on International Agendas
Eckholm, *Down to Earth*, chapter 1 (book on reserve)
*Soroos, "Trends in the Perception of Environmental Problems in the UN General
    Debates" (available from instructor)
*Caldwell, *In Defense of Earth*, 1972.
*UN Environment Programme, *The World Environment: 1972-1982*, 1982.

January 27   Tragedy of the Commons (Game)
Hardin, "The Tragedy of the Commons" (photocopy on reserve)
Brown, chapter 11
*Hardin, *New Ethics for Survival*, 1972.
*Hardin and Baden, *Managing the Commons*, 1977.

II. The Politics of Population and Food
Is the world becoming "overpopulated?" Is "overpopulation" the root of other
ecological problems? Are hunger and starvation manifestations of overpopulation?
Most Americans would respond "yes" to all three questions. These viewpoints
have, however, been challenged for failing to distinguish "overpopulation" from
poverty, inequality, and exploitation. Equally controversial has been the subject of
alternative international population and food policies that could be adopted by the
United States, especially Garrett Hardin's proposed "lifeboat ethics."

February 1   Global Population Trends
Marden et al., chapters 1,5
*Ehrlich, *The Population Bomb*, 1968.
**Scientific American*, special issue on "The Human Population."
*Salk and Salk, *World Population and Human Values*, 1981.
***Tragedy of the Commons Paper is Due*

February 3   National and International Population Policies
Brown, chapter 7
Mardin et al., chapters 3, 4
*Brown, *In the Human Interests*, 1972.
**Policy Studies Journal*, Winter 1977, special issue entitled "Symposium on Popu-
    lation."
*Salas, *International Population Assistance: The First Decade*, 1979.

February 8   The Malthusian Predicament: How Immediate Is It?
Brown, chapters 2, 5
Hopkins et al., chapters 1, 5
*Borgstrom, *The Hungry Planet*, 1972.
*Eckholm, *Losing Ground*, 1976.
*Bryson and Murray, *Climates of Hunger*, 1977.

February 10   Simulation Game: "Baldicer"

February 15   The "Lifeboat" Debate
Soroos, "Lifeboat Ethics Versus One Worldism in International Food and Resource
   Policy," chapter 7 in Orr/Soroos, *The Global Predicament*, 1979.
*Paddock and Paddock, *Times of Famines*, 1976.
*Lucas and Ogletree, *Lifeboat Ethics: the Moral Dilemma*, 1976.
*Brown, *Food Policy: The Responsibility of the United States in Life and Death
   Choices*, 1976.

February 17   Food Policies of the Developed Countries
Hopkins, et al., chapter 3
International Organization, entire Summer 1978 issue on "The Global Political
   Economy of Food."
*Talbot, *The World Food Problem and US Food Politics and Policies*, 1975.
*Lappé, Collins, and Kinley, *Aid as Obstacle: Twenty Questions about our Foreign
   Aid and the Hungry*, 1981.

February 22   Food Politics in the Developed World
Hopkins et al., chapter 4
*George, *How the Other Half Dies*, 1977.
*Dahlberg, *Beyond the Green Revolution*, 1979.
*Alamgir, *Famine in South Asia: Political Economy of Mass Starvation*, 1979.
*Lappé and Collins, *Food First*, Revised 1979.

February 24   Midterm Examination

III. Resources: Issues of Scarcity, Price, and Security
Energy and mineral resources are prerequisites to economic development and the
modern industrial lifestyle. Impending scarcities of certain key resources, such as
petroleum, increase the potential for international conflict. The price of resources
has also been a major issue with the rise of OPEC and the demands of developing
countries for more stable prices for their exports. Finally, consideration will be
given to the problem that the expanding use of nuclear power poses for controlling
the spread of nuclear weapons.

March 1   Fossil Fuels and Minerals: How Limited Are They?
Brown, chapter 4
*Tilton, *The Future of Nonfuel Minerals*, 1977.
*Workshop on Alternative Energy Strategies, *Energy: Global Prospects, 1985-2000*,
   1977.
*Ridgway, *Who Owns the Earth*. 1980.
*Rifkin, *Entropy*, 1980.

March 3   Resources, Interdependence, and National Security
Shafer, "Mineral Myths," *Foreign Policy,* Summer 1982 (photocopy on reserve)
Yergen, *Global Insecurity,* 1982, chapter 1 (book on reserve)
*Choucri, *International Politics of Energy Interdependence,* 1976.
*Garvey and Garvey (eds.), *International Resource Flows,* 1976.
*Doran, *Myth, Oil, and Politics,* 1977.
*Eckes, *The United States and the Global Struggle for Minerals, 1979.*
Orbis, Winter 1980, special issue on oil politics.
*Deese, *Energy and Security,* 1980.
*Clark and Page, *Energy, Vulnerability, and War,* 1981.

March 15   Cartels: The Rise and Decline of OPEC
Winberg, "Resource Politics: the Future of International Markets for Raw Materials," chapter 9 in Orr/Soroos, *The Global Predicament,* 1979 (book on reserve).
*Engler, *The Brotherhood of Oil,* 1977.
*Odell, *Oil and World Powers,* 1979.
*Safer, *International Oil Policy,* 1979.
*Allen, *OPEC Oil,* 1979.

March 17   Nuclear Power and the Potential for Proliferation
*Wonder, *Nuclear Fuel and American Foreign Policy,* 1977.
*Wohlstetter et al., *Nuclear Policies, Fuel without the Bomb,* 1978.
*Kapur, *International Nuclear Diplomacy,* 1979.

March 22   Resource Problems of the Third World
Brown, chapters 8-9
*Tinbergen, *Reshaping the International Order,* 1976.
*Leontief et al., *The Future of the World Economy,* 1977.
*Reynolds, *International Commodity Agreements and the Common Fund,* 1978.
*Rothstein, *Global Bargaining: UNCTAD and the Request for a New International Economic Order,* 1979.
*Brandt Commission, *North-South: A Program for Survival,* 1980.
*Dolman, *Resources, Regimes, and World Order,* 1981.

March 24   The Steady-State and Alternative Technologies
Brown, chapter 10
*Schumacher, *Small is Beautiful,* 1973.
*Daly, *Toward a Steady-State Economy,* 1973.
*Ophuls, *Ecology and the Politics of Scarcity,* 1977.
*Pirages, *The Sustainable Society,* 1977.
*Stokes, *Helping Ourselves: Local Solutions to Global Problems,* 1981.
*Soroos, "From Bullocks to Nuclear Power: Meeting India's Energy Needs," 1982.

IV. Managing the Resources of Non-national Areas
Decisions have been recently made at the United Nations Conference on the Law of the Seas regarding how the vast natural wealth of the oceans should be managed. Conflicts have also arisen over the resources of other non-national areas, in particular over those of Antarctica and space.

March 29   The Law of the Seas Conference and Seabed Resources
Lewis Alexander, "The New Geography of the World's Oceans Before and After the
  Law of the Sea," *Columbia Journal of World Business*, Winter 1980.
International Organization, Spring 1977 issue on "Restructuring Ocean Re-
  gimes."
*Walsh, *The Law of the Sea: Issues in Resource Management*, 1977.
*Luard, *The Control of the Seabed*, 2nd edition, 1977.
*Barkenbus, *Deep Seabed Resources*, 1979.
*Eckert, *The Enclosure of Ocean Resources: Economics and the Law of Sea*, 1979.
Columbia Journal of World Business, Winter 1980 issue on UNCLOS.
*Hollick, *U.S. Foreign Policy and the Law of the Seas*, 1981.

March 31   The Living Resources of the Ocean (and Land)
Brown, chapter 3
Eckholm, *Down to Earth*, chapters 5, 10. (book on reserve)
*Knight, *Managing the Seas Living Resources*, 1977.
*Schmidhauser and Totten, *The Whaling Issue in US-Japanese Relations*, 1978.
*Myers, *The Sinking Arc*, 1979.
*Allen, *Conservation and Management of Whales*, 1980.
*Ehrlich and Ehrlich, *Extinction: the Causes and Consequences of the Disappear-
  ance of Species*, 1981.
*Bordman, *International Organization and the Conservation of Nature*, 1981.
*McNally, *So Remorseless a Havoc: Of Dolphins, Whales, and Men*, 1981.

April 5   Resources of Antarctica and Outer Space
Mitchell, "The Politics of Antarctica," *Environment*, Jan/Feb 1980, pp. 12-20.
*O'Neill, *The High Frontier*, 1977.
*Smith, *Space Stations and International Law and Policy*, 1979.
*Auburn, *Antarctic Law and Politics*, 1982.
*Soroos, "The Commons in the Sky," *International Organization*, Summer 1982.

V. Pollution: Cleaning up the Planet
Energy concerns pushed pollution problems into the background as we began the
decade of the 1980's. Pollution is, however, becoming more serious both as a
transboundary phenomenon and in global commons, such as the oceans, in addition
to being a local problem. The pollution policies of both the international community and several countries will be examined.

April 7   Controlling Pollution Internationally
Rosencranz, "The Problem of Transboundary Pollution," *Environment*, July 1980,
  pp. 15-20. (photocopy on reserve)
Eckholm, *Down to Earth*, chapters 4, 6, 7. (book on reserve)
*Teclaff and Utton, *International Environmental Law*, 1974.
*Mostert, *Supership*, 1974.
*Eckholm, *The Picture of Health*, 1977.
*Schneider, *World Public Order of the Environment*, 1979.
*M'Gonigle and Zacher, *Pollution, Politics, and International Law: Tankers at Sea*,
  1979.
*Silverstein, *Superships and Nation States*, 1979.
*Weir and Shapiro, *Circle of Poison: Pesticides and People in a Hungry World*,
  1981.

April 12 Comparative Pollution Policies
*Enloe, *The Politics of Pollution in a Comparative Perspective*, 1975.
*Kelley et al., *The Economic Superpowers and the Environment: The U.S., USSR, and Japan*, 1976.
*Rosenbaum, *The Politics of Environmental Concern*, second edition, 1977.

VI. Simulation Exercise
The class will take part in a World Conference on the Human Environment, an ad hoc simulation exercise developed for the course. It is designed to be a representation of the recent international conferences on environmental problems that are discussed during the semester. It will offer the class an opportunity to put forth some integrated proposals for coming to grips with planetary ecological problems.

April 14, 19, 21, 26 World Conference on the Human Environment
**Term Paper is Due* (April 22)

VII. The Future
In the final session an effort will be made to pull together some of the directions that mankind may take in the next 25 to 50 years. A few selected term papers may be presented.

April 28   Scenarios of Ecological Futures
Brown, chapter 13
*Callenback, *Ecotopia* (a novel), 1975.
*Kahn, *The Next 200 Years*, 1976.
*Boulding, *Ecodynamics*, 1978.
*North, *The World that Could Be*, 1980.
*Mische and Mische, *Toward a Human World Order*, 1978.
*O'Neill, *2081: A Hopeful View of the Future*, 1981.

Environmental Ethics

L. Shannon Jung   *Fall 1983*
Religion 381/Concordia College/Moorhead, MN 56560

Purposes of the Course

1. To facilitate the participants' ability to think clearly, logically, and imaginatively. I take it that this is the primary purpose of the liberal arts and thus of this course as well.
2. To become aware of the growing interdependence of the regions and peoples of the world, the increasing interrelatedness of its problems (food, population, industrial growth, energy, nonrenewable resources, etc.), and the necessity of interdisciplinary approaches to these problems.
3. To investigate and evaluate the religious and cultural roots and values which lie behind the rise of modern technological civilization and which have contributed to the problems generated by consumption and growth.
4. To explore what solutions to these problems our religious and cultural resources might suggest.
5. To look in some depth at two particularly troublesome ecological crises: that of nuclear war and the ecological and economic difficulties that face the farmers of our nation.

Requirements of the Course

1. Two tests.
2. A group project. Rather than assigning individual papers which often receive no further hearing, I am asking you to initiate a project which will be presented to some group and have an impact beyond that of the writer and the evaluator. That might take several forms—chapel, presentation to a lay group in a church, slide show, preparation of a grant proposal, etc. While the instructor will be glad to assist you in this project, the primary responsibility for it will be the student's. I am asking each individual to keep a record of her or his own reading, planning time.
3. A short (7 page) paper which represents the culmination of your reasoning about ecological matters. This paper should be a tight argument which takes a position on an issue central to environmental concerns and defends it. Organize in teams of two and present your argument to the class during the last two class sessions.

Texts

Ian G. Barbour, ed. *Western Man and Environmental Ethics*. Reading, Mass.: Addison-Wesley Publishing Company, 1973.

Loren Wilkinson, ed. *Earthkeeping: Christian Stewardship of Natural Resources*. Grand Rapids, Mich.: Eerdmans, 1980.

Ground Zero, *Nuclear War: What's In It For You*. New York: Pocket Books, Simon and Schuster, 1982.

8

30

Jonathan Schell, *The Fate of the Earth.* New York: Alfred A. Knopf, 1982.
Charles P. Lutz, *Farming the Lord's Land: Christian Perspectives on American Agriculture.* Minneapolis: Augsburg, 1980.
E.F. Schumacher, *Small is Beautiful: Economics as if People Mattered.* New York: Harper & Row, 1973.

Organization of Course

I. An Historical/Attitudinal Overview of the Ecological Situation

August 30   Introduction

September 1   The Logic of Argument
Film: "The Tragedy of the Commons"
Barbour, 1-42

September 3   Historical Roots and Attitudes
Barbour, 43-64

September 6   Historical Roots and Attitudes
Barbour, 66-115

September 8   Ecology in America
Barbour, 115-155

September 10   The Current Debate over Wilderness
Deadline: Decide on Semester Project
Barbour, 156-186

September 13   Technology as Environmental Culprit
Barbour, 188-242

September 15   Global Ecology
Barbour, 243-276

September 17   Local Issues in the Red River Valley

II. A Case Study in the Preservation of the Environment: Nuclear Armament and War

September 20   How It Might Happen and the Facts
Nuclear, pp. 1-121
Schell, pp. 1-96

September 22   Consequences, Solutions, and Fallout Shelters
Nuclear, pp. 125-195
Schell, pp. 99-178

September 24   The Future of the Planet
Nuclear, pp. 199-249
Schell, pp. 181-231

September 26, 27   Concordia Conference on National Security and Nuclear Arms
"Problems in Contemporary War: A Just War Critique," Dr. James Johnson, Christian ethicist

"U.S. Policy for Peace," Dr. Ronald Lehman, Dept. of Defense
"The Defense Budget: Is It Really Buying Security?" Dr. Gordon Adams, Economist

September 28   Processing the Conference: Christian Ethics on War and Peace

September 29   Wrap-up and Review

October 1   Test #1

III. Christian Perspectives on the Environment

October 11   Dimensions of the Crisis: Population
Films and Discussion
Wilkinson, 1-48

October 13   Dimensions: Rich and Poor Nations
Possible film; discussion
Wilkinson, 49-98

October 15   Focus on the Third World
Jung and Jon Evert, a local farmer, to meet with Hovde's Political Science class

October 20   Attitudinal Roots in the Western World: A Contrast in Eastern Orthodoxy
Wilkinson, 101-143

October 22   Where We Are Today
Wilkinson, 143-199

October 25   The Stewardship Model
Wilkinson, 200-252

October 27   An Alternative Christian Model: Global Interdependence
Paper by Jung

October 29   Towards a Christian Solution, or Solutions in Christian Perspective
Wilkinson, 255-292; 301-309

IV. A Case Study on the Preservation of the Environment; Farming the Land

November 1   Farming and Food for People
Lutz, 7-40

November 3   Family Farming
Lutz, 41-78

November 5   Corporate Farming: Agribusiness—Blessing or Curse?
TBA

November 8   The Structure of U.S Farming
Lutz, 79-121

November 10-12   The Ecology of Farming
Lutz, 123-164
Lutz, 165-199

November 15   The Land Ethic

V. Alternate Views on the Environment from a Religious Perspective

November 17   An Alternative from the East: Buddhist Economics
Schumacher, 1-75

November 19   Buddhist Economics
Schumacher, 79-159

November 22-24   Economic Conservationism: The Pro's and Con's of Schumacher's Position
Schumacher, 1-159
Schumacher, 163-220

November 29   Native American Perspectives on Ecology
Schumacher, 223-297

December 1   Native American Religious Perspectives

December 3   Testing some Conclusions
Film: Limits to Growth
Student response papers in search of closure

December 6   Test #2

December 8   Team Presentations (4 teams)

December 10   Team Presentations (3 teams)

December 13   Revised presentation papers due

Social Ecology

Joseph Miller   *Spring 1983*
Psychology 333D/St. Mary's College/Notre Dame, IN 46556

This course is designed to provide us with a forum to conduct a relatively intense, multidisciplinary analysis of a variety of social and environmental problems, and an opportunity to explore a number of alternative "solutions" to such problems. Attention will be devoted to the diverse effects of large corporations on our lives and the lives of Third World peoples, and to socialization practices and psychological processes that are contributing to our current problems. Problems to be addressed in the course include nuclear energy and wastes; chemicalization of our air, land, water, and food; world food and hunger; abuses in our business and health systems; masculist values and the technological imperative; and groupthink and dehumanization. Potential "solutions" to be addressed include alternative energy, agriculture, and community strategies; conservation and energy efficiency; intermediate/appropriate technologies; simple/self-sufficient living strategies; citizen awareness and education; and public-interest groups and citizen activism.

Nuclear Energy: Resources

Browne, Corinne and Munroe, Robert. *Time Bomb: Understanding the Threat of Nuclear Power*. William Morrow, 1981.
Faulkner, Peter. *The Silent Bomb: A Guide to the Nuclear Energy Controversy*. Vintage Books/Friends of the Earth, 1977.
Freeman, Leslie. *Nuclear Witnesses: Insiders Speak Out*. W.W. Norton, 1981.
Gofman, John W. *Radiation and Human Health*. Sierra Club, 1981.
Gyorgy, Anna. *No Nukes: Everyone's Guide to Nuclear Power*. South End Press, 1979.
Nader, Ralph and Abbotts, John. *The Menace of Atomic Energy*. (Revised Edition), Norton, 1979.
Stephenson, Lee and Zachar, George. *Accidents Will Happen: The Case Against Nuclear Power*. Perennial Library/Environmental Action Foundation, 1979.
Sternglass, Ernest. *Secret Fallout*. McGraw Hill, 1981.
Wasserman, Harvey; Solomon, Norman; Alvarez, Robert; and Walters, Eleanor. *Killing Our Own: The Disaster of America's Experience with Atomic Radiation*. Delacorte, 1982.

Nuclear Energy: Topics and Readings

January 17
Faulkner, Introduction
Faulkner, Chapter 1, "The Incident at Brown's Ferry"

Faulkner, Chapter 2, "Malignant Giant: The Nuclear Industry's Terrible Power and How It Silenced Karen Silkwood"

January 20
Faulkner, Chapter 3, "We Almost Lost Detroit"
Gyorgy, Section 1, Chapter 2, "Atomic Power, Nuclear Plants"
Gyorgy, Section 1, Chapter 3, "The Nuclear Fuel Cycle"

January 24
Freeman, Chapter 3, "Ernest J. Sternglass, Physicist"
Freeman, Chapter 4, "John W. Gofman, Medical Physicist"

January 27
Freeman, Chapter 2, "Rosalie Bertell, Medical Researcher"
Schwartz, Loretta. "Uranium Deaths at Crown Point," *Ms.*, October, 1979.
Wasserman, et al., Chapter 9, "Uranium Milling and the Church Rock Disaster"

January 31
Gyorgy, Section 1, Chapter 4, "Health Dangers"
Gyorgy, Section 1, Chapter 5, "Safely Along the Fuel Cycle"
Faulkner, "Reactor Safety Study and Reactor Safety Problems," 145-163.
Harding, Jim. "Steam Generator Corrosion Plagues Nuclear Reactors," *Not Man Apart*, November, 1981.
Harding, Jim. "Nuclear Headaches for the New Year," *Not Man Apart*, February/March, 1982.

February 3
Film: "America, From Hitler to MX"
Soft Energy Path Preview Articles
Morgan, Richard and Talbot, David. Appendix. In Morgan, Richard and Talbot, David, *Power and Light: Political Strategies for the Solar Transition*.
Talbot, David. "Conservatopia, U.S.A.," *Mother Jones*, August, 1979, 37-41.
Harding, Jim. "The Conservation Connection," *Not Man Apart*, January, 1983.

February 7
Wasserman, et al., Chapter 13, "Animals Died at Three Mile Island"
Wasserman, et al., Chapter 14, "People Died at Three Mile Island"
Wasserman, et al., Chapter 15, "Conclusion: Surviving the New Fire"

February 10
Faulkner, Chapter 9, "The Silent Bomb: Radioactive Wastes"
Faulkner, Chapter 10, "Theft and Terrorism"
Faulkner, Chapter 12, "Insurance and Nuclear Power Risks"
Warnock, Donna. "Waving Goodbye to the Bill of Rights," In Stephenson and Zachar, 162-174.
Wasserman, Harvey. "Radiation Roulette," *Mother Jones*, August, 1979.

Energy Alternatives: Resources

Coates, Gary (Ed.). *Resettling America: Energy, Ecology and Community*. Brick House Publishing Company, 1982.
Commoner, Barry. *The Politics of Energy*. Knopf, 1979.

Courrier, Kathleen (Ed.). *Life After '80: Environmental Choices We Can Live With.* Solar Lobby/Brick House, 1982.

Farallones Institute. *The Integral Urban House: Self-Reliant Living in the City.* Sierra Club Books, 1979.

Harding, Jim. *Tools for the Soft Path.* Friends of the Earth/Brick House, 1982.

Lovins, Amory. *The Energy Controversy: Soft Path Questions and Answers.* Friends of the Earth, 1979.

Merrill, Richard and Gage, Thomas. *Energy Primer—Solar, Water, Wind, and Biofuels* (updated and Revised Edition). Delta/Portola Institute, 1978.

Morgan, Richard and Talbot, David. *Power and Light: Political Strategies for the Solar Transition.* Pilgrim Press, 1981.

Morris, David. *Self-Reliant Cities: Energy and the Transformation of Urban America.* Sierra Club, 1982.

Ridgeway, James. *Energy-Efficient Community Planning.* JG Press/The Elements, 1979.

Todd, Nancy (Ed.). *The Book of the New Alchemists.* E.P. Dutton, 1977.

Energy Alternatives: Topics and Readings

February 2
Soft Energy Path Preview Articles

February 14
"The Plowboy Interview: Amory Lovins," *Mother Earth News,* November/December, 1977.

"The Plowboy Interview: Dr. E.F. Schumacher," *Mother Earth News,* November/December, 1976.

Broad, William. "The Chaos Factor," *Science 83,* January/February, 1983.

February 17
Gyorgy, Section 3, Chapter 1, "Conservation"
Gyorgy, Section 3, Chapter 2, "Recycling"
Gyorgy, Section 3, Chapter 4, "Energy Sources, Now and for the Future"

February 21
Guest speaker to present the "pro" side of nuclear energy and other hard energy paths.

February 24
Morgan, Richard and Talbot, David. "A Place in the Sun." In Morgan and Talbot, *Power and Light: Political Strategies for the Solar Transition.*

Morris, David. "First Steps." In Morris, David, *Self-Reliant Cities,* 109-136.

Grossman, Richard. "Energy and Jobs." In Lyons, Stephen (Ed.), *SUN: A Handbook for the Solar Decade.* Friends of the Earth, 1978, 68-94.

February 28
Morris, David. "Humanly Scaled Energy Systems." In Morris, David, *Self-Reliant Cities,* 137-177.

Morris, David. "The Ecological City." In Morris, David, *Self-Reliant Cities,* 204-221.

March 3
Reece, Ray. "The Solar Blackout," *Mother Jones*, September/October, 1980.
Hochschild, Adam. "Shuttling Manhattans to the Sky," *Mother Jones*, May, 1978.
Chernow, Ron. "The Day We Set New York on Fire," *Mother Jones*, January, 1977.
Rapoport, Roger. "The Dark Side of Diesel Chic," *Mother Jones*, February/March, 1980.

Agriculture, Agribusiness, and Hunger—Issues and Alternatives: Resources

Ahmed, Karim; Scherr, S. Jacob; and Richter, Robert. *Pills, Pesticides and Profits: The International Trade in Toxic Substances.* North River Press, 1982.
Berry, Wendell. *The Unsettling of America: Culture and Agriculture.* Sierra Club Books, 1977.
Burbach, Roger and Flynn, Patricia. *Agribusiness in the Americas.* Monthly Review Press, 1980.
Jackson, Wes. *New Roots for Agriculture.* Friends of the Earth, 1980.
Lappé, Frances Moore. *Diet for a Small Planet* (10th Anniversary Edition). Ballantine, 1982.
Lappé, Frances Moore and Collins, Joseph. *World Hunger: Ten Myths* (Revised Edition). Institute for Food and Development Policy, 1979.
Lappé, Frances Moore and Collins, Joseph. *Food First.* Institute for Food and Development Policy, 1977.
Merrill, Richard (Ed.) *Radical Agriculture.* Harper and Row, 1976.
Nelson, Jack. *Hunger for Justice: The Politics of Food and Faith.* Orbis Books, 1980.
Valentine, William and Lappé, Frances Moore. *What Can We Do. Food and Hunger: How You Can Make a Difference.* Institute for Food and Development Policy, 1980.
Weir, David and Shapiro, Mark. *Circle of Poison: Pesticides and People in a Hungry World.* Institute for Food and Development Policy, 1981.

Agriculture, Agribusiness, and Hunger—Issues and Alternatives: Readings

March 7
Zwerdling, Daniel. "The Day of the Locust," *Mother Jones*, August, 1977.
Garcia, Richard and Dahlsten, Donald. "The Price of Pesticides," *Not Man Apart*, September, 1980.
Mazzora, Maria. "Farm Workers Live Under the Spray Gun," *Not Man Apart*, September, 1980.
Collins, Joseph and Lappé, Frances Moore. "Still Hungry After All These Years: The Not-so-Grand Opening of the Global Supermarket," *Mother Jones*, August, 1977.
Lappé, Frances Moore and Collins, Joseph. "Isn't Nature Neutral?" From *Food First.*

March 10
Weir and Schapiro, Chapter 1, "The Circle of Poison;" Chapter 2, "A Victim Every Minute;" Chapter 3, "Dumping: Business as Usual;" Chapter 4, "The Pesticide Bommerang;" Chapter 5, "Pesticides to Feed the Hungry".

March 21
Weir and Schapiro, Chapter 6, "The Global Pesticide Supermarket;" Chapter 7,

"Lubricating the Sales Machine;" Chapter 8, "With the Advice and Consent of Government;" Chapter 9, "Breaking the Circle of Poison."

Scherr, S. Jacob. "Reagan to U.S. Exporters: Dump Away," *Multinational Monitor*, July, 1982.

March 24

Dybdahl, Tom. *The Cornucopia Project: Organic Paths to Food Security*. Rodale Press.

Cook, Kenneth. "Organic Gains Ground," *Environmental Action*, May, 1981, 4-9.

Goldstein, Jerome. "Organic Force." In Merril, Richard (Editor), *Radical Agriculture*, Harper Colophon, 1976, 212-223.

Ecology Action of the Midpeninsula. "Biodynamic/French Intensive Agriculture: High Yields and Higher Hopes," *Mother Earth News*, May, 1976.

Cole, Barbara and Goldman, "M.C. Community Gardens Come to the City," *Organic Gardening and Farming*, March, 1978.

March 28

Ehrenreich, Barbara; Dowie, Mark; and Minkin, Stephen. "The Charge: Gynocide— The Accused: The U.S. Government," *Mother Jones*, November, 1979.

Silverman, Milton; Lee, Philip; and Lydecker, Mia. "How the Drug Companies Kill One Million People A Year." Excerpt from *Prescriptions for Death: The Drugging of the Third World*, University of California Press, 1982, in the *Multinational Monitor*, July, 1982.

Beardshaw, Virginia and Medawar, Charles. "Health Activists Seek UN Code on Drug Company Marketing Practices," *Multinational Monitor*, July 1982.

Garson, Barbara. "The Bottle Baby Scandal: Milking the Third World for all it's Worth," *Mother Jones*, December, 1977.

Ehrenreich, Barbara and Fuentes, Annette. "Life on the Global Assembly Line," *Ms.*, January, 1981.

Schapiro, Mark. "Seeds of Disaster," *Mother Jones*, December, 1982.

April 7

Selected Readings from Lappé (1982) and Valentine and Lappé (1980).

Chemicalization of Air, Land, Water, and Food: Resources

Brown, Michael. *Laying Waste: The Poisoning of America by Toxic Chemicals*. Pantheon, 1980.

Chen, Edwin. *PCB: An American Tragedy*. Prentice Hall, 1979.

Green, Mark and Massie, Robert Jr. *The Big Business Reader: Essays on Corporate America*. The Pilgrim Press, 1980.

Environmental Defense Fund and Boyle, Robert. *Malignant Neglect*. Knopf, 1979.

Epstein, Samuel. *The Politics of Cancer*. Sierra Club, 1978.

Hall, Ross. *Food for Naught: The Decline in Nutrition*. Vintage Books, 1974.

Hightower, Jim. *Eat Your Heart Out: Food Profiteering in America*. Vintage Books, 1975.

Hunter, Beatrice. *Food Additives and Federal Policy: The Mirage of Safety*. Scribner, 1976.

Keough, Carol. *Water Fit to Drink*. Rodale, 1980.

Nader, Ralph; Brownstein, Ronald; and Richards, John. *Who's Poisoning America? Corporate Polluters and their Victims in the Chemical Age*. Sierra Club, 1981.

Norwood, Christopher. *At Highest Risk: Environmental Hazards to Young and Unborn Children.* McGraw-Hill, 1980; Penguin, 1981.

Pim, Linda. *The Invisible Additives.* Doubleday (Toronto), 1981.

Powledge, Fred. *Water: The Nature, Uses, and Future of our Most Precious and Abused Resource.* Farrar Straus Giroux, 1982.

Robbins, William. *The American Food Scandal.* William Morrow and Co., 1974.

Toxic Nightmare—Environmental Perspectives. Data Center, 1982. (Three Volumes)

Toxics Training Program. *Training Manual on Toxic Substances: Tools for Effective Action.* Sierra Club, 1981. (Two Volumes)

Verrett, Jacqueline and Carper, Jean. *Eating May Be Hazardous to Your Health.* Anchor Books, 1975.

Yudkin, John. *Sweet and Dangerous.* Bantam Books, 1972.

Chemicalization of Air, Land, Water, and Food: Readings

April 11

Brownstein, Ronald. "The Toxic Tragedy." In Nader et al., pp. 1-59.

April 14

Rubenstein, David. "The Synergy Factor," *Not Man Apart,* June, 1981.

Epstein, Samuel. "Industry's Game for Testing Chemicals," *Not Man Apart,* September, 1980.

Castleman, Michael. "Why Johnny Can't Have Kids," *Mother Jones,* April 1982.

Foster, Douglas and Dowie,Mark. "The Illusion of Safety, Part I," *Mother Jones,* June, 1982.

IOS Team. "The Illusion of Safety, Part II: A Daring Rescue," *Mother Jones,* July, 1982.

MacRobert, Alan. "Look What They've Done to the Rain," *Mother Jones,* December, 1977.

Gold, Michael. "The Radiowave Syndrome," *Science 80,* Premier Issue.

April 18

Powledge, Fred. "Water: The Substance and Crisis." In Powledge, Fred, pp. 3-11.

Harty, Sheila. "Hucksters in the Classroom," *Social Policy,* September/October, 1981, 38-42.

Jacobsen, Michael. "Nutrition and the Politics of Food," In Green and Massie, 123-130.

Zwerdling, Daniel. "The Food Monsters," *The Progressive,* March, 1980.

Harris, Michael. "Eating Oil: From the Kitchens of Amoco Comes Petroleum Protein, the New 'Natural' Food," *Mother Jones,* August, 1977.

Reading on Irradiated Foods TBA

Bunin, Greta. "Does Everything Cause Cancer?" *Nutrition Action,* May, 1979.

April 21

Environmental Defense Fund and Boyle, Robert. "The Solution to the Problem," In the Environmental Defense Fund and Boyle, Robert, 211-232.

"Nutrients that Team Up Against Pollution," *Prevention,* August, 1978.

Sherman, Car. "Vitamin A—A Kind of Internal Gas Mask," *Prevention,* June, 1979.

Gottlieb, Bill. "A and C: Vitamins For a Toxified World," *Prevention,* February, 1980.

Feltman, John. "Antioxidants, Aging and Cancer," *Prevention*, July, 1978.
Uhlaner, Jonathan. "Selenium, a Mineral Made to Fight Cancer," *Prevention*, February, 1980.
"Vitamin E Lubricates the Circulation," *Prevention*, April, 1978.
Yates, John. "Lecithin Works Wonders," *Prevention*, February, 1980.
Reading on Fiber TBA

April 25
Nader, Ralph. "Conclusion: We Are Not Helpless," In Nader et al., 311-357.

Health Care: Resources

Arms, Suzanne. *Immaculate Deception: A New Look at Women and Childbirth in America*. Bantam Books, 1977.
Corea, Gena. *The Hidden Malpractice: How American Medicine Treats Women as Patients and Professionals*. Jove/HBJ Book, 1977.
Dreifus, Claudia. *Seizing our Bodies: The Politics of Women's Health*. Vintage, 1978.
Ehrenreich, Barbara and English, Deidre. *For Her Own Good: 150 Years of the Experts' Advice to Women*. Anchor Press/Doubleday, 1978.
Ehrenreich, Barbara and Ehrenreich, John. *The American Health Empire: Power, Profits, and Politics*. Vintage Books, 1970.
Illich, Ivan. *Medical Nemesis: The Expropriation of Health*. Bantam Books, 1976.
Lappé, Marc. *Germs That Won't Die*. Doubleday, 1982.
Seaman, Barbara and Seaman, Gideon. *Women and the Crisis in Sex Hormones*. Rawson, 1977; Bantam Books, 1978.

Health Care: Readings

April 28
Spake, Amanda. "The Drugging Industry." In Green and Massie, 139-147.
Arms, Suzanne. "The New, Improved, Quick-and-Easy, All-American Hospital Birth." In Arms, 62-104.
Gordon, James and Haire, Doris. "Alternatives in Childbirth." In Hastings, Arthur; Fadiman, James; and Gordon, James (Eds.), *Health for the Whole Person: The Complete Guide to Holistic Medicine*. Westview Press, 1980.

May 2
Seaman, Barbara and Seaman, Gideon. "The Amazing Story of DES." From *Women and the Crisis in Sex Hormones*.
Minkin, Stephen. "Nine Thai Women Had Cancer . . . None of Them Took Depo-Provera: Therefore, Depo-Provera is Safe. This is Science?" *Mother Jones*, November, 1981.
Bruck, Connie. "Menopause," *Human Behavior*, April 1979.
Dowie, Mark and Marshall, Carolyn. "The Benedectin Cover-Up," *Mother Jones*, November, 1980.

Social Change Careers and Information

Aptakin, Karen (Ed.). *Good Works: A Guide to Social Change Careers*. Center for the Study of Responsive Law, 1980.

International Politics and the Physical Environment

David Rosen   *Spring 1982*
Department of Human Ecology/Ramapo College of New Jersey/
Mahwah, NJ 07430

This course examines the constellation of issues defined by the interactions among the global society, national decision-making structures and the physical environment. Among the topics considered will be population, growth, energy policy, the control of oil, nuclear power and proliferation, adequacy and control of mineral supplies, food and hunger, international control of pollution, and the regulation of ocean exploitation. The readings are drawn from a broad range of disciplines and nations. The perspectives we will examine range from the apocalyptic to the Panglossian, from the revolutionary to the complacent.

Texts

Jeremy Rifkin, *Entropy: A New World View*, Bantam, 1981 (hereafter: Rifkin).
Julian L. Simon, *The Ultimate Resource*, Princeton University Press, 1981 (hereafter: Simon).
David W. Orr and Marvin S. Soroos, eds., *The Global Predicament: Ecological Perspectives on World Order*, University of North Carolina Press, 1979 (hereafter: TGP).
The requirement for the course shall be the writing of at least four seminar papers during the course of the semester.

Course Outline

January 26   Some Underlying Concepts and Issues
G. Hardin, "The Tragedy of the Commons," *Science*, Dec. 13, 1968, 1243-1248.
B. Crowe, "The Tragedy of the Commons Revisited," in L. Roos, ed., *The Politics of Ecosuicide*, 29-40.
A. D'Amato, "The Politics of Ecosuicide," in L. Roos, *The Politics of Ecosuicide*, 10-28.
G. Hardin, *"Carrying Capacity as an Ethical Concept,"* in G.R. Lucas, et al., *Lifeboat Ethics*.
G. Hardin, "Lifeboat Ethics: The Case Against Helping the Poor," *Psychology Today*, Sept., 1974.
M. Soroos, "Lifeboat Ethics versus One-Worldism in International Food and Resource Policy," in *TGP*, 131-149.

February 2   Perspectives on Growth and Scarcity
Rifkin, 1-59, 261-269.
Simon, 3-29.

"Intro," *TGP*, 3-14.

J. Randers and W. Behrens, "Watch for the Foothills: Signaling the End of Growth in a Finite World," in *TGP*, 18-38.

M. Soroos, "Exploring Global Ecological Futures," in *TGP*, 39-53.

D. Orr, "Modernization and the Ecological Perspective," in *TGP*, 75-86.

M. Soroos, "Ecology and the Time Dimension in Human Relationships," in *TGP*, 327-346.

R. North, "Toward a Framework for the Analysis of Scarcity and Conflict," *International Studies Quarterly*, Dec., 1977, 569-592.

February 9   Population, Growth and Scarcity

Rifkin, 63-94.

Simon, 30-50, 144-215.

J. Galtung, "The Limits to Growth and Class Politics," *Journal of Peace Research*, 1973, 101-114.

R. Clinton, "Population Dynamics and Future Prospects for Development," in *TGP*, 57-74.

W. Oltmans, ed., *On Growth*, pp. 1-6 (U Thant), 26-34 (Toynbee), 65-71 (Kaysen), 119-125 (Nordhaus), 192-197 (Strong), 216-231 (Forrester), 284-291 (Chomsky), 291-299 (Clark), 313-326 (Kahn), 334-338 (Marcuse), 385-390 (Rawls), 448-456 (Falk).

February 16   Energy

Rifkin, 99-113, 196-203. Simon, 90-126.

A. Lovins, "Energy Policy: The Road Not Taken," *Foreign Affairs*, Oct., 1977, 65-96.

L. Schipper and A. Lichtenberg, "Efficient Energy Use and Well-Being: The Swedish Example," *Science*, 1976, 1001-1013.

R. Lieber, "Europe and America in the World Energy Crisis," *International Affairs*, 1979, 531-545.

D. Bobrow and R. Kurdle, "Energy R&D: In Tepid Pursuit of Collective Goods," *International Organization*, 1979, 149-175 (see also related correspondence in *10*, Autumn, 1980, 641-649).

T. Berrie and D. Leslie, "Energy Policy for Developing Countries," *Energy Policy*, 1978, 119-128.

J. Krenz, "The Nation's Energy Dilemma," *Bulletin of Atomic Scientists*, May, 1981, 31-33.

February 23   Oil, OPEC and World Politics

C. Doran, "Oil Politics and the Rise of Codependence," in *TGP*, 195-208.

D. Bobrow, et al., "Contrived Scarcity: The Short-Term Consequence of Expensive Oil," *International Studies Quarterly*, 1977, 619-645.

W. Levy, "Oil and the Decline of the West," *Foreign Affairs*, Summer, 1980, 999-1015.

J. Amuzegar, "OPEC and the Dollar Dilemma," *Foreign Affairs*, 1978, 740-750.

F. Singer, "Limits to Arab Oil Power," *Foreign Policy*, 1978, 53-67.

J. Nye, "Energy Nightmares," *Foreign Policy*, Fall, 1980, 132-154.

M. Khail, "The Oil Price in Perspective," *International Affairs*, 1979, 517-530.

H. Maull, "The Control of Oil," *International Journal*, Spring, 1981, 271-293.

R. Keohane, "The International Energy Agency: State Influence and Transnational Politics," *International Organization*, 1978, 929-952.

March 2   Nuclear Power as an Energy Source
H. Bethe, et al., "Six Views of Atomic Energy," *Bulletin of Atomic Scientists*, March, 1977, 59-69.
V. Gilinsky, et al., (several articles on Three Mile Island), *Bulletin of Atomic Scientists*, Jan., 1980, 18-37.
R. Purple, "U.S. Nuclear Policy and the European Energy Market," *Energy Policy*, Dec., 1978, 277-284.
I. Bupp, "The Actual Growth and Probable Future of the World-Wide Nuclear Industry," *International Organization*, Winter, 1981, 59-76.
B. Flowers, "Nuclear Power," *Bulletin of Atomic Scientists*, March, 1978, 21-26, 54-57.
E. Radford, "Cancer Risks From Ionizing Radiation," *Technology Review*, Nov.-Dec., 1981, 66-78.

March 9   Civilian Nuclear Power and Weapons Proliferation
P. Lellouche, "Breaking the Rules Without Quite Stopping the Bomb: European Views," *International Organization*, Winter, 1981, 39-58.
A. Lovins, et al., "Nuclear Power and Nuclear Bombs," *Foreign Affairs*, Summer 1980, 1137-1177.
L. Dunn, et al., "Proliferation Watch, " *Foreign Policy*, Fall, 1979, 71-104.
L. Scheinman, "Multinational Alternatives and Nuclear Proliferation," *International Organization*, Winter, 1981, 77-102.
R. Gomer, et al., (commentaries on bombing of Osirak reactor), *Bulletin of Atomic Scientists*, Aug./Sept., 1981, 7-15.
S. Moglewer, "IAEA Safeguards and Non-Proliferation," *Bulletin of Atomic Scientists*, Oct., 1981, 24-29.
R. Richter, "Testimony From a Former Safeguards Inspector," *Bulletin of Atomic Scientists*, Oct., 1981, 29-36.
G. Handel, "Managing Nuclear Wastes: The International Connection," *Natural Resources Journal*, April, 1981, 267-314.
N. Call, "Atoms for Brazil, Dangers For All," *Bulletin of Atomic Scientists*, June, 1976, 4-9, 41-48.
K. Gottstein, "Nuclear Energy for the Third World," *Bulletin of Atomic Scientists*, June, 1977, 44-48.

March 16   Minerals, Resources and Power
Rifkin, 114-119, 123-127.
Simon, 216-239.
A. Winberg, "Resource Politics: The Future of International Markets for Raw Materials," in *TGP*, 178-194.
P. Crewson, "Dependency on Non-Fuel Minerals," *International Affairs*, Jan., 1978, 48-59.
H. Hveem, "Militarism of Nature: Conflict and Control Over Strategic Resources and Some Implications for Peace Research," *Journal of Peace Research*, 1979, 1-26.
S. Okita, "Natural Resource Dependency and Japanese Foreign Policy," *Foreign Affairs*, 1974, 714-725.

Z. Mikdashi, et al., "One, Two, Many OPEC's . . . ," *Foreign Policy*, Spring, 1974, 57-90.

P. Abelson and A. Hammond, "The New World of Materials," *Science*, Feb. 20, 1976, 633-636. (Note: Useful articles by Landsberg, Fried, Hayes and others in same issue.)

March 30   Food, Hunger and Politics
Rifkin, 138-142.
Simon, 70-89.
N. Jensen, "Limits to Growth in World Food," *Science*, 1978, pp. 317-320.
R. Hopkins and D. Puchala, "Perspectives on the International Relations of Food," *International Organization*, 1978, 581-616.
H. Bergesen, "A New Food Regime: Necessary But Impossible," *International Organization*, Spring, 1980, 285-302.
T. Sloan, "A Look at America's Potential Roles in Global Food Crisis," in *TGP*, 110-130.
S. Rosenfield, "The Politics of Food," *Foreign Policy*, Spring, 1974, 17-29.
C. Billo and L. Brown, "An Exchange on Food," *Foreign Policy*, Spring, 1974, 30-34.
O. Holsti, "Global Food Problems and Soviet Agriculture," in *TGP*, pp. 150-175.
N. Islam, "Food Aid: Conscience, Morality and Politics," *International Journal*, Spring, 1981, 353-370.
D. Kowalewski, "Transnational Corporations and the Third World's Right to Eat."
M. Doxey, "Oil and Food as International Sanctions," *International Journal*, Spring, 1981, 311-334.

April 6   Global and Transnational Pollution Policies
K. Mingst, "Evaluating Public and Private Approaches to Environmental Disputes: Statist and Transnational Alternatives From North America and Northern Europe," unpublished paper.
L. Juda, "International Environmental Concern: Perspectives and Implications for Developing States," in *TGP*, 90-107.
D. Piper, "Unilateral Acts of States with Regard to Environmental Protection," in *TGP*, 264-281.
R. d'Arge and A. Kneese, "State Liability for International Environmental Degradation: An Economic Perspective," *Natural Resource Journal*, July, 1980, 428-450.
H. Jacobson and D. Kay, "The Environmental Protection Activities of International Organizations."
M. Wilcher, "Transnational Environmental Problems," in David A. Kay and Eugene B. Skolnikoff, *World Eco-Crisis: International Organizations in Response*, Madison: Univ. of Wisconsin Press, 1972.
J. Howell, "An Approach to the Development of International Jurisdiction to Deal with Environmental Problems," unpublished paper.
M. Tolba, et al., (several articles on global environmental issues), *E.P.A. Journal*, June, 1978, 5-16.

April 13   Oceans, Resources and the Law of the Sea
G. Kent, "Ocean Fisheries Management," in *TGP*, 232-248.
J. Barkenbus, "The Politics of Ocean Resource Exploitation," *International Studies Quarterly*, 1977, 675-699.

R. Hudson, "The International Struggle For a Law of the Sea," *Bulletin of Atomic Scientists*, Dec., 1977, 14-20.

M. Hardy, "The Implications of Alternative Solutions for Regulating the Exploitation of Seabed Minerals," *International Organization*, 1977, 313-342.

R. Frank, "Jumping Ship," *Foreign Policy*, Summer, 1981, 121-138.

R. Mandel, "Transnational Resource Conflict: The Politics of Whaling," *International Studies Quarterly*, March, 1980, 89-127.

April 20   Scarcity and the New Economic Order

Rifkin, 185-193.

Simon, 240-288.

T. Moran, "The Multinational Corporations and Dependency," *International Organization*, 1978, 79-100.

W. Morehouse, "Separate, Unequal, But More Autonomous: Technology, Equity and World Order in the Millennial Transition," World Order Models Project, Working Paper #16, NY: World Policy Institute, 1981.

R. Kothari, "Environment and Alternative Development," World Order Models Project, Working Paper #15, NY: World Policy Institute, 1981.

R. Friedheim and W. Durch, "The International Seabed Authority and the New International Economic Order, " *International Organization*, 1977, 343-384.

V. Bye, "Nationalization of Oil in Venezuela: Redefined Dependence and the Legitimization of Imperialism," *Journal of Peace Reseach*, 1979, 57-78.

April 27   Toward Resolution

Rifkin, 203-256.

Simon, 291-348.

J. Taulbee, "Law, Organization and Environmental Concern," in *TGP*, 249-263.

A. Scott, "The Logic of International Interaction," in *TGP*, 284-307.

D. Orr and S. Hill, "Leviathan, The Open Society, and the Crisis of Ecology," in *TGP*, 308-326.

Environmental Policy Analysis

Richard Andrews   *Spring 1982*
Environmental Studies 252/University of North Carolina/
Chapel Hill, NC 27514

This course is designed to provide an intensive introduction to the structure and dynamics of U.S. environmental policymaking, and to the analysis of selected current environmental policies and regulations. It is intended primarily for students in the applied environmental professions, such as environmental management, planning, engineering, law, and health.

The central purpose of the course is to provide students in the various applied environmental professions with an understanding of the political and policy context in which they will work. The course material focuses, therefore, first on the structure and political dynamics of the U.S. federal government, and especially on the questions of how and why particular environmental problems have come to be the subject of various sorts of government policies. Within this context, the second half of the course material focuses on the critical examination of various current and proposed instruments of environmental policy.

Readings

Reading for this course will be relatively substantial, but will, I hope, be worth the effort. Most are contained in a duplicated course pack which will be available for purchase; in addition, you should purchase a copy of Charles Schultze's book *The Public Use of Private Interest*, which should be available in paperback at the medical school bookstore.

In general, many of the best readings both on the government framework and on policy analysis are not necessarily specific to environmental policy issues. Throughout the course, therefore, the reading assignments will reflect a mixture of these more general readings with some more specific to particular environmental policy issues; and we will use writing assignments as a vehicle for each student's deeper exploration of a particular issue of interest.

Written Assignments

The central written assignment of the course will be preparation of an "issue paper" on an environmental policy issue of particular interest to the student. This paper will be developed, however, in a series of more specific assignments due approximately every other week over the course of the term, in order to provide opportunities both for careful attention to each element of the paper, and for feedback from the instructor and revision where appropriate.

Outline and Reading List

January 13   Introduction: Policy Analysis and Political Environment

Thomas Dye, *Understanding Public Policy* (Englewood Cliffs, New Jersey: Prentice-Hall, 1972), pp. 1-37 (Chapters 1 & 2).

Peter Woll, "Models of the Policy Process." From his *Public Policy*, 1974, Chapter 2, pp. 21-52.

Hugh Heclo, "Issue Networks and the Executive Establishment." From Anthony King (editor), *The New American Political System* (Washington, D.C.: American Enterprise Institute, 1978, 87-124.

January 18   Guest Speaker

Dr. Dennis Meadows, Director, Center for Resource Policy Analysis, Dartmouth University.

January 20   Environmental "Problems": Identification, Criteria and Priorities

John Passmore, *Man's Responsibility for Nature: Ecological Problems and Western Traditions* (New York: Charles Scribner's Sons, 1974), pp. 43-45, 1971.

Sterling Brubaker, "A Summary and Prospect." From his *To Live on Earth* (Baltimore: Johns Hopkins University Press, 1972), Chapter 8, pp. 179-190.

Paul Slovic, Baruch Fischhoff, and Sarah Lichtenstein, "Facts Versus Fears: Perceived Risks and Opposition to Nuclear Energy." Paper presented at the annual meeting of the American Association for the Advancement of Science, Washington, D.C., January 4, 1982.

U.S. Council on Environmental Quality et al., *The Global 2000 Report to the President* (Washington, D.C.: U.S. Government Printing Office, 1980), Executive Summary, pp. 1-5.

Herman Kahn et al., "Four Characteristic Views . . ." from their *The Next 200 Years* (New York: William Morrow & Co., 1976), pp. 9-25.

(For further reading: remainder of *Global 2000* and Kahn works; U.S. Council on Environmental Quality, *Environmental Quality 19*—annually since 1970; U.S. Environmental Protection Agency, *Environmental Outlook* 1980; U.S. Department of Health, Education and Welfare, *Health 1978*; U.S. Council on Environmental Quality, *Environmental Trends*, 1981, and other basic census and statistical data on status and trends in environmental quality and its effects).

Assignment 1 due.

January 25   Solution Systems: Markets and Governments

Charles L. Schultze, *The Public Use of Private Interest* (Washington, D.C.: The Brookings Institution, 1977).

Richard A. Musgrave, "A Multiple Theory of The Public Household." From his *Theory of Public Finance* (New York: McGraw-Hill, 1959), Chapter 1, pp. 3-27.

Samuel Mermin, "Functions of Law." From his *Law and the Legal System* (Boston: Little, Brown, 1973), Chapter 1, pp. 5-10.

Thomas Dye, "Limits of Public Policy." From his *Understanding Public Policy*, pp. 228-229.

Burton A. Weisbrod, "Problems of Enhancing the Public Interest: Toward a Model of Governmental Failures." From his *Public Interest Law: An Economic and Institutional Analysis* (Berkeley: University of California Press, 1978), Chapter 3, pp. 30-41.

January 27   U.S. Environmental Policy I: Constitutional Powers and Constraints
Milton S. Heath, Constitutional Considerations for Natural Resources." (mimeo—
1 page).
The Constitution of the United States.
J. Gordon Arbuckle et al., "Constitutional Law." From their *Environmental Law
Handbook* (Washington, D.C.: Government Institute, Incorporated, 1976), pp. 26-
38.

February 1   Guest speaker
Dr. H. Stanley Bennett (former member, U.S. President's Science Advisory Com-
mittee).
Assignment 2 due.

**February 3   U.S. Environmental Policy II: Political Mobilization of Environmental
Interest**
Norman J. Ornstein and Shirley Elder, "Theories about Groups." From their
Interest Groups, Lobbying and Policy Making (Washington, D.C.: CQ Press,
1978), Chapter 1, pp. 7-21.
Gary D. Brewer, "Some Key Participants and Their Perceived Problems" (mimeo).
Robert S. Gilmour, "Private Interest and Public Lands," *Current History*, Volume
59 (1970), pp. 36-52.
Anthony Downs, "Up and Down with Ecology—the 'Issue—Attention Cycle'," *The
Public Interest* (Summer 1972), pp. 38-50.
Jeffrey M. Berry, "Tactics of Advocacy . . . and the Strategies of Influence." From his
Lobbying for the People (Princeton, New Jersey: Princeton University Press,
1977), Chapters 8 and 9, pp. 212-285.
(Further reading: remainder of Ornstein and Elder book.)

February 8   U.S. Environmental Policy III: The Congress
Raymond A. Bauer et al., "The Job of the Congressman" and "Congress as a Social
System." From their *American Business and Public Policy* (Chicago: Aldine,
1972), Chapters 29 and 31, pp. 403-413 and 425-432.
Wiliam J. Keefe, "The Impact of Recent Reforms." From his *Congress and the
American People* (Englewood Cliffs, New Jersey: Prentice-Hall, 1980).
Howard Margolis, "The Politics of Auto Emissions," *The Public Interest* (Fall
1977), pp. 3-21.
Bruce A. Ackerman and William T. Hassler, "Beyond the New Deal." From their
Clean Coal/Dirty Air (New Haven: Yale University Press, 1981), Chapter 1, pp. 1-
12.

February 9   Special Session with Former Senator Gaylord Nelson

**February 10   U.S. Environmental Policy IV: The President and the Executive
Office**
Thomas E. Cronin, "The Braking of the Presidency" and "The Swelling of the
Presidency." From his *The State of the Presidency* (Boston: Little, Brown, 1975),
Chapters 4 and 5, pp. 85-152.
James O. Edwards, "U.S. Forest Policy: The Role of the Office of Management and
Budget." From F.E. Convery and J.E. Davis, *Centers of Influence and U.S. Forest
Policy* (Durham, North Carolina: School of Forestry and Environmental Studies,
Duke University, 1977), pp. 37-47.

George Eads, "Harnessing Regulation: The Evolving Role of White House Oversight," *Regulation* (May/June 1981), pp. 19-26.

February 15   Guest Speaker
Assignment 3 due.

February 17   U.S. Environmental Policy V: Departments and Agencies
"Environmental Protection Agency." (mimeo).
Harold Seidman, "The Politics of Government Organization." From his *Politics, Position and Power: The Dynamics of Federal Organization* (New York: Oxford University Press, 1970), pp. 15-37.
Francis E. Rourke, "Variations in Agency Power." From his *Bureaucracy, Politics and Public Policy* (Boston: Little, Brown, 1969), pp. 63-86.
Sally K. Fairfax, "Lawyers in the Bureaucracy: the Power and the Glory." From Convery and Davis, *Centers of Influence and U.S. Forest Policy*, pp. 92-97.
Richard B. Stewart, "The Reformation of American Administrative Law," *Harvard Law Review*, Volume 88 (June 1975), pp. 1669-1688, 1805-1813.
Richard N.L. Andrews, "Environment and Energy: Implications of Overloaded Agendas," *Natural Resources Journal*, Volume 19 (July 1980), pp. 487-503.

February 22   U.S. Environmental Policy VI: The Judiciary
David L. Bazelon, "The Judiciary: What Role in Health Improvement?" *Science* (22 February 1981), pp. 792-93.
"The Administrative Procedure Act." (5 U.S. Code Section 551 and following). From *The Federal Regulatory Directory* 1979-80 (Washington, D.C.: CQ Press, 1979), pp. 721-729.
W. Gellhorn and C. Byse, "Scope of Judicial Review." From their *Administrative Law: Cases and Comments*, pp. 379-389, 478-483.
Martin Shapiro, "Courts Versus Administrative Agencies—A False Vision." From his *Supreme Court and Administrative Agencies* (New York: Free Press, 1968), pp. 91-103.
Robert H. Jackson, "Government by Lawsuit." Abridged from his *Struggle for Judicial Supremacy* (New York: Knopf, 1941).
Samuel Mermin, "Limits of Law." From his *Law and the Legal System*, pp. 11-30.

February 24   Federal-State Relations
Joseph L. Sax, "Federal Authority and States' Rights." (mimeo of a lecture delivered at the University of Michigan).
William A. Campbell, "Federal-State Relations in Environmental Policy," *Environmental Science and Technology*, Volume 14, No. 3 (March 1980), pp. 264-268.
Edward Flattau, "The Necessary Evil," *Conservation News*, Volume 40, No. 23, pp. 2-3.

March 1   Guest Speaker
Dr. Lester Lave (Economist, The Brookings Institution).
Assignment 4 due.

March 3   Environmental Professions in a Political Context: Roles and Ethics
Lawrence Susskind, "The Uses of Negotiation and Mediation in Environmental Impact Assessment." (mimeo).
Eric Ashby, "What Price the Furbish Lousewort?" (mimeo).

(Further reading: Martin Rein, *Social Science and Public Policy*, especially pages 254-268, "Dilemmas").

Spring Break

March 15   Policy Analysis: Approaches and Issues

Edith Stokey and Richard Zeckhauser, "Putting Analysis to Work," From their *Primer for Policy Analysis* (New York: Norton, 1978), Chapter 15, pp. 320-329.

Robert Dorfman, "Methods of Policy Analysis." (mimeo).

Irvin L. White and Mary Hamilton, "Policy Analysis in Integrated Impact Assessment." (mimeo).

Further reading: Lawrence Lynn, *Designing Public Policy* (Goodyear, Santa Monica, 1980).

March 17   Instruments of Environmental Policy

Joseph F. Coates, "Instruments of Governments." (mimeo).

Blair T. Bower et al., "Implementation Incentives for Environmental Quality Management." From International Joint Commission on the Great Lakes, *Workshop on Economic and Legal Enforcement Mechanisms* (Windsor, Ontario: IJC 1977), Report No. R-77-1, pp. 17-45.

March 22   Guest speaker

Dr. Clair Patterson (California Institute of Technology)

Assignment 5 due.

March 24   U.S. Environmental Policy Instruments I: Policy and Resource Allocation

"Major Environmental and Resource Conservation Laws," *National Journal*, January 19, 1980, pp. 96-97.

The National Environmental Policy Act of 1969 (mimeo).

Edward R. Fried et al., "Investing in the Physical Environment," from their *Setting National Priorities—The 1974 Budget* (Washington, D.C.: The Brooking Institution, 1973), Chapter 6.

March 29   U.S. Environmental Policy Instruments II: Regulatory Legislation

A. Myrick Freeman, III, "Air and Water Pollution Policy." From Paul R. Portney et al., *Current Issues in U.S. Environmental Policy* (Baltimore: John Hopkins, 1978), Chapter 2, pp. 12-18.

Federal Legislation and Regulations for Toxic Substances (2 mimeos).

Ronald Brickman and Erica Jasanoff, article on comparative international approaches to toxic substances control.

March 31   Issues in Environmental Quality Regulation

U.S. Senate Committee on Governmental Affairs, "Overview." From its *Study on Federal Regulations*, Volume VI, *Framework for Regulation*, December 1978, pp. xi-xxvii.

William Lilley III and James C. Miller III, "The New 'Social Regulation'," *The Public Interest*, No. 47, (Spring 1977), pp. 49-61.

U.S. General Accounting Office, "Improving the Scientific and Technical Information Available to the EPA," Report No. CED-79-115 (September 21, 1979), pp. 1-2, 4-12.

"Models for Developing Air and Water Quality Standards." (mimeo, 1 page).

Robert Dorfman, "The Lessons of Pesticide Regulation." Duke University: Center for the Study of Business Regulation, Paper No. 67, May 1981.

April 5   Guest speaker
Assignment 6 due.

April 7   Regulatory Reform I: Economic Incentives Versus Direct Regulation
Douglas M. Costle, "Efficiency and Compassion: Regulatory Reform," *EPA Journal*, September 1980, pp. 2-3.
Robert Reich, "Warring Critiques of Regulation," *Regulation*, 1980.
A. Myrick Freeman III and Robert H. Haveman, "Clean Rhetoric and Dirty Water." From A.C. Enthoven and A.M. Freeman III, *Pollution, Resources, and the Environment* (New York: Norton, 1973), pp. 122-137.
David R. Zick, "A Criticism of the Effluent Charge." From Enthoven and Freeman, pp. 138-140.
Robert W. Crandall, "Environmental Control is Out of Control," *Chemical and Engineering News*, April 23, 1979, pp. 29-33.
Gary Hart, "A Law Maker's View," *EPA Journal*, January 1979, pp. 7, 8, 26.
William Drayton, Jr., "Economic Law Enforcement," *EPA Journal*, January 1979, p. 26.
Stephen R. Kelman, "Economists and the Environmental Muddle," *The Public Interest*, 1981.
Frederick R. Anderson et al., *Environmental Improvement Through Economic Incentives*; Theodore Lowi, *The End of Liberalism* (Norton, New York, 1969).

April 12   Holiday

April 14   Regulatory Reform II: Analytical Requirements—Risk Assessment, Environmental Impact Assessment, and Benefit Cost Analysis
Lester Lave, "Eight Frameworks for Regulation." From his *Strategy of Social Regulation* (Washington, D.C.: The Brooking Institution, 1981), Chapter 2.
Paul Slovic, Baruch Fischoff, and Sarah Lichtenstein, "Rating the Risks," *Environment*, 1980.
Articles by Kletz, McGinty, and Ravetz on Risk Assessment from *New Scientist*.
Administration of Ronald Reagan, *Executive Order 12291*.
Richard N.L. Andrews, "Will Benefit Cost Analysis Reform Regulation?" *Environmental Science and Technology*, September 1981.
Richard Ayres, "Trading Health for Dollars."
(Further reading: William Lawrance, *Of Acceptable Risk*; Arthur Vander, *Nutrition, Stress, and Toxic Chemicals* (University of Michigan Press, 1981); James Miller and Bruce Yandle, *Benefit Cost Analyses of Social Regulation* (American Enterprise Institute, Washington, D.C., 1979).

April 19   Regulatory Reform III: Changes in Decision Processes and Authority
(Re-read Eads article from February 10).
Randall L. Calvert and Barry R. Weingast, "Congress, The Bureaucracy, and Regulatory Reform." Paper presented at the annual meeting of the Association for Public Policy Analysis and Management, Boston, October 1980, pp. 1-7, 18-24, 30-end.
"That Legislative Veto," *The Washington Post*, May 14, 1980.

April 21   Other Current Environmental Policy Issues
Terrence K. Pierson, "State and Local Hazardous Waste Management—A Framework for Action?" *Carolina Planning*, Volume 7, No. 1 (Spring 1981), pp. 16-25.

April 26   Guest speaker

International Law and Organization

Nuclear Weapons Policy and International Law
Lee Meyrowitz, Cardoza Law School

Semester on the United Nations
Douglas Simon, Drew University

International Law
Pavel Machala, Amherst College

Public International Law
Christopher C. Joyner, George Washington University

International Law and Organization
Lawrence S. Finkelstein, Northern Illinois University

The Dynamics of International Law
Karen Mingst, University of Kentucky

Nuclear Weapons Policy and International Law

Lee Meyrowitz   *Spring 1983*
Cardoza Law School/Yeshiva University/New York, NY 10033

The prevalent belief among the general public, as well as policy-makers, is that nuclear weapons are legal. This belief is based on the assumption that a state may do whatever it is not expressly forbidden from doing. The legality of nuclear weapons, however, cannot be judged solely by the existence or non-existence of a treaty rule specifically prohibiting or restricting their use. Any reasonable legal analysis must take into account all the recognized sources of international law, international treaties, international custom, general principles of law, judicial decisions and the writings of the most qualified publicists. Of particular relevance to the legality of nuclear weapons are the many treaties and conventions which limit the use of any weapons in war, the traditional distinction between combatant and non-combatant, and the principles of humanity, including the prohibition of weapons and tactics that are especially cruel and cause unnecessary suffering. A review of these basic principles supports a conclusion that the threat and use of nuclear weapons is illegal under international law.

Historically, the principles of humanity have been one of the primary sources of law limiting the violence permissible in war. Ever since the Declaration of St. Petersburg of 1868, the principles of humanity have been asserted as a constraint upon military necessity. The Declaration embodies what may be the twin ground rules of the laws of war: that "the right to adopt means of injuring the enemy is not unlimited" and that "the only legitimate object which States should endeavor to accomplish during a war is to weaken the military forces of the enemy..."

A basic source of the laws of war is the Hague Conventions of 1907, particularly the Regulations embodied in Hague Convention IV. The United States Air Force, in its most recent official publication (1976) on international law and armed conflict, states that these Regulations "...remain the foundation stones of the modern law of armed conflict." A fundamental tenet the Regulations is the prohibition of wanton or indiscriminate destruction. The Regulations forbid, for example, "the attack or bombardment, by whatever means, of towns, villages, (and even individual) dwellings or buildings which are undefended."

The universally-accepted Geneva Conventions of 1949 updated and greatly strengthened the 1907 Regulations. In particular, the Convention on "the Protection of Civilian Person in Time of War" imposes additional detailed obligations on all belligerents to ensure the essential requirements for the health, safety and sustenance of the civilian population. A primary objective of these Conventions is to assure that "disinterested (outside) aid (can be) given without discrimination to all victims of war, including members of the armed forces who, on account of their wounds, capture, or shipwreck, cease to be enemies but become suffering and helpless human beings."

We will go to the Genocide Convention of 1948, which made the destruction of groups on racial, religious, or nationality grounds an international crime. We will also examine the important law-making treaty, the United Nations Charter, and a further substantial body of fundamental humanitarian principles.

Yet, there is an influential school of thought which would deny the applicability of the existing laws of war to nuclear warfare. This school asserts that in an era of "total war" even the most fundamental rules can be disregarded if this enhances the chances for victory. This argument was urged in another context by some of the Nuremberg defendants, and indignantly rejected by the International Tribunal. The Tribunal's judgment warns that this "nazi conception" of total war would destroy the validity of international law altogether. Ultimately, the legitimacy of such a view would exculpate Auschwitz.

In sum, if the goal of the laws of war—to set limits on permissible violence—is to be realized to any serious degree, and if the fundamental principles of humanity are to be of continuing relevance to their interpretation, then it must be concluded that any threat of use of nuclear weapons is illegal. Global "survivability" is so elemental that the prohibition of nuclear weapons can be reasonably inferred from the existing laws of war. To conclude differently would be to ignore the barbaric and nefarious character of the use of nuclear weapons. As the laws of war embody the minimum demands of decency, exempting nuclear weapons from that body of laws would be abandoning even this minimum standard.

Goals

This course has two basic objectives: (1) to consider whether the basic concepts underlying strategic nuclear doctrine are consistent with the international law of armed conflict and (2) to analyze and evaluate the implications of the international law of armed conflict for the arms control process. More than any other technological development in military weaponry, the advent of nuclear weapons has challenged the relevance of the law of armed conflict to modern warfare. Consequently, nuclear weapons pose two legal questions: Are nuclear weapons by their very nature lawful, and if so, can they be used lawfully in various military situations? Posing these questions for investigation is particularly appropriate now as the United States formulates new national strategies for the use of nuclear weapons and new negotiating proposals for arms control. An understanding of the complexities of the nuclear weapons issue will provide a basis of clearer understanding of these questions and help develop a basis for judgement. Furthermore, such a legal perspective provides an important means for stimulating and framing the debate.

Initially, the seminar will provide the law student with a framework for understanding the trends and patterns of international conflict with particular attention given to the nuclear weapons dimension of international conflict. The seminar will also examine the character of international law with emphasis placed on its limits as well as its achievements.

Furthermore, the seminar will examine the rules and doctrines of nuclear weapons. The course will also deal with a range of issues relating to the past, present and future legal efforts to control, reduce and eliminate nuclear weapons. Finally, an effort will be made to interpret the relationship between international law and the changing role of force in international relations. Consequently, attention will be placed on the links between law and politics, and law and justice, by making an evaluation of past and present efforts to establish a viable, stable structure for peace in international affairs.

Requirements: Each student will be required to write a seminar paper of approximately 20-25 pages on a subject relating to the course.

Readings

A. The Nature of the International System: Conflict and Coercion
Hedley Bull, *The Anarchical Society* (New York, Columbia University Press, 1977), pp. 3-52

Richard Falk, *A Study of Future Worlds* (New York, Free Press, 1975), pp. 56-57 and 97-103

Alexander George, ed., *The Limits of Coercive Diplomacy* (Boston, Little, Brown, 1971), intro and pp. 1-35

Hedley Bull, "The State's Positive Role in World Affairs," in *Toward a Just World Order*, edited by Falk, Kim & Mendlovitz (Boulder, CO, Westview Press, 1982), pp. 60-74

Richard Falk, *This Endangered Planet* (New York, Random House, 1971), pp. 93-213

Friedrich Kratochwil, *International Order and Foreign Policy* (Boulder, CO, Westview, 1979), pp. 1-66

Thomas C. Schelling, *Arms and Influence* (New Haven, Yale University Press, 1966), pp. 1-34 and 126-189

B. Nuclear Deterrence: An Overview of Strategic Doctrine
Philip Green, *Deadly Logic* (New York, Schocken Books, 1968), pp. 3-92 and 255-276

Harry Rowen, "The Evolution of Strategic Doctrine," in Laurence Martin, ed., *Strategic Thought in Nuclear Age* (Baltimore, Johns Hopkins University Press, 1979), pp. 131-157

Alexander George and Richard Smoke, *Deterrence in American Foreign Policy* (New York, Columbia University Press, 1974), pp. 11-83

David Gompert, Michael Mandelbaum, et al., *Nuclear Weapons and World Politics* (New York, McGraw-Hill, 1978), pp. 1-80

Colin Gray and Keith Payne, "Victory is Possible," *Foreign Policy*, Summer 1980, pp. 14-27

Leon V. Sigal, "Rethinking the Unthinkable," *Foreign Policy*, Spring 1979, pp. 35-51

Fred C. Ikle, "Can Nuclear Deterrence Last Out the Century?" *Foreign Affairs*, Vol. 51, No. 2, January 1973, pp. 267-85

Robert J. Pranger and Roger P. Labrie, eds., *Nuclear Strategy and National Security* (Washington, D.C., American Enterprise Institute, 1977), "Official Documents and Statements," pp. 85-202

Louis Rene Beres, *Nuclear Strategy and World Order*, (New York, World Policy Institute), World Order Models Project, Working Paper No. 23, 1982

Recommended Readings
Michael Mandelbaum, *The Nuclear Question: The U.S. and Nuclear Weapons*
Louis Rene Beres, *Apocalypse: Nuclear Catastrophe in World Politics*
Sidney Lens, *The Day Before Doomsday*
Herman Kahn, *Thinking the Unthinkable*
Herman Kahn, *On Thermonuclear War*
George Quester, *Nuclear Diplomacy: The First 25 Years*

C. Internal Law and Control of Force: Reality, Effectiveness and Limits

J.L. Brierly, *The Law of Nations*, 6th Ed. (New York, Oxford University Press, 1963), pp. 1-93 and 397-432

Hedley Bull, "Order or Justice in International Society," *Political Studies*, XIX (1971), pp. 269-83

Weston, Falk, D'Amato, eds., *International Law and World Order* (St. Paul, Minn., West Publishing Co., 1980), Chapters II & III

Stanley Hoffman, "International Law and the Control of Force," in Richard Falk and Samuel Kim, eds., *The War System: An Inter-Disciplinary Approach* (Boulder, Westview Press, 1980), pp. 588-612

William Geberding, "International Law and the Cuban Missile Crisis," in L. Scheinman and Wilkinson, eds., *International Law and Political Crisis* (Boston, Little Brown & Co., 1968), pp. 175-210

Abram Chayes, *The Cuban Missile Crisis* (New York, Oxford University Press, 1974)

D. The Effects and Consequences of Nuclear Weapons

Office of Technology Assessment, *The Effects of Nuclear War* (Washington, D.C., US Government Printing Office, 1979), pp. 63-106

Jonathan Schell, *The Fate of the Earth* (New York, Alfred Knopf, 1982), pp. 1-96

Herbert L. Abrams and William Von Kaenel, "Medical Problems of Survivors of Nuclear War," *American Journal of Public Health*, 70:9, September 1980, pp. 1226-1232

Ruth Adams and Susan Cullen, eds., *The Final Epidemic* (Chicago, University of Chicago Press, 1981), pp. 7-34, 93-168 and 169-222

Arthur Katz, "Economic and Social Consequences of Nuclear Attacks on the United States," testimony prepared for the Joint Committee on Defense Production of the Congress of the United States (Washington, D.C., US Government Printing Office, 1979), pp. 1-27

E. Nuclear Weapons and International Law

Falk, Meyrowitz, Sanderson, *Nuclear Weapons and International Law* (Center of International Studies, Princeton University, 1982)

Carl H. Builder and Morlie H. Graubard, *The International Law of Armed Conflict: Implications for the Concept of Assured Destruction*, Rand Corporation

John Fried, "International Law Prohibits the First-Use of Nuclear Weapons," *Revue Belge De Droit International* (to be published)

Ian Brownlie, "Some Legal Aspects of the Use of Nuclear Weapons," *International Comparative Law Quarterly* 14, pp. 437-451 (1965)

George Schwarzenberger, *The Legality of Nuclear Weapons* (London, Stevens & Sons, 1958)

Department of the Army, *The Law of Land Warfare, FM 27-10*, 1956 (Washington, D.C., US Government Printing Office, 1956), p. 18, para 35

Myres McDougal, "The Hydrogen Bomb Tests and the International Law of the Sea," 49 *American Journal of International Law*, 356 (1955)

Richard Falk, "The Shimoda Case," in *Legal Order in a Violent World* (Princeton, Princeton University Press, 1968), pp. 374-413

F. The Potential of the International System for Future Conflict: Trends and Alternatives

Robert Johansen, *Toward a Dependable Peace: A Proposal for an Appropriate Security System*, World Policy Institute, World Order Models Project, Working Paper No. 8, pp. 1-50

Richard Falk, *Nuclear Policy and World Order: Why Denuclearization*, World Policy Institute, World Order Models Project, Working Paper No. 2

Louis Rene Beres, *Apocalypse: Nuclear Catastrophe in World Politics* (Chicago, Univ. of Chicago Press, 1980), pp. 197-264

Leslie Gelb, "The Future of Arms Control...A Glass Half Full," *Foreign Policy*, Fall 1979, pp. 21-32

Richard Burt, "The Future of Arms Control...or Half Empty," *Foreign Policy*, Fall 1979, pp. 34-48

Barry Blechman, "Do Negotiated Arms Limitations Have A Future?" *Foreign Affairs*, Fall 1980, pp. 102-125

Edward Luttwak, "Why Arms Control Has Failed," *Commentary*, January 1978, pp. 19-28

Suggested Topics for Seminar Paper

1. An analysis of Truman's decision to drop the atomic bomb on Hiroshima and Nagasaki from a legal-historical perspective.

2. An analysis of post-World War II efforts in the United Nations to control nuclear weapons, especially the effort to outlaw nuclear weapons.

3. An analysis of the impact of weapons technology on the laws of war in the 19th and 20th Century (the airplane, long range artillery, missiles, submarines, chemical and biological weapons, etc.).

4. A comparative analysis of the views of international legal scholars on the status of nuclear weapons under international law (Falk, Weston, McDougal, Stone, Schwarzenberger, Singh, Rosas, Castren, etc.).

5. An analysis of the arms control process as a legal process, i.e. the relations between commitments made for arms control, which have pronounced as its goal disarmament, and an obligation to nuclear disarmament.

6. The military use of outerspace—do President Reagan's proposals violate existing treaties?

7. Is there a connection between nuclear war, human rights and the right to existence?

8. Are the laws of war (armed conflict) relevant at all in the 20th Century to nuclear weapons?

9. The status of United Nations' treaties and resolutions concerning nuclear weapons.

10. What is the impact and meaning of the McCloy-Zorin agreement on the question of arms control and nuclear disarmament?
11. Toward a legal regime for the elimination of nuclear weapons—how do we make the transition from the arms control process to the nuclear disarmament stage?
12. Is there a legal connection between first-strike weapons and the prohibition against preparing to wage an aggressive war?
13. History of the no first-use proposal.
14. Is deterrence a legal regime?

Bibliography

Bilder, Richard. "Distinguishing Human Rights and Humanitarian Law: The Issue of Nuclear Weapons," 31 *American University Law Review*, pp. 959-963 (1982)

Bright, Fred. "Nuclear Weapons as a Lawful Means of Warfare," 30 *Military Law Review* 1 (1965)

Brownlie, Ian. "Some Legal Aspects of the Use of Nuclear Weapons," 14 *International and Comparative Law Quarterly*, p. 437 (1965)

Builder, Carl H. and Graubard, Morlie H. *The International Law of Armed Conflict: Implications for the Concept of Assured Destruction*, Santa Monica, California, The Rand Corporation (1982)

Castren, Erik. "The Illegality of Nuclear Weapons," *Toledo Law Review*, Fall/Winter, p. 89 (1971)

Department of Air Force, AFP 110-31. *International Law—The Conduct of Armed Conflict and Air Operations*, pp. 5-6 (1976)

Department of the Army, FM 27-10. *The Law of Land Warfare*, para. 35, p. 18 (1956)

Department of the Army, Pam. 27-161-2. *International Law* (Vol. II), pp. 42-43 (1962)

Falk, Richard, Meyrowitz, Lee, and Sanderson, Jack. "Nuclear Weapons and International Law," 20 *Indian Journal of International Law* 541 (1980); also published by the Center of International Studies of Princeton University, Occasional Paper No. 10 (1981)

Falk, Richard. "The Shimoda Case," in *Legal Order in a Violent World*, Princeton, New Jersey, Princeton University Press, 1968, pp. 374-413

Falk, Richard. "Toward a Legal Regime for Nuclear Weapons," *McGill Law Review* (1983).

Fried, John H. E. "International Law Prohibits the First Use of Nuclear Weapons," 1 *Revue Belge de Droit International*, pp. 33-52 (1981-1982)

Fujita, Hisakazu. "First Use of Nuclear Weapons: Nuclear Strategy versus International Law," 3 *Review of Law and Politics* (Kansai University), pp. 57-86 (1982)

Greenspan, Morris. *The Modern Law of Land Warfare*, Berkeley, University of California Press, 1959, pp. 368-375

Kalshoven, Frits. *The Law of Warfare*, Leiden, A.W. Sijthoff, 1973, pp. 93-97

Kunz, Josef. "The Laws of War," 50 *American Journal of International Law*, pp. 313, 333 (1956)

Lauterpacht, Hersh, ed. *Oppenheim's International Law*, 7th ed., Vol. II, Disputes, Wars and Neutrality, London, Longmans and Co., 1952, pp. 350-352

Lee, Luke T. "The Legality of Nuclear Tests and Weapons," 18 *Osterreichische Zeitschrift Fur Offentliches Recht* 307 (1968)

Maggs, Peter B. "The Soviet Viewpoint on Nuclear Weapons and International Law," 29 *Law and Contemporary Problems* 956 (1964)

McDougal, Myres S. and Feliciano, Florentine P. "International Coercion and World Public Order: The General Principles of the Law of War," 67 *Yale Law Journal* 771 (1958)

McDougal, Myres S. and Feliciano, Florentino P. *Law and Minimum Public Order*, New Haven, Yale University Press, 1961, pp. 659-668

Meyrowitz, Henri. "Les Juristes Devant L'Arme Nucleaire," 67 *Revue Generale International Public* 820 (1963)

Note. "The United States' Nuclear First Strike Position: A Legal Appraisal of its Ramifications," 7 *California Western International Law Journal* 508 (1977)

O'Brien, William V. "Legitimate Military Necessity in Nuclear War," 1 *Yearbook of World Policy* 109 (1957)

O'Brien, William V. "Some Problems of the Law of War in Limited Nuclear War," 14 *Military Law Review* 1 (1961)

Paust, Jordan J. "The Nuclear Decision in World War II—Truman's Ending and Avoidance of War," 8 *The International Lawyer* 160 (1974)

Rosas, Allan. "International Law and the Use of Nuclear Weapons," in *Essays in Honour of Erik Castren*, Finnish Branch of the International Law Association, Helsinki, 1979, pp. 73-95

Sack, Alexander. "ABC—Atomic, Biological, Chemical Warfare in International Law," 10 *Lawyers Guild Review* 161 (1950)

Schwarzenberger, George. *The Legality of Nuclear Weapons*, London, Stevens and Sons, 1958

Singh, Nagendra. *Nuclear Weapons and International Law*, New York, Praeger, 1959

Spaight, J. M. *Air Power and War Rights*, 3rd ed., London, Longmans, 1974, pp. 275-77

Stowell, Ellery C. "The Laws of War and the Atomic Bomb," 39 *American Journal of International Law* 784 (1945)

Thomas, Elbert. "Atomic Bombs in International Society," 39 *American Journal of International Law* 736 (1945)

Tucker, Robert W. *The Law of War and Neutrality at Sea*, Naval War College, International Law Studies, Vol. 50, 1955

U.S. Naval War College. *The United States Law of Naval Warfare*, International Law Studies, 1955, p. 410

Weston, Burns H. "Nuclear Weapons versus International Law: A Contextual Reassessment," *McGill Law Review* (1983).

Semester on the United Nations

Douglas Simon   *Fall 1983*
Political Science 170 (6 credits)/Drew University/Madison, NJ 07940

Unless noted otherwise on the schedule, classes will be held in Drew University's conference facility at 777 United Nations Plaza in New York City. With certain variations dictated by the nature of the subject matter, or by the vicissitudes of speaker scheduling, a "typical" day in New York will look like this: We will board the bus for New York and will arrive on U.N. Plaza about 9:15 a.m.; you may receive a mini-lecture, short film, etc; at 10:00 you will hear your first speaker or staff lecture; a discussion will follow; at about 11:30 we will break for lunch; you will hear your second speaker, etc., at 2:00 p.m.; a discussion will follow; at 3:30 we will all return to the bus and will arrive back at Drew University.

Texts
Bennett, A. Leroy, *International Organizations.*
Blake, David H. and Walters, Robert S., *The Politics of Global Economic Relations.*
Stoessinger, John G., *The United Nations and the Superpowers.*

In addition there will be a limited number of articles on reserve in the library. They are specified in the following schedule under required reading.

Section I—The United Nations and Its Constituents

Sept. 8   Introduction/Tour of the United Nations
Staff Lectures:
The League of Nations and its Antecedents
Some Nuts and Bolts of the United Nations
Reading:
Bennett, Chap. 1 "By Way of Introduction," Chap. 2 "A Great Experiment—The League of Nations," and Chap. 3 "The Genesis of the United Nations"

Sept. 13   Background Briefings
A.M. The International System
    The Political Development of the U.N.
P.M. The U.N. and the Development of International Norms
    U.N. Caucusing Groups—The Way Things Work at the U.N.
Reading:
Bennett, Chap. 8 "The Search for Justice Under the Law"

Sept. 15   The General Assembly/The Security-Council
Reading:
Bennett, Chap. 4 "Basic Principles and Organization of the U.N."
Stoessinger, Chap. 1 "The Security Council: The Veto and the Superpowers" and Chap. 2 "The G.A.: China and the Rise of the Third World"

Sept. 20   International Civil Service/The Secretary General
Reading:
Bennett, Chap. 15 "International Administration and the Search for Leadership"
Stoessinger, Chap. 3 "The Secretary-General: The American and Soviet Attacks on the Secretariat"

Sept. 22   ECOSOC/Metropolitan Museum of Art Visit
Reading:
Bennett, Chap. 10 "Promoting Economic Welfare"

Sept. 27   Specialized Agencies/Free Afternoon
Reading:
Bennett, Bottom of 244 to 247, 279-301.

Sept. 29   General Assembly Meeting/Mission Visit/Report on Research Topics

Oct. 4   First Examination/Mandatory Research Consultations

Section II—The U.N. and the Maintenance of Peace and Security

Oct. 6   Background Briefings
Lectures: The Political Functions of the United Nations
        "What You See is Not Necessarily What You Get: The Role of the U.N. Security Council"
Reading:
Bennett, Chap. 6 "Peaceful Settlement of Disputes" and Chap. 7 "Collective Security and its Alternatives—Theory and Practice"
Haas, Ernst. "Regime Decay: Conflict Management and International Organizations, 1945-1981," *International Organization*, Spring 1983, pp. 189-246. (Xeroxed and on Reserve)

Oct. 11   Peacekeeping
Reading:
Rikhye, et al. *The Thin Blue Line*, Chap. 5, Case Study 1—Middle East. (Xeroxed and on Reserve)
Stoessinger, Chap. 5 "The Congo Crisis and the U.N. Operation in the Congo"
Film: "Man in the Middle: Peacekeeping in Lebanon"

Oct. 13   The U.N. and the Middle East
Reading:
Stoessinger, Chap. 4 "The Middle East Crises of 1956, 1967 and 1973 and U.N. Peacekeeping Forces"
"The Middle East and the Superpowers" Annual Editions: *World Politics* (Xeroxed and on Reserve)
"The Arab-Israeli Conflict: Basic Documents" Annual Editions: *World Politics* (Xeroxed and on Reserve)

Oct. 18   The U.N. and the Middle East Cont./Discussions

Oct. 25   The U.N. and Southern Africa
Reading:
Thatcher, Gary. "South Africa's Archipelago," *The Christian Science Monitor*, Sept. 14-18, 1981 Condensed. (Xeroxed and on Reserve)

Grundy, Kenneth. "Namibia in International Politics," *Current History*, March 1982 (Xeroxed and on Reserve)

Cowell, Alan. "U.S. Policy and Africa," *New York Times*, Nov. 18, 1982 (Xeroxed and on Reserve)

Films: "The White Laager"
　　　"Namibia: A Trust Betrayed"

Oct. 27 The U.N. and Southern Africa Cont./South Street Seaport Museum Visit

Nov. 1 Cyprus and the U.N./Research Designs Due

Reading:

Rikhye, et al. *The Thin Blue Line*, Chap. 7, Case Study—Cyprus (UNFICYP) (Xeroxed and on Reserve)

Nov. 3 The U.N. and Arms Control—Background Briefing/Research Consultations

Reading:

Bennett, Chap. 9 "Controlling the Instruments of War"

Stoessinger, Chap. 8 "The Superpowers and Arms Control"

Nov. 8 The U.N. and Arms Control Cont./Free Afternoon

Nov. 10 Second Examination

Section III—The U.N. and the Management of Global Development

Nov. 15 Background Briefings/Films

Lectures: "The Theory of Functionalism"
　　　　"U.N. Development Machinery: An Overview"

Reading:

Bennett, Chap. 10 "Promoting Economic Welfare" and Chap. 12 "The 1970s: A Decade of World Conferences"

Films: "A New Bargain"
　　　"The Marginal People"

Nov. 17 UNDP/International Trade

Reading:

Blake and Walters, Chap. 2 "World Trade Dilemmas," Chap. 5 "Aid Relations Between Rich and Poor States," and Chap. 6 "Technology Transfer and International Relations"

Nov. 22 Transnational/The World Bank

Reading:

Blake and Walters, Chap. 4 "The Multinational Corporation: Challenge to the International System," and Chap. 3 "The Global Monetary Order"

Nov. 29 U.S. Mission Visit: U.S. Economic Policy

Dec. 1 Energy/Roundtable Discussion

Reading:

Blake and Walters, Chap. 7 "OPEC and Other Strategies for States in the Periphery of the Global Political Economy"

Dec. 6 Population/Refugees

Reading:

Bennett, pp. 282-289 and 303-305.

Dec. 8   Human Rights/Free Afternoon
Reading:
Bennett, pp. 274-279

Dec. 12   Free Day

Semester on the United Nations Research Paper

The research paper should be considered a major scholarly piece. The faculty is more interested in scholarly analysis, explanation and prescription than it is in the simple description of an event or process. Scores of topics are both researchable and appropriate. The faculty asks only that the topic be linked directly to the current activities of the United Nations or the behavior of Member States in the organization.

Students are encouraged to give this matter serious thought; they should ask themselves not only what topic interests them most, but also how it might result in exploiting to the fullest their presence at the United Nations. The actual format of the paper is flexible and will depend upon the nature of the subject.

Many of you may not have experience designing and executing a formal research project of this magnitude. The faculty recognizes this and will spend considerable time explaining how to construct a "Statement of the Problem" and a "Research Design." The attached sample should help to answer many of your general questions. In addition, the faculty and library staff will acquaint you with techniques regarding utilization of U.N. documents and other specialized sources.

Students are expected to conduct at least one interview for their paper. You will be briefed on this in greater detail.

Students will find it helpful to consult colleagues working on topics similar or related to their own. Indeed, we suggest that you double-up on interviews where possible in order to minimize any burden on the very busy U.N. personnel.

Samples

Statement of the Problem

The purpose of the paper will be to assess the effectiveness of the United Nations Centre on Transnational Corporations (CTC).

The Centre on Transnational Corporations was established by the Economic and Social Council in 1974 and became operational in November 1975. Its creation stemmed from a growing concern over the behavior of multinational corporations throughout the world, particularly in developing countries. The immediate catalyst was the outrage expressed by many states over the behavior of International Telephone and Telegraph (ITT) in Chile during the pre- and post-election period of Salvadore Allende.

The Centre is the administrative or "working arm" of the intergovernmental Commission on Transnational Corporations also established in 1974. The Centre performs a number of tasks including the collection of information on transnationals, writing of corporate profiles, assessments of the impact of transnationals on various sectors of the economy, the conduct of workshops for government officials, the sending of advisory teams to countries requesting assistance in dealing with the large corporations and assisting the Commission in drafting a Code of Conduct, setting behavioral guidelines for the corporations and the countries that host them.

How effective are these operations? Does the Centre have enough manpower and access to information to thoroughly examine TNC behavior? Are member states cooperative with the CTC? Do TNCs cooperate with the CTC? While the methodology for answering these and other questions has yet to be developed, they do constitute the direction of research for this paper.

Research Paper

I. Statement of the Problem

It is the central hypothesis of this research paper that the United Nations Centre for Transnational Corporations (CTC) has met with what can only be described as partial effectiveness since becoming operational in 1975. An elaboration of this hypothesis can be made by the following evaluations of its principal functions:

A. *Collection of Information on Transnationals.* In this area, the CTC is severely limited by the lack of cooperation by the transnationals themselves. The accounting books are not completely open to public scrutiny so the CTC must rely on information available to the public, much of it offered by the TNCs themselves.

B. *Writing Corporate Profiles.* Again, there are limitations for the same reason given for item A.

C. *Assessment of Impact of Transnationals on Various Sectors of the Economy.* There is a growing body of quantitative and non-quantitative data in this area. Developing countries are willing to share some information on the impact of TNCs in their countries and scholarly research on this subject is flourishing, making the job of the CTC much easier.

D. *Advising Functions.* Perhaps in no other area has the CTC had greater success. Highly trained advisory teams have been sent to a variety of countries and been helpful in assessing the need for TNC ventures and in assisting countries in negotiating and drafting contracts.

E. *Drafting a Code of Conduct.* To be sure, there will be a Code of Conduct for TNC and host country behavior. But the guidelines will be voluntary and there seems little doubt the document will be considerably weaker than anticipated

II. Importance of the Problem

A. *The Problem of TNC's.* The growth in size and power of transnational corporations (TNC's) over the past twenty to thirty years has been nothing less than phenomenal. Depending on how one defines a transnational, estimates as to the number range from 800 to 5000. Many of these corporations, with ownership principally in the Western industrial countries, have GNPs significantly higher than the GNP's of scores of nation-states.

While nobody will deny that TNC's can supply badly needed employment and capital, provide the means to extract valuable resources and generally assist in development efforts, the reality is that many of these corporations have done as much damage as they have good. Some have accomplished this by removing excess profits from a country without adequate compensation; others have thwarted efforts of indigenous economic enterprises to thrive; some have dodged existing tax laws through devices like transfer pricing. A few TNC's have been accused of being socially irresponsible as in the case of the Nestle Company which aggressively markets baby formula in developing countries creating an unnecessary and perhaps dangerous demand. Finally, some TNC's have meddled in the internal political affairs of host countries.

It has now been slightly over five years since the CTC was created and because TNCs continue to grow more powerful, a sound analysis of the Centre's operation seems appropriate.

B. *Literature.* A great deal has been written over the last decade about the growth and behavior of TNC's.[1] There has not, however, been a great deal of scholarly work assessing the role of the U.N. in this area.[2] It is for this reason that this report is being prepared.

III. Methodology

A. *General Approach.* The study will generally be narrative in style. Determining the effectiveness of the CTC will rely heavily on the opinions of government, corporate and U.N. personnel. At particular junctures, quantifiable data may be used. Examples that come to mind are changing patterns of tax structures in countries seeking U.N. advice, fluctuations in investment levels by both the corporations and governments as in the case of joint ventures, increases or decreases in TNC investment in basic infrastructure in host countries.

B. *Sources.* In terms of the excesses of transnationals, there is an abundance of material. Evaluative studies from sources outside the U.N. are hard to come by but I am conducting a thorough search of publications such as *Fortune, Business Week, The Economist, Barron's, The Wall Street Journal, New York Times* and *The Christian Science Monitor.*

There is a plethora of United Nations documents dealing with the operation of the CTC including its own publication, *The CTC Reporter.* Many of these contain self-criticism and should prove useful.

Extensive interviews will be conducted. Two employees of the CTC itself have been contacted and will provide interviews. I plan to seek interviews with at least two representatives of TNC's who are familiar with CTC operations and personnel from host countries. For the latter, I would like to interview not only representatives from dissatisfied countries but also someone from a country which is favorably effected by TNCs. Singapore is perhaps the best example of this.

IV. Preliminary Outline
Chapter 1: Introduction
   A. Statement of the Problem

---

[1]Richard Barnet and Ronald E. Muller, *Global Reach*, (New York: Simon and Schuster, 1974); Jack Behrman, *National Interests and the Multinational Enterprise*, (Englewood Cliffs, N.J.: Prentice-Hall, 1970); Robert Gilpin, *U.S. Power and the Multinational Enterprise in Transition*, (Princeton, N.J.: Darwin Press, 1972); Stefan Robock and Kenneth Simmonds, *International Business and Multinational Enterprises*, (Homewood, IL: Irwin, 1973); Sidney Rolfe and Walter Damm, eds., *The Multinational Corporation in the World Economy*, (N.Y.: Praeger, 1970); Christopher Tugendhat, *The Multinationals*, (London: Eyre and Spottiswoode, 1971); Raymond Vernon, *Sovereignity at Bay*, (N.Y.: Basic, 1974).

[2]A few exceptions to this include: James Grant, "Capital Punishment: The U.N. Finds Multinationals Guilty as Charged," *Barron's* (May 15, 1978, p. 7); Paul Hoeffel, "U.N. Study Sees Dulling of MNC's Bargaining Edge as LDC's Assert Themselves," *Business International* (June 23, 1978, pp. 194-195); "Questionable Methodology Casts Doubt on Findings of U.N. Advertising Study," *Business International* (June 22, 1979, pp. 194-195); "Individual Profiles Being Drawn Up by U.N.: Present Dilemma for Firms," *Business International* (July 18, 1980, pp. 225-226).

B. Importance of the Problem
C. Methodology
D. Limits of the Study

Chapter 2: The TNC Problem
A. Short Chapter summarizing the growth and power of the TNC's and types of behavior that led to the creation of the CTC

Chapter 3: The Establishment and Work of the CTC
A. Creation and Mandate
B. Basic Organization
C. Activities

Chapter 4: Evaluation of the Work of the CTC
A. Collection of Information
B. Corporate Profiles
C. Assessment of Impact of TNC's
D. Advising Functions
E. Code of Conduct

Chapter 5: Conclusion

V. Preliminary Bibliography

Behrman, Jack N. *National Interests and the Multinational Enterprise.* Englewood Cliffs, N.J.: Prentice-Hall, 1970.

Chudson, Walter A. *The International Transfer of Commercial Technology to Developing Countries.* New York: United Nations Institute for Training and Research, 1971.

Gilpin, Robert. *U.S. Power and the Multinational Corporations: The Political Economy of Foreign Direct Investment.* New York: Basic, 1975.

Hymer, Stephen. "The Multinational Corporation and the Law of Uneven Development," in Jagdish N. Bhagwati, ed. *Economics and World Order.* New York: Macmillan, 1972.

Kapoor, Ashok, and Phillip Grub, eds. *The Multinational Enterprise in Transition.* Princeton, N.J.: Darwin Press, 1972.

Litrak, Isaiah A., and Christopher J. Maule, eds. *Foreign Investment: The Experience of Host Countries.* New York: Praeger, 1970.

Robock, Stefan H., and Kenneth Simmonds. *International Business and Multinational Enterprises.* Homewood, IL: Irwin, 1973.

Rolfe, Sidney E. and Walter Damm, eds. *The Multinational Corporation in the World Economy.* New York: Praeger, 1970.

Said, Abdul A. and Luiz R. Simmons, eds. *The New Sovereigns: Multinational Corporations as World Powers.* Englewood Cliffs, N.J.: Prentice-Hall, 1975.

Stopford, John M. and Louis T. Wells, Jr. *Managing the Multinational Enterprise.* New York: Basic, 1972.

Tugendhat, Christopher. *The Multinationals.* London: Eyre and Spottiswoode, 1971.

United Nations. *Restrictive Business Practices: The Operations of Multinational U.S. Enterprises in Developing Countries, Their Role in Trade and Development.* N.Y.: United Nations, 1972.

United Nations. *Multinational Corporations in World Development*. New York: United Nations, 1973.

United Nations. *Report of the Group of Eminent Persons to Study Impact of Multinational Corporations on Development and on International Relations.* N.Y.: United Nations, 1974.

United Nations. E/C.10/L.2. "Areas of Concern Which Could Be Used as a Basis for Preliminary Work for a Code of Conduct to be Observed by Transnational Corporations," (April 14, 1975) pages 1-6.

United Nations. E/C.10/61. "Report on the Activities of the Centre on Transnational Corporations," (April 4, 1980) pages 1-27.

United Nations. St/CTC/13. "Users Guide to the Information System on Transnational Corporations." UNECOSOC, (1980).

Numerous issues of the *CTC Reporter*.

International Law

Pavel Machala   *Spring 1982*
Political Science 38/Amherst College/Amherst, MA 01002

Materials to be Read

Burns H. Weston, Richard A. Falk, Anthony A. D'Amato, eds., *International Law and World Order* (St. Paul, MN: West Publishing Co., 1980)

Burns H. Weston, Richard A. Falk, Anthony A. D'Amato, eds., *Basic Documents in International Law and World Order* (St. Paul, MN: West Publishing Co., 1980).

Stanley Hoffman, *Duties Beyond Borders* (Syracuse, NY: Syracuse University Press, 1981).

Charles R. Beitz, *Political Theory and International Relations* (Princeton, NJ: Princeton University Press, 1979).

Michael Walzer, *Just and Unjust Wars* (NY: Basic Books, 1977).

Books recommended for purchase are marked (P); materials to be found only on reserve are marked (R). Readings compiled in multilithed form are marked (M); the entire packet can be purchased in the Political Science office, Clark House, Room 103. The cost of the multilith is $6.50.

I. Law and Justice in International Affairs

1. Introduction to Course

2. The International Legal System
(a) Can there be international law when states consider themselves sovereign political entities?
(b) How are international legal norms created?
(c) Are the rules that are contained in the Charter of the United Nations and other UN documents legally binding?

Readings:
Burns H. Weston, *International Law and World Order*, pp. 4-255; 1026-1067; 1122-1131; 1162-72. (P)

Documents:
Charter of the United Nations in Basic Documents [BD], pp. 6-23.
Statute of the International Court of Justice, in BD, pp. 23-29.
Vienna Convention on the Law of Treaties, in BD, pp. 59-75.

3. Ethics and International Affairs
(a) What is meant by "ethical standards"?
(b) What is the relationship between "legal" and "ethical" standards?
(c) What is the function of "ethical standards" in international relations?
(d) What is the ethical status of states' rights?

Readings:
Stanley Hoffman, *Duties Beyond Borders*, chap. 1. (P)

Charles Beitz, *Political Theory and International Relations*, part I. (P)

Geoffrey Stern, "Morality and International Relations," in Alan James, *The Bases of International Order*, pp. 133-55. (R)

Hedley Bull, "Order versus Justice in World Politics," in *The Anarchical Society*. (R)

Richard A. Falk, "The Domains of Law and Justice," *International Journal* 31 (1) Winter 1975-76, pp. 1-13. (M)

Julius Stone, "Justice in International Law and Organization," in *Legal Control of International Conflicts*, pp. 50-56. (M)

Documents:

Charter of the United Nations, in BD

4. The International Protection of Individual Rights

(a) What has been the status of "basic individual rights" in international law?

(b) Are there any specific individual rights that "ought" to have universal moral validity?

(c) What is the implication of the idea of "universal individual rights" for a state's sovereignty?

Readings:

Stanley Hoffman, *Duties Beyond Borders*, chap. 3. (P)

Weston, *International Law and World Order*, pp. 466-536; 578-580; 585-593; 595-614; 621-650. (P)

Jeane Kirkpatrick, "Dictatorships and Double Standards," *Commentary*, 68 (5) November 1979, pp. 34-45. (M)

Mariano Grondona, "Reconciling International Security and Human Rights," *International Security*, Vol. 80, pp. 3-9. 1977. (M)

Louis Henkin, "Rights: American and Human," *Columbia Law Review*, 79 (3) April 1979, pp. 405-425. (M)

Goronwy J. Jones, "The Principle of Non-Intervention in the Internal Affairs of States, With Special Reference to the Implications of Human Rights," *International Relations* (London), 6 (6) November 1977, pp. 154-161. (M)

M.G. Kaladharan Nayar, "Human Rights and Economic Development: The Legal Foundations," *Universal Human Rights*, 2 (3) July-Sept. 1980, pp. 55-81. (M)

Paul Streeten, "Basic Needs and Human Rights," *World Development*, Vol. 8, pp. 107-111. (M)

Maurice Cranston, *What Are Human Rights?* chaps. 1, 3, 4, 5, 6, 8. (R)

Documents:

Universal Declaration on Human Rights, in BD, pp. 161-164.

International Covenant on Economic, Social and Cultural Rights, in BD, pp. 196-200.

Optional Protocol to the International Covenant on Civil and Political Rights, in BD, pp. 210-211.

Declaration on Territorial Asylum, in BD, pp. 211-213.

5. The International Protection of Human Rights

(a) What has been the status of "basic ethnic rights" in international law?

(b) Are there any specific ethnic rights that "ought" to have universal moral validity?

(c) What is the implication of "basic ethnic rights" for either a state's sovereignty or "basic individual rights"?

(d) Does the South African policy of "Bantustanization" violate any international legal norms?

Readings:

Burns H. Weston, *International Law and World Order*, pp. 265-281; 537-562; 615-620; 789-791. (P)

Charles Beitz, *Political Theory and International Relations*, part II. (P)

Stanley French and Andres Gutman, "The Principle of Self-Determination," in Virginia Held, *Philosophy, Morality and International Affairs*. (R) (M)

Michael Walzer, *Just and Unjust Wars*, pp. 53-58. (P)

Lee C. Buchheit, *Secession: The Legitimacy of Self-Determination*, pp. 1-137. (R)

Henry J. Richardson, "Self-Determination, International Law and South African Bantustan Policy," *Columbian Journal of International Law*, 17 (2), 1978, pp. 185-204. (M)

D.H.N. Johnson, "Sanctions against South Africa? The Legal Aspect," in Ronald Segal, *Sanctions Against South Africa*, pp. 62-93. (M)

Documents:

Declaration on the Granting of Independence to Colonial Countries and Peoples, in BD, pp. 177-78.

International Convention on the Elimination of All Forms of Racial Discrimination, in BD, pp. 190-195.

UN Security Resolution 232, in BD, pp. 195-196.

UN Security Resolution 253, in BD, pp. 213-216.

International Convention on the Suppression and Punishment of the Crime of Apartheid, in BD, pp. 233-236.

II. Regulating War

6. International Laws of War: "Just War" and "Aggression"

(a) What has been the place of the "just war" doctrine in international law?

(b) What is the meaning of aggression in the contemporary international legal system?

(c) Does a "preemptive strike" constitute aggression?

(d) Should "humanitarian" intervention be considered as an act of aggression?

(e) Was American military intervention in Southeast Asia a form of aggression?

Readings:

Weston, *International Law and World Order*, pp. 1110-1122; 281-388; 905-922. (P)

Lynn H. Miller, "The Contemporary Significance of the Doctrine of Just War," *World Politics*, 16 (2) January 1964, pp. 254-286. (P)

Michael Walzer, *Just and Unjust Wars*, chaps. 1, 2, 4, 4, 6, 7, 15 and Afterword. (P)

Department of State, "The Legality of United States Participation in the Defense of Vietnam," *Yale Law Review*, 75 (7) June 1966, pp. 1085-1108. (M)

John Norton Moore, "The Lawfulness of Military Assistance to the Republic of Vietnam," in Richard A. Falk, *The Vietnam War and International Law*, Vol. 1, pp. 237-270. (M)

Charles Chaumont, "A Critical Study of American Intervention in Vietnam," in Richard A. Falk, *The Vietnam War and International Law*, Vol. 2, pp. 127-157. (M)

Richard A. Falk, "International Law and the United States Role in the Vietnam War," in Richard A. Falk, *The Vietnam War and International Law*, pp. 362-400. (M)

Jean-Pierre L. Fonteyne, "Forcible Self-Help by States to Protect Human Rights: Recent Views from the United Nations," in Richard B. Lillich, *Humanitarian Intervention and the United Nations*, pp. 197-221. (M)

Stanley Hoffman, *Duties Beyond Borders*, chap. 2.(P)

Documents:

Kellogg-Briand Pact, in BD, pp. 93-94.

Uniting for Peace Resolution, in BD, pp. 116-117.

Declaration on the Inadmissibility of Intervention in the Domestic Affairs of States, in BD, pp. 119-121.

Resolution on the Definition of Aggression, in BD, pp. 136-138.

7. The International Law of Warfare

(a) What is the rationale behind international laws of warfare?

(b) Do the Israeli "reprisals" against the Palestinians violate any international law of warfare? Can they be "morally" justified?

(c) Can guerilla fighters be "bound" by the same rules as regular troops?

(d) Did U.S. troops violate any rules of war in Vietnam?

Readings:

Weston, *International Law and World Order*, pp. 281-388; 905-922. (P)

Michael Walzer, *Just and Unjust Wars*, chaps. 3, 8, 9, 11, 12, 13, 14, 16, 17. (P)

Guenter Lewy, *America in Vietnam*, pp. 223-33, 242-70, 299-306. (R)

Derek Bowett, "Reprisals Involving Recourse to Armed Force," *American Journal of International Law*, 66 (1) January 1972, pp. 1-36. (M)

Milton Leitenberg, "America in Vietnam: Statistics of a War," *Survival* 14 (6) November-December 1972, pp. 268-274. (M)

William V. O'Brien, "The *Jus in Bello* in Revolutionary War and Counterinsurgency," *Virginia Journal of International Law*, 18 (2) Winter 1978, pp. 193-242. (M)

Stanley Hoffman, *Duties Beyond Borders*, pp. 85-93. (P)

Documents:

"Convention on Respecting the Laws and Customs of War on Land," in BD, pp. 88-92.

Geneva Protocol, in BD, pp. 92-93.

"Convention for Amelioration of the Condition of Wounded and Sick in Armed Forces in the Field," in BD, pp. 98-104.

"Convention Relative to the Treatment of Prisoners of War," in BD, pp. 109-112.

"Convention Relative to the Protection of Civilian Persons in Time of War," in BD, pp. 112-116.

8. International War Crimes: Collective or Individual Responsibility?

(a) What is the international legal significance of the Nuremberg trials?

(b) Should an individual soldier be held legally responsible for executing the orders of his superiors?

(c) Can an entity such as a "nation" be held morally responsible for international crimes?

Readings:
Weston, *International Law & World Order*, pp. 63-68, 76-80, 195-198. (P)
Michael Walzer, *Just and Unjust Wars*, chaps. 18, 19. (P)
David Cooper, "Responsibility and the 'System'," in Peter French, *Individual and Collective Responsibility*, pp. 83-100. (M)
William V. O'Brien, "The Nuremberg Principles," in Richard A. Falk, *The Vietnam War and International Law*, Vol. 3, pp. 193-247. (M)
Telford Taylor, "Nuremberg and Vietnam: Who is Reponsible for War Crimes?" in Richard A. Falk, *The Vietnam War and International Law*, Vol. 3, pp. 379-396. (M)
Stanford Levinson, "Responsibility for Crimes of War," in Marshall Cohen, *War and Moral Responsibility*, pp. 104-133. (M)

III. Regulating Global Material Inequalities

9. International Economic Law in Historical Perspective

(a) Historically, what kind of international legal standards have been used to regulate the flow of material goods and capital among states?
(b) What "ethical" principles support these legal standards?
(c) What is the international legal status of the claims contained in the so-called "new international economic order"?
(d) What "ethical" principles support these claims?
(e) What is the international legal status of economic embargo?

Readings:
Weston, *International Law and World Order*, pp. 674-748; 768-787; 792-796; 799-801; 802-803; 814-824; 828-833. (P)
Wil D. Verwey, *Economic Development and International Law*, pp. 236-281. (M)
Jordan J. Paust and Albert P. Blaustein, "The Oil Weapon—A Threat to International Peace," in Paust and Blaustein, *The Arab Oil Weapon*, pp. 67-96. (R)
Ibrahim F.I. Shihata, "Destination Embargo of Arab Oil: Its Legality Under International Law," in Paust and Blaustein, *The Arab Oil Weapon*, pp. 97-133. (R)

Documents:
"Statute of the Organization of the Petroleum Exporting Countries," in BD, pp. 43-50.
"Articles of Agreement on the International Bank for Reconstruction and Development," in BD, pp. 247-258.
"Resolution on Permanent Sovereignty over Natural Resources," in BD, pp. 259-261.
"Protocol Amending the General Agreement on Tariffs and Trade," in BD, pp. 261-265.
"OECD Guidelines for Multinational Enterprises," in BD, pp. 296-300.
"Convention on the Settlement of Investment Disputes," in BD, pp. 265-272.

10. International Charity and "Lifeboat Justice"

(a) Should the existence of global material inequalities be perceived as an ethical problem or is it merely a matter of prudential concern?
(b) What are the empirical and ethical assumptions behind the claim that massive food aid to all starving people in the world would be "immoral"?
(c) Is a plea for "charity" the strongest moral claim people in less developed

countries can make for themselves in the eyes of the developed societies?

Readings:
Peter Singer, "Famine, Affluence, and Morality," in Aiken and LaFollette, pp. 22-36. (R)
John Arthur, "Rights and Duty to Bring Aid," in Aiken and LaFollette, pp. 37-48. (R)
Jan Narveson, "Morality and Starvation," in Aiken and LaFollette, pp. 49-65. (R)
Garrett Harding, "Lifeboat Ethics: The Case Against Helping the Poor," in Aiken and LaFollette, *World Hunger and Moral Obligation*, pp. 11-21. (R)
Joseph Fletcher, "Give If it Helps but Not If it Hurts," in Aiken and LaFollette, pp. 103-14. (R)
Janet Besecker and Phil Elder, "Lifeboat Ethics: A Reply to Hardin," in William R. Burch, Jr., *Readings in Ecology, Energy and Human Society*, pp. 225-230.

11. International Retributive Justice
(a) What constitutes "exploitation"?
(b) Can "reparation" be owed to groups?
(c) What is the international legal status of "reparation"?

Readings:
Tord Hoivik, "Three Approaches to Exploitation: Markets, Products and Communities," *Journal of Peace Research* 10 (3) 1972, pp. 261-69. (M)
Barnard R. Boxill, "Morality of Reparation," *Journal of Social Issues*, 28 (1) 1972, pp. 113-23. (M)
Joel Kassiola, "Compensatory Justice and the Moral Obligation for Preferential Treatment of Discriminated Groups," *Polity* 11 (1) Fall 1978, pp. 46-66. (M)
Robert W. Tucker, *The Inequality of Nations*, pp. 115-126. (R)

Documents:
"Charter of Economic Rights and Duties of States," in BD, pp. 289-295.
"Declaration on the Establishment of a New International Economic Order," in BD, pp. 273-276.
"Programme of Action on the Establishment of a New International Economic Order," in BD, pp. 276-288.

12. International Distributive Justice (I)
(a) What is "distributive justice"?
(b) Can distributive justice be applied internationally?

Readings:
Charles Beitz, *Political Theory and International Relations*, Part III. (P)
James Rachels, "Killing and Starving to Death," *Philosophy*, 54 (208) April 1979, pp. 159-171. (M)
Stanley Hoffman, *Duties Beyond Borders*, chap. 4. (P)

13. International Distributive Justice (II)
(a) What would constitute a "just standard of living" and a "just level of economic development" and "just prices" at the global level?
(b) What would constitute "equality of opportunity" at the global level?

Readings:
Oscar Schachter, *Sharing the World's Resources*, pp. 4-34 and 87-95. (M)

Oscar Schachter, "A Normative Framework for Reducing Economic Inequalities,"
in G. Dorsey, *Equality and Freedom*, Vol. III, pp. 973-990. (M)
David Miller, *Social Justice*, pp. 122-150. (M)
Robert W. Tucker, *The Inequality of Nations*, pp. 126-158. (R)

Some Suggested Paper Topics:

Israel, the West Bank and international law
A case study of a claim to national self-determination
Human rights and foreign policy
The right of asylum in the contemporary international legal system
A case study of a specific theory of international law—scholar or country (example:
Julius Stone, Richard Falk, G.I. Tunkin, Soviet, South African, Indian, etc.)
The United States position towards the international Law of the Sea Treaty
International law and civil war (revolution)
International legal aspects of terrorism

Public International Law

Christopher C. Joyner   Fall 1983
Political Science 244/George Washington University/
Washington, DC 20052

The chief purpose of this course is to survey the field of international law, focusing especially on world order issues of legal importance. Since the legitimacy of international law *qua* law has sometimes been called into question, it will be necessary first to examine carefully the major principles and concepts of international law as gleaned from multilateral conventions, court decisions, and the writings of publicists. Having done this, attention will then be directed to specific legal problems found in contemporary international relations, particularly the law relating to ocean space, outer space, human rights, transnational terrorism and economic development, as well as the evolving status of law in a multicultural world.

Assigned Reading Materials

The following texts comprise much of the reading required for this course, and they are available for purchase at the Marvin Center bookstore:

Akehurst, Michael. *A Modern Introduction to International Law*, 4th edition. London: George Allen, 1982.

Bozeman, Adda B. *The Future of Law in a Multicultural World*. Princeton: Princeton University Press, 1971.

Cohen, Raymond. *International Politics: The Rules of the Game*. New York: Longman, 1981.

Dolman, Antony J. *Resources, Regimes, World Order*. New York: Pergamon Press, 1981.

Several selected readings will also be placed on reserve in the Gelman Library, and daily reading of the *New York Times* or *Washington Post* is strongly encouraged.

Course Requirements

1. A final examination, essay in format and comprehensive in coverage, to determine the student's understanding and mastery of lecture materials and assigned readings (40%);
2. A scholarly research paper, approximately 25 pages in length dealing with a topic related to this course. It is strongly suggested that you discuss your topic preference with the professor prior to commencing the research (40%). Papers due no later than December 3, 1983.
3. Regular attendance and meaningfully active class participation (20%).

Course Outline and Reading Assignments

Part I: International Law as Law
Week 1 Introduction
Akehurst, Chaps. 1, 2

Week 2 Sources and Sanctions of International Law
Akehurst, Chaps. 3, 4
C. Joyner, "U.N. General Assembly Resolutions and International Law: Rethinking the Contemporary Dynamics of Norm Creation," *California Western International Law Journal*, Vol. 11 (Summer 1981), pp. 445-478.

Week 3 Subjects of International Law
Akehurst, Chaps. 5, 6

Week 4 International Law and the Individual
Akehurst, Chaps. 6, 7
J. Donnelly, "Human Rights and Human Dignity: An Analytic Critique of Non-Western Conceptions of Human Rights," *American Political Science Review*, Vol. 76 (June 1982), pp. 303-316.

Week 5 Territorial Questions
Akehurst, Chaps. 8, 9, 11, 12

Week 6 International Agreements
Akehurst, Chap. 10
Cohen, entire volume

Week 7 Use of Force
Akehurst, Chaps. 13, 14

Week 8 War
Akehurst, Chaps. 15, 16, 17
G. Aldrich, "New Life for the Laws of War," *American Journal of International Law*, Vol. 75 (1 October 1981), pp. 764-783.

Part II: Contemporary Issues in International Law

Week 9 National Attitudes and International Law
Articles on Reserve:
W. Levi, Ch. 7, "Inequality," and Ch. 8, "Cultural Heterogeneity and International Law," in *Law and Politics in the International Society* (1976), pp. 121-150.
S. Kim, "The People's Republic of China and the Charter-Based International Legal Order," *American Journal of International Law*, Vol. 72 (April 1978), pp. 317-349.
C. Osakwe, "Contemporary Soviet Doctrine on the Sources of General International Law," American Society of International Law *Proceedings*, Vol. 73 (1979), pp. 310-323.
R. Dean, "Beyond Helsinki: The Soviet View of Human Rights in International Law," *Virginia Journal of International Law*, Vol. 21 (Fall 1980), pp. 55-96.

Week 10 International Law and Economic Development
Dolman, entire volume
Article on Reserve:
B. Weston, "The Charter of Economic Rights and Duties of States and the Depriva-

tion of Foreign-Owned Wealth," *American Journal of International Law*, Vol. 75, (July 1981), pp. 437-475.

Week 11   Law of the Sea
Akehurst, Ch. 18
San Diego Law Review, entire issue
Articles on Reserve:
J.T. Swing, "Who Will Own the Oceans?" *Foreign Affairs*, Vol. 54 (April 1976), pp. 527-546.
Comptroller General, *Impediments to U.S. Involvement in Deep Ocean Mining Can Be Overcome* (February 3, 1982), entire report.

Week 12   Common Space Resource Regimes: Air and Outer Space
Akehurst, Ch. 19
Articles on Reserve:
C. Christol, "The Common Heritage of Mankind Provision in the 1979 Agreement Governing the Activities of States on the Moon and Other Celestial Bodies," *International Lawyer*, Vol. 14 (Spring 1980), pp. 429-465.
C. Christol, "International Liability for Damage Caused by Space Objects," *American Journal of International Law*, Vol. 74 (April 1980), pp. 346-372.
M. Rothblatt, "Satellite Communication and Spectrum Allocation," *American Journal of International Law*, Vol. 76 (January 1982), pp. 56-77.
S. Gorove, "The Geostationary Orbit: Issues of Law and Policy," *American Journal of International Law*, Vol. 73 (July 1979), pp. 444-461.
J. Freeman, "Direct Broadcast Developments and Directions: The National Sovereignty and Cultural Integrity Positions," American Society of International Law *Proceedings*, Vol. 74 (1980), pp. 302-311.

Week 13   Common Space Resource Regimes: Polar Space
Articles on Reserve:
L. Bloomfield, "The Arctic: Last Unmanaged Frontier," *Foreign Affairs*, Vol. 60 (Fall 1981), pp. 87-105.
R. Bilder, "The Present Legal and Political Situation in Antarctica," in J. Charney, editor, *The New Nationalism and the Use of Common Spaces* (1981), pp. 167-205.
C. Joyner, "The Exclusive Economic Zone and Antarctica," *Virginia Journal of International Law*, Vol. 21 (Summer 1981), pp. 691-715.
C. Joyner, "Antarctica and the Law of the Sea: Rethinking the Current Legal Dilemmas," *San Diego Law Review*, Vol. 18 (1981), pp. 415-442.

Week 14   Crimes in International Law
Articles on Reserve:
B. Ferencz, "The Beginning of Wisdom," in *An International Criminal Court: A Step Towards World Peace* (Vol. II, 1980), pp. 1-100.
"Terrorism and Political Crimes in International Law," American Society of International Law *Proceedings*, Vol. 67 (1973), pp. 87-104.

Week 15   Conclusion
Bozeman, entire volume
Article on Reserve:
J. Fried, "International Law—Neither Orphan Nor Harlot, Neither Jailor Nor Never-Never Land," in K. Deutsch and S. Hoffman, editors, *The Relevance of International Law* (1971), pp. 124-176.

International Law and Organization

Lawrence S. Finkelstein   *Spring 1982*
Political Science/Northern Illinois University/DeKalb, IL 60115

International law and international organization are instruments or means for the conduct of relations across national boundaries and are seen as mechanisms for the regulation of the behavior of nation states. The course will seek to explore how the performance of these functions by international law and international organizations depends upon, is influenced by and, in turn, influences the international political order. The course will rely heavily on careful advance preparation of "problems," particularly the developments of "issue outlines" from the "coursebook" in international law on which much of the work will be based. There will thus be active class participation in the learning process, to supplement lectures by the instructor. The workload will be heavy. Timely and intensive preparation will be demanded of all students.

Course Requirements

There will be no midterm examination. Instead, "issue outlines" will be assigned for two of the hypothetical cases in the "coursebook," as set forth in the schedule below. These outlines will require advance preparation and each will be due on the class day when class discussion of the subject of the case is to begin. Students should prepare two copies of each outline, one as an aid to participation in class discussion and the other to be turned in for evaluation and grading by the instructor. Timely submission of the outlines is required and will be a criterion for grading. Late submission, unless authorized by the instructor ahead of time on grounds of incapacity, such as major illness, will be penalized; a late outline will be "docked" one full letter grade.

The issue outlines should be based on the "Recommended Writing Assignment" which will be found in Section 3.B of the relevant chapter of the coursebook. The outlines should present in a logical and succinct fashion the principal arguments on both sides of the main issues raised by the case, taking account of the "Discussion Notes/Questions" to be found in connection with each case in the coursebook. The outlines should also synopsize the conclusions you favor, with summaries of your reasons. Please note that the assignment will require that you read, not only the textual matter and readings in the coursebook, but also the readings referred to in the accompanying volume of *Basic Documents*. Please assume that the coursebook's references to the *Basic Documents* are always included in the assigned readings in the course outline which follows below.

N.B.: Graduate students, in addition to following the above instructions about the issue outlines, should also carry out the "Reflective Assignment" to be found in Section 3.D of the relevant chapter of the coursebook. Do so in outline form in not more than five additional pages.

There will be a final exam. Different exams will be given to graduate and to undergraduate students. The nature of the exam(s) will be discussed later in the term and guidance will be given as to how graduate and undergraduate students may best prepare for the exam(s).

Schedule

First issue outline
    Begin preparation no later than February 11
    Due as basis for class discussion on February 23
Second issue outline
    Begin preparation no later than March 18
    Due as basis for class discussion on March 30
Final exam—May 1, 3-4:30 P.M.

Assigned Texts

Please purchase the following:
Weston, Falk and D'Amato, *International Law and World Order: A Problem-Oriented Casebook*
Weston, Falk and D'Amato, *Basic Documents in International Law World Order*
Jacobson, *Networks of Interdependence: International Organizations and the Global Political System*

Course Outline

January 12   Politics and International Law and Organization
Introduction by the Instructor

January 14   The Concept of International Law
Read: Weston, Falk and D'Amato coursebook (Hereinafter referred to as "Coursebook"), Part I, Introduction and Chap. 1.

January 19 and 21   Sources of International Law
Read: Coursebook, Chap. 2.

January 26 and 28   The Force and Effect of International Law
Read: Coursebook, Chap. 3.
Begin preparation of Kilimanjaro case. Read: Coursebook, Problem 5-1, pp. 259-410; and Jacobson, Part III, pp. 147-203.

February 2 and 4   The Nature of International Organizations
Read: Jacobson, Chaps. 1, 3, 5, 6, pp. 3-20, 33-63, 83-143. Continue preparation of Kilimanjaro case.

February 9 and 11   The Kilimanjaro Case
Begin preparation of *Issue outline* on Nuclear Testing in Sharaq, Problem 5-2. Read: Coursebook, pp. 410-465.

February 16 and 18   The Kilimanjaro Case continued
Continue preparation of Sharaq issue outline.

February 23 and 28   The Sharaq Case
Issue outline due. Begin preparation of Militarism and Economic Growth in Hispania, Problem 6-2. Read: Coursebook, pp. 595-651; Jacobson, Part V, pp. 315-389.

March 2 and 4   The Sharaq Case continued
Continue preparation of Hispania case.

March 9 and 11   Spring Break

March 16 and 18   The Hispania Case
Begin preparation of *Issue Outline* on Economic Development in Tukulor, Problem 7-2. Read: Coursebook, pp. 768-834; Jacobson, Part IV, pp. 219-311.

March 23 and 28   The Hispania Case continued
Continue preparation of Tukulor issue outline.

March 30 and April 1   The Tukulor Case
Issue outline due. Begin preparation of The Sea Around Antilla and Costa Grande, Problem 8-1. Read: Coursebook, pp. 835-960.

April 6 and 8   The Tukulor Case continued
Continue preparation of the Sea Around Antilla and Costa Grande.

April 13, 15, 20 and 22   The Sea Around Antilla and Costa Grande

April 27 and 29   Interdependence and World Order
Read: Jacobson, Chap. 16, pp. 393-424; Coursebook, Part III, Introduction and Chaps. 9, 10, 11, pp. 1026-1147.

May 1   Final Exam

The Dynamics of International Law

Karen Mingst   *Fall 1983*
Political Science 437/University of Kentucky/Lexington, KY 40506

To the casual newspaper reader international relations appears random, chaotic, anarchic. While this cliche has some truth to it, it also suffers from serious defects. First of all, it is based upon ideas about law gleaned only from our immediate cultural experience. The more closely law is studied— the more we see the biases implicit in conventional ideas about it. In the second place, such a view rests upon the assumption that law and conflict are irreconcilable opposites. This viewpoint is a vast oversimplification. In the course of this semester, we will be examining what role, if any, law plays in structuring the relationships among states, individuals and states, states and multinational businesses, and states and international organizations.

Books to be purchased

Akehurst, Michael. *A Modern Introduction to International Law*, 4th ed., fully revised (London: George Allen and Unwin, 1982)

Chayes, Abram. *The Cuban Missile Crisis. International Crisis and the Role of Law* (New York: Oxford University Press, 1974).

Taylor, Telford. *Nuremburg and Vietnam. An American Tragedy* (New York: Times Books). No longer in print; sections on reserve.

McWhinney, Edward. *Conflict and Compromise. International Law and World Order in a Revolutionary Age* (New York: Holmes and Meier, 1981).

Reserved reading on 2 hour restricted circulation

Xerox: Vienna Convention on the Law of Treaties.

Xerox: Treaty on Principles Governing the Activities of States in the Exploration and Use of Outer Space, Including the Moon and Other Celestial Bodies. Convention on International Liability for Damage Caused by Space Objects.

Xerox: Bozeman, Adda. *The Future of Law in a Multicultural World*, pp. 34-49; 140-186.

Xerox: Witkin, Merrie. "Transkei: An Analysis of the Practice of Recognition— Political or Legal?" *Harvard International Law Journal* 18 (1977), pp. 605-627.

Xerox: Handl, Gunther. "An International Legal Perspective on the Conduct of Abnormally Dangerous Activities in Frontier Areas: The Case of Nuclear Power Plant-Siting," *Ecology Law Quarterly* 7 (1978), pp. 1-50.

Humphrey, John H. "The Implementation of International Human Rights Law," *New York Law School Law Review* 24 (1978), pp. 31-61.

Buergenthal, Thomas. "International and Regional Human Rights Law and Institutions: Some Examples of Their Interaction," *Texas International Law Journal* 12 (1977), pp. 321-330.

Grading and Assignments

1. First examination, 20% of grade. In class written exam, given at the end of about six weeks, end of C.1c on the syllabus. The exact date will be announced at least one week in advance.
2. Second examination, 20% of grade. Will be given after D.2a on the syllabus.
3. One legal brief, 5% of grade. Students will select one case from those "Cases for Student Reports" on the syllabus. Students will be prepared for presentation of the case to the class. The briefs are due in class the day that the case is to be discussed. In most cases, the original citation for the cases is given in the syllabus. Excerpts from the cases are found in the law books on reserve in the library. (Consult the hand-out on International Legal Research for details.)
4. Paper, 25% of grade. Students will have a choice. Hypothetical cases will be distributed. Students may choose one of these cases, research the issues, and write a paper on the case. Or students may choose their own research topic in international law. Both assignments will require students to use the law library, write a coherent paper of approximately 10-15 pages (typewritten), with proper footnoting and bibliography. The paper is due November 18.
5. Final examination, 25%. The final exam will be comprehensive, however, the last section of the syllabi will be intensively tested. The exam will be held during the regularly scheduled exam period.

A. The Nature and Functions of International Law
McWhinney, Chap. 1, 2

1. The Functions of Law
Akehurst, Chapter 1

2. The Feasibility of International Law
Akehurst, Chapter 2

3. Sources of International Law
Akehurst, Chapter 3
Cases distributed in class:
    a. Asylum Case (Columbia v. Peru) 1950 ICJ Reports 271
    b. The Scotia, (U.S. Supreme Court) 14 Wall (81 US) 1770

4. The View of International Law from States
Bozeman, (xerox)

B. International Law and the International System

1. The International System
Chayes (whole book)

2. International Legal Institutions
Akehurst, pp. 206-215
International Court of Justice
International Law Commission

3. The Role of Law in U.S. Policy Formulation

C. Subjects of International Law

1. States and Government
Akehurst, Chapters 4, 5
a. Relations Between International Law and Municipal Law
Cases distributed in class:
West Rand Central Gold Mining Co., Ltd. v. the King
Great Britain King's Bench Division 1905 (1905) 2K.B. 391

The Paquette Habana; The Lola
U.S. Supreme Court, (1900) 175 U.S. 677

b. Recognition
Witkin (xerox)
Cases for student reports:
1. Tinoco Arbitration (Great Britain-Costa Rica) 1923
1 UN Reports of International Arbitral Awards 369
2. Bank of China v. Wells Fargo Bank and Union Trust Co.
U.S. District Court, 1952; 104 F. Supp. 59
3. The Sapphire (U.S. Supreme Court)
11 Wallace 164

c. Treaties
Akehurst, Chapter 10
Vienna Convention on the Law of Treaties (Lib. xerox)

U.S. Practice
Cases for student reports:
1. Missouri v. Holland (1920) 252 U.S. 416
2. Asakura v. City of Seattle (1924) 265 U.S. 332
3. Sei Fuji v. The State of California (1952) 242 p. 2d 617

2. Individuals
a. Nationality
Akehurst, pp. 81-86
Case distributed in class:
1. Nottebohm (Liechtenstein v. Guatemala) 1955 (ICJ Rep. 4)
Cases for student reports:
1. U.S. v. Wong Kim Ark, U.S. Supreme Court, 1898; 169 U.S. 649
2. Perkins v. Elg (1938) 307 U.S. 325

b. State Responsibility to Aliens
Akehurst, Chapter 7
Cases for student reports:
1. Laura Janes (U.S.A. v. United Mexican States (1926)
4 U.N. Reports on International Aribitral Awards 82
2. U.S. (B.E. Chattim Claim) v. United Mexican States (1927)
4 U.N. Reports on International Arbitral Awards 282

c. Extradition
Akehurst, Chapter 8
Case for student report:
1. Jimenez v. Aristequieta (1962) U.S. Court of Appeals, Fifth Circuit; 311 F2d
547

d. Immunity from Jurisdiction
Akehurst, Chapter 9
Distributed in class:
  1. Convention on Diplomatic Relations
     Signed at Vienna, 1961; Force April 1964
     UN Document A/CONF. 20/13, 16 April 1961
  2. Vienna Convention on Consular Relations
     signed at Vienna 1963
     UN Document A/CONF. 25/12, 23 April 1963

3. International Organizations
Akehurst, Chapter 6
Cases distributed in class:
  a. Reparation for Injuries Suffered in the Service of the United Nations
  b. Certain expenses of the United Nations
     (Art. 17, Par. 2 of the Charter)

D. Persistent Issues of International Law

1. Management of Violence
Taylor (selected reserve)
a. Peaceful Settlement of Disputes
   Akehurst, Chap. 14; Review Chayes
b. Wars
   Akehurst, Chaps. 15, 16

2. Territorial Problems
McWhinney, Chaps. 5, 6
a. Land
   Akehurst, Chaps. 11, 12, 17
   Cases distributed in class:
     1. The Island of Palmas (Miangas) Arbitration
        (U.S.—The Netherlands), Tribunal of the Permanent Court of Arbitration, 1928
     2. Preah Vihear Temple Case (Cambodia v. Thailand)
     3. The Corfu Case (United Kingdom v. Albania)
     4. Case Concerning Right of Passage Over Indian Territory (Portugal v. India) 1960

b. The Law of the Sea
   Akehurst, Chapter 18
   Case distributed in class:
     1. Fisheries Jurisdiction Cases
        (UK v. Iceland) 1974; (Germany v. Iceland) 1974

c. Air Space and Outer Space
   Akehurst, Chapter 19
   Documents on reserve (xerox)
     1. Treaty on Principles Governing the Activities of States in the Exploration and Use of Outer Space, Including the Moon and Other Celestial Bodies, Jan. 27, 1967 (610) U.N.T.S. 205,(18 U.S.T. 2410)

2. Convention on International Liability for Damage Caused by Space Objects (Gen. Ass. REs. 2777 (XXVI) Nov. 29, 1971)

3. Business Relationships
Akehurst, review pp. 71-74
Case distributed in class:
   a. Case Concerning the Barcelona Traction, Light and Power Co., Ltd. (Belgium v. Spain) 1970 (I.C.J.) 3

Cases for student reports:
   a. Banco Nacional de Cuba v. Sabbatino (1964)
      US Sup. Court 376 U.S. 398
   b. Banco Nacional de Cuba v. Farr (1965)
      U.S. District Court 243 F. Supp. 957
   c. American Banana Co. v. United Fruit (1909)
      213 U.S. 347/29 S. Ct. 511

Control of International Business   OECD on MNC's (xerox, reserve)

E. Developing International Law
McWhinney, Chap. 7, 8, 9

1. Human Rights
Akehurst, pp. 74-81
Cases for student reports:
   a. Lawless Case (merits)
      European Court of Human Rights, 1961
      56 *American Journal of International Law*, 171
   b. Attorney General v. Eichmann
      Jerusalem District Court of Israel, 1961
      56 *American Journal of International Law*, 805-845

Evaluation of Human Rights Area   Humphrey (xerox); Buergenthal (xerox); Handl (xerox)

2. Environment
Case distributed in class:
   a. Nuclear Test Cases
      (Australia v. France 1974) (New Zealand v. France 1974)

Case for student report:
   a. Trail Smelter Case (US v. Canada)
      III U.N. Rep. International Arb. Awards, 1905, 1907 (1949)

F. The Future of International Law
Student Contributions

Human Rights and Social Justice

Social Policy and Social Justice:
Global Perspectives on Social Welfare
Lois Martin, Salem State College

Disarmament, Development and Human Rights
Jim Zwick and Amy Hubbard, Syracuse University

Victims of Politics:
The State of Human Rights
Louis Furmanski, Virginia Polytechnic Institute

International Freedom of the Press
Howard H. Frederick, Mary Baldwin College

Global Challenges to Human
Dignity: Human Rights
Thomas E. McCoullough, Duke University

Aggression, Suppression, Holocaust:
Lessons for Students
Jutta Bendremer, University of Akron

International Human Rights
Robert Elias, Tufts University

Human Rights and International Organizations
E. Thomas Rowe, University of Denver

Social Policy and Social Justice: Global Perspectives on Social Welfare

Lois Martin   *Spring 1984*
Social Service 400/Salem State College/Salem, MA 01970

Course Objectives

1. To increase students' awareness of social welfare issues in the lives of Third World peoples.
2. To enlarge students' understanding of the inter-relatedness of domestic and global social welfare issues.
3. To acquaint students with widely accepted standards by which to define violations of human rights.
4. Using hunger as a case study, to provide students with information and tools of analysis by which to assess the roles of global institutions and policies in creating or perpetuating injustice.
5. To help students determine the kind of world in which they want to live.
6. To help students identify avenues for action through which they as individuals and/or future professionals will be able to work toward a more just society.
7. To encourage students to seek out communication from Third World peoples, e.g., through literature.
8. To improve students' ability to communicate through technical writing, creative writing and orally about global social welfare issues.

Structure of Course

Although a full range of global social welfare issues are of concern in this course, analytical focus will be sharpened through particular emphasis on world hunger. Classes will be conducted primarily as a seminar using required readings and student assignments #1 and #2 as points of departure. Student participation will be maximized and instructor lectures minimized. The instructor expects to serve as a facilitator, a resource for information or guidance in finding information, and as a co-learner. Students are urged to use the instructor's conference hours to discuss their ongoing work on assignments. They are also encouraged to bring to class new items which relate to course content.

Required Readings

McGinnis, James B. *Bread & Justice* (NY: Paulist Press, 1979).
Kidron, Michael & Segal, Ronald. *The State of the World Atlas* (NY: Simon & Schuster, 1981).
The New International Economic Kit (Cambridge, MA: American Friends Service Committee, 1976).
Ajami, Fouad. *Human Rights and World Order Politics* (NY: World Policy Institute, 1978).

Ashbrook, Tom. "Scramble for Jobs has Become Worldwide," *The Boston Globe*, Sept. 26, 1983.

Brown, Lester. "Too Many People? Yes," *Food Monitor*, May/June, 1983.

Commins, Stephen. "Too Many People? No," *Food Monitor*, May/June, 1983.

Ehrenreich, Barbara & Fuentes, Annette. "Life on the Global Assembly Line," *Ms.*, January, 1981.

Forsberg, Randall. "Behind the Facade: Nuclear War and Third World Intervention," in *The Deadly Connection: Nuclear War & U.S. Intervention* (conference transcripts) (Cambridge, MA: American Friends Service Committee, 1982).

Freire, Paulo. "The Role of the Social Worker in the Process of Change." Unpublished translation of *O papel do trabalhado social no proceso de mudanca*. Rio de Janeiro: Acao Cultural Para a Liberdade e Outros Ensaids, 1977.

George, Susan. "Scholarship, Power and Hunger," *Food Monitor*, Nov./Dec., 1981.

Harrington, Michael. *The Vast Majority: A Journey to the World's Poor* (NY: Simon & Schuster, 1977).

Holland, Joe & Henriot, Peter, S.J. *Social Analysis: Linking Faith and Justice* (Maryknoll, NY: Orbis Books, 1983).

"The International Monetary Fund and the Third World," *Hunger* #22. Interreligious Taskforce on U.S. Food Policy, Feb., 1980.

Checole, Kassahun. "South Africa and the Threat of Second Tier Nations," in *The Deadly Connection: Nuclear War & U.S. Intervention* (conference transcripts) (Cambridge, MA: American Friends Service Committee, 1983).

Kohler, Gernot. *Global Apartheid* (NY: World Policy Institute, 1978).

Lappé, Frances Moore & Collins, Joseph. *Food First* (NY: Ballantine, 1982).

Means, Russell. "Fighting Words on the Future of the Earth," *Mother Jones*, Dec., 1980.

Planas, Charito. "The Deadly Connection: A View From the Philippines," in *The Deadly Connection: Nuclear War & U.S. Intervention* (conference transcripts) (Cambridge, MA: American Friends Services Committee, 1983).

Sivard, Ruth L. *World Military and Social Expenditures 1983* (Wash., DC: World Priorities, 1983).

Universal Declaration of Human Rights (NY: United Nations).

World Hunger: Facts (Boston, MA: Oxfam America).

Course Outline

The following outline projects an estimated nine weeks' work. It does not reflect the time which will be devoted to student assignments (#2) and to intermittent student presentations (#3). These additions are expected to expand the work outlined to the full semester.

Week 1: Defining our Investigative Framework

Instructor's conception of course.

Our individual interests and biases.

Paulo Freire's model for critical analysis.

Standards:

Universal Declaration of Human Rights (& Covenants)

Statements from religious sources.

Professional social values.

Becoming familiar with information sources and course assignments.
Readings:
Univ. Declaration of Human Rights.
Holland & Henriot, pp. 21-45.
Article, book or chapter of your choice.

Week 2: Describing the Problem
Some disturbing facts and their interpretations.
Value bases which shape different interpretations: political, religious, ethnic/cultural experience, professional.
Orientations toward need for change: traditional, liberal, radical.
Readings:
McGinnis, Preface through p. 36.
Harrington, Chaps. 3 & 7
World Hunger: Facts
Ajami; Means; Brown; Commins.

Penetrating the Problem

Week 3: Principles of the New International Economic Order: The Components of Justice
Messages from the Third World.
Readings:
McGinnis, pp. 39-53.
NIEO Kit: (Sect. I) NIEO Declaration; Study Guide; From Confrontation to Negotiation.
Third world poem, interview, story of your choice.

Week 4: Underpinnings of Injustice
Historical roots: colonial to modern hunger.
Racism and sexism, silently fueling oppression.
Readings:
Lappé, Part III and Part IV through #16.
Kohler; Ehrenreich
NIEO Kit: (Sect. I) Diagnosis Incomplete; (Sect. II) Bangladesh.

Week 5: International Trade, Aid, Finance: By Whom & For Whom?
Export cropping and Third World dependence.
International lending institutions.
When does aid help?
Readings:
Lappé, Part IX, #40, #41, #42, & #45.
McGinnis, pp. 55-135.
NIEO Kit: (Sect. I) UNCTAD report.
The IMF & the Third World.

Week 6: Multinational Corporations: The World as a Single Economic Unit
The GNP as a measure of progress.
Citizens' confrontations with transnational power.
Readings:
McGinnis, pp. 137-234.

NIEO Kit: (Sect. II) Multinationals.
Ashbrook.

Week 7: Increasing Militarization
Third World connections.
Effects on social welfare.
Readings:
Sivard; Checole; Planas.
NIEO Kit: (Sect. II) World Military.

Weeks 8 and 9: Making Changes
Reaffirmation of personal & professional value bases.
Models for alternative development.
Action models: personal & professional responses.
Readings:
McGinnis, pp. 235-331.
George; Freire.
NIEO Kit: (Sect. II) Planning I & II, How Much is Enough?; Land & Water; Corp.
    Charters, (Sect. III) (all articles).
Holland & Henriot, pp. 46-63.

Assignments

1. Third World Literature Assignment
Objectives:
a. To learn from Third World people speaking from their own life experience.
b. To expand students' ability to make public issue/private trouble connections in
    environments foreign to their own.
c. To increase student appreciation of both cultural difference and shared human
    experience globally.

Book selection:
Each student is asked to read one book, fiction or autobiographical, written by a
Third World writer. Several which are available in the college bookstore and/or the
instructor's library are listed on the accompanying bibliography. However, a student may select an alternative book with the instructor's permission.

Written assignment (to be typed on ditto masters for copy distribution to class
    members):
    I. A concise book report.
    II. Using the *Universal Declaration of Human Rights* as a guide, list the human
    rights issues which you find raised in the lives of those about whom the book is
    written. Try to state them in the order of their importance to these people.
    III. Prepare a summary statement or outline of the national context in which this
    book is set, highlighting historical or systemic factors which you find most
    relevant to the private troubles of the book's characters. Exhaustive research is
    not expected for this statement. Rather, your *State of the World Atlas* and other
    readily available reference sources, e.g., the UN's *World Statistics in Brief*,
    encyclopedia, can serve as your principal sources.

    If more than one student choose to read the same book, they have the choice of working separately or together to prepare this assignment; if together, a group grade will be given.

Copies of this assignment should be made in the Social Service office for distribution to all class members. Two or three class periods will be devoted to discussion and comparison of the life experiences revealed in this literature.

2. Research Paper and Presentation
Objectives:
a. To allow each student opportunity to investigate in depth a subject of particular interest to her/him.
b. To give students opportunities to teach and learn from each other through class presentation.
c. To provide students an experience in writing and presenting a technical report.

Students are asked to select and research a subject relating to global social welfare issues. Much latitude is intended in selection of a topic. To illustrate a possible range of interest areas: human rights issues on campus; governmental or voluntary aid programs; an ecological problem; a thorough social analysis of a country (e.g. that in which your assign. #1 was set); the life and work of a particular human rights activist; Third World protest poetry; the role of a particular international agency. Whatever subject the student chooses, she should *first submit to the instructor a brief written statement* identifying the intended topic.

Students will be expected to share their reports orally with the class. Therefore, it will be necessary for each student to schedule this presentation with the instructor—this may be arranged at any point during the semester.

3. Personal Creative Work (Optional assignment)
Students may earn an additional 10 points (extra credit) by writing a poem, short story or song based on a theme relating to the course content. Anyone completing this assignment will receive the full 10 points, as the quality of this work is not the issue. Rather, what is sought is the student's effort to communicate about global social welfare issues in a form other than "academese,"—a form that is more nearly universal.

Bibliography

Third World Novels and Autobiographies
Achebe, Chinua. *Things Fall Apart* (Greenwich, CT: Fawcett, 1959).
Armah Ayi Kwei. *The Beautiful Ones Are Not Yet Born* (London: Heinemann, 1969).
Barrios de Chungara, Domitila. *Let Me Speak!* (NY: Monthly Review Press, 1978).
Bulosan, Carlos. *America Is in the Heart* (Seattle: U. of Wash., 1943).
de Jesus, Carolina. *Child of the Dark* (NY: E.P. Dutton & Co., 1962).
Emecheta, Buchi. *In the Ditch* (London: Allison & Busby, 1972).
Ngugi wa Thiong'o. *Devil on the Cross* (London: Heinemann, 1982).
Roumain, Jacques. *Masters of the Dew* (London: Heinemann, 1944).
Sembene, Ousmane. *God's Bits of Wood* (Garden City, NY: Doubleday & Co., 1970).

Poetry & Short Literary Pieces from the Third World
Boullata, Kamal, ed. *Women of the Fertile Crescent* (Wash., DC: Three Continents Press, 1981).
Brutus, Dennis. *Letters to Martha* (London: Heinemann, 1968).
Hughes, Langston. *Selected Poems* (NY: Random House, 1959).
Marquez, Robert. *Latin American Revolutionary Poetry* (NY: Monthly Review Press, 1974).
Moraga, Cherrie & Anzaldua, Gloria, eds. *The Bridge Called My Back* (Watertown, MA: Persephone, 1981).
Neruda, Pablo. *A Call for the Destruction of Nixon and Praise of the Chilean Revolution* (Cambridge, MA: West End Press, 1980).
Neruda, Pablo. *Fully Empowered* (NY: Farrar, Straus & Giroux, 1967).
Randall, Margaret, ed. *Breaking the Silences* (Vancouver: Pulp Press, 1982).
White, Margaret B. & Quigley, Robert, eds. *How the Other Third Lives . . .* (Maryknoll, NY: Orbis, 1977).

Suggested Additions to Required Readings
Barnet, Richard & Muller, Ronald. *Global Reach* (NY: Simon & Schuster, 1974).
Falk, Richard, Kim, Samuel & Mendlovitz, Saul, eds. *Toward a Just World Order*, Vol. 1 (Boulder, CO: Westview Press, 1982).
Freire, Paulo. *Pedagogy in Process* (NY: Continuum, 1983).
Freire, Paulo. *Pedagogy of the Oppressed* (NY: The Seabury Press, 1974).
Fuentes, Annette & Ehrenreich, Barbara. *Women in the Global Factory* (Boston, MA: South End Press, 1983).
George, Susan. *Feeding the Few: Corporate Control of Food* (Wash. DC: Institute for Policy Studies, 1983).
Hartmann, Betsy & Boyce, James. *Needless Hunger: Voices From a Bangladesh Village* (San Francisco, CA: Institute for Food & Development Policy, 1979).
Hinton, William. *Fanshen: A Documentary of Revolution in a Chinese Village* (NY: Vintage Books, 1966).
Huston, Perdita. *Third World Women Speak Out: Interviews in Six Countries on Change, Development, and Basic Needs* (NY: Praeger, 1979).
King, Martin Luther, Jr. *Where Do We Go From Here: Chaos or Community.* (Boston, MA: Beacon, 1967).
Lappé, Frances Moore, Collins, Joseph & Kinley, David. *Aid As Obstacle* (San Francisco, CA: Institute for Food & Development Policy, 1981).
Lernoux, Penny. *Cry of the People* (NY: Doubleday, 1980).
Morgan, Dan. *Merchants of Grain* (Middlesex, England: Penguin, 1979).
Pope Paul VI. *Development of Peoples* (Boston, MA: St. Paul's Editions, 1967).
Pope John Paul II. *On Human Work* (Boston, MA: St. Paul's Editions, 1978).
Toton, Suzanne, C. *World Hunger* (Maryknoll, NY: Orbis, 1982).

Periodicals
Issues of *Multinational Monitor* and of *Food Monitor*, available from the instructor's library, contain many relevant articles.

Disarmament, Development and Human Rights

Jim Zwick and Amy Hubbard   *Spring 1984*
Public Affairs 204/Syracuse University/Syracuse, NY 13210

This course will introduce the theory and practice of nonviolent social change while exploring three issues of great concern in the modern age in which social change is currently under way. Students should gain a basic understanding of the three issues and the various approaches used (or suggested) for addressing them. Students will also be challenged to develop their own perspectives and understandings of the issues and to use these to evaluate the social change methods introduced.

Requirements and Grading

Three short position papers dealing with the issues covered in the course will be required. Each paper should address: 1) the problems to be solved, 2) your interpretation of what solution is needed, and 3) what appropriate actions might be taken to reach the solution you are proposing. Papers will be graded on the basis of clarity, sophistication of analysis, understanding of readings and lectures, and originality and potential effectiveness of solutions. Each paper will be worth 25% of your final grade.

Three short quizzes on materials covered in the readings and lectures will be administered in the first discussion section following the sections on Disarmament and Development and in the first part of the last class period.

Course Outline
(**indicates reserve readings)

Part I: Introduction

Week 1: Overview of the World Situation
Readings (full citations can be found under Reserve Readings):
Rajni Kothari, "On Violence"**
Burns Weston, "General Introduction: The Machines of Armageddon"

Week 2: Introduction to Violence and Peace
Readings:
Gene Sharp, *Power and Struggle*, Chapters 1-2.

Part II: Disarmament

Week 3: National Security, the International System and Military Power
Readings:
Harold Freeman, "Imagine One Nuclear Bomb" or Jonathan Schell, "A Republic of Insects and Grass"

Hedley Bull, "The Prospects for Deterrences"
Allan Krass, "Deterrence and its Contradictions"
Robin Luckham, "Myths and Realities of Security"
Robert Donaldson, "Soviet Conceptions of Security"
Walter Clemens, "National Security and U.S.-Soviet Relations
Lloyd Dumas, "Military Spending and Economic Decay"

Week 4: Arms Race Dynamics and Nuclear Arms Proliferation
Slideshow: "The Buddha is Smiling" (Center for Development Policy)
Readings:
U.S. International Communications Agency, "Soviet Perceptions of the U.S.:
    Results of a Surrogate Interview Project"
George Arbatov, "Relations Between the U.S. and the USSR: The Accuracy of U.S.
    Perceptions"
George Kennan, "Two Views of the Soviet Problem"
Bruce Russett, "Why Do Arms Races Occur?"
Robert Johansen, *SALT II: A Symptom of the Arms Race*
Fred Kaplan, *Dubious Specter: A Skeptical Look at the Soviet Nuclear Threat*

Week 5: Arms Control and Disarmament Proposals
Readings: •
Robert Johansen, "Toward an Alternative Security System"
Jerome Frank, "Psychological Aspects of Disarmament and International Negotia-
    tions"
Charles Osgood, "Disarmament Needs GRIT"
G.F. Kennan, "A Modest Proposal"
Mary Kaldor, "Disarmament: The Armament Process in Reverse"

Week 6: Movements for Disarmament
Readings:
Randall Forsberg, "Call to Halt the Nuclear Arms Race"
Nigel Young, "The Contemporary European Anti-Nuclear Movement: Experi-
    ments in the Mobilization of Public Power"**
Jonathan Dean, "Beyond First Use"
National Conference of Catholic Bishops, "Pastoral Letter on War and Peace—The
    Challenge of Peace: God's Promise and Our Response"
Rajni Kothari, "Survival in an Age of Transformation"

Part III: Development

Week 7: Introduction to Problems of Development
Slideshow: "Taking Charge: The Struggle for Economic Justice" (AFSC)
Readings:
Heraldo Munoz, "The Various Roads to Development"
J. Samuel Valenzuela and Arturo Valenzuela, "Modernization and Dependency:
    Alternative Perspectives in the Study of Latin American Underdevelopment"
Mahbub ul Haq, "Negotiating a New Bargain with the Rich Countries"

Week 8: Spring Vacation

Week 9: Decolonization, the NIEO and Beyond
Readings:
Gustavo Lagos, "The Revolution of Being: A Preferred World Model"
Johan Galtung, "The Politics of Self-Reliance"

Week 10: Development and Over-Development
Film: "To Sing Our Own Song" (BBC)
Readings:
Nathan Keyfitz, "World Resources and the World Middle Class"**
"The Dai Dong Declaration: Independent Declaration on the Environment"**
Rodolfo Stavenhagen, "The Future of Latin America: Between Underdevelopment and Revolution"
Kenneth Hal and Byron Blake, "Collective Self-Reliance: The Case of the Carribean Community (CARICOM)"

Week 11: Movements for Development
Readings:
Denis Goulet, "Development as Liberation: Policy Lessons from Case Studies"** or Ernesto Cardenal, "Revolution and Peace: The Nicaraguan Road"**
Miles Wolpin, "Egalitarian Reformism in the Third World vs. the Military: A Profile of Failure"** or Miles Wolpin, "Civilian and Military Reformism: The Pattern of Destabilization"**
C.B. Macpherson, "Participatory Democracy"** or Marjorie Hope and James Young, "Movement for a New Society"**

Part IV: Human Rights

Week 12: International Human Rights: An Introduction
Readings:
Jose Zalaquett, *The Human Rights Issue and the Human Rights Movement*, pp 7-29.
"Declaration of Independence"
"Universal Declaration of Human Rights"
"Universal Declaration of the Rights of Peoples"
Amnesty International, *Amnesty International Report*

Week 13: Development, Militarism and Human Rights
Slideshow: "Roots of the Crisis: Central America in the 1980's" (AFSC)
Readings:
Eqbal Ahmad, "The Neo-Fascist State: Notes on the Pathology of Power in the Third World"**
Jim Zwick, "Militarism and Repression in the Philippines"** or Robert Denemark and Howard Lehman, "South African State Terror: The Costs of Continuing Repression"**
Amnesty International, *Amnesty International Report* (cont.)

Week 14: The Human Rights Movement: A Typology and Assessment of Prospects
Readings:
Jose Zalaquett, *The Human Rights Issue and the Human Rights Movement*, pp. 30-65.

Stephen Marks, "The Peace-Human Rights-Development Dialectic"**
Amnesty International, *Amnesty International Report* (finish)

Week 15: Disarmament, Development and Human Rights: An Agenda for Action

Required Texts
Gene Sharp, *Power and Struggle* (Boston, MA: Porter Sargent, 1973).
Burns Weston (ed.), *Toward Nuclear Disarmament and Global Security* (Boulder, CO: Westview Press, 1984).
Heraldo Munoz (ed.), *From Dependency to Development: Strategies to Overcome Underdevelopment and Inequality* (Boulder, CO: Westview Press, 1981).
Jose Zalaquett, *The Human Rights Issue and the Human Rights Movement* Background Information 1981/3 (Geneva: Commission of the Churches on International Affairs of the World Council of Churches, 1981).
Amnesty International, *Amnesty International Report 1983* (London: Amnesty International, 1983).

Reserve Readings
Rajni Kothari, "On Violence," in Rajni Kothari, *Footsteps into the Future* (New York: The Free Press, 1974) pp. 79-117.
Nigel Young, "The Contemporary European Anti-Nuclear Movement: Experiments in the Mobilization of Public Power," *Peace and Change* 9:1 (Spring 1983) pp. 1-16.
Nathan Keyfitz, "World Resources and the World Middle Class," in Richard Falk, Samuel S. Kim and Saul H. Mendlovitz (eds.), *Toward a Just World Order* (Boulder, CO: Westview Press, 1982) pp. 297-314.
"The Dai Dong Declaration: Independent Declaration on the Environment," in Falk, Kim and Mendlovitz (eds.), *Toward a Just World Order*, pp. 492-496.
Denis Goulet, "Development as Liberation: Policy Lessons from Case Studies," *World Development* 7:6 (June 1979) pp. 555-566.
Ernesto Cardenal, "Participatory Democracy," in C.B. Macpherson, *The Life and Times of Liberal Democracy* (New York: Oxford University Press, 1977) pp. 93-115.
Marjorie Hope and James Young, "Movement for a New Society," in Marjorie Hope and James Young, *The Struggle for Humanity* (Maryknoll, NY: Orbis Books, 1977) pp. 11-39.
Miles Wolpin, "Egalitarian Reformism in the Third World vs. the Military: A Profile of Failure," *Journal of Peace Research* 15:2 (1978) pp. 89-107.
Miles Wolpin, "Civilian and Military Reformism: The Pattern of Destabilization," in Miles Wolpin, *Militarism and Social Revolution in the Third World* (Totowa, NJ: Allanheld, Osmun & Co., 1981) pp. 43-67.
Eqbal Ahmad, "The Neo-Fasist State: Notes on the Pathology of Power in the Third World," in Falk, Kim and Mendlovitz (eds.), *Toward a Just World Order*, pp. 74-83.
Jim Zwick, "Militarism and Repression in the Philippines," in Michael Stohl and George A. Lopez (eds.), *The State as Terrorist: The Dynamics of Governmental Violence and Repression* (Westport, CT: Greenwood Press, 1984).
Robert A. Denemark and Howard P. Lehman, "South African State Terror: The Costs of Continuing Repression," in Stohl and Lopez (eds.), *The State as Terrorist*.

Stephen Marks, "The Peace-Human Rights-Development Dialectic," *Bulletin of Peace Proposals* 11:4 (1980) pp. 339-347.

Amnesty International Report 1983—Required Readings

Week 12

Preface	Iran
Amnesty International—A Worldwide Campaign	Lebanon
United States of America	Yemen
United Kingdom	Saudi Arabia
Union of Soviet Socialist Republics	Egypt
Yugoslavia	Angola
Japan	Kenya
Albania	Mozambique
Czechoslovakia	Guinea-Bissau
Uruguay	Chad
Spain	

Week 13

Italy	Argentina
Greece	Philippines
Hungary	Turkey
France	Poland
Switzerland	Malaysia
Israel	Chile
South Africa	Guatemala
German Democratic Republic	El Salvador
Federal Republic of Germany	

Week 14

Cuba	Zimbabwe
Mexico	Ethiopia
Venezuela	Korea (Demo. Republic of)
Nicaragua	Korea (Republic of)
Honduras	Indonesia and East Timor
China	Costa Rica
Taiwan	Grenada
Vietnam	Tanzania

Discussion Questions: Week 1

Kothari presents a rather dismal picture of the world. He discusses the arms race, trade in weapons, unequal development, the alienation of people from their work, and ecological problems. He also discusses potential for change and has some controversial ideas about the relationship between violence and nonviolence in global social change.

1. What are the main global problems (terms of violence) that Kothari identifies?
2. What are the sources of these problems? (Who or what is causing or creating violence in the world?)
3. It is commonly accepted in the U.S. and other developed countries that population growth in the Third World is a major cause of poverty and resource depletion

in the Third World. After reading Kothari (especially pp. 85-88), do you agree with this assessment? Why or why not?

4. When might violence contribute to a more nonviolent world? Do you think violence is "legitimate" under the situations described by Kothari? Might there be other times when it would be justified to use violence to achieve nonviolent goals?

5. Is the nuclear arms race presenting the greatest threat to the people of the world? Or do some of the issues raised by Kothari represent greater immediate threats? How might you approach making a decision about which issue you would spend your career working on (assuming that you were choosing between the arms race, unequal development, or human rights)? Is it necessary to make a choice?

Discussion Questions: Week 2
Chapter 1 of Gene Sharp's book deals with the nature of State power (and power generally). He argues that power resides not in those who hold State power, but in those *who allow them* to hold that power. He argues that power (including the power of States) is not monolithic. However, in the lecture on January 31 several other views of the State were presented which disagree with Sharp. In particular, the advances in technology of recent years may be making the state more monolithic (as in Orwell's *1984)* or that real power is not held by the State but by classes, both nationally and internationally.

1. Which of these views of State power do you agree with?

2. What are the implications of each of these theories for developing social change strategies? In particular, what do these theories imply, if anything, about using resistance, reform or revolution as social change strategies? (see Chapter 2 for examples of these)

3. Does the distinction between structural violence and personal violence imply a need for different strategies to remove them? Or should the main choice of strategy come from analysis of the particular issue you are trying to address?

Discussion Questions: Week 3
The readings for this week outline the effects a nuclear war would have on the world, the problems and potential of deterrence as a means of avoiding nuclear war, and various conceptions of "national security." In addition, the lecture this week presented both the main arguments for the necessity of preserving national security through building up military forces and several critiques of these arguments.

1. How do you personally define "security" in your life?

2. To what extent is your security guaranteed by the State (including local, state and national branches of the State)?

3. To what extent do global conflicts affect your security? Can you imagine a situation in which you would support policies which risked nuclear war but had potential to ensure your personal security?

4. In the international system, can all countries achieve security simultaneously? How or why not? How does a person's view of the world affect their position on military policy?

5. How do you respond to feelings of insecurity? To whom can you address your grievances? What power do you have to change policies which affect your security?

Discussion Questions: Week 4

There are many inter-related factors which need to be examined to understand the nuclear arms race and nuclear proliferation. The U.S. and USSR are certainly primary actors in the arms race, and each seems to be irreversably opposed. But other States have also gained nuclear weapon capacity and, as Weston notes, India, Israel, South Africa and Pakistan might be able to produce nuclear weapons in a matter of months. Argentina, Brazil, Libya, Iraq, Taiwan and South Korea may also have this capacity soon.

1. To what extent does the international system (of States holding unlimited sovereignty) influence the nature of the nuclear arms race and arms proliferation?
2. What factors do you think are most important in explaining the arms race: U.S.-USSR ideological differences, perceptions of threat, technological momentum, "swaggering," personal ambitions of those in power, other? Why?
3. What might be done to control or reverse the arms race and nuclear proliferation to ensure against possible accidents or nuclear terrorism?
4. Whose security is being ensured by the arms race? (Note that Pakistan's leader promised to gain nuclear weapons even if his people "have to eat grass" but that this was to save them from a potential nuclear attack from India.) How would you balance the "guns or butter" issue?

Discussion Questions: Week 5

From 1945-1960 arms control proposals made by both the US and USSR were geared toward nuclear disarmament. From the 1960's onward, the idea of disarmament had been abandoned until President Reagan proposed the Strategic Arms Reduction Talks (START). Johansen has argued that SALT II actually institutionalized the arms race.

1. What were the reasons for the shift in goals of arms control talks after 1960? In what ways was this a reflection of changes in the arms race? In the international goals of the U.S. and USSR?
2. How would you evaluate the relative importance of the psychological aspects of disarmament negotiations outlined by Frank and Osgood and the more economically-focused aspects outlined by Kaldor? Do our perceptions of "the enemy" make disarmament impossible even though we would gain many economic benefits through disarming?
3. Do you think that the "action-reaction" elements of the arms race might be reversed to achieve disarmament?
4. What changes in the international system do you think are necessary to achieve disarmament? Can you imagine a disarmed world? What would it look like?

Discussion Questions: Week 6

The decision by NATO to modernize nuclear forces in Europe, the strong rhetoric of the Reagan Administration, and the failure of the Second U.N. Special Session on Disarmament all contributed to greatly increased worldwide concern about the danger of nuclear war and sparked a very rapid development of anti-nuclear movements in North America, Europe and Asia. While these movements have had considerable influence in raising and shaping debate on nuclear issues, they have not so far succeeded in changing the military policies of the nuclear States.

1. What are the specific goals of the U.S. Nuclear Freeze Movement, the movement

for European Nuclear Disarmament, and the Nuclear Free Pacific movement? In what areas do they conflict? In what ways are they similar?

2. How would you explain their inability to change military policy? Are there issues in the nature of the arms race they do not satisfactorily address? Are they naive about the nature of State power? Are they naive about the nature of global conflicts?

3. How do the movements for disarmament address the issue of security? How does this differ from the view of national security used by military planners?

4. If you were to design a disarmament movement, how would you proceed? How might the disarmament movements be made more effective?

Discussion Questions: Week 7
Valenzuela & Valenzuela describe the reasons for concern about Third World development following World War II and then go on to contrast two prevalent methodologies for studying the problems of poverty in the Third World. Both methodologies have explicit assumptions which shape the kinds of policies advocated as a result of their findings.

1. Why was there a sudden concern about Third World development following WW II?
2. What are some of the main assumptions of the modernization perspective?
3. What link is there between these assumptions and the backgrounds of the scholars who developed the perspective?
4. What policy implications do their assumptions have?
5. What are some of the main assumptions of the dependency perspective?
6. What policy implications do their assumptions have?

Discussion Questions: Week 9: The Development Debate
You are to choose (or be assigned—to even out the groups) one of the following positions to argue and defend in the development debate:

1. The Modernization View (Walt Rostow) see article by Valenzuela and Valenzuela.
2. The New International Economic Order View (Mahbub ul Haq) see his article.
3. The Self-Reliance View (Johan Galtung) see his article.

To prepare for the debate, outline answers to the following questions. These will serve mainly as reminders to you during the debate so they do not have to be long. You may also get together with others who will be arguing the same position to formulate responses.

1. What are the main assumptions of the view I am arguing?
2. What policies does it advocate?
3. What are its strong and weak points?
4. What are the main assumptions of the other two positions?
5. What policies do they advocate?
6. What are their weak points? (in other words, how can you tear them apart during the debate?)

Discussion Questions: Week 10
The film "To Sing Our Own Song" vividly presented the conditions of uneven

development, militarism and human rights violations in the Philippines as well as both legal and revolutionary movements which have developed to change the situation. It ended with a request that people in developed countries take action to change our own government's support for the status quo in the Philippines. Stavenhagen's article also addressed the issue of revolutionary change as an alternative to uneven development. Keyfitz addressed the issue of global disparities in income and resource consumption which reinforces situations like those in the Philippines and Latin America.

1. What relations were drawn in the film between uneven development, militarism, human rights violations and revolution?
2. To what degree is "over-development" dependent on underdevelopment in other parts of the world?
3. The demands of the world's poor are, in part, for a more equitable distribution of world resources. What changes in the international system would be needed to meet these demands? What specific institutions would need to be changed?
4. What sacrifices (in income, consumption of food and luxuries, in lifestyle) do you think would need to take place for a more even distribution of goods and resources to take place? What sacrifices are you willing to make?
5. Is the Philippines situation one where Kothari would say that revolutionary violence is "legitimate"? Is there any other viable means of change which Sharp might propose?
6. Johan Galtung, in his article "A Structural Theory of Revolution," argues that violent revolution may be less costly in human terms than slow changes of exploitative social structures. How would you evaluate the relative merits of violent and nonviolent social change in light of this argument and the readings for this week?

Discussion Questions: Week 11
Goulet's and Cardenal's articles both present case studies of (at least partially) successful movements for development. Wolpin presents cases where movements for reform in the Third World were overthrown by national and/or international actors opposed to the reforms. Macpherson's and Hope & Young's articles outline movements for development in already developed countries.

1. How would you evaluate these proposals for development in light of your understanding of the various positions taken in "The Development Debate"? What kind of change do you think is necessary and most likely to succeed?
2. Can national movements for development succeed? Is international support necessary? What are the national and international obstacles to development?
3. How do theories of the State affect positions on how movements for development should proceed? How is this related to whether violence or nonviolence is used in the social change process?
4. If you were to design a movement for development, how would you proceed? How might development movements be made more effective?

Discussion Questions: Week 12
The following is a list of rights that have been affirmed in the Universal Declaration of Human Rights. They cover a wide range of concerns, from the right to life to the right to rest and leisure. It is often argued that not all of these rights can be enjoyed by everyone in the community because (1) some people's rights may conflict with other's rights, (2) political or economic development may not allow rights to be

exercised, or (3) the national interest may call for some individual rights not to be recognized during certain times of crisis. Which of these rights is most important to you? Which would you demand to have no matter what?

1. Rank the rights from 1-14 (1 being the most important, 14 being the least important. How do you make evaluations of rights?)
2. Put an * next to the 5 rights you would not want to lose under any circumstances.
____ Right to a fair trial
____ Freedom of religion
____ Right to life, liberty and security of the person
____ Right to work with equal pay
____ Right to marry and found a family
____ Right to participate in the cultural life of the community
____ Freedom from torture
____ Freedom of peaceful assembly and association
____ Right to education
____ Right to rest and leisure
____ Right to participate in the government of your country
____ Right to social security
____ Right to a standard of living adequate for health & well-being
____ Right to own property
____ Freedom of opinion and expression
3. Put an "?" next to any rights that you think are actually not human rights (i.e., any rights that you think are not required as something that makes the development of people as people possible or are rights that are confered to people on the basis of merit or service and not just because they are human).
4. How have international human rights gained recognition historically? What do you do when your rights are violated? Does it matter who violates them?
5. How does the concept of human rights affect the concept of unlimited sovereignty of States?

Discussion Questions: Week 13
Eqbal Ahmad describes 5 characteristics of the contemporary "neo-fascist State." He refers to the Philippines as an example of a neo-fascist State but does not include South Africa in the article. Note the specific characteristics of the Philippine or South African States which do or do not correspond to Ahmad's characteristics of the Neo-fascist State listed below. (In other words, why is the Philippines included and South Africa not included?)

1. They are marked by a fundamental shift in the use of organized terror.
2. They are "neo-fascist" as opposed to "fascist."
3. They share a similar ideological base.
4. They share a similar "model" of development.
5. They all have symbiotic external ties.
6. In what ways are the characteristics of the neo-fascist States a product of the same international dynamics that have led to the arms race?
7. In what ways are the regimes' choice of development models associated with the nature of the neo-fascist States?
8. In what ways are the global arms race, uneven development, and human rights violations linked?

Discussion Questions: Week 14

Amnesty International (AI) is the international non-governmental human rights organization with the largest active membership throughout the world. Its "mandate" is limited to specific civil and political rights, however, and it addresses symptoms of human rights violations rather than the causes of them. Zalaquett notes that the human rights movement has not effectively addressed the causes of human rights violations because to do so would require more political (ideological) conformity within the movement than currently exists. To work on causes of human rights violations might lead to a decrease in active involvement in the movement.

1. How would you assess the strengths and weaknesses of Amnesty International's methods of addressing the human rights problem?
2. How would you assess the strengths and weaknesses of the human rights movement more generally? Are the International League for Human Rights or the International League for the Rights and Liberation of Peoples any more effective than Amnesty International?
3. What generation of rights (civil & political; economic, social & cultural; rights of peoples) do you think priority should be placed on by the international human rights movement?
4. What is (or should be) the relationship between national human rights organizations (such as the American Civil Liberties Union or Task Force Detainees Philippines) and international organizations? Is one type more effective than the other? Or do they have separate or complementary functions?
5. How would you design a movement for human rights? Is it possible to address all three generations of rights in one organization? Is it best to address symptoms (and have more support) or causes (and possibly have more lasting effect)? What changes will be necessary in the international system to ensure respect for human rights?
6. In what ways would success in movements for disarmament, development *or* human rights affect the potential for success of the other movements? What similarities are there in the obstacles they face? What changes in the international system would benefit all three movements?

Songs, Films & Novels

Action for social change takes place in the cultural as well as political and economic realms. Many of the topics to be discussed this semester have been addressed by contemporary musicians. Since social change through popular culture is not significantly addressed in any of the readings for this course, a song will be played each week before the discussion section meeting begins for those who arrive early. The songs for each week are:

Week 2: The Gang of Four, "Why Theory?" *Solid Gold*, Warner Bros. Records, 1981.

Week 3: The Clash, "London Calling," *London Calling*, Epic, 1979.

Week 4: XTC, "Living Through Another Cuba," *Black Sea*, Virgin Records, 1980.

Week 5: XTC, "Melt the Guns," *English Settlement*, Virgin Records, 1982.

Week 6: Holly Near & Ronnie Gilbert, "Singing for Our Lives," *Lifeline*, Redwood Records, 1983.

Week 7: Bob Marley and the Wailers, "War/No More Trouble," *Babylon by Bus*, Islands Records, 1978.

Week 9: Talking Heads, "Listening Wind," *Remain in Light*, Sire Records, 1980.

Week 10: The Members, "Off-shore Banking Business."

Week 11: Frankie Armstrong, "Anti-Carol," *Out of Love, Hope and Suffering.*

Week 12: Peter Gabriel, "Biko," *Peter Gabriel*, Geffen Records, 1980.

Week 13: Holly Near and Ronnie Gilbert, "Hay Una Mujer Desaparecida," *Lifeline*, Redwood Records, 1983.

Week 14: Peter Tosh, "Equal Rights," *Equal Rights*, Columbia Records, 1977.

Week 15: Holly Near & Ronnie Gilbert, "No More Genocide," *Lifeline*, Redwood Records, 1983.

You may also want to see the following films which will be shown on campus by the NVS Film Series:

"In Our Hands" (on the June 12 rally in support of the UN Special Session on Disarmament, 1982)

"Under Fire" (a fictional—Hollywood—account of the Nicaraguan Revolution)

Novels related to this course include Ursulla LeGuin, *The Dispossessed;* Ariel Dorfman, *Widows;* George Orwell, *1984;* and Nadine Gordimer, *Burgher's Daughter.*

Victims of Politics: The State of Human Rights

Louis Furmanski   *Winter 1983*
International Studies 3112/Virginia Polytechnic Institute/
Blacksburg, VA 24061

This course intends to examine the current status of human rights as a concern fundamental to the advancement of global peace and solidarity. It will deal with the historical development of the concept of human rights from an interdisciplinary perspective, encompassing political, cultural, religious, and economic factors which define the universe of human rights. Our intention here will be to critically consider the various values which attempt to explain the definition of human rights and consequently, the various factors which mitigate against their full realization. In particular, we will examine the relation of political and economic systems to the compliance and/or violation of human rights throughout the world. We will also examine the various methods at the disposal of the international community which oversee the status of human rights and which attempt to further their observance, especially actions by international organizations and non-governmental bodies such as Amnesty International. A related concern will be to explore the relevancy and effectiveness of International Law as a focus for the implementation of human rights. Finally, the question of human rights as a proper focus for U.S. foreign policy will be critically assessed for what we can learn concerning the possible "future" state of human rights concerns in the interstate environment.

The guiding principle of this course will be that the state of human rights is a proper, if not the most proper standard, by which to assess and judge contemporary governments. Consequently, our perspective will necessarily be a critical one, but one tempered by acknowledgement of the role, function, and necessity of governmental restrictions on absolute individual freedom.

Requirements

Each of you will be required to select a particular country and become an "expert" on the human rights situation within. You will explore the underlying reasons for the observance or non-observance of human rights in your country by analyzing its normative values, cultural traditions, ideological developments, and sociopolitical and economic conditions. Analysis of major institutions such as the military, government, religious organizations, labor unions, and political parties and their relationship to the status of human rights is expected to be an important part of your critical evaluation.

Reading Materials
David P. Forsythe, *Human Rights and World Politics*, University of Nebraska
Press, 1983.
Penny Lernoux, *Cry of the People*, Penguin Books, 1982.

Topic Sequence and Dates of Coverage

January 4 Introductory Comments

January 6 Human Rights: The Basic Norms
Readings: Forsythe, Chapter 1

January 9 The Political Philosophy of Human Rights
Readings: Forsythe, Chapter 5

January 11 The Theological Perspective on Human Rights

January 13 Human Rights Violations: Sexual Discrimination
Readings: K. Barry, *Human Rights Quarterly*, Vol. 3, #2

January 18 Human Rights Violations: Race—South Africa
Readings: South Africa: *Time Running Out*, Study by U.S. Commission on South
Africa, 1983.

January 20 Human Rights Violations: Race—United States
Readings: *Christianity and Crisis*, Vol. 41, pp. 67-74
Oates, *Let the Trumpet Sound*, pp. 55-112—on reserve

January 23 Human Rights Violations: Torture and Extrajudicial Executions
Readings: M. Lippman. *Universal Human Rights*, Vol. 1, #4
E. Kaufman and P.W. Fagen, *Human Rights Quarterly*, Vol. 3, #4

January 25 Human Rights and Economic Development
Readings: J.D. Sethi, *Human Rights Quarterly*, Vol. 3, #3

January 27 Political Ideologies and Human Rights

January 30 Authoritarianism and Human Rights Violations

February 1 Responses to Human Rights Violations

February 3 Formal and Informal Methods of Human Rights Implementation
Readings: Forsythe, Chapters 2 and 4

February 6 Amnesty International and Human Rights

February 8-10 International Law and Human Rights

February 13 Human Rights, US Foreign Policy and the Catholic Church

February 15-17 Catholic Church in Latin America
Readings: Forsythe, Chapter 3
Lernoux, entire book

February 20-March 7 Student Reports

March 9 Concluding Remarks
Readings: Forsythe, Chapter 6

International Freedom of the Press

Howard H. Frederick   *Spring 1983*
Communication 320/Mary Baldwin College/Staunton, VA 24401

Most upperdivision and graduate courses on press freedom taught in the United States explore the history and philosophical foundations of the free press doctrine. Typically they examine the social transformation in Europe in the 17th century which became known as liberalism, proceed through the challenges to liberalism in the last century, and conclude with the continuing debates today on such issues as pornography and censorship.

This approach is important in that much of the philosophical underpinnings of the Western free press doctrine arose within European liberalism. But it is also short-sighted and Euro-centric, for advances and refinements on freedom of the press, articulations that correspond to the unique and changing national cultures around the world, have given rise to a number of other competing conceptions of a free press. These new concepts have put the Western free press doctrine increasingly on the defensive. Indeed, the emergence and gradual definition of the New International Information and Communication Order (NIICO), as debated in UNESCO, have put the free press concept on the agenda for world debate.

This course is part of Mary Baldwin College's continuing efforts to internationalize its Communication Program. International Communication Studies examines the flow of attitudes, values and information among and between nation-states and cultures, as well as the institutions and ideologies that motivate this flow. This Seminar will prepare the student to face the changing international environment in which the world's press systems operate and to participate consciously as an actor in this international debate.

Course Requirements

There will be a mid-term examination and a comprehensive final examination (which may not be substituted for other work). Students will prepare occasional short essays as assigned by the instructor. One 10-page country profile will be assigned. In a seminar, class participation counts more than in other courses. In addition, each student will make at least two scholarly presentations to the rest of the class.

Required Texts
You must subscribe to one of the following: *The Washington Post, Christian Science Monitor*, and/or *Wall Street Journal, Richmond Times-Dispatch* (all delivered daily in Staunton).

One of the following four books:
Bob Woodward and Carl Bernstein, *All the President's Men*. Warner Books, 1976.
Larry Collins and Dominique LaPierre, *Freedom at Midnight*. Avon Books, 1976.
I.F. Stone, *I.F. Stone's Weekly Reader*. Neil Middleton (ed.). Random House, 1971.
Gunter Walraff, *The Undesirable Journalists*. London: Pluto Press, 1977.
Vladimir I. Lenin, *What is to Be Done?* USSR: Progress Pubs, 1973.
Maurice Cullen, *Mass Media and the First Amendment*. William C. Brown, 1981.
Theodore S. Seibert et al. *Four Theories of the Press*. Univ. of Illinois Press, 1963.
John Milton, *Areopagitica*. Saifer, 1972 (reprint of 1644 edition).
John S. Mills, *On Liberty*. Penguin, 1983.
C.L. Jackson et al. *Newspapers and Videotex: How Free a Press?* Modern Media
   Institute, 1981.
American Heritage Magazine, Vol. 33, No. 6, "The American Press."

Course Outline

I. The Mind and Milieu of the Professional Communicator

The course begins in a unique fashion. Students will be divided into four sections and will work together in these sections to prepare presentations to the whole class. In addition to the four books, relevant articles provide background material.

In these selections we have four different approaches to the press and to press freedom. Gunter Walraff is a master of deceit and infiltrates into elite power circles through journalistic subterfuge. Woodward and Bernstein, in the classic "big scoop" tradition, reveal to a disbelieving public the most devastating story ever of a U.S. President. I.F. Stone, through perseverance, common sense and seeing the obvious, rocked the ship of state for two decades. And finally, the story of Mohandas K. Gandhi's struggle against Britain is seen through the eyes of journalists who witnessed his campaigns.

Each student section will be responsible for presenting the substance of the material to the rest of the class through dramatic readings, role play or another format. In addition, each student will write a four-page integrative essay drawing together all of the readings and presentations in section I.

A. Four Styles of Journalistic Reportage and Ethics

Introduction to the course. Lecture on conflicting conceptions of freedom and press coverage. International perspectives on press freedom. How to be a student in a seminar.

Section 1—Gunter Walraff, *The Undesirable Journalist*

Abbie Hoffman, "Undercover in New Germany," *Mother Jones*, February/March 1979, pp. 44-54.
"Ten Theses of Power Structure Research," *NACLA Research Methodology Guide*, 1970. (to be handed out in class)

Section 2—Bob Woodward and Carl Bernstein, *All the President's Men*

James McCartney, "The Washington Post and Watergate: How Two Davids Slew Goliath," *Columbia Journalism Review*, July/August 1973, pp. 8-22.
Nat Hentoff, "Woodward, Bernstein and 'All the President's Men'," *Columbia Journalism Review*, July/August 1974, pp. 10-15.

Section 3—I.F. Stone, *I.F. Stone Weekly Reader*
Andrew Kopkind, "The Importance of Being Izzy," *Ramparts,* May 1974, pp. 39-44.
I.F. Stone, "Izzy on Izzy," *New York Times Magazine,* January 22, 1978, pp. 12-13 +.

Section 4—Larry Collins and Dominique LaPierre, *Freedom at Midnight*
Kosum Singh, "Gandhi and Mao as Mass Communicators," *Journal of Communication* 29, Summer 1979, pp. 94-101.
Louis Fisher, "Across India With A Camera and A Typewriter," *Saturday Review,* June 25, 1949, pp. 12-13.
Margaret Bourke-White, "Gandhi Didn't Want to Live," *Journal American,* February 15, 1946, p. xx.
Margaret Bourke-White, "Mahatma Gandhi," in W. Yelen and K.S. Giniger, eds., *Heroes of Our Times,* pp. 88-109.
Photographs by Margaret Bourke-White, *Life Magazine,* 1946: May 27, pp. 101-7; July 15, p. 17; September 9, pp. 38-39, 134-137; September 30, pp. 47-49. 1947: May 19, 16ff; February 9, pp. xx; February 16, pp. xx. Study questions due on January 19.
Films: "I.F. Stone's Weekly," "All the President's Men," "Gandhi."

II. Press Freedom: Historical Perspectives on Liberalism and Enlightment

Scientific as well as geographical discoveries in the 15th and 16th centuries influenced the way humans saw themselves and their roles on this planet. Rather than relying on some mystical and undependable divinity, women and men were forced to rely on themselves for power and authority. A growing middle class (bourgeoisie), emboldened by newly accumulated wealth, challenged the right of kings to decide whose views got into print. Limits were placed on sovereign power. Popular rights and demands became laws. Diversity of religious and political beliefs were tolerated. Individual initiative was valued highly in economic enterprise. It was only logical that as the fetters of the mind were dropped, so too were the restrictions on published thought. But who did freedom of the press benefit?

Students must write a three-page essay on "What is Liberalism and the Libertarian Press Theory?" An examination will be given on all of the readings and presentations in Section II.

A. Historical Background of the First Amendment. Lectures: Political Theory of the Liberal Revolution. What is Democracy? What is Democratic Communication?

Films: "Mightier Than the Sword—Zenger and Freedom of the Press" "Rights, Wrongs and the First Amendment" or "Our Bill of Rights."
Audio Tape Presentation: "Media Power," by National Public Radio.
Cullen, Chapter 1, "Historical Background on the First Amendment," and Chapter 2, "Mass Media Responsibility."
Special issue of *American Heritage,* "The Press: Its Power and Its Enemies," pp. 16-73.

B. Objectivity and Press Freedom: The Impossible Ideal?

Cullen, Chapter 3. "Reporting the News."
Ben Bagdikian, "First Amendment Revisionism," *Columbia Journalism Review,* May/June 1974, pp. 39-48.
John C. Merrill and Ralph L. Lowenstein, "Objectivity: An Attitude," in *Media*

Messages and Men: New Perspectives in Communication, pp. 202-214.

E.W. Kenworthy, "Agnew Says TV Networks Are Distorting the News," *New York Times*, November 14, 1969, p. 1.

Revolutionary Left Movement, "On Journalism and Objectivity," in *Communication and Class Struggle, 1. Capitalism and Imperialism*, edited by Armand Mattelart and Seth Siegelaub, pp. 130-135.

C. Classics and Critics of the Libertarian Tradition of Press Freedom

John Milton, *Areopagitica*, all.

John Locke, *A Letter Concerning Toleration* (1689).

Fred S. Siebert, "The Libertarian Theory of the Press," in *Four Theories of the Press*, pp. 39-71.

William G. Harley, "Mass Media and Society: An American Viewpoint," *UNESCO Courier*, April 1977, pp. 28-31.

Herbert I. Schiller, "Genesis of the Free Flow of Information Principle," in Richstad and Anderson, eds. *Crisis in International News*, pp. 161-183.

Spiro T. Agnew, "Transcript of Address by Agnew Criticizing Television on Its Coverage of the News," *New York Times*, November 14, 1969, p. 24.

J.S. Mill, *On Liberty.*

Selected readings from Thomas Jefferson.

James Mills, *Liberty of the Press.*

Jeremy Bentham, *On the Liberty of the Press.*

Audiotape: "Why Do We Study Communication?" Debate between Herbert I. Schiller and Ithiel de Sola Pool.

Videotape: CBS "Sixty Minutes" on Happy Talk News.

Films: "Absence of Malice," "The First Freedom," "The First and Essential Freedom," and "The Front Page" (1931).

D. The Libertarian Theory Makes A Mid-Course Correction: Social Responsibility and the Press

Theodore Peterson, "The Social Responsibility Theory," in *Four Theories of the Press*, pp. 73-103.

E.W. Kenworthy, "Commission on Freedom of the Press," *A Free and Responsible Press.*

"Three Concepts of Responsibility," in *Responsibility in Mass Communication.* Edited by William L. Rivers, Wilbur Schramm and Clifford G. Christians, pp. 30-50.

John C. Merrill, "Political Theories and the Press," in *The Imperative of Freedom: A Philosophy of Journalistic Autonomy*, pp. 23-43.

III. Challengers to Western Press Freedom: Communism, Authoritarianism, Development Journalism, "Freedom to Communicate," Democratic Communication

A number of doctrines have challenged the Western concept of press freedom. In the democracies of the West, so goes the Soviet-Cuban argument, freedom of the press belongs *to the press*, not to the people. The press has become an instrument of power for the dominant classes who own and control the presses and use them as an instrument of antagonism directed at the lower, disenfranchised classes.

Authoritarian political structures, sometimes even in the name of socialism, also suppress freedom of the press. Throughout the world today, dozens of nations suffer the burden of authoritarian or dictatorial regimes who grant "freedom" only within strict guidelines and under the pain of militarist repression.

More positive alternatives to the present Western doctrine have been articulated throughout the world. One now hears the call for more democratic communication structures, ones that enhance public participation, enfranchise people as self-conscious political actors, and give voice to the weak, the poor, and the oppressed. An intractable dilemma arises, though when, in the name of these utopian ideals, certain countries suppress democratic communication.

An indigenous, Third World Press approach has been formulated within the cauldron of nationalist revolution over the past three decades. Radical, non-communist "critical approaches" to mass society have challenged prevailing doctrine in Europe. Even a human rights position, the "freedom to communicate," has been elaborated in international fora. Whatever their name, these new approaches today increasingly confront the libertarian doctrine.

A. Communist Theory of the Press. Lecture: A Primer on Materialist Philosophy and Its Relation to Press Freedom

Communist press doctrine views the press as an agitator, propagandizer and mobilizer harnessed to the engine of national development. Within the agreed upon bounds of a nation's goals, journalists experience a degree of freedom to criticize. But outside of these bounds, criticism is met with repression. As Fidel Castro once said, "Within the revolution everything, outside the revolution nothing." Communist press theory thus relies as much on perceived controls (peer pressure, ideological upbringing, and the socialist "emulation" system) as on actual controls (censorship, governmental control, patent monopolies) to determine the content of communication.

Karl Marx, Preface to *A Contribution to the Critique of Political Economy* (1859), all.

John G. Gurley, "The Materialist Conception of History," in *Challengers to Capitalism: Marx, Lenin, Stalin and Mao,* pp. 8-21.

"Throughout the world today, dozens of nations suffer the Marxist Critique," No. 69, Human Rights Series, Red Feather Institute for Advanced Studies, 1980.

Werner Ullrich, "The Question of Press Freedom," *The Democratic Journalist,* (9, 1973), pp. 1-3.

Yassen N. Zasursky, "The Mass Media and Society: A Soviet Viewpoint," *UNESCO Courier,* April 1977, pp. 24-27.

Wilbur Schramm, "The Soviet Communist Theory of the Press," in *Four Theories of the Press,* pp. 105-46.

Vladimir I. Lenin, *What is to Be Done?* All.

Leon Trosky, "The Newspaper and Its Readers," in *Problems of Everyday Life and Other Writings on Culture and Science,* pp. 120-28.

Karl Marx, "Debates on Freedom of the Press and Publications," in *On Freedom of the Press and Censorship,* pp. 3-48.

Allen Hutt, "Karl Marx as Journalist," *Marxism Today,* May, 1966.

V.Korobeinikov, "What is Behind the 'Freedom of Information' Concept," *Democratic Journalist* (9, 1976).

Film: "Soviet TV: Heroes, Workers and the Party Line," from the *World* Series.

B. Authoritarian Theory of the Press. Lecture: Is There a Distinction Between Communism and Totalitarianism?

From Plato to Pinochet, authoritarian philosophers and politicians have believed that the state is the highest expression of social organization. In direct opposition to libertarian doctrines, authoritarianism suppresses individual liberties and aspirations at the expense of the glorification of the state. Such regimes use patents, monopolies, governmental control, censorship, prosecution and subterfuge to control press content.

"The Authoritarian Theory of the Press," *Four Theories of the Press*, pp. 9-37.

Plato's *Republic*.

Machiavelli, *The Prince*.

Karl R. Pepper, *The Open Society and its Enemies*. Volume I on Plato, Chapters 6, 7, 8.

Derrick Sington and Arthur Weidenfeld, "Broadcasting in the Third Reich," in Mattelart and Siegelaub, eds., *Communication and Class Struggle*, pp. 272-280.

Derrick Sington and Arthur Weidenfeld, *The Goebbels Experiment: A Study of the Nazi Propaganda Machine*. London: John Murrary, 1943.

Robert A. Brady, "The Art and Education as Tools of Propaganda," in Mattelart and Siegelaub, eds., *Communication and Class Struggle*, pp. 268-272.

Carl J. Friedrich and Zbigniew Brzezinski, "Propaganda and Monopoly in Mass Communication," in *Totalitarianism, Dictatorship and Autocracy*, pp. 129-147.

Alexander F. Kiefer, "Government Control of Publishing in Germany," *Political Science Quarterly* 57 (March 1942), pp. 73-97.

C. Towards New Approaches to Press Freedom. Development Journalism vs. Developmental Journalism: A Third World Alternative

One recent innovation arising from the developing world is a doctrine known as development journalism. It holds that the economic, political and social development of a poor country are too important to permit outright, independent criticism of a government's policies. Development journalism places the focus on the positive aspects of a country's development—on dams, agrarian reform, and transportation successes—rather than on the failings of these programs. Western critics have seen this as just another form of press suppression. A free press, they argue, is the only guarantor of successful development.

John Lent, "Mass Media in the Developing World: Four Conundrums."

John Lent, *The Use of Development News*.

Narinder K. Aggarwala, "Statement Before the New York Law School International Law Society," May 21, 1982.

Narinder K. Aggarwala, "Press Freedom: A Third World View," *Exchange*, Winter 1978, pp. 18-20.

Jim Richstad, "Third World vs. the Fourth Estate," East-West Communication Institute, Honolulu.

B.G. Verghese, "A Philosophy for Development Communication," *Media Asia* (1981), pp. 24-34.

Dana Bullen, "A Free Press Means Better Development," in *The Media Crisis . . . A Continuing Challenge*. World Press Freedom Committee, pp. 35-38.

D. Another Alternative? Non-Communist "Critical" (Mass Society) Theories from Europe

"Critical" sociological theory arose in the crucible of Nazi Germany in the so-called "Frankfurt School" of scholars around the Institute of Social Research. These include Herbert Marcuse, Theodor Adorno and others who attempted to reform the objectionable aspects of Marxism-Leninism into a doctrine that would appeal to European progressive circles. These "Neo-Marxists" of the pre-World War II era spawned a vigorous group of disciples whose analysis has much relevance to media in mass societies in the West.

Jurgen Habermas, "The Public Sphere," in *Communication and Class Struggle, 1. Capitalism and Imperialism*, pp. 198-201.

Hans Magnus Enzensberger, "Constituents of a Theory of the Media," *New Left Review* 64, November/December 1980, pp. 13-36.

Herbert Marcuse, "Repressive Tolerance," in *A Critique of Pure Tolerance*, pp. 81-117.

Oscar Negt, "Mass Media: Tools of Domination or Instruments of Liberation?" *New German Critique* 14, 1978, pp. 61-80.

E. Recent Contributions on Democratic Communication

"The Willow Declaration: A Call for Democratic Communications," Drafted by members of the Union for Democratic Communication, Willow, New York, August 1981.

Howard Frederick, "Democratic Communication in Theory and Practice," *Chasqui* (Quito), forthcoming.

Robert White, "Contradictions in Contemporary Policies for Democratic Communication." Presented at the International Association of Mass Communication Research, Paris, 1982.

Robert White, "Comunicacíon Popular: Language of Liberation," *Media Development* 3/1980.

Fernando Reyes Matta, "A Model for Democratic Communication," *Development Dialogue* (2, 1981), pp. 79-97.

Juan Somavi, "The Democratization of Communication," *Development Dialogue* (2, 1981), pp. 14-30.

F. On the Freedom to Communicate

Jean D'Arcy, "The Right to Communicate," in Richstad and Anderson, eds. *Crisis in International News: Policy and Prospects*, pp. 117-136.

Leo Gross, "Some International Law Aspects of the Freedom of Information and the Right to Communication," in Schiller and Nordenstreng, eds., *National Sovereignty and International Communication*, pp. 195-216.

Wolfgan Kleinwaechter, "Internal and International Aspects of the Right to Communicate," Institute for International Studies, Karl Marx University, Leipzig, GDR.

IV. The New International Information Order and Press Freedom

A. Who Are the Actors?

Academy for Educational Development, "Specific Fora: United Nations, UNESCO, International Telecommunications Union, Non-Aligned Movement," in *The United States and the Debate Over the New World Information Order*, pp. 17-54.

Daniel Patrick Moynihan, "Freedom of the Press: At Issue," Speech to the American Newspaper Publishers Association, September 21, 1982.

"Declaration of Talloires," in *The Media Crisis . . .* pp. 143-7.

Fletcher School of Law and Diplomacy, *Voices of Freedom: A World Conference of Independent Mass Media.* Working Papers, Talloires, France, May 15-17, 1981.

Amadou-Mahtar M'Bow, "Statement Before the Talloires (Voices of Freedom) Conference," May 16, 1981.

"World Press Freedom Committee Story," in *The Media Crisis . . .* , pp. 149-50.

"The Unknown World of Information: The Long Reach of Freedom House," *Boletin Informativo de la Comision Nacional Cubana de la UNESCO* (Havana) 17, No. 77, September/October 1978, pp. 32-33.

Freedom House, *Annual Report,* 1982.

M.L. Mueller, "Warnings of a Western Waterloo: The International Organization of Journalists on the Evolution of the New International Information Order," Murrow Reports: Occasional Papers of the Edward R. Murrow Center of Public Diplomacy, Tufts University, Medford, MA, April 1982.

Elise Burroughs, "Degree of Freedom Varies for 'Free Press'," *Presstime: The Journal of the American Newspaper Publishers Association,* April 1982, pp. 4-8.

Mary A. Gardner, "Evolution of the Inter-American Press Association," in Heinz Dietrich Fischer and John C. Merrill, *International and Intercultural Communication,* pp. 392-404.

A.M. Rutkowski, "United States Policy Making for Public International Forums on Communication," *Syracuse Journal of International Law and Economics* 8, Summer 1981, pp. 95 + .

Film: "The Reality of the Media—One Menu for the Whole World," NOVIB, The Hague, Holland.

B. New International Information Order: Basic Concepts

Richard Dill, "Who May Say What To Whom?—A Short Introduction to the New World Information Order (NWIO)," in Dieter Bielenstein, *Toward a New World Information Order: Consequences for Development Policy,* pp. 53-58. Bonn, FRG: Institute for International Studies, 1980.

Mustapha Masmoudi, "The New World Information Order," in *Crisis in International News,* pp. 77-96.

Elie Abel, "Communication for an Interdependent, Pluralistic World," in *Crisis in International News,* pp. 97-116.

International Commission for the Study of Communication Problems [MacBride Commission], "Recommendations," in *One World, Many Voices,* pp. 253-272.

"Communication in the Service of Man," Paragraphs 3001-3048, and "Information Systems and Access to Knowledge," Paragraphs 7001-7057, in *Medium Term Plan of UNESCO for 1984-1989.*

Academy for Educational Development, "Issue Areas," in *The United States and the Debate Over the 'New World Information Order,'* pp. 55-107.

Enrique Gonzalez-Manet, "The International Information System: A Critical Analysis for the Next Decade." Havana: Cuban National Commission for UNESCO, c. 1981.

Tran Van Dinh, "Nonalignment and Cultural Imperialism," in Schiller and Nordenstreng, eds., *National Sovereignty and International Communication,* pp. 261-276.

World Press Freedom Committee, *The Media Crisis . . . A Continuing Challenge*, all.

Miguel Angel Granados Chapa, "Freedom of Expression and Responsibility within the Framework of the New International Information Order," *The Democratic Journalist*, November 1982, pp. 12-23.

C. The Crucial Free Press Issue: Licensing of Journalists

Pierre Gaborit, "Project for the Establishment of an International Commission and Periodical International Conference for the Protection of Journalist," Paris: UNESCO, February 16-17, 1981.

"Rights and Responsibilities of Journalists," *One World, Many Voices* [MacBride Report], pp. 233-38.

Curtis Prendergast, "No Licensing in the Name of Protection," in *The Media Crisis . . .* , pp. 93-6.

Hans Treffkorn, "Do Journalists Need Protection?" *Democratic Journalist*, May 1981, pp. 5-6.

"Global First Amendment War," *Time*, October 6, 1980, pp. 62-63.

Rosemary Righter, "Battle of the Bias," *Foreign Policy*, 34, Spring 1979, pp. 121-38.

Ithiel de Sola Pool, "The Communications Revolution in an Interdependent World: A Growing Flow and Attempts to Restrict It." Research Program on Communications Policy, Massachusetts Institute of Technology, November 15, 1979.

A. McBarnet, "Disciplining the Journalists," *Media, Culture and Society*, Vol. 1, No. 2.

Articles dealing with journalists imprisoned or detained abroad.

"Statement of the Committee to Protect Journalists."

V. New Technologies and Press Freedom

Charles L. Jackson, Harry M. Shooshan III, Jane L. Wilson, *Newspapers and Videotex: How Free a Press?*

Donald N. Soldwedel, "Kenaf Newsprint: An Idea Whose Time Has Come," in *The Media Crisis . . .* , pp. 131-135.

Ithiel de Sola Pool, "Technology and Change in Modern Communications," *Technology Review*, Nov/Dec 1980, pp. 64-75.

Daniel Bell, "The Social Framework of the Information Society," in Tom Forester, ed., *The Microelectronic Revolution.*

Herbert I. Schiller, *Who Knows? Information in the Age of the Fortune 500.*

Videotape: "The Canadian Telidon Experiment."

Film: "New Technologies from Holland."

Selected Bibliography

Academy for Educational Development. *The United States and the Debate Over the 'New World Information Order'*. Washington: International Communication Agency, 1979.

Aggarwala, Narinder K. "Press Freedom: A Third World View," *Exchange*, Winter 1978, pp. 18-20.

Agnew, Spiro T. "Transcript of Address by Agnew Criticizing Television on Its Coverage of the News," *New York Times*, November 14, 1969, p. 24.

"The American Press," Special issue of *American Heritage Magazine*, Vol. 33, No. 6, 1982.

Anderson, Michael H. and Richstad, Jim, eds. *Crisis in International News: Policies and Prospects.* New York: Columbia University Press, 1981.

Arthur, William R. and Crossman, Ralph L. *The Law of the Newspapers.* New York: McGraw-Hill Book Company, Inc., 1940.

Bagdikian, Ben. "First Amendment Revisionism," *Columbia Journalism Review,* May/June 1974, pp. 39-48.

Barney, Ralph D. and Merrill, John C., eds. *Ethics and the Press.* New York: Hastings House Publishers.

Barron, Jerome A. *Freedom of the Press for Whom?* Indiana: Indiana University Press, 1973.

Bartlett, Jonathan, ed. *The First Amendment in a Free Society.* The Reference Shelf, Vol. 50, No. 6. New York: The H.W. Wilson Company, 1979.

Bielenstein, Dieter, ed. *Toward a New World Information Order: Consequences for Development Policy.* Bonn, FRG: Institute for International Studies, 1980.

Brennan Jr., William J. "Why Protect the Press?" *Columbia Journalism Review* (January/February, 1980): 59-62.

Brzezinski, Zbigniew K. and Friedrich, Carl J. "Propaganda and Monopolization in Mass Communication," in *Totalitarian Dictatorship and Autocracy,* pp. 129-147. New York: Praeger Publishers, 1966.

Bullen, Dana. "Unesco and Press Freedom: The Acapulco Conference," *Index on Censorship,* March, 1982, pp. 24-28.

Burroughs, Elise. "Degree of Freedom Varies for 'Free Press'," *Presstime: The Journal of the American Newspaper Publishers Association,* April 1982, pp. 4-8.

Collins, Larry and LaPierre, Dominque. *Freedom at Midnight,* 1974.

Commission on Freedom of the Press. *A Free and Responsible Press;* 1947, Midway reprint, 1974.

"The C.I.A., the F.B.I., and the Media," *Columbia Journalism Review,* July/August 1976, pp. 37-42.

Cox, Archibald. *Freedom of Expression.* Cambridge: Harvard University Press, 1981.

Cullen, Maurice R. *Mass Media and the First Amendment.* Dubuque, Iowa: Wm. C. Brown, Company Publishers, 1981.

Devol, Kenneth S., ed. *Mass Media and the Supreme Court.* 3rd ed. New York: Hastings House Publishers, 1982.

Douglas, William O. *Freedom of the Mind.* Reading for an Age of Change, No. 3. New York: American Library Association, 1962.

Drier, Peter and Weinberg, Steve. "Interlocking Directorates," *Columbia Journalism Review,* November/December, 1979, pp. 51-68.

Enzensberger, Hans Magnus. "Constitutents of a Theory of the Media," *New Left Review* 64, November/December 1970, pp. 13-36.

Fletcher School of Law and Diplomacy. *Voices of Freedom: A World Conference of Independent Mass Media.* Working Papers, Talloires, France, May 15-17, 1981.

Francois, William E. *Mass Media Law and Regulation.* 3rd ed. Columbus, OH: Grid Publishing, Inc., 1982.

Franklin, Marc A. *Cases and Materials on Mass Media Law.* 2nd ed. New York: The Foundation Press, Inc., 1982.

Franklin, Marc A. *The First Amendment and the Fourth Estate.* 2nd ed. New York: The Foundation Press, Inc., 1981.

Frederick, Howard H. "Democratic Communication in Theory and Practice," *Chasqui*, 1984.

Friedman, Robert. "The United States vs. the Progressive," *Columbia Journalism Review*, July/August, 1979, pp. 27-35.

Friendly, Fred W. *The Good Guys, the Bad Guys, and the First Amendment*. New York: Vintage Books, 1976.

Gaborit, Pierre. "Project for the Establishment of an International Commission and Periodical International Conference for the Protection of Journalists." Paris: UNESCO, February 16-17, 1981.

Gardner, Mary A. "Evolution of the Inter-American Press Association," in Heinz Dietrich Fischer and John C. Merrill, *International and Intercultural Communication*, pp. 392-404.

Gaynes, Martin J., and Zuckman, Harvey L. *Mass Communications in a Nutshell*. St. Paul: West Publishing Co., 1977.

"Global First Amendment War," *Time*, October 6, 1980, pp. 62-3.

Gonzalez-Menet, Enrique. "The International Information System: A Critical Analysis for the Next Decade." Havana: Cuban National Commission for UNESCO, 1981.

Gora, Joel M. *The Rights of Reporters*. New York: Avon Books, 1974.

Gordon, David. *Problems in Law of Mass Communications*. Mineola, NY: The Foundation Press, Inc., 1982.

Grandaos-Chapa, Miguel Angel. "Freedom of Expression and Responsibility Within the Framework of the New International Information Order," *The Democratic Journalist*, November 1982, pp. 12-23.

Gross, Gerald, ed. *The Responsibility of the Press*. New York: Fleet Publishing Corporation.

Hanson, Jim. "The Political Economy of Free Speech: A Marxist Critique," No. 69, Human Rights Series, Red Feather Institute for Advanced Studies, 1980.

Harley, William G. "Mass Media and Society: An American Viewpoint," *UNESCO Courier*, April 1977, pp. 28-31.

Hentoff, Nat. "Woodward, Bernstein and 'All the President's Men'," *Columbia Journalism Review*, July/August 1974, pp. 10-15.

Hentoff, Nat. "Woodstein in the Movies," *Columbia Journalism Review*, May/June, 1976, pp. 46-47.

Hoffman, Abbie. "Undercover in the New Germany," *Mother Jones*, February /March 1979, pp. 44-54.

Hogan, Paul M. "Ohio: Printing the Obscenity," *Columbia Journalism Review*, July/August 1975, pp. 15-17.

Horton, Philip C., ed. *The Third World and Press Freedom*. New York: Praeger, 1978.

Hughes, Frank. *Prejudice and the Press*. New York: The Devin-Adair Company, 1950.

Hutt, Allen. "Karl Marx as a Journalist," *Marxism Today* (London), May 1966.

Jackson, C.L. et al. *Newspapers and Videotex: How Free a Press?* St. Petersburg, FL: Modern Media Institute, 1981.

Kenworthy, E.W. "Agnew Says TV Networks Are Distorting the News," *New York Times*, November 14, 1969, p. 1.

Kiefer, Alexander F. "Governmental Control of Publishing in Germany," *Political Science Quarterly* 57, March 1942, pp. 73-97.

Kleinwaechter, Wolfgang. "Internal and International Aspects of the Right to Communicate." Leipzig, GDR: Institute for International Studies, Karl Marx University.

Kopkind, Andrew. "The Importance of Being Izzy," *Ramparts*, May 1974, pp. 39-44.

Korbeinikov, V. "What is Behind the Freedom of Information Concept," *Democratic Journalist*, September 1976, pp. 18-21.

Lendvai, Paul. *The Bureaucracy of Truth.* London: Burnett Books, 1981.

Lenin, V.I. *What is to be Done?* Moscow: Progress Publishers, 1973.

Lent, John. "Mass Media in the Developing World: Four Conundrums." Paper presented at the Conference of International Association of Mass Communication Research, Caracas, Venezuela, 1980.

Lent, John. "The Use of Development News," *Studies in Third World Societies* (College of William and Mary), No. 9-10.

Liebling, A.J. *The Press.* 2nd ed. New York: Ballantine Books, 1975.

Lofton, John. *The Press as Guardian of the First Amendment.* Columbia, SC: University of South Carolina Press, 1980.

Loory, Stuart H. "The CIA's Use of the Press: a Mighty Wurlitzer," *Columbia Journalism Review*, September/October 1974, pp. 9-18.

M'Bow, Amadou-Mahtar, "Statement Before the Talloires 'Voices of Freedom' Conference," May 16, 1981.

McCartney, James. "The Washington Post and Watergate: How Two Davids Slew Goliath," *Columbia Journalism Review*, July/August 1973, pp. 8-22.

Marcuse, Herbert. "Repressive Tolerance," in *A Critique of Pure Tolerance*, pp. 81-117. Boston: Beacon Press, 1975.

Marx, Karl. *On Freedom of the Press and Censorship.* The Karl Marx Library, Vol. IV. New York: McGraw-Hill, 1974.

Matellart, Armand and Siegelaub, Seth. *Communication and Class Struggle, Vol. 1, Capitalism and Imperialism.* New York: International General, 1979.

Matta, Fernando Reyes. "A Model for Democratic Communication," *Development Dialogue*, 2, 1981, pp. 79-97.

Merrill, John C. and Lowenstein. "Objectivity: An Attitude," in *Media Messages and Men: New Perspectives on Communication,* pp. 202-214.

Merrill, John C. "Political Theories and the Press," in *The Imperatives of Freedom: A Philosophy of Journalistic Autonomy*, pp. 23-43.

Mill, John Stuart. *On Liberty.* Edited by Elizabeth Rappaport. Indianapolis: Hackett Publishing Company, Inc., 1978.

Milton, John. *Areopagitica and of Education.* Edited by George H. Sabine. New York: Appleton-Century-Crofts, Inc., 1951.

Minogue, Kenneth R. *The Liberal Mind.* New York: Vintage Books, 1968.

Moynihan, Daniel Patrick. "Freedom of the Press: At Issue." Speech Before the American Newspaper Publishers Association, September 21, 1982.

Mueller, M.L. "Warnings of a Western Waterloo: The International Organization of Journalists on the Evolution of the New International Information Order," Murrow Reports: Occasional Papers of the Edward R. Murrow Center of Public Diplomacy, Tufts University, Medford, MA., April 1982.

Negt, Oscar. "Mass Media: Tools of Domination or Instruments of Liberation?" *New German Critique* 14, 1978, pp. 61-80.

Nelson, Harold L. *Law of Mass Communications.* 4th ed. New York: The Foundation Press, Inc., 1982.

Petrusenko, Vitaly. *A Dangerous Game.* Translated by Nicolai Kozelsky and Vladimir Leonov. Prague: Interpress, c1980.

Pool, Ithiel de Sola. "The Communications Revolution in an Interdependent World: A Growing Flow and Attempts to Restrict It." Research Program on Communications Policy, Massachusetts Institute of Technology, November 15, 1979.

Pool, Ithiel de Sola. "Technology and Change in Modern Communications," *Technology Review,* November/December 1980, pp. 64-75.

Popper, Karl R. *The Open Society and Its Enemies.* Princeton: Princeton University Press, 1966.

"Protecting Two Vital Freedoms: Fair Trial and Free Press," *Columbia Journalism Review,* March/April 1980, pp. 75-84.

Richstad, Jim and Anderson, Michael H., eds. *Crisis in International News: Policies and Prospects.* New York: Columbia University Press, 1981.

Righter, Rosemary. "The Battle of the Bias," *Foreign Policy* 34, Spring, 1979, pp. 121-38.

Righter, Rosemary. "UNESCO and Press Freedom: the Next Round," *Index on Censorship,* March 1982, pp. 21-28.

Rips, Geoffrey. *The Campaign Against the Underground Press.* Foreword by Allen Ginsberg. San Francisco: City Lights Books, 1981.

Rivers, William L.; Schramm, Wilbur and Christians, Clifford G. *Responsibility in Mass Communication.* New York: Harper and Row, 1980.

Rohrer, Daniel Morgan. *Freedom of Speech and Human Rights.* Dubuque, Iowa: Kendall/Hunt Publishing Company, 1979.

"Role of Journalists in the Struggle for Peace, Understanding Among Nations, Humanism and Social Progress," *The Democratic Journalist,* 28, 1981, p. 23.

Rubin, Barry. "International Censorship," *Columbia Journalism Review,* September/October 1975, pp. 55-58.

Rutkowski, Anthony M. "United States Policy Making for Public International Forums on Communication," *Syracuse Journal of International Law and Economics* 8, Summer 1981, pp. 95 + .

Schiller, Herbert I. and Nordenstreng, Kaarle. *National Sovereignty and International Communication.* Norwood, NJ: Ablex Publishing Corporation, 1979.

Schiller, Herbert I. *Who Knows? Information in the Age of the Fortune 500.* Norwood, NJ: Ablex Publishing Corporation, 1982.

Schramm, Wilbur. *Communications in Modern Society.* Urbana: University of Illinois Press, 1948.

Seldes, George. *Freedom of the Press.* New York: The Bobbs-Merrill Company, 1935.

Seldes, George. *You Can't Print That!* New York: Garden City Publishing Company, Inc., 1929.

Somavia, Juan. "The Democratization of Communication," *Development Dialogue* 2, 1981, pp. 14-30.

"Statement on 'The Progressive' H-Bomb Issue," *Columbia Journalism Review,* September/October 1979, pp. 84-85.

"Statement on Search and Seizure," *Columbia Journalism Review,* May/June 1979, pp. 90-91.

Stevenson, Robert L. "The Western News Agencies Do Not Ignore the Third World," *Editor and Publisher,* July 5, 1980, pp. 11-32.

Stone, I.F. *The I.F. Stone's Weekly Reader.* New York: Random House, 1971.

Treffkorn, Hans. "Do Journalists Need Protection?" *Democratic Journalist,* May 1981, pp. 5-6.

Trotsky, Leon. "The Newspaper and Its Reader," in *Problems of Everyday Life and Other Writings on Culture and Science,* pp. 120-28.

Ullrich, Werner. "The Question of Press Freedom," *The Democratic Journalist 9,* 1973, pp. 1-3.

UNESCO. *List of Documents and Publications in the Field of Mass Communications.* Paris: UNESCO, 1981.

UNESCO. *One World, Many Voices.* New York: Unipub, 1980.

UNESCO. *Right to Communicate: Legal Aspects.* Paris: UNESCO, 1982.

Verghese, B.G. "A Philosophy for Development Communication," *Media Asia,* 1981, pp. 24-34.

Wallraff, Gunter. *Wallraff: the Undesirable Journalist.* Translated by Steve Gooch and Paul Knight. London: Pluto Press, 1977.

Whalen, Jr., Charles W. *Your Right to Know.* New York: Vintage Books, 1973.

White, Robert. "Contradictions in Contemporary Policies for Democratic Communication." Presented at the International Association for Mass Communication Research, Paris, 1982.

White, Robert. "Comunicacíon Popular: Language of Liberation," *Media Development,* 3/1980, pp. 3-9.

Williams, Raymond. *Keywords.* New York: Oxford University Press, 1976.

"The Willow Declaration: A Call for Democratic Communication," Drafted by members of the Union for Democratic Communication, Willow, New York, August 1981.

Woodward, Bob and Bernstein, Carl. *All the President's Men.*

Wise, David. *The Politics of Lying.* New York: Vintage Books, 1973.

Yoakum, Robert. "The Great Hustler Debate," *Columbia Journalism Review,* May/June 1977, pp. 53-58.

Zasursky, Yassen N. "The Mass Media and Society: A Soviet Perspective," *UNESCO Courier,* April 1977, pp. 24-7.

Global Challenges to Human Dignity: Human Rights

Thomas E. McCoullough   *Spring 1983*
History 109/Political Science 160/Religion 156/Sociology 175/
Duke University/Durham, NC 27706

Course Objectives

1. To examine the nature, scope and justification of human rights.
2. To study the development of statements of human rights, particularly in the history of the U.N., its Charter, the Universal Declaration of Human Rights and International Covenants.
3. To examine and compare in cultural context those views of human rights stressing individual liberty and those giving priority to collective welfare.
4. To examine the relation of the U.S. to the U.N. in regard both to the statements and practices of the U.S. in the area of human rights.
5. To investigate human rights violations and conditions hindering or fostering respect for the dignity of persons in the contemporary world, focusing on selected countries.
6. To discover channels and means of action on behalf of those whose rights are violated or jeoparized.

Required Readings
Donald P. Kommers and Gilbert D. Loescher, *Human Rights and American Foreign Policy*, University of Notre Dame Press, 1979.
Kenneth W. Thompson, ed. *The Moral Imperatives of Human Rights: A World Survey*, University Press of America, 1980.
Report on Human Rights in El Salvador, Vintage Books, 1982.

Requirements
A term paper of 12-15 pages. A one page overview of the subject with an accompanying annotated bibliography. Select either (a) or (b):
a. Select a particular country and become an "expert" on the situation there.
b. Select a topic on human rights, in consultation with your teaching assistant.

Course Outline

January 10 Orientation

January 12 Human Rights: Today and Tomorrow   Thomas Buergenthal
Thomas Buergenthal, "Codification and Implementation of International Human Rights"
Thomas Buergenthal, "Human Rights and the U.S. National Interest"
Kommers and Loescher, Part One

Historical-Conceptual

Western

January 14 Religious   Charles Long
Thompson, pp. 1-38, 229-235

January 17 Philosophical   Martin Golding
Martin Golding, "Towards a Theory of Human Rights"
Martin Golding, "Justice and Rights: A Study in Relationship"
Kommers and Loescher, Part Two
Paper due: Define human rights

Eastern

January 19 Islam: Africa, Asia, Middle East   Bruce Lawrence
Read: Thompson, pp. 139-167

January 21 Discussion Groups

January 24 Hindu and Sikh   Richard Fox

January 26 China   Creighton Lacy
Read: Thompson, pp. 81-107

January 28 Overview

Women's Rights

January 31 Women's Rights: West   Amanda Smith
Paper due: Are human rights universal?

February 2 Women's Rights: East   Laila Moustapha

February 4 Discussion groups

Selected Countries

February 7 Latin America   Edmundo Vargas
Read: Thompson, pp. 169-227

February 9 El Salvador   Jose Siman
Read: *Report on Human Rights in El Salvador*

February 11 Overview

February 14 Poland   Magnus J. Krynski
Paper due: What role should human rights play in U.S. foreign policy toward El
  Salvador?

February 16 U.S.S.R.   Jerry F. Hough and Warren Lerner
Read: Kommers and Loescher, Part Four
Thompson, pp. 69-80

February 18 Discussion groups

February 21 South Africa   Sheridan Johns

Read: Kommers and Loescher, Part Three
Thompson, pp. 123-138

February 23 Amnesty International James David Barber

February 25 Overview

The United Nations

February 28 International Law and Human Rights A. Kenneth Pye
Read: Kommers and Loescher, Part Five and U.N. Declaration of Human Rights
John W. Halderman, "Advancing Human Rights Through the United Nations"
Paper due: Overview of selected country or topic

March 2 The Role of the U.N. and Protection of Human Rights
John W. Halderman

March 4 International Human Rights Programs in Europe
John W. Halderman

United States

Domestic

March 14 Civil Rights C. Eric Lincoln

March 16 The Black Sharecropper's Struggle for Human Rights
Sydney Nathans

March 18 Discussion groups

Foreign Policy

March 21 The United States and Latin America Lars Schoultz
Kommers and Loescher, Parts Six and Seven and Appendices (Carter and Vance)
Jeane Kirkpatrick, "Dictatorship and Double Standards," and "Establishing a Viable
   Human Rights Policy"
Ch. 13, "Legal Restrictions on U.S. Involvement Abroad," *Report on Human Rights
in El Salvador*
Paper due: Should the U.S. intervene in other countries on behalf of human rights?

March 23 U.S. Foreign Policy and Human Rights
Patricia Derain, first Assistant Secretary of State for Human Rights and Humanitarian Affairs

March 25 Discussion groups

Food and Resource Policy and Human Rights

March 28 Nutritional Requirements Henry Kamin
Read: Julius K. Nyerere, *Freedom and Development*

March 30 The Politics of Hunger Nick Kotz

April 1 Overview

April 4 Multinationals and Food Policy   Sheridan Johns
Paper due: Should priority to be given to the satisfaction of basic human needs over civil/political rights?

April 6 The Common Heritage of Mankind   Horace B. Robertson, Jr.

April 8 Discussion Groups

Emerging Rights

Aprill 11 Children's Rites: Values in Conflict   Carol Hague

April 13 The Rights of the Aging   Carol Hague

April 15 Discussion Groups

April 18 The Strategic Arms Race   Joseph J. Kruzel
Read: Kermit D. Johnson, "The Nuclear Reality: Beyond Niebuhr and the Just War"

April 20 The Right to Survival   Major-General Kermit D. Johnson, Chief of Chaplains, U.S. Army, Retired

April 22 Overview

Selected Bibliography on Human Rights

I. Historical-Conceptual

Bartell, Joyce J., *Rights and Responsibilities: International, Social, and Individual Dimensions*, 1978.
Braybrooke, David, *Three Tests for Democracy*, 1968.
Brownlie, Ian, ed., *Basic Documents on Human Rights*, 1971.
Duchacek, Ivo D., *Rights and Liberties in the World Today*, 1973.
Henkin, Alice H., ed., *Human Dignity*, 1979.
Hollenbach, David, *Claims in Conflict: Retrieving and Renewing the Catholic Human Rights Tradition*, 1979.
Laqueur, Walter and Barry Rubin, *The Human Rights Reader*, 1979.
Nelson, Jack L., and Vara M. Green, *International Human Rights: Contemporary Issues*, 1980.
O'Grady, Ron, *Bread and Freedom*, 1979.
Pennock, J. Roland, and John W. Chapman, eds., *Human Rights;* Martin P. Golding, "From Prudence to Rights: A Critique," 1981.
Pollis, Adamantia, and Peter Schwab, eds., *Human Rights: Cultural and Ideological Perspectives*, 1979.
Rosenbaum, Alan S., ed., *The Philosophy of Human Rights: International Perspectives*, 1980.
Seymour, James D., ed., *The Fifth Modernization*, 1980.
Symposium on the International Law of Human Rights, 1965.

II. Women's Rights

Boulding, Elise, *Women in the Twentieth Century World*, 1977.
Duchacek, Ivo D., *Rights and Liberties in the World Today*, "Status of Women," pp. 89-95, 1973.

III. Latin America

Dominguez, Jorge I., Nigel S. Rodley, Bryce Wood, Richard Falk, *Enhancing Global Human Rights*, 1979.

Hennelly, Alfred T. and John Langan, eds., *Human Rights in the Americas: The Struggle for Consensus*, 1982.

Schoultz, Lars, *Human Rights and United States Policy Toward Latin America*, 1981.

Vogelgesang, Sandy, *American Dream, Global Nightmare*, 1980.

IV. Selected Countries

Buergenthal, Thomas, and Judith R. Hall, eds., *Human Rights, International Law and the Helsinki Accord*, 1977.

Amnesty International *Reports*, 1982.

The following on reserve in Public Documents and Maps:

Organization of American States, InterAmerican Commission on Human Rights. *Country Reports*.

Organization of American States, InterAmerican Commission on Human Rights. *Annual Reports, 1978* and **1979-1980**.

U.S. Congress. *Human Rights Conditions in Selected Countries and U.S. Responses*.

U.S. Congress. *Human Rights and U.S. Foreign Policy*. 1979.

U.S. Congress. *Country Reports on Human Rights Practices for 1979, 1980, 1981*.

U.S. Congress. *Human Rights and the Phenomenon of Disappearances*. 1979.

Yearbook on Human Rights for 1975-1976.

Yearbook of the United Nations 1978.

V. Amnesty International

Amnesty International *Reports*, 1982.

Power, Jonathan, *Amnesty International*, 1981.

VI. United Nations

Halderman, John W., *The Political Role of the United Nations*, 1981.

Jacobs, Francis Geoffrey, *The European Convention on Human Rights*, 1975.

Moskowitz, Moses, *The Politics and Dynamics of Human Rights*, 1968.

Sohn, Louis B., and Thomas Buergenthal, eds., *Basic Documents on International Protection of Human Rights*, 1973.

Stuber, Stanley I., *Human Rights and Fundamental Freedoms in Your Community*, 1968.

Tuttle, James C., ed. *International Human Rights: Law and Practice*, 1978.

Van Dyke, Vernon, *Human Rights, the United States, and World Community*, 1970.

Williams, Paul, ed., *The International Bill of Human Rights*, 1981.

VII. United States

Brown, Peter G. and Douglas McLean, eds., *Human Rights and U.S. Foreign Policy*, 1979.

Lillich, Richard B., eds., *U.S. Ratification of the Human Rights Treaties*, 1981.

Mower, A. Glenn, Jr., *The United States, The United Nations, and Human Rights*, 1979.

Nanda, Ved P., James R. Scarritt, and George W. Shepherd, Jr., eds., *Global Human Rights: Public Policies, Comparative Measures, and NGO Strategies*, 1981.

Newberg, Paula R., *The Politics of Human Rights*, 1980.

Rubin, Barry M., and Elizabeth P. Spiro, eds., *Human Rights and U.S. Foreign Policy*, 1979.

Said, Abdul Aziz, ed., *Human Rights and World Order*, 1978.

Wiarda, Howard J., *Human Rights and U.S. Human Rights Policy*.

VIII. Food and Resource Policy and Human Rights

Crahan, Margaret E., ed., *Human Rights and Basic Needs in the Americas*, 1978.

IX. Emerging Rights

Boulding, Elise, *Children's Rights and the Wheel of Life*, 1979.

Joyce, James Avery, *The New Politics of Human Rights*, 1979.

Said, Abdul Aziz, ed., *Human Rights and World Order*, "Children's Rights," Elise Boulding, pp. 31-9, 1978.

Aggression, Suppression, Holocaust: Lessons for Students

Jutta Bendremer   *Summer 1982*
Summer Workshop/Department of English/University of Akron/
Akron, OH 44325

This workshop has been geared to meet the needs of teachers and others in all disciplines to use value concepts to enhance their teaching and/or sensitivity to human rights issues. By examining the Holocaust from a literary and historical point of view, students will be exposed to the tools with which to develop an interdisciplinary unit on a humanitarian topic. Examples of failures to meet or implement human rights issues abound in history, including the Armenian massacres, Cambodian exterminations, Argentinian repressions, and, of course, the Holocaust.

Textbooks

The Jewish Catastrophe in Europe—J. Pilch, ed.
Out of the Whirlwind—A. Friedlander, ed.
The Holocaust: A Study of Genocide—Board of Education of the City of New York

Assignments for all students
Each student will write a brief theme (critical essay) on one of the following topics, using the required texts, books from the supplementary reading list and the numerous handouts. Suggested topics are: European Jewry in the 30's; Ghetto Existence; A Day in the Life of a Concentration Camp Inmate; Social, Moral, Humanitarian Aspects of the "Final Solution;" Life in DP Camps; The Role of the Righteous; The Case for the Palestinian Refugee; Could the Armenian Massacres Have Been Prevented?; Recent Argentinian Horrors; The *Refusniks* Speak Out in Russia. Other topics may be selected. Please discuss selection of topic other than the ones cited with the instructor.

Unit Reports
For students seeking an "A" grade, a brief unit on teaching the Holocaust or some other human rights issue will be required. A 2-3 page unit in outline form will suffice. The text, *The Holocaust*, will prove most helpful; other source material may also be used. Undergraduates will fulfill this requirement through the preparation of a brief unit; graduate students are expected to add two, detailed daily lesson plans to their units, to be presented on the last day of the workshop.

Annotated Bibliographies
Those students seeking an "A" grade who *do not* wish to prepare a teaching unit, may instead, prepare an annotated bibliography. Undergraduates may fulfill this assignment by using 5 books listed on the supplementary reading list or the handout, *Books on the Holocaust*. Graduate students are expected to critique one article in addition to their bibliographies. When preparing these bibliographies, students are expected to write 3-5 sentences about each book (or article), including

the central idea of the written material, and the audience the writer intended to reach.

Oral Report on Article

All students are expected to present an oral report on one or more of the articles given to you. This report should be brief (5-10 min.). Undergraduates should select a fairly short article; graduate students should select a longer article or two short articles. Students are required to complete at least four media evaluations. Forms will be provided.

Workshop Syllabus

Monday, June 21

Student introduction. Introduction of syllabus, aims and objectives.

Film: "Night and Fog"—discussion.

Questions frequently asked about the Holocaust.

Reading assignment for 6/22: *Whirlwind*, pp. 11-19; 133-154; *Catastrophe*, pp. 11-38. Discussion of the economic, political, and cultural conditions in Europe.

Tuesday, June 22

Lici Calderon—survivor.

Students are encouraged to ask questions.

Discussion of previous day's assignment. Read for 6/23: *Whirlwind*, pp. 309-329; *Catastrophe*, pp. 40-86. (Evian Conference, race issues). Dr. Saslaw

Wednesday, June 23

"The Camera of my Family"—18 min. filmstrip. Brief discussion. Record: "Concentration Camp Horrors"—40 min.

Discussion of Evian Conference and rest of assignment. Use handout. Reading assignment for 6/24: *Whirlwind*, pp. 24-67. (Two views of prison camp behavior.)

Thursday, June 24

Rose Kaplovitz—survivor. Students are urged to ask questions.

Discussion of previous day's assignment.

Film: "Lili Meier at Auschwitz." Reading assignment: *Whirlwind*, pp. 181-192, 227-258. (Life in camps, etc.)

Friday, June 25

Reminder! All short essays are due today.

Jeff Lautman—Survivor's Child. He will do a presentation using slides and the film "Tomorrow Came Much Later." Discussion.

Discussion of previous day's assignment. Dr. Saslaw

Reading assignment for 6/28: *Whirlwind*, pp. 353-370; *Catastrophe*, pp. 138-141. (The Righteous)

Monday, June 28

Film: "Playing for Time." Discussion.

Discussion of previous day's assignment.

Reading assignment: *Whirlwind*, pp. 259-282; *This Shall Tell All Ages*. (Art and music).

Tuesday, June 29

James Barnett—Concentration camp liberator.

Record on liberation of survivors.
Art and music of Holocaust. Reading assignment: *Catastrophe*, pp. 88-137.

Wednesday, June 30
Continue art and music.
Filmstrip on resistance.
Discussion of assignment. Read: *Whirlwind*, pp. 465-521; *Catastrophe*, pp. 205-225.
   (Silent world and theological questions raised by Holocaust)

Thursday, July 1
Discussion of previous assignment. Dr. Saslaw

Friday, July 2
Scheduling of students who are presenting bibliographies on human rights units.
Oral presentations on articles. To save time and organize more accurately, we will
try to arrange reports to fall under the following headings:
   Views on the Holocaust (Writers)
   Heroes of the Holocaust
   Children of the Holocaust
   Holocaust Fiction
   Psychological Aspects of the Holocaust
   Everpresent Anti-Semitism
Other headings may be needed.
Evaluations and other written works should be turned in at this time.
Film: "The Twisted Cross."

Reading List

Views on the Holocaust
1. Wiesel, E., Friedlander and Hilberg. "The Holocaust: Three Views," *ADL Bulletin*, 1977.
2. Checinski, M. "How Rumkowski Died," *Commentary*, May 1979.
3. Burgess. "Prime Time for Hitler," *Saturday Review*, 1979.

Human Rights
1. Knovitz, M.R. "From Jewish Rights to Human Rights," *Congress Monthly*, 1979.
2. *Sh'ma*. "Shall We Encourage Jewish Communities in Germany?"

Psychological Aspects
1. Selzer, Michael. "The Murderous Mind," *The New York Times*, 1977.
2. Anderson, Jack. "Tracking the Fiendish Nazi Doctor," *Parade*, November 1978.
3. "The Demjanjuk Trial: A Moment in History," Educational Supplement by *The Cleveland Jewish News*.
4. Gottlieb, M. "The Hunt for Ivan the Terrible," *Cleveland Magazine*, 1979.
5. Charny, I.W. *A Pilot Project for a Genocide Early Warning System*.
6. Epstein, H. "Children of the Holocaust," *The National Jewish Monthly*, April 1979.

Historical Evidence of Holocaust
1. Slappey, S.G. "History's Most Incriminating Evidence," *The American Legion*, February 1980.

2. Wyman, D.S. "Why Auschwitz Was Never Bombed," *Commentary*, May 1978.
3. Fischhoff, B. "Warsaw: Forty Years After," *Reform Judaism*, October 1978.
4. O'Toole, T. "Photos Revealed Auschwitz A Year Before End of War," *The Miami Herald*, February 1979.
5. Friedrich, O. "The Kingdom of Auschwitz," *The Atlantic Monthly*, September 1981.
6. *The Holocaust and Resistance: Growth of Anti-Semitism.*
7. Feingold, H.L. *Determining the Uniqueness of the Holocaust: The Factor of Historical Balance.*
8. **Cahnman, W.J.** "Ju dengasse: The Reconstruction of Eleventh-Century Jewish Presence on the Rhine," *The National Jewish Monthly*, June 1978.
9. Friedlander, R. "Jews: The European and American Historical Experience," *Chitty's Law Journal*, Vol. 28, 1980.

Revisionist Literature and Comments

1. Butz, A.R. "The International 'Holocaust' Controversy," *The Journal of Historical Review*, July 1980.
2. Reprint from *Spotlight*, December 1979.

Anti-Semitism and Neo-Nazi Movement

1. Dick, C.H. "Neo-Nazi Surge Alarms Prober," *Chicago Tribune*, 1977.
2. Shapiro, E.S. "American Anti-Semitism Reconsidered," *Congress Monthly*, January 1980.
3. Leonard, J. "Why We Love to Hate Jews," *Penthouse*, November 1976.

Education—Holocaust

1. Hyman, P.E. "New Debate on the Holocaust," *The New York Times*, 1979.
2. Eliach, Y. "Despair in Search of a Method," *The Jewish Spectator*, Spring 1977.
3. Raphael, M.L. *Yom Ha—Shoah and Holocaust Education in an Israeli High School.*
4. Baron, L. *Teaching the Holocaust to Non-Jews.*

Theological Aspects

1. Pastor Hauerwas Sermon on Holocaust and Reader's Response.

Additional Reading Material for English Majors

1. Primo, Levi. "Iron A Memoir," *Commentary*, Aug. 1977.
2. Terrence, Des Pres. "Goodness Incarnate," *Harpers*, May 1979.
3. Herbert, Mitgang. *Publishing: The Holocaust.*
4. *Sh'ima: A Journal of Jewish Responsibility*, April 1977.
5. "What are the writers doing to the Holocaust?" *Sh'ima: A Journal of Jewish Responsibility*, April 29, 1977.
6. Rosenfeld, Alvin. "Poetics of Expiration: Reflection on Holocaust Poetry," *The American Poetry Review*, Nov./Dec. 1978.
7. Langer, Lawrence. "The Writer and the Holocaust Experience," *Congress Monthly*, May, 1979, Vol. 46.
8. Wouk, Herman. *War and Remembrance.*
9. Arendt, Hannah. "The Jew as Pariah." *We Refugees*, January 1943.
10. **Hux, Samuel,** "The Holocaust and the Survival of Tragedy," *Worldview* XX/Oct. 1977.

International Human Rights

Robert Elias   *Fall 1983*

Political Science 132/Tufts University/Medford, MA 02155

This course provides an interdisciplinary examination of international human rights, drawing from fields such as international relations, political theory, cross-culture studies, history, law, literature, administration, communications, education, economics, and citizen participation. It critically evaluates the state of global human rights, the fundamental sources of human rights violations, and the alternatives. It emphasizes the international relations context of human rights enforcement, the interconnectedness between peace and human rights, the need for consensus on basic human rights, and the value of world order politics.

The course begins with a literary introduction to human rights violations, then considers the impact of the prevailing world order. It examines the historical, philosophical, and documentary foundations of human rights. It considers the major and diverging cultural, ideological and religious conceptions of human rights, with special attention to political/civil versus economic/social/cultural/development rights, and suggests their impact on setting human rights norms and priorities. Then, the course examines the various methods of human rights enforcement or implementation, ranging from sanctions to bilateral, regional, and international mechanisms. Nongovernmental organizations receive special attention, particularly the impact of multinational corporations and the role of human rights groups. The role and impact of human rights information is also considered. Then, the materials examine selected violations in some detail, including hunger and food policy, torture and killings, sexism and racism, environmental decay, migrant work and wage slavery, underdevelopment and imperialism, terrorism, and peace. Next, the course considers the impact of foreign policy, particularly of the superpowers, on human rights, with special attention to Latin America and Eastern Europe. Domestic human rights policies and practices of the superpowers are also examined. Finally, the course stresses the role of citizen activism in promoting human rights.

Course Outline

1) Introduction
Baraheni, *God's Shadow*, pp. 11-26, 54-59
Chi Ha, *Cry of the People* (optional)
Garbayevskaya, *Fourteen Poems* (optional)
Davis, *Political Prisoners* (optional)
Victor Jara, Albums . . . (optional) (New York: Monitor Records)

2) The International Relations Context
Falk, "Theoretical Foundations of Human Rights" (Newberg)
Beitz, *Political Theory & International Relations*, pt. I, III, Concl.
Bull, "Order Versus Justice in World Politics" (Bull)
Hoffman, *Duties Beyond Borders*, ch. 1,4
Falk & Kim, "An Approach to World Order Studies & The World System" (WOMP)
Mische, "The National Security State" (Mische)
Ajami, "Human Rights & World Order Politics" (WOMP)

3) Historical, Philosophical & Documentary Foundations
Minogue, "The History of the Idea of Human Rights" (Lacquer & Rubin)
Pennock, "Rights, Natural Rights, and Human Rights" (Pennock & Chapman)
Forsythe, *Human Rights & World Politics*, pp. 1-25
Lacquer & Rubin, "International Agreements," "The Helsinki Agreement," *The Human Rights Reader*, pp. 197-263, 282-291
"Universal Declaration of the Rights of Peoples" (Mimeo)
Falk, 'The Algiers Declaration & the Struggle for Human Rights" (Falk)

4) Sources, Norms & Priorities
Bay, "Universal Human Rights Priorities" (Nelson & Orum)
Dominguez, "International Human Rights Norms" (Dominguez)
Forsythe, *Human Rights & World Politics*, pp. 25-40

5) Political & Civil Rights
Van Dyke, "Civil and Political Rights" (Van Dyke)
Joyce, "Mobilization of Shame," pp. 87-108, (Joyce)

6) Economic, Social, Cultural and Development Rights
Shue, "Security & Subsistence" (Shue)
Van Dyke, "Economic, Social & Cultural Rights" (Van Dyke)
Joyce, "Self Determination in the Third World," pp. 154-65, 171-76 (Joyce)
McGinnis, "Basic Principles of the New Intl. Economic Order" (McGinnis)
Wren, "The Marks of Cultural Oppression" (Wren)
Eide, "Choosing the Path to Development" (optional) *Bulletin of Peace Proposals* (1980), p. 349

7) Comparative Perspectives: Cultural, Ideological, Religious
Pollis, "Liberal, Socialist, & Third World Perspectives" (Schwab & Pollis)
Pollis & Schwab, "Human Rights: A Western Construct with Limited Applicability" (Pollis & Schwab)
Mojekwu, "International Human Rights: The African Perspective" (Pollis & Schwab)
Said, "Human Rights in Islamic Perspective" (Pollis & Schwab)
Huang, "Human Rights in a Revolutionary Society: The Case of the People's Republic of China" (Pollis & Schwab)
Hueman, "A Socialist Conception of Human Rights" (Said)

8) Implementation
Forsythe, "Protecting Human Rights" (Forsythe)
Joyce, "Ways & Means," pp. 205-19 (Joyce)

9) Nongovernmental Organizations; MNCs & Human Rights Groups
Sklar, *Trilateralism,* Overview, ch. 9

McGinnis, "The Impact of Multinational Corporations" (McGinnis)

Lernoux, "Multinational Skulduggery in Central America," pp. 81-123; "U.S. Capitalism & The Multinationals" (Lernoux)

Christian Conference of Asia, "Asian People's Struggle for Economic Freedom— Impact of TNCs" (Christian Conf. of Asia)

Schoultz, *Human Rights & U.S. Policy Toward Latin America,* ch. 2

Wiseberg & Scoble, "Monitoring Human Rights Violations: The Role of Nongovernmental Organization" (Kommers & Leescher)

Lernoux, "Repression—The Recognition of Human Rights (churches)" (Lernoux)

10) Information, Intellectuals & the Media
Chomsky, "Foreign Policy & the Intelligensia" (Chomsky)

Herman, "Semantics & the Role of Terrorism," "Role of Mass Media" (Herman)

Chomsky, "Brainwashing Under Freedom," pp. 66-83 (Chomsky & Herman)

Salzberg, "Monitoring Human Rights Violations: How Good is the Information?" (Brown & MacLean)

11) Selected Violations
A) Hunger

Read:

Lappe & Collins, *World Hunger: Ten Myths*

Burbach & Flynn, *Agribusiness in the Americas,* ch. 3-5

Christensen, "The Right to Food: How to Guarantee" (WOMP)

B) Torture & Death

Amnesty International, "Political Killings by Governments" (AI)

Amnesty International, "What Is A Disappearance?" (AI)

C) Sexism & Racism

Leghorn & Parker, "The Personal Is Economic" (Leghorn & Parker)

Segal, "The Race War" (Segal)

Joyce, "Slavery" & "The Black Hole of South Africa," pp. 13-20, 115-123 (Joyce)

Svennson, "Comparative Ethnic Policy on the American & Russian Frontiers," *J. International Affairs* (1983), p. 83

D) Environmental Decay

Falk, "The Ecological Imperiative" (Falk-2)

Gowan, "Environmental Crisis" (Gowan)

Ophuls, "Ecological Scarcity & International Politics" (Ophuls)

E) Migrant Work & Wage Slavery

Portes, "Why Illegal Migration: A Human Rights Perspective" (Said)

Berger, *A Seventh Man: Migrant Workers in Europe* (optional)

F) Underdevelopment & Imperialism

Hayter, *On the Creation of World Poverty,* pp. 9-49, 82-96, 109-117

Gowan, "Exported Plague" (Gowan)

Mische, "Liberation for Being" (Mische)

Schiller, "Cultural Domination" (Schiller)

Kothari, "Human Rights as a North-South Issue," *Bull. of Peace Proposals*, II (1981), p. 331

Galtung, "Towards A New International Technological Order" (optional) (WOMP)

G) Terrorism

Herman, "The Lesser & Mythical Terror Networks" (Herman)

Pottenger, "Liberation Theology: Its Methodological Foundation for Violence" (Rappoport & Alexander)

Gerstein, "Do Terrorists Have Rights?" (Rappoport & Alexander)

H) Peace

Sakamoto & Falk, "A World Demilitarized: A Basic Human Need," *Alternatives* 6 (1981), 1

Russett, "Disarmament, Human Rights and Basic Human Needs"

Marks, "The Peace-Human Rights-Development Dialectic," *Bulletin of Peace Proposals* 11 (1981) pp. 339

Thompson, "Human Rights & Disarmament"

Raskin and Wilcox, "The U.S. Intl. War & Preservation of Human Rights," (Hevener)

Bilder, "The Individual & the Right to Peace," *Bulletin of Peace Proposals* 11 (1980), 387

Alston, "Peace as a Human Right," (optional) *Bulletin of Peace Proposals*, 11 (1980), 319

Schell, *The Fate of the Earth* (optional)

12) Impact of Foreign Policy

A) American

Herman, *The Real Terror Network*, ch. 3, 5

Lernoux, *Cry of the People*, ch. 3, 5, 6, 8

Chomsky, *Washington Connection & Third World Fascism*, pp. 32-66

Klare & Arnson, *Supplying Repression*, ch. 1, 6

Wolfe, "Exporting Repression" (Wolfe)

Farer, "Exaggerating the Communist Menace" (Said)

CAMINO, *El Salvador*, ch. 9, 10

Borosage, "Domestic Consequences of U.S. Human Rights Policies" (Hevener)

Shue, "Some Priorities for U.S. Foreign Policy" (Shue)

Hoffman, "An American Policy for World Order: Human Rights" (Hoffman)

Kissinger, "Continuity & Change in American Foreign Policy" (Lefever)

Lefever, "Morality versus Moralism in Foreign Policy" (Lefever)

Kirkpatrick, "Dictatorships & Double Standards" (Wiarda)

Drinan, "Human Rights & The Reagan Administration," *America*, 5 March 1983

Abrams, "Human Rights & The Reagan Administration: Another View," *America*

B) Soviet

Chaliand, *Report from Afghanistan*, ch. 1, 3, 5; pp. 73-87

Singer, *The Road to Gdansk*, pp. 157-95, 239-74

Masterman, "Poland: Eyewitness to Terror," *Inquiry*, 15 Feb 1982, p. 22

Starski, "Martial Law & Beyond" (Starski)

Vogelgesang, "Soviet Union: Exile for Political Protest" (Vogelgesang)

Riese, *Since the Prague Spring: Charter '77 & the Struggle for Human Rights in Czechoslovakia*, pp. 3-8, 11-14, 155-77, 189-201 (opt.)

13) Domestic Policy
A) American
Parenti, *Democracy for the Few*, ch. 7-9
Wolfe, *Seamy Side of Democracy: Repression in America*, ch. 4-6

B) Soviet
Sakharov, "Peace, Progress and Human Rights" (Sakharov)
Mowrer, "Human Rights in the Soviet Union" (Said)
Joyce, "The Soviet Enigma" (Joyce)
Medvedev, *On Socialist Democracy*, ch. 8-10

14) Cross National Comparisons
Falk, "Comparative Protection of Human Rights in Capitalist and Socialist Third
    World Countries" (Falk- 1)

15) Citizen Activism & Human Rights Promotion
Alger, "Foreign Policies of U.S. Publics," *Intl. Studies Q.* 21 (1977), 277
Mische, "Strategies for a Just World Order" (Mische)
Galtung, *True Worlds*, ch. 9
Bay, *Strategies for Political Emancipation*, ch. 5-6
Boyte, "The Formation of the New Peace Movement," *Social Policy* 13 (1982), 4
Henderson, "Citizens Movement for Greater Global Equality" (Henderson)
McGinnis, *Bread & Justice*, ch. 11
Gowan, "Organizing for Social Transformation" (Gowan)

16) Future Directions
Fromm, *To Have Or To Be?*, ch. 4, 5, 9
Wolfe, "Building A Non-Repressive Society" (Wolfe)
Kothari, "On Justice" (Kothari)
Johansen, "Building A Just World Order" (Johansen)

Bibliographic Sources
Reza Baraheni, *God's Shadow* (Bloomington, Indiana U Press, 1979)
Kim Chi Ha, *Cry of the People*(Brookline, MA: Autumn Press, 1974)
Natalya Garbayevskaya, *Fourteen Poems*
Angela Davis, *Political Prisoners*
Richard Falk, *Human Rights and State Sovereignty* (NY: Holmes & Meier Pub.
    1981) (1)
Charles Beitz, *Political Theory and International Relations* (Princeton: Princeton
    U. Press, 1979)
Hedley Bull, *The Anarchical Society: A Study of Order in World Politics* (NY:
    Columbia U. Press, 1977)
Stanley Hoffman, *Duties Beyond Borders* (Syracuse: Syracuse U. Press, 1981)
Gerald & Patricia Mische, *Toward a Human World Order* (NY: Paulist Press, 1977)
Walter Lacquer & Barry Rubin, *The Human Rights Reader*
J. Roland Pennock & John W. Chapman, *Human Rights* (NY: NYU Press, 1981)
David Forsythe, *Human Rights and World Policies* (Lincoln: U. Nebraska Press,
    1983)
Jorge Dominguez, et al., *Enhancing Global Human Rights* (NY: McGraw-Hill,
    1979)

Paula Newberg, (ed.), *The Politics of Human Rights* (NY: NYU Press, 1980)

Vera Green & Jack Nelson (eds.), *International Human Rights* (Pine Plains, NY: E. Coleman Pub., 1980)

Richard Claude, *Comparative Human Rights* (Baltimore: J. Hopkins Press, 1976)

Richard Lillich & Frank Newman, *International Human Rights* (Boston: Little Brown, 1979)

Vernon Van Dyke, *Human Rights, The U.S. and the World Community* (NY: Oxford U. Press, 1978)

James Joyce, *The New Politics of Human Rights* (NY: St. Martins Press, 1978)

Henry Shue, *Basic Rights: Subsistence, Affluence & U.S. Foreign Policy* (Princeton: Princeton U. Press, 1980)

James McGinnis, *Bread & Justice: Toward a New Intl. Economic Order* (NY: Paulist Press, 1979)

Brian Wren, *Education for Justice* (Maryknoll, NY: Orbis, 1977)

Adamantia Pollis & Peter Schwab (eds.), *Human Rights: Cultural & Ideological Perspectives* (NY: Praeger, 1979)

Peter Schwab & Adamantia Pollis (eds.), *Toward A Human Rights Framework* (NY: Praeger, 1982)

Abdul Said, *Human Rights and World Order* (NY: Praeger, 1977)

Judith Sklar, *Trilateralism* (Boston: South End Press, 1980)

Penny Lernoux, *Cry of the People* (Garden City, NY: Doubleday, 1980)

Christian Conf. of Asia, *In Clenched Fists of Struggles: Impact of TNCs in Asia* (Hong Kong Christian Conf. on Asia, 1981)

Lars Schoultz, *Human Rights and U.S. Policy toward Latin America* (Princeton: Princeton U. Press, 1981)

Noam Chomsky, *Human Rights and American Foreign Policy* (Nottingham: Spokesman Books, 1978)

Edward Herman, *The Real Terror Network: Terrorism in Fact & Propaganda* (Boston: South End Press, 1982)

Frances Moore Lappe & Joseph Collins, *World Hunger: Ten Myths* (San Francisco: Inst. for Food & Development Policy, 1979)

Frances Moore Lappe, *Aid as Obstacle* (San Francisco: Inst. for Food & Development Policy, 1980)

Roger Burbach & Patricia Flynn, *Agribusiness and the Americas* (NY: Monthly Review Press, 1980)

Arthur Simon, *Bread for the World* (NY: Paulist Press, 1975)

Jack Nelson, *Hunger for Justice* (Maryknoll, NY: Orbis Books, 1980)

Amnesty International, *Political Killings by Governments* (London: Amnesty Intl., 1983)

Amnesty International, *Disappearances* (NY: Amnesty Intl., 1981)

Lisa Leghorn & Katherine Parker, *Women's Worth* (Boston: Routledge & Kegan Paul, 1980)

Sheila Rowbotham, *Man's World, Women's Consciousness* (Baltimore: Penguin Books, 1973)

Susan George, *Feeding the Few: Corporate Control of Food* (Washington: Inst. for Policy Studies, 1979)

Susan George, *How The Other Half Dies* (Montclair, NJ: Allanheld, Osman Pub., 1977)

Ronald Segal, *The Race War* (NY: McGraw-Hill, 1966)

Richard Falk, *This Endangered Planet* (NY: Vintage Books, 1972) (2)

Williams Ophuls, *Ecology and the Politics of Scarcity* (San Francisco: W.H. Freeman, 1977)

Susanne Gowan, et al., *Moving Toward a New Society* (Philadelphia: New Society Press, 1976)

John Berger, *A Seventh Man: Migrant Workers in Europe* (London: Writers & Readers Pub., 1982)

Teresa Hayter, *On the Creation of World Poverty* (London: Pluto Press, 1981)

Teresa Hayter, *Aid as Imperialism* (Baltimore: Penguin Books, 1971)

Willy Brandt, *North-South* (London, Pan Books, 1981)

Herbert Schiller, *Communication and Cultural Domination* (White Plains, NY: M.E. Sharpe, 1976)

Johan Galtung, *True Worlds* (NY: Free Press, 1980)

Myres McDougal, et al., *Human Rights and World Public Order* (New Haven: Yale Univ. Press, 1980)

Stanley Hoffman, *Primacy or World Order* (NY: McGraw-Hill, 1978)

David Rappoport & Yonah Alexander (eds.), *The Morality of Terrorism* (NY: Pergamon, 1982)

E.P. Thompson, *Beyond the Cold War* (NY: Pantheon, 1982)

E.P. Thompson & Dan Smith, *Protest and Survive* (NY: Monthly Review Press, 1981)

Natalie Kaufman Hevener (ed.), *The Dynamics of Human Rights in U.S. Foreign Policy* (New Brunswick, NJ: Transaction, 1981)

Jonathan Schell, *The Fate of the Earth* (NY: Vintage, 1983)

Robert Jay Lifton & Richard Falk, *Indefensible Weapons* (NY: Basic Books, 1982)

Helen Caldicott, *Nuclear Madness* (NY: Bantam, 1978)

Noam Chomsky & Edward Herman, *Washington Connection & Third World Fascism* (Boston: South End Press, 1979)

Michael Klare & Cynthia Arnson, *Supplying Repression* (Washington: Inst. for Policy Studies, 1977)

Tom Farer (ed.), *Toward A Humanitarian Diplomacy* (NY: NYU Press, 1980)

CAMINO, *El Salvador* (Cambridge, Central American Information Office, 1982)

Ernest Lefever (ed.), *Morality and Foreign Policy* (Washington: Ethics & Public Policy Center, 1977)

Ernest Haas, *Global Evangelism Rides Again* (Los Angeles: Univ. So. Calif. School Intl Affairs, 1978)

Howard Wiarda (ed.), *Human Rights and U.S. Human Rights Policy* (Washington: Amer. Enterprise Inst. for Public Policy Research, 1982)

Gerard Chaliand, *Report from Afghanistan* (NY: Viking Press, 1980)

Daniel Singer, *The Road to Gdansk* (NY: Monthly Review Press, 1981)

Stanislaw Starski, *Class Struggle in Classless Poland* (Boston: South End Press, 1982)

Hans-Peter Riese, *Since the Prague Spring: Charter '77 & Human Rights in Czechoslovakia.* (NY: Vintage 1979)

Sandy Vogelgesang, *American Dream, Global Nightmare* (NY: W.W. Norton, 1980)

Donald Kommers & Gilbert Loescher (eds.), *Human Rights & American Foreign Policy* (Notre Dame: U. Notre Dame Press, 1979)

Human Rights and International Organization

E. Thomas Rowe   *Winter 1983*
International Studies 19494.5/University of Denver/Denver, CO 80208

This course will explore the changing roles of international organizations in efforts to protect and promote human rights. The activities of international intergovernmental and nongovernmental organizations will be examined at both the global and regional levels. Particular attention will be given to the issues of whether or not, and if so under what circumstances, such activities have an impact on the actual observance of human rights.

Readings

All required readings are on reserve. Any difficulties in obtaining the materials should be reported immediately to the instructor so that alternative arrangements can be made.

F. Ajami, *Human Rights and World Order Politics* (New York: World Policy Institute, 1978).

L. Henkin, ed., *The International Bill of Rights* (New York: Columbia University Press, 1981).

A. Said, ed., *Human Rights and World Order* (New Brunswick, N.J.: Transaction Books, 1978).

Reading Assignments

January 4 Introduction and Organization of the Seminar

January 11 International Action on Human Rights

H. Bergesen, "Human Rights—The Property of the Nation State or a Concern of the International Community?" *Cooperation and Conflict*, 14 (1979), 239-254.

V. Chkhikvadzi, "Human Rights and Non-Interference in the Internal Affairs of States," *International Affairs* (Moscow), 12 (December 1978), 22-30.

H. Espiell, "The Evolving Concept of Human Rights," and J. Freymond, "Human Rights and Foreign Policy," in B. Ramcharan, ed., *Human Rights: Thirty Years After the Universal Declaration* (The Hauge: Nijhoff, 1979).

R. Gastil, "Human Rights and U.S. Policy," and E. Lefever, "Human Rights and United States Foreign Policy," in U.S. Congress, House of Representatives, *Human Rights and U.S. Foreign Policy*, Hearings before the Subcommittee on International Organizations of the Committee on Foreign Affairs, 96th Congress, 1st Session.

H. Kissinger, "Continuity and Change in American Foreign Policy," A. Said, "Pursuing Human Dignity," and D. Riesman, "Prospects for Human Rights," in A. Said, ed., *Human Rights and World Order* (New Brunswick, N.J.: Transaction Books, 1978).

J. Nelson and V. Green, eds., *International Human Rights* (Stanfordville, New York: Human Rights Publishing Group, 1980), pp. 5-95.

January 18 The United Nations and Related Agencies

P. Alston, "UNESCO's Procedure for Dealing with Human Rights Violations," *Santa Clara Law Review,* 20 (1980), 665-695.

T. van Boven, "The United Nations and Human Rights," in B. Rubin and E. Spiro, eds., *Human Rights and U.S. Foreign Policy* (Boulder: Westview, 1979).

J. Donnelly, "Recent Trends in UN Human Rights Activity: Description and Polemic," *International Organization,* 35:4 (Autumn 1981), 633-656.

T. Gardeniers, H. Hannun and J. Kruger, "The UN Sub-Commission on Prevention of Discrimination and Protection of Minorities: Recent Developments," *Human Rights Quarterly,* 4:3 (Summer 1982), 353-370.

E. Luard, "The Origins of International Concern over Human Rights," and C. Macartney, "League of Nations Protection of Minority Rights," in E. Luard, ed., *The International Protection of Human Rights* (London: Thames and Hudson, 1967).

A. Mower, "Implementing United Nations Covenants," in A. Said, ed., *Human Rights and World Order.*

B. Ramcharan, ed., *Human Rights: Thirty Years After the Universal Declaration* (The Hague: Nijhoff, 1979), pp. 21-37, 83-107, 159-231.

January 25 Regional Intergovernmental Organizations

L. LeBlanc, *The OAS and the Promotion and Protection of Human Rights* (The Hague: Martinus Nijhoff, 1977), 41-171.

A. Mower, "The Effectiveness of an International Human Rights Program," *International Organization,* 29:2 (Spring 1975), 545-556.

B. Ramcharan, "The Role of Regional, National and Local Institutions: Future Perspectives," in B. Ramcharan, ed., *Human Rights: Thirty Years After the Universal Declaration.*

A. Robertson, *Human Rights in Europe* (2nd ed., Manchester: Manchester University Press, 1977), pp. 1-25, 139-267, 278-293.

C. Welch, "O.A.U. and Human Rights: Towards a New Definition," *Journal of Modern African Studies,* 19 (September 1981), 401-20.

E. Kannyo, *Human Rights in Africa: Problems and Prospects* (New York: Human Rights Working Paper, International League for Human Rights, May 1980).

February 1 Nongovernmental Agencies and Human Rights

A. Cassese, "Progressive Transnational Promotion of Human Rights," in B. Ramcharan, ed., *Human Rights: Thirty Years After the Universal Declaration.*

D. Forsythe, *Humanitarian Policies* (Baltimore: Johns Hopkins University Press, 1977), pp. 1-56, 222-248.

J. Green, "NGOs;" and L. Wiseberg and H. Scoble, "Human Rights as an International League," in A. Said, ed., *Human Rights and World Order.*

International League for Human Rights and the Federation Internationale des Droits de L'Homme, *Report of the Conference on Strategies for Strengthening the Implementation of Human Rights* (October 1979), pp. 4-41.

D. Weissbrodt, "The Role of International Nongovernmental Organizations in the Implementation of Human Rights," *Texas International Law Journal,* 12 (1977), 293-320.

L. Wiseberg and H. Scoble, "Transnational Actors in the Promotion and Protection of Human Rights: An Analysis of the Role and Impact of Non-Governmental Organizations" (Paper presented at the International Political Science Association World Congress, August 14, 1979, Moscow, USSR).

February 8 Group Rights: Selected Issues
G. Bennet, *Aboriginal Rights in International Law* (London: Royal Anthropological Institute, Occasional Paper No. 37, 1978).
A. Cassese, "The Self-Determination of Peoples," in L. Henkin, ed., *The International Bill of Rights*.
V. Dinstein, "Collective Human Rights of Peoples and Minorities," *International and Comparative Law Quarterly*, 25 (1976), 102-120.
D. Goulet, "In Defense of Cultural Rights: Technology, Tradition, and Conflicting Models of Rationality," *Human Rights Quarterly*, 3:4 (Fall 1981), 7-18.
L. Sohn, "The Rights of Minorities," in L. Henkin, ed., *The International Bill of Rights*.

February 15 Rights of Special Categories of Individuals: Selected Issues
E. Boulding, "Children's Rights," in A. Said, ed., *Human Rights and World Order*.
J. Comas, "The International Fight Against Racism: Words and Realities," *Human Organization*, 37:4 (Winter 1978), 334-344.
M. Galey, "Promoting Nondiscrimination Against Women: The UN Commission on the Status of Women," *International Studies Quarterly*, 23:2 (June 1979), 273-302.
F. Hosken, ed., "Symposium: Women and International Human Rights," *Human Rights Quarterly*, 3:2 (Spring 1981), 1-52.
B. Ramcharan, "Equality and Nondiscrimination," in L. Henkin, *The International Bill of Rights*.
D. Weisberg, "The Concept of the Rights of the Child," *The Review, International Commission of Jurists*, 21 (December 1978), 43-51.

February 22 Individual Rights: Selected Issues
Amnesty International, *Report on Torture* (New York: Farrar, Strauss and Giroux, 1975), 13-113.
Amnesty International, *Disappearances: A Workbook* (New York: AI/USA, 1981), 1-4, 75-165.
Y. Dinstein, "The Right to Life, Physical Integrity and Liberty," in L. Henkin, ed., *The International Bill of Rights*.
D. Forsythe, "Political Prisoners: The Law and Politics of Protection," *Vanderbilt Journal of Transnational Law*, 9 (1976).
International Commission of Jurists, and Swiss Committee Against Torture, *Torture: How to Make the International Convention Effective* (Geneva: ICJ, 1980).
E. Kaufman and P. Fagen, "Extrajudicial Executions: An Insight into the Global Dimensions of a Human Rights Violation," *Human Rights Quarterly*, 3:4 (Fall 1981), 81-100.
M. Lippman, "The Protection of Human Rights: The Problem of Torture," *Universal Human Rights*, 1:4 (October/December 1979).
K. Partsch, "Freedom of Conscience and Expression, and Political Freedoms," in L. Henkin, ed., *The International Bill of Rights*.

March 1   Economic Rights: Selected Issues

V. Dimitrijevic, "The Right to Develop," Paper prepared for delivery at the International Studies Association 23rd Annual Convention, March 1982, Cincinnati.

J. Donnelly, "The Right to Development: An Exposition and Critique," Paper prepared for delivery at the International Studies Association 23rd Annual Convention, March 1982, Cincinnati.

A. Fields, "Human Rights and World Resources," in A. Said, ed., *Human Rights and World Order.*

D. Forsythe, "Socioeconomic Human Rights: The United Nations, the United States and Beyond," *Human Rights Quarterly*, 4:4 (Fall 1982), 439-449.

E. de Kadt, "Some Basic Questions on Human Rights and Development," *World Development*, 8:2 (February 1980).

J. Sethi, "Human Rights and Development," *Human Rights Quarterly*, 3:3 (Summer 1981).

P. Streeten, "Basic Needs and Human Rights," *World Development*, 8:2 (February 1982).

March 8   Conclusions

F. Ajami, *Human Rights and World Order Politics* (New York: World Policy Institute, 1978).

Writing assignment for January 11

Write a brief essay of about 3 pages on *one* of the following:

1. Are there enough common elements across major cultures to allow for a truly internationally defined set of standards for human rights?

2. Does the pursuit of human rights through international action make sense?

Writing assignment for January 18

Write a brief essay of about three pages on one of the following:

1. Do you think the political character of the United Nations, and the fact that some bias is very probable, destroys the utility of the organization for the promotion or protection of human rights?

2. Do you think the principle of national sovereignty, combined with the weak enforcement capabilities of the United Nations, destroys the utility of the U.N. in the area of human rights?

Writing assignment for January 25

Write a brief essay of about three pages on one of the following:

1. To what would you attribute the relatively highly developed regional human rights machinery in Western Europe as compared with other regions in the world?

2. Do you think regional institutions are more likely to be effective in the promotion and protection of human rights than universal institutions? What are the strengths and weaknesses of each.

Writing assignment for February 1

Write a brief essay of about three pages on one of the following:

1. What would your assessment be of the relative utility or effectiveness of the various strategies used by major nongovernmental human rights agencies?

2. Do you think the relationships which presently exist between nongovernmental and intergovernmental organizations could be changed or developed to produce a more effective international human rights system? If so, in what ways?

World Political Economy and Economic Justice

Political Economy of Race, Gender and Class
Angela Gilliam, State University of New York
at Old Westbury

The Dispossessed of the Earth:
Land Reform and Economic Development
Steve Fisher, Emory and Henry College

Contemporary World Development
Andre Gunder Frank and David Seddon, University of East Anglia

Alternative Paradigms in Economics
Francisco Bataller M., Kenyon College

Cross-Cultural Perspectives on Development
J.A. Mestenhauser, University of Minnesota

Development Conflict and Political Change
Guy Gran, The American University

Problems of Poverty, Promises
of Development, Prospects for Humanity
Jasper Ingersoll, Catholic University

Economic and Social Development
James Lobenstine, School for International Training

Senior Seminar: Political Economy
Manning Marable, Fisk University

Continued on next page

Political Economy of the Third World
Gloria Young Sing, State University of New York
at Old Westbury

Natural Resources in the World Economy: Control and Conflict
Jerald Barnald, University of Iowa

Third World Development
Girma Kebbede, Mount Holyoke College

Political Economy of Race, Gender and Class

Angela Gilliam   *Spring 1984*
Politics and Economics 323/State University of New York/Old Westbury, Long Island, NY 11568

In the Western industrial world, the interlocking relationships of race, gender and class must be discussed within the context of the major debate of the current period concerning the control, access and distribution of the world's resources. Part of this discussion is connected to the relationship between societal rewards and punishment and the question of who suffers the sociological burden of structured inferiorization and/or inequality in a given society.

Hence, cultural, political and gender equality cannot be separated from the political economy and profound socio-economic change. This relates to one of the methodological principles of the course—that development and underdevelopment are part of a single process.

This lower division course has as its objective the examination of these issues from the perspective of that which is normally excluded—the view of the dominated peoples in those societies which are characterized by differential and unequal access to power. An ancillary purpose is an incipient overview of the effects of multinational institutions on the reproduction of racism, gender and class discrimination.

Given the scope of this goal, the course will focus on six major case studies or areas through which to focus the two themes:

Theme #1—Plantation Economies: Two Case Studies in Culture
               Contact
  Case Study #1—United States
  Case Study #2—Cuba

Theme #2—National and Ethnic Resistance to Resource Plunder
  Case Study #1—Bolivia, Guatemala
  Case Study #2—South Africa, Nambia

To achieve this understanding, we will utilize an interdisciplinary approach covering Economics, History, Political Science, Sociology and Anthropology. In addition, this methodology will be reinforced through cinematic examples for each section.

I. The Atlantic Slave Trade and its Impact on Social Relations in the Plantation Economy

Case Study #1 The Plantation Economy and the Convergence of Racial, Economic and Gender Oppression in the United States
Readings:
Women, Race and Class by Angela Davis, Random House, 1981. The chapter entitled, "Myth of the Black Rapist" will be integrated with the discussion of economic oppression and its relationship to "crime as big-business."
How Capitalism Underdeveloped Black America by Manning Marable, South End Press, 1983.
Caste, Class and Race: A Study in Social Dynamics by Oliver C. Cox, Monthly Review Press, 1959.
"The Myth of the Black Matriarchy" by Robert Staples in *The Black Woman Cross-Culturally*, edited by Filomena Steady, Schenkman Publishers, 1981.
Film:
"Ashes and Embers" by Haile Gerima (Distributor: Mypheduh Films, Inc., Washington, D.C.) An Afro-American Vietnam veteran returns home to the U.S. to question who he went to fight and why. This two-hour film shows one man's attempt to deal with racism—in himself and others.

Case Study #2 Transculturation and Cultural Transformation: The Heritage of Slavery and National Reconstruction in Cuba
Readings:
Marriage, Class and Colour in Nineteenth Century Cuba: A Study of Racial Attitudes and Sexual Values in a Slave Society by Verena Martinez-Alier, Cambridge University Press, 1974.
"Women in Cuba: The Revolution Within the Revolution" by Johnnetta B. Cole in *Comparative Perspectives of Third World Women* edited by Beverly Lindsay, Praeger, 1980.
The following work will be presented in translation during class time: *Nación y Mestizje en Nicolás Guillén* [Nation and Race Mixture in Nicolás Guillén] by Nancy Morejón, Union of Writers and Artists in Cuba [UNEAC], 1982. This book has a good treatise on transculturation, race mixture, the concept of nationality and the race question in contemporary Cuba.
Film:
"The Other Francisco" by Sergio Giral, ICAIC, Havana (Distributor: UNIFILM, New York)
"Portrait of Teresa" by Pastor Vega, ICAIC, Havana (Distributor: UNIFILM, New York)

II. National Resistance in the Americas: Twentieth Century "Indian" Wars

Case Study #3 Multinational Corporations and the People's Resistance
Readings:
Let Me Speak: A Woman of the Bolivian Mines by Domitila Barrios de Chungara with Moema Viezzer, Monthly Review Press, 1978.

Film:

"The Courage of the People" by Jorge Sanjinés and the Ukamau Collective (Distributor: UNIFILM, New York) After protesting multinational and United States control of the economy, tin miners and their families are attacked in the massacre of San Juan at the Cataví mines.

Case Study #4 Guatemala and the Struggle for Human Rights
Readings:

Guatemala, edited by Susanne Jonas and David Tobis for the North American Congress on Latin America, NACLA, 1974.

"Classes, Colonialism and Acculturation" by Rodolfo Stavenhagen in *Masses in Latin America* edited by Irving Horowitz, Oxford University Press, 1970.

Film:

"The Cost of Cotton" by Luis Argueta (Distributor: UNIFILM, New York)

"Controlling Interest: The World of the Multinationals" (Distributor: California Newsreel) The export of basic commodities and the need to retain a favorable investment climate—cheap labor, new markets, abundant resources, and a political climate to assure the first three—are the root cause of continued problems of the world's human resources.

III. Southern Africa and Settler Colonialism

Case Study #5 Minerals, Militarism and Multinational Corporations in Southern Africa
Readings:

"Social Inequality: The South Africa Case" by B. Magubane in *Social Inequality* edited by G. Gerreman, Academic Press, 1981.

"Plunder of Namibian Uranium: Major Findings of the Hearings on Namibian Uranium"—Held by the United Nations Council for Namibia in July, 1980, UN Publications, 1982.

How Europe Underdeveloped Africa by W. Rodney, Bogle L'Ouverture Publication/Tanzania Publishing House, London, 1972.

Film:

"South Africa Belongs to Us," and "Crossroads: South Africa" (Distributor: California Newsreel) Women speak out about the impact of apartheid on family structure.

Case Study #6 Deculturation and Apartheid in Namibia: The !Kung San Dilemma
Readings:

"Bushmen: The Hunters Now Hunt Guerrillas" by Gary Thatcher in *Anthropology 83/84* edited by Elvio Angeloni, Dush Publishers.

Namibia: The Effects of Apartheid on Culture and Education, UNESCO, 1977.

Film:

"!N'ai: A Woman of the Kalahari" (Distributor: Documentary Educational Resources, Watertown, MA) A woman is tossed between her traditional culture and the market economy, as her kinsmen join the South African army.

The Dispossessed of the Earth: Land Reform and Economic Development

Steve Fisher   *Spring 1983*
Global Studies/Emory and Henry College/Abingdon, VA 24210

This course focuses upon land reform as an integral part of the strategy and policy of economic development. It attempts to provide a synthesis, in an interdisciplinary and global framework, of the theories and policies in land reform. The course begins with a discussion of the concepts of development and underdevelopment, and the role of land reform in development strategies. It then examines the case for land reform and looks at land redistribution efforts around the world. Finally, through comparative analysis, it identifies the key variables for a successful land reform program. Guest speakers, videotapes, slides, films and Lyceum programs will complement course readings and lectures.

Rationale

Land reform is not, of course, a modern phenomenon. Rural people have throughout the centuries agitated and fought for more control over the land they tilled. Yet land reform as an explicit and strategic development issue has gained new prominence since the disintegration of the colonial empires following World War II. Over the next two decades the number of rural people lacking secure access to farmland will approach one billion, and the conflict rooted in the inequality of landownership will become more acute in nation after nation.

It is difficult to overstate the importance of the land reform issue. Throughout history, patterns of landownership have shaped patterns of human relations in nearly all societies. They have, as Erik Eckholm points out,

> helped determine the possibility and pace of economic change. In agrarian societies, land is the primary productive asset, the tangible expression of economic and hence political power. Some tenure patterns have manifested and solidified social inequality while others have promoted social mobility or even something approaching equality. Some tenure patterns have blocked technological progress while others have encouraged it. And invariably, changing the relationship of people to the land has meant changing the relationship of people to one another—the stuff of political struggles and sometimes of war or revolutions.

Many of the international community's widely shared goals are not likely to be achieved without radical changes in the ownership and control of the land. Three examples should suffice.

1. *Hunger.* Analyses of the world hunger problem consistently identify two imperatives: firstly, more and different types of food must be produced in developing countries, and secondly, it must be more widely distributed. Land reform can often contribute to the achievement of the first goal and can always contribute to the achievement of the second.
2. *Poverty.* Land reform is not a one-time cure-all for poverty. But clearly a more equitable distribution of farmland would provide a base for a development strategy that would maximize employment and economic opportunities and give the dispossessed a chance to work their way out of extreme poverty.
3. *Lack of political stability and democracy.* Redistributing the land, thereby enlarging the class of small owners, would appear to be a crucial step toward political democracy and the reduction of conflict between classes.

In sum, land reform is an issue of global significance. It illustrates the commonality and interdependence of the human condition. It is an issue that will help students come to understand the existence of a world system and the kind of future they can look forward to in that system. It will help students to develop skills of comparison and to understand the necessity for, as well as the process of, change. But, perhaps most importantly, it is a global issue because the needs of the world's poorest people cannot be met without the world coming to grips with the land reform issue. It is a delusion to think that the dispossessed of the earth will watch their numbers grow and their plights worsen without protesting. The issue of land reform will not go away.

Outline

A. Introduction
1. Why Are We Here? Where Are We Going?
2. The Global Framework
   a. Global Studies: What Is It and Why Is It Important?
   b. Global Studies and Land Reform
3. The Nature and Urgency of the Problem: The Food, Population, Resources, Ecological and Poverty Crisis

B. Why Poor People Stay Poor: The Political Economy of Development
1. Concepts of Development and Underdevelopment
2. History of Development and Underdevelopment
3. The Human Costs of Underdevelopment
4. The Role of Land Reform in Development Strategies

C. Land Reform in Principle and Practice
1. Principles
   a. Fundamental Features of the Man-Land Relationship
   b. Evolution and the Concept of Land Reform
   c. Land Reform and the Organization of Agriculture
   d. The Case for Land Reform
2. Practice
   a. Early Historical Examples—England, France, Russia
   b. Land Reform in Latin America
   c. Land Reform in Asia

d. Land Reform in Africa
e. Land Reform in the Middle East
f. Case Study: China
g. Case Study: United States
3. Comparative Analysis
   a. Reform Background: Prerequisites for a Land Reform Movement
   b. Reform Objectives and Processes
   c. General Effects and Evaluation
   d. Political Effects
   e. Administration: Keeping What's Been Won

D. Conclusion
1. The Relation to Development Reconsidered: Land Reform and Sustainable Development
2. Toward a General Theory of Land Reform

Selectively Annotated Bibligraphy

Amin, Samir. *Unequal Development: An Essay on the Social Formations of Peripheral Capitalism.* Trans. by Brian Pearce. NY: Monthly Review Press, 1976.

Barnes, Peter (ed.) *The People's Land: A Reader on Land Reform in the United States.* Emmaus, PA: Rodale Press, 1975.

Belden, Joe; Edwards, Gibby; Guyer, Cynthia; and Webb, Lee (eds.). *New Directions in Farm, Land and Food Policies: A Time for State and Local Action.* Wash., DC: Agricultural Project, Conference on Alternative State and Local Policies, 1978. Excellent summary of reform efforts at the state and local level.

Bergmann, Theodor. *Farm Policies in Socialist Countries.* Trans. by Lux Furtmüller. Lexington, MA: Lexington Books, 1975. Provides a helpful discussion of Marxist agrarian theory. Includes a useful bibliography (pp. 273-85).

Blair, Thomas L. *The Land to Those Who Work It: Algeria's Experiment in Worker's Management.* Garden City, NY: Anchor, 1969.

Cehelsky, Marta. *Land Reform in Brazil: The Management of Social Change.* Boulder, CO: Westview Press, 1979.

Constant, Florence. *Land Reform: A Bibliography.* Cambridge, MA: Center for Community Economic Development, 1972. Nine-page bibliography.

Dore, Ronald P. *Land Reform in Japan.* London: Oxford Univ. Press, 1959.

Dorner, Peter. *Land Reform and Economic Development.* Baltimore: Penguin Books, 1972. Treats land reform as an integral part of the strategy and policy of economic development. Includes a useful bibliography (pp. 149-57).

Eckholm, Erik. *The Dispossessed of the Earth: Land Reform and Sustainable Development.* Wash., DC: Worldwatch Institute, 1979.

Faux, Geoffrey. "Reclaiming America," *Working Papers,* 1 (Summer 1973), pp. 31-42. Frequently cited article on land reform in the U.S.

Feder, Ernest. *The Rape of the Peasantry: Latin America's Landholding System.* Garden City, NY: Anchor Books, 1971. Analysis of the characteristics and functioning of Latin America's latifundia agriculture and the "so-called" land reforms of the 1960's.

Food and Agricultural Organization of the United Nations. *Land Reform: Annotated Bibliography of FAO Publications and Documents (1945—April 1970).* NY: Unipub, Inc., 1971. Valuable reference for non-U.S. sources.

FAO. *Land Reform, Land Settlement and Cooperatives.* Issued semi-annually. No. 1 (1968-Present). A medium for dissemination of information and views on land reform and related subjects.

Francisco, Ronald A.; Laird, Betty A.; and Laird, Roy D. (eds.). *The Political Economy of Collectivized Agriculture: A Comparative Study of Communist and Non-Communist Systems.* NY: Pergamon Press, 1979.

Frank, Andre Gunder. *Capitalism and Underdevelopment in Latin America: Historical Studies of Chile and Brazil.* NY: Monthly Review Press, 1969.

Griffin, Keith. *Land Concentration and Rural Poverty.* NY: Holmes and Meier, 1976. Focus on North Africa, Latin America, and Asia.

Heath, Dwight B.; Erasmus, Charles J.; and Buechler, Hans C. *Land Reform and Social Revolution in Bolivia.* NY: Praeger, 1969.

Hinton, William. *Fanshen: A Documentary of Revolution in a Chinese Village.* NY: Vintage, 1968. Important and easy-to-read account of land reform in China after the revolution.

Hopkins, Raymond F.; Puchala, Donald J.; and Talbot, Ross B. (eds.). *Foods, Politics, and Agricultural Development: Case Studies in the Public Policy of Rural Modernization.* Boulder, CO: Westview Press, 1979. Includes essays on the Soviet Union, China, Taiwan, South Korea, Iran, Pakistan, Black Africa, and the U.S.

International Independence Institute. *A Community Land Trust: A Guide to a New Model for Land Tenure in America.* Cambridge, MA: Center for Community Economic Development, 1972.

Jacoby, Erich H. in collaboration with Charlotte F. Jacoby. *Man and Land: The Essential Revolution.* NY: Knopf, 1971. Describes current conditions of the man-land relationship and makes the case for land reform. Includes a useful bibliography (pp. 372-91).

Jalée, Pierre. *The Pillage of the Third World.* Trans. by Mary Klopper. NY: Monthly Review Press, 1968. Focuses on the economic relations between the Third World and imperialism by looking at changes and trends in the relations between Third World and industrialized capitalist countries.

Johnston, Bruce F. and Kilby, Peter. *Agriculture and Structural Transformation: Economic Strategies in Late-Developing Countries.* NY: Oxford Univ. Press, 1975. Analyzes agricultural development in the context of its relationship with other economic sectors and discusses a development strategy. Historical chapters highlight relevant aspects of the experiences of Japan, U.S., Taiwan, Mexico and the Soviet Union.

King, Russell. *Land Reform: A World Survey.* Boulder, CO: Westview Press, 1977. Examines land reform in Latin America, Asia, Africa, and the Middle East.

Lappé, Frances Moore and Collins, Joseph, with Cary Fowler. *Food First: Beyond the Myth of Scarcity.* Boston: Houghton Miflin, 1977. Attacks myths about land reform and makes a strong case for such reform.

Lehmann, David (ed.). *Peasants, Landlords and Governments: Agrarian Reform in the Third World.* NY: Holmes and Meier, 1974. Essays on Latin America, China and India.

Lippit, Victor D. *Land Reform and Economic Development in China: A Study of Institutional Change and Development Finance.* NY: M.E. Sharpe, 1975.

Lipton, Michael. *Why Poor People Stay Poor: Urban Bias in World Development.* Cambridge, MA: Harvard Univ. Press, 1977. Forceful argument that a developed

mass agriculture is needed before you can have widespread successful development in other sectors.

Melville, Thomas, and Melville, Majorie. *Guatemala: The Politics of Land Ownership*. NY: Free Press, 1971.

Migdal, Joel S. *Peasants, Politics, and Revolution: Pressures toward Political and
Social Change in the Third World*. Princeton: Princeton Univ. Press, 1974.

Morgan, W.B. *Agriculture in the Third World: A Spatial Analysis*. Boulder, CO:
Westview Press, 1978. Major review of the economic, developmental and anthro-
pological literature dealing with the characteristics of Third World agriculture.
Includes a useful bibliography (pp. 259-78).

O'Hagan J.P. (ed.). *Growth and Adjustment in National Agricultures: Four Case
Studies and an Overview*. Pub. by arrangement with the FAO of the UN.
Montclair, NJ: Allanheld, Osmun/Universe Books 1978. FAO studies of Japan,
Poland, Sweden and the Sudan.

Petras, James. *Critical Perspectives on Imperialism and Social Class in the Third
World*. NY: Monthly Review Press, 1978. Effort at a synthesis of "dependency"
and class analysis.

Senior, Clarence O. *Land Reform and Democracy*. Gainesville, FL: Univ. of Florida
Press, 1958; reprint ed., NY: Greenwood. 1974.

Strong, Ann L. *Land Banking—European Reality, American Prospect.*. Baltimore·
Johns Hopkins Univ. Press, 1979. Examines the European examples and specu-
lates on the potential for land banking in the U.S.

Tai, Hung-Chao. *Land Reform and Politics: A Comparative Analysis*. Berkeley,
CA: Univ. of California Press, 1974. Comparative analysis of the political pro-
cesses and effects of the land-reform programs of 8 developing countries (Taiwan,
Philippines, India, Pakistan, Iran, Egypt, Columbia, and Mexico).

Tuma, Elias H. *Twenty-six Centuries of Agrarian Reform: A Comparative Analysis*. Berkeley, CA: Univ. of California Press, 1965. Provides an interesting and
useful classification of land reform movements. Based on Greek, Roman, English,
French, Russian, Mexican, Japanese and Egyptian reforms. Includes a useful
bibliography (pp. 287-97).

Warriner, Doreen. *Land Reform in Principle and Practice*. Oxford: Clarendon Press,
1969. Designed as a general introduction.

Wilber, Charles K. (ed.). *The Political Economy of Development and Underdevelopment*. 2nd ed. NY: Random House, 1979. Important collection focusing on
alternative strategies of economic growth.

Wong, John. *Land Reform in the People's Republic of China: Institutional Transformation in Agriculture*. NY: Praeger, 1973.

Contemporary World Development

Andre Gunder Frank and David Seddon   *Autumn 1982*
School of Development Studies/University of East Anglia/
Norwich, England

This course is intended to offer a global perspective on selected contemporary world development and Third World problems. Emphasis is on contemporary development on a world scale and particularly on the world economic, social and political crisis of the 1970's and 1980's.

A brief review of postwar development shows that rapid industrial growth and trade as well as primary and terciary sector developments significantly raised incomes and welfare in the industrial capitalist countries of the West, developed the Socialist economies in the East, but despite rapid sectoral advances, left the (under)developing countries in the South with vast problems of poverty and social tension. The Club of Rome, United Nations and other "futures" projections to be examined predict the aggravation of these problems in the "Third World" unless there is much faster growth with redistribution towards and within the South.

Since the 1960's, however, world capitalist (and recently also socialist) development has apparently entered another major structural crisis with reduced and sometimes negative growth rates and tendencies to accentuate inequalities between and within countries. The theory and praxis of the this crisis of development is to be analysed and projected in the West, East and South. In the West, the crisis of capital accumulation is traced through its cyclical development with declining profits, credit creation and inflation, stagnating but job reducing investment, growing unemployment, (stagflation or slumpflation), and (in the absence also of adequate theory to guide them) the so far inadequate national and international economic, social, and political policy responses and unresolved tensions. The detente with the East and de facto US-China alliance, the "transideological enterprise," and accelerating economic integration of "socialist" economies in the capitalist international division of labour are examined in the context of the growing social and political crisis within and between the socialist countries and in relation to the world crisis as a whole. In the South, unequal Third (Fourth? Fifth?) World development is examined in many countries and their participation in the new international division of labour through export promotion (of manufactures and minerals and through agribusiness) is analysed. Particular attention is devoted to the concomitant reliance on and transformation of the state and the recent growth and institutionalisation of internal political repression (emergency rule, martial law, military government, etc.) and the increase of international wars around the Third World.

Throughout, the diverse currrent natural resource, technological, economic, social, cultural, national, (especially growing nationalism), ideological, political and military developments are to be analysed in relation to each other and as parts of a single world historical process. For this reason and because the emphasis is deliberately on current development on a world scale, evidence and material can be drawn only in part from books (by E. Mandel and unpublished by A.G. Frank) but must rely heavily on current official publications (by United Nations, OECD, GATT, World Bank, IMF, and other international institutions), some recent journal articles and unpublished monographs, and very importantly on current press reports or analyses, as well as on class members' own personal experience.

The course will be taught substantially as a seminar and students (individually and collectively) are expected to participate actively in the examination of current material, their presentation and discussion in class, and their analyses in writing, all of which will bear on their assessment. This course complements those on transitions to capitalism, international relations, Britain and the world economy, and social policy.

Texts

Each week, read the first listed reading first and supplement it with as many other readings as possible more or less in the priority order of their listing below. Use the questions posed for each week/topic as guides to your own reading (if possible, clip and bring to class) of current press items related to each topic.

Frank, Andre Gunder. *Crisis: In the World Economy*, Heinemann Education.
Frank, Andre Gunder. *Crisis: In the Third World*, Heinemann Education.
Mandel, Ernest. *The Second Slump*, New Left Books/Verso.
Amin, Samir; Giovanni Arrighi, Andre Gunder Frank and Immanuel Wallerstein. *Dynamics of Global Crisis*, Monthly Review Press.
Current Press: *Financial Times, Times, Guardian, International Herald Tribune, Economist, Far Eastern Economic Review, Time.*

The World Today (Session #1) The World Today as Seen by Ourselves and the Press
Frank, A.G. Conclusion Chapter in *World Economy* or *Third World, World Economy*, Chapter 1.
Introduction to the Course and Discussion of Current World Affairs based on: Participant Reports of Reality and Views in their Respective Counties; Participant Reports/Readings of Recent Press Clippings; Participant Comments on Course Content and Organisation.

Week 1 (Session #2) The World Economy Today as Seen by Official Institutions and the Press
Each student is to report on one official institution's report(s) to be selected in Session 1 for report/comparison/discussion in Session 2, and/or relevant current press reports on world political economy (if possible clippings to be brought to class).

Each participant need read the general/introductory/or summary section of only *one* official institution report to be selected from the following; but it would be very useful if two or three years successive reports by (some of) these institutions could be read and reported on by one or more participants, in order to see whether and how the institutions have changed its/their views over time. We will then compare the different institutional and press accounts (or of personalities cited by the press) of the world political economy today. Some of the questions below can guide your reading and our discussion.

Readings Week 1
BIS/Bank for International Settlements. *Annual Report,* 1982, 1980/1979.
GATT/General Agreements on Tariffs, and Trade. *International Trade 1980-81* (Note: Do not use GATT Director's Report).
IMF/International Monetary Fund. *World Economic Outlook* 1982, (do not use Director's Annual Report).
WB/World Bank. *World Development Report 1982, 1979,* (not Annual Report).
OECD/Organisation for Economic Cooperation and Development. *Economic Outlook,* December 1981, July 1982.
UNCTAD/United Nations Conference on Trade and Development. *Report of the Director,* 1982, 1981.
UNECOSOC/United Nations Economic and Social Commission. *World Economic Survey,* 1982, 1981.
UNECE/United Nations Economic Commission for Europe. *Economic Survey of Europe,* 1982, 1981.

Questions
What is the time dimension of the present crisis? From when to when?
What is the space dimension of the present crisis? What areas are included/excluded?
What is the depth of the present crisis? How can we define or measure the depth?
What do we mean by crisis, as distinct, for instance, from recession?
How is the perception of the crisis changing from one year to another?
What is the difference in the definition/perception of the crisis among institutions?
What went wrong—according to one institution and another?

Week 2 The New Economic Crisis in the West
Frank, A.G. *World Economy,* Chapter 2.
Mandel, E. *Second Slump,* Chapters 1, 2, 3.
Mandel, E. "The Second Postwar World Recession," *International Viewpoint,* No. 8, June 7, 1982.

Questions
Continuation of questions from previous week; and
What has been the development of the present crisis?
What are the prospects of future development and resolution of the present crisis?
What are the international ramifications of the crisis?
What is the cause and remedy for inflation?
What is the cause and remedy for unemployment?

Week 3 Political Economic Response to Crisis in the West
Frank, A.G. *World Economy,* Chapter 3.

OECD. *The Welfare State in Crisis*, pp. 5-40.

Frank, A.G. "After Reaganomics and Thatcherism, What?" *Contemporary Marxism*, No. 4, Winter 1981/82.

Questions

Success and/or failure of Keynesianism? Why?

Decline of the Welfare State?

Political polarization? In whose favor?

Resurgence of militarism?

Implications of "new" social movements of new right, religion, nationalism, regionalism, minorities, women, etc.?

Week 4 World Political Economy and International Political Economic Relations

Frank, A.G. "Atlantic Alliance to European Detente" (mimeo).

Arrighi, G. "Crisis of Hegemony," in S. Amin, G. Arrighi, A.G. Frank and I. Wallerstein, *Dynamics of Global Crisis.*

Parboni, R. *The Dollar and its Rivals*, pp. 7-24, 99-140, 169-207.

Wolfe, A. *The Rise and Fall of the 'Soviet Threat.'*

Kaldor, M. *The Decline of the West.*

Radice, H. (ed.) *International Firms and Modern Imperialism.*

United Nations. *Report on Transnational Enterprises.*

Questions

Are transnationals independent of state power, use it, in conflict with it?

Is U.S. hegemony declining? Replaced by whom or what? With what consequences?

What are the reasons and dangers of war?

Is economic bloc formation possible? What (membership) blocs?

What are the threats and potential consequences of protectionism?

What is the impact of technological change and its political economic use?

Week 5 A New International Division of Labour and World Industrialization
  Third World Newly Industrializing Countries and Export Led Growth

Frank, A.G. *Third World*, Chap. 1 "Unequal Development," especially pp. 1-27; Chap. 3 "Export Promotion," only pp. 96-111; Chap. 5 "Superexploitation," especially pp. 160-173.

Warren, B. *Imperialism, Pioneer of Capitalism*, Chapter 8. "The Illusion of Underdevelopment," especially pp. 186-224, 241-255.

ILO Asian Employment Programme. *Export-Led Industrialisation and Development* (edited by Eddy Lee), pp. 1-21 (An Overview).

Lall, S. "Export Manufacturing by Newly Industrialized Countries," *Economic and Political Weekly*, Dec. 6 & 12, 1980, pp. 2051-2062, 2103-2112.

Fröbel, F., Heinrichs, J., & Kreye, O. *The New International Division of Labour*, Introduction and Part III.

UNIDO. *World Manufacturing Since 1960.*

Questions

What is new about the new international division of labour?

Are the newly industrializing countries (NICS) industrializing?

Why runaway shops?

Why promotion of "non-traditional (manufacturing)" exports?

What are the costs and benefits and to whom?

What obstacles are there, e.g., protectionism, technological change, etc.?

Week 6 World Agribusiness and the Third World
Frank, A.G. *Third World*, Chapter 2.
FAO. *World Food and Agriculture* 1981.
OECD. *Study of Trends in World Supply and Demand in Major Agricultural Commodities.*
George, Susan. *How the Other Half Dies*, Montclair, N.J.: Allanheld, 1977. Or *Feeding the Few*, Washington, D.C.: Institute for Policy Studies, 1981.
Lappé, Frances Moore and Collins, Joe. *Food First*, parts IV-VIII, (San Francisco, CA: Institute for Food and Development Policy), or *World Hunger, Ten Myths*, or *Aid as Obstacle.*
Burbach, Roger and Flynn, Patricia. *Agribusiness in the Americas* (Monthly Review Press).

Questions
What are world trends in supply, demand and prices of major agricultural commodities?
How does agriculture compare to any other business?
What are some important policies toward agriculture?
What are the consequences of agribusiness spread in the Third World?
What are the causes and—if any—the remedies for hunger?
Note: Similar examination of mineral and fuels to be in CW II.

Week 7 Third World Aid and Finance, Debt and the IMF
Frank, A.G. *Third World*, Chapter 5, "Third World Debt."
Engellau, P. and Nygren, N. *Lending Without Limits*—on International Lending and Developing Countries.
OECD/DAC. *Development Cooperation Efforts and Policies*, 1980, pp. 13-28.
Development & Finance, Vol. 19, No. 1, March 1982, pp. 13-16, debt in developing countries. Vol. 18, No. 2, June 1981, pp. 14-21, conditionality.
World Development, Vol. 7, No. 7, February 1979, Issue on International Indebtness.
Development Dialogue, 1980: No. 2 (Dag Hammarskjold Foundation, Uppsala, Sweden).
World Development Report 1981, 1982.
Third World Debt and the IMF (University of East Anglia Development Monograph).
IMF. *World Economic Outlook 1981*, 1982.

Questions
Why are balance of payments deficits and debt increasing? What is the role of oil?
What is the source, nature and proposed solutions to the 1980-81-82 financial crisis?
What is the role of the IMF and how is it changing?
Who bears the cost?
What is the relation between the financial system/flows/pressures and the international division of labour?

Week 8 Third World State, Repression, Warfare and Liberation

Frank, A.G. *Third World*, Chapter 6 (Repression), Chapter 7 (State), Chapter 8 (Arms and War).

Collier, David (ed.) *The New Authoritarianism in Latin America* (Princeton, NJ, 1979), Chapters 1, 2, 3, 7, 9.

Chossodovsky, Michael. "Capital Accumulation and State Violence in the Third World" (mimeo), or "Transnationalization and the Development of Peripheral Capitalism" (mimeo).

Chomsky, Noam and Herman, Edward S. *The Political Economy of Human Rights*, Vol. I, The Washington Connection and Third World Fascism. Vol. II. (Boston, MA: South End Press, 1982.)

Review of African Political Economy, No. 7, 1976; No. 8, 1977.

Insurgent Sociologist, Vol. VII, No. 2, Spring 1977, Special Issue on Imperialism and the State.

Student Reports?

Questions

What is the political economy and economic rationale/function of political repression?

How and why is the Third World State being transformed?

What are the foreseeable political prospects in the Third World?

Why and where/when war in the Third World?

Week 9 The Socialist Countries in the World Economy

Frank, A.G. *World Economy*, Chapter 4, "Transideological Enterprise . . ."

Mandel, E. *Second Slump*, Chapter 4.

Mandel, E. "Impact of the World Capitalist Recession on Eastern Europe," *Intercontinental Press*, 14 July 1980.

Bahro, Rudolph. *The Alternative*, summary in *New Left Review* 106, Nov-Dec 1977.

Corrigan, Philip, H. Ramsay and D. Sayer. *Socialist Construction and Marxist Theory*.

Monthly Review, July-August 1978—"China Since Mao."

Carr. E.H. "The USSR and the West." *New Left Review*, No. 111.

Szymanski, A. *Is the Red Flag Flying?*

Nove, A. (ed) *The East European Economies in the 1970s*, especially Chapters 1, 2, 3, 4.

Bulletin of Concerned Asian Scholars, Special China Issues, Vol. 13, No. 2, June 1981, especially pp. 2-40. Vol. 13, No. 3, July-Sept 1981, especially pp. 2-41.

Chossodovsky, M. *Capitalist Restoration in China*, 1982.

Singer, D. *Road to Gdansk*, second edition, 1981.

Questions

Are the socialist countries in or out of the world capitalist system and its crisis?

Does the law of value operate in the socialist economies?

What is happening in Poland and why?

Is China taking a great leap backwards, fowards, sideways, not at all?

Alternative Paradigms in Economics

Francisco Bataller M.   *Fall 1982*
Economics 91/Kenyon College/Gambier, OH 43022

The point of departure of this course is to put into question the fundamental axiom of neoclassical economics that positive economics as a science is value-free and that its tools are valid for the understanding of human behavior across time, space and culture. The course takes as a working tool the assumption that economics as "a study of Man" might be defined and approached from alternative perspectives depending on the cultural background and the ideological stance of the observer or thinker. Kenneth Boulding pointed this out a few years ago:

> "The subculture of economists as it has existed now for nearly two hundred years is very far from being a random sample of human populations or human cultures. It bears the genetic stamp of its British origin, of its eighteenth century birth date, of its connection with the larger scientific culture, and of its origins in what might be called the intellectual middle class. The important thing is would economics have been any different if it had originated, let us say, in China or in India or if its practitioners were less middle class, or if the economic structure of the profession, divided as it is between education, business, and government institutions had been different? . . . It has been argued, for instance, that the classical division of factors of production into land, capital and labor reflected the peculiar social circumstances of eighteenth—or nineteenth—century Britain with its land-holding aristocracy, its rising merchant-capitalist middle class and its rather clearly defined lower class of workers. These three classes were separated quite sharply from each other by forms of speech, manners, religion, and other cultural characteristics, and hence it is not surprising that the classical economists perceived them as associated with three different factors of production. If economics had grown up in India, there might have been a factor for each caste . . ." (Boulding, "Is Economics Culture-Bound?"), *AER Paper, and Proceedings,* May 1970, pp. 407 and 408).

Objectives

1. To improve students ability to read carefully and critically works of political economy. Students should be able to distance themselves from what is being read to look for the hidden assumptions in order to identify the image of man and the ethical and political biases that are implicit in those works.
2. To acquaint students with other modes of thought and of reasoning different from that of our culture or from that of neoclassical economics. For this reason a major emphasis in the readings will be on the influence of theology, ideology and culture in the formulation of economic ideas and models.

3. To improve students use of the tools and understanding of the usefulness and limitations of neoclassical economics.

As it should be obvious from those objectives the core premise in this course is the questioning of one's beliefs and acquired knowledge. The questioning assumes the form of both the reading and class discussion of a diversity of works with different ideological foundations and of the writing of a paper which reflects that questioning premise. In practical terms this means that, during their readings and during the presentation of their papers, students should try to justify and/or explain the validity and cultural or "economic" consistency of any given viewpoint that emerges in the texts or in class. It further means that that critical view should be incorporated in the papers in an explicit and clear manner. This will involve in most occasions the comparison between a certain viewpoint and neoclassical economics. Let us suppose, for example, that someone is interested in the Islamic view of man and how it relates to Islamic economic principles and institutions. This, by itself, would not constitute a paper acceptable for this course. That paper should go further than that either by attempting to show the limitation that those principles imply for economic growth or alternatively by attempting to show the limitations of neoclassical theory when its principles are used to interpret Islamic behavior.

Course requirements
The first part of the course will concentrate on the reading and class discussion of works representative of the philosophy of supply side economics, Austrian economics, radical economics, Islamic economics, etc. The fundamentals of the methodology of neoclassical economics will also be discussed.

Texts
Required:
Blaugh, *The Methodology of Economics* (Cambridge)
Hunt and Sherman, *Economics: An Introduction to Traditional and Radical Views* (Harper and Row)
Novak, *Capitalism and Socialism: A Theological Inquiry* (American Enterprise Insitute)
Gilder, *Wealth and Poverty* (Bantam)
Littlechild, *The Fallacy of the Mixed Economy* (Cato)

Suggested:
Hutt, *A Rehabilitation of Say's Law* (Ohio University)
Ackerman, *Reaganomics: Rhetoric Vs. Reality* (South End)
Esposito, *Islam and Development* (Syracuse)
Wanniski, *The Way the World Works* (Simon and Schuster)
Laffer and Seymour, *The Economics of the Tax Revolt* (Harcourt, Brace)
Schumacher, *Small is Beautiful: Economics as if People Mattered* (Harper and Row)
Luntz and Lux, *The Challenge of Humanistic Economics* (Benjamin/Cummings)
Ward, *The Economic World Views* (Basic)

The second part of the course will consist of student in-class presentations of the papers written for the seminar.

Cross-Cultural Perspectives on Development

J.A. Mestenhauser   *Spring 1984*
International Relations 5-XXX/University of Minnesota/
Minneapolis, MN 55455

The purpose of this course is to give students an opportunity to examine analytically and critically various aspects of development of the "Third World" countries as seen from the perspectives of nationals of these countries. Emphasis will be on cross-cultural, comparative and inter-disciplinary analyses. Three countries from different continents and of varying social, cultural, religious, historical, governmental, economic, and educational backgrounds will be selected for discussion. These countries are Turkey, Nigeria, and Thailand. At present, the University does not offer courses about these countries. The expected outcomes of this course will be: 1) minimal familiarity with relatively little-known countries which are nevertheless very important to United States foreign policy; 2) understanding of development; 3) understanding of cross-cultural analysis, which includes the role of perceptions, culture-contact, transfer of knowledge, and different thinking styles; 4) understanding of developmental issues from a global rather than single country perspective, since the three countries represent three major continents; 5) development of some cross-cultural skills in interviewing foreign students, and 6) gaining of broader understanding of the role of the United States with respect to the North-South dialogue.

Course Content

Lecture 1 Introduction to course
Role of perceptions in cross-cultural analysis; Bafa-Bafa; lecture and simulation game

Lecture 2 What are cross-cultural perspectives; global perspectives
Practical application: relating to foreign students; nature of cross-cultural communication; lecture and demonstration

Lecture 3 Common American perceptions about development
Concepts about development prevailing in social sciences; general issues related to transfer of technology; lecture and demonstration

Lecture 4 Third World views about development
Perspectives about transfer of technology, dependency theories, and monopoly of knowledge; lecture

Lecture 5 Turkey I. Slides, general introduction and overview

Lecture 6 Turkey II. Contemporary issues and their historical perspectives
Nature of foreign relations; panel of selected foreign students and scholars from Turkey

Lecture 7 Turkey III. Economics of development in Turkey
Turkish students or scholars from economics and business administration; panel

Lecture 8 Nigeria I. Slides, general introduction and overview

Lecture 9 Nigeria II. Contemporary issues and their historical perspectives
Nature of Nigeria's foreign relations; panel of Nigerian students and scholars

Lecture 10 Nigeria III. Politics of development in Nigeria
Panel of Nigerian students and scholars

Lecture 11 Thailand I. Slides, general introduction and overview

Lecture 12 Thailand II. Contemporary issues and their historical perspectives
Nature of Thailand's foreign relations; panel of Thai students and scholars

Lecture 13 Thailand III. Social, cultural and religious issues of development
Panel of Thai students and scholars

Lecture 14 Special topic of development I. Role of education in development
Lecture and panel of foreign students and scholars from education

Lecture 15 Special topic of development II. Role of technology and technology transfer
Lecture and panel of foreign students and scholars from technological fields

Lecture 16 Special topic of development III. Role of health and welfare in development
Basic human needs; lecture and panel of foreign students and scholars from the fields of medicine, public health and social services

Lecture 17 Special topic of development IV. Leadership and administration of development programs
Developing cross-cultural approaches to leadership; developing voluntarism and participation; lecture

Lecture 18 Development and U.S. response
Lecture and discussion

Lecture 19 Summary and synthesis; Star Power Game
Lecture, discussion and simulation game

Lecture 20 Final examination
Papers and journals are due.

Readings

Amnvay, Tapingkae. *Education in Thailand: Some Thai Perspectives.* Washington, DC: Education and Welfare Pub. No. (OE) 72-61, U.S. Government Printing Office, 1973.

Area Handbook for Nigeria.

Area Handbook for Thailand.

Area Handbook for the Republic of Turkey.

Asian Survey.

Barrows, Thomas S. *College Students' Knowledge and Beliefs, A Survey of Global Understanding.* New Rochelle, NY: Changing Magazine Press, 1981.

Bhalla, A.S., Ed. *Towards Global Action for Appropriate Technology.* Elmsford, NY: Pergamon Press, Inc., 1979.

Brzezinski, Zbigniew. "America in a Hostile World," *Foreign Policy,* May, 1977.

Cochrane, Glynn. *The Cultural Appraisal of Development Projects.* NY: Praeger Publishers, 1979.

de Souza, Anthony and Philip Porter. *The Underdevelopment and Modernization of the Third World.* Washington, DC: Association of American Geographers, 1974.

Erb, Guy F. and Valeriana Kallab, Eds. *Beyond Dependency: The Developing World Speaks Out.* Washington, DC: Overseas Development Council, 1975.

Fieg, John P. *The Thai Way.* Washington, DC: Meridian House International, 1976.

The Global 2000 Report to the President: Entering the Twenty-First Century. Washington, DC: U.S. Government Printing Office, 1980.

Hansen, Roger D. *Beyond the North-South Stalemate.* NY: McGraw-Hill, 1979.

Hardin, Garrett. "The Tragedy of the Commons," in *Ekistics,* 1969.

Jervis, Robert. *Perception and Misperception in International Politics.* Princeton, NJ: Princeton University Press, 1976.

Kumar, Krishna, Ed. *Bonds Without Bondage: Explorations in Transcultural Interactions.* Honolulu, Hawaii: University Press of Hawaii, 1979.

McLaughlin, Martin M., et al. *The United States and World Development Agenda 1979.* NY: Praeger Publishers, 1979.

National Research Council. *U.S. Science and Technology for Development: A Contribution to the 1979 U.N. Conference.* Washington, DC: Department of State, 1979.

Nafziger, E. Wayne. "The Economic Impact of the Nigerian Civil War," *Journal of Modern African Studies,* 1972.

Nisbett, Richard E. and Timothy DeCamp Wilson. "The Halo Effect: Evidence of Unconscious Alteration of Judgment," in *Journal of Personality and Social Psychology,* 1977.

North-South: A Program for Survival. The Report of the Independent Commission on International Development Issues under the Chairmanship of Willy Brandt. Cambridge, MA: The MIT Press, April, 1980.

Rothko Chapel Colloquium. *Toward a New Strategy for Development.* NY: Pergamon Press, 1979.

Sardar, Ziauddin. *Science, Technology and Development in the Muslim World.* Atlantic Highlands, NJ: Humanities Press, 1977.

In addition to these books and journals, there will be at least one book or article for each country, (in English) selected by the foreign students and scholars.

Development Conflict and Political Change

Guy Gran   *Spring 1983*
Government and Public Administration 53.631/The American
University/Washington, DC 20016

This course will explore the nature of local and regional politics in the
Third World to lay bare the conflictual realities with which national and
international development activities must contend. Conflict will be studied as a function of the mode of production, political processes, bureaucratic imperatives, and culture. We shall be particularly concerned with how
and why conflict is created, how elites mystify its essence, and how a less
conflictual, more developmental future could be created.

The course begins with a brief review of the generic conflicts created by
elite interests (Marx) and organizational imperatives (Weber) in the world-
system (Wallerstein). The nature of capitalist modernization on the periphery is then explored: how rural areas were incorporated; how processes of
stratification are maintained; and how the rural poor in Bangladesh, as a
case study, have adapted to the larger system. The nature of socialist
modernization is introduced. An overview of major aid agency efforts leads
into an extended study of rural development as it appears from above and
from below in capitalist and socialist models. Participatory development
will then be explored as the operational alternative to these conflictual
environments. Urban micropolitical conflict is the concluding section
with a role playing session placing you in Nairobi. Illich and other 21st
century visions are the finale.

Requirements

Two papers and several kinds of class participation will be expected. Papers will be
12 page take-homes, handed out the week in advance. Required reading is marked
by an *.

All titles will be discussed in class, and new ones added as discovered. My own
volume, *Development by People*, contains a development studies guide with a
global bibliography of 2000 items through the end of 1982.

Course Outline

January 11 Conflict in the World-System: An Introduction
D. Chirot, *Social Change in the 20th Century* (Harcourt Brace, 1977).
L.S. Stavrianos, *The Global Rift: The Third World Comes of Age* (Morrow, 1981).
I. Wallerstein, *The Capitalist World Economy* (Cambridge, 1980).

January 18 Theories of Organizations
*B. Abrahamsson, *Bureaucracy or Participation* (Sage, 1977).
R. Hummel, *The Bureaucratic Experience* (St. Martin's, 1977).
W.G. Scott and D.K. Hart, *Organizational America* (Houghton Mifflin, 1979).
M.A. Lutz and K. Lux, *The Challenge of Humanistic Economics* (Benjamin/Cummings, 1979).

January 25 Capitalist Modernization and its Microconflicts
*C. Elliott, *Patterns of Poverty in the Third World* (Praeger, 1975, on reserve).
R. Palmer and N. Parsons, *The Roots of Rural Poverty in Central and Southern Africa* (Univ. of California, 1977).
A. Warman, *We Come to Object* (Mexico) (Johns Hopkins, 1981).
K.E. Sharpe, *Peasant Politics* (Dominican Republic) (Johns Hopkins, 1977).

February 1 Confidence Mechanisms and Other Conflict Mystifiers
Discussion of Elliott
C. Obbo, *African Women* (Zed Press, 1981).
B. Ribes, *Domination or Sharing?* (UNESCO, 1981).
G. Therborn, *What Does the Ruling Class Do When it Rules?* (NLB, 1978).

February 8 Modernization as Export-Led Growth—Rural Asian Conflict
*W. Van Schendel, *Peasant Mobility: The Odds of Life In Rural Bangladesh* (1981).
K. Griffin et al., *Poverty and Landlessness in Rural Asia* (ILO, 1977).
B. Kerkvliet, *The Huk Rebellion* (Univ. of California, 1977).
D.S. Gibbons et al., *Agricultural Modernization, Poverty and Inequality* (Saxon House, 1980).

February 15 State Socialist Modernization and Its Microconflicts
E. Croll, *The Family Rice Bowl: Food and the Domestic Economy in China* (UNRISO, 1982).
B.P. Harzard, *Peasant Organization and Peasant Individualism . . .* (China) (Verlag Breitenbach, 1982).
W. Hinton, *Fanshen* (Vintage, 1966).
G. Gran, "Vietnam in Pursuit of Development: Socialist Promise, Natural Calamities, and Permanent Learning," *Cultures et developpement* (XI, 2:261-81, 1979).

February 22 Creating the Official Future and Mystifying Conflict—Aid Agencies in the Third World, 1950-80
First Exam Due
R. Packenham, *Liberal America and the Third World* (Princeton, 1973).
H. Brookfield, *Interdependent Development* (Univ. of Pittsburgh, 1975).
C. Payer, *The World Bank* (Monthly Review, 1982).
W. Bello et al., *Development Debacle: The World Bank in the Philippines* (IFDP, 1982).

March 1 Rural Development Conflict I: The World Food System as a Whole
*A. deJanvry, *The Agrarian Question and Reformism in Latin America* (Johns Hopkins, 1981).
J. Heyer et al., *Rural Development in Tropical Africa* (St. Martins, 1981).
R.W. Franke and B. Chasen, *Seeds of Famine* (Allanheld, Osmun, 1980).
A. Pearse, *Seeds of Plenty, Seeds of Want* (Oxford Univ. Press, 1980).

March 15 Rural Development Conflict II: State Socialism in Action
*J Collins, *What Difference Could a Revolution Make.* (Nicaragua) (IFDP, 1982).
T. Walker, ed. *Nicaragua in Revolution* (Praeger, 1982).
EPICA, *Grenada—The Peaceful Revolution* (EPICA Task Force, 1982).
A. Coulson, *Tanzania—A Political Economy* (Oxford Univ. Press, 1982).

March 22 Rural Development—View From Below
*B. Head, *Serowe: Village of the Rainwind* (Heinemann, 1981).
J. Scott, *The Moral Economy of the Peasant* (Yale Univ. Press, 1977).
A. Fugelsang, *About Understanding* (Dag Hammarskjold, 1982).
J. Berger, "Towards Understanding Peasant Experience," *Race and Class,* XIX (4:345-359, 1978).
A. Adams, "The Senegal River Valley: What Kind of Change?" *Review of African Political Economy,* (10:33-59, 1977).

March 29 Rural Participatory Development
*B. Galjart and D. Buijs, eds., *Participation of the Poor in Development* (Univ. Leiden, 1982).
A. Bhaduri and M.A. Rahman, eds., *Studies in Rural Participation* (Oxford Univ. Press, 1982).
G.V.S. de Silva et al., "Bhoomi Sena: A Struggle for People's Power," *Development Dialogue,* (2:3-70, 1979).
M.R. Hollnsteiner, "Mobilizing the Rural Poor Through Community Organization," *Philippine Studies,* 27, (3:387-411, 1979).
D.C. Korten, "Community Organization and Rural Development: A Learning Process Approach," *Public Administration Review,* 40, (5:480-511, 1980).

April 5 Urban Micropolitics in the Third World
Second Exam Due
*R. Sandbrook, *The Politics of Basic Needs* (Univ. of Toronto, 1982).
J. Perlman, *The Myth of Marginality* (Univ. of California, 1976).
R. Bromley and C. Gerry, eds., *Casual Work and Poverty in Third World Cities* (Wiley, 1979).
J. Abu-Lughod and R. Hay, eds., *Third World Urbanization* (Methuen, 1980).
N. Mahfouz, *Midaq Alley* (Heinemann, 1966).

April 12 Inside a World Bank Sites and Services Project: Acting Out Conflict in Nairobi
*Case materials to be distributed
*R. Bromley and C. Gerry, op. cit., Ch. 10 and 14 (on reserve).

April 19 Unresolved Problems of Development in a Conflictual Environment: Rethinking Organization versus People
*I. Illich, *Shadow Work* (Marion Boyars, 1980).
J. Galtung, *The True Worlds* (Free Press, 1980).
B. Horvat, *The Political Economy of Socialism* (M.E. Sharpe, 1981).
E.P. Thompson, *The Poverty of Theory* (Monthly Review, 1978).
G. Gran, *Development by People: Citizen Construction of a Just World* (Praeger, 1983).

Problems of Poverty, Promises of Development, Prospects for Humanity

Jasper Ingersoll   *Fall 1982*
Anthropology/Catholic University/Washington, DC 20064

The focus of this course is on human issues of world poverty and development. We shall review the distribution, theories and nature of poverty; theories, policies and practices of development; and the problems and future prospects for human survival. The emphasis in the course is anthropological, but the issues are global and multidisciplinary. Several anthropological perspectives are pertinent, but the issues of poverty and development are so complex as to require contributions from many disciplines and professions combined with the practical knowledge and experience of the host people. Social scientists can usefully participate, but only by sustained efforts to relate our limited contributions to those of others.

Framework

The following anthropological perspectives (not mutually exclusive) can contribute to development analysis and action:

holistic: anthropologists approach reality as a whole composed of many diverse but interacting parts, but we have normally done our field work alone; development is interdisciplinary work.

cross cultural: peoples do differ in their experience and in their definitions of experience; we can help identify significant differences.

contextual: project designs and monitoring activities require direct *in situ* information which we can obtain from study of every day life.

comparative: comparisons within and between countries provide essential, practical understanding of particular project experience.

evolutionary: development is incremental, based on previous experience and organization; it cannot begin with a clean slate; we can help reconstruct pertinent features of the local past on which to build.

adaptation: people's own coping mechanisms in their own social and natural settings are central to their development.

cognitive: their indigenous organization of their experience and knowledge is an essential resource and constraint in their development.

symbolic: the meanings they attach to their experience is similarly an integral strand in their development.

These perspectives, however, can be useful in development work only if anthropologists face the limitations of our discipline in an arena of awesome complexity. The problems of world poverty and development can be grasped and acted upon only through extraordinary syntheses of thought and action. The issues of resource depletion, exploitation, justice and meaning in life all require concerted efforts by humanists, social and natural scientists, and service professionals together with farmers and workers as well as rural landless and unemployed people.

In this complex setting, the traditional dichotomy between basic and applied research—indeed, between research and action—dissolves into a single process of theory-analysis-planning-action. All of these parts of the process test and inform each other. Theories interpret and guide action, as action tests and refines theories; and results—in the improved capacities of people to sustain their own well-being— constitute the ultimate judgment of theories and action.

Further, in such a setting, the unworldly ideal of value-free analysis is stripped of utility and meaning. Analysis and appropriate action in a world-wide sea of poverty and a few scattered islands of wealth are not value neutral; they can be carried on only in explicit relation to the values which seem to justify and support a viable global human order through more equitable world development. The alternative courses available to a given people and the various implications for them of each option can be analyzed carefully and factually, but the actual implications for the people are *not* value-free at all.

Adequate understanding and action in any development setting are thus possible only in relation to some standard of common values for sustained world order and human well-being. The standard presented in this course (always open to argument) is the set of values embedded in the world order premises of peace, ecological sustainability, economic well-being and social justice. They will be used as a value standard for judging our data and theories of world poverty and development.

Course Outline
(Items marked with * are general readings for everyone)

I. Poverty (September)

A. Global Distribution of Poverty and Wealth
 1. Past trends and current patterns
 2. Contrast with world order premises
 3. Implications for peace and war
*Brandt Commission, *North-South.*
*Falk, Richard et al., *The Strategy of a Just World Order*, esp. Part I.
*Haq, Mabub ul, *The Poverty Curtain: Choices for the Third World.*
Morris, M., *Measuring the Condition of the World's Poor: The Physical Quality of Life Index.*
Scientific America, special issue, September 1980.
Smith, C., "What We Got for What We Gave: The American Experience with Foreign Aid" in *American Heritage*, April-May 1978.
Unesco Courier, November 1979 and March 1977.
*World Bank, *World Development Report*, 1980.

B. Theories of Poverty and Impoverishment
 1. The spread of development as a powerful ideology
 2. Capitalist theories: factors of production, distribution
 3. Socialist theories: dependency, world system

Hopkins, N., "Modern Agriculture and Political Centralization: A Case from Tunisia" in *Human Organization*, No. 1, 1978.

*Nash, June, "The World System" in *Annual Review of Anthropology*, 1981.

Powelson, John, "Why are the Poor so Poor in Less Developed Countries?" in *Human Organization*, No. 1, 1975.

Wallerstein, I., *The Modern World System*, 2 vols. NY: Academic Press, 1974.

*Weaver, James and Kenneth Jameson, *Economic Development: Competing Paradigms, Competing Parables.*

Wolf, Eric, "Types of Latin American Peasantry: A Preliminary Discussion" in Yehudi Cohen, *Man in Adaptation: The Cultural Present.*

C. The Process and Structure of World Poverty and Wealth

1. Dimensions of Asymmetrical Global Interdependence:

   Physical: biosphere; energy flows; entropy; pollution; desertification; resource distribution; depletion and conflicts.

   Material: technological and economic growth; depletion of nonrenewable resources; patterns of world trade and debt.

   Military: magnitude of armaments escalation and nuclear threat; resulting distribution of debts.

   Information: organization of information flows; distribution of knowledge and R&D as resources.

   Demographic: trends in population growth; global distribution of these trends.

   Political: national and multi-national centers of power; asymmetrical participation.

   Socio-cultural: social hierarchies and provincial social identities; real tribal identities vs. abstract human solidarity; socially unequal access to resources; power; influence and prestige; marginalization of peoples; from global to local levels.

Adams, R.N, *Energy and Structure: A Theory of Social Power.*

*Barnet, Richard, "The World's Resources . . . I-The Lean Years; II-Minerals, Food and Water; III-Human Energy" in *The New Yorker*, March 17, March 31, and April 7, 1980.

Bozeman, Adda, *The Future of Law in a Multi-Cultural World.*

*Davis, Shelton and Robert Mathews, *The Geological Imperative: Anthropology and Development in the Amazon Basin of South America.*

Dirks, R., "Social Responses During Severe Food Shortages and Famine" in *Current Anthropology*, No. 1, 1980.

Dobyns, Henry et al., *Peasants, Power and Applied Social Change: Vicos as a Model.*

Eckholm, Eric, *Losing Ground.*

Epstein, Scarlett, "Productive Efficiency and Customary Systems of Rewards in Rural South India" in Daniel Bates and Susan Lees, *Contemporary Anthropology: An Anthology*, 80/81.

Frank, R. "Miracle Seeds and Shattered Dreams in Java" in *Annual Editions in Anthropology*, 80/81.

*Geertz, Clifford, "Two Types of Ecosystems" in his *Agricultural Involution.*

Gross, Daniel, "The Great Sisal Scheme" in Daniel Bates and Susan Lees, *Contemporary Anthropology: An Anthology.*

Anderson, E.N., "The Life and Culture of Ecotopia" in Del Hymes, *Reinventing Anthropology*.

Haney, E.B. and W.C., "Social and Ecological Consequences of Community Development and Rural Modernization in a Columbian Peasant Community" in *Human Organization*.

Lappé, Frances and Joseph Collins, "Why Can't People Feed Themselves?" in *Annual Editions in Anthropology* 80/81.

Mendonsa, Eugene, "The Failure of Modern Farming in Sisala-land, Northern Ghana, 1967-1977" in *Human Organization*, No. 3, 1980.

Unesco Courier, special issue on the arms race, April 1979.

Willings, John, "Cross Cultural Communication: Possibility or Pipedream?" in *Unesco Courier*, April 1977.

II. Development Theories and Policies (October)

A. Capitalist
Economic growth.

B. Socialist
Political economy approach; revolution and redistribution; new international economic order.

C. Recent Syntheses
Growth with equity; employment generation; basic human needs; integrated rural development; participatory development; diffusing innovation vs. improving indigenous systems; delivering services vs. enabling people to improve their own.

Baker, Randall, "Development and the Pastoral People of Karamoja, North-Eastern Uganda: An Example of the Treatment of Symptoms" in *Contemporary Anthropology: An Anthology*, D. Bates and S. Lees (eds).

*Berger, Peter, *Pyramids of Sacrifice: Political Ethics and Social Change*.

*Galtung, J., *The North-South Debate: Technology, Basic Human Needs and the New International Economic Order*, NY: World Policy Institute, 1980.

*Goulet, Denis, "On the Ethics of Development Planning," Overseas Development Council.

Grant, James, "Meeting Basic Human Needs," Overseas Development Council.

Hagen, Everett, *On The Theory of Social Change: How Economic Growth Begins*.

Munoz, *Beyond Dependency*.

Owens, Edgar and Robert Shaw, *Development Reconsidered: Bridging the Gap Between Government and People*.

*Streeton, Paul (ed), *First Things First*.

Weaver, James and Kenneth Jameson, *Economic Development: Competing Paradigms, Competing Parables*.

D. Sociocultural Dimensions of Development
Development as a process of interrelated shifts among interacting systems in the natural and human environments, in which sociocultural dimensions are also interacting.

*Adams, R.N. "Harnessing Technological Development" in J. Poggie and R. Lynch (eds). *Rethinking Modernization: Anthropological Perspectives*.

*Bartlett, Peggy, "Adaptive Strategies in Peasant Agricultural Production" in *Annual Review of Anthropology*, 1980.

*Brokensha, David et al. (eds), *Indigenous Knowledge Systems and Development*.

Cochrane, Glynn, *What We Can Do For Each Other: An Interdisciplinary Approach to Development Anthropology*.

Foster, George, *Traditional Societies and Technological Change*, 1973.

Gillette, Cynthia, "Maize Production in a Traditional African Society: Economic Rationality Revisited" in *Human Organization*, #2, 1980.

*Goulet, Denis, *The Uncertain Promise: Value Conflicts in Technology Transfer*.

*Hardin, Garrett and John Baden (eds), *Managing the Commons*.

Holmberg, Allan, "The Research and Development Approach to the Study of Change" in T. Weaver (ed), *To See Ourselves: Anthropology and Modern Social Issues*.

Houston, Perdita, *Third World Women Speak Out*.

Lansing, Stephen, "Economic Growth and 'Traditional Society': A Cautionary Tale from Bali" in *Human Organization*, #4, 1978.

Mesthene, E., *Technological Change: Its Impact on Man and Society*.

Nash, Manning (ed), *Essays on Economic Development and Cultural Change in Honor of Bert E. Hoselitz*.

Okpala, Donatus, "Towards a Better Conceptionalization of Rural Development: Empirical Findings from Nigeria" in *Human Organization*, #2, 1980.

*Peattie, Lisa, *Thinking About Development*.

III. Development Practice (November)

A. "Unplanned" Process of Growth and Development

Boserup, E., *The Conditions of Agricultural Growth: The Economics of Agrarian Change Under Population Pressure*.

Graves, Nancy and Theodore, "The Impact of Modernization on the Personality of a Polynesian People; or, How to Make an Uptight, Rivalrous Westerner out of an Easygoing, Generous Pacific Islander" in *Human Organization* #2, 1978.

Nag, Moni, "How Modernization can also Increase Fertility" in *Current Anthropology*, #5, 1980.

Sharp, Lauriston, "Steel Axes for Stone-Age Australians" in *Human Organization* #1, 1952, and in Y. Cohen (ed), *Man in Adaptation: The Cultural Present*.

Turnbull, Colin, "The Mountain People," in *Readings in Anthropology 80/81*.

B. Programs and Projects

*Agency for International Development, *Implementation of "New Directions" in Development Assistance* . . . (esp. the first section).

*Baum, "The project cycle," World Bank, reprint.

Lele, Uma, *The Design of Rural Development Programs: Lessons from Africa*.

*McNamara, Robert, "Address to the Board of Governors," Nairobi, 1973, World Bank.

C. The Project Process

A series of (not always separate) phases: identification, analysis, preparation or design, appraisal, funding agreement, implementation, monitoring and evaluation; sociocultural aspects of the project process; project soundness or feasibility.

Alexander, Paul, "Innovation in a Cultural Vacuum: the Mechanization of Sri Lanka Fisheries" in *Human Organization*, #4, 1975.

Almy, Susan, "Anthropologists and the Development Agencies" in *American Anthropologist*, June 1977.

Climo, Jacob, "Capitalism and Unemployment on a Collective Farming (Ejido) Development Project in Southern Yucatan, Mexico" in *Human Organization* #4, 1979.

DeWalt, Bilie, "Alternative Adaptive Strategies in a Mexican Ejido: A New Perspective on Modernization and Development" in *Human Organization*, #2, 1979.

Ingersoll Jasper, Mark Sullivan and Barbara Lenkerd, *Social Analysis of Aid Projects: Review of the Experience.*

Oliver-Smith, Anthony, "Disaster Rehabilitation and Social Change in Yungay, Peru" in *Human Organization*, Spring 1977.

Swetnam, John, "Disguised Employment and Development Policy in Peasant Economies" in *Human Organization*, #1, 1980.

Thompson, Laura, "An Appropriate Role for Post Colonial Applied Anthropologists" in *Human Organization*, #2, 1976.

Trimble, Joseph, "Forced Migration: Its Impact on Shaping Coping Strategies" in George Coelho and Paul Ahmed (eds), *Uprooting and Development: Dilemmas of Coping With Modernization.*

Whyte, Wm. F. and Allan Holmberg, "Human Problems of U.S. Enterprise in Latin America" in T. Weaver (ed), *To See Ourselves: Anthropology and Modern Social Issues.*

IV. Process of Poverty and Development: Problems, Promises, Prospects (December)

A. Global Interdependence and Human Solidarity

Review of trends and patterns in relation to principles of world order.

B. The Global Village

Belshaw, Cyrus, *The Sorceror's Apprentice.*

Bohannan, Paul, "Beyond Civilization: On the Past, Present and Future of Man" in *Anthropology: Contemporary Perspectives*, David Hunter and Phillip Whitten (eds).

Clarke, Wm. C., "The Structure of Permanence: The Relevance of Self-Subsistence Communities for World Ecosystem Management" in D. Bates and S. Lees (eds), *Contemporary Anthropology: An Anthology.*

*Council on Environmental Quality, *The Global 2000 Report to the President: Entering the Twenty-First Century.*

Downing, Theodore, "Ecodevelopment: An Alternative Future?" in *Human Organization*, #2, 1978.

*Goulet, Denis, *Global Interdependence: Smokescreen or Hope?*

Huxley, Julian, "A Philosophy for Unesco" in *Unesco Courier*, March, 1976.

M'Bow, Amadou-Mahtar, "UNESCO and the World Outlook Tomorrow," *Unesco Courier*, March 1976.

Mische, Patricia, *Women, Power and Alternative Futures.*

*Morehouse, Ward, *Separate, Unequal but More Autonomous*, 1982.

Pirages, Dennis (ed), *The Sustainable Society: Implications for Limited Growth.*

Economic and Social Development

James Lobenstine   *Fall/Winter 1983*
School for International Training/Brattleboro, VT 05301

Although the Reagan administration has moved the Cold War back to center stage, barring a nuclear holocaust the issues which will dominate the next quarter century are those surrounding how the world will cope with a population 50% larger than today's, with an increasing number of "absolute poor." Although the search for a new paradigm is increasing, no country has yet found an alternative to continued growth as the only way to provide for its people. The primary goal of this course is to try to find out why. Individual research on the strategies of different developing countries will develop research, writing and oral presentation skills. Visits in the Brattleboro economic area will develop field research and interviewing skills, economic and sociological analysis, and communication skills.

Building on the type of experience you had on the drop-off, and on the concepts and techniques learned in the Community Development course, we will continue the study of development by seeking a much more in-depth understanding of one small economic system. Each student will visit a few farms, factories, wholesale distributors, retail stores, educational and health establishments, government offices, or private voluntary organizations seeking to meet some of the Brattleboro area's perceived problems. This will be done during the Practicum/Evaluation period. This course will begin with a systematic economic, political and social analysis of the area, based on your findings.

Next we will look at the concepts of "underdevelopment" and "development," review a variety of development theories, and examine the limits of growth—all in terms accessible to the non-economist. We will then examine the question of whether "development" can be measured—as economists and governments are wont to do—and if so, how. Following up on the International Economics session on trade and international investment, we will study the degree to which these can assist development, as well as the different theories and strategies of "foreign aid." Finally, we will examine the "South's" demands for systemic change, and examine some of the efforts to articulate a new development paradigm.

In order to make these theories more concrete, each student will research the development strategy of a developing country, prepare a paper describing and analyzing that strategy, and give a brief oral report to the class summarizing it. We will then seek to draw some conclusions from these different experiences.

Research Paper and Report
Each student is to research the development strategy (or strategies—some countries have followed several different strategies at different times) of one developing country. The purpose is to understand different development strategies—not to prepare an exhaustive economic history or other kind of descriptive report. For the purposes of this study, a few articles in recent journals will often be of more help than several books.

Obviously, you will need to know a good deal about the country, and in particular its economic, social and political structures before you can begin to understand its development strategy (often a good place to start is the *Encyclopedia of the Third World*).

Course Syllabus and Schedule

November 29 Introduction to Economic and Social Development Course
Case Study: Brattleboro Area: Reports

December 2 Case Study: Brattleboro Area: Analysis and Conclusions

December 6, 7 What is "underdevelopment"?
Read:
Galbraith, John Kenneth, "The Causes of Poverty," ch. II in *Economic Development*, 1964.
Harrington, Michael, " 'The Development of Underdevelopment'—Why Poor Nations Stay Poor," *Christianity and Crisis*, Oct. 3, 1977, pp. 211-220.
Gutierrez, Gustavo, "Liberation and Development," ch. 2 in *A Theology of Liberation*, 1973.
Goulet, Denis, "The Shock of Underdevelopment," ch. 1 in *The Cruel Choice: A New Concept in the Theory of Development*, 1975.
Suggested additional reading:
Goulet, Denis, "Introduction" to *ibid.*
Due at beginning of seminar sections: personal goal statement.
Due in conference with me this week: choice of country and initial bibliography for research paper and report.

December 9, 10 What is "development"?
Read:
Gurley, John G., "Capitalist and Maoist Economic Development," in *America's Asia: Dissenting Essays on Asian-American Relations*, 1971, pp. 324-339 only.
Weaver, James H, and Jameson, Kenneth P., *Economic Development: Competing Paradigms—Competing Parables*, 1978.
"Dimensions of Development," ch. 2 in *North-South*.
Due this week: outline of research paper.

December 13, 14 What is a "development strategy"?
Read:
Owens, Edgar and Shaw, Robert, "Development Reconsidered," ch. 1 in *Development Reconsidered: Bridging the Gap Between Government and People*, 1974.

Hughes, Helen, "Private Enterprise and Development—Comparative Country Experience," in *Economic Development and the Private Sector, Articles Prepared for Finance and Development*, Sept. 1981, pp. 36-39.
Continue discussion of Weaver and Jameson.
Due this week (sign up for appointment): outline of research paper.

December 16 Are there limits to "development" or "growth"?
Review: Ophuls, William, *Ecology and the Politics of Scarcity*, 1977.
Read (or review if read for Environmental Studies): Daly, Herman, "Toward a Stationary-State Economy," ch. 14 in John Harte and Robert H. Socolow, eds., *The Patient Earth*, 1971.
What are the costs of development? How will these be affected by "the politics of scarcity"?
Read:
Hewlett, Sylvia Ann, "Tragic Trade-Offs," ch. 1, and "Historical Perspectives," ch. 2 in *The Cruel Dilemmas of Development: Twentieth-Century Brazil*, 1980.

January 3, 4 How should "development" be measured? Can it be?
Read:
ODC Staff, "Statistical Note," "Glossary," and Table "B-4. Economic and Social Indicators of Development," *U.S. Foreign Policy and the Third World: Agenda 1982*, 1982.

January 6 Can development be assisted from the outside? a) Trade?
Review:
"Commodity Trade and Development," ch. 9, and "Industrialization and World Trade," ch. 11 in *North-South*.
"Changing International Specialization and U.S. Imports of Manufactures," ch. 6 in *The Challenge of the New International Economic Order*.

January   10, 11 b) Private Investment; Technology Transfers; Transnational Corporations
Review:
Cohen, Robert and Jeffry Frieden, "The Impact of Multinational Corporations on Developing Nations," ch. 9 in *The Challenge of the New International Economic Order*.
Read:
Bell, Carl, "Promoting Private Investment: the Role of the International Finance Corporation," in *Economic Development and the Private Sector, Finance and Development*, Sept. 1981, pp. 6-9.
May, Stacy and Galo Plaza, "United Fruit's Contribution to National Development," ch. 11 in *Dialectics of Third World Development*, 1980.
Tobis, David, "United Fruit's Contribution to Underdevelopment," ch. 12 in *ibid.*

January 13 c) Aid theories and strategies
Read:
"Development Finance: Unmet Needs," ch. 14 in *North-South*.
Wiener, Mervyn L., "International Assistance Worked?" *Ms.*, July 20, 1982.
Review:
"A New Approach to Development Finance," ch. 15 in *North-South*.

Siegman, Charles J., "Developing Countries and the International Finance System," ch. 10 in *The Challenge of the New International Economic Order.*

Familiarize yourself with: Overseas Development Council Staff, Tables F-2, 3, 5, 6, 8, 9, 12, 16, 17, 20 in *U.S. Foreign Policy and the Third World: Agenda 1982,* 1982.

January 17, 18 d) Systemic change—the New International Economic Order
Review:
North-South, all sections previously read.
Reuben, Edwin P., ch. 1 and 13 of *CNIEO.*
Read:
Leipziger, Danny M., "The Basic Needs Approach and North-South Relations," ch. 12 in *CNIEO.*
United Nations General Assembly, "Resolutions on the NIEO," ch. 2 in *CNIEO.*

January 20, 21 Development strategies
Student reports on individual country strategies.

January 24 Analysis of development strategies

January 27 Are new development paradigms emerging?
Review:
Brandt, Willy, "A Plan for Change: Peace, Justice, Jobs—an Introduction" to *North South.*
Daly, Herman E., "Toward a Stationary-State Society," ch. 14 in *The Patient Earth.*
Read:
Ward, Barbara, " 'Where There is no Vision, the People Perish,' " *International Development Review* 1980/4.

January 31 Conclusions and Evaluation

Senior Seminar: Political Economy

Manning Marable   *Spring 1983*
Management 498/Race Relations Institute/Fisk University/
Nashville, TN 37203

Political economy involves the study of the relationship between the states (the agencies of civil and political order, the government, political organizations, etc.) and the means of production, ownership and distribution (economics). The class will explore some of the more important paradigms of modern political economy: Marxism (Karl Marx); neoclassical economics (Milton Friedman, Thomas Sowell); Keynesian economics (John Maynard Keynes, John Kenneth Galbraith); modern orthodox Marxists (Ernest Mandel, Paul Sweezy); underdevelopment economic theory (Walter Rodney, André Gunder Frank); and the New Left "Radicals" (William Tabb, Samuel Bowles, David Gordon).

Required Texts

1) Milton Friedman, *Capitalism and Freedom* (Chicago: University of Chicago Press, 1962).
2) Pierre Jalée, *How Capitalism Works*, (New York: Monthly Review Press, 1977).
3) Union for Radical Political Economics, eds., (David M. Gordon, William Tabb, et al.), *U.S. Capitalism in Crisis* (New York: Union for Radical Political Economics, 1978).
4) Ernest Mandel, *An Introduction to Marxist Economic Theory* (New York: Pathfinder Press, 1970).
5) Manning Marable, *How Capitalism Underdeveloped Black America* (Boston: South End Press, 1983).

Other texts which will be used and will be available on library reserve include: Paul Sweezy, *Modern Capitalism* (New York: Monthly Review Press, 1972); Michael Harrington, *Socialism* (New York: Bantam, 1972); M.C. Howard and J.E. King, eds., *The Economics of Marx* (New York: Penguin, 1976); John Kenneth Galbraith, *Economics and the Public Purpose* (New York: Houghton-Mifflin, 1973); Walter Rodney, *How Europe Underdeveloped Africa* (London: Bogle-L' Ouverture, 1972); Thomas Sowell, *Markets and Minorities* (New York: Basic Books, 1981); Robert Lekachman, *The Age of Keynes* (New York: McGraw-Hill, 1966).

Section I What is Political Economy?

Week I Introduction: Theoretical Problems Discussed in the Seminar
Readings:
1) Paul Sweezy, *Modern Capitalism*, "Modern Capitalism," pp. 3-14.

Week II The Origins of Capitalism
Readings:
1) Pierre Jalée, *How Capitalism Works*, pp. 7-48.
2) Ernest Mandel, *An Introduction to Marxist Economic Theory*, pp. 7-28.

Week III Capitalism: Class Development and the Process of Accumulation
Readings:
1) Ernest Mandel, *An Introduction to Marxist Economic Theory*, pp. 29-53.
2) Pierre Jalée, *How Capitalism Works*, pp. 49-80.

Week IV Capitalism and the State
Readings:
1) Ernest Mandel, *An Introduction to Marxist Economic Theory*, pp. 54-78.
2) Pierre Jalée, *How Capitalism Works*, pp. 81-122.

Section II Modern Theories of Political Economy

Week V Marx
Readings:
1) Michael Harrington, *Socialism*, Chapter 4, "The Unknown Karl Marx," pp. 65-90; Chapter 5, "Das Kapital," pp. 91-129.
2) David McLellan, *Karl Marx*, "Capital," pp. 334-359.
3) Howard and King, eds., *The Economics of Marx*, "Theoretical Underpinnings," pp. 77-113.

Week VI Marx vs. Neoclassical Economists
Readings:
1) Milton Friedman, *Capitalism and Freedom*, "Economic Freedom and Political Freedom;" "Government in a Free Society;" "The Control of Money;" "The Role of Government in Education;" pp. 7-55; 85-107.
2) Thomas Sowell, *Markets and Minorities*, "The Economics of Discrimination," pp. 19-35.

Week VII The Neoclassical Tradition
Readings:
1) John Kenneth Galbraith, *Economics and the Public Purpose*, pp. 11-18.
2) Milton Friedman, *Capitalism and Freedom*, "Capitalism and Discrimination;" "The Distribution of Income;" "Social Welfare Measures;" "Alleviation of Poverty;" pp. 108-118; 161-195.
3) Thomas Sowell, *Markets and Minorities*, "The Economics of Slavery;" "Government and Minorities;" pp. 83-124.

Week VIII Keynes and the General Theory
Readings:
1) John Kenneth Galbraith, *Economics and the Public Purpose*, pp. 19-28; 207-241.
2) Robert Lekachman, *The Ages of Keynes*, "Preface;" "The General Theory;" "The New Deal;" pp. iii-x; 78-143.

Week IX Neokeynesians: Galbraith
Readings:
1) John Kenneth Galbraith, *Economics and the Public Purpose*, pp. 3-10; 242-313.

2) Paul Sweezy, *Modern Capitalism*, "Keynesian Economics," pp. 79-91.
3) Robert Lekachman, *The Age of Keynes*, "Inflation: Classic and Modern," pp. 246-265.

Week X Orthodox Marxists
Readings:
1) Paul Sweezy, *Modern Capitalism*, "Theory of Monopoly Capitalism;" "Toward a Critique of Economics;" "Theories of the New Capitalism;" "Thoughts on the American System;" pp. 25-78, 110-123.
2) Harry Magdoff and Paul Sweezy, *The End of Prosperity*, "Keynesian Chickens Come Home to Roost;" "Banks: Skating on Thin Ice;" "Keynesianism: Illusions and Delusions;" pp. 21-54; 125-136.

Week XI Underdevelopment Theory: Focus on Africa
Readings:
1) Walter Rodney, *How Europe Underdeveloped Africa*, "Some Questions on Development;" "Colonialism as a System for Underdeveloping Africa;" pp. 9-39; 223-261.
2) André Gunder Frank, *Reflections on the World Economic Crisis*, "World Crisis and Underdevelopment;" "Imperialism, Crisis and Superexploitation in the Third World;" pp. 39-65.

Week XII Underdevelopment Theory: Focus on Black America
Readings:
1) Manning Marable, *How Capitalism Underdeveloped Black America*, Introduction, Chapters 2, 4 and 8.

Section III Contemporary Problems in the U.S. Political Economy

Week XIII The Crisis of Workers
Readings:
1) Manning Marable, *How Capitalism Underdeveloped Black America*, Chapters 1 and 3.
2) Harry Magdoff and Paul M. Sweezy, *The End of Prosperity*, "Capitalism and Unemployment," pp. 77-90.
3) URPE, ed., *U.S. Capitalism in Crisis*, pp. 55-110.

Week XIV Capital Flight: Sectors in Crisis
Readings:
1) URPE, ed., *U.S. Capitalism in Crisis*, pp. 122-143; 174-204.
2) Manning Marable, *How Capitalism Underdeveloped Black America*, Chapter 5.

Week XV The Possibilities For Change
Readings:
1) URPE, eds., *U.S. Capitalism in Crisis*, pp. 331-342.
2) Manning Marable, *How Capitalism Underdeveloped Black America*, Section III, "The Question of Genocide," Chapters 9 and 10.
3) Pierre Jalée, *How Capitalism Works*, pp. 123-126.

Note: Other required readings may be assigned during the course. The outline above includes over 90 percent of all anticipated sources which will be assigned.

Political Economy of the Third World

Gloria Young Sing

Spring 1983

Politics and Economics 400-1/State University of New York/
Old Westbury/Long Island, NY 11568

This course undertakes an interdisciplinary social science analysis of the problems of the "Third World"—the "underdeveloped" nations of Asia, Africa, and Latin America. Central to the course will be an investigation of "Third World" poverty in its economic, social, and political dimensions— the role of colonialism, and of the internal structures and institutions which evolved under it in perpetuating conditions of dependence and "underdevelopment." Alternative theories (orthodox and radical) that attempt to explain the causes of "Third World underdevelopment" will be examined as the analysis is brought up to date to address the present reality of international inequality and the demand of the "Third World" for a new international economic order. Finally, one Latin American and one African case study will be used to add specificity to the general analysis, to assess, at the level of an individual country, "Third World" strategies of development and the internal and external constraints to its realization.

Discussion topics

1. The "Third World", what is it? The origin and shortcomings of the term; the concepts of "underdevelopment", "unequal exchange", "center/periphery" relations etc.; accepted indices of development and their limitations.
2. Historical overview of the development of the international economy from mercantilism, through industrial capitalism to imperialism.
3. The contemporary world economy: the role and function assigned to the "Third World;" critique of existing international economic arrangements and institutions; the "Third World's" proposal for a new international economic order; present crisis in the world economy, and growing "Third World" debt; "aid" and imperialism.
4. Poverty, political protest, and repression in Latin America; U.S. policy vis-a-vis authoritarian regimes; the growing activist role of the Catholic Church in Latin America.
5. *Case Study 1:* The Brazilian model of development: the evolution from classic dependence to dependent development; the relationships among multi-national corporations, local capitalists and state-owned enterprises in Brazil since the military coup of 1964.
6. *Case Study 2:* Ghana: the failure of conventional development strategies which emphasize continued dependence on imported capital and continued specialization on the production of raw materials for external markets; Ghana's desperate and unsuccessful adoption of so-called "socialist" planning to correct the failure, culminating in its first military coup.

Required Texts
1. Anell, L. and Nygren, B., *The Developing Countries and the World Economic Order*, Methuen
2. Lernoux, Penny, *Cry of the People*, Penguin
3. Evans, Peter, *Dependent Development—The Alliance of Multi-National, State and Local Capital in Brazil*, Princeton University Press
4. Fitch, Bob, and Oppenheimer, Mary, *Ghana: End of an Illusion*, Monthly Review

Research Assignment
A short research paper of 10-15 pages on any one of the following:
1. Though there is ample evidence to show that the present international order creates numerous external constraints to Third World development, in the final analysis the internal constraints emanating from the socio-political structures of these countries may be far more critical in the development process. Evaluate the above with reference to any one specific country in Africa, Asia, or Latin America.
2. "The abyss that exists in Latin America between the well-being of the few and the misery of the many is infinitely greater than in Europe or the United States. Hence the methods necessary to maintain it are much more ruthless." (Galeano). Examine the economic basis of repression in any one Latin American country.
3. "The IMF operates consciously to block certain development options and paths a Third World country may wish to pursue, while pressuring these countries to adopt other strategies of a more traditional kind. It plays this role on behalf of the international banking system, the transnational corporations, and the major industrial capitalist countries." (Girvan and Bernal). Critically assess this statement.
4. "One of the most serious indictments of the World Bank, and the developed capitalist governments which support and control it, is that it consistently uses its considerable financial resources to block the forces of progressive change." (Payer). Evaluate.
5. Conventional wisdom in metropolitan countries holds that the transnational (or global, or multinational) corporation is a vehicle for transferring needed capital and technology to the Third World and therefore is an important contributor to Third World development. Third World critics, on the other hand, see the transnational corporation as a contributor to continued underdevelopment. Discuss.
6. Critically evaluate the experience of either Chile or Tanzania in attempting a socialist approach to the resolution of the problems of underdevelopment.

Selected References
1. Amin, S., *Imperialism and Unequal Development*, Monthly Review, 1977
2. Barnet, R., and Muller, R., *Global Reach*, Simon & Schuster, 1974
3. Emmanuel, A., *Unequal Exchange*, Monthly Review, 1972
4. Fanon, F., *The Wretched of the Earth*, Grove Press, 1968
5. Frank, A.G., *Lumpenbourgeoisie; Lumpendevelopment*, Monthly Review, 1972
6. Galeano, E., *Open Veins of Latin America*, Monthly Review, 1973
7. Hayter, T., *Aid as Imperialism*, Penguin, 1971
8. Jalée, P., *Imperialism in the Seventies*, Third Press, 1972

9. Lenin, V.I., *Imperialism: the Highest Stage of Capitalism*, International Publishers, 1972
10. Nkrumah, K., *Class Struggle in Africa*, International Publishers, 1970
11. Payer, C., *The Debt Trap: the IMF and the Third World*, Monthly Review, 1975
12. Petras, J., and Morley, M., *The U.S. and Chile: Imperialism and the Overthrow of the Allende Government*, Monthly Review, 1975
13. Rodney, W., *How Europe Underdeveloped Africa*, Bogle l'Ouverture, 1972
14. Sweezy, P., and Magdoff, H. (eds.), *Revolution and Counter-Revolution in Chile*, Monthly Review, 1974
15. Wachtel, H., *The New Gnomes: Multinational Banks in the Third World*, Transnational Institute, 1977
16. Worsley, P., *The Third World*, U. of Chicago Press, 1970

Natural Resources in the World Economy: Control and Conflict

Jerald Barnald   *Fall 1982*
Industrial Relations and Human Resources/University of Iowa/
Iowa City, IA 52242

The objectives of the course are to examine the economic issues connected with the "new scarcity" in natural resources (primary commodities) in the world economy and the application of the tools of economic analysis to the problems of market control, implications for economic growth and development, and potential conflict among nations. The course will seek to provide a synthesis of economic theory and examine the political economy of the current issues of natural resource development and current and future trade relations in the world economy, especially between the so-called developed and less-developed countries. It will bring students to an understanding of the role of prices in resource use and discovery, or market coalitions and strategies, of the role of technological advance, and probable market strategies and protection measures. Finally, the course will examine conflict situations among nations, the impact of cost of adjustments in consumption versus the cost of conflict, and economic policies that may influence world peace.

Reading Materials and Assignments

Textbook: Howe, Charles W., *Natural Resource Economics*, John Wiley & Sons, Inc., New York, 1979
Reading assignments marked with an * are assigned. Other materials included under the same topic heading are for further reading. Full citations for each work can be found in the bibliography.

Course Outline and Reading Assignments

1. Introduction
1.1 Survey of issues connected with natural resources in the world economy
1.2 Rapid depletion of scarce resources and intensifying competition among countries to protect access to external supplies
1.3 Commodities involved, trade relationships, and country response
*Bergsten, "The New Era in World Commodity Markets," *Challenge*
Resources, "An Abundance of Shortages"
*Brubaker, *In Command of Tomorrow*, Preface and Chapter 1 (pp. ix-22)
*Bhagwati, "Economics and World Order from the 1970's to 1990's: The Key Issues," in *Economics and World Order*

*Meadows, et al., *The Limits of Growth*
*Gordon, L., "Limits of Growth Debate," *Resources*, Summer 1976
*Leontief, et al., *The Future of the World Economy*, pp. 1-11

2. Relevant Theory
2.1 Overview
*Howe, *Natural Resource Economics*, Chapters 1, 2, 3
2.2 Economic theory of natural resources exploitation and conservation stock and
    flow resources, resources in economic growth, and optimal use over time
*Howe, *Natural Resource Economics*, Chapters 4, 5, 8, 11, 13
Heady, Chapter on "Intertemporal Production Relationships in Conservation," pp.
    768-781, *Economics of Agricultural Production and Resource Use*
*Howe, *Natural Resource Economics*, Chapter 12
Dorfman, "The Technical Basis for Decision Making," *The Governance of Com-
mon Property Resources*
2.3 Oligopoly
*Mansfield, Chapter 11, "Price and Output Under Oligopoly," *Microeconomics*

3. Supply and Demand in the World Economy
3.1 Supply and demand of primary commodities
*Howe, *Natural Resource Economics*, Chapters 6, 9, 10
*Leith, Furness, and Lewis, *World Minerals and World Peace*, pp. 8-101
*Schanz, J.J., "Mineral Economics—Perspective of the Past, Present and Future,"
    Resources for the Future, Reprint 138
*University of California Food Task Force, *A Hungry World: The Challenge to
    Agriculture*
*Leontief, et al., *The Future of the World Economy*, pp. 13-64
*Breimeyer, Harold F., "Outlook for Food Supply," *Challenge*, Vol. 24, (3)
3.2 Control and conflict: Types of markets, market coalitions and alternative
    market strategies
*Mikesell, "More Third World Cartels Ahead," *Challenge*
*Bergsten, "The New Era in World Commodity Markets," *Challenge*
*Perlo, "Behind the U.S.-OPEC Conflict," *Challenge*, Sept./Oct. 1975
*Bergsten, "A New OPEC in Bauxite," *Challenge*
McDivitt and Manners, *Minerals and Men*
3.3 Role of technological advancement and resource discovery
*Howe, *Natural Resource Economics*, Chapter 7
*Chynoweth, "Materials Conservation—A Technologist's Viewpoint," *Challenge*
3.4 Primary commodities, inflation and growth prospects in the world economy
*Cooper and Lawrence, "The 1972-75 Commodity Boom," *Brookings Paper on
    Economic Activity*, 3:1975
*Chenery, "Restructuring the World Economy," *Foreign Affairs*
*Henry, J.P., et al., "World Energy: A Manageable Dilemma," *Harvard Business
    Review*, May/June 1979
*Rosenstein-Rodan, "The Have and the Have Nots Around the Year 2000," *Eco-
nomics and World Order*

4. Adjustments to Resource Scarcity
4.1 Conflict situations among nations

*Harrison, *China, Oil and Asia: Conflict Ahead*
*Nakhleh, *Arab-American Relations in the Persian Gulf*
*Levy, "World Oil Cooperation or International Chaos," *Foreign Affairs*
4.2 Cost of adjustment vs. cost of conflict
*Kagan, Sioma, "A New International Economic Order: What is the Price Tag?"
*Brubaker, *In Command of Tomorrow*, Chapters 4, 5, 7, 8
*Leith, Furness & Lewis, *World Minerals and World Peace*, pp. 185-206
*Committee for Economic Development, *International Economic Consequence of High Priced Energy*
*Gordon, Lincoln, "Environment, Resources and Directions of Growth," *World Development*, Vol. 3, pp. 131-121, Feb./Mar. 1975
*Mason, "Natural Resources and Environmental Restrictions to Growth," *Challenge*, Jan./Feb. 1978
4.3 Responsible natural resources policy and the world economy
*Howe, *Natural Resource Economics*, Chapter 16
*Joskow, Paul L., "America's Many Energy Futures—A Review of Energy Future; Energy, The Next Twenty Years; and Energy in America's Future," *The Bell Journal of Economics*, Vol. 12, 1981, pp. 377-398
Tinbergen, et al., *RIO—Reshaping the International Order*

Bibliography

Books

Bhagwati, Jagdish N., *Economics and World Order: From the 1970's to the 1990's*, The Free Press, New York, 1972

Brubaker, Sterling, *In Command of Tomorrow: Resource and Environmental Strategies for Americans*, Resources for the Future, Inc., Johns Hopkins University Press, Baltimore, MD, 1975

Committee for Economic Development, *International Consequences of High Priced Energy*, Committee for Economic Development, New York, 1975

Haefele, Edwin T., *The Governance of Common Property Resources*, Resources for the Future, Inc., The Johns Hopkins University Press, Baltimore, MD, 1974

Harrison, Selig S., *China, Oil and Asia: Conflict Ahead*, Columbia University Press, New York, 1977

Heady, Earl O., *Economics of Agricultural Production and Resource Use*, Prentice-Hall, Inc., Englewood Cliffs, N.J., 1952

Howe, Charles W., *Natural Resource Economics*, John Wiley & Sons, Inc., New York, 1979

Johnson, D. Gale, *World Food Problems and Prospects*, American Enterprise Institute for Public Policy Research, Washington, D.C., 1975

Landsberg, Hans, H., *Natural Resources for U.S. Growth: A Look Ahead to the Year 2000*, Resources for the Future, Inc., The Johns Hopkins University Press, Baltimore, MD, 1964

Leith, C.K., J.W. Furness, C. Lewis, *World Minerals and World Peace*, The Brookings Institution, Washington, D.C., 1943

Leontief, W., A.P. Carter and P. Petri, *The Future of the World Economy*, Oxford University Press, New York, 1977

Mansfield, Chapter 11, "Price and Output Under Oligopoly," *Microeconomics*, 1970

McDivitt, James F. and G. Manners, *Minerals and Man*, Resources for the Future, Inc., The Johns Hopkins University Press, Baltimore, MD, 1965

Meadows, Donella, et al., *The Limits to Growth*, Universe Books, New York, 1972

Mitchell, Edward J., *Dialogue on World Oil*, American Enterprise Institute for Public Policy Research, Washington, D.C., 1974

Nakhleh, Emile A., *Arab-American Relations in the Persian Gulf*, American Enterprise Institute for Public Policy Research, Washington, D.C., 1975

Tinbergen, Jan, et al.,*RIO—Reshaping the International Order: A Report to the Club of Rome*, E.P. Dutton & Co., Inc., New York, 1976

University of California Food Task Force, *A Hungry World: The Challenge to Agriculture*, Division of Agricultural Sciences, University of California, Berkeley, CA, 1974

Journal Papers and Articles

Adelman, H.A., "Oil Import Quota Auctions," *Challenge*, Vol. 18, No. 4, pp. 17-22, Jan./Feb., 1976

Bergsten, C. Fred, "The New Era in World Commodity Markets," *Challenge*, Vol. 17, No. 4, pp. 34-42, Sept./Oct., 1974

Bergsten, C. Fred, "A New OPEC in Bauxite," *Challenge*, Mar./Apr., 1977

Brown, Lester R. and Erik F. Eckholm, "Food and Hunger: The Balance Sheet," *Challenge*, Vol. 17, No. 4, pp. 12-24, Sept./Oct., 1974

Breimeyer, Harold F., "Outlook for Food Supply," *Challenge*, Vol. 24 (3), July/Aug., 1981

Carter, H.O., "World & U.S. Food Trends . . .," *AEI Studies . . .*

Chenery, H.B., "Restructuring the World Economy," *Foreign Affairs*, Vol. 53, pp. 242-63, Jan., 1975

Chynoweth, A.G., "Materials Conservation—A Technologist's Viewpoint," *Challenge*, Vol. 18, No. 6, pp. 34-42, Jan./Feb., 1976

Cooper, Richard N. and Robert Z. Lawrence, "The 1972-75 Commodity Boom," *Brookings Papers on Economic Activity*, Vol. 3, pp. 671-715, 1975

Eckert, Ross D., "Exploitation of Deep Ocean Minerals: Regulatory Mechanisms and United States Policy," *Journal of Law and Economics*, Vol. 17, pp. 143-77, April, 1974

Gordon, L., "Limits to Growth Debate," *Resources*, Summer, 1976

Gordon, L., "Environmental Resources and Directions of Growth," *World Development*, Vol. 3, pp. 113-121, Feb./Mar., 1975

Heilbroner, R.L., "Second Thoughts on the Human Prospect," *Challenge*, Vol. 18, pp. 21-28, May/June, 1975

Henry, John P., V. Eugene Harless, and Jay B. Kopelman, "World Energy: A Manageable Dilemma," *Harvard Business Review*, Vol. 57, No. 3, May/June, 1979

Joskow, Paul L., "America's Many Energy Futures—A Review of Energy Future; Energy: The Next Twenty Years; and Energy in America's Future," *The Bell Journal of Economics*, Vol. 12, pp. 377-398, 1981

Kagan, Sioma, "A New International Economic Order: What is the Price Tag," *Business Economics*, Vol. 13, No. 2, March, 1978

Levy, W.J., "World Oil Cooperation or International Chaos," *Foreign Affairs*, Vol. 52, pp. 690-713, July, 1974

Third World Development

Girma Kebbede   *Fall 1982*
Geography and Geology/Mount Holyoke College/South Hadley, MA 01075

This course involves an examination of major issues related to Third World development problems. It includes such issues as growth, development, and underdevelopment, physical environment and economic development, population, food crises, multinational corporations, and the New International Economic Order. Students will be required to (1) complete required readings, (2) actively participate in class discussions, (3) complete a number of assignments including literature reviews, and (4) complete a term paper on some aspect of Third World development problems. The term paper topic should be selected and approved by the instructor.

Course Outline

Week 1 Introductory Discussion. The Third World: Similarity and Diversity
Readings:
Vogeler, Ingolf and de Souza, Anthony R. (eds.) *Dialectics of Third World Development*. Montclair, NJ: Allanheld, Osmun, 1980, pp. 1-52.
Todaro, Michael P. *Economic Development in the Third World*. NY: Longman, 1981, pp. 23-45.

Weeks 2-4 Growth, Development, and Underdevelopment: Theoretical Issues
Readings:
deSouza, Anthony and Porter, Philip W. *The Underdevelopment and Modernization of the Third World*. AAG Resource Paper No. 28, 1974, pp. 1-23 and 25-52.
Baran, Paul. "On the Political Economy of Backwardness," in Wilber, (ed.) *The Political Economy of Development and Underdevelopment*. NY: Random House, 1979, 97-102.
Frank, Andre Gunder. "The Development of Underdevelopment," in Cockroft, James D., et al. (eds.) *Dependence and Underdevelopment: Latin America's Political Economy*. NY: Anchor Books, pp. 3-17.
"Sociology of Development and Underdevelopment Sociology," in Cockcroft, pp. 321-397.
Rostow, W.W. *The Stages of Economic Growth: A Non-Communist Manifesto*. NY: Cambridge University Press, 1971.
Amin, Samir. "Underdevelopment and Dependence in Black Africa: Origin and Contemporary Forms," in Abu-Lughod, Janef and Hay, Richard (eds.). *Third World Urbanization*. NY: Methuen, 1977, pp. 140-150.
Goulet, Denis. *The Cruel Choice: A New Concept in the Theory of Development*. Antheneum, 1971, especially pp. 23-108.
Todaro, pp. 67-76.

Recommended:

Rodney, Walter. *How Europe Underdeveloped Africa.* Washington, D.C.: Howard University Press, 1979.

Baran, Paul. *The Political Economy of Growth.* NY: Monthly Review Press, 1957.

Roxborough, Ian. *Theories of Underdevelopment.* Atlantic Highlands, NJ: Humanities Press, 1979.

Petras, James P. *Class, State and Power in the Third World.* Montclair, NJ: Allanheld, 1981.

Amin, Samir. *Neo-colonialism in West Africa.* NY: Monthly Review Press, 1973.

Week 5 Geographic Factors and Economic Development

Readings:

Kamarck, Andrew M. *The Tropics and Economic Development.* Baltimore, MD: The Johns Hopkins University Press, 1976, pp. 3-42; 53-80.

Huntington, Ellsworth. "Huntington's Climatic Theory of Underdevelopment," in Vogeler and de Souza, *Dialectics of Third World Development*, pp. 55-65.

Hodder, B.W. "A Liberal Critique of Environmental Determinism," in Vogeler and de Souza, *Dialectics of Third World Development*, pp. 66-69.

Szentes, Tamas. "The Political Economy of Resource Exploitation," in Vogeler and de Souza, *Dialectics of Third World Development*, pp. 70-76.

Ginsberg, Norton. "Natural Resources and Economic Development," *Annals of the Association of American Geographers*, 47 (September 1957), pp. 196-212.

Franke, Richard W. and Chasin, Barbara H. *Seeds of Famine: Ecological Destruction and the Development Dilemma in the West African Sahel.* Montclair, NJ: Allanheld, Osmun, 1978, pp. 1-38.

Pearson, Charles and Pryor, Anthony. *Environment: North and South: An Economic Interpretation.* NY: Wiley, 1978.

Weeks 6, 7 Population

Readings:

Hardin, Garrett. "Lifeboat Ethics: A Malthusian View," in Vogeler and de Souza, (eds.), *Dialectics of Third World Development*, pp. 171-185.

Commoner, Barry. "Poverty Breeds Overpopulation," in Vogeler and de Souza, pp. 186-195.

Harvey, David, "A Marxian Analysis of the Population-Resource Problem," in Vogeler and de Souza, pp. 202-227; also in *Economic Geography*, 50, (July 1974), 256-277.

Mamdani, Mohmood. *The Myth of Population Control: Family, Caste, and Class in an Indian Village.* NY: Monthly Review Press, 1972.

"The Ideology of Population Control" in Karen L. Michaelson (ed.) *And The Poor Get Children: Radical Perspectives on Population Dynamics.* NY: Monthly Review Press, 1981, pp. 39-49.

Michaelson, Karen L. "Introduction: Population Theory and the Political Economy of Population Processes," in Karen (ed.), pp. 11-35.

George, Susan. *How the Other Half Dies.* Montclair, NJ: Allanheld, 1977, pp. 31-45.

Zelinsky, Wilbur. "The Geographer and His Crowding World; cautionary notes toward the study and population pressure in the 'Developing Lands'," in Demko, George J., Rose, Harold M., and Schnell, George A. *Population Geography: A Reader.* NY: McGraw-Hill, 1970, pp. 487-503.

Weeks 8, 9 The Food Crisis
Readings:
Lappe, F.M. and Collins, J. *Food First: Beyond the Myth of Scarcity.* NY: Ballantine, 1978.
George, Susan. *How the Other Half Dies.* 1977.
Reutlinger, Schlomo. "Malnutrition: A Poverty or a Food Problem," *World Development*, 5, 8 (August 1977), pp. 715-724.
Lappe, F.M. *Diet for a Small Planet.* NY: Ballantine, 1971.
Brown, Lester. *By Bread Alone.* NY: Praeger, 1974.
Sinha, Radha. *Food and Poverty—The Political Economy of Confrontation.* NY: Holmes and Meier, 1976.
Recommended:
Shepherd, Jack. *The Politics of Starvation.* NY: The Carnegie Endowment for International Peace, 1976.
Dumont, René and Cohen, N. *The Growth of Hunger.* Boston: Marion Boyars, 1974.
Lappe, F.M., Collins, J. and Kinley, D. *Aid as Obstacle.* San Francisco: Institute for Food and Development Policy, 1980.
Franke and Cashin. *Seeds of Famine*, pp. 165-227.

Weeks 10, 11 Multinational Corporations and the Third World
Senghaas, D. "Multinational Corporations and Third World," *Journal of Peace Research*, 12 (1975), pp. 257-274.
Lall, S. "Transnational Domestic Enterprise and Industrial Structure in Host LDCs: A Survey," in Livingstone, pp. 148-163.
Muller, Ronald. "The Multinational Corporation and the Underdevelopment of the Third World," in Wilber, pp. 151-178.
Drucker, Peter F. "Multinationals and Developing Countries: Myths and Realities," *Foreign Affairs*, 53, 1 (October 1974), pp. 121-134.
Recommended:
Turner, Louis. *Multinational Corporations and the Third World.* London: Allen Lane, 1974.
Vernon, Raymond. *Storm over the Multinationals: The Real Issues.* Cambridge: Harvard University Press, 1977.

Weeks 12, 13 The New International Economic Order and The Third World
Ul Haq, Mahbub. "The Inequalities of the Old Order," in Wilber, pp. 179-187.
Islam, Nurul. "Revolt in the Periphery," in a Rothko Chapel Colloquium, *Toward a New Strategy for Development.* NY: Pergamon Press, 1979, pp. 171-197.
Cooper, Richard N. "Developed Country Reactions to Calls for a New International Economic Order," in Rothko Chapel Colloquium, pp. 243-274.
Amin, Samir. "Self-reliance and the New International Order," *Monthly Review*, 29, 3 (August 1977), pp. 1-21.
Recommended:
Ward, Barbara, "Another Chance for the North," *Foreign Affairs*, 59, 2 (Winter 1980/81), pp. 386-397.
McGinnis, James B. *Bread and Justice: Toward a New International Order.* NY: Paulist Press, 1979.

Militarism and the Arms Race

The Technological Imperative of the Arms Race:
A Search for Appropriate Solutions
Steven Slaby, Princeton University

The Political Economy of Military Spending
David Gold, The New School for Social Research

Nuclear Weapons and U.S. Foreign Policy
Daniel Ellsberg, Stanford University

Problems of War and Peace
Carolyn Stephenson and Kenneth Boulding,
Colgate University

Social Change in a Militarized Economy
Tony Mullaney, Boston College

Aspects of the Post WWII U.S.— U.S.S.R.
Military Confrontation
Milton Leitenberg, Swedish Institute of
International Affairs

The Threat of Nuclear War:
Looking for Creative Responses
George W. Morgan, Brown University

Science, Technology and Arms Control
Lester Paldy, State University of New York at Stony Brook

Military Force and Disarmament
Randy Forsberg, Boston University

Continued on next page

Nuclear Weapons and Nuclear War
Eric Markusen and John Harris, University of Minnesota

Problems in a Technological Society:
Modern Warfare and Arms Control Problems
Avron Blumberg, DePaul University

The Legality and Morality of War
Robert Rodes, Robert Webster, James Sterba, John Yoder,
Simon Harek, King Pfeiffer, University of Notre Dame

The Technological Imperative of the Arms Race: A Search for Appropriate Solutions

Steven Slaby   *Spring 1984*
Engineering 314/Princeton University/Princeton, NJ 08544

The following is a statement (including a guide-outline) suggesting the main thrust of this seminar and a description of the general format to be followed during the course of our work this term. Please note that the major purpose of the outline is to suggest general guidelines for the efforts that we set for ourselves within the format and time-limitations of a one-term course. The outline is not inviolate, and can and should be jointly revised, adjusted, added to and subtracted from, as is necessary to accomplish your research and writing done in the seminar.

Problem

To study and research the general area of the technological imperative of the arms race and to search for and propose appropriate solutions to this problem; to critically analyze and evaluate the role and developments of technology in the arms race including economic, political, social, psychological and cultural implications; to develop a critical understanding of the relationship between technology, political power, and the arms race, and the role that U.S. institutions of higher learning play in this relationship; to derive some insights into the causes of war, and to attempt to understand how (or if) the arms race can be stopped and ultimately reversed through appropriate means—means that must be defined; and finally, to see and understand the above developments in micro and macro perspectives as they relate to the welfare and well-being of humanity and the earth.

Goal

To produce a comprehensive, jointly written, Final Research Report on: The Technological Imperative of the Arms Race: A Search for Appropriate Solutions.

This is a special seminar which cannot accomplish goals set without substantial commitments and contributions from every participant; preparation is not simply an individual prerogative, as it is in a standard lecture course. Each seminar member has an additional responsibility to every other member in what is a joint learning endeavor. Failure to actively and regularly participate in the seminar and its related sessions, meetings, and schedules may result in a failing grade, even with a passing grade on written work.

Team Projects

The seminar group will be divided into research-writing "dialogical" teams. Each team will be responsible for the development of the equivalent of one chapter in the Final Research Report.

Each team will develop its own internal organization and schedule (tied into the master schedule) and will select and identify a Coordinator whose responsibilites will include the coordination of the work of her or his team members (arranging team meetings, division of labor, overseeing work progress, keeping in contact with the Coordinators of the other teams, etc.). The Coordinators will also act as liaisons between the seminar Director and each Team to develop a coordinated effort towards the development of the Final Report. In addition, each Team will select one of its members to act as the Team Editor of the Chapter.

Required Common Readings

Read Week of January 30: (discuss week of February 6)
a) Engineering 314 seminar format, schedules, and guide outline.
b) "Science, Technology and the Arms Race," Panofsky, W.K.H., *Physics Today*, American Institute of Physics, N.Y., June 1971, pp. 32-41.
c) *Autonomous Technology*, Winner, L., M.I.T. Press, Cambridge, Mass., 1980 (Read first half of book).

Read Week of February 6: (discuss week of February 13)
a) *Scientists, the Arms Race and Disarmament*, Rotblat, J. (ed.) Taylor & Francis Ltd., London, 1982, pp. 1-32.
b) "Recollections of Max Born," Barn, M., *Bulletin of Atomic Scientists*, Nov. 1969.
c) *Autonomous Technology*, Winner, L., M.I.T. Press, Cambridge, Mass., 1980 (Read second half of book).

Read Week of February 13: (discuss week of February 20)
a) *Scientists and War: The Impact of Science in Military and Civil Affairs*, Zuckerman, S. (Ch. 2, pp. 1-2 and Ch. 1, pp. 1-25).
b) *Future Fire: How the New Technology is Leading to War*, Cunningham, A.M. and Fitzpatrick, M., Warner Books, N.Y., 1983.

Read Week of February 20: (discuss week of February 27)
a) "The Nature of Conflict," Wright, Q., in *The War System: An Interdisciplinary Approach*, Falk, R. & Kim S. (eds.), Westview Press, Boulder, Co. 1980, pp. 317-333.
b) *A Study of War*, Wright, Q., The University of Chicago Press, Chicago, 1964:
"The History of War," pp. 20-26.
"Modern Warfare," pp. 51-87.
"Causes of War Under Socialism," pp. 303-307.
"Causes of War Under Capitalism," pp. 307-316.
c) "The First Modern War," Catton, B., *American Defense Policy in Perspective*, Connor, R.G.O. (ed.), John Wiley & Sons, N.Y., 1965, pp. 102-107.
d) *The Age of Imperialism*, Magdoff, H., Monthly Review Press, N.Y., 1969.

Read Week of February 27: (discuss week of March 5)
a) *Race to Oblivion*, York, H.F., Simon and Schuster, N.Y., 1970.
b) *The Warfare State*, Cook, F.J., Collier Books, N.Y., 1962.

Read Week of March 5: (discuss week of March 19)
a) *The Permanent War Economy*, Melman, S., Simon and Schuster, N.Y. 1974.
b) "The Myths of Edward Teller," VonHipple, F., *The Bulletin of Atomic Scientists*, March 1983, pp. 2-6, April 1983, pp. 42-44.
c) "The Consequences of a Limited Nuclear War in East and West Germany," Arkin, W., VonHippel, F., and Levi, B.G., *AMBIO*, 1983, pp. 163-174.
d) "Limited Nuclear War," VonHippel, F., and Drell, S.O., *Scientific American*, Nov. 1976, pp. 27-37.

Read Week of March 19: (discuss week of March 26)
American Journal of Public Health, Sept. 1980:
"The Pseudo-Environment of National Defense," Yankver, A., pp. 949-950.
"The Nuclear Arms Race: Sociopsychological Aspects," Frank, J., pp. 950-952.
"On the Social Cost of U.S. Militarism," Melman, S., pp. 953-955.

Read Week of March 26: (discuss week of April 2)
The War Economy of the United States, Melman, S., (ed.):
"Convertability of Military Industry to Civilian Economy," Melman, S., pp. 201-207.
"U.S. Industrial Economy Unprepared for Peace," Melman, S., pp. 207-209.
"Arms Firms See Postwar Spirit," Nassiter, B.C., pp. 209-214.
"Conversion and the Impact Problem," Ullman, J.E., pp. 215-225.
"Economic and Social Consequences of Disarmament," United Nations, pp. 255-299.
"Economic Report of the President, 1969," pp. 229-230.
"Impact of Deep Cuts in Defense," pp. 231-234.
"How to Give Up the Economy of Death and Keep Prosperity," Barnet, R.J., pp. 234-240.
"Nonviolent Economics: Next Task for Mankind," Schumacher, E.F., pp. 240-243.

Read Week of April 2: (discuss week of April 9)
a) "More Bang, More Bucks: $450 Billion for Nuclear War," *The Defense Monitor*, Vol. XII, No. 7, 1983, Center for Defense Information, Washington, D.C.
b) *Agreement for Arms Control: A Critical Survey*, Goldblat, J. Stockholm International Peace Research Institute, Taylor & Francis Ltd., London, 1982, pp. 354-366.

Read Week of April 9: (discuss week of April 16)
Protest and Survive, Smith, D. and Thompson, E.P. (eds.), Monthly Review Press, N.Y., 1981.
For weeks April 16 to the end of the semester, readings and discussions will be based on research and writing being done by students in this seminar.

The Technological Imperative of the Arms Race Guide-Outline

I. Causes of War—Sociological Analysis
A. Physical, political, ideological, and legal unresolved conflict
B. Sequence of events

1. Existence of disparities and inconsistencies in wealth, religion, ideology, etc.
2. Increase of tensions from:
   a. Mounting power and/or energy behind various groups
   b. Technological developments intensifying contact
3. Anxiety, power accumulation, and conflict
4. War
C. Sequence can be halted by
   1. Tolerance, understanding of inconsistencies and cultural differences
   2. No increase of tensions
   3. Nonviolent settlement of conflict by diplomacy, education, adjudication, conciliation, compromise, and many other channels
D. Role of armed conflict among nations
   1. Resources, trade, prestige, elements of desired lifestyle
   2. Territorial gains
   3. Only known means of dispute settlement (competition is generally viewed as inevitable, but does that mean war is also inevitable?)
E. Fronts of war
   1. Military
   2. Economic
   3. Diplomatic
   4. Psychological
F. Factors conducive to expansion of international conflict to total war
   1. Psychological displacement of internal conflict upon an external party: scapegoating
   2. Political tendencies towards bipolarization of world
      a. Balance of power among larger nations
      b. Need for protection of smaller nations
   3. Equality of parties in power and determination
   4. Communications and transportation technology increasing contact
   5. Advances in weaponry as increasing tension
      a. Increased destructive capability
      b. Improved guidance systems
G. Additional analytic approaches to study of war: moral/philosophical, psychological, cultural, anthropological, socioeconomic, normative, historical

II. History of Warfare in the U.S.
A. The colonies
   1. Militia system; emphasis on manpower over weaponry
   2. Arms/equipment provided by each militiaman
B. Revolutionary War—1775
   1. Government under Articles of Confederation
      a. Congress could just request states to raise troops
      b. Congress could not raise taxes
   2. Strategy based on swiftness and secrecy, which was dependent on lack of communications technology
C. Congressional delegation of power—1789
   1. Congressional powers
      a. To declare war
      b. To levy taxes

      c. To raise and support army and navy

      d. To call forth the militia

   2. Presidential powers

      a. As Commander-in-Chief

      b. As leader in foreign policy-making

      c. As advised by Presidential Cabinet

D. War of 1812

   1. Demonstrated need for centralized military organization

   2. Led to creation of first non-civilian naval administrative posts

E. Mexican War—1846

   1. Demonstrated reliance upon militia/volunteers in emergency

      a. Outnumbered regular army in the war

      b. Organized on democratic principles

   2. Increased U.S. territory by one third

   3. Involved "Manifest Destiny"

F. Civil War—1861—The First Modern War

   1. Unpredictability

   2. Massive destruction

   3. Dehumanization

      a. Old weapons conducive to personal assault

      b. New weapons (rifles) with longer effective range conducive to distant assault, lack of contact

   4. All or nothing stakes

   5. Total war

      a. Anything goes—social, economic, and psychological warfare

      b. Aim to incapacitate enemy, not just make war too costly

      c. Link between industry and military

   6. Change in Congressional attitude

      a. Pre-Civil War reluctance to appropriate money for military

      b. Post-1861 enlargement of appropriations and forces

   7. Accelerated mobilization because of railroad and telegraph

G. Spanish-American War—1898

   1. Acquisition of overseas empire

   2. Increased importance of navy

   3. Increased foreign obligations

H. World I—1917

   1. Preparedness debate before U.S. entrance

   2. National Defense Act—1916

   3. Total war

   4. Enlarged role of weapons technology

      a. Submarine warfare

      b. Aircraft

      c. Tanks

      d. Poison gas

   5. Acceleration of age of mechanization

      a. Precision engineering

      b. Mass production

      c. Petro-chemicals

      d. Internal combustion engine

I. World War II—1941
   1. Rearmament after inter-war reductions
   2. Total war
   3. Enlarged area of warfare
      a. Communications technology: radio broadcasting
      b. Development of airplane as fighter and bomber
   4. New technologies
      a. Tanks—improved from WWI—German Blitzkrieg
      b. Operations research
      c. Radar
      d. Computers—for decoding and for bombing tables
      e. Nuclear fission
   5. Role of industries
      a. Multinational corporations with multinational interests
      b. I.G. Farben—products for warfare, Auschwitz branch
      c. General Motors—role in Allied and in Nazi war efforts
   6. First atomic bomb
      a. Manhattan Project—begun 1941
      b. Hiroshima and Nagasaki bombed—1945
J. Cold War
   1. U.S.S.R. first atomic bomb explosion—1949
   2. Korean War—1952
      a. Limited war, by political decisions
      b. Increased proportion of technical specialists in units
   3. "Bomber gap"—1955-58
      a. Intercontinental Ballistic Missiles (ICBM's) development
   4. "Missile gap"—1957-61
      a. Sputnik launching
      b. U.S. ballistic missiles' placement in Europe
      c. U.S. ICBM and Polaris strategic missile programs
   5. Cuban Missile Crisis—1962
   6. Limited Test Ban Treaty, U.S., U.S.S.R., U.K.—1963
   7. Antiballistic Missile Systems (ABM's) race
   8. Non-Proliferation Treaty—1968
   9. Multiple Independently-Targeted Reentry Vehicle (MIRV) technology development—"counterforce capability"
   10. Vietnam War
      a. Increased collusion of Joint Chiefs of Staff on actions
      b. Agent Orange
      c. Cambodian secret bombings—computer use in cover-up
      d. Question of accountability
K. SALT I signed and ratified—1972
L. SALT II signed, not ratified—1979

III. Technologies of the Arms Race
(Separation of technologies is superficial. They are all related.)
A. Nuclear weapons
   1. A-bomb, fission
   2. H-bomb, fusion

    3. Bombers
        a. U.S.: B-52, B-1
        b. U.S.S.R.: Backfire, Tupolev-160
    4. Ballistic missiles
        a. Landbased ICBM's
            U.S.: Atlas, Titan, Minuteman, MX
        b. Submarine-launched (SLBM's)
            U.S.: Polaris, Poseidon, Trident
        c. Maneuverable Reentry Vehicles
        d. MIRV's
    5. Anti-Ballistic Missiles (ABM's)
    6. Cruise Missiles
    7. Anti-Submarine Warfare
B. Chemical and biological weapons
    1. Precedent: mustard gas, WWI
    2. Binary chemical weapons, a new form of nerve gas
    3. Neutron bomb
C. Particle beam/laser weapons
D. Conventional weapons
E. Computers
    1. Guidance systems in weapons
    2. Early warning defense systems
    3. Command and control systems
    4. Simulations
        a. Weapons evaluation
        b. Strategy evaluation
F. Operations Research
    1. Analysis of past and present
    2. Projective research
    3. Cost-effectiveness
    4. Scenario analysis
G. Surveillance technology
H. Weapons detection system
I. Weapons testing technology
J. Uranium/plutonium mining and production technology
K. Communications technology
        a. Digital transmissions
        b. Satellites
L. Espionage technologies
M. Bureaucracy—technology of control
N. Transportation technologies
O. Civil defense technologies

IV. Present Arms Build-up
A. Arsenals
    1. U.S.
    2. U.S.S.R.
    3. "Middle-power nations"
B. Risk of nuclear war

    1. Accidental initiation
    2. Purposeful, aggressive initiation
C. Consequences of nuclear war
    1. Immediate effects
        a. Casualties
        b. Physical destruction of environment from bombing
        c. Fires from thermal radiation
    2. Aftermath
        a. Radioactive fallout
        b. Food shortage
        c. Loss of utilities
        d. Inadequate medical care
        e. Damage to government; anarchy
        f. Psychological damage

V. Forces in the Arms Races
A. Politics
    1. Prestige, power of nuclear superiority
    2. Desire to "bargain from strength" as reasoning for arms build-up
    3. Difficulty of abandoning formerly important "bargaining chips" in arms limitations negotiations
    4. Role of technology/military policy in national elections e.g.: Role of "missile gap" in 1960 Presidential election
B. Doctrine
    1. Common strategy
        a. Strategic forces—triad concept
        b. Tactical/theater forces
    2. Deterrence—demonstration to potential initiator of nuclear war that he faces an unacceptable outcome—massive retaliation
    3. Flexible Response—capability to respond to variety of warfares—nuclear or conventional
    4. Counterforce strategy—aim to destroy enemy's nuclear forces
    5. Mutually Assured Destruction
    6. Action-reaction
    7. Mirror-imaging
C. Economics
    1. The war economy (Seymour Melman analysis)
    2. Military expenditures at expense of civilian industry
    3. Supply/demand imbalance resulting from willingness to spend any amount for top quality
    4. International arms trade
    5. Inflation
    6. Structural unemployment
    7. Influence of American big business on American foreign policy
    8. Role of multinational corporations in actual war efforts
D. Social-institutional forces
    1. Interdependency of military-industrial-governmental-educational complex
        a. Power structure/decision-making structure/bureaucracy
        b. Communications

      c. Computer networks
- 2. Governmental structure
  - a. Departments
  - b. Presidential cabinet
  - c. Joint Chiefs of Staff
  - d. Appropriations procedure
- 3. Dialectic of military spending (Ravenal analysis)
- 4. Weapons acquisitions process
  - a. No-bid contracts
  - b. Cost-plus
  - c. "Gold-plating"—demand for weapons performance beyond that required by current defense policy
- 5. Commercial investment and employment in military technology
  - a. Creating jobs for scientists within military complex rather than non-military
  - b. Spending money on military rather than human needs technology
- 6. Convertability and linkage of industry to war production; e.g.: automobile industry

E. Psychological forces
- 1. Sprawling military-industrial-academic bureaucracy, leading to decreasing feeling of politicians' individual responsibility for doctrines and dynamics of the arms race
- 2. Citizens' growing feeling of impotency to stop the race
- 3. Less security in the long-term
- 4. Nationalism—good guys vs. bad guys image of world
- 5. Fear of the unknown—the enemy
- 6. Scientists' egos—fascinations with technological tinkering, and protection of "progress"
- 7. Belief in the "technical fix"

F. International relations
- 1. Secrecy
  - a. Little exchange of ideas and information
  - b. Military build-up because of insecurity and large best/worse case differential
  - c. Knowledge of opponent's system only in final stages of testing and deployment
- 2. Nuclear weapons proliferation
  - a. More nations in the arms race (horizontal proliferation)
  - b. Increased danger of nuclear war
  - c. Proportionally large military expenditures in developing countries

G. Technology
- 1. Destabilizing technology
  - a. "Technically sweet" (J. Robert Oppenheimer)
  - b. Creates own momentum
  - c. Increases insecurity in other nations
  - d. Decreases willingness to negotiate limitations
  - e. High accuracy ballistic missiles
  - f. MIRV's
- 2. Nuclear energy

      a. Research and development of energy used as source of information for weapons research and development

      b. Plutonium byproducts of fuel cycle suitable for use in weapons

  3. Decision-making technology: Worst case analysis

      a. Tendency to overreact to potential threat

      b. Exaggeration of worst case

      c. Uncertainty and lack of knowledge

      d. Long lead time to develop weapons

  4. Technical installations as targets for opposition

  5. Increased dependency on foreign resources needed for technologies

      a. Increased demand for "national security"

      b. Example: oil for automobiles

  6. Question of accountability for technology

      a. Responsibility of scientist, of engineer, of user, of bureaucrat

      b. Example: Who is responsible for what a computer program does?

VI. Past and Present Efforts to Stop the Arms Race

A. Early efforts to avoid an arms race after WWII

  1. Franck Report to President Truman before first atomic bomb dropping

  2. Debate over H-bomb, including efforts of Oppenheimer

  3. Baruch Plan

      a. Place all nuclear technology under U.N. control, 1946

      b. Rejected by U.S.S.R.

B. Arms control treaties

  1. Limited Test Ban Treaty—U.S., U.S.R.R., U.K.—1963

  2. Non-Proliferation Treaty—1968

  3. SALT I—1972

      a. ABM Treaty

      b. Interim Agreement

  4. SALT II—signed, not ratified—1979

C. Scientific and academic movements

  1. Federation of American Scientists

      a. Founded 1946

      b. Publishes *Bulletin of Atomic Scientists*

      c. Concerned with ethics

  2. World Federation of Scientific Workers

      a. Founded 1946

      b. Concerned with social implications of science and technology

  3. Pugwash Movement

      a. Founded 1957

      b. Concerned with problems of the arms race and disarmament

      c. Sponsors Pugwash Conferences of Scientific and World Affairs

  4. Peace research institutes (over 500 worldwide)

      a. U.S. Agency for Arms Control and Disarmament

      b. U.S.S.R. Scientific Research Council on Peace and Disarmament

      c. International Peace Research Institute (Oslo)

      d. International Peace Research Association

      e. Stockholm International Peace Research Institute

D. Non-scientific professional movements

1. Physicians (Physicians for Social Responsibility)
2. Lawyers
3. Religious leaders
4. Engineers

E. Grassroots movements
   1. Freeze campaigns in U.S. and Europe
   2. Campaign for Nuclear Disarmament in U.K.
   3. Direct action by women's groups (Peace Links, Women's Action for Nuclear Disarmament, Greenham Common Women's Peace Encampment)
   4. Nuclear Free Zones in South Pacific, the Netherlands, and elsewhere

F. Evaluation of past and present arms control efforts
   1. Positive aspects
      a. Provide a first step
      b. Decrease risk of war by accident or by miscalculation
      c. Increase understanding among states
      d. Decrease suspicion and secrecy
   2. Negative aspects/problems
      a. SALT not given priority, but held hostage to vicissitudes of U.S./U.S.S.R. relations
      b. Prohibited weapons not important
      c. Important weapons not prohibited, e.g.: MIRV
      d. Parity not possible because build-ups not symmetrical
      e. Lack of domestic harmonizing of politically developed arms control strategies with militarily developed national security requirements
      f. Emphasis on precise numbers and technical performance of weapons
      g. Narrow scope of negotiations
      h. Presupposition of continued existence of national military establishments
      i. Continuance of motives for arms build-up: overseas obligations, national security and insecurity
      j. Lack of public awareness of issues and dangers
      k. Lack of adequate verification process before final phases of testing and deployment

VII. Future Alternatives

A. Arms control negotiations, with changed priorities
   1. Make necessary distinctions in types of arms control
      a. Conventional/non-conventional weapons
      b. Qualitative/quantitative reductions
      c. Horizontal/vertical reductions
   2. Enlarge scope of negotiations
   3. Reduce linkage to other negotiations
   4. Incorporate doctrine of sufficiency—have weapons sufficient for national defense, but not to reply in kind to any attack
   5. Supplement governmental negotiations with non-governmental conferences
   6. Create more nuclear free zones
   7. Stop production of weapons-grade fissionable materials

B. Reciprocal unilateral restraints
   1. Gradual and reciprocated initiatives on tension reduction (GRIT)

2. Freeze—by prior moratorium—temporary unilateral restraint subject to reciprocation
3. Elimination of redundant weapons
4. Elimination of First Strike weapons
5. Decrease production of weapons-grade fissionable materials
C. Confidence-Building Measures (CBM's)—make military intentions explicit
D. Action by Non-Nuclear-Weapons States (NNWS's)
   1. Disarmament conference of NNWS's
   2. Watchdog committee to oversee NNWS's negotiations
E. Increased United Nations' involvement
   1. Action through UNESCO
   2. Establishment of an international verification agency
   3. Establishment of an international reporting system of military expenditures
F. Increased control of technologies
   1. Non-development of weapons which increase instability and insecurity
   2. Decreased bureaucracy
   3. Increased awareness of and limitation of other military technologies
   4. Decreased incentives for "gold-plating"
G. Transformation of the military-industrial-educational complex to meet human needs
   1. Changed priorities
      a. Appropriations
      b. Employment
      c. Structure
   2. Change within each sector
      a. Government
      b. Industry
      c. Universities
   3. Decreased interdependency
H. Use of science and technology for arms control and peacekeeping
   1. Development of tools for verification
   2. International communication and cooperation between scientists
I. Strengthening and expansion of social movements
   1. Stress on awareness of issues and dangers
   2. Unity and action to increase political influence
   3. International cooperation among national movements
   4. Lobbying
   5. Rallies and demonstrations
   6. Publications and publicity
   7. Professional, religious, and labor movements
J. Action by individuals: Nonviolent approaches and civil disobedience
   1. Gandhi's tactics and strategies
   2. Thoreau's approach
   3. Voting to put pressure on policy-makers
   4. Participation in political campaigns and in grassroots movements
   5. Refusal to participate in arms research or production

General Reference List

Adams, Ruth and Cullen, Susan, eds. *The Final Epidemic: Physicians and Scientists on Nuclear War.* Chicago: Educational Foundation for Nuclear Science, Inc., 1981:
 *Chap. 3: "Buying Death with Taxes"—Victor W. Sidel
 *Chap. 4: "Economics of the Arms Race—and After"—John Kenneth Galbraith
 *Chap. 5: "A Clear and Present Danger—West"—Herbert Scoville, Jr.
Adams, Ruth and Rabinowitch, Eugene I., eds. *Debate the Antiballistic Missile.* Chicago: BAS, 1967.
American Security Council, National Strategy Committee. *The ABM and the Changed Strategic Military Balance.* 2nd ed. Washington, D.C.: Acropolis Books, 1969.
Arkin, William M. *Research Guide to Current Military and Strategic Affairs.* Washington, D.C.: The Institute for Policy Studies, 1981.
Arkin, William and Levi, Barbara G., and VonHippel, Frank. "The Consequences of a 'Limited' Nuclear War in East and West Germany," *AMBIO,* 1982.
York, Herbert Frank. *Arms Control: Readings from the Scientific American.* San Francisco: W.H. Freeman, 1973.
Barnet, Richard J. *Real Security: Restoring American Power in a Dangerous Decade.* Washington, D.C.: Institute for Policy Studies, 1982.
Barnet, Richard J. and Falk, Richard, eds. *Security in Disarmament.* Princeton: Princeton University Press, 1965.
Barnet, Richard and Muller, Ronald. *Global Reach: The Power of the Multinational Corporations.* NY: Simon and Schuster, 1974.
Borkin, Joseph. *The Crime and Punishment of I.G. Farben.* NY: The Free Press, 1978.
Brown, Thomas, A., et al. *Swords from Ploughshares: The Military Potential of Civilian Nuclear Energy.* Chicago: U. of Chicago Press, 1979.
Buchan, Alastair. *War in Modern Society: An Introduction.* London: C.A. Watts & Co. Ltd, 1966.
Carlton, David and Schaerf, Carlo, eds. *The Dynamics of the Arms Race.* NY: Wiley, 1975.
Chayes, Abram and Wiesner, Jerome B., eds. *ABM: An Evaluation of the Decision to Deploy an Antiballistic Missile System.* NY: Harper, 1969.
Carlam, Robert F. *Illusions of Choice: The F-111 and the Problems of Weapons Acquisition Reform.* Princeton: Princeton University Press, 1977.
Endicott, John and Stafford, Roy, Jr., eds. *American Defense Policy,* 4th ed. Baltimore: Johns Hopkins U. Press, 1977.
Enthoven, Alain C. and Smith, K. Wayne. *How Much Is Enough? Shaping the Defense Program, 1961-69.* NY: Harper, 1971.
Epstein, William and Feld, Bernard T., eds. *New Directions in Disarmament.* NY: Praeger Publishing, 1981.
Falk, Richard and Kim, Samuel S., eds. *The War System: An Interdisciplinary Approach.* Boulder, CO: Westview Press, 1980.
Falk, Richard and Lifton, Robert. *Indefensible Weapons: The Political and Psychological Case Against Nuclearism.* NY: Basic Books, 1982.
Falk, Richard, Tucker, Robert C., and Young, Oran R. *On Minimizing the Use of Nuclear Weapons.* Princeton: Princeton U. Center for International Studies, 1966 (research monograph 23).

Fallows, James. *National Defense.* NY: Random House, 1981.

Feld, B., Greenwood, T., Rathjens, G.W., and Weinberg, S., eds. *The Impact of New Technologies of the Arms Race.* Cambridge, MA: MIT Press, 1971.

Fox, J.E. *Arming America: How the U.S. Buys Weapons.* Cambridge, MA: Harvard University Press, 1974.

Gilpin, Robert S. *American Scientists and Nuclear Weapons Policy.* Princeton: Princeton U. Press, 1962.

Goldblat, Josef. *Agreements for Arms Control—A Critical Survey.* (Stockholm International Peace Research Inst.) Cambridge, MA: Oelgeschlager, Gunn & Hain, Inc., 1982.

Gompert, David, et al. *Nuclear Weapons and World Politics: Alternatives for the Future.* NY: McGraw-Hill, 1977.

Ground Zero. *Nuclear War: What's in it for You?* NY: Pocket Books, 1982.

Halperin, Morton H. *Bureaucratic Politics and Foreign Policy.* Washington, D.C.: The Brookings Inst., 1974.

Halperin, Morton H. *Limited War: An Essay on the Development of the Theory and an Annotated Bibliography.* Cambridge, MA: Center for International Affairs, Harvard Univ., 1963.

Halperin, Morton, H. *National Security Policy-making: Analyses, Cases and Proposals.* Lexington, MA: Lexington Books, 1975.

Halperin, Morton, et al. *The Political Economy of the Military-Industrial Complex.* Berkeley, CA: Inst. of Business and Economic Research, 1973.

Hornig, D.F. *Science Advice to the President.* London: Pergamon, 1980.

International Peace Research Association. *Studies in Peace Research (#8): Elements of World Instability: Armaments, Communication, Food, International Division of Labor.* Frankfurt, NY: Campus, 1981.

International Assembly on Nuclear Weapons. *The Control of Proliferation: Three Views.* London: Inst. for Strategic Studies, 1966.

Janowitz, Morris. *Military Conflict: Essays in the Institutional Analysis of War and Peace.* Beverly Hills, CA: Sage Publications, 1975.

Janowitz, Morris. *The Professional Soldier: A Social and Political Portrait.* NY: Free Press, 1960.

Janowitz, Morris. *Sociology and the Military Establishment,* rev. ed. NY: Russell Sage Foundation, 1965.

Kanter, Arnold and Halperin, Morton. *Readings in American Foreign Policy: A Bureaucratic Perspective.* Boston, MA: Little, Brown, 1973.

Killian, J.R., Jr. *Sputniks, Scientists and Eisenhower.* Cambridge, MA: MIT Press, 1977.

Kings, John Kerry, ed. *International Political Effects of the Spread of Nuclear Weapons.* Washington, D.C.: U.S. Gov't Printing Office, 1979.

Kistiakowsky, G.B. *A Scientist at the White House.* Cambridge, MA: Harvard Univ. Press, 1976.

Labrie, Roger P. and Pranger, Robert J. eds. *Nuclear Strategy and National Security: Points of View.* Washington, D.C.: American Enterprise Inst. for Public Policy Research, 1977.

Labrie, Roger P., ed. *SALT Handbook: Key Documents and Issues, 1972-79.* Washington, D.C.: American Enterprise Inst. for Public Policy Research, 1979.

Long, Franklin A., and Rathjens, George W., eds. *Arms, Defense Policy, and Arms Control Essays.* NY: Norton, 1976.

Long, Franklin A., and J. Reppy, eds. *The Genesis of New Weapons: Decision Making for Military R&D.* London: Pergamon, 1980.

Long, F.A. "The Process of New Weapons Development," paper given at 36th Pugwash Symposium, London, 10-12 December, 1980.

Mandelbaum, Michael. *The Nuclear Question: The U.S. and Nuclear Weapons, 1946-1976.* NY: Cambridge U. Press, 1979.

Melman, Seymour. *The Defense Economy: Conversion of Industries and Occupations to Civilian Needs.* NY: Praeger, 1970.

Melman, Seymour. *Pentagon Capitalism: The Political Economy of War.* NY: McGraw-Hill, 1970.

Melman, Seymour. *The War Economy of the United States: Readings on Military Industry and Economy.* NY: St. Martin's Press, 1971.

Myrdal, Alva. *The Game of Disarmament: How the U.S. and Russia Run the Arms Race.* NY: Pantheon Books, 1976.

O'Connor, Raymond Gish, ed. *American Defense Policy in Perspective from Colonial Times to the Present.* NY: Wiley, 1965.

Potter, William C. *Nuclear Power and Nonproliferation: An Interdisciplinary Perspective.* Cambridge, MA: Oelgeschlager, Gunn & Hain, Inc., 1982.

Primack, Joel and von Hippel, Frank. *Advice and Dissent: Scientists in the Political Arena.* NY: Basic Books, 1974.

U.S. Senate Committee on Governmental Affairs. Subcommittee on Energy, Nuclear Proliferation and Federal Services. *Reader on Nuclear Nonproliferation.* Washington, D.C.: U.S. Gov't Printing Office, 1978.

Raskin, Marcus, ed. *The Federal Budget and Social Reconstruction.* Washington, D.C.: Institute for Policy Studies.

Reichart, John F. and Sturm, Steven R. *American Defense Policy,* 5th ed.

Ridgeway, James. *The Closed Corporation—American Universities in Crisis.* NY: Random House, 1968.

Roberts, Chalmers, McGeagh. *The Nuclear Years: The Arms Race and Arms Control, 1945-70.* NY: Praeger, 1970.

Segal, Gerald, et al. *Nuclear War and Nuclear Peace.* NY: St. Martin's Press, 1983.

Sivard, Ruth Leger. *World Military and Social Expenditures 1980.* Leesberg, VA.: World Priorities, Inc., 1980.

Stockholm International Peace Research Institute. *SIPRI Yearbook.* London: Taylor & Francis, Ltd, annual.

Art, Robert J. and Waltz, Kenneth N., eds. *The Use of Force: International Politics and Foreign Policy.* Boston, MA: Little, Brown & Co., 1971.

Wiesner, Jerome B. *Where Science and Politics Meet.* NY: McGraw-Hill, 1965.

Williams, William A. *The Tragedy of American Diplomacy,* 2nd ed. NY: Dell, 1972.

Winner, Langdon. *Autonomous Technology: Technics-out-of-Control as a Theme in Political Thought.* Cambridge, MA: MIT Press, 1977.

Wright, Quincy. *A Study of War.* Chicago: U. of Chicago Press, 1942.

Yager, Joseph A., ed. *Nonproliferation and U.S. Foreign Policy.* Washington, D.C.: The Brookings Institute, 1980.

York, Herbert Frank. *The Advisors: Oppenheimer, Teller, and the Superbomb.* San Francisco: W.H. Freeman, 1976.

Zuckerman, Sir Solly. *Beyond the Ivory Tower: The Frontiers of Public and Private Science.* London: Weidenfeld & Nicolson, 1970.

The Political Economy of Military Spending

David Gold   *Summer 1983*
Economics SS136/ New School for Social Research/ New York, NY 10011

Books

Jacques Gansler, *The Defense Industry*, MIT Press, 1980.
Gordon Adams, *The Iron Triangle: The Politics of Defense Contracting*, Transaction Books and Council on Economic Priorities, 1981.
James Fallows, *National Defense*, Random House, 1981.
Seymour Melman, *The Permanent War Economy*, Touchstone, 1974.
Robert DeGrasse, Paul Murphy and William Ragen, *The Costs and Consequences of Reagan's Military Buildup*, Council on Economic Priorities, 1982.

Topics and Readings

I. Overview of Military Spending in the United States
Gansler, ch. 1
Fred Block, "Economic Instability and Military Strength: The Paradoxes of the 1950 Rearmament Decision," *Politics & Society*, 1980
James Cypher, "The Basic Economics of 'Rearming America,' " *Monthly Review*, November 1981

II. Producing and Selling Weapons
Gansler, ch. 2-6, 9-10, 12; Fallows, ch. 1-4
William Perry, "Fallows' Fallacies," *International Security*, Spring 1982
Adams, ch. 1-15; Gansler, ch. 8
William Hartung, "Weapons for the World," *Council on Economic Priorities Newsletter*, 1981

III. The Volunteer Army
Fallows, ch. 5

IV. Economic Impacts of Military Spending
Melman, ch. 1-6, 10; DeGrasse, pp. 13-24
Michael Reich, "Does the U.S. Economy Require Military Spending"? *American Economic Review*, May 1972
Ernest Mandel, *Late Capitalism*, New Left Books, 1975, ch.9

V. Empirical Issues
Ronald P. Smith, "Military Expenditure and Investment in OECD Countries, 1957-1973," *Journal of Comparative Economics*, 1980
R.P. Smith, "Military Expenditure and Capitalism," *Cambridge Journal of Economics*, March 1977; and *Comments*, September 1978

VI. The Reagan Rearmament and Beyond
DeGrasse, pp. 1-12, 25-44; Melman, ch. 7-9
Articles by Lester Thurow, Herbert Stein, others (on reserve)

Nuclear Weapons and U.S. Foreign Policy

Daniel Ellsberg   *Spring 1982*
Undergraduate Special 45/Stanford University/ Stanford, CA 94305

What are U.S. nuclear weapons for? Why have we acquired 30,000 of them, and why are we still adding more? Why the current programs for new "counterforce" weapons and the neutron warheads? Various interpretations will be explored in the light of history that has been largely secret: the numerous specific occasions when U.S. Presidents—every one of them, in every term of office since Hiroshima—have seriously contemplated or secretly threatened imminent U.S. initiation of nuclear war.

In nearly every case, the fact of urgent Presidential consideration of U.S. first-use of nuclear weapons has been kept secret from the American public and scholars—though not from adversaries—both at the time and for years afterward. (This also applies to the history—to be examined—of strategic bombing doctrine and practice in World War II, and to the political considerations leading to the urgent use of atomic bombs on both Hiroshima and Nagasaki in early August, 1945). Recent revelations in memoirs and studies based on newly declassified documents, therefore, put in question most available analyses of U.S. foreign and strategic policy.

Sketchy as these data are, they refute the important popular beliefs:

—that the U.S. has at any time adopted policy constraints on "no first use" of nuclear weapons, or of "no first strike" against the Soviet Union;
—that U.S. nuclear weapons are for "deterrence only;" either solely to deter nuclear attacks or respond to them, or, as sole significant addition, to deter or repond to major conventional attack against our NATO allies;
—or that there has been at any time, including the present, real danger of imminent Soviet strategic nuclear superiority or of significant Soviet first-strike capability against the U.S.

Most of the instances recently revealed involve confrontations outside the NATO area, in which Presidents have contemplated U.S. initiation of nuclear operations against Third World adversaries who did not possess nuclear weapons: with further consideration, in case of Soviet response in support of their ally, of a possible U.S. first strike against the Soviet Union. The simple policy premise that the U.S. should retain and improve capabilities for such "options" in the future leads plausibly to the conclusion of the current buildup, and that what must be added are precisely the weapons designed for first-strike or first-use now being programmed for development and production: Trident, Missile X, cruise missiles, Mark 12A warheads, and enhanced radiation warheads.

What are the implications of Soviet weapons programs for such U.S. capabilities and possible intentions? How is the recent Russian expansion to be understood, in the light of the past crises and policies: given possible tendencies of the Soviets, and others, to imitate as well as to counter U.S. practices? Must the mutual buildup of nuclear weapons persist? If it does, will we?

Lecture Topics

I. Secret Crisis: The historical record of unannounced U.S. threats of, or preparations for, imminent U.S. first-use of nuclear weapons.

Nixon's Vietnam strategy: the "secret plan ... to end the war and win the peace"—by threats of escalation including possible use of nuclear weapons. 1969: the "madman theory" and the November ultimatum. 1972: the spring offensive, the December bombing.

The current record of earlier secret nuclear crises: Berlin, 1948; Korea, 1950-51, 1953; Dienbienphu, 1954; Tachen Islands, 1955 (Guatemala, 1954? Lebanon, 1958?); Quemoy, 1958; Laos, 1961; Vietnam, 1964-65; Khe Sanh, 1968; Korea, 1969; Jordan, 1970? And "public nuclear crises": Berlin, 1961; Buca, 1962; Middle East, October War, 1973.

Why have the crises—in particular, the November ultimatum in 1969—not led to nuclear wars?

II. The Art of Coercion: Theory and Practice of Blackmail. Hitler as thinker: the political uses of madness. Recent pupils: how it sounds in English.

III. The Strangelove Era: The construction of the Doomsday machine. U.S. strategic nuclear force posture and planning, from the H-bomb to the Cuban Missile Crisis. Bomber and missile gaps; counterforce doctrine; proposals and preparations for a U.S. first strike. BNSP, JSCP, and SIOP. Delegation of Presidential authority to execute nuclear war plans to field commanders and below. "Dr. Strangelove" as documentary. Khrushchev's bluff. Falling bombs.

IV. Sowing the Wind: Strategic Bombing and the First Use of Nuclear Weapons. The Allies' discovery: "Hitler exists: therefore everything is permitted." Cities, economies and whole populations come to be targets for mass destruction. The lessons of Rotterdam and Coventry are applied to worker's housing in Hamburg, Dresden and Tokyo. The whirlwind's first harvest: Hiroshima and Nagasaki. Last shots of World War or the first of the Cold War?

V. Strategic Terrorism: Bombing-and-Negotiating in Vietnam. U.S. officials' private prescriptions for success: "the 'water-drip' technique;" "one more turn of the screw;" "the will of the DRV as the real target." The paradigm of torture. Dams and dikes as targets in Korea and Vietnam. Underlying options from 1961 on: invasion of North Vietnam, population bombing, destruction of dikes, confrontation and detente with Russia and China, nuclear weapons. New data on Johnson's ultimatums, 1964-65 and the Tonkin Gulf dissimulation.

VI. NATO Strategy: Alliance as Suicide Pact. The Western responses to Soviet conventional superiority (and to official exaggerations of it, along with underestimation of Soviet buildup of theater nuclear forces): the decision to build the H-bomb (with no attempt to forego it bilaterally); German rearmament; formal U.S. commitment to nuclear first-use and first-strike, "when necessary." Theories of and preparations for limited nuclear war and for limited strategic war, from Kissinger to Schlesinger and Brown.

VII. Small 'Clean' Bombs and Dirty Little Wars: The neutron warhead and U.S. involvement in the Third World. A case study of the manipulation of public discussion. Characteristics of a weapon preeminently adapted to kill people in nations lacking nuclear retaliatory power, as contrasted to its public image of an anti-tank weapon intended exclusively against Soviet forces in Europe. The enhanced radiation warheads as first-use-only weapons, whose effects will likely be felt mainly in the Third World. Their potential for commencing (if it does not begin otherwise) the global era of routine combat use of nuclear weapons; their evidence of Carter's reaffirmation of the U.S. policy of readiness for first-use of nuclear weapons.

In light of U.S. weapons development and threatened use, of our Vietnam experience and of revelations on U.S. covert operations, a new look at "revisionist" versus orthodox theories of U.S. foreign policy. Democratic ideology and counter-revolutionary practice: how are they managed together?

VIII. U.S. First Strike Capabilities in the 1980's: The Russian strategic and tactical buildup, and its implications for U.S. nuclear retaliatory, first strike, and localized first-use capabilities. Alternative interpretations of the Soviet programs, and alternative U.S. reponses. The implications of the current U.S. weapons development programs—Trident, cruise missiles, Missile X, Mark 12A warhead, enhanced radiation warheads, and antisubmarine warfare systems for various U.S. capabilities and for underlying policy. The relation of a "not incredible first-strike capability" to a policy using first-use threats or limited nuclear operations.

IX. Will We Survive Our Defense? Prospects for a future markedly different from the U.S./Soviet practices of the last 30 years; i.e., prospects for a future. Alternatives to the arms race and proliferation, to SALT and to the current weapons programs on all sides. Lessons from the movements against nuclear testing, the Vietnam War, nuclear energy and nuclear weapons. The need for government secrecy from the public, the Bill of Rights, and these dissenting movements as obstacles to governmental programs. The road to Watergate and the ending of the bombing and the war. The role of the public understanding, and of bodies on the tracks.

Reading Assignments

Week I   Secret Crises
A) Nixon's Secret Strategy of Escalation
Required:
   Richard Nixon, *Memoirs*: 256-57, 322-29, 340-341, 347-351, 380-382, 390-414, 430-432, 445-469, 583-608, 557, 687-751, 864, 866-867, (esp. 390-414).
   H.R. Haldeman, *The Ends of Power:* 117-124, 139-140.
   Jeb Stuart Magruder, *An American Life:* 92-98.

Richard Whalen, *Catch the Falling Flag:* 3-5, 10-15, 25-59, 91, 96, 128-132, 184-191, 137-144, (optional 72-77, 84-87, 91-95, 184-191, 211-212, 283-294.)

Marvin Kalb and Bernard Kalb, *Kissinger:* 142-214 (optional, but see esp. 142, 147-153, 165-169, 214), 224-254 (esp. 335, 339, 342), 467-478.

Tad Szulc, *The Illusion of Peace:* 148-156.

Daniel Ellsberg, *Papers on the War:* 253-274.

Roger Morris, *Uncertain Greatness:* 163-171.

B) Other Unannounced Nuclear Crises
Required:

Nixon, *Memoirs:* 150-155, 382-385, 476-485, 485-489, 937-940.

Dean Acheson, *Present at the Creation:* 478-485, 513-517.

Robert J. Donovan, *Eisenhower: The Inside Story:* 114-125.

Roscoe Drummond, and Gaston Coblentz, *Duel at the Brink:* 69, 180-181, 111-114, 115-123, 124-129, 191-196, 205, 210, 235, 236.

Barry M. Blechman and Stephen S. Kaplan, *Force Without War:* 50-52, 98-101, 131-138, 255-256.

Optional:

Morton Halperin, *The Taiwan Straits Crisis* (unpublished study).

Further Required:

George and Smoke, *Deterrence in American Foreign Policy:* 235-262, 304-306.

James Shepley, "How Dulles Averted War," *Life,* Jan. 16, 1966: 70-80.

Peter Lyon, *Eisenhower: Portrait of the Hero:* 534-536.

Week II   The Art of Coercion

Daniel Ellsberg, Lowell Lectures, 1959 (copyrighted manuscript, on reserve).

Week III   Strangelove Era: The Construction of the Doomsday Machine

Required:

York, *Race to Oblivion:* 9-48, 156-239.

Albert Wohlstetter, "The Delicate Balance of Terror," in *Problems of National Strategy,* and *Foreign Affairs,* Jan. 1959.

Kahn, *On Thermonuclear War:* vii-xxiv, 138-160, 239-240, 205-210.

Maxwell Taylor, *The Uncertain Trumpet:* 23-79.

Optional:

Bottome, *The Balance of Terror.*

Week IV   Sowing the Wind

A) Strategic Bombing
Required:

F.M. Sailagar, *The Road to Total War: Escalation in World War II.* (RAND Report R-455-FR, April 1960).

Further Optional Reading:

Bernard Brodie, *Strategy in the Missile Age:* 3-144.

George Quester, *Deterrence Before Hiroshima.*

C.P. Snow, *Science and Government:* 47-53.

B) The U.S. First Use of Nuclear Weapons
Required:

Barton J. Bernstein, *The Atomic Bomb: The Critical Issues.*

Gar Alperovitz, *Cold War Essays:* 51-73.

Further Optional Reading:
  Gar Alperovitz, *Atomic Diplomacy.*
  Nuel Pharr Davis, *Lawrence and Oppenheimer.*
  John Hersey, *Hiroshima.*
  Martin Sherwin, *A World Destroyed.*
  Herbert York, *The Advisors: Oppenheimer and Teller.*
Articles required:
  Barton J. Bernstein, "Energy and Conflict: The Life and Times of Edward Teller: A Review," *Bulletin of the Atomic Scientists,* May, 1978, pp. 51-53.
  Bernstein, "New Light on the A-Bomb Race," *The Nation,* Sept. 16, 1978, pp. 238-242.
  Bernstein, "Doomsday II," *New York Times Magazine,* July 27, 1975.

Week V   Strategic Terrorism in Vietnam
See earlier reading under Nixon's secret strategy of escalation.
In addition:
  Ellsberg, *Papers on the War:* 1-131, 275-309, 234-252.
  Nixon, *Memoirs:* 386-390, 357-358, 469-475, 508-515, 687-757, 786, 813-814, 823-824, 864, 977, 997.
  Haldeman, *The Ends of Power:* 125-169.
  Magruder, *An American Life:* 208-213, 243-247, 268-269.
  Pentagon Papers, Gravel edition, Vol. 3: 64, 65, 172-177, 238, 519-520. Vol. 2: 320-323.
  Morton Halperin, "The Lessons Nixon Learned," *The Legacy of Vietnam,* ed. Anthony Lake: 411-428.
Optional:
  Chomsky, *For Reasons of State:* Intro and 1-171.

Weeks VI and VII   First Strike Capabilities, NATO Strategy, and the Current Arms Race
Required:
  John G. Hubbell, "Needed Now: A New, Mobile ICBM Force," *Readers Digest,* Jan. 1979, pp. 65 69.
  Radomir Bogdanov and Lev Semeiko, "Soviet Military Might: A Soviet View," *Fortune,* Feb. 26, 1979, 46-84.
  Richard Pipes, "Why the Soviet Union Thinks It Could Fight and Win a Nuclear War," *Commentary,* July, 1977, 21-34.
  Paul H. Nitze, "Deterring our Deterrent," *Foreign Policy,* Winter 1976-77, pp. 195-210.
  Paul H. Nitze, "Assuring Nuclear Stability in an Era of Detente," *Foreign Affairs,* Jan. 1976.
Plus the following:
  Robert C. Aldridge, *The Counterforce Syndrome* (TNI Pamphlet No. 7).
  Fred Kaplan, *Dubious Specter* (TNI Pamphlet No. 6).
  Gompert, et al., *Nuclear Weapons and World Politics: Alternatives for the Future:* only pp. 255-298 required.
Optional:
  Gompert, et al., *Nuclear Weapons and World Politics: Alternatives for the Future:* rest of book.

Herman Kahn, *On Thermonuclear War:* vii-xxviii, 126-308, 2-116, 200-210, 470-476, 500, 456, 457.

Daniel Yergin, "The Arms Zealots," *Harpers*, June, 1977, 64-76.

Philip Morrison and Paul F. Walker, "A New Strategy for Military Spending," *Scientific American*, Oct. 1978.

Frank Barnaby, "The Mounting Prospects of Nuclear War," *The Bulletin of Atomic Scientists*, Vol. 33, No. 6, June, 1977, 11-19.

Daniel Yergin, "The Terrifying Prospect," *The Atlantic*, 47-65.

G.B. Kistiakowsky, "False Alarm Over Salt," *The New York Review of Books*, March 22, 1979, 33-38.

Alain Enthoven and K. Wayne Smith, *How Much is Enough?* pp. 174-164, 165-184.

Required:

Michael Klare, "Making Nuclear War 'Thinkable'," *The Nation*, April 13, 1974, pp. 461-466.

Michael Klare, "Humane Nuclear War?" *Sane World*, May, 1974.

Paul H. Nitze, "Civil Defense-The New Debate," *Worldview*, Jan.-Feb. 1979, pp. 40-41.

Sidney D. Drell and Frank von Hippel, "Limited Nuclear War," *Scientific American*, Nov. 1976, 27-37.

Optional:

George E. Lowe, *The Age of Deterrence.*

Richard S. Leghorn, "No Need to Bomb Cities to Win War," *U.S. News and World Report*, Jan. 28, 1955, 78-94.

Week VIII   The Neutron Bomb and The Third World

Required:

Daniel Ellsberg, "There Must Be No Neutron Bomb," *The Nation*, May 27, 1978, 632-633.

George B. Kistiakowsky, "Weaponry: The Folly of the Neutron Bomb," *The Atlantic*, June, 1978, Vol. 241, No. 6, pp. 4-14.

Samuel H. Day, Jr., "The Neutron Bomb Lives After All," *The Progressive*, Oct., 1978, 28-29.

Robert Sam Anson, "The Neutron Bomb," *New Times*, Aug. 5, 1977, 24-32.

Sam Cohen, interview with, *People*, Aug. 8, 1977, 34-38.

S.T. Cohen, "Enhanced Radiation Warheads: Setting the Record Straight," *Strategic Review*, Winter 1978, 9-17.

Colin S. Gray, "NATO Strategy and the 'Neutron Bomb'," *Policy Review*, Winter, 1979, 7-26.

Week IX   Revisionist Theories of U.S. Foreign Policy

Required:

Alperovitz, *Cold War Essays* (Chapter on the Cold War): 75-121.

Noam Chomsky, "Human Rights and American Foreign Policy."

Chomsky and Edwards, "The United States versus Human Rights in the Third World," *Monthly Review*, July-August, 1977, 22-45.

Optional:

Carl Oglesby, *Containment and Change:* 3-176.

L. Shoup and W. Minter, *Imperial Brain Trust.*

Problems of War and Peace

Carolyn Stephenson and Kenneth Boulding   *Fall 1983*
University Studies 211/ Colgate University/ Hamilton, NY 13346

Materials to be Obtained

Berryman, Phillip, *What's Wrong in Central America and What to do About It.* (Philadelphia: American Friends Service Committee, 1983).

Boulding, Kenneth E., *Stable Peace* (Austin: University of Texas Press, 1978) or *National Defense Through Stable Peace* (International Institute for Applied Systems Analysis: Laxenburg, Austria, 1983).

CDI, "Soviet Geopolitical Momentum: Myth or Menace?" *The Defense Monitor*, 9.1 (Washington: Center for Defense Information, 1980).

CDI, "A World at War: Small Wars and Superpowers Intervention," *The Defense Monitor*, 8.10 (Washington: Center for Defense Information, 1979).

Jamgotch, Nish, Jr., *Soviet Security in Flux.* (Muscatine, Iowa: Stanley Foundation, 1983).

Johansen, Robert C., *Toward a Dependable Peace.* (New York: World Policy Institute, 1978).

Kennan, George F., "A Proposal for International Disarmament," (Albert Einstein Peace Prize, Washington, D.C., 1981).

Morrison, Philip and Walker, Paul F., "A New Strategy for Military Spending," *Scientific American* 239.4 (October 1978).

Schell, Jonathan, *The Fate of the Earth.* (New York: Avon, 1982).

Sivard, Ruth Leger, *World Military and Social Expenditures, 1983.* (Leesburg, VA: World Priorities Inc., 1983).

Stephenson, C.M., Boulding, K.E., and Reardon, W.A., eds., *Problems of War and Peace: A Book of Readings.* (Hamilton, NY: Colgate University, 1983). Noted as *Manual.*

Stephenson, C.M., ed., *Alternative Methods for International Security.* (Washington, D.C.: University Press of America, 1983). Noted as *AMIS.*

Syllabus of Assignments

September 8   Introduction

I. War as a Moral Question

Is war moral? Are there certain circumstances when the use of armed force is justified, and others when it is not? How does an individual choose which war to support? Is there such a thing as a "just war" using modern means of warfare?

September 13
Film: "Hiroshima/Nagasaki"

Potter, "The Moral Logic of War," *Manual,* 1-5.

National Conference of Catholic Bishops, "The Challenge of Peace: God's Promise and Our Response," *Manual,* 6-13.

International Meeting of Latin American Bishops, "Nonviolence: A Power for Liberation," *Manual*, 14-22.
Schell, skim parts I and II, 1-178.

September 15
Horsburgh, "Critique of Armed Forces as an Instrument of Justice," *Manual*, 23-29.
Tolstoy, "Advice to a Draftee," *Manual*, 30-31.
Robert Seeley, "Registration and Resistance," *Manual*, 32-37.

II. Theories of Conflict, Violence and War

What are the causes of conflict, violence and war? Some believe that war is the result of innate human tendencies, while others believe that it is a social invention used to achieve certain ends. Is war implicit in the nation-state system, or can nation-states exist without war? Will there always be wars while oppression exists?

September 20
Film: "Obedience"
Wright, "Analysis of the Causes of War," *Manual*, 39-46.
Corning, "Human Violence: Some Causes and Implications," *Manual*, 47-59.
Mead, "Warfare is Only an Invention—Not a Biological Necessity," *Manual*, 60-63.

September 22
Hobbes, "On the Natural Condition of Mankind," *Manual*, 64-68.
Niebuhr, "The Morality of Nations," *Manual*, 69-78.
Barnet, "Farewell to the Nation-State," *Manual*, 79-80.
Schelling, "The Diplomacy of Violence," *Manual*, 81-89.
Boulding, K.E., "Power in Society," *Manual*, 90-94.

September 26
Film: "Battle of Algiers"

September 27
Dedijer, "Guerilla Warfare: The Poor Man's Power," *Manual*, 95-99.
Beckett, "Algeria vs. Fanon," *Manual*, 100-104.
Pierre, "The Politics of International Terrorism," *Manual*, 105-114.
Curle, diagram, *Manual*, 115.

III. The Economy of War

War preparation has become a big business, so big that it has possibly led to the development of an economic and social system that is guided by military needs rather than civilian needs. How do our institutions influence our ways of thinking, and vice versa? How have the vast sums of money spent on the military affected the American economy? Can we convert from military spending to civilian production without hurting the economy? What are the trade-offs between military spending and social services? How do arms sales affect the developing nations?

September 29
Eisenhower, "Farewell Address," *Manual*, 117-119.
Dumas, "Thirty Years of the Arms Race," *Manual*, 120-131.
Melman, "Ten Propositions on the War Economy," *Manual*, 132-137.

Pilisuk and Hayden, "Is There a Military-Industrial Complex that Prevents Peace?" *Manual*, 139-152.
Paper #1 Due

October 4
Barron, "How Grumman Spends its Campaign Fund," *Manual*, 153-154.
Winpisinger, "Planned Economic Conversion," *Manual*, 155-156.
Holtzman, "Useful Work: The Lucas Aerospace Workers' Conversion Campaign," *Manual*, 157-160.
Morrison and Walker, "A New Strategy for Military Spending," *Scientific American* 239.4 (October 1978), 1-19.
Sivard, *World Military and Social Expenditures, 1983*.

October 6
C.D.I., "A World at War: Small Wars and Superpower Military Intervention," *Defense Monitor* 8.10 (1979).
SIPRI, "Tables on Weapons Exports and Imports, *Manual*, 161.
Boulding, "Introduction," from Boulding and Mukarjee, *Economic Imperialism*, *Manual*, 163-168.

IV. Defense, Deterrence, the Arms Race and Nuclear War

Arising out of the Cold War, deterrence theory has guided much of the foreign policies of the superpowers over the last thirty years. Does deterrence work, or is it merely a cover for a massive arms race? Is there really a "Russian threat" that justifies ever-larger American weapons systems? Can American weapons meet their supposed missions, or have their missions changed from deterrence to first strike? What would a nuclear war mean to our allies, and to the rest of the world?

October 11
Morgenthau, "Origins of the Cold War," *Manual*, 170-181.
Iklé, "What it Means to be Number Two," *Manual*, 182-193.
ACDA, SALT Glossary, *Manual*, 194.
Johansen, "Building a New International Security Order: Policy Guidelines and Recommendations," in *AMIS*.

October 12
Film: "The War Game"
Patterson, "A Historical View of American Security," in *AMIS*.
McNamara, "Mutual Deterrence," *Manual*, 195-198.
Gray and Payne, "Victory is Possible," on library reserve.
NYT, "Pentagon Draws Up First Strategy for Fighting a Long Nuclear War," *Manual*, 199-201.
Fromm, "Paranoia and Policy," *Manual*, 202-203.
Keys, "The Abolition of War: Neglected Aspects," in *AMIS*.

October 18
Kaldor, "Is There a Soviet Military Threat?" *Manual*, 204-211.
C.D.I., "Soviet Geopolitical Momentum: Myth or Menace?" *Defense Monitor* 9.1 (1980). Read pp. 1, 3-7; regional summaries of Africa, Middle East, South Asia, East Asia, Latin America, and two countries.

October 20
First Hour: Mid-Term Exam
Second Hour: Schell, skim parts I and II again, 1-178.

October 25
Schell, Part III, 181-231.

V. Case Studies in U.S. Intervention

While there has not been a direct military confrontation between the superpowers, there have been 130 wars with combined casualties of 30 million since World War II. Many of these wars have occurred in the former colonial nations of the Third World. This section looks at the relation between two of these wars and American intervention. Why did America become involved in Vietnam and Central America and what are the implications for future American policies in similar situations?

October 26
Film: "Hearts and Minds"

October 27
Millett, "Chronology of the War for Vietnam," *Manual,* 213-217.
Thomson, "How Could Vietnam Happen?" *Manual,* 218-224.
Klare, "War Without End," *Manual,* 225-233.

October 31
Film: "El Salvador—Another Vietnam?"

November 1
Romero, "Letter to President Carter," *Manual,* 234.
Schultz, "Strengthening Democracy in Central America," *Manual,* 235-239.
Berryman, *What's Wrong in Central America and What to do About It.* 1983.

VI. Arms Control and Disarmament

The previous sections have given us an idea of some of the problems created by the world's dependence upon military force. The remaining sections will explore some alternatives to the use of military force and some ways to begin instituting these changes. This section presents some of the methods and problems of instituting arms control and disarmament measures, especially in the light of the spreading proliferation of nuclear weapons in the world.

November 3
Myrdal, "Arms Control and Disarmament Agreements, 1959-1975," *Manual,* 241-242.
Barnet, "The Promise of Disarmament," *Manual,* 243-246.
Yergin, "The Terrifying Prospect: Atomic Bombs Everywhere," *Manual,* 247-261.
Myrdal, "The High Price of Nuclear Arms Monopoly," *Manual,* 262-268.
York, "A Little Arms Control Can Be a Dangerous Thing," *Manual,* 269-272.

November 8
Reagan, "Paths Toward Peace: Deterrence and Arms Control," *Manual,* 273-277.

Andropov, "The USSR—Buttress of the Great Cause of Peace and Freedom of the Peoples," *Manual*, 278-280.

Kennan, "A Proposal for International Disarmament," 1-4.

Kennedy and Hatfield, "Joint Resolution on Nuclear Weapons Freeze and Reductions," *Manual*, 281-284.

Johansen, *Toward a Dependable Peace*, read 29-58, skim remainder.

VII. Alternative International Security Systems

How can alternatives to the use of violence be institutionalized in our global system? Can the United Nations settle conflicts and maintain peace in the world? Will a global legal system enforced by the world government bring security? Or would a world government be too unwieldy to work? Can alternative security systems arise from smaller cooperative efforts already being used by nations?

November 10
Stephenson, "Alternative International Security Systems: An Introduction," and Table, page 209, in *AMIS*.
"United Nations Charter," *Manual*, 286-288.
"The Structure of the United Nations," *Manual*, 289.
Stanford, "The U.N. as Peacemaker and Peacekeeper," *Manual*, 290-293.
Hollister, "World Organizations and Peace," *Manual*, 294-299.
Lall, "Disarmament and International Security," in *AMIS*.

November 15
Boulding, *Stable Peace*, or "National Defense Through Stable Peace."

November 17
Mitrany, "The Functional Alternative," *Manual*, 300-304.
Russett, "Causes of Peace," in *AMIS*.
Yarrow, "Unofficial Third Party Conciliation in International Conflicts," in *AMIS*.
Kriesberg, "Noncoercive Inducements in International Conflict," in *AMIS*.

November 22
Clark, "Introduction to World Peace Through World Law," *Manual*, read 305-306, 314-317 carefully; skim 307-313.
Claude, "World Government," *Manual*, 218-239.
Mische, "Revisioning National Security: Toward a Viable World Security System," in *AMIS*.

VIII. Nonviolence

Is nonviolence a viable alternative to the use of violent force for settling conflicts? Must nonviolence be based upon a firm moral background, or can it be used as a means to some ends? Can nonviolent civilian defense provide security for a nation?

November 29
Film: "Gandhi"
"An Introduction to Nonviolence," *Fellowship* 46.34 (March/April 1980), *Manual*, 331-334.
Gandhi, "On Nonviolence," *Manual*, 335-336, 337-338.
Gandhi, "Satyagraha or Passive Resistance," *Manual*, 339-340.

Gandhi, "Some Picketing Rules," *Manual*, 341.
Horsburgh, "The Bases of Satyagraha," *Manual*, 342-346.

December 1
Woodward, "Nonviolent Struggle, Defense, and Peacemaking," in *AMIS*.
Sharp, "Civilian-based Defense as a Peace Strategy," in *AMIS*.
Sharp, "Examples of Nonviolent Resistance," *Manual*, 347-350.
Schelling, "Some Questions on Civilian Defense," *Manual*, 351-354.
Paper #2 Due

IX. Individual Action for Social Change

How does an individual begin to take action if she/he wants to change the direction of our society. Where are the best places to take action, and what are the methods? Is action for social change really an individual effort, or does it involve working in community with others?

December 6
Walzer, "Strategic Choices," *Manual*, 356-357.
Beitz and Washburn, "On Choosing a Social Change Vocation," *Manual*, 359-363.
Washburn and Wehr, "Working for Peace and Social Justice," *Manual*, 364-369.

December 8
Thoreau, "On the Duty of Civil Disobedience," *Manual*, 371-377.
Pickus and Woito, "What Can I Do? 23 Answers," *Manual*, 378-381.
Carroll, et al., "Organizing for Social Transformation," *Manual*, 382-385.
Beitz and Washburn, "Questions for Yourself and Others . . .," *Manual*, 386-387.
Berrigan, "The Price of Peace," *Manual*, 388.

Social Change in a Militarized Economy

Tony Mullaney   *Spring 1982*
Sociology 270/ Boston College/ Chestnut Hill, MA 02167

This course will examine the nature and extent of the impact of military spending on the U.S. economy. Social dimensions of the impact will be emphasized.

A brief description and critique of the "arms race" will serve as an introduction since this is necessary background to an understanding of the kind and amount of military spending authorized by Congress.

The course will also explore some of the current efforts for social change known as economic conversion. This refers to the transfer of labor, capital and other productive resources from military use to alternative, civilian-oriented activity. In addition to a discussion of legislative and trade union efforts, case studies of various conversion projects will be presented.

Course Requirements

- active participation in the experiences provided by the class.
- required readings.
- critical issue review: a paper of approximately 10 pages which will be in effect an annotated outline of a critical issue raised in the course. It should indicate a familiarity with a number of primary sources and a skill with the methodology to handle them. Some possibilities will be discussed early in the course.
- final exam.
- students are also encouraged to keep a journal throughout the course, a series of reactions or responses to materials read or otherwise experienced. The creation of parables or fables or similar efforts may be substituted for the critical issue review. This should be discussed beforehand with the course coordinator.

Course Outline

January 22   Overview and Definitions
Annual Report. Department of Defense, Fiscal Year 1981, Chapter on Budget Summary.
Development and the Arms Race. Robert S. McNamara. Address at University of Chicago, May 22, 1979.
North-South: A Program for Survival. MIT Press, Cambridge, 1980. Introduction and Ch. 7: Disarmament and Development.
Lovins, Amory and Lovins, Hunter. "Nuclear Weapons/Nuclear Power," *Foreign Affairs*, Fall, 1980.

January 29   The Arms Race: Present Situation
Film: "War Without Winners."
Aldridge, Robert C. *The Counterforce Syndrome*, IPS, Washington, D.C., 1979.

Military Implications of the Treaty on the Limitation of Strategic Offensive Arms and Protocol Thereto. Part III. Senate Armed Services Committee Hearing, Oct. 9-11, 16, 1979. Testimony of Paul Nitze, Fred Iklé, and Richard Pipes.

"Pentagon Rebuts Charges of U.S. Military Weakness," *Defense Monitor*, Nov. 1980.

February 5   The Arms Race: U.S. Foreign and Military Policy
Questions and Answers on the Soviet Threat and National Security. American Friends Service Committee, Philadelphia, 1980.

Nitze, Paul. "Strategy in the 1980s," *Foreign Affairs*, Sept., 1980, 82-101.

"Soviet Geopolitical Momentum: Myth or Menace?" *Defense Monitor*, Jan. 1980.

Resource person: Randall Forsberg, Director, Institute of Defense and Disarmament Studies.

February 12   The Arms Race: The "Soviet Threat"
Melman, Seymour. *The Permanent War Economy.* Ch. 1-3 incl.

Fox, J. Ronald. *Arming America: How the U.S. Buys Weapons.* Ch. 5: The Pentagon.

Margiotta, Col. Franklin. *Evolving Strategic Realities.* Ch. 5: The Growing Importance of Economics: Can the U.S. Manage the Problem? National Security Affairs Institute, 1980, pp. 73-100 and pp. 185-190.

Gansler, Jacques. *The Defense Industry.* Ch. 1: Defense Industry and the U.S. Economy, pp. 9-28.

Resource person: Prof. Mark Solomon, History Department, Simmons College.

February 26   The Militarized Economy: Overview/Special Characteristics
The Pentagon Tax: The Impact of the Military Budget on Major American Cities. Employment Research Associates, Lansing, Mich., 1979.

Melman, Seymour. *The Permanent War Economy.* Ch. 5.

Sivard, Ruth Leger. *World Military and Social Expenditures 1980.* World Priorities, Inc, 1980.

Resource person: Jan Swanbeck, librarian, Government Documents.

March 5   The Militarized Economy: Effect on Civilian Needs/The Opportunity Cost
Testimony of David A. Gold. Massachusetts State Legislature, April 5, 1979.

Anderson, Marion. *The Empty Pork Barrel.* ERA, Lansing, Mich., 1978.

Anderson, Marion. *The Impact of Military Spending on the Machinists Union.* ERA, Lansing, Mich., 1979.

Hong, B.Y. *Inflation Under Cost Pass-along Management.* Ph.D. Dissertation, Columbia U., 1978. Chapter 5: Conclusions.

March 12   The Militarized Economy: Effects on Employment and Inflation
McGovern, George. "Unprofitable War," *Harper's*, Oct., 1980.

Barnet, Richard. *The Lean Years.* Ch. 8, Scarce Resources and the New International Military Order, pp. 216-235.

March 19   The Militarized Economy: Summary/Implications for the Social Economy and Introduction to Conversion
Birchard, Bruce. "Human Security and National Defense: the Question of Conversion." *J. Sociology and Social Welfare*, Jan.-March, 1977.

"Prosperity in a Demilitarized Economy: A Program for Conversion," *Defense Monitor*, Dec., 1978.

Testimony of Lloyd Dumas. Massachusetts State Legislature, April 5, 1979.

Resource person: Dr. Robert Case, Member of Energy Panel of National Council of Churches, and of Mathematics Dept. of Northeastern U.

March 26   Economic Conversion: Overview of Issues

Daniels, Marta. *Jobs, Security, and Arms in Connecticut.* American Friends Service Committee, 1980.

Creating Solar Jobs. Report from Mid-Peninsula Conversion Project. Mountain View, CA, 1979.

Economic Conversion: What Should Be the Government's Role? Congressional Budget Office, Jan., 1980.

Film: "We've Always Done It This Way."

April 2   Economic Conversion: Case Studies

"Feminism: The Hope for a Future," *Peacework*, April, 1980.

Bianchi, Eugene and Reuther, Rosemary. *From Machismo to Mutuality.* Paulist Press, 1976.

Film: "Between Men."

April 9   Economic Conversion: Some Obstacles

Zanotti, Barbara. *Militarism and Violence: Feminist Perspective.* Address at Riverside Disarmament Conference, Oct., 1979.

Lifton, Robert J. *The Broken Connection.* Ch. 22, Nuclear Distortions; Ch. 23, Nuclearism, pp. 335-387.

Resource person: Barbara Zanotti, Lecturer, Harvard Divinity School.

April 23   Summary

Slide presentation: "The Last Slide Show."

Possible Questions to Serve as a Basis for the Issue Reviews

Is there any evidence to suggest that the arms race, at least in part, is itself an "economic weapon?" That is, do some nations engage in an arms race as a way to "bleed the economy" of a present or potential antagonist?

Is there a "cowboy" or "macho" element in foreign and military policy? Is there a growing reliance on the military solution to political problems that can be traced at least to some degree to these variables?

What are the influences which shape American public opinion towards the USSR?

What purposes are served by a "cold war mentality?" Is there such a phenomenon? What can we learn from the origins of the Cold War?

What psychological factors might be operating to sustain the perception of "the Soviet threat?"

The relationship between inflation and military spending levels: Has it been consistent? Is it of concern at the national level? What attitudes are expressed?

What are the various impacts of military spending on the social economy, e.g., productivity, employment, balance of payments, value of the dollar, distribution of income, human services spending, etc.?

What ethical systems support the present arms race? with critique.

What are the steps leading to an alternative use plan for a given facility, e.g., General Dynamics in Quincy?

Aspects of the Post-WWII US-USSR Military Confrontation

Milton Leitenberg   *Fall 1982*
Swedish Institute of International Affairs 46.521/11128
Stockholm, Sweden

Books Assigned

Arms Control Readings from Scientific American, W.H. Freeman and Co., San Francisco, 1979

How Much is Enough?, Shaping the Defense Program, 1961-1969, A.C. Enthoven, K.W. Smith. Harper Colophon Books, New York, 1971

Current Issues in U.S. Defense Policy, D.T. Johnson and B.R. Schneider (eds.). Praeger, New York, 1976

The Atomic Bomb, The Critical Issues, B.J. Bernstein (ed.). Little, Brown and Co., Boston, 1976

"Arms, Defense Policy and Arms Control," *Daedalus*, Journal of the American Academy of Arts and Sciences. Cambridge . Summer 1975

Bureaucratic Politics and Foreign Policy, M.H. Halperin et al. The Brookings Institution, 1974

The Cold War Years: American Foreign Policy Since 1945, P.Y. Hammond. Harcourt, Brace and World, Inc., New York, 1969

America, Russia and the Cold War, 1945-1975, (third edition), Walter LaFeber, J. Wiley and Sons, Inc., New York, 1976

American Strategy in the Nuclear Age, D.W. Tarr. MacMillan Co., New York, 1966

General Background Assignment

If you have had no previous course work which provided a knowledge of nuclear weapons and their effects, you must look at the following papers and books, certainly before topics 6-7.

The Effects of Nuclear Weapons, S. Glasstone, ed., U.S. DOD and U.S. AEC, February 1964, 730 pages.

"Review of Nuclear Weapons Effects," H.L. Brode, *Annual Review of Nuclear Science*, 18, 1968, pp. 153-202.

Topic 13; Item No. 9.

"Nuclear Strategy and Nuclear Weapons," B. Carter, *Scientific American*, 230, No. 5, May 1974, pp. 20-31.

"Limited Nuclear War," S.D. Drell, F. Von Hippel, *Scientific American*, 235, No. 5, November 1976, pp. 27-37.

1. The 1945 U.S. Decision on the First Use of a Nuclear Weapon

Required Reading:

The Atomic Bomb, the Critical Issues, B.J. Bernstein, (ed.), 1976.

"The Atomic Bomb and the Origins of the Cold War," M.J. Sherwin, *American Historical Review*, October 1973, pp. 947-968.

"Atomic Diplomacy Revisited," T.T. Hammond, *Orbis*, 19, No. 4, Winter 1976, pp. 1403-1428.

Recommended:

Atomic Diplomacy, Gar Alperovitz, Simon and Schuster, 1965.

A World Destroyed: the Atomic Bomb and the Grand Alliance, M.J. Sherwin, Knopf, 1975.

The Atomic Bomb and the End of WWII, Herbert Feis, PUP, 1966.

"The Decision to Use Atomic Weapons Against Hiroshima and Nagasaki," K.M. Glazier, *Public Policy*, 18, No. 4, Summer, 1970, pp. 464-516.

2. Early Negotiations
a) The "Baruch Plan"
Required Reading:

The Baruch Plan: U.S. Diplomacy Enters the Nuclear Age, Lenice Wu, Congressional Research Service, August 1972, for the Committee on Foreign Affairs, U.S. House of Representatives, 67 pages.

Atomic Shield, 1947/52 Vol. II, A History of the United States Atomic Energy Commission, R.G. Hewlett and F. Duncan, 1969.

Postwar Negotiations for Arms Control, B.G. Bechhoefer, the Brookings Institution, 1961.

Atlantic Monthly, July 1946, 178, No. 1, "Stopping the Atomic Armament Race," (three articles), pp. 37-45.

b) The Stassen negotiations and their outcome

"The Quest for Disarmament since World War II," W.R. Frye, in *Arms Control: Issues for the Public*, (ed.) Louis Henkin, Spectrum, Prentice Hall, 1961, pp. 18-48.

All references to Stassen in *Postwar Negotiations for Arms Control*, B.G. Bechhoefer, 1961.

c) Miscellaneous proposals related to the building up and deployments of specific weapons

Chronology of major disarmament efforts, 1945 to mid-1969, *SIPRI Yearbook*, 1968/69, pp. 280-320.

Who Wants Disarmament? R J Barnet, Beacon 1960, 140 pages.

3. The Nuclear Test Ban Treaty
Required Reading:

Arms Control, pp. 109-153, 283, 302, and 346-348.

Nuclear Weapon Testing Programs, 1945-1968, *SIPRI Yearbook, 1968/69*, pp. 241-258.

SIPRI Yearbook, 1970, pp. 384-387.

The Test Ban, *SIPRI Yearbook, 1972*, pp. 389-437, 461-469, 523-532.

SIPRI Yearbook, 1975, pp. 405-415.

SIPRI Yearbook, 1976, pp. 306-310.

"A Comprehensive Nuclear Test Ban, Technical Aspects, 1957 to 1967," M. Leitenberg and C. Hohenemser, *Scientist and Citizen*, 9, No. 8, pp. 197-217, October 1967.

Recommended:

Diplomats, Scientists and Politicians: The United States and the Nuclear Test Ban Negotiations, H.K. Jacobson and E. Stein, University of Michigan Press, 1966.

4. CW, BW and the BW Treaty

Required Readings:

Development in Chemical and Biological Warfare, *SIPRI Yearbook, 1968/69*, pp. 112-134, 271-275, 334-336.

Arms Control, pp. 303-317.

"The Special Case of Chemical and Biological Weapons," J.P. Robinson, *Bulletin of the Atomic Scientists*, 31, No. 5, pp. 17-23.

Scan Vol. I (1971) and Vol. II (1973) of *The Problem of Chemical and Biological Warfare* (SIPRI)

SIPRI Yearbook, 1969/70, pp. 185-205, 438-452.

SIPRI Yearbook, 1972, pp. 501-522.

SIPRI Yearbook, 1973, pp. 383-390.

SIPRI Yearbook, 1974, pp. 370-383.

SIPRI Yearbook, 1975, pp. 426-431.

Recommended:

Chemical and Bacteriological Weapons and the Effects of their Possible Use, United Nations, 1969, 100 pages.

Health Aspects of Chemical and Biological Weapons, World Health Organization, 1970, 132 pages.

The Control of Chemical and Biological Weapons, Carnegie Endowment, 1971, 130 pages.

Chemical and Biological Weapons, A Special Issue, *Scientist and Citizen*, 9, No. 7, August-September, 1967, 59 pages.

Chemical and Bacteriological Warfare, Chapter 3, in *Armaments and Disarmament in the Nuclear Age: A Handbook*, SIPRI, 1976, pp. 108-33.

5. Military Aspects of the Ocean, the Seabed, ASW, and the Seabed Treaty

Required Readings:

Submarine Launched Ballistic Missiles, *SIPRI Yearbook, 1968/69*, pp. 96-111, 144-147.

The Militarization of the Deep Ocean, the Sea Bed Treaty, *SIPRI Yearbook 1969/70*, pp. 92-184, 425-437.

Prospects for Arms Control in the Ocean, SIPRI Research Report No. 7, October 1972, 25 pages.

Antisubmarine Warfare, *SIPRI Yearbook, 1974*, pp. 303-325.

Tactical and Strategic Anti-submarine Warfare, SIPRI Monograph, 1974, 148 pages.

World Stock of Fighting Vessels, 1950-74, *SIPRI Yearbook, 1975*, pp. 255-307.

World Stock of Fighting Vessels, *SIPRI Yearbook, 1969-70*, pp. 307-330.

Arms Control, pp. 235-259.

The Control of Naval Armaments: Prospects and Possibilities, B.M. Blechman. (Studies in Defense Policy Series) The Brookings Institution, 1975, 100 pages.

Soviet Naval Power: Challenge for the 1970's, Norman Polmar. Crane, Rusak, and Co. (Revised Edition, 1974), 126 pages.

Recommended:

The Future of the Sea-Based Deterrent, K. Tsipis et al., (eds.) MIT Press (1973). (Note: the best papers on the Soviet Navy are probably those of MccGwire in past issues of *Brasseys Annual* and *ISS Survival*, and his two edited volumes, *Soviet*

Naval Developments: Context and Capability, Dalhousie, 1973 and *Soviet Naval Policy: Objectives and Constraints,* Dalhousie, 1975.)

6-7. The Acquisition of Nuclear Weapons and their Delivery Systems, Strategic and Tactical, by the US and the USSR, 1945-1976

Required Reading:

Strategic Weapons: An Introduction, N. Polmar. Crane, Russak & Co., Inc., 1975, 170 pages.

Nuclear Diplomacy: The First Twenty Five Years, G.H. Quester. The Dunellen Co., 1970.

Nuclear War: The Impending Strategic Deadlock, Neville Brown. Pall Mall Press, 1964.

Race to Oblivion: A Participant's View of the Arms Race, Herbert F. York. Simon and Schuster, 1970.

Look at any recent copy of:
a) *Janes Weapon Systems*
b) *Janes Fighting Ships*
c) *Janes All the World's Aircraft*

SIPRI Yearbook, 1969/70, pp. 376-383.

SIPRI Yearbook, 1974, pp. 97-102.

SIPRI Yearbook, 1976, pp. 24-28.

"The Debate Over the Hydrogen Bomb," H. York, *Scientific American,* 233, No. 4, pp. 106-130.

"The Present State of the World's Arms Race," M. Leitenberg, *Bulletin of the Atomic Scientists,* 28, No. 1, January 1972, pp. 15-21.

Military Application of Nuclear Technology, Hearings, Parts I and II, Subcommittee on Military Applications, Joint Committee on Atomic Energy, U.S. Congress, 1973, 54 pages and 134 pages.

U.S. Security Issues in Europe: Burden Sharing and Offset, MBFR, and Nuclear Weapons, A Staff Report, Committee on Foreign Relations, U.S. Senate, September 1973, 27 pages.

8. The Weapons Acquisition Process

Required Reading:

How Much is Enough? Shaping the Defense Program 1961-1969, A.C. Enthoven & K.W. Smith. Harper-Colophon Books, N.Y., 1971.

Bureaucratic Politics and Foreign Policy, M.H. Halperin et al. Brookings Institution, 1974.

Current Issues in U.S. Defense Policy, D.T. Johnson and B. Schneider, (eds.) Praeger, 1976.

Arming America: How the U.S. Buys Weapons, J.R. Fox. H.U.P., 1974.

"Arms, Defense Policy and Arms Control," *Daedalus,* Summer, 1975.

Resources Devoted to Military Research and Development, *SIPRI Yearbook, 1972,* pp. 149-239; also, *SIPRI Yearbook, 1968/69,* pp. 90-96.

"The Dynamics of Military Technology Today," M. Leitenberg, *International Social Science Journal,* 25, No. 3, 1973, pp. 336-357.

European Defense Industries: National and International Implications, Mary Kaldor. ISIO Monograph, Series 1, No. 8, 1972.

Military R&D, (item 6 on list), *SIPRI Yearbook, 1973,* pp. 252-296.

Reduction in Military Budgets, *SIPRI Yearbook, 1975*, pp. 103-118.
Estimating Soviet Military Expenditure, *SIPRI Yearbook, 1974*, pp. 172-204.
Papers by James Kurth:
  a) "A Widening Gyre, the Logic of American Weapon Procurement," *Public Policy*, 19, Summer 1973, pp. 373-404.
  b) "Why We Buy the Weapons We Do," *Foreign Policy*, No. 11, Summer 1973.
  c) "The Political Economy of Weapons Procurement: The Follow-on Imperative," *The American Economic Review*, 62, No. 2, May 1972, pp. 296-311.

9. Crisis Deployments, Long-term Targeting Policies and Nuclear Threats
(Note: The literature is *particularly* deficient in this area. Very recent and excellent papers by Blechman and Kaplan (Brookings-ARPA), Mahoney (Center for Naval Analysis) and Atkeson (U.S. Army) are not generally available. Academic volumes such as George and Smoke contain next to nothing. Bits and pieces can at times be gotten from volumes such as Hillsman's or Sorenson and Schlessinger on J.F.K.)
Required Reading:
Deja Vu: The Return to Counterforce in the Nixon Administration, Desmond Ball. California Seminar on Arms Control and Foreign Policy, December 1974, 73 pages.
Bulletin of the Atomic Scientists, 30, No. 7, September 1974, pp. 12-16.

10. Interventions (US & USSR) Overt and Covert
Required Reading:
The United States Against the Third World: Antinationalism and Intervention, Melvin Gurtov. Praeger, 1974.
"U.S. Military Policy, Limits to Intervention," G. Allison et al. *Foreign Affairs*, 48, No. 2, January 1970, pp. 245-261.
"The CIA in Africa: How Central? How Intelligent?" *The Journal of Modern African Studies*, 14, No. 3, 1976, pp. 401-426.
Also select several from among:
"To Intervene or Not to Intervene," H.J. Morgenthau, *Foreign Affairs*, 1967, pp. 425-436.
"Future Small Wars: Must the United States Intervene?" L. Bloomfield, *Orbis*, 12, No. 3, Fall 1968, pp. 669-683.
"The Dominican Intervention in Retrospect," A.F. Lowenthal, *Public Policy*, 18, No. 1, Fall 1969, pp. 133-153.
"Political Outcomes of Foreign Assistance, Influence, Involvement or Intervention," H. Wriggins, *Journal of International Affairs*, 22, No. 2, 1968, p. 217.
"American Foreign Policy and the Decision to Intervene," A. Yarmolinsky, *Journal of International Affairs*, 22, No. 2, 1968, pp. 231-235.
Inside the Company: CIA Diary, Philip Agee. Bantam, 1975, 1976.
Recommended Papers by Frederic Pearson:
  a) "A Perceptual Framework for Analysis of International Military Intervention," *Peace Research Reviews*, 1974.
  b) "Foreign Military Interventions and Domestic Disputes," *International Studies Quarterly*, 18, No. 3, September 1974, pp. 259-290.
  c) "Foreign Military Intervention by Large and Small Powers," *International Interactions*, 1, 1974, pp. 273-278.

d) "Geographic Proximity and Foreign Military Intervention: 1948-1967," *Journal of Conflict Resolution*, 18, No. 3, September 1974, pp. 432-459.

e) "American Military Intervention Abroad: A Test of Economic and Noneconomic Explanations," Chapter 2 in S. Raicher and C. Liske, eds., *The Politics of Aid, Trade and Investment*, J. Wiley and Sons, 1976, pp. 37-62.

11. Military Assistance, Arms Transfers, and Trade

Required Reading:

The Arms Trade with the Third World, SIPRI, 1971, *(at least* p. 271).

Arms Trade Registers: Arms Trade with the Third World, SIPRI, 1975, pp. 149-176 (and 131-148).

The Arms Trade and International Systems, R.E. Harkavy. Ballinger Pub. Co., 1975.

World Military Expenditures and Arms Trade, 1963-1973, U.S. Arms Control and Disarmament Agency, 1975, pp. 1-12. *World Military Expenditures and Arms Trade, 1965-1974, 1976*, pp. 1-11.

"The Study of International Trade in Arms and Peace Research," U. Albrecht, *Journal of Peace Research*, 9, No. 2, 1972, pp. 165-178.

"Arms Trade with the Third World as an Aspect of Imperialism," *Journal of Peace Research*, 12, No. 3, pp. 213-234.

"The Political Economy of Arms Sales," M.T. Klare, *Bulletin of Atomic Scientists*, 32, No. 9, November 1976, pp. 11-18.

Recommended:

International Transfer of Conventional Arms: A Report to the Congress, U.S. Arms Control and Disarmament Agency, April 12, 1974, Committee on Foreign Affairs, U.S. House of Representatives.

Economic Issues in Military Assistance, Hearings, Joint Economic Committee, U.S. Congress, January, February, 1971.

International Security Assistance Act of 1976

a) *Hearings, and Report*, Committee on International Relations, House, 1976.

b) *Hearings, and Report*, Committee on Foreign Relations, Senate, 1976.

12. The Strategic Arms Limitation Talks (SALT)

Required Reading:

Advanced Strategic Missiles: A Short Guide, Ian Smart, Adelphi Papers, No. 63, December 1969, IISS, 31 pages.

Offensive Missiles, K. Tsipis, Stockholm Paper 5, SIPRI, 1974, p. 33.

"All You Ever Wanted to Know About MIRV and ICBM Calculations But Were Not Cleared to Ask," L.E. Davis, W.R. Schilling, *Journal of Conflict Resolution*, 17, No. 2, June 1972, pp. 207-242.

"Two Legs Do Not a Centipede Make," Cong. R.L. Leggett, *Armed Forces Journal International*, February 1975, pp. 30-32.

"SALT II, The Race to Oblivion; the Superpowers Talk Peace While Preparing for War," M. Leitenberg, *Bulletin of the Atomic Scientists*, 30, No. 7, September 1974, pp. 8-20.

"The Salt II Ceilings and Why They Are So High," M. Leitenberg, *British Journal of International Studies*, 2, No. 2, 1976, pp. 149-163.

"Strategic Vulnerability, The Balance Between Prudence and Paranoia," J.D. Steinbrunner and T.M. Garwin, *International Security*, 1, No. 1, Summer 1976, pp. 138-181.

SIPRI Yearbook, 1968/69, pp. 29-44.
SIPRI Yearbook, 1969/70, pp. 36-63, 358-375.
SIPRI Yearbook, 1972, pp. 1-50.
SIPRI Yearbook, 1973, pp. 1-59.
SIPRI Yearbook, 1974, pp. 103-122.
The Future of the Strategic Arms Race: Options for the 1970s, G.W. Rathjens, The Carnegie Endowment, 1969.
Towards a Strategic Arms Limitation Agreement, H. Scoville Jr., The Carnegie Endowment, 1970.
Nuclear Arms Control Agreements: Process and Impact, G.W. Rathjens et al., 1974, 69 pages.

13. Nuclear Proliferation
Required Reading:
The Near Nuclear Countries and the Non-Proliferation Treaty, *SIPRI Yearbook, 1972*, pp. 283-388. Also, *SIPRI Yearbook, 1975*, pp. 16-37; *SIPRI Yearbook, 1976*, pp. 363-391.
Commercial Nuclear Power and Nuclear Proliferation, Steven Baker, Occasional Papers, No. 5, Cornell University, Peace Studies Program, 1975, 66 pages.
"Peaceful Nuclear Explosions," F.L. Long, *Bulletin of the Atomic Scientists*, 32, No. 8, October 1976, pp. 18-28.
Perspective on the NPT Review Conference, Mason Willrich, Occasional Paper No. 7, Stanley Foundation, 1975, 17 pages.
Retrospective on the NPT Review Conference: Proposals for the Future, W. Epstein, Occasional Paper No. 9, Stanley Foundation, 1975, 26 pages.
"The Proliferation of Nuclear Weapons," W. Epstein, *Scientific American*, 232, No. 4, April 1975, pp. 18-33.
"Failure at the NPT Review Conference," W. Epstein, *Bulletin of the Atomic Scientists*, 31, No. 7, September 1975, pp. 46-48.
NPT: Paradoxes and Problems, A. W. Marks, ed. Arms Control Association, Carnegie Endowment, 1975, 106 pages.
Effects of the Possible Use of Nuclear Weapons and the Security and Economic Implications for States of the Acquisition and Further Development of These Weapons, Report of the Secretary General, United Nations, 1968, 76 pages.
Nuclear Energy and Nuclear Weapons, Michael Nacht. Aspen Conference Report, 1976, 22 pages.

14. Weapons Development To Come
Required Readings:
"The Evolution of Weaponry in the Next Half Century," D. Brennan, in *Tomorrow's World: Challenges to U.S. Diplomacy*, Headline Series, No. 189, June 1968, pp. 34-58.
"Controlling Future Arms," Abt, C.C., *Disarmament and Arms Control*, No. 1, Spring 1965, pp. 19-40.
"Effective Military Technology for the 1980's," R.L. Garwin, *International Security*, 1, No. 2, Fall 1976, pp. 50-77.
Unless Peace Comes, Nigel Calder (ed.), Allen Lane, The Penguin Press, 1968.
"How to Avoid Monad, and Disaster," *Foreign Policy*, No. 24, Fall 1976, pp. 172-201.

At least one ARPA and one DDR&E summation, in an annual U.S. Defense Budget
Hearing Volume. (any one of the four)

"Wars Fourth Dimension," *Newsweek*, Nov. 29, 1976, pp. 46-48.

"The Requirements of Military Technology in the 1970's," No. 5 in *Defense,
Technology and the Western Alliance*, IISS, 1967.

Precision Guided Weapons, James Digby, Adelphi Papers, No. 118, IISS, Summer
1975.

The Automated Battlefield, *SIPRI Yearbook, 1974*, pp. 326-360.

Drones and RPVs, *SIPRI Yearbook*, 1975, pp. 339-377.

Reconnaissance Satellites, *SIPRI Yearbook, 1973*, pp. 60-102.

SIPRI Yearbook, 1974, pp. 287-302.

SIPRI Yearbook, 1975, pp. 378-404.

SIPRI Yearbook, 1976, pp. 102,-122.

Environmental and Ecological Warfare, *SIPRI Yearbook, 1976*, pp. 72-86.

Reconnaissance, Surveillance and Arms Control, Ted Greenwood, Adelphi Papers,
No. 88, 1972, 28 pages, (also in *Arms Control*, pp. 223-234).

Long Range Cruise Missiles, *SIPRI Yearbook, 1975*, pp 311-338.

Recommended:

The Other Arms Race, New Technologies and Non-Nuclear Conflict, G. Kemp et
al. (eds.), Lexington Books, D.C. Heath and Co., 1975.

Impact of New Technologies on the Arms Race, B.T. Feld, et al. (eds.), MIT Press,
1971.

Controlling the Conventional Arms Race, Report, UNA-USA, 1976.

The Threat of Nuclear War: Looking for Creative Responses

George W. Morgan   *Spring 1984*
University Course/Brown University/Providence, RI 02912

The topic will be examined from a wide range of perspectives, including factors generally in the forefront of attention to nuclear arms and war, as well as underlying dimensions of human existence that bear upon them. The instructor hopes that the study will lead to participants' greater understanding of the matters discussed and, at the same time, to their greater ability to prepare themselves for thoughtful action aimed at diminishing the likelihood of nuclear war.

Conducted as seminar. Class discussion on the basis of common readings. Each student will choose one of the major topics for special study and, together with others working on the same topic, will be responsible for selecting a significant portion of the common readings.

I. The Threat of Nuclear War
War making potentials—weapons
Plans for increasing U.S. nuclear weapons power
Consequences of nuclear war
Historical summary of nuclear arms build-up

II. Attitudes Toward the Threat
Apathy, denial, and repression
Confronting the threat
What is hope? May we hope?

III. Theorizing about National Security
Security doctrines
Assessments of the balance of power
Significance of "Who's ahead?"

IV. Some Forces Behind the U.S. Nuclear Arms Build-up
Economic factors
Political factors
Psychological factors
Bureaucratic factors
Science and technology—R and D

V. Language, Reason, and Nuclear War
The use of estranging language—the abstract and the concrete
Language, deception, and self-deception
Appeals to rationality by "hawks" and "doves"
Different kinds of reason

VI. Moral Issues
Value conflicts arising from war
Special problems connected with nuclear arms
Individual moral responsibility with respect to nuclear war

VII. Our Relation to the "Other"
The adversarial stance
The enemy
Aggressiveness and control
Trust and mistrust
Dialogue and negotiation

VIII. Nuclear Weapons in our Life
Psychological impact
Impact on our sense of meaning and absurdity
Impact on our relation to mortality
Impact on confidence in the future
Impact on democratic politics

IX. Diminishing the Likelihood of Nuclear War
Assessments of arms control
Calls for more far-reaching steps
Rethinking the meaning of national security
What individuals can do

Science, Technology and Arms Control

Lester Paldy   *Fall 1983*
Department of Technology and Society/State University of New York/
Stony Brook, NY 11794

Technology, defined as the organization of knowledge and material re-sources to achieve specific goals, has contributed to warfare over a period that predates recorded history. The potential that technology holds for improving the capacity of nations to use force to achieve political ends has been recognized and exploited all too well. We know far more about techniques of mass destruction than we do about the technology of peace-keeping. In the 20th century, scientific technology, or technology that is firmly based on scientific concepts, has been ingeniously applied to warfare and violence in ways that few could have foreseen.

Scientific technology is now routinely harnessed for military purposes. Virtually all new weapons systems employ scientific technology in sophis-ticated forms. Yet, despite our experience with the application of technolo-gy for military purposes, many questions have not yet been fully answered. To what extent does what has been called autonomous technology gener-ate powerful new weapons systems which may have the paradoxical effect of reducing national security? Can technology really be autonomous, or is this a concept that has been invented to provide a rationale for ill-conceived human action?

What has been the impact of the widespread application of scientific technology to military purposes on Third World development? Is there a relationship between the arms trade and the fact that so many developing nations have military, non-democratic governments?

How might scientific technology make a comparable contribution to the maintenance of peace and genuine world security? Have technological resources been allocated in reasonable proportion for peacekeeping pur-poses? To what extent is the contemporary scientific-technological enter-prise fueled by its military applications?

These are questions which need to be addressed by persons who seek to understand the time in which we live, and who seek to create and shape the future. The network of relationships linking science, technology, national security issues, foreign policy, world development, international law and the maintenance of peace should be the subject of intensive study. Con-cepts from both the natural and social sciences must be applied. These issues and problems must also be viewed in the light of knowledge and insights gained from the study of the humanities: ethical and value consid-erations influence technological choices; technology may exert a signifi-cant influence on the development of social, cultural and individual values.

The relationship between technology, peace and war is so complex that neither theorists or governments have succeeded very well in shaping it in ways that minimize the probability of conflict. Many academic departments find it difficult to offer courses addressing this relationship. The necessary scientific and technological content may not be considered accessible by social scientists and humanists, while complex political, social, and value considerations cause natural science and engineering departments to be reluctant to participate. Further, the lack of powerful conceptual models which describe these complex interactions reduces the attractiveness of the field to potential scholars and researchers. Nevertheless, the relationship linking technology, peace and war is being increasingly recognized as a fundamental one worthy of serious study at many institutions.

This course provides an opportunity for students to study the role of scientific technology in national defense policy, arms control and disarmament negotiations and the maintenance of peace. It begins with an overview of the manner in which technology has been used to support military purposes in history. It examines the military research and development process and the ways in which new weapon systems are conceived, developed and acquired by the defense establishment.The conceptual origins, engineering design and effects of nuclear weapons are studied in some detail, followed by a survey of strategic nuclear doctrine, or the ways in which nuclear weapons are designed to be used or brandished as threats to deter attack or achieve national political goals. This section of the course ends with an introduction to the objectives, processes and institutions of arms control.

The second half of the course explores important military technologies and existing arms limitation agreements. The proliferation of nuclear weapons is presented as a problem that must be dealt with in both a political and technical context. The international trade in arms and the development and improvement of conventional weapons technologies is reviewed in sufficient detail to enable students to interpret and analyze news accounts and official reports released by government agencies.

Course Requirements

1. Seven 30-minute examinations with essay questions and problems based on lectures and readings administered at bi-weekly intervals are designed to provide students with frequent opportunities to assess their progress.
2. Term paper, 12 to 15 pages on a topic related to one of the major issues studied.

Reading List

Texts
1. B. Russett and B. Blair, *Progress in Arms Control?* Readings from *Scientific American*, W.H. Freeman & Co., San Francisco, 1979.

2. J.H. Barton and L. Weiler, *International Arms Control*, Stanford University Press, Stanford, CA 1976.
3. H. York, ed. *Arms Control*, Readings from *Scientific American*, W.H. Freeman, San Francisco, 1973.

Reprints, *Scientific American*
1. W. Foley and V. Soedel, "Ancient Oared Warships," April 1982.
2. V. Soedel and W. Foley, "Ancient Catapults," March 1979.
3. K. Lewis, "The Prompt and Delayed Effects of Nuclear War," July, 1979.
4. B. Feld and K. Tsipis, "Land-Based Intercontinental Ballistic Missiles," Nov. 1979.
5. J. Wit, "Advances in Antisubmarine Warfare," Feb. 1981.
6. K. Tsipis, "Laser Weapons," Dec. 1981.
7. J. Parmentola and K. Tsipis, "Particle Beam Weapons," April 1979.
8. W. Epstein, "A Ban on the Production of Fissionable Material for Weapons," July 1980.
9. P. Morrison and P. Walker, "A New Strategy for Defense Spending," Oct. 1978.
10. H. Meselson and P.J. Robinson, "Chemical Warfare and Chemical Disarmament," April 1980.
11. D. Olander, "The Gas Centrifuge," Aug. 1980.
12. P. Walker, "Precision-Guided Weapons," Aug. 1981.

Reading and Study Assignments

August 30   Introduction: Course Objectives, Resources
No reading assignment is due for this class but you should begin immediately on assignment no. 2.

September 1   Science, Technology and Warfare: From Antiquity to World War I
Read:
Scientific American Reprints (SARP)
1. W. Foley and V. Soedel, "Ancient Oared Warships," April 1981.
2. V. Soedel and W. Foley, "Ancient Catapults," March 1979.
Study Questions:
1. Describe one of the major design problems confronting the builders of oared warships. How was it solved? Explain how the development of new weapons systems designed for shipboard use may have forced a change in naval tactics of the time. Describe a contemporary change in modern naval tactics forced by new technology.
2. Explain how the demand for engineers in Ancient Greece may have been influenced by advances in military technology. What were some of the associated political effects?
3. Should the work of Greek catapult engineers be described as "scientific?" Why? What is meant by "scientific?"
4. How might issues which arose in connection with the development of the oared warship and catapult be said to anticipate issues that we now confront when studying the relationship between science and technology and their links to warfare and society?

September 8   Military R&D and The Research University: The Genesis of New Weapons Systems

Read:

Progress in Arms Control: Articles 3 and 4 (Rathjens, York)

Arms Control: 1-7 (Newman, Wilson, Morrison, Newman, Blackett, Ridenour,
   Barnard) (numbers refer to articles listed on the contents page of these books)

Study Questions:

1. How is military research justified in university settings? What are the major
   criticisms leveled against such research? What are the rebuttal arguments?
2. Trace the path between basic research and its military application. What are the
   strengths and weaknesses of the system?

September 13   Basic Concepts of Atomic and Nuclear Physics

Read:

"Nuclear Fission," *Encyclopaedia Britannica,* pages 301-306.

Study Questions:

1. Summarize the evolution of our conceptual model of atoms and nuclei citing key
   observations, experiments and theoretical advances.
2. What are isotopes?
3. What is radioactivity?
4. What is meant by "mass defect" or "binding energy?"

September 15   Uranium Technology: Mining, Conversion and Enrichment

Read:

Scientific American Reprint: D. Olander, "The Gas Centrifuge," August 1980.

Study Questions:

1. Describe in general terms how uranium is mined and milled.
2. What is the isotopic composition of natural uranium and why is this of significance in connection with nuclear weapons?
3. What environmental problems are associated with uranium mining and milling
   operations and how are they controlled?
4. Outline the gaseous diffusion of gas centrifuge enrichment processes. Why was
   the latter process developed?

September 20   The Design of Fission Weapons

Read:

"Nuclear Weapons," *Encyclopaedia Britannica,* Vol. 13, pages 324-325.

"Nuclear Weapons," *Encyclopaedia Americana,* pages 518-528.

Optional: John McPhee, *The Curve of Binding Energy,* Ballantine Books, 1974.

Study Questions:

1. Sketch the design of a gun-type and implosion-type fission weapon.
2. Why must its fissile components be assembled rapidly for a fission weapon to
   work?
3. Give an explanation of the term "critical mass."
4. About how much 99% pure U^{235} is needed to make a bomb? Plutonium U^{239}?
   What are the dimensions of such masses?

September 22   The Effects of Fission Weapons

Read:

International Arms Control (IAC), pages 46-53.

Scientific American Reprint: K. Lewis, "The Prompt and Delayed Effects of
   Nuclear War," July 1979.

AC: Articles 12, 13 and 14 (Loutit, Beadle, Newman)
"The Effects of Nuclear War," Office of Technology Assessment, pages 1-12.
Study Questions:
1. IAC, chapter 4, nos. 1-7.
2. What are the principal effects of radiation exposure on humans? How is such exposure measured? In what units? What is meant by "LD-50?"
3. Describe the physical effects of a nuclear explosion, contrasting air and surface bursts.
4. What are some of the major long-term environmental effects of nuclear explosions in the atmosphere?

September 29   The Development of Thermonuclear Weapons
Read:
AC: Articles 8-11 (Ridenour, Bethe, Bacher, Szent-Gyorgyi)
Progress in Arms Control (PIAC): 1. (York)
Study Questions:
1. Sketch a design of a simple thermonuclear weapon.

October 4   U.S. Strategic Doctrine for the Use of Nuclear Weapons
Read:
PIAC: Articles 11 and 12 (Carter, Drell)
IAC: Pages 123-150.
Study Questions:
1. *IAC:* Chapter 2; 1-4, 5, 6, 8, 9, 10.
2. What is meant by "strategic warfare?" Where did the term originate?
3. Outline what is meant by the following terms: counterforce vs. countervalue attacks; first strike vs. second strike capacities; mutual assured destruction.
4. Explain the United States policy bearing on "no first use."
5. Explain the following statement: "nuclear weapons are not meant to be used."
6. Outline the Soviet "first strike against our missile forces" scenario advanced by persons who believe that U.S. forces are vulnerable to Soviet attack. What counter-arguments are presented by those who do not believe that this scenario is realistic?
7. One justification for the U.S. MIRV was the Soviet ABM. Why wasn't MIRV scrapped after the U.S. and U.S.S.R. signed the ABM Treaty?
8. Why did MIRV become feasible in the 1970s? Discuss this in terms of the relationship between a missile's accuracy, yield, and effectiveness. For example, if the accuracy of the missile is improved by a factor of 2, how much can the yield of a weapon be reduced to have the same probability of success that the missile had before improvement? Note that the blast pressure created at a distance from the detonation of a nuclear weapon varies approximately as the inverse cube of the distance.
9. The Department of Defense report "Soviet Military Power" published in the fall of 1981 states that "each warhead of the 10 SS-18 re-entry vehicles has a better than 50% chance of destroying a Minuteman silo." If this is true, how many warheads would have to be launched at a single silo to assure at least a 90% probability that the silo is destroyed?

October 6   Arms Control: Objectives, Processes and Institutions
Read:
IAC: Pages 1-45, 66-93, 151-171
AC: Articles 15-18 (Wiesner, Bullard, Treaties)
Study Questions:
IAC: Chapter 5 questions 4-7; Chapter 8 questions 1-4, 5, 7, 8.

October 11   Land-based ICBM and MIRV Technology
Read:
PIAC: Article 10. (York)
SARP: Bernard Feld and K. Tsipis, "Land-based Intercontinental Ballistic Missiles,"
   November 1979.
Study Questions:
1. Why are MIRV systems regarded as potentially destabilizing? How did the SALT
   II Treaty attempt to deal with MIRV systems?
2. What is meant by a "cold launch"-ICBM? What problems do such systems pose
   for arms control? How might the reload time factor be considered important in
   discussions of force levels?
3. Explain the concept of CEP.
4. What is meant by missile "fratricide?"

October 13   Missile Firing Submarines and Anti-submarine Warfare
Read:
PIAC: Articles 6 and 7. (Scoville, Garwin)
SARP: J. Wit, "Advances in Antisubmarine Warfare," February 1981
Study Questions:
1. How do submarines attempt to evade detection? What technologies are used to
   locate them? Contrast active and passive sonar systems.
2. Why might an exceptionally effective anti-submarine warfare system be regarded
   as destabilizing?
3. What is the technical basis of the command and control problem posed by the
   need to communicate with submerged submarines? How does the Department
   of Defense attempt to deal with this problem?
4. Describe a Trident submarine's strike capacity giving the numbers of missiles,
   warheads, yields and ranges.

October 18   Manned Aircraft and Cruise Missile Technologies
Read:
PIAC: Article 15. (Tsipis)
SARP: P. Walker, "Precision-Guided Weapons," August 1981.
Study Questions:
1. What technical characteristics of cruise missiles make them attractive to
   military planners? What problems do they pose for arms limitation agreements?
2. If you heard a claim that the U.S. and U.S.S.R. were placing cruise missiles on
   orbiting satellites for potential use against targets on earth, how could this be
   dismissed on technical grounds alone?
3. Explain the differences between active and passive radar systems used on
   precision-guided weapons.

October 20   Antiballistic Missile Technology
Read:
AC: Article 19. (Garwin and Bethe)
Study Questions:
1. Since an ABM system is purely defensive, how can it be construed as a destabilizing weapon?
2. Why was the prototype U.S. ABM system abandoned?

October 25   Strategic Arms Limitation Talks (SALT)
Read:
PIAC: Article 14. (Scoville)
AC: Article 27. (ABM Treaty)
Study Questions:
1. What are the major features of SALT II?
2. What are the merits and deficiencies of the SALT II Treaty as argued by supporters and critics? How would you vote on the Treaty if you were a senator? Why?
3. Show why it is difficult to compare U.S. and U.S.S.R. strategic weapons systems if one relies solely upon simple numerical comparisons.
4. Give rough numerical estimates of the U.S.-U.S.S.R. "strategic balance" citing your sources.

October 27   The MX Basing Mode Debate
Study Questions:
1. Describe several alternative deployment systems for the MX, presenting the rationales of their designers.
2. How would you vote on MX development funds? Why?

November 3   Military Technology in Space
Read:
SARP: 1. K. Tsipis, "Laser Weapons," December 1981; 2. J. Parmentoal and K. Tsipis, "Particle Beam Weapons," April 1979.
PIAC: Article 8 (Greenwood)
Study Questions:
1. What characteristics of laser and particle beam weapons make them of interest to defense planners? What disadvantages are cited as making them inappropriate for ABM systems?
2. What is the NAVSTAR system and why might it pose a problem for arms control?
3. Explain the physics of satellite motion in qualitative terms. What keeps them up? What is a "synchronous" satellite?
4. How is information from reconnaissance satellites returned to earth?

November 8   Strategic Arms Reduction Talks (START)
Study Questions:
1. Outline President Reagan's initial proposal for strategic arms reductions.
2. Outline and explain the initial Soviet response. (*NY Times*, 8-1-82)

November 10   Plutonium Technology
Read:
AC: Articles 34 and 35 (Weinberg, Seaborg)

November 15   Proliferation of Nuclear Weapons
Read:
PIAC: Articles 16, 17 and 19 (Epstein, Rose, NP Treaty)
IAC: pages 288-309.
SARP: W. Epstein, "A Ban on the Production of Fissionable Material for Weapons,"
 July 1980.
Study Questions:
1. *IAC:* Chapter 14; 2, 5, 7, 8, 9.
2. What are the major features of the nonproliferation treaty?
3. What is the position of the U.S. Nuclear Regulatory Commission regarding the
 effectiveness of IAEA safeguards?
4. What are the incentives for a non-nuclear weapon state considering the acquisition of nuclear weapons? What are the disincentives?

November 17   Nuclear Weapons Testing and Detection Technologies
Read:
AC: Articles 16 and 28 (Bullard, Myers)
PIAC: Article 2 (York)
Study Questions:
1. How are underground nuclear explosions detected? What are the major technical
 features of the limited test ban treaty? What is the current limit on the yields of
 nuclear weapons tested underground? What is meant by "decoupling" a nuclear
 explosion?

November 22   New Technologies and Conventional Weapons
Read:
AC: Article 33
IAC: pages 271-287.
Study Questions:
1. *IAC:* Chapter 13; 1-7.

November 24   The International Arms Trade
Read:
IAC: pages 228-248.
Study Questions:
1. What justifications are usually given for arms sales abroad whether by the U.S. or
 U.S.S.R.? How do such sales affect U.S. defense expenditures?

Military Force and Disarmament

Randy Forsberg   *Summer 1980*
Political Science 578 B1/Boston University/Boston, MA 02156

Purpose

The structure, rationales and likely future development of world military forces; the obstacles to disarmament; and the alternatives before us.

History

1. Nature & Effects of Nuclear Weapons

July 2   Introduction to course
Effects 1-45, 276-304

July 3   Read *Hiroshima*
Effects, 154-206

July 5   Design of nuclear weapons
Effects, 324-353, 387-450

July 6   Effects of nuclear weapons
Effects, 541-628

2. Nonnuclear Military Force in the Modern World

July 9   Relation of nuclear and conventional arms
Price of Defense, 1, 2, 5; Quiz 1

July 10   Armies
U.S. Troops in Europe, 1-10

July 11   Air Forces
Price of Defense, 3, 4, 9

July 12   Navies
U.S. Nuclear Weapons in Europe

July 13   Tactical nuclear weapons
Price of Defense, 10-12

3. The Strategic Nuclear Arms Race

July 16   War in 20th century; nuclear-conventional
Race to Oblivion, 1-59; Quiz 2

July 17   U.S.-Soviet strategic arms, 1945-60
Race to Oblivion, 75-105, 144-146

July 18   U.S.-Soviet strategic arms, 1960-1972
Race to Oblivion, 147-239

July 19   U.S.-Soviet strategic arms, 1972-85
Nacht & Greenwood photocopy

July 20   Nuclear warfare scenarios; escalation

4. Arms Control Negotiations

July 23-24   Review of 20th century arms control & disarmament negotiations
Arms Control and Disarmament Agreements, 33-39, 55-59, 77-83, 124-131, 136-
137; Quiz 3

Explanation
5. Exploring the Reasons for the World Arms Buildup

July 25   Trends & projections of world arms
Milbal & *WMSE* photocopies

July 26   Dove vs. Hawk interpretations
AFSC & Pipes photocopies

July 27   Ideology vs. International economics
Magdoff photocopy; Quiz 4

July 30   Domestic economics & politics

July 31   Elite theory and bureaucratic politics

Aug. 1   Comparing accounts of the arms race

Alternative Futures

Aug. 2   Defining goals for future of world arms

Aug. 3   Obstacles to arms control & disarmament
Rathjens, Ruina handout

Aug. 6   Unilateral vs. negotiated action

Aug. 7   Timing and international interaction

Aug. 8   Possible wars in the late 20th century

Aug. 9   Information & public opinion in formation of military policy

Aug. 10   Discussion of goals and means

Military Force and Disarmament Literature List
Department of Energy and Department of Defense, *Effects of Nuclear Weapons,*
U.S. Government Printing Office, 1977.
John Hersey, *Hiroshima,* Knopf, 1958.

Boston Study Group, *The Price of Defense*, New York Times Publishing Co., 1979.

John Newhouse, et al., *U.S. Troops in Europe*, Brookings Institution, 1971.

Jeffrey Record, *U.S. Nuclear Weapons in Europe*, Brookings Institution, 1974.

Herbert York, *Race to Oblivion*, Simon & Schuster, 1970.

Michael Nacht and Ted Greenwood, "The New Nuclear Debate: Sense or Nonsense?" *Foreign Affairs*, July 1974.

U.S. Arms Control & Disarmament Agency, *Arms Control and Disarmament Agreements*, 1977.

International Institute for Strategic Studies, *Military Balance 1978-79* (few excerpts).

Harry Magdoff, *The Age of Imperialism*, Monthly Review Press, 1969.

George Rathjens, Jack Ruina and Abram Chayes, *Nuclear Arms Control Negotiations: Process and Impact*, Carnegie Endowment for International Peace, 1974.

Course Outline

Lecture 1.   Introduction

Lecture 2.   U.S. Defense Budget and Military Forces
Schultze, Charles, et al. *Setting National Priorities: The 1971 Budget.* Brookings Institution, 1970; *The 1972 Budget.* Brookings, 1971. *The 1973 Budget.* Brookings, 1972.

Fried, E.R., A.M. Rivlin, C.L. Schultze, N.H. Teeters. *Setting National Priorities: The 1974 Budget.* Brookings, 1973.

Blechman, B.M., E.M. Gramlich, R.W. Hartman. *Setting National Priorities: The 1975 Budget.* Brookings, 1974; *The 1976 Budget.* Brookings, 1975.

Owen, H. and C.L. Schultze, eds. *Setting National Priorities: The Next Ten Years.* Brookings, 1976.

Pechman, J. *Setting National Priorities: The 1978 Budget.* Brookings, 1977.

U.S. Department of Defense. *Annual Report—Fiscal Year 1979.*

U.S. Department of Defense. *Research, Development, Test, and Evaluation—Fiscal Year 1979.*

U.S. Department of Defense. *Manpower Report—Fiscal Year 1979.*

U.S. Department of Defense. *Selected Manpower—1978 Statistics.*

Lecture 3.   Nature and Effects of Nuclear Weapons
Brodie, B. and F. Chapter 9, "The Nuclear Revolution," pp. 233-267 in *From Crossbow to H-Bomb.* Indiana University Press, 1973 edition.

Foster, J.S. "Nuclear Weapons," *Encyclopedia Americana*, 1972, Vol. 20, pp. 518-528.

Glasstone, S. and P.J. Dolan. *The Effects of Nuclear Weapons*, 3rd edition, 1977. Prepared and published by U.S. Department of Defense and U.S. Department of Energy.

Hersey, J. *Hiroshima.* Knopf, 1958.

York, H.F. "The Debate over the Hydrogen Bomb," *Scientific American*, October 1975.

York, H.F. *The Advisors: Oppenheimer, Teller and the Superbomb.* W.H. Freeman, 1976.

Lecture 4. U.S. and Soviet Strategic Weapons, Early Period

York, H.F. Chapters 1-8, pp. 1-172 in *Race to Oblivion: A Participant's View of the Arms Race.* Simon and Schuster, 1970.

Bottome, E.M. Chapters 1-3, pp. 1-73 in *The Balance of Terror.* Beacon, 1972.

Lecture 5. U.S. and Soviet Strategic Weapons, Later Period

Forsberg, R. "U.S. and Soviet Strategic Nuclear Forces, 1964-1974" (1966-1976, 1967-1977, 1968-1978) in *World Armaments and Disarmament: SIPRI Yearbook 1974* (1976, 1977, 1978), Stockholm; various publishers, same years.

Johnson, D.T. and B.R. Schneider, eds. *Current Issues in U.S. Defense Policy.* Praeger Publishers, 1976. (Published in cooperation with the Center for Defense Information): pp. 129-175; Chapters: 8—Leader, S.H., and B.B. Schneider, "U.S.-Soviet Strategic Forces: SALT and the Search for Parity." 9—Stanford, P., "Nuclear Missile Submarines and Nuclear Strategy." 10—Berman, R., "The B-1 Bomber."

York, H.F. ed. *Arms Control: Readings from Scientific American.* W.H. Freeman, 1973: pp. 159-259; Chapters: Garwin and Bethe, "Anti-Ballistic Missile Systems;" Rathjens, "The Dynamics of the Arms Race;" York, "Military Technology and National Security;" Rathjens and Kistiakowsky, "The Limitation of Strategic Arms;" Scoville, "The Limitations of Offensive Weapons;" Greenwood, "Reconnaissance and Arms Control;" Scoville, "Missile Submarines and National Security." Garwin, "Antisubmarine Warfare and National Security."

Quanbeck, A.H., and B.M. Blechman. *Strategic Forces: Issues for the Mid-Seventies.* Brookings, 1973.

Quanbeck, A.H., and A.L. Wood. *Modernizing the Strategic Bomber Force: Why and How.* Brookings, 1973.

Tsipis, K. "Accuracy of Strategic Missiles," *Scientific American,* July 1975.

Scoville, H. "The SALT Negotiations," *Scientific American,* August 1977.

Lecture 6. U.S. Army, Marines, Air Force and Reserves

White, W.D. *U.S. Tactical Air Power: Missions, Forces and Costs.* Brookings, 1974.

Newhouse, J. et al. *U.S. Troops in Europe: Issues, Costs and Choices.* Brookings, 1971.

Lawrence, R.D., and J. Record. *U.S. Forces Structure in NATO: An Alternative.* Brookings, 1974.

Binkin, M., and J. Record. *Where Does the Marine Corps Go from Here?* Brookings, 1976.

Binkin, M. *U.S. Reserve Forces: The Problem of the Weekend Warrior.* Brookings, 1974.

Johnson & Schneider, *Current Issues;* Chapter 14.

Whitaker, B.W. "U.S. Tactical Air Forces: Technology Outpaces Management."

Lectures 7 & 8. U.S. Navy and Tactical Nuclear Weapons

Kuzmack, A.M. *Naval Force Levels and Modernization: An Analysis of Shipbuilding Requirements.* Brookings, 1971.

Blechman, B.M. *The Control of Naval Armaments: Prospects and Possibilities.* Brookings, 1975.

Record, J. *U.S. Nuclear Weapons in Europe: Issues and Alternatives.* Brookings, 1975.

Johnson & Schneider, *Current Issues;* Chapters: Schneider, B.R., "U.S. Tactical Nuclear Weapons: A Controversial Arsenal;" Schneider, B.R., "Tactical Nuclear Weapons: Four Peacetime Safety Dilemmas."

Lecture 9.   Soviet Conventional Forces and Tactical Nuclear Weapons
Blechman, B.M. *The Changing Soviet Navy.* Brookings, 1973.
Record, J. *Sizing Up the Soviet Army.* Brookings, 1975.
International Institute for Strategic Studies. *The Military Balance 1977-78.* London, 1977.
International Institute for Strategic Studies. *Strategic Survey, 1976.* London, 1977.
Aspin, L. *Are the Russians Really Coming?* 1976.

Lectures 10 & 11.   Military Forces of Other Countries
I.I.S.S., *The Military Balance 1977-78,* and *Strategic Survey, 1976.*

Lecture 12.   World Summary of Military Forces and Spending and Projections
U.S. Arms Control & Disarmament Agency. *World Military Expenditures and Arms Transfers, 1966-1975.* Washington, D.C.: U.S. Government Printing Office, December 1976.
Sivard, R.L. *World Military and Social Expenditures 1977.* WMSE Publications, 1977.
Stockholm International Peace Research Institute. *World Armaments and Disarmament: SIPRI Yearbook 1973.* New York: Humanities Press, 1973: Chapter 10. Landgren-Backstrom, S., "Domestic Defense Production in Third World Countries," pp. 343-379.
Forsberg, R., "Resources Devoted to Military Research and Development," *An International Comparison,* Stockholm: Stockholm International Peace Research Institute. New York: Humanities Press, 1972.

Lectures 13 & 14.   Nuclear Exchange Models
Brodie, B. Part II, pp. 147-409, in *Strategy in the Missile Age.* Princeton paperback edition, 1965.
Kahn, H. *On Escalation: Metaphors and Scenarios.* Penguin paperback, 1968.
Tsipis, K. *Offensive Missiles.* Stockholm International Peace Research Institute, 1974.
Pipes, R. "Why the Soviet Union Thinks It Could Fight and Win a Nuclear War," *Commentary,* 64:1, July 1977.
Nitze, P.H. "Assuring Strategic Stability in an Era of Detente," *Foreign Affairs,* July 1974.
Davis, L. *Limited Nuclear Options: Deterrence and the New American Doctrine,* Adelphi Paper #121. International Institute for Strategic Studies, London, 1976.
Schilling, W. and L. Davis. "All You Ever Wanted to Know About MIRV and ICBM Calculations But Were Not Cleared To Ask," *Journal of Conflict Resolution,* 17:2, June 1973.
Greenwood, T., and M. Nacht. "The New Nuclear Debate: Sense or Nonsense?" *Foreign Affairs,* January 1976.
York, H.F. *Race to Oblivion,* Chapters 9-12, pp. 173-240.

Lecture 15.   Major Conventional War

Enthoven, A.C., and K.W. Smith. Chapter 4, pp. 117-164, and Chapters 6 & 7, pp. 197-266, in *How Much Is Enough?* Harper Colophon paperback, 1972.

Clough, Ralph. *Deterrence and Defense in Korea: The Role of U.S. Forces.* Brookings, 1976.

Lecture 16.   Other Wars

Parker, W.D. *A Concise History of the United States Marine Corps, 1775-1969.* U.S. Marine Corps Headquarters, Historical Division, Washington, D.C., 1970.

Lectures 17-19.   The Cold War as the Rationale for the Arms Race

Huntington, S.P. Chapters 1-8, pp. 1-122, in *The Common Defense.* Columbia University Press paperback edition, 1966.

Fulbright, J.W. *The Arrogance of Power.* Vintage paperback, 1966.

Magdoff, H. *The Age of Imperialism.* Monthly Review Press, 1969.

Kolko, G. *The Politics of War: The World and United States Foreign Policy, 1943-1945.* Vintage paperback, 1970.

Maddox, R.J. *The New Left and the Origins of the Cold War.* Princeton University Press, 1973.

Lectures 20 & 21.   Postulating Disarmament

No reading.

Lecture 22.   The History of Arms Control and Disarmament Negotiations

Barton, J.H., and L.D. Weiler, eds. *International Arms Control: Issues and Agreements.* Stanford University Press, 1976.

U.S. Arms Control and Disarmament Agreements. Washington, D.C., 1977.

Schilling, W., P. Hammond and G. Snyder. *Strategy, Politics and Defense Budgets.* Columbia University Press, 1962: Hammond, P., "The B-36—Carrier Controversy."

Huntington, *The Common Defense,* Chapters 9-21 and 28-30, pp. 123-283 and 369-425.

Rathjens, G.W., J. Ruina and A. Chayes. *Nuclear Arms Control Negotiations: Process and Impact.* New York, Carnegie Endowment for International Peace, 1974.

Lecture 24.   The Alternatives Before Us

No reading.

Nuclear Weapons and Nuclear War: A Multimedia Study Course

Eric Markusen and John Harris   *Fall 1983*
International Relations 3105 and Sociology 3960/
University of Minnesota/Minneapolis, 55455

Student enrollment in this course has risen steadily since it was first offered in 1980—a reflection of the growing interest in the nuclear war controversy. In preparing this course, we have tried to incorporate suggestions from our former students. We have also attempted to include what we are constantly learning about these difficult times.

Several premises underlie our efforts to offer this course to as wide a range of students as possible. First, the threat of nuclear war is the most fateful issue of our age. Second, until very recently, American citizens have tended to be indifferent to and ignorant of facts and issues concerning nuclear war. Third, teaching about nuclear war must be an urgent priority of our nation's educational institutions. Our democratic political system is meaningless in the absence of an informed, concerned citizenry. Finally, education about nuclear war must be balanced and comprehensive. Students should be exposed to divergent points of view in order to fairly examine a broad range of issues.

Objectives

1) To provide you with a basic introduction to facts and issues concerning nuclear weapons and nuclear war. Upon completing this course, it is hoped that you will have attained "nuclear literacy"—the abilities to follow current debates about nuclear weapons policy; to evaluate political candidates and their platforms on nuclear war issues; and to recognize a wide range of approaches to reducing the threat of nuclear war.
2) To stimulate creative thinking about means to reduce the threat of nuclear war, this course examines past and present efforts to control the nuclear arms race, and provides a factual basis for evaluating candidates for political offices and their proposed policies.
3) To encourage you to participate as politically active citizens in efforts to evaluate present nuclear weapons policies and reform them where advisable.

Broadcast Schedule

"The Day After," written by Edward Hume, directed by Nicholas Meyer and produced by Robert Papazian for ABC Circle Films, will be broadcast over KSTP-TV (Channel 9) from 7:00 to 9:15 p.m. on Sunday, Nov. 20, 1983.

"Viewpoint," a televised panel discussion hosted by Ted Kopel will follow immediately on the same channel (from 9:15 to 10:00 p.m.)

Required Textbooks: An Introduction

Adams, Ruth and Susan Cullen, editors. *The Final Epidemic: Physicians and Scientists on Nuclear War.* Chicago: The Educational Foundation For Nuclear Science, 1982. Based on talks presented at various symposia offered during 1980-1981 by Physicians for Social Responsibility (PSR). PSR is an organization of physicians and other health professionals dedicated to educating the public about the medical consequences of nuclear war. (One such symposium was held on the University of Minnesota campus in November 1982).

Carnesale, Albert, et al. (The Harvard Nuclear Study Group). *Living With Nuclear Weapons.* New York: Bantam Books, 1983. Written by a group of Harvard arms control experts, most of whom have been working on nuclear weapons and related issues for a large part of their professional lives. They bring a tremendous amount of expertise to the subject, as demonstrated through the breadth of the book. Nevertheless, the book has a definite political message to which you should be sensitive. It was written largely as a means to "bridge" the gap between the Nuclear Weapons Freeze Campaign and the Reagan Administration. The authors perceive themselves as exploding some of the "myths" perpetuated by each side in this public debate and as advocating moderate, responsible positions on such issues as nuclear warfighting.

Ground Zero. *Thinking About Preventing Nuclear War.* Washington, D.C. 1982. Offers a convenient categorization of the ways in which a nuclear war might begin, and helps us to think about what techniques or "firebreaks" might be introduced to block these paths to holocaust. Ground Zero is a non-partisan organization based in Washington D.C. with state chapters nationwide. It has mounted a major effort to educate the American public about nuclear weapons issues, and has published *Nuclear War: What's in it for You?* and *What About the Russians and Nuclear War?* (parts of which you'll read for this course).

Johansen, Robert. *Toward an Alternative Security System.* World Policy Paper No. 24. New York: World Policy Institute, 1983. Johansen offers something of a more radical—and more visionary—analysis of the nuclear dilemma. Johansen is highly skeptical of partial or incremental solutions to the nuclear threat. He advocates a program with nuclear disarmament as its basic objective, in which security is maintained by a more just and equitable world order. Johansen's concept of "global security" is a marked departure from most of the deterrent and arms control proposals we encounter in the course, which define security as national defense.

Leaning, Jennifer. *Civil Defense in the Nuclear Age.* Cambridge, MA: Physicians for Social Reponsibility, 1982. Another outgrowth of Physicians for Social Responsibility's efforts. This is, to our knowledge, the most comprehensive and devastating critique of crisis relocation's potential contribution to long-term survival after a nuclear war.

Mayers, Teena. *Understanding Nuclear Weapons and Arms Control.* Arlington, VA: Arms Control Research, 1983. Selected as a basic introduction to nuclear weapons and the history of the Soviet-American nuclear arms competition. A list of acronyms and glossary are helpful in translating some of the difficult terminology used in this course.

Union of Concerned Scientists. *Solutions for the Nuclear Arms Race: Briefing Manual.* 1982. A compilation of various articles related to nuclear weapons systems, strategy, and arms control issues. We draw liberally on the *Briefing*

Manual for readings in several lessons. You should pay particular attention to the articles assigned which discuss the Freeze and other arms control proposals.

Required Cassettes (Ten C-60 audio cassette tapes)
The programs for this course were originally broadcast over KUOM radio, 770 AM, and have been adapted for your use in conjunction with "The Day After." The 20 half-hour radio programs have been recorded on audio cassettes that you may either purchase from the Department of Independent Study or check out and listen to at the Learning Resources Center, Minneapolis campus, University of Minnesota.

Course Requirements
To complete this course successfully, you must do the required readings from your texts, this study guide, and the appendices, watch the televised programs "The Day After" and "Viewpoint," listen to 20 programs which comprise the audio component of this course, and submit three written assignments and a questionnaire.

Audio Programs
Always complete the required reading prior to listening to the assigned audio programs. As you will see, each audio program and lesson subject usually correspond.

Course Outline
This course is comprised of twenty study guide lessons, readings, corresponding audio programs and a television drama immediately followed by a televised panel discussion. Each lesson has a reading assignment in the form of study notes, selections from the textbooks, and reprints in the study guide appendices.

Lesson 1 Themes of the Nuclear Age
Required Reading:
The Final Epidemic, pp. vii-xi., 1-3, 7-20.
Living with Nuclear Weapons, pp. ix-xvii, 3-21, 71-73, 77.
Listening Assignment: Program 1

Lesson 2 Nuclear Weapons and Their Effects
Required Reading:
The Final Epidemic, pp. 93-109. Appendix 1.
The Final Epidemic, pp. 110-116, 117-150.
Understanding Nuclear Weapons and Arms Control, pp. 24-50.
Listening Assignment: Program 2

Lesson 3 The Consequences of Nuclear War
Required Reading:
Appendices 2 and 3
The Final Epidemic, pp. 169-218.
Listening Assignment: Program 3

Lesson 4 The Issue of Civil Defense
Required Reading:
Appendices 4 and 5
Civil Defense in the Nuclear Age
Listening Assignment: Program 4

Lesson 5 The Search for Security in the Nuclear Age
Required Reading:
Appendix 6
UCS *Briefing Manual,* pp. 52-58, Appendices 7, 8, and 9.
Toward An Alternative Security System, pp. 1-32.
Listening Assignment: Program 5

Lesson 6 The Evolution of U.S. Nuclear Strategy
Required Reading:
Understanding Nuclear Weapons and Arms Control, pp. 1-23.
Appendices 10, 11, 6, (begin with Strategic Nuclear Policy Under Reagan) 12, 13.
Listening Assignment: Program 6

Lesson 7 The Evolution of Strategic Arsenals
Required Reading:
The Final Epidemic, pp. 76-85.
UCS *Briefing Manual,* pp. 1-3, skim 18-25, read pp. 26-40, 45-51.
Appendix 14
Listening Assignment: Program 7

Lesson 8 The U.S./Soviet Strategic Nuclear Weapons Balance
Required Reading:
Living With Nuclear Weapons, pp. 115-126.
Appendix 15
UCS *Briefing Manual,* pp. 12-15.
Appendices 16 and 17
Listening Assignment: Program 8
Written Assignment 1: Suggested Due Date: January 3, 1984

Lesson 9 The Threat of Nuclear War in Europe
Required Reading:
Appendix 18
Living With Nuclear Weapons, pp. 126-132, 165-170.
UCS *Briefing Manual,* pp. 123-139.
Appendix 19
Listening Assignment: Program 9

Lesson 10 The Soviet Union and Nuclear Weapons
Required Reading:
Appendix 20
Listening Assignment: Program 10

Lesson 11 The Proliferation of Nuclear Weapons
Required Reading:
Living With Nuclear Weapons, pp. 215-231.
Appendices 21 and 22
Listening Assignment: Program 11

Lesson 12 Paths to Nuclear War
Required Reading:
Living With Nuclear Weapons, pp. 47-68.
Thinking About Preventing Nuclear War

Appendices 23, 24, and 25
Listening Assignment: Program 12

Lesson 13 Past Efforts to Control the Arms Race
Required Reading:
Living With Nuclear Weapons, pp. 188-202.
UCS *Briefing Manual*, pp. 59-68, 75-84.
Understanding Nuclear Weapons and Arms Control, skim 1-23, read pp. 53-70.
Appendix 26
Listening Assignment: Program 13
Written Assignment 2: Suggested Due Date: January 24, 1984

Lesson 14 Political and Economic Causes of the Arms Race
Required Reading:
Living With Nuclear Weapons, pp. 102-114.
Appendices 27, 28, 29, 30, and 31.
Listening Assignment: Program 14

Lesson 15 Psychological Forces Aggravating the Nuclear Threat
Required Reading:
The Final Epidemic, pp. 27-34.
Appendix 32
Listening Assignment: Program 15

Lesson 16 Lessons of the Holocaust for the Nuclear Age
Required Reading:
Appendices 33, 34, 35, 36, and 37
Listening Assignment: Program 16

Lesson 17 Moral and Ethical Issues
Required Reading:
Appendices 38 and 39
Listening Assignment: Program 17

Lesson 18 Costs of the Arms Race
Required Reading:
The Final Epidemic, pp. 21-26, 35-47, 48-57.
Appendix 40
Listening Assignment: Program 18

Lesson 19 Current Proposals to Reduce the Risk of Nuclear War
Required Reading:
Living With Nuclear Weapons, pp. 203-214.
UCS *Briefing Manual*, pp. 85-141, skim pp. 86-87, 89-90, 123-139.
The Final Epidemic, pp. 223-236.
Thinking About Preventing Nuclear War (review)
Listening Assignment: Program 19

Lesson 20 An Agenda for Human Survival and Continuity
Required Reading:
Living With Nuclear Weapons, pp. 232-255.
Toward an Alternative Security System

Appendices 41 and 42
Listening Assignment: Program 20, December 7
Written Assignment 3: Suggested Due Date: February 10, 1984

Appendix/Title
Each appendix number and the title represents a larger, integrated document in that subject area:
  1 General Description of Effects
  2 The Continuing Body Count at Hiroshima and Nagasaki
  3 Three Attack Cases and Other Long-term Effects
  4 Civil Defense
  5 Selling Civil Defense
  6 The Reagan Nuclear Strategy
  7 MAD vs. NUTS: The Mutual Hostage Relationship of the Superpowers
  8 Flexibility: The Imminent Debate
  9 PD-59: A Strategic Critique
  10 The Policy War: Brodie vs. Kahn
  11 Counterforce Targeting: How New? How Viable?
  12 Nuclear Combat: The Five Year Defense Plan
  13 Nuclear Warfighting as an Issue for Public Education
  14 Soviet Military Power 1983
  15 Paths Toward Peace: Deterrence and Arms Control
  16 U.S. Strategic Vulnerability
  17 Summary
  18 Nuclear Weapons in Europe
  19 No First Use: A View From the United States
  20 What About the Russians and Nuclear War?
  21 Nuclear Power and Nuclear Weapons: The Connection is Dangerous
  22 Nuclear Power and Nuclear Weapons: The Connection is Tenuous
  23 Command and Control: Use It or Lose It?
  24 First Strike: Myth or Reality
  25 On Strategic Uncertainty
  26 Detente and Arms Control: Constructing a Positive Reaction Cycle
  27 The Process of Government Policy-making in this Area
  28 The Iron Triangle: The Politics of Defense Contracting
  29 Defense Dependency: Grumann and the Long Island Economy
  30 The B-1: Bomber for all Seasons?
  31 Liberty is at Stake: A Farewell Address
  32 The Bureaucratization of Homicide
  33 Atrocities and other Conditions in Concentration Camps in Germany
  34 Rudolf Hess Affidavit
  35 Hermann Graebe Affidavit
  36 Kurt Gerstein Affidavit
  37 Walter Neff Testimony
  38 Nuclear Weapons: What is the Moral Response?
  39 Catholic Debate and Division on Deterrence
  40 Defense Spending and the Economy
  41 A Nuclear Education Campaign
  42 Steps Toward a New Planetary Identity

Problems in a Technological Society: Modern Warfare and Arms Control Problems

Avrom Blumberg   *Spring 1983*
Chemistry 200/DePaul University/Chicago, IL 60604

Rationale & Goals of the Division of Natural Science & Mathematics

The natural sciences are our principal means of discovering and describing physical reality. The work of scientists consists of making careful observations (including measurements) and of creating models which describe more or less perfectly these observations. The total set of successful thus accepted models is what we know of physical reality. Whenever possible, scientists use the concise and precise methods of mathematics to describe their results. Like artists, scientists are interested in the designs or patterns of nature; unlike artists, scientists validate their models by experimentation. Mathematicians, who often work closely with scientists, are concerned with the nature of patterns and designs.

Together natural science and mathematics are great adventures of the human intellect and properly belong in any program of general or liberal studies. One cannot be truly educated without knowing something about these subjects. Our curiosity about the way things happen provided, from the very beginning of human history, an important role for science and mathematics. Early efforts to mark the seasons, tides, and celestial phenomena; to plot out land areas; to extract metals from their ores and to make alloys; to preserve food and convert hides and fibers into clothing; and to heal sickness, are some of the roots upon which these modern disciplines are based.

But there is another reason for the importance of science and mathematics to an undergraduate curriculum and that is the relationship between these and technology. Where science and mathematics are used to describe natural phenomena or to discover the character of these descriptions, technology is used to manipulate natural processes. We live in a highly technological age. Almost all the material things and comforts we enjoy and also the matters we worry about have their roots in science and technology. The problems of our society cannot be fully understood, nor can solutions to these problems be obtained, without some knowledge of how the natural sciences, mathematics and technology operate.

The Division of Natural Science & Mathematics has these broad goals: to acquaint a student with her scientific heritage, the methods, fundamental knowledge and achievements of science and mathematics; to increase her ability to reason quantitatively, analytically and with symbols; and to examine the relation of natural science and mathematics to technology and the problems our society has connected to these endeavors.

Purpose of this Course

The subject of this course (modern warfare, the arms race, arms control and disarmament) is an important and attractive one for accomplishing these goals. The importance of science and mathematics to defense matters can be judged from the fact that one fourth of our scientists and engineers work on weapons-related jobs. Modern weapons, both nuclear and conventional, their delivery systems, and reconnaissance and surveillance methods, have seriously affected the character of armed conflict and of preventing wars. Conversely, by providing their expertise, scientists have been able to influence national security and attempts to control arms. The importance of these issues to scientists can be assayed by the very frequent appearance of arms-control articles in *Scientific American* magazine (where these are always the first articles of that issue), in *Science* (the official publication of the American Association for the Advancement of Science) and in other similar periodicals. Accordingly, the account of the role of science and mathematics in warfare and national security is an excellent way in which to show how problems arise from science and how solutions to these are approached.

The student will, in addition, become familiar with the scientific basis and nature of conventional, chemical, biological and nuclear weapons, and risk-evaluation and monitoring systems. Ample opportunities are provided to sharpen her analytical and expository skills by applying natural science, basic arithmetic and elementary algebra and symbolic reasoning to selected diverse topics. She will become a more informed and wiser citizen by seeing how it is that serious problems rooted in science and technology seldom have easy or simple solutions.

Resources

These texts will be referred to in the detailed list of objectives by their identifying codes:

MX—Scoville, *MX: Prescription for Disaster*
MR—Meselson & Robinson, *Chemical Warfare and Chemical Disarmament*
P—Parmentola, *Particle-beam Weapons*
WY—Wiesner & York, *National Security & the Nuclear Test Ban*
These will be on reserve in the library:
RTO—York, *Race to Oblivion* (Simon & Schuster 1971)
AWIC—Littauer, *Air War in Indochina* (Beacon Press 1972)
CBW—Cookson, *A Survey of Chemical and Biological Warfare* (Monthly Review Press, 1969)
F&F—Blumberg & Stanley, *Form & Function* (McGraw-Hill 1972)
MOM—Young, *The Mystery of Matter* (Oxford 1965)
ACDA—Some Arms Control Treaty Booklets
These single articles from *Scientific American*:
M—Meyers, "Extending the nuclear test bank" (January 1972)
HS—Scoville, "The SALT negotiations" (August 1977)

LA—Aspin, "The verification of the SALT II agreement" (February 1979)
MW—Morrison & Walker, "A new strategy for military spending" (October 1978)
EB—Bullard, "The Detection of underground explosions" (July 1966)
PMSB—Blackett, "The role of two scientists in government" (April 1961)
JW—Wit, "Advances in antisubmarine warfare" (February 1981)
MH—Hellman, "The mathematics of public-key cryptography" (August 1979)
DO—Olander, "The gas centrifuge" (August 1978)
RL—Rose & Lester, "Nuclear power, nuclear weapons and international stability"
    (April 1978)
FS—Foley & Soedel, "Ancient oared warships" (April 1981)
SF—Soedel & Foley, "Ancient catapults" (March 1979)
Other background material can be obtained from these:
Lanchester, "Mathematics in warfare," in *The World of Mathematics*, Jame R.
    Newman, ed. Simon & Schuster 1956, volume 4, pp. 2138-57
Morse & Kimball "How to hunt a submarine," *ibid.*, pp. 2160-79
In addition, there will be occasional hand-outs and references to current literature,
and some audio-visual presentations.

Course Outline

A. From Antiquity through the First World War
How were sieges broken by the attackers in ancient times? What was the common
means of powering ancient warships, and what methods of combat were used
between warships? What kind of artillery was used in ancient times and in the
middle ages? How did the cross bow affect warfare? In terms of the Lanchester N-
square law, what naval tactics were adopted by the British? Give one famous
example. Be able to perform a very simple calculation based on the N-square law to
illustrate its significance. What nineteenth and early twentieth century technologies are associated with these persons: Richard Jordan Gatling, Alfred B. Nobel,
Orville & Wilbur Wright, Fritz Haber? How did these technological innovations
affect wars? Describe two methods used to overcome the static nature of trench
warfare. What different types of poison gas were used, and for what purposes? What
roles were played by blockades, submarines, propaganda, aircraft, and intelligence
in World War I? (FS, SF, Lanchester)

B. The Evolution of Military Technology during World War II
Tactical, strategic & interdiction bombing; radar; ballistic & cruise missiles; V-1, V-
2 weapons, firestorm. What factors led to the decision on strategic bombing of
German targets, and what roles were played by Tizard, Blackett, Lindemann,
Galbraith & Nitze? Who were Dornberger and von Braun? (AIWC 197-206; RTO,
75-79, 181; RL; F&F 450, 460; PMSB)

C. The Development and Use of the First Nuclear Weapons
Element, atom, nucleus, proton, neutron, electron, isotope, stability & radioactivity; alpha, beta & gamma rays & half-life (be able to do a simple half-life problem);
neutron capture, fission, transuranium elements, chain reaction, critical size or
mass, implosion, enrichment, gas diffusion, Manhattan Project, Quebec Agreement
(1943), Alamogordo. What roles were played here by these: the Curies, Rutherford,
Fermi, Hahn, Meitner, Frisch, Bohr, Wheeler, Wigner, Szilard, Einstein, Oppenheimer, Leslie Groves? How are wavelength, frequency, energy and temperature of

emitting source all related? Electromagnetic spectrum; Wien displacement law; Stefan-Blotzmann law. List the effects, in proper time sequence, of a nuclear weapon. Prompt radiation, fireball, thermal radiation, blast, fallout, worldwide or delayed fallout or radiation; crater; tenth-value thickness. How do the intensities of these effects vary or differ among high-altitude, low-altitude and ground-level bursts? How are the distances or ranges of damage, the area affected, and the size or yield of a weapon related to each other? Mega, kilo; Franck report. Give some reasons why such weapons were used on Hiroshima & Nagasaki. Give some reasons why Germany failed to develop these weapons. What was the principal reason the US, with its allies, decided to develop this kind of weapon? (F&F 16-18, 138, 187, 212, 218-227, 230-237, problems 5.13 & 5.14, 404-407, 432-439, 442-462, problems 8.11 and 8.12; RTO chapters one & two; MOM 190-2 and glossary) (read MX, chapter 5, pp. 35-50)

D. Early Postwar Decision
FAS, Baruch plan, May-Johnson bill, McMahon bill, AEC. Compare US and Soviet views on international control. How was the first Soviet nuclear weapon detected, by whom, and by whom was this information first made public? Booster, thermonuclear process, fusion. What roles did Bethe, Teller, Borden & Oppenheimer play in developing a fusion weapon? What role did secrecy play here? Fission-fusion-fission weapons; clean, dirty & salted weapons. Compare absolute and relative fallout from these weapons. (RTO, passim)

E. The Sputnik Crisis and its Consequences
How did this crisis come about? What effect did this have on public or federal support for science & technology? Compare Soviet & American accomplishments in the space race. What effect did this crisis have on US policy toward arms control? What is meant by the military-industrial complex and when was this term introduced? Conference of Experts; verification (EB); monitoring; disarming & inspecting; low-yield detection; seismometry; decoupling; single-to-noise ratio; seismic array; core shadow; earthquake/explosion discrimination; satellite reconnaissance. SAINT. (RTO, passim; M)

F. The Limited Test Ban Treaty
Why are strontium-90, iodine-130 and -131 of special concern? What roles do these play in human bodies? Compare the roles of Pauling and Teller in the arguments over open-air testing. Give specific points of their arguments. What is the origin of the symbol: ☣. Linear- and S-shaped response curves; LD-50; threshold, LTBT, TTBT, CTBT. In what way is the LTBT limited & why? Pugwash conferences; moratorium; ACDA. What important nations are not party to the LTBT; what event in the summer of 1973 involved one of these nations? (MOM 578-605; WY; M; EB; MX pp. 41-45)

G. Deterrence
Massive retaliation; counterforce, countervalue; first & second strike capabilities; hostages; deterrence; MAD; TRIAD (MX chapter 7); stability; worst case analysis; pre-emptive strike; damage-limitation and assured destruction (MX chapter 8, pp. 71-88); overkill; horizontal & vertical proliferation; reliability; accuracy; CEP; arms-race and crisis instabilities; nth country problem; kill probability; guidance; multi RVs; balance of terror. How can stability be upset? PD-59 (MX, chapter 6).

CEP problem, algebra & map. (F&F 463-69; WY; MX Chapter 6, pp. 51-58 and glossary, page 219ff.)

H. The Anti-Ballistic Missile Debate and SALT

ABM, MSR, PAR, Spartan, Sprint, discrimination, chaff, decoys, fragments, jamming, blackout, penetration aids, FOBS, RV, MRV, CLAW, MIRV, MARV, terminal guidance, Sentinel, Safeguard, light ABM, shell game, proliferation, mobile launchers, superhardening, launch-on-warning (or launch-under-attack), absurdities arising from these weapons. State in detail the arguments pro & con ABM systems, Tallinn, B-70; action-reaction cycle. Given the kill probability of a single RV destroying a single target, be able to calculate the chance that several RVs directed to a single target will destroy it; and from this, to be able to estimate the fraction of a set of targets, and the absolute number in this set, which will survive an attack with one and with several RVs directed to each target. What effect does the introduction of MRV and MIRV have on the stability of our deterrence systems? What is the nature of SALT I and of the Interim Agreement? Superiority, parity, sufficiency, equivalence. Compare US and Soviet strengths & weaknesses in the different areas of nuclear weapons technology. Fallacy of the last move. What factors delayed the first SALT agreement and what factors made the agreement possible? ENDC, CCD, bargaining chip. What areas were not covered in the 1972 treaties? What is the etymology of the word 'minuteman' and how does it affect stability? (RTO; HS; F&F 463-69, problem 8, 9, answer on page 671; MX chapter 7, also see index for specific topics)

I. Submarines

Compare the vulnerabilities of the three parts of our TRIAD. What are the several missions of submarines? SLBM, ULMS, Polaris, Poseidon, Trident. Compare SLBMs as first- and second-strike weapons. What is transit time & how can it be reduced? Compare US & Soviet strategic submarines and state how these differences lead to asymmetries in the Interim Agreement. What is ASW; active & passive detection; SONAR; LORAN; NAVSTAR; ELF? How did operations research affect the competition between submarines & convoys during the second World War? (JW, also see index in MX)

J. Intelligence, Reconnaissance & Surveillance

Inferential data and direct data; U-2 overflights; SAINT; data transmission; Kepler's laws; multispectral photography; Big Bird, orbits, periods, elevations; early warning satellites; national technical means of verification; OTH radar; signature, seismology; black boxes; on-site inspections; Elint; types & functions of military satellites; verification for compliance and military intelligence. Codes, ciphers, cryptanalysis, public-key ciphers; Enigma; Ultra; MK-Ultra. (EB; RL)

K. New Military Technology

Enhanced radiation weapons, neutron bomb, CM, SLCM, ALCM, non-BM defense of ICBMs; NAVSTAR, pro & con; MX & MAPS, the factors promoting this technology, its various suggested forms, basing, limitations or arguments against, economic & ecological implications, alternatives to; laser and charged-particle weapons; radiological weapons. (P; MW; MX, except chapters 5 through 8)

L. Chemical & Biological Warfare

CBW; ABC; persistent & non-persistent gases; role of these in the two world wars; Geneva Protocol; biological weapons; toxins; lachrymators; vesicants; nerve gases; herbicides; defoliants; LD_{50}; LC_{50}; Ct factor; lethal and incapacitating agents & possible criterion to distinguish between these; inversions; list some uses for CW agents; where have anti-plant agents been used? Where have CW agents been used after the 1925 Geneva Protocol? Compare ABC weapons as to effective dose level; detection & defenses against, length of time area is affected. Why did the US not sign the Geneva Protocol in the 1920s, and why not in the 1960s & early 1970s? What are binary weapons and why are they said to be needed? Have biological weapons ever been used? Have there ever been charges concerning their alleged use? (CBW; MR)

M. SALT II & Other Arms Control Agreements

In a general rather than in a specific, detailed manner, be familiar with what is covered in each of these treaties or agreements: Geneva Protocol, Antarctica, Hotline; LTBT; Outer-space; Prohibition of nuclear weapons in Latin America; Nonproliferation; Seabed; BW convention; SALT I; Interim Agreement; ABM protocol; TTBT; PNE. Detente; linkage; Jackson amendment; Vladivostok agreement. List some arguments pro & con SALT II. What is SCC and how has it been involved in arms control treaties? What arguments have been made about our not having to match conventional manpower and weapons with the Soviet Union (MW)? (LA; MW; and some ACDA booklets on reserve)

N. The Indochina War

Capital-intensive & labor-intensive warfare; electronic battlefield; interdiction; contingent bombing; standoff capability; fire-free zone; iron bombs; CBU; napalm; flechettes; daisy cutter; smart bombs, gravel mines; plastic shrapnel. How did these new technologies affect adherence to accepted rules of war? What role did Congress play in this war, what role for news media? How did popular support for this war change when the conversion from a ground- to an air-war was made? (AWIC)

O. Military-Industrial Complex and the Scientific-Technological Elite

What is the origin of the phrase which is the title of this section? List some reasons why the defense industry and the Defense department are interested in overseas arms sales, and list some disadvantages in these sales. How is it that the DoD budget seems to be wasteful? What role does military work play in the activities of scientists & engineers? Comment on the possibilities of keeping scientific research pure and not used for military purposes. What roles did scientists play within Germany 1933-45? And in the US since 1938? Mention some technology which has helped to contain the arms race or to allay anxiety. (RTO)

The Legality and Morality of War

Robert Rodes (Law), Robert Webster (AROTC), James Sterba (Philosophy), John Yoder, (Theology), Simon Harek (GA), King Pfeiffer (U.S. Navy-Retired)   *Fall 1982*
Philosophy 249/Theology 381/The University of Notre Dame/
Notre Dame, IN 46556

The University of Notre Dame has one of the largest contingents of ROTC students on the campus of any university in the U.S. It is also one of the most important among the North American universities which wish to continue to make much of their Roman Catholic character, in a generation when Catholic character is increasingly being defined as including elements of concern for political and social justice.

The course entitled the "Legality and Morality of War" has been offered five times since the fall of 1978, with a teaching team of four persons representing theology, philosophy, law, and military science. The following is the syllabus for the fall 1982, but the form had not changed much since its beginning. The major question about the aptness of the present form has to do with whether the mock court portion should be retained, and with technical details of fair grading when a course has several instructors. In the spring of 1983 the course ran for the first time without the mock courts and with a smaller teaching team.

Course Objectives: General Objective of NDU and the College of Arts and Letters

The student who has taken this course should be more qualified than before to respond with a formed and informed conscience:
a) when as citizen he/she participates in public discernment regarding the nation's military policies;
b) when in a position of command responsibility he/she is called on to make choices where legal and moral principles are at stake;
c) when in a context of vocational choice or in response to conscription he/she decides whether/how to serve the nation's government militarily.

Specific Objectives of the Course as Theology
The forming of conscience shall be illuminated by acquaintance with biblical, historical and contemporary faith perspectives on the violence of war as a perennial moral issue concerning which most Christian communities have made normative commitments.

Specific Objectives of the Course as Philosophy
The forming of conscience shall be illuminated by acquaintance with competing

moral theories, their underlying justification, and the implications they have for action.

Readings: Books to purchase (in Bookstore under theology)
Michael Walzer, *Just and Unjust Wars* (Basic Books)
Malham M. Wakin (ed.) *War, Morality, and the Military Profession* (Westview)
Available on loan: Army Field Manual 27-10 *The Law of Land Warfare*
Other readings will be distributed in xeroxed form.

Course Outline

August 31 Introduction
Entire team of instructors and course concepts, the distinct nature and concern of each discipline, makeup of the student group, course structure, and requirements.

Perspectives of History and Theology (Yoder)

September 2 The Pacifism of the Early Christians
Readings: Xeroxes from Marrin

September 7 The Constantinian Change

September 9 The Just War Tradition: Grotius Prolegomena
Readings: Walzer, Chs. 1-3

September 14 The Changes in Just War Thought

September 16 Modern Alternatives
Written Review

Philosophical Perspectives (Sterba)

September 21 Moral Approaches to Warfare
Essential characteristics and examples of such approaches

September 23 Moral Approaches to Warfare
The justification of moral approaches
Readings: Walzer, Ch. 1

September 28 Just War Theory
Just causes/just means and their relationship to moral approaches
Readings: Wakin, Ch. 21

September 30 Nuclear Deterrence
Arguments against nuclear deterrence
Readings: Lackey, handout

October 5 Nuclear Deterrence and Defense Spending
Arguments for nuclear deterrence and arguments for and against increased defense spending
Written review

Legal Perspectives (Rodes)

October 7 History and Background of the Laws of War

Discussion question: Jefferson Davis believed that a citizen of a southern state who joined the Union Army and was captured could be punished as a traitor to his state instead of being treated as a prisoner of war. What would Grotius think of this view? What would Lieber?

Readings: Grotius, handout, pp. 1-24; Lieber, Instructions, handout, pp. 25-34; Articles 14-16, 20-25, 27-30, 37, 40-41, 56-57, 67-68, 153-54

October 12 Classical *Jus in Bello*

Discussion questions: (1) Sam and Charlie, enemy soldiers, both put on American uniforms and pass through the American lines. Sam blows up an ammunition dump. Charlie steals the plans for a new bomber. Both return to their lines and are later captured. How will they be treated differently? (2) You are the leader of a highly mobile raiding force operating deep inside the enemy's territory. You have taken by surprise an enemy force slightly larger than your own whose commander has sent a message offering to surrender to you. What options are legally open to you? How do Lieber's Instructions differ from the Hague Rules on this point? (3) In 1864, Confederate General Early led a force on a wide swing through Pennsylvania and Maryland. In Frederick, MD, he demanded a large cash contribution from the city officials, threatening to burn the city if they didn't pay. They paid. Later, he made a similar demand of the city of Chambersburg, Pennsylvania. They could not pay, and he burned down the city. Supposing after the war he were sued by the city of Frederick and by the owner of a building in Chambersburg?

Readings: Lieber,Instructions, handout, pp. 25-34, Hague Rules 1907, handout, pp. 35-40; Walzer, pp. 127-75, 207-22

October 14 Terrorism and Irregular Warfare

Discussion questions: (1) Certain members of the IRA, the Black Panthers, etc. have claimed the right to be dealt with according to the laws of war instead of according to the regular criminal law. What would happen to them if this claim were accepted? (2) Would the Northern Ireland legislation, supra, have worked against the FLN in the Battle of Algiers? (3) Can you suggest amendments to Article 4 of the Geneva Convention in the light of the considerations developed by Walzer?

Readings: Northern Ireland (Emergency Provisions) Act, handout, pp. 42-51; Geneva Convention, 1949, handout, p. 41; Lieber, supra, articles 81-85, 90-92, 148; Hague Rules, supra, articles 1-3, 22-26, 42, 46, 47, 5c; Walzer, pp. 176-206

October 19 Bombs, Submarines and Technology

Discussion question: How, if at all, would you modify the above rules in the light of Walzer's arguments or in the light of experience during and after World War II?

Readings: Proposed Rules of Air Warfare, 1923, handout, pp. 52-54; Treaty Relating to Submarines and Noxious Gases, handout, pp. 55-56; Walzer, pp. 147-51, 157-59, 251-83

October 21 Jus ad Bellum and the Punishment of War Crimes

Discussion questions: Assume a tribunal like those established in the above materials, with power to try American leaders for their actions in Vietnam War,

and assume Walzer's description of those actions on pp. 97-101 and 188-96 of his book is accurate, what American leaders could be charged with what crimes?
Readings: Nuremberg Charter, handout, pp. 57-62; Control Council Law #10, handout, pp. 63-65; Hostage Case, handout, pp. 66-86; Walzer, pp. 51-108, 287-327

Command Perspectives (Webster)

November 2 Purpose and Function of War
Historical aims of war, legitimate aims of war, the Christian and the Soldier, the types of warfare and problems of command during wartime
Required Reading: Walzer, Ch. 2, 3; Wakin, Ch. 1
Recommended: Walzer, Ch. 19, pp. 304-309; Wakin, pp. 3-11, 107-127, 143-160, 179-188, 245-257, 285-298

November 4 Responsibility in War
Commissar Case Study, Malmedey Case Study, Rules from Nuremberg, Geneva Convention, Code of Conduct, the Law of Land Warfare
Required Reading: Walzer, Ch. 19, pp. 316-325; Wakin, Ch. 25, 28
Recommended: Walzer, Ch. 14; Wakin, Ch. 9, 22, 24; Scan FM 27-10 for content

November 9 Mass Destruction Weapons and Siege
Case studies on Leningrad, War of the Three Emperors, The Lines of Torres Vedas, WWI Blockades, Introduction to NBC
Required Reading: Walzer, Ch. 10, 16; Wakin, Ch. 31

November 11 Impact of Technology on War
Chemical and Biological Warfare, Nuclear Warfare, Deterrence, Unilateral Disarmament
Required Reading: Wakin, Ch. 30; Handout, "A Rational Approach to Nuclear Disarmament," Weinberger

November 16 Problems of Irregular Warfare
Hostages, Assassinations, Terrorism, Psychological Operations, Vietnam
Required Reading: Walzer, Ch. 6, 11, 12

December 9 Review from the Perspectives of Theology and Philosophy

December 14 Course Summary (All Instructors)
The "December" calendar is flexible—it will probably provide for two evening sessions for the "mock court" events, and some daytime sessions will drop out.

Religious Perspectives on Justice and Peace

Religion and Power
Margaret E. Crahan, Occidental College

Christian Responsibility for Peace and Justice
Jay Losher, Garrett-Evangelical Theological Seminary

Global Issues and World Churches
Charles Chatfield, Wittenberg University

Perspectives on Liberation Theology
John Mullaney, Boston College

War, Peace and Disarmament
John Langan, Yale Divinity School

Seeking Peace: Spiritual Resources for Living under the Nuclear Arms Race
G. Clarke Chapman, Moravian College

War, Peace and Revolution
Wilmer Cooper, Earlham College School of Religion

Religion and Power

Margaret E. Crahan   *Spring 1983*
Religious Studies 66/Occidental College/Los Angeles, CA 90041

The purpose of this course is to gain an understanding of the interplay of religion and power in the modern world. Emphasis will be on the role of institutionalized religions in promoting and reacting to political change. The course will begin with an overview of ways in which major religions are reacting to political pressures in various areas of the world, e.g., Poland, the Middle East, the Indian subcontinent, and Latin America. We will then focus on a single Church, the Roman Catholic, and how it has reacted to pressures for political, economic, and social change since World War II. The Catholic Church in Latin America will serve as a case study of a complex bureaucratic institution responding to pressures for internal democratization and general societal change. In order to do this, new theological formulations, organizational modes, and patterns of behaviour of clergy will be examined. These will include the theology of liberation, base Christian communities, and changes in clerical behaviour. The overall aim is not only to provide an understanding of the relationship between churches and the exercise of political, economic, social, and moral power in the contemporary world, but also to increase each student's ability to analyze complex phenomena and describe them accurately and clearly, both verbally and in writing. As a consequence, heavy emphasis will be placed on written assignments, as well as class discussions.

Course Requirements

1. One-third of the final grade will be based on the quality of analysis expressed in class discussions.
2. There will be a two-hour mid-term essay exam on April 25. The grade received will constitute one-third of your final grade.
3. There will be a term paper (no more than 15 pages) focusing on the role of a major religion in a single country of the world and answering the following questions:
   a. Does this religion play a conservative or progressive role with respect to political, economic, and social change in X country?
   b. What are the specific historical reasons for this role?
   c. What are the theological bases for the role that this religion is currently playing in X country?
   d. What are the political reasons for the role that this religion is currently playing in X country?
   e. What do you think will be the consequences for this religion of the role it is currently playing in X country?

Required readings

Gremillion, J. *Gospel of Peace and Justice: Catholic Social Teaching Since John XXIII*. New York: Maryknoll, Orbis Books, 1976.

Levine, Daniel H., ed. *Churches and Politics in Latin America*. Beverly Hills: Sage Publications, 1980.

Miguez Bonino, José. *Doing Theology in a Revolutionary Situation*. Philadelphia: Fortress Press, 1975.

Novak, Michael, ed. *Capitalism and Socialism: A Theological Inquiry*. Washington: American Enterprise Institute, 1979.

Torres, Sergio and Eagleson, John, eds. *The Challenge of Basic Christian Communities*. Maryknoll, New York: Orbis Books, 1981.

*Article on Library Reserve. Crahan, Margaret E. *Varieties of Faith: Religion in Revolutionary Nicaragua*.

Lecture Topics and Reading Assignments

March 30   Introduction to the Course

April 4   How Do Religions Exercise Power in the Modern World? Some Examples:
A. Poland.
B. Middle East.
C. India/Pakistan.
D. United States.

April 6   Churches as Political Actors
A. Multilaterally, e.g. World Council of Churches.
B. Unilaterally, e.g. Vatican.
Reading Assignment: Gremillion, pp. 3-124.

April 11   Changing Catholic Social Doctrine
A. Nineteenth century roots.
B. Early twentieth century developments.
C. Contemporary developments.
Reading Assignment: Gremillion, pp. 125-138; 143-241.
Final paper topic and thesis due.

April 13   The Second Vatican Council
A. Background.
B. Major decisions.
Reading Assignment: Gremillion, pp. 243-377; 387-415

April 18   Impact of Vatican II on Latin America
A. Theologically.
B. Organizationally.
C. Politically.
Reading Assignment: Levin, pp. 7-107.
Outline and preliminary bibliography due.

April 20   Impact of Changing Catholic Social Doctrine on Political Behaviour
A. Of Roman Catholic Church.
B. Of individuals.
Reading Assignment: Levine, pp. 109-194.

April 25   Mid-Term
Study questions:
1. Describe the role in the last twenty years of a major religion in the political life of any one country in the world. Focus on specific attempts by the religious group to influence government and the reasons for such attempts.
2. Analyze the evolution of Roman Catholic social doctrine since 1960 in terms of its impact on Catholic theology.
3. Analyze the impact of Vatican II on the political behaviour of the Roman Catholic Church in Latin America.

April 27   The Theology of Liberation: The Liberation of Theology?
A. Roots.
B. Utilization of the Social Sciences.
Reading Assignment: Miguez Bonino, pp. vii-xxviii; 2-83.

May 2   Critiques of Liberation Theology
A. Theological.
B. Ideological.
C. Social scientific.
Reading Assignment: Bonino, pp. 86-174.

May 4   New Ecclesial Forms: Base Christian Communities
A. Organization and function.
B. Theological bases.
Reading Assignment: Torres and Eagleson, pp. 13-23; 46-61; 77-188; 197-210.

May 9   Critiques of Base Christian Communities
A. From within the Catholic Church.
B. From without the Catholic Church.
Reading Assignment: Torres and Eagleson, pp. 213-281, Levine, pp. 225-237.
Revised outline and bibliography due.

May 11   Other Patterns of Innovation: Women
A. Women religious.
B. Lay women.
Reading Assignment: Levine, pp. 198-224; Torres and Eagleson, pp. 24-37.

May 16   The Roman Catholic Church in Revolutionary Cuba: An Historical Evaluation
A. The Catholic Church in Cuba in historical perspective.
B. Impact of the Revolution.
Reading Assignment: Levine, pp. 238-266.

May 18   The Roman Catholic Church in Revolutionary Nicaragua
A. Participation in the Sandinista Movement.
B. Current Church—State conflict.
Reading Assignment: *Crahan; Torres and Eagleson, pp. 62-73; 189-196.

**May 23   The Theological Debate Over Capitalism and Socialism:
    A North American View**
A. Roots of Capitalism and Socialism.
B. Theological critiques of Capitalism.
Reading Assignment: Novak, pp. 1-84.

May 25   Capitalism and Socialism: Some Assessments
A. Religion and Capitalism.
B. Religion and Socialism.
Reading Assignment: Novak, pp. 85-128.

May 30   Is Capitalism Religiously Sanctioned?
A. Empirically.
B. Morally.
Reading Assignment: Novak, pp. 152-174.

June 1   Is Socialism Religiously Sanctioned?
A. Empirically.
B. Morally.
Reading Assignment: Novak, pp. 176-186.
Final paper due. No extensions.

Supplementary Bibliography

I. General Works: Theory, Classics, and Major Theologians

Eisenstadt, S.N., ed. *The Protestant Ethic and Modernization: A Comparative View.* New York, 1984.

Gerschenkron, A. *Economic Backwardness in Historical Perspective.* New York, 1962.

Gilkey, Langdon. "The Political Dimensions of Theology," *Journal of Religion,* 59 (April, 1979), 154-168.

Green, Robert W. *Protestantism, Capitalism, and Social Science: The Weber Thesis Controversy.* 2nd ed. Lexington, Mass., 1973.

Gremillion, Jos. B. *Food/Energy and the Major Faiths.* Maryknoll, N.Y., 1978.

Gremillion, J., ed. *The Gospel of Peace and Justice: Catholic Social Teaching Since Pope John XXIII.* Maryknoll, N.Y., 1976.

Gremillion, Jos. and Ryan, Wm., eds. *World Faiths and the New World Order.*

Moltman, Jurgen. *Religion, Revolution and the Future.* New York, 1969.

Murvar, Vatro. "Integrative and Revolutionary Capabilities of Religion," *Sociological Inquiry,* 49, 2-3 (1979), 74-86.

Portelli, Hugues. *Gramsci et la question religigieuse.* Paris, 1974.

Smith, Donald E. *Religion, Politics and Social Change in the Third World: A Sourcebook.* New York, 1971.

Tillich, Paul. *A History of Christian Thought, from Its Judaic and Hellenistic Origins to Existentialism.* New York, 1972.

II. Religion and Politics in Asia

Barkat, Anwar M. "Church-State Relations in an Ideologically Islamic State," *Ecumenical Review,* 29 (1977), 39-51.

Braswell, George W. "Civil Religion in Contemporary Iran," *Journal of Church and State,* 21 (Spring, 1979), 223-246.

Ichikawa, Akira. "Compassionate Politics: Buddhist Concepts as Political Guide," *Journal of Church and State,* 21 (Spring, 1979), 247-263.

Stasser, Steven, et al. "The Khomeini Contagion: Political Turmoil in the Islamic World," *Newsweek,* 94 (December 17, 1979), 39-41.

Wall, James W. "Moralists, Politicists and the Middle East," *Christian Century*, 96 (October 17, 1979), 995-996.

III. Religion and Politics in Latin America

Bruneau, Thomas C. "Power and Influence: Analysis of the Church in Latin America and the Case of Brazil," *Latin American Research Review*, VIII, 2 (Summer, 1973), 25-51.

CELAM. *La Iglesia en la actual transformacion de America Latina a la luz del Concilio.* 1968.

CELAM. *Conferencia General del Episcopado Latinoamericano en Puebla: La Evangelizacion en el Presente y en el Futuro de America Latina.* 1979.

Cesar, Waldo. *Protestantismo e imperialismo en America Latina.* Petropolis, 1968.

Della Cava, Ralph. "Catholicism and Society in Twentieth Century Brazil," *Latin American Research Review*, XI, 2 (1976), 7-50.

Dodson, Michael. "The Catholic Church in Contemporary Argentina," in *New Perspectives of Modern Argentina*, edited by Alberto Ciria. Bloomington, 1972.

d'Epinay, Christian Lalive. *El refugio de las masas: estudio sociológico del protestantismo chileno.* Santiago, 1968.

Levine, Daniel. "Authority in Church and Society: Latin American Models," *Comparative Studies in Society and History*, 20 (October, 1978), 517-544.

Levine, Daniel H., ed. *Churches and Politics in Latin America.* Beverly Hills: Sage Publications, 1979.

Romano, Roberto. *Brasil: Igreja contra Estado.* Sao Paulo: Kairos, 1979.

Smith, Brian H. "Religion and Social Change: Classical Theories and New Formulations in the Context of Recent Developments in Latin America," *Latin American Research Review*, X, 2 (Summer, 1975), 3-34.

Sanks, T. Howland and Smith, Brian H. "Liberation Ecclesiology: Praxis, Theory, Praxis," *Theological Studies*, 38, 1 (March, 1977), 3-38.

IV. Religion and Politics in North America

Bennett, John L. "Watergate and Civil Disobedience," *Christianity and Crisis*, 33, 11 (1973).

Brownfield, Allan C. "The Decline of Principle in American Politics," *Religion and Society*, 6, 1 (1973), 2-7.

Flowers, Ronald B. "The 1960s: A Decisive Decade in American Church-State Relationship," *Encounter*, 40 (Summer, 1979), 287-304.

Hitchcock, James. "Catholics and Liberals: Decline of Detente," *America*, 130, 10 (1974), 186-190.

Hudson, Winthrop Still. *Nationalism and Religion in America: Concepts of American Identity and Mission.* Magnolia, 1971.

Smith, Elwyn Allen. *Religious Liberty in the U.S.: Development of Church-State Thought Since the Revolutionary Era.* Philadelphia, 1972.

Wuthnow, Robert. "The Current Moral Climate: What Pastors Think," *Theology Today*, 36 (July, 1979), 239-250.

Zaretsky, Irving L. and Leone, Mark P. *Religious Movements in Contemporary America.* Princeton, 1974.

Christian Responsibility for Peace and Justice

Jay Losher   *Spring 1982*
Theology (9)21-614/Garrett-Evangelical Theological Seminary/
Evanston, IL 60201

This course is a general introduction to the ethical study of war, justice and peace. We will focus on (but not necessarily resolve) the major problems involved in these areas.

This is an interdisciplinary study. We will utilize two diverse sets of methodologies because the problem of war cannot be fully understood from any single perspective. War is both a moral and a social problem—to understand it we will use 1) the methods of social science, principally international relations, and 2) the methods of philosophical and Christian ethics. This course is intended to be an introduction to ethics for students of the social sciences and simultaneously an introduction to international relations for theological students. It is hoped that the two perspectives will be represented among the students so that a true cross-disciplinary dialogue may develop.

Texts

Aldridge, Robert, *The Counterforce Syndrome: A Guide to US Nuclear Weapons and Strategic Doctrine* (Institute for Policy Studies, 1978).

Bainton, Roland, *Christian Attitudes Toward War and Peace* (Abingdon, 1960).

Beer, Francis, *Peace Against War: The Ecology of International Violence* (W.H. Freeman, 1981).

Walzer, Michael, *Just and Unjust Wars: A Moral Argument with Historical Illustrations* (Basic Books, 1977).

A Packet of Reprints and Copies

Center for Defense Information, "Soviet Geopolitical Momentum: Myth or Menace?" (January 1980 *Defense Monitor*) and "Measure of the Nuclear Arms Race."

Sojourners reprints: Billy Graham, "A Change of Heart" (August, 1979), Mernie King, "Peace by Peace" (September, 1980) and George Zabelka, "A Turn to Peacemaking: A Personal Story" (August, 1980).

Philip Morrison and Paul Walker, "A New Strategy for Military Spending," *Scientific American*, October, 1978.

Richard Barnet, "The Search for National Security," *New Yorker*, (April 27, 1981). This article contains most of the material in Barnet's *Real Security*.

Richard Watts, "How To Preach Peace (Without Being Tuned Out)," *The Pastor's Letter*, October, 1981.

IMPACT Hunger #'s 22 (February, 1980) and 25 (November, 1980): "The International Monetary Fund and the Third World" and "Which Way the Third Development Decade?"

"Chronology of the Arms Race: 1945-1977," Appendix II from *A Call to Faithfulness: The Arms Race and the Gospel of St. Mark.*

Bibliographies prepared by members of the Peace and Justice Institute of GETS.

Books on Reserve

Beitz, Charles and Theodore Herman, eds., *Peace and War (PW)* (W.H. Freeman, 1973).

Dougherty, James and Robert Pfaltzgraff, *Contending Theories of International Relations (D&P)* (J.B. Lippincott, 1971) 1st Edition.

Falk, Richard and Saul Mendlovitz, eds., *Toward a Theory of War Prevention (F&M)* (World Policy Institute, 1966).

McSorley, Richard, *New Testament Basis of Peacemaking (NTBP)* (Georgetown University Center for Peace Studies, 1979).

Niebuhr, Reinhold, *Moral Man and Immoral Society (MMIS)* (Scribner's Sons, 1932).

Sharp, Gene, *The Politics of Nonviolent Action, Part One (PNA)* (Porter Sargent, 1973).

Smith, Clagett, ed., *Conflict Resolution: Contributions of the Behavioral Sciences (CR)* (Notre Dame, 1971).

Smith, Donald, *Religion, Politics and Social Change in the Third World (RPSC)* (Free Press, 1971).

Wasserstrom, Richard, ed., *War and Morality (WM)* (Wadsworth, 1970).

Yoder, John Howard, *The Politics of Jesus (POJ)* (Eerdmans, 1972).

Articles on Reserve

James Stegenga, "Dunbar's Bremen," *Christianity and Crisis,* January 19, 1981, 371-380.

Alexander Haig and Raymond Hunthausen, "Documentation: Two Mentalities," *Christianity and Crisis,* August 17, 1981, 219 and 226-231.

John Bennett, "Soviet Aims and Priorities: The Need for a New Debate," *Christianity and Crisis,* October 19, 1981, 275-279.

"A Proper Peace Establishment," *Engage/Social Action,* April, 1981, 10-43.

Roger Shinn, M.M. Thomas and Martin Stohr on "Just Revolution," *The Ecumenical Review,* October, 1978, 317-345.

George Kennan, "Two Views of the Soviet Problem," *New Yorker,* November 2, 1981, 54-62.

John Lambelet, "Do Arms Races Lead to War?" *Journal of Peace Research,* 12.2 (1970), 123-128.

Johan Galtung, "A Structural Theory of Imperialism," *Journal of Peace Research,* 13.2 (1971), 81-117.

Sam Nunn, "SALT and National Security: Where Do We Go From Here?" *Congressional Record,* November 2, 1979.

Lloyd Dumas, "Thirty Years of the Arms Race: The Deterioration of Economic Strength and Military Security," *Peace and Change,* 4.2 (Spring, 1977).

Seymour Melman, "Ten Propositions on the War Economy," *The American Economic Review,* May 1977.

"An Introduction to Nonviolence," *Fellowship*, 46.3-4 (March/April, 1980).

Charles Beitz and Michael Washburn, "On Choosing a Social Change Vocation," *Creating the Future* (Bantam, 1974).

Robert Pickus and Robert Woito, "What Can I Do? Twenty-three Answers," *Peacemaking*, ed. by Barbara Stanford (Bantam, 1976).

Assignments

Essay #1—Due March 29. Is War Inevitable? The purpose of this assignment is for you to decide and justify a basic understanding of war. This should be a closely reasoned essay—stating a clear thesis and defending it with evidence from the readings and beyond. Be definite with your terms: if war is inevitable, in what sense? If not, how is it to be avoided? On what evidence do you base your conclusion, social or theological or both? Do not assume that there will be a major change in human nature unless you can come up with a reason for the change.

Essay #2—Due May 17 (Seniors Due May 3). The purpose of this assignment is for you to define a theoretical approach and to apply it to a particular question based on your own interests and focus.Theoretical analysis should reflect either ethical analysis or social science methods. Hopefully you will demonstrate wider reading on the topic you choose than merely having sat in on the class discussions. Bibliography on various subjects will be circulated as the course progresses. Suggested topic could include: defining national security, the ethics of terrorism/just revolution or the feasibility of non-violent resistance. This essay could take the form of a thorough literature review since much of this material might be unfamiliar. In a literature review, the purpose is to cover the major works in a field, to identify the major theoretical approaches to the subject and to describe the major problems in the field.

Course Outline

March 1   Introduction: Definitions and Methods in Social Ethics

I. The Nature of War and Peace

March 3   Searching for the Causes of War
F&M, pp.124-141—Quincy Wright, "Analysis of the Causes of War;" Beer, ch's 1-2
D&P, ch 5—"The Older Theories of Conflict"

March 8   Innate Theories
PW, pp.112-143—Margaret Mead, "Warfare Is Only an Invention—Not a Biological Necessity," and Peter Corning, "Human Violence: Some Causes and Implications"
D&P, ch 7—"Microcosmic Theories of Conflict"

March 10   Economic Theories of War: Structuralists and Marxists
D&P, ch 6—"Economic Theories of Imperialism and War"
Johan Galtung, "A Structural Theory of Imperialism"

March 15   Revolution
D&P, ch 8—"Macrocosmic Theories of Conflict: Revolution"

PW, pp.50-68—Kenneth Grundy, "The Cause of Political Violence"
CR, pp.272-293—Johan Galtung, "A Structural Theory of Aggression"

March 17 Polarization
Beer, ch 4
John Bennett, "Soviet Aims and Priorities: The Need for a New Debate"
George Kennan, "Two Views of the Soviet Problem"

March 22 Interventionism
Richard Barnet, "The Search for National Security"
CDI, "Soviet Geopolitical Momentum: Myth or Menace?"

March 24 Arms Races/Militarization
Beer, ch 5
Lloyd Dumas, "Thirty Years of the Arms Race"
John Lambelet, "Do Arms Races Lead to War?"
"Chronology of the Arms Race: 1945-1977"
Film: "War without Winners"

II. The Morality of War

March 29 Christological Pacifism
Bainton, ch's 1-5
Essay #1 Due

March 31 Nonresistance
Yoder, ch's 1, 2, 4, 5 and 12

April 5 and 7 Easter Break

April 12 Nonviolent Resistance
Walzer, pp. 329-335
Bainton, ch's 10-12
"An Introduction to Nonviolence," *Fellowship*
PNA, pp. 75-97—Gene Sharp, "Examples of Nonviolent Resistence"

April 14 Just War
Bainton, ch's 6-9
Walzer, ch's 1-3

April 19 Just Revolution
Shinn, et al., "Just Revolution," *The Ecumenical Review*
Walzer, ch's 11-12
RPSC, ch 10—"Religion and Revolutionary Change"

April 21 Situational Pacifism and Choices (American Mission Conference)
Beer, ch 6
Billy Graham, "A Change of Heart" and George Zabelka, "A Turn to Peacemaking: A Personal Story"
James Stegenga, "Dunbar's Bremen"
WM, pp. 15-41—John Ford, "The Morality of Obliteration Bombing"

III. Prevention of War

April 26   Realist Solutions I: Niebuhr and National Interest Theory
MMIS, ch 4—Reinhold Niebuhr, "The Morality of Nations"
NTBP, ch 6—Richard McSorley, "Answers to Objections"
D&P, ch 3 and pp.30-36—"Political Realism at the International Level"

April 28   Realist Solutions II: Balance of Power and Deterrence
D&P, ch 9—"Nuclear Deterrence and Arms Control"
Walzer, ch 17

May 3   Idealist Solutions I: Pacifism and Disarmament
Bainton, ch's 13-15
F&M, pp.55-60—Richard Barnet, "Preparations for Progress"
Alexander Haig and Raymond Hunthausen, "Documentation: Two Mentalities"
Seniors Essay #2 due

May 5   Idealist Solutions II: World Government and Regional Integration
F&M, pp.3-13—Kenneth Boulding, "The Prevention of World War III"
D&P, ch 10—"Theories of International Integration, Regionalism and Alliance
   Cohesion"
Beer, ch 3
F&M, pp.111-116—Pope John XXIII, "Pacem in Terris, Part IV"

**May 10   Reformist Solutions I: Arms Control and New International Economic
   Order**
Aldridge, *The Counterforce Syndrome*
Impact Hunger #'s 22 and 25
Sam Nunn, "SALT and National Security"

May 12   Reformist Solutions II: Appropriate Security and Conflict Resolution
PW, pp. 316-340—Arthur Burns, "The Defense Sector: An Evaluation of Its Eco-
   nomic and Social Impact" and John Galbraith, "Controlling the Military"
Philip Morrison and Paul Walker, "A New Strategy for Military Spending: A Proper
   Peace Establishment" from *Engage/Social Action*
Seymour Melman, "Ten Propositions on the War Economy"

May 17   Parish Peacemaking and Conflict Resolution
PW, pp. 415-424—Sue Carroll, et al., "Organizing for Social Transformation"
Richard Watts, "How to Preach Peace (Without Being Tuned Out)"
Mernie King, "Peace by Peace"
Charles Beitz and Michael Washburn, "On Choosing a Social Change Vocation"
Robert Pickus and Robert Woito, "What Can I Do? Twenty-three Answers"
Essay #2 Due

May 19   Peace Education
No Readings
Viewing films "The Last Slideshow," "Shalom," "Guess Who's Coming to Break-
   fast" and "The Race Nobody Wins"
Examining Peace Curricula

Global Issues and World Churches

Charles Chatfield
Summer Study Program in Geneva/Wittenberg University/
Springfield, OH 45501

Utilizing the resources of Geneva, Switzerland, this program explores the roles of world churches as they interact with international and non-governmental organizations to deal with critical global problems. The study program is only part of living in Geneva for six weeks, but it is the core part, the raison d' etre for our coming together. It is the part of our experience that is introduced in this syllabus.

Syllabus for the Course of Study

The course of study is the heart of our program. It is designed to integrate religious, political science, and historical approaches. It offers two course credits of academic work which can be chosen from the three related emphases of our study:

1. Religion: Ecumenism in the Contemporary World, the Churches' Roles
Underlying the politics and programs of world church bodies are various strands of theology, missiology, ethics, and social-political assumptions which involve questions of faith and order. An essential question is: What is the mission of the ecumenical church in light of its plural heritage and organization and its interaction with the contemporary world?

2. Political Science: International Organization and Religious NGOs
Whether or not their beliefs are true, world churches are important nongovernmental organizations (NGOs) which interact with other international organizations and with nations. Essential questions are: How do religious NGOs function in relation to other international agencies, and how are they affected by their international roles?

3. History: Evolution of World Ecumenism
The organization of church work and belief on an ecumenical and worldwide scale is part of the history of both international organization and twentieth-century thought. Essential questions are: What factors have shaped ecumenical thought and organization, and to what extent is ecumenism part of an emerging global civilization?

The three emphases of this course of study enable us to explore the interactions and relationships of beliefs and institutions on a global scale. Because we undertake our exploration in Geneva, we are able to consult with people who are involved in the life and work of international agencies and world church bodies, notably the World Council of Churches and the Lutheran World Federation.

Objectives
This course of study does not presume the prior study of theology, church history,

or international relations. It is an introduction to these three subjects as they are related to one another. It does presume the commitment of each student to pursue the subject aggressively and to help everyone think through the issues we encounter. The Student should expect:

- To become familiar with the structure and functions of the world church bodies, especially the WCC & LWF;
- To become familiar with the operations of international organizations in Geneva, especially as they relate to NGOs;
- To know the outlines of the historic development of organized transnational ecumenism;
- To appreciate the ways in which world churches interact with the modern world and address its future;
- To be able to think through the relationship of theology and ecumenical action;
- To be able to appreciate the relationships between Christian and secular perspectives on mission;
- To come into personal contact with men and women who are shaping ecumenism and are wrestling with the issues mentioned above;
- To organize information and ideas, to write clearly about them, and to share with his/her colleagues in the learning experience.

Elements of the Study Program

Seminars will be held with executives of world church bodies and international organizations. Preparation through reading and prior discussion will enable you to get beyond the obvious with your speakers.

Director's Seminars will be held occasionally in order to provide background and interpretation of seminars and to integrate them.

Group Meetings will be held occasionally in order to process what we have heard in seminars, and to deal with details of living and traveling together.

Conversations will be held occasionally in the evening with guests who may be invited to dinner by the director or yourselves.

Individual Study Time will be available during which you may read, schedule individual interviews, or write.

Research is included in the program in order to enable you to pursue an issue or program of your own interest. It should enable you to integrate the emphases of the program in a single, coherent study. Essentially, this is an extended abstract and bibliography for a research paper, the full writing of which time will not permit.

Requirements (Remember that you are earning two course credits)

1) *Preparation and Participation in Seminars*
   Preparation includes reading in advance as indicated.
   Participation is the heart of the learning experience.

2) *A Personal Journal*
   The journal can take any form that conveys your reflection upon your study and other experience. Begin your journal *before leaving home* by writing down your objectives for the program and the course of study.

3) *Interpretive Papers*
   Four papers are required as indicated in the Course of Study. These enable you to integrate the seminar experience and readings in each major unit of study. Review the questions from which each paper is to be developed at the beginning of the respective unit of the course.

4) *A Final Examination*

A written examination will be given at the end of the program and will be based on the questions listed in the syllabus. You will choose questions in relation to the fields in which you take academic credit.

5) *A Research Project*

Early in the program you will select a specific topic of research. You will work out a schedule of research with the director and will explore your subject using written resources and individual consultations.

The Course of Study

This course begins with a week of orientation to the relation of religious NGOs to international organizations and issues in New York and Paris, and with a similar week of orientation to the international organizations in Geneva. This should acquaint us with the scale of our study and the groups involved, and it should enable us to begin to see how various agencies relate to one another and to international issues.

Southern Africa becomes a case study of interrelated issues and programs in the second unit of our study. It helps us to see how all issues are related to one another, how local, national, regional, and global levels are connected, and how involvement in southern Africa affects relationships among the WCC, the LWF, and their constituent churches.

With that background, we will examine specific international programs directed to the problems of human rights, refugees, and relief. We will study both church and secular agencies working in these areas. We will then turn to alternative approaches to human and social development and to a consideration of programs designed to change social structures. We will learn how refugee and relief work, world politics, and the very conceptions of human rights and Christian mission affect programs in social and economic development.

This will lead us to consider programs designed to promote dialogue among people of living faiths and ideologies, within the Christian world community and between it and other religions. Throughout these units of study we will be introduced, also, to the historical development of international ecumenism and to issues of church mission and ecumenism. These considerations will become particularly important in our contact with Roman Catholic agencies and in our reflections upon the meaning of our study for ourselves.

1. Orientation to International Organization and Religious NGOs

World church bodies such as the WCC and the LWF are religious, interdenominational, nongovernmental organizations. NGOs constitute an important block of nonstate actors in world relations. Like other actors, they have their own belief systems, interests, agendas, and constituencies.

Our course of study begins, therefore, by demythologizing the world church bodies. That is to say, we will make a case for the importance and feasibility of studying them whether or not the theology of ecumenism is true.

In New York we will be introduced to the Lutheran World Ministries (LWM), a nationally federated church body which represents several national U.S. churches and forms their link to the LWF. We will be introduced to the roles played by the

LWF, the U.S. Commission of the WCC, and similar groups in the U.N., and we will tour the U.N. We will consult with representatives of several constituencies in southern Africa.

In Paris we will be introduced to the world of Unesco, especially with respect to its relationship with NGOs. In Geneva we will become acquainted with the cluster of United Nations agencies, the International Council of Voluntary Agencies, the WCC, the LWF, and other Christian church bodies. We will watch especially for the functions of these organizations, for the beliefs and constituencies they represent, and for their attitudes to and interaction with one another.

Seminars

Lutheran World Ministries andLutheran World Relief
Assignment: Ans J. van der Bent, *What in the World is the World Council of Churches?* and material distributed at these sessions

Lutheran World Federation, U.S. Comm. of the World Council of Churches, etc.
Tour of the U.N.

Consultations with Representatives of Southern African Constituencies
Assignment: Background Papers on Southern Africa

Director's Seminar
Unesco, Overall Programs and Work with NGOs
United Nations Agencies in Geneva
Assignment: Background Papers on U.N. Agencies in Geneva; material distributed at these sessions

International Council of Voluntary Agencies
WCC: Churches' Commission on International Affairs; Commission on World Mission and Evangelism; WCC History, Theology, and Organization; Library of Ecumenical Center
Assignment: Visser 'T Hooft, *Has the Ecumenical Movement a Future?* pp. 11-30; "CCIA Related Matters: Public Issues" (August 1980), mimeographed; *Arms Race in Europe* (1980/3), 36 pp.; scan *The Churches in International Affairs, Reports 1974-78*, 231 pp.; materials distributed at these sessions

WCC: Refugee Service
LWF: Theology and Organization
Christian World Communions
(Note: for the lake tour of Lac Leman, reading of Visser 'T Hooft, "The 1927 Lausanne Conference in Retrospect," in *Lausanne* 77, pp. 4-20.)

II. A Case in Point: Southern Africa

A case of what? The interrelationship of all issues: human rights—refugees—relief—political affairs—social and economic development—conflicts among living faiths and ideologies. The relationships of local, national, regional, and international politics. The relationship of religious and secular agencies and programs. The relationship of controversial interpretations of mission to the organization of the WCC and to its image. And, ethically, the relationship of means and ends.

We can only glimpse the turmoil in the vortex that is called Africa, but it is important that we try. And the resources for learning about this continent are great in Geneva.

The stage will be set for our study by the reading of two books: Ernest Lefever's *Amsterdam to Nairobi* (61pp), and Barbara Roger's *Race: No Peace Without Justice* (93pp). They describe and interpret the way in which the Program to Combat Racism (PCR) of the WCC polarized the Christian community. With that background, we will turn to the study of the problems, issues, and programs which have involved the world church bodies in southern Africa, and to the questions they raise.

Seminars
Introduction through Film and Discussion
Assignment: Lefever, *Amsterdam to Nairobi*; Rogers, *Race: No Peace Without Justice*; *Namibia: The Strength of the Powerless* (IDOC, 1980), 135pp

Africa
Assignment: *LWF World Service*, 23pp; Report, *Zambia Christian Refugee Service, 1979*; Report, *Botswana Refugee Programme, 1978*; "Director's Report: LWS in Mozambique" (1980)

Director's Seminar: WCC and Africa
United Nations Work in regard to Southern Africa
LWF and WCC Task Forces on Africa
LWF: Communications and Africa
Assignment: Recent issues of *Lutheran World Information*

WCC: Program to Combat Racism in Africa and in the World
Assignment: *A Small Beginning: An Assessment of the First Five Years of the PCR* (1974), "The Historical Context," pp. 3-10, "Policy and Programme," pp. 11-38

III. Organized Responses to the Challenges of Human Rights, Refugees, and Relief

In many respects, the WCC had origins in relief and humanitarian/Christian services provided to civilian and military refugees in World Wars One and Two. Similarly, the challenge to human rights during the Nazi period was instrumental in giving the WCC its sense of mission.

An estimated 9 to 15 million persons are refugees today, and the world churches minister to them in important ways. The world churches also address the problems of the violation of human rights in virtually all societies. In addressing the violation of human rights, the international community has encountered various conceptions of rights which have broadened the ethical agenda of the Christian community.

In addressing the problems of refugees and relief, the international community has encountered the social structures of oppression and disparate development. Accordingly, the WCC and LWF—with similar organizations—have coupled their relief efforts with work on behalf of social and economic development.

Seminars
LWF and Human Rights, Questions of Theological and Religious Imperative, Violence and Nonviolence

Assignment: Ron O'Grady, *Bread and Freedom: Understanding and Acting on Human Rights* (1979), 75pp.

WCC: CCIA and Human Rights
Assignment: "Report of Working Group I" (1981 CCIA), 14pp.; "A Decade of Human Rights in the World of the WCC" (1981), 10pp.; "Note on WCC-CCIA Actions Related to Human Rights, 1979-1980," 9pp.
Director's Seminar
WCC: Refugee Service
LWF: Refugees and Development, LWS
Assignment: Materials distributed at these sessions

United Nations Disaster Relief
World Health Organization
United Nations High Commissioner for Refugees

IV. Organized Responses to the Challenges of Social and Economic Development

As we will have noted, problems of relief and human rights relate to social, economic, and political structures as well as to immediate conditions. In order to address the long-range causes of misery and dislocation, the international community has to encounter the future in the form of alternative paths of societal change.

Social and economic development, as a condition for peace and justice, has been a priority of the U.N. and most world powers for at least a generation. In that time, however, the understanding of development and the changes that are required for it has been a subject of controversy. We will begin with a study prepared for the WCC by Richard Dickinson, and then consider various approaches to development.

Seminars
Assignment: Richard D.N. Dickinson, *To Set at Liberty the Oppressed* (1975), 193pp.
United Nations Conference on Trade and Development
International Labor Organization
Director's Seminar: Impact of War, Cold War, and Third World on Ecumenism
Assignment: *Towards a Church in Solidarity with the Poor* (1980), 38pp.; *CCPD Activity Report No. 7* (1980), 27pp.; Koson Srisang, "On Religion and Politics in Thailand," "Recovering the Power of Life," and "Sharing the Cup of Suffering"
Christian Medical Commission
LWF: Community Development Service
Assignment: *CDS: Community Development Service* (1977); a recent issue of *DEF: Development Education Forum*
Institut Universitaire d'etudes Special Committee on UN Development

V. Organized Responses to the Challenges of Creating Dialogue among People of Living Faiths and Ideologies

Institutions reflect systems of belief. Accordingly, institutional conflict, whether over social and economic development, human rights, or national interest, takes the form of ideological conflict in many cases. It often involves hidden values and assumptions. The resolution of conflict requires the recognition and reconciliation of values and beliefs. That is one of the assumptions of the WCC and LWF programs— to create dialogue among people of living faiths and ideologies.

We will study these programs as they are created within the Christian community and between it and other religious communities. We will want to be attentive to the process of dialogue as well as to its purpose and achievements.

Seminars
Christian World Communions
Assignment: *Guidelines on Dialogue* (1979), 22pp.; Carl F. Hallencrentz, *Dialogue and Community* (1977), 109pp.

Director's Seminar
Interfaith Dialogue
Assignment: Nils Ehrenstom & Gunther Gassmann, *Confessions in Dialogue* (1975), "Methods and Procedures," pp. 122-41, "Descriptive Accounts," pp. 14-52, and "Concluding Reflections," pp. 237-55.
Christian-Marxist Dialogue
Assignment: Ans J. van der Bent, *Christians and Communists* (1981), 67pp.

Roman Catholic-Protestant Dialogue
Secretariat for Christian Unity, Rome, Italy

VI. Review and Reflections

It is possible to diagram our study in terms of two intersecting planes. One plane is constituted by the ecumenism of the Christian community. The other plane is constituted by humanity. This is the double vision of ecumenism.

For most of our study we have approached these planes as though the WCC and LWF were at the center of their intersection. This week we review our studies and draw conclusions about the functional interactions of these two communities. But we also have to place ourselves individually at the center of the ecumenical intersection and ask, what are its implications for our own faith, life, and work?

Seminars
Conversation with Visser 'T Hooft
Assignment: Ernst Lange, *And Yet It Moves . . . Dream and Reality of the Ecumenical Movement* (1979), 173pp.

Director's Seminar on Ernst Lange
Review of the Course of Study
Assignment: Final Examination

Interpretive Papers
During the course of study, four interpretive papers will be prepared in which you will form your understanding of particular programs into a coherent presentation. You will draw upon your reading, our seminars and group discussions, and any individual conversations you have.

Your papers should be probably 6-10 pages, and should be written clearly on lined paper. They should be finished pieces of work. Quotations should be cited as to source, and you should add a bibliography of works consulted. If you have had interviews or consultations on an individual basis, in addition to our seminars, list them.

1. A Case in Point: Southern Africa (due July 3)
Explain the perspectives of Ernest Lefever and Barbara Rogers respectively: what does each argue and what does each assume?
What is the essential issue (or issues) that divides them; of what is this a case in point?
Offer a resolution of their difference(s) or defend one of their points of view in terms of your study and contacts in Geneva.

2. Human Rights (due July 10)
Identify the alternative interpretations of human rights as Ron O'Grady develops them.
What understanding(s) of human rights underlie the international programs you have studied? To what extent do alternative approaches to human rights produce tensions in international programming?

3. Social and Economic Development (due July 17)
Identify the various approaches to social and economic development as Richard Dickinson discusses them.
What understanding of social and economic development underlies the programs of the WCC and LWF? How do these organizations relate to other international organizations in the promotion of development, and to what extent do alternative approaches produce tensions in international programming?

4. Dialogue (due July 31)
What theological assumptions underlie programs for dialogue?
How do these programs contribute to the functions of the WCC in relation to the Christian community and to the international community respectively?
In what respects are these authentic expressions of ecumenical mission?

Individual Project
This is designed to be an instrument through which you can integrate the various emphases of the program in terms of a subject of interest to you. It should represent the research and thought required for a term paper, although it will not be written in full because of the limitations in time.

Form
Précis, or abstract: identify the subject, issue, program or problem you have studied and the questions it raises for our understanding; state your conclusion in thesis form; develop a succinct summary of your research; define the subject in historical and international contexts, explain the functional responses of church bodies as NGOs and the organizational problems resulting therefrom, explain what this has to do with current theologies of ecumenism and Christian responsibility, and draw an extended conclusion from your work.
Bibliography: list all written sources consulted and all interviews conducted (with a full identification of your consultant and the date and place of the interview).
Process: during the week of June 29-July 5 you will consult with the director regarding a choice of subject which will be significant for you and will be feasible to research.

Perspectives on Liberation Theology

John Mullaney   *Spring 1982*
Theology 256/Boston College/Chestnut Hill, MA 02167

The Theology of Liberation is the product of recent theological reflection on the conditions of political and economic oppression that exist in Latin America. By theological reflection we mean the way one understands faith in light of experience. Less than twenty years old, this method of reflection has given rise to a prophetic Church that is increasingly critical of political and economic structures that perpetuate economic bondage for three quarters of the worlds population. Liberation theology poses a challenge to not only the governments in Latin America, but to the U.S. government as well—a challenge that is not without controversy.

The purpose of this course is to examine the phenomenon of Liberation Theology as theological reflection on the factors that limit or keep human-kind from self fulfillment and the exercise of his/her freedom. In the process, three basic questions will need to be answered: a) What is this faith I am attempting to understand? b) What do I believe? and c) How do I participate in the incarnation of these beliefs in my world? To ground ourselves, we will examine the Biblical themes which are central to liberation theology. From the Old Testament, the concepts of "Justice" and "Salvation," the Exodus, Moses and the imagination of the Prophets are of particular interest. From the New Testament, the person of Jesus, the meaning of Eucharist and the concept of Church will be discussed at length. Running parallel to the discussion of these themes will be practical examples of the activity of the Church in Latin America as it struggles with a faith that carries a mandate for the liberation of oppressed peoples.

Requirements

A journal to be submitted every two weeks should include your own reflections on liberation in your own life or on a theme of particular interest. There will be 1 short mid-term examination, 1 final examination, and a research/reflection paper. The paper can be on one of two options:

1. Choose a developing country and discuss the role of the Church or Churches in the struggle for political and economic reforms.
2. Choose an instance of injustice in your own experience or in this country and discuss the role of the church in this issue as well as your own reflections on the subject given your understanding of Jesus as liberator. Examples of topics: the role of women in the Church, feminism, racism, materialism, homosexuality, Reaganomics and the like.

Readings
Tissa Balasuriya, *The Eucharist and Human Liberation*, Orbis Press, 1981
Walter Bruggerman, *The Prophetic Imagination*, Fortress Press, 1980
Ernesto Cardenal, *The Gospel of Solentiname*, Orbis Press, 1977
Penny Lernoux, *The Cry of the People*, Doubleday, 1980
Sebastian Kappen, *Jesus and Freedom*, Orbis, 1980
Jon Sobrino, *The Community Called Church*, Orbis, 1979

Course Outline

January 19   Introductory Remarks
Handout: Gutierrez, "The Process of Liberation in Latin America," from *A Theology of Liberation*

January 21   Liberation Theology   What is it?
a. Colonial History of Latin American Economic Development
b. "Dependence" Models of Development
Reading: Penny Lernoux, *The Cry of the People*, Chapter 1-2

January 26   The Role of The Church in the Development of Latin America
a. Vatican Documents "Populorum Progressio," "Gaudiem et Spes"
b. Medellin and Puebla—The Latin American Bishops Call for Review
c. The New Martyrs

January 28   Biblical Foundations for Liberation Theology
a. Exodus, Covenant, Moses
b. Justice, Salvation in the OT
c. Moses the Alternative Consciousness
Reading: Bruggerman, *The Prophetic Imagination*, Chapter 1-2.

February 2   The Prophet as Harbinger of Liberation
a. Israel the Nation State
b. The Royal Consciousness
c. Isaiah
Reading: Bruggerman, Chapter 3-4

February 4   Contemporary Prophets
a. The Problem of Superficial Religiosity
Readings: Lernoux, Chapter X, pp. 363-388
Monica Helwig, "Christology and Social Structures" from *Above Every Name*, Woodstock Theological Center, 1981

February 9   Search for the Historical Jesus
a. Jesus through history
b. The Cult of Jesus
Readings: Stephan Kappen, *Jesus and Freedom*, Chapter 1-2

February 11 The Challenge of Jesus as Liberator
Readings: Kappen, Chapter 3; Bruggerman, Chapter 5

February 16, 19   Holiday—No class

February 23   The Critical Consciousness of Jesus
Readings: Bruggerman, Chapter 5-6

February 25   Jesus and the Economic Order

March 2   Jesus Christ—The Message of Liberation
Readings: Kappen, Chapter 4-5-6

March 4   Continued Discussion

March 9   In class Mid-term Examination

March 11   The Meaning of Eucharist and Liberation
Reading: Balasuriya, *The Eucharist and Human Liberation*, Chapter 1-5

March 16   Political Interpretations of Eucharist
Readings: Balasuriya, Chapters 7 and 10
John Haughey, "The Eucharist at Corinth: You are the Christ," from *Above Every Name*

March 18   The Meaning of Church
Readings: Segundo, *The Community Called Church* (selected chapters)

March 23, 25   The Mission of the Prophetic Church
Readings: Segundo, (selected chapters); Lernoux, Chapter 3

March 30, April 1   The Consequences of "Liberation Theology"
a. Return to Persecution
Reading: Lernoux, Chapter 4

April 6, 8   A Global Church in a Global Village
a. Latin America Challenges the United States
Readings: Lernoux, Chapters 5, 6, 7, 9 and remainder of 10

April 13   Film "Controlling Interests"

April 15   A Church Divided: Liberation Theology, a Spiritual Witness or Political Ideology
Reading: Shubert M. Ogden, "The Concept of a Theology of Liberation: Must a Christian Theology Today Be So Conceived?"

April 20   The Message of Liberation Theology for the First World
Reading: Dorothy Soelle, "Thou Shalt Have No Other Jeans Before Me" (Levi's Advertisement, Early Seventies): The Need for Liberation in a Consumerist Society

April 22   Continued topic
Choice of Readings on: Black Theology of Liberation; Feminist Theology of Liberation; or Liberation and Politics

April 29   Where do we go as Members of a Church?
Reading: David Hollenbach, "A Prophetic Church and the Catholic Sacramental Imagination"

War, Peace and Disarmament

John Langan   *Spring 1983*
Yale Divinity School/Yale University/New Haven, CT   06520

The goal of the course is to achieve familiarity with both the current state of debate in the churches on the question of Western defense policy and the main historic forms of Christian response to the problem of achieving justice and peace in a violent and divided world.

Format

The course will meet once a week for two hours. Students will be expected to show both familiarity with the texts under discussion and an ability to relate these in a critical fashion to contemporary debates.

Requirements

a) Active class participation
b) Assigned readings
c) A 5-8 page critical review of a recent article or document—due March 1
   Among the items suitable for critical review are:
   "God's Hope in a Time of Fear" (U.S.C.C. draft, June 1982)
   "The Challenge of Peace: God's Promise and our Response" (U.S.C.C. draft, November 1982)
   "Nuclear Weapons and Christian Conscience" (Church of England draft, April 1982)
   John Langan, "The American Hierarchy and Nuclear Weapons," *Theological Studies* 43 (September 1982), 447-467
   David Hollenbach, "Nuclear Weapons and Nuclear War," *Theological Studies* 43 (December 1982), 577-605
   Leon Wieseltier, "Nuclear War, Nuclear Peace," *The New Republic*, January 10-17, 1983, 7-38
   Michael Howard, "Reassurance and Deterrence," *Foreign Affairs* 61 (Winter 1982-83), 309-324
   Stanley Hoffman, *Duties Beyond Borders*, ch. 2
d) A 20-page term paper on a topic approved by the instructor

Required Texts

Jonathan Schell, *The Fate of the Earth*
Thomas Shannon (ed.), *War or Peace?*
Roland Bainton, *Christian Attitudes Toward War and Peace*
Alan Geyr, *The Idea of Disarmament*
Michael Walzer, *Just and Unjust Wars*

Syllabus

January 11   Introduction and Overview

January 18   The Present Crisis and Our Choices

January 25   Christianity and War to 1500
Bainton, chs. 1-7

February 1   Christianity and War since 1500
Bainton, chs. 8-15

February 8   Pacifism Today
Essays by Deats and Lammers in Shannon
James Douglas, *The Non-Violent Cross*, ch. 7
John Howard Yoder, *The Politics of Jesus*, chs. 4, 5, 10

February 15   Just War Theory and the Modern Mind
Walzer, chs. 1-4, 7

February 22   Just War Theory as Theory
Walzer, ch. 8
Essays by Hehir and Childress in Shannon

March 1   Just War Theory as Casuistry
Walzer, chs. 6, 9-14

March 22   Just War Theory and the Nuclear Age
Walzer, chs. 16-17
James Stegenga, "Dunbar's Bremen," *Christianity and Crisis*, January 19, 1981

March 29   The Problem of Deterrence
Geyer, chs. 1-4

April 5   The Task of Disarmament
Geyer, chs. 5-8

April 12   The Problem of Limited Nuclear War

April 19   The Mission and Responsibility of the Church—An Assessment of the Catholic and Anglican Debate

Seeking Peace: Spiritual Resources for Living under the Nuclear Arms Race

G. Clarke Chapman
Religion J-823/Moravian College/Bethlehem, PA 18018

Spring 1983

This course was taught in January, 1983, as a 4 week special "January term" course at Moravian College. Three objectives were announced in advance. 1) To become knowledgeable about the current arms race (through an intensive series of readings, lectures, and some guest speakers). 2) To develop a personal spiritual discipline (through a succession of non-sectarian meditation techniques, which were practiced in class and also assigned for daily use individually). 3) To construct a multi-dimensional concept of "peace" as inner, societal, intrapersonal, and global (through readings, discussions, and group dynamics exercise). One evening each week was devoted to relevant films and subsequent discussion; for this, non-class members and the community at large were also invited.

The problem of psychic numbing

Having taught such a course before, I know how overwhelming the subject matter can be to the average student. Several elements accordingly were added to this course in an attempt to minimize psychic numbing, a retreat into apathy and fatalism:

1. Careful selection of readings for their reliability, yet readability and some perspective of hope.
2. Emphasis on some classical spiritual disciplines: open-ended meditation periods in each class session as well as assigned for individual use.
3. Emphasis on a holistic vision of peace, *shalom*, encompassing all the dimensions of life.
4. Affective learning and personal involvement of students: peace-envisioning (collages and drawings, buzz groups), "cooperation-squares" exercise, a simulation game on the problems of trust and verification in disarmament, a nuclear mapping exercise, and some journaling.
5. Group-building efforts: a daily round of introductions, frequent buzz groups, class involvement in procedural decisions and in compilation of crucial definitions ("peace," "security") as well as lists of suggestions.

Evaluation of the course

1. Strengths—e.g., the film series (especially an alarmist documentary from the American Security Council, "The S.A.L.T. Syndrome," with explicit rebuttals from the Center for Defense Information read aloud at intervals while the film was halted), the simulation game (e.g., the issue arose: "may we cheat on verification in order to save the world?"), and the mapping exercise. Most

students mastered the basic concepts and manifested a wholesome balance of conviction and mutual tolerance.
2. Weaknesses—e.g., the dilemma of how to handle the belligerent class dissenter, a widespread laxity in individual daily practice in meditation, and an insufficient integration of the informational, attitudinal and meditational dimensions of the course. Unfortunately, the optimal level of esprit de corps never developed. One wonders, to what extent can this whole topic, with its complexity and many personal ramifications, be effectively taught in the confines of academia?

Some suggestions for revisions and improvement
1. More attention to the need for group-building measures outside the classroom, encouraging trust and interaction through, e.g., convivial social occasions.
2. More emphasis on individual responses in writing both in and outside the classroom.

Textbooks
Nigel Calder, *Nuclear Nightmares: An Investigation into Possible Wars.* New York, Penguin Books, 1981.
The Defense Monitor, Vol. IX, No. 5, "American Strength, Soviet Weakness."
The Defense Monitor, Vol. IX, No. 8, "Pentagon Rebuts Charges of U.S. Military Weakness."
Effects of Nuclear War: Official U.S. Appraisal; An Appeal to Conscience: What You Can Do. (Reprint) State College, PA: The Sycamore Community, 1981.
Mary Lou Kownacki, ed., *A Race to Nowhere: An Arms Race Primer for Catholics.* Chicago: Pax Christi—USA, 1981.
Lawrence LeShan, *How to Meditate: A Guide to Self-Discovery.* New York: Bantam, 1975.
A Matter of Faith: A Study for Churches on the Nuclear Arms Race. Washington, DC: Sojourners, 1981.
James A. Stegenga, "Dunbar's Bremen: A Morality Play for the Nuclear Age," *Christianity and Crisis*, Vol. 40, No. 22 (Jan. 19, 1981), pp. 371-80.
Also, select one of the following to be used in personal reflection:
Elizabeth O'Connor, *Search for Silence*. Waco, TX: Word, 1972.
Thomas Merton, *New Seeds of Contemplation.* New York: New Directions, 1972.

Schedule of Readings

I. Background on the Arms Race (Jan. 6)
Calder, chapter 1;
A Race to Nowhere, pp. 1-14;
A Matter of Faith, pp. 5-20, 84-85;
LeShan, pp. 1-18 and browse.

II. Europe and Modern War (Jan. 8)
Calder, chapter 2;
A Matter of Faith, pp. 58-60, 86-87.

III. Is There a Soviet Threat? (Jan. 11)
A Race to Nowhere, pp. 15-26;
A Matter of Faith, pp. 21-28, 66-69;

The Defense Monitor, both issues: "American Strength, Soviet Weakness," and "Pentagon Rebuts Charges of U.S. Military Weakness"; George F. Kennan, "The Soviet Threat: How Real?" *Inquiry* (March 17, 1980), and the Albert Einstein Peace Prize speech of May 19, 1981.

IV. Problems of Proliferation (Jan. 13)
Calder, chapter 3;
A Race to Nowhere, pp. 42-51;
Thomas Merton, "The Root of War" and "Red or Dead: The Anatomy of a Cliche," xeroxed reprints;
Michael T. Klare, "The Political Economy of Arms Sales," in *The Riverside Disarmament Reader*, pp. 250-57 (on reserve shelf).

V. The Effects of Nuclear War (Jan. 18)
A Matter of Faith, pp. 32-37, 63;
Effects of Nuclear War, pp. 3-12, 15-46, 63-75, 81-90, 94-100, 109-15, 124-138;
(Recommended also: *Riverside Disarmament Reader*, pp. 141-49, on reserve shelf).

VI. Recent Strategic Doctrine and Weaponry (Jan. 20)
Calder, chapters 4 and 5;
A Matter of Faith, p. 64;
Robert Aldridge, *The Counterforce Syndrome*, pp. 1-13 and then browse.

VII. The Effects of Preparing for War (Jan. 22)
A Race to Nowhere, pp. 28-40;
A Matter of Faith, pp. 29-31, 80-82; review pp. 62-69;
Lloyd J. Dumas, "30 Years of the Arms Race: The Deterioration of Economic Strength & Military Security," *Riverside Disarmament Reader*, pp. 266-77 (on reserve shelf);
Alan Geyer, "Some Theological Perspectives on Militarism," *Colleague* (Summer, 1981), pp. 6-12 (xerox copies of reserve shelf).

VIII. The Response of Faith (Jan. 25)
A Race to Nowhere, pp. 54-68;
A Matter of Faith, pp. 44-57, and review pp. 84-87;
James Stegenga, "Dunbar's Bremen: A Morality Play for the Nuclear Age," *Christianity and Crisis*, 40:22 (Jan. 19, 1981), pp. 371-80;
Theodore Roszak, "A Just War Analysis of Two Types of Deterrence," *Riverside Disarmament Reader*, pp. 315-26 (on reserve shelf).

IX. The Response of Faith at Work (Jan. 27)
A Race to Nowhere, pp. 69-85;
A Matter of Faith, pp. 72-79, 88-93, 98-102.

Extra Projects
There is the option of writing a factual report or research paper and/or making a class presentation on topics pertinent to the course. These extra-credit projects should be negotiated with me no later than Jan. 18.

Spiritual Disciplines
This course is intended to be non-sectarian, open to people of any religious background, but who believe that spirituality must be at least part of the answer to

the nuclear threat. By enrolling for this course you have agreed to attempt to practice some sort of meditation for 20 minutes daily. This may not be easy, but after several weeks your patience and efforts should pay off. During each of the daytime class sessions we will spend some minutes as a group in an exercise in meditation (usually drawn from LeShan). In addition, you should set aside 20 minutes daily for your own spiritual discipline, using the resources provided (in LeShan, or O'Connor or Merton's books). At least 5 minutes of that time should be in silent meditation, and gradually this may be increased. Take notes and re-evaluate from time to time (some may prefer daily "journaling"). Your purpose is to attain more inner tranquility.

Terms to Learn
Here are at least some of the terms to watch out for and learn to define:
strategic nuclear weapons, tactical nuclear weapons, theater nuclear weapons, mutually assured destruction, counterforce, minimum deterrence, damage limitation, strategic triad, SALT, first-strike capability, ICBM, SLBM, warhead, MIRV, MARV, kiloton, megaton, direct nuclear radiation, thermal radiation, fallout, rems, psi, electromagnetic pulse, fire storm, lethality, yield, SS-20, MX, Trident, Pershing II, cruise missile, neutron bomb, proliferation, nuclear freeze, the just war theory, economic conversion, ABM, firebreak, forward defense strategy of NATO, warfighting capability, launch-on-warning policy, Minuteman vulnerability (or "window of vulnerability"), idolatry, moratorium, deterrence.

Questions to think about
In the next several weeks, give some time to reflect on the following questions (and you will need to come back to them several times, at least!):
1. What is "peace"?
2. What is "security"?
3. As best as I can now see, what must happen within the next ten years, if either peace or security is to become a reality? Within the next five years? Now?
4. What part will I play in all this?

War, Peace and Revolution

Wilmer Cooper   *Fall 1983*
Theology 50/Earlham College School of Religion/Richmond, IN 47374

This is a new course in Peace Studies at ESR. The purpose of the course is to examine the peace witness in relationship to the issues of war and peace in revolutionary situations. Both Christian pacifist and non-pacifist positions will be considered as alternative ways of dealing with revolutionary conflict. An attempt will also be made to place these conflicts in global perspective in relationship to political, economic and social structures which have the seeds of revolution and war in them.

The course will examine options of dealing with these issues from a Christian ethical point of view. A major problem here is to what extent the Church should become involved in Christian action related to war and peace issues. What are the arguments for and against such organized and institutional involvement of Christians concerned about peace and social justice?

Objectives

1. Examine the peace witness in relationship to some of the central issues of war, violence and revolution:
   • Nature and meaning of revolution in today's world
   • Relationship of power, force and violence
   • Meaning of the just war and just revolution, and how these relate to the concepts of holy war and crusades
   • How our views of human nature and society affect the possibility of ridding the world of war and violence
   • How nonresistance and nonviolent resistance are related
   • How faithfulness (principle) and effectiveness (results) are related
2. Acquaint students with some of the complexities of war, peace and revolution as they relate to poverty, world hunger, over-population, depletion of natural resources and energy, world economic development, human rights, nuclear policy and disarmament, etc.
3. How are we to understand war, peace and revolution from the perspective of Christian and biblical ethics?
4. What should be the relationship of the church and state concerning issues of war, peace and revolution? Specifically, what is the role of the church?
5. Is Christian nonviolence a viable alternative to military approaches to problems of war, violence and revolution in society?

Methodology
1. Introduce students to a sampling of contemporary authors and literature concerning issues of war, peace and revolution.

2. Help students develop a bibliography of material they can use on issues of war, peace and revolution.
3. Have students prepare critical book reviews *or* do a research paper to be presented and discussed in class.
4. Have students work in teams of two to make presentations to the seminar and lead class discussions. This is intended to be a learning experience in the dynamics of organization, communication and teaching.

Organization of the Course

The course will be offered in the form of a seminar. This assumes that the class will be relatively small and that students will become involved in a major way in presenting material for class discussion. Although a general framework will be provided by the instructor, and certain objectives and guidelines for the course will be made clear, it is the intent that students help develop the details of the course and that they provide the main input for the class. The role of the instructor is to be a resource person and be the moderator for class discussion and debate.

Requirements of the Course

The following books will provide the core for the Seminar's study and work. They should be read in the order given.

John Howard Yoder, *The Politics of Jesus,* Grand Rapids, MI: Wm. Eerdmans Publishing Co., 1972.

Ronald J. Sider, *Christ and Violence,* Scottsdale, PA: Herald Press, 1979.

J.R. Davis, *Christians, Politics and Violent Revolution,* Maryknoll, NY: Orbis Books, 1976.

James W. Douglass, *The Non-violent Cross,* New York: Macmillan Publishing Co., 1966.

Brandt Commission, *North-South: A Program for Survival,* Cambridge, MA: The MIT Press, 1980.

Edward Norman, *Christianity and the World Order,* Oxford: Oxford University Press, 1979.

Charles Elliott and others, *Christian Faith and Political Hopes: A Reply to E.R. Norman,* London, Epworth Press, 1979

During the first class session we will organize ourselves for the term's work. Depending on the number in the class, students will be paired off in teams to work together. They will be responsible for systematic presentations of material from the assigned books and lead discussions during class.

Paper Assignments

The class will have a choice of one or two paper assignments: Either four critical book reviews *or* a special research project with a 4000 to 5000 word term paper. The critical book reviews will include the following from among the required readings for the course:

John Howard Yoder, *Politics of Jesus*
J.G. Davis, *Christians, Politics and Violent Revolution*
James W. Douglass, *The Non-violent Cross*
Edward Norman, *Christianity and World Order,* and the compendium *Reply to E.R. Norman: Christian Faith and Political Hopes*

If you do a research project and term paper, your topic is to be picked in consultation with the instructor. For example, you might research the Just War theory and its relevance for war, peace and revolution both historically and today. Or you might want to go more deeply into the subject of violence and non-violence in relationship to war, peace and revolution.

Bibliography

Radical Reformation Witness
Donald Durnbaugh, *The Believers' Church*, Macmillan, 1968
Arthur Gish, *The New Left and Christian Radicalism*, Eerdmans, 1970
John Howard Yoder, *The Christian Witness and the State*, Faith & Life Press, 1964
John Howard Yoder, *Nevertheless*, Herald Press, 1971
The Original Revolution, Herald Press, 1970

Nonviolence and Revolution
Peter Berger and Richard Neuhaus, *Movement and Revolution*, Doubleday, 1970
Anders Boserup and Andrew Mack, *War Without Weapons*, Schocken, 1975
James Douglass, *Resistance and Contemplation*, Doubleday, 1972
John Ferguson, *The Politics of Love*, Attic Press
Richard B. Gregg, *The Power of Nonviolence*, Lippincott, 1934
Paul Hare and Herbert Blumberg, *Liberation Without Violence*, Rowman & Littlefield, 1977
Stephen Hall-King, *Defense in a Nuclear Age*, Gollanez, 1963
Cecil Hinshaw, *Nonviolent Resistance*, Pendle Hill Pamphlet #88
Marjorie Hope and James Young, *Struggle for Humanity*, Orbis, 1977
George Lakey, *Nonviolent Action: How It Works*, Pendle Hill Pamphlet #129
George Lakey, *Strategy for a Living Revolution*, Freeman, 1968
Bradford Lyttle, *National Defense Through Nonviolent Resistance*, AFSC, 1958
Martin Marty and David Peerman eds., *New Theology* No. 6
Rosemary Ruether, *The Radical Kingdom*, Harper & Row, 1970
Gene Sharp, *Exploring Nonviolent Alternatives*, Sargent
Gene Sharp, *The Politics of Nonviolent Action*, Sargent, 1973

Just War Theory
Paul Ramsey, *The Just War,*Scribners, 1968
LeRoy Walters, *Five Classic Just War Theories*
Michael Walzer, *Just and Unjust Wars*, Basic Books, 1977

Church and State
Oscar Cullmann, *The State in the New Testament*, SCM Press, 1963
Thomas G. Sanders, *Protestant Concepts of Church and State*, Doubeday, 1964
  (especially chapters on Anabaptists and Quakers)

Liberation Theology
James Cone, *Black Theology of Liberation*, Lippincott, 1970
Gustavo Gutierrez, *A Theology of Liberation*, Orbis, 1973
Jose Miguez-Bonino, *Doing Theology in a Revolutionary Age*, Fortress, 1975
Juan Luis Segundo, *The Liberation of Theology*, Orbis 1976

Community, Cultures, Values and Change

Global Systems
Elise Boulding, Dartmouth College

Acquiring a Multicultural Perspective Through the Writing Process
Teresa M. Castaldi, Stockton State College

Alienation
Melvin Gurtov, University of California at Riverside

Quality of Life
Lester W. Milbrath, State University of New York at Buffalo

Political Mobilization
Jeane Grassholtz, Mount Holyoke College

The Third World Through Film
Angela Gilliam, State University of New York at Old Westbury

Poverty and Culture
Dan Rosenberg, Earlham College

Global Systems

Elise Boulding   *Fall 1983*
Sociology 12/Dartmouth College/Hanover, NH 03755

The purpose of this course is to look at the development of world community as a complex of social processes, dependent on skills of conflict regulation and peacemaking, and on the development of a sense of shared interests and common fate, at all levels from the local to the global. We will view the planet as a sociosphere, the sphere of human transactions involving social structures, institutions and persons-in-roles in continuous interaction, kept in motion by inter-generational socialization processes and images of the past and future, generated out of partly shared, partly conflicting values and aspirations. The conditions for peace and justice and the viability of various means of peacekeeping will be considered from statist, UN and NGO perspectives, in the context of images of desired futures and development goals for diverse social groups within the international system.

This is an elective ten week, introductory-level course fitting in with a new cluster in international sociology. Typically the course size is 35-50 students, including international and minority students.

Texts

Werner Feld and Roger Coate, *The Role of International Nongovernmental Associations in World Politics.* Learning Package #17 of the ISA Consortium for International Studies.
Paul Wehr, *Conflict Regulation.* Boulder, CO: Westview Press, 1979.
Saul H. Mendlovitz, *On the Creation of a Just World Order.* NY: The Free Press, 1975.

Topics and Readings

I. The Individual and the Global Perspective

Week 1 Introduction to Global Perspectives
Bergesen's "From Utilitarianism to Globology: The Shift from the Individual to the World as a Whole as the Primordial Unit of Analysis" in Bergesen's *Studies of the Modern World System*
Ramchandra Gandhi, "Notes From the Metaphysical Underground" in *Gandhi Marg,* Journal of the Gandhi Peace Foundation, Vol. IV, No. 2 & 3 (May-June 1982)

The Transnationals
Feld and Coate, Section 1; Ex. No. 1 in Coate due Week 2

Week 2 Growth of NGO's
Feld and Coate, Section 2, Ex. No. 2 will be done in class today

How NGO Networks Facilitate Global Action Locally
Feld and Coate, Sections 3 and 4
E. Boulding, "Global Altruism and Everyday Behavior," Chapter 2 in *Humatriotism: Human Interest in Peace and Survival*, Theodore F. Lentz, Editor. St. Louis: The Futures Press, 1976, pp. 39-65
"Family" NGO map due week 4

Week 3 The Working of Integrative Processes
Chs 1 and 2 in Philip Jacob and James Toscano, eds., *The Integration of Political Communities*

II. The Changing International Order

The UN and its National Missions
R.G. Feltham, *Diplomatic Handbook*, whole book. Note #1: Identify and obtain UN reports for the current "UN Year," i.e. 1983 is World Communications Year. 1986 will be International Peace Year. Note #2: Each student will choose a country and nationality to "adopt" for the remainder of the term in doing the remaining assignments. Get the basic facts about "your" country from the current *World Almanac*. Follow the news events concerning it in the *New York Times* and 1 newspaper published outside the U.S. Write to "your" national mission at the UN for information
Progress report on "your" country in the changing international order. Due week 6

Week 4 The New International Economic Order
Chs. 1-7 and Annex 1, Summary of Recommendations, in *North-South: A Programme for Survival*, Report of the Brandt Commission.
Optional: E. Boulding, "Learning to Learn: The North Responds to the New Economic Order," *Alternatives*, Vol. IV, No. 3, 1979

The New International Security Order
Chs. 1, 4 and 6 in *Common Security: A Blueprint for Survival*, Report of the Palme Commission; or, Chs. 5, 6, and the Conclusion in Mary Kaldor's *Baroque Arsenal*. Compare figures on military and social expenditures in your country with those for the rest of the world, by an inspection of Ruth Sivard's *World Military and Social Expenditures*, current annual edition

Week 5 The New International Information Order, and the New International Cultural Order
Many Voices, One World, The UNESCO commissioned MacBride Report, pp. 137-200
Herbert Shore, *Cultural Policy: UNESCO's First Cultural Development Decade*, published by U.S.Commission for UNESCO

Human Rights and the International Order
Asbjorn Eide, "The Right to Peace," in *Bulletin of Peace Proposals*, No. 2, 1979

Week 6 Disarmament and Development
A speaker from the UN

III. Alternative Futures

Imaging Preferred Worlds

Boulding, Elise. "A Disarmed World: Problems in Imaging the Future," *Journal of Sociology and Social Welfare*, Vol. IV, No. 3 & 4, Jan/Mar 1977, pp. 656-668

Introduction by Mendlovitz and Chapter by Ali Mazrui in Mendlovitz, *On the Creation of a Just World Order*

Optional: Chs. 9-11 in *Indefensible Weapons* by Robert Lifton and Richard Falk

Week 7 Preferred Worlds continued

Chapters by Rajni Kothari and Johan Galtung in Mendlovitz

Workshop on Imaging a World Without Weapons

Class will last from 2 to 6 PM. Workshop exercises taken from Warren Ziegler's mindbook for *Imaging a World Without Weapons*, available from Futures Invention Associates, 2026 Hudson St., Denver, CO

Papers describing the world you image. Due week 8

IV. Conflict, Peacekeeping and Peacemaking

Week 8 Models of Conflict Processes

Wehr, Ch 1 and 2

Transnational Peace Education Networks

Read 2 or more articles in Peace Education issue of the *Bulletin of Peace Proposals*, No. 4, 1979

Week 9 Self-Limiting Conflict

Wehr, Chs. 3-5; optional additional reading: Bondurant, *Conquest of Violence*, Chs. 2 and 3 on Satyagraha, precepts and practices

Adam Roberts, *Civilian Resistance as a National Defense*, any chapters

In-class mediation workshop: 2 to 6 PM

"Intermediaries and Mediation," Ch. 7 in Louis Kriesberg's *Social Conflicts*

James Laue, "Conflict Intervention," Ch. 4 in *Handbook of Applied Sociology*, Marvin Olsen and Michael Micklin, eds.

John Burton, "The Second Track," Part II of *Dear Survivors*

Week 10 UN and Nongovernmental Peacekeeping

Read one of the following:

Charles Moskos, *Peace Soldiers*

Indar Rikhye, et al. *The Thin Blue Line*

Materials on the Shanti Sena and the World Peace Brigade from the ISTNA packet of "Readings on Nonviolent Alternatives," available from: ISTNA, Box 515, Waltham, MA 02254

Two page description of the international dimensions of your own intended career.

Training for New Peacemaking Roles

Summary Section in the Report of the National Peace Academy Commission (U.S. Gov't Printing Office)

Current issue of *Coping with Conflict*, annual review of the work of the International Peace Academy, 777 UN Plaza, NY 10017

Optional: UN report on the UN University for Peace, Costa Rica

Projects

#1 Exercise
Follow instructions for Parts 1 and 2 only, in Feld and Coate.

#2 Family NGO Membership Map
List all memberships in INGO's (international nongovernmental organizations) for yourself and other members of your immediate family. Look 3 of these organizations up in a recent volume of the *Handbook of International Organizations*, recording the official aims and purposes of each NGO. Show the distribution of the NGO country memberships on the map provided you, developing a coding system which clearly distinguishes between different NGO's. Attach a sheet to the map showing the name, headquarters location, list of member countries and purposes of each NGO. Write 2 pages of suggestions on how these NGO linkages might be used to deal with a global problem that concerns you. Pay particular attention to the type of country coverage each NGO offers. What countries do not have sections, and how does this limit what the NGO can do?

#2a Alternative: Your Community in the World
The basic premise behind the Community in the World/the World in the Community type of project, which originated in Columbus, Ohio and is currently being carried out in a number of American cities, is that individuals and community organizations in local communities are making and carrying out foreign policy every day in the course of their normal transactions. This is because these transactions have international dimensions not always fully recognized or articulated; these international dimensions may contribute to the enhancement or diminution of social welfare at home and abroad, without ever touching directly on governmental foreign policy transactions. The export and import policies of Hanover (New Hampshire) businesses may be an important source of international goodwill. The activities of local leadership training programs channeled through International Rotary, may enhance leadership potentials in Third World countries. The activities of local churches and programs for youth, through scholarships, leadership training, and development aid programs, are channeled through international church bodies and may directly affect levels of living among Third World poor.

All of these types of contacts and transactions contribute to the development of an alternative set of ways for human beings to help one another across national boundaries. These activities are supplementary to inter-state inter-actions and may indeed create a stronger climate of cooperation than formal inter-governmental interactions are able to do.They are therefore significant to national and international well-being, as well as to the welfare of the community.

Each member of the class will seek the cooperation of one (Hanover) organization to explore the actual or potential international dimensions of that group's activities, reporting back both to the organization itself and to the class. The tools for exploration are developed in the Feld and Coate booklet and also in *You and Your Community in the World* by Alger and Hoovler. (Obtainable through Mershon Institute, Ohio University, Columbus OH.) The class will divide into groups for this project, according to whether they have chosen business, civic or church organizations to study. Individual papers will be chapters in a class report to the community.

#3 "Country" Reports

Using the country perspective you have chosen, write a report on how the objectives promoted in the reports on the international economic, security, information and cultural orders are viewed in "your" country, and what progress, if any, is being made in achieving them. The most recent UN *Statistical Yearbook* will provide you with social and economic data about your country. The current *World Almanac* contains concise country descriptions, including brief histories.

#4 Your Image of a World Without Arms

Use the notes you develop during the workshop, and build on them. The following description of the workshop is taken from an invitation to a two-day residential workshop. We will utilize the approach in a limited 4-hour version.

The workshop uses a futures-invention technique already utilized in a wide range of public policy arenas to facilitate break-throughs on the part of decision makers facing apparently intractable policy problems, but not applied before to disarmament. The participants will begin by thinking about what a disarmed world without war would be like. The assumptions behind the exercises are that we cannot get to a substantially disarmed world if we can't or won't imagine what human society would look like under those conditions. Warren Ziegler is the author of the futures invention technique and director of Futures Invention Associates.

#5 International Dimensions of your own Career

Describe what you see as the international dimensions of your own possible future career, and explore its conflict resolution and tension reduction aspects. What do you see as the larger implications for the future social order of the career choice you are now trying to make?

Acquiring a Multicultural Perspective Through the Writing Process

Teresa M. Castaldi   *Spring 1983*
General Studies 2120/Stockton State College/Pomona, NJ 08240

This course will focus on the customs, lifestyles and social structures of various cultural groups throughout the world. Students will have the opportunity to explore the framework and boundaries of their own particular subculture through a variety of readings and their own writings.

Methodology

Interactions with my students demonstrate that the majority are unable to understand experience from perspectives other than the singular and personal. I have discovered that many students find it difficult to move from an ego-centered model of reality to a more expansive world view. On a higher level, students, as well as many people in the general population, have a limited sense of other cultures and are caught up in a web of ethnocentric biases without quite knowing how and why these biases exist. My interest, then, is to provide a structure in which individual experiences can be shaped into larger mental patterns and articulated, as either similar to or different from other cultural modes in the world.

The same set of tools required in all education is necessary for learning with a global perspective. Insight, the capacity to communicate ideas clearly, and critical thinking constitute the skills and awareness necessary for discerning, perceptive citizens to function in a community. Students can be aided in developing a global perspective at the same time as they are acquiring reasoning and communication abilities. I have designed, therefore, a sequence in which critical analysis and writing are integrated into a framework to enable students to first, identify their own private point of view, second, familiarize them with other perspectives, and finally, move them toward a larger field of cultural and historical awareness. This model, a "continuum of awareness," is structured according to the marked development stages of cognitive, abstractive and communication capacities.

Because writing is intrinsically involved with content, I have designed writing exercises with an anthropological base. The underlying assumptions within the field are ideally suited to the acquisition of multi-cultural perspectives. The general structure of each exercise could also be easily applied to other disciplines.

Culture can be defined as the learned, shared meanings and behavior used as a basic means of survival within a group. The inherent movement from egocentricity to a larger, more encompassing societal view necessary for human coexistence can, therefore, be exploited to encourage a global perspective. In other words, if our young can be taught the cultural codes to survive in domestic societies, we can take them several steps beyond to teach them about world society.

Exercises

The first exercise in my sequence assigned to students is quite simple: I ask them to go out and observe the opposite sex, after we have spent a considerable amount of time reading and discussing non-verbal communication. They are asked not to focus exclusively on their own age group. After collecting their "data," they are asked to formulate the hypotheses about their observations. As expected, these hypotheses, often consisting of grand generalizations, elicit class responses ranging from agreement with the observer to total discord. The purpose of this activity is to have the students become actively engaged in the process of thinking about who they are and what it might be like to be someone else. It succeeds on two levels: the students have the opportunity to sharpen their observational skills through writing, as they widen their angle of vision of the world.

The second writing heuristic in my model allows the student to explore his or her own ideas and those of others through a peer collaborative learning activity. Students identify an inner perspective and then branch outward through discussion of what I call "culturally loaded" words. This exercise could also be used both before and after a class unit on a specific country or culture or a unit on a particular period in history to determine if preconceived notions changed after class instruction and discussion. Students could also create their own "loaded words" or think of words in common usage that have both connotative and denotative meanings. Temporal change in language could be examined by gathering words from different time periods which have similar dictionary meanings but have come to have different connotations through time. An example of this could be words such as bum, vagabond, urchin, tramp, hobo, bag lady, ragamuffin, vagrant, panhandler, etc. Are these words all recognizable to the average student?

The three excerpts I have included in my "continuum of awareness" expose students to anthropological literature. Exercises to increase multicultural awareness stemming from these or similar readings could include the writing and discussion about (1) the similarities and differences among people across time and space; (2) the notion of exploitation; and (3) inferences made by both the reader and the writer. Content cannot be divorced from the writing process and contributes to the students' knowledge base as well as fostering abstract thinking. Students master content through writing. The use of sequential stages in heuristics is important if one intends to consciously move students toward a larger scheme of reality.

Again, the strategies I have presented are not discipline specific and can be used in psychology, sociology, history, economics, English literature, journalism and composition classes. I would particularly like to emphasize their use with students who have had little or no awareness of the values and customs of other cultures or countries. They, especially, need to shed the state of blissful oblivion in which they have become mired.

Required Texts

Edward T. Hall, *The Silent Language*
Edward Angeloni, *Annual Editions: Anthropology 82/83*
Edward Corbett, *The Little English Handbook*
Elizabeth W. Fernea, *Guests of the Shiek*
Elenore Smith Bowden, *Return to Laughter*

Joanna Stratton, *Pioneer Women*
Pauli Murray, *Proud Shoes*
Jean Itard, *The Wild Boy of Aveyron*
John McPhee, *The Pine Barrens*

A Continuum of Awareness

Collaborative Learning Exercise: "Culturally" Loaded Words

Samples: sexism, marriage, poverty, Iran, racism, communism, abortion, nationalism, energy, feminism.
After introducing yourselves to each other, agree on one person to record the views
expressed by the group and any decisions the group makes collectively. The
recorder will speak for the group.
1. One person who is not the recorder will read each word (concept) aloud.
2. Spend 2 to 3 minutes jotting down the first impressions that come to your mind
   on the index cards provided after hearing a word read.
3. Discuss your impression of the word with the group.
4. Discuss what you think the same word would mean to your family.
5. Discuss what you think the same word would mean to the average American.
6. Discuss what you think the same word would mean to someone from another
   culture.
7. Contrast your initial impressions of the word with your opinions after discussing
   it with the rest of the group.
8. Have any of the ideas/arguments presented changed or modified your definition
   of the word in question?

Writing Assignment

Write a paragraph on your original perception of one of the words/concepts
discussed and how new insights through collaborative learning caused you to
change or remain the same.

I. An Insider Looking In

". . . When you are a child, you play at nothing things. You build little huts and
play. Then you come back to the village and continue to play . . . If people bother
you, you get up and play elsewhere.

Once we left a pool of rain water where we had been playing and went to the little
huts we had made. We stayed there and played at being hunters. We went out
tracking animals and when we saw one, we struck it with make-believe arrows.

We made believe about everything. We made believe we cooked food and then we
took it out of the fire. We had a trance dance, and we sang and danced and danced
and sang and the boys made believe they were curing us.

One day when I was fairly big, I went with some of my friends and with my
younger brother and sister away from the village into the bushes. As we were
walking, I saw the tracks of a baby kudu in the sand. I called to everyone and
showed them. As we followed the tracks around, we saw in the shade of a tree the
little kudu dead asleep. I jumped and tried to grab it. I hadn't really caught it well.
We started following the new tracks. I ran ahead of everyone. I came on it, jumped
on it and then killed it. I grabbed its legs and carried it back. When I came to where
the rest of them were, my older cousin said to me 'My cousin, my little cousin

killed a kudu! The rest of you here, what are you doing? How come the men didn't kill the kudu? This young girl has so much run in her that she killed the kudu' . . ."

From Shostak, Marjorie, "A !Kung Woman's Memories of Childhood" in *Kalahari Hunter-Gatherers* edited by R. Lee and I. DeVore, Harvard University Press, 1976.

Suggested Writing Exercises
A. Write a paragraph with yourself as the insider, e.g., yourself within your family (now or in the past), your peer group, or another particular environment in which you have been comfortable.
B. Write about the similarities and differences among people across space and time.
C. Discuss the notion of self as expressed by the !Kung woman. Compare it to your own.

II. An Outsider Looking In

" . . . We arrived at the village and docked the boat along the muddy bank at the terminus of the path used by the Indians to fetch their drinking water. It was hot and muggy and my clothing was soaked with perspiration. The small, biting gnats were out in astronomical numbers, for it was the beginning of the dry season. My face and hands were swollen from the venom of their numerous stings. In just a few moments, I was to meet my first Yanomamo, my first primitive man. What would it be like? I had visions of entering the village and seeing 125 social facts running about calling each other kinship terms and sharing food, each waiting and anxious to have me collect his genealogy. I would wear them out in turn. Would they like me? This was important to me; I wanted them to be so fond of me that they would adopt me into their kinship system and way of life, because I had heard that successful anthropologists always get adopted by their people.

My heart began to pound as we approached the village and heard the buzz of activity within the compound. The entrance to the village was covered with brush and dry palm leaves. We pushed them aside to expose the low opening to the village. The excitement of meeting my first Indians was almost unbearable as I duck-waddled through the low passage into the village clearing. I looked up and gasped when I saw a half dozen burly, naked, filthy, hideous men staring at us down the shafts of their drawn arrows! Immense wads of green tobacco were stuck between their lower teeth and lips making them look even more hideous, and strands of dark green slime dripped or hung from their noses. My next discovery was that there were a dozen or so vicious, underfed dogs snapping at my legs, circling me as if I were going to be their next meal. I just stood there helpless and pathetic. What sort of welcome was this for the person who came here to live with you and learn your way of life, to become friends with you? . . . ," from Chagnon, Napoleon, *The Yanomamo: The Fierce People.*

Suggested Writing Exercises
A. In a paragraph, react to a situation where you were the outsider. For example, you could write about your experiences during the first few weeks of your freshman year of college when you were the outsider discovering new situations. Or you could react to a scene on a bus, a discussion among friends when you were just observing or your impressions of a different country or part of the United States.
B. What does Chagnon infer about Indians?

III. An Insider's Response to an Outsider's Perception

" . . . Into each life, it is said, some rain must fall. Some people have bad horoscopes, others take tips on the stock market. Indians have anthropologists.

Every summer when school is out a veritable stream of immigrants heads into Indian country. From every rock and cranny in the East they emerge, as if responding to some primevil fertility rite, and flock to the reservations. They are the anthropologists. They are the most prominent members of the scholarly community that infests the land of the free, and in the summer time, the home of the brave.

Each summer there is a new battle cry, which inspires new insights into the nature of the 'Indian problem.' One summer Indians will be greeted with the joyful cry of 'Indians are bilingual!' The following summer this great truth will be expanded to 'Indians are not only bilingual, they are bicultural!' Biculturality creates great problems for the opposing anthropological camp. So the opposing school of thought cries 'Indians are a folk people!' Thus go the anthropological wars, testing whether this school or that school can endure longest. And the battlefields, unfortunately, are the lives of Indian people.

You may be curious as to why the anthropologist never carries a writing instrument. He never makes a mark because he already knows what he is going to find. He need not record anything except his daily expenses for audit, for he has found his answer in the books he read the winter before. No, the anthropologist is only out to verify what he has suspected all along—Indians are a very quaint people who bear watching.

The fundamental thesis of the anthropologist is that people are objects for observation; people are then considered objects for experimentation, for manipulation and eventual extinction. The anthropologist furnishes the justification for treating Indian people like so many chessman available for anyone to play with. The massive volume of useless knowledge produced by anthropologists attempting to capture the real Indians in a network of theories has contributed substantially to the invisibility of the Indian today. Indian people begin to feel that they are merely shadows of a mythical super-Indian. Many anthropologists spare no expense to reinforce this sense of inadequacy in order to further support their influence over Indian people. Over the years, anthropologists have succeeded in burying Indian communities so completely beneath the mass of irrelevant information that the total impact of the scholarly community on Indian people has become one of simple authority . . . ," from Deloria, Vine. *Custer Died for Your Sins.* Macmillan Publishing Co., 1969.

Suggested Writing Exercises

A. Respond in a paragraph to someone who has recently evaluated you. This could be a reaction to a teacher or employer's evaluation of your performance, a friend or relative's response to you, or your reaction to a newspaper article, editorial or a book focusing on your ethnic background, race, religion, or area of residence. Your paper should first address what you think their perceptions are of you and then focus on a response.

B. According to Deloria, what do anthropologists infer about Indians?

C. How does one use knowledge to exploit? How is a particular group exploited by another?

Alienation

Melvin Gurtov   *Fall 1982*
Humanities and Social Sciences 108/University of California/
Riverside, CA 92521

Reflections

"We are born into a world where alienation awaits us. We are potentially men [and women], but are in an alienated state, and this state is not simply a natural system. Alienation as our present destiny is achieved only by outrageous violence perpetrated by human beings on human beings."—R.D. Laing, *The Politics of Experience*

"Let me say, with the risk of appearing ridiculous, that the true revolutionary is guided by strong feelings of love. It is impossible to think of an authentic revolutionary without this quality."—Che Guevara

"The success of the human species is due notably to its biological diversity. Its potential lies in this diversity. The diversity of human beings must be carefully preserved. From it stems the need to respect the other person and the differences in social life—all the more since cultural diversity, which in the course of the development of humanity has had an even more important role than genetic diversity, is seriously threatened today by the model imposed by industrial civilization."—Francois Jacob, 1965 Nobel prize-winner

"I am sure all of us, however lowly or however intellectual we are, want to find a way of life that is orderly, full of beauty and great love. That has been the search of man for thousands of years. And instead of finding it he has externalised it, put it out there, created gods, saviours, priests with their ideas and so he has missed the whole issue. One must deny all that, deny totally the acceptance that there is heaven through another, or by following another. Nobody in the world or in heaven can give you that life. One has to work for it—endlessly . . . It is in our daily life that we have to bring about a change and not in some ideological future world.—Krishnamurti

This is a course in which feelings, experiences, and intuitions are as valid as thoughts. We are not merely trying to understand the idea of alienation; we also want to explore what it feels like and what we can do to overcome it. We are learning about alienation because each of us is alienated in some way. And since alienation is not something "out there" for other people to worry about, our learning has the personal and collective objective of helping us to survive and be powerful. We all have a certain measure of expertise on the subject, and the most important work each of can contribute to the class consists in sharing our emotional and intellectual energies.

We meet with a positive vision of human possibilities. Cynicism and defeatism create one reality, powerfulness and alternative thinking, another. We aim to construct a humane environment.

Texts
Peter Hawken, *The Magic of Findhorn*
Mel Gurtov, *Making Changes*
Paul Williams, *Das Energi*
Marge Piercy, *Woman on the Edge of Time*
Carl Rogers, *On Personal Power*

The major work expected of you is to integrate what you have learned from the course with personal experience. This can be accomplished in a journal, poetry, essay, or tape recording.

Course Outline

1. What is Alienation? (October 6)
We will explore ways in which alienation is manifested in our own and other people's lives.
*Eric Fromm, *The Sane Society*, esp. pp. 102-37;
*S. & G. Putney, *The Adjusted American*, esp. chs. 1-3;
*R.S. Gilmour and R.B. Lamb, *Political Alienation in Contemporary America*, esp. chs. 1-2;
*R. Pirsig, *Zen and the Art of Motorcycle Maintenance.*
(*All starred books are on reserve.)

2. Values and Change (October 13)
P. Williams, *Das Energi;*
M. Gurtov, *Making Changes*, chs. 1-3;
*(Charles Reich, *The Sorcerer of Bolinas Reef*, and Philip Slater, *The Pursuit of Loneliness*, are highly recommended);
Film: "What You Are Is . . . ," by Morris Massey, on our values.

3. Exploring and Healing Ourselves (October 20)
Rogers, Introduction, and ch. 1;
*Alexander and Leslie Lowen, *The Way to Vibrant Health*, introduction.

4. Alienation On the Job (October 27)
For all to read:
*Studs Terkel, *Working* (read as many of the personal stories as you can); Gurtov, ch. 5; Rogers, ch. 5;
Film: "The Willmar Eight." Eight previously nonpolitical women in a conservative town unionize in response to sexist practices at their bank. The results say as much about mutual support as about sexual politics.

5. Alienation and Education (November 3)
For all to read:
Gurtov, ch. 4; Rogers, ch. 4;
Recommended:
*Jonathan Kozol, *The Night is Dark and I am Far From Home;*

†Carl Rogers, *On Becoming a Person*, chs. 1 & 14-15 (on self-motivated learning and creative teaching);
*Paolo Freire, *Pedagogy of the Oppressed*, esp. the first few chapters on the "banker concept" of learning. (Carl Rogers discusses Freire's book in chapter 6);
On this subject, however, we are our own best resource.

6. Community (November 10)
Hawken, *Magic Of Findhorn*;
Sharing skills: bring your creativity;
Recommended:
Nancy Seifer, *Noboby Speaks For Me: Self-Portraits of American Working Women.*

7. Violence (November 17)
Rogers, chs 6-7.
*J. Vasconcelles, "Violence Prevention: Our Responsibility;"
*J.W. Prescott, "Body Pleasure and the Origins of Violence;"
*C. Steiner, ed., *Readings in Radical Psychiatry*, chs. 6-7 (on "Warm Fuzzies" and other things).

8. Aging and Alienation (November 24)
*Maggie Deutschmann, "Grandma's Leaving;"
*D. Christiansen, "Dignity in Aging," *Journal of Humanistic Psychology*;
Recommended:
Carobeth Laird's memoir of survival in a nursing home *Limbo*;
The Measure of My Days, by Florida Scott-Maxwell, age 82 when she wrote it;
*Sharon Curtin, *Nobody Ever Died of Old Age.*

9. "Friction in the System": A New Politics (Dec. 1)
Complete Gurtov, and read Rogers, chs. 8-13;
Recommended and on reserve:
*John Vasconcellos, "Humanizing Politics," *New Age*, Oct. 1978;
*Wells and Commons, "Moving Politics With Spirit," *New Realities*, June 1979;
Recommended:
Marilyn Ferguson, *The Aquarian Conspiracy.*

10. A Society Without Alienation? (Dec. 8)
Please read: *Marge Piercy, Woman on the Edge of Time.*

Quality of Life

Lester W. Milbrath   Spring 1982
Environmental Studies Center 777/State University of New York/
Buffalo, NY 14261

We all desire quality of life; it is an important policy objective in all societies. But what is it? How can it be conceptualized and measured? Over the past decade social scientists have done considerable thinking about quality of life and have tried to measure it in several ways. The topic also is developing a body of literature. These developments are significant and should be shared with students.

Early attempts at measuring quality of life used economic indices and other aggregate societal indicators; these efforts will be evaluated for their conceptual adequacy and their reliability and validity. Several large-scale studies using subjective indicators of quality of life have recently have been completed. We will read several of these. We also will read brief reports on similar studies conducted in England, Scandinavia, Canada, and Hungary.

Format

Class discussion of conceptual problems will be crucial; hence it is important to attend the seminar regularly. Students will write a brief(10 page) paper on some conceptual problem, measurement problem, or specific quality of life study. There also will be a take-home final.

Texts

Campbell, Converse and Rogers, *The Quality of American Life*. NY: Russell Sage, 1976.
Andrews and Withey, *Social Indicators of Well-Being*. NY: Plenum, 1976.
UNESCO, *Indicators of Environmental Quality and Quality of Life*. Paris, 1978.
Campbell, *The Sense of Well-Being in America*. NY: McGraw Hill, 1981.
Szalai and Andrews, eds., *Quality of Life: Comparative Studies*. Beverly Hills: Sage, 1981.

January 12   Quality of Life

Rising public interest in the concept. Various approaches toward defining it and measuring it.
Read:
"Quantifying the Unquantifiable" from *Mosaic* (to be distributed); Milbrath, "A Brief Statement of Some Major Thrusts of Research on Quality of Life in the U.S."

January 19   Quality of Life: We all know what it is, but how do you define it?

Read:
Milbrath, "Indicators of Environmental Quality" in UNESCO volume.
Milbrath, "Final Report" in UNESCO volume.

Campbell, "Subjective Measures of Well Being."
Milbrath, "Policy Relevant Quality of Life Research," *Annals*, July 1979.

January 26 A Comprehensive Matrix of Human Needs
Read:
Mallmann, "Research Priorities and Holistic Knowledge."
Scheer, "Conceptualizing the Quality of Life" *Labour and Society*, January 1978.
Hankiss, "Quality of Life Models" in the UNESCO volume.
Campbell, Converse & Rogers, Ch. 1, pp. 1-18.
Campbell, Ch. 1, pp. 1-9.

February 2 Concepts, Definitions and Methods
Read:
Campbell, Converse and Rogers, Chs. 2-4, pp. 21-133.
Allardt, "The Question of Interchangeability of Objective & Subjective Social
    Indicators of Well-Being" (on reserve).
Campbell, Chs. 2-3, pp. 11-38.
Milbrath, "A Conceptualization and Research Strategy for the Study of Ecological
    Aspects of the Quality of Life."

February 9 Concepts, Definitions and Methods (cont'd)
Read:
Campbell, Converse and Rogers, Chs. 5-6, pp. 135-210.
Campbell, Chs. 4-6, pp. 39-93.

February 23 Satisfaction with Aspects of Living
Read:
Campbell, Converse & Rogers, Chs. 7-11, pp. 213-388.
Campbell, Chs. 7-11, pp. 95-174.

March 2 Special Life Situations, Personal Characteristics, Conclusions
Read:
Campbell, Converse & Rogers, Chs. 12-14, pp. 391-508.
Campbell, Chs. 12-14, pp. 175-238.

March 9 Spring Recess

March 16 Quality of Life Studies in Scandinavia and Canada
Read:
Allardt: "Dimensions of Welfare in a Comparative Scandinavian Study," 1975.
Moum, "Environmental Quality and Quality of Life in Two Norwegian Communi-
    ties."
Atkinson and Murray, "Values, Domains and the Perceived Quality of Life" (on
    reserve).
Atkinson, "Trends in Life Satisfaction Among Canadians, 1967-1977" (on reserve).
Atkinson, "Public Perceptions of the Quality of Life" (on reserve).
Stevenson and Ornstein, "The Political Response to the Quality of Life: Canada in
    Comparative Perspective" (on reserve).

March 23 Measuring Quality of Life
Read:
Andrews & Withey—Chs. 1-3, pp. 1-106.
Szalai, "An Overview of Comparative Studies of Life Quality" Ch. 1 in Szalai and Andrews.

March 30 Predicting "Global" Well Being
Read:
Andrews & Withey—Chs. 4-6, pp. 107-217.
Szalai & Andrews, Chs. 9-11.

April 6 Evaluating Well-Being in the U.S.
Read:
Andrews & Withey, Chs. 7-11, pp. 219-357.

April 13 Quality of Life on the Niagara Frontier
Read:
Milbrath, "Quality of Life on the Magara Frontier."
Milbrath, "Values, Lifestyles and Basic Beliefs as Influences on Perceived Quality of Life."

April 20 Quality of Life Studies in Comparative Perspective
Read:
Hall, "Subjective Measures of Quality of Life in Britain 1971-75; Some Developments and Trends," *Social Trends*, No. 7, 1976 (on reserve).
Hankiss, "Second Generation Comparisons" Ch. 3 in Szalai and Andrews, and Quality of Life Newsletter.
Moum, "Toward a Non-Psychological Need Concept in Quality of Life Research" (on reserve).
Moum, "The Role of Values and Life Goals in Quality of Life."

April 27 Comparative Quality of Life Research
Read:
Doh Shin, Hongkoo Lee and Kyong Kim, "Value Preferences and Quality of Life in Korea" (on reserve).
Szalai and Andrews, Chs. 2, 4, 5, 6, 7 & 8.

May 4 Comparative Quality of Life Research
Read:
Szalai and Andrews, Chs. 12-17.

Political Mobilization

Jeane Grassholtz   *Spring 1983*
Politics 342/Mount Holyoke College/South Hadley, MA 01075

Texts to be Purchased

Wini Breines, *Community and Organization in the New Left 1962-68. The Great Refusal.* New York Praeger, 1982.
Sara Evans, *Personal Politics: The Roots of Women's Liberation in the Civil Rights Movement and the New Left.* New York: Random House (Vintage), 1980.
Susan Schecter, *Women and Male Violence: The Visions and Struggles of the Battered Women's Movement.* Boston: South End Press, 1982.
Lynne Jones, editor, *Keeping the Peace: A Women's Peace Handbook.* London: The Woman's Press, 1983.
Frances Fox Pivin and Richard Cloward, *Poor People's Movements.*
Harry Boyt, *Backyard Revolution.*

Course Outline

Section I Introduction
Goals, strategies, organization and tactics. Who gets organized and why? What determines the strategies adopted?
Governmental Response: Cooptation, Repression, or ? Why one and not the other? What is success and who determines it?
Film: "From Montgomery to Memphis."

Section II Movements Growing Out of the Civil Rights Movement and their Experience
A. The Student Movement of the Sixties
  Read: Wini Breines, *Community and Organization*
B. The Urban Poor
  Read: Frances Fox Pivin and Richard Cloward, *Poor People's Movements*
C. The Women's Movement
  Read: Sara Evans, *Personal Politics*
  Susan Schecter, *Women and Male Violence*
  Film: Keynote Speech at NCADV Meeting, 1982
D. The Peace Movement
  Read: Lynne Jones, editor, *Keeping the Peace*
  Speaker: Frances Crowe, American Friends Service Committee
E. The Liberal Reform Movement
  Read: To be announced
F. The Radical Right
  Read: Various Xeroxed Materials on Reserve under Radical Right

Section III Organizers—What They Do and How They Do It
Three women presently engaged in political organizing in the United States will discuss with students the nature of their work.

The Third World Through Film

Angela Gilliam   *Fall 1983*

Politics, Economics and Society/State University of New York/
Old Westbury, Long Island, NY 11568

The basic objective of this lower division course is to show students how the ideas of state power can be reflected in the films that receive support of the major institutions. Thus, film can serve many functions. For the most part, students will be introduced to the view of power as expressed by the powerless. This broad theme is particularly important as it relates to the question of "development" and "underdevelopment."

This course will analyze three major themes: a) how can one detect the mechanisms of propaganda in films? How do lighting and sound factors contribute to influencing an audience? b) what are the socio-political concerns that have guided Third World film makers in confronting the cinematic paradigms of the West? c) how have some American film makers integrated their efforts with the lessons from Third World film makers to represent visually the interests of working people?

Format

Each discussion topic has a film to exemplify the critical points to be learned. Most films have readings that accompany them so real familiarity with some respect of the films can be absorbed at the student's own pace. In this way, the visual and printed course materials reinforce the teacher's contributions in class lectures.

Students will be divided into seminar teams which will be responsible for leading discussion following the film. Each seminar discussion will automatically begin with a discussion of aforementioned points of this section. All are expected to have read the pertinent written material before viewing the film. In this way, classroom discussion will be lively as well as informed. Students should familiarize themselves with the journals, *Cineaste* and *Jump Cut*, in the library.

Supplementary Texts
The Pretend Indians by G. Bataille and C. Silet
Toms, Coons, Mulattoes, Mammies and Bucks by D. Boyle
"Asian Images in the Media" in *Bridge* magazine—Vol. 3, Number 2, April 1974

Topic I Introduction
In the first two class sessions, a broad overview of the accepted definitions of "Third World" will be given. In addition, students will discuss "development" and "underdevelopment," propaganda, and the relationship between film hardware and ideology.

Topic II The Conditioning and Dispersal of Values
(Achieved by what is *not* shown as much as by what is.)
For best pedagogical results, the content of this film should not be made known to students before the viewing. It is the positive depiction of a young man who was born with thalidomide-generated defects. In most films about the disabled, the physically able usually perform the roles, but this is a dramatized story starring Terry Wiles as himself. Students should be encouraged to confront their own response after viewing.
Film: "On Giant's Shoulders" Produced by British Broadcasting Corporation (Distributor: Films, Inc. Chicago)

Topic III Bias in Defining National Culture: Cinematic Elitelore as Political Paradigm
Case Study I: Nazi Germany: The Manipulation of Sound and Lighting to Express Ideology
Film: "When Germany Awakes." Illustrates how the Nazi's ideas were integrated into the schools and minds of youth by subliminal use of lighting.
Reading: *From Caligari to Hitler: A Psychological History of the German Film* by Siegfried Kracauer, Princeton University Press, 1947. (In spite of its contribution, this book has examples of racism, i.e. page 279.)

Topic IV The Third World Confronts the Multinational Control of Mass Media: The Struggle for a New Information Order
Film: "Controlling Interest: The World of the Multinational" (Distributor: California Newsreel, San Francisco, California)
Reading: *Multinational Corporations and the Control of Culture: The Ideological Apparatuses of Imperialism* by Armand Mattelart, Humanities Press, 1979.

Topic V Bias in Defining U.S. National Culture: Cinematic Elitelore as Political Paradigm
Film #1: "Birth of a Nation" (Distributor: Films, Inc.)
Reading: *The Clansman* by Thomas Dixon. This is the book that inspired *Birth of a Nation* reprint of 1905 edition, Gordon Press, 1973.
From Sambo to Superspade: The Black Experience in Motion Pictures by Daniel Leab, Houghton Mifflin, 1975.
Film #2: "If You Love This Planet." The alternative view as "propaganda." (Distributor: Direct Cinema Limited, Los Angeles)

Topic VI The Origins of Algerian Cinema: Confronting the Motion Picture Export Company of America
Film: "Battle of Algiers" directed by Gillo Pontecorvo. (Distributor: Films, Inc.)
Reading: *The Algerian Cultural Policy*, NY: UNESCO, 1977.
Gillo Pontecorvo's 'The Battle of Algiers', Editor, Pier Nico Solinas, Scribner's Sons, 1973.

Topic VII Women as Part of the Collective in the Cinematic Process: The Ukamau Film Collective in Bolivia
Film: "Courage of the People" by J. Sanjines (Distributor: UNIFILM, N.Y.). This film is invaluable for demonstrating the relationship between mineral resources and the struggles of miners for economic equality. The organization of miners'

wives to support the miners is a critical component of the film. The supplementary reading material cited below is written by one of the miner's wives.

Reading: *Let Me Speak* by Domitila Barrios de Chungara with Moema Viezze, Monthly Review Press, 1981.

Topic VIII Filming the Dynamics of Neo-Colonialism: The African Experience

Film: "Xala" by Ousmane Sembene (Distributor: New Yorker Films, New York City). The film maker uses sexual impotence as metaphor in demonstrating the relationship between national corruption and neo-colonialism.

Reading: Charles Larson's Introduction in *Tribal Scars and Other Stories* by Ousmane Sembene, Black Orpheus/Inscape Pub., 1980.

Topic IX The Impact of the Western Hero/Fantasy Paradigm: The 'Slave' as Hero

Film: "El Rancheador" (The Bounty Hunter) by Sergio Giral of Cuba (Distributor: UNIFILM, New York City). This is the second film in a trilogy by Sergio Giral that confronts Cuba's past as a plantation economy. The "form" of this confrontation is a film that uses the direct (Hollywood) approach of "god guys versus bad guys," yet redefines the concept of "hero." This film demonstrates how the food production in runaway slave communities ("palenques") threatened the Spanish Crown's monopoly.

Reading: *Autobiography of a Runaway Slave* by Esteban Montejo with Miguel Barnet.

Topic X Use of Oral History to Confront the Negative Images and Reinterpret History

Case Study I: The Impact of World War II on the people of Papua New Guinea

Film: "Angels of War" (narrated by John Waiko, author of the reading cited below) (Distributor: The Museum of Modern Art Department of Film).

Reading: "Binandere Oral Tradition" by J. Waiko in *Oral Traditions in Melanesia*, ed., Nenoon, D. and Lacey, R. Institute of Papua New Guinea Studies, 1981.

Case Study II: An African Epic Examines the Painful Past—Christian and Muslim missionaries and African participation in the Atlantic Slave Trade.

Film: "Ceddo" by Ousmane Sembene (Distributor: New Yorker Films)

Reading: "The Role of Culture in the Liberation Struggle" by Amilcar Cabral in *Return to the Source.*

Topic XI Independent Film makers in the United States: New Form and New Message

Film: "Clarence and Angel" by Robert Gardner (Distributor: Texture Films, New York)

Film: "I Am a Man." A documentary about the strike by black sanitation workers in Memphis, Tenn. (Distributor: CSEA Education and Training Department, Albany, N.Y.)

Reading: "An Analysis of the Memphis Garbage Strike of 1968" by Thomas Collins in *Public Affairs Forum*, 1974.

Film: "Puerto Rico—Our Right to Decide" by Stanley Nelson (Distributor: Stanley Nelson, United Methodist Church, New York)

Film: "G.I. Jose" by Norberto Lopez (Distributor: California Newsreel)

Film: "The Klan: A Legacy of Hate in America" (Distributor: Guggenheim Productions/Klanwatch Project, Montgomery, Alabama)

Reading: *My Life in the Klan* by Jerry Thompson, Putnam, 1982.

Topic XII Aboriginals and Non-Aboriginals: Developing Non-Exploitative Film Making

Film: "Two Laws" directed by Carolyn Strachan. Two non-Aboriginal film makers were approached by the Borroloola people to help them make a film about their laws and history. The cinematography utilized new approaches to hardware, and filmic rhythm, i.e. the use of wide-angle lens to depict the extended family collective aspect of Borroloola culture. The professional film makers taught others to use the equipment, and editing and consultation was part of the cinematic process from beginning to end.

Reading: *The Jigalong Mob: Aboriginal Victors of the Desert Crusade* by Robert Tonkinson, Benjamin/Cummings Publishing Company, 1974.

Poverty and Culture

Dan Rosenberg   *Term III 1983*
Sociology/Anthropology 70/Earlham College/Richmond, IN 47374

This course focuses on cultural systems as key survival mechanisms among the poor. In addition to this emphasis on social adaptations to inequality and consequent scarcity, we will give attention to the historical and structural sources of poverty and inequality, the political economic position of poor people in the world market system, and the impact of social intervention (such as welfare and housing programs) on the lives of the poor. Theories of poverty will be examined and applied to case studies.

Texts

Needless Hunger: Voices from a Bangladesh Village, Betsy Hartmann and James Boyce (NH)

We Eat the Mines and the Mines Eat Us: Dependency and Exploitation in Bolivian Tin Mines, June Nash (Mines)

The Urban Poor of Puerto Rico: A Study in Development and Inequality, Helen Safa (Safa)

Rastafari: A Way of Life, Tracy Nicholas and Bill Sparrow (Rasta)

Poverty Amid Plenty: A Political and Economic Analysis, Harrell R. Rodgers, Jr. (Amid)

Drylongso: A Self-Portrait of Black America, John Gwaltney (Dry)

Format

The course material lends itself well to discussion, and you are asked to prepare carefully for class by completing the reading assignments on time. There will be two exams based on readings, lectures and class discussions. A paper will be required, and course grades will reflect positive participation in class discussion. We will discuss possible alternatives to the course organization at the first class, including discussion leaders, group projects, guest speakers, and exam options.

This project affords class members the opportunity to explore a special interest loosely related to our topic. You may wish to choose a topic that evaluates a theoretical approach (such as "culture of poverty" theory), investigates the impact of a specific commodity (such as oil or sugar) on a group or region, examines a form of resistance to poverty (such as a socio-political movement), or analyzes a specific population or region (such as a Native American tribe, Appalachia, Appalachian migrants to Dayton or Richmond, single mothers on AFDC, or Guatemalan Indian peasants). You may wish to focus on a period of change, such as the transformation of an indigenous economy, the droughts in Northeastern Brazil, or the Sahel, the development of welfare in the U.S., or the "War on Poverty". Those interested in field research projects will find the surrounding region offers abundant research opportunities on the subject.

Course Outline

March 24 Introduction

March 28-31 Origins and Persistence of Poverty
NH: entire book
Mines: Preface and Introduction
Film: "The Turtle People"

April 4 Exploitation and Cultural Adaptation
Mines: 2-3

April 7 Consciousness: Class and Religion
Mines: 4-5

April 11 Relations of Production
Mines: 6-7

April 14 Support Group Organization
One page project prospectus

April 18 Class Conflict and Consciousness
Mines: 8-9

April 21 The Shantytown
First Exam; Safa: Intro., 1-2

April 25 Social Organization in the Shantytown
Safa: 3-4

April 28 Impacts of Social Intervention and Development
Safa: 5-6

May 2 The Poetry of Despair and Hope: Movements; Nativist, Nationalist, Messianic, Revitalization
Rasta: entire book

May 5 Film: "Rastafari Voices"

May 8 Poverty and Culture in the U.S.
Amid: 1-4

May 12 Welfare
Amid: 5-6; Film: "Welfare"

May 16 Bandages and Alternatives; Poor People's Movements
Amid: 7-9

May 19 Second Exam
Dry: TBA

May 21 Ideology and Coping; Perspectives on Poverty
Papers Due

May 26-30 Perspectives on Poverty: What Can Be Done?
Dry: TBA

Regional Studies

Ethnonationalism in Ireland, Wales and Scotland
Andrew A. Reding, Princeton University

America and Vietnam
George Lopez, Earlham College

The Soviet Union
Roberta Manning, Boston College

Peace in the Southern Philippines
Robert McAmis, Mindanao State University

The Political Economy of Africa
Michael Ford, Fran White and Frank Holmquist,
Hampshire College

Contours of the Current Crisis in Central America
José Jorge Simán, University of North Carolina at Chapel Hill

Ethnonationalism in Ireland, Wales and Scotland

Andrew A. Reding   *Spring 1980*
Politics/Princeton University/Princeton, NJ 08544

This course is an intensive historical, literary, religious and political exploration of the development and expression of nationalism among the Irish, Welsh and Scottish peoples over the last seven centuries. These three national movements are treated as case-studies for a more general examination of the phenomenon of nationalism in global politics. Theories of nationalism are tested against the experiences of the four nations (including England) that inhabit the "British Isles." Special attention is devoted to several particular themes: the interrelationship between structural and physical violence; the conflict between assimilation, xenophobic retrenchment, and universalistic liberation as response to political and cultural subjugation; and the personal, cultural, and world order implications of the shift from the statist to ethnonational identification.

Required Books

G.W.S. Barrow, *Robert Bruce and the Community of the Realm of Scotland* (Edinburgh: Edinburgh U. Press, 1976).

Martin Buber, *Moses: The Revelation and the Covenant* (New York: Harper, 1958).

George Dangerfield, *The Damnable Question: One Hundred and Twenty Years of Anglo-Irish Conflict* (Boston: Atlantic-Little, Brown, 1976).

Gwynfor Evans, *Wales Can Win* (Llandybie, Wales: Christopher Davies, 1973).

Abraham Joshua Heschel, *The Prophets: An Introduction* (New York: Harper, 1969).

R. Tudur Jones, *The Desire of Nations* (Llandybie, Wales: Christopher Davies, 1974).

Hugh MacDiarmid, *A Drunk Man Looks at the Thistle* (Amherst: U. of Mass., 1971).

John A. Murphy, *Ireland in the Twentieth Century* (Dublin: Gill and MacMillan, 1975).

Jean-Jacques Rousseau, *The Social Contract* (South Bend, Indiana: Gateway, 1954).

William Stringfellow, *An Ethic for Christians and Other Aliens in a Strange Land* (Waco, Texas: Word, 1973).

Leon Uris, *Trinity* (New York: Bantam, 1977).

John Howard Yoder, *The Politics of Jesus* (Grand Rapids, Mich.: Eerdmans, 1972).

Part I Introduction

Note: All numbered reading is required. Asterisk (*) indicates highly recommended supplementary reading.

Intersession: Introductory Popularization of the Irish Conflict
Leon Uris, *Trinity* (1977)

Week 1 Statism and Nationalism—Definitions and Theories
1. Benjamin Akzin, *State and Nation* (1964), Chs. 1-5
2. Hans Kohn, *The Idea of Nationalism* (1944), Ch. 1
3. R. Tudur Jones, *The Desire of Nations* (1974), Chs. 1-5, 8
Elie Kedourie, *Nationalism* (1966)
Karl Deutsch, *Nationalism and Social Communication* (1953)
Anthony Smith, *Theories of Nationalism* (1971)

Part II Ireland

Week 2 Ireland Under English Occupation
1. Liam de Paor, *Divided Ulster* (1971), intro., Chs. 1, 2
2. Conor Cruise O'Brien, *States of Ireland* (1974), Chs. 1, 2
3. George Dangerfield, *The Damnable Question* (1976), Chs. 4-13
*Conor Cruise O'Brien, *Parnell and His Party* (1957)
Leon O'Broin, *The Unfortunate Mr. Emmet* (1958)

Week 3 The Imagined Past, The Literary Revival, and the Development of Irish Nationalism
1. William Irwin Thompson, *The Imagination of an Insurrection* (1967), preface, Chs. 1-3, Chs. 4-5 (pp. 115-24, 145-50, 154-9)
2. William Butler Yeats, "Cathleen ni Houlihan," *The Collected Plays of W.B. Yeats*, pp. 50-57
3. Yeats, *Collected Poems* (MacMillan), pp. 105-7, 177-82, 184-5, 202-3, 276-9, 304-7

Week 4 The Rising, Sinn Fein, and Evolution of the Twenty-Six County Republic
1. Dangerfield, *The Damnable Question*, Chs. 14-18, Part V
2. John A. Murphy, *Ireland in the Twentieth Century* (1975), Chs. 2-7, (pp. 32-154)
*Earl of Longford and Thomas P. O'Neill, *Eamon de Valera* (1970)

Week 5 Partition, Orange and Catholic States, and Chronic Civil War
1. De Paor, *Divided Ulster*, Chs. 4-7
2. Cruise O'Brien, *States of Ireland*, Ch. 6 (pp. 110-27), Chs. 8-9, Ch. 11 (p. 243-64, 270-80), Ch. 12 (pp. 295-303), Epilogue, Appendix
*Bernadette Devlin, *The Price of My Soul* (1969)
*Frantz Fanon, *The Wretched of the Earth* (1961)
*Sean Cronin and Richard Roche, *Freedom the Wolfe Tone Way* (1973)
*Eugene Kennedy, "The End of the Fairytale Kingdom," in *St. Patrick's Day with Mayor Daly* (1976)
*J.H. Whyte, *Church and State in Modern Ireland* (1971)
Albert J. Menendez, *The Bitter Harvest: Church and State in Northern Ireland* (1973)

Part III Biblical Nationalism

Week 6 Zion as Light to the Nations—Covenants, the Kingdom of God, and the Jubilee

1. Kohn, *The Idea of Nationalism*, Ch. 2, (pp. 27-50)
2. Martin Buber, *Moses: The Revelation and the Covenant* (1946), esp. pp. 20-2, 28-9, 31, 35-55, 62-4, 69-73, 80-5, 101-9, 111-15, 122-46, 172-81
3. John Howard Yoder, *The Politics of Jesus* (1972), Chs. 1-3, 8
*Richard J. Cassidy, *Jesus, Politics, and Society* (1978)
*Erich Fromm, *You Shall Be As Gods* (1966)
*Arthur I. Waskow, *God-Wrestling* (1978), Ch. 11
*Arthur I. Waskow, *The Bush is Burning* (1971)

Week 7 A Fallen Vision—Zion's Idolatrous Shadow
1. Abraham Joshua Heschel, *The Prophets* (1962), esp. pp. 3-33, 39-51, 57, 59-73, 78-9, 92-7, 104-5, 128-39, 145, 155-64, 166-8, 183-6, 199-200, 209-10, 212-13, 216
2. William Stringfellow, *An Ethic for Christians and Other Aliens in a Strange Land* (1973)
*Daniel Berrigan, *The Words Our Savior Gave Us* (1978)
*Daniel Berrigan, *Lights On In The House Of The Dead* (1974)
*Erich Fromm, *Escape From Freedom* (1941)

Part IV Scotland, Wales, and Decentralist Politics

Week 8 Medieval Manifestations of Nationhood
1. Jones, *The Desire of Nations*, Ch. 6
2. G.W.S. Barrow, *Robert Bruce* (1976).
3. *The Declaration of Arbroath*, 1320

Week 9 The Scottish Poets—Irreverent Celebrants of the Extraordinary in the Ordinary
1. Robert Burns, *Poems and Songs* (Oxford, 1969), pp. 44 (#45), 101-2 (#69), 156-7 (#83), 353 (#240), 369 (#259), 511-12 (#375), 561-2 (#425), 580-1 (#451), 602-3 (#484)
2. Roderick Watson, "The Symbolism of A Drunk Man Looks at the Thistle," in Duncan Glen, ed., *Hugh MacDiarmid: A Critical Survey* (1972), pp. 94-116
3. Hugh MacDiarmid, *A Drunk Man Looks at the Thistle*
4. Grieve and Scott, *The Hugh MacDiarmid Anthology* (1972), pp. 159, 196-201, 233-7, 247-50, 286-7

Week 10 Assimilation and Ethnocide
1. Akzin, *State and Nation*, Ch. 6
2. Gwynfor Evans, *Wales Can Win*, (1973), Chs. 1, 2
3. Jones, *The Desire of Nations*, Chs. 7, 9-10
4. J.M. Reid, *Scotland's Progress* (1971), Chs. 12-14
Christopher Harvie, *Scotland and Nationalism* (1977)

Week 11 Formation and Rise of the Scottish National Party and Plaid Cymru
1. Jack Brand, *The National Movement in Scotland* (1978), Chs. 1-10, 14-15
2. Evans, *Wales Can Win*, Ch. 3
*H.J. Hanham, *Scottish Nationalism* (1969)
Billy Wolfe, *Scotland Lives: The Quest for Independence* (1973)

Week 12 The Politics of Communitarian Democracy

1. Isabel Lindsay, "Nationalism, Community, and Democracy," in Gavin Kennedy, ed., *The Radical Approach* (1976), pp. 21-6
2. Gynfor Evans, "Nonviolent Nationalism" (1973)
3. Jean-Jacques Rousseau, *The Social Contract*, Bk. I, chs. 1-6, 9
4. Scottish National Party policy documents on "Land Ownership and Use," "The Crofting Counties," "The Environment"
5. Rousseau (cont.), Bk. II, chs. 9-11, Bk. III, chs. 1, 3-6, 15, Bk. IV, ch. 2
6. Evans, *Wales Can Win*, Ch. 4, Chs. 5, 6 (pp. 128-45)
7. Akzin, *State and Nations*, Ch. 11
8. Jones, *The Desire of Nations*, Ch. 11
*Richard A. Falk, "Anarchism and World Order," in J. Roland Pennock and Joan W. Chapman, eds., *Anarchism* (New York: N.Y.U. Press, 1978), pp. 63-87
*Ivan Illich, *Deschooling Society* (1971)
Leopold Kohr, *The Breakdown of Nations* (1957)
*John Osmond, *The Centralist Enemy* (1974)

America and Vietnam

George Lopez   *Spring 1981*
Peace Studies 80/Earlham College/Richmond, IN 47374

Why a Senior Year Integrative Seminar entitled "America and Vietnam?" A number of important reasons come to mind. First, the intellectual benefits derived from such a topic are enormous for majors in the social sciences. The U.S. involvement in and ultimate withdrawal from Vietnam occurs against the background of the influence of a number of prevalent social science theories, widely held by both the general public and governmental officials. Thus any understanding of the American epoch in Vietnam must be undertaken through an examination of such theories as Rostow's stage of growth, the dissent in the bureaucracy, the role of morality in public affairs, Kissinger's realpolitik and even the Vietnamese concept of Ngoui Thoung Dan. As the culminating experience as social science majors, this course examines, in their own terms and during their own time, important theories which influence policy.

Secondly, the seminar topic permits extensive investigation of a complex policy issue. The U.S. involvement in Southeast Asia posed a number of social, economic and political dilemmas. Moreover, these problems were of a continually changing nature, which means that "solutions" to the U.S. in 1966 did not equal the "solutions" expressed in 1965. Our "presence" and the evolution of the entire situation changed the nature of the problem even as new policies were being developed.

Thirdly, the Vietnam era was winding down as each of you entered your political, social and intellectual maturity. The current "man-on-the-street" assessments of Vietnam tend to dichotomize the epoch as either a mistake (of will not to win or of involvement in somebody else's problems) or a consciously chosen immoral policy. How valid are any of these claims? What evidence exists to substantiate any claim?

Finally, and related, but in a more individual way, to the last point, Vietnam poses issues of personal and national choices. What choices would you have made? Why? What choices lie ahead, especially in an era where current political debate asks, "Will El Salvador become another Vietnam?"

It is our hope that as a group we can bring these four rationales together in a stimulating, high level, professional environment as we come to deeply know one of the most tragic and perplexing eras of our history. If we meet the challenge to its fullest we may emerge free (as is the goal of liberal education) from what the poet Robert Bly described in his assessment of the American personality's inability to reflect on the Vietnam era: "We're engaged in a vast forgetting mechanism and from the point of view of psychology, we're refusing to eat our grief, refusing to eat our dark side, we won't absorb it."

Requirements

It is also important to note that, as a Senior Year Integrative Course, the ethos and pedagogical themes of the course are a bit distinct from other Earlham courses. In particular, we have a high set of expectations for individual participation in the seminar. We expect a high degree of professionalism; a commitment to close consultation with the instructor on progress in individual projects; a shared set of experiences in public speaking skills and an honest strategy for assessing and developing one's liberal arts skills. We will discuss each of these during the first meeting of the seminar. These translate to the following course requirements:

1. *Reading:* The course contains a fairly heavy dose of material. Our hope is to move you away from the dependence developed as an undergraduate of reading with a "highlighter" to reading for speed, retention and pleasure.
2. *Attendence and participation:* Each person is to be thoroughly enthralled by the seminar. To be specific, you need to push one another, call each other and the instructor, question, and refuse to tolerate lack of preparedness in ways which you have been reluctant to do in other classes. In addition, persons who miss two sessions for reasons other than death will fail the course.
3. *A project:* Each of you will undertake research on a topic of your choice. However, to better prepare for the environs of the "real world," you will not be expected, unless you so choose, to report your research in traditional term paper format. If you do elect the later, we expect to work closely with you in the drafting of the paper in a way which you have not yet experienced in your undergraduate career.

If you choose an alternative approach, here are some of the options:
- write a report to Congress on a particular aspect of the war and list particular policy recommendations
- develop an annotated bibliography
- write a "citizen's guide to the war" which might contain 30 central questions and answers
- write two or three shorter essays, as in the style of a magazine article for *Harper's* or the *New Yorker*, about an aspect of the war
- write the position paper that a particular group might take on the war and defend that position (such groups might be a church, a union, an ethnic group)

Some of the topics for study are:
- analysis of the causes and consequences of particular events (the failure to hold elections in 1956; the fall of Diem; the Gulf of Tonkin resolution; the '68 Tet Offensive)
- a discussion of the theories of limited (or guerilla) war and Vietnam
- a consideration of a social, political or economic theory in terms of the Vietnam happenings (containment—before and after)
- Vietnam and the Elections of ('62 through '72)
- War crimes and Vietnam
- Military expenditures and Vietnam

- the legality of U.S. involvement in Vietnam (may be done in conjunction with International Law)
- the role of universities in the Vietnam era
- Vietnam and the rights of citizens vs. the state
- Vietnam and the right of selective conscientious objection
- Vietnam and the right of political protest
- U.S. public opinion and Vietnam

Reading

The core texts of the course are:
Frances Fitzgerald, *Fire in the Lake*. Vintage Books, 1973.
Leslie Gelb, *The Irony of Vietnam: The System Worked*. Brookings, 1978.

There will be a number of readings from *Foreign Affairs* and other sources for each class session. These are designed to provide a flavor of the way in which analysts from the late forties through the seventies viewed Vietnam.

Class Schedule

September 10   Course Introduction: "Why a Senior Integrative Seminar on Vietnam?"

This will be a discussion of our vision and hopes for the course in both its substantive and methodological foci. In the former, we will address the "nature of the Vietnam problem" to those who examine it in hindsight and why it constitutes a fertile topic for social science/liberal arts students to investigate. In the latter, we will discuss the style of operation of the seminar, its emphasis on liberal arts skills, in particular public speaking, and why your education has inadequately prepared you for the tasks ahead in the next 40 years.
Readings: Substantive on Vietnam:
Gelb, Introduction and Chapter 1
Fitzgerald, Chapters 1 and 2
Methods of the Course:
Len Clark, "Terror: A Generation Unprepared," Earlham Baccalaureate Address, 1978
George Lopez, "Sowing the Seeds of . . . Cynicism or Sophistication?" Earlham Baccalaureate Address, 1979
Michael Nelson, "What's Wrong With Political Science," *Washington Monthly*, 1978
Carter Daniels, "Notes on a Dissenting Commencement Address," *Chronicle of Higher Education*, May, 1979

September 14 Politics, Democracy and World Views

What was the perspective of the U.S. on the "nature of" the world environment after World War II? What was the view of political democracy in this context, particularly the role of American democracy? In what way was there a unified perspective? What context is formed between 1945 and the mid-fifties which might predispose leaders and the American people to organize their information about Vietnam a particular way?

Readings:
'X', "The Sources of Soviet Conduct," *Foreign Affairs*, July, 1947
Stanley Hoffman, "Contemporary Theory in International Relations," *Foreign Affairs*
Walt W. Rostow, "The United States in the World Arena," *Foreign Affairs*
John Lewis Gaddis, "Was the Truman Doctrine Really a Turning Point?" *Foreign Affairs*, January, 1974
Gelb, Chapters 2 and 6

September 17 Perspectives on National Development
What were the theories of the process of national economic and political development prevalent during the post war era? What role was ascribed to U.S. foreign aid in this process? Given these dual sets of expectations, what were the contours of thinking about the process of change occuring in Vietnam?
Readings:
Selections assigned from Walt Rostow, "Politics and the Stages of Economic Growth"
Harlan Cleveland, "The Caricature of Foreign Aid"
John K. Galbraith, "Economic Development: Rival Systems and Comparative Advantages"
Edward C. Banfield, "American Foreign Aid Doctrines"
Chester Bowles, "Foreign Aid: The Essential Factors of Success"

September 21, 24 Vietnam in its World, Asian and Local Context
How might we interpret events in Vietnam from the early thirties through 1954? What can be said of Asian Communism? Of the relationship between the Vietnamese and Chinese as peoples, as Communists? How did the Asia patterns and local Vietnamese cultures fit into the world views and perspectives on national development previously discussed?
Readings:
Kahin and Lewis, *The U.S. and Vietnam*, Chapters 1 and 2
Fitzgerald, Chapters 3 and 4
Davis Bobrow, "Chinese Views on Escalation"
George A. Carver, Jr. "The Real Revolution in South Vietnam," *Foreign Affairs*, April 1965, pp. 387-408
Harrison E. Salisbury, "Image and Reality in Indo-China," *Foreign Affairs*, April 1971, pp. 381-394

September 28 The Geneva Conference of 1954 and its Aftermath
What happened at Geneva in 1954? What operated in the minds of U.S. policymakers? Did the U.S. consciously undermine the conference and/or the fullfillment of the agreement after the signing of the accords?
Readings:
Kahin and Lewis, Chapter 3
Berkowitz, et al., Chapter 4, "The Decision Not to Intervene in Indochina in 1954" in *The Politics of American Foreign Policy: The Social Context of Decisions*
Frank C. Zagare, "The Geneva Conference of 1954: A Case of Tacit Deception," *International Studies Quarterly*, Sept. 1979, pp. 390-411
Fitzgerald, Chapters 5-10

October 5 Americanizing the War: Kennedy

How did Kennedy view the Vietnam problem? What stage did he set for Johnson? What sets of thinking (about war, strategy and communism) were in place that prompted U.S. behavior?

Readings:

Robert E. Osgood, "The Theory of Limited War"

Sir Robert G.K. Thompson, "Basic Principles and Operational Concepts of Counterinsurgency"

Bernard B. Fall, "The Theory and Practice of Insurgency and Counterinsurgency"

Paul Keckskeneti, "Insurgency as a Strategic Problem"

Gelb, Chapter 3

October 8 War Escalation Under Johnson: I

Herman Kahn, "Escalation as a Strategy"

Bernard Fall, "Vietnam in the Balance," *Foreign Affairs,* October, 1966, pp. 1-18

McGeorge Bundy, "The End of Either/Or," *Foreign Affairs,* January, 1967, pp. 191-201

Gelb, Chapters 4 and 5

October 12 Johnson and Escalation: II

What was the linkage between all the programs the U.S. was conducting in Vietnam and the decisions made in Washington? What of the infrastructure of intelligence, foreign policy reporting, etc.—was there large disagreement or bureaucratic unanimity?

Readings:

General William Westmoreland, "The Year of Decision—1968" and "Rolling Thunder" in *A Soldier Reports*

Fitzgerald, Chapters 11-15

Gelb, Chapters 8, 9, 11, 12

October 15 Public Opinion and the War

What was the attitude of the general public toward war in Vietnam as it developed? Did certain groups, like American business, support it more than others? Did the public demonstrations make a difference in war policy?

Readings:

Gelb, Chapter 7

John Vasquez, "A Learning Theory of the American Anti-War Movement," *Journal of Peace Research* (13)4: 299-314

Craig McCormick, "Public Opinion" (reprint)

October 19 Nixon, Kissinger and the War

How are we to view the Administration that both brought the war to a conclusion and also expanded it to other sections of Indochina? Did we get "peace with honor?" Did the Vietnamese in the south ever really have a chance to defend their territory?

Readings:

Fitzgerald, Chapters 16 and 17

R.H. Johnson, "Vietnamization: Can It Work?" *Foreign Affairs,* July, 1970: 629-647

H.A. Kissinger, "The Vietnam Negotiations," *Foreign Affairs,* Jan. '69: 211-234

Gelb, Chapter 13

Selections from William Shawcross, *Sideshow: Nixon, Kissinger and the Destruction of Cambodia*

October 22 The Impact of the War on American Life
The experience of Vietnam changed many things in America, but exactly what changed? By how much? What of the impact on the institution which ultimately had to bear the burden of the continuation of the war—the Presidency? Was Vietnam one of the key elements in building an Imperial Presidency or is the Presidency weaker than ever before because of Vietnam?
Readings:
Gelb, Chapter 10
Selections from Keith Nelson, *The Impact of War on American Life*

October 26 The Lessons of Vietnam I
What are we to learn from the Vietnam era in our study and participation in social and political life? What does our experience this term mean for the application of social theory to social life? Is there agreement about what Vietnam meant for America? Should we be cautious about positing "history" and "lessons" from Vietnam, lest we "overlearn" from the experience, as was the case with the "fall" of China and the "loss" of Korea in the forties and fifties?
Readings:
Gelb, Chapter 13
Richard Falk, "What We Should Learn From Vietnam," *Foreign Policy*, 1: 98-114
Ole Holsti and James Roserau, "America's Foreign Policy Agenda: The Post-Vietnam Beliefs of American Leaders" in Kegley and McGowan, *Challenges to America*
Earl C. Ravenal, "The Ultimate Strategic Lessons" in Ravenal's *Never Again*

October 29 Lessons II
Ellen Nissenbaum, "The Lessons of Vietnam: An Exploration of the 'Lessons' Literature." (reprint)

All of November is devoted to student research projects.

The Soviet Union

Roberta Manning
History 273/Boston College/Chestnut Hill, MA 02167

Fall 1982

The Brezhnev generation of Soviet leaders which has governed the USSR since the end of the 1930s is currently in the process of passing from the political scene. What were the formative historical experiences of this unique leadership group? How do these experiences differ from those of the men and women who will replace them at the helm of the Soviet government? What political issues, both domestic and foreign, are likely to figure prominently in the political transition? And how are these issues likely to be resolved?

This course will attempt to answer these questions by showing the contributions of history to current politics. We will seek to place current Soviet political developments in the context of other industrial and developing nations. We will study the Brezhnev generation and their most likely political successors and then go on to investigate current Soviet policy debates as reflected in the mass media, in a number of areas of interest to the class. Topics to be covered include: Soviet attitudes on foreign policy; the politics of disarmament and prospects for peace; decentralization of the decision-making process (which will include the question of the professionalization or bureaucratization of the Soviet political elite); the state of the Soviet economy (stagnation or continued growth); the impact of high technology ("the scientific-technological revolution" as the Soviets call it); the ongoing (but changing) problems of the Soviet agriculture; economic equality and economic incentives (can the two be reconciled?); the role of the mass media; the position of Soviet minority groups; Soviet dissent (a current issue or a past phenomenon?); social services (or are the Soviets cutting back too?); energy policies (crisis or Soviet advantage?); human rights in the USSR (the problems of Soviet legality); new trends in Soviet culture; the state of Soviet education; the crisis of the Soviet family and the position of women; and contemporary youth culture in the USSR (and/or opportunities for youth). The actual list of topics selected will depend on the interests of class members.

Course Requirements

Two short papers will be required. The first of these entails an 8-10 page analysis of the U.S. and Soviet white papers on the arms race: *Soviet Military Power* (a U.S. Defense Dept. publication) and *Whence the Threat to Peace* (the Soviet government white paper). The second paper is a 10-12 page media project comparing any recent issue of the Soviet pictorial monthly *The Soviet Union* with the same month's edition of its approximate U.S. counterpart *Life Magazine*. A description of the media project follows at the end of this syllabus. Students who have a strong background in Soviet studies and/or have undertaken similar assignments with me before might want to substitute a research paper delineating current Soviet policy debates (as displayed in the Soviet press) on some issue of contemporary concern in place of one of the papers.

Readings

Brezhnev, "Speech to the Congress of the CPSU," February 23, 1981

Shukshin, *Snowball Berry Red and Other Stories*. Ann Arbor, MI: Ardis Press, 1979

Trifonov, "The Exchange" (1969), *Russian Literary Triquarterly*, No. 5, Winter 1973

Karl W. Ryavec, *Soviet Society and the Communist Party*

"Protecting the Environment in 1981—1985," *Current Digest of the Soviet Press*, Vol. 34, No. 12

Jerry Hough and Merle Fainsod, *How the Soviet Union is Governed*

S. Bialer, *Stalin's Successors*

U.S. Dept. of Defense, *Soviet Military Power*. Washington, DC: U.S. Government Printing Office, 1981

Soviet Ministry of Defense, *Whence the Threat to Peace*. Chicago, IL: Imported Publications, 1982

The Soviet Union (Soviet English language edition monthly—any issue)

The USSR Today—fifth edition

Rasputin, "The French Lesson" in *Soviet Russian Stories of the 1960's and 1970's* Moscow: Progress Publishers, 1977

Course Outline

Intro: The State of Soviet Studies and the Soviet Succession (September 9)

The Nature of the Russian Revolution: New Directions in American Scholarship (September 14)

Stalin and the Stalin Revolution (September 17, 21)

Krushchev and the Thaw (September 24, 28)

Brezhnev: The Man and the System (September 30, October 5)

Institutional Arrangements in Soviet Politics of the Post-Stalin Period (Oct. 7, 12)

The Locus of Power and Implications for the Future (October 19)

Mid Term Examination (October 21)

The Post Brezhnev Successions: Prospects and Peculiarities (October 26, 28)

Discussion: Two Prospects for the Soviet Future—Soviet and Western (Nov. 2)

Soviet Foreign Relations: The U.S., Third World and Europe: Linkage and Detente (November 4, 9)

U.S.—Soviet Relations: The Military Dimension (November 16)

Paper #1 due

Soviet Economic Prospects for the Eighties: Continued Growth or Stagnation (November 18)

The Soviet Energy Crisis: Real or Nonexistent (November 23)

Environmental Protection: The Soviet Record (November 30)

The Soviet Mass Media: The Case of The Soviet Union (December 2)
Media Project Due

Women and the Family (December 7)

The Multi-National Character of the Soviet Union: Destablizing Factor or a Political Advantage (December 9)

Media Project
a. Pick a topic of current interest to you and follow it in the American and Soviet presses by following it in the newspaper and in *The Current Digest of the Soviet Press* or through one of the major news weeklies and their Soviet counterpart, *New Times*. The *Current Digest* is an anthology of articles from the Soviet press, selected and translated by the American Association for the Advancement of Slavic Studies. *New Times* is the English edition of the major mass circulation Soviet journal on foreign affairs.

Since the *Current Digest* is an anthology, the editors often save articles on a given subject (like the position of women) and publish them in batches so you should consult this journal for the last 4 to 6 months to obtain a sufficiently broad selection of articles. Conscientious students will probably want to go back one-two years.

Suggested topics include disarmament, foreign relations (with particular countries or regions of the world, Afghanistan, Iran, the Middle East, Africa, why the two sides think the Cold War is reviving, Soviet views of the U.S., U.S. views of the U.S.S.R.), domestic affairs (the position of women, the energy crisis, the crisis of the family, the economy, current literary controversies or cultural trends), the role, attitude toward the United Nations, policies toward national minorities, attitudes toward crime. Some times the best media projects have been quite off-beat ones. Historical projects are also possible—like Czechoslovakia in 1968, Cuban missile crisis, the impact of the 20th party congress (1956). In the case of domestic affairs, you might want to compare Soviet media coverage of a given topic, i.e. the role of women, with U.S. articles on U.S. women, and U.S. policies towards women, etc.

b. Take several issues of the *Current Digest of The Soviet Press* (2-3) and a couple of issues of a major U.S. newsweekly *(Time, US News, Newsweek)* and discuss the types of issues, concerns, attitudes and intellectual orientation of these two samples of the Soviet and American press. An alternate version for those primarily interested in foreign policy would be to take the foreign affairs sections of several issues of a major American newsweekly and compare them with coverage in issues of the Soviet foreign affairs weekly *New Times* for the same time period.

Note: Because of delays in translating Soviet periodicals and transporting *New Times*, you will want to check your dates *closely* to make sure that the issues used cover roughly the same time.

In analyzing this material you want to consider the following factors:

a. The types of issues and concerns expressed by the two presses
b. The kinds of issues covered and omitted—similarities and differences in both the kinds of stories covered and the coverage given them
c. What kinds of issues and topics are covered in one press and not the other?
d. Assess the strengths and weaknesses of each as a source of information—i.e. the quality and comprehensiveness of coverage
e. Based on these publications, what kinds of problems and concerns do Soviet and American society share in common? On what issues (or kinds of issues) do they appear to diverge the most?
f. How well does each press support its arguments with facts—which documents their allegation most soundly?
g. What issues are best handled in your opinion by each slant or perspective of each press?
h. How much does the press of each country appeal to emotions and how much to reason?
i. How much space is devoted to the discussion of personalities and how much to policies and issues?
j. How do they see us? How do we see them?
k. How do these two examples of the mass media deal with individuals? What kinds of individuals are singled out for recognition? What aspects of their lives are stressed?

English language editions of Soviet periodicals or anthologies of articles from the Soviet press:

Current Digest of the Soviet Press (CCDSP)
New Times (leading Soviet foreign affairs weekly)
Moscow News (English language news daily)
Soviet Education
Soviet Law and Government (BPL)
Soviet Neurology and Psychiatry
Soviet Psychology
Soviet Sociology
Soviet Studies in History
Soviet Studies in Literature
Soviet Studies in Philosophy
Soviet Reprints (contains recent speeches of Soviet leaders)
Soviet Review (the best from Soviet Sociology, Soviet Psychology, Soviet Educations, Soviet Law and Government, etc.)
Soviet Statutes and Decisions
Soviet Woman
Soviet and Eastern European Foreign Trade
Sputnik
USSR
Russian Library Triquarterly (for recent fiction and poetry, though increasingly focuses solely upon dissident writers to the neglect of the many excellent Soviet writers who are not dissidents)

Peace in the Southern Philippines

Robert McAmis   *Summer 1982*
Southern Philippines Center for Peace Studies/Mindanao State University/
Marawi City, Philippines

The Philippine government, during the height of the conflict in the 1970s, adopted a two-pronged approach of conciliation and development for the southwestern Philippines. The conciliation policy involves open dialogues with all groups engaged in the rebellion to thresh out problems and arrive at acceptable solutions. The policy of development commits the resources of the national government to the provision of economic, social, cultural and educational facilities and the expansion of citizen participation in nation-building (*Southwestern Philippine Question*, 2nd ed., p. 3).

The Mindanao State University is actively participating in the challenge to bring about lasting peace in the Southern Philippines. The Board of Regents in 1979 unanimously approved the creation of the Southern Philippines Center for Peace Studies with four goals: study, information, discussion, and visitation. Under the objective "study," the Center shall suggest new courses on understanding causes and resolutions of conflict.

Objectives

The course is multi-disciplinary in approach with the following objectives:
1. Expose the layperson and students to theories on peace education as a tool in understanding conflict resolution;
2. Present more objective and reliable facts regarding the history and possible causes of the conflict in Southern Philippines; and,
3. As an alternative approach to bring about lasting peace, love and understanding among peoples in Southern Philippines.

Course Outline

1. Rationale
1.1 Why Peace?
1.2 Definitions of Peace
  —Western and Islamic

2. Survey of Theories on Peace Education
2.1 Survey and discussion of the several theories on peace and world order education

3. An Overview of Southern Philippine History
3.1 Philippine history with special emphasis on Southern Philippines
3.2 Discussion of the Moro province to the present autonomous government (Region IX and XII)

4. Survey of Several Dimensions of the Conflict in Southern Philippines
4.1 Educational Dimensions
    a) Philippine educational system b) madrasah schools, and c) innovations, studies geared toward Muslim education
4.2 Economic Dimensions
    a) economic policies initiated by government to uplift Muslim conditions, b) bank (Amanah) and loan privileges to Muslims, and c) infrastructure projects
4.3 Inter-Ethnic Dimensions
    a) majority-minority relations in Southeast Asia, especially the Philippines, b) studies on the problems/causes and suggestions on ethnic relations, and c) possibilities for smooth inter-ethnic relationship
4.4 Historical Dimensions
    a) controversies written about Muslim history, b) the need to rewrite Philippine history, and c) other studies with respect to Muslim history
4.5 Political Dimensions
    a) attempts for self-government (from Moro province to autonomous government), b) conflict between traditional government and civilian government and c) areas of accommodation and complementation
4.6 Religious Dimensions
    a) area of conflict, b) Muslim-Christian basis of common understanding, and c) suggestions for unity, respect, tolerance and understanding
4.7 International Dimensions
    a) RP—Middle-East foreign policies, b) foreign policies and the Southern Philippine issue, and c) actions adopted by Philippine government to minimize conflict
4.8 Southeast Asian Dimensions
    a) RP relations with ASEAN countries, b) issues like claim to Sabah and Muslim refugees in Sabah, and c) policies adopted regarding the above
4.9 Integration of the above
    a) areas of conflict and b) accommodation for national unity

5. Strategies for Peace in Southern Philippines
5.1 Theories on how peace can be attained utilizing Philippine materials
5.2 The Role of State Universities/Private Institutions/Research Centers
    a) state universities like MSU, KFCIAS, Islamic Institute, U.P., Western Mindanao State University, b) URC, Peace Center, Dansalan Research Center, NDC (Cotabato City) etc.
5.3 Government Institutions and Offices
    a) Southern Philippine Development Authority, b) Ministry of Muslim Affairs, c) Islamic Affairs, Ministry of Foreign Affairs, d) Philippine Pilgrimage Authority
5.4 Autonomous Government
    —Region IX and XII
5.5 Rebel Returnees Program
    —Problems and solutions adopted
5.6 Infrastructure Projects
    —Survey of the infrastructure projects in Southern Philippines
5.7 Symposia, Conferences and Dialogues
    a) Annual seminar on Mindanao and Sulu cultures, b) policy conferences,

c) peace talks, d) Muslim-Christian dialogues
5.8 Law and Order
—Muslim Personal Code (Shariah Courts)
—PDs, LOI on the Muslims
5.9 Summation

Readings
1. Abubakar, Asiri J. "Muslim Philippines: With Reference to the Sulus, Muslim-Christian Contradictions, and the Mindanao Crisis," *AS* 11/1 (Apr 1973), 112.
2. Asani, Abdurassad. "Moros-Not Filipinos," *The Diliman Review*, 29/2 (Mar-Apr 1981), 27.
3. "An Investment in the Future of Mindanao," *Salam* 111/2 (Apr-Dec 1976), 32.
4. Baradas, David B. "Conflict in the 'Land of promise'," *PSR*, 20/4 (Oct 1972), 363.
5. Beckett, Jeremy. "The Datus of the Rio Grande de Cotabato under Colonial Rule," *AS* 15 (Apr-Aug-Dec 1977), 46.
6. Boransing, Manaros B. Policy of Total Development as an Approach to the Bangsa Moro Problem: An Alternative to Autonomy. (12th Annual Seminar on Mindanao and Sulu Cultures, Mindanao State University, Marawi City), November 16-18, 1979.
7. Bruno, Juanito A. *The Social World of the Tausog: A Study in Culture and Education*. Centro Escolar U., Mla., 1973.
8. Casiño, Eric. "Integration and the Muslim-Filipinos," *PSR*, 20/4 (Oct 1972), 360.
9. Casiño, Eric. "Structuralism in Philippine Cultural Universities," *Solidarity*, 10/6 (Jl-Aug 1975), 18.
10. Castro, Emilio M. "Muslim Integration: Its Implications on National Security," *NSR*, 1/4 (Dec 1973), 40.
11. "Characteristics of the Mindanao Economy," *The Diliman Review*, 29/2 (Mr-Apr 1981), 17.
12. Chavez, Martiniano V. "The Problem of Ethnic Integration: Muslim Filipinos," *NSR*, 1/4 (Dec 1973), 40.
13. Demetrio, Francisco R. "Religious Dimensions of the Moro Wars," in the *Southern Philippines Issue*, 1979: 58.
14. Dirawatun, M.B. "Reaction to Jalahuddin de los Santos' Paper," *Philippine Political Science Journal* 7 (Je 1978), 15.
15. "Editorial: Peace a Prerequisite of Progress," *Salam* 2/5 (Jl-De 1975), 1.
16. Enrile, Juan P. "The National Security Situation," *FTP Yearbook*, 1980: 80.
17. Espidol, Artemio S. "The Integration of Our Muslim Communities and its Relation to Peace and Order," *National Security Review*, 1/4 (Dec 1973), 8.
18. Fabella, Armand V. "Government Reorganization: A Continuing Thrust Towards Administrative Development," *FTP Yearbook*, 1980: 300.
19. Glang, Alimuddin C. "Islam and Agricultural Development," *Notre Dame Journal* 10/2 (Oct 1980), 5.
20. Glang, Alunan C. "A Constitution for the Muslims," *Solidarity* 6/9 (Sept 1971), 8-16.
21. Glang, Alunan C. "Realities and Illusions in the Muslim Conflict," *National Security Review* 1/4 (Dec 1973), 34.
22. Glang, Alunan C. "Why the Shooting Won't Stop," *Solidarity*, 7/4 (Apr 1972), 6.
23. Gowing, Peter G. "Christian-Muslim Relationship in Insular Southeast Asia," *Solidarity*, 10/6 (Jl-Aug 1975), 2.

24. Gowing, Peter G. *Muslim-Filipinos—Heritage and Horizon.* New Day Publication, Quezon City, 1979.

25. Gowing, Peter G. *Mandate in Moro Land: The American Government of Muslim-Filipinos 1899-1920.* Philippine Center for Advanced Studies, Quezon, 1977.

26. Gowing, Peter G. and Robert D. McAmis. "Introd: Irresistable Forces, Immovable Objects," in *The Muslim Filipinos: Their History, Society and Contemporary Problems,* edited by Gowing, Peter G. and Robert D. McAmis. Solidaridad Publishing House, Manila, 1974, vii.

27. Guerrero, Leon Ma. "Encounters of Cultures: The Muslims in the Philippines," in *The Southern Philippines Issue,* Tiamson and Cañeda, 1979: 19-57.

28. Hassoubah, Ahmad Mohammad. Teaching Arabic as a Second Language in Southern Philippines: Problems and Possibilities. (MA in Education, College of Education, MSU, Marawi City, November 1980), 166pp.

29. Hunt, Chester L. "Ethnic Stratification and Integration in Cotabato," in *The Muslim Filipinos,* Gowing and McAmis, 1974: 194.

30. Isidro, Antonio. *Trends and Issues in Philippine Education.* Alemar-Phoenix Pub. House, Inc., Quezon City. 1969. See Chapter IX, p. 209; Chapter XIII, p. 313.

31. Jubaira, Almuzrin B. "600 Years of Islam in the Philippines," *1980 Fookien Times Philippines Yearbook,* 52.

32. Khan, Mohammad Z. *Islam—Its Meaning for Modern Man.* Routledge and Kegan Paul.London and Henley, 1980. See Chapter 18, "International Relations: Peace," p. 164.

33. Kiefer, Thomas M. "The Tausug of Jolo and the Modern Philippines," in *The Muslim Filipinos,* Gowing and McAmis, 1974: 100.

34. "King Faisal Institute of Islamic and Arabic Studies," *Salam* 1/1 (Mr 1974), 21.

35. Madale, Abdullah T. Educating the Muslim Child: The Philippine Case. (Paper read in the International Seminar on the Future of the Muslim Child, al Azhar University, Cairo Egypt, May 7-9, 1977).

36. Madale, Nagasura T. "My Marriage: An Encounter of Two Cultures," *WHC* (Ja 30/75), 16 19.

37. Madale, Nagasura T. The Concept of Power and the Mindanao Conflict (UGAT 4th National Conference, Silliman University, Dumaguete City), April 2, 1981.

38. Madale, Nagasura T. "Preliminary Notes on the Bangsa Moro and the Philippine Nation-State," *Asian Viewpoint,* 1/3 (Mr 1981), 13-14, 19-20.

39. Madale, Nagasura T. (ed.) *The Muslim Filipinos: A Book of Readings.* Alemar-Phoenix Publishing House, Quezon City, 1981.

40. Mahmoud, Mohammad Fatthy. "The Muslims in the Philippines: A Bibliographic Essay," *AS* 12/1-3 (Ag-De 1974), 173.

41. Magdalena, Federico V. "Intergroup Conflict in Southern Philippines: An Empirical Analysis," in Tiamson and Cañeda (eds.), *The Southern Philippines Issue,* 1979: 274.

42. Majul, Cesar A. *Muslims in the Philippines.* Asian Center, University of the Philippines Press, Quezon City, 1973.

43. Majul, Cesar A. "Islam in Relation to Change and Development," in *Islam and Development: A Collection of Essays.* OCIA Publications, 1980, 91.

44. Majul, Cesar A. "The Islamic Attitude Towards Development," in Majul, Cesar A. (ed.) *Islam and Development*, 1980, 79.

45. Majul, Cesar A. "Problems in the Implementation of Sharia Personal Laws in Muslim Minority Countries in the Far East," in *Islam and Development*, 153.

46. Majul, Cesar A. "The Role of Islam in the History of the Filipino People," *AS* 4/2 (Ag 1966), 303.

47. Majul, Cesar A. "The General Nature of Islamic Law and Its Application in the Philippines, in *Islam and Development*, 155.

48. Mapanao, Portia R. "Cotabato Rural Uplift Movement," *Solidarity*, 7/4 (Apr 1972), 10.

49. Marcos, Ferdinand E. "The Philippines in the last 15 years," *1980 Fookien Times Philippines Yearbook*, 28.

50. Marcos, Ferdinand E. "The President's Report on Southern Philippines," in *The Southern Philippine Issue*, Tiamson and Cañeda, 1979: 139.

51. Mastura, Michael O. "Reaction to Jalahuddin delos Santos' Paper," *PPSJ* 7 (Je 1978), 20.

52. Mastura, Michael O. and Musib Buat. "Maguindanaon Hopes and Fears from the Constitutional Convention," *Solidarity*, 7/4 (Apr 1972), 18.

53. Mastura, Michael O. and Musib Buat. "The Introduction of Muslim Law into the Philippine Legal System," *Solidarity*, 10,6 (Aug 1972), 47.

54. Mednick, Melvin. "Sultans and Mayors: The Relation of a National to an Indigenous Political System," in *The Muslim Filipinos* 1974: 225.

55. Ministry of Foreign Affairs. "Brief Historical Background to the Southern Philippine Issue," in *Philippine Issue*, 1979: 175.

56. "Moro History Re-Examined," *Mindanao Journal* 3/1 (Jl-Se 1976), Proceedings of the 9th Annual Seminar on Mindanao and Sulu Cultures.

57. "New Concept of Education: MSU," *Salam* 1/1 (Mr 1974), 18.

58. Noble, Cela. "The Muslim-Christian Conflict—Its Religious Background," *Solidarity* 11/2 (Mr-Apr 1977), 19.

59. Orosa, Sixto Y. *The Sulu Archipelago and Its People.* (Enlarged and Updated Edition with a Supplement 1st Ed. 1923), 2nd ed. 1970. World Book Co., Yonkers-on-Hudson, New York. Reprinted in the Philippines, New Mercury Printing Press, 1970.

60. Pendaliday, Usop K. "The Problems and Prospects of Maguidanaons: Economic Development," *Solidarity* 7/4 (Apr 1972), 9.

61. "Philippine Foreign Policy Reorientation," *Salam* 1/1 (Mr 1974), 18.

62. *Philippine Majority-Minority Relationship and Ethnic Attitudes.* Filipinas Foundation Inc., 1975. See Chapter I, pp. 52-96; Chapter IV, pp. 157 and 162; Chapter V, pp. 194-208.

63. Proceedings: Americans in Mindanao and Sulu 1899-1946. MSU-IIT and Mindanao State University, Marawi City, Ag 20-22, 1981.

64. Rachagan, Sothi S. and Richard F. Dorall. The Conflict in Mindanao: Perspectives from South of the Border (4th UGAT Annual National Conference, Silliman University, Dumaguete City), April 2-4, 1981.

65. Rasul, Jainal D. *Muslim-Christian Land—Ours to Share.* Alemar-Phoenix Publishing House Inc., Quezon City. 1969. See Chapter IV, p. 209; Chapter XIII, p. 313.

66. "Reconstruction and Development Programs in Muslim Mindanao," *Salam* 1/1 (Mr 1974), 14.
67. "Religious Dimensions of Moro History." *Mindanao Journal,* 1/3 (Ja-Mr 1975), Proceedings of the 7th Annual Seminar on Mindanao and Sulu Cultures.
68. Romula, Carlos P. "A Shift in Perspective," *1980 Fookien Times Philippines Yearbook,* 66.
69. Saber, Mamitua. "Majority-Minority Situations in the Philippines," *Solidarity* 10/6 (Ag 1975), 36.
70. Saber, Mamitua. The Transition from a Traditional to a Legal Authority System: A Philippine Case (Ph. D. dissertation) University of Kansas, 1967.
71. Saleeby, Najeeb M. "Studies in Moro History, Law and Religion," *Notre Dame Journal* 6/1 (Apr 1975) reprint.
72. Santos, Jalahuddin delos. "Liberation and Separatist Movements and Their Impact on Political Integration and National Development," *Philippine Political Science Journal* 7 (Je 1978), 8.
73. Sherfan, Andrew D. *The Yakans of Basilan Island: Another Unknown and Exotic Tribe of the Philippines.* Fotomatic (Phils) Inc., Cebu City, 1976.
74. Shih-fu,Lo. "The Moro Rebellion: Its History and Background," in *The Southern Philippines Issue,* 1979: 139.
75. Sicat, Gerardo P. "Philippine Development Strategy for the 1980s," *1980 Fookien Times Philippines Yearbook,* 114.
76. Sinsuat, Mama S. "Problems and Prospects of Maguidanaon Integration," *Solidarity* 7/4 (Apr 1972), 13.
77. Stauffer, Robert B. "The Politics of Becoming: The Mindanao Conflict in a World-System Perspective," *The Diliman Review* 29/21 (Mr-Apr 1981), 20.
78. Stewart, Schlegel A. "The Cotabato Conflict: Impressions of an Outsider," *Solidarity* 7/4 (Apr 1972), 31.
79. Stone, Richard L. "Intergroup Relations Among the Tausug, Samals and Badjaos of Sulu," in *The Muslim Filipinos,* Gowing and McAmis, 1974: 74.
80. "Strengthen our Ties with the Muslim World," *Salam* 111/2 (Apr-Dec 1976), 22.
81. Tadem, Eduardo. "Mindanao: Patterns of Underdevelopment," *The Diliman Review* 29/2 (Mr-Apr 1981), 1, 15.
82. Tamano, Mamintal. "The Expectations of Muslims as Philippine Citizens," *Solidarity,* 10/6 (Jl-Ag 1975), 30.
83. Tamano, Mamintal. "How to Solve the Muslim Problem Without Bullets," *Solidarity* (De 1973), 17-26.
84. Tamano, Mamintal. "Problems of the Muslims: A National Concern," *Solidarity* 4/3 (1969), 13-23.
85. Tan, Samuel K. "A Historical Perspective for National Integration," *Solidarity* 10/2 (Mr-Apr 1976), 3.
86. "The Church and Islam in History," in *Notre Dame Journal* 9/1 (Apr 1979).
87. "The Maguindanaons: Resources and Prospects for Development," *Notre Dame Journal* 10/2 (O 1980), 2.
88. "The Philippine Amanah Bank," *Salam* 1/1 (Mr 1974), 22.
89. "The Philippines and the Muslim South," *Salam* 1/1 (Mr 1974), 3.
90. "The Prophet of God Jesus," in *Notre Dame Journal* 9/2 (Oct 1979).
91. *The Southwestern Philippine Question,* 2nd ed., Ministry of Foreign Affairs, Manila, n.d.

92. Tiamson, Alfredo T. and Cañedo, Rosalinda N. (eds.) *The Southern Philippine Issue: Readings in the Mindanao Problem.* Vol. 1. Peace Center, Mindanao State University, Marawi City, Nov. 16-18, 1979.

93. Tiamson, Alfredo T. *The Muslim Filipinos: An Annotated Bibliography,* Filipinas Foundation, Inc., Makati, 1979.

94. Tillah, Ide C. "The Role of Islam (Muslim Religion) in the New Society," *NSR* 1/4 (Dec 1973), 45.

95. Tongson, Vincente S. "Our Muslim Policy: What Went Wrong?" *NSR* 1/4 (Dec 1974).

96. "Towards Closer Philippine-Arab Relations," *Salam* 1/1 (Mr 1974), 5.

97. "Training Returnees Into Executives," *Salam* (English version), 1/4 (Jl-Dec 1975), 18.

98. Utrecht, Ernst. "The Separatist Movement in the Southern Philippines," in *The Southern Philippines Issue,* Tiamson and Cañeda, 1979: 156.

99. Waltz, Kenneth N. *Man, The State and War: A Theoretical Analysis.* Columbia University Press, New York, 1954.

100. "Workshop on Issues and Problems of Southern Philippines," *PPSJ* 7 (Je 1978), 30.

101. *Zamboanga Peace Talks.* Sowescom, Zamboanga City, April 17-19, 1975.

The Political Economy of Africa

Michael Ford, Frank White and Frank Holmquist *Spring 1982*
Social Sciences 257/Hampshire College/Amherst, MA 01002

The intent of the course is to provide a basic understanding of past and present African political economy and processes of social and material development. We will try to be theoretically conscious and abreast of current debate, yet at the same time empirical enough to touch base in the real world.

Evaluations for the course will be based on a 25:75 fashion on contribution's to class discussions and a research paper (roughly 20 pages) on a topic discussed in advance with one or all of the instructors.

A special series of visiting scholars will run parallel to the course, and, to provide some visual grasp of the historical subject matter, a trilogy of films on Kenya will be shown. Further bibliographic help beyond the syllabus may be found in our texts as well as in regularly published bibliographies in *The Review of African Political Economy*, and *Current African Bibliography* and *International African Bibliography*.

Required Books

Nancy Hafkin and Edna Bay, *Women in Africa*
Anthony Hopkins, *An Economic History of West Africa*
J. Forbes-Munro, *Africa and the International Economy*, 1800-1960
Robert Price, *U.S. Foreign Policy in Sub-Saharan Africa*
Richard Sandbrook and Jack Arn, *The Labouring Poor and Urban Class Formation: The Case of Greater Accra*
Ousmane Sembene, *God's Bits of Wood*
Claude Ake, *A Political Economy of Africa*
Dennis Cohen and John Daniel, *Political Economy of Africa: Selected Readings*

1. Introduction

Questions
What is the present political-economic situation in Africa?
    Course theme: to *explain* the current situation
Why don't we understand Africa?
    U.S. historical, racial and cultural factors
    Recent evolution of academic analysis

Bibliography
Stavrianos, L.S. *Global Rift: The Third World Comes of Age*. N.Y.: Wm. Morrow, 1981.
International Studies Quarterly (special issue on "World System Debates") 25:1 (March 1981).

Szymanski, Albert. *The Logic of Imperialism*, 1981.

Warren, Bill. *Imperialism: Pioneer of Capitalism.* London: New Left Books, 1980.

Katz, Stephen. *Marxism, Africa and Social Class: A Critique of Relevant Theories.* Montreal: Centre for Developing-Area Studies, McGill U., 1980.

Gutkind, Peter C.W. and Immanuel Wallerstein (eds.) *The Political Economy of Contemporary Africa.* Beverly Hills: Sage, 1976.

Meillassoux, Claude. "Introduction," in Meillassoux (ed.), *The Development of Indigenous Trade and Markets in W. Africa.*

Klein, Martin. "The Decolonization of West African History," *Interdisciplinary History* 6:1 (1975).

Hansen, Wm. and B. Shulz. "Dependency Theory, Social Class and Development," *Africa Today* 28:3 (1981).

Rodney, Walter. "Problems of Third World Development," *Ufahamu* 11:1 (Summer 1981).

Killick, Tony. "Trends in Development Economics and Their Relevance to Africa," *J. of Modern African Studies* 18:3 (Sept. 1980).

Evans, Peter and M. Timberlake. "Dependence, Inequality and the Growth of the Tertiary: A Comparative Analysis of Less Developed Countries," *ASR* 45 (Aug. 1980).

Smith, Sheila. "The Ideas of Samir Amin: Theory or Tautology?" *J. of Development Studies* 17:1 (October 1980).

Roxborough, Ian. *Theories of Undervelopment*, 1979.

Chenery, Hollis. et al. *Redistribution with Growth*, 1975.

Wallerstein, Immanuel. *The Capitalist World Economy*, 1979.

Amin, Samir. *Class and Nation, Historically and in the Current Crisis*, 1980.

Petras, James. *Critical Perspectives on Imperialism and Social Class in the Third World*, 1979.

Frank, Andre G. *Dependent Accumulation and Underdevelopment*, 1979.

"State and Social Formation in the Capitalist Periphery" (symposium), *Insurgent Sociologist* 9:24, Spring 1980.

"Facing the 1980's: New Directions in the Theory of Imperialism" (symposium) *Review of Radical Political Economics* 11:4, Winter, 1979.

Caporaso, J.A. (ed.) "Dependence and Dependency in the International System," *International Organization* 32:1, 1978.

Warren, Bill. "Imperialism and Industrialization," *New Left Review*, No. 81 (1973).

Petras, James and Robert Rhodes. "Industry in the Third World," *New Left Review*, No. 85, May-June 1979.

Journal of Contemporary Asia 7:1 (1977): Special Issue on Development and Underdevelopment. See especially the article by Colin Leys.

Phillips, Anne. "The Concept of Development," *Review of African Political Economy*, #8, January-April, 1977.

Snyder David and Edward Rich. "Structural Position in the World System and Economic Growth, 1955-1970," *American Journal of Sociology* 84:5, 1979.

McGowan, Patrick J. "Economic Dependency and Economic Performance in Black Africa," *Journal of Modern African Studies* 14:1 (March 1976).

Lehman, David (ed.) *Development Theory: Four Critical Studies*, 1979.

Smith, L. "The Underdevelopment of Development Literature," *World Politics* 31, 1979.

Stein, L. "Dependency Theories and Underdevelopment," *Journal of Economic Studies* 31, 1979.

Mack, A., et al., (ed.) *Imperialism, Intervention and Development*, 1979.

Mahler, Vincent A. *Dependency Approaches to International Political Economy: A Cross-National Study*, 1980.

Magdoff, Harry. *Imperialism: From the Colonial Age to the Present*, 1978.

2. Pre-Colonial Africa in the Creation of World Economy

Questions

What was the nature and impact of trade and slavery between Europe and Africa?

What were the similarities and differences between E., W., Central and Southern Africa?

Why didn't Africa develop as fast as Europe?

Bibliography

Kno'nui, Helge. *Ecology Control and Economic Development in East African History*, 1977.

Crummey, Donald, and C.C. Stewart (eds.) *Modes of Production in Africa: The Pre-Colonial Era*, 1981.

Lovejoy, Paul E. "Long-Distance Trade and Islam: The Case of the 19th C. Gausa Kola Trade," *J. of the Historical Society of Nigeria*, 5 (1971).

Akinjogbin, J.A. *Dahomey and its Neighbors*, 1708-1818.

Anstey, Roger T. "Capitalism and Slavery: A Critique," *Economic History Review* 21 (1968).

Curtin, Philip D. *The Atlantic Slave Trade: A Census.*

Curtin, Philip D. "Pre-Colonial Trading Networks and Traders: The Diakhals," in C. Meillassoux (ed.) *The Development of Indigenous Trades and Markets in West Africa.*

Curtin, Philip D. *Economic Change in Pre-Colonial Africa: Senegambia in the Era of the Slave Trade*, 1975.

Person, Y. "Ethnic Movements and Acculturation in Upper Guinea Since the 15th C.," *African Historical Studies*, 4, 1971.

Horton, Robin. "Stateless Societies in the History of West Africa," in J.F. A. Ajayi and M. Crowder (eds.), *History of W. Africa*, Vol. 1, 1971.

Thornton, John. "The Slave Trade in Eighteenth Century Angola: Effects of Demographic Structures," *Canadian J. of African Studies* 14:3 (1980).

Fage, J. "Slaves and Society in Western Africa, c. 1445-1700," *J. of African History* 21: 3 (1980).

Patterson, Orlando. "Slavery in Human History," *New Left Review* #117, (1979).

Cooper, F. "The Problem of Slavery in African Studies," *J. of African History* 20:1, (1979).

3. Colonialism

Questions

What are the theories explaining the imperial "scramble for Africa"?

What was the nature and impact of African resistance?

What were colonial development strategies in agriculture, industry or trade?

How did the class and gender structure evolve?

Bibliography

Cordell, Dennis and J.W. Gregory. "Historical Demography and Demographic History in Africa: Theoretical and Methodological Considerations," *Canadian J. of African Studies* 14:3 (1980).

Review (Special Issue: "The Incorporation of Southern Africa into the World Economy, 1800-1940") 3:2 (Fall, 1979).

Hill, Polly. "The Migrant Cocoa Farmers of Southern Ghana," *Africa* 31 (1961).

Cohen, Abner. *Custom and Politics in Urban Africa: A Study of Hausa Migrants in Yoruba Towns*, 1969.

Flint, J.E. "Economic Change in W. Africa in the 19th C.," in J.F.A. Ajayi and M. Crowder (eds.), *History of West Africa*, Vol. 2.

Afigbo, A.E. "The Establishment of Colonial Rule," in J.F.A. Ajayi and M. Crowder (eds.), *History of West Africa*, Vol. 2.

Johnson, G. Wesley. "African Political Activity in French West Africa, 1900-1940," in J.F.A. Ajayi and M. Crowder (eds.), *A History of West Africa*, Vol. 2.

Skinner, David E. *Thomas George Lawson: African Historian and Administrator in Sierra Leone*, 1980.

Kaplow, Susan B. "The Mudfish and the Crocodile: Underdevelopment of a West African Bourgeoisie," *Science and Society* 41 (1977).

Fetter, Bruce. *Colonial Rule in Africa: Readings from Primary Sources*. Madison: U. of Wisc., 1979.

Kaniki, M.H.Y. (eds.) *Tanzania Under Colonial Rule*. London: Longmans, 1980.

Robinson, Ronald. "The Moral Disarmament of African Empire: 1919-47," in Norman Hillmer and P. Wigley (eds), *The First British Commonwealth: Essays in Honour of Nicholas Mansergh*, London: Cass, 1980.

Rhoda, Howard. "Formation and Stratification of the Peasantry in Colonial Ghana," *J. of Peasant Studies* 8:1 (Oct. 1980).

Jones, Douglas H. "The Catholic Mission and Some Aspects of Assimilation in Senegal, 1817-1852," *J. of African History* 21:3 (1980).

Stickter, Sharon. "Trade Unionism in Kenya, 1947-52: The Militant Phase," in Peter C.W. Gutkina et al. (eds.). *African Labor History*. Beverly Hills: Sage, 1978.

Bryceson, D.F. "Changes in Peasant Food Production and Food Supply in Relation to the Historical Development of Commodity Production in Pre-colonial and Colonial Tanganyika," *J. of Peasant Studies* 7:3 (1980).

Vail, L. and L. White. *Capitalism and Colonialism in Mozambique*. London: Heinemann, 1980.

Davies, R.H. *Capital, State and White Labour in S. Africa 1900-60*. Brighton: Harvester, 1979.

van Zwenenberg, R.M.A. *Colonial Capitalism and Labour in Kenya: 1919-1939*, 1975.

Wolff, Richard. *Britain and Kenya: 1870-1930*, 1974.

Lonsdale, J.M. "The Politics of Conquest; The British in Western Kenya: 1894-1908," *Historical Journal* 20:4, Dec. 1977.

Lonsdale, J.M. and Bruce Berman. "Coping with Contradictions: The Development of the Labor Control System in Kenya, 1895-1914," *Journal of African History* 20, 1979.

J.M. Lonsdale. "Crisis of Accumulation, Coercion, and the Colonial State: The Development of the Labor Control System of Kenya, 1919-1929," *Canadian Journal of African Studies* 14:1, 190.

Iliffe, John. *A Modern History of Tanzania*, 1979.

Brett, E.A. *Colonialism and Underdevelopment in East Africa.*

Lenin, V. *Imperialism: The Highest Stage of Capitalism.*

Owen, R. and B. Sutcliffe (eds.) *Studies in the Theory of Imperialism*, 1972.

Brown, Michael Barratt. *The Economics of Imperialism.*

Low, D.A., and A. Smith (eds.) *History of East Africa*, Vol. 3, 1976.

Mamdani, Mahmood. *Politics and Class Formation in Uganda.*

Rimmer, D. "The Economics of Colonialism in Africa," *Journal of African History* 19:2, 1978.

Rodney, Walter. *How Europe Underdeveloped Africa.*

Dewey, Clive and A.G. Hopkins (eds.) *The Imperial Impact: Studies in the History of Africa and India*, 1978.

4. A View of Colonialism Through the Novel

Required: Ousmane Sembene, *God's Bits of Wood*, 1962.

5. Nationalism and Decolonization

Questions

How did protest evolve? Role of Pan-Africanism? Describe the evolution from elite to mass-based protest? Role of women?

What was nationalist ideology? What was the program? Was it populist?

What was the nature of the economy in late colonialism?

What was the "independence bargain" between colonizer and colonized?

Bibliography

Gropeter, John J. and Warren Weinstein. *The Pattern of Decolonization: A New Interpretation.* Syracuse: Maxwell School, Syracuse U., 1973.

Langley, J.A. *Pan-Africanism and Nationalism in West Africa: 1900-1945*, 1973.

Urdang, Stephanie. *Fighting Two Colonialisms.*

Rivkin, Elizabeth Thaele. "The Black Woman in South Africa: An Azanian Profile," in Steady (ed.), *The Black Woman Cross-Culturally*, 1981.

Rhode, Howard. "Differential Class Participation in the Ghana Cocoa Boycott, 1937-38," *Canadian J. of African Studies*, 10:3 (1976).

Gordon, David F. "Colonial Crisis and Administrative Response: Kenya, 1946-60," *Journal of African Studies* 6:2, Summer, 1979.

Bates, Robert. "The Issue Basis of Rural Politics in Africa," *Comparative Politics*, 10:3, April 1978.

Cliffe, L. "Nationalism and Reaction of Enforced Agricultural Change in Tanganyika During the Colonial Period," in Cliffe and Saul (eds.), *Socialism in Tanzania*, Vol. I.

Post, K.W. J. "Peasantization and Rural Political Movements in Western Africa," *European Journal of Sociology* 13:2 (1972).

Stichter, Sharon. "Workers, Trade Unions, and the Mau Mau Rebellion," *Canadian Journal of African Studies* 9:2 (1975.)

Lonsdale, John. "Some Origins of Nationalism in East Africa," *Journal of African History* 11:1 (1968).

Barnett, Donald and Karari Njama. *Mau Mau from Within*, 1966.

Rosberg, Carl and John Nottingham. *The Myth of Mau Mau: Nationalism in Kenya.* The best overall account of Mau Mau and Kenyan Nationalism.

Newsinger, John. "Revolt and Repression in Kenya: The 'Mau Mau' Rebellion, 1952-60," *Science and Society* 45:2 (Summer 1981).

6. Independence and After: A Theoretical Interlude

Questions

What are the basic features of the contemporary economy?

What are the basic features of the contemporary class structure?

How do we understand the relation between the state and the broader society and international forces?

Bibliography

Markakis, John and Nega Ayele. *Class and Revolution in Ethiopia.* Nottingham: Spokesman, 1978.

Davidson, Basil. *The People's Cause: A History of Guerillas in Africa.* Essex: Longman, 1981.

Mohiddin, Ahmed. *African Socialism in Two Countries.* Totowa, N.J.: Barnes and Noble, 1981.

Swainson, Nicole. *The Development of Corporate Capitalism in Kenya: 1918-1977.* Berkeley: Univ. of Cal., 1980.

O'Brien, Rita Cruise. *The Political Economy of Underdevelopment: Dependency in Senegal,* 1979.

Africa Today (Special issue: "The Sudan: 25 Years of Independence") 28:2 (1981).

Africa Today (Special issue: "Return to Civilian Rule in Ghana and Nigeria") 28:1 (1981).

Gran, Guy. *Zaire: The Political Economy of Underdevelopment,* N.Y.: Praeger, 1979.

Ibingira, Grace Stuart. *African Upheavals Since Independence.* Boulder, CO: Westview Press.

Marenin, Otwin. "Essence and Empiricism in African Politics," *J. of Modern African Studies* 19:1 (March 1981).

Schatzberg, Michael. "The State of the Economy: The 'Radicalization' of the Revolution," *Canadian J. of African Studies.* 14:2 (1980) (Zaire).

Gould, David. "Patrons and Clients: The Role of the Military in Zairian Politics," in I.J. Mowoe (ed.), *The Performance of Soldiers vs. Governors.* Wash, D.C.: Univ. Press of America, 1980.

Kitching, Gavin. *Class and Economic Change in Kenya: The Making of an African Petite-Bourgeoisie, 1905-1970.* New Haven: Yale U., 1980.

Ahmad, Eqbal. "Post-Colonial Systems of Power," *Arab Studies Q.* 2:4.

"Nigeria" (Special issue) *Review of African Political Economy* #11 (Jan.-April 1978).

"Debate on Dependency in Kenya" (several writers) *Review of African Political Economy* #17 (Jan.-Apr. 1980).

Bienen, H and V.P. Drejomaoh. *The Political Economy of Income Distribution in Nigeria.* N.Y.: Africana Pub., 1981.

Green, Reginald et al. *Economic Shocks and National Policy-Making: Tanzania in the 1970s.* Res. Report #8. The Hague: Inst. of Social Studies, 1980.

Bienen, H. *Armies and Parties in Africa*, 1978.

Sklar, Richard. "The Nature of Class Domination in Africa," *Journal of Modern African Studies*, 17:4 (Dec. 1979).

Samoff, Joel. "The Bureaucracy and the Bourgeoisie: Decentralization and Class Structure in Tanzania," *Comparative Studies in Society and History* 21:1 (Jan. 1979).

Chazan, Naomi. "African Voters at the Polls: Re-examination of the Role of Elections in African Politics," *J. of Commonwealth and Comparative Politics* 17:2 (July 1979).

Amey, Alan and David Leonard. "Public Policy, Class and Inequality in Kenya and Tanzania," *Africa Today* 26.4 (1979).

Kwan, Kim et al. (eds.) *Papers on the Political Economy of Tanzania*, 1979.

Leys, Colin. *Underdevelopment in Kenya*, 1974.

Coulson, A.C. (ed.) *African Socialism in Practice: The Tanzanian Experience*, 1979.

Mwanoasu, B. and C. Pratt (eds.) *Towards Socialism in Tanzania*, 1979.

Wolpin, Miles D. *Militarism and Social Revolution in the Third World*. Totowa, N.J.: Littlefield, Adams & Co., 1981.

Jackson, Robert H. and C.G. Rosberg (eds.) *Personal Rule in Black Africa: Prince, Autocrat, Prophet, Tyrant*. Berkeley: U. of Cal., 1981.

7. Neo-Colonial Culture and Reaction

Questions

What is neo-colonial culture? How is it maintained? What is the impact? What are some strategies to overcome it?

Bibliography

(Few sources on education systems are cited although they are very important)

Jules-Rosette, B. "Women in Indigenous African Cults and Churches," in F.C. Steady (ed.), *The Black Woman Cross-Culturally*, 1981.

Sudiakasa, Niara. "Female Employment and Family Organization in West Africa," in F.C. Steady (ed.), *The Black Woman Cross-Culturally*, 1981.

Langley, A.J. *Ideologies of Liberation in Black Africa, 1856 1970, Documents on Modern African Political Thought from Colonial Times to the Present*. Totowa, N.J.: Rowman and Littlefield.

Chabal, Patrick. "The Social and Political Thought of Cabral: A Reassessment," *J. of Modern African Studies* 19:1 (March 1981).

Hinzen, H. and V.A. Hunadorfer (eds.) *The Tanzanian Experience: Education for Liberation and Development*. London: Evans Brothers, 1980.

Stabler, E. "Kenya and Tanzania: Strategies and Realities in Education and Development," *African Affairs* 78 (1979).

Chinweizu. *The West and the Rest of Us: White Predators, Black Slavers and The African Elite*, 1975.

Mattelart, Armand. "Cultural Imperialism, Mass Media and Class Struggle," *The Insurgent Sociologist* 9:4, Spring, 1980.

Mattelart, Armand. *Mass Media, Ideologies and Revolutionary Movement*.

Mattelart, Armand. *Multinationals and Systems of Communication*.

Mattelart, Armand and Seth Siegelamb (eds.) *Mass Communications Media and Class Struggle*, 1979.

Constantino, Renata. *Cultural Imperialism.*
Fanon, Frantz. *The Wretched of the Earth.*
Fanon, Frantz. *Black Skins, White Masks.*

8. Ethnicity

Questions
Are ethnic loyalties timeless or do they come and go—if so, why?;
    i.e., how do we *explain* ethnicity?
How do ethnic, class and other loyalties interact?
What is the political impact of ethnic ideology?

Bibliography
Cohen, Almer. *Urban Ethnicity,* 1974.
Kanicki, Martin. "Attitudes of Reactions Towards the Lebanese in Sierra Leone
    During the Colonial Period," *Canadian J. of African Studies* 7 (1973).
Shock, Wm. and Elliot Skinner (eds.) *Strangers in African Societies,* 1979.
Harrell-Bond, Barbara, Allen Howard and David Skinner. *Community Leadership
    and the Transformation of Freetown,* 1978.
Cohen, R. "Ethnicity: Problem and Focus in Anthropology," *Annual Review of
    Anthropology* 7 (1978).
Lyon, J.M. "Marxism and Ethno-Nationalism in Guinea-Bissau: 1956-76," *Ethnic
    and Radical Studies* 3:2 (1980).
Blunt, Peter. "Bureaucracy and Ethnicity in Kenya: Some Conjectures for the
    1980s," *J. of Applied Behavioral Science* 16 (1980).
Ake, Claude. "Explaining Political Instability in New States," *Journal of Modern
    African Studies* 11:3 (Sept. 1973).
Nelson, Robert and Howard Wolfe (eds.) *Nigeria: Modernization and the Politics of
    Communalism,* 1971.
Lemarchand, Rene. "Political Clientelism and Ethnicity: Competing Solidarities in
    Nation-Building," *American Political Science Review* 66: (March 1972).
Young, Crawford. *The Politics of Cultural Pluralism,* 1976.
Barrows, Walter. "Ethnic Diversity and Political Stability in Africa," *Comparative
    Political Studies* 9:2 (July 1976).
Enloe, C.H. "Ethnicity, Bureaucracy and State-Building," *Ethnic and Racial Stud-
    ies* 1:3, 1978.

9. Peasants, Food and Rural Development

Questions
Who is a peasant?
Peasant society is not homogenous. Explain.
What are some basic features of peasant politics, political consciousness, and
    relations to the State?
How do we explain the contemporary crisis in agriculture?

Bibliography
McHenry, Dean E. Jr. *Ujamaa Villages in Tanzania: A Bibliography.* Uppsala:
    Scandinavian Institute of African Studies, 1981.

Lappe, Frances Moore and Adele Baccar-Varela. *Mozambique and Tanzania: Asking the Big Questions.* San Francisco: Institute for Food and Development Policy, 1980.

Franke, Richard W. and B. Chasin. *Seeds of Famine: Ecological Destruction and the Development Dilemma in the West African Sakel.* Montclair, N.J: Allanheld, Osman & Co.

Hyden, Goran. *Beyond Ujamaa in Tanzania: Underdevelopment and the Uncaptured Peasantry.* Berkeley: U. of Cal., 1980.

Young, Sherilynn. "Fertility and Famine: Women's Agricultural History in Southern Mozambique," in Robin Palmer and Neil Parsons (eds.), *The Roots of Rural Poverty in Central and Southern Africa.* Berkeley: U. of Cal., 1977.

Jeusiewicki, B. "Political Consciousness Among the African Peasantry in the Belgian Congo," *Review of African Political Economy* 19 (Sept.-Dec. 1980).

Spittler, Gerd. "Peasants and the State in Niger," *Peasant Studies* 8:1 (Winter 1981).

Allen, Rob. "Agriculture & Industry: A Case Study of Capitalist Failure in Northern Nigeria," *J. of Modern African Studies* 18:3 (Sept. 1980).

Bryceson, Deborah F. "The Proletarianization of Women in Tanzania," *Review of African Political Economy* #17 (Jan.-Apr., 1980).

Bates, Robert and M.F. Lofchie (eds.) *Agricultural Development in Africa: Issues of Public Policy.* N.Y.: Praeger, 1980.

Fortmann, Louise. *Peasants, Officials and Participation in Rural Tanzania: Experience with Villagization and Decentralization.* Ithaca: Center for International Studies, Cornell U., 1980.

VonFreyhold, Michael. *Ujamaa Villages in Tanzania: Analysis of a Social Experiment.* N.Y.: Monthly Review, 1979.

Liisa-Swartz, M. *Women in Development.* London: Hurst, 1980.

Turshen, Meredith. *Women, Food & Health in Tanzania.* London: Onyx, 1980.

Carlsen, John. *Economic and Social Transformation in Rural Kenya.* Uppsala: Scandinavian Institute of African Studies, 1980.

Bager, Torben. *Marketing Cooperatives and Peasants in Kenya.* Uppsala: Scandinavian Institute of African Studies, 1980.

Verhagen, K. "Changes in Tanzania's Rural Development Policy, 1975-78," *Development and Change* 11 (1980).

Bondestam, Lars and S. Bergstrom (eds.) *Poverty and Population Control.* London: Academic Press, 1980.

Hunt, Diana. "Chayanov's Model of Peasant Household Resources Allocation," *Journal of Peasant Studies* 6:3 (April 1979.)

Bates, Robert. "People in Villages: Micro-level Studies in Political Economy," *World Politics,* 1978.

Payer, Cheryl. "The World Bank and The Small Farmers," *Journal of Peace Research* 16:4, 1979.

Ranger, Terence. "Growing From the Roots: Reflections on Peasant Research in Central and Southern Africa," *Journal of Southern African Studies* 5:1, Oct., 1978.

Brown, David. "The Political Response to Immiseration: A Case Study of Rural Ghana," *Geneve-Afrique* 18:1 (1980).

Lee, Eddy. "Export-led Rural Development: The Ivory Coast," *Development and Change* 11:4 (Oct. 1980).

Caplan, Patricia and J. Bujra (eds.) *Women United, Women Divided: Comparative Studies of Ten Contemporary Cultures*, 1979.

Huston, Perdita. *Third World Women Speak Out*, 1979.

Kongstad, Per and M. Monsted. *Family, Labour and Trade in Western Kenya.* Uppsala: Scandinavian Institute of African Studies, 1980.

Bates, Robert H. *Market and States in Tropical Africa: The Political Basis of Agricultural Policies.* Berkeley: U. of Cal., 1981.

Obbo, Christine. *African Women: Their Struggle for Economic Independence.* Westport, Conn.: Lawrence Hill, 1981.

Cliffe, Lionel. "Rural Class Formation in East Africa," *Journal of Peasant Studies*, 4:2 (Jan. 1977).

Uma, Lele. *The Design of Rural Development: Lessons from Africa*, 1975.

Chambers, Robert. *Managing Rural Development: Ideas and Experience from East Africa*, 1974.

Berry, Sara. *Cocoa: Custom and Socioeconomic Change in Rural Western Nigeria*, 1975.

Williams, Gavin. "Political Consciousness Among the Ibadan Poor," in E. deKadt and C. Williams (eds.), *Sociology and Development*, 1974. A rare study of peasant ideology.

Coulson, Andrew. "Agricultural Politics in Mainland Tanzania," *Review of African Political Economy* #10, Sept.-Dec. 1977.

Klein, Martin (ed.) *Peasants in Africa: Historical and Contemporary Perspectives*, 1980.

Lofchie, Michael. "Political and Economic Origins of African Hunger," *Journal of Modern African Studies* 13:4 (Dec. 1975).

Palmer, R. and N. Parsons (eds.) *The Roots of Rural Poverty in Central and Southern Africa*, 1977.

Schumacher, E.J. *Politics, Bureaucracy and Rural Development in Senegal*, 1975.

Briggs, John. "Villagization and the 1974-6 Economic Crisis in Tanzania," *Journal of Modern African Studies* 17:4, Dec. 1979.

Raikes, Phil. *State and Agriculture in Tanzania*, 1980.

Raikes, Phil. "Rural Differentiation and Class Formation in Tanzania," *Journal of Modern African Studies* 17:4, Dec. 1979.

Lofchie, Michael. "Agrarian Crisis and Economic Liberalization in Tanzania," *Journal of Modern African Studies* 16:3, 1978.

Raikes, Phil. "Agrarian Crisis and Economic Liberalization in Tanzania: A Comment," *Journal of Modern African Studies* 17:2, 1979.

Samoff, Joel. "Underdevelopment and its Grass Roots in Africa," *Canadian Journal of African Studies* 14:1, 1980.

Clayton, Eric. "Kenya Agriculture and the I.L.O. Employment Mission—Six Years After," *Journal of Modern African Studies* 16:2, June 1978.

Steeves, Jeffrey. "Class Analysis of Rural Africa: The Kenya Tea Development Authority," *Journal of Modern African Studies* 16:1, March 1978.

Anthony, Kenneth. *Agricultural Change in Tropical Africa*, 1979.

Bernstein, Henry. "African Peasantries: A Theoretical Framework," *Journal of Peasant Studies* 16:4, July 1979.

Tosh, John. "The Cash-Crop Revolution in Tropical Africa: An Agricultural Reappraisal," *African Affairs*, 79, 314, Jan. 1980.

10. Industrialization, Cities and the Working Class

Questions
What was the nature of historical industrialization to the present?
Who is the working class, i.e., long-term residents, ethnic make-up, gender?
Describe contemporary living standards for different classes in cities.
What is a "labor aristocracy"? Is there one? So what?
How would you describe the political consciousness of the working class? What is
their critique? What do they want?

Bibliography

Jeffries, Richard. *Class, Power and Ideology in Ghana: The Railwaymen of Se-kondi.* N.Y.: Cambridge U., 1979.

Africa (special issue on "Small Towns in African Development") 49:3 (1979).

Bhagavan, M.R. *Inter-relations Between Technological Choices and Industrial Strategies in Third World Countries.* Res. Rpt. #49. Uppsala: Scandinavian Institute of African Studies, 1979.

Cohen, Robin. "Resistance and Hidden Forms of Consciousness Among African Workers," *Review of African Political Economy* 19 (Sept.-Dec. 1980).

Cunningham, Simon. *The Copper Industry of Zambia: Foreign Mining Companies in a Developing Country.* N.Y.: Praeger, 1981.

Nnoli, Okwudiba. "Ethnicity and the Working Class in Africa: Consciousness and Praxis," *Ufahamu* 10:1 and 2 (Fall and Winter, 1980-81).

Todd, David. "The Informal Sector and Zambian Employment Crisis," *J. of Modern African Studies* 18:3 (Sept. 1980).

Shildkrout, Enid. "Women's Work and Children's Work: Variations Among Moslems in Kano," in Sandra Wallman (ed.), *Social Anthropology of Work.* London: Academic Press, 1979.

Ferraro, Gary P. "Nairobi: Overview of an East African City," *African Urban Studies* 3 (1978-79).

Temple, Frederick T. and Nelle W. Temple, "The Politics of Public Housing in Nairobi," in Merillee Grindle (ed.), *Politics and Policy Implementation in the Third World,* Princeton: Princeton U., 1980.

Strobel, Margaret. *Muslim Women in Mombasa, 1900-1975.* New Haven: Yale Univ., 1979.

Sandbrook, Richard. *Proletarians and African Capitalism: The Kenyan Case 1960-1972,* 1975.

Sabot, R. *Economic Development and Urban Migration: Tanzania, 1900-1971,* 1979.

Elkan, Walter. "Is a Proletariat Emerging in Nairobi?" *Economic Development and Cultural Change* 24:4, July 1976.

Sandbrook, R. and R. Cohen (eds.) *The Development of an African Working Class.*

Gutkind, Peter. "The View from Below: Political Consciousness of the Urban Poor in Ibadan," *Cahiers d'Etudes Africaines* #57.

VanOnselen, C. *Chibaro: African Mine Labour in Southern Rhodesia 1900-1933,* 1976.

Gutkind, Peter, et al., (eds.). *African Labor History,* 1979.

Bienefeld, M.A. "Trade Unions, the Labour Process and the Tanzanian State," *Journal of Modern African Studies* 17:4, Dec., 1979.

11. Foreign Relations: MNCs, Aid, Trade, and the U.S.A.

Questions
What is the role and impact on MNCs?
Aid and trade: Why must Africa "run faster" in order to "stand still"?
U.S. policy toward Africa? from Carter to Reagan; the French connection; the "underside"—mercenaries, CIA, and the arms sales.
Why are the USSR and Cuba in Africa? To what extent are they?

Bibliography
LeoGrande, William M. *Cuba's Policy in Africa: 1959-1980*, 1980.

Libby, Ronald T. *Toward an Africanized U.S. Policy for Southern Africa: A Strategy for Increasing Political Leverage*, 1980.

Klare, Michael T. *Beyond the "Vietnam Syndrome": U.S. Interventionism in the 1980s*, 1981.

Klare, Michael T. and Cynthia Arnson. *Supplying Repression: U.S. Support for Authoritarian Regimes Abroad*, 1981.

Rothstein, Robert L. *The Third World and U.S. Foreign Policy: Cooperation and Conflict in the 1980s*, 1981.

Report of the Study Commission on U.S. Policy Toward Southern Africa. *South Africa: Time Running Out*. Berkeley: U. of Cal., 1981.

Halliday, Fred. *Soviet Policy in the Arc of Crisis*. Wash, D.C.: Institute for Policy Studies, 1981.

Bon, Daniel and Karen Mingst. "French Intervention in Africa: Dependence or Development," *Africa Today* 27:2 (1980).

Churchill, Ward. "U.S. Mercenaries in Africa: The Recruitment Network," *Africa Today* 27:2 (1980).

Adelman, Kenneth L. *African Realities*, 1980.

Weinstein, Warren and T.H. Henriksen (eds.) *Soviet and Chinese Aid to African Nations*. N.Y.: Praeger, 1980.

Bissell, Richard and Chester Crocker (eds.) *South Africa into the '80s*. Boulder, CO: Westview, 1980.

Ottaway, Marina. *Soviet and American Influence in the Horn of Africa*. N.Y.: Praeger, 1982.

Heldman, Dan C. *The USSR and Africa: Soviet Foreign Policy Under Krushchev*. N.Y.: Praeger, 1981.

Baade, R. and J. Calloway. "Economic Sanctions Against S. Africa: Policy Options," *Alternatives* 4:4 (1979).

Albright, David E. (ed.) *Communism in Africa*. Bloomington: Indiana U., 1980.

Kraus, Jon. "American Foreign Policy in Africa," *Current History* 80:464 (March 1981).

Kaplinsky, R. "Foreign Capital, Employment and Accumulation in Kenya," *Development and Change* 12 (1981).

Kaplinsky, R. *Multinationals in Kenya*.

Langdon, Steven W. "Export-Oriented Industrialization Through the Multinational Corporation: Evidence from Kenya," in Aamed Iaris-Soven et al., (eds.), *The World as a Company Town: Multinational Corporation and Social Change*. The Hague: Mouton, 1978.

Bender, Gerald. "Angola: Left, Right and Wrong," *Foreign Policy* (Summer 1981).

Klinghoffer, A.J. "The Soviet Union and Angola," in R.H. Donaldson (ed.), *The Soviet Union and the Third World*. London: Croom and Helm, 1980.

Biersteker, Thomas J. "Self-Reliance in Theory and Practice in Tanzanian Trade Relations," *International Organization* 34 (1980).

Mittelman, James H. "International Monetary Institutions and Policies of Socialism and Self-Reliance: Are They Compatible? The Tanzanian Experience," *Social Research* 47 (1980).

Stein, Leslie. *The Growth of East Africa Exports and Their Effect on Economic Development*. London: Croom and Helm, 1979.

Kaplinsky, R. "Export-Oriented Growth: A Large International Firm in a Small Developing Country," *World Development* 7 (1979).

Wachtel, Howard. "A Decade of International Debt," *Theory and Society* 9:3 (May 1980).

Aronson, Jonathan (ed.) *Debt and Less Developed Countries*, 1979.

Arnold, Guy. *Aid in Africa*, 1979.

Lappé, Frances Moore et al. *Aid as an Obstacle*, 1980.

Curry, R. "Africa's External Debt Situation," *J. of Modern African Studies* 17:1 (1979).

Lemarchand, Rene (ed.) *American Policy in Southern Africa: The Stakes and the Stance*. Wash., D.C.: U. Press of America, 1981.

Howe, R.W. "U.S. Policy in Africa," *Current History*, March 1979.

Whitaker, J.S. (ed.). *Africa and the U.S.*, 1978.

Cotter, William. "How AID Fails to Aid Africa," *Foreign Policy* 34, Spring, 1979.

Weissman, Stephen. "CIA Covert Action in Zaire and Angola: Patterns and Consequences," *Political Science Quarterly* 94:2, Summer 1979.

Brayton, Abbot. "Soviet Involvement in Africa," *Journal of Modern African Studies* 17:2, June 1979.

Gould, David. "The Problem of Seepage in International Development Assistance: Why U.S. Aid to Zaire Goes Astray," *Civilizations* 29, 3/4.

Ottaway, David. "Africa: U.S. Policy Eclipse," *Foreign Affairs* 58:3, 1980.

Bissell, Richard. "Soviet Policies in Africa," *Current History* 77:450, Oct. 1979.

Crocker, Chester and William Lewis. "Missing Opportunities in Africa," *Foreign Policy* #35, Summer 1979.

Macebah, Stanley. "Misreading Opportunities in Africa," *Foreign Policy* #35, Summer 1979.

Lemarchand, Rene. "The CIA in Africa," *Journal of Modern African Studies* 14:3, Sept. 1976.

Singleton, Seth. "Soviet Policy and Socialist Expansion in Asia and Africa," *Armed Forces and Society* 6:3, Spring 1980.

12. Strategies for Development and the Future of Africa

Questions

What is the contemporary situation again?

What are current economic strategies? How effective are they?

   —socialist Tanzania

   —capitalist Kenya

What is politically progressive in contemporary independent Africa?

Africa in the year 2000—what do you think it will look like?

Bibliography

Resnick, Idrian N. *The Long Transition: Building Socialism in Tanzania*, 1981.

Toward a New Strategy for Development (collection of papers). N.Y.: Pergamon Press, 1979.

Legum, Colin, et al. (eds.) *Africa in the 1980s: A Continent in Crisis*, N.Y.: McGraw-Hill, 1979.

Rosberg, Carl G. and Thomas Callaghy (eds.) *Socialism in Sub-Saharan Africa: A New Assessment*. Berkeley: Institute of International Studies, U. of Cal., 1979.

Aaby, Peter. *The State of Guinea-Bissau: African Socialism or Socialism in Africa?* Res. Report #45, Scandinavian Institute of African Studies, 1978.

Carter, Gwendolen and Patrick O'Meara (eds.) *Southern Africa: The Continuing Crisis*. Bloomington, Ind.: Indiana U., 1979.

Palmberg, Mai (ed.) *Problems of Socialist Orientation in Africa*. Uppsala: Scandinavian Inst. of African Studies, 1978.

Babu, Mohamed. *African Socialism or Socialism in Africa?* London: Zed Press, 1981.

Beckman, Bjorn. "Imperialism and Capitalist Transformation: Critique of a Kenyan Debate," *Review of African Political Economy* 19 (Sept.-Dec. 1980).

Barkan, Joel with John Okuma (eds.) *Politics and Public Policy in Kenya and Tanzania*. N.Y.: Praeger, 1979.

Price, Robert and C.G. Rosberg. *The Apartheid Regime*. Berkeley: Institute of International Studies, U. of Cal.

Brayton, Abbott. "The Future of Zimbabwe: An Overview," *Africa Today* 27:4 (1980).

Warr, Michael. "The Process of Class Conflict in Ethiopia," *Ufahamu* 10:1 and 2, (Fall and Winter, 1980-81).

Makgetta, Neva and Ann Seidman. *Outposts of Monopoly Capitalism: Southern Africa in the Changing Global Economy*. London: Lawrence-Hill, 1980.

Adam, Heribert. "Minority Monopoly in Transition: Recent Policy Shifts of the Southern African State," *J. of Modern African Studies* 18:4 (Dec. 1980).

Southall, Aidan. "Social Disorganization in Uganda: Before, During and After Amin," *J. of Modern African Studies* 18:4 (Dec. 1980).

Cohen, John M. "Analyzing the Ethiopian Revolution: A Cautionary Tale," *J. of Modern African Studies* 18:4 (1980).

Southall, Rodger. "New Perspectives on South Africa," *J. of Modern African Studies* 18:4 (December 1980).

Samoff, Joel. "Crises and Socialism in Tanzania," *J. of Modern African Studies* 19:2 (June 1981).

Carter, Gwendolyn. *Which Way is South Africa Going?*, 1980.

Davidson, Basil. *Crossroads in Africa*. Nottingham: Spokesman, 1980.

Clarence-Smith, W.G. "Class Structure and Class Struggles in Angola in the 1970s," *J. of Southern Africa Studies* 7:1 (Oct. 1980).

Marakakia, John. "No Longer a Hidden War: Recent Writers on the Eritrean Nationalist Struggle," *J. of Modern African Studies* 19:2 (1981).

Freud, William. "Class Conflict, Political Economy and the Struggle for Socialism in Tanzania," *African Affairs* 80:321 (Oct. 1981).

Sandbrook, Richard. "Is Socialism Possible in Africa?" *J. Commonwealth and Comparative Politics* 19:2 (July 1981).

Contours of the Current Crisis in Central America

José Jorge Simán   *Spring 1982*
Latin American Studies 90/University of North Carolina/
Chapel Hill, NC 27514

There is every indication that in the years ahead Central America will remain of crucial significance to the study of Latin America and U.S.-Latin American relations. The region not only reflects many of the traditional problems of development in the Third World, but has also assumed strategic importance as a social laboratory for competing ideologies of change.

With the interest of opening some windows on such actual topics, this seminar intends to present for discussion the issues and instruments that will help in better understanding such an explosive situation.

This seminar will introduce the participants into a basic working knowledge of the Central American region. We will explore together the different scenarios and actors, from distinct perspectives. Experts from the region and the Institute of Latin American Studies at UNC will lecture, illustrating some of the topics on which we will focus. It is my purpose to present balanced readings of the many different visions of the Central American reality.

The study of the people of Central America is the underlying core and force of the seminar, even if the people of the region do not appear explicitly named as the actors. The course will attempt to foster empathy to the people of the isthmus.

Required texts

1. Ralph Lee Woodward, Jr., *Central America—A Nation Divided* (New York: Oxford University Press), 1976.
2. Marvin E. Gettleman et al., (editors), *El Salvador: Central America in the New Cold War* (New York: Grove Press), 1981.
3. *Latin American Perspectives*, Issues 25 and 26, Spring and Summer, 1980.
4. Richard R. Fagen, *The Nicaraguan Revolution, A Personal Report* (Washington, D.C.: Institute for Policy Studies), 1981.
5. Hector M. Dada Hirezi, *Why The Christian Democrats of El Salvador Abandoned The Government and Their Party*, (Washington, D.C.: Epica), 1981.

For the participants who can read Spanish, there will be for their voluntary use material on each of the units. The participants in the seminar should research every week a topic that will be assigned at the beginning of the course in the following periodicals: *Salpress, Agencia Independiente de Prensa*, FBIS *(Foreign Broadcast*

Information Service), *Christian Science Monitor*, *New York Times*, *Washington Post*, and *The Weekly Edition of the Manchester Guardian*. There will be a five minute presentation every other class by the participants.

Course Outline
Introduction (January 13)

Unit 1 Historical Overview (January 18)

Unit 1.1 Historical Viewpoint
Required Readings:
*R.L. Woodward, Ch. 1, *The Isthmus* (17 pages)
*T.D. Allman, *Rising to Rebellion* (16 pages)
*U.S. Department of State, *El Salvador: The Search for Peace* (11 pages)
*Rep. Gerry E. Studds, "Central America, 1981—A Report to the House Committee on Foreign Affairs" (39 pages)
*E. Torres-Rivas, *Seven Keys to Understanding the Central American Crisis* (12 pages)
*A. Riding, *Central America from the Inside* (12 pages)
En Español:
Gregoria, Selser en *Centroamérica en Crisis*, "Centroamerica entre la atrocidad y la esperanza" (21 pages)

Unit 2 Failure of the Union (January 20)

Unit 2.1 The Honduras-El Salvador War
Required Readings:
*R.L. Woodward, *The Failure of Reunification*, Ch. 9 (9 pages)
*T.L. Karnes, *Background of Separatism, A Judgment*, Ch. I, XI (21 pages)
*C. Castillo, Ch. 7 (8 pages)
*F.D. Parker, *The Futból Conflict and Central American Unity* (15 pages)
*J. Mallin, *Salvador-Honduras War, 1969: The Soccer War* (5 pages)
*E. Richter, *Latin American Perspectives*, "Social Classes, Accumulation, and the Crisis of 'Overpopulation' in El Salvador" (26 pages)
*W.H. Durham, *Conclusion*, Ch. VI (15 pages)

Unit 3 Mass-Media Overview (January 25-27)

Unit 3.1 Mass-Media Structures in the Region and Their Influence

Unit 3.2 How the Mass-Media Informs about the Region in the United States
Required Readings:
*C. Brown and F. Moreno, *The Press and El Salvador* (6 pages)
*J.E. Maslow and A. Arana, *Operation El Salvador* (6 pages)
*J.E. Maslow, *The Junta and the Press: A Family Affair* (6 pages)
*"Forgotten Trabajadores," *The Wall Street Journal*, October 19, 1981.
*A. Neier, "Drawing the Line at the W.S.J.," *The Nation*, November 14, 1981.
*A.J. Cruz, "Nicaragua Needs U.S. Tolerance," *The New York Times*, December 9, 1981.
*"The 'No Choice' Hustle," *The Wall Street Journal*, December 10, 1981.

Unit 4 Socio-Economic Development (February 1-3)

Unit 4.1 The Central American Common Market
Required Readings:
*E. Torres-Rivas, "The Central American Model of Growth: Crisis for Whom?" in *Latin American Perspectives* (20 pages)
*I. Cohen and G. Rosenthal, *The International Aspects of the Crisis in Central America* (39 pages)
*C.M. Castillo, Chs. 4, 5, 6 and 7 (40 pages)
*I. Cohen Orantes, Chs. 3 and 6 (17 pages)
E. Galeano, "Introduction," pp. 11-21 (8 pages) and "King Sugar and other Agricultural Monarchs," pp. 119-129 (10 pages) in *Open Veins of Latin America*
Recommended Readings:
Ph.C. Schmitter, *Autonomy or Dependence as Regional Integration Outcomes: Central America* (77 pages)
F. Villagran-Kramer, *Central America in Transition From the 60's to the 80's* (25 pages)
En Español:
R. Mayorga Q., *Centroamérica en los años ochenta* (17 pages)
R. Mayorga Q., *El crecimiento desigual en Centroamérica (1950-1980)* (176 pages)
CEPAL, Notas sobre el transfondo histórico del desarollo económico (41 pages)
CEPAL, Centroamerica: Evolución económica desde la postguerra (118 pages)
CEPAL, Antecedentes para el estudio sobre la pobreza, satisfacción de necesidades basicas y distribucion del ingreso en el itsmo centroamericano. Una approximación inicial (38 pages)

Unit 5 The Agrarian Question (February 8-10)

Unit 5.1 El Salvador's Case—Agrarian Reform: Pros and Cons
Required Readings:
*R. Prosterman et al., *Land Reform and the El Salvador Crisis* (21 pages)
*W.C. Thiesenhusen, *El Salador's Land Reform: Was it Programmed to Fail?* (5 pages)
*J.C. Stephens, Jr. (ed.), *Conference on Land Tenure in Central America*, March 23, 1981 (48 pages)
C. Castillo, Ch. 3, pp. 29-37 (8 pages)
*M. Chapin, *A Few Comments on Land Tenure and the Course of Agrarian Reform in El Salvador* (mimeo) (43 pages)
*M.E. Gettleman et al. (eds.), *El Salvador: Central America in the New Cold War* #23-28, pp. 157-188
Recommended Readings:
R.L. Woodward, *Coffee Republics and Banana Republics*, Ch. 6-7, (54 pages)
L.R. Simon and J.C. Stephens, Jr., *El Salvador Land Reform 1980-1981*, impact audit (70 pages)
G. Huizer, "A Field Experience in Central America: The Rationality of Distrust," *The Revolutionary Potential of Peasants in Latin America*, pp. 21-30 (9 pages)
D. Browning, *El Salvador: Landscape and Society* (Especially chapters 3, 5, 6, and 7)
R. Adams, *Crucifixion by Power* (Especially pp. 353-380; 394-407)
T. and M. Melville, *Guatemala: The Politics of Land Ownership* (Especially 107-119; 61-74; 390-401)
P. Wheaton, *Agrarian Reform in El Salvador: A Program of Rural Pacification* (21 pages)

Roy L. Prosterman et al., "Land Reform in El Salvador: The Democratic Alternative," *World Affairs*, Vol. 144, #1 (Summer 1981), pp. 36-54
En español:
ECA 356/357 and 335/336 *Guatemala: Drama y Conflicto Social y Transformacion Agraria*

Unit 6 The Agro-Export Oligarchy (February 15)
Take Home Exam
Required Reading:
*W. LeoGrande and Carla A. Robbins, *Oligarchs and Officers: The Crisis in El Salvador* (11 pages)
*M. Ayau, *What to do about El Salvador?* (3 pages)
*R. Mayorga Q., *El Salvador: Between Tragedy and Hope* (23 pages)
*P. Heath Hoeffel, *The Eclipse of the Oligarchs* (9 pages)
Recommended Readings:
Testimony of Dr. Cleto DI Giovani, Jr., before the Latin American Affairs Subcommittee—U.S. House of Representatives, May 20, 1980 (4 pages)
Statement by Mario Sulit, Member, Board of Directors, American Chamber of Commerce in El Salvador before House Foreign Affairs Subcommittee, April 29, 1980, (5 pages)
Statement of Enrique Altamirano before the House Appropriation Foreign Operations Subcommittee, April 29, 1981, (12 pages)

Unit 7 The Church (February 17-22)

Unit 7.1 Monsignor Romero
Take home exam due February 22
Required Readings:
*C. Jerez S.J., "The Church in Central America" (20 pages)
*B. Bonpane, "The Church and Revolutionary Struggle in Central America," *Latin American Perspectives* (12 pages)
*J.J. Simán, "Romero: 'Building God's Kingdom Here' " (4 pages)
*T. Quigley, "Remembering a Bishop" (3 pages)
*Richard R. Fagen, "Nicaraguan Bishops," *The Nicaraguan Revolution on Socialism* (1 page)
*P. Edmonds, "Oklahoma Priest Murdered in Guatemala" (4 pages)
*P. Lernoux, "Notes on a Revolutionary Church: Human Rights in Latin America," *Latin America—Crisis of the Old Order and a Non-Violent Revolution* (16 pages)
*M. d'Escoto, "Nicaragua and the World" (8 pages)
*M.E. Gettleman et al. (eds.), *El Salvador: Central America in the New Cold War*, Ch. IV, pp. 188-213, #29-33
P. Lernoux, "Be a Patriot (in El Salvador) and Kill a Priest," Ch. 3, pp. 61-81, *Cry of the People* (20 pages)
Recommended Readings:
G. Gutierrez, M., "From the Colonial Church to Medellin" (9 pages)
J. Sobrino S.J., "The Witness of the Church in Latin America" (26 pages)
K. Greenhalg and M. Gruenke, editors, "The Guatemala: Church Martyred" (38 pages)
O. Romero and A. Rivera Dama, "The Church, Political Organization and Violence" (14 pages)

M. Dodson, "Prophetic Politics and Political Theory in Latin America" (21 pages)

G. Arroyo, "The Ideological and Cultural Action of the Church" (6 pages)

Nicaraguan Bishops, "Christian Commitment for a New Nicaragua" (5 pages)

M. Lange and R. Iblacker, "Campesinos in Central America and God came to El Salvador" (36 pages)

P. Lernoux, *Cry of the People*, "The Church Role, Ch. X, pp. 363-408 and "The Church Divided," Ch. XI , pp. 409-448

T.S. Montgomery, "The Church in El Salvador: Profile of a Country in Revolution"

D. Keogh, *Romero: El Salvador's Martyr*, Chs. 2-5

Unit 8 Doctrine of National Security (February 24)
Required Readings:

*A. Nina, *Nueva Sociedad*, "The Doctrine of National Security and Latin America Integration" (15 pages)

*P. Lernoux, *Cry of the People*, "The Doctrine of National Security—Terror—The U.S. Teaches Latin America How," Ch. 6 (48 pages)

*N. Chomsky and E. Herman, *The Washington Connection and Third World Fascism—The Political Economy of Human Rights*, Vol. 1, pp. 242-263

En español:

J. Comblin, La doctrina de la seguridad nacional (8 pages)

F. Flores Pinel, El estado de seguridad nacional en El Salvador, un fenómeno de crisis hegemónica (26 pages)

Film (March 1)

Unit 9 The Military (March 3)

Unit 9.1 Condeca, Personal Dictators, Southern Command (March 17)
Required Readings:

*J. Saxe-Fernandez, *Latin American Radicalism*, "The Central American Defense Council and Pan Americana," pp. 75-101

*Gil et al., "From Oligarchy Republic to Personal Dictators," pp. 9-17

*M.E. Gettleman et al. (eds.), *El Salvador: Central America in the New Cold War*, #5, 33-34-38, 39, 40, 41, 48, pp. 216-229, 263-282, 327-333

Recommended Readings:

R. Millet, *Guardians of the Dynasty*, Chs. 7, 10, 11, pp. 145-169, 223-267.

R. Adams, "The Development of the Military," *Crucifixion by Power*, pp. 238-278

D.L. Etchison, *The United States and Militarism in Central America*, pp. 1-50

C. Arnson, *The Salvadoran Military and Regime Transformation*

D. Miller and C. Arnson, *Background Information on El Salvador and U.S. Military Assistance to Central America, 1980*

C. Arnson, *Background Information on El Salvador and U.S. Military Assistance to Central America, 1981*

D. Miller, C. Arnson and R. Seeman, *Background Information on Guatemala and U.S. Military Assistance to Central America, 1981*

U.S. Military Involvement in El Salvador 1947-1980 (28 pages)

William R. Thompson, "Regime Vulnerability and Military Takeovers," *Comparative Politics*, vii, 4 (July 1975)

William R. Thompson, "Systematic Change and the Latin American Military Coup," *Comparative Policy Studies*, vii, (Jan. 1975), pp. 441-59

Karen Remmer, "Evaluating The Policy Impact of Military Regimes in Latin America," *LARR* (Summer 1978)

Richard Rawkin, "The Expanding Institutional Concerns of the Latin American Military Establishments: A Review Article," *LARR* (Spring 1974)

Alain Rouquie, "Military Revolution and National Independence," in a volume edited by Phillippe Schmitten, *Military Rule in Latin America* (Sage, 1973)

Spring Break (March 8-10)

Mid-Term Exam (March 15)

Unit 10 The External Actor: International Relations—United States (March 22-24)

Unit 10.1 Intervention?
Required Readings:
*C. Fuentes, "Where Anglos Should Fear to Tread" (3 pages)
*L. Tambs, "Guatemala, Central America and the Caribbean" (7 pages)
*E. Kenworthy, "The U.S. and Latin America: Empire vs. Social Change" (11 pages)
*A. Cavalla Rojas, "U.S. Military Strategy in Central America: From Carter to Reagan" (17 pages)
M.E. Gettleman, et al. (eds.), *El Salvador: Central America in the New Cold War*, pp. 229-263, 380-390, 35-38, 54
Dissent Paper on El Salvador and Central America (16 pages)
Ph. Agee, "Critique of State Department White Paper" (25 pages)
*FDR-FMLN, "On Elections and Political Solution" (5 pages)
C. Menges, "Central America and Its Enemies" (7 pages)
M. Williams, "U.S. Chances Missed in El Salvador" (5 pages)
Recommended Readings:
P. Lernoux, *Cry of the People*, "The U.S. Connection," pp. 449-459 and "U.S. Capitalism and the Multinationals," pp. 203-236
T.R. Whelan, *Through the American Looking Glass: Central America's Crisis* (87 pages)
E. Galeano, *Guatemala: Occupied Country*, pp. 69-83, 103-115
E. Feinberg, "Central America: No Easy Answers," in *Foreign Affairs*, Spring, 1981, pp. 1121-1146
Prepared statement of Dr. William LeoGrande before the Subcommittee on Foreign Affairs, U.S. House of Representatives, March 5, 1981 (14 pages)
Prepared statement by Robert S. Leiken, before the Subcommittee on Inter-American Affairs, U.S. House of Representatives, September 24, 1981 (47 pages)
T. Gilbert and P. Joris, "American Involvement in Latin America," *Global Interference: The Consistent Pattern of American Foreign Policy*, pp. 21-34
F.J. Devine, *El Salvador: Embassy under Attack*, pp. 35-43, 122-130, 151-167
Fachres, *Symposium on El Salvador and U.S. Policy in the Region* (38 pages)
H. Gonzales, "When Is Military Aid Justified? The Case of El Salvador," *InterAmerican Economic Affairs*, Autumn, 1981, pp. 71-83
L. Schoultz, "Conclusions," *Human Rights and U.S. Policy Toward Latin America*, pp. 344-381
A. Hadar, *El Salvador: The Struggle for Democracy and U.S. Involvement* (25 pages)

Unit 11 Political Participation: Political Actions

Unit 11.1 Popular Organization, Political Parties, Political Military Groups
Required Readings:
*C. Forches, "El Salvador: An Aide Memoire" (9 pages)
*H. Dada Hirezi, "Why the Christian Democrats of El Salvador Abandoned the Government and their Party" (23 pages)
V. Navarro et al., "A Report on the Meeting of the Permanent Tribunal of the Peoples on the Violation of Human Rights in El Salvador" (13 pages)
*Gil et al., "The Salvadoran Model of 1948-1972" (53 pages)
*Gil et al., "Perspectives on Democracy in Guatemala," pp. 8-26
*Gil et al., "Political Groups in Somoza's Nicaragua," pp. 49-68
*M.E. Gettleman et al., (eds.), *El Salvador: Central America in the New Cold War*, #5-22, pp. 57-157
Recommended Readings:
Ch. W. Anderson, "Central American Political Parties: A Functional Approach," *Western Political Quarterly*, XV (1962), (14 pages)
T.S. Montgomery, *El Salvador: Profile of a Nation in Revolution*, "The Revolutionary Organizations"
En Español:
H. Assmann (ed.), *El Juego de los reformismos frente a la Revolucion en Centroamerica*
CEDAL, "La Situacion política de Centroamerica"

Film (April 5)

Unit 12 The "Dominoes" in Central America (April 7)
Required Readings:
M.E. Gettleman et al. (eds.), *El Salvador: Central America in the New Cold War*, #1-5; 42-47; 49 pp. 3-57; 283-318; 327-333
Committee of SantaFe, "A New Inter-American Policy for the Eighties," (53 pages)

Unit 13 Revolution and Counterinsurgency: El Salvador—Guatemala (April 14-19)

Unit 13.1 Revolution in Nicaragua
Required Readings:
*R.R. Fagen, "The Nicaraguan Revolution—A Personal Report" (32 pages)
*R. Mauro Maurini, "The Nicaraguan Revolution and the Central American Revolutionary Process" (5 pages)
G. Aguilera P., "Terror and Violence as Weapons of Counterinsurgency in Guatemala" *Latin American Perspectives*, (22 pages)
*A. Riding, "Guatemala: Revolution and Reaction in Central America" (10 pages)
*M.E. Gettleman et al., *El Salvador: Central America in the New Cold War*, #50-53, pp. 339-380
Recommended Readings:
T. Anderson, "Matanza: El Salvador's Communist Revolt in 1932"
Latin American Perspectives, "The Nicaraguan Revolution," Issue 29, Vol. VIII, No. 2, Spring, 1981
Information Bulletin, "Political Diplomatic Commission FMLN-FDR," October 16, 1981 (13 pages)
Organization of American States Human Right's Commission, *Report on Guatemala*, October 14, 1981, (134 pages)
"Revolution," *El Salvador: From Coordination to Unity* (35 pages)

Panel Discussion (April 21)

Recommended Reserved Reading List

Adams, Richard. *Crucifixion by Power* (Austin: University of Texas Press), 1971.

Anderson, Thomas P. *Matanza: El Salvador's Community Revolt of 1932* (Lincoln: Nebraska Press), 1981.

Anderson, Thomas P. *The War of the Dispossessed: Honduras and El Salvador 1969,* (Lincoln: Nebraska Press), 1981.

Browning, David. *El Salvador, Landscape and Society* (Oxford: Clarendon Press), 1971.

Castillo, Carlos M. *Growth and Integration in Central America* (New York: Praeger), 1966.

Chomsky, Noam and Edward S. Herman. *The Washington Connection and Third World Fascism: The Political Economy of Human Rights,* Vol. 1 (Boston: South End Press), 1979.

Cohen, Isaac Orantes. *Regional Integration in Central America* (Lexington: D.C. Heath and Company), 1973.

Devine, Frank J. *El Salvador: Embassy Under Attack* (New York: Vantage Press), 1981.

Durham, William H. *Scarcity and Survival in Central America* (Stanford: Stanford Press), 1979.

Ethison, Don L. *The United States and Militarism in Central America* (New York: Praeger), 1975.

Galeano, Eduardo. *Guatemala: Occupied Country* (London: Monthly Review Press), 1973.

Gilbert, Tony and Pierre Joris. *Global Interference: The Consistent Pattern of American Foreign Policy* (London: Liberation), 1981.

Greenhalgh, Kurt and Mark Gruenke (editors). *The Church Martyred: Guatemala* (Minneapolis: Guatemala Solidarity Committee of Minnesota), 1981.

Gutierrez, Merino Gustavo. *From the Colonial Church to Medellin* (Washington, D.C.: CECOP), 1970.

Hadar, Arnon. *El Salvador: The Struggle for Democracy and U.S. Involvement* (San Francisco: Casa El Salvador), 1981.

Hadar, Arnon. *Revolution in El Salvador: from Coordination to Unity* (San Francisco: Popular Press), 1981.

Horowitz, Irving Louis, Josue de Castro and John Gerassi. *Latin American Radicalism* (New York: Vintage Books), 1969.

Huizer, Gerrit. *The Revolutionary Potential of Peasants in Latin America* (Lexington: D.C. Heath and Company), 1972.

Iblacker, Reinhold and Martin Large. *Witnesses of Hope: The Persecution of Christians in Latin America* (Maryknoll: Orbis Books), 1981.

Karnes, Thomas L. *The Failure of Union* (Chapel Hill: UNC Press), 1961.

Keogh, Dermot. *Romero: El Salvador's Martyr.* (Dublin: Dominican Publications), 1981.

Lernoux, Penny. *Cry of the People* (New York: Doubleday), 1980.

Lernoux, Penny. *Notes on a Revolutionary Church: Human Rights in Latin America* (Alice Patterson), 1978.

Melville, Marjorie and Thomas. *Guatemala: The Politics of Land Ownership* (New York: The Free Press), 1971.

Millett, Richard. *Guardians of Dynasty* (Maryknoll, Orbis Book), 1977.

Montgomery, Tommie Sue. *El Salvador: Profile of a Nation in Revolution.*

Nicaraguan Bishops. *Christian Commitment for a New Nicaragua* (London: CIIR), 1981.

Nueva Sociedad, Special Issue 1977. (San Jose: Nuevo Sociedad, 1977).

Parker, Franklin D. *The Central American Republics* (New York: Oxford University Press), 1964.

Romero, Oscar and Arturo Rivera Damas. *The Church, Political Organization and Violence* (London: CIIR), 1979.

Schmitter, Philippe C. *Autonomy and Dependence as Regional Integration Outcomes: Central America* (Berkeley: University California Press), 1972.

Schoultz, Lars. *Human Rights and United States Policy Toward Latin America* (Princeton, Princeton Press), 1981.

Simon, Lawrence R., and James C. Stephens, Jr. *El Salvador Land Reform 1980-1981 Impact-Audit* (Boston: Oxfam), 1981.

Sobrino, Ion S.J. *The Witness of the Church in Latin America* (Maryknoll: Orbis Books, 1981).

Stephens, James C., Jr. (coordinator)*Conference on Land Tenure in Central America* (Johns Hopkins University, Washington, D.C.: WOLA), 1981.

Symposium on El Salvador and U.S. Policy in the Region held at University of California, Berkeley, (San Francisco: Solidarity Press), 1981.

U.S. Military Involvement in El Salvador 1947-1980 (San Francisco: Solidarity Press), 1981.

Webre, Stephen. *Jose Napoleon Duarte and the Christian Democratic Party in Salvadoran Policies, 1960-72* (Baton Rouge: Louisiana State University Press), 1979.

Wheaton, Philip. *Agrarian Reform in El Salvador: A Program of Rural Pacification* (Washington, D.C.: EPICA), 1980.

Whelan, James R. *Through the American Glass: Central America's Crisis* (Washington, D.C.: Council for Inter-American Security), 1980.

Alternative Futures

Future Society
Lester Milbrath, State University of New York at Buffalo

The Relations of Humanity
Chadwick Alger, Ohio State University

Alternative Urban Futures
Jeanne Howard, Virginia Polytechnic Institute

The Future
Richard K. Curtis, Indiana University

Imaging
Roy King, Wittenberg University

Toward a Human World Order
Gerald and Patricia Mische, College of Saint Teresa

Alternative Visions
Joseph Miller, Saint Mary's College

Alternative World Futures
Christine Sylvester, Gettysburg College

Future Society

Lester Milbrath   *Spring 1982*
Environmental Studies 778/State University of New York/
Buffalo, NY 14261

Students of society are confronted with many predictions about the future, some dire and some optimistic. Most futurists seem to agree that there will be change and that it probably will be swift. How do futurists arrive at their predictions? What assumptions do they make? What models do they employ? What time frame do they use? What physical space (geographic or extraterrestrial) do they use?

The course will be divided into four parts. The first part will focus on futures forecasting methods. The best overview of these methods is contained in a book edited by Jib Fowles and titled, *Handbook of Futures Research.*

Part two will examine several widely known forecasts (forecasting traditions) for their characteristics and validity. Some of this material is contained in the Fowles *Handbook* but Jones, *Options for the Future: A Comparative Analysis of Policy Oriented Forecasts* speaks directly to the topic. Magda McHale's *Ominous Trends and Valid Hopes* also compares several well-known recent forecasts.

Part three of the course will address the most prominent debate about the future: Can we continue to grow in population and economic activity or must we limit our growth? A subsidiary question is: Can we develop a sustainable society and how would such a society work? William Catton's new book, *Overshoot: The Ecological Basis of Revolutionary Change* speaks to the issue.

The fourth part of the course will be devoted to student research reports. Preparation for and writing the report will constitute the "research paper" requirement of the course.

Required Texts
Fowles, ed., *Handbook of Futures Research*
Catton, *Overshoot: The Ecological Basis of Revolutionary Change*
Jones, *Options for the Future*
McHale, *Ominous Trends and Valid Hopes*

Part I Futures Forecasting Methods
January 25 Introduction to the seminar, futures forecasting, futures centers, futures publications, bibliography
Jib Fowles, "An Overview of Social Forecasting Procedures."
Note also the appendix to the *Handbook of Futures Research,* pp. 803-806 which cites journals, periodic reports, graduate programs, and orgnizations.

Set of excerpts from *Congressional Record* by Toffler, Kahn, Forrester, Schumacher, Mead.

February 1, 8   Methods for Future Forecasting
Futures Handbook, preface and pp. 1-66, 67-224.
Three articles on "The Futures Field" by Roy Amara in *The Futurist*

February 22, March 1   Methods (continued)
Futures Handbook, pp. 225-328, 329-448.
Jones, *Options*, pp. VII-XII, and 1-67, 68-110.

March 8, 15   Substantive Futures Research
Futures Handbook, pp. 449-570, 571-692.
Jones, *Options*, pp. 111-143.
McHale, *Ominous*, Part I, "Critical World Trends," pp. 9-64.

March 22   No Class—Mid-Semester Recess

March 29   The Future of Futures Research
Futures Handbook, pp. 693-801.
Jones, *Options*, pp. 147-187.

April 5   Overshoot
Catton, *Overshoot*, pp. VII-XVII and 1-92.

April 12   Ecological Understanding
Catton, *Overshoot*, pp. 93-180.

April 19   Growth or Sustainable Society?
Catton, *Overshoot*, pp. 181-209.
Jones, *Options*, pp. 188-304.

April 26   Living with a New Reality
Catton, *Overshoot*, pp. 211-270.
Yankelovich, "New Rules" (on reserve in ESC).

May 3   Options for the Future
McHale, *Ominous*, pp. 66-131.
Jones, *Options*, pp. 305-311.
Yankelovich and Lefkowitz, "The New American Dream" from *The Futurist*, (Aug. 1980) (on reserve in ESC).

Bibliography

Adams, D., *Conceptual Blockbusting*, San Francisco, Freeman, 1974. An exploration of the creative process including individual and group exercises.

Baier, K., Rescher, N., *Values and the Future*, New York, Free Press, 1969. The role of human values in our transition to the future. Essays by prominent futurists.

Bandura, A., *Social Learning Theory*, Englewood Cliffs, Prentice-Hall, 1977.

Bateson, G. *Steps to An Ecology of Mind*, New York, Ballantine, 1972. A revolutionary approach to man's understanding of himself, a book which develops a new way of thinking about the nature of order and organization in living systems. A book that is, unfortunately, more discussed than read.

Bell, D., *The Coming of the Post-Industrial Society*, New York, Basic Books, 1973.

A venture in social forecasting. One of the more frequently cited books in the futurist literature.

Boulding, K., *Eco-Dynamics*, Beverly Hills, Sage Publications, 1978. A new theory of societal evolution.

Brown, Harrison, *The Human Future Revisited: The World Predicament and Possible Solutions*, New York, Norton, 1978. An updating of his earlier classic, *The Challenge of Man's Future:* focuses on resources and society.

Conway, F., Siegelman, J., *Snapping*, Philadelpia, Lippincott, 1978. Deals with the phenomenon of apparent instant conversions, sudden personality changes, and the theories and dynamics that help us understand these bewildering personal alterations.

Cornish, E., *The Study of the Future*, Washington, World Future Society, 1977. An excellent introduction to the historical development of the future's movement and to current methods of exploring the future.

de Chardin, T., *The Phenomenon of Man*, New York, Harper and Row, 1965. A theological analysis of the evolution of the universe and of man.

de Jouvenel, B., *The Art of Conjecture*, New York, Basic Books, 1967. A classic futurist work by the man many consider to be the father of the futurist movement. A thought provoking work.

Deutsch, K., Fritsch, B., Jaquaribe, H., Markovits, A., *Problems of World Modeling*, Cambridge, Mass., Ballinger, 1977. A compilation of papers from a conference on World Modeling.

Edmunds, S., *Alternative U.S. Futures*, Santa Monica, Goodyear, 1978.

Falk, Richard A., *A Study of Future Worlds*, New York, The Free Press, 1975. An examination of the present world and a design for a new world order.

Fuller, B., *Ideas and Integrities*, New York, Collier, 1963. A rich assortment of ideas from the wide ranging mind of Bucky Fuller, a perennial futurist.

Galtung, Johan, *The True Worlds: A Transnational Perspective*, New York, The Free Press, 1980. Written by a Norwegian sociologist, it is an examination of why the world is the way it is and what it's likely to be like in the future.

Hamrin, Robert, *Managing Growth in the 1980's: Toward a New Economics*, New York, Praeger, 1980. One of the few books by an economist that escapes the "economics paradigm."

Harman, W., *An Incomplete Guide to the Future*, San Francisco, San Francisco Book Co., 1976. A concise work by the former Director of the Stanford Research Institute. Willis Harman is a prominent futurist.

Henderson, H. *Creating Alternative Futures*, New York, Berkley, 1978. A series of essays forecasting revolutionary changes in our economic thinking.

Highwater, J., *The Primal Mind*, New York, Harper and Row, 1981. A contrast and critique of western civilization's modes of thought by an American Indian author raised in both traditions.

Hofstadter, D.R., *Godel, Escher, Bach*, New York, Vintage, 1979. This is an intellectual fugue; a brilliant explanation of formal systems and a joyful tour of some challenging intellectual mazes.

Kahn, H., Brown, W., Martel, L., *The Next 200 Years*, New York, Morrow, 1976. A rosy look at the future by the world's most famous optimistic futurist.

Kothari, Rajni, *Footsteps Into the Future: Diagnosis of the Present World and a Design for an Alternative*, New York, The Free Press, 1974. Written by an Indian social scientist from a Third World perspective.

Lakein, A., *How to Get Control of Your Time and Your Life*, New York, Signet, 1973. A personal exercise in planning your own life, which has the added benefit of revealing how inept individuals and institutions are at planning and setting priorities for the future.

Leff, H.L., *Experience, Environment and Human Potential*, New York, Oxford, 1978. A text for Environmental Psychology from the perspective of a futurist.

McHale, J., *The Future of the Future*, New York, Ballantine Book, 1969. An excellent introduction to an ecological perspective by the late Director of the Center for Integrative Studies which is now based at SUNYAB.

McHale, John, *World Facts and Trends*, New York, Collier Books, 1972, updated 1979. An excellent introductory walk through a world perspective and its ancillary data.

Mead, M., *Culture and Commitment*, New York, Columbia University Press, 1978. On the new relations between the generations in the 1970's.

Mead, M., *New Lives for Old*, New York, Morrow, 1975. An account of how one primitive tribe accomplished the transition to modern society in a twenty-five year period.

Platt, J., *The Step to Man*, New York, Wiley, 1966. This book is concerned with the evolving nature of man, social and intellectual, what he is and what he may become.

Ridker, Ronald G., and William Watson, *To Choose a Future: Resource and Environmental Consequences of Alternative Growth Paths.* Baltimore, John Hopkins University Press, 1980. A methodological and data contribution to the growth debate constituting a refutation of the "Limits to Growth" projections.

Robertson, J., *The Sane Alternative*, St. Paul, River Basin, 1980.

Sargeant, W., *Battle for the Mind*, New York, Harper & Row, 1973.

Schumacher, E., *Small is Beautiful*, New York, Harper and Row, 1973. Economics as if people mattered.

Stanford Research Institute, *Changing Images of Man*, Menlo Park, California, 1974. A monograph offering an interdisciplinary analysis of the historical development of our images of man, and the effects such images have on our views of the future.

Pirages, Dennis C., ed., *The Sustainable Society: Implications for Limited Growth*, N.Y. Praeger, 1977. Collected papers from a conference on this topic. Good selection.

Toffler, A., *Future Shock*, New York, Random House, 1970. The "Pop" version of futurist thinking. Nevertheless, it is stimulating and mind stretching.

Weinberg, G., *An Introduction to General Systems Thinking*, New York, Wiley, 1975. A meta-level perspective of laws about laws.

Waddington, C., *Tools for Thought*, New York, Basic Books, 1977. How to understand and apply the latest scientific techniques of problem solving.

Wolfe, Alan, *America's Impasse: The Rise and Fall of the Politics of Growth*, New York, Pantheon Books, 1981. An historical analysis of American politics, post World War II, assessing the origins of the current impasse in American society.

The Relations of Humanity

Chadwick Alger   *Winter 1982*
Political Science 760/Ohio State University/Columbus, OH 44115

The purpose of this seminar is to enable participants to pose alternative futures, from a global perspective, for relations among large human groups based upon knowledge about past and present experience. The first part of the seminar will develop perspectives necessary for this task under the following topics:

1. *Some Historical Perspectives,* beginning with relations between civilizations across the Eurasian continent, trade, migration, spread of religions and inventions, etc., in the early Christian era.
2. *The Search for Units of Analysis* for perceiving and studying relations of humanity by anthropologists, economists, geographers, historians, political scientists and sociologists (e.g., community, culture, ecumene, ecumenopolis, intelligible fields, nation-state, world society, world system, etc.).
3. *Evolving Paradigms through which U.S. Political Scientists View the World,* as reflected in the slow modification of the traditional nation-state paradigm in the study of international relations by the addition of what has customarily been called "transnational relations."
4. *Boundaries, Borders, Frontiers,* in the light of a world perceived to consist of a diversity of overlapping units, such as nations, cultures, states, societies, systems, etc. Are borders barriers or hinges?
5. *Participation* in relations of humanity in the context of nations, ethnic groups, local communities, citizen movements, etc. Particular concern will be devoted to the possibility for creating widely expanded educational programs and organized opportunities for self-conscious citizen participation in the relations of humanity.

In the second part of the seminar the broad perspective developed in the first part will be employed in exploration of a number of "laboratories" in which the relations of humanity occur:

6. *Regions, Provinces, Cities and Towns.*
7. *Social Science.*
8. *Voluntary Development Agencies.*
9. *Transnational Corporations.*
10. *Labor.*
11. *Information.*
12. *Tourism.*

Written Assignments
A paper of 5 to 10 pages responsive to the readings assigned through February 1.
A prospectus (including outline and a few items of bibliography) for a paper of 20 to

30 pages that deals with a specific kind of activity or problem in the relations of humanity. This paper will include three elements: (1) be placed in the context of *past, present* and *future*, (2) be inclusive of an array of units, from *local* to *global*, and (3) deal with *participation* issues.

March 10. Paper described above is due.

Course Outline

Introduction and Overview (January 4)

1. Some Historical Perspectives (January 6)

"I deplore the effort to dissociate humanity's deeper past from the contemporary encounter with the world." (William H. McNeill, *The Human Condition*, p. 5).

"Our century is a huge cauldron in which all historical eras are boiling and mingling." (Octavio Paz).

William H. McNeill, *The Human Condition: An Ecological and Historical View.* Princeton, NJ: Princeton University Press, 1980.

Peter Farb, *Humankind,* Part II Human Adaptations, p. 83-184:
  Chapter 5, The Hunting-Gathering Adaptation
  Chapter 6, Food Production and its Consequences
  Chapter 7, The Perennial Peasants
  Chapter 8, Urban Influences
  Chapter 9, Modernization: Toward the World City

Marshall G.S. Hodgson, "The Interrelations of Societies in History," in Louis Kriesberg (ed.), *Social Processes in International Relations.* New York: John Wiley, 1968, p. 24-36.

January 13

William H. McNeill, *The Rise of the West.* Chicago: University of Chicago Press, 1963:
  Chapter 7, "Closure of the Eurasian Ecumene, 500 B.C.—200 A.D.," especially p. 295-298, 316-317, 351-360.
  Chapter 10, "Steppe Conquerors and the European Far West, 100-1500 A.D.," especially p. 484-494 (second closure of ecumene).
  Chapter 11, "The Far West's Challenge to the World, 1500-1700 A.D.," especially p. 569-578, 652 (closure of global ecumene).
  Chapter 13, "The Rise of the West: Cosmopolitanism on a Global Scale," especially p. 726-730 (from ocean centered to polar centered ecumene).

Daniel Chirot, *Social Change in the Twentieth Century:*
  Chapter 1, "Comparative Sociology: Past Failures and New Ideas," p. 3-17.
  Chapter 2, "The Capitalist System in the Early Twentieth Century," p. 18-54.

2. Searching for Units of Analysis (January 20)

"The intelligible field of historical study is neither nation-state nor mankind as a whole but a certain grouping of humanity which we have called a society—five are in existence today." (Arnold J. Toynbee, *A Study of History*, p. 11).

" . . . I abandoned the idea altogether of taking either the sovereign state or that vaguer concept, the national society, as the unit of analysis. I decided that neither was a social system and that one could only speak of social change in social systems. The only social system in this scheme was the world system." (Immanuel Wallerstein, *The Modern World System*, p. 7).

Eucumene
Gordon W. Hewes, "The Ecumene as a Civilizational Multiplier System," *The Kroeber Anthropological Papers*. Fall 1965, No. 25, Berkeley, California, p. 73-100.

Intelligible Fields
Arnold Toynbee, *A Study of History*, abridgement of Vol. 1-vi, D.C. Somervell, NY: Oxford University Press, 1947:
Chapter 1, "The Unit of Historical Study," p. 1-11.
Chapter 2, "The Comparative Study of Civilization," p. 12-34.
Chapter 3, "The Comparativity of Societies," p. 35-47.

Groups Exercising Independent Power or Initiative
Quincy Wright, *The Study of International Relations*. NY: Appleton-Century-Crofts, 1955. Chapter 1, "The Meaning of International Relations," p. 3-8.

World Society
John Burton, "International Relations or World Society," in John Burton, et al., *The Study of World Society*, Pittsburgh: International Studies Association, 1974, p. 3-29.

World System
Immanuel Wallerstein, *The Modern World System*. NY: The Academic Press, 1974:
Introduction: "On the Study of Social Change," p. 3-11.
Chapter 7, "Theoretical Reprise," p. 347-357.

Ecumenopolis
C.A. Doxiadis, *Building Entopia*. NY: W.W. Norton, 1975. Part one, "The Concept of Entopia," especially p. 2-19. Chapter 15, "Ecumenopolis," p. 231-239.

Culture
Roy Preiswerk, "The Place of Intercultural Relations in the Study of International Relations."

Authoritative Allocations of Values
David Easton, *The Political System*. NY: Alfred A. Knopf, 1953. "The Concept of the State," p. 106-115.

3. Evolving Paradigms through which U.S. Political Scientists View the World (January 25)
"A theory of politics can be elaborated that reunites the disparate and artificial divisions among international, comparative, American or other national theories of politics." (Mansbach and Vasquez, p. 69).
" . . . the conventional distinction between 'domestic' and 'international' politics may become spurious in cases of multi-national states and multi-state nations . . . the conventional concept of 'nation-state' is inapplicable to about half of the states in the global state system." (Nielsson, p. 5).

The Westphalian System in Historical Perspective
Edward L. Morse, *Modernization and the Transformation of International Relations*. NY: The Free Press, 1976.

Linkage Politics

James Rosenau, *Linkage Politics*. NY: The Free Press, 1969:
Chapter 3, "Toward the Study of National-International Linkages," p. 44-66.

Transnational Relations (January 27)
Robert O. Keohane and Joseph S. Nye, *Transnational Relations and World Politics*.
Cambridge: Harvard University Press, 1972 (Also in *International Organization*,
Summer 1971.): Introduction and Conclusion.

Complex Interdependence
Robert O. Keohane and Joseph S. Nye, *Power and Interdependence*. Boston: Little
Brown, 1977: Chapter 2, "Realism and Complex Interdependence," p. 23-37.

Complex Conglomerate System
Richard W. Mansbach, Y.H. Ferguson and D.E. Lampert. *The Web of World Politics:
Nonstate Actors in the Global System*. Englewood Cliffs, NJ: Prentice-Hall, Inc.,
1976:
Chapter 2, "The Growing Irrelevance of the State-Centric Model," p. 20-31.
Chapter 3, "Towards a New Conceptualization of Global Politics," p. 32-45.

Issues
Richard W. Mansbach and John A. Vasquez, *In Search of Theory: A New Paradigm
for Global Politics*. NY: Columbia University Press, 1981:
Chapter 3, "The Elements of a New Paradigm," p. 68-86.

Nation (ethnic) Groups
Gunnar P. Nielsson, "Toward Systematic Comparative Analysis of Nation-Groups
as a Unit of Analysis in the Study of Intra-State Political Integration and Inter-
State Relations," School of International Relations, University of Southern California, 1980.

4. Boundaries, Borders, Frontiers (February 1)
"Time and mankind patiently strive to put together again what treaties and
systems of law once tore asunder to meet the requirements of a particular type of
political organization." (P.Orianne).
"One chance for Europe must surely be its frontier regions, with local and
regional representatives playing the leading role." (J.P. Delamuraz).
"Forget about the borders dividing the United States, Canada, and Mexico, those
pale barriers thoroughly porous to money, immigrants, and ideas . . . Consider the
way America really works. It is Nine Nations . . . Most important, each nation has a
distinct prism through which it views the world." (Joel Gareau, *The Nine Nations
of North America*, p. 1, 2).
Raimondo Strassoldo, "Boundaries in Sociological Theory: A Reassessment."
Raimondo Strassoldo and Renzo Gubert, "The Boundary: An Overview of its
Current Theoretical Status." In Institute of International Sociology, *Boundaries
and Regions*, p. 29-57.
J.W. House, "The Frontier Zone: A Conceptual Problem For Policy Makers,"
International Political Science Review. Vol. 1, No. 4, 1980, p. 456-477.
Joel Garreau, *The Nine Nations of North America*. Boston: Houghton Mifflin, 1980,
p. 1-13.

Participation (February 3)
"The quest for self-determination, at its core, is not a national or any other group

aspiration, but the aspiration of the individual human being to the vague notions of 'freedom' and the 'the good life.' " (Dov Ronen, *The Quest for Self-Determination*, p. 9).

"The forces of progress also further a multinationalization of previously domestic activities and intensify the intermeshing of decision-making in multinational frameworks. This inherently expansive process could in the name of economic advancement, efficiency, and interdependence ultimately undermine our Western systems of democracy unless we develop new forms of democratic control." (Karl Kaiser).

Dov Ronen, *The Quest for Self-Determination*. New Haven: Yale University Press, 1979.

Lee C. Buchheit, *Secession: The Legitimacy of Self-Determination*. New Haven: Yale University Press, 1978:
Chapter 4, "The Standards of Legitimacy," p. 216-248.

Richard Falk, "Anarchism and World Order," xerox.

February 8

Hazel Henderson, "Citizen Movements for Greater Global Equity," *International Social Science Journal*, Vol. 28, No. 4, 1976, p. 773-788.

Gerald and Patricia Mische, *Toward a Human World Order*," p. 298-329.

William O. Chittick, "The Group Perspective in Foreign Policy: A Report on U.S. World Affairs Organizations" (NGOs). Athens: University of Georgia, 1977, p. 1-77.

Karl Kaiser, "Toward a Theory of Multinational Politics," in Keohane and Nye, *Transnational Relations and World Politics*. Cambridge: Harvard University Press, 1972.

Johan Galtung, *The True Worlds: A Transnational Perspective*. NY: The Free Press, 1980:
Chapter 7, "The Nonterritorial System," p. 305-340.
Chapter 9, "Individual Action," p. 393-429.

6. Regions, Provinces, Cities and Towns (February 10)

"Cities of the world unite, you have nothing to lose but your slums, your poverty, and your military expendability." (Kenneth Boulding, p. 1123).

"The Region, then, speaks of democratic involvement in societal decision making (participation) and in efficient societal control over the allocation of resources (planning). The nation-state smells of rules, armies, history, blood; the Region recalls geography and rational administration. (Raimondo Strassoldo and Renzo Gubert, p. 32).

Regions

Council of Europe, *The Conference of Local and Regional Authorities of Europe: Twenty Years' Work for Local and Regional Authorities*. Strasbourg: Council of Europe, 1977.

Council of Europe, *Report of Transfrontier Co-operation in Europe*. Strasbourg: Council of Europe, 24 March 1980.

States (Provinces)

John W. Outland, "Yes, Virginia, Foreign Policy Means You," *Virginia Social Science Journal*, Vol. 9, No. 2 (Nov. 1974), p. 34-42.

Thomas J. Price, "State Development Agencies as Transnational Actors: A First Observation," The University of Texas at El Paso, 1978.

James Harwell, "The States Go International," State Government, Winter 1975, p. 2-5. (Other related articles attached).

Carol S. Goldsmith, "Sister-State Relations," The China Business Review, July-August 1980.

Cities

Kenneth E. Boulding, "The City as an Element in the International System," Daedalus, 1968, p. 1111-1123.

Norman D. Palmer, "Philadelphia As a Transnational Actor," Philadelphia Transnational Project, Philadelphia: University of Pennsylvania, 1977.

M. Lal Goel, "Pensacola and the World: A Study of International Linkages of the Pensacola Community," Pensacola: University of West Florida.

Chadwick F. Alger, "A World of Cities or Good Foreign Policies Begin at Home," Columbus in the World Project, Transnational Intellectual Cooperation Program, Mershon Center, Ohio State University, Columbus, Ohio, June 1976.

Carolyn Stephenson, The International Relations of a Metropolitan Area: San Diego in the World. Ph.D. dissertation, Ohio State University, 1980.

David A. Heenan, "Global Cities of Tomorrow," Harvard Business Review, May-June 1977, p. 79-92.

7. Social Science (February 15)

"The less understandable and less readable a given work is, the more scientific it pretends to be." (Longin Pastusiak).

". . . . corresponding to the existence of a transnational class there also exists a transnational social science, but there is nothing scientific, objective or ethically-neutral about their methods of science, and nothing universal, secular or pontifical about their espousal for the causes of peace, order, justice, equality, freedom, development, or what have you . . . . they turn out ultimately to be rationalizations for certain class interests that are indeed transnational in character." (Tandon, p. 32).

"No one in his right mind should go into cross-national (collaborative) research— if he is looking for an ego trip or an easy and efficient way to utilize his intellectual talents . . . The need for such cross-national research in social relations and public policy escalates exponentially as the technological revolution chains the world together in interdependence, while demands of burgeoning populations strain its physical resources." (Jacob and Jacob, p. 85, 100).

Overview

C. Alger and Gene M. Lyons, "Social Science as a Transnational System."

Kinhide Mushakoji, "Scientific Revolution and Inter-Paradigmatic Dialogues," UN University, Project on Goals, Processes and Indicators of Development, Tokyo, 1979.

Contending Perspectives

Krishna Kumar, "Indigenization and Transnational Cooperation in the Social Sciences," in Krishna Kumar (ed.), Bonds Without Bondage: Explorations in Transcultural Interactions. University of Hawaii Press, 1979, pp. 103-120: Okwudiba Nnoli, "The African Social Scientist as a Transnational Man."

Longin Pastusiak, "The Development of Social Science Knowledge in World Perspective."

Aldo E. Solari, "The Role of Ideologies in the Situation of Social Science in Latin America."

Y. Tandon, "Nationalism and Transnationalism in the Making of a Political Scientist."

Organized Collaboration

Gene Lyons, "Globalizing the Social Sciences," Dartmouth College.

Betty M. Jacob and Philip E. Jacob, "The Diplomacy of Cross-National Collaboration," in Krishna Kumar (ed.), *Bonds Without Bondage*, p. 85-102:

Raimo Vayrynen, "Transnational Coordination and Development of Peace Research."

8. Voluntary Development Agencies (February 17)

"The development of contemporary concepts of social ethics has made it clear that compassion expressed in remedial acts of love cannot be a legitimate substitute for a passion for justice." (Bruno Muetzelfeldt, cited by Lissner, p. 280).

"the development of the international autonomous entity is a reaction to the incapacities of that type of State which dominates the international scene; to the incapacity to solve the basic problems of life in an international community: war, hunger, hatred, waste, ignorance, greed." (Eva Senghass-Knobloch, cited by Lissner, p. 208).

Jorgen Lissner, *The Politics of Altruism: A Study of the Political Behavior of Voluntary Development Agencies*. Geneva: Lutheran World Federation, 1977.

9. Transnational Corporations (February 22)

"The large private corporation fits oddly into democratic theory and vision. Indeed, it does not fit." (Charles E. Lindblom, *Politics and Markets*, 356).

"It is not very clear what the Canadian people—who are among the richest in the world—would stand to win if the 'center of decision' moved from . . . Manhattan to . . . Montreal, or what the people of India—among the most poverty-stricken of the world—would stand to lose further if her capitalists handed over their factories to others holding a Japanese or German passport." (Arghiri Emmanuel, in Kumar, p. 149).

" . . . multinational commercial and industrial firms have been among the major carriers of knowledge from the industrial world to the less developed countries . . . How can the knowledge so created or exchanged be mobilized to reduce the economic and cultural dependency of the Third World upon industrial nations? *This is the imperative of decolonization.* (Ali Mazrui, in Kumar, p. 227).

TNC as an Actor

Werner J. Feld, *International Relations: A Transnational Approach*. Sherman Oaks, CA: Alfred Publishing Co., 1979, chapter 13.

Overall Viewpoints

Werner J. Feld, chapter 14.

Otto Kreye, "Perspectives for Development Through Industrialization in the 1980s: An Independent Viewpoint on Dependency," Tokyo: The United Nations University, Project on Goals, Processes and Indicators of Development, 1980.

Arghiri Emmanuel, "The Multinational Corporations and Inequality of Development," in Krishna Kumar, *Transnational Enterprises: Their Impact on Third
World Societies and Cultures.* Boulder: Westview Press, 1980, p. 137-164.

Impact of TNC

Ali Mazrui, "The Impact of Transnational Corporations on Educational Processes
and Cultural Change: An African Perspective," in Kumar, *Transnational Enterprises,* p. 207-230.

Linda Y.C. Lim, "Women Workers in Multinational Corporations: The Case of the
Electronics Industry in Malaysia and Singapore," in Kumar, *Transnational Enterprises,* p. 109-136.

Controls and Codes of Conduct

P.G. Bock, "Controlling the Transnational Corporation: The Issue of Codes of
Conduct," University of Illinois, Urbana. Prepared for presentation at the International Studies Association Annual Meeting, Washington, D.C., February 22-25,
1978.

Amos Yoder, "UN Monitoring of Transnational Corporations," University of
Idaho, Moscow, Idaho. Prepared for International Studies Association Convention, 1980.

10. Labor (February 24)

"It is not the workers' interests that bring workers of the North and South into
conflict with each other . . . This conflict is the result of the expansionist logic of
the capitalist system and the international division of labour which it produces
. . . Top priority must be given to demystification and information." (Edmond
Maire, p. 13).

"Workers much more than managers and entrepreneurs have local roots and, if
they are not forced to migrate, tend to spend most of their lives in a restricted
horizon of work and community life . . . The transnational strategy of organizing
production on a world scale, however, can also create conditions for common
wokers' interests and coordinated action." (Martinelli, p. 85).

"The American unions themselves are already paying a high price for their
national chauvinism. The absence of a class solidarity with Latin America means
that USA-based TNCs are able to take advantage of the low wages and shift their
investment there." (Transnationals Information Exchange, p. 110).

Folker Fröbel, Jurgen Heinrichs and Otto Kreye, *The New International Division of
Labour: Structural Unemployment in Industrialized Countries and Industrial-
ization in Developing Countries.* New York: Cambridge University Press, 1980:
Chapter 1: "The New International Division of Labour in the World Economy," p.
1-23.
Chapter 2: "The New International Division of Labour: A Phase in the Develop-
ment of the World Capitalist System," p. 24-48.
Chapter 9: "Conclusion to Part I," (The Development of the Federal German
Textile and Garment Industry as an Example of the New International Division
of Labour) p. 176-182.
Chapter 13: "The Economic and Political Determinants and Consequences of
Increased Production Abroad," p. 276-294.
Chapter 17: "The Impact of World Market Oriented Industrialisation on the

Socio-Economic Development of Developing Countries," p. 365-391. (Scan pages 291-364).

Alberto Martinelli, "Contradictions Between National and Transnational Planning: The Role of Labour Unions," *IFDA Dossier* 11, September, 1979, p. 75-86.

Edmond Maire, "The Solidarity of the International Labour Movement as an Essential Element in the Establishment of a New International Order," *IFDA Dossier* 4, February 1979, p. 12-16.

War on Want, "North-South Workers' Solidarity," *IFDA Dossier* 12, October 1979, p. 107-110.

Transnationals Information Exchange, "Labour Movement Tourism Won't Stop Multinationals," *IFDA Dossier* 19, September/October 1980, p. 108-110.

11. Information (March 1)

". . . eighty-one of the largest-selling transnational corporations control up to 75 percent of the flow of international communication. . . . The free flow of information as a principle of international cultural exchange does not exist in contemporary global reality—the flow of cultural products, be it art, scientific knowledge, or entertainment, goes freely only from the economically and organizationally most powerful metropolitan centres to those socio-cultural entities where the cultural-exchange potential is less developed in terms of media power, international marketing, or dominant criteria of quality." (Littunen, p. 287, 298).

"Sri Lanka's Press Trust (in collaboration with Reuters) is among ninety national agencies which are ill-disguised branch offices linked in a subservient and colonial relationship to their dominant partner in the former imperial headquarters. Reuters of London still dictates the shape, substance and stress bestowed on every item of news flowing both inwards and outwards from Sri Lanka." (Fred de Silva, p. 57).

Herbert I. Schiller, "Genesis of the Free Flow of Information," *Current Research on Peace and Violence*, 2/1975, p. 75-87.

Herbert I. Schiller, "The Transnational Corporation and the International Flow of Information: Challenges to National Sovereignty," *Current Research on Peace and Violence*, 1/1979, p. 1-11.

Herbert I. Schiller, "Advertising and International Communications," *Current Research on Peace and Violence*, 4/1976, p. 175-182.

International Social Science Journal, "Dilemmas of Communication: Technology versus Community," Vol. XXXII, No. 2, 1980, p. 195-322. See especially: Majid Tehranian,"The Curse of Modernity: The Dialectics of Modernization and Communication," 247-263; and Yrjo Littunen, "Cultural Problems of Direct Satellite Broadcasting," 283-303.

"The New International Information Order: Who Wants It? What Is It?" *Issues of the 80's*, UNA-USA.

John E. Fobes, "Acting to Improve Information and Communications Systems in the World," 31 August 1981 (author is former Deputy Director General of UNESCO).

12. Tourism

"It is perfectly legitimate to compare tourists with barbarian tribes. Both involve the mass migration of peoples who collide with cultures far removed from their own. There is, however, one major difference. The old Golden Horde was a nomadic, non-monetary people which threatened the settled urban civilisations of

Europe. Today the pattern is reversed. Tourists come from the industrialised centres but, this time, it is they who are fanning out through the world, swamping apparently less dynamic societies, including the few pre-industrial ones which still remain." (Turner and Ash, p. 11)

"While corporate domination of world tourism has made new destinations accessible, it has also packaged the tourist and, in a sense, sterilized him. It has minimized rather than maximized the intercultural experience of the consumer, and at an ever-rising price. . . . The struggle for economic rewards continues to dominate the politics of tourism, and politics continues to be an exercise in *who gets what*." (Harry G. Matthews, p. 93).

"The Anatomy of Tourism," *International Social Science Journal*, XXXII, No. 1, 1980, p. 7-150.

Lanfant,"Introduction: Tourism in the Process of Internationalization," p. 14-43.

Harry G. Matthews, *International Tourism: A Political and Social Analysis.* Cambridge, Mass.: Schenkman Publishing Co., 1978.

Louis Turner and John Ash. *The Golden Hordes: International Tourism and the Pleasure Periphery.* London: Constable, 1977: Chapter 17, "The Future," p. 280-292.

E. Cohen, "Toward a Sociology of International Tourism," *Social Research*, Vol. 39, 1972, p. 164-182.

Dean MacCannell, *The Tourist: A New Theory of the Leisure Class.* New York: Schocken, 1976.

George Young, *Tourism, Blessing or Blight?* Harmondsworth: Penguin, 1973.

Progress Reports on Class Papers (March 8, 10)

Alternative Urban Futures

Jeanne Howard   *Summer 1983*
Environmental and Urban Systems 4130/Virginia Polytechnic Institute/
Blacksburg, VA 24061

EUS 4130, which has the catalogue designation "Planned Innovative Communities," is in reality the course entitled "Alternative Urban Futures,"
which has been taught several times in the past. The elements of innovative community planning and of utopian thought are definitely to be
included in the course material, but the course will spend the majority of
the time considering non-utopian versions of the future.

The course deals with a subject-matter which has not happened yet, and
so assumes a greater desire on the part of students to think speculatively
than does the usual college course. The course syllabus, therefore, is
designed more as a framework for the consideration of questions and
alternatives, than as a straight-jacket of material which must be considered. It is designed to provide some guidance for speculation, while closing
off as few avenues as possible.

It is assumed that you like to read. (A futures course should perhaps
dispense with the outdated, fifteenth-century print medium; an instructor
who is a known audio-visual enthusiast should probably accept as a
challenge a student with a disinclination toward print. Nevertheless, there
is hardly any way around the necessity to read extensively and broadly.)
The reading we will be doing will deal with three rather generally defined
areas, moving from the largest scale to the small scale (or, from the
universe to you): first, a study of general, long-range, planetary future
scenarios, including both pessimistic and optimistic ones; then a study of
specifically urban alternatives; and finally a consideration of the lives of
individuals in the future and of the role of alternative human values in
shaping the urban future. Important in all our considerations will be the
range of alternative choices in such dimensions as high/intermediate
technology; equality/inequality; conservative/liberal/radical political outlooks; economic growth/"steady-state" economics, etc. Students will be
encouraged not only to explore alternatives, but to formulate preferences.

Readings

Three books have been ordered for this class and should be available at the
bookstore: Robert Heilbroner's *An Inquiry into the Human Prospect*; Herman
Kahn's *World Economic Development: 1979 and Beyond*; and Alvin Toffler's *The
Third Wave*. Additionally, three articles will be required: Sam Cole, Jay Gershuny,
and Ian Miles, "Scenarios of World Development" (*Futures*, Feb. 1978); James A.
Dator, "Beyond the Nation-State?" (from the World Future Society *Bulletin*, No-

vember 1981); and Willis Harman, "The Coming Transformation" (from the *Futurist*, Feb.-April 1977). Students will be responsible for assigned readings from these, and will be evaluated on the basis of a mid-term exam and a final examination.

Suggested Course Calendar

June 21   Introduction. Five possible future scenarios

June 22   Film/scenario, "1985"

June 23   Techniques for forecasting future scenarios

June 24   "Disaster—Unless" scenarios: the Club of Rome

June 25   Discussion of Robert Heilbroner's "Human Prospect" scenario
(Reading for Week I: Heilbroner's *Inquiry into the Human Prospect* (all) and the article, "Scenarios for World Development")

June 28   Optimistic scenarios: Herman Kahn; Daniel Bell's post-industrial society

June 29   Extremely optimistic, high-tech scenarios: F.M. Esfandiary; Gerard O'Neill
(Related reading, for contrast: Jonathan Schell, "The Fate of the Earth")

June 30   Long-range economic cycles and their impact on forecasting future scenarios: Kondratieff cycles; Jay Forrester's models

July 1   Forecasting a known future: scenarios for the USSR and China

July 2   Midterm exam
(Reading for Week II: Herman Kahn's *World Economic Development, 1979 and Beyond*, pp. 7-34, 53-111, 113-126, 139-177, 208-219, 231-252)

July 5   Technology (high and intermediate) and the future

July 6   Built "utopias"—the Archigram group, Soleri's Arcosanti, etc.

July 7   The future urbanization in western Europe: Project Europe 2000; the Third Garden City

July 8   Issues of centralization vs. decentralization; regional shifts in the U.S.

July 9   Discussion of "Beyond the Nation-State?"
(Reading Week III: Alvin Toffler's *The Third Wave*, chapters 1-5, 7, 8, 9, 10, 11, 12, 16, 17, 19, 20, 21, 22; and the article, "Beyond the Nation-State?")

July 12   "Paradigm Shifts" and transformational scenarios

July 13   Final exam, part 1 (in-class)

July 14   Local futures-oriented projects
(Related reading: Clement Bezold, ed., *Anticipatory Democracy*)

July 15   Professionals and "inventing the future"

July 16   Final exam, part 2: discussion
(Reading for week IV: Willis Harman, "The Coming Transformation")

The Future

Richard K. Curtis   *Spring 1983*
Speech, Theatre and Communications J444/Indiana University/
Indianapolis, IN 46202

The purpose of this course is to engage the student, whether graduate or undergraduate, in a meaningful study of the future to the end that he or she will be capable of exerting a more rational control over the course of events.

I. Methodology of the Course
A. Films will be viewed, generally each week, with an open discussion to follow. Each of the continuing faculty will try to take diverse points of view to stimulate perceptive questions from the class leading to fruitful discussion.
B. Lectures will be given, both by the continuing faculty and by visiting lecturers, in areas of their respective expertise. There will be opportunity for questions and buzz sections in keeping with these, with the continuing faculty leading out with "hard" questions.
C. Reading will be required, averaging 200 pages a week, drawn largely from the appended suggestive bibliography, dealing with the week by week subjects.
D. Term paper will be written as an in-depth presentation to the class on a specific subject of interest to the student.
E. Notebook will be kept of class notes, outside reading, handouts, etc.

II. Schedule for the Course

Week I. Why Study the Future?
Class 1. Films
a. "6, 5, 4, 3, 2, 1" McGraw-Hill Documentary. The countdown for the future continues; can we ever hope to relax without being blasted into a new era of change? (7")
b. "Time Is" McGraw-Hill Documentary. The impact of accelerated change jars loose our conceptions of time, relativizing past, present, and future into a single NOW. (30")
c. "Futurists" McGraw-Hill Documentary. Specialists in all fields have now made it respectable to inquire scientifically of tomorrow. (25")
d. Discussion, led by teaching team.

Class 2. Lectures by teaching team, with discussion following.
a. The need for delineating general developmental possibilities.
b. The need for delineating long-range goals.
c. Emergence of a new science for futurology.

Week II. The Nature of the Predictive Process
Class 1. Films
a. "Goodnight, Socrates" McGraw-Hill Documentary. When progress threatens an ethnic group with social change, which way should the individual choose? (34")

b. "Ishi in Two Worlds" McGraw-Hill Documentary. The Aborigine who steps from the Stone Age into modern life dies a symbolic death from the pressure of social change. (19")
c. Discussion, led by teaching team.

Class 2. Guest symposium, with open discussion following.
a. The factor of time in relating cause and effect and reason.
b. Prediction within the natural sciences.
c. Prediction within the social sciences.
d. Prediction within the arts and humanities.

Week III. Methodological Considerations in the Study of the Future
Class 1. Films
a. "Homo Sapiens" McGraw-Hill Documentary. Man's ability to adapt is both a blessing and a curse. (10")
b. "Of Holes and Corks" McGraw-Hill Documentary. Under the shock of the future, some try to resist change by fatuously attempting to contain it. (10")
c. "Anti-Darwin Theory" McGraw-Hill Documentary. Perhaps Darwin was wrong, and we are reversing our own evolution, diminishing consciousness to a more primitive level. (20")
d. "Games Futurists Play" CBS Documentary. Even games can reduce the shock of the future on our lives. As ordinary modes of planning fail, chance factors come into play, helping us to simulate situations we cannot predict. (20")
e. Discussion, led by teaching team.

Class 2. Lectures by teaching team, followed by discussion.
a. General guidelines for studying the future.
  1) Guidelines for forecasting the future.
  2) Guidelines for creating the future.
b. Specific techniques for studying the future.
  1) Techniques of conjecture.
  2) Quantitative techniques.

Week IV. Forecasts of the Future
Class 1. Films
a. "Stranger than Science Fiction" CBS Documentary. Science fiction, both in its earliest forms, and in recent films, has proven amazingly accurate in its predictions of tomorrow . . . today. (30")
b. "Bats, Birds and Bionics" McGraw-Hill Documentary. Bionics, a new science connecting biology, mathematics and engineering, and reaching into medicine, psychology and communications, applies the principles through which animal systems adjust to change. (25")
c. "001763" McGraw-Hill Documentary. When our values collide with machinery of change, which gives way? (9")
d. Discussion, led by teaching team.

Class 2. Interviews by teaching team of guests, with discussion.
a. Forecasts based on a sample surveys.
b. Forecasts based on individual opinion.
  1) Forecasts of mankind's future.
  2) Forecasts of the future of Western man.

3) Forecasts of the developing nations' future.

Week V. Forecasts of the Future (cont.)
Class 1. Films
a. "Cosmic Zoom " NFBC Documentary. Awareness of change in the macrocosm of the universe and the microcosm of the organism can give us the needed overview to cope well. (8")
b. "Replay" McGraw-Hill Documentary. The generation gap seems cyclical, but it is in reality a symptom of social change and the growing impermanence of social bonds. (8")
c. "Future Shock" McGraw-Hill Documentary. Orson Welles, host and narrator: "Our modern technology has achieved a degree of sophistication beyond our wildest dreams. But this technology has exacted a pretty heavy price. We live in an age of anxiety, a time of stress; and with all our sophistication we are, in fact, the victims of our own technological strength. We are the victims of shock." (42")
d. Discussion, led by teaching team.

Class 2. Symposium forum, with guests and teaching team, followed by open discussion.
a. Change and stress.
b. Disease and stress.
c. Aging and stress.

Week VI. Forecasts of the Future—Communication
Class 1. Films
a. "An American Time Capsule" Pyramid Documentary. Kaleidoscopic views of still pictures summarizes 200 years of American history. (3")
b. "This Is Marshall McLuhan: The Medium is the Message." NFBC Documentary. Communications technology immerses us in a flowing stream of information which, without our knowing it, changes our natures. (55")
c. Discussion, led by teaching team.

Class 2. Lectures by teaching team, followed by discussion.
a. The nature and importance of communication.
b. Pitfalls in communications.
c. Toward communication hygiene.
d. The possibilities of a universal language.

Week VII. Forecasts of the Future—Cybernetics
Class 1. Films
a. "A Matter of Survival." NFBC Documentary. As we approach the limits to our tolerance of change, we are forced to ask if the computer cannot adapt better than we? (26")
b. "Cybernetics" McGraw-Hill Documentary. Control systems now enable machines to learn, to master environments in ways ever closer to human behavior. (22")
c. Discussion, led by teaching team.

Class 2. Debate forum, with guest debaters.

a. Subject: "Resolved, that further automation of industry should cease as being dehumanizing."

b. Open discussion.

Week VIII. Forecasts of the Future—Medical Electronics
Class 1. Films.

a. "Medical Electronics" CBS Documentary. Technology touches man intimately through medicine. (26")

b. "Miracle of the Mind" CBS Documentary. Chemistry profoundly alters functions, even one's I.Q. (26")

c. Discussion, led by teaching team.

Class 2. Symposium forum, with guests, followed by open discussion.

a. To what extent is I.Q. hereditary and fixed?

b. What changes can we anticipate at IUPUI as a result of combining electronics with medicine?

Week IX. Forecasts of the Future—Organ Transplants
Class 1. Films

a. "Man-Made Man" CBS Documentary. We are already learning to rebuild the human body, organ by organ. (25")

b. "Can We Live to be 100?" CBS Documentary. Transplants push back the boundaries of human existence. (26")

c. Discussion, led by teaching team.

Class 2. Guest lectures.

a. What limitations are there in the eventual replication of a human being? Organ by organ?

b. What are the consequences legally, morally and socially of continuing transplantation?

Week X. Forecasts of the Future—the Governance of Men
Class 1. Films

a. "Quest for Freedom" Churchill Documentary. Development of democracy in different countries, from the Stone Age to the American Revolution, and the documents that resulted. (16")

b. "Demokratia" McGraw-Hill Documentary. Change threatens to reverse the development of many complex and beautiful institutions in our own day; how does democracy fare? (9")

c. "Sweden" McGraw-Hill Documentary. Modern Sweden and the social, economic, and political problems which a highly-socialized country faces. (20")

d. Discussion, led by teaching team.

Class 2. Debate-forum. "Resolved, that the proposed Tugwell Constitution come to replace our present form in the U.S."

Week XI. Forecasts of the Future—Crime and Punishment
Class 1. Films

a. "Crime and the Courts" Carousel Documentary. The mounting crime wave; the proportion of juvenile crime; drugs in criminal motivation; probation reform; and prison as a deterrent. (37")

b. "A Night in Jail, A Day in Court" CBS Documentary. Two cases, from arrest to final disposition, show the complexities and pitfalls of our criminal justice system. Filmed in Indianapolis. (52")

Class 2. Colloquy, with guests
a. Subject: "Resolved, that more attention be paid to be the victim than to the criminal."
b. Open discussion, following debate and cross examination.

Week XII. Forecasts of the Future—War and Peace
Class 1. Films
a. "Ten Seconds That Shook the World" FI Films. The atom bomb's development. The work of scientists Fermi and Einstein, the Manhattan Project, how the bomb was perfected, the work of the crew of the bomber, 'Enola Gay,' the decision of Truman to drop the bomb, and the destruction of Hiroshima. (53")
b. "Very Nice, Very Nice." NFBC Documentary. The shadow of the atomic bomb hangs over a generation, its stresses generating extremes of anxiety and apathy. (10")
c. "The Hole" McGraw-Hill Documentary. The ultimate irrationality lies in the possibility that nuclear war could occur by some absurd chance which, whether willed or not, would be equally effective in abolishing life. (15")
d. Discussion, led by teaching teams.

Class 2. Colloquy, with guest.
a. Subject: "Resolved that the U.S. should pare at least 15 billion dollars from its defense budget for domestic problems."
b. Open discussion, following debate and cross-examination.

Week XIII through Week XV
a. Presentation of term papers to each member of the class.
b. Oral summary of each.
c. Questions from teaching team and class.

Imaging

Roy King   *Winter 1983*
Future Studies 100/Wittenberg University/Springfield, OH 45501

Purposes of the Course

To serve as an introduction to the discipline of Future Studies by discussing
in detail one important theory about how change takes place—through
the development of pictures about possible new forms of reality.

To show how human beings form images and how these images can
influence behavior.

To suggest that a very significant element of any reality consists of the
pictures we have of it.

Texts

Boulding, *The Image*
Kuhn, *The Structure of Scientific Revolutions*
Various handouts from lecturers

Course Outline

Week I: On the Nature of Images and Imaging
Photographic Images (Steichen's *The Family of Man*)
Discussion of Cultural Change Chart and images it embodies
Boulding, Chapter 1
Poetic Images (Imogene Bolls)

**Weeks II, III: Images and Values (Images Challenge, Clarify, Change, Support
Values)**
Rituals and Sacraments as Affirmations of Values (Graef)
Life-Boat Ethics (Copeland)
Images of Conflict (2 days) (Chatfield)
The Nuclear Issue (2 days) (Kent Dixon)
Discussion of *The Idols of the Mind*, Francis Bacon (Handout)
Boulding, Chapter 2

Week IV: Figures and Pictures—How Images Clarify Abstractions
From Chart to Picture (Brown)
Information Science: the Present State of the Art (Entorf)
Abstracting: There is a range of levels at which an issue can be discussed, and as a
discipline develops, discussion tends to leave behind more and more concrete
details and to "draw out" only the essential features, which are presented as
images or symbols. The image orients us to the level at which appropriate
discussion can take place, and without a capacity to handle images and symbols,
we cannot get beyond the elementary stage of any field to the place where the
action is. Sometimes discussion of a topic is facilitated by changing the level and

dealing with other images. Success in the academic world depends on learning how to handle currently productive images/abstractions.
Boulding, Chapter 3

Week V: Discussions of Kuhn, The Structure of Scientific Revolutions
Robert Cutler (History)
William Buscemi (Political Science)
Louis Laux (Biology)
Richard Graef (Religion)
Boulding, Chapter 8

Week VI: Images of Time and Space as Orienting Mechanisms
Urban Geography (Brown)
The Middle Eastern City (King)
Boulding, Review Chapter 1
Images of Time (Chatfield)

Week VII: Imaging and Re-imaging as Futuristic Tools
Imaging a World Without War (Chatfield)
(This will be an evening session from 6:30-9:30, time to be arranged)
The Designed Environment (Laux)
Urban Design (Ramsay)
Energy Transformations (Sartoris)
Social Planning (McEvoy)

Week VIII: Pictures of Ourselves
Industrial Self-Portraits: the Rise of the *Logo* (Ramsay)
Images of Self-Transcendence (Graef)
Inter-cultural Problems in Self-Imaging (King, Brown)
Boulding, Chapters 4, 9

Week IX: Images in Art—the Affective Element
Images and Emotion in Poetry (Imogene Bolls)
Images in the Graphic Arts (Ramsey)
The Emotional Content of Music (Walters)

Week X: Wrap-Up
Boulding, Chs. 10, 11
Concluding Panel Discussions

Toward a Human World Order

Gerald and Patricia Mische   *Spring 1983*
Interdisciplinary Studies 305/College of Saint Teresa/Winona, MN 55987

The general goal of this course is to enable participants to deepen their awareness of critical issues on our interdependent planet, to analyze the strengths and constraints of existing world systems, to put forward and evaluate world order alternatives and strategies and to explore the spiritual and faith dimensions of a more human world order.

Objectives

1. Explore the signs of the times and alternative futures within a historical context of global interdependence and major transformation.
2. Examine the linkages between local and global concerns.
3. Analyze threats to national and world security, including the arms race, world economic trends, competition for scarce resources and environmental dangers and the prospect and constraints of existing national and world systems to manage them.
4. Explore and assess the strengths and weaknesses of various models of world order alternatives.
5. Explore the spiritual, inner dimensions of a more human world order.
6. Become familiar with some of the documents from the Christian Churches and other world faith communities related to a more just and peaceful world order.

The learning methods include lectures, group discussions, journal-keeping, research reading, and film/film scripts. Grades will be based on participation in group discussion and a research-reflection paper.

Course Outline
Is there a realistic basis of hope in today's world of escalating military, economic and environmental crisis? This lecture series considers this question within a historical and analytic framework that transcends simplistic ideological or doomsday answers. Examining the dangers and opportunities of global interdependence, it provides a practical basis for hope and local initiatives.

March 10: Crisis of Growth: A Period of Global Transformation

March 17: The National Security Straitjacket

March 24: State of the Arms Race and its Effects

April 7: How Can We Be More Secure? U.S. and Soviet Security Dilemmas

April 24: Disarmament and International Security: World Order Approaches

April 21: Biblical and Church Perspectives on World Order

April 28: Economic Security in an Interdependent World

May 5: Global Spirituality

May 12: World Environmental Issues

May 19: Strategies for a More Human World Order

Texts
Required:
Gerald and Patricia Mische. *Toward a Human World Order.* New York/Ramsey, N.J.: Paulist Press, 1977.
Robert C. Johansen. *Toward A Dependable Peace: A Proposal for An Appropriate Security System.* New York: World Policy Institute, 1978.

Recommended:
Willy Brandt, et al. *North-South: A Programme For Survival.* Cambridge, Mass: MIT Press, 1980
Helen Caldicott. *Nuclear Madness.* New York: Bantam, 1978.
James McGinnis. *Bread and Justice.* New York. Paulist Press, 1979.
Patricia Mische. "Global Spirituality" in *The Whole Earth Papers,* No. 16, E. Orange, N.J.: Global Education Associates.
Patricia Mische. "Women, Power and Alternative Futures." Parts I and II, *The Whole Earth Papers,* No. 8 & 9.
Earthscope: Transitions Toward World Order. A special issue of the *Whole Earth Papers* (No. 12), featuring articles by Thomas Berry, Robert Muller, Pat Mische and Robert Manley on global transformation.
Land and World Order: The Whole Earth Papers, No. 17, 1982.
Jonathan Schell. *The Fate of the Earth.* New York: Knopf, 1982.
J. Carter Swaim. *War, Peace and the Bible.* Maryknoll, New York: Orbis Books, 1982.
Mendlovitz, Saul H., editor. *On the Creation of a Just World Order.* New York: Free Press, 1975.

Alternative Visions

Joseph Miller   *Fall 1982*
Psychology 209E/Saint Mary's College/Notre Dame, IN 46556

This course is designed to provide us with a forum to explore various
alternative visions that have been investigated by groups and communities
to the ways in which society is currently dealing with problems relating to
energy, housing, food production, health care, etc. In general, the format in
each area will be to first briefly discuss society's current response to the
problem, and to then in greater depth discuss the various positive alternative "solutions" that have been offered, and the pros and cons of such
"solutions." The course will operate on an almost exclusively discussion
oriented format, and grades will be assigned on the basis of participation
and completion of the readings and a readings log (see the next section).

Course Schedule

Attitudes and Values (September 13, 20)
Elgin, Duane and Mitchell, Arnold. "Voluntary Simplicity: Life-style of the Fail-
    ure?" In *Alternative Celebrations Catalog*, 4th Edition, Alternatives, 1978, 20-39.
Shippee, John. "Simple Living: Personal and Political Change." In Simple Living
    Collective, *Taking Charge: Personal and Political Change Through Simple
    Living*, Bantam, 1975, 10-30.
McRobie, George, "E.F. Schumacher: on Technology for a Democratic Society." In
    McRobie, George, *Small is Possible*, Harper & Row, 1981, 1-15.
"The Plowboy Interview. Dr. E.F. Schumacher." *Mother Earth News*, November,
    1976, 9-18.
Hayes, Denis. Foreword. In Coe, Gigi, *Present Value: Constructing a Sustainable
    Future*, Friends of the Earth, 1979, 1-4.
Bender, Tom. "New Values." In deMoll, Lane and Coe, Gigi, *Stepping Stones:
    Appropriate Technology and Beyond*, Schocken Books, 1978, 47-51.

Overview: Alternative Organizations and Emphases (September 27)
McRobie, George. "Technology: The Critical Choice." In McRobie, George, *Small
    is Possible*, 75-85.
McRobie, George. "A Guided Tour of Alternative Organizations in the U.S.A." In
    McRobie, George, *Small is Possible*, Harper and Row, 1981, 127-163.

Energy and Self-Reliant Communities (October 4, 11, 18)
Sale, Kirkpatrick. "Energy: The Sun King." In Sale, Kirkpatrick, *Human Scale*,
    Coward, McCann and Geoghegan, 1980, 209-228.
Morgan, Richard and Talbot, David. Appendix. In Morgan, Richard and Talbot,
    David, *Power and Light: Political Strategies for the Solar Transition*, Pilgrim
    Press, 1981.
Talbot, David. "Conservatopia, U.S.A.," *Mother Jones*, August, 1979, 37-41.
Foster, Lee. "The Integral Urban Home." In the Berkeley Holistic Health Center's

The Holistic Health Lifebook, And/Or Press, 1981, 319-325.

Morris, David. "Independent Cities: Changing the Nature of Economic Development." In deMoll, Lane and Coe,Gigi, *Stepping Stones: Appropriate Technology and Beyond*, 158-173.

Morris, David. "Neighborhood Power," *The Ecologist*, Aug./Sept., 1977.

Morris, David. "First Steps." In Morris, David, *Self-Reliant Cities: Energy and the Transformation of Urban America*, Sierra Club, 1982, 109-136.

Morris, David. "Humanly Scaled Energy Systems." In Morris, David, *Self-Reliant Cities: Energy and the Transformation of Urban America*, 204-221.

Morris, David. "The Ecological City," In Morris, David, *Self-Reliant Cities: Energy and the Transformation of Urban America*, 204-221.

Potpourri (November 1)

Henderson, Hazel. "The Emerging 'Counter-Economy'." In Henderson, Hazel, *Creating Alternative Futures: The End of Economics*. Berkeley, 1978, 381-398.

Rofsky, Mitch and Thompson, David. "Cooperatives Deserve Credit." In Green, Mark, and Massie, Robert, *The Big Business Reader: Essays on Corporate America*, Pilgrim Press, 1980, 537-549.

Fritsch, Albert. "Moving from Reflection to Action." In Frisch, Albert, *Environmental Ethics: Choices for Concerned Citizens*, Anchor Books, 1980, 257-276.

Agriculture and Food Alternatives (November 8, 15)

Rifkin, Jeremy. "Agriculture." In Rifkin, Jeremy, *Entropy: A New World View*, Viking, 1980, 136-140.

Cook, Kenneth. "Organic Gains Grounds," *Environmental Action*, May, 1981, 4-9.

Goldstein, Jerome. "Organic Force." In Merrill, Richard (Editor), *Radical Agriculture*, Harper Colphon, 1976, 212-223.

Van der Ryn, Sim. "Ecotopia Now." In the Berkeley Holistic Health Center's, *The Holistic Health Lifebook*, 335-343.

Friend, Gil. "Nurturing a Responsible Agriculture." In deMoll, Lane and Coe , Gigi, *Stepping Stones: Appropriate Technology and Beyond*, 146-157.

Ecology Action of the Midpeninsula. "Biodynamic/French Intensive Agriculture: High Yields and Higher Hopes," *Mother Earth News*, May, 1976.

Cole, Barbara and Goldman, M.C. "Community Gardens Come to the City," *Organic Gardening and Farming*, March, 1978.

Selected Readings from Valentine, William and Lappe, Frances Moore, *What Can We Do? Food and Hunger: How You Can Make a Difference*, Institute for Food and Development Policy, 1980.

Selected Readings from *People Power: What Communities are Doing to Counter Inflation*, U.S. Office of Consumer Affairs, 1980.

Health Alternatives (November 22, 29; December 6)

Ferguson, Tom. "Medical Self-Care: Self-Responsibility for Health." In Hastings, Arthur; Fadiman, James; and Gordon, James (Editors), *Health for the Whole Person: The Complete Guide to Holistic Medicine*, Westview Press, 1980.

Sale, Kirkpatrick. "Health: Heal Thyself." In Sale, Kirkpatrick, *Human Scale*, 266-277.

Ferguson, Marilyn. Excerpt from "Healing Ourselves." In Ferguson, Marilyn, *The Aquarian Conspiracy: Personal and Social Transformation in the 1980's*, Tarcher/Houghton Mifflin, 1980, 244-248.

Hartsough, Jan. "Health Care." In the Simple Living Collective's *Taking Charge: Personal and Political Change Through Simple Living*, Bantam, 1977, 198-219.

Cousins, Norman. "Prelude: What I Learned from 3000 Doctors." In the Berkeley Holistic Health Center's *The Holistic Health Lifebook*, xiii-xviii.

Ardell, Donald. Excerpt from Holistic Health Planning. In the Berkeley Holistic Health Center's, *The Holistic Health Handbook*, 404-409.

Carlson, Rick. "Holistic Health: Will the Promise Be Realized?" In the Berkeley Holistic Health Center's, *The Holistic Health Lifebook*, 354, 358.

Environmental Defense Fund and Boyle, Robert. "The Solution to the Problem." In EDF and Boyle, Robert, *Malignant Neglect*, Knopf, 1979, pp. 211-232.

"Nutrients that Team Up Against Pollution," *Prevention*, August, 1978.

Sherman, Carl. "Vitamin A—A Kind of Internal Gas Mask," *Prevention*, June, 1979.

Gottlieb, Bill. "A and C: Vitamins For a Toxified World," *Prevention*, February, 1980.

Feltman, John. "Antioxidants, Aging and Cancer," *Prevention*, July, 1978.

Uhlaner, Jonathan. "Selenium, a Mineral Made to Fight Cancer," *Prevention*, February, 1980.

"Vitamin E Lubricates the Circulation," *Prevention*, April, 1978.

Yates, John. "Lecithin Works Wonders," *Prevention*, February, 1980.

Epstein, Samuel. Preface (and) "What You Can Do to Prevent Cancer." In Epstein, Samuel, *The Politics of Cancer*, Sierra Club Books, 1978, 1-3 and 429-468.

Catch-up, Additions, and Wind-up. (December 13)

Alternative World Futures

Christine Sylvester

Gettysburg College/Gettysburg, PA 17325

January 1983

In the words of one scholar (Richard Falk) we live on an "endangered planet." We are endangered by structures which encourage a global war system, gross development disequilia, ecological abuse, the violation of human rights, and a "we-they" view of the species. We are also endangered by our seeming inability or disinclination to think seriously and creatively about our options. We are impaled in a world of structural injustice and intellectual paralysis.

The purposes of this course are as follows: 1) to foster a politics of species identity; 2) to highlight our collective sources of endangerment; 3) to gain an appreciation of alternative approaches to global management; and 4) to encourage creative, systematic thought on the future. To these ends, the course is divided into four thematic sections each built around a unique set of learning experiences.

To pass the course, students must attend class daily, participate in discussions, and complete all assignments on time. Participation is of the utmost importance—this is not a standard lecture course.

Required Texts

The Third Wave by Alvin Toffler (William Morrow and Company, Inc., 1980).
The Dispossessed by Ursula LeGuin.
Toward a Just World Order by Richard Falk, Samuel Kim, and Saul Mendlovitz (Westview, 1982).
Mankind at the Turning Point by Mihajlo Mesarovic and Edward Pestel (E.P. Dutton & Co., 1974).
The Communist Manifesto by Karl Marx and Frederick Engels (Pathfinder Press, 1978).
New York Times—daily

Reserve Readings

"Religion, Futurism, and Models of Social Change" by Elise Boulding.
"Outline for a Normative Forecasting/Planning Process" by Michael Washburn.
"Constructing Models of Presents, Futures, and Transitions: An Approach to Alternative World Futures" by Harry R. Targ.
You and Your Community in the World by Chadwick Alger and David Hoovler, Chapters 1 (intro) and 2 (individual foreign policies).

Course Outline

Week 1: The Global Problematique

This week, we consider four interrelated problems or issues in the current global system: direct violence, poverty, injustice, and ecological balance. Students are to prepare one 2-3 page "reaction" paper on each topic. This exercise encourages integration of classroom work with the topical readings. Be creative; use any format you please. A fifth synthesizing reaction paper is also required in which students look for connections between issue-areas as a way of broadening vision and encouraging holistic thinking.

January 3 Introduction to Course
Film: "Voyage to Next"

January 4 Our Capacity for War
Film: "The War Game"
Falk, Kim, Mendlovitz, Section 4, (Peace) pp. 219-271

January 5 Our Capacity to Underdevelop Others
Film: "The Tuaregs" or "Controlling Interest"
Falk, Kim, Mendlovitz, Section 5, (Economic well-being)

January 6 Our Capacity to Deny Human Rights
Film: "Come Back Africa"
Falk, Kim, Mendlovitz, Section 6, (Social Justice)

January 7 Our Capacity to Disrupt Eco-Systems
Film: "On the Edge of the Forest"
Falk, Kim, Mendlovitz, Section 7, (Ecological Balance); Before preparing fifth
  reaction paper, read Falk, Kim, and Mendlovitz, Section 1

Week 2: A Look at the Sources of and Proposed Solutions to the Global Problematique

We move now into the realm of holistic assessment by evaluating ongoing and alternative strategies of world order. Students will compile an annotated list of the institutions or organizational processes, public policy bottlenecks and successes in the contemporary global system. This exercise enables you to appreciate the complexities of the system and the myriad issues of social organization which must be taken into account when constructing an alternative world. Ideas are to be taken from the readings (especially the *NYT*) and from personal observation/experience.

January 10-11 How We Got Into This Mess
Falk, Kim, Mendlovitz, Section 2 (The Sovereign State and the World System)
Toffler, Chapters 1-10. Boulding (reserve)

January 12 Solutions
Current Strategies:
Falk, Kim, Mendlovitz, pp. 271-284
Marx
Toffler, Chapters 11-28

January 13 Utopian Images
LeGuin

January 14 Social Engineering
Mesarovic and Pestal
Falk, Kim, Mendlovitz, pp. 505-535

January 15 Humanistic Transformation

Falk, Kim, Mendlovitz, Section 3, (Approaches to World Order)
For next Monday, read Falk, Kim, Mendlovitz, pp. 537-end
Washburn (reserve), Targ (reserve)
Short paper placing the ideas of those writers in the context of the list on social
   functions, etc. you have prepared.

Week 3: Designing Global Futures: The Methodologies

By now, your growing appreciation for the intricacies of global society and the
possibilities for change may elicit feelings of confusion and helplessness. It is time,
therefore, to think systematically about the ways in which the institutions,
processes, bottlenecks, and policy successes you have been tracing could be altered.
The readings for this week focus on the methods of constructing alternative world
orders: where to begin, how to decide what is important, how to generate consensus. Your assignment, besides completing the readings, to draft a questionnaire
designed to tap attitudes on change and/or the future and administer is to at least 8
residents of Adams County. This exercise will help to broaden your appreciation of
the unity and the diversity of viewpoints that must be taken into account as you
design an alternative world. You may work in teams if you wish.

January 17 Issues of Methodology

*Alger/Hoovler, Chapters 1 (intro), 2 (individual foreign policies) (reserve)
Using ideas from class and additional reading by Alger and Hoovler, develop your
   questionnaire.

January 18 Questionnaire Approval (Individual Conferences)

January 19-20 Questionnaire Administration and Data Analysis

January 21 Student Presentations

Week 4: Constructing Alternative Worlds: Praxis

During this final week of class, students will form groups and design alternative
world orders. Each group is free to structure its time and discussions as it pleases.
However, all final products must address the problems discussed the first week,
specify the philosophy of change informing the project, note the processes and
institutions that will be affected by the new philosophy, and trace the process of
transition to the future world. Each student is to keep a daily journal of events in his
or her group—topics covered, points of agreement and disagreement, final decisions. It is very important that the student indicate how his/her preferences in a
given discussion differs or accords with the decisions reached by the group. In
modelling the future, strive for comprehensiveness and try to anticipate critics.
Each group must present and defend its alternative world to the class.Students from
last year's class will be invited to assist in critiquing and evaluating each alternative. A final reaction paper is due January 29.

January 24 Group Assignments

January 24-26 Student-Initiated Meetings to Construct Alternative Futures

January 27-28 Student Presentations; Evaluation

January 29 Final Reaction Paper Due

Conferences with instructor to determine grade. Be prepared to suggest a grade for
yourself and to defend your choice.

III
Case Studies

A sampling of Peace and World Order Studies Programs in the U.S.

The case study articles that follow describe the rationale, intellectual content, goals, history and curriculum design of selected Peace and World Order Programs. Space does not permit a full representation of all social justice and peace studies programs in the U.S.

The programs have been chosen for inclusion because they are formal majors, minors, concentrations or cluster arrangements. In addition, they use the globe as their primary unit of analysis. They are structural or systemic in their definition of world problems, and favor fundamental transformation of the international system. Finally, the programs engage students in the search for universal normative goals of preventing and eventually eliminating war, establishing a healthy global ecology, achieving economic justice and advancing human rights.

- City College of New York
- Warren Wilson College
- Pennsylvania State University
- St. Bonaventure University
- Gustavus Adolphus College
- State University of New York
  —Old Westbury
- St. Joseph's University
- Syracuse University
- Boston College
- Southern Illinois University
  —Edwardsville
- Bethel College
- Colgate University
- Guilford College
- Kent State University
- The School for International
  Training

- Berkshire Community College
- Juniata College
- Wilmington College
- Earlham College
- Wayne State University
- Wittenberg University
- West Chester University
- University of Akron
- Catholic University
- Chapman College
- Donnelly College
- Georgetown University
- University of Missouri—Columbia
- Goshen College
- Manchester College
- Manhattan College

International Studies, City College of the City University of New York

Founded in 1847, City College is the oldest municipally-financed college in the U.S. Over 75% of the College's current 12,367 students are Black, Hispanic, Asian, or Native American. Given this composition of the student body, the College's International Studies program aims to serve as a vehicle for the advancement of members of minority groups and of lower-middle and working-class backgrounds into foreign policy positions. Thus, the main thrust is toward the development of problem-solving and policy-making skills. Also among the program's stated objectives are: to coordinate international activities that draw on the resources of the college and community; to respond more fully to the international needs of local groups; to better integrate foreign language learning into the study of foreign areas; to assist the foreign student population; to increase participation in co-curricular activities such as study abroad and internship programs; to enhance faculty competence and research; and to introduce a significant international dimension into the general College curriculum.

The central themes of the program are established in an introductory survey course that examines global problems, including the danger of war, imbalances in the international political economy, and the critical importance of Africa, Asia, and Latin America in the present world. Competing world views are evaluated in the light of key concepts such as state, power, race, ethnicity, class, imperialism, and revolution, and are developed through case studies. The future world order and alternative stratagems of transformation are also considered.

International Studies is essentially an honors major. Fourteen to nineteen courses are needed to fulfill the major. There are seven specific course requirements: an introductory international studies course, a two-semester seminar which examines the long-term policy implications of one major world problem per semester, a two-semester senior essay, a writing course in English, and a quantitative skills course. Students must demonstrate competency in a foreign language and must, with the approval of an advisor, do at least a semester's internship for credit in an organization concerned with international affairs. At the end of the semester, students must write a critical term paper evaluating their experience in the light of relevant literature.

City College students must take eight elective courses in four fields; they must choose three courses from two of the fields and one course from each of the other two fields. The four fields are the following: History/Political Science; Anthropology/Philosophy/Sociobiology; Economics; and Area Studies. This latter field offers courses from ten departments on Africa, Asia, the Middle East, the Caribbean, the U.S.S.R., Latin America, Europe, Israel, and Puerto Rico. Majors must also take four low-level core courses in the Division of Social Science, which is comprised of Social Sciences, Area

Studies, History, Political Science, and Economics. Finally, study abroad is encouraged. It may consist of courses at a foreign institution, independent field work, or intensive language training.

City College also offers a concentration in International Studies for which a student takes only seven courses.

In addition to its formal curricula, the International Studies program sponsors a series of special events for the general student body featuring lunchtime lectures by and discussions with faculty members, government officials, and representatives of various international non-governmental organizations.

International Studies has been primarily dependent on College funds. The initial monies came through a program called LAPP (Liberal Arts, Pre-Professional Programs, and Public Policy). LAPP was established with a $500,000 Mellon Foundation grant to CUNY to serve as an apparatus for developing new programs at City College. A small grant was awarded by the Transnational Academic Program of the Institute for World Order (now the World Policy Institute) to assist in the development of the introductory course. Although additional funds have been sought from other sources, no sizeable grants have been received to date.

Because of its origins in the LAPP program, the rationale for International Studies at City College has been oriented toward skills and career development from the start. A current LAPP brochure states that students completing the International Studies major may pursue "a number of career options, including work in a wide variety of government agencies, international businesses, multinational corporations, international banks, the international press, and teaching positions." The major's value as preparation for graduate study is emphasized.

Contact: Sherry Baver, Director, International Studies Program. City College of New York, Convent Ave. at 138th Street, New York, NY 10031; (212) 690-6909.

International Development, Warren Wilson College

The International Development program at Warren Wilson College is designed to increase global awareness in the college as a whole. Special emphasis is placed upon what constitutes a world citizen approach to education, what technologies are appropriate in other cultures as well as in our own, and what kinds of lifestyles and communities are desirable in today's changing world. The program provides groups of students and staff with the opportunity to work as volunteers for eight weeks in overseas village development projects.

Warren Wilson College is a small liberal arts college in southern Appalachia. The college has a work program which involves resident students in maintaining all aspects of the college, from farming and gardening to plumbing and secretarial work. Students contribute 15 hours a week in exchange for room and board. The college also has a long tradition of service to the region and of maintaining itself as a small but diverse international community of students and staff. Seventeen percent of the college's students come from Asia, Africa, or Latin America.

The International Development program, elected in addition to a student's major, was initiated in 1982 to combine Wilson's patterns of work, study, and service. A small Department of Education grant helped commence the program by adding a technical advisor to establish contact with local projects and to train students in appropriate technology. The program was built on existing courses in intercultural studies. The required preparatory courses for the program are "Global Issues," "International Development and Appropriate Technology," and Spanish. There are also a number of recommended courses: "Intercultural Communications," "Economic Development," "Self-Instructional Language Study," area courses such as "Introduction to Mexico, Central America, and the Caribbean," "Nutrition," "Appropriate Technology," "Horticulture," and "Community Field Studies."

These courses are followed by eight weeks of overseas project work with locally-initiated non-governmental projects. Groups of about ten students, led by a staff member, participate in a local work project, devise and carry out additional service projects, and live and commune with the local people. The program emphasizes that the students participate in the project to learn from the indigenous people and not to teach them. Two groups have already completed their work: helping to build a community of 70 hurricane-proof earth block houses, garden, and market in a village in the Dominican Republic, and aiding villagers in central Mexico to construct an education center. The next two groups will help build a medical mission in Yucatan, Mexico, and work with the Sarvodaya movement in Sri Lanka.

During the work project, each student is required to maintain a journal of his/her experiences and a personal diary. Upon return to Warren Wilson at the end of the eight weeks, the students help to orient others for their own overseas projects and share their experiences with the wider Warren Wilson community. Returning students also write two papers which report on their field work and on a researched topic.

A major goal of the program is to keep costs of travel, food, and lodging low—at around $500—so that the program is open to all students. Training is planned so that students from different majors can participate. The program has involved students majoring in social work, sociology, intercultural and environmental studies, English and music. Future plans include integrating the groups' work more fully into daily college life. As an example, students will be using their appropriate technology skills to build a 1000-square-foot structure on the campus. The program is also being developed to include service projects in local rural and urban areas.

Contact: Glenn Mitchell, Department of Social Sciences. Warren Wilson College, Swannanoa, NC 28778; (704) 298-3325.

Center for the Study of World Problems, Pennsylvania State University

In 1969 Penn State, with an enrollment of over 30,000, was like most large universities in the U.S., beset by student unrest and malaise as the Vietnam era drew to a close. In 1970, the University put into operation the first stages of a plan for a Center for the Study of World Problems. At that time, it was hoped that the new Center would capture the interests of protesting students and help unite the 12 separate colleges of the campus in a common, centrally-funded and administered instructional program. Two years later the nascent program was defunct. The purpose of this case study is to describe the plans for the Center, its two years of operation, and the reasons for its demise.

In 1969, it was apparent that very few courses at Penn State adequately reflected the fact that relations between nations had become increasingly multilateral and that social problems and issues had become global rather than simply international in impact. Although problem-oriented courses had been taught for years, mostly in the graduate schools, virtually all of them had been oriented towards domestic problems, specific disciplines, or problems of certain geographical locations abroad.

Consequently, the Center was created to seek out professors and sponsor their work in developing and teaching new courses dealing with transnational problems. The Center provided a modest sum of money to support the development of new courses, assisted in the acquisition of course materials, and identified resource persons such as area specialists, visiting foreign scholars and students.

During the two-year life of the Center, two courses were developed. "Problems of Rural Development" was taught in the College of Agriculture and dealt with the worldwide problem of mass exodus from rural regions. "World Problems of Education," offered in the College of Education, dealt with the widespread problems of student unrest, unemployed school leavers, discrimination against women, and illiteracy, among other topics.

Courses developed but not taught were "World Hunger" (College of Agriculture), "The Social Impact of Science and Technology" and "War and Peace" (College of Liberal Arts). In preliminary planning stages were "Pollution Across International Boundaries" and "Control of Nuclear Power" (College of Science).

During the Center's life, over 75 students were exposed to the World Problems course; an estimated 17 professors from varying disciplines participated as course developers, consultants, or visiting professors. Over 20 foreign scholars and 30 foreign students were involved in presenting multicultural views. Virtually all participating students and professors were enthusiastic about the approach and the substance of these courses. Why, then, was the Center terminated?

While the Center was successful in enlisting the support of a number of professors, administrative support in terms of official endorsement and funding for course development was never forthcoming. The death of a provost resulted in a new policy of decentralization; administrative responsibilities were shifted from the president's office to those of the deans of the separate colleges. It, therefore, became impossible to generate small grant funds for a university-wide program from the individual budgets of the 12 separate colleges.

The central lesson to be learned from the demise of the Penn State Center on World Problems is that while creative, innovative, energetic, pioneering professors are certainly the heart of a new program, the wholehearted support of top-level policy makers who control resources and create a general climate conducive to innovation is essential.

Contact: Howard B. Leavitt (former director), Vice President, Consortium for International Cooperation in Higher Education. National Center for Higher Education, 1 Dupont Circle, NW, Washington, DC 20036; (202) 659-4197.

Peace Studies Program, St. Bonaventure University

St. Bonaventure University was founded as a Catholic College on the feast day of St. Francis of Assisi, a man canonized for his preaching and practicing of nonviolence and peace. The University was named after the patron Saint of Franciscan Studies and Learning. The school offers an undergraduate degree in theology and maintains a graduate institute for Franciscan studies which it calls a "principal American center for Franciscan research." The school requires that all students take three courses in both philosophy and theology in order to graduate.

The University also has four programs sponsored by the United States Armed Services. These programs allow students to train for the army or marines while studying for an undergraduate degree; they also allow servicemen and veterans to complete or commence their undergraduate degrees while serving at the local army base.

Faced with such a dissonant climate, in 1980 Friar Mathias Boyle, President of the University, established a Committee on the Purpose and Identity of the University. This Committee recognized that the Catholic and Franciscan heritage of the University included a strong tradition of promoting peace and justice. A year later in December of 1981, the Faculty Senate Curriculum Committee approved a proposal for a secondary concentration—much like a minor—in peace studies.

The Peace Studies Program is designed to be fundamentally multidisciplinary. Courses are team-taught. The Program also includes "integrating seminars" in which three or four lecturers participate in a discussion format with the students.

At present, there are four core courses: "Integrating Seminar," "Problems of War and Peace," "Nonviolence and Conflict Resolution," and "Peace and World Order". In addition to these four courses, students must choose three electives of the six that have been approved by the coordinating committee thus far: "History of War," "American Military History," "Geography of Food and Famine," "Management and the Behavioral Sciences," "Christianity and Society" and "International Organization." The Program is willing to approve other existing courses as electives if the professors teaching those courses allow the Peace Studies students to consider the course material in light of peace or social justice issues.

Most funding for the Program came from the University itself, although COPRED, the Institute for World Order (now the World Policy Institute), and the Poverello Fund of the Friars of Holy Name Province contributed additional funds.

Contact: Sister Mary Hamilton, Coordinator, Peace Studies Program. St. Bonaventure University, St. Bonaventure, NY 14778; (716) 375-2520.

Peace Education Program, Gustavus Adolphus College

The Peace Education Program at Gustavus Adolphus College was initiated in 1973. The objectives of the program are 1) to infuse the concerns of peace and justice into the existing curriculum and campus life and 2) to acquaint faculty and the 2,200 students with the issues and problems that relate to promoting nonviolence and social justice.

There is no Peace Studies major, department, or course. It was always felt that to segregate peace studies so that it becomes a competing bureaucratic component would be contradictory to the entire concept of the discipline. Rather, the effort should be an informal one, so that as people learn more about the issues and confront their own values, they become more concerned and knowledgeable about peace and justice issues. While it is difficult to measure its impact on the College, the Program's success is reflected in the greater concern for peace and justice issues in the curriculum and campus life in general.

In its early years, the Program was directed by Dr. Bernard Lafayette, Jr. During this time, many faculty members took leaves of absence which allowed them to study peace and justice issues more closely. Visiting professors of Peace Studies and a variety of outside speakers presented the concerns and issues of the program. In 1976, the Consortium on Peace Research, Education, and Development (COPRED) moved its national headquarters to Gustavus for two years, and Dr. Norman Walbek joined the faculty as director of COPRED and part-time member of the political science department.

Funding for the program has come from different sources. The U.S. Office of Education funded a World Development Program in which the faculty received stipends to study peace and justice issues during the summer, the results of which were presented in public and course lectures. The World Development Program resulted in a variety of January term courses and over 100 guest lectures.

With the help of a private contribution, the College presented its first May Day Conference on the arms race in 1982 and a similar forum in 1983. The College will continue to support faculty leaves, develop conferences, bring in guest speakers, and provide other services and activities related to peace through the Mardag Foundation.

In addition to the variety of courses and peace themes that exist throughout the curriculum, there is an active Hunger Awareness group on campus, a Peace and Social Issues student group, an Amnesty International chapter and a Political Issues forum. Supporters believe that these groups have grown out of the activities of the Peace Education Program.

Contact: Professor Norman V. Walbek, Political Science Department, Gustavus Adolphus College, St. Peter, MN 56082; (507) 931-7676.

Politics, Economics and Society Program, State University of New York at Old Westbury

The program in Politics, Economics and Society (PES), established in 1971 at SUNY/Old Westbury, is in a unique and somewhat enviable situation in that it enjoys an unusual degree of support from students and faculty. As one PES professor remarked, "It's safe to say that the whole campus is concerned." The main reason for the enlightened sensitivity at the college is a combination of the student body composition and a concerted effort on the part of the faculty to emphasize the issues of social injustice.

The students of the college are made up of over half women, and half minorities, and have an average age of 28; in short, it is a student body that has been "historically by-passed by higher education." Furthermore, its faculty is ethnically and culturally diverse and is "dedicated to teaching in a context that promises to redress some of society's ills." The College's stated mission for the 1980's and beyond is to encourage a sense of moral and social responsibility for constructive social change, to develop and implement a curriculum that, among other things, addresses contemporary issues and the social forces that shape students' lives, to encourage interdisciplinary study, to include bilingual programs, and to encourage students to participate in experimental field studies and internships.

The goals of the PES major can be summed up as examining the "needs, problems, issues, and concerns of a student body that is comparatively older, poorer, multi-cultural, multi-lingual, multi-racial and from a variety of educational backgrounds and circumstances." The PES curriculum is organized around a core of five courses which all PES majors are required to complete in sequence: "Political Economy I and II" is an interdisciplinary analysis of pressing social problems and developmental tendencies of modern capitalism, imperialism, and anti-capitalist socialist revolution; "Introduction to the Third World" surveys the problems facing the Third World today, as well as these areas' history of colonialism, neo-colonialism, capitalism, and struggle for independence; "History of Social Theory I or II" are historical social science theory courses with emphasis on the interaction between political and economic changes in society and social theories. Finally, students must take a senior seminar which provides both an integrated approach to examining current theory and methodology in the social sciences, as well as guidance and supervision on senior projects.

The second part of the PES program consists of three concentrations: Political Economy/Economics, Political Sociology, or Anthropology. The key courses in the Political Economy/Economics concentration are "Micro- and Macro-Economics," "Statistics," "Introduction to Econometrics," and "Advanced Micro- (or Macro-) Economic Theory." The main courses in the Political Sociology concentration are "People, Power and Politics," "Ideology and Social Class," "Comparative Political Systems," and "Political Power and Social Class." Finally, the key courses in the Anthropology concentration are "Foundations of Modern Anthropology," "Political Anthropology," and "Introduction to Society."

There are also a variety of electives which fall into the three categories of international, area, and ethnic courses, and do not need to be taken in any particular combination. Students are also encouraged to double major; in the past four years, about 12-15 PES students have done so. Each year, about 20 of the program's 100 plus majors graduate. In an effort to provide the sort of social justice which the program advocates, the core courses are offered every year, both during the day and at nights; elective and concentration courses are also offered during both day and night classes. The Old Westbury program has been successful because of both the faculty and student commitment to it.

There has been above average student participation in both the major and related campus events. The PES remains highly visible on campus.

Contact: Angela Gilliam, Convener, PES. SUNY/Old Westbury, Box 210, Old Westbury, Long Island, NY 11568; (516) 876-3000.

Faith-Justice Institute, St. Joseph's University

St. Joseph's University is an independent, Jesuit liberal arts institution with a student body that is over 80% Catholic and native Philadelphian. Such a homogeneous student body makes for a rather provincial and non-worldly campus atmosphere. The University believes that "Christ and His teachings should inform its activities and inspire reverence and love for God and His creation." The Faith-Justice Institute was created to be a direct route for the reflection and implementation of these ideas. Yet, despite the religious background on the campus, the Institute receives little student support.

The program of studies of the Faith and Justice Institute provides an opportunity for students to relate their academic courses to important contemporary problems. The focus of the Institute is to explore the ethical implications of major contemporary human problems and point the way to solutions and responses based on the Judeo-Christian value of justice-right relationship. The approach is problem-centered and interdisciplinary, stressing student experiential work as an integral part of the program.

Students completing the Faith-Justice Program are awarded a certificate. The Program is much like a minor, except that students may count the Program's courses towards their major or towards the general requirements of the University.

Students are required to take three courses. "Hunger For Justice" and "Humanity Challenged: War or Peace" are both interdisciplinary seminars which probe the ethical dimension of specific contemporary issues. By reviewing political, economic, and technical factors and studying philosophical, esthetic, and theological approaches, the courses try to illicit a personal response to their content. Students must take a theology course, which is approved by the director of the Institute. They must also do some sort of field work in order to provide them with more realistic insights into the human dynamics of specific justice issues in contemporary society.

Students must take five electives. The electives are clustered according to the student's major. There are three clusters: sociology, psychology, and international business. As an example, those students who are majoring in international business must take the following courses as their electives: "Government and Business," "Seminar in International Finance," "Management of Human Resources," "Business, Society, and Ethics," and "Moral Philosophy." Appropriate course groupings may be developed in other majors.

The Institute also sponsors community programs, such as a 10-mile Run for Hunger, Hunger Awareness Week, and volunteer work at local hospices and soup kitchens. In addition, it sponsors open forums in which corporate, government, and military policies "that seem to victimize people" are probed and Christian/moral responses are sought.

Contact: Father Donald Clifford., S.J., Director, Faith and Justice Institute. St. Joseph's University, 5600 City Ave., Room 300 B/L, Philadelphia, PA 19131; (215) 879-7300.

Program in Nonviolent Conflict and Change, Syracuse University

The Program in Nonviolent Conflict and Change (PNCC) was created in 1970 to study creative, peaceful ways of dealing with conflict. Since its inception, PNCC has participated in nationwide efforts to develop and expand peace education and research. The basis of these efforts is an examination of the theory, history, and dynamics of nonviolent movements and techniques, including an inquiry into their social-psychological and political dimensions. Courses focus on alternative means of waging and managing conflict on all levels, from interpersonal to international, and on the methods of conflict intervention.

Syracuse University is one of the largest private universities in the United States, with approximately 10,000 undergraduate students and 5,000 graduate students on the main campus. Every year, about 600 undergraduate students enroll in PNCC courses. There are approximately 15 graduate students pursuing doctorates with a peace or nonviolent focus.

PNCC is part of the Maxwell School of Citizenship and Public Affairs, which is the social science division of Syracuse University. The Maxwell School, established in 1924, has long been an internationally recognized center for teaching and research in public policy, training for public service, and general citizenship education. In addition to the usual academic departments, the Maxwell School includes a wide variety of interdisciplinary and professional programs, including Foreign and Comparative Studies, Social Science, and Metropolitan Studies.

The requirements for an undergraduate major in nonviolent conflict and change are six core courses and a minimum of five additional courses in related disciplines, such as Public Affairs, Sociology, Political Science, and History. The six core courses are the following: "Nonviolent Action and the Nature of Social Change," which compares, among other topics, the efficacy of nonviolent and violent behavior in effecting change; "Nonviolent Change in America," an historical investigation of social movements such as the suffragettes, early labor movements, and Native Americans; "Nonviolent Action: What it is and How it Works" considers the variety, range, dynamics, effectiveness, and implications of nonviolent actions; "Nonviolent Conflict Intervention" emphasizes theories and skills of listening, problem-solving, negotiation, conflict management, and mediation; "Selected Topics in International Peace" and the "Senior Research Seminar" are both in-depth examinations of particular theme-related topics such as feminism and nonviolence, or nuclear power and nuclear weapons protests. Students may fulfill requirements as part of a dual major or combine several disciplines in order to examine such subjects as race or labor relations, law, or social change. Each student, in consultation with the director of PNCC, plans her or his course of study.

The Program in Nonviolent Conflict and Change believes its educational service to the greater Syracuse community is one of its most important functions. In the past, outreach programs have included workshops, a highly successful three-course summer institute on conflict management, a film series, and aid to local teachers on curriculum development. PNCC staff and students have also led discussions about nonviolence and conflict resolution with community organizations, lectured, and done draft counseling.

Contact: Professor Neil Katz, Director, Program in Nonviolent Conflict and Change. 249 Physics Building, Syracuse University, Syracuse, NY 13210; (315) 423-3870.

Program for the Study of Peace and War, Boston College

Respect for the dignity of persons and the "faith that does justice" motto are the underlying philosophies of this Jesuit-affiliated college. It is difficult to single out just one facet of Boston College that inspires students to study and act upon peace and human rights issues; the urgent problems of war, economic inequity and global resource shortages are current themes in dozens of campus activities and are stressed in many courses.

With a middle- to upper-class student population of over 14,000—the highest full-time enrollment of any U.S. Catholic college—B.C. is introducing large numbers of young people to global problems and their possible solutions from a broad spectrum of disciplines. The Program for the Study of Peace and War, initiated in 1971 through the impetus of a highly motivated group of undergraduates, attempts to address these global concerns.

The Program directly sponsors four courses which serve as the core of a Peace Studies concentration which students are invited to design for themselves; at this point there is no formal majors program. The courses place dual emphases on the East-West strategic confrontation and the economic relationship between industrialized and developing countries.

"Perspectives on War, Aggression and Conflict Resolution, I and II" is a two-semester interdisciplinary course which examines the causes of war from the perspectives of history, psychology, economics, sociology and political science. "Perspectives on World Hunger" studies the political and economic roots of global hunger. "Social Change in a Militarized Economy" discusses the tensions that the military buildup creates for a government dedicated to the good of its people. "Perspectives on Liberation Theology" examines the theology that has emerged from recent social teachings of the Catholic Church and its activities within the existing political/economic climate of Latin America.

Students create their own major utilizing these core courses and one of five pre-designed sets of electives or "clusters" which are offered in various departments and arranged around the following themes: sources and causes of conflict; human rights; violence in society; conflict resolution; nonviolence.

Sponsors of the Program aim to encourage students to affirm and act upon their ideals and values through this academic reference. The program sponsors numerous extracurricular activities such as films and lectures, and conferences on issues of interest to the Boston College community. In addition, social service opportunities are made available through other B.C.-affiliated groups, including: World Hunger Committee; Haley House, which offers community living to a limited number of people, lectures, films, workshops and other events; PULSE, which enables part-time off-campus social service field work; and the International Volunteers program, which provides placement for students in Haiti, Nicaragua, Mexico, Jamaica and Peru.

Contact: Rev. Robert J. Daly, SJ, Program for the Study of Peace and War. Theology Department, Carney 418, Boston College, Chestnut Hill, MA 02167; (617) 969-0100 ext. 3880.

Peace Studies, Southern Illinois University at Edwardsville

The Peace Studies program at the Southern Illinois University at Edwardsville (SIUE) got off to a grand start when demand for its core course suddenly—through a change in college course requirements—exceeded the capacity to staff it. In one year, 453 students crowded into the course "The Problem of War and Peace"; enrollment is now over 600. In 1974 a Peace Studies minor was approved. At the same time, Ronald J. Glossup, the motivating force behind the Peace Studies program, petitioned the University to allow the United Nations flag to fly daily on one of the campus flagpoles. Glossup believed that the flag would serve as a daily reminder that all the students are part of a world community and are thus world citizens.

The goal of the Peace Studies minor is to allow students to take related courses from several different departments. The goal of the core course, "The Problem of War and Peace," is to provide students with a political awareness of contemporary events and to better evaluate the proposals and actions of politicians. The main pedagogic thrust is an understanding of the nature of the war problem, and a critical appreciation of the ideas which have been put forth about how to solve it.

There are four other required: "Introduction to International Relations", "History of American Diplomacy (since 1919)", and either "International Organizations" or "Public International Law." Students also must take one course on recent economic thought and two electives. Electives include courses in Economics, Political Science, History, Philosophy, Anthropology, Government, Sociology and the Interdisciplinary department. Students must elect the minor in addition to a major, which can be totally unrelated to Peace Studies. However, no courses counted toward graduation requirements for the major may also be counted as requirements for the minor.

The Program has no budget of its own and, consequently, depends on support from the departments involved, primarily Philosophical Studies, Government, and History. Although its core course has a consistently large enrollment, as of August 1982, only three students have graduated with a Peace Studies minor. These two disparate factors could endanger the future of the Program. In addition, Mr. Glossup maintains that the Program will not be expanded until more students elect it. Until then, however, SIUE will continue to provide at least a one-course glimpse into Peace Studies to a great number of students.

Contact: Ronald J. Glossup, Chair, Peace Studies Program. Room 3212, Peck Building, SIUE Edwardsville, IL 62026; (618) 692-2250.

Peace Studies Program, Bethel College

Bethel College is a residential Christian liberal arts college in North Newton, Kansas. The college, which has approximately 625 students, was
founded in 1887 by Mennonites who came to Kansas committed to working
for freedom and peace through "feeding the hungry, clothing the naked, and
loving the enemy." Today, Bethel College organizes its curriculum and
plans its campus life around the values of justice, reconciliation, and peace.
In 1974, the Fund for the Improvement of Postsecondary Education awarded
a federal grant to develop the college around peacemaking and conflict management.

The "peace" objective is further pursued on campus in many ways. College committees which govern such things as student life, policies, and
procedures have representation from faculty, students, and administrators.
These same groups work together to develop skills in confrontation,
rational dialogue, and reconciliation. Approximately 20% of the students
are engaged in some form of community-based voluntary service, in addition to the students who interrupt their formal studies with internships or
periods of full-time voluntary service. Many campus events focus on peace
issues: twice-weekly campus-wide meetings, four annual lectures, the
peace film series, and special short term seminars, which are sometimes led
by visiting professors.

The Peace Studies major at Bethel is the academic complement to this
goal of peace and freedom. Peace Studies is a multidisciplinary major
designed to help students understand the nature and causes of human
conflict, the factors contributing to peace with justice, and the processes by
which conflict can be managed creatively to bring about fundamental social
change. The program includes study of global relationships, conflicts between groups and institutions, and conflicts among individuals. The Peace
Studies major is granted only to students who have majored in another
academic discipline.

In addition to the 30 hours of regular course work, Peace Studies majors
are required to participate in an off-campus internship which integrates
peacemaking with students' other academic major. Students are encouraged
to take special courses and seminars at other institutions engaged in peace
research; some students have gained credit through the programs connected
with the Canadian Peace Research Institute.

In the view of the college, Peace Studies is not just a specialized field of
study, but a central issue to be dealt with in all disciplines. Consequently,
Bethel College faculty members from all academic divisions have worked
for two years to bring their own competencies and academic disciplines to
bear on the problems of conflict and prospects of peace.

*Contact: Peace Studies Program, Bethel College, North Newton, KS 67117;
(316) 283-2500.*

Peace and World Order Studies, Colgate University

The Peace and World Order Studies Program (originally Peace Studies) was established at Colgate University in 1970, making it one of the oldest programs of its kind in the United States. The program, which received initial financial support from the Institute for World Order (now the World Policy Institute), the Fund For Peace and a New York State Department of Education grant, is highly visible on campus and seeks to engage students, faculty and others in an active vocational quest to create a "world community freed from organized violence and based upon a just and viable system of peace."

In 1971, Colgate University established the first chair of Peace Studies at an undergraduate institution in the U.S. Named for the late Dag Hammarskjold, Secretary General of the United Nations 1953-61, the chair was made possible through the personal gift of George Cooley, Class of '21. The college also set up a residence hall, the Ralph Bunche House, where 36 of the school's 2,600 students can live and share their interests in peace, social justice, and community.

The academic program offers multidisciplinary, team-taught courses shared by the faculties of Political Science, Philosophy, Economics, History, and Geography. Students may major or concentrate in Peace and World Order Studies, the latter option functioning essentially like a minor.

The major requires seven basic and three elective courses, as well as an internship. There are two required introductory courses, as well as an internship. On average, 40 students attend "Problems of War and Peace," which presents the moral, political, and social dimensions of modern war and weaponry, with some discussion of alternative means of conflict resolution. "Problems of World Community" examines resource competition and the economic and political disparities that threaten human survival, with some discussion of alternative kinds of world organization.

Students must also select one course on ethical perspectives, two in international affairs and three elective courses. Examples of courses are "Social and Political Ethics," "International Organization," and "Problems of Arms Control and Disarmament." In addition, students participate in a methods course (either the "Seminar in Nonviolence and Conflict Resolution" offered through the program or an independent study), an off-campus January term internship, and an upper-level research seminar, all of which reflect the "action" orientation of the peace program.

The Ralph Bunche House serves as the residential education center of the program. Named for the late Ralph J. Bunche, former Undersecretary General of the U.N. and Nobel Peace Prize recipient, the House offers many programs through the initiatives of its members and the resident advisor, panels, lectures, films, workshops and special events. A resident noted that the house "keeps everybody together" and makes peace studies visible on campus.

The resident advisor for Ralph Bunche is usually the "peace intern," a graduating senior who is selected through competition to serve various teaching and administrative functions. The intern, who is funded by an outside grant, facilitates the peace studies program on campus, lectures occasionally, and joins weekly faculty meetings, among other tasks.

Contact: Director, Peace and World Order Studies Program. Colgate University, Hamilton, NY 13346; (315) 824-1000.

Peace and Justice Studies, Guilford College

The Quaker faith stresses "candor, integrity, tolerance, simplicity, and strong concern for social justice and world peace." A peace and justice studies program is offered at Guilford College, a liberal arts college nestled in the suburbs of Greensboro, North Carolina. Guilford, the oldest co-educational institution in the South, does not attempt to indoctrinate its Quakerism, but the Society of Friend's traditional concern with peace and social change enriches the college environment. Approximately nine percent of the school's 1000 students and 20 percent of the faculty and administration are Quakers.

The Quaker heritage of a global perspective in learning is infused into the general curriculum. Foreign language study and a course in intercultural study is required for practically all baccalaureate degree candidates. The intercultural courses, which are divided regionally, examine the patterns of thought, religious and philosophical traditions, modes of artistic expression, political and social structures, economic systems, and lifestyles found in cultures other than our own. Interdisciplinary studies are also required of most majors. Interdisciplinary Studies 101, a freshman requirement, is taught in small discussion groups and led by a team of professors from various disciplines. The course explores a single major theme; in 1981-82, for example, the theme was "freedom."

Peace and Justice Studies is a minor concentration which encourages students and faculty to consider the complex interdependence of human life with our natural and sociopolitical environments. The peace and justice minor requires two specific courses—"Social Problems" and a choice between a capstone course "Interdisciplinary Studies," mentioned above, or an independent study. "Social Problems" is the core course for the concentration. Its major objectives: 1) to develop a frame of reference for the study of certain social problems, as rooted in the complex interdependence of personal and social systems; 2) to investigate and propose possible solutions to social problems that seem particularly ominous, evaluating both the positive and negative consequences of such solutions; and 3) to encourage students to "image" and act on their preferred futures.

In addition, four elective courses must be chosen from a selection of 32 offered within the departments of Sociology, Philosophy, Chemistry, Economics, Political Science, Religion, Psychology, Geology and History.

Contact: Cyrus Johnson, Program Director, Peace and Justice Studies. Guilford College, Archdale 206, 5800 West Friendly Avenue, Greensboro, NC 27410; (919) 292-5511.

Integrative Change Major, Kent State University

The Integrative Change major at the 25,000-student Kent State University is offered through the Center for Peaceful Change in cooperation with the College of Arts and Sciences. The program, formerly the Peaceful Change Major, seeks to develop "human change agents" who can think sensitively about human needs and who have the vision to see the world as a community. It is a transdisciplinary program in which personal development and experiental learning are integral. The major provides an excellent background for careers in public and private service organizations.

The Center for Peaceful Change (CPC) is a "living" memorial to the May 1970 Kent State tragedy. Established in May 1971, the Center is an academic unit reporting directly to the Office of the Academic Vice President and Provost. The Center operates as a regular academic department and relies upon university funding.

The Center offers five core requirements which all Integrative Change majors must take. "Anatomy of Peaceful Change" provides an introduction to the scope and nature of peace studies; acquaints the student with some methods of peaceful change at various levels; and examines the role and potentional impact of an agent of social change. "Theories of Change" examines various theories of social and individual change from a variety of points of view. "Concepts of Nonviolence" explores the philosophical, psychological, sociological, and political implications of differing concepts of nonviolence. "Techniques of Nonviolent Change" and "Seminar in Peaceful Change" both examine the elements of peaceful change in human systems.

In addition, students are required to fulfill an independent study course and a field study. The remaining half of the necessary credits are earned through electives offered in 17 college departments chosen in consultation with an advisor from the Center for Peaceful Change.

Although relatively few students at Kent State elect to major in Integrative Change, on average over 100 students a year enroll in the courses offered through the Center. In general, the program has low visibility, but among certain members of the Board of Trustees, administrators, faculty and students, support is strong. Advocates of the program point out that their efforts have caused the Ohio State Statistics Board to establish a code number for Peace Studies.

Administrators of the program see their major problems to be material. Procuring adequate funding is a long-standing difficulty and the lack of an adequate textbook creates much work for faculty. Efforts are now being made to compile an introductory text for the "Anatomy of Peaceful Change" course.

Contact: Dennis Carey, Director, Center for Peaceful Change. Kent State University, Kent, OH 44242; (216) 672-3143.

World Issues Program,
The School for International Training

The School for International Training (SIT) was founded in 1964 in response to a demand from people interested in pursuing international careers. The school offers intercultural training in a non-traditional undergraduate and graduate environment in which there are irregular semesters, highly-individualized programs, and no departments. Each student's program combines classroom and internship work in a rigorous and demanding experience-based education.

Students at SIT are 19-45 years of age and from diverse cultural and international backgrounds. Undergraduate students, all of whom study in the World Issues Program, transfer to SIT after two years of undergraduate work at other institutions. They must be willing to play an active role in determining the course and success of their own learning.

The World Issues Program offers only an undergraduate degree in International Studies. It offers four major areas to which all its students are exposed: Peace Studies and Conflict Resolution, Environment and Ecology, Population and Family Planning, and Social and Economic Development. In addition, there are a number of skills which are specifically stressed: management (project design and evaluation), research, verbal (public presentations, interviewing skills), group skills (leadership, organization), cross-cultural (awareness of different values and norms) and language. During the first "semester," which actually lasts eight months, World Issues students are trained in all of the above areas and skills. Training methods consist of intensive three-week "classes," language laboratory work and classroom instruction, short internships, community meetings, and independent study.

Some of the courses which students take during the first semester are: "Perspectives in Foreign Policy," "International Economics," "Community Development," "Environmental Studies," "Economic and Social Development," "Peace and Conflict Studies," and "Cross-Cultural Communications."

During the second and third "semesters," which can last around 30-50 weeks, students work on internships abroad. Before they depart for these jobs, they work with an advisor to define their areas of interest and learning goals. They must also begin to develop plans for their senior projects. In the past students have gone to countries all over the world and have worked in a variety of organizations. Some examples are: Save the Children, Inc., Indonesia; United Nations Development Forum, Switzerland; National Park Service of Costa Rica; Ministry of Agriculture, Egypt; Gandhi Peace Foundation, India; Minority Rights Group, England; Peace Corps Language Development, Botswana; U.S. Public Health Service, Alaska.

All internships are full-time activities with organizations whose purposes are consistent with both the student's career goals and the priorities of the World Issues Program's. Financial arrangements vary greatly, but most students receive compensation of some sort.

In the fourth and final semester, students must participate in a re-entry seminar, which is described as "cross-cultural debriefing." They share their experiences with the community in a day-long presentation which covers the substantive learning and issues of the internship. Finally, they must research and write a thesis. Fourth-semester students also participate in seminars and workshops on career choice. They help tutor first-semester students and work on group projects. The goals of the fourth semester are to synthesize learning accomplished during the internships, to develop theoretical perspectives on internship experiences, and to prepare for graduate study or professional careers.

The World Issues Program graduates about 25 students a year. The Program has no serious monetary problems; student tuitions provide the bulk of annual funding.

Contact: Shaun Bennett, Director, World Issues Program. The School for International Training, Brattleboro, VT 05301; (802) 257-7751.

Peace and World Order Studies, Berkshire Community College

The Peace and World Order Studies Program was begun at the 3,000-student Berkshire Community College in 1982 to provide students with an understanding of global problems from the perspective of the world order values of peace, social justice, economic well-being and ecological balance, with a strong emphasis on political activism. Peace and World Order Studies is a non-degree-granting concentration within the Selected Studies and Liberal Arts programs. The coordinator of the Program, Professor Don Lathrop, says that the main educational concern of peace studies is to expand student views and to prepare them to pursue further degrees in Peace Studies, History, Political Science, and Religion. He describes the program as an "activist workshop."

Courses related to peace studies are included in the Departments of Business Administration, Accounting, Physics, Human Resources, History, and Political Science. Optional courses in these departments may be taken to complement the four required for the concentration. The introductory course "Peace, World Order, and War" examines the causes of war, the obstacles to peace, superpower military preparedness, corporate activities, the military economy, and strategies for peace and world order. Pursuant to the Program's activist goals, course participants are required to both write letters concerning these issues to relevant persons in the media and government and to complete an independent project, which might involve organizing a conference or drafting a conversion proposal for local industries involved with the military.

"Models for Human Community," the second course in the concentration, focuses on alternative images of human society based on political, economic, and social justice. "Literature of Peace and War" includes sections from a variety of sources, including the Old Testament, Thucydides, Thoreau, and Tolstoy. "The Peace and World Order Practicum," the final course in the series, is individually designed independent study. Projects might include internships with established peace groups, research on nonviolence, and teaching peace studies to area high school students. All four peace studies courses fulfill liberal arts requirements at the college and can thus be taken by non-majors to fill distribution requirements.

In addition to the Practicum and other course requirements, activism is stressed by the many campus and public events sponsored jointly by the Program and the Global Issues Resource Organization (GIRO), a student peace group. GIRO has independently educated both the college and the public communities through workshops, conferences, and publications concerning nonviolent problem-solving, disarmament, world unity, ecology, world hunger, and other globally-oriented problems. GIRO stresses active political participation and serves as an information center for peace-related events. Individual students enrolled in Peace and World Order Studies have also organized forums independently of GIRO. For example, some students organized a forum with local rifle associations addressing the connection between handgun proliferation and the arms race, and have presented films on the dangers of militarism and nuclear weapons to members of a local army base and to several hundred area high school students.

A wide range of students, including older professionals and returning students, Air Force veterans, high school students, and college-aged students from all disciplines have enrolled in the concentration.

According to Don Lathrop, one of the Program's greatest strengths is that it gives students the expertise and analytical tools necessary both to engage in informed dialogue with participants of the military-industrial complex and to confront feelings of powerlessness. Little criticism of the Program has been heard on campus, although some faculty members are opposed to it on ideological grounds and have argued against the emphasis on activism.

However, Lathrop met with no resistance when he recently proposed new courses for the program. The Program is financed completely by the college but retains control over its allocations.

Contact Donald Lathrop, Director, Peace and World Order Studies. Berkshire Community College, West Street, Pittsfield, MA 01201; (413) 499-4660, ext. 351.

Peace and Conflict Studies, Juniata College

At Juniata College, Peace and Conflict Studies (PACS) is more than a discipline. It is an idea of "applied liberal arts" which allows each discipline to contribute toward an understanding of the problem of war. PACS students are encouraged to consider ways to delegitimize war and to discover alternative ways to solve conflicts. With roots in the Church of the Brethren, Juniata's religious heritage has always included the peace tradition. Although the PACS program encourages an interdisciplinary—and not necessarily a religious—basis for peace studies, this Brethren background provides underlying support for the program.

Specific support is supplied by Dr. and Mrs. John C. Baker, whose generous endowment funds all programming expenses of the PACS program. PACS's financial strength makes it possible for students to participate in the greater peace network. For example, students have visited government agencies such as the Arms Control and Disarmament Agency and the Pentagon, met with foreign diplomats and discussed policy with special-interest groups such as the National Peace Academy Campaign and the Center for Defense Information. Juniata also actively participates in the New Call to Peacemaking Conferences which are sponsored by Brethren, Mennonite and Quaker colleges in Pennsylvania and Virginia.

Juniata features "programs of emphasis" (POE) in place of traditional majors. The POE encourages students to tailor their courses to their particular interests, even if that means crossing departmental lines. This concept works especially well for PACS students, who generally follow one of three tracks. The vocational track is for students who are committed to peacemaking as a lifestyle, though their specific career choice is in another field. The graduate student tailors his or her POE to the requirements of graduate school. Students of these tracks supplement their regular courses with related PACS courses. Finally, the student pointed towards a career in peacemaking would include all types of PACS courses and would specialize in one aspect of PACS.

Juniata has eight courses specifically designed for PACS: "Introduction to Peace and Conflict Studies" and a "Peace and International Studies Internship," which are nondepartmental courses; "Introduction to War"; "Trials of the Major Nazi War Criminals"; "Religion, Rebellion, and Pacifism";

"Studies in Historic Peace Churches"; "Conflict and Social Change"; and "War and Conscience in America." There are eight other PACS related courses from varying departments as well as two special topics seminars: "Disarmament and Soviet-American Relations" and "South Africa."

There are a number of special opportunities for PACS students: field trips, independent studies, simulation games, student exchanges, the most recent of which was to Japan; weekly World Issues luncheons; and a series of distinguished guest lectures. Freshman PACS students are eligible for the $1,000 Baker Peace Scholarship, which is awarded annually and is renewable.

PACS students have the opportunity to serve, with an administrator and six professors, on the committee which administers the program. These student members have equal standing with the faculty members, and are involved in programming, budget, and policy decisions.

Contact: Rev. Andrew Murray, PACS Director. Juniata College, Huntington, PA 16652; (814) 643-4310.

Peace Studies, Wilmington College

Wilmington College seeks to equip students for leadership roles within its Quaker tradition of peace, service, and inner direction. The College's Peace Studies program, initiated in 1979, was developed in order to prepare students for careers in agencies and organizations dedicated to peacemaking activities. The program also hopes to "enable those entering other careers to become effective as lay leaders and to fulfill their responsibilities as citizens."

Wilmington is a small liberal arts college with approximately 1,400 students. In its third year, the Peace Studies program had seven declared majors and 13% of the student population enrolled in its courses. Peace Studies is a multidisciplinary major which is often elected as a double major. Students must take three core courses: "War and Peace," "Social and Political Thought," and "International Conflict." "War and Peace" surveys such topics as the roots of war, why nations go to war, liberation ethics, and war resistance. "Social and Political Thought" is an introduction to major classical and modern theorists. "International Conflict" describes and compares international systems, foreign policies, and the conflicts that arise from these sources.

In addition to these three courses, the College stresses that any student who wishes to prepare for a career in "the field of peace" must elect a human relations laboratory. This course entails both the study of interpersonal and intergroup relations and an internship with an agency devoted to peacemaking. Finally, the Peace Studies major must develop a plan of concentrated study appropriate to her or his goals. This concentration is planned around existing Peace Studies electives. Examples of the variety of electives are "Philosophies of Self-Reliance," "Model United Nations," "Management as if People Mattered," "The World in Crisis," "Communication and Conflict," and "Foundations and Methods of Peace Education."

The program is funded by private grants. The Director of the program has free reign in budgetary matters.

From 1981 to 1984, the Peace Studies and Agriculture departments co-sponsored the Food, Peace and International Development Program. The goal of this Program, which was funded partially by a Kellogg Company grant, was to study the interrelated conditions required to foster sustainable food systems in both the U.S. and in the Third World. The Program also looked into how resource shortages can lead to conflict and how problems of this sort can be prevented and resolved. The Program also built bridges between the Peace Studies and Agriculture departments; and allowed the Agriculture department to develop courses which moved away from its previous "agribusiness" focus.

Adjacent to the Wilmington campus is the Peace Resource Center which serves as the focal point for peace-related research, and as a meetinghouse for small groups to engage in dialogue and fellowship. The Center also houses the Hiroshima/Nagasaki Memorial Collection. This collection focuses on the explosion of the atomic bomb over the cities of Hiroshima and Nagasaki and on the after effects of these events on human life and thought. This collection consists of books (in Japanese and English), magazine and newspaper articles, films, slides, photographs, and other objects. In addition, the Garland Library of War and Peace is housed in the college library and is available to students pursuing Peace Studies. Finally, the Woolman Peace Institute is the newest development at Wilmington. When completed, the Institute will integrate peace issues into the rest of the campus, serve as a resource, information, and outreach center, and assist the Peace Studies majors.

Contact: Earl W. Redding, Coordinator, Peace Studies Program. Pyle Center, Box 1243, Wilmington College, Wilmington, OH 45177; (513) 382-6661.

Peace and Global Studies, Earlham College

Earlham's Quaker heritage, which places a high value on nonviolence and social justice, makes the college an especially appropriate place for the study of peace and conflict. Peace and Global Studies (PAGS) at Earlham is an interdepartmental program which combines the perspectives of various disciplines on social justice, war, nonviolence and the prospects for building peace on a global scale.

Students who wish to participate in the program may pursue one of three options. One option is the PAGS Certificate program which allows students to gain competence in peace-related issues while majoring in another field. Requirements are the four PAGS core courses, an internship, and 45 hours of human relations laboratories. As a second route, students major in Peace and Global Studies jointly with another field. A plan of study is worked out by the student and the three-person committee the student selects to oversee his or her program. Finally, the student may major in PAGS alone, with requirements similar to that of the co-major.

The PAGS major consists of four core courses, a variety of elective upper-division courses, human relations laboratories, a senior seminar and an off-campus internship with an organization actively working for peace and social change.

The core courses were designed to satisfy distribution requirements at the college and can thus be taken by students who are not formally associated with a PAGS program. "Culture and Conflict," is offered jointly by the Sociology/Anthropology Department. "Political Violence and World Order," a Political Science/PAGS class, incorporates the traditional study of comparative politics and international relations with a systematic analysis of the global issues of arms, security and food. "Political Economy of Global Relations" is an economics course which introduces students to the basic concepts and methods of political economy. "Food Ethics and Policy" is an introductory philosophy course which examines the global issues of food and hunger, through the perspective of classical and contemporary thinkers.

Eighteen other courses in Peace and Global Studies are available, including "Religious Responses to War and Violence," "American Foreign Policy," and "Conflict Resolution." Approximately 15 professors from eight departments are involved in the PAGS program; consequently, Earlham can claim that it has the largest teaching faculty of the 56 programs of its kind in the country.

For the PAGS internship, students participate in a conflict-related program either within or outside the U.S. Recent internships have included work with the Council on Economic Priorities' Military Conversion Project, the North American Congress on Latin America, the Institute for Policy Studies, as well as with groups in Northern Ireland, Jerusalem, Mexico, Nicaragua, and Hong Kong. Opportunities are also available with the Center for Social Change in India and other organizations in the United States.

A number of peace-related extracurricular activities are made available through the efforts of the campus chapters of Hunger Action Coalition, American Friends Service Committee, and Amnesty International. The Earlham Volunteer Exchange coordinates programs with local groups providing legal aid and other services to local residents.

Contact: George Lopez, Peace and Global Studies. Box 105, Earlham College, Richmond, IN 47374; (317) 962-6561.

Center for Peace and Conflict Studies, Wayne State University

Wayne State University in Detroit is Michigan's largest urban university, with a student population of 30,000. The student body is largely comprised of commuting students, many of whom work in order to pay for their education. The University is a reflection of the ethnic make-up of the Greater Detroit metropolitan area, with a large number of minority students and foreign nationals from more than one hundred nations. The University has a long history of involvement with social programs and a deep sense of community responsibility.

Wayne State's Center for Peace and Conflict Studies was dedicated in 1965 and was one of the first university centers in the country devoted to peace education and research. The co-major in Peace and Conflict Studies was organized by the Center in 1977. The goals of the program are to integrate the approaches to human conflict now being presented in the University, to provide a framework within which students might develop tools and expertise needed to study, analyze, manage, resolve and compare conflict, and to provide opportunities for co-majors to work on projects in the community that require conflict resolution. Central to the program is the concept that war has become dysfunctional as a means of solving conflict.

From its inception, the Center's organizers saw their main objective to be the legitimization of peace education in primary and secondary schools, in college and university courses, and in the field of adult education. Although the co-major is the Center's main focus, additional projects concentrate on teacher in-service education, outreach programs to local schools and community programs, and the Detroit Council for World Affairs, a peace institute which regularly sponsors lectures, films, workshops and other events. All co-majors receive an honorary one-year membership in the Council and are invited to participate in all Center and Council activities.

There are at present two required courses for the co-major: "Introduction to Peace and Conflict Studies" and a "Senior Seminar in Conflict Studies." These courses cover the topics of nuclear war, arms control, disarmament, sources of conflict, labor-management conflict, revolution, world order and peacekeeping. Co-majors must also take any three of the following courses: "Nuclear War," "World Politics," "Psychology and Union-Management Relations," "Foreign Relations," "Social Movements and Collective Behavior," or "Philosophy of Peace." Students also choose from a broad range of electives from the departments of Political Science, Economics, Sociology, Physics, Education, and Anthropology. Finally, a senior research paper is required. The co-major is usually elected with a Political Science or History major.

The co-major is now in its 6th year. Although it has not had tremendous success in numbers, the core classes are extremely popular. The introductory course in Peace and Conflict Studies seems to have stabilized at approximately 40 students a semester, who represent a cross-section of the

University population. The Center is developing both a clearinghouse and library of periodicals, journals, clippings, curricula and books. The library is run by a professional librarian and volunteer students.

Contact: Lillian Genser, Director, Center for Peace and Conflict Studies. Wayne State University, 5229 Cass Ave., Detroit, MI 48201; (313) 577-3453.

Global Studies, Wittenberg University

Wittenberg University is an independent undergraduate liberal arts institution in Springfield, Ohio. Its 3,200 full-time resident students come from 33 states and 13 countries and represent widely diverse cultural, ethnic, and religious backgrounds.

The Global Studies minor at Wittenberg University was created after a 1981 survey of the Wittenberg faculty yielded a set of learning objectives. These included awareness and basic understanding of cultural pluralism and ethnocentrism, functional language competence, deepened and comparative understanding of other cultures and social systems, and ability to relate the skills of a discipline to its international context. The minor was approved in the fall of 1982 after it became clear that over the past decade Wittenberg had developed significant resources in international education, but had no comprehensive institutional plan to define its international emphasis. Therefore, the Global Studies minor was created to institutionalize an already-existing but unorganized global perspective.

In addition to the general learning objectives, the minor was created to fulfill two other objectives. The first of these is to enhance cross-cultural courses and to create global issues courses that contribute to a global perspective. The second objective is to strengthen cross-cultural learning and global frameworks in the departments of Business Administration, Sociology, Education and Languages.

Before the Global Studies minor was created, Wittenberg already had a mandatory "transdisciplinary" requirement. This consists of two courses in either inter-area studies, which is "designed to deal with the great issues, ideas, concerns of humankind in its past, present, and future," foreign cultures, or study abroad. There is also a two-course language requirement. The Global Studies minor complements these institutional requirements.

The minor is elected, but not required, in addition to a student's major. Students must take one course in six different categories: non-Western culture; global issues; comparative culture, society or politics; history, culture and society of an area of the world served by the student's second language; international systems, and foreign language at the advanced intermediate level. Students are also expected to study abroad for at least a semester unless extenuating circumstances prevent their doing so.

A multidisciplinary faculty team created six courses for the Global Studies minor. "Imaging" introduces students to global perspectives and to Future Studies through the development of pictures, or images, about possible new forms of reality. "Emerging Global Systems" attempts to develop a planetary view of contemporary problems by utilizing faculty from the departments of Geology, Geography, Biology, History, Business, Library Science, Political Science, and Religion. The four other courses are "Modernization and Cultural Change," "International Politics," "Human Ecology," and "Economic and Social Development," with attention to the North-South dialogue.

In developing these six courses, the faculty identified several important international themes and educational goals. The themes that were stressed pertained to human rights, equity and justice; system interaction and interdependence; and social conflict and conflict resolution. The educational goals identified are awareness of ethical issues, the use of images in problem-solving, and ethnocentrism and its analysis.

The faculty committee which developed these courses did so with the second major in mind. Thus, the departments of Business Administration, Sociology, Education, and Languages have hired consultants and have devised other ways to make their departments more compatible with global studies.

The program was funded by two federal grants, college budgetary support, and a progressive faculty development committee which agreed to release its funds for a variety of workshops, consultations, travel, and individual experimentation, all of which helped to establish the minor.

Contact: Lila Wangoes, Director of International Education. Wittenberg University, P.O. Box 720, Springfield, OH 45501; (513) 327-6314.

Peace and Conflict Studies, West Chester University

West Chester University is located in West Chester, PA and enrolls approximately 8,000 students. Its Peace and Conflict Studies minor has helped make West Chester unique among the Pennsylvania state schools, and has helped draw students to the rural college. The Program was established after a poll showed that 30-40% of the student body was interested in peace-related courses. Using this data, a small core of professors was able to persuade the administration of the need for a Peace Studies minor.

The minor in Peace and Conflict Studies was initiated in 1982. Its stated goals were the following: to understand the causes, structures, and dynamics of social conflict; to learn cooperation and conflict resolution in group settings; to develop skills necessary for studying issues and taking nonviolent action; and to understand and appreciate factors which contribute to peace with justice and processes by which conflict may be managed.

The core course which brings these objectives together is "Introduction to Conflict Studies." Offered for the first time in the spring of 1982, the class had seventeen vocal students. The Director of the Program, Richard Webster, considers the enrollment and activity in the course quite good "especially since its initial appearance had so little publicity and a virtually secret listing in the schedule of classes."

The minor requires five other courses in specific areas. For example, students must take one course in "Themes and Special Approaches." They are given the choice of "Applied Social Change," "Science and Human Values," or "Psychology of Aggression." The other areas are "Global Perspectives" and "Experimental Learning." In this latter category, students either choose an internship or develop an experiential course which is equivalent to life experience.

Students round out the minor by choosing two electives from an interdisciplinary selection of courses, from the departments of History, Psychology, Economics, Sociology, Political Science, and Philosophy. Examples of elective courses are "International Economics," "American Foreign Policy," "The Arab and the Jew," "Racial and Ethnic Understanding" and "Introduction to Ethics."

Towards the end of their work for the minor, students must write a paper which synthesizes the varying aspects of the minor. The paper can be accomplished as part of the courses for the minor, and thus must be worked out on an individual basis.

The college also sponsors an annual summer conference on Peace and Conflict Resolution. Usually a two-day affair, the conference draws particularly important people as speakers. It typically includes workshops, lectures, and group meetings. The Peacemakers, a student activist and study group, helps to organize the conferences. The group, which is very active on campus, also helps recruit students for the minor and designed the initial brochure for the program.

Contact: Professor David S. Eldredge, Co-convener, Peace and Conflict Studies. Wayne Hall, Room 325, West Chester University, West Chester, PA 19383; (215) 436-2286.

Peace Studies, University of Akron

The University of Akron is a co-educational, state-run institution with more than 22,000 full-time and part-time students. The Center for Peace Studies, established in 1970, sponsors peace-related courses and activities on the campus. The objective of the Center is to help students through education, public service and research, to formulate solutions to many of the world-wide problems of overpopulation, food shortages, terrorism and the threat of nuclear war.

One means of achieving this goal is the interdisciplinary certificate program in Peace Studies, which is designed to give the student an opportunity to develop a minor area of specialization in peace issues outside of the major field of study. Five courses must be completed from a list of approved courses, distributed among at least three separate departments and including two required courses. Students must also complete a substantial paper or project.

"Peace, War, and Mankind," one of the core courses, presents theories of peace and war, from ancient to modern times, ending with the problems of the nuclear age and alternative international systems. "Value Concepts on Peace and War" explores perspectives on these topics from various fields of knowledge; speakers and authors have included a philosopher on the morality of war, a physicist on the responsibility of scientists to conceive of weapons, and a former leader of student protest movements.

Between 1975 and 1980, 27 students received the Peace Studies certificate. Enrollments in classes have increased over the years and now average 25 students per class, most of whom are not formally affiliated with the certificate program. Administrators at the Center attribute this increase to the growing concern about the danger of nuclear war and the survival of the human species.

In addition to sponsoring the certificate program, the Center for Peace Studies actively promotes consideration of war problems through several kinds of activities. Teacher-training workshops have been offered, and each fall the Center schedules a one-credit "Special Topics" course, discussing an issue such as nuclear war. Lectures are offered periodically throughout the year, a "Peace Day" has been organized, and there is a regular film series that offers peace- and war-related movies.

The Center also maintains an extensive file of materials in the forms of pamphlets, paperback books, tapes of lectures, and literature on international and peace societies; these are available to students, faculty, and members of the community. The Center conducts independent research projects and cooperates with the Akron Council on World Affairs, the American Friends Service Committee of Northeast Ohio, and the Greater Akron Alternatives to War Committee in planning programs and activities in the community. Finally, the *International Peace Studies Newsletter* is published by the Center. The *Newsletter*, with a national circulation of over 3,000, reports on peace programs in colleges and universities throughout the country.

The Center is funded completely by the university and has an advisory board of students and faculty members to help plan its activities.

Contact: Warren F. Kuehl, Director, Center for Peace Studies. The University of Akron, Akron, OH 44325; (216) 375-7008.

Peace and World Order Studies, Catholic University

Catholic University of America (CUA) is the graduate university of the national Roman Catholic Church. Located in Washington, D.C., the university enrolls 7,000 students, 2,000 of which attend the undergraduate liberal arts college. The interdisciplinary Peace and World Order Studies (PWOS) program, initiated in 1979, is offered within the undergraduate college of arts and sciences.

The PWOS program has three primary objectives: 1) to enable students to explore the moral, philosophical, and religious conceptions of justice, peace, and world order, and to pursue a variety of studies focused on these topics; 2) to promote a transdisciplinary, multilevel and integrated approach to the analysis of the nature of conflict and the causes—personal and structural—of violence, and 3) to cultivate in the students, regardless of their major concentration, an awareness of the dimensions of violent conflict and a commitment to its just and peaceful resolution.

The student may choose one of three options within the PWOS program. The first is the subconcentration, which is similar to a minor. Three core courses are required of all students: "Introduction to Peace Research"; which is the introductory course to the subconcentration; "The Church and Social Issues," which looks at contemporary problems of war, revolution, poverty, development, human rights, and nonviolence from a theological perspective; and "Conflict and Conflict Resolution," usually taken in the senior year and requiring a term paper based on field work. In addition, students must choose three electives, taken from a list of eight basic courses dealing with economics, cultural anthropology, ethics, domestic society and politics, and arms control, among other topics.

Honor students may design an interdisciplinary program utilizing PWOS courses. Other students who want to take PWOS classes without committing themselves to a formal program may do so. Such courses are available as elective credit in the departments of Anthropology, History, Law, Religion, and Sociology.

In order to limit expenses, maximum use was made of existing Catholic University courses which could serve the program with little or no modifications. Some newly developed PWOS classes were introduced as electives to avoid the need for special funding from the university. Also, a grant from the Institute for World Order (now World Policy Institute) permitted the development or redevelopment of five courses.

As of 1981, nine students had enrolled in the introductory course, though greater numbers had taken other PWOS courses offered as electives in regular departments. As a subconcentration, PWOS is not a full-fledged department, though a coordinator has been selected to administer the program.

The academic program is complemented by the student-initiated and -operated CUA Peace Studies Group, which was the original impetus for the formation of the academic program on campus. The Peace Studies Group helps to link study with action by sponsoring informational and promotional events on campus and by cooperating with off-campus social action groups. The PWOS faculty, in conjunction with interested faculty in other Washington-area universities, formed a Peace Studies Committee. The Committee co-sponsors an annual peace studies institute and has conducted workshops and an intra-Committee research project.

Contact: Rev. Joseph Komonchak, Coordinator, Peace and World Order Studies Program. Department of Religion and Religious Education, The Catholic University of America, Washington, DC 20064; (202) 635-5700.

Peace Studies, Chapman College

Chapman College is a four-year liberal arts college located in one of the more politically conservative areas of the United States. The stated goal of the school is to "educate men and women who will take from Chapman an understanding of the problems and complexities of human existence." The Peace Studies minor is one representation of the College's objective to create a caring, value-centered community within which students can foster their respect for all forms of life.

The proposal for the minor, which was approved in 1981, was largely a product of the student initiative that had also formed a Peace Club in the fall of 1980. Chapman had already included peace-related courses in its curriculum, and these were expanded in order to form the minor.

The Peace Studies minor is an interdisciplinary, problem-centered program based on the premise that a fair-minded analysis of the issues of war and peace can only be achieved through the synthesis of insights from various fields of knowledge. Peace here is understood to be not merely the absence of war, but social justice, economic well-being and ecological stability as well.

The study of peacemaking at Chapman has the following goals: 1) to examine the most prevalent conflicts found between and within individuals, groups, races, nations and ideologies; 2) to examine, in a theoretical and participatory way, various methods and ethical models by which conflicts have been and may be resolved; 3) to provide the opportunity to become informed and effective peacemakers by choosing from among these models and applying them through personal commitment and action.

"Peace, Justice and World Order" is the required introductory course to the minor. The various disciplinary approaches to the study of nonviolent conflict resolution are applied to a range of political and social conflicts occurring on micro- and macro-levels. Students are also required to serve an internship which allows them to test their theories and techniques of reconciliation in a practical setting.

In addition, students must choose a minimum of two courses from a variety of electives. "Alternative World Futures," "History of Peace Movements," "War and Peace in the Nuclear Age," and "International Human Rights" are some examples of the 14 related courses offered through seven departments.

The Peace Studies minor is the major focus of the program, but other activities are sponsored as well. The annual Peace Lecture Series invites two guests each year to interact through lectures, debate, and coffee sessions with students and faculty on a variety of issues relevant to peace. In addition, the Peace Club sponsors lectures and special events throughout the year.

The Peace Studies Program is administered by a committee composed of faculty members, administrators and students, including the officers of the Peace Club. The committee chairperson is the Program Coordinator. Funding is provided by the College for courses, the lecture series, and general overhead; the Peace Club is funded by the Associated Student Body.

Contact: Dr. Barbara E. G. Mulch, Program Coordinator, Peace Studies Committee. Chapman College, Orange, CA 92666; (714) 997-6621.

World Studies, Donnelly College

Donnelly is a two-year, independent, co-educational community college affiliated with the Catholic Church and sponsored by the Archdiocese of Kansas City in Kansas. Donnelly is one of only two institutions in the Kansas City region that has an intensive "English as a Second Language" program and hence has a high proportion of international students. World Studies is an offshoot of these demographics and the institutional goal is "to create an open, aware, and respectful environment, capitalizing on the rich mix of persons, backgrounds and beliefs within the Donnelly College community."

The total curriculum of the College emphasizes the need for global international awareness; many courses include an international dimension and every student must fulfill a second-language requirement. Two Associate of Art degrees relating to world education were initiated in 1979: World Studies-Economics and International Relations. Both degrees require 64 hours of coursework, or a minimum of 20 courses, including two world civilization classes, "International Ethics" and "International Problems."

The World Studies academic program evolved from the "One World Program" between 1977 and 1979. The Program, supported by a grant from the U.S. Office of Education, was designed by the faculty to incorporate the international dimension into the whole curriculum. During the first year, four new courses with international emphasis were added, nine underwent major revision, and most other courses on campus interjected a global topic where possible.

Two other special programs on campus complement the World Studies program. The World Languages Program, another spinoff of the One World Program and supported by a grant from the National Endowment for the Humanities, is a self-instructional program in which the student works with tapes and text, practices before a tutor and is tested for academic credit. The Refugee Certificate Program is offered to refugees with minimal English and emphasizes basic competency skills to help the student adapt to living in the United States.

In addition to these academic programs, there is an Intercultural Center which supplies course and career counseling to international students and helps promote intercultural understanding on campus. Once a year an International Fair enables students from over 25 countries to share their rich cultural heritages with members of the local community.

The World Studies program is overseen by a Steering Committee, made up of teachers and interested community members who are responsible for monitoring, evaluating and improving the program. The program is considered to be quite a success. Thirteen nearby four-year institutions responded favorably to the new degree programs and facilitate the transfer of students. Course enrollments, officially limited to 25 students, regularly overflow to 30 or 40 in some classes. Supporters of the World Studies program say there has been no faculty resistance to the program because of the international composition of the student body.

Contact: Sr. Martha Ann Linck, Director, World Studies Program. Donnelly College, 1236 Sandersky Avenue, Kansas City, KS 66102; (913) 621-6070, ext. 36.

Peace Studies, Georgetown University

The Peace Studies program at Georgetown University, the oldest Catholic university in the country, was established in 1965. It was begun in response to Vatican II's statement to educators "to regard as their most weighty task to instruct all in a new understanding of peace" and in recognition of the appeal from the U.S. Catholic Bishops to work towards developing an "entirely new attitude" towards war and peace.

The goal of the Peace Studies program is to help develop among students and faculty an understanding of the process of war and peace, examining past and present methods of peacemaking and conflict resolution.

Students can either major or minor in the interdisciplinary Peace Studies program. The major is normally begun in the junior year following the completion of all general education requirements and the maintenance of a 3.3 cumulative average at the time of application. A minimum of 36 credits, or 12 upper division courses, must be taken to complete the major. Of these

12, four are required and eight are elected from a list of 22. In addition, the student majoring in Peace Studies must attend a seminar, research tutorial or internship program related to the discipline and write a research paper about his or her experience. The student minoring in Peace Studies is required to take two core courses and four electives.

One of the core courses in the program is "War and Peace," offered through the Theology Department and taught by the director of the program, Richard McSorley, S.J. The course develops six issues: nuclear, biological and chemical destructive capacity; theorists of war and peace; morality; the economics of war; Vietnam; and the history of peacemaking. Examples of elective courses are "Power and Politics in Biblical Tradition" (from the Theology department), "News Media and Society" (Sociology), "The Artist as Political Actor" (English), and "The New International Economic Order" (Economics).

Associated with the program is the Washington Consortium of Universities, through which students may take peace-related courses at five other local universities and receive credit in their major or minor. Georgetown University also has a Peace Studies Center which serves as a general resource center. In addition, there are many local peace- and defense-related organizations through which students can become knowledgeable about the issues.

Contact: Richard T. McSorley, S.J., Director, Center for Peace Studies. 2 O'Gara, Georgetown University, Washington, DC 20057; (202) 625-4240.

Peace Studies, University of Missouri at Columbia

The Peace Studies major at the University of Missouri at Columbia is an interdisciplinary program which requires participants to devise their own concentration of study. This approach was adopted because it was felt that no one existing department or discipline had all the insights or methods which the program needed. The faculty members who administer the program believe that "by concentrating their study in peace, students contribute to the growing awareness that war is not necessary but a condition born in the minds of men and women." The emphasis of the entire program is on peace studies as they relate to the United States, and not as they relate to the rest of the world.

There are a number of suggested concentrations that students can follow. Some include: "History of Pacifism and Nonviolent Resistance," "War and Peace Problems of a Specific Geographic Area," "International Agencies of World Law and World Order," "War and Peace in Literature and the Humanities," "Economics of War and Peace," "Understanding and Rechanneling Aggression," and "Disarmament Logistics." A student's proposed area of concentration is evaluated by an advisory committee of two faculty members, one of whom serves as the student's advisor.

All students must take four courses—"Introduction to Peace Studies" and three seminars. The seminars explore the psycho-biological, intersocietal, political, economic, sociological and cultural bases for conflict and aggression. In addition, students must write a senior thesis. The advisory committee evaluates the thesis, presides over the student's oral defense of the thesis, and determines its acceptability and grade.

From over 150 courses in a variety of departments, the student must choose nine or ten electives. Aside from the "typical" departments which offer Peace Studies courses, the departments of Agricultural Economics, Germanic and Slavic Studies, Speech and Dramatic Art, Biology, Nuclear Engineering, Finance, Mechanical and Aerospace Engineering, Rural Sociology, and Journalism all provide Peace Studies courses.

The program is funded by 160 regular contributors who make up The Friends of Peace Studies and the Peace Studies Program. The faculty committee which coordinates the program has complete control over its funds. Nevertheless, faculty members who teach the core courses must do so on a voluntary basis because the funding is not sufficient to compensate for their work. This situation produces either low-morale, "burnt-out" teachers or very dedicated ones, and it limits the faculty that will get involved in the program. Despite these problems, the program is well-received on campus. It is very visible and its public events are normally rewarded with large attendances.

Contact: Director, Peace Studies Program. Room 22, Middlebush Hall, University of Missouri, Columbia, MO 65211; (314) 882-2840.

Peace Studies, Goshen College

Goshen College is a four-year liberal arts college located 120 miles east of Chicago in north-central Indiana. The college was founded in 1894 by the Mennonite Church, a Christian denomination with roots in the Anabaptist movement of the 16th century and, along with the Society of Friends (Quakers) and Church of the Brethren, one of the three historic peace churches. From its parent church, Goshen College derives a spirit of peace and simplicity, mutual support and biblically-based service to others. Of the 1,200 men and women who study at the college, approximately 75 percent come from Mennonite-related backgrounds.

Peace-related studies have been offered at Goshen College since the 1940's, and a minor has been part of the curriculum since 1972. The minor program was preceded by the establishment of a peace collection in the library, the development of a peace studies course called "War, Peace, and Nonresistance," and the birth of the Peace Society, which sponsors workshops, conferences, and other events in order to promote interest in peace and justice issues. All of these are still present on campus. There is also an annual peace oratorical contest which involves students in peace-related issues outside the classroom.

A student may combine peace studies with any academic major to form a co-major, such as Art-Peace, English-Peace, History-Peace, Biology-Peace, etc. This is not the same as a double major, as only a minimum of 15 hours in the PAXCOM (peace co-major) is required. The program was designed so as not to consume too many of the student's available credit hours and to allow both students and professors to fuse peace concerns with their own interests and expertise. The College contends that keeping students connected with an established discipline provides fine academic training and enhances the prospect of the student being employed, and thus working effectively for peace after graduation.

PAXCOM has three requirements. The first is comprised of two compulsory core courses. "War, Peace, and Resistance" is an introduction to the theory and practice of Christian pacifism, with theological, ethical, historical, and sociological perspectives on peacemaking. "Violence and Nonviolence" is an interdisciplinary study of the nature, causes, scope and pathology of violence in contemporary society, combined with an examination of nonviolent alternatives.

The student must also take a minimum of three related courses selected from a multidisciplinary listing of courses which deal with the problems of conflict and peace. Some examples are "Christian Ethics," "Rise of Totalitarianism," "Studies in Drama: Peace Plays" and "The Politics of World Human Need."

Finally, students complete Senior Advanced Work, an exercise which may be a seminar, field experience or some kind of advanced study, combining the students' major with a peace-related issue.

According to the Peace Program Coordinator, PAXCOM is not well-known, partly because it is not well-publicized. The coordinator, Don Blosser, would like to see the number of students enrolling in the core PAXCOM courses—currently 100 annually—grow. He would also like to have other aspects of the peace studies program, including library resources and internships, strengthened and expanded; consequently, there is an endowment drive underway with a goal of $500,000.

The Peace Studies program is administered by the College which, in turn, is accountable to the Mennonite Board of Education. On campus the decision-making bodies which affect the program are the Peace Studies Advisory Committee (with three students and seven professors), the Goshen College Board of Overseers (which includes nine students), and the Mennonite Board of Education (with 19 student, faculty and community members). The program, which receives some university funding, is directly overseen by the Peace Program Coordinator.

Contact: Don Blosser, Director, Peace Studies. Goshen College, Goshen, IN 46526; (219) 533-3161, ext. 452.

Peace Studies, Manchester College

Founded in 1948, Manchester College's Peace Studies program is the oldest in the United States. It was shaped according to a 1950 report on the assumption that "the war-peace problem is not a problem for a narrowly-trained specialist, but if we are to see it in all its many facets, we must have first of all liberally educated men [sic]." The Manchester program started the interdisciplinary focus which has characterized almost all subsequent peace studies programs. The program was also predicated on the realization that more than institutional changes, such as the League of Nations, were essential for world peace. Therefore, in addition to the study of theology and biology, politics and international relations, the program included study of the philosophy of peace as understood in other cultures, the techniques of peacemaking (mediation, conciliation, nonviolence) and the ideas of Gandhi, Tolstoy, Bunche and others.

Today, the Peace Studies program still emphasizes the interdisciplinary and cross-cultural approach. Current brochures suggest that those with "a concern for world peace, a reverence for life, and a desire to be of service to others" should major in the program. It is stressed that Peace Studies is eminently compatible with other interests and co-majors. The program provides a list of possible career paths that Peace Studies majors can follow, and is the only program in the country which has inventoried its graduates to assess their career histories.

The emphasis of the major has changed little since 1948. The biology and theology courses are no longer required, but politics, international relations and peace techniques still comprise the integral part of the program. There are now seven core courses. "Current Issues in Peace and Justice" is concerned with different and changing topics and may thus be taken repeatedly. "Philosophy of Civilization" explores the ideas of political analysts and philosophers on how society may best be ordered, what causes the development and breakdown of civilization, the nature of historical analysis, and the role of the individual both as thinker and actor in historical development.

The other courses are the following: "Conflict Resolution"; "Analysis of War and Peace"; "Peace Issues," which deals with Gandhi and the thought of Martin Luther King, human rights, and racial justice; "Religions and War," which examines the religious traditions of East and West and "modern ideological pseudo-religions," such as Communism and nationalism. The final course is a choice between "International Politics" and "International Law and Organization."

Five electives are required. Elective concentrations for majors are developed in consultation with each student. The concentrations are structured from a student's interest in a traditional discipline to which Peace Studies can be applied. There is no specific list of courses, although the majority of electives are within the areas of Political Science and Sociology.

Majors are encouraged to take advantage of practical work opportunities during the summers in overseas or service-oriented agencies. Many majors have spent their junior year abroad, studying with the Brethren Colleges Abroad program or independently. Independent study credits are often arranged for a variety of extracurricular experiences. There are also January term programs both on and off campus which Peace Studies students utilize to further their extracurricular learning.

Finally, there is a Peace Studies Institute which sponsors college-wide conferences, visiting lecturers, workshops for vocational groups, colloquia with campus peace and international relations groups, and evening and summer classes on war and peace problems.

Contact: Dr. Kenneth L. Brown, Director, Program of Peace Studies. Manchester College, North Manchester, IN 46962; (219) 982-2141.

Peace Studies Institute, Manhattan College

The interdisciplinary Peace Studies major was initiated at New York City's Manhattan College in 1971. The college, with a total enrollment of approximately 5,000 students, most from New York state, began formal course offerings in Peace Studies in 1967 through the efforts of a few faculty members who wished to put Pope John XXIII's *Pacem in Terris* pronouncement into practice in the field of education. According to Dr. Joseph Fahey, the current director of the Peace Studies Institute which sponsors the major, the first course "The Anatomy of Peace" was team-taught, "partially because no one faculty member knew enough to offer a full course and also because it was recognized from the beginning that Peace Studies was at heart a multidisciplinary area of study." During the next few years courses were added in Biology, Religious Studies and Economics and Government, and a student-initiated proposal resulted in the formal major in 1971.

The Peace Studies major is dedicated to the academic and moral search for solutions to the problems of war, revolution and human injustice, with particular attention to the nonviolent resolution of conflict. To these ends, five problem areas are examined: war and the arms race; social justice; conflict resolution; nonviolent strategies; and world order.

Peace Studies is available as an independent major but students are encouraged to pursue a dual major in such fields as Economics, Government, Language, Psychology, and Religious Studies so as to have in-depth training in a traditional discipline. A minimum grade of "C" is required for course credit towards the major.

Thirty credits or ten courses are required to complete the major; three are mandatory and the remaining seven are selected from an interdepartmental list of peace-related classes. "Problems of Peace and Social Issues" is *the* required introductory seminar that exposes students to the nature, scope, and methodology of peace studies and research, as well as explores some major contemporary problems which threaten peaceful and just relations between groups or nations. The Peace Studies Field Project enables students to experience practical field training in reconciliation, mediation and nonviolent conflict resolution. Considered to be a strong feature of the overall program, this requirement has resulted in domestic placement of students at the United Nations, the American Arbitration Association and the American Friends Service Committee, among others, and international experience in Northern Ireland, Jamaica and Peru. The "Senior Seminar in Peace Studies" is designed to integrate the students' course work and field experience into an academic framework which enables them to appreciate the "holistic" nature of Peace Studies.

In addition to the undergraduate major, a Certificate in Peace Studies is offered as a one year or one semester program for those who already have their degree but who wish to spend some time developing expertise in peace studies for their ministry. One can also obtain an M.A. degree in Religious Studies with a concentration in Social Justice and Peace, with half of the 30 credits necessary for the M.A. falling into the latter category. To facilitate these graduate and undergraduate programs, the Cardinal Hayes Library on campus has collected and printed a useful bibliography of published material on peace topics, entitled "Library Resources in Peace Studies."

As of 1981, 80 individuals had graduated as Peace Studies majors and gone on to graduate school in law, theology, communications, government, social work, management and Peace Studies. As a salient benefit of the program, over 6,000 non-majors have taken one or more of the peace studies courses.

Dr. Fahey, in reflecting on the first ten years of the major, credits the following factors for the survival of the program: a strong academic focus; the constant support of the college administration; continued faculty involvement and dedication; the support of the college library; student interest and concern; and a Catholic environment.

Contact: Dr. Joseph J. Fahey, Director, Peace Studies Institute. Manhattan College, Riverdale, N.Y., 10471; (212) 920-0305.

IV
Resources

Funding Sources

Filmography

Periodicals

Organizations

Bibliography

Funding Sources

WHERE TO FIND FOUNDATION INFORMATION
FOUNDATION CENTERS

The Foundation Center
79 Fifth Avenue
New York, NY 10003
(212) 620-4230

The Foundation Center
1001 Connecticut Ave. NW
Washington, DC 20036
(202) 331-1400

The Foundation Center
Kent H. Smith Library
739 National City
Bank Building
629 Euclid
Cleveland, OH 44114
(216) 861-1933

The Foundation Center
312 Sutter Street
San Francisco, CA 94108
(415) 397-0902

(There are also other contributing regional Foundation Centers.)

GUIDES

The Foundation Directory
Loren Renz, Editor. Compiled by The Foundation Center, New York, 1983 (periodic updates and supplements)

The Grantseekers Guide: A Guide for Social & Economic Justice Projects
by Jill R. Shellow
Chicago: National Network of Grantmakers and The Interreligious Foundation for Community Organization, 1981

The Grass Roots Fund-Raising Book
by Joan Flanigan
Chicago: Swallow Press, 1977
Available from: The Youth Project, National Office,
1555 Connecticut Ave. NW, Washington, DC 20036. •$5.25

The Grass Roots Organization: Getting Started & Getting Results
Chicago: Contemporary Press, 1981

Research Activities & Funding Programs
Volume 5 of Encyclopedia Of Associations
Detroit: Gale Research Company, 1983

POSSIBLE FUNDING SOURCES FOR PEACE
AND SOCIAL JUSTICE EDUCATION

This list is a sampling of funding organizations which may consider requests for support of peace and social justice education efforts. It is by no means a definitive listing nor can it be guaranteed that the funding source will consider your request. It is strongly suggested that each funding source be fully researched prior to application.

Foundation Name	Areas of Interest Include	Limitations Include
Aetna Life & Casualty Corporate Contributions Programs, and Aetna Life and Casualty Foundation, Inc. 151 Farmington Avenue Hartford, CT 06156 (203) 273-3340 Contact: Edwin B. Knauft Robert H. Roggeveen	1) human services/urban problems 2) education (not a priority) 3) arts & culture, humanities	1) tax-exempt organizations in U.S. 2) no funds for schools outside Hartford area
Agape Foundation 85 Carl Street San Francisco, CA 94117 (415) 566-2710 Contact: Diane Spaugh Dorie Wilsnack	1) nonviolence as a philosophy 2) direct action against injustice & violence, specifically militarism, sexism, & racism	1) Western US & Hawaii 2) low-budget 3) grounded in nonviolent philosophy 4) unable to get traditional funds 5) must promote nonviolence
Arca Foundation 1425 21st Street, NW Washington, DC 20036 (202) 822-9193 Contact: Margery Tabankin	1) communication between organizations 2) democratic outlook 3) stress social issues 4) especially funds environmental issues 5) loosely falls under other issues	Application deadlines: March 15 & September 15
The Boehm Foundation 500 5th Avenue New York, NY 10036 (212) 354-9292 Contact: Robert Boehm	1) war & peace issues 2) nuclear power 3) civil rights & liberties	1) no geographic limitations 2) range: $1,000-10,000
The Bydale Foundation 60 East 42nd Street Rm. 5010 New York, NY 10017 (212) 682-4052 Contact: Milton D. Solomon	1) foreign policy 2) peace issues 3) disarmament 4) world order	1) tax-exempt organizations 2) no grants to individuals 3) range: $250-$50,000

Foundation Name	Areas of Interest Include	Limitations Include
Cabot Corporation Foundation 125 High Street Boston, MA 02110 (617) 423-6000	1) higher education 2) broad purposes	1) no individual or medical/scientific projects 2) primarily community giving near Cabot installations
Capp Street Foundation 294 Page Street San Francisco, CA 94102 (415) 552-0860 Contact: Arthur W. Simon	1) public education 2) legal training 3) litigations of major public interest issues 4) human rights on international & national levels	1) must be community-based grassroots projects supporting social change 2) low-budget projects

Robert Sterling Clark
  Foundation
112 East 64th Street
New York, NY 10021
(212) 308-0411
Contact:
  Margaret C. Ayers
	1) better management of cultural institutions
	2) improved performance of public institutions
		1) no grants to individuals, building or endowment funds

Columbia Foundation 1090 Sansome Street San Francisco, CA 94111 (415) 986-5179 Contact: Susan Clark Silk	1) world peace & international understanding 2) public information programs that focus on the interdependence of nations 3) projects that promote an awareness of national & international strategies for peace	1) limited to San Francisco area 2) prefer projects not in fields of health, religion or scientific research 3) no building, individuals or ordinary operating budgets 4) ordinarily will consider grants to organizations certified by IRS as public charities

Common Capital Fund
2706 Ontario Rd., NW
Washington, DC 20009
(202) 265-1305
Contact:
  Tim Siegel
  Phyllis Jones
	1) support groups that educate community about social & economic issues
	2) bring people together for social change
		1) no businesses or human services linked with larger institutions
		2) only DC area

Compton Foundation Ten Hanover Square New York, NY 10005 (212) 635-3205 Contact: Randolph P. Compton	1) to coordinate family giving to community, national & international programs, including peace, world order and higher education	1) no grants to individuals, or building funds
CS Fund 469 Bohemian Highway Freestone, CA 95472 (707) 829-5444 Contact: Marty Teitel	1) immediate dangers to the earth, i.e. nuclear material 2) abuses of power by major corporations	1) will support new groups without track records 2) range: $2,000-30,000 but average grants are $5,000-10,000

Foundation Name	Areas of Interest Include	Limitations Include
Cummins Engine Foundation Box 3005 Columbus, IN 47202 (812) 379-8617 Contact: Diana Chambers Leslie	1) public institutions 2) local programs with emphasis on minorities & urban problems	1) no individual grants 2) priority to communities where Cummins has major facilities
Dyer-Ives Foundation 200 G Water Building Grand Rapids, MI 49503 (616) 454-4502 Contact: Judy Hooker	1) innovative grassroots organizations; educational, social & cultural fields 2) assists groups in seeking funds elsewhere	1) Grand Rapids area 2) no annual drives, building funds, scholarships, or support of ongoing programs
Lucius & Eva Eastman Fund, Inc. 133 East 64th Street New York, NY 10021 (212) 861-2211 Contact: Lucius R. Eastman	1) grassroots organizations specifically relating to women, arts, litigation & civil rights	1) must have specific, well-focused project
Exxon Education Foundation 111 West 49th Street New York, NY 10020 (212) 398-2273 Contact: Robert L. Payton	1) aid to higher education through integrative studies, research, writing, etc.	1) no grants to individuals, building or endowment funds
Booth Ferris Foundation 30 Broad Street New York, NY 10004 (212) 269-3850 Contact: Robert J. Murtagh	1) higher education 2) local social agencies	1) must be located in US
Field Foundation 100 East 85th Street New York, NY 10028 (212) 535-9915 Contact: Richard Boone	1) race relations including civil rights & liberties 2) world peace 3) poverty within the U.S. 4) reduction of nuclear armaments and military spending 5) education 6) child welfare	1) tax-exempt 2) usually limited to domestic concerns 3) no expense budgets of health and welfare agencies or building funds
Film Fund 80 East 11th Street New York, NY 10003 (212) 475-3720 Contact: Terry Lawler	1) supports films that examine social issues	1) tax-exempt groups 2) 2/3 of grants given to projects that will be ready in one year or less

Foundation Name	Areas of Interest Include	Limitations Include
Ford Foundation 320 East 43rd Street New York, NY 10017 (212) 573-5000 Contact: Howard R. Dressner	1) national affairs 2) education & public policy 3) international perspectives	1) most given to organizations 2) no undergraduate scholarships 3) 1979: 22,000 proposals, 960 grants awarded
Fund for Investigative Journalism 1346 Connecticut Ave., NW Washington, DC 20036 (202) 462-1844 Contact: Howard Bray	1) investigative journalism	1) all grants to individual reporters
Fund for New Jersey 57 Washington St. E. Orange, NJ 07017 (201) 676-5905 Contact: Robert P. Corman	1) inform people in order to allow them to be effective participants in all levels of government 2) emphasis on public policy research, oversight of government activities, citizen action programs	1) tax-exempt (will sometimes help obtain tax exemption) 2) only in New Jersey 3) no individuals, capital projects, day care centers, curricular changes in education, health care, or scholarships
Funding Exchange 135 East 15th Street New York, NY 10003 (212) 691-91552 Contact: June Makela	1) equitable distribution of power 2) society without discrimination 3) minorities and international issues priorities	1) average grant: $1,000-5,000

Frank Gannett
   Newspaper Carrier
   Scholarships, Inc.
Lincoln Tower
Rochester, NY 14604
(716) 262-3315
Contact:
   Debra B. Jansen
	1) College scholarships for newspaper carriers of participating Gannett newspapers	

Wallace Alexander
   Gerbode Foundation
470 Columbus Avenue,
   Suite 201
San Francisco, CA 94133
(415) 391-0911
Contact:
   Thomas C. Layton
	1) innovative programs
	2) education
		1) San Francisco Bay area
		2) no individuals, budgets, endowments, films, religious projects, or scholarships

Foundation Name	Areas of Interest Include	Limitations Include
DS & RH Gottesman Foundation 100 Park Avenue New York, NY 10017 Contact: Ira D. Wallach	1) broad purposes 2) general giving with emphasis on higher education, local Jewish welfare funds, museums and world peace organizations	1) grant range: $100-130,000
George Gund Foundation One Erieview Plaza Cleveland, OH 44114 (216) 241-3114 Contact: James S. Lipscomb	1) broad purposes 2) priority for education projects with emphasis on new concepts & methods in teaching 3) social programs for the disadvantaged, including improved economic opportunities & housing for minorities 4) supports ecology, civic affairs, & arts	1) grants mainly in Ohio 2) no building programs, endowments, normal operating budgets, or individuals 3) Deadlines Jan. 15, Apr. 15, Aug. 15, Oct. 15
Haymarket People's Fund 25 West Street Boston, MA 02111 (617) 426-1909 Contact: Joellen Lamblotte	1) "oppressed" populations 2) provides funds for groups organized around issues in a specific community, institution, or workplace	1) New England area 2) community work 3) involving working-class and/or Third World people in the area 4) interested in giving grants to informational work on international issues 5) no businesses, human services, or groups linked to larger institutions
Edward W. Hazen Foundation 16 E. 34th Street New Haven, CT 06511 (212) 889-1616 Contact: Richard Magat	1) junior & senior high school levels concerned with their value systems 2) work environments of young people 3) competence of teachers	1) no building funds, operating budgets, propaganda, efforts to influence legislation, medicine or health, or individuals
Honeywell Foundation P.O. Box 524 Minneapolis, MN 55440 (612) 870-6821 Contact: Patricia Hoven	1) broad interests 2) higher education 3) community funds	1) no individuals, endowment funds, or operating budgets 2) only communities where Honeywell has major facilities 3) new contributions suspended 1984

Foundation Name	Areas of Interest Include	Limitations Include
George Frederick Jewett Foundation 1 Maritime Plaza The Alcoa Building, Suite 1340 San Francisco, CA 94111 (415) 421-1351 Contact: Mrs. Sara Fernandez	1) higher education 2) conservation of natural resources	1) primarily Pacific Northwest 2) no grants to individuals
Joyce Foundation 135 South LaSalle Street Chicago, IL 60603 (312) 782-2464 Contact: Charles Daly	1) interested in cultures, education & government accountability	1) Midwest USA
Max & Anna Levinson Foundation 1318 Beacon Street, Rm. 6 Brookline, MA 02146 (617) 731-1602 Contact: Sidney Shapiro	1) regional, national or global concerns 2) social change funding, energy, equal rights, law & government, economics, & development	1) prefers tax-exempt 2) favors groups that can't get traditional funding
Liberty Hill Foundation PO Box 1074 Venice, CA 90291 Contact: Mary Jo von Mach	1) funds educational & charitable projects that unite people for progressive social change 2) supports grassroots organizations	1) Los Angeles Area 2) Supports change nationally and internationally through membership in the NY-based Funding Exchange
Limantour Fund 88 First Street, Rm. 210 San Francisco, CA 94105 Contact: Victor Honig	1) community-based projects 2) nuclear issues 3) education	1) San Francisco area 2) donations, i.e.: Agape, Capp Street Foundation, San Francisco Women's Health Center
McKenzie River Gathering 454 Willamette Eugene, OR 97401 (503) 485-2790 Contact: Peter Jenson or 408 SW Second Avenue Portland, OR 97204 (503) 228-7009 Contact: Bonnie Tinker or 1204 Smith Tower Seattle, WA 98104 (206) 622-2267 Contact: Kim Ewing	1) challenge social & economic inequalities 2) support social change nationally & internationally 3) promote democratic nonviolent society 4) promote grassroots organizations working against violence	1) funds Washington region 2) unlikely to give funds elsewhere 3) no food co-ops, health centers, or alternative schools unless promoting social change

Foundation Name	Areas of Interest Include	Limitations Include
Stewart R. Mott Associates 1133 Fifth Avenue New York, NY 10028 (212) 289-0006 Contact: Deni Frand or 122 Maryland Avenue, NE Washington, DC 20002 (202) 546-3732	1) supports political candidates 2) population control 3) arms limitations	1) average grant for 1979: $5,000
Ms. Foundation for Women 370 Lexington Avenue New York, NY 10017 (212) 639-3475 Contact: Julia R. Scott	1) survival issues 2) women's health 3) non-discrimination 4) models for other groups working on survival issues	1) no individual, research, arts-related or litigation projects 2) generally tax-exempt groups
New World Foundation 100 East 85th Street New York, NY 10028 (212) 249-1023 Contact: David Ramage	1) the avoidance of war 2) how children are taught & teachers are trained	1) will not consider requests for building funds, capital investment, general budgets, individuals, or programs in the arts 2) must be action- or policy-oriented
New York Community Trust 415 Madison Avenue New York, NY 10017 (212) 758-0100 Contact: Herbert B. West	1) special programs for NYC area 2) community funds	1) no individuals, building or endowment funds

North Star Fund
135 E. 15th Street
New York, NY 10003
(212) 460-5511
Contact:
  Toby D'Oench
  Lois Ross
  John Silva
	1) educating community on social issues nationally & internationally	1) New York City area

Ottinger Foundation 370 Lexington Avenue New York, NY 10017 (212) 532-0617 Contact: David R. Hunter	1) advocates democracy, social justice, ecological balance, & civil rights	1) no individual, capital campaigns, or operating budgets

Foundation Name	Areas of Interest Include	Limitations Include
Peace Development Fund 274 N. Pleasant Street PO Box 270 Amherst, MA 01004 Contact: Meg Gage	1) promotes global demilitarization, world peace & nonviolent conflict resolution 2) primary goals: halting & reversing the arms race—developing broader base to peace movement	1) peace through peaceful means 2) tax-exempt 3) must submit reports to PDF
Pittsburgh Bridge & Iron Works Charitable Trust 1310 Commonwealth Bldg. Pittsburgh, PA 15222 (412) 471-7500 Contact: George Klingelhofer or PO Box 247 Sun Valley, Idaho 83353	1) social change 2) women's issues 3) environment	1) Western PA & Idaho 2) no individuals
Playboy Foundation 919 N. Michigan Avenue Chicago, IL 60611 (312) 751-8000 Contact: Margaret Standish	1) advance human rights & freedom 2) government surveillance	1) Only US projects
Public Welfare Foundation 2600 Virginia Avenue, NW, Rm. 505 Washington, DC 20037 (202) 965-1800 Contact: Charles Glenn Ihrig	1) grass roots organizations	1) no individuals, religious purposes, arts, films, building, endowments, scholarships, graduate work, foreign study, research, or conferences
Charles H. Revson Foundation 444 Madison Avenue New York, NY 10022 (212) 935-3340 Contact: Ell N. Evans	1) changing role of women 2) organizations whose programs are designed to demand strong participation of women	1) no individuals, local health appeals, art groups, general budget, building or construction
Rockefeller Family Fund 1290 Avenue of Americas New York, NY 10104 (212) 397-4844 Contact: Director	1) to promote responsive relationships between individuals & institutions 2) arms control	1) no individuals, building or endowments

Foundation Name	Areas of Interest Include	Limitations Include

Samuel Rubin Foundation
777 UN Plaza
New York, NY 10017
(212) 697-8945
Contact:
  Cora Weiss
	1) programs for peace &
	   justice
	2) social, economic &
	   political rights
		1) no individuals or
		   building funds

Shalan Foundation
680 Beach Street
Suite 498
San Francisco, CA 94109
(415) 673-8660
Contact: Loni Hancock
	1) tax reform
	2) redistribution of wealth
	3) safety
	4) appropriate
	   development of
	   resources
		1) Western US
		2) tax-exempt
		3) project should be more
		   than 10% & less than
		   30% of budget

Stern Fund, et al.
370 Lexington Avenue
Rm. 1801
New York, NY 10017
(212) 532-0617
Contact:
  David R. Hunter
	1) open government
	2) economic democracy
	3) social justice
	4) expose abuse of power
	5) work for institutional
	   change
		1) no individuals or
		   building funds

A Territory Resource
Lloyd Building, Rm. 304
6th & Stewart
Seattle, Washington 98101
(206) 624-4081
Contact:
  Greg Caplan Tuke
	1) social change
	   activities—supports
	   training & start-up
	   costs
	2) promoting justice,
	   equality, &
	   humaneness
		1) projects must address
		   fundamental issues
		   facing Northwest &
		   Northern Rockies
		2) no individuals or
		   government agency
		   sponsored services

Tides Foundation
873 A Sutter Street
San Francisco, CA 94109
(415) 771-4308
Contact:
  Drummond Pike
	1) oriented toward
	   progressive social
	   change
		1) primarily Southwest,
		   Pacific West, & Rocky
		   Mountain Region

Vanguard Public
  Foundation
4111 24th Street
San Francisco, CA 94114
(415) 285-2005
Contact:
  Evelyn Shapiro
	1) working toward
	   redistribution of wealth
	   & power
	2) supports projects that
	   address national &
	   international issues
		1) San Francisco Bay area
		   counties
		2) supports social change
		   nationally and
		   internationally through
		   the Funding Exchange

Youth Project
National Office
1555 Connecticut Ave., NW
Washington, DC 20036
(202) 483-0030
Contact:
  Karen Pajet
  (also has regional offices)
	1) supports groups
	   interested in promoting
	   social, political and
	   economic change
		1) tax-exempt status

Filmography

The following is a select list of audio-visual resources that have been successfully used in the classroom. Rental prices are quoted here and are subject to change. For other materials, we suggest you consult the following organizations, film guides and libraries:

Guides and Libraries

American Friends Service Committee, 2161 Massachusetts Avenue, Cambridge, MA 02140, (617) 497-5273;

American Friends Service Committee, 1501 Cherry St., Philadelphia, PA 19102, (215) 241-7171;

Audio Brandon Films, 34 MacQueston Parkway South, Mt. Vernon, NY 10550, (914) 664-5051;

Audio-Visual Resources on Global Issues, Unitarian Universalist UN Office, Inc., 777 UN Plaza, New York, NY 10017;

Black Filmmaker Foundation/Distribution Service, 1 Centre St., New York, NY 10002, (212) 891-8240;

Black Women Artists Film Series, 14 Beacon St., Boston, MA 02108;

Bull Frog Films, Oley, PA 19547; (215) 779-8226

California Newsreel, 630 Natoma, San Francisco, CA 94103, (415) 621-6196;

Cambridge Documentary Films, Priscilla France, P.O. Box 385, Cambridge, MA 02139, (617) 354-3677;

Center For Documentary Media, c/o New Times Films Library, P.O. Box 315, Franklin Lakes, NJ 07417, (201) 891-8240;

Churchill Films, 662 N. Robertson Blvd., Los Angeles, CA 90069, (213) 657-5110;

Corinth Films, 410 E. 62nd St., New York, NY 10021, (212) 421-4770;

Direct Cinema, P.O. Box 315, Franklin Lakes, NJ 07417, (201) 891-8240;

Disarmament: A Select Film Bibliography, The Riverside Church Disarmament Program, 490 Riverside Dr., New York, NY 10027, (212) 222-5900;

Extension Media Center, U. of California, 2223 Fulton St., Berkeley, CA 94720, (415) 642-0460;

Films Inc., 1213 Wilmette Ave., Wilmette, IL 60091, (800) 323-4222;

Films of the United Nations Family 1980-81, UN Information Center, New York, NY 10017;

First Run Features, 153 Waverly Pl., New York, NY 10014, (212) 243-0600;

Green Mountain Post Films, P.O. Box 229, Twiner Falls, MA 01376, (413) 863-4754;

Icarus Films, 200 Park Ave. So., Ste. 1319, New York, NY 10003, (212) 674-3375;

International Films Bureau, Inc., 332 S. Michigan Ave., Chicago, IL 60604, (312) 427-4545;

Iris Films, P.O. Box 5353, Berkeley, CA 94705, (415) 549-3192;

Kartemquin Films, 1901 W. Wellington, Chicago, IL 60657, (312) 472-4366;

La Operacion, P.O. Box 735, Chelsea Station, New York, NY 10011, (212) 864-6564;

Learning Corporation of America, 1350 Ave. of the Americas, New York, NY 10019, (212) 397-9365;

Maryknoll Films, Maryknoll, NY 10545, (914) 941-7590 ext. 577;

Michigan Media, 416 Fourth St., Ann Arbor, MI 48109, (313) 764-5360;

Media Network, 208 W. 13th St., New York, NY 10011, (212) 620-0878;

The Museum of Modern Art, Department of Film Circulating Programs, 11 W. 53rd St., New York, NY 10019, (212) 956-4204;

New Day Films, P.O. Box 315, Franklin Lakes, NJ 07417, (201) 891-8240;

New York University Film Library, 26 Washington Place, New York, NY 10003, (212) 598-2250;

Oxfam America, 115 Broadway Ave., Boston, MA 02116, (617) 482-1211;

Packard Manse Media Project, P.O. Box 450, Stoughton, MA 02072, (617) 344-3259;

Phoenix Films, 468 Park Ave. So., New York, NY 10016, (212) 684-5910;

Public Media, Inc., Sydney Levine, 119 W. 57th St., Ste. 1511, New York, NY 10019, (212) 247-8050;

Resolution, 630 Natoma St., San Francisco, CA 94103, (415) 621-6198;

SANE, 318 Massachusetts Ave., NE, Washington, DC 20002, (202) 546-7100;

Second Decade, P.O. Box 1482, Franklin Lakes, NJ 07147, (212) 222-1185;

Star Film Library, 120 Boylston St., #708, Boston, MA 02216, (617) 426-1912;

Third World Newsreel, 160 Fifth Ave., Ste. 911, New York, NY 10010, (212) 243-2310;

Time-Life Video, 100 Eisenhower Dr., P.O. Box 644, Paramus, NJ 07652, (201) 843-4545;

Unifilm, 419 Park Ave. So., New York, NY 10016, (212) 686-9890;

War, Peace Film Guide, 1980; John Dowling, World Without War Publications, 67 E. Madison, Ste. 1417, Chicago, IL 60603, (717) 662-4275.

Titles

Abaphucine—The Dispossessed. Color, 40 min., 1980, ($60). Southern Africa Media Center, California Newsreel, 630 Natoma St., San Francisco, CA 94103. Analysis of how apartheid functions to produce and maintain a cheap, controlled labor force. '

Acid Rain: Requiem or Recovery? Color, 30 min., 1983, ($50). Canadian Travel Film Library, 1251 Ave. of the Americas, New York, NY 10019. Examines the cause and effect of acid rain and what should be done to stop it.

Act Now! Because Nobody Wants A Nuclear War. 3/4" video, Color, 35 min., 1982, ($35). New Century Policies, P.O. Box 963, Boston, MA 02103. A training film for activists whose thrust is that public opinion about the arms race can only affect public policy through political activism.

The Afrikaaner Experience. Color, 35 min., 1978, ($40). Learning Corp. of America, 1350 Ave. of the Americas, New York, NY 10019. Traces the history of South Africa's apartheid policies.

Alternatives to Violence Video Forum. 3/4" video, 60 min., 1982, ($50). WTL, Box 351 (D), Primos, PA 19018. A five-part program with a 147-page Learner's Guide for use in promoting alternatives to violence in conflict situations.

America—From Hitler to M-X. Color, 90 min., 1982, ($115). Parallel Films, 314 W. 91st St., New York, NY 10024. A new anti-war feature documentary about the present military aims of the United States, including its long-standing first-strike policy and the escalating threat of worldwide annihilation.

America's Twentieth Century Foreign Policy: Crisis in Diplomacy. Six color filmstrips, 7 cassettes, Guide, 1981, ($141). Social Studies School Service, 10,000 Culver Blvd., Dept. 13, Culver City, CA 90230. Chronicles the development of U.S. foreign policy from McKinley to Reagan. Sections include: 1) isolation and expansion; 2) from neutrality to war; 3) between world wars; 4) evolution of the Cold War; 5) Third World rumblings; and 6) the world arena.

American Constitutional Convention. Simulation game. Subject: Political Science, U.S. History. Number of Players: 32-49 in 13 teams. Playtime: 2-6 hours. Science Research Association, 259 E. Eric St., Chicago, IL 60611. Players adopt the roles of delegates to the 1787 Philadelphia Convention and learn about the conditions surrounding the writing of the U.S. Constitution, political issues contained within it and its role in the development of the American political system.

Americas in Transition. Color, 29 min., 1982, ($50). Icarus Films, 200 Park Ave., Ste. 1319, New York, NY 10003. Provides an excellent introduction to U.S. relations with Latin America and the underlying causes of unrest in that region.

And Who Shall Feed This World? Color, 47 min., 1975, ($65). Films, Inc., 733 Green Bay Rd., Wilmette, IL 60091. Does the U.S. have an obligation to provide food for the rest of the world? This film tries to answer that question.

As If People Mattered. Color, 16 min., 1977, ($28.50). Bullfrog Films, Oley, PA 19547. Presents arguments for small-scale, appropriate technologies, and a more humane, decentralized economy, with special reference to the world energy situation.

Back to Kampuchea. Color, 57 min., 1982, ($100). First Run Features, 144 Bleecker St., New York, NY 10012. Documents the difficult but determined struggle of the people of Kampuchea (formerly Cambodia) to rebuild their country after the destruction of Vietnam and the despotic rule of the Khmer Rouge.

Bam: Beyond Baikal. Color, 28 min., 1982, ($55). First Run Features, 144 Bleecker St., New York, NY 10012. Edward Lamb, an industrialist from Toledo, Ohio was invited by the radio and TV industry of the Soviet Union to record ongoing development of Eastern Siberia which is rich in mineral wealth. This film is a result of that invitation.

Banking on S. Africa. Color, 20 min., 1982, ($35). Packard Manse Media Project, P.O. Box 450, Stoughton, MA 02072. Demonstrates that bank loans by U.S. and Canada to the government of S. Africa support apartheid. Suggests ways to pressure banks to withdraw this support.

Belgian Congo Independence. Color, 20 min., 1981, ($39). Filmstrip Social Studies School Service, 10,000 Culver Blvd., Dept. 13, P.O. Box 802, Culver City, CA 90230. The independence and Africanization of the modern state of Zaire is studied.

Black and White in Color. Color, 91 min., 1976, ($250). Corinth Films, 410 E. 62nd St., New York, NY 10021. Story set in colonial West Africa in 1914 of a mini-war fought by France and Germany which uses local black tribesman as soldiers. Portrays the horrors and absurdity of war.

Black Waters. Color, 28 min., 1980, ($55). Green Mountain Post Films, P.O. Box 229, Turner Falls, MA 01376. Focuses on Marvin Kammerer, a South Dakota rancher and leading community organizer, and examines his reasons for active opposition to uranium mining. Includes rebuttals by a Union Carbide public relations spokesman.

Blood and Sand: War in the Sahara. Color, 58 min., 1981, ($100). First Run Features, 144 Bleecker St., New York, NY 10012. First film to examine the conflict between the Polisario guerillas fighting for the liberation of their land and the Kingdom of Morocco, and U.S. involvement through arms sales.

Blood of the Condor. B&W, 72 min., 1969, ($100). Unifilm, 419 Park Ave. So., New York, NY 10016. Examines U.S. involvement in population control programs for Latin Americans, which frequently involve sterilization.

Bomb. Color, 55 min., 1975, ($24). University of Illinois Film Center, 1325 S. Oak St., Champaign, IL 61820. Examines the decision to drop the bomb, arguing that its use was primarily for diplomatic and political reasons rather than military ones.

Bombs Will Make the Rainbow Break. Color, 17 min., 1982, ($45). Films, Inc., 1213 Wilmette Ave., Wilmette, IL 60091. Documents the Children's Campaign for Nuclear Disarmament and their letter-writing campaign to Ronald Reagan.

Bottle Babies. Color, 26 min., 1975, ($30). California Newsreel, 630 Natoma St., San Francisco, CA 94103. An award-winning documentary that first brought the dangers of infant formula malnutrition to public attention.

Brinkmanship: Holocaust or Compromise. Simulation game. Subject: History, International Relations. Age: High School. Number of players: 20-40 in 2 teams. Playtime: 3-5 hours. History Simulations, P.O. Box 2775, Santa Clara, CA 95051. Players experience the difficulties of negotiation during a crisis as they act as representatives of two world powers dealing with Cold War conflicts.

Budgetary Politics and Presidential Decision-Making. Simulation game. Subject: Political Science. Age: College. Number of players: one. Science Research Association, 259 E. Erie St., Chicago, IL 60611. Player is involved in the budget process of the American government.

The Bull's Eye War. Color, 52 min., 1980, ($75). Films, Inc., 1144 Wilmette Ave., Wilmette, IL 60091. This film examines the technology and intelligence applications of precision-guided weapons, and analyzes the implications for the future.

But What Do We Do? Color, 22 min., 1969, ($18). University of California, Extension Media Center, 222 Fulton St., Berkeley, CA 94720. True story of an engineer who quits his military analyst job to join the Peace Corps.

Cabinets in Crisis. Simulation game. Subject: International Relations. Age: High School. Number of Players: 15-30 in 3 teams. Playtime: 4 classroom sessions. WGBH Educational Foundation, 125 Western Avenue, Boston, MA 02124. TV foreign affairs simulation in which representatives from the U.S., Soviet Union and Yugoslavia work to resolve a famine crisis in Yugoslavia.

A Call For Peace. Color, 30 min., 1983, ($45). Conference on the Fate of the Earth, 1045 Sansome St., San Francisco, CA 94111. A compelling analysis and moving plea by Congressmember Ronald V. Dellums, Chair of the Military Construction Subcommittee of the House Armed Services Committee, to stop our suicidal drift toward nuclear war and change U.S. priorities from arms for war to jobs for peace.

Caltech Political Military Exercise. Simulation game. Subject: International Relations. Age: College/Adult. Number of players: 30-100 in 12 teams. Playtime: 2 days in 1-2 hour rounds. E.S. Munger, Bernice Abell, Willard Manning, Jr., California Institute of Technology, Pasadena, CA 91109. Players assume the roles of leaders of various countries in order to deal with hypothetical and real international crises.

Cambodia: Year Zero. Color, 60 min., 1979, ($25). American Friends Service Committee, 2161 Massachusetts Ave., Cambridge, MA 02140. The incredible story of Cambodia from 1975-1979. The brutality of the Pol Pot years is starkly portrayed, but within a sound historical and political context.

Ceddo. Color, 120 min., 1977, ($125 classroom rental only). Third World Newsreel, 160 Fifth Ave., New York, NY 10010. Banned in Senegal due in part to the explicit treatment of taboo topics such as African complicity in the provision of slaves for the Western Hemisphere, the traditionally low status of women in Africa, and "Islamic colonialism."

The Changing Middle East. Color, 25 min., 1975, ($19). Michigan Media, 416 Fourth St., Ann Arbor, MI 48109. Background on a dozen Middle Eastern countries.

Choice or Chance. Color, 20 min., 1982, ($20). American Friends Service Committee, 2160 Lake St., San Francisco, CA 94121. Provides the facts young people need to make an informed response to registration and the draft.

The CIA Case Officer. Color, 30 min., 1978, ($50). Center for Documentary Media, c/o New Times Films Library, P.O. Box 315, Franklin Lakes, NJ 07417. Portrait of former CIA official, John Stockwell, who served in the CIA for 12 years, primarily in Africa and Vietnam. Reveals much information about CIA practices and policies.

Collision Course. Color, 35 min., 1977 (FREE). Mennonite Central Committee, Audio-Visual Library, 21 S. 12th St., Akron, PA 17501. Explores the effects of repression by the Marcos government of the Filipino people.

Colonialism Has Fallen. B&W, 24 min., 1980, ($40). Icarus Films, 200 Park Ave. So., New York, NY 10003. Filmed in a small rural village in Mozambique, the film shows the local impact of illiteracy, political isolation, and the oppression of women.

Come Back Africa. B&W, 83 min., 1959, ($100). Icarus Films, 200 Park Ave. So., New York, NY 10003. First film to present to the outside world the grim reality of apartheid.

Community Game of South East Asia. Simulation game. Subject: Economics, International Relations. Age: Adult. Number of players: 8. Peace Corps, International Voluntary Service, Lancaster, England. The gameboard is a large map of a typical village, with rice paddies, a local temple, and other landmarks. Each player draws a number of picture cards representing rice, schools, wells, roads, hospitals and then takes his turn trying to build what the village needs most, discovering opportunities for cooperation and the dangers of poor planning.

Conflict. Simulation game. Subject: International Relations. Age: Adult. Number of players: 24-36 in 3 teams. Simile II, 1150 Silverado Rd., La Jolla, CA 92037. Designed to encourage students to focus on potential dangers embedded in the international political system, and to help them investigate the problems of disarmament by raising questions about its feasibility.

Conflict in the Middle East. Simulation game. Subject: International Relations. Age: College. Number of players: 45-60, 9-11 teams. Playtime: 4 hours, in 1-hour rounds. Lincoln Filene Center for Citizenship and Public Affairs, Tufts University, Medford, MA 02155. Provides better understanding of the complexity of decision-making in foreign policy. Oriented around the situation in the Middle East.

Conscience and War Taxes. Color slideshow, 15 min., 1977, ($10). American Friends Service Committee, 407 S. Dearborn, Chicago, IL 60605. Discusses the possibility of creating a legal alternative for taxpayers who are opposed to funding the military establishment.

Conscience in Conflict. Color, 34 min., 1973, ($40). Learning Corp. of America, 1350 Ave. of the Americas, New York, NY 10102. Focuses on the extent to which people should hold fast to their principles.

Controlling Interest. Color, 40 min., 1978, ($25). American Friends Service Committee, 2161 Massachusetts Ave., Cambridge, MA 02140. A stimulating and insightful look at the impact of multinational corporations on the economic and political development of the U.S. and the Third World.

Co-op: Moses Coady. Color, 58 min., 1979, ($60). Bullfrog Films, Oley, PA 19547. About Reverend Moses Coady, who spearheaded Canada's cooperative movement from 1929 to 1950. Today Third World students attend Coady College to learn about his principles.

A Crime to Fit the Punishment. Color, 46 min., 1982, ($75). First Run Features, 144 Bleecker St., New York, NY 10012. Examines the relationship between politics and filmmaking with a chilling indictment of the abuse of authority during the McCarthy era.

Crisis. Simulation game. Subject: International Relations, Economics. Age: High School/Adult. Number of players: 18-35 in 6 teams. Playtime: 2-4 hours in 30 minute rounds. Simile II, 1150 Silverado Rd., La Jolla, CA 92037. Simulation of international conflict in which players form teams to manage the affairs of 6 fictional nations. The nations, which vary in strength and military capacity, are faced with the problem of resolving a tense situation in a mining area of enormous importance.

A Cry For Freedom. Color, 20 min., 1981, ($25). Ausburg A-V Dept., 57 E. Main St., Columbus, OH 43215. Describes the plight of the Namibian people under South African rule.

Dangerous Parallel. Simulation game. Subject: International Relations. Age: Adult. Number of players: 18-36 in 6 teams. Playtime: 3-7 hours in 40 minute rounds. Scott, Foresman and Co., 1900 E. Lake Ave., Glenview, IL 60025. A foreign policy simulation in which students play ministerial roles in six countries facing a situation similar to that of the Korean War.

Daniel Ellsberg Speaks on America's Nuclear Policy. Color, 55 min., 1983, ($35). Original Face Video, P.O. Box 447, Grass Valley, CA 95945. Ellsberg, principal civilian architect of U.S. nuclear war plans under President Kennedy, discloses a hidden history of American nuclear supremacy as an instrument of coercive diplomacy.

Dark Circle. Color, 90 min., 1982, (apply for rental). New Yorker Films, 16 West 61st St., New York, NY 10023. Interweaves dramatic personal stories with rare, recently declassified footage of reactor meltdowns, bomb assembly lines and a sales convention for nuclear weapons.

The Decision to Drop the Bomb. B&W, 82 min., 1965, ($125). Films, Inc., 1144 Wilmette Ave., Wilmette, IL 60091. A film that discusses foreign policy decision-making, war, and its alternatives.

The Deep Cold War. Color, 50 min., 1980, ($75). Films, Inc., 1144 Wilmette Ave., Wilmette, IL 60091. A report on the secret and silent struggle between NATO's anti-submarine forces and the Soviet submarine fleet.

Democracy: Use It! or Lose it in a Nuclear War. 3/4″ video, color, 40 min., 1982, ($35). New Century Policies, P.O. Box 963, Boston, MA 02103. Another election skills-training tape which discusses why Congress is important to arms race decisions, how members of Congress view advocacy groups, and techniques for effective campaigning.

Developing Nations Series. Color, 40 min., 1980, ($25). International Films Bureau, Inc., 332 S. Michigan Ave., Chicago, IL 60604. This series chronicles the development of Papua, New Guinea as an independent nation.

The Development Game. Simulation game. Subject: Economics. Age: Adult. Number of players: 24-60 in 2-4 teams. Playtime: 1 day. Oxfam Education Department, 247 Banbury Rd., Oxford OX 2 707, England. Participants play the role of governments of developing countries. Each team draws up a 3-5 year development plan and a prospectus for one major project needing support.

Development Without Tears. Color, 27 min., 1978, ($25). Michigan Media, 416 Fourth St., Ann Arbor, MI 48109. Interviews with development experts from Africa, Asia, and Latin America, who stress the importance of political action in assisting material progress in developing countries.

A Dialogue for Human Survival with Ram Davis and Daniel Ellsberg. Video, color, 45 min., 1982, ($35). Original Face Video, P.O. Box 447, Grass Valley, CA 95945. Joins spiritual understanding and political acumen in a common quest: the avoidance of nuclear war.

Direct Action. Color, 45 min., 1978, ($50). Green Mountain Post Films, P.O. Box 229, Twiner Falls, MA 01376. History and documentary footage of the Diablo Canyon civil disobedience movement. Good for discussion.

The Discarded People. Color, 30 min., 1981, ($50). California Newsreel, 630 Natoma St., San Francisco, CA 94103. An updated report on the conditions of "reformed" apartheid rule in South Africa.

Ecocide: A Strategy of War. Color, 23 min., 1981, ($55). Green Mountain Post Films, P.O. Box 229, Twiner Falls, MA 01376. Between 1969 and 1973, Dr. E.W. Pfeiffer, a zoologist, made five trips to Indochina to study and document the ecological effects of the war in Vietnam. This film is a result of that study.

Ecology. Simulation game. Subject: National Resources. Age: Adult. Number of players: 5-10. Playtime: 1-3 hours. Urban System Inc., 1033 Massachusetts Ave., Cambridge, MA 02138. Players attempt to lead a population safely through a history of conflict between man's inventive genius and the environment.

Egypt. Color, 16 min., 1979, ($45). Films, Inc., 733 Green Bay Rd., Wilmette, IL 60091. Examines Sadat's peace initiatives and how the U.S. is caught in the three-sided dispute between Israel, Egypt and Saudi Arabia.

Eight Minutes to Midnight. Color, 60 min., 1981, ($100). Direct Cinema Ltd., P.O. Box 315, Franklin Lakes, NJ 07417. Profile of Dr. Helen Caldicott alerting the public to the ramifications that a nuclear war would have on the medical world.

El Salvador: Another Vietnam. Color, 53 min., 1981, ($40). Michigan Media, 416 Fourth St., Ann Arbor, MI 48109. Examines the civil war in El Salvador in light of the Reagan Administration's decision to "draw the line" against "Communist interference" in Central America.

El Salvador: The Seeds of Liberty. Color, 30 min., 1981, ($50). Icarus Films, 200 Park Ave. So., Ste. 1319, New York, NY 10003. Focuses on the murder of four North American missionaries and the role of the church in El Salvador.

End of Innocence. Color, 29 min., 1982, ($55). First Run Features, 144 Bleecker St., New York, NY 10012. Examines the impact of the execution of Julius and Ethel Rosenberg on a small Jewish boy, his family, and community.

Fable Safe. Color, 9 min., 1971, ($20). Museum of Modern Art, Circulating Film Program, 11 W. 53rd St., New York, NY 10019. Animated satire pointing out the folly of the spiralling arms race.

The Face of Famine. Color, 75 min., 1982, ($125). Films, Inc., 733 Green Bay Rd., Wilmette, IL 60091. This film shows how enormous quantities of grain are used to feed livestock in the West and the repercussions of such a system on starving people all over the world.

Facing Up to The Bomb. Color, 52 min., 1982, ($90). Films, Inc., 733 Green Bay Rd., Wilmette, IL 60091. Examines the nuclear freeze movement and discusses alternatives to nuclear arms control.

Factories for the Third World: Tunisia. Color, 43 min., 1979, ($75). Icarus Films, 200 Park Ave. So., Ste. 1319, New York, NY 10003. Examines the history of the union movement in Tunisia.

$1,000,000,000,000 For Defense. 3/4" video, color, 60 min., 1980, ($60). WNET Media Service, 356 W. 58th St., New York, NY 10019. Portrays a visit to an annual arms fair where manufacturers like Singer, G.E., Ford and RCA exhibit their latest high-technology weapons systems.

For Export Only. Color, 112 min., 1982, ($100). Richter Prods., 330 W. 42nd St., New York, NY 10036. This film shows how products banned or restricted in the West, because of their danger to humans, are knowingly exported to the Third World by multinational corporations.

Foreign Policy Decision-Making Exercise. Simulation game. Subject: International Relations. Age: College. Number of players: 5-45 in 3 teams. Playtime: 3-4 hours. Markham Pabe Co., 3322 W. Peterson Ave., Chicago, IL 60645. Focuses on the role of intellectual and ideological factors in foreign policy-making.

Forget Not Our Sisters. Color, 39 min., 1982, ($20). American Friends Service Committee, 2161 Massachusetts Ave., Cambridge, MA 02140. An overview of the apartheid system of South Africa, focusing on the impact of apartheid on Black women.

Fundi: The Baker Story. Color, 60 min., 1980, ($75). New Day Films, P.O. Box 315, Franklin Lakes, NJ 07417. An inspiring film about the days of the civil rights movement and a great but little-known figure who was at its core.

The Game of Mice. Simulation game. Subject: International Relations. Age: High School. Number of players: 30 or more. Playtime: 6 weeks. Richard Eastridge, Antwerp High School, Antwerp, OH 45813. Players, assuming the roles of delegates to the U.N., act upon the problematic Arab-Israeli confrontation.

Gathering Wealth Like Eggs. Color, 15 min., 1983, ($15). United Methodist Communications, 810 12th Ave. So., Nashville, TN 37203. Presents the hidden costs of transnational corporations and examines the need for corporate responsibility.

Generations of Resistance. Color, 52 min., 1980, ($70). Southern Africa Media Center, California Newsreel, 630 Natoma St., San Francisco, CA 94103. Provides the framework necessary for understanding apartheid and the events exploding in South Africa today.

George Kennan: A Critical Choice. Color, 58 min., 1982, ($90). Blackwood Prods., 251 W. 57th St., New York, NY 10019. The former American ambassador to the USSR assesses present East-West relations and possible alternatives to the dilemmas presented by the arms race.

The Gift That Multiplies. Color, 20 min., 1976, (FREE). Mennonite Central Committee, Audio-Visual Library, 21 S. 12th St., Akron, PA 17501. Tells about the work of the Heifer Project Inc. in helping the hungry in many countries help themselves with food-producing animals.

Gods of Metal. Color, 27 min., 1982, ($25). Maryknoll Films, Maryknoll, NY 10545. The arms race is analyzed from a Christian perspective, showing the economic and social effects on people in the U.S. and the Third World, especially the poor.

The Good Society Exercise. Simulation game. Subject: Political Science. Age: Adult. Number of players: 23. Playtime: 2-3 hours. International Relations Program, Simulated International Processes Project, Northwestern University, Evanston, IL 60601. Represents a society where the guidelines are Order and Justice, but where the reality does not measure up to the principles. Maintaining stability and order while promoting change is the dynamic purpose of this game.

The Great Lakes: No Free Lunch. Color, 29 min., 1981, ($20). Michigan Media, 419 Fourth St., Ann Arbor, MI 48109. Irreversible damage of blind and rampant "progress" will be one of the key national problems at the close of this century. This film looks at the Great Lakes where some of these problems are being confronted now.

Ground Zero. 3/4" video, color, 50 min., 1981, ($22.50). Michigan Media, 416 Fourth St., Ann Arbor, MI 48109. Takes a close look at what would happen if a 15-megaton bomb is dropped on SAC headquarters near Omaha.

Growing Dollars. Color, 27 min., 1978, ($25). Michigan Media, 416 Fourth St., Ann Arbor, MI 48109. Looks at several examples of cash crop production in Third World countries and the involvement of multinational corporations in rural development.

Guatemala (My Country Occupied). B&W, 30 min., 1971, ($50). Third World Newsreel, 160 5th Ave., Ste. 911, New York, NY 10010. Traces the life of one Guatemalan woman as she deals with life in a corporately-controlled Guatemalan village.

Guatemala...Personal Testimonies. Video, color, 20 min., 1982, ($50). Icarus Films, 200 Park Ave. So., Ste. 1319, New York, NY 10003. Eyewitness accounts of the continuing pattern of human rights abuses by the U.S.-backed military government.

Guess Who's Coming to Breakfast? Color, 20 min., 1982. ($35). Packard Manse Media Project, P.O. Box 450, Stoughton, MA 62072. Spotlights Gulf and Western presence in the Dominican Republic as a model of multinational domination of Third World nations.

Guide to Armageddon. Color, 25 min., 1982, ($50). Public Media Inc., Sydney Levine, 119 W. 57th St., Ste. 1511, New York, NY 10019. Depicts the aftermath of a projected one-megaton nuclear bomb explosion on St. Paul's Cathedral in London. It demonstrates the absurdity of civil defense.

Habbanaae: The Animal of Friendship. Color, 20 min., 1980, ($35). Packard Manse Media Project, P.O. Box 450, Stoughton, MA 02072. Describes the African herders' adaptation to the Sahel and their capacity for self-reliance.

Hearts and Minds. Color, 112 min., 1975, ($82). Extension Media Center, 2223 Fulton, Berkeley, CA 94720. Powerful documentary that examines the American military and political consciousness that led to U.S. involvement in Vietnam.

Hiroshima: A Document of the Atomic Bombing. Color, 28 min., 1970, ($17). Michigan Media, 416 Fourth St., Ann Arbor, MI 48109. One of the best documentations of the bomb's effects on Hiroshima.

Hiroshima—Nagasaki! August 1945. B&W, 17 min., 1970, ($35). Museum of Modern Art, Circulating Film Program, 11 W. 53rd St., New York, NY 10019. Uses Japanese film, withheld from the public for 20 years, to show the results of the bombing.

The Hopeful Revolution: Nicaragua. Color, 16 min., 1979, ($35). Packard Manse Media Project, P.O. Box 450, Stoughton, MA 02072. Analyzes the principles, problems, and needs of the new Sandinista government.

Hostage at Hell's Bottom. Color, 19 min., 1982, ($85), Packard Manse Media Project, P.O. Box 450, Stoughton, MA 02072. Demonstrates connections between increased military spending and unemployment, inflation, social service cutbacks and national security.

How Much Is Enough? Color, 58 min., 1982, ($85). Documerica Films, P.O. Box 315, Franklin Lakes, NJ 07417. History of the U.S. nuclear arms buildup over the past two decades, with interviews of highly-placed policymakers from Kennedy to Reagan.

I Can Hear Zimbabwe Calling. Color, 50 min., 1981, ($80). Icarus Films, 200 Park Ave. So., Ste. 1319, New York, NY 10003. Focuses on the foundations laid during long years of struggle to reconstruct a new Zimbabwean society.

If You Love This Planet. Color, 26 min., 1982, ($26). Michigan Media, 416 Fourth St., Ann Arbor, MI 48109. Dr. Helen Caldicott lectures to students in Plattsburgh, NY about weapons used during the 1940's and those used today.

Imperialism. Color, 20 min., 1981, ($22.50). Social Studies School Service, 10,000 Culver Blvd., Dept. 13, P.O. Box 802, Culver City, CA 90230. Examines the inadequacy of existing theories in explaining superpower behavior and outlines efforts of contemporary writers to develop new concepts and explanations.

India Today. Color, 17 min., 1980, ($22.50). International Film Bureau, 332 S. Michigan Ave., Chicago, IL 60604. Presents many facets of life in India.

In Our Defense. Color, 25 min., 1983, ($65). Public Media Inc., 119 W. 57th St., New York, NY 10019. Examines the effects of the nuclear arms buildup on employment.

In Our Own Backyard. 3/4" video, color, 59 min., 1982, ($50). Bullfrog Films, Oley, PA 19547. Examines the ways Love Canal residents understood and responded to developments at Love Canal, combining footage of public events and interviews with the participants in those events.

In Our Water. Color, 58 min., 1982, ($100). Transit Media, P.O. Box 315, 779 Susquehanna, Franklin Lakes, NJ 07417. Examines chemical pollution in U.S. drinking water, and focuses on the problems wrought by one of an estimated 50,000 toxic waste dumps in the U.S.

In The Minds of Men. Color, 29 min., 1982, ($55). Public Media Inc., Sydney Levine, 119 W. 57th St., Ste. 1511, New York, NY 10019. A history of war, produced in response to a U.N. General Assembly resolution.

In the Nuclear Shadow: What Can the Children Tell Us? Color, 26 min., 1982, ($40). Educational Film and Video Project, 1725 B Seabright Ave., Santa Cruz, CA 95062. Features 25 children from around the world, expressing their thoughts and feelings on the nuclear issue.

Inter-Nation Simulation. Simulation game. Subject: International Relations. Age: Adult. Number of Players: 20-36 in 6 teams. Playtime: 6-10 hours. Science Research Assoc., 259 E. Erie St., Chicago, IL 60611. Creates real or fictional nations in past, present, and future times. Teams of 5 players interact in efforts to maintain and strengthen their country's economy and international prestige.

International Trade. Simulation game. Subject: International Relations, Economics. Age: Adult. Number of players: 6. Playtime: 2-4 hours. Science Research Assoc., 259 E. Erie St., Chicago, IL 60611. Through simulation, participants have a chance to observe, analyze, and solve problems in a critical part of the economy.

Into the Mouths of Babes. Color, 30 min., 1978, ($40). California Newsreel, 630 Natoma St., San Francisco, CA 94103. A CBS documentary narrated by Bill Moyers about the sale of infant formula to Third World countries.

Iran. Color, 22 min., 1979, ($50). Films, Inc., 733 Green Bay Rd., Wilmette, IL 60091. An overview of U.S. policy in Iran.

Israel. Color, 13 min., 1979, ($40). Films, Inc., 733 Green Bay Rd., Wilmette, IL 60091. Discusses the question of how the U.S. reconciles its historical and moral ties to Israel along with its need for Arab oil, and how the problem must be solved.

The Last Epidemic. Color, 36 min., 1981, ($21). Michigan Media, 416 Fourth St., Ann Arbor, MI 48109. Highlights the 1980 San Francisco symposium on the medical consequences of nuclear war.

Latin American Studies. Color, (6 filmstrips, 20 min. each), 1982, ($144). Social Studies School Service, 10,000 Culver Blvd., Dept. 13, P.O. Box 802, Culver City, CA 90230. This film helps students understand the upheavals taking place in this region.

La Operacion. Color, 40 min., 1982, ($100). Anna Maria Garcia, P.O. Box 735, Chelsea Station, New York, NY 10011. Over one-third of the women in Puerto Rico have been sterilized. This film is a moving and highly informative account of how this happened.

Linus Pauling: Crusading Scientist. Color, 60 min., 1977, ($150). Corinth Films, 410 E. 62nd St., New York, NY 10021. This film sketches Pauling's contribution to science and his work to stop nuclear weapons tests.

Louder Than Our Words: Women and Civil Disobedience. 3/4" video, color, 36 min., 1983, ($35). Lydia Dean Pilcher, 801 Union St., Brooklyn, NY 11215. An historical and current overview of women and civil disobedience, which also addresses the relationship between feminism, nonviolent resistance, and other critical political issues.

Lovins on the Soft Path. Color, 36 min., 1982, ($28.50). Michigan Media, 416 Fourth St., Ann Arbor, MI 48109. Amory and Hunter Lovins outline their analysis of the energy problem.

Maxwell International Development Simulation. Simulation game. Subject: International Relations, Business. Age: Adult. Playtime: 1 day. ERIC Document Reproduction Svce., P.O. Drawer P, Bethesda, MD 20014. Designed for seminars for mid-career officials from the Agency for International Development. Three areas of learning are addressed—policy and issues, inter- personal and intercultural relations, and managerial skills.

The Migrants. Color, 52 min., 1980, ($65). Films, Inc., 733 Green Bay Rd., Wilmette, IL 60091. Documents the fact that the plight of America's itinerant farm workers has improved very little in the last decade.

Missiles of October. Color, 155 min., 1974, ($75). Learning Corp. of America, 1350 Ave. of the Americas, New York, NY 10019. Dramatization of the cuban missile crisis and of Kennedy's and Khruschev's thoughts, tactics, and logic in dealing with the crisis.

Molly Rush: Turning Swords into Plowshares. 3/4" video, color, 28 min., 1982, ($40). Green Mountain Post Films, P.O. Box 229, Turner Falls, MA 01376. Examines the motives and convictions that led Molly Rush to enter a nuclear missile assembly plant and destroy unarmed nuclear warheads.

The Mondragon Experiment. Color, 55 min., 1981, ($75). California Newsreel, 630 Natoma St., San Francisco, CA 94103. A BBC documentary about the world's largest and most successful venture in worker-owned production located in Spain.

Mythia. Simulation game. Subject: Political Science, International Relations. Age: College. Number of players: 8 or more in 8 teams. Playtime: 1 hour-2 weeks. American Institute for Research. A world affairs simulation in which 8 countries strive to survive and prosper by resolving economic and political crises in a cooperative manner.

The Myth of Nationalism. Color, 30 min., 1976, ($30). International Film Bureau, 3325 Michigan Ave., Chicago, IL 60604. Clarifies the confusing period between the Franco-Prussian War and World War I.

Nepal Series. Color, 30 min., 1968, ($90). International Film Bureau Inc., 3325 S. Michigan Ave., Chicago, IL 60604. Provides an understanding of the Nepalese and their political and economic environment.

New Zimbabwe. Color, 28 min., 1982, ($25). Maryknoll World Films, Maryknoll, NY 10545. Documents the building of a fledgling nation based on reconciliation, equality, and cooperation.

Nicaragua Libre. B&W, 20 min., 1981, ($65). Packard Manse Media Project, P.O. Box 450, Stoughton, MA 02072. Depicts the struggle and dreams of the Nicaraguan people as they rebuild their society.

No Act of God. Color, 28 min., 1980, ($35). Bullfrog Films, Oley, PA 19547. Tackles the central issues of nuclear power.

No First Use: Preventing Nuclear War. Color, 30 min., 1982. ($30). Union of Concerned Scientists, Publications Dept., 1384 Massachusetts Ave., Cambridge, MA 02238. Examines how an attempt by NATO to stop a Russian tank assault could rapidly escalate into global nuclear war.

No Immediate Danger. 3/4" video, B&W, 30 min., 1982. ($50). Gerald Saldo and Joan Engel, 250 Mulberry St., New York, NY 10012. Documents the crisis and struggle that occurred in a small-town community when residents discover a 70-year-old radioactive waste dump in their midst.

...No Other Generation. Video, color, 30 min., 1983, ($35). Original Face Video, P.O. Box 447, Grass Valley, CA 95945. This film was largely recorded at the 1982 Meeting of Ways Conference.

The Nuclear Battlefield. 3/4" video, color, 50 min., 1981, ($22.50). Michigan Media, 416 Fourth St., Ann Arbor, MI 48109. Examines the efforts of the superpowers to develop tactics for fighting nuclear war and what would happen to Europe if it became a battlefield.

Nuclear Countdown. Color, 28 min., 1978, ($40). Journal Films Inc., 930 Pitner Ave., Evanston, IL 60202. Designed to raise public awareness about the disarmament imperative by sketching the dangers of the arms race and of nuclear proliferation.

Nuclear Nightmares. 3/4" video, color, 52 min., 1980, ($175). Corinth Films, 410 E. 62nd St., New York, NY 10021. Examines hypothetical scenarios that could lead to nuclear war.

Nuclear Power: War and Profit. Color, 22 min., 1982, ($70). Parallel Films, 314 W. 91st St., New York, NY 10024. Connects the hazards of nuclear power production to the international arms race.

Nuclear War: The Incurable Disease. 3/4" video, color, 60 min., 1982, ($90). Films, Inc., 733 Green Bay Rd., Wilmette, IL 60091. The hour-long discussion between the U.S. and Soviet physicians on the medical effects of nuclear war which was broadcast in both countries.

Oil and American Power Series: Saudi Arabia. Color, 18 min., 1979, ($45). Films, Inc., 733 Green Bay Rd., Wilmette, IL 60091. Saudi Arabia, having the largest known oil reserves, is a key factor in America's economic well-being and foreign policy.

On Our Land. Color, 55 min., 1983, ($100). Icarus Films, 200 Park Ave., So., Ste. 1319, New York, NY 10003. This film centers on Umm el-Fahm, the largest Arab village in Israel, and shows Palestinian men and women speaking freely about their lives under Israeli rule.

On the Edge of the Forest. Color, 32 min., 1979, ($38.50). Bullfrog Films, Oley, PA 19547. A message by E.F. Schumacher to get people to pay attention to the disastrous consequences of the doctrine of limitless growth.

The Palestinian People Do Have Rights. Color, 48 min., 1979, ($75). Icarus Films, 200 Park Ave. So., Ste. 1319, New York, NY 10003. Presents a comprehensive examination of the Palestinian/Israeli conflict.

Papua New Guinea—A Model. Color, 40 min., 1980, ($85). International Film Bureau Inc., 332 S. Michigan Ave., Chicago, IL 60604. Raises issues and concerns of the developing nations.

Passing The Message. Color, 47 min., 1983, ($85). Icarus Films, 200 Park Ave. So., Ste. 1319, New York, NY 10003. Traces the development of the trade union movement in South Africa and its confrontation with the apartheid regime.

Paul Jacobs and the Nuclear Gang. Color, 60 min., 1979, ($25). Riverside Church Disarmament Program, 490 Riverside Dr., New York, NY 10027. Focuses on the effects of radiation from the atom bomb tests of the 1950's.

Power and Corruption. Color, 34 min., 1973, ($40). Learning Corp. of America, 1350 Ave. of the Americas, New York, NY 10102. Concerned with why men are attached to power and what influence power has upon their natures.

Pressure Points: Oman, N. Yemen, S. Yemen. Color, 21 min., 1979, ($50). Films, Inc., 733 Green Bay Rd., Wilmette, IL 60091. Examines U.S. relationship with the nations of the Arabian peninsula.

The Price of Change. Color, 26 min., 1982, ($50). Icarus Films, 200 Park Ave. So., Ste. 1319, New York, NY 10003. Presents a picture of changing attitudes toward work, family, and sex in Egyptian society.

A Problem of Power. Color, 45 min., 1970, ($15). United Methodist Film Svce., 1525 McGavock, Nashville, TN 32703. Depicts the desperation of Columbian peasants and their problems with large landowners and the government.

Prophecy. Color, 41 min., 1983, ($60). Public Media Inc., Sydney Levine, 119 W. 57th St., Ste. 1511, New York, NY 10019. Made in Japan, with footage bought from the United States government in "$10 a foot" fundraising campaign.

The Race Nobody Wins. Slideshow, 15 min., 1981, ($20). American Friends Service Committee, 2161 Massachusetts Ave., Cambridge, MA 02140. A presentation on the dangers and costs of the international arms race.

Race To Oblivion. Color, 40 min., 1982, ($50). Physicians for Social Responsibility, Film Library, 5707 Douglas Fir Rd., Calabasas, CA 91302. Burt Lancaster interviews a Hiroshima survivor.

Resurgence. Color, 54 min., 1982, ($100). First Run Features, 144 Bleecker St., New York, NY 10012. Focusing on a strike at a chicken-processing plant, this film examines the efforts of union and civil rights activists to achieve social and economic justice.

The Rising Tide. Color, 44 min., 1977, ($80). Icarus Films, 200 Park Ave. Ste. 1319, New York, NY 10003. Uses historical footage to trace the source of today's crisis in South Africa to its colonial roots.

Roses in December: The Story of Jean Donovan. Color, 55 min., 1982, ($100). First Run Features, 144 Bleecker St., New York, NY 10012. Chronicles the brief life of Jean Donovan, a lay missionary killed in El Salvador along with three American nuns.

Sandino, Today and Forever. Color, 55 min., 1981, ($85). Icarus Films, 200 Park Ave. So., Ste. 1319, New York, NY 10003. Depicts the Sandinista movement through the eyes of a small farmer and member of an agricultural cooperative.

Sarvodaya Shramadana. Color, 40 min., 1978, ($25). Oxfam America, Resource Librarian, 115 Broadway, Boston, MA 02116. Story of the 24-year-old grassroots movement in Sri Lanka that combines economic, political, and spiritual development while seeking to build a self-reliant nation.

Seeds of Revolution. Color, 28 min., 1979, ($50). Icarus Films, 200 Park Ave. So., Ste. 1319, New York, NY 10003. Examines various sectors of Honduran society from corporate representatives to peasants and the conflicts simmering beneath the surface of Honduran life.

Sharing Global Resources: Toward a New Economic Order. Slideshow, 35 min., 1978, (FREE). Maryknoll Justice and Peace Office, Maryknoll, NY 10545. Asks some hard questions, particularly of North Americans, who consume nonrenewable global resources provided by transnational corporations from developing countries.

Simuland. Simulation game. Subject: Political Science. Andrew Scott, Univ. of N.C., Chapel Hill, NC 27514. Simulates the interplay of various political and economic factors.

Simulated Community Training Game. Simulation game. Subject: Natural Resources. Age: College. Number of players: 1-30 in 6 teams. Playtime: 1-3 hours, in 1-hour sessions. Ray F. Weston, Lewis Lane, Westchester, PA 19380. Players work to optimize air quality and minimize cost in making environmental policy decisions.

Simulation. The Decision Making Model. World Affairs Council of Philadelphia, 1300 Market, Philadelphia, PA 19107. Students play the role of decision-makers for 5 hypothetical countries seeking to improve their nation's domestic and international position by proper allocation of economic resources.

Simulex. Simulation game. Subject: International Relations. Age: College. Number of players: 20-30. Playtime: Optional. Dept. of Political Science, University of N.H., Durham, NH 03824. Participants formulate national policy in a simulated international situation.

So Far from India. Color, 60 min., 1982, ($75). Filmmaker's Library, 133 East 58th St., Room 7A, New York, NY 10022. A moving portrait of Ashor, a recent immigrant to America who struggles to maintain his identity.

Soldier Girls. Color, 90 min., 1982, ($150). A true story of women in boot camp and what they must go through.

South Africa Belongs to Us. Color, 57 min., 1980, ($65). Icarus Films, 200 Park Ave. So., Ste. 1319, New York, NY 10003. Depicts the struggle of Black women for human dignity in the face of apartheid.

South Africa: The Nuclear File. Color, 54 min., 1979, ($39). Michigan Media, 416 Fourth St., Ann Arbor, MI 48109. Shows how, with the help of business and military interests in the U.S., South Africa obtained the material and technology to build an atomic device.

South East Asian Studies. Color, 80 min., 1980. ($104). Social Studies School Service, 10,000 Culver Blvd., Dept. 13, P.O. Box 802, Culver City, CA 90230. A wide-ranging profile of the land and peoples of Laos, Kampuchea, Thailand, and Vietnam.

Survival or Suicide. Color, 27 min., 1979, ($10). AFSC Rocky Flats Project, 1660 Lafayette, Denver, CO 80218. About the strategic military forces of the U.S. and the USSR.

Survivors. Color, 58 min., 1965, ($200). First Run Features, 144 Bleecker St., New York, NY 10012. Hiroshima and Nagasaki victims speak about what they saw and felt on the day of the Bomb, and how their lives were affected.

Tanzania: Education for Self-Reliance. Color, 30 min., 1978, ($50). Icarus Films, 200 Park Ave. Ste. 1319, New York, NY 10003. Demonstrates how educators from outside can help create a self-sufficient community, in this case in housing needs.

Target Nicaragua: Inside a Covert War. Color, 40 min., 1982, ($60). New Time Films Library, P.O. Box 315, Franklin Lakes, NJ 07417. Documents the new developments of the Nicaraguan civil war, and CIA involvement with former Somoza guardsmen.

The Temptation of Power. Color, 43 min., 1977, ($75). Icarus Films, 200 Park Ave. So., Ste. 1319, New York, NY 10003. Examines the social and economic development policies of the Iranian government during the period of the White Revolution, 1962 to 1978.

Thank God and the Revolution. Color, 50 min., 1981, ($75). Icarus Films, 200 Park Ave. So., Ste. 1319, New York, NY 10003. Looks at the role of the church in rebuilding Nicaragua.

There But For Fortune. Color, 60 min., 1982, ($100). First Run Features, 144 Bleecker St., New York, NY 10012. Combines footage of Joan Baez in impromptu concerts on her Latin American tour, and her subsequent efforts in the U.S. to find answers to the injustices she witnessed.

Thinking Twice: Living in The Nuclear Age. Color, 60 min., 1982, ($40). Skye Pictures, Inc., 1460 Church St. NW, Washington, DC 20005. Looks at how American families have adjusted to the realities of living in a world with nuclear weapons.

The Third World: In Search of U.S. Policy. Color, 20 min., 1983, ($32). Social Studies School Service, 10,000 Culver Blvd., Dept. 13, P.O. Box 802, Culver City, CA 90230. Examines U.S. foreign policy toward Third World countries from World War II up to the Reagan administration.

To Die, To Live: The Survivors of Hiroshima. Color, 65 min., 1975, ($90). Films, Inc. 733 Green Bay Rd., Wilmette, IL 60091. Documents survivors' reactions to the A-Bomb.

Todos Santos Cuchumatan: A Report from a Guatemalan Village. Color, 41 min., 1982, ($75). Icarus Films, 200 Park Ave. So., Ste. 1319, New York, NY 10003. Illustrates changes underway in Guatemala and responses of the Indian people to governmental policies.

Together We Can Stop the Bomb. Color, 25 min., 1981, ($25). American Friends Service Committee, 2161 Massachusetts Ave., Cambridge, MA 02140. Very upbeat portrayal of the speeches, music, march, and rally in London on October 24, 1981 in Hyde Park in which 250,000 people participated.

To Live in Freedom. Color, 54 min., 1975, ($80). Icarus Films, 200 Park Ave. So., Ste. 1319, New York, NY 10003. Produced by a Palestinian and Israeli collective, the film presents a comprehensive critique of the Israeli reality.

To Love, Honor, and Obey. Color, 55 min., 1980, ($85). Third World Newsreel, 160 5th Ave., Ste. 911, New York, NY 10010. Explores the social, psychological, and cultural factors that contribute to violence against women in the home and in society.

Training for Non-Violence. B&W, 20 min., 1978, ($45). Green Mountain Post Films, P.O. Box 229, Turner Falls, MA 01376. A documentary about the theories and preparation for peaceful direct action.

The Tuaregs. Color, 46 min., 1974, ($75). Icarus Films, 200 Park Ave. So., Ste. 1319, New York, NY 10003. Examines the struggles of a proud, warrior tribe in Niger to adapt to the twentieth century.

Vietnam Requiem. Color, 90 min., 1982, ($150). Direct Cinema, P.O. Box 315, Franklin Lakes, NJ 07417. This film is the sad story of five men who were given medals in Vietnam and are now in prison for violent crimes.

The War Game. Color, 49 min., 1968, ($150). Films, Inc., 733 Green Bay Rd., Wilmette, IL 60091. A classic portrayal of the medical and social catastrophe resulting from a nuclear war.

The War Machine. 3/4" video, color, 50 min., 1981, ($22.50). Michigan Media, 416 Fourth St., Ann Arbor, MI 48109. Investigates whether sophisticated American weapons will function in a military conflict and looks at the military-industrial complex, including Pentagon and Congress.

War Without Winners II. Color, 28 min., 1982, ($50). Films, Inc., 1144 Wilmette Ave., Wilmette, IL 60091. American and Russian people express their fears, thoughts, and hopes about the future in the nuclear age.

Water Crisis. Color, 57 min., 1981, ($36). Michigan Media, 416 Fourth St., Ann Arbor, MI 48109. Amory and Hunter Lovins outline their analysis of the water problem.

We've Always Done It This Way. Color, 52 min., 1978, ($70). California Newsreel, 630 Natoma St., San Francisco, CA 94103. Documents innovative efforts of union stewards at a British multinational defense contractor to promote socially useful employment by linking workers' skills to production for social instead of military needs.

We've Got the Power. Slideshow, 26 min., 1980, ($20). American Friends Service Committee, 2161 Massachusetts Ave., Cambridge, MA 02140. A lively and informed look at the urgent energy choice this country faces.

What About the Russians?. Color, 26 min., 1983, ($50). Educational Film and Video Project, 1725 B Seabright Ave., Santa Cruz, CA 95062. This film examines the Soviet position in the arms race.

What Could You Do With A Nickel?. Color, 26 min., 1982, ($55). First Run Features, 144 Bleecker St., New York, NY 10012. Tells the story of two hundred Black and Hispanic women in the South Bronx who formed the first U.S. domestic workers' union.

When The Almsgiving Stops. Slideshow, 22 min., 1980, ($20). American Friends Service Committee, 2161 Massachusetts Ave., Cambridge, MA 02140. An introduction to the issues of world hunger and overpopulation.

Who Owns the Sky?. Slideshow, 25 min., 1978, ($20). American Friends Service Committee, 2161 Massachusetts Ave., Cambridge, MA 02140. A presentation of how large companies from developed countries take advantage of the politically weaker Third World in order to expand their power.

Whose Budget Is It Anyway?. Color, 20 min., 1982, ($15). NARMIC/AFSC, 1501 Cherry St., Philadelphia, PA 19102. Focuses on the loss of jobs, educational programs, and other human services due to the Reagan budget's enormous increases in military spending.

Who Will Feed the World?. B&W, 30 min., 1975, ($20). Ecufilms, 810 12th Ave. South, Nashville, TN 37203. An ABC documentary about concrete steps that can be taken towards feeding the world's hungry.

Women in Vietnam. Slideshow, 45 min., 1973, ($20). American Friends Service Committee, 2161 Massachusetts Ave., Cambridge, MA 02140. Historical portrayal of the development of the Vietnamese resistance movement and the critical role played by women in that movement.

Women of Nicaragua. Color, 59 min., 1980, ($25). American Friends Service Committee, 2161 Massachusetts Ave., Cambridge, MA 02140. A down-to-earth film on the Nicaraguan revolution and women's role in it.

Women of the World. Color, 96 min., 1975, ($100). ROA Films, 1696 N. Astor St., Milwaukee, WI 53202. Designed to bring recognition to the contributions of women to societies around the world.

Women Under Siege. Color, 26 min., 1982, ($50). Icarus Films, 200 Park Ave. So., Ste. 1319, New York, NY 10003. Explores the lives of six Palestinian women and the role they play in their beseiged community on the Israeli border in Southern Lebanon.

The World Game. Simulation game. Subject: Natural Resources, Economics. Age: Adult. Spaceship Earth Exploration by Design Science, P.O. Box 909, Carbondale, IL 62901. Object is to work out ways to "make the world work" while simultaneously promoting human values.

You Have Struck a Rock. Color, 28 min., 1981, ($50). Southern Africa Media Center, California Newsreel, 630 Natoma St., San Francisco, CA 94103. About the spirit and perseverance of black South African women in their struggle for freedom.

Periodicals

Africa Today. Quarterly. Africa Today Associates, c/o Graduate School of International Studies, University of Denver, Denver, CO 80208. U.S., Canada, Pan Am., Institution: $15; Individual: $10; Single copies:$3. Elsewhere, Institution: $17; Individual: $12; Single copies: $3.25.

African Affairs. Quarterly. Oxford University Press, Walton Street, Oxford OX2 6DP, UK. $42/yr. Single copy: $12.

Agenda. Monthly. Agency for International Development, Office of Public Affairs, Washington, DC 20523. Free upon request.

Alternatives. Quarterly. World Policy Institute, 777 UN Plaza, New York, NY 10017.
   Area 1: North America, Europe, Japan, Australia, New Zealand, South Africa, Israel. Individual: $16/yr; $28/2 yrs. Institution: $30/yr.
   Area 2: The Caribbean, Central America, South America. Individual: $9/yr. Institution: $15/yr.
   Area 3: Africa, West Asia, South Asia, Southeast Asia. Individual: $6/yr. Institution: $9/yr. Order from: Centre for Developing Societies, 29 Rajpur Road, Delhi 110054, India.

Alternatives. Quarterly. c/o Trent University, Peterborough, Ontario, K9J 7B8. Individual: $10/yr. Institution: $15/yr.

American Journal of Sociology. Bi-monthly. The University of Chicago Press, P.O. Box 37005, Chicago, IL 60637. Institution: $55/yr. Individual: $30/yr.

Anthropology and Humanism Quarterly. American Anthropological Association, 1703 New Hampshire Ave., NW, Washington, DC 20402. $30.50/yr.

Arab Studies Quarterly. Association of Arab-American University Graduates, 556 Trapelo Road, Belmont, MA 02178. Individual: $16/yr. Institution: $35/yr.

Arms Control Reporter. Monthly Supplements. Institute for Defense and Disarmament Studies, 2001 Beacon St., Brookline, MA 02146. $120/yr.

Arms Control Today. Monthly. Arms Control Association, 11 Dupont Circle, NW, Washington, DC 20036. Individual: $20/yr. Institution: $25/yr.

Asian Survey. Monthly. University of California Press, Berkeley, CA 94720. Individual: $30/yr. Institution: $55/yr.

Buddhists for Peace. Quarterly. ABCP Headquarters, Gangdanthekchenling Monastery, Ulan Bator, Mongolian People's Republic. Available on request.

Bulletin of the Atomic Scientists. 10 issues/yr. 5801 S. Kenwood, Chicago, IL 60637. Individual: $19.50/yr. Institution: $25/yr.

Bulletin of Concerned Asian Scholars. Quarterly. Post Office Box W, Charlemont, MA 01339. Individual: $9/yr. Institution: $14/yr.

Bulletin of Peace Proposals. Quarterly. Universitarsforlager, Journals Dept., P.O. Box 2959, Tøyen, Oslo 6, Norway. $22/yr.

Bulletin of the Peace Studies Institute. 2 issues/yr. The Manchester College Bulletin of the Peace Studies Institute, North Manchester, IN 46962. Individual: $3/yr.

Caribbean Quarterly. Department of Extra-Mural Studies, University of the West Indies, Mona, Kingston 7, Jamaica. Jamaica: J$ 24/yr. Eastern Caribbean: J$ 28/yr. U.S.A.: $22/yr.

The China Quarterly. Contemporary China Institute, School of Oriental and African Studies, Malet Street, London WC1E 7HP, England. $30/yr; $15/yr for students.

Christianity and Crisis: A Christian Journal of Opinion. Monthly. Bi-weekly during July, August, January. P.O. Box 1163, Fort Lee, NJ 07024. $21/yr.

Christianity Today. Monthly. 465 Gunderson Drive, Carol Stream, IL 60187. $21/yr.

Coevolution Quarterly. Point Foundation, Box 428, Sausalito, CA 94965. $12/yr.

Co-existence. Quarterly. 9/11 South Park Terrace, Glasgow G12 8 LO, Scotland. Individual: £15/yr. Institution: £20/yr.

Commonsense. Quarterly. Republican National Committee, 310 First St., SE, Washington, DC 20003. $12/yr.

Connexion: An International Women's Quarterly. Peoples Translation Service, 4228 Telegraph Ave., Oakland, CA 94609. Individual: $10/yr. Institution: $20/yr.

Cooperation and Conflict: A Nordic Journal of International Politics. Quarterly. Universitetsforlager, P.O. Box 2959 Tøyen, Oslo 6, Norway. Individual: $17/yr. Institution: $22/yr. Students: $10/yr.

Cultural Survival Quarterly. Cultural Survival Inc., 11 Divinity Ave., Cambridge, MA 02138. $15/yr.

Current Research on Peace and Violence. Quarterly. Tampere Peace Research Institute, P.O. Box 447, 33101 Tampere 10, Finland. Individual: $12.50/yr. Institution: $13/yr.

Current Thought on Peace and War. Quarterly. Dept. of Political Science, Wisconsin State University, Oshkosh, WI 54901. Individual: $15/yr. Institution: $20/yr.

Daedalus: A Journal of the American Academy of Arts and Sciences. Quarterly. 1440 Main Street, Waltham, MA 02254. $16/yr.

The Defense Monitor. 10 issues annually. Center for Defense Information, 122 Maryland Ave., NE, Washington, DC 20002. $15/yr.

Department of State Bulletin. Monthly. The Office of Public Communication. U.S. Govt. Printing Office, Washington, DC 20402. $19/yr. Single copies: $3.25.

The Developing Economies. Quarterly. Maruzen Co., P.O. Box 5050, Tokyo International 100-31, Japan. $50/year, with postage.

Development and Change. Quarterly. SAGE Publications Ltd., 28 Banner Street, London EC 14 8QE, England. Individual: £12.50/yr. Institution: £28/yr.

Development and Peace. Hungarian Peace Council, H-1360 Budapest, P.O. Box 6, Hungary. Available on request.

Development and Socio-Economic Progress. Quarterly. Afro-Asian People's Solidarity Organization, 89, Abdel Aziz Al-Saoud Street, Manial El-Roda, Cairo, A.R.E.

Development Dialogue. 2 issues/yr. The Dag Hammarskjold Foundation, Ovreslottsgatan 2, S-752 20 Uppsala, Sweden.

Development Forum. Monthly. U.N. Division for Economic and Social Information, Palais des Nations, Geneva CH 1211, Switzerland. 15Fr/mth.

Development Quarterly. Society for International Development, Palazzo Civilta del Lavaro, 00144 Rome, Italy. Individual: $25/yr. (High-Income Countries), $6/yr. (Low-Income Countries). Institutions can become members by paying annual dues of $200.

Disarmament Times. 8 issues/yr. World Conference on Religion and Peace, Room 7B, 777 UN Plaza, New York, NY 10017. USA and Canada: $4/yr. Overseas: $8/yr.

Dissent. Quarterly. Foundation for the Study of Independent Social Ideas Inc., 521 5th Ave., New York, NY 10017. Individual: $14/yr. Institution: $19/yr. Students: $9/yr.

East-West Outlook. Bi-monthly. American Committee on East-West Accord, 109 Eleventh Street SE, Washington, DC 20003. $12/yr.

The Ecologist: Journal of the Post-Industrial Age. Subscription Dept., Worthyvale Manor Farm, Camelford, Cornwall PL32 9TT, England. Individual: $28. Institution: $36. $12 extra for foreign airmail.

Economist. Weekly, P.O. Box 2700, Woburn, MA 01888. $55/yr. $150/2 yrs. Student: $51/yr.

Education Research Quarterly. University of Southern California, School of Education WPH 703, Los Angeles, CA 90089. $36/yr; $7.25 single issue.

Ekistics: The Problems and Science of Human Settlements. Monthly. Athens Center of Ekistics of The Athens Technological Organization, P.O. Box 471, Athens, Greece, U.S.: $48/yr. Student: $36/yr.

Environmental Ethics. Quarterly. Dept. of Philosophy and Religion, University of Georgia, Athens, GA 30602. Individual: $18/yr. Institution: $24/yr.

Feminist Studies. 3 issues/yr. Womens's Studies Program, University of Maryland, College Park, MD 20742. Individual: $15/yr. Institution: $30/yr.

Food Monitor. Bi-monthly. World Hunger Year Inc., 350 Broadway, Suite 209, New York, NY 10013. Individual: $12.95/yr. Institution: $18/yr.

Food Policy. Quarterly. MAGSUB Lt., Oakfield House, Perrymount Road, Haywords Heath RH 16 3DH, Sussex, UK. $116.60/yr. Single copies: $34.90.

Foreign Affairs. 5 issues/yr. Foreign Affairs Reader Services, 58 East 68th St., New York, NY 10021. $22/yr.

Foreign Policy. Quarterly. P.O. Box 984, Farmingdale, NY 11737. Individual: $17/yr. Institution: $25/yr.

Future: Development Perspectives on Children. Quarterly. Unicef House, 73 Lodi State, New Delhi 110003, India. India: Rs. 30/yr. Asia and Africa: $9/yr. Europe: $11/yr. US: $13/yr.

Futures: The Journal of Forecasting and Planning. 6 issues/yr. IPC Science and Technology Press Ltd., Box 63, Westbury House, Bury Street, Guildford, Surrey GU2 5BH, England. $104/yr.

Gandhi Marg. Monthly. N. Vasudevan for The Gandhi Peace Foundation, 221-223 Deen Dayal Upadhyaya Marg, New Delhi, 110002. India or South Asia: Rs 30/yr. Elsewhere: $12/yr.

Human Rights Internet Reporter. Bi-monthly. 1338 G St., SE, Washington, DC 20003. Individual: $35/yr. Institution: $50/yr.

Human Rights Quarterly. The Johns Hopkins University Press, Journals Division, Baltimore, MD 21218. Individual: $18/yr. Institution: $36.50/yr.

The Humanist. 6 issues annually. 7 Harwood Drive, Amherst, NY 14226. US: $15/yr; $25/2 yrs; $35/3 yrs. $3 extra for foreign postage and handling.

IDOC Bulletin. International Documentation and Communication Center, Via S. Maria dell'Anima, 30-00186 Rome, Italy. $15/yr.

IFOR Report. The International Fellowship of Reconciliation, Hof Van Sonoy 15-17, 1811 LD Alkmaar, The Netherlands. $15/yr.

In These Times. Weekly. Institute for Policy Studies, 1300 W. Belmont Ave., Chicago, IL 60657. $17.50/yr.

Indian Journal of International Law. Quarterly. The Indian Society of International Law, 7-8, Scindia House, Kasturba Gandhi, New Delhi 110001. India: Rs. 100/yr. Abroad: $35/yr.

Instant Research on Peace and Violence. Quarterly. Tampere Peace Research Institute, Tammelanpuistokatu 58 B, 33100 Tampere 10, Finland. Individual: $5/yr. Institution: $7/yr.

Intercom. 3 issues/yr. Global Perspectives in Education, 218 East 18 St., New York, NY 10003. $18/yr. $7/single issue.

Interdependent. 8 issues/yr. United Nations Association, 300 East 42 St., New York, NY 10017. $10/yr.

International and Comparative Public Policy. 1 issue/yr. International Public Policy Institute, Graybar Building, Suite 354, 420 Lexington Ave., New York, NY 10017. Individual: $12/yr. Institution: $18/yr.

International Interactions. Quarterly. Gordan and Breach Science Publishers Ltd., 42 William IV Street, London WC 2N 4DE, England. Individual: $46/yr. Institution: $85/yr.

International Labor Review. Quarterly. ILO Publications, International Labor Office, CH 1211 Geneva 22, Switzerland. $25.50/yr.

International Organization. Quarterly. M.I.T. Press Journals, 28 Carleton Street, Cambridge, MA 02142. Individual: $18/yr. Institution: $36/yr.

International Peace Research Newsletter. Quarterly. International Peace Research Foundation, Faculty of Law, Univ. of Tokyo, Bunkyoku Tokyo 113, Japan. Individual: Swiss Fr 30/yr. Low-income: Swiss Fr 10/yr. Institution: Swiss Fr 90/yr.

International Social Science Journal. Quarterly. 7-9 Place de Fontenoy, 75700 Paris, France. $23/yr.

International Studies Quarterly. Butterworth and Co., Ltd., Borogh Green, Seven Oaks, Kent, England TN 15 8 PH. $50/yr.

Journal of Asian-Pacific and World Perspectives. Semi- annually. Asian-Pacific Services Institute, 2115 Oahu Avenue, Honolulu, HI 96822. $7/yr.

The Journal of Conflict Resolution: Research on War and Peace Between and Within Nations. Quarterly. Sage Publications, 275 South Beverly Drive, Beverly Hills, CA 90212. Individual: $28/yr. Institution: $60/yr. Add $4 for foreign airmail.

Journal of Contemporary Asia. Quarterly. P.O. Box 49010, Stockholm 49, Sweden. Institution or Library: $30/yr. Individual: $18/yr. Govt. Agency or Business Firm: $40/yr. Third World citizen: $15/yr.

Journal of Defense and Diplomacy. Monthly. The Journal Building, 6819 Elm St., McLean, VA 22101. $24/yr.

The Journal of Environmental Education. Quarterly. Helen Dwight Reid Educational Foundation, 4000 Albemarle St. NW, Washington, DC 20016. $25/yr; outside US add $5 postage.

Journal of Environmental Systems. Quarterly. Baywood Publishing Company Inc., 120 Marine Street, P.O. Box D, Farmingdale, NY 11735. Individual: $21/yr. Institution: $51/yr.

Journal of Gandhian Studies. Quarterly. Indian Society of Gandhian Studies, University of Allahabad, Gandhi Bhawan, Allahabad, India.

The Journal of Modern African Studies. Quarterly. Cambridge University Press, 32 East 57th St., New York, NY 10022. Individual: $39.50/yr. Institution: $82.50/yr.

Journal of Palestine Studies: A Quarterly on Palestinian Affairs and the Arab-Israeli Conflict. P.O. Box 19449, Washington, DC 20036. Individual: $24/yr; $46/2 yrs; $67/3 yrs. Student: $17/yr. Additional airmail postage: $12/yr. for Mexico, Canada & Central America; $18/yr. for Europe, North Africa & South America; $24/yr. for Middle East, Africa & Asia.

Journal of Peace Research. Quarterly. Universitetsforlaget, Journals Dept., P.O. Box 2959 Tøyen, Oslo 6, Norway. $28/yr.

Journal of Political & Military Sociology. Semi-annually. c/o Sociology Department, Northern Illinois University, Dekalb, IL 60115. Individual: $14/yr. Institution: $18.50/yr. Student: $9/yr. Add $2 for foreign postage. Airmail delivery: $8 extra for Europe, Mexico, Canada and South America; $11 for all other countries.

Latin American Perspectives. Quarterly. Box 792, Riverside, CA 92502. Individual: $16. Student & Low-income: $13. Educational Institution: $24. Corporation & Government Agency: $46/yr.

Middle East Research & Information Project (MERIP) Reports. 9 issues annually. P.O. Box 1247, New York, NY 10025. Individual: $17/yr. Institution: $28/yr.

Middle East Review. Quarterly. Transaction Periodicals Consortium, Rutgers University, New Brunswick, NJ 08903. US and Canada: $12/yr.; $22/2 yrs; $30/3 yrs. Other countries: $15/yr.; $27/2 yrs.; $37/3 yrs. Student: $10/yr.

Millenium: Journal of International Studies. 3 issues annually. The Millenium Publishing Group, The London School of Economics, Houghton Street, London WC2A 2AE, England. Student: $10.50/yr. in US; $13/yr. in Canada. Individual: $20/yr. in US; $25/yr. in Canada. Institution: $40/yr. in US; $50/yr. in Canada.

Minerva: Quarterly Report on Women and the Military. Linda Grant De Pauw, 1101 Arlington Ridge Road, Arlington, VA 22202. $30/yr.

Modern Times. Monthly. 186 Hampshire Street, Cambridge, MA 02139. Individual: $18/yr., $33/2 yrs., $45/3 yrs. Institution: $24/yr. Add $3 for Canadian subscription, and $6 for all other countries.

Monthly Review: An Independent Socialist Magazine. Monthly (bimonthly in July and August). 155 West 23rd St., New York, NY 10011. US: $18/yr.; $13/yr. for students and senior citizens. Foreign: $22/yr.; $15/yr. for students and senior citizens. Libraries and Institutions: $30/yr. in US; $33/yr. overseas.

Multinational Monitor. Monthly. Ralph Nader's Corporate Accountability Group, 1346 Connecticut Ave., Washington, DC 20036. US: Individual $15/yr.; Non-profit Organization $20/yr.; Business $30/yr. Add $5/yr. postage for Canada and Mexico; $8/yr. for all other countries.

NACLA: Report on the Americas. Bi-monthly. North American Congress on Latin America, 151 West 19th St., 9th Floor, New York, NY 10011. Individual: $15/yr.; $28/2 yrs.; $39/3 yrs. Institution: $29/yr.; $54/2 yrs., $75/3 yrs. For airmail subscription add: $6/yr. in US and Canada; $9 in Central America and Caribbean; $12 in Europe and South America; $14 in all other countries.

The Nation. Weekly (except for first week in January, and bi-weekly in July and August). 72 Fifth Ave., New York, NY 10010 Individual: $35/yr.; $65/2 yrs.; $17.50/6 months. Add $7/yr. postage in Canada and Mexico; $13/yr. postage all other foreign.

New African. Monthly. IC Magazines Ltd., P.O. Box 261, Carlton House, 69 Great Queen St., London WC2B 5B2, England. $2.50 per issue.

New Left Review. Quarterly. 7 Carlisle St., London W1V 6NL, England. Individual: $22/yr. Institution: $40/yr.

New Outlook: Middle East Monthly. 10 issues annually. 107 Hahashomonaium St., Tel Aviv 67011, Israel. Individual: $33/yr. Student: $26/yr. Institution: $42/yr.

New Political Science: Quarterly Journal of the Caucus for a New Political Science. NPS Editorial Collective, Caucus for a New Political Science, Columbia Univ., 420 West 118th St., Room 733, New York, NY 10027. Individual: $15/yr. Low-Income: $10/yr. Institution: $25/yr.

Nuclear Times. 10 issues annually. 298 5th Avenue, Room 512, New York, NY 10001. $15/yr.; $2 single copy. Add $7/yr. postage for Mexico and Canada; $7/yr. surface and $17/yr. airmail for all other foreign countries.

Pacific Issues. 6 issues annually. Justice, Human Development and Peace, Commission for World Mission, Uniting Church in Australia Center, 130 Lt. Collins St., Melbourne 3000, Australia. $1/issue.

Peace and Change: A Journal of Peace Research. Quarterly. Center for Peaceful Change, Kent State University, Kent, OH 44242. Individual: $15/yr. Institution: $21/yr.

Peace and the Sciences. Irregular. Gazzetta, Ges.m.b.H., fur den Inhalt verantwor-lich, DDr.Dr.h.c. Geog Fuchs, samtliche, Mollwaldplatz 5, A-1040 Wien, Austria. AS 80 per issue; AS 240/yr plus postage.

Peace Education: An International Journal. Irregular. D. 61/23 Rajvila, Siddhgiribag, Varanasi-221001, India. Rs 10 per single copy, or $3.

Peace News: For Nonviolent Revolution. Fortnightly. 5 Caledonian Road, London N1, England. Britian: £12/yr., £6.50/6 months, £2 for 5-issue trial. Foreign: £13/yr., £7/6 months, £2.50 for 5-issue trial.

Peace Research: The Canadian Journal of Peace Studies. Quarterly. M.V. Naidu, Brandon University, Brandon, Manitoba, Canada R7A 6A9. Individual: $9/yr. Institution: $18/yr.

Peace Research Reviews. 6 issues per volume. Peace Research Institute, 25 Dundana Ave., Dundas, Ontario, Canada. $20 per volume; $14 per volume with paid order.

Philosophy and Public Affairs. Quarterly. Princeton Univ. Press, Box PPA, 3175 Princeton Pike, Lawrenceville, NJ 08648. US and Canada: Individual $14.50/yr.; Institution $22.50/yr.; Student $9/yr. All other countries: Individual $18.25/yr.; Institution $28/yr.; Student $11/yr. Add $3.50 foreign postage.

Population and Development Review. Quarterly. The Population Council, One Dag Hammarskjold Plaza, New York, NY 10017. $14/yr. or $24/2 yrs.

Population Bulletin. Quarterly. Circulation Dept., Population Reference Bureau, 1337 Connecticut Ave. NW, Washington, DC 20036. Individual: $25/yr. in US; $32.50 for overseas. College teachers: $15/yr. in US; $19.50 overseas. School teachers: $10/yr. in US; $13 overseas. Students: $5/yr. in US; $6.50 overseas. Libraries: $30/yr. in US; $39 overseas. Institutions: $100/yr. in US; $130 overseas.

The Progressive. Monthly. 409 East Main Street, Madison, WI 53703. US, Canada and Mexico: $20/yr.; $35/2 yrs. Foreign: $25/yr.; $45/2 yrs. Students: $12/yr. Libraries and Institutions: $20/yr. for domestic, $29 if foreign.

Race & Class: A Journal for Black and Third World Liberation. Quarterly. Institute of Race Relations, 247-9 Pentonville Road, London N1, England. Institutions: $30/yr. Individuals: $16/yr.

Radical Teacher. Quarterly. Kendall P.O. Box 102, Cambridge, MA 02142. Institution: $11/yr. Regular: $8/yr employed; $4/yr. part-time, unemployed and retired.

Review: A Journal of the Fernand Braudel Center for the Study of Economies, Historical Systems, and Civilizations. Quarterly. Fernand Braudel Center, SUNY, Binghamton, NY 13901. Institution: $52/yr. Individual: $22/yr. Add $4/yr. for foreign postage. Third World citizens: $10/yr.

Review of African Political Economy. 3 issues annually. 341 Glossop Road, Sheffield S10 2HP, England. UK and Africa: £6/yr. or £11/2 yrs. for individuals; £14/yr. or £25/2 yrs. for institutions. Other countries: $15/yr. or $24/2 yrs. for individuals; $35/yr. or $60/2 yrs. for institutions. Students £4.50/yr. Airmail postage: add £3/yr. in Europe, £5/yr. for other countries.

Review of Radical Political Economics. Quarterly. Union for Radical Political Economics, 41 Union Square West, Room 901, New York, NY 10003. URPE members: $50/yr. contributing; $35/yr. regular; $20/yr. low-income; $10/yr. for URPE newsletter only. Non-members: $25/yr. Libraries and Institutions: $45/yr.

Signs: Journal of Women in Culture and Society. Quarterly. The University of Chicago Press, Journals Division, P.O. Box 37005, Chicago, IL 60637. Institution: $45/yr. Individual: $25/yr. Student: $18/yr. Add $3/yr. for overseas postage.

Social Alternatives. Quarterly. c/o Division of External Studies, University of Queensland, St. Lucia, Qld. 4067, Australia. Individual: $14/yr. or $25/2 yrs. Institution: $20/yr. or $36/2 yrs.

Social Development Issues. 3 issues annually. Managing Editor, Social Development Issues, School of Social Work, The University of Iowa, Iowa City, IA 52242. Individual: $12/yr. Institution: $18/yr. Overseas: Individual $19/yr.; Institution $27/yr.

Social Education: Official Journal of the National Council for the Social Studies. 7 issues annually. 3501 Newark St. NW, Washington, DC 20016. $35/yr.

Social Policy. Quarterly. 33 West 42nd St., New York, NY 10036. Student: $8/yr. Individual: $15/yr. or $27/2 yrs. Institution: $20/yr.

Socialist International Women Bulletin. Bi-monthly. 85a St. Johns Wood High St., London NW8 7SJ, England. $12/yr.

Socialist Review. Bi-monthly. Center for Social Research and Education, 3202 Adeline Street, Berkeley, CA 94703. Individual: $19.50/yr.; $22 overseas. Institution: $39/yr.; $41.50 foreign.

Sojourners. Monthly (except in June/July). P.O. Box 29272, Washington, DC 20017. Domestic: $12/yr., $22/2 yrs., $32/3 yrs. Canada, Mexico and all other foreign countries: $15/yr., $28/2 yrs., $39/3 yrs.

Solidarity: Magazine of the Czechoslovak Committee for Solidarity with the Nations of Africa and Asia. 6 issues annually. Slavickova 5, Prague 6, 160 00, Czechoslovakia. $0.90 an issue, or equivalent.

South: The Third World Magazine. Monthly. South Publications Ltd., Suite 319, 230 Park Ave., New York, NY 10169. $28/yr.

Southeast Asia Chronicle. 6 issues annually. Southeast Asia Resource Center, P.O. Box 4000D, Berkeley, CA 94704. Regular: $12/yr. Low-income: $9/yr. Institution: $25/yr. Foreign surface mail: $15/yr. Foreign airmail or domestic first class: $25/yr. Sustaining: $30/yr.

Southern Africa. Monthly (except when bi-monthly in Jan/Feb and Aug/Sept). The Southern Africa Committee, 198 Broadway, New York, NY 10038. Individual: $10/yr. Institution: $18/yr. Add $3 for foreign subscriptions.

Southern Exposure. Bi-monthly. P.O. Box 531, Durham, NC 27702. Individual: $16/yr. Institution: $20/yr.

Studies in Comparative International Development. Quarterly. Transaction Periodicals Consortium, Rutgers University, New Brunswick, NJ 08903. Individual: $18/yr. Institution: $24/yr. Student: $12/yr.

Studies in Political Economy: A Socialist Review. 3 issues annually. Box 4729, Station E, Ottawa, Ontario K1S 5H9, Canada. Individual: $13/yr. Institution: $23/yr.

Teachers College Record. Quarterly. Teachers College, Columbia University, 525 West 120 Street, New York, NY 10027. Institution: $30/yr., $45/2 yrs. Individual: $20/yr., $32/2 yrs. Add $2/yr. for foreign postage.

Third World Quarterly. Third World Foundation for Social and Economic Studies, New Zealand House, 13th Floor, 80 The Haymarket, London SW1Y 4TS, England. Institution: $30/yr. Individual: $20/yr. Student: $16/yr.

Ufahamu. 3 issues annually. African Activist Association, African Studies Center, University of California, Los Angeles, CA 90024. Individual: $8/yr.; $10/yr. foreign. Institution: $12/yr. Add $7.50 for overseas airmail.

Women's International Network (WIN) News. Quarterly. Fran Hosken, 187 Grant Street, Lexington, MA 02173. Individual: $20/yr. Institution: $30/yr. Add $3 surface or $9 airmail overseas postage.

Women's Studies International Forum. Bi-monthly. Pergamon Press, Journals Division, Maxwell House, Fairview Park, Elmsford, NY 10523. Individual: $30/yr. Student: $18.50/yr. Institution: $95/yr.

World Affairs: A Quarterly Review of International Problems. American Peace Society, Room 100, 4000 Albemarle St. NW, Washington, DC 20016. $18/yr.; add $5 for foreign postage.

World Development. Monthly. Pergamon Press Inc., Maxwell House, Fairview Park, Elmsford, NY 10523. Library: $225/yr. Special rates for students and individuals.

World Marxist Review: Problems of Peace and Socialism. Monthly. Central Books Ltd., 14 The Leather Market, London SE1 3ER, England. 50p single issue; £7 annual subscription.

World Policy Journal. Quarterly. World Policy Institute, 777 United Nations Plaza, New York, NY 10017. Individual: $18/yr. Institution: $24/yr.

World Politics: A Quarterly Journal of International Politics. Princeton University Press, 3175 Princeton Pike, Lawrenceville, NJ 08648. US and Canada: Individuals $16.50/yr., $26.50/2 yrs., $39/3 yrs.; Institution $25/yr. Foreign Countries: Individual $20.50/yr., $33/2 yrs., $48.50/3 yrs.; Institution $31/yr. Add $3.50/yr. for foreign postage and handling.

World Press Review: News and Views from the Foreign Press. Monthly. Subscription Dept., Box 915, Farmingdale, NY 11737. US and Possessions: $17.95/yr., $29.95/2 yrs. In Canada add $2.50; other foreign countries add $7, or $25 for airmail.

Worldview. Monthly. Council on Religion and International Affairs, Subscription Dept., P.O. Box 1935, Marion, OH 43305. Regular: $17.50/yr., $33/2 yrs., $47/3 yrs. Student: $8.75/yr. Add $5/yr. for overseas postage.

Organizations

African Institute for Economic Development and Planning, United Nations, Economic Commission for Africa, B.P. 3186, Dakar, Senegal. A subsidiary of the United Nations Economic Commission for Africa, IDEP researches the economic development and the economic environment of Africa to devise appropriate economic planning for individual nations.

American Committee on East-West Accord, 109 11th Street, S.E., 2003, Washington, DC 20003. Involved in strengthening public understanding of initiatives to control and to reduce nuclear arms and to encourage mutually beneficial programs in science, culture, and non-military trade between the U.S. and the U.S.S.R.

American Friends Service Committee (AFSC), 1501 Cherry St., Philadelphia, PA 19105; (215) 241-7000. Dedicated to the search for nonviolent solutions to human problems, AFSC is involved in peace education, human rights work, refugee relief and community development in a variety of countries.

American Committee on Africa (ACOA), 198 Broadway, New York, NY 10038; (212) 962-1210. Originally founded to support African independence movements, ACOA provides information on Africa, mobilizes political action in support of African struggles, and lobbies in the U.S. Congress for a more progressive U.S. foreign policy towards Africa.

American Committee on East-West Accord, 227 Massachusetts Avenue, N.E. #300, Washington, DC 20002. Involved in strengthening public understanding of initiatives to control and to reduce nuclear arms and to encourage mutually beneficial programs in science, culture, and non-military trade between the U.S. and the U.S.S.R.

American Friends Service Committee (AFSC), 1501 Cherry St., Philadelphia, PA 19102; (215) 241-7000. Dedicated to the search for nonviolent solutions to human problems, AFSC is involved in peace education, human rights work, refugee relief and community development in a variety of countries.

American Peace Society, 4000 Albernarle St., N.W., Washington, DC 20016. Promotes judicial methods and other peaceful means to remedy differences between nations.

Amnesty International-USA, 304 W. 58th St., New York, NY 10019; (212) 582-4440. An internationally-based advocacy group working for the release of prisoners of conscience.

Arms Control Association, 11 Dupont Circle, N.W., Washington, DC 20036. Devoted to security for the general public, while concentrating on influencing Washington officials, the national media, and the higher education community.

Baystate Conversion Group, 120 Bellvue Rd., Watertown, MA 02171. Views military spending as detrimental to the world economy. The organization attempts to direct interest away from military-defense spending toward civilian-based production.

Blacks Against Nukes (BAN), 3728 New Hampshire Ave., N.W. #2021, Washington, DC 20010. A multiracial education and action group exposing the tradeoffs between massive military spending and meeting social needs, and the potential use of nuclear weapons in Third World arenas.

Bread for the World, 802 Rhode Island Ave., N.E., Washington, DC 20018. A Christian citizens' movement which publishes a newsletter and educational materials, sponsors conferences, and monitors current U.S. legislation and foreign food issues.

Campaign Against Nuclear War, 122 Maryland Avenue, N.E., Washington, DC 20002. CANW offers Americans ways to become involved with various existing organizations working on peace and disarmament issues. Outreach includes a toll free telephone number, a publication, and the creation and operation of a name bank.

Canadian Peace Research Institute, 119 Thomas St., Oakville, Ontario, Canada L6J 3A7; (416) 845-9370. A private research institute concerned with peace, civil and international conflicts and attitudes. CPRI provides training, documentation, research promotion, publications (CPRI News Report), and policy-making.

Carnegie Endowment for International Peace, 11 Dupont Circle N.W., Suite 900, Washington, D.C. 20036. Stressing the need for peace, CEIP promotes research on international law and international organization. Publications include the *Foreign Policy* journal, bulletins, monographs and progress-reports.

Center of Concern, 3700 13th St., N.E., Washington, DC 20017; (202) 635-2757. Engaged in social analysis, religious reflection and public education on social justice and human rights issues.

Center for Defense Information, 600 Maryland Ave., S.W., Washington, DC 20024; (202) 484-9490. Publishes information and conducts research on defense, arms control, and disarmament issues.

Center for Disarmament Education (CDE), P.O. Box 23790, Baton Rouge, LA 70893; (504) 927-6127. A member of Clergy and Laity Concerned network, CDE works to abolish nuclear weapons, provide alternatives to military solutions of international conflict, and protect human rights.

Center for International Policy, 120 Maryland Ave., N.E., Washington, DC 20002. Conducts research on U.S. foreign policy toward the Third World, particularly the relationship of economic and military assistance to the status of human rights.

Centre for the Study of Developing Societies, 29 Rajpur Road, Delhi 110054, India. A major research institute working on issues of international equity, economic dependence, militarism, as well as on problems of developing countries.

Citizens Against Nuclear War, 1201 16th St., N.W., Washington, DC 20016. A coalition and information forum of national membership organizations that express their view on issues of nuclear arms control.

Citizen's Energy Council, Box 285, Allendale, NJ 07401. This group of concerned citizens develops workshops and training programs on community organization. They also have a speaker's bureau and library to educate the public on the hazards of nuclear war.

Citizens for Common Sense in National Defense, 2000 P St., N.W., Washington DC 20026. Holds individual senators and congressmen accountable for their anti-peace votes, primarily on the nuclear freeze.

Clergy and Laity Concerned (CALC), 198 Broadway, New York, NY 10038; (212) 964-6730. An ecumenical organization concerned about social justice issues, including human rights, arms proliferation, Indochina conflict and military conversion.

Coalition for a New Foreign and Military Policy, 120 Maryland Ave., N.E., Washington, DC 20002. Mobilizes grassroots attention towards Congressional attempts to conduct a non-interventionist, humane, and open U.S. foreign policy.

Committee for National Security, 2000 P Street, N.W., Suite 515, Washington, DC 20036; (202) 833-3140. Concerned individuals united by a mutual goal to change the direction of national security policy, CNS seeks to develop public knowledge of present threats, redirect national security policy, and devise new ways to augment the strength and confidence of the nation in today's global community.

Common Cause, 2030 M St., N.W., Washington, DC 20036. Committed to improving the government's actions with emphasis on national security, arms control, and tax reform.

Communications for Nuclear Disarmament, 44 Hunt St., Watertown, MA 02172. Engaged in imploring the public outreach and increasing the effectiveness of educational materials for other disarmament organizations.

Conference on Peace Research in History, c/o Prof. Wm. Hoover, Dept. of History, University of Toledo, OH 42606. Encourages and coordinates peace research among historians and social scientists.

Congressional Caucus for Peace through Law (CPL), Room 3538, House Annex 11, U.S. House of Representatives, Washington, DC 20515. Bipartisan group of Congressmen and women concerned about world peace, CPL is working to increase Congressional commitment to human rights, arms control, and more effective foreign aid.

Consortium on Peace, Research, Education and Development (COPRED), University of Illinois at Urbana-Champaign, 361 Lincoln Hall, 702 Wright St., Urbana, IL 61801. A network and catalyst for peace research, education and advocacy, both within professional and social change constituencies.

Corporacion Integral para el Desarrollo Cultural y Social (CODECAL), Apartado 20439, Bogota, Colombia. An institute and network of educators involved in social education, with emphasis on involvement with peasants and the urban poor for justice and peace.

Council for the Development of Economic and Social Research in Africa, B.P. 3304, Dakar, Senegal. Primarily concerned with the socio-economic development of African nations, the council studies rural development, population policy, industrialization and income distribution, and economic integration and cooperation.

Council on Economic Priorities, Conversion Information Center, 30 Irving Place, New York, NY 10003; (212) 420-1133. Provides information on the defense industry and conversion efforts.

The Data Center, 464 19th St., Oakland, CA 94612. A library and information center which provides data on the U.S. and its role in world political economy.

Educators for Social Responsibility, 23 Garden Street, Cambridge, MA 02138. A national alliance of educators and parents working for nuclear arms reduction through school and community action/education projects. They also devise curriculum materials which help students to think critically and to reason morally.

Facing History and Ourselves National Foundation, Inc., 25 Kennard Rd., Brookline, MA 02146. Provides teachers and students with resources for studying topics that are complex and controversial, intellectually and emotionally challenging, particularly the origins of nuclear arms.

Fellowship of Reconciliation, P.O. Box 271, Nyack, NY 10960; (914) 358-4601. An international, ecumenical organization promoting the use of nonviolence and pacifism in conflict resolution. Also politically active in disarmament, human rights, and disaster-relief efforts.

Foundation for the Arts of Peace, 1918 Bonita Ave., Berkeley, CA 94704. Devoted to educating the public about the need to cultivate a peaceful world and to encouraging other groups to use communications media to stress the need for peace.

Foundation Reshaping the International Order (RIO), P.O. Box 299, 3000A6 Rotterdam, The Netherlands. Engaged in research in areas of international politics and disarmament, RIO devises new international development strategies for the achievement of international peace and cooperation between nations.

Friends of the Earth, 1045 Sansome, San Francisco, CA 94111; (415) 433-7373. A membership organization engaged in research, education and advocacy on environmental and ecological issues, including environmentally sound energy and development policies.

The Fund for Peace, 345 E. 46th St., New York, NY 10017; (212) 661-5900. A multi-project institution dedicated to the survival of human life on earth under conditions that make life worth living in a socially and economically just world.

Fundacion Bariloche, Casilla de Correa 138, 8400 San Carlos de Bariloche, Province de Rio Negro, Argentina. Involved in research and education emphasizing the importance of basic needs in national and international development strategies.

Geneva International Peace Research Institute, 41, rue de Zurich, CH-1201 Geneva, Switzerland. Conducts scientific and transdisciplinary research in the field of peace and security in order to contribute to the establishment of true peace.

Gandhi Peace Foundation, 2221-223 Deen Dayal, Upadhyaya Marg, New Delhi 110002 India. Devoted to both research and constructive activities in the field of peace, nonviolence, and social economic reconstruction.

Global Education Associates, 552 Park, E. Orange, NJ 07017; (201) 675-1409. An educational organization which facilitates the efforts of concerned people of diverse cultures, talents and experience in contributing to a more human and just world order.

Global Learning, Inc., 40 S. Fullerton Ave., Montclair, NJ 07042; (201) 783-7616. Through in-service training, workshops and development of curriculum materials, Global Learning seeks to facilitate the study of global issues in area secondary schools.

Global Perspectives in Education, Inc., 218 E. 18th St., New York, NY 10003; (212) 475-0850. A nonpartisan educational effort, building upon American democratic traditions, to prepare youth for the challenges of national citizenship in a global age. (Publishes two key directories.)

Goals, Processes and Indicators of Development, United Nations University, c/o UNITAR, Palais des Nations, 1211 Geneva 10 Switzerland. A UNU research network engaged in a series of international studies ranging from development strategies and energy to alternative life-styles.

Greenpeace U.S.A./Disarmament Project, 2007 R St., N.W., Washington, DC 20009. Engaged in an international campaign to stop nuclear weapons testing as the first step toward disarmament, Greenpeace works to protect the environment from the disposal of toxic and nuclear wastes into oceans, seas, and rivers.

Ground Zero, 805 15th St., N.W., Suite 515, Washington, DC 20005. Provides education on the problem of nuclear war with the objective of bringing private citizens into more active participation in national security decisions.

Health and Energy Learning Project, 236 Massachusetts Ave., N.E. #506, Washington, DC 20002. Conducts research and provides education to the public about the effects of radiation from nuclear weapons and nuclear power technology.

Human Rights Internet, 1338 G St. S.E., Washington, DC 20003. Serves as a clearinghouse of information for human rights educators and advocates throughout the globe.

Institute of the Black World, 87 Chestnut St., S.W., Atlanta, GA 30314; (404) 523-7805. Conducts and stimulates research and analysis, education and publication on the history and prospects of the black freedom struggle through a professional staff and network of teachers, artists, scholars, writers and consultants.

Institute for Defense & Disarmament Studies, 2001 Beacon St., Brookline, MA 02146; (617) 734-4216. Established with the view that the principles of democracy and the rule of law, not the use of force, should prevail within and among nations, the Institute studies the nature and purposes of military forces and the obstacles to and opportunities for disarmament.

Institute for East/West Security Studies, 304 E. 45th St., New York, NY 10017. A research center established to explore the dynamics of security and international policy options for the future.

Institute for Food and Development Policy, 1885 Mission St., San Francisco, CA 94103; (415) 864-8555. A research, documentation, and education center focusing on food and agricultural issues, in particular the role of governments and corporations in the struggle to provide food security.

Institute for Global Education, 415 Ethel St., Grand Rapids, MI 49506. Devoted to increasing public awareness and understanding of international issues, particularly peace and disarmament, IGE emphasizes the importance of global interdependence through seminars and conferences.

Institute for International Education, 809 UN Plaza, New York, NY 10017. Seeks to build international understanding and promote international development through the interchange of scholars and students, knowledge and skills.

Institute for Peace and Justice, 4144 Lindell Blvd. #400, St. Louis, MO 63108. Provides educational resources and services in social justice and peacemaking for individuals, families, schools, educators and religious communities.

Institute for Policy Studies, 1901 Que St., N.W., Washington, DC 20009. A transnational research and education center which provides alternative strategies and analyses of domestic policy, national security, international economics, and human rights.

Institute for the Study of Labor and Economic Crisis, 2701 Folsom St., San Francisco, CA 94110; (415) 550-1703. Committed to encouraging rational debate about the current world situation, with research programs and seminars focusing on: the crisis in the world capitalist economy; contradictions in the construction of socialism; the growth of austerity capitalism and the role of transnational corporations; U.S. foreign policy; the attack on labor; the rise of the New Right; and repression.

Institute of International Law, 82 Avenue du Castel, 1200 Brussels, Belgium. Primarily concerned with questions of international law, international relations and peace.

Interfaith Center on Corporate Responsibility, 475 Riverside Dr., Rm. 566, New York, NY 10027; (212) 876-2293. Sponsored by the National Council of Churches, ICCR is engaged in research, education and action on such corporate issues as economic conversion, agribusiness, and the operations of transnational corporations in South Africa and Third World countries.

Interfaith Center to Reverse the Arms Race, 132 N. Euclid, Pasadena, CA 91101. Its focus is to reverse the arms race via a speaker's bureau, a library, films, organizing rallies and vigils, and producing resource and educational materials.

Interfaith Hunger Coalition, 1010 S. Flower #404, Los Angeles, CA 90015; (213) 746-7500. A network of groups in Southern California working on education and action programs concerning domestic and global hunger.

International Center for Research on Women, 1717 Massachusetts Ave., N.W., Suite 507, Washington, DC 20036; (202) 797-0007. Focuses on women's work in Third World countries and expands their work and strategies through public information, public education, and technical assistance.

International Coalition for Development Action, Bedford Chambers, Covent Garden, London WC2E 8HA, England. A network of development-oriented action groups and agencies located in industrialized countries, bound together by a commitment to achieve a more just and equitable international order.

International Commission of Jurists, American Association for, 777 United Nations Plaza, New York, NY 10017; (212) 972-0883. Drawn from all sectors of the legal community, the Commission is dedicated to the rule of law and the independence of the judiciary to uphold and strengthen the observance of human rights.

International Food Policy Research Institute, 1776 Massachusetts Avenue, N.W., Washington, DC 20036. Conducts research on the world food problem through an integrated approach examining the interrelationships of technological change, agricultural growth, overall economic growth and social welfare for improving the equity of distribution.

International Foundation for Development Alternatives (IFDA), 2 Place du Marche, 1260 Nyon, Switzerland. Concerned with finding more equitable and humane development strategies at the local, national and global levels, IFDA sponsors research on development questions and acts as a network for scholars, educators, and public interest organizations throughout the world.

International Institute for Peace, Mollwaldplatz 5, A-1040 Vienna, Austria. A research and educational institute concerned with questions of international relations, peace, and disarmament.

International Human Rights Law Group, 1346 Connecticut Ave., N.W., Washington, DC 20036; (202) 659-5023. Provides legal services and conducts educational programs in the field of international human rights.

International League for Human Rights, 236 E. 46th St., New York, NY 10017; (212) 972-9554. Through the publication of special reports, the submission of documented complaints to governmental and intergovernmental bodies, and the organization of investigative commissions, the League works toward the protection of the rights of individuals.

International Peace Academy, 777 United Nations Plaza, New York, NY 10017. Devoted to furthering the practical skills and procedures for dispute settlement, peacekeeping, peacemaking, mediation and conflict management, as well as the broader concerns of human rights and peace.

International Peace Bureau, 41 rue de Zurich, 1201 Geneva, Switzerland. An international federation of peace organizations concentrating on the evaluation and formulation of proposals for world disarmament.

International Peace Research Association, c/o Chad Alger, Mershon Center, 199 West 10th Ave., Columbus, OH 43201; (614) 422-1681. Founded for the purpose of advancing interdisciplinary research into the conditions of peace and the causes of war, IPRA conducts research, organizes conferences and publishes a newsletter for peace research educators and scholars.

International Physicians for the Prevention of Nuclear War, 635 Huntington Avenue, 2nd Floor, Boston, MA 02115. Citizens united to educate the public on the dangers of nuclear war and to disseminate information on nuclear power alternatives.

International Student Pugwash, 505B Second Ave., N.E., Washington, DC 20002. Structured around an array of nuclear age topics, science, technology and responsibility issues, the group seeks to educate and to sensitize students through conferences, publications and courses.

The Lawyers Committee on Nuclear Policy, Inc., 225 Lafayette Street, Suite 207, New York, NY 10012; (212) 334-8044. An organization of lawyers, law professors, legal workers and law students which advises on the legal implications of defense policies and the prospects for strengthening norms against the resort to violence in international relations, and dedicated to the abolition of nuclear weapons through legal mechanisms and the legal community.

Lindisfarne Association, Baca Grande Ranche, Baca Grande, Ca. Devoted to building a new planetary culture through the synthesis of new age consciousness and modern insights into culture and science.

Meadowcreek Project, Fox, Arkansas 72051. A model appropriate technology community research/educational center equipped with laboratory facilities, conference center, and housing for researchers, visiting scholars, and interns. It aims toward a balance between humanity and nature, ecology and economy, and centralization and decentralization.

Mid-Peninsula Conversion Project, 867 W. Dana St., Mt. View, CA 94041; (415) 968-8798. Engages in research and education related to the conversion of the military industry to socially useful production and to the escalation of nuclear energy and weapons throughout the globe.

MIT: Program in Science and Technology for International Security, Dept. of Physics, Rm. 20A011, Cambridge, MA 02139. Performs research, technical analysis, evaluation and assessment of emerging new weaponry, provides the results for Congress, policy makers, the public, and international scholars.

Mobilization for Survival, 853 Broadway, Rm. 2109, New York, NY 10003; (212) 533-0008. A national organization involved in coalition-building and education for stopping nuclear power, banning nuclear weapons, ending the arms race, and funding human needs.

National Action-Research on the Military Industrial Complex (NARMIC), 1501 Cherry St., Philadelphia, PA 19102; (215) 241-7175. Conducts intensive sustained research on the links between industry and the military, and disarmament, militarism, human rights and Southern Africa.

National Audubon Society, 950 Third St., New York, NY 10022; (212) 832-3200. Dedicated to the wise use and conservation of renewable resources, and to educating the public regarding ecological interdependence.

National Center For Economic Alternatives (NCEA), 2000 P St., N.W., Washington, DC 20036; (202) 483-6667. To develop practical economic alternatives for the coming decades—reorganizing the American economy in order to make it more decentralized, more democratic and more supportive of a sense of community in America.

National Center For Jobs and Justice, 413 8th Street, S.E., Washington, DC 20003; (202) 547-9292. A research and advocacy organization representing the interests of unemployed, underemployed, and low-wage workers.

National Nuclear Weapons Freeze Campaign, 4144 Lindell Blvd., #404, St. Louis, MO 63108. Monitors, facilitates, and coordinates hundreds of local freeze groups across the U.S. by collecting and disseminating information concerning freeze activities.

National Wildlife Federation, 8925 Leesburg Pike, Vienna, VA 22180; (703) 790-4244. A nationwide conservation education organization deriving direction and strength from a broad-based membership concerned about conserving natural resources and preserving a quality environment.

National Women's Studies Association, University of Maryland, College Park, MD 20742; (301) 454-3557. Comprised of twelve regional associations, NWSA promotes programs in social and political development areas in women studies and feminist education, and sponsors an annual conference.

Natural Resources Defense Council/Nuclear Non-proliferation Project, 1725 I St., N.W., Suite 600, Washington, DC 20006. Through litigation, public education, and political action the council works to influence U.S. governmental action to protect the environment and to reduce the deployment of nuclear weapons.

Nautilus, 541 W. 113 St., #6c, New York, NY 10025; (212) 666-1327. Engages in research on the social, political and economic issues relating to the development of nuclear energy, and on alternative energy options in Third World countries.

Network, 806 Rhode Island Ave., N.E., Washington, DC 20018; (202) 526-4070. Concerned with social justice and human rights issues, Network seeks to effect systemic change by influencing national legislation.

Nigerian Institute of International Affairs, Kofo Abayomi Road, Victoria Island, G.P.O. Box 1727, Lagos, Nigeria. Concerned with international relations and international affairs in Africa, as well as the global community. NIIA provides research conferences-organization and publications.

Non-Government Organization (NGO) Committee on Disarmament, 777 UN Plaza, New York, NY 10017. Brings together officially designated NGO's to educate the public and bring pressure to bear on the UN system to achieve disarmament.

North American Congress on Latin America (NACLA), 151 W. 19th., 9th Fl., New York, NY 10011; (212) 989-8890. Founded in response to the U.S. invasion of the Dominican Republic in 1965, NACLA conducts research and analysis on the impact of U.S. policies on Latin America.

Nuclear Control Institute, 1000 Connecticut Avenue, N.W., Suite 406, Washington, DC 20036. Alerts the public, Congress, and the public interest community to civilian nuclear policies and programs that cause the global spread of nuclear weapons. (membership organization).

Nuclear Freeze Foundation, 324 4th St., N.E., Washington, DC 20002. Supports a mutual, verifiable nuclear weapons freeze followed by major reductions in the current arsenals on both sides. Constitutency includes members of Congress, freeze activists, and nation-wide freeze supporters.

Nuclear Information and Resource Service (NIRS), 1346 Connecticut Ave., N.W., #401, Washington, DC 20036; (202) 296-7552. Provides current information, advice, and organizational assistance to grassroots anti-nuclear power groups, and speakers to those trying to halt nuclear power plants and find alternatives to nuclear power.

Nuclear Network, 1346 Connecticut Avenue, N.W., Washington, DC 20036. To establish a world safe from the threat of a nuclear war through participation in the anti-nuclear movement and study of the question of national security.

Nukewatch: Project on Campus Militarism, 315 W. Gorham, Madison, WI 53703. A project of the Progressive Foundation, Nukewatch is interested in educational work in the area of nuclear weapons and nuclear power. Constituency includes peace activists, educators, environmentalists, and other concerned citizens.

Overseas Development Council, 1717 Massachusetts Ave., N.W., Washington, DC 20036; (202) 234-8701. Seeks to promote understanding of development issues by the American public, policymakers, specialists, educators, and the media through its research, conferences, publications, and liaison with U.S. organizations interested in U.S. relations with the developing world.

Oxfam-America, 115 Broadway, Boston, MA 02216; (617) 482-1211. A private, voluntary organization which provides relief services to famine-stricken areas, stricken areas, organizes and funds self-reliant economic development projects in the Third World, and conducts educational programs on food and economic development.

Pacific Concerns Resource Center, in support of the Nuclear Free and Independent Pacific Movement, P.O. Box 27692, Honolulu, HI 96827; (808) 538-3522. A politically active, cohesive group of Third World and First World people pursuing a nuclear-free and independent Pacific, PCRC is the parent institute of the U.S. Nuclear Free Pacific Network (USNFPN). USNFPN acts as liaison between domestic groups and the pan-Pacific movement.

Pacific Studies Center, 222 B View St., Mountainview, CA 94041; (415) 969-1545. A public interest information center involved with U.S./Asian relations and the development of high technology electronics. Publications include the *Pacific Research* journal and a newsletter "Global Electronics Information."

Pax Christi International, Kerkstratt 150, 2000 Antwerp, Belgium; Tel 35.02.72. USA: 3000 N. Mango Ave., Chicago, IL 60634. An internationally-based peace movement, Pax Christi seeks to promote peace and justice through educational and networking programs.

Peacelinks: Women Against Nuclear War, 723½ 8th St., S.E., Washington, DC 20003. Supplies mainstream American women with information and materials to prevent nuclear war.

Peace Research Institute, 25 Dundas, Ontario L9H 4E5 Canada. Conducts research on the obstacles to and conditions for peace, including international trade, disarmament and the United States.

Peaceworkers, 3565 Mt. Diablo Blvd., Box 2, Lafayette, CA 94549; (415) 283-6500. Building a roster of volunteers who are willing to serve in a UN Peaceworkers service, if and when one is established, and to train for such a service in laboratory projects in urban areas.

Peace Through Law Education Fund, 2700 Virginia Avenue, N.W. #807, Washington, DC 20037. Seeks to provide the entire Congress, its staff, and the U.S. public with information and alternative approaches to the problems of international cooperation and security. Affiliate of Congressional Caucus for Peace Through Law.

Physicians for Social Responsibility, 639 Massachusetts Avenue, Cambridge, MA 02139. Doctors, dentists, and medical students working to educate the public about the threat of nuclear war.

The Population Council, 1 Dag Hammarskjold Plaza, New York, NY 10017; (212) 644-1300. Committed to the improvement of human welfare, the Council focuses on health and family planning and conducts social science research useful to the understanding of population policy issues. Facilities include a library and biomedical labs for the development and improvement of contraceptives.

Population Reference Bureau, 2213 M Street, N.W., Washington, DC 20037; (202) 785-4664. PRB is a private/non-profit organization that compiles surveys surveys of population issues, plans, and trends; a public resource center provides additional population statistics. The Bureau also publishes a newsletter "Population Today."

Progressive Foundation, 315 W. Gorham St., Madison, WI 53703. Promotes public awareness and debate about public concerns and especially the dangers of nuclear power.

Promoting Enduring Peace, P.O. Box 5103, Woodmont, CT 06460; (203) 878-4769. A religious, educational, non-political group promoting international peace and understanding; PEP sponsors the Gandhi Peace Award annually, conducts international peace seminars, and reprints and distributes free materials to those interested in the peace/nuclear disarmament movement.

Riverside Church Disarmament Program, 490 Riverside Dr., New York, NY 10027; (212) 222-5900. Organizes conferences and provides speakers and resources on disarmament education.

SANE (The Committee for a SANE World), 911 G Street, S.E., Washington, DC 20003; (202) 546-7100. Mobilizes grassroots support for American initiatives for peace and disarmament, SANE explores alternatives for shifting away from nuclear weapons towards human welfare.

Sojourners Fellowship, 1309 L St., N.W., Washington, DC 20036; (202) 636-3637. A religious oriented citizens' group actively involved in the struggle of the poor in the local DC area as well as in international issues concerning the nuclear arms race, human rights, abortion, biblical feminism, and justice issues.

The Stanley Foundation, 420 E. 3rd St., Muscatine, IA 52761. Promotes peace education with heavy emphasis on arms control and disarmament. Topics selected stem from current U.S. foreign policy questions and issues at the UN and other international organizations.

Stockholm International Peace Research Institute, Sveagen 166, S-113 46 Stockholm, Sweden. An independent institution for research into problems of peace and conflict, with particular attention to the problems of disarmament and arms regulation.

Tampere Peace Research Institute, Tammeian puistokatu 58B, 33100 Tampere 10, Finland. Conducts interdisciplinary and international scientific research on the problems of war and peace.

Tranet, Transnational Network for Appropriate Alternative Technologies, P.O. Box 567, Rangley, ME 04970. A network of individuals and groups developing new, sustainable technologies, lifestyles and economic patterns.

Transnational Institute (TNI), Paulus Potterstraat 20, 1017DA Amsterdam, The Netherlands. Drawing researchers from throughout the world, TNI conducts research on human rights, development, militarism and disarmament, international law and the new international economic order.

Union for Radical Political Economics, 41 Union Square West, Rm. 901, New York, NY 10003; (212) 691-5722. A membership organization, URPE is an interdisciplinary association oriented towards development and application of political/economic analysis to social problems. Publications include a journal and a newsletter. Also sponsors two national conferences annually.

Union of Concerned Scientists, 26 Church Street, Cambridge, MA 02238. Seeks to conduct widespread education on issues that shape national security and arms control policy.

United Campuses to Prevent Nuclear War, 1346 Connecticut Avenue, Washington, DC 20036. Organizes meetings, forums, and debates on campuses nationwide to prevent nuclear war.

United Nations Association of the USA, 300 E. 42nd St., New York, NY 10017. Seeks to familiarize the U.S. public with the essential role of the UN and other international organizations as well as some of the serious issues facing the UN and world community.

United Nations Education, Scientific and Cultural Organization (UNESCO), Division of Human Rights and Peace, 7 Place de Fontenoy, 75700 Paris, France. In addition to sponsoring peace research, the Division of Human Rights and

Peace currently is establishing an International Peace Research Information System aimed at improving the exchange of information and documentation among peace researchers and assisting the creation and development of peace research centres in developing countries.

United Nations Institute for Training and Research, 801 United Nations Plaza, New York, NY 10017. UN agency engaged in and supporting research on global issues, including security, development, and future modeling.

U.S. Nuclear Free Pacific Network (formerly the Bay Area Coalition for a Nuclear Free Pacific), 944 Market St., #712, San Francisco, CA 94102; (415) 434-2988. Unites Third and First World people and serves as a resource and information center to educate, organize, support, and act around issues of land rights in the Pacific Basin, struggles of indigenous people, resistance to the nuclear fuel cycle and nuclear waste dumping in the Pacific region, opposition to the militarization of Micronesia and many other priority issues.

War Resisters League, 339 Lafayette St., New York, NY 10012; (212) 228-0450. Particularly concerned with the rights of the individual to refuse military service, WRL is based on the principles of nonviolence and pacifism.

Women's Action for Nuclear Disarmament Education Fund, Inc., 691 Massachusetts Avenue, Arlington, MA 02174. Provides information and educational materials to the public on nuclear weapons to prevent the holocaust of nuclear war.

Women's Action for Nuclear Disarmament, Inc., P.O. Box 153 New Town Branch, Boston, MA 02258. By organizing women and men at the grassroots level, the group hopes to induce the end of the arms race. It focuses on specific bills in Congress via Congressional Action alerts.

Women's International League for Peace and Freedom (WILPF), 1213 Race St., Philadelphia, PA 19107; (215) 563-7110. Founded in 1915 to achieve peace, freedom and justice through non-violent means, WILPF publishes current analysis on disarmament and social justice issues, often with special reference to the actions of Congress and international organizations.

Women's International Tribune Center, Inc., 777 United Nations Plaza, 3rd Fl., New York, NY 10017. Extensive library/resource center in support of women's development. Provides information on films, books, organizations, etc.

Women Strike for Peace, 201 Massachusetts Avenue, N.E., #102, Washington, DC 20002. Nationwide activist group dedicated to ending the nuclear arms race and preventing nuclear war.

World Council for Curriculum and Instruction, School of Education, Indiana University, Bloomington, IN 47405; (812) 337-1086. With the general goal of facilitating transnational cooperation among educators, WCCI seeks to develop curriculum for international cooperation, peace, and global community building.

World Hunger Education Service, 1317 G Street, N.W., Washington, DC 20005; (202) 347-4441. Facilitates the exchange of information and insights on world food and development issues through citizen education and support for policies and actions that will help all people live in sufficiency and dignity.

World Federalists Association, 418 Seven St., S.E., Washington, DC 20003; (202) 546-3950. Promotes the voluntary establishment of a world government and concurrently encourages the growth of global institutions which can effectively deal with today's interdependent world.

World Future Society (WFS), 4916 St. Elmo Ave., Washington, DC 20014. Through a series of workshops and publications, WFS seeks to contribute to a reasoned awareness of the future and of the importance of its study, without advocating particular ideologies and engaging in political activities.

World Future Studies Federation, Caesella Postage 6203, Roma Prati, Rome 00195, Italy. Promotes and encourages future studies from all disciplines, facilitates networking of individuals and organizations involved in future studies and organizes conferences and workshops on specific issues of concern to futurists.

World Information Service on Energy International (WISE), 2e Weteringplantsoen 9, 1017 ZD Amsterdam, Netherlands. USA: 1536 16th St., N.W., Washington, DC 20036. Provides information relevant to the transnational antinuclear movement against nuclear power and a technocratic, centralized, authoritarian, undemocratic form of society.

World Peace Council, Lonnnrotinkatu 25 A 6krs. 00180 Helsinki 18, Finland. Facilitates cultural, educational and scientific cooperation between peace research institutes throughout the globe.

World Peacemakers, 2852 Ontario Rd., N.W., Washington, DC 20009. Faith-oriented network dedicated to activating people on security issues.

World Policy Institute, 777 United Nations Plaza, New York, NY 10017; (212) 490-0010. The Institute is a non-profit, international public policy and research organization founded in 1948. Key projects include *World Policy Journal*, a new quarterly; The Security Project, a 5 year effort to develop a new, comprehensive economic and security agenda; and a Curriculum Development Program, a continuing service to educators and students

World Without War Council, 175 Fifth Ave., New York, NY 10010; (212) 674-2085. A national organization whose overall purpose is to help end war through the peaceful change of U.S. foreign policy and the strengthening of international institutions. Its activities include workshops, conferences, professional training, publications, and networking with peace organizations.

Worldwatch Institute, 1776 Massachusetts Ave., N.W., Washington, DC 20036. An independent research organization created to analyze and focus attention on global problems.

Bibliography

The following is a list of books and articles deemed basic to a peace and world order studies library. As the Third Edition of *Peace and World Order Studies* included books published before 1981, this list concentrates most heavily on books published since then. Books appearing on the list which do not fit into this criterion have been selected because they are particularly important works in their subject areas.

The bibliography is divided into sections to correspond as closely as possible with the syllabi headings of the book. In many cases, the entries which fall under a particular heading are also suitable for study of other topics.

A. World Systems and Alternative Futures

Alger, Chadwick F. "Role of People in the Future Global Order," *Alternatives* 4 (October 1978): 232-62.

Amin, Samir, Giovanni Arrighi, et al. *Dynamics of Global Crisis*. NY: Monthly Review Press, 1982.

Angell, Robert C. *The Quest for World Order*. Ann Arbor, MI: Univ. of Michigan Press, 1979.

Barnet, Richard J., and Ronald E. Muller. *Global Reach: The Power of Multinational Corporations*. NY: Simon and Schuster, 1976.

Bay, Christian. *Strategies of Political Emancipation*. Notre Dame, IN: Univ. of Notre Dame Press, 1981.

Beitz, Charles R. *Political Theory and International Relations*. Princeton, NJ: Princeton Univ. Press, 1979.

Bell, Daniel, ed. "The Future World Disorder: The Structural Context of Crisis," *Foreign Affairs*, No. 27 (Summer 1977): 109-135.

Beres, Louis Rene and Harry R. Targ. *Constructing Alternative World Futures: Reordering the Planet*. Cambridge, MA: Schenkman, 1977.

Beres, Louis Rene and Harry R. Targ, eds. *Planning Alternative World Futures: Values, Methods, and Models*. NY: Praeger, 1975.

Bergesen, Albert, ed. *Studies of the Modern World-System*. NY: Academic Press, 1980.

Bertsch, Gary K., ed. *Global Policy Studies*. Beverley Hills, CA: Sage Publications, 1982.

Boulding, Kenneth. *The Meaning of the Twentieth Century*. NY: Harper Colophon Books, 1964.

Camilleri, Joseph A. *Civilization in Crisis: Human Prospects in a Changing World*. NY: Cambridge Univ. Press, 1976.

Clark, Ian. *Reform and Resistance in the International Order*. NY: Cambridge Univ. Press, 1980.

Cornish, Edward, *The Study of the Future*. Washington, DC: The World Future Society, 1977.

Dolman, Anthony J. *Resources, Regimes, World Order*. NY: Pergamon Press, Inc., 1981.

Domhoff, William G. *The Powers That Be: Processes of Ruling Class Domination in America*. NY: Vintage Books, 1979.

Domhoff, William G. *Who Rules America?* Englewood Cliffs, NJ: Prentice-Hall, 1967.

Falk, Richard. *A Study of Future Worlds*. NY: The Free Press, 1975.

Falk, Richard, Samuel S. Kim, and Saul H. Mendlovitz, eds. *Studies on a Just World Order, Vol. I: Towards a Just World Order*. Boulder, CO: Westview Press, 1982.

Fuller, Buckminster. *Operating Manual for Spaceship Earth*. Carbondale, IL: Southern Illinois Univ. Press, 1969.

Fuller, Buckminster. *Utopia or Oblivion*. NY: Bantam Books, 1969.

Galtung, Johan. *The True Worlds: A Transnational Perspective*. NY: The Free Press, 1980.

Heilbroner, Robert I. *An Inquiry into the Human Prospect*. NY: W.W. Norton, 1975.

Henderson, Hazel. *Creating Alternative Futures: The End of Economics*. NY: Berkeley Publishers, 1978.

Johansen, Robert C. *The National Interest and the Human Interest*. Princeton, NJ: Princeton Univ. Press, 1980.

Kedron, Michael and Ronald Segal. *The State of the World Atlas*. NY: Simon and Schuster, 1981.

Keohane, Robert O. and Joseph S. Nye. *Power and Interdependence: World Politics in Transition*. NY: The Free Press, 1975.

Kim, Samuel S. *The Quest for A Just World Order*. Boulder, CO: Westview Press, 1983.

Lagos, Gustavo and Horatio Godoy. *Revolution of Being: A Latin American View of the Future*. NY: The Free Press, 1977.

Mandlebaum, Michael. *The Nuclear Revolution: International Politics Before and After Hiroshima*. NY: Cambridge Univ. Press, 1983.

Mazrui, Ali A. *A World Federation of Cultures: An African Perspective*. NY: The Free Press, 1977.

Mendlovitz, Saul H., ed. *On the Creation of a Just World Order*. NY: The Free Press, 1977.

Mendlovitz, Saul H. *The Struggle for a Just World Order: An Agenda of Inquiry and Praxis for the 1980's*. Working Paper #20. NY: World Policy Institute, 1982.

Mesarvoic, Mihajlo and Eduard Pestel. *Mankind at the Turning Point*. The Second Report to the Club of Rome. NY: Signet, 1976.

Mills, C. Wright. *The Power Elite*. NY: Oxford Univ. Press, 1956.

North, Robert. *The World That Could Be*. NY: W.W. Norton, 1976.

Pirages, Dennis. *The New Context for International Relations: Global Ecopolitics*. North Scituate, MA: Duxbury Press, 1978.

Reisman, Michael and Burns H. Weston, eds. *Toward World Order and Human Dignity*. NY: The Free Press, 1976.

Sklar, Holly. *Trilateralism: the Trilateral Commission and Elite Planning for World Management*. Boston, MA: South End Press, 1980.

Stavrianos, L.S. *The Promise of the Coming Dark Age*. San Francisco, CA: W.H. Freeman, 1976.

Wallerstein, Immanuel. *The Modern World System*. NY: Academic Press, 1974.

Wagner, Warren. *Building the City of Man: Outlines of a World Civilization*. NY: Grossman Publishers, 1971.

B. International Organization and Law

Akehurst, Michael. *A Modern Introduction to International Law*, 4th Edition. London: George, Allen, and Unwin, 1982.

Baxter, Richard R. "Humanitarian Law or Humanitarian Politics? The 1974 Diplomatic Conference on Humanitarian Law," *Harvard International Law Journal* 16 (Winter 1975): 1-26.

Bennet, LeRoy. *International Organizations: Principles and Issues*. 2nd Edition. Englewood Cliffs, NJ: Prentice-Hall, 1980.

Boeck, Alvard. *The Economic Essentials of International Arbitration*. San Bernadino, CA: Borgo Press, 1982.

Castaneda, Jorge: *Legal Effects of United Nations Resolutions*. Trans. Alba Amoia. NY: Columbia Univ. Press, 1969.

Clark, Grenville and Louis B. Sohn. *Introduction to World Peace Through World Law*. Chicago, IL: World Without War Publications, 1973.

Clark, Grenville and Louis B. Sohn. *World Peace Through World Law*. 3rd Edition, rev. Cambridge, MA: Harvard Univ. Press, 1966.

Cox, Robert W. "The Crisis of World Order and the Problem of International Organization in the 1980s," *International Journal* 35 (Spring 1979): 257-302.

Elements of United Nations Reform. Wayne, NJ: Center for United Nations Reform Education, 1980.

Falk, Richard, Friedrich Kratochwil, and Saul H. Mendlovitz, eds. *Studies on a Just World Order Series, Volume II: International Law and Just World Order*. Boulder, CO: Westview Press, forthcoming 1985.

Falk, Richard, Samuel Kim and Saul H. Mendlovitz, eds. *Studies on a Just World Order Series, Volume III: The United Nations and a Just World Order*. Boulder, CO: Westview Press, forthcoming, 1985.

Falk, Richard, Lee Meyrowitz, and Jack Sanderson. *Nuclear Weapons and International Law*. Occasional Paper #10, World Order Studies Program, Center of International Studies. Princeton, NJ: Princeton Univ. Press, 1981.

Fischer, Dana D. "Reporting Under the Covenant on Civil and Political Rights: The First Five Years of the Human Rights Committee," *The American Journal of International Law* 76 (January 1982): 142-53.

Holsti, K.J. *International Politics: A Framework for Analysis*. 4th Edition. Englewood Cliffs, NJ: Prentice Hall Inc., 1983.

Jack, Homer A. *Disarm Or Die: The Second U.N. Special Session on Disarmament*. NY: World Conference on Religion and Peace, 1983.

Kim, Samuel S. *China, the United Nations and World Order*. Princeton, NJ: Princeton Univ. Press, 1979.

Knorr, Klaus E. and Sidney Verba, eds. *The International System: Theoretical Essays*. Westport, CT: Greenwood Press, 1982.

Luard, David Evan Trent. *International Agencies: The Emerging Framework of Interdependence*. London: Macmillan for the Royal Institute of International Affairs, 1977.

McWhinney, Edward. *Conflict and Compromise: International Law and World Order in a Revolutionary Age*. NY: Holmes and Meier Inc., 1981.

M'Gonigle, Michael and Mark W. Zacher. *Pollution, Politics and International Law*. Berkeley, CA: Univ. of California Press, 1979.

Rittberger, Volka. *Evolution and International Organization: Toward a New Level of Sociopolitical Integration*. Dan Haag, Netherlands: Martinus Nijhoff, 1973.

Thant, U. *View From the U.N.* NY: Doubleday Books, 1978.

Weston, Burns H., et. al., eds. *International Law and World Order*. St. Paul, MO: West Pub. Co., 1980.

Weston, Burns H. "Nuclear Weapons Versus International Law: A Contextual Reassessment," *The McGill Law Journal*, Vol. 28, No. 3 (1983).

Woito, Robert. *To End War: A New Approach to International Conflict*. NY: Pilgrim Press, 1982.

Yeselson, Abraham and Anthony Gaglione. *A Dangerous Place: The U.N. as a Weapon in World Politics*. NY: Grossman Pubs., 1974.

Zagladin, V.V. and I.T. Frolov. "Global Problems as Areas of International Cooperation," *International Social Science Journal* 34 (1982).

C. Peacemaking and Nonviolence

Agreements: Texts and Histories of Negotiations. Washington, DC: US Arms Control and Disarmament Agency, 1982.

Alston, Philip. "Peace as a Human Right," *Bulletin of Peace Proposals* 11 (December 1980): 319-30.

Alternative Defense Commission. *Defense Without the Bomb*. NY: International Publications Service, Taylor Francis Inc., 1983.

Arms Control Association. "Verification: No Obstacle to Arms Control," *Arms Control Today*, Vol. 13, No. 5, June 1983.

Arendt, Hannah. *On Revolution*. NY: Viking Press, 1963.

Arendt, Hannah. *On Violence*. NY: Harcourt, Brace, and World, 1970.

Bandura, Albert. *Aggression: A Social Analysis*. Englewood Cliffs, NJ: Prentice-Hall, Inc., 1973.

Beer, Francis A. *Peace Against War: The Ecology of International Violence*. San Francisco, CA: W.H. Freeman, 1981.

Berkowitz, Leonard. *Aggression: A Social Psychological Analysis*. NY: McGraw Hill, 1962.

Bondurant, Joan. *Conquest of Violence: The Gandhian Philosophy of Conflict*, Rev. ed., Berkeley, CA: Univ. of California Press, 1971.

Boulding, Kenneth. *Stable Peace*. Austin, TX: Univ. of Texas Press, 1978.

Brock, Peter. *Twentieth-Century Pacifism*. NY: Van Nostrand Reinhold, 1970.

Bruyn, Sevryn T. and Paula Rayman, eds. *Nonviolent Action and Social Change*. NY: Irvington Publishers, 1979.

Bunn, George. "Nuclear Arms Control: Obstacles to Agreement," published paper prepared for the 42nd Pugwash Symposia, 1983.

Carver, Field Lord Marshall. *A Policy for Peace*. London: Faber and Faber, 1982.

Charny, Israel W., ed. *Strategies Against Violence: Design for Nonviolent Change*. Boulder, CO: Westview Press, 1978.

Claude, Inis L. Jr. *Swords into Plowshares*. 4th Edition. NY: Random House, 1971.

Common Security: A Blueprint for Survival, Independent Commission on Disarmament and Security Issues. NY: Simon and Schuster, 1983.

Cooney, Robert, Helen Michalowski, et al., eds. *Power of the People: Active Nonviolence in the United States*. Culver City, CA: Peace Press, 1977.

Dellinger, Dave. *Revolutionary Nonviolence: Essays*. Indianapolis, IN: Bobbs-Merrill, 1970.

A Disarmament Chronology. NY: United Nations Chronicle, June 1982, Vol. 19, No. 6.

Erikson, Erik. *Gandhi's Truth: On the Origins of Militant Nonviolence*. NY: W.W. Norton and Co., 1969.

Falk, Richard and Saul H. Mendlovitz, eds. *The Strategy of World Order, Vols. 1, 2, 3 and 4*. NY: World Policy Institute, 1966.

Fisher, Roger and William Ury. *Getting To Yes—Negotiating Agreement Without Giving In*. 1981.

Gallie, W.B. *Philosophers of Peace and War*. NY: Cambridge Univ. Press, 1978.

Gandhi, Mohandas K. *For Pacifists*, Bharatan Kumarappa, ed. San Diego, CA: Greenleef Classics, 1981.

Gandhi, Mohandas K. *Nonviolence in Peace & War*. NY: Garland, 1971.

Green, Martin. *The Challenge of the Mahatmas*. NY: Basic Books, Inc., 1978.

Hoffman, Paul. *Peace Can Be Won*. Garden City, NY: Doubleday, 1951.

Huntington, Samuel P. *The Soldier and the State*. Cambridge, MA: Belknap, 1957.

Huxley, Aldous. *What Are You Going to Do About It? The Case for Constructive Peace*. London: Chatto and Windus, 1936.

Johansen, Robert C. *Toward a Dependable Peace: A Proposal for an Appropriate Security System*. World Policy Paper #8. NY: World Policy Institute, 1983.

"Joint Statement of Agreed Principles for Disarmament Negotiations" of the Soviet Union and the United States (McCloy-Zorin Agreement), Sept. 20, 1961, in *Disarmament and Economic Development*, Vol. 4, in *The Strategy of World Order*, Richard Falk and Saul H. Mendlovitz, eds. NY: World Policy Institute, 1966.

Kant, Immanuel. *Perpetual Peace: A Philosophic Essay*. (Eng. trans.). Los Angeles, CA: Westwood Village, 1932.

Kaldor, Mary and Dan Smith, eds. *Disarming Europe*. London: The Merlin Press, 1982.

King, Martin Luther, Jr. *Stride Toward Freedom*. NY: Harper and Row, 1968.

Lewin, Leonard C. *Report from Iron Mountain on the Possibility and Desirability of Peace*. NY: The Dial Press, 1967.

Likert, R. and J. *New Ways of Managing Conflict*. NY: McGraw Hill, 1976.

Magri, Lucio. "The Peace Movement and Europe," in *Exterminism and Cold War*, ed. by *New Left Review*. London: Verson Editions and NLR, 1982.

Merton, Thomas. *The Nonviolent Alternative*. Gordon C. Zahn, ed. NY: Farrar, Strauss, Giroux, 1980.

Muste, A.J. *The Essays of A.J. Muste: The Individual Conscience*. Indianapolis, IN: Bobbs-Merrill, 1967.

Robinson, Randall. *Military Research for Arms Reduction*. Washington, DC: TransAfrica, 1983.

Rockman, Jane, ed. *Peace in Search of Makers*. Valley Forge, PA: Judson Press, 1978.

Russell, Bertrand. *The Autobiography of Bertrand Russell*. NY: Simon and Schuster, 1969.

Sakamoto, Yoshikazu and Richard Falk, eds. "A World Demilitarized: A Basic Human Need," *Alternatives* (Winter 1980-81).

Schweitzer, Albert. *Peace or Atomic War*. NY: Holt, 1958.

Sharp, Gene. *Exploring Nonviolent Alternatives*. Boston, MA: Porter Sargent, Publishers, 1970.

Sharp, Gene. *Gandhi as a Political Strategist*. Boston, MA: Porter Sargent Publishers, 1979.

Sharp, Gene. *Making the Abolition of War a Realistic Goal*. NY: World Policy Institute, 1981.

Sharp, Gene. *Making Europe Unconquerable: A Civilian-Based Deterrence and Defense System*. NY: Taylor Francis, 1985.

Sharp, Gene. *The Politics of Non-Violent Action*. Boston, MA: Extending Horizon Books, 1973.

Shere, Waris, ed. *In Search of Peace*. NY: Exposition Press, 1980.

Sibley, Mulford. *The Quiet Battle: Writings on the Theory and Practice of Non-Violent Resistance*. Boston, MA: Extending Horizon Books, 1973.

Stanford, Barbara, ed. *Peacemaking: A Guide to Conflict Resolution for Individuals, Groups, and Nations*. NY: Bantam Books, 1976.

Stephenson, Carolyn M., ed. *Alternative Methods for International Security*. Washington, DC: Univ. Press of America, 1982.

Thompson, E.P. and Daniel Smith, eds. *Protest and Survive*. NY: Monthly Review Press, 1981.

Tolstoy, Leo. *The Kingdom of God and Peace Essays*. Trans. Aylmer Maud. London: Oxford Univ. Press, 1936.

Tolstoy, Leo. *Tolstoy's Writings on Civil Disobedience and Non-Violence*. Atlantic Highlands, NJ: Humanities Press, Inc. 1967.

Tuchman, Barbara. "Is There an Alternative to Arms Control?" *Radcliffe Quarterly*, March, 1983.

Wallis, Jim. *Waging Peace: A Handbook for the Struggle to Abolish Nuclear Weapons*. NY: Harper and Row, 1982.

Wehr, Paul. *Conflict Regulation*. Boulder, CO: Westview Press, 1979.

Zacharias, Jerrold, Myles Gordon and Saville R. Davis. *Common Sense and Nuclear Peace*. Newton, MA: Education Development Center, Inc., 1983. Reprinted in *The Bulletin of the Atomic Scientists*, Vol. 39, No. 4 (April 1983).

D. International Political Economy, Economic Justice and Development

Adelman, Irma. "Development Economics—A Reassessment of Goals," *American Economic Review* 65 (May 1975): 302-309.

Adler-Karlson, Gunnar. "Eliminating Absolute Poverty: An Approach to the Problem," in *Reducing Global Inequities*, Howard Wriggins and Gunnar Adler-Karlson, eds. NY: McGraw Hill, 1978.

Amin, Samir. "Self Reliance and the New International Economic Order," *Monthly Review*, (July/August 1977).

Amin, Samir. *Unequal Development*. NY: Monthly Review Press, 1976.

Amuzegar, Jahangir. "Oil Wealth: A Very Mixed Blessing," *Foreign Affairs* 60 (Spring 1982).

Anderson, Marion. *Bombs or Bread: Black Unemployment and the Pentagon Budget*. Lansing, MI: Employment Research Associates, 1981.

Anderson, Marion. *Converting the Work Force: Where the Jobs Would Be*. Lansing, MI: Employment Research Associates, 1980.

Anderson, Marion. *The Empty Pork Barrel: Unemployment and the Pentagon Budget*. 1982 Edition. Lansing, MI: Employment Research Associates, 1982.

Annell, Lars and Birgitta Nygren. *The Developing Countries and the World Economic Order*. NY: St. Martin's Press, 1980.

Arndt, H.W. "The Trickle Down Myth," *Economic Development and Cultural Change*, 32 (1) (October 1983).

Ashley, Richard K. *The Political Economy of War and Peace: The Sino-Soviet American Triangle and the Modern Security Problematique*. NY: Nicholas Publishing Co., 1980.

Bagchi, Amiya K. *The Political Economy of Development and Underdevelopment*. NY: Random House Inc., 1979.

Baran, Paul. *The Political Economy of Growth*. NY: Monthly Review Press, 1957.

Barnet, Richard J. "The Profits of Hunger," *The Nation*, Vol. 230, No. 5 (Feb. 9, 1980).

Barraclough, Geoffrey. "Wealth and Power: The Politics of Food and Oil," *New York Review of Books*, (August 7, 1975).

Beitz, Charles R. "Economic Rights and Distributive Justice in Developing Societies," *World Politics* 33 (April 1981): 321-46.

Bergsten, C. Fred. *Toward a New International Economic Order*. Lexington, MA: Lexington Books, 1975.

Bhagwati, Jagdish, ed. *Economics and World Order from the 1970's to the 1990's*. NY: MacMillan Inc., 1972.

Bhagwati, Jagdish. *The NIEO: the North-South Debate*. Cambridge, MA: MIT Press, 1977.

Block, Fred. *The Origins of International Economic Disorder*. Los Angeles, CA: Univ. of California Press, 1977.

Bluestone, Barry and Bennett Harrison. *The Deindustrialization of America: Plant Closings, Community Abandonment, and the Dismantling of Basic Industry*. NY: Basic Books, Inc., 1982.

Blumberg, Paul. *Inequality in an Age of Decline*. NY: Oxford Univ. Press, 1980.

Bornschier, Volker. "The World Economy in the World-System: Structure, Dependence and Change," *International Social Science Journal* 34 (1982): 37-59.

The Brandt Commission. *Common Crisis: North-South Cooperation for World Recovery*. London: Pan Books, Ltd., 1983.

Browne, Robert S., Robert J. Cummings. *The Lagos Plan of Action vs. the Berg Report*. The African Studies and Research Program, Howard University, Washington, DC., 1983.

Camps, Miriam. *Collective Management: The Reform of Global Economic Organizations*. NY: McGraw Hill, 1981.

Cardoso, Fernando Henrique and Enzo Faletto. *Dependency and Development in Latin America*. Berkeley, CA: Univ. of California Press, 1979.

Chichilnisky, Graciela. *Basic Needs and the North/South Debate*. Working Paper #21. NY: World Policy Institute, 1982.

Christensen, Cheryl. *The Right To Food: How to Guarantee*. Working Paper #6. NY: World Policy Institute, 1978.

CIDA. *Self-Reliance and Global Interdependence*. Ottawa, 1978.

Clark, Robert P. *Power and Policy in the Third World*. 2nd Edition. NY: John Wiley and Sons, 1982.

Cockcroft, James, et al., eds. *Dependence and Underdevelopment: Latin America's Political Economy*. NY: Anchor Books, 1982.

Davis, Shelton H. *Victims of the Miracle: Development and the Indians of Brazil*. NY: Cambridge Univ. Press, 1977.

Daly, Herman E. *Steady-State Economics: The Economic of Biophysical Equilibrium and Moral Growth*. San Francisco, CA: W.H. Freeman and Co., 1977.

Duller, H.J. *Development Technology*. London: Routledge and Kegan Paul, 1982.

Erb, Guy, Valerina Kallab, eds. *Beyond Dependency: The Developing World Speaks Out*. Washington, DC: Overseas Development Council, 1975.

Foster-Carter, Aidan. "From Rostow to Gunder Frank: Conflicting Paradigms in the Analysis of Underdevelopment," *World Development* 4 (3) (March 1976).

Frank, Andre Gunder. *Crisis in the World Economy and Crisis in the Third World*. NY: Homes and Meier, 1981.

Galtung, Johan. *The North/South Debate: Technology, Basic Human Needs and the New International Economic Order*. Working Paper #12. NY: World Policy Institute, 1980.

Galtung, Johan, Roy Preiswerk, et al., eds. *Self Reliance, A Strategy for Development*. A publication of the Institute for Development Studies, Geneva. London: Bogle-L'Ouverture Pub., 1980.

George, Susan. *How the Other Half Dies: The Real Reasons for World Hunger*. Montclair, NJ: Allenheld-Osmun, 1977.

Gilpin, Robert. *U.S. Power and the Multinational Corporation: The Political Economy of Foreign Direct Investment*. NY: Basic Books, 1975.

Gordon, David M., William Tabbe, et al., eds. *US Capitalism in Crisis*. NY: Union for Radical Political Economics, 1978.

Gran, Guy. *Development by People*. NY: Praeger Pubs., 1983.

Gussow, Joan Dye. *The Feeding Web*. Palo Alto, CA: Bull Pub. Co., 1978.

Hammarskjold Foundation, Dag. *What Now—Another Development*. Uppsala, *Development Dialogue*, 1975.

Harris, Richard. *The Political Economy of Africa*. NY and London: Monthly Review Press, 1975.

Hartman, Betsy, and James Boyce. *Needless Hunger: Voices from a Bangladesh Village*. San Francisco, CA: Institute for Food and Development Policy, 1979.

Hoogvelt, Ankie M.M. *The Third World in Global Development*. London: Macmillan Inc., 1982.

Hopkins, Raymond, et al. *Global Food Interdependence: Challenge to American Foreign Policy*. New York: Columbia Univ. Press, 1980.

International Monetary Fund. *World Economic Outlook*. Washington, DC: International Monetary Fund, 1982.

Kamath, M. V. "A South-South Strategy," *Indian Express*, India, March 21, 1982.

Kratochwil, Friedrich V. "On the Notion of 'Interest' in International Relations," *International Organization* 36 (Winter 1982).

Lappé, Francis Moore. *Diet for a Small Planet*. rev. edition. NY: Ballantine Books, 1975.

Lappé, Francis Moore and Joseph Collins. *Food First*. Boston, MA: Houghton Mifflin Co., 1977.

Lappé, Francis Moore and Joseph Collins, et al. *Aid as a Obstacle*. San Francisco, CA: Institute for Food and Development Policy, 1980.

Marable, Manning. *How Capitalism Underdeveloped Black America*. Boston, MA: South End Press, 1983.

Mathieson, John A. *Basic Needs and the New International Economic Order: An Opening for North/South Collaboration in the 1980's*. Working Paper #14. Washington, DC: Overseas Development Council, 1981.

Melman, Seymour. *Pentagon Capitalism: The Political Economy of War*. NY: McGraw Hill, 1970.

Morehouse, Ward. *Separate, Unequal, But More Autonomous: Technology, Equity, and World Order in the Millenial Transition*. World Order Models Project, Working Paper #16. NY: World Policy Institute, 1981.

Myrdal, Gunnar. *A World Anti-Poverty Program in Outline*. NY: Pantheon, 1970.

Nerfin, Marc, ed. *Another Development*. Uppsala, Sweden: Hammarskjold Foundation, 1977.

North-South: A Program for Survival. Report of the International Commission on International Development Issues. Cambridge, MA: MIT Press, 1980.

Paalberg, Robert. "A Food Security Approach for the 1980's: Righting the Balance," in *US Foreign Policy and the Third World: Agenda 1982*. NY: Praeger. Published for the Overseas Development Council, 1982.

Perkins, Edwin J. *The World Economy in the Twentieth Century*. Cambridge, MA: Schenkman, 1982.

Pierre, Andrew J. *The Global Politics of Arms Sales*. Princeton, NJ: Princeton Univ. Press, 1981.

Organization for Economic Cooperation and Development. *Development Cooperation: 1982 Review*. Paris, 1983.

Organization for Economic Cooperation and Development. *World Economic Interdependence and The Evolving North-South Relationship*. Paris, 1983.

Reich, Robert B. *The Next American Frontier*. NY: New York Times Books, 1983.

Ruggie, John Gerard, ed. *The Antinomies of Interdependence*. NY: Columbia Univ. Press, 1983.

Sandbrook, Richard. *The Politics of Basic Needs: Urban Aspects of Assaulting Poverty in Africa*. Toronto: Univ. of Toronto Press, 1982.

Schumacher, E.F. *Small is Beautiful*. NY: Harper and Row, 1979.

Sen, Amartya. *Poverty and Famines: An Essay on Entitlement and Deprivation*. NY: Oxford Univ. Press, 1982.

Sinha, Radha. *Food and Poverty—the Political Economy of Confrontation*. NY: Holmes and Meier, 1976.

Sommer, John. *Beyond Charity: US Voluntary Aid for a Changing Third World*. Washington, DC: Overseas Development Council, 1977.

Stevens, Charles J. *Confronting the World Food Crisis*. Occasional Paper #27. Muscatine, Iowa: The Stanley Foundation, 1981.

Stohl, Michael and Harry R. Targ. *Global Political Economy in the 1980's: The Impact on the New International Economic Crisis*. Cambridge, MA: Schenkman, 1982.

Streeten, Paul, et al. *First Things First: Meeting Basic Human Needs in Developing Countries*. A World Bank Publication. NY: Oxford Univ. Press, 1981.

Wilbur, Charles K. *The Political Economy of Development and Underdevelopment*. NY: Random House Inc., 1979.

ul Haq, Mahbub. "Negotiating the Future," *Foreign Affairs* (Winter 1980/81).

UNCTAD. *Arusha Programme for Collective Self-Reliance & Framework for Negotiations*. Manila: May 1979, Fifth Session, May 7, UN document TD/236, 2/28/79.

United Nations. "The Relationship Between Disarmament and Development: A Summary," Fact Sheet No. 21. NY: United Nations, 1982.

Valentine, William and Frances Moore Lappé. *What Can We Do? Food and Hunger: How You Can Make a Difference*. San Francisco, CA: Institute for Food and Development Policy, 1980.

Wallerstein, Immanuel. *The Capitalist World-Economy*. NY: Cambridge Univ. Press, 1979.

Weerakoon, A.C.J. "Development for Whom?" *Sunday Observer*, Colombo, Sri Lanka, December 1980.

Weisskopf, Thomas E. "Capitalism, Underdevelopment, and the Future of the Poor Countries," in *Economics and World Order: from the 1970's to the 1990's*, J. Bhagwati, ed. NY: Macmillan Inc., 1972.

Weisskopf, Thomas E. "The Current Economic Crisis in Historical Perspective," *Socialist Review*, (May-June, 1981) 11:3.

World Bank. *World Development Report 1983*. NY: Oxford Univ. Press, 1983.

E. Human Rights

Amnesty International Report 1983. London: Amnesty International Publications, 1983.

Arnold, Millard, ed. *Steve Biko*. NY: Random House Inc., 1978.

Biko, Steve. "Black Consciousness and the Quest for a True Humanity," In *I Write What I Like*. NY: Harper and Row, 1978.

Brownlie, Ian, ed. *Basic Documents on Human Rights*. 2nd Edition. NY: Oxford Univ. Press, 1981.

Bossong, Ken and Scott Denman. *Nuclear Powers and Civil Liberties: Can We Have Both?* 2nd Edition. Citizens Energy, 1981.

Charny, Israel. *How Can We Commit the Unthinkable: Genocide: The Human Cancer*. Boulder, CO: Westview Press, 1982.

Chomsky, Noam and Edward S. Herman. *The Political Economy of Human Rights. Vol. I: The Washington Connection and Third World Fascism*; Vol. II: *After the Cataclysm: Postwar Indochina and the Reconstruction of Imperial Ideology*. Boston, MA: South End Press, 1979.

Dominquez, Jorge I., et al., *Enhancing Global Human Rights*. NY: McGraw Hill, 1979.

Donnelly, Jack. "Human Rights and Human Dignity: An Analytic Critique of Non-Western Conceptions of Human Rights," *American Political Science Review* 76 (June 1982).

Dworkin, Ronald. *Taking Rights Seriously*. Cambridge, MA: Harvard Univ. Press, 1978.

Falk, Richard. *Human Rights and State Sovereignty*. NY: Holmes and Meier, 1982.

Fanon, Frantz. *The Wretched of the Earth*. NY: Grove Press, 1968.

Feinberg, Joel. *Rights, Justice and the Bounds of Liberty*. Princeton, NJ: Princeton Univ. Press, 1980.

Goldstein, Robert Justin. *Political Repression in Modern America*. Cambridge, MA: Schenkman, 1978.

Gross, Bertram. *Friendly Facism: The New Face of Power in America*. Boston, MA: South End Press, 1983.

Herman, Edward. *The Real Terror Network*. Boston, MA: South End Press, 1982.

Hertzberg, Sanra. *The Protection of Human Rights in the Criminal Process Under International Instruments and National Constitutions*. Eres, 1981.

Hopkins, Raymond F. "Food as a Global Issue," in *Food in the Global Arena*. James E. Harf and B. Thomas Trout, eds. NY: Holt, Rinehart and Winston, 1982.

"Human Rights and United States Policy in Central America." Transcript of Stanford University Symposium, Jan. 13, 1983. Stanford, CA: Stanford Central American Action Network, 1983.

"Human Rights: Women's Rights and Development." Proceedings of the Ad Hoc Group For Equal Rights For Women, Vienna International Centre, March 8, 1982.

Jacobsen, Harold K. "The Global System and the Realization of Human Dignity and Justice," *International Studies Quarterly* 26 (Sept. 1982).

Johansen, Robert C. "Human Rights in the 1980's: Revolutionary Growth or Unanticipated Erosion?" *World Politics* 35 (2) (Jan. 1983).

Kamenka, Eugene and Alice Ehr-Soon Tay, eds. *Human Rights*. NY: St. Martin's Press, 1978.

Moore, Barrington, Jr. *Reflections on the Causes of Human Misery and Upon Certain Proposals to Eliminate Them*. Boston, MA: Beacon Press, 1972.

Moore, Barrington, Jr. *Injustice: The Social Bases of Obedience and Revolt*. White Plains, NY: M.E. Sharpe, 1978.

Nanda, Ved P., James R. Scarritt, and George W. Shepherd Jr., eds. *Global Human Rights: Public Policies, Comparative Measures, and NGO Strategies*. Boulder, CO: Westview Press, 1981.

Neilser, Neils C. *The Crisis of Human Rights: An American Christian Perspective*. Nashville, TN, 1978.

Nelson, Jack. *Hunger for Justice: The Politics of Food and Faith*. Maryknoll, NY: Orbis Books, 1980.

Newberg, Paul R., ed. *The Politics of Human Rights*. NY: New York Univ. Press, 1980.

NOMOS XXIII and XXIV: *Human Rights*. NY: New York Univ. Press, 1981.

Parenti, Michael. *Democracy for the Few*. 4th Edition. NY: St. Martin's Press, 1983.

Randle, Michael. "Militarism and Repression," *Alternatives* Vol. VII, No. 1 (Summer 1981).

Rawls, John. *A Theory of Justice*. Cambridge, MA: Harvard Univ. Press, 1971.

Shue, Henry. *Basic Rights: Subsistence, Affluences and US Foreign Policy*. Princeton, NJ: Princeton Univ. Press, 1980.

Solzhenitsyn, Aleksandr I. *The Gulag Archipelago*. Three volumes. Trans. Thomas P. Whitney. NY: Harper and Row, 1974-78.

Vasek, Karel. *The International Dimensions of Human Rights. Vol. I and II*. Westport, CT: Greenwood Press, 1982.

F. Ecological Balance

Allen, Robert. *How to Save the World: Strategy for World Conservation*. Totowa, NJ: Littlefield, Adams and Co., 1981.

Anderson, Marion. *American Jobs From Alcohol Fuel*. Lansing, MI: Employment Research Associates, 1981.

Barkenbus, J. "The Politics of Ocean Resource Exploitation," *International Studies Quarterly*, Vol. 21, 34 (1977).

Barnet, Richard J.. *Lean Years: Politics in the Age of Scarcity*. NY: Simon and Schuster, 1980.

Bensen, David W. and Arnold H. Sparrow, eds. *Survival of Food Crops and Livestock in the Event of Nuclear War*. Washington, DC: US Atomic Energy Commission, 1971.

Brown, Lester R. *Building a Sustainable Society*. NY: W.W. Norton and Co., 1981.

Carson, Rachael. *Silent Spring*. Boston, MA: Houghton Mifflin, 1962.

Clark, Wilson and Jake Page. *Energy, Vulnerability, and War: Alternatives for America*. NY: W.W. Norton and Co., 1981.

Commoner, Barry. *The Closing Circle: Nature, Man and Technology*. 2nd Edition. NY: Bantam Books, 1974.

DeSilva, Res. "The Battle for the Ocean's Riches," *Sun*, Colombo, Sri Lanka, December 12, 1982.

Deudney, Daniel. *Renewable Energy: The Power to Choose*. NY: W.W. Norton and Co., 1983.

Eckholm, Erik. *Down to Earth: Environment and Human Needs*. NY: W.W. Norton and Co., 1982.

Ehrlich, Paul R., and Anne H. *Population, Resources, Environment: Essays in Human Ecology*. San Francisco, CA: W.H. Freeman, 1970.

El-Hinnawi, Essam E., ed. *Nuclear Energy and the Environment*. NY: Pergamon Press, 1980.

Enloe, Cynthia H. *The Politics of Pollution in a Comparative Perspecive*. NY: David McKay, 1975.

Environment and Health. Washington, DC: Congressional Quarterly, Inc., 1981

Flowers, Sir Brian, Chairman. *Nuclear Power and the Environment*, Sixth Report of the Royal Commission of Environmental Pollution. London: Her Majesty's Stationery Office, September 1976, p. 76.

Falk, Richard. *This Endangered Planet*. NY: Vantage Books, 1972.

Galtung, Johan. *Environment, Development and Military Activity: Towards Alternative Security Doctrines*. NY: Columbia Univ. Press, 1984.

Gilinsky, Victor. "Plutonium, Proliferation, and Policy," *Technology Review*, (February, 1977): 58-65.

Goldberg, Edward D. *The Health of the Oceans*. Paris: UNESCO, 1976.

Gorz, Andre. *Ecology as Politics*. Boston, MA: South End Press, 1980.

Hardin, Garrett and John Baden, eds. *Managing the Commons*. San Francisco, CA: W.H. Freeman, 1977.

Holgate, Martin, Mohamed Kassas and Gilbert White. "World Environment Trends between 1972 and 1982," in *Environmental Conservation*, Spring issue, 1983.

Hveem, H. "Militarization of Nature: Conflict and Control Over Strategic Resources and Some Implications for Peace Research," *Journal of Peace Research* Vol. XXI, No. 1 (1979).

Keeny, Spurgeon M., Seymour Abrahamson, et al. *Nuclear Power Issues and Choices*, Report of the Nuclear Energy Policy Study Group of the Ford Foundation. Cambridge, MA: Ballinger, 1977.

Kelly, Brian and Mark London. *Amazon*. San Diego, CA: Harcourt, Brace, Jovanovich, 1983.

Kothari, Rajni. *Environment and Alternative Development*. Working Paper #15. NY: World Policy Institute, 1981.

Long-Term Worldwide Effects of Multiple Nuclear Weapons Detonations Washington, DC: National Academy of Sciences, 1975.

Lovins, Amory B. and L. Hunter. *Energy/War: Breaking the Nuclear Link*. Harper Colophon Books, 1980.

Marx, Wesley. *The Oceans: Our Last Resource*. San Francisco, CA: Sierra Club Books, 1981.

Meadows, Donelle H., et al. *The Limits to Growth*. NY: Signet Books, 1972.

Orr, David W. and Martin S. Soroos, eds. *The Global Predicament: Ecological Perspectives on World Order*. Chapel Hill: Univ. of North Carolina Press, 1979.

Pirages, Dennis, ed. *The Sustainable Society*. NY: Praeger Pubs., 1977.

Regenstein, Lewis. *America The Poisoned: How Deadly Chemicals are Destroying our Environment, Our Wildlife and Ourselves, and How We Can Survive!* Washington, DC: Acropolis Books, 1983.

Sale, Kirkpatrick. *Human Scale*. NY: Perigee Books, Putnam's Sons, 1980.

Schachter, Oscar. "International Equity and Its Dilemmas," in *Sharing the World's Resources*. NY: Columbia Univ. Press, 1977.

Shrader-Frechette, K.S. *Environmental Ethics*. Pacific Grove, CA: Boxwood Press, 1983.

Sivard, Ruth Leger. *World Energy Survey*. Washington, DC: World Priorities Inc., 1983.

United Nations. *Review of Major Achievements in the Implementation of the Action Plan for the Human Environment*. Report of the Executive Director. UNDOC UNEP/GC(SCC)/INF.1 (26 Jan., 1982).

United Nations. *The State of the World Environment 1972-82*. Report of the Executive Director. UNDOC UNEP/GC.10/3 (29 Jan., 1982)

. United Nations. *World Conservation Strategy: Living Resource Conservation for Sustainable Development*. NY: UNIPUB, 1980.

Weapons of Mass Destruction and the Environment. Stockholm International Peace Research Institute. London: Taylor & Francis, 1977.

Weir, David and Mark Schapiro. *Circle of Poison: Pesticides and People in a Hungry World*. San Francisco, CA: Institute for Food and Development Policy, 1981.

White, L. Jr. "The Historical Roots of Our Ecologic Crisis," *Science* (March 10, 1967) Vol. 155, No. 3767.

G. Culture, Community, Values and Change

Beres, Louis Rene. *People, States and World Order*. Itasca, IL: F.E. Peacock, 1981.

Berrigan, Daniel and Robert Coles. "Youth, Problems and Dissent," in *The Geography of Faith*. Boston, MA: Beacon Press, 1971.

Brown, Claude. *Manchild in the Promised Land*. NY: Macmillan, 1965.

Dewey, John. *Individualism: Old and New*. NY: G.P. Putnam's Sons, 1929.

Earth's Answers, Explorations of Planetary Culture at the Lindisfarne Conferences. NY: Harper and Row, 1977.

Elgin, Duane. *Voluntary Simplicity: Toward a Way of Life That is Outwardly Simple, Inwardly Rich*. NY: William Morrow Co., 1981.

Frank, Jerome D. *Sanity & Survival in the Nuclear Age: Psychological Aspects of War and Peace*. Reissue of the 1968 work. NY: Vintage Books, 1968.

Fromm, Erich. *To Have or To Be?* NY: Harper and Row, 1976.

Hall, Edward. *Beyond Culture*. Garden City, NY: Doubleday Anchor Books, 1977.

Harrington, Michael. *The Twilight of Capitalism*. NY: Simon and Schuster, 1976.

Huxley, Aldous. *Ends and Means: An Inquiry Into the Nature of Ideals and Into Methods Employed for Their Regulation*. NY: Greenwood Press, 1969.

Huxley, Aldous. *Island*. NY: Harper and Row, 1962.

Jung, Carl Gustav. *The Undiscovered Self*. Boston, MA: Little, Brown, 1958.

Keyes, Ken. *The Hundredth Monkey*. St. Mary, KY: Vision Books, 1982.

Lifton, Robert J., "Beyond Psychic Numbing: A Call to Awareness," *American Journal of Orthopsychiatry* Vol. 52, No. 4 (Oct. 1982).

Mazrui, Ali A. *The Moving Cultural Frontier of World Order: From Monotheism to North/South Relations*. Working Paper #18. NY: World Policy Institute, 1982.

McLuhan, T.C., ed. *Touch the Earth: A Self-Portrait of Indian Existence*. NY: Simon and Schuster, 1971.

Mead, Margaret. *Culture and Commitment*. Garden City, NY: Natural History Press, 1979.

Pirsig, Robert M. *Zen and the Art of Motorcycle Maintenance: An Inquiry Into Values*. NY: Bantam Books, 1974.

Roszak, Theodore. *Person/Planet: The Creative Disintegration of Industrial Society*. NY: Anchor, 1979.

Said, Edward W. *Orientalism*. NY: Vintage Books, 1978.

Slater, Philip. *Earthwalk*. Garden City, NY: Anchor Press/Doubleday, 1974.

Slater, Philip. *The Pursuit of Loneliness: American Culture at the Breaking Point*. Boston, MA: Beacon Press, 1970.

Thompson, William Irwin. *The Time Falling Bodies Take to Light: Mythology, Sexuality, and the Origins of Culture*. NY: St. Martin's Press, 1981.

Turnbull, Colin. *The Human Cycle*. NY: Simon and Schuster, 1983.

Walker, R.B.J. *World Politics and Western Reason: Universalism, Pluralism, Hegemony*. Working Paper #19. NY: World Policy Institute, 1982.

H. World Order Education

Adams, F. *Unearthing Seeds of Fire: The Idea of Highlander*. Winston-Salem, NC, 1975.

Becker, J., ed. *Schooling for a Global Age*. NY: McGraw Hill, 1979.

Botkin, James W., Mahdi Elmandjra, and Mirecea Malitza. *No Limits to Learning: Bridging the Human Gap*. NY: Pergamon Press, 1979.

Boulding, Elise. "Learning About the Future," *Bulletin of Peace Proposals* 12 (May 1981): 172-177.

Boyer, William. "World Order Education: What Is It?" *Phi Delta Kappan* (April 1975).

Branson, Margaret and Judith Torney-Puria. *International Human Rights, Society and the Schools*. Washington, DC: National Council for the Social Studies, 1982.

Buergenthal, Thomas and Judith Torney. *International Human Rights and International Education*. NY: US National Commission for UNESCO, 1976.

Burns, Robin. *Development Education and Peace Education: From Conflict to Cooperation*. United Nations Development Education Paper No. 22. UNICEF, 1981.

Butwell, Richard. "Why Don't Americans Study Anyone Else?" *The Christian Science Monitor* (May 28, 1980).

Deutsch, Morton. "Conflict Resolution: Theory and Practice." Inaugural lecture as Edward Lee Thorndike Professor of Psychology and Education, Teachers College, Columbia Univ. (April 22, 1982).

Education for Responsible Citizenship. The Report of the National Task Force on Citizenship Education. NY: McGraw Hill, 1977.

Elements of a Network to Educate for World Security. NY: World Policy Institute, 1981.

Falk, Richard and Samuel S. Kim. *An Approach to World Order Studies and the World System*. Working Paper #22. NY: World Policy Institute, 1982.

Food First College Curriculum Guide. San Francisco, CA: Institute for Food and Development Policy, 1984.

Freire, Paulo. *Pedagogy in Process*. NY: Seabury Press, 1978.

Freire, Paulo. *Pedagogy of the Oppressed*. NY: Continuum Publishing Corporation, 1981.

Freire, Paulo. *Education for Critical Consciousness*. NY: Seabury Press, 1973.

Greene, Maxine. *Teacher As a Stranger: Educational Philosophy for the Modern Age*. Belmont, CA: Wadsworth Pubs., 1973.

Greene, Maxine. *Landscapes of Learning*. NY: Teachers College Press, 1978.

Haavelsrud, Magnus. *Approaching Disarmament Education*. Woburn, MA: Butterworth Pubs., 1981.

Harari, M. *Internationalizing the Curriculum and the Campus*. Washington, DC: American Associates of State Colleges and Universities, 1981.

Hayden, Rose Lee. "The World and You: Global Education is the Answer," *International Brief Series* No. 6 (1979), Washington, DC: Town Affiliation Association of the US.

Marshaka, Robert E. "The Global Mission of American Higher Education," *The Key Reporter*, Vol. XLVIII, No. 1 (Autumn 1982).

McGinnis, James B. *Bread and Justice*. NY: Paulist Press, 1979.

"Militarism and Education—Racism, Sexism and Militarism: The Links," *Interracial Books for Children Bulletin*, Vol. 13, Nos. 6 and 7. (1982).

Murray, Andrew M. *Peace and Conflict Studies as Applied Liberal Arts: A Theoretical Framework for Curriculum Development*. Huntington, PA: Juniata College, 1980.

National Task Force on Education and the World View. New Rochelle, NY: Council on Learning, 1981.

"Nuclear Disarmament Before It's Too Late," *Radcliffe Quarterly* (March, 1983).

"Nuclear War Education," *Journal of College Science Teaching*, State Univ. of New York, Stony Brook (April 1983).

"Peace and Justice Education," *Current Issues in Catholic Higher Education*, Association of Catholic Colleges and Universities, Vol. I, No. 2 (Winter, 1981).

"Peace Studies," *The Forum for Liberal Education*, Vol. V., No. 4 (March, 1983).

"Peace Studies," *Radical Teacher*, issue #26 (Spring 1984).

Peace and World Order Studies: A Curriculum Guide. 3rd Edition. NY: World Policy Institute, 1981.

Reardon, Betty. *Militarization, Security and Peace Education: A Guide for Concerned Citizens*. NY: United Ministries in Education, 1982.

Riemer, Neal. *Political Science: An Introduction to Politics*. NY: Harcourt, Brace, Jovanovich, 1983.

Rifkin, Jeremy. *Entropy: A New World View*. NY: The Viking Press, 1980.

Saxon, David S. "A Role for Universities in Ending the Arms Race," *The Chronicle of Higher Education* (July 6, 1981).

Shor, Ira. *Critical Teaching and Everyday Life*. Boston, MA: South End, 1980.

Simmons, Adele Smith. "Colleges Must Speak Out on War and Peace," *The Chronicle of Higher Education* (June 23, 1982).

Simmons, John, ed. *The Education Dilemma: Policy Issues for Developing Countries in the 1980's*. NY: Pergamon Press, 1980.

Sloan, Douglas, ed. *Education for Peace and Disarmament: Toward a Living World*. NY: Teachers College Press, 1984.

Taylor, Harold. *The World as Teacher*. Garden City, NY: Doubleday, 1969.

Thomas, Barb. *Working with Teachers Against Racism*. Ontario, Canada: Cross-Cultural Communication Centre, 1983.

Vandenberg, Donald. *Human Rights in Education*. NY: Philosophical Library, 1983.

Weston, Burns. "Contending With a Planet in Peril and Change: An Optimal Educational Response," *Alternatives* Vol. V, No. 1 (June 1979).

Wolf-Wasserman, Miriam and Linda Hutchinson. *Teaching Human Dignity*. Minneapolis, MI: Education Exploration Center, 1978.

Wren, Brian. *Education for Justice*. Maryknoll, NY: Orbis Books, 1977.

I. Women and World Order

Anderson, Marion. *Neither Jobs Nor Security: Women's Unemployment and the Pentagon Budget*. Lansing, MI: Employment Research Associates, 1982.

Berkin, Carol R. and Clara Lovett, eds. *Women, War and Revolution*. NY: Holmes and Meier, 1980.

Bethel, Lorraine and Barbara Smith, eds. *Conditions 5: The Black Women's Issue* (Autumn 1979).

de Beauvoir, Simone. *The Second Sex*. NY: Vintage Books, 1974.

"Economic Development and the Sexual Division of Labor," *Signs* 7 (2), 1981.

Boulding, Elise. *The Underside of History*. Boulder, CO: Westview Press, 1976.

Boulding, Elise. *Women in the Twentieth Century World*. NY: Halstead Press, 1977.

Blumberg, R.L. *Stratification: Socioeconomic and Sexual Inequality*. Dubuque, IA: William Brown, 1978.

Brock-Utne, Birgit. "The Role of Women as Mothers and as Members of Society in the Education of Young People for Peace and Mutual Understanding," PRIO Publications S-12/81.

Burns, Robin. "Development, Disarmament and Women: Some New Connections," *Social Alternative* 2 (5) (1982).

Buvinic, Mayra and Margaret Lycette. *Women and Poverty in the Third World*. Baltimore, MD: Johns Hopkins, 1982.

Chapkis, W., ed. *Loaded Questions: Women in the Military*. Washington, DC: Institute for Policy Studies, 1982.

Davis, Angela. *Women, Race and Class*. NY: Random House, 1981.

Ehrenreich, B. and A. Fuentes. "Life on the Global Assembly Line," *Ms.* 9 (7): 52-59, 71.

Elshtain, J.B. "Women, War and Feminism," *Nation* 230: 705, June 14, 1980.

Etienne, Mona and Eleanor Leacock, eds. *Women and Colonization: Anthropological Perspectives*. NY: Praeger Pubs., 1980.

Feminism: The Hope for the Future. Cambridge, MA: American Friends Service Committee, 1981.

Flexner, Eleanor. *Century of Struggle: The Women's Rights Movement in the United States*. rev. edition. Cambridge, MA: Harvard Univ. Press, 1975.

Gelpi, Barbara C. "Special Issue: Development and the Sexual Division of Labor," *Signs*, Vol. 7, No. 2 (1981).

Gornick, Vivian. *Essays in Feminism*. NY: Harper and Row, 1978.

Hooks, Bell. *Ain't I a Woman*. Boston, MA: South End Press, 1981.

Hull, Gloria, Patricia Bell Scott and Barbara Smith. *All the Women are White, All the Blacks are Men, but Some of Us are Brave: Black Women's Studies*. Old Westbury, NY: The Feminist Press, 1981.

Huston, Perdita. *Third World Women Speak Out*. Published in cooperation with the Overseas Development Council. NY: Praeger Pubs., 1979.

Johansen, Ruthann Knechel. *Coming Together: Male and Female in a Renamed Garden*. Elgen, IL: The Brethren Press, 1977.

Jones, Lynne, ed. *Keeping the Peace: A Woman's Peace Handbook*. London: The Woman's Press, 1983.

Joseph, Gloria. "The Incompatible Menage a Trois: Marxism, Feminism and Racism," in *Women and Revolution*, L. Sargent, ed. Boston, MA: South End Press, 1981.

Joseph, Gloria and Jill Lewis. *Common Differences: Conflicts in Black and White Feminist Perspectives*. Garden City, NY: Anchor Press, 1983.

Koedit, Ann, et al., eds. *Radical Feminism*. NY: Quandrangle, 1973.

Keely, Gail P. and Carolyn Elliot. *Women's Education in the Third World: Comparative Perspectives*. NY: State Univ. of NY Pub., 1982.

Latin American and Caribbean Women's Collective. *Slaves of Slaves: The Challenge of Latin American Women*. London, 1980.

Leghorn, L. and K. Parker. *Women's Worth: Sexual Economics and the World of Women*. Boston: Routledge & Kegan Paul, 1981.

Lindsay, Beverly, ed. *Comparative Perspectives of 3rd World Women: The Impact of Race, Class and Sex*. NY: Praeger Pubs., 1980.

Lipman-Blueman, Jean and Jesse Bernard. *Sex Roles and Social Policy*. Beverly Hills, CA: Sage Pub., 1979.

McAllister, Pam. *Reweaving the Web of Life: Feminism and Nonviolence*. Philadelphia, PA: New Society Pub., 1982.

Mische, Patricia. *Women and World Order*. Whole Earth Papers. East Orange, NJ: Global Education Associates, 1978.

Morage, Cherrie and Gloria Anzaldua. *This Bridge Called My Back: Writings by Women of Color*. Watertown, MA: Persephone Press, 1981.

Omvedt, Gail. *We Will Smash This Prison! Indian Women in Struggle*. London: Zed Press, 1980.

Reardon, Betty. *Sexism and the War System*. NY: Teachers College Press, 1985.

Reiter, Rayna R., ed. *Toward an Anthropology of Women*. NY: Monthly Review Press, 1975.

Rowbotham, Sheila. *Woman's Consciousness, Man's World*. NY: Pelican Books, 1973.

Rogers, Barbara. *Domestication of Women: Discrimination in Developing Societies*. NY: Methuem, Inc., 1981.

Rubinson, Richard. "Production and Reproduction of Everyday Life," *Dynamics of World Development*, SAGE Publications, Vol. 4 (1981).

Saadawi, Nawal. *The Hidden Face of Eve*. Boston: Beacon Press, 1982.

Spivak, Gayatri. "French Feminism in an International Frame," *Yale French Studies* #62 (1981).

Strange, Heather. *Rural Malay Women in Tradition and Transitions*. NY: Praeger Pubs., 1981.

Tabari, Azar and Nahid Yeganeh. *In the Shadow of Islam: The Women's Movement in Iran*. London: Zed Press, 1982.

Tinker, Irene and Michele Bo Bramsen. *Women and World Development*. Washington, DC: Overseas Development Council, 1976.

Touris, Carol and Carole Offin. *The Longest War: Sex Differences in Perspective*. NY: Harcourt Brace Jovanovich, 1977.

Woolf, Virginia. *Three Guineas*. NY: Harcourt Brace and World, 1938.

J. War, Militarism, the Arms Race and Disarmament

Acimovic, L.J. *Problems of Security and Cooperation in Europe*. Germantown, PA: Sijthoff and Noordhoff International Pubs., 1981.

Adams, Gordon, et al. *Controlling Weapons Costs: Can the Pentagon Reforms Work?* NY: Council on Economic Priorities, 1983.

Adams, Gordon. *The Iron Triangle: The Politics of Defense Contracting*. NY: Council on Economic Priorities, 1981.

Aldridge, Robert C. *The Counterforce Syndrome*. Washington, DC: Institute for Policy Studies, 1979.

Arkin, William M. *Research Guide to Current Military and Strategic Affairs*. Washington, DC: Institute for Policy Studies, 1981.

Barnaby, Frank. "The Mounting Prospects for Nuclear War," *Bulletin of Atomic Scientists* 33 (June 1977): 10-19.

Barnet, Richard. "The Illusion of Security," *Foreign Affairs* No. 3 (Summer 1971).

Barnet, Richard. *Real Security*. NY: Simon and Schuster, 1981.

Barnet, Richard. *The Roots of War: The Men and the Institutions Behind U.S. Foreign Policy*. Baltimore, MD: Penguin, 1971.

Beres, Louis Rene. *Apocalypse: Nuclear Catastrophe in World Politics*. Chicago, IL: Univ. of Chicago Press, 1980.

Beres, Louis Rene. *Nuclear Strategy and World Order: The US Imperative*. Working Paper #23. NY: World Policy Institute, 1982.

Beres, Louis Rene. *Mimicking Sisyphus: America's Countervailing Nuclear Strategy*. Lexington, MA: Lexingon Books, 1983.

Bertram, Christopher. "Arms Control and Technological Change," in *Armaments, Arms Control and Disarmament*, Marek Thee, ed. Paris: The UNESCO Press, 1981.

Blechman, Barry M., ed. *Rethinking the US Strategic Posture*. Cambridge, MA: Ballinger Pub. Co., 1982.

Bundy, McGeorge, George F. Kennan, et al. "Nuclear Weapons and the Atlantic Alliance," *Foreign Affairs*, Vol. 60, No. 4 (Spring 1982).

Buteaux, Paul. *Strategy, Doctrine and the Politics of Alliance: Theatre Nuclear Force Modernization in NATO*. Boulder, CO: Westview Press, 1983.

Caldicott, Helen. *Nuclear Madness*. Brookline, MA: Autumn Press, 1979.

Clarke, Duncan L. and Hans G. Brauch. *Decision-Making for Arms Limitations in the 1980's: Assessments and Prospects*. Cambridge, MA: Ballinger Pub., 1982.

Clemens, Walter C., Jr. *National Security and U.S. Soviet Relations*. Rev. edition. The Stanley Foundation, Occasional Paper 26, 1982.

Crable, Cecil V. Jr. *American Foreign Policy in the Nuclear Age*. 4th edition. NY: Harper and Row, 1982.

Cunningham, Ann Marie and Mariana Fitzpatrick. *Future Fire: How the New Technology is Leading Us to War*. NY: Warner Communications, 1983.

The Death of Deterrence. Amherst, MA: Deterrence Study Project, 1984.

DeGrasse, Robert Jr. *The Costs and Consequences of Reagan's Military Buildup*. NY: The Council on Economic Priorities, 1982.

Dumas, Lloyd, ed. *The Political Economy of Arms Reduction: Reversing Economic Decay*. Boulder, CO: Westview Press, 1982.

Dunn, Lewis A. *Controlling the Bomb: Nuclear Proliferation in the 1980's*. Hartford, CT: Yale Univ. Press, 1982.

Epstein, William & Lucy Webster, eds. *We Can Avert a Nuclear War*. Cambridge, MA: Oelgeschlager, Gunn & Hain Pubs., 1983.

Falk, Richard. *Normative Initiatives and Demilitarization: A Third System Approach*. Working Paper #13. NY: World Policy Institute, 1982.

Falk, Richard. "Nuclear Weapons and the End of Democracy," *Praxis International* Vol. 2, No. 1 (April 1982).

Ford, Daniel, et al, eds. *Beyond the Freeze: The Road to Nuclear Sanity*. Cambridge, MA: The Union of Concerned Scientists, 1982.

Forsberg, Randall. "A Bilateral Nuclear-Weapon Freeze," *Scientific American*, Vol. 247, No. 5 (Nov. 1982).

Forsberg, Randall. *Seeds of Promise: The First Real Hearings on the Nuclear Arms Freeze*. Andover, MA: Brick House Pub. Co., 1983.

Gaddis, John L. *Strategies of Containment: A Critical Appraisal of Postwar American National Security Policy*. NY: Oxford Univ. Press, 1982.

Goldblat, Josef. *Agreements for Arms Control: A Critical Survey*. London: Taylor and Francis Ltd., 1982.

Goldman, Ralph M. *Arms Control and Peacekeeping*. NY: Random House, 1982.

Ground Zero. *Nuclear War: What's In It For You*. NY: Pocket Books, 1982.

Hoffman, Stanley. *Primacy or World Order: American Foreign Policy Since the Cold War*. NY: McGraw-Hill Book Co., 1978.

Ireland, Timothy P. *Creating the Entangling Alliance: The Origins of the North Atlantic Treaty Organization*. Westport, CT: Greenwood Press, 1981.

Irwin, Bob and Beverly Woodward. *US Defense Policy: Mainstream Views and Non-violent Alternatives*. Waltham, MA: International Seminars on Training for Non-Violent Action, 1982.

Jasani, Bhupendri and Stockholm International Peace Research, eds. *Outer Space: A New Dimension of the Arms Race*. England: Oelgeschlager, 1982.

Johansen, Robert C. "How to START," *World Policy Journal*, Vol. I, No. 1. NY: World Policy Institute, 1983.

Johansen, Robert C. *Toward An Alternative Security System: Moving Beyond the Balance of Power in the Search for World Security*. World Policy Paper #24. NY: World Policy Institute, 1983.

Kaldor, Mary. *The Baroque Arsenal*. NY: Hill and Wang, 1981.

Kaldor, Mary. *The Disintegrating West*. NY: Hill and Wang, 1978.

Kaplan, Fred M. *Dubious Specter: A Skeptical Look at the Soviet Nuclear Threat*. Washington, DC: Institute for Policy Studies, 1977.

Kaplan, Fred. *The Wizards of Armageddon*. NY: Simon and Schuster, 1983.

Kennan, George. *The Nuclear Delusion*. NY: Pantheon Books, 1982.

Kennan, George. *Two Views of the Soviet Problem*," *The New Yorker*, Vol. 57, No. 37 (2 Nov., 1981).

Kidron, Michael and Dan Smith. *The War Atlas: Armed Conflict—Armed Peace*. NY: Simon and Schuster, 1983.

King, J.K., ed. *International Political Effects of the Spread of Nuclear Weapons*. Washington, DC: US Government Printing Office, April 1979.

Kistiakowsky, George B. "False Alarm: The Story Behind SALT II," *New York Review of Books*, 1979, 26, 4: 33-38.

Lifton, Robert J. *Death in Life: Survivors of Hiroshima*. NY: Basic Books, 1982.

Lifton, Robert Jay, and Richard Falk. *Indefensible Weapons: The Political and Psychological Case Against Nuclearism*. NY: Basic Books, 1982.

Markey, Edward. *Nuclear Peril: The Politics of Proliferation*. Cambridge, MA: Ballinger Pub. Co., 1982.

Melman, Seymour. *The Permanent War Economy: American Capitalism in Decline*. NY: Simon and Schuster, 1974.

Myrdal, Alva. *The Game of Disarmament*, rev. and updated. NY: Pantheon Books, 1982.

Owen, Henry. "Peace or War," *Setting National Priorities: The Next Ten Years*. Washington, DC: Brookings, 1976.

Pierre, Andrew J. *The Global Politics of Arms Sales*. NJ: Princeton Univ. Press, 1982.

Ravenal, Earl C. "No First Use: A View from the United States," *The Bulletin of Atomic Scientists*, Vol. 39, No. 4 (April 1983).

Rothschild, Emma. "Delusions of Deterrence," *The New York Review of Books*. Vol. 30, No. 2 (April 14, 1983).

Sanders, Jerry. "Elites, Public Opinion and Empire: On Lions, Foxes and Mass Politics in the Post-Vietnam Era," *Alternatives: A Journal of World Policy*, (Summer, 1982) 8:1.

Sanders, Jerry W. *Empire at Bay: Containment Strategies and American Politics at the Crossroads*. World Policy Paper #25. NY: World Policy Institute, 1983.

Sanders, Jerry. *Peddlers of Crisis: The Committee on the Present Danger and the Politics of Containment*. Boston, MA : South End Press, 1983.

Scheer, Robert. *With Enough Shovels: Reagan, Bush and Nuclear War*. NY: Random House, 1982.

Schell, Jonathan. *The Fate of the Earth*. NY: Alfred A. Knopf, 1982.

Sivard, Ruth Leger. *World Military and Social Expenditures*. Leesburg, VA: World Priorities, annual.

Snow, Donald. *The Nuclear Future: Toward a Strategy of Uncertainty*. University, AL: Univ. of Alabama Press, 1983.

Swedish International Peace Research Institute. *Armaments or Disarmament?* Stockholm: SIPRI, 1982.

Swedish International Peace Research Institute. *World Armaments and Disarmament*. Stockholm: SIPRI yearbook, annual.

Thee, Marek. *Armaments, Arms Control and Disarmament, a UNESCO Reader for Disarmament Education*. Paris: UNESCO, 1981.

Tobias, Sheila, Peter Goudinoff, et al. *What Kind of Guns Are They Buying for Your Butter? A Beginner's Guide to Defense, Weaponry and Military Spending*. NY: William Morrow and Co., 1982.

Vance, Cyrus. *Common Security*. NY: Simon and Schuster, 1982.

Weston, Burns, ed. *Toward Nuclear Disarmament and Global Security: A Search for Alternatives*. Boulder, CO: Westview Press, 1984.

Williams, William Appleman. *Empire as a Way of Life*. NY: Oxford Univ. Press, 1980.

Wolfe, Alan. *The Rise and Fall of the Soviet Threat*. Washington, DC: Institute for Policy Studies, 1980.

Yergin, Daniel. *Shattered Peace: The Origins of the Cold War and the National Security State*. Boston: Houghton Mifflin, 1977.